CONNECT WITH MATHS

JUNIOR CYCLE HIGHER LEVEL

FREE e-book with Digital Resources

Revised and fully in line with the NEW JUNIOR CYCLE SPECIFICATION

FREE digital resources · ...ts, videos and more

Edco

John McKeon with Michelle Kelly and Gillian Russell

First published 2019
The Educational Company of Ireland
Ballymount Road
Walkinstown
Dublin 12
www.edco.ie

A member of the Smurfit Kappa Group plc

ISBN 978-1-84536-838-8

Editor: Eric Pradel
Proofreaders: Judith Paskin, Eric Pradel, Christine Vaughan
Design and layout: Compuscript, Liz White
Cover Design: emc design, Shutterstock/Kertu
Artwork: Compuscript, Angeles Peinador (Beehive Illustration)
Photograph and other acknowledgements:
Alamy, Big Stock, cso.ie, Irish Rail, istockphoto, Roger Fereday, Brendan Howard, Meunierd, recycledproducts.com, Science Photo Library, Shutterstock, Thaves

05M20

Contents

Note from the authors

The authors would particularly like to thank Meike Sommer of Edco for her wonderful professionalism, patience and great good humour in bringing this whole package to its completion.

We would also to thank Martina Harford, Declan Dempsey, Julie Glennon, Emer Ryan and all at Edco whose support and expertise were so important at critical stages.

Thanks also to Eric Pradel, Judith Paskin and Christine Vaughan for their painstaking editing and proofreading.

A special mention to the students and staff of Maynooth Post Primary School, past and present. Many happy hours of teaching there have contributed hugely to this book.

Dedications

To Emily, my wife and best friend down all the years, and to our wonderful sons, Robert, Barry, Stephen and Kevin. For Adi, Isla, Cora, Sean, Doug and Frank and remembering little Charlie. – John

To my family, especially my husband, Oscar, thank you all for your support and guidance through this process. – Gillian

To my family and friends who have been very patient and supportive, in particular David, Jack, Katie and Conor. – Michelle

Introduction

Connect with Maths – Junior Cycle Higher Level is a two-year course in mathematics for students in second and third year in second-level schools. It builds on *Connect with Maths – Introduction to Junior Cycle*, which students will have studied in first year.

The sequence of topics in the *Connect With Maths* series follows closely the suggested sequence in the Teacher Handbooks on the **Maths Development Team's** website (**www.projectmaths.ie**).

Teachers can access a full suite of **digital activities** at **www.edcolearning.ie**. Further information is available in the **Teacher's Resource Book**.

The *Connect with Maths* series of books follows the aims and objectives of the new specification and associated assessment specifications, with an emphasis on:

- Teaching and learning for understanding by investigation and discussion
- Developing problem-solving skills
- Making connections between all strands of the syllabus so that students are able to transfer their skills from one topic to other seemingly unrelated topics
- Making mathematics relevant to everyday life
- Making the learning of mathematics as enjoyable as possible given that some students find the subject challenging

Connect with Maths has the following features:

- A Learning Intentions section at the start of each chapter
- Connections boxes, where feasible, linking the topic to other strands
- Plenty of well-constructed, graded activities so that students of different ability levels are challenged
- Class activity boxes to encourage class discussion
- Blue definition boxes to highlight key points
- Key information boxes to emphasise important information
- Revision activities for each chapter
- Exam-style questions at the end of each chapter
- Key words and phrases at the end of each chapter

A **Student Activity Book** comes free with *Connect with Maths – Junior Cycle Higher Level.* This has activities related to each chapter and can be used independently of the main book for revision, class tests or extra class work. The Activity Book can be used at any stage of the Junior Cycle once the relevant chapter in *Connect with Maths* has been studied.

A separate **Teacher's Resource book** is provided for teachers and contains chapter notes and fully worked-out solutions for every activity in *Connect with Maths – Junior Cycle Higher Level.*

Additional teacher resources, including a full suite of digital activities and fully worked-out solutions for the textbook, are available online at **www.edcolearning.ie**.

Many years of teaching experience and a lot of effort and consultation have gone into the writing of this book. We hope that students and teachers enjoy working with it together.

John McKeon, Gillian Russell, Michelle Kelly

Digital Resources

The *Connect with Maths – Junior Cycle Higher Level* digital resources will enhance classroom learning by encouraging student participation and engagement. They support the New Junior Cycle Specification's emphasis on the use of modern technology in the classroom and are designed to cater for different learning styles.

To provide guidance for the integration of digital resources in the classroom and to aid lesson planning, they are **referenced throughout the textbook** using the following icons:

 Highly adaptable **Interactive Tools** that allow students to create their own activities

 A series of stimulating **videos**, covering a variety of different topics, allowing students to observe maths in action

 Editable **PowerPoint** presentations providing step-by-step solutions to a selection of activity questions

 Dynamic curriculum based **Animated Constructions**.

Teachers can access the *Connect with Maths* digital resources, including **digital activity suggestions, weblinks** and **team projects**, via the *Connect with Maths* interactive e-book, which is available online at **www.edcolearning.ie**.

Learning Outcomes

Number strand

Students should be able to:

N.1 investigate the representation of numbers and arithmetic operations so that they can:

a. represent the operations of addition, subtraction, multiplication, and division in $\mathbb{N}$, $\mathbb{Z}$, and $\mathbb{Q}$ using models including the number line, decomposition, and accumulating groups of equal size

b. perform the operations of addition, subtraction, multiplication, and division and understand the relationship between these operations and the properties: commutative, associative and distributive in $\mathbb{N}$, $\mathbb{Z}$, and $\mathbb{Q}$ **and in $\mathbb{R}\backslash\mathbb{Q}$, including operating on surds**

c. explore numbers written as a^b (in index form) so that they can:

I. flexibly translate between whole numbers and index representation of numbers

II. use and apply generalisations such as $a^p a^q = a^{p+q}$; $(a^p)/(a^q) = a^{p-q}$; $(a^p)^q = a^{pq}$; and $n^{1/2} = \sqrt{n}$, for $a \in \mathbb{Z}$, and $p, q, p-q, \sqrt{n} \in \mathbb{N}$ **and for $a, b, \sqrt{n} \in \mathbb{R}$, and $p, q \in \mathbb{Q}$**

III. use and apply generalisations such as $a^0 = 1$; $a^{p/q} = \sqrt[q]{a^p} = (\sqrt[q]{a})^p$; $a^r = 1/(a^r)$; $(ab)^r = a^r b^r$; and $(a/b)^r = (a^r)/(b^r)$, for $a, b \in \mathbb{R}$; $p, q \in \mathbb{Z}$; and $r \in \mathbb{Q}$

IV. generalise numerical relationships involving operations involving numbers written in index form

V. correctly use the order of arithmetic and index operations including the use of brackets

d. calculate and interpret factors (including the highest common factor), multiples (including the lowest common multiple), and prime numbers

e. present numerical answers to the degree of accuracy specified, for example, correct to the nearest hundred, to two decimal places, or to three significant figures

f. convert the number p in decimal form to the form $a \times 10^n$, where $1 \leq a < 10$, $n \in \mathbb{Z}$, $p \in \mathbb{Q}$, and $p \geq 1$ **and $0 < p < 1$**

N.2 investigate equivalent representations of rational numbers so that they can:

a. flexibly convert between fractions, decimals, and percentages

b. use and understand ratio and proportion

c. solve money-related problems including those involving bills, VAT, profit or loss, % profit or loss (on the cost price), cost price, selling price, compound interest for not more than 3 years, income tax (standard rate only), net pay (including other deductions of specified amounts), value for money calculations and judgements, **mark up (profit as a % of cost price), margin (profit as a % of selling price), compound interest, income tax and net pay (including other deductions)**

N.3 investigate situations involving proportionality so that they can:

a. use absolute and relative comparison where appropriate

b. solve problems involving proportionality including those involving currency conversion and those involving average speed, distance, and time

N.4 analyse numerical patterns in different ways, including making out tables and graphs, and continue such patterns

N.5 explore the concept of a set so that they can:

a. understand the concept of a set as a well-defined collection of elements, and that set equality is a relationship where two sets have the same elements

b. define sets by listing their elements, if finite (including in a 2-set or **3-set** Venn diagram), or by generating rules that define them

c. use and understand suitable set notation and terminology, including null set, Ø, subset, $\subset$, complement, element, $\in$, universal set, cardinal number, #, intersection, $\cap$, union, $\cup$, set difference, \, $\mathbb{N}$, $\mathbb{Z}$, $\mathbb{Q}$, $\mathbb{R}$, and $\mathbb{R} \backslash \mathbb{Q}$

d. perform the operations of intersection and union on 2 sets **and on 3 sets**, set difference, and complement, including the use of brackets to define the order of operations

e. investigate whether the set operations of intersection, union, and difference are commutative and/or associative

Geometry and trigonometry strand

Students should be able to:

GT.1 calculate, interpret, and apply units of measure and time

GT.2 investigate 2D shapes and 3D solids so that they can:

a. draw and interpret scaled diagrams

b. draw and interpret nets of rectangular solids, **prisms (polygonal bases), cylinders**

c. find the perimeter and area of plane figures made from combinations of discs, triangles, and rectangles, including relevant operations involving pi

d. find the volume of rectangular solids, cylinders, **triangular-based prisms, spheres,** and combinations of these, including relevant operations involving pi

e. find the surface area and **curved surface area (as appropriate)** of rectangular solids, **cylinders, triangular-based prisms, spheres,** and combinations of these

GT.3 investigate the concept of proof through their engagement with geometry so that they can:

a. perform constructions 1 to 15 in *Geometry for Post-Primary School Mathematics* **(constructions 3 and 7 at HL only)**

b. recall and use the concepts, axioms, theorems, corollaries and converses, specified in *Geometry for Post-Primary School Mathematics* (section 9 for OL **and section 10 for HL**)

I. axioms 1, 2, 3, 4 and 5

II. theorems 1, 2, 3, 4, 5, 6, 9, 10, 13, 14, 15 **and 11, 12, 19**, and appropriate converses, including relevant operations involving square roots

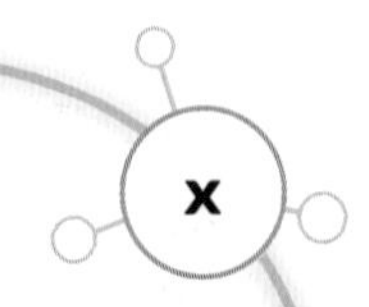

III. corollaries 3, 4 **and 1, 2, 5** and appropriate converses

c. use **and explain** the terms: theorem, proof, axiom, corollary, converse, and implies

d. create and evaluate proofs of geometrical propositions

e. display understanding of the proofs of theorems 1, 2, 3, 4, 5, 6, 9, 10, 14, 15, **and 13, 19**; and of corollaries 3, 4, **and 1, 2, 5** (full formal proofs are not examinable)

GT.4 evaluate and use trigonometric ratios (sin, cos, and tan, defined in terms of right-angled triangles) and their inverses, involving angles between 0° and 90° at integer values **and in decimal form**

GT.5 investigate properties of points, lines and line segments in the co-ordinate plane so that they can:

a. find and interpret: distance, mid-point, slope, point of intersection, and slopes of parallel **and perpendicular** lines

b. draw graphs of line segments and interpret such graphs in context, including discussing the rate of change (slope) and the y intercept

c. find and interpret the equation of a line in the form $y = mx + c$; $y - y_1 = m(x - x_1)$; **and $ax + by + c = 0$** (for $a, b, c, m, x_1, y_1 \in \mathbb{Q}$); including finding the slope, the y intercept, and other points on the line

GT.6 investigate transformations of simple objects so that they can:

a. recognise and draw the image of points and objects under translation, central symmetry, axial symmetry, and rotation

b. draw the axes of symmetry in shapes

Algebra and functions strand

Students should be able to:

AF.1 investigate patterns and relationships (linear, quadratic, doubling and tripling) in number, spatial patterns and real-world phenomena involving change so that they can:

a. represent these patterns and relationships in tables and graphs

b. generate a generalised expression for linear **and quadratic** patterns in words and algebraic expressions and fluently convert between each representation

c. categorise patterns as linear, non-linear, **quadratic, and exponential (doubling and tripling)** using their defining characteristics as they appear in the different representations

AF.2 investigate situations in which letters stand for quantities that are variable so that they can:

a. generate and interpret expressions in which letters stand for numbers

b. find the value of expressions given the value of the variables

c. use the concept of equality to generate and interpret equations

AF.3 apply the properties of arithmetic operations and factorisation to generate equivalent expressions so that they can develop and use appropriate strategies to:

a. add, subtract and simplify

I. linear expressions in one or more variables with coefficients in $\mathbb{Q}$

II. quadratic expressions in one variable with coefficients in $\mathbb{Z}$

III. expressions of the form $\frac{a}{(bx + c)}$, where $a, b, c \in \mathbb{Z}$

b. multiply expressions of the form

I. $a(bx + cy + d)$; $a(bx^2 + cx + d)$; and $ax(bx^2 + cx + d)$, where $a, b, c, d \in \mathbb{Z}$

II. $(ax + b)(cx + d)$ **and $(ax + b)(cx^2 + dx + e)$,** where $a, b, c, d, e \in \mathbb{Z}$

c. divide quadratic **and cubic expressions** by linear expressions, where all coefficients are integers and there is no remainder

d. flexibly convert between the factorised and expanded forms of algebraic expressions of the form:

I. axy, where $a \in \mathbb{Z}$

II. $axy + byz$, where $a, b \in \mathbb{Z}$

III. $sx - ty + tx - sy$, where $s, t \in \mathbb{Z}$

IV. $dx^2 + bx$; $x^2 + bx + c$; **and $ax^2 + bx + c$,** where $b, c, d \in \mathbb{Z}$ **and $a \in \mathbb{N}$**

V. $x^2 - a^2$ **and $a^2 x^2 - b^2 y^2$,** where $a, b \in \mathbb{Z}$

AF.4 select and use suitable strategies (graphic, numeric, algebraic, trial and improvement, working backwards) for finding solutions to:

a. linear equations in one variable with coefficients in $\mathbb{Q}$ and solutions in $\mathbb{Z}$ **or in $\mathbb{Q}$**

b. quadratic equations in one variable with coefficients and solutions in $\mathbb{Z}$ **or coefficients in $\mathbb{Q}$ and solutions in $\mathbb{R}$**

c. simultaneous linear equations in two variables with coefficients and solutions in $\mathbb{Z}$ **or $\mathbb{Q}$**

d. linear inequalities in one variable of the form $g(x) < k$, and graph the solution sets on the number line for $x \in \mathbb{N}$, $\mathbb{Z}$, and $\mathbb{R}$

AF.5 generate quadratic equations given integer roots

AF.6 apply the relationship between operations and an understanding of the order of operations including brackets and exponents to change the subject of a formula

AF.7 investigate functions so that they can:

a. demonstrate understanding of the concept of a function

b. represent and interpret functions in different ways—graphically (for $x \in \mathbb{N}$, $\mathbb{Z}$, and $\mathbb{R}$, [continuous functions only], as appropriate), diagrammatically, in words, and algebraically — using the language and notation of functions (domain, range, co-domain, $f(x) =$, $f{:}x \mapsto$, and $y =$) (drawing the graph of a function given its algebraic expression is limited to linear and quadratic functions at *OL*)

c. use graphical methods to find and interpret approximate solutions of equations such as $f(x) = g(x)$

and approximate solution sets of inequalities such as $f(x) < g(x)$

d. make connections between the shape of a graph and the story of a phenomenon, including identifying and interpreting maximum and minimum points

Statistics and probability strand

Students should be able to:

SP.1 investigate the outcomes of experiments so that they can:

a. generate a sample space for an experiment in a systematic way, including tree diagrams for successive events and two-way tables for independent events

b. use the fundamental principle of counting to solve authentic problems

SP.2 investigate random events so that they can:

a. demonstrate understanding that probability is a measure on a scale of 0–1 of how likely an event (including an everyday event) is to occur

b. use the principle that, in the case of equally likely outcomes, the probability of an event is given by the number of outcomes of interest divided by the total number of outcomes

c. use relative frequency as an estimate of the probability of an event, given experimental data, and recognise that increasing the number of times an experiment is repeated generally leads to progressively better estimates of its theoretical probability

SP.3 carry out a statistical investigation which includes the ability to:

a. generate a statistical question

b. plan and implement a method to generate and/or source unbiased, representative data, and present this data in a frequency table

c. classify data (categorical, numerical)

d. select, draw and interpret appropriate graphical displays of univariate data, including pie charts, bar charts, line plots, histograms (equal intervals), ordered stem-and-leaf plots, **and ordered back-to-back stem-and-leaf plots**

e. select, calculate and interpret appropriate summary statistics to describe aspects of univariate data. Central tendency: mean **(including of a grouped frequency distribution),** median, mode. Variability: range

f. evaluate the effectiveness of different graphical displays in representing data

g. discuss misconceptions and misuses of statistics

h. discuss the assumptions and limitations of conclusions drawn from sample data or graphical/numerical summaries of data

Unifying strand

Elements	Students should be able to:	
Building blocks	U.1	recall and demonstrate understanding of the fundamental concepts and procedures that underpin each strand
	U.2	apply the procedures associated with each strand accurately, effectively, and appropriately
	U.3	recognise that equality is a relationship in which two mathematical expressions have the same value
Representation	U.4	represent a mathematical situation in a variety of different ways, including: numerically, algebraically, graphically, physically, in words; and to interpret, analyse, and compare such representations
Connections	U.5	make connections within and between strands
	U.6	make connections between mathematics and the real world
Problem solving	U.7	make sense of a given problem, and if necessary mathematise a situation
	U.8	apply their knowledge and skills to solve a problem, including decomposing it into manageable parts and/or simplifying it using appropriate assumptions
	U.9	interpret their solution to a problem in terms of the original question
	U.10	evaluate different possible solutions to a problem, including evaluating the reasonableness of the solutions, and exploring possible improvements and/or limitations of the solutions (if any)
Generalisation and proof	U.11	generate general mathematical statements or conjectures based on specific instances
	U.12	generate and evaluate mathematical arguments and proofs
Communication	U.13	communicate mathematics effectively: justify their reasoning, interpret their results, explain their conclusions, and use the language and notation of mathematics to express mathematical ideas precisely

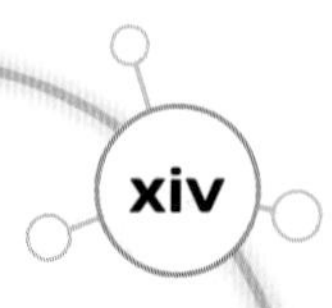

Ratio and Proportion

Chapter 1

Learning Intentions

In this chapter, you will learn about:

- Ratio and proportion
- Direct proportion and inverse proportion
- Drawing and understanding scaled diagrams

LO: U.4, U.5, U.6, N.2(b), N.3(a), GT.2(a)

Section 1A Ratio and Proportion

John is mixing sand and cement to make a concrete path. He has sand and cement in bags of equal size. John wants the mixture to have five bags of sand for every one bag of cement. This will give him the strength of concrete he needs.

In mathematics we say that John wants the **ratio** of sand to cement to be **5 : 1**.

When we compare €36 to €12, using the idea of **how many times** €36 is bigger than €12, we call this **the ratio 36 : 12**.

€36 is three times €12.

We can write many pairs of numbers in the same ratio as 36 : 12.

We get ratios equivalent to 36 : 12 by **multiplying or dividing** each number in the ratio by the same number.

For example, 36 : 12 = 72 : 24 = 18 : 6 = 12 : 4 = 9 : 3 = 6 : 2 = 3 : 1.

Connections

- You will remember that we use the very same method to write **equivalent fractions**, e.g. $\frac{3}{4} = \frac{6}{8} = \frac{9}{12} = \frac{12}{16}$ etc. Fractions are also ratios.

A **ratio** is the quotient of two numbers giving their relative size.

Ratios can be written in different forms: $\frac{a}{b} = a : b$

For example, 3 : 5 means that for every 3 portions of the first amount you have, you have 5 portions of the second amount. This ratio can also be written as $\frac{3}{5}$ or we can say '3 is to 5'.

Ratios (just like fractions) are usually written in the lowest terms, i.e. 15 : 3 = 5 : 1.

When we have a statement of equivalent ratios, we have a **proportion**.
This is sometimes called **direct proportion**.

A famous ratio found in nature is the **golden ratio**, φ (pronounced phi), which is approximately 1 : 1.618. It is found in the natural world such as in snowflakes or plants, in architecture and in the ratio of measurements of humans.

Indeed, it has even been claimed that the golden ratio is the mathematics behind beauty.

Example 1

Rewrite each of the following ratios in its simplest form.

(i) 10 : 25 (ii) 36 : 42 : 60 (iii) 450 g : 1 kg (iv) $\frac{1}{4} : \frac{1}{6}$

Solution

(i) 10 : 25 = 2 : 5 ... divide each part by 5

(ii) 36 : 42 : 60 = 6 : 7 : 10 ... divide each part by 6

(iii) 450 g : 1 kg ... convert each part to the same unit

= 450 g : 1000 g ... divide each part by 50

= 9 : 20

(iv) $\frac{1}{4} : \frac{1}{6}$

Convert each fraction to a whole number by multiplying each fraction by the LCM.

The LCM is 12.

Therefore: $(12)\frac{1}{4} : \frac{1}{6}(12) = 3 : 2$

Number	Multiples
4	4, 8, 12, 16, ...
6	6, 12, 18, ...

Example 2

In an election, Siobhán got three votes for every two votes that Thomas got. Siobhán got 72 votes. How many votes did Thomas get?

Solution

Write the ratios as fractions.

Siobhán's votes : Thomas's votes

= 3 : 2 = 72 : x

Write an equivalent ratio for 3 : 2 to make the first part = 72

3 : 2 = 72 : 48 ... multiply both parts by 24

⇒ 72 : 48 = 72 : x

⇒ x = 48

Hence, Thomas got 48 votes.

Example 3

Alan, Brian and Cathy share a prize fund of €500 in the ratio 5 : 3 : 2.

Find each person's share.

Solution

- Write down the total number of parts.

  5 + 3 + 2 = 10 parts
- Write each part of the ratio as a fraction of the total number of parts.

  $\frac{5}{10} : \frac{3}{10} : \frac{2}{10}$
- Multiply €500 by each fraction to find the value of each share.

  Alan: $\frac{5}{10} \times €500 = €250$

  Brian: $\frac{3}{10} \times €500 = €150$

  Cathy: $\frac{2}{10} \times €500 = €100$

Therefore, the money will be shared out in the ratio €250 : €150 : €100.
(Alan) (Brian) (Cathy)

Example 4

In a Youth Club, the ratio of boys to girls is 3 : 5. If there are 18 boys in the club, how many girls are there in the club?

Solution

- From the given ratio

  3 : 5 = 18 boys : x girls

  So we know that 3 parts = 18 boys

  5 parts = x girls
- Calculate the number of members which are equal to one part.

  3 parts = 18 boys … divide both sides by 3

  1 part = $\frac{18}{3}$ = 6 members of the club

  5 parts = 6 × 5 = 30 girls

  30 = x girls

  So there are 30 girls in the club.

Example 5

Marie can do 30 star jumps in 1 minute and Laura can do 150 star jumps in 5 minutes. Are these ratios of star jumps to time equal? In other words, **do they represent the same proportion**? Explain your answer.

Solution

Marie's ratio ⇒ number of star jumps : time taken = 30 : 1

Laura's ratio ⇒ number of star jumps : time taken = 150 : 5 = 30 : 1

As the ratios in their simplest form are equal, then these ratios represent the same proportion.

Keeping different quantities in **correct proportion** is very important. For example, when:

- baking or cooking: the taste and texture depends on the **proportion** of ingredients
- diluting juices
- enlarging photographs
- making tea or coffee
- mixing cement
- manufacturing pharmaceuticals (making medicines).

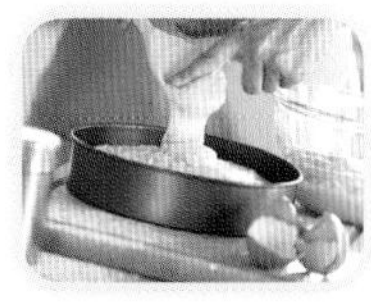

Example 6

A production line in a factory can make 80 pens in 10 minutes. How many pens can be made in 1 hour?

Solution

Ratio given ⇒ pens : minutes
= 80 : 10
= 8 : 1

Calculate how many pens can be made in 1 hour.

We know: 8 pens in 1 minute

So: 60 × 8 pens in 60 minutes … multiply both sides by 60

480 pens in 1 hour

The factory can make 480 pens in 1 hour.

Example 7

Find the value of x in the proportion $15 : 45 = 5 : x$

Solution

Method 1

$15 : 45 = 5 : x$

$15 : 45 = 5 : 15$ … divide both parts of the ratio by 3

$\Rightarrow 5 : 15 = 5 : x$

$\Rightarrow x = 15$

Method 2

$15 : 45 = 5 : x$

Write each ratio as a fraction.

$15 : 45 = \frac{15}{45}$ $\quad 5 : x = \frac{5}{x}$

Equate the fractions and solve for x.

$\frac{15}{45} = \frac{5}{x}$ … multiply both sides by $45x$, the LCM

$(45x)\left(\frac{15}{45}\right) = (45x)\left(\frac{5}{x}\right)$

$15x = 5(45)$

$15x = 225$ … divide both sides by 15

$x = 15$

Example 8

Find the value of x in the proportion $4 : 5 = x : 80$

Solution

Method 1

$4 : 5 = x : 80$

Write an equivalent ratio for $4 : 5$ where the second part = 80

$4 : 5 = 64 : 80$ … multiply both parts by 16

$\Rightarrow 64 : 80 = x : 80$

$\Rightarrow x = 64$

Method 2

$4 : 5 = x : 80$

Write each ratio as a fraction.

$4 : 5 = \frac{4}{5}$ $\quad x : 80 = \frac{x}{80}$

Equate the fractions and solve for x.

$\frac{4}{5} = \frac{x}{80}$ … multiply both sides by 80

$(80)\left(\frac{4}{5}\right) = (80)\left(\frac{x}{80}\right)$

$64 = x$

We can use a **ratio table** to help identify patterns when problem solving. Each ratio in the table will be equivalent to all the other ratios. We can also represent the ratios on a graph.

Example 9

A bakery uses 1 kg of flour to make 8 cakes, and 3 kg of flour to make 24 cakes.

(i) Using the information given, complete the ratio table.

Amount of flour	0 kg	1 kg	2 kg	3 kg	6 kg	10 kg
Number of cakes	0	8	16	24	48	180

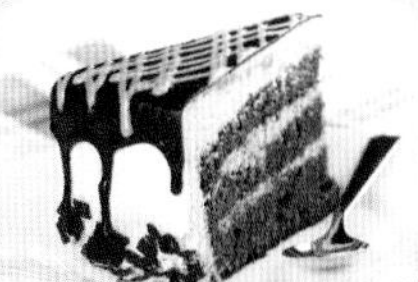

(ii) Using the pattern found in part (i), find how many cakes could be made with 25 kg of flour.

(iii) Draw a graph showing the relationship between the amount of flour and the number of cakes.

Solution

(i) We know that: 1 kg = 8 cakes

$\therefore$ 2 kg = 8 cakes × 2 = 16 cakes

$\therefore$ 3 kg = 8 cakes × 3 = 24 cakes

$\therefore$ 6 kg = 8 cakes × 6 = 48 cakes

$\therefore$ 10 kg = 8 cakes × 10 = 80 cakes

Amount of flour	0 kg	1 kg	2 kg	3 kg	6 kg	10 kg
Number of cakes	0	8	16	24	48	80

(ii) Using the pattern above:

Number of cakes made from 25 kg of flour = 8 cakes × amount of flour

= 8 cakes × 25

= 200 cakes

(iii)

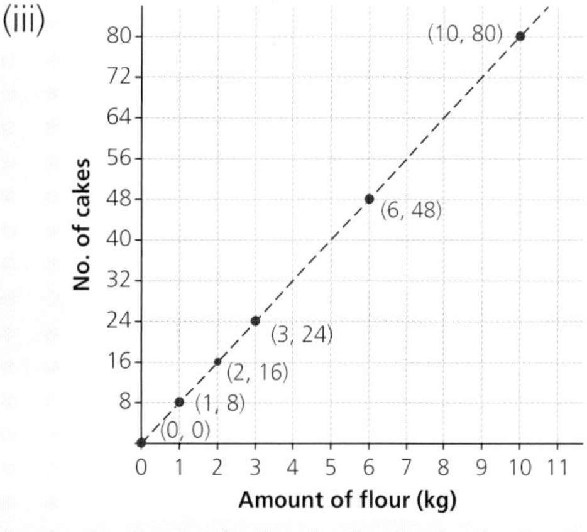

Key Point

The graph in Example 9 showing the relationship between the flour amounts and the number of cakes is a straight line which **passes through** (0, 0). This is true of all (directly) **proportional relationships**.

Activity 1.1

1 The ratio of boys to girls in a class is 4 : 5. How many boys are there in the class if there are 15 girls in the class? Explain your answer.

2 A car manufacturer can make 12 cars in 2 hours. How many cars can be made in a 24-hour period?

3 Simplify each of the following ratios.

(i) 5 : 55
(ii) 3 : 15 : 30
(iii) 27 : 9
(iv) 25 : 5 : 50
(v) 7 : 28 : 14
(vi) 8 : 10 : 12
(vii) 10 : 80 : 100
(viii) 4 : 20 : 80
(ix) 12 : 72 : 36
(x) 20 : 100 : 300

4 Write each of the following ratios in their simplest form.

Hint

› Make sure all values have the same units.

(i) 30 minutes : $\frac{1}{5}$ of an hour
(ii) 8 months : $\frac{1}{6}$ year
(iii) $\frac{1}{3} : \frac{1}{6}$
(iv) 3 km : 21 km
(v) $\frac{1}{4} : \frac{1}{5} : \frac{1}{6}$
(vi) $2\frac{1}{5} : 3\frac{4}{5}$
(vii) 4 hours : 1 day
(viii) $\frac{2}{7} : \frac{3}{5}$
(ix) 110 mm : 4 cm
(x) $\frac{4}{9} : \frac{2}{5} : \frac{1}{3}$

5 Write each of the following ratios in their simplest form.

Hint

› Make sure all values have the same units.

(i) 25 cent : €2.50
(ii) 35 seconds : 1 minute
(iii) $2\frac{1}{2} : 3\frac{1}{4}$
(iv) 250 g : 1.5 kg
(v) 30 cm : 1.5 m
(vi) $\frac{9}{4} : \frac{7}{3}$
(vii) $\frac{1}{3} : 2\frac{2}{6}$
(viii) 520 kg : 1 tonne

6 Divide each of the following quantities in the given ratio.

	Quantity	Ratio
(i)	€465	3 : 2
(ii)	$583	4 : 7
(iii)	6391 grams	5 : 6
(iv)	380 minutes	1 : 4
(v)	€4850	7 : 3
(vi)	392 metres	1 : 2 : 5
(vii)	522 kg	2 : 7 : 9
(viii)	£6410	5 : 3 : 2
(ix)	216 cent	4 : 3 : 2
(x)	9720 centimetres	1 : 4 : 5

7 Find the value of x for each of the following proportions.

	Proportion
(i)	$4 : 5 = x : 25$
(ii)	$8 : 11 = 24 : x$
(iii)	$9 : 13 = x : 39$
(iv)	$6 : 7 = x : 42$
(v)	$30 : 40 = 3 : x$
(vi)	$x : 7 = 4 : 14$
(vii)	$1 : x = 6 : 60$
(viii)	$x : 5 = 9 : 15$
(ix)	$2 : x = 8 : 24$
(x)	$x : 40 = 3 : 8$

8 At a basketball game, Susan, Maeve and Aoife scored in the ratio 1 : 3 : 4. If the three girls scored a total of 48 points, find out how many baskets each girl scored. (Note: Each basket is worth 2 points.)

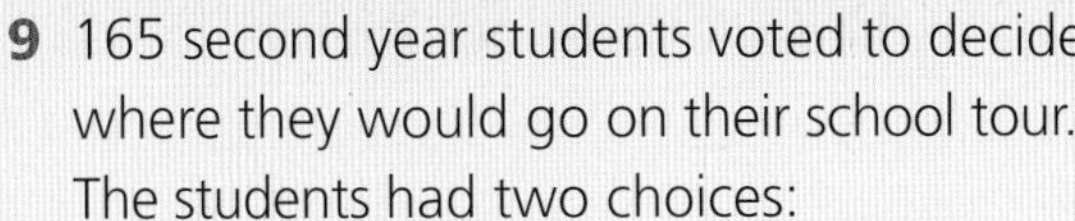

9 165 second year students voted to decide where they would go on their school tour. The students had two choices:

- go shopping and to the cinema, or
- go to an outdoor pursuits centre.

The results were split in the ratio 7 : 4 in favour of going to an outdoor pursuits centre.

(i) How many students voted to go shopping and to the cinema?

(ii) How many students voted to go to the outdoor pursuits centre?

10 The year head for sixth year checks absenteeism every Friday. On a given Friday, 18 students out of a total of 162 students were absent.

(i) What is the ratio of the number of absent students to the number of students present on the Friday mentioned?

(ii) If 12 students came in late and were then marked present, how would this affect the answer in part (i)?

11 A junior and a senior waiter in a café have agreed to divide their tips in the ratio 5 : 7. If the junior waiter receives €25, how much does the senior waiter receive?

12 A builder wants to build a house and landscape a garden on a site of area 561 m^2. The ratio of the area needed for the house to the garden is 3 : 8.

(i) What is the area of the house?

(ii) What is the area of the garden?

13 Gráinne drove 300 km in 2.5 hours, and Brendan drove 240 km in 2 hours.

Are these ratios of distance to time proportional? Explain your answer.

14 A recipe states that to make 48 cookies you need 2 cups of flour.

Another recipe states that to make 60 cookies you need 6 cups of flour.

Are these ratios of cookies to quantities of flour proportional? Explain your answer.

15 A farmer divides his field in the ratio 1 : 3 : 4 to grow potatoes, carrots and parsnips, respectively. The area used to sow parsnips is 48 m^2.

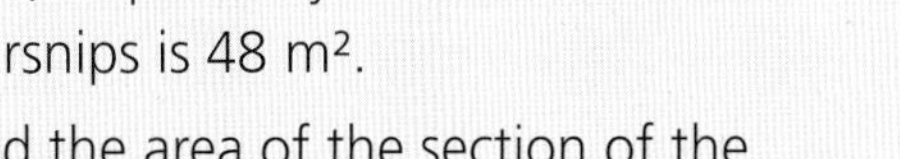

(i) Find the area of the section of the field used to plant potatoes.

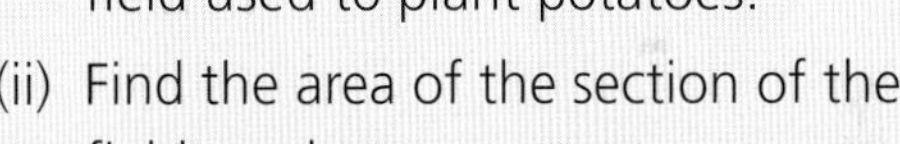

(ii) Find the area of the section of the field used to sow carrots.

16 John makes 45 cups of coffee from every 100 g jar of instant coffee. If John buys 4 jars of the same coffee, he can make 180 cups of coffee.

(i) Use the pattern to complete this ratio table.

Amount of instant coffee	0 g	100 g	200 g	400 g	700 g	800 g
Number of cups		45		180		

(ii) Using the pattern found in part (i), how many cups of coffee can John make if he buys 1 kg of instant coffee?

(iii) Draw a graph showing the relationship between the coffee amounts and the number of cups.

17 A car travels 53 km in 1 hour. If the car continues at the same speed for 3 hours, it will travel 159 km.

(i) Use the pattern to complete the ratio table.

Time taken	0 hour	1 hour	2 hours	3 hours	7 hours	10 hours
Distance travelled (km)		53		159		

(ii) Using the pattern found in part (i), find the distance travelled in 6.5 hours.

(iii) Draw a graph showing the relationship between the time taken and the distance travelled.

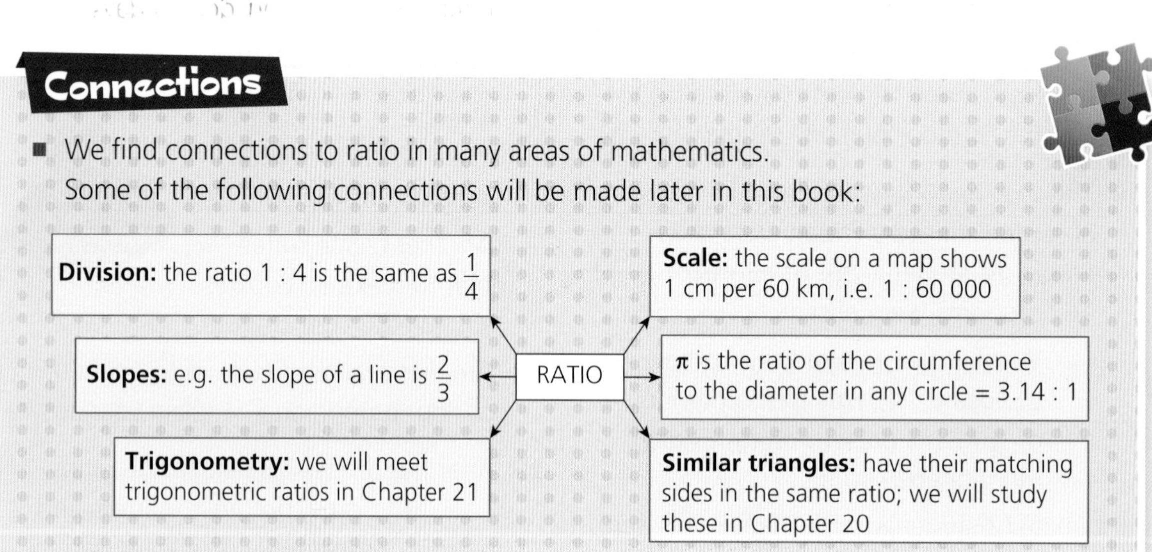

Connections

- We find connections to ratio in many areas of mathematics. Some of the following connections will be made later in this book:

Section 1B Inverse Proportion

Michael wants to hire a taxi to go to a show. The taxi fare is €12.

If Michael goes on his own, he pays €12. If he shares the taxi with his friend Grace, then the cost for each is €6. If Emily goes with them as well, each person will pay €4.

We see that as the number of passengers **increases**, the cost per head **decreases proportionally**. This is an example of **inverse proportion**.

If we draw a table, we can see the pattern of the costs per passenger.

Number of passengers	1	2	3	4
Cost of taxi	€12	€12	€12	€12
Cost per person	$\frac{12}{1}$ = €12	$\frac{12}{2}$ = €6	$\frac{12}{3}$ = €4	$\frac{12}{4}$ = €3

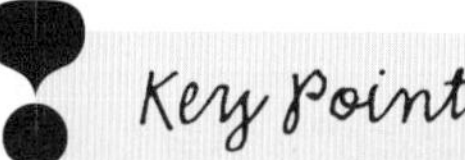

Key Point

When we multiply the number of passengers by the cost per person, we always get 12. This is the way we recognise inverse proportion.

Inverse proportion is used in stock control, project management and financial services.

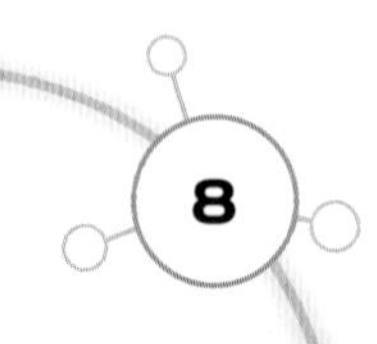

Example 1

It takes 12 builders four days to complete the brickwork for a house.

(i) How long would the same job take if 4 of the builders didn't turn up for work? (Assuming that all of the builders work at the same rate.)

(ii) If the homeowner said he needed the brickwork done in 3 days, how many builders would be needed for the job?

Solution

(i) Ratio given ⇒ 12 builders: 4 days

- Calculate how long 1 builder would take to complete the brickwork.

  This is inverse proportion: as the number of builders decreases, the time taken increases proportionally.

  12 builders : 4 days

  1 builder : 4 days × 12

  1 builder : 48 days

- Now work out how long it will take 8 builders to do the work.

  8 builders : $\frac{48}{8}$ days

  8 builders : 6 days

  It will take 6 days to complete the brickwork with 8 builders.

(ii) Ratio given ⇒ 12 builders: 4 days

- Calculate how many builders are needed to complete the work in 1 day.

  12 builders : 4 days

  4 × 12 builders : 1 day

  48 builders : 1 day

- Work out how many builders are needed to complete the work in 3 days.

  $\frac{48}{3}$ builders : 3 days

  16 builders : 3 days

  To get the job done in 3 days would require 16 builders.

Example 2

(i) Complete the table below to show the time taken by a car for a journey of 120 km at various speeds.

Speed (km/h)	30	40	60	120
Distance (km)	120	120	120	120
Time (h)	$\frac{120}{30} = 4$			

(ii) What is the pattern of the times as the speed increases?

(iii) What would be the time for a speed of 90 km?

Solution

(i)

Speed (km/h)	30	40	60	120
Distance (km)	120	120	120	120
Time (h)	$\frac{120}{30} = 4$	$\frac{120}{40} = 3$	$\frac{120}{60} = 2$	$\frac{120}{120} = 1$

(ii) The time taken for the journey is **inversely proportional** to the speed of the car. When the speed is multiplied by the time, the answer is always 120 km (the distance).

(iii) At a speed of 90 km/h, the time would be $\frac{120}{90} = 1\frac{1}{3}$ hours = 1 hour 20 minutes.

Activity 1.2

1 The prize in a lottery is €12,000.

(i) Copy and complete the table showing the amount won per person for different numbers of winners.

Number of winners	1	2	3	4
Lottery prize	€12,000	€12,000	€12,000	€12,000
Amount won per person				

(ii) What is the pattern of the 'Amount won per person' as the number of winners increases?

(iii) If there were 5 winners, how much would each receive?

(iv) If there were 10 winners, how much would each receive?

2 A builder has agreed to build a garage in 10 days. He needs 3 bricklayers to build the garage in this time period.

(i) If the builder had to build the garage in 5 days, how many bricklayers would he need?

(ii) If only one bricklayer was employed, how long would it take him to build the garage?

(iii) If the builder had only 2 bricklayers available to work, how long would it take them to build the garage?

3 A team of five chefs takes 3 hours to prepare a meal for 150 guests at a function.

(i) If two of the chefs don't turn up for work, how long will it take the other three chefs to prepare the meal?

(ii) If the meal needs to be prepared in $1\frac{1}{2}$ hours, how many chefs would be needed to get the meal ready in time?

4 A 1.5 metre length of material costs €18.

(i) What is the price of 1 metre of this material?

(ii) What is the price of 5 metres of this material?

(iii) If a customer spent €108 buying this material, how much material did the customer buy?

5 Two painters can paint a house in six days.

(i) How long would it take six painters to paint the same house?

(ii) If the same house needs to be painted in just two days, how many painters would be required?

6 A man earns €410 if he works a 40-hour week. How much will he earn if he works only 25 hours?

7 The cost of hiring a bus for a school match is €300.

(i) Copy and complete the table below to show the cost per student for different numbers of students.

Number of students	30	35	40	45	50
Cost of bus	€300	€300	€300	€300	€300
Cost per student					

(ii) What is the pattern of the 'Cost per student' as the number of paying students increases?

(iii) If there were 52 students, how much would each have to pay?

(iv) The cost per student was €12.50. How many students went on the bus?

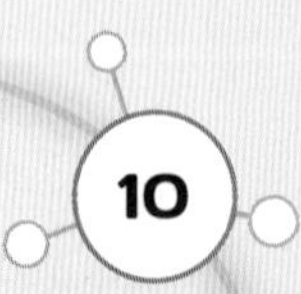

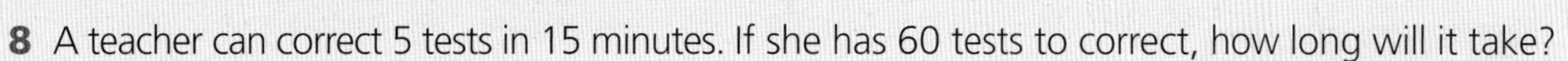

8 A teacher can correct 5 tests in 15 minutes. If she has 60 tests to correct, how long will it take?

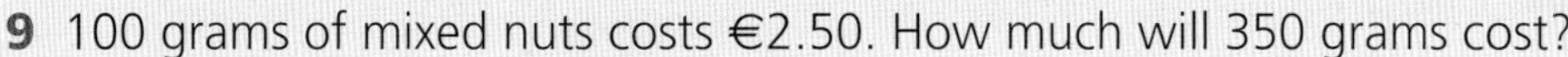

9 100 grams of mixed nuts costs €2.50. How much will 350 grams cost?

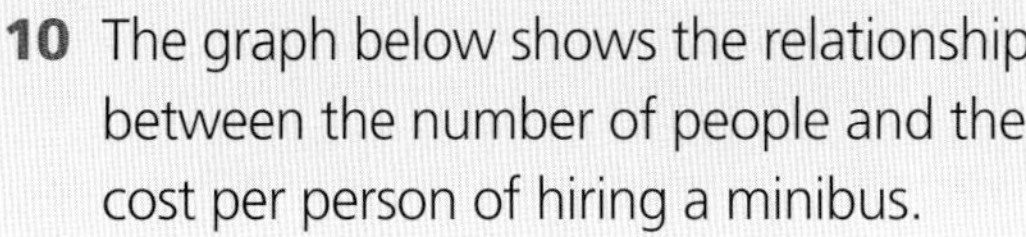

10 The graph below shows the relationship between the number of people and the cost per person of hiring a minibus.

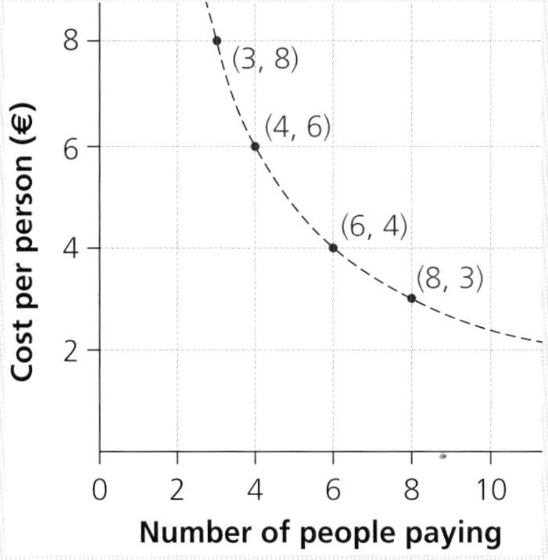

(i) Explain what the point (6, 4) means in this context.

(ii) If there were 8 people, what would be the cost per person?

(iii) Can you see any pattern in the relationship between the co-ordinates of each point?

(iv) What is the cost of hiring the minibus? Explain your answer.

Section 1C Scaled Diagrams

The picture on the right shows a model of a car which is a replica of the real car. Models like these were originally made as toys to fit into a matchbox.

The scale is 1 : 87.

This means that the real car is 87 times the size of the model car.

The model is 7 cm long, so the length of the real car is $7 \times 87 = 609$ cm.

The picture is an example of a **scaled diagram**.

> Scaled diagrams have the same shape as the real object but a different size.

Architects and engineers use scaled drawings of buildings and roads so that the builder can construct them properly.

When we look at a map or a house plan, we are looking at a scaled diagram.

Example 1

The diagram shows a plan for an extension to a house.

The scale used is 1 : 50.

(i) Find the actual dimensions of the rooms.

(ii) If the sitting room in the house is 5.7 m by 4.5 m, what would be the dimensions of this room on the plan?

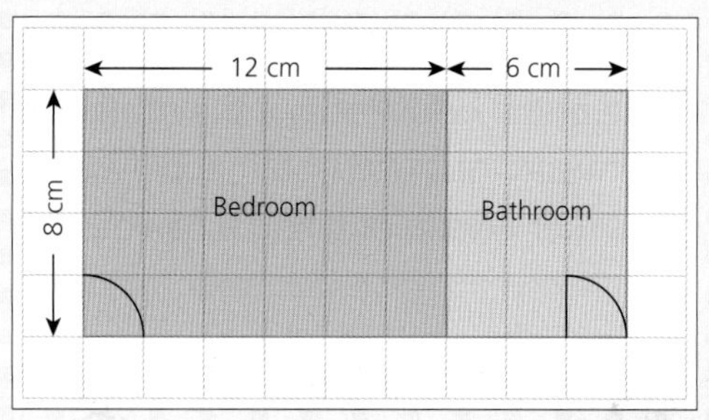

Solution

(i) The scale is 1 : 50

1 cm on the plan = 50 cm in reality

8 cm on the plan = (8 × 50) cm in reality = 400 cm

12 cm on the plan = (12 × 50) cm in reality = 600 cm

6 cm on the plan = (6 × 50) cm in reality = 300 cm

Hence, the bedroom measures 600 cm by 400 cm or 6 m by 4 m.

The bathroom's dimensions are 300 cm by 400 cm or 3 m by 4 m.

(ii) The sitting room is 5.7 m by 4.5 m = 570 cm by 450 cm

$\frac{1}{50}$ cm on the plan = 1 cm in reality

1 cm on the plan = 50 cm in reality

Divide each measurement by 50 to get the plan measurements:

Dimensions on the plan = $\frac{570}{50}$ by $\frac{450}{50}$ = 11.4 cm by 9 cm.

Example 2

This is a scaled map of Ireland using the scale 1 : 6 000 000.

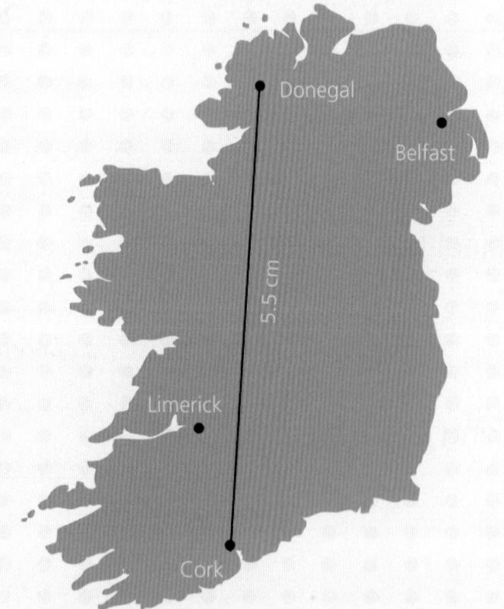

(i) Using the information on the scaled diagram, calculate the straight line distance from Cork to Donegal, to the nearest kilometre.

(ii) If the direct distance between Limerick and Belfast is 276 km, what distance would this measure on the diagram?

Solution

The scale reads: 1 cm = 6 000 000 cm

So, each 1 cm on the diagram represents an actual distance of 6 000 000 cm.

As we normally measure distances in km, we need to convert 6 000 000 cm into km.

- To change cm to metres, divide by 100: $\frac{6\,000\,000}{100} = 60\,000$ m
- To change metres to kilometres, divide by 1000: $\frac{60\,000}{1000} = 60$ km

Scale: 1 cm = 60 km

(i) The distance from Cork to Donegal on the map is 5.5 cm.
Actual distance is $5.5 \times 60 = 330$ km.

(ii) The straight line distance between Limerick and Belfast is 276 km.

The scale for the diagram is 1 cm = 60 km, so to find the distance on the map we need to divide 276 by 60: $\frac{276}{60} = 4.6$ cm.
The distance between Limerick and Belfast on the map should be 4.6 cm.

Activity 1.3

1 Copy and complete this sentence:
'A scale of 1 : 200 on a diagram means that 1 cm on the diagram represents ________ in reality.'

2 The scale on a map is 1 : 12 000.
How big are the following in real life?
- (i) a distance of 2 cm on the map
- (ii) a distance of 20 cm on the map
- (iii) a distance of 70 cm on the map
- (iv) a distance of 4.5 cm on the map

3 Lines are drawn on a diagram with a scale of 1 : 75. Find the length in reality of each of the following lines on the diagram.
- (i) 9 cm
- (ii) 3.5 cm
- (iii) 150 mm
- (iv) 15 cm

4 Find the actual height of the giraffe and the elephant, given the scale for each.

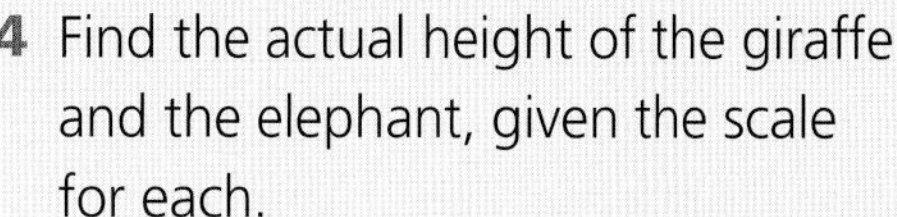

(i) 1 : 70 (ii) 1 : 90

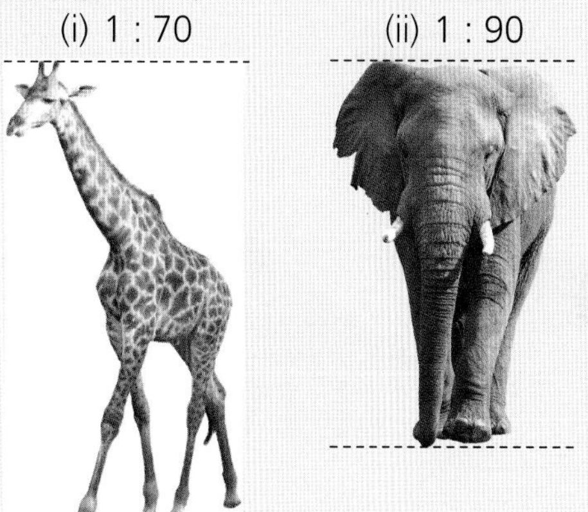

5 Here is the plan of a house.

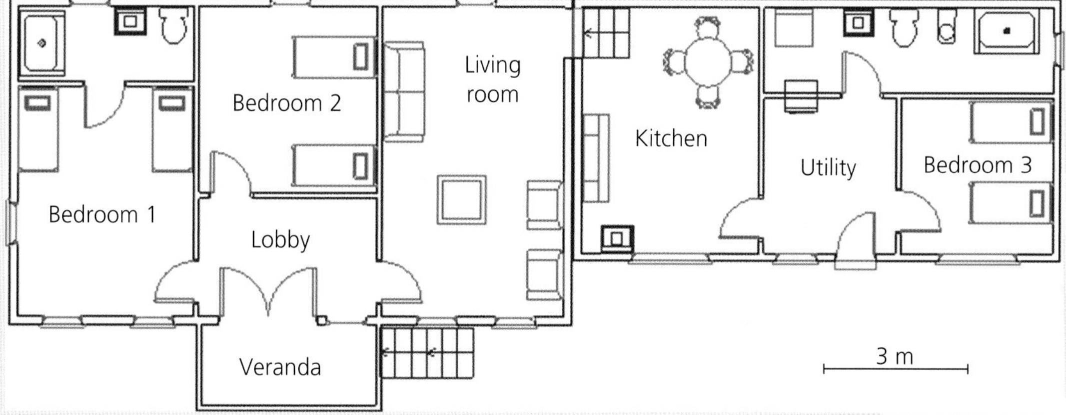

Using the scale for 3 m given, find:
- (i) The length and width of the living room
- (ii) The floor area of the kitchen
- (iii) The perimeter of the house.

6 The diagram shows a scaled drawing of a tennis court.

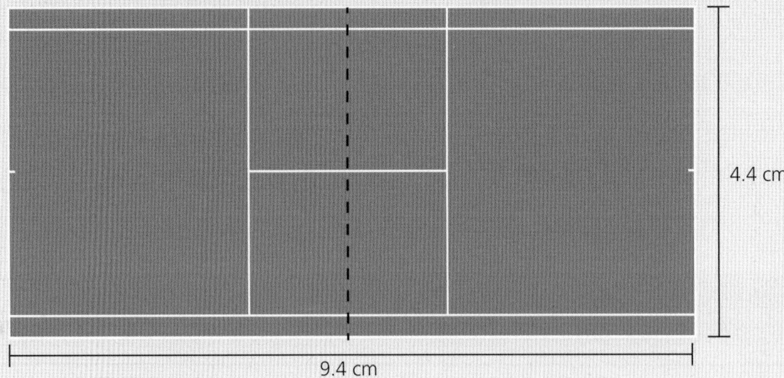

Using the scale 1 : 250, find the actual length and width of the tennis court.

7 Estimate the actual height and length of the dinosaur using the scale provided.

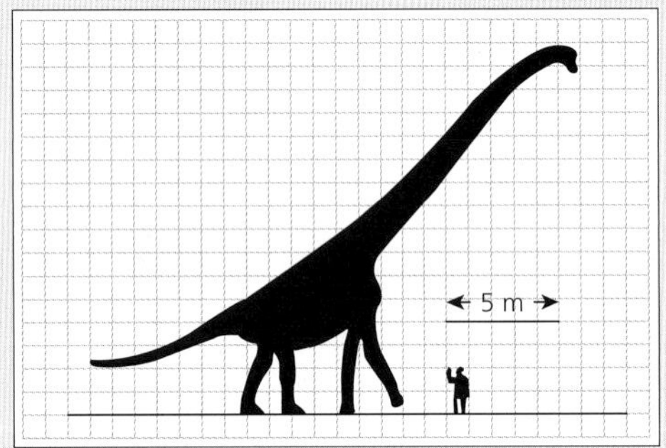

8 Draw each of the following shapes using a suitable scale. Indicate the scale on your diagram.

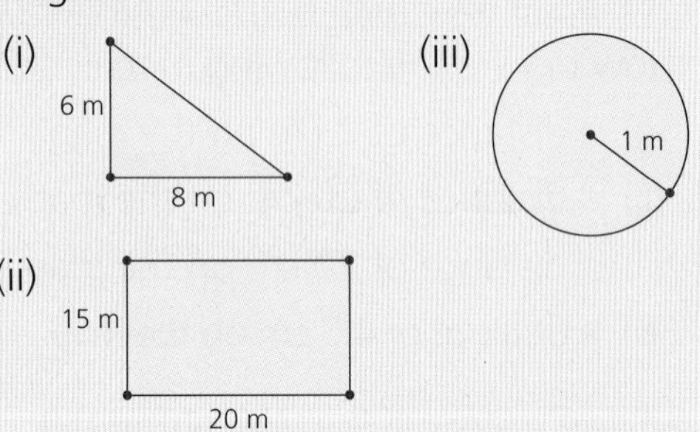

9 Using the map and scale, approximate the straight line distances between:

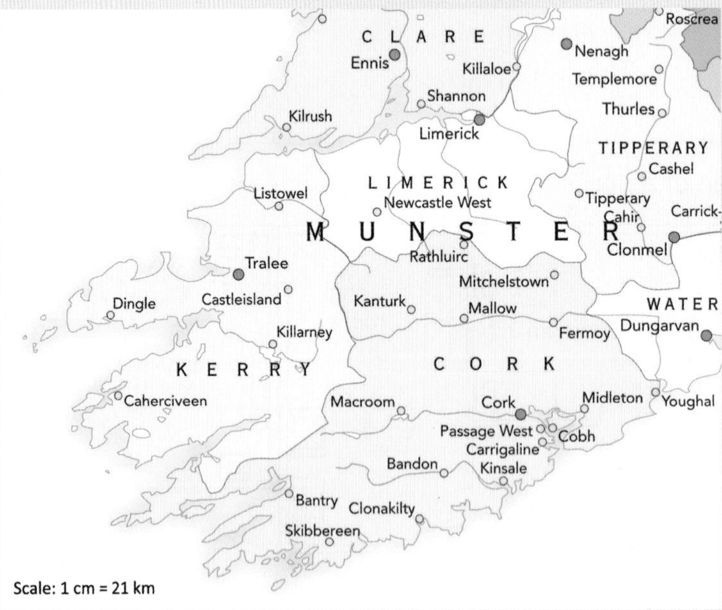

(i) Tralee and Cork

(ii) Dungarvan and Limerick

(iii) Ennis and Nenagh

(iv) Killarney and Clonmel.

Give your answers correct to the nearest kilometre.

10 This is a map of Ireland using the scale 1 : 7 500 000.

Using the information on the map, calculate the following.

(i) The distance from Dublin to Sligo to the nearest kilometre.

(ii) The distance from Belfast to Galway to the nearest kilometre.

(iii) If the direct distance between Sligo and Waterford is 210 km, what distance would this measure on the map?

Revision Activity 1

1 (a) Divide 1.5 km in the ratio 7 : 8.

(b) Divide €1050 in the ratio $\frac{1}{2} : \frac{1}{4} : \frac{1}{6}$.

(c) Divide 300 minutes in the ratio 2 : 4.

(d) Divide €1500 in the ratio 3 : 1 : 2.

(e) Divide 200 sweets in the ratio 2 : 3 : 5.

(f) Divide 40 cm in the ratio: $\frac{1}{2} : \frac{1}{5}$.

2 A drink is made up of 15% orange concentrate and 85% water.

(i) Write the ratio of orange concentrate to water in its simplest form.

(ii) If 300 ml of orange concentrate is used, how much water is needed?

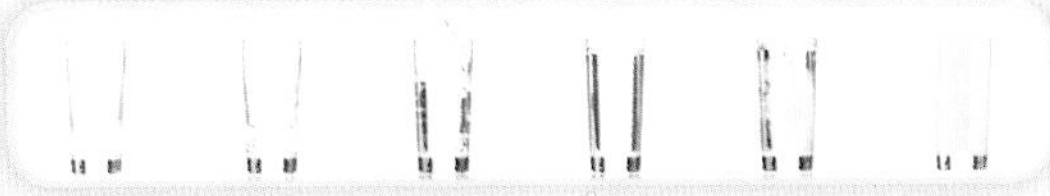

3 A football coach buys a 1 litre bottle of concentrated blackcurrant juice. The concentrated juice is mixed with water in the ratio 125 ml of concentrate to 1 litre of water.

Hint

› 1 litre = 1000 ml

(i) What is the ratio of concentrate to water in its simplest form?

(ii) If the coach uses all the concentrate, how much blackcurrant drink will he have made?

(iii) If he used 6 litres of water, how much concentrate would he have used?

Hint

› Make sure all values have the same units.

4 A fruit farmer employs seasonal workers to pick fruit. Each worker is expected to pick 45 kg of fruit every three hours.

(i) How much fruit can be picked in 8 hours?

(ii) How long would it take a worker to pick 210 kg of fruit?

(iii) If the farmer needs 1 to be picked in 1 hour, workers will he need?

Interactive Tool 1.1

1

Ratio and Proportion

Exam-style Question

1 *Fruitex* and *Juicy* are each made from mixing fruit juice and water.
In *Fruitex*, the ratio of fruit juice to water is 3 : 7.

(a) Find how many litres of fruit juice are in 20 litres of *Fruitex*.

20 litres of *Fruitex* is mixed with 40 litres of *Juicy*.
In this 60-litre **mixture**, the ratio of fruit juice to water is 7 : 8.

(b) Find the ratio of fruit juice to water in *Juicy*. Give your answer in its simplest form.

JCHL 2017

KEY WORDS AND PHRASES

- **Ratio**
- **Proportion**
- **Direct proportion**
- **Inverse proportion**
- **Scaled diagram**

Chapter Summary 1

- When we compare €36 to €12, using the idea of **how many times** €36 is bigger than €12, we call this the ratio 36 : 12.
- We get ratios equivalent to 36 : 12 by **multiplying or dividing** each number in the ratio by the same number.
- Ratios can be written in different forms: $\frac{a}{b} = a : b$, or a to b.
- When we have a statement of equivalent ratios, we have a **proportion**. This is sometimes called **direct proportion**, e.g. a proportion for 12 : 8 is 12 : 8 = 6 : 4 or 12 : 8 = 3 : 2 etc.
- **Indirect proportion** is a ratio where one quantity increases as another decreases proportionally, e.g. if one is doubled, the other is halved.
- On a **scaled diagram** a scale of 1 : 20 means that 1 cm on the diagram represents 20 cm in reality.

Chapter 2

Algebra 1

Learning Intentions

In this chapter, you will learn about:

LO: U.5, U.6, U.7–U.10, AF.3

- Algebraic expressions
- Evaluating expressions
- Simplifying terms
- Multiplying terms
- Multiplying expressions including the use of brackets and the distributive law
- Factorising:
  - Expressions with a common factor across all terms
  - Expressions where grouping is necessary
  - Quadratic expressions with three terms (trinomials)
  - The difference of two squares
- Dividing terms
- Dividing expressions

Historical Background

The German mathematician Carl Friedrich Gauss is widely acknowledged as one of the three greatest mathematicians of all time. The other two are Newton and Archimedes.

In his first arithmetic class, Gauss' teacher gave the students a task to keep them busy. The problem was to add up all the natural numbers from 1 to 100. Gauss had the answer almost immediately.

Carl Friedrich Gauss (1777–1855)

What problem-solving strategy did he employ?

Can you work out how he did it? He saw that:

$(100 + 1) = 101$

$(99 + 2) = 101$

$(98 + 3) = 101$ … etc.

Thus the sum $= (101 \times 100) \div 2 = 5050$

But then, after all, Gauss was a genius!

Section 2A Review

You have already met the following words and phrases in your study of algebra.

Variable: The letters which stand for unknown numbers in algebra, e.g. x, y, z.

Constant: A term whose value never changes, e.g. 5, -32, $\frac{1}{2}$.

Term: When a constant and a variable(s) are multiplied together, e.g. $13p$, $3x^2$.

Coefficient: The constant multiplied by the variable in a term, e.g. in the term $23x^2$, 23 is the coefficient of x^2.

Expression: A set of terms which are added or subtracted, e.g. $5x - 7$ is a linear expression; $3x^2 - 5x + 6$ is a quadratic expression.

Binomial: An expression with two terms, e.g. $3a + b$ or $7x^2 - 6$.

Trinomial: An expression with three terms, e.g. $x^2 - x + 7$ or $b^3 - 6b^2 + 4$.

Like terms: Terms with the same variables and the same powers, e.g. $5x^2$ and $7x^2$ both involve the same variable x, raised to the same power, 2.

Equivalent expressions: Expressions which can be written in different forms but have the same value, e.g. $x^2 + 2x$ and $x^2 + 3x - x$.

Key Points

- Only like terms may be added or subtracted.
- When adding like terms, the powers of the variables do not change.
- Expressions can be multiplied using the Distributive Law.
- The Distributive Law says multiplication is distributive over addition and subtraction.

Activity 2.1

1 $5x + 6$ is a linear expression.

(i) Write down the coefficient of x.

(ii) What is the constant term?

2 $3x^2 - 4x - 7$ is a quadratic expression.

(i) Write down the coefficient of x^2 and the coefficient of x.

(ii) What is the constant term?

3 $3ab - 5ac - 6$ is an algebraic expression.

(i) Name the variables in the expression.

(ii) Write down the coefficient of ab and the coefficient of ac.

(iii) What is the constant term?

4 (i) Copy and complete the diagram below, by writing $3m^2 - 6m + 2$ in ten different ways.
Note: these are all **equivalent expressions** for $3m^2 - 6m + 2$.

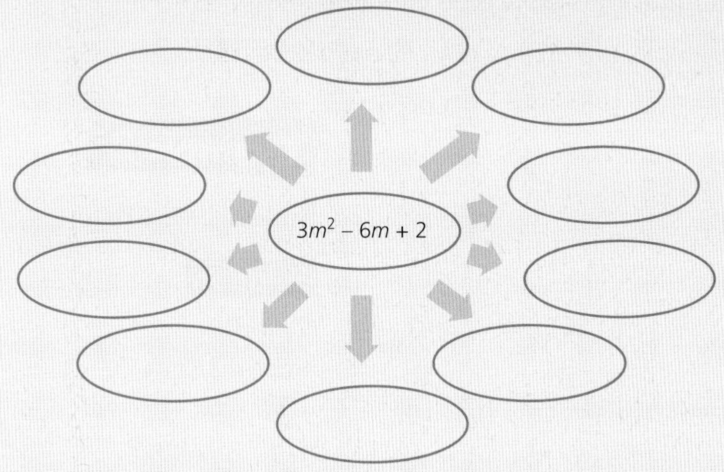

(ii) Which expression is the most compact?

In questions **5–17**, use the distributive law to remove the brackets, then simplify each expression as far as possible.

5 $5(3x + 2y)$

6 $-2(3a - b)$

7 $7(3 - 2q - r)$

8 $5a(3a - 2b)$

9 $5x - 2(3x - y)$

10 $5 - 2(3x - 2) + 4(5 - x)$

11 $6 + 3(2a - 5) - 7a$

12 $3x(2x - 3y) - x(x + 10y)$

13 $7a(3b - c) - 3b(2a + c)$

14 $x^2(x^3 - x^2 - x - 2)$

15 $4(p + 2q - 5) - (2p - 3q)$

16 $x(3x + 2) - (x^2 - x - 5)$

17 $x^3(x^2 - x) - 3x(x^2 - 2x + 1)$

18 Simplify each of the following.
(i) $5x^2 - 4x + 8 + 3x^2 + 4x - 7$
(ii) $a^3 - 4a^2 - 6a + 3a^3 + 6a^2 - a$
(iii) $-2x(3x + 5) - (6x - 2)$
(iv) $-5x(2x + 1) - 2(3x + 4)$

19 Given that $a = x^2 - 2x$ and $b = x^2 + 3x + 4$, write each of the following in terms of x.
(i) $a + b$ (ii) $a - b$ (iii) $5a - 2b$ (iv) $5a + 2b$

20 Write each of the following in its simplest form.
(i) $\frac{a^5}{a}$ (ii) $\frac{4a^3}{2a^2}$ (iii) $\frac{5a^2b^4}{ab^2}$ (iv) $\frac{8x^5y^2}{12x^3y^3}$ (v) $\frac{4xy^3}{3y}$ (vi) $\frac{16(-a^2)^2}{(-4a)^2}$ (vii) $\frac{3xy}{x} \div \frac{6xy}{x^2}$ (viii) $\frac{9(x^2y^3)^2}{xy} \div \frac{3x^2y}{2(xy)^3}$

21 Express in its simplest form:
$2x - [3 - (4 - 3x)] + 6$

22 Express in its simplest form:
$5a - [4 - (6 - 32a)] - 2$

Section 2B Multiplying Expressions

A **binomial** is an expression with two terms.

For example, $(x + 3)$ and $(2x - 7)$ are binomials.

Example 1

Multiply $(4x + 3)(3x - 4)$.

Solution

$(4x + 3)(3x - 4)$
$= 4x(3x - 4) + 3(3x - 4)$
$= 12x^2 - 16x + 9x - 12$ … the distributive law
$= 12x^2 - 7x - 12$

Example 2

Expand $(2x + 3)^2$.

Solution

$(2x + 3)^2$
$= (2x + 3)(2x + 3)$
$= 4x^2 + 6x + 6x + 9$
$= 4x^2 + 12x + 9$

Example 3

Expand $(ax + b)^2$.

Solution

$(ax + b)^2$
$= (ax + b)(ax + b)$
$= a^2x^2 + abx + abx + b^2$
$= (ax)^2 + 2abx + b^2$

Note: In Examples 2 and 3, there is a clear pattern to be seen when we **square a binomial**:

(first + second)^2
= (first)^2 + 2(first)(second) + (second)^2

If you practise this method, you will find it very convenient and quick.

Example 4

If $(2x + 5)(3x - a) = 6x^2 + 11x - 10$, find the value of a.

Solution

$(2x + 5)(3x - a) = 6x^2 + 11x - 10$
$\Rightarrow 6x^2 - 2ax + 15x - 5a = 6x^2 + 11x - 10$
Equating the constant terms gives
$-5a = -10$
$\Rightarrow a = \frac{-10}{-5} = 2$
We can check this by equating the terms with x:
$-2ax + 15x = 11x$
$\Rightarrow \quad -2a + 15 = 11$
$\Rightarrow \quad -2a = 11 - 15$
$\Rightarrow \quad -2a = -4$
$\Rightarrow \quad a = \frac{-4}{-2} = 2$ ✓

Activity 2.2

1 Copy and complete the following multiplication arrays. Simplify your answers as far as possible.

(i)

×	2x	–3
5x		
+2		

$(5x + 2)(2x - 3) =$

(ii)

×	–4x	–4
5x		
–1		

$(5x - 1)(-4x - 4) =$

(iii)

×	−3a	−3
3a		
−3		

$(3a - 3)(-3a - 3) =$

(iv)

×	2p	−6
−p		
+5		

$(-p + 5)(2p - 6) =$

In questions **2–14**, expand (multiply out) and simplify each expression as far as possible.

2 $(x + 2)(x + 5)$

3 $(a + 4)(a + 6)$

4 $(y - 1)(y - 5)$

5 $(3x - 2)(x + 4)$

6 $(3x - 4)(2x - 5)$

7 $(5p + 1)(2p + 3)$

8 $(5x + 2y)(3x - y)$

9 $(7x - y)(3x + y)$

10 $(5a - 2b)(5a + 2b)$

11 $(x - 1)(x + 3)(2x - 5)$

12 $(x - 2y)(x^2 + 2xy + y^2)$

13 $x(x - 3)(5x - 4)$

14 $(x + 4)(x^2 - x - 1)$

15 Multiply out $(3x - 1)(2x^2 + x - 4)$.

16 If $(3x + 2)(2x + a) = 6x^2 + x - 2$, find the value of a.

17 If $(x - 2)(3x + a) = 3x^2 - 8x + 4$, find the value of a by filling in the array.

×	3x	+a
x	$3x^2$	
−2		

18 If $(x - 3)$ is one factor of $x^2 + x - 12$, find the other factor.

19 Find the area of this rectangle in terms of x.

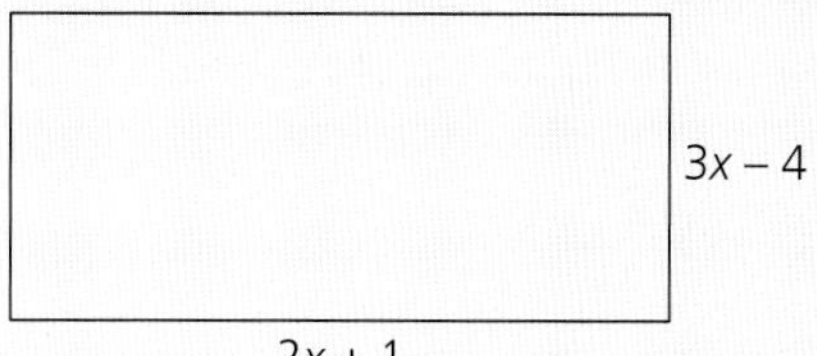

20 Expand:

(i) $(x + y)^2$ (ii) $(x - y)^2$

21 Use your answers to question **20** to expand each of the following.

(i) $(x + 2)^2$ (iv) $(a - 5)^2$
(ii) $(x - 3)^2$ (v) $(p - 6)^2$
(iii) $(a + 4)^2$ (vi) $(x + 7)^2$

22 Expand:

(i) $(ax + b)^2$ (ii) $(ax - b)^2$

23 Use your answers to question **22** to expand each of the following.

(i) $(3x + 2)^2$ (iv) $(4m + 3)^2$
(ii) $(4x - 1)^2$ (v) $(2p - 6)^2$
(iii) $(2a - 5)^2$ (vi) $(2x + 1)^2$

Section 2C Evaluating Expressions

To find the value of an expression for particular value(s) of the variables, **substitute** the value(s) into the variables in the expression.

Example 1

If $p = -5$ and $q = 3$, find the value of the following.

(i) $-5pq$ (ii) $3p^2 - 2p - 8$ (iii) $-q^2 - 4q + 7$ (iv) $\frac{-p - 3q}{5p - 2q}$

Solution

(i) $-5pq = -5(-5)(3) = -5(-15) = 75$

(ii) $3p^2 - 2p - 8 = 3(-5)^2 - 2(-5) - 8 = 3(25) + 10 - 8 = 75 + 2 = 77$

(iii) $-q^2 - 4q + 7 = -(3)^2 - 4(3) + 7 = -9 - 12 + 7 = -21 + 7 = -14$

(iv) $\dfrac{-p - 3q}{5p - 2q} = \dfrac{-(-5) - 3(3)}{5(-5) - 2(3)} = \dfrac{5 - 9}{-25 - 6} = \dfrac{-4}{-31} = \dfrac{4}{31}$

Example 2

Find the value of $3x^2 - 5x + \frac{4}{x}$ when $x = \frac{2}{3}$.

Solution

$3x^2 - 5x + \frac{4}{x}$ when $x = \frac{2}{3}$

$= 3\left(\frac{2}{3}\right)^2 - 5\left(\frac{2}{3}\right) + \dfrac{4}{\left(\frac{2}{3}\right)}$

$= 3\left(\frac{4}{9}\right) - \left(\frac{10}{3}\right) + \frac{4}{(1)} \times \frac{3}{2}$

$= \frac{12}{9} - \frac{10}{3} + \frac{6}{1}$

$= \frac{12 - 30 + 54}{9}$ ... LCM is 9

$= \frac{36}{9}$

$= 4$

Activity 2.3

1 If $x = 3$ and $y = -6$, find the value of each of the following.

(i) $5x - 2y$
(ii) $-2x - y$
(iii) $-y^2 + 6y$
(iv) $-2y^2 + 2x$
(v) xy
(vi) $(x - 3)^2$
(vii) $y^2 - 6$

2 If $a = 4$ and $b = -3$, find the value of each of the following.

(i) $5ab$
(ii) $a^2 + 3a + 5$
(iii) $-b^2 - b + 2$
(iv) $\dfrac{-3a - b}{a + b}$

3 If $x = -2$ and $y = -4$, find the value of each of the following.

(i) $-3xy$
(ii) $x^2 - xy$
(iii) $y^2 - 3y + 5$
(iv) $\dfrac{5x + y}{3x - 2y}$
(v) $\dfrac{4x - 3y}{-2x - y}$
(vi) $\dfrac{3x + 2y}{-x + 2y}$

4 If $m = -1$, $p = -5$ and $q = 3$, find the value of each of the following.

(i) mpq
(ii) $3pq$
(iii) $2p^3 + 3q^2$
(iv) $p^3 + q^3$
(v) $m^3 + m^2 - m$
(vi) $p^3 - q^3$

5 If $a = -2$, $b = -3$, and $c = -1$, find the value of each of the following.

(i) $a^3 - bc$
(ii) $2a^2c$
(iii) $2b^2 - 4c^2$
(iv) $2a - 3b + c$
(v) $3a^2b^2c^2$
(vi) $a^2 + b^2 + c^2$

6 Find the value of each of the following expressions when $x = -4$.

(i) $3x^2 - 2x + 4$
(ii) $x^3 - 3x^2 - 4x + 2$
(iii) $2x^3 - 4x^2 - x + 7$
(iv) $5 - 4x - 3x^2 - 2x^3$

7 When $x = \frac{1}{3}$, find the value of

$\frac{3}{x+1} + \frac{4}{x+5}$.

8 When $x = \frac{1}{2}$, find the value of

$\frac{3}{x+2} - \frac{1}{2x+4}$.

9 Given that $y = \sqrt{2x - a}$, find the value of y when $x = 4$ and $a = -1$.

10 Given that $x = 3t - 2$ and $y = \frac{1}{3}t - 4$, express $2x - 3y - 8$ in terms of t, in its simplest form.

11 When $m = \frac{2}{5}$ and $n = \frac{3}{2}$, find the value of $\frac{1}{2m} - \frac{2}{n}$. Write your answer in the form $\frac{a}{b}$, where $a, b \in \mathbb{Z}$.

12 Find the value of $3x^2 - 5x + \frac{4}{x}$, when $x = \frac{2}{3}$.

13 Find the value of $\frac{1}{a - c}$ when $a = 1\frac{1}{2}$ and $c = 2\frac{1}{3}$.

Section 2D Factors Type 1: Taking Out a Common Factor

We have already worked with factors of numbers.

For example: $3 \times 4 = 12$, so 3 and 4 are a pair of factors of 12.

Now we want to find factors for algebraic expressions, because this will help us solve a lot of maths problems later.

$(3x)(2y) = 6xy$, so **3*x* and 2*y* are factors of 6*xy***.

When a common factor can be found for all terms, always look for the highest common factor (HCF) of the expression.

Example

Factorise:

(i) $2b^2 + 5bc$ (ii) $3x^2 + x$ (iii) $8a^2 - 16a^3$ (iv) $5x^2y - 15xy^2$

Solution

(i) $2b^2 + 5bc$

b is the highest common factor of b^2 and bc

$\therefore 2b^2 + 5bc = b(2b + 5c)$

(ii) $3x^2 + x$

x is the highest common factor of x^2 and x

$\therefore 3x^2 + x = 3x^2 + 1x = x(3x + 1)$

(Notice that you need a 1 here and remember that x means $1x$.)

(iii) $8a^2 - 16a^3$

8 is the highest common factor of 8 and 16

a^2 is the highest common factor of a^2 and a^3

$\therefore 8a^2 - 16a^3 = 8a^2(1 - 2a)$

(iv) $5x^2y - 15xy^2$ … HCF $= 5xy$

$= 5xy(x - 3y)$

Activity 2.4

Copy and complete these equations. Always check to see if the expression is a 'Type 1' first.

Check your answers by mentally multiplying out the right-hand side.

1 $4x + 8y = 4(\quad)$

2 $5a + 15b = 5(\quad)$

3 $12p + 18q = 6(\quad)$

4 $14a + 21b = 7(\quad)$

5 $12a - 15b = 3(\quad)$

6 $30x - 50y = 10(\quad)$

7 $3x + xy = x(\quad)$

8 $p^2 - pq = p(\quad)$

9 $10x^2 - 5x = 5x(\quad)$

10 $15xy - 10xy^2 = 5xy(\quad)$

11 $10a^2 - 15ab = 5a(\quad)$

12 $14x^2 - 21xy = 7x(\quad)$

13 $12ab - 18ac = 6a(\quad)$

14 $45p^2 - 30pq = 15p(\quad)$

15 $p^3 + p^2 = p^2(\quad)$

16 $25xy - 125px = 25x(\quad)$

17 $5x - 15y + 20z = 5(\quad)$

18 $x^4 + x^3 - x^2 = x^2(\quad)$

Factorise each of the following expressions. Mentally check your answers by multiplying back.

19 $3x + 6$

20 $2p + 10$

21 $3b - 9$

22 $6x - 36$

23 $12y + 8$

24 $24x + 36$

25 $27x - 18$

26 $18 - 6p$

27 $15k + 35$

28 $9 - 27q$

29 $3a + 3b + 3c$

30 $4p + 4q + 4$

31 $6p^2 + 8pq$

32 $24p^2 + 30pq$

33 $16t^2 - 24t^3$

34 $6x^3 - 18x^2$

35 $9j^3 + 3j^2$

36 $5x^3 + 10x^2 - 15x$

37 $4x^3 + 8x^2 - 8x$

38 $3p - 3p^2 - 6p^3$

39 $8a - 12a^2 - 20a^3$

40 $15p - 5pq - 20pq^2$

41 $3a^2 + 3ab + 3a^2b$

42 $4a^3 - 4b^2 - 4b$

43 $7p^3d^2 - 14p^2d^3$

44 $a^2b - ab^2$

45 $4mn^2 - 9m^2n$

46 $9a^2 - 12a + 3a^3$

47 $2a^2b + 8ab - 12ab^2$

48 $21x^2y + 7xy - 14x^2y^2$

49 $p^3 + p$

50 $x^5 - x^4 - x^3$

51 Find the missing side of each rectangle.

(i) $3b$ | Area = $3ab + 9b$

(ii) x | Area = $x^2 + x$

(iii) $7x$ | Area = $35x^2 + 42x$

(iv) 2 | Area = $4x^2 + 2x + 2$

---

52 Factorise:

(i) $ay + by$ (ii) $a(y + 1) + b(y + 1)$

Check your answers by multiplying back.

53 Factorise:

(i) $3x + ax$ (ii) $3(x + 2) + a(x + 2)$

Check your answers.

54 Factorise:

(i) $ad + bd$ (ii) $a(d - 4) + b(d - 4)$

Check your answers.

55 Factorise:

(i) $px - qx$ (ii) $p(x + 7) - q(x + 7)$

Check your answers.

Section 2E Factors Type 2: Grouping to Get a Common Factor

Some expressions do not have a common factor for all terms.

This type usually has four terms (we could call it a 'gang of 4').

Group the terms into pairs that have common factors.

Example 1

Factorise the following and check your answers.

(i) $ax + ay + bx + by$

(ii) $3ax - bx + 3ay - by$

(iii) $xy + x - y^2 - y$

(iv) $10de - df - 5ef + 2d^2$

Solution

(i) $ax + ay + bx + by$

$= (ax + ay) + (bx + by)$ ... split into two pairs with common factors

$= a(x + y) + b(x + y)$ ... factorise the pairs separately (the brackets should have identical terms)

$= (x + y)(a + b)$

- Check: Work backwards → multiply out the answer.

  $(x + y)(a + b) = x(a + b) + y(a + b)$

  $= ax + bx + ay + yb$ ✓

  Remember: yb and by are the same, just as $(2)(6) = (6)(2)$.

(ii) $3ax - bx + 3ay - by$

$= x(3a - b) + y(3a - b)$

$= (3a - b)(x + y)$

- Check: $(3a - b)(x + y) = 3a(x + y) - b(x + y)$

  $= 3ax + 3ay - bx - by$ ✓

(iii) $xy + x - y^2 - y$ ... note the (–) sign before y^2 and before y

$= x(y + 1) - y(y + 1)$ ... see how the sign in the bracket has become +

$= (y + 1)(x - y)$

- Check: $(y + 1)(x - y) = y(x - y) + 1(x - y)$

  $= xy - y^2 + x - y$ ✓

(iv) $10de - df - 5ef + 2d^2$

$= 10de - 5ef + 2d^2 - df$ ... re-grouping

$= 5e(2d - f) + d(2d - f)$

$= (2d - f)(5e + d)$

Example 2

Factorise $6c + 12bd - 8d - 9bc$.

Solution

$6c + 12bd - 8d - 9bc$

$= 6c - 8d - 9bc + 12bd$ ... regroup to get pairs with common factors

$= 2(3c - 4d) - 3b(3c - 4d)$ ... note the sign change

$= (3c - 4d)(2 - 3b)$ ... factorise

Check: Work backwards → multiply out the answer

$(3c - 4d)(2 - 3b) = 6c - 9bc - 8d + 12bd$ ✓

Notice that when regrouping, the coefficients of the pairs are in the same ratio, e.g. $6:8 = 9:12$ in Example 2 above. Can you see another way that we could have regrouped in Example 2?

Activity 2.5

Multiply out these brackets.

1 $-5(x + y)$

2 $-2(3a + b)$

3 $-4(3a - 2)$

4 $-10(x^2 - x + 1)$

Copy these equations and fill in the brackets in each case.

5 $-2x - 2y = -2(\quad)$

6 $-12a - 4b = -4(\quad)$

7 $-5x + 10y = -5(\quad)$

8 $-a - b = -1(\quad)$

9 $-12x + 6 = -6(\quad)$

10 $-8m - 4n = -4(\quad)$

Factorise the following. Check your answer each time by multiplying back.

11 $mx + my + nx + ny$

12 $pa + pb + qa + qb$

13 $5a + 5b + pa + pb$

14 $wa + wb + 7a + 7b$

15 $ac + 5c + ab + 5b$

16 $mx + my + 7x + 7y$

17 $am + an + 4m + 4n$

18 $p^2 + py + 2p + 2y$

19 $x^2 + 2x + xy + 2y$

20 $mp + 3np + mt + 3nt$

21 $p^2 - p + 4pq - 4q$

22 $ax - bx + am - bm$

23 $ax^2 - bx + apx - bp$

24 $xy - y^2 + 7x - 7y$

25 $7m - 21n + m^2 - 3mn$

26 $20x^2 - 16xy + 15x - 12y$

27 $x^2 + x - xy - y$ (be careful with signs)

28 $8ax + 4bx - 6ay - 3by$ (be careful with signs)

29 $cx - dx - cy + dy$

30 $p^2x - 2px - pq + 2q$

31 $pq + ps - 8q - 8s$

32 $3ax - 2ax^2 + 18p - 12px$

Factorise the following expressions. You may need to regroup the terms.

33 $3a - ax + bx - 3b$

34 $3x - 15a + 5ab - bx$

35 $4c^2 - 3d - 2cd + 6c$

36 $ax - 3 - a + 3x$

37 $2x - kx + ky - 2y$

38 $3a - b + 3ab - b^2$

39 $3xy - 10x - 10b + 3by$

40 $5x^2 - 10xy - 2y + x$

41 $6ap - 4b - 12bp + 2a$

42 $x^2 - ab - bx + ax$

Section 2F Factors Type 3: Quadratic Trinomials

A quadratic expression is an expression of the form: $ax^2 + bx + c$, where $a \neq 0$.

Examples are $2x^2 + 5x + 10$ and $3x^2 - 2x$.

We want to factorise expressions like $x^2 + 4x + 5$ or $6x^2 + 13x + 5$ etc.

Remember that factorising is the opposite of multiplying out.

For example:

$$(5x + 3)(2x - 1) = 5x(2x - 1) + 3(2x - 1)$$
$$= 10x^2 - 5x + 6x - 3$$
$$= 10x^2 + x - 3$$

Hence, the factors of $10x^2 + x - 3$ are $(5x + 3)(2x - 1)$.

This means that the factors for these expressions look like $(ax + b)(cx + d)$ where a, b, c and d are numbers which could be + or –.

Notice that the middle term ($+x$) in the expression $10x^2 + x - 3$ is found by combining the factors of $10x^2$ and -3 (the first and last terms) like this:

$$(5x + 3)(2x - 1)$$

middle term is $(5x)(-1) + (3)(2x) = -5x + 6x = +x$

Example 1

Factorise $6x^2 + 13x + 5$.

Solution

Method 1

Break up the middle term ($+13x$) into two terms so that we have a 'gang of 4' terms.

To do this, our guide number is $(6)(5) = +30$.

- Find all the factors of +30:

(30)(1)
(–30)(–1)
(15)(2)
(–15)(–2)
(3)(10)
(–3)(–10)
(5)(6)
(–5)(–6)

- Only one pair of these factors will add to give the middle coefficient (+13).
  These are +3 and +10. So we write $+13x$ as $(+3x + 10x)$:

  $6x^2 + 13x + 5 = 6x^2 + 3x + 10x + 5$ ... use Type 2 method from here

  $= 3x(2x + 1) + 5(2x + 1)$

  $= (2x + 1)(3x + 5)$

  Check: $(2x + 1)(3x + 5) = 6x^2 + 10x + 3x + 5$

  $= 6x^2 + 13x + 5$ ✓

Method 2

Factorise $6x^2 + 13x + 5$.

Guess and test: We need factors of $6x^2$ to work with factors of +5 (the first and last terms) in order to get $+13x$ in the middle.

Trial 1: $(6x + 5)(x + 1)$ ... wrong ×

Trial 2: $(2x + 5)(3x + 1)$ ... wrong ×

Trial 3: $(2x + 1)(3x + 5)$ ... correct ✓

So $6x^2 + 13x + 5 = (2x + 1)(3x + 5)$

Example 2

Factorise $14x^2 - 17x - 6$.

Solution

Method 1

Break up the middle term $(-17x)$ into two terms so that we have a 'gang of 4' terms.

To do this, our guide number is $(14)(-6) = -84$.

- Find all the factors of -84:

(84)(–1)	(4)(–21)
(–84)(1)	(–4)(21)
(42)(–2)	(6)(–14)
(–42)(2)	(–6)(14)
(3)(–28)	(7)(–12)
(–3)(28)	(–7)(12)

- Only one pair of these factors will add to give the middle coefficient (–17). These are +4 and –21. So we write $-17x$ as $(+4x - 21x)$:

$14x^2 - 17x - 6 = 14x^2 - 21x + 4x - 6$ ... use Type 2 method from here

$= 7x(2x - 3) + 2(2x - 3)$

$= (2x - 3)(7x + 2)$

Check: $(2x - 3)(7x + 2) = 14x^2 + 4x - 21x - 6$

$= 14x^2 - 17x - 6$ ✓

Method 2

Factorise $14x^2 - 17x - 6$.

Guess and test: We need factors of $14x^2$ to work with factors of –6 (the first and last terms) in order to get $-17x$ in the middle.

Trial 1: $(7x + 6)(2x - 1)$ ... wrong ×

Trial 2: $(7x + 3)(2x - 2)$ ... wrong ×

Trial 3: $(7x + 2)(2x - 3)$ ... correct ✓

So $14x^2 - 7x - 6 = (2x - 3)(7x + 2)$

Although Method 2 may seem difficult at first, you may find it more efficient with a little practice.

Activity 2.6

Factorise each expression in questions **1–45**.

1 $x^2 + 11x + 18$

2 $p^2 - 11p + 18$

3 $m^2 + 11m + 10$

4 $a^2 + 11a + 24$

5 $a^2 - 18a + 81$

6 $a^2 + 29a + 100$

7 $x^2 - x - 12$

8 $x^2 + x - 12$

9 $x^2 - 4x - 12$

10 $x^2 + 4x - 12$

11 $p^2 + 7p - 18$

12 $a^2 + 13a - 30$

13 $x^2 - 5x - 6$

14 $x^2 + 5x - 6$

15 $p^2 - p - 2$

16 $p^2 + p - 2$

17 $a^2 - 3a - 70$

18 $x^2 + 11x - 60$

19 $a^2 - 15a + 56$

20 $x^2 + 0x - 16$

21 $a^2 + 5a + 6$

22 $x^2 - x - 6$

23 $a^2 - 3a - 88$

24 $m^2 + 11m - 42$

25 $x^2 + 5x - 66$

26 $a^2 - 5a - 66$

27 $5x^2 - 6x + 1$

28 $3x^2 + x - 2$

29 $10x^2 + 11x - 6$

30 $12x^2 - 23x + 10$

31 $6x^2 + x - 35$

32 $11x^2 + 75x - 14$

33 $6x^2 + 7x - 10$

34 $9m^2 - 24m + 16$

35 $25x^2 - 30x + 9$

36 $24x^2 + 2x - 15$

37 $36x^2 - 7x - 4$

38 $10x^2 - 17x - 20$

39 $12x^2 - 11x - 5$

40 $12x^2 - 61x + 70$

41 $13x^2 - 35x - 12$

42 $5x^2 + 13x - 6$

43 $12x^2 - 17x + 6$

44 $6x^2 + x - 22$

45 $4x^2 - 63x - 16$

Section 2G Factors Type 4: The Difference of Two Squares

Expressions of the form $x^2 - y^2$ are called **the difference of two squares**.

Once again, remember that factorising is the opposite of multiplying out.

Consider these factors: $(x - 5)(x + 5)$ ... notice the opposite signs

When we multiply out, we get $x(x + 5) - 5(x + 5)$

$= x^2 + 5x - 5x - 25$

$= x^2 - 25$ ... because $5x - 5x = 0$

$= x^2 - 5^2$ ... this is 'the difference of two squares'

So the factors of $x^2 - 5^2$ are $(x - 5)$ and $(x + 5)$.

Note that $1^2 = 1$.

Also, you may recall that because $2^2 = 4$, $3^2 = 9$, etc., these numbers are called square numbers.

In general, $x^2 - y^2 = (x + y)(x - y)$
There must be a '–' sign between the squares. We don't have factors for $x^2 + y^2$ with real numbers.

Example 1

Factorise each of these expressions and check your solution.

(i) $x^2 - 49$

(ii) $36 - m^2$

(iii) $25x^2 - 1$

Solution

(i) $x^2 - 49$

$= x^2 - 7^2$ .... difference of two squares

$= (x + 7)(x - 7)$

Check: $(x + 7)(x - 7) = x(x - 7) + 7(x - 7)$

$= x^2 - 7x + 7x - 49$

$= x^2 - 49$ ✓

(ii) $36 - m^2$

$= 6^2 - m^2$

$= (6 + m)(6 - m)$

Check: $(6 + m)(6 - m)$

$= 6(6 - m) + m(6 - m)$

$= 36 - 6m + 6m - m^2$

$= 36 - m^2$ ✓

(iii) $25x^2 - 1 = (5x)^2 - (1)^2$

$= (5x + 1)(5x - 1)$

Check: $(5x + 1)(5x - 1)$

$= 5x(5x - 1) + 1(5x - 1)$

$= 25x^2 - 5x + 5x - 1$

$= 25x^2 - 1$ ✓

Example 2

Use factors to evaluate:

(i) $(1001)^2 - (999)^2$ (ii) $(50.1)^2 - (49.9)^2$

Solution

(i) $(1001)^2 - (999)^2$

$= (1001 + 999)(1001 - 999)$

$= (2000)(2)$

$= 4000$

(ii) $(50.1)^2 - (49.9)^2$

$= (50.1 + 49.9)(50.1 - 49.9)$

$= (100)(0.2)$

$= 20$

Activity 2.7

Copy and complete the following table of square numbers.

$1^2 =$	$6^2 =$	$11^2 =$	$16^2 =$
$2^2 = 4$	$7^2 =$	$12^2 =$	$17^2 =$
$3^2 =$	$8^2 =$	$13^2 =$	$18^2 =$
$4^2 =$	$9^2 =$	$14^2 =$	$19^2 =$
$5^2 = 25$	$10^2 =$	$15^2 =$	$20^2 = 400$

These numbers are often referred to as 'perfect squares'. You will find this table of square numbers very useful when factorising the differences of two squares.

Activity 2.8

For **1** to **16**, factorise each expression. Check your answers by multiplying back.

1 $x^2 - y^2$

2 $a^2 - b^2$

3 $m^2 - n^2$

4 $p^2 - q^2$

5 $x^2 - 5^2$

6 $a^2 - 36$

7 $x^2 - 81$

8 $a^2 - 121$

9 $m^2 - 196$

10 $b^2 - 400$

11 $256 - y^2$

12 $144 - a^2$

13 $a^2 - 10\,000$

14 $(5x)^2 - 36$

15 $(7x)^2 - 1$

16 $(3x)^2 - 100$

17 Show that $(3x)^2 = 9x^2$. Use this to factorise $9x^2 - 4^2$.

18 Express $16a^2$ as a perfect square. Use your answer to factorise $16a^2 - 9$.

19 Factorise $25x^2 - 4$.

20 Factorise $49x^2 - 36y^2$.

21 Use factors to evaluate these.

(i) $51^2 - 49^2$

(ii) $101^2 - 99^2$

(iii) $79^2 - 81^2$

(iv) $(9.1)^2 - (0.9)^2$

(v) $(8.6)^2 - (1.4)^2$

(vi) $(17.1)^2 - (16.9)^2$

22 $25x^2 - 36y^2$

23 $49a^2 - 16b^2$

24 $144x^2 - 9y^2$

25 $169p^2 - 144$

26 $m^2 - 10000$

27 $(x + y)^2 - z^2$

28 $(a + b)^2 - 1$

29 $2x^2 - 18$ (3 factors)

30 $(x - 2)^2 - 36y^2$

31 $(3x + 1)^2 - (2x - 1)^2$

Section 2H Miscellaneous Factors

You need to be able to factorise any of the four types of expression.

A quick summary:

	Type	Example
1	Take out a common factor	$3x^2 + 6x$
2	Group to get a common factor (gang of 4)	$ax + bx + ay + by$
3	Quadratic with three terms	$x^2 + 6x + 8$
4	Difference of two squares	$p^2 - q^2$

Note: Always check to see if the method of Type 1 works first.

Key Points

A **linear** expression has a highest power of 1 on the variable, e.g. $7x - 3$.

A **quadratic** expression has a highest power of 2 on the variable, e.g. $5x^2 - 3x$.

Example 1

Find three factors of $3x^2 - 27$.

Solution

First, this is a Type 1 factor:

$3x^2 - 27 = 3(x^2 - 9)$ ... taking out 3, the highest common factor

Inside the bracket we have the difference of two squares:

$$3x^2 - 27 = 3(x^2 - 3^2)$$
$$= 3(x - 3)(x + 3)$$

Example 2

Write down four linear expressions that have $(x - 6)$ as a factor.

Solution

Multiplying by any constant will give a new linear multiple of $(x - 6)$:

$2(x - 6)$ $34(x - 6)$

$15(x - 6)$ $-23(x - 6)$

Example 3

Write down four quadratic expressions that have $(x - 4)$ as a factor.

Solution

Multiplying by any other linear expression will give a quadratic multiple of $(x - 4)$:

$x(x - 4)$	$(15x - 7)(x - 4)$
$3x(x - 4)$	$(22x + 5)(x - 4)$

Activity 2.9

Factorise each expression in questions **1–10**. Check your answers by multiplying out.

1 $x^2 - 25$

2 $x^2 - 49$

3 $ab - 2ax + mb - 2mx$

4 $144 - y^2$

5 $x^2 - x - 20$

6 $2x - 2y + cx - cy$

7 $5cd + 7d$

8 $7a^2 - 28$ (3 factors)

9 $ax + 3ay + 4x + 12y$

10 $2a^2 - 18$ (3 factors)

11 Write down a linear expression in x that has $(x + 2)$ as a factor.

12 Write down four linear expressions that have $(x - 3)$ as a factor.

13 Write down a quadratic expression that has $(x - 3)$ as a factor.

14 Write down three quadratic expressions that have $(x + 4)$ as a factor.

15 $x^2 - k$ is a quadratic expression in x that has $(x - 10)$ as a factor. What is the value of k?

16 $x^2 - k$ is a quadratic expression where k is a number.

For what value of k will $x^2 - k$ have $(x + 3)$ as a factor?

17 Simplify $(3 - 4x)^2 - (3 - 5x)^2$.

18 Simplify $(7x - 2)(7x + 2) - (5x + 4)(5x - 4)$ and fully factorise the simplified expression.

19 Use factors to simplify $\dfrac{8x^2 - 12x}{4x^2 - 12x + 9}$.

20 Simplify $\dfrac{6x^2 - 17x + 12}{3x - 4}$.

21 Simplify $(2x + a)(4x - 2a) - (3y + a)(6y - 2a)$ and fully factorise the simplified expression.

22 Factorise
(i) $17y - 5y^2$
(ii) $6a^2 - 19a + 10$

23 Simplify $(2a - 1)^2 - (a - 1)^2$.

24 (a) Factorise $4x - 12$ and $3x - 9$.

If A and B are variable quantities, we say that ***A* is proportional to *B*** if the fraction $\dfrac{A}{B}$ is constant.

(b) Using your answers to part (a) above, show that $4x - 12$ is proportional to $3x - 9$.

(c) Is $x^2 + 4x - 5$ proportional to $3x + 3$?

Section 2I Adding and Subtracting Algebraic Fractions

We can add, subtract, multiply and divide fractions in **algebra** in the same way that we do in arithmetic. However, we cannot simplify algebraic fractions on a calculator!

Example 1

(i) Add these fractions: $\frac{2}{9} + \frac{5}{6}$.

(ii) Now write these algebraic fractions as a single fraction: $\frac{2x}{9} + \frac{5x}{6}$.

Solution

(i) $\frac{2}{9} + \frac{5}{6}$

$= \frac{2(2)}{18} + \frac{3(5)}{18}$ ... LCM of 9 and 6 = 18

$= \frac{4}{18} + \frac{15}{18}$

$= \frac{4 + 15}{18}$

$= \frac{19}{18}$

Answer: $\frac{19}{18}$

(ii) $\frac{2x}{9} + \frac{5x}{6}$

$= \frac{2(2x)}{18} + \frac{3(5x)}{18}$

$= \frac{4x}{18} + \frac{15x}{18}$

$= \frac{4x + 15x}{18}$

$= \frac{19x}{18}$

Answer: $\frac{19x}{18}$

Example 2

Write the following expression as a single fraction: $\frac{5x + 2}{3} - \frac{4x + 3}{4}$.

Solution

$\frac{4(5x + 2)}{12} - \frac{3(4x + 3)}{12}$ ... the LCM of the denominators is 12

$= \frac{4(5x) + 4(2)}{12} - \frac{3(4x) + 3(3)}{12}$ ... expand the brackets

$= \frac{20x + 8 - (12x + 9)}{12}$ ... subtract the numerators

$= \frac{20x + 8 - 12x - 9}{12}$ ... simplify

$= \frac{8x - 1}{12}$

Example 3

Express in its simplest form $\frac{3a-1}{4} - \frac{5a+4}{3} - \frac{2a-7}{6}$.

Solution

The lowest common denominator is 12.

$$\frac{3a-1}{4} + \frac{5a+4}{3} - \frac{2a-7}{6} = \frac{3(3a-1) + 4(5a+4) - 2(2a-7)}{12}$$ … always use brackets in the numerator

$$= \frac{9a - 3 + 20a + 16 - 4a + 14}{12}$$

$$= \frac{25a + 27}{12}$$

Example 4

Write as a single fraction $\frac{1}{2x} + \frac{5}{4x}$.

Solution

The lowest common denominator is $4x$.

$$\frac{1}{2x} + \frac{5}{4x}$$

$$= \frac{2+5}{4x}$$

$$= \frac{7}{4x}$$

Example 5

Express in its simplest form $\frac{3}{2x+1} + \frac{5}{3x+4}$.

Solution

The lowest common denominator is $(2x + 1)(3x + 4)$.

$$\frac{3}{2x+1} + \frac{5}{3x+4} = \frac{3(3x+4) + 5(2x+1)}{(2x+1)(3x+4)}$$ … always use brackets

$$= \frac{9x + 12 + 10x + 5}{(2x+1)(3x+4)}$$

$$= \frac{19x + 17}{(2x+1)(3x+4)}$$

Activity 2.10

Write each of the expressions in questions **1–28** as a single fraction.

1 $\frac{8x}{9} + \frac{x}{3}$

2 $\frac{5a}{8} - \frac{3a}{4}$

3 $\frac{y}{2} - \frac{2y}{7}$

4 $\frac{4b}{5} + \frac{2b}{3}$

5 $\frac{3c}{4} - \frac{4c}{5}$

6 $\frac{11x}{3} + \frac{x}{5}$

7 $\frac{8y}{3} - \frac{3y}{14}$

8 $\frac{12x}{7} + \frac{7x}{12}$

9 $\frac{13x}{2} - \frac{x}{13}$

10 $\frac{x}{20} - \frac{3x}{5}$

11 $\frac{x+2}{4} + \frac{x+3}{2}$

12 $\frac{6x+1}{3} + \frac{2x+2}{4}$

13 $\frac{5x-3}{5} + \frac{x-7}{2}$

14 $\frac{7x-1}{3} + \frac{2x+8}{5}$

15 $\frac{9x-2}{4} - \frac{x-3}{2}$

16 $\frac{2x-9}{8} - \frac{5x+6}{2}$

17 $\frac{5x-4}{3} - \frac{3x-7}{2}$

18 $\frac{3x-1}{2} - \frac{4-x}{5} + (x-3)$

Hint: Remember that $(x-3) = \frac{(x-3)}{1}$

19 $4x - \frac{5x-1}{4} + \frac{x}{12}$

20 $\frac{3p-1}{7} - \frac{2p+7}{14} + 7p$

21 $\frac{k}{4} + \frac{3k-2}{3} - \frac{2k-5}{12}$

22 $\frac{1}{x} + \frac{3}{2x}$

23 $\frac{5}{3k} - \frac{2}{5k}$

24 $\frac{5}{x} + \frac{3}{2x+1}$

25 $\frac{5}{3x-2} + \frac{6}{2x+3}$

26 $\frac{3}{3x+1} - \frac{1}{2x-4}$

27 $\frac{2}{3p-5} - \frac{5}{p+1}$

28 $\frac{5}{3x+2} - \frac{4}{3x-2}$

29 Show that $\frac{1}{x-3} - \frac{1}{x}$ can be written in the form $\frac{p}{x^2-3x}$ where $p \in \mathbb{N}$ and find the value of p.

30 Show that $\frac{5}{2x-6} + \frac{7}{3x-9}$ can be written in the form $\frac{k}{6(x-3)}$ where $k \in \mathbb{N}$ and find the value of k.

31 (i) Show that $\frac{1}{x-2} = \frac{-1}{2-x}$.

(ii) Write $\frac{5}{x-2} + \frac{4}{2-x}$ in the form $\frac{p}{x-2}$ where $p \in \mathbb{N}$.

32 Write $\frac{6}{x-3} + \frac{4}{3-x}$ as a single fraction. Verify your answer by letting $x = 10$.

33 Write $\frac{3}{x-4} + \frac{7}{4-x}$ as a single fraction. Verify your answer by letting $x = 2$.

34 Express as a single fraction $\frac{3}{2x+5} + \frac{1}{x+5}$.

35 Show that $\frac{4}{3x-12} + \frac{3}{2x-8}$ can be written in the form $\frac{k}{6(x-4)}$ where $k \in \mathbb{N}$ and find the value of k.

Section 2J Algebraic Division

Key Points

- Division is the inverse (opposite) of multiplication.
- When dividing indices with the same variable (base), subtract the indices:

$$\frac{a^m}{a^n} = a^{m-n}$$

- $(3x)(2) = 6x$ so: $\frac{6x}{3x} = 2$ and $\frac{6x}{2} = 3x$

> Recall: Subtract the indices to divide when the bases are the same.

- $(x^2)(x^3) = x^5$ so: $\frac{x^5}{x^3} = x^2$ and $\frac{x^5}{x^2} = x^3$
- $(5xy)(3xy) = 15x^2y^2$ so: $\frac{15x^2y^2}{5xy} = 3xy$ and $\frac{15x^2y^2}{3xy} = 5xy$
- $(3x^2y)(6xy^2) = 18x^3y^3$ so: $\frac{18x^3y^3}{3x^2y} = 6xy^2$ and $\frac{18x^3y^3}{6xy^2} = 3x^2y$

Example 1

Use an array model to multiply $(x + 2)(x + 3)$.

Solution

Array model

Multiply $(x + 2)(x + 3)$ by completing the **array** below.

×	x	$+3$
x	x^2	$+3x$
$+2$	$+2x$	$+6$

... collect terms from the highlighted boxes: $x^2 + 2x + 3x + 6$

$(x + 2)(x + 3) = x^2 + 2x + 3x + 6$

Answer: $x^2 + 5x + 6$

Key Points

- Notice the position of the x^2 term and +6 in the array (the first and last terms).
- Notice how $5x$ comes from the array by adding the two like terms together (x terms).

Example 2

(i) Divide $x^2 + 5x + 6$ by $(x + 2)$, using the array model.

(ii) Divide $x^2 + 5x + 6$ by $(x + 2)$, by long division.

Solution

Note: this is Example 1 in reverse.

Method 1

(i) **Division using the array model**

Divide $x^2 + 5x + 6$ by $(x + 2)$, using the array model.

×	**?**	**?**
x	x^2	
+2		+6

To get the term x^2, x must be multiplied by x. So **?** = x.
To get the term +6, 2 must be multiplied by +3. So **?** = +3.
So the factor is $(x + 3)$.
To check that the factor we found is correct:

- Multiply the two factors in the array, filling in all boxes.
- Check that the answer is $x^2 + 5x + 6$.

Check:

×	x	+3
x	x^2	$+3x$
+2	$+2x$	+6

Collect terms from the highlighted boxes: $x^2 + 2x + 3x + 6$

$(x + 2)(x + 3) = x^2 + 2x + 3x + 6 = x^2 + 5x + 6$ ✓

Method 2

(ii) **Using long division**

Divide $x^2 + 5x + 6$ by $(x + 2)$, using long division.

$$
\begin{array}{r|l}
 & x + 3 \\
x + 2 & x^2 + 5x + 6 \\
 & -(x^2 + 2x) \\
 & \quad 3x + 6 \\
 & \quad -(3x + 6) \\
 & \qquad 0 \quad 0
\end{array}
$$

... dividing x into x^2 gives x
... multiply x by $(x + 2)$
... subtract and bring down +6
... multiply 3 by $(x + 2)$
... subtracting gives 0

So the factor is $(x + 3)$.

The following examples use Method 2: Long division

Example 3

Divide $15x^2 + 4x - 32$ by $3x - 4$.

Solution

$$\begin{array}{r l}
5x + 8 \quad & \text{... divide } 3x \text{ into } 15x^2 \Rightarrow 5x \text{ on top line (answer)} \\
3x - 4 \overline{)15x^2 + 4x - 32} & \text{... multiply } 5x \text{ by } (3x - 4) \Rightarrow 15x^2 - 20x \\
\underline{15x^2 - 20x} \qquad & \text{... subtract} \Rightarrow 24x\text{; bring down } -32 \\
24x - 32 & \text{... divide } 3x \text{ into } 24x \Rightarrow +8 \text{ on top line (answer)} \\
\underline{24x - 32} & \text{... multiply 8 by } (3x - 4) \Rightarrow 24x - 32 \\
0 & \text{... subtract} \Rightarrow 0
\end{array}$$

Answer = $5x + 8$

Example 4

Divide $x^3 - x^2 - 11x + 15$ by $x - 3$.

Solution

$$\begin{array}{r l}
x^2 + 2x - 5 \quad & \\
x - 3 \overline{)x^3 - x^2 - 11x + 15} & \text{... divide } x \text{ into } x^3 \Rightarrow x^2 \text{ on top line (answer)} \\
\underline{x^3 - 3x^2} \qquad\qquad & \text{... multiply } x^2 \text{ by } (x - 3) \Rightarrow x^3 - 3x^2 \\
2x^2 - 11x \qquad & \text{... subtract} \Rightarrow 2x^2\text{; bring down } -11x \\
\underline{2x^2 - 6x} \qquad & \text{... divide } x \text{ into } 2x^2 \Rightarrow +2x \text{ on top line (answer)} \\
-5x + 15 & \text{... multiply } 2x \text{ by } (x - 3) \Rightarrow 2x^2 - 6x \\
\underline{-5x + 15} & \text{... subtract} \Rightarrow -5x\text{; bring down } +15 \\
0 & \text{... repeat these 3 steps once more}
\end{array}$$

Answer = $x^2 + 2x - 5$

Example 5

Divide $6x^3 - 15x + 9$ by $3x - 3$.

Solution

There is no x^2 term in the numerator, so we write the numerator as $6x^3 + 0x^2 - 15x + 9$.

$$\begin{array}{r l}
2x^2 + 2x - 3 \quad & \\
3x - 3 \overline{)6x^3 + 0x^2 - 15x + 9} & \text{... divide } 3x \text{ into } 6x^3 \Rightarrow 2x^2 \text{ on top line (answer)} \\
\underline{6x^3 - 6x^2} \qquad\qquad & \text{... multiply } 2x^2 \text{ by } (3x - 3) \Rightarrow 6x^3 - 6x^2 \\
6x^2 - 15x \qquad & \text{... subtract} \Rightarrow 6x^2\text{; bring down } -15x \\
\underline{6x^2 - 6x} \qquad & \text{... divide } 3x \text{ into } 6x^2 \Rightarrow +2x \text{ on top line (answer)} \\
-9x + 9 & \text{... multiply } 2x \text{ by } (3x - 3) \Rightarrow 6x^2 - 6x \\
\underline{-9x + 9} & \text{... subtract} \Rightarrow -9x\text{; bring down } +9 \\
0 & \text{... repeat these 3 steps once more}
\end{array}$$

Answer = $2x^2 + 2x - 3$

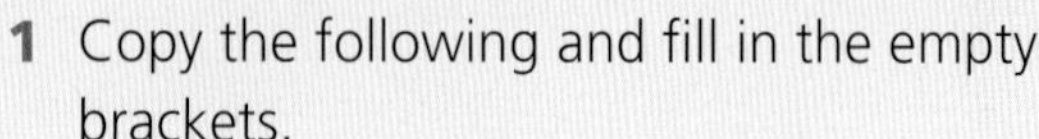

Activity 2.11

1 Copy the following and fill in the empty brackets.

(i) $(3x^2)(\quad) = 12x^4$

(ii) $\dfrac{16x^2}{(\quad)} = 4x$

(iii) $\dfrac{25x^2}{5x} = (\quad)$

(iv) $(5x^2)(2x^3) = (\quad)$

(v) $(\quad)(3x) = 12xy$

(vi) $\dfrac{20xy}{4x} = (\quad)$

(vii) $\dfrac{2a}{a} = (\quad)$

(viii) $\dfrac{4ab}{(\quad)} = 2b$

(ix) $\dfrac{8xyz}{4xy} = (\quad)$

(x) $\dfrac{25m^2n}{5mn} = (\quad)$

(xi) $\dfrac{20a^2b^2}{4ab} = (\quad)$

(xii) $\dfrac{5ab}{ab} = (\quad)$

2 Simplify each of the following algebraic fractions:

(i) $\dfrac{8x^2}{4}$

(ii) $\dfrac{24y^3}{3}$

(iii) $\dfrac{27x^2}{9}$

(iv) $\dfrac{18a^2}{3}$

(v) $\dfrac{12x^2}{4x}$

(vi) $\dfrac{20x^3}{4x^2}$

(vii) $\dfrac{10x^2y}{5y}$

(viii) $\dfrac{16x^3}{8x^2}$

(ix) $\dfrac{25x^2y^3}{5xy}$

(x) $\dfrac{16x^2y^3z^2}{8xy^2z}$

3 (i) Divide $x^2 + x - 2$ by $(x + 2)$.

×	?	?
x	x^2	
+2		−2

(ii) Divide $2a^2 + 9a - 5$ by $(2a - 1)$.

×	?	?
$2a$	$2a^2$	
−1		−5

(iii) Divide $3x^2 + 5x - 12$ by $(x + 3)$.

×	?	?
x	$3x^2$	
+3		−12

4 The area of a rectangular field is $(x^2 - 17x + 30)$ square metres.

The length of the field is $(x - 2)$ m.

Find the width of the field in metres.

$(x - 2)$ m

Area of the field = $(x^2 - 17x + 30)$ m^2

(Width) m

5 $(x + 3)$ is one factor of $3x^2 + 11x + 6$.

(i) Explain how division will allow you to get the other factor.

(ii) Divide $3x^2 + 11x + 6$ by $(x + 3)$ to get the other factor.

6 One factor of $2x^2 + 3x - 5$ is $(x - 1)$. Use division to find the other factor.

7 One factor of $3x^2 + 7x - 20$ is $(x + 4)$. Use division to find the other factor.

8 Divide

(i) $x^2 - x - 6$ by $(x - 3)$

(ii) $6a^2 + a - 2$ by $(2a - 1)$

(iii) $3x^2 - 17x - 28$ by $(x - 7)$

(iv) $15p^2 - 7p - 4$ by $(5p - 4)$

(v) $6x^2 - 11x - 10$ by $(2x - 5)$

(vi) $x^2 - 64$ by $(x - 8)$

(vii) $12x^2 + 7xy - 10y^2$ by $(3x - 2y)$

(viii) $3 - 10x - 8x^2$ by $(1 - 4x)$

9 Divide $x^3 - 2x^2 - 24x - 27$ by $(x + 3)$.

10 Divide $2x^3 - 9x^2 - 10x + 25$ by $(x - 5)$.

11 Divide $a^3 - 6a^2 - 12a + 17$ by $(a - 1)$.

12 One factor of $6a^3 + 5a^2 - 25a - 28$ is $(3a + 4)$. Find the other factor.

13 Simplify by division $\dfrac{4p^3 - 4p^2 - 7p - 20}{2p - 5}$.

14 Divide $6k^3 + 7k^2 - 18k + 5$ by $(2k + 5)$.

15 One factor of $2x^3 - 7x^2 + 4x + 3$ is $(2x - 3)$. Find the other factor.

16 The length of one side of a rectangle is $x + 12$. The area of the rectangle is $x^2 + 16x + 48$. Find an expression in x for the other side.

$x + 12$

? $x^2 + 16x + 48$

17 Simplify by division $\frac{3k^3 - 4k - 16}{k - 2}$.

18 $6x^3 - 17x^2 + 2x + 15 = (2x - 3)(ax^2 + bx + c)$ for all values of x.

Find the values of a, b and c.

19 (i) Simplify by division $\frac{x^3 - 7x^2 + 12x}{x - 4}$.

(ii) Use factors to check your answer to part (i).

20 Divide $x^3 - 8$ by $(x - 2)$.

21 Divide $3 - 8x + 3x^2 + 2x^3$ by $(1 - x)$.

Revision Activity 2

1 Factorise fully

(a) $20xy - 4x^2$

(b) $5x^2 - 9x - 2$

(c) $6x^2 - 24y^2$

2 Find the value of $x^2 - 2xy + 3$ when $x = \frac{1}{2}$ and $y = \frac{2}{3}$.

3 Multiply out and simplify $(3x - 4)(2x^2 + 5x - 2)$.

4 (a) Factorise $x^2 - ab - bx + ax$.

(b) Simplify $(4x - 2a)(2x + a) - (3y + a)(6y - 2a)$ and fully factorise the simplified expression.

5 (a) Multiply out $(5x - 2)(3x^2 + x - 6)$.

(b) Evaluate your answer to part (a) when $x = -1$.

6 Factorise

(a) $9x^2 - 15x$

(b) $9x^2 - 24x + 15$

(c) $3y - 3x - 4xy + 4x^2$

7 Express in its simplest form $\frac{5}{x - 3} - \frac{3}{x - 2}$.

8 Simplify $\frac{2p^2 + 4p - 30}{p - 3}$.

9 Express as a single fraction $\frac{x + 7}{5} + \frac{3 - x}{4}$.

10 Find the value of each expression when $a = -1$, $b = -4$ and $c = 5$.

(a) $\frac{a^2}{bc}$

(b) $\frac{a^2 - b}{c + 3}$

(c) $\frac{a + c}{4bc}$

(d) $\frac{a + b^3}{b^3 + c}$

Exam-style Questions

1 (a) Express in its simplest form

$$\frac{5-x}{5} + \frac{x-4}{4}$$

(b) Divide $2x^3 + x^2 - 13x + 6$ by $(x + 3)$.

JCHL 2013 Paper 1

2 Factorise fully each of the following expressions.

(a) $5x^3 - 10x^2$ (b) $4x^2 - 81y^2$ (c) $a^2 - ab + 3a - 3b$

JCHL 2012 Paper 1

KEY WORDS AND PHRASES

- **Algebra**
- **Variable**
- **Factor**
- **Equivalent expressions**
- **Indices**
- **Term**
- **Coefficient**
- **Constant**
- **Expression**
- **Division**
- **Distributive Law**
- **Substitution**
- **Long division**
- **Factors**
- **Factorise**
- **Common factor**
- **Quadratic expression**
- **Linear expression**
- **Difference of two squares**
- **Algebraic fractions**

Chapter Summary 2

- $5(3x - 2y) = 15x - 10y$ by the Distributive Law.
- $(x + y)^2 = x^2 + 2xy + y^2$
- Factors
  - Type 1: take out the HCF from each term, e.g. $5x^2y^3 - 10x^3y^2 = 5x^2y^2(y - 2x)$
  - Type 2: group to get a common factor, e.g. $ax + by + cx + dy = a(x + y) + b(x + y) = (x + y)(a + b)$
  - Type 3: quadratic trinomials, e.g. $x^2 - x - 6 = (x - 3)(x + 2)$
  - Type 4: difference of two squares, e.g. $9x^2 - 16y^2 = (3x)^2 - (4y)^2 = (3x + 4y)(3x - 4y)$
- Express two algebraic fractions as one fraction.
- Divide expressions (long division).

Financial Maths

Chapter 3

Learning Intentions

In this chapter, you will learn about:

- Currency exchange
- Percentage profit and loss
- Mark-up and margin
- Value Added Tax
- Discounts
- Value-for-money calculations and judgements
- Household bills and meter readings
- Income tax and net pay
- Compound interest

LO: U.5, U.6, N.2(c), N.3(b)

Section 3A Currency Exchange

There are many occasions when you may need to change one kind of currency into another, e.g. when travelling abroad or buying products online.

Throughout Europe, the most common currency in use is the euro (€). Other countries have their own currencies, such as the British pound (£), the US dollar ($) and the South African rand (R).

At most financial institutions such as banks, post offices and the Bureau de Change, we can exchange one currency for another. The currency exchange rates change daily. When currency is being exchanged, the customer is often charged a **commission**, which is is a percentage charge on the amount converted and is paid to the financial institution for the service provided.

Example 1

Before going on holiday to Japan and Australia, Frank changed €1000 to Japanese yen (¥) and €2500 to Australian dollars (A$).

The exchange rates were €1 = ¥1.24 and €1 = A$1.29.

(i) How many yen did Frank get?

(ii) How many Australian dollars did he get?

Solution

(i) Exchange rate: €1 = ¥1.24

⇒ €1000 = ¥(1.24 × 1000)

= ¥1240

(ii) Exchange rate: €1 = A$1.29

⇒ €2500 = A$(1.29 × 2500)

= A$3225

To convert from another currency to euro takes more steps. The '**unitary method**' is the best way to convert, as the following examples show.

Example 2

Peter travelled to England for the weekend and took £300 spending money with him. If the exchange rate was €1 = £0.80, what was the equivalent amount in euro?

Solution

Exchange rate: €1 = £0.80

$\Rightarrow € \frac{1}{0.80} = £1$ ... unitary method (find the value of £1)

$\Rightarrow € \frac{300}{0.80} = £300$ ... multiply both sides by 300

$= €375$

Peter changed €375.

Example 3

Mary took $2000 to the USA on holiday. The exchange rate was €1 = $1.33. How much did this cost Mary in euro?

Solution

Exchange rate: €1 = $1.33

$\Rightarrow € \frac{1}{1.33} = \$1$ ... unitary method (find the value of $1)

$\Rightarrow € \frac{2000}{1.33} = \$2000$ ... multiply both sides by 2000

To the nearest cent, it cost Mary €1503.76 to buy $2000.

Activity 3.1

Give all answers correct to the nearest cent, i.e. to two decimal places.

1 On a given day, the exchange rate between the euro and sterling is €1 = £0.86.

Calculate:

(i) the value of €250 in sterling

(ii) the value of £445 in euro.

2 A breadmaker costs $75 to buy online. The exchange rate is €1 = $1.25.

(i) Calculate the cost in euro.

(ii) If the postage charge is €10.20, calculate the postage cost in $.

3 A family went on holiday to Sweden. They exchanged €2500 for Swedish kronor. The exchange rate was €1 = 9.10 kronor.

(i) How many kronor did the family take on holiday?

(ii) They spent 19,565 kronor while in Sweden and changed the remainder back into euro at the airport. How many euro did they receive?

4 On returning from a holiday to Canada, Tim changes $200 into euro at the airport Bureau de Change. The exchange rate was €1 = $1.28. How many euro did Tim get?

5 Ciara orders a special Manga book from a Japanese publisher's website. The cost of the book is ¥2500 and overseas postage is ¥1000.

(i) How much does the book plus postage cost in euro if the exchange rate is €1 = ¥124.8?

(ii) Ciara's credit card provider charges 1.5% commission on foreign currency transactions.

How much is the commission?

6 A shop imports goods from China. They spend €25,000 and get 208,500 Chinese yuan worth of goods. What is the exchange rate of euro to Chinese yuan?

7 A toy shop imports goods from different countries. Using the table below, answer the following questions.

(i) What is the total cost of 100 action figures and 500 action figure accessory packs in euro?

(ii) What is the cost of 200 miniature toy cars in euro?

(iii) The shop places an order for the following items:

- 20 action figures and an accessory pack for each one
- 500 miniature toy cars
- 50 model planes.

What is the total cost of this order in euro?

Item	Country of origin	Cost per item	Exchange rate
Action figure	USA	\$9.17	€1 = \$1.31
Action figure accessory pack	USA	\$6.55	€1 = \$1.31
Miniature toy cars	England	£2.40	€1 = £0.86
Model plane	France	€1.25	

8 A couple book a honeymoon to South Africa. Their costs are:

- Flights: €2300
- Hotel: 15,903 South African rand
- Spending money: 20,520 South African rand.

(i) What is the total cost of the holiday in euro, based on the exchange rate €1 = 11.64 rand?

(ii) The couple spend an extra €300 to upgrade their hotel room. What is the new cost of the hotel in rand?

(iii) The couple have 4084 rand at the end of their honeymoon and exchange it for euro in the airport's Bureau de Change, at an exchange rate of €1 = 10.21 rand.

How many euro will they get?

9 Livia wants to buy a pair of runners. She can buy them online from a shop in Wales for £48.65. The currency conversion rate is €1 = £0.87.

(i) Convert £48.65 to euro. Give your answer to the nearest cent.

(ii) The same runners are for sale in the local sports shop for €62. Livia has a voucher for 15% off anything she buys in this shop.

How much will the runners cost Livia if she uses this voucher?

10 Linda has £300 and wishes to convert this money to US dollars ($).

The exchange rates are shown below:

€1 = £0.91

€1 = $1.14

Work out how many US dollars ($) Linda got for her £300.

Give your answer correct to the nearest cent.

Section 3B Percentage Profit and Loss

Knowing whether a business makes a profit or loss is very important for the long-term success of any business.

If the **cost price** is less than the **selling price**, then there is a **profit**:

Profit = Selling price – Cost price = positive amount

If the cost price is more than the selling price, then there is a **loss**:

Loss = Selling price – Cost price = negative amount

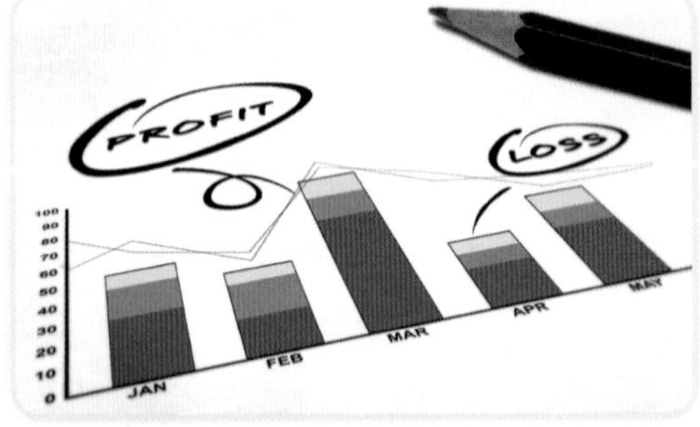

Profit or loss can be expressed as a percentage of the cost price.
The **percentage profit or loss** formulae are:

$$\%\text{ profit} = \frac{\text{profit amount}}{\text{cost price}} \times 100\%$$

$$\%\text{ loss} = \frac{\text{loss amount}}{\text{cost price}} \times 100\%$$

Example 1

A house was bought for €213,200 and sold for €260,000 seven years later. Find the percentage profit (as a percentage of the cost price).

Solution

Profit = €260,000 – €213,200 = €46,800

$$\%\text{ profit} = \frac{46\,800}{260\,000} \times 100\% = 18\%$$

The seller made a profit of 18%.

Example 2

A bicycle was bought for €425 and later sold at a profit of 15% of the cost price. Find the selling price.

Solution

The cost price (the **first** transaction) is **always 100%**.

- Work out what percentage the bicycle is now worth.

  The bicycle is now worth 100% + 15%, i.e. 115% of the cost price.

- Calculate 1% of the original cost.

$$100\% = €425$$

$$1\% = \frac{€425}{100}$$

$$= €4.25$$

$$115\% = €4.25 \times 115 = €488.75$$

The bicycle was sold for €488.75.

Example 3

A car is sold for €3525 at a loss of 25% of the cost price. What was the original price of the car?

Solution

The cost price (the **first** transaction) is **always 100%**.

The car was sold for 75% of the cost price.

$$75\% = €3525$$

$$1\% = \frac{€3525}{75}$$ ... divide both sides by 75

$$100\% = \frac{€3525}{75} \times 100$$ ... multiply both sides by 100

$$= €4700$$

The original price of the car was €4700.

Activity 3.2

Give all answers correct to the nearest cent.

1 The table shows the cost price and selling price of various second-hand cars in a garage. Calculate the percentage profit/loss in each case as a percentage of the cost price.

Car	Cost price	Selling price
A	€1450	€1508
B	€6700	€7169
C	€11,120	€10,008
D	€13,200	€12,276
E	€18,560	€21,344

2 Find the **selling price** of each of the following items based on the cost price and the percentage profit or loss in each case.

Cost price of each item	% profit or loss (as a percentage of the cost price)
Waffle iron: €36	20% profit
TV: €160	35% profit
Oven: €450	12% loss
Coffee table: €210	5% loss
Suite of furniture: €1125	15% profit
Bookcase: €360	8% loss

3 Grace bought two tickets for a music concert at a cost of €60 each. She then discovered that she was unable to attend.

(i) She sold one of the tickets to her brother for €48.
What percentage loss was this (as a percentage of the cost price)?

(ii) She sold the other ticket at a profit of 15%. What was the selling price of this ticket?

(iii) Write down the cost price and the selling price of the two tickets combined. What percentage profit or loss (as a percentage of the original cost) did Grace make overall?

4 Alan sells a second-hand bike for €150 at a loss of 25% of the cost price.

(i) If Alan's cost price is 100%, what percentage represents his selling price?

(ii) What price did Alan pay for the bike?

5 Pádraig bought a laptop. He sold it a year later for €360 at a loss of 40% of the cost price.

How much did Pádraig pay for the laptop originally?

6 An electrical shop buys the following products and sells them all at 8% profit (as a percentage of the cost price).

(i) Find the cost price of each item.

(a) washing machine: €216

(b) oven: €334.80

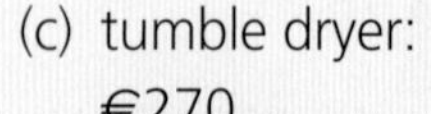
(c) tumble dryer: €270

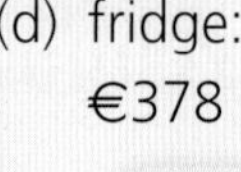
(d) fridge: €378

(ii) One weekend, the shop sold:

- 13 washing machines
- 7 tumble dryers
- 9 ovens
- 3 fridges

How much profit did the shop make?

7 A pet shop sells a variety of dog kennels at the following prices.

Kennel size	Selling price (€)	% profit (as a percentage of the cost price)
Small	81	20%
Medium	122	22%
Large	150	25%

(i) What is the cost price of each dog kennel?

(ii) The pet shop has a sale and the price of a particular kennel is reduced from €65 to €42.25. What is the percentage reduction offered in the sale?

8 Find the **cost price** of each of the following items based on the selling price and the percentage profit or loss made in each case.

Item	Selling price (€)	% profit or loss (as a percentage of the cost)
Leather Jacket	€132	10% profit
Skirt	€41.04	8% profit
Blouse	€27.26	6% loss
Shoes	€58.80	2% loss
Jeans	€35.65	15% profit

Mark-up and Margin

In business situations, we generally wish to make a profit on all the products we sell. However, in some situations, a business may record a loss on product(s).

The following situations can affect the profit made by a business:

- 'Sales' when products are marked down in price
- Discounts for employees
- A 'loss leader', where a company makes a decision to sell a product at a loss to generate sales for other products
- The launch of a new product
- Inventory shrinkage due to water or fire damage
- Selling an older version of a product, when a new product line is launched.

Key Points

We can use **mark-up** or **margin** to analyse a company's ability to make a profit or not.

- **Mark-up**
  Mark-up is the profit as a percentage (%) of the **cost price**.

$$\text{Mark-up} = \frac{\text{Profit}}{\text{Cost price}} \times 100\%$$

- **Margin**
  Margin is the profit as a percentage (%) of the **selling price**.

$$\text{Margin} = \frac{\text{Profit}}{\text{Selling price}} \times 100\%$$

Example 4

Caroline imports handheld tied flowers at a cost of €25 per bunch. She sells the flowers for €40 per bunch.

(i) Calculate the profit Caroline makes on each bunch of flowers.
(ii) Calculate the mark-up.
(iii) Calculate the margin.
(iv) What do you notice about the value of the margin compared with the mark-up?
Can you explain why this is the case?

Solution

(i) Cost price = €25 and
Selling price = €40
Profit = €40 – €25
= €15

(ii) $$\text{Mark-up} = \frac{\text{Profit}}{\text{Cost price}} \times 100\%$$
$$= \frac{15}{25} \times 100\%$$
$$= 60\%$$

(iii) $$\text{Margin} = \frac{\text{Profit}}{\text{Selling price}} \times 100\%$$
$$= \frac{15}{40} \times 100\%$$
$$= 37.5\%$$

(iv) The mark-up is greater than the margin because a profit was made.

As a result

$$\frac{\text{Profit}}{\text{Cost price}} > \frac{\text{Profit}}{\text{Selling price}}$$

In this case, the ratios are:

$$\frac{15}{25} > \frac{15}{40} \Rightarrow \frac{3}{5} > \frac{3}{8}$$

Example 5

A retailer sells a notebook for €4.50 with a profit margin of $33\frac{1}{3}\%$. Find:

(i) the profit made selling the notebook

(ii) the cost price of the notebook.

Solution

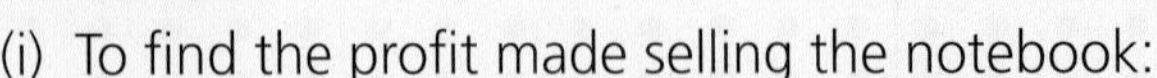

(i) To find the profit made selling the notebook:

- Write down all the information you know:

  Selling price = €4.50

  Margin = $33\frac{1}{3}\%$

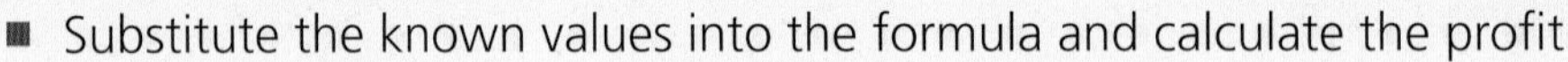

- Substitute the known values into the formula and calculate the profit.

$$\text{Margin} = 33\frac{1}{3}\% = \frac{1}{3} = \frac{\text{Profit}}{\text{Selling price}}$$

$$\Rightarrow \frac{1}{3} = \frac{\text{Profit}}{4.50}$$

$$\Rightarrow 3 \times \text{Profit} = 4.50$$

$$\Rightarrow \text{Profit} = \frac{4.50}{3} = €1.50$$

The profit made on the notebook is €1.50.

(ii) Cost price = Selling price − Profit

= €4.50 − €1.50

= €3.00

Example 6

A hardware store buys wooden picnic tables at a cost price of €140 each.

Find the selling price of one table if it is sold with:

(i) a 32% mark-up

(ii) a 32% margin, correct to the nearest cent.

Solution

(i) 32% mark-up

Cost price = €140

Mark-up = 32%

Let P = Profit

- Substitute the known values into the formula and calculate the Profit.

$$\text{Mark-up} = 32\% = 0.32 = \frac{\text{Profit}}{\text{Cost price}}$$

$$\Rightarrow 0.32 = \frac{P}{140}$$

$$\Rightarrow \quad P = 0.32 \times 140 = €44.80$$

- Calculate the selling price of one picnic table.

$\therefore$ Selling price = Cost price + Profit
= €140 + €44.80
= €184.80

(ii) 32% margin

Cost price = €140

Margin = 32%

Let P = Profit

- Substitute the known values into the formula and calculate the Profit.

$$\text{Margin} = 32\% = 0.32 = \frac{\text{Profit}}{\text{Selling price}}$$

$$0.32 = \frac{P}{P + 140}$$

$$\Rightarrow 0.32(P + 140) = P$$

$$\Rightarrow 0.32P + 44.80 = P$$

$$\Rightarrow 0.68P = 44.80$$

$$\Rightarrow P = \frac{44.80}{0.68} = €65.88$$

$\Rightarrow$ Selling price = 140 + €65.88
= €205.88

Example 7

A shop sells shirts at a mark-up of 25%.

Find the margin for these shirts.

Solution

$$\text{Mark-up} = 25\% = 0.25 = \frac{\text{Profit}}{\text{Cost price}} = \frac{P}{C}$$

$$\Rightarrow P = 0.25C$$

$$\Rightarrow \text{Selling price } (S) = C + P = 1.25C$$

$$\Rightarrow \text{Margin} = \frac{P}{S} = \frac{0.25C}{1.25C} = \frac{1}{5} = 20\%$$

Activity 3.3

1 In the case of each of (i), (ii) and (iii) in the table below, calculate the:

(a) profit

(b) mark-up

(c) margin.

Write all answers correct to two decimal places.

	Cost price (€)	Selling price (€)
(i)	10.00	12.50
(ii)	6.00	7.20
(iii)	45.00	63.00

2 Calculate the cost price of each of the following products to the nearest cent.

	Product	Selling price (€)	Margin
(i)	DVD	19.99	30%
(ii)	Computer game	49.99	35%
(iii)	Headphones	150.00	60%

3 Calculate the selling price of each of the following products to the nearest cent.

	Item	Cost price (€)	Mark-up
(i)	Shirt	12	15%
(ii)	Jumper	15	20%
(iii)	Jeans	49	30%

4 A coffee machine has a cost price of €444.31. The mark-up is 17.5%.

(i) Calculate the selling price of the coffee machine, to the nearest cent.

(ii) Calculate the margin for the coffee machine, correct to the nearest percentage.

(iii) What do you notice about the value of the mark-up compared with the margin? Can you explain why this is the case?

5 A 40″ television is sold for €899.99. The margin is 42%.

(i) Calculate the cost price of the television, to the nearest cent.

(ii) Calculate the mark-up, correct to two decimal places.

6 A tablet is sold for €609.53.

(i) If the margin is 59%, find the cost price of the tablet to the nearest cent.

(ii) Calculate the mark-up, correct to the nearest percentage.

7 Milk is bought from a farmer at 34 cent per litre. The milk is subsequently sold at an average price of €1.20 per litre. Calculate:

(i) the profit per litre

(ii) the mark-up

(iii) the margin.

(iv) What do you notice about the value of the mark-up compared with the margin? Can you explain why this is the case?

8 A new car is sold for €19,000.

(i) If the dealer's mark-up is 7%, calculate the cost price of the car from the manufacturer to the nearest euro.

(ii) Find the cost price of the car, if the mark-up is 15% to the nearest euro.

9 A meat factory buys beef from a farmer for €4 per kilogram. The beef is subsequently sold by a butcher at an average price of €15 per kilogram. Calculate:

(i) the profit per kg

(ii) the mark-up

(iii) the margin to the nearest %.

10 A jeweller buys gold rings at a cost price of €210 each. Calculate the selling price of a ring, correct to the nearest cent, if it is sold with a:

(i) 34% mark-up

(ii) 34% margin.

11 A toy store buys children's bikes for €76. Calculate the selling price of one bike if it is sold with a:

(i) 28% mark-up

(ii) 28% margin, correct to the nearest cent.

12 A boutique sells jackets at a mark-up of 20%. Find the margin for these jackets.

13 A shop sells televisions at a mark-up of 60%.

Find the margin for these televisions, correct to the nearest percent.

Section 3C Value Added Tax

Value **A**dded **T**ax is usually referred to as VAT, which is a sales tax that the government applies to the sale of most goods and services. VAT is expressed as a percentage and it is added to the selling cost of an item or service.

VAT is charged every time a product is sold.

- The term **VAT inclusive** means that the price quoted includes VAT.
- The term **VAT exclusive** means that the price quoted does not include VAT.

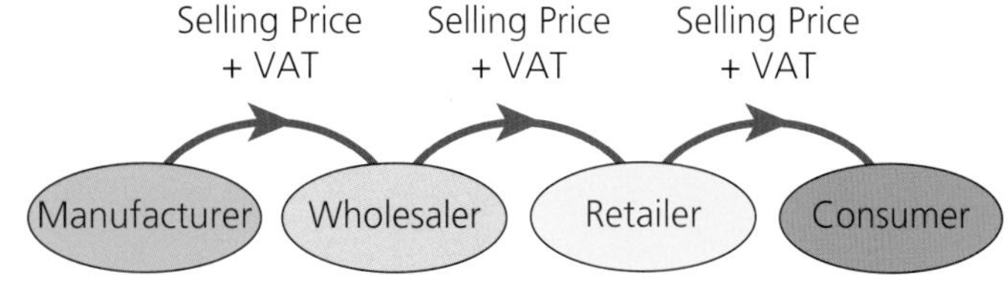

Example 1

Mary buys a new washing machine. The shop quotes the price of the washing machine as €400 + VAT. The VAT rate on the washing machine is 23%.

What price does Mary pay for the washing machine?

Solution

Calculate 23% of €400:

Let 100% = €400

Find 1% of the amount:

$1\% = \frac{€400}{100} = €4$

23% = €4 × 23 = €92 ... the VAT amount

Price paid = €400 + €92 = €492

Alternatively:

Selling price = original price + 23% VAT

= 100% + 23%

= 123% of the price quoted.

Using a Casio calculator, press:

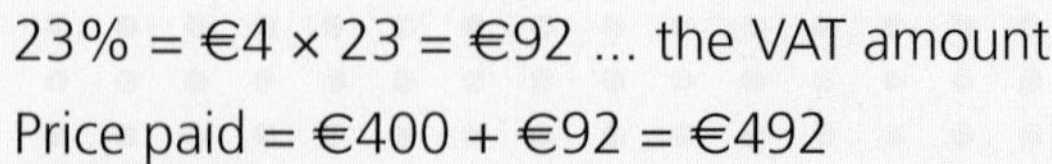

492 will appear on the screen, so the selling price for the washing machine is €492.

Example 2

Peter, a mechanic, charges €140 plus VAT for the work done on a customer's car. What amount is the customer billed including VAT at 9%?

Solution

Peter charges €140 for fixing the car: this is 100%.

If Peter includes 9% VAT, then the bill is represented by 109%.

We know: 100% = €140

$1\% = \frac{€140}{100} = €1.40$ ... divide both sides by 100

109% = €1.40 × 109

= €152.60

The customer is billed €152.60 including 9% VAT.

Example 3

Sophie buys a television at Christmas for €492 including VAT. The VAT rate paid on electrical goods is 23%. How much VAT did Sophie pay?

Solution

We know: price of television (100%) + 23% VAT = €492

123% = €492

$1\% = \frac{€492}{123} = €4$ ... divide both sides by 123

23% = €4 × 23 ... multiply both sides by 23

23% = €92

Sophie paid €92 in VAT.

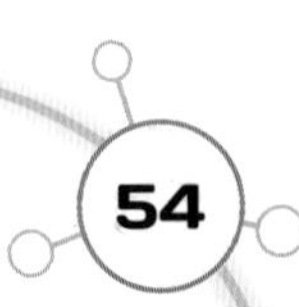

1 VAT is charged at 23% for each of the following items. Find the actual retail price (including VAT) for each item.

(i) Mobile phone: €109
(ii) PC: €345
(iii) TV: €288
(iv) Kettle: €25
(v) Juicer: €67

2 A bill for a meal came to €177.50 excluding VAT. What is the total bill for the meal if VAT is charged at 9%?

3 A shopkeeper buys 250 toasters at a cost of €2000 excluding VAT.

(i) If VAT is charged at 13.5%, find the VAT charged for each toaster.
(ii) What is the total cost of the 250 toasters, including VAT?
(iii) If the shopkeeper wants to make 10% profit on each toaster, how much should he sell each toaster for?

4 Sam bought a laptop for €516.60 including VAT at 23%.

(i) Find the original price of the laptop before VAT was added.
(ii) Find the VAT paid on the laptop.

5 A retailer (shop) buys a product from a wholesaler for €122 including VAT.

(i) If VAT is charged at 22%, calculate the amount of VAT paid by the retailer.

The retailer then sells the product to a customer for €180 including VAT.

(ii) Find the amount of VAT paid by the customer.

6 The following prices include VAT charged at 23%. Calculate the price of each item before VAT.

	Price (VAT inclusive)
(i)	€715.86
(ii)	€41.82
(iii)	€79.95
(iv)	€246.00
(v)	€105.78

7 The rate of VAT charged on food served in a restaurant is 9%. Copy and complete the table below.

Table number	Bill – excluding VAT	VAT amount	Bill – including VAT
1	€68	€6.12	
2		€12.78	€154.78
3		€16.74	
4		€10.89	
5		€23.85	

8 The cost of a dishwasher was €480 including €96 VAT. Calculate the VAT rate.

Section 3D Value for Money and Household Bills

A **discount** is a reduction in the selling price of an item or service. A discount can be given as a percentage of the selling price 50% OFF or as a flat amount €30 Discount.

To calculate the percentage discount, use the formula: % discount = $\left(\frac{\text{discount}}{\text{selling price}} = \times 100\%\right)$

Example 1

A sports store offers a 20% discount off all stock in a sale. Jimmy buys a pair of trainers which cost €80 before the sale. How much do the trainers cost now?

Solution

Let the original price be 100%.

As the discount is 20%, Jimmy must pay 80%.

We know 100% = €80 ... divide both sides by 100

$1\% = \frac{€80}{100} = €0.80$ ... unitary method

$80\% = €0.80 \times 80 = €64$ ... multiply both sides by 80

Jimmy pays €64 for the new trainers.

Alternatively:

Jimmy pays 80% of the original price.

80% of €80 = €80 × 0.8 = €64

Example 2

Ciarán buys Christmas presents in a toy store. The toy store is offering a cashback amount for purchases over €200. Ciarán spends €225 in the store and gets €20 back. Calculate the percentage discount that Ciarán gets.

Solution

Amount spent = €225

Discount = €20

$$\% \text{ discount} = \frac{\text{discount}}{\text{amount spent}} \times 100\%$$

$$= \frac{20}{225} \times 100\% = 8.89\%$$

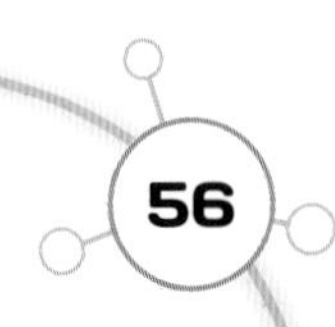

Value for Money

Most products are packed and sold in multiple units or weights. A common example of this is a soft drink, which can be purchased in various containers such as:

- a 330 ml aluminium can
- a 500 ml plastic bottle
- a 1 litre plastic bottle
- a 1.5 litre plastic bottle
- a 2 litre plastic bottle.

To decide which container gives us the best 'value for money', we need to **calculate the lowest common unit price** and compare these prices.

Example 3

Jennifer buys some orange juice for her party. In the shop she has three options:

Option A: A 500 ml plastic bottle costing €0.80

Option B: A 1.5 litre plastic bottle costing €2.05

Option C: A twin pack of 1.5 litre plastic bottles costing €3.

Based on the information given:

(i) Calculate the cost per 100 ml for each option.

(ii) Determine which option is the best 'value for money'.

Solution

Make sure all measurements are in the same unit, in this case, millilitres.

(i) **Option A**

We know: 500 ml = €0.80 (divide both sides by 5)

$$100\text{ ml} = \frac{€0.80}{5} = €0.16$$

Option B

We know: 1.5 litres = €2.10

1500 ml = €2.10 ... 1 litre = 1000 ml

$$100\text{ ml} = \frac{€2.10}{15} = €0.14 \quad \text{... divide both sides by 15}$$

Option C

We know: 2 × 1.5 litres = €3

3000 ml = €3

$$100\text{ ml} = \frac{€3}{30} = €0.10 \quad \text{... divide both sides by 30}$$

(ii) As Option C is the cheapest price per 100 ml, it is the best value.

Household Bills

All households have a range of bills for various products and services such as electricity, gas, oil, groceries, phones and insurance.

When we work with usage-based bills, we follow these steps:

- Calculate the amount of the service used.
- Calculate the total cost of the amount of the service used.
- Add any service or standard charge.
- Calculate the VAT and add to get the total bill amount.

Example 4

Calculate the values of A, B, C and D for the electricity bill below.

MyPower

Electricity Bill

Account B7846321

Charge Period: June to July

Invoice Date 08/08/2018

Meter Reading:

	Previous	Current	Units Used	Rate	Amount
Standard	A	54 071	1422	€0.17	B
Standing Charges/Fixed Charges					€22.00
Government Levy (Public Service Obligation)					€4.64
Total charges included in bill					C
VAT Applied to total charges				13.50%	€36.23
Total Due					D

Solution

Value A – The number of **Previous Standard Units** recorded from the meter.

$$\text{Number of Previous Standard Units} = \text{Current Units} - \text{Units used}$$
$$= 54\,071 - 1422$$
$$= 52\,649 \text{ units}$$

Value B – **Amount (€)** is the cost of the number of standard units used.

$$\text{Amount (€)} = \text{Units used} \times \text{Rate}$$
$$= 1422 \times €0.17$$
$$= €241.74$$

Value C – **Total charges** included in this bill:

$$\text{Amount B} + €22.00 + €4.64 = €268.38$$

Value D – **Total Due** is the total charge including VAT:

$$€268.38 + €36.23 = €304.61$$

Activity 3.5

1 Calculate the discounted amount for each item below:

	Selling price	% Discount
(i)	€875	10%
(ii)	€180	12%
(iii)	€230	5%
(iv)	€496	12.5%
(v)	€1500	25%

2 Calculate the percentage discount offered on each of the following items.

	Selling price (before discount)	Discount amount
(i)	€580	€46.40
(ii)	€248	€12.40
(iii)	€6800	€408
(iv)	€2750	€330
(v)	€69	€2.07

3 A bookshop gives an 8% discount on all school books. Calculate the discount given if the school books previously cost:

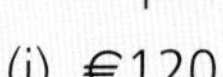

(i) €120 (ii) €85 (iii) €165 (iv) €38 (v) €65

4 A pizzeria offers a 12% discount to students if they buy the €15 meal deal.

(i) What is the cost of a student's meal deal with the discount applied?

On Thursday, the pizzeria sold 20 meal deals, of which 12 were sold to students.

(ii) What was the income of the pizzeria on Thursday?

5 A shop has the following special offers:

Offer	Product	Price
A	6 cans of soft drink	€4.20
B	9 cans of soft drink	€5.85
C	18 cans of soft drink	€9.00

(i) What is the cost per can for each offer?

(ii) Which offer gives the best 'value for money'?

(iii) What is the **percentage discount** for each offer, based on a selling price of €0.80 per can?

6 Susan decides to book a family holiday to Portugal. Two 'packages' appeal to her:

- Package A: 1-week stay in a hotel costing €371, plus 2 day trips costing €70 in total.
- Package B: 2-week stay in the same hotel costing €672, plus 4 similar day trips costing €95 in total.

(i) Calculate the cost per night for each package.

(ii) Calculate the cost of one day trip for each package.

(iii) Based on your calculations, which package offers the best 'value for money'?

7 In a fruit and vegetable shop, the following vegetables are on offer:

Bags of carrots:
1.5 kg for €1.80
or 4 kg for €4.40

Bags of potatoes:
2.5 kg for €3.50
or 6 kg for €8.16

(i) Calculate the price per kg of carrots for each offer.

(ii) Which bag of carrots offers the best 'value for money'?

(iii) Calculate the price per kg of potatoes for each offer.

(iv) Which bag of potatoes offers the best 'value for money'?

8 Dry cat food comes in a range of sizes:

(A) small bag: 375 g for €1.95

(B) medium bag: 950 g for €4.75

(C) large bag: 2 kg for €9.80.

(i) Find the price per 100 g for each bag.

(ii) Which size offers the best 'value for money'?

9 A fashion boutique has a sale on all stock. Nicola likes three different dresses:

- a pink dress with a price tag of €70 which has 30% off
- a purple dress with a price tag of €90 which has 40% off
- a blue dress with a price tag of €60 which has 50% off.

Which dress has the biggest discount (in euro) in the sale?

10 A popular breakfast cereal comes in two box sizes: Regular (360 g) and Large (900 g). A standard portion of cereal is 30 g.

(i) How many portions are there in each size of box?

(ii) A Regular box costs €0.96 and a Large box costs €2.25. Using the number of portions per box, or otherwise, find which size is better value.

Give all answers correct to the nearest cent.

11 Calculate the values of A, B, C and D for this mobile phone bill.

Mobile Phone Bill

MyComms

Account		A1234561
Period		Mar 2018
Invoice Date		04/04/2018
Usage:		
All Network Minutes Used:	358	
Less 180 Free Minutes	A	
Minutes to charge @ €0.24/min		€42.72
All Network Text Messages	176	
Less 150 free texts	B	
Texts to charge @ €0.08/text		C
Total Usage charge		€44.80
Standing charge		€26.00
Total charges		€70.80
VAT charged VAT rate = 23%		D
Total Due		€87.08

12 Calculate the values of A, B, C and D for this electricity bill.

MyPower

Electricity Bill | **Account** C6534214

Charge Period: August to September | **Invoice Date** 11/10/2018

Meter Reading:

	Previous	Current	Units Used	Rate	Amount
Standard	5698	6645	A	€0.17	B
Standing Charges/Fixed Charges					€22.00
Government Levy (Public Service Obligation)					€4.64
Total charges included in bill					C
VAT Applied to total charges				13.50%	D
Total Due					€212.96

Section 3E Income Tax

Everybody who has an income has to pay tax. This tax is used by the government to provide schools, hospitals, roads and many other services. The rate of tax varies from year to year and country to country.

- Income before tax is called **gross income** or **gross pay**.
- You do not pay tax on everything you earn. Each earner gets **tax credits** depending on the amount of allowable expenses they have. Tax credits are deducted from your tax bill.
- Income tax in Ireland is charged at two rates: **standard rate** and **higher rate.**
- To calculate the **take-home pay** (also called **net income/pay**), **we subtract the tax payable** (also called tax due) **from the gross income**.

Example 1

Pat's gross income is €28,000. He pays all his tax at the standard rate of 20% and has tax credits of €2500.
Find Pat's net pay for the year.

Solution

Gross tax = 20% of €28,000
= 0.2 × €28,000
= €5600

Tax payable = gross tax – tax credits
= €5600 – €2500
= €3100

Net pay/income = gross income – tax payable
= €28,000 – €3100
= €24,900

Standard Rate Cut-Off Point (SRCOP)

Two rates of income tax apply in Ireland:

- The standard rate which applies to the lower part of income up to a certain level
- The higher rate which applies to income above this level.

The Standard Rate Cut-Off Point (SRCOP) is the amount of income up to which a person pays tax at the standard rate.

The lower rate of tax is 20% and the higher rate is 40%. The standard rate cut-off point for a single person is €35,300 (2019 figures).

For example, a single person earning €45,000 will pay:

- 20% tax on the first €35,300; and
- 40% on the remainder, i.e. €45,000 – €35,300 = €9700.

Visually, this information can be represented as:

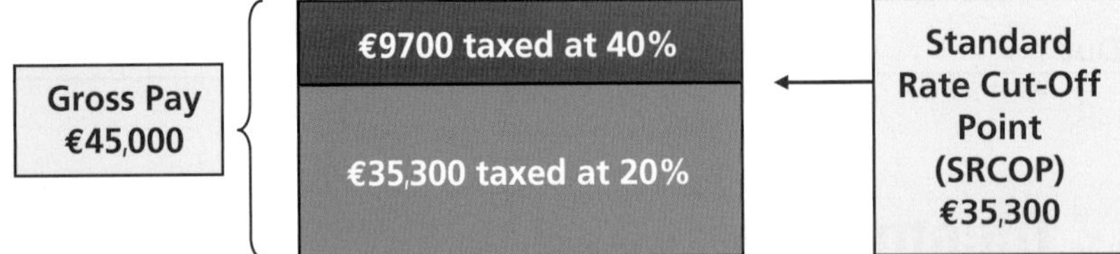

The example below shows how to calculate the net pay for a couple who earn more than the standard rate cut-off point.

Example 2

A couple earn a total of €87,000 per annum. The standard rate cut-off point is €65,600 and their tax credits total €3300.

(i) Calculate their gross tax for the year.
(ii) Calculate their tax payable for the year.
(iii) Calculate their net income for the year.

Solution

(i) The gross tax is calculated as shown below:

Tax rate	Amount charged at this rate	Gross tax due
Standard rate of tax @ 20%	€65,600	€65,600 × 20% = €13,120
Higher rate of tax @ 40% on the balance	Balance: €87,000 – €65,600 = €21,400	€21,400 × 40% = €8560
Gross tax due		€13,120 + €8560 = €21,680

(ii) Tax payable = gross tax – tax credits
= €21,680 – €3300 = €18,380

(ii) Net income/pay = gross pay – tax payable
= €87,000 – €18,380 = €68,620

Other Deductions

- **PRSI** stands for Pay Related Social Insurance. A PRSI contribution is paid by employers and employees (normally 4% for Class A1 workers) towards social welfare benefits, State old age pensions and a National Training Fund levy.
- **USC** stands for Universal Social Charge and replaced the health and income levies from 2011. These charges cover employees for various social welfare benefits and medical benefits. USC is charged at different rates.

Example 3

Peter earns €50,500. Peter pays PAYE, PRSI and USC statutory deductions on his gross pay.

(i) Find his PAYE/gross tax for the year, by completing the table below:

PAYE rate	Amount charged at this rate	PAYE due
Standard rate of tax @ 20%	€35,300	
Higher rate of tax @ 40% on the balance		
Total Gross tax		

(ii) Find the tax payable for the year, if his tax credits are €1650.

(iii) Find his PRSI for the year by completing the table below:

PRSI rate	Amount charged at this rate	PRSI due
4% on Gross Income over €18,304		

(iv) Find his USC for the year, by completing the table below:

USC rate	Amount charged at this rate	USC due
0.5% up to €12,012		
2% on the next €7862		
4.5% on the next €50,126		
8% on the balance		
Total USC due		

(v) Calculate the total deductions for the year.

(vi) Calculate Peter's net income for the year.

Solution

(i) PAYE/Gross Tax is charged at 20% for the first €35,300 earned and 40% on the balance.

PAYE rate	Amount charged at this rate	Tax due
Standard rate of tax @ 20%	€35,300	€35,300 × 20% = €7060
Higher rate of tax @ 40% on the balance	Balance: €50,500 – €35,300 = €15,200	€15,200 × 40% = €6080
Total Gross tax		**€13,140**

(ii) Tax payable = gross tax – tax credits = €13,140 – €1650 = €11,490

(iii) PRSI charges:

PRSI Rate	Amount charged at this rate	PRSI due
4% on gross income over €18,304	€50,500 – €18,304 = €32,196	€32,196 × 4% = €1287.84

Answer: PRSI for the year is €1287.84

(iv) USC charges:

USC Rate	Amount charged at this rate	USC due
0.5% up to €12,012	€12,012	€12,012 × 0.5% = €60.06
2% on the next €7862	€7862	€7862 × 2% = €157.24
4.5% on the next €50,126	€50,500 – (€12,012 + €7862) = €30,626	€30,626 × 4.5% = €1387.17
8% on the balance	€0	€0
Total USC due		**€1604.47**

Answer: USC for the year is €1604.47

(v) Total deductions = €11,490 + €1287.84 + €1604.47 = €14,382.31

(vi) Net income = €50,500 – €14,382.31 = €36,117.69

Example 4

Livia has a **gross** income of €60,000 for the year.

The standard rate cut-off point is €44,300.

The standard rate of income tax is 20% and the higher rate is 40%.

As a result of a pay rise, her **net** income for the year increases by €1800.

Find Livia's new **gross** income for the year.

Solution

Since Livia's gross income is above the standard rate cut-off point, all of her increase will be taxed at 40%.

$\Rightarrow$ €1800 = 60% of increase in gross income

$\Rightarrow$ 1% of increase in gross income = $\frac{1800}{60}$ = €30

$\Rightarrow$ 100% of increase in gross income = €30 × 100 = €3000

$\Rightarrow$ new gross income = €60,000 + €3000 = €63,000

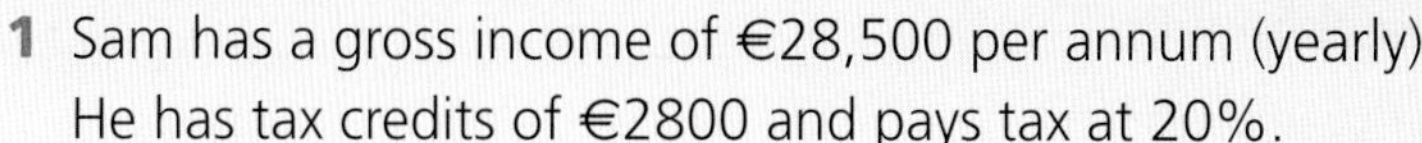

Activity 3.6

1 Sam has a gross income of €28,500 per annum (yearly).
He has tax credits of €2800 and pays tax at 20%.

(i) Calculate the tax payable by Sam in one year.

(ii) Calculate his annual net income.

2 Aoife has a gross income of €35,000. She has tax credits of €4100 and pays tax at 20%.

(i) Calculate her annual gross tax.

(ii) What is her annual take home pay?

Note: when dealing with money in this section, we always round answers to the nearest cent, i.e. two decimal places.

Use the following table to help answer the questions below, if necessary.

Tax rate	Amount charged at this rate	Gross tax due
Standard rate of tax @ 20%		
Higher rate of tax @ 40% on the balance		
Gross tax due		

3 A married couple with one income earn a total of €1450 per week. The standard rate cut-off point is €1262 and their tax credits total €63.46 per week.

(i) Calculate the gross tax per week.

(ii) Calculate the tax payable per week.

(iii) Calculate the net income per week.

(iv) Calculate the couple's net income for the year.

4 For each of the situations described in the table below:

(i) calculate the gross tax for the year

(ii) calculate the tax payable for the year

(iii) calculate the net income for the year.

Scenario	Income details
A	Niamh is a solicitor who earns a total of €93,000 per annum. She is the sole earner of a married couple. Her standard rate cut-off point is €44,300 and her tax credits total €3300.
B	A farmer earns a total of €47,000 per annum. He is the sole earner of a married couple. The standard rate cut-off point is €44,300 and his tax credits total €3300.
C	A couple have a combined income of €72,000. Their standard rate cut-off point is €70,600 and their tax credits total €3300.

5 For each of the situations described in the table below:

(i) calculate the gross tax per week/month
(ii) calculate the tax payable per week/month
(iii) calculate the net income per week/month.

Scenario	Income details
A	John's weekly wage is €570 and he has tax credits of €31.73. His standard rate cut-off point is €678.85 per week.
B	A carpenter earns a total of €3800 per month. The standard rate cut-off point is €3691.60 and his tax credits total €275 per month.
C	A couple have a combined income of €5990 per month and tax credits of €550. They have a standard rate cut-off point of €5883.30.

6 Siobhán has tax credits of €1650. She pays €7000 income tax. Her standard rate cut-off point is €35,300. The standard rate of tax is 20% and the higher rate is 40%.

(i) Calculate the total amount of her income charged at the higher rate of 40%. Give your answer to the nearest cent.
(ii) Calculate her gross income.

7 A woman pays income tax of €11,000 and her tax credits are €3300. She is the sole earner of a married couple. Her standard rate cut-off point is €44,300. The standard rate of tax is 20% and the higher rate is 40%.

(i) Calculate the total amount of her income charged at the higher rate of tax. Give your answer to the nearest cent.
(ii) Calculate her salary before any deductions.

8 Orla has a standard rate cut-off point of €35,300 and tax credits of €1650 for the year. She has a gross income of €38,650 for the year. The standard rate of income tax is 20% and the higher rate is 40%.

(i) What is Orla's net income for the year?
(ii) Orla's net income changes to €33,500. What is Orla's new gross income for the year?

9 Martin's gross income is €38,000 and his gross income tax amounts to €8692. The standard rate cut-off point is €35,300. The standard rate of tax is 20% and the higher rate is 40%. Martin's take-home pay is €30,958.

(i) What are Martin's tax credits for the year?

Martin gets an increase in gross pay such that his gross income tax amounts to €10,455.

(ii) Calculate Martin's new gross income.
(iii) What is Martin's new take-home pay for the year?

10 Kathy has a gross income of €75,000. The standard rate of tax is 20% and the higher rate is 40%. The SRCOP is €39,300 and she has a tax credit of €1650.

(i) What is Kathy's net tax for the year?
(ii) What is Kathy's take-home pay for the year?

Kathy's take-home pay increases to €57,404.

(iii) Calculate Kathy's new gross income.

Use the following tables as a guide in questions **11** to **13**.

PRSI rate	Amount charged at this rate	PRSI due
4% on gross income over €18,304		

USC rate	Amount charged at this rate	USC due
0.5% up to €12,012		
2% on the next €7862		
4.5% on the next €50,126		
8% on the balance		

11 Calculate how much (a) PRSI and (b) USC each of the following people pays per year.

(i) Susan is a part-time hairdresser who earns €18,000 per year.

(ii) Conor is an apprentice radiologist who earns €26,000 per year.

(iii) Mark is an engineer who earns €59,000 per year.

(iv) Clare is an accountant who earns €87,000 per year.

12 Peter earns €57,350. He pays PAYE, PRSI and USC statutory deductions on his gross pay. His pay is subject to a non-statutory deduction of €1350 per annum on private health insurance. PAYE is charged at standard 20% on his standard rate cut-off point of €39,300 and the remainder of his income is charged at 40%.

(i) Find his PAYE/gross tax for the year.

(ii) Find the tax payable for the year, if his tax credits are €1650.

(iii) Find his PRSI for the year, by copying and completing the PRSI table given above.

(iv) Find his USC for the year, by copying and completing the USC table given above.

(v) Calculate the total deductions for the year.

(vi) Calculate Peter's net income for the year.

13 Luke has a **gross** income of €50,000 for the year.
The standard rate cut-off point is €44,300.
The standard rate of income tax is 20% and the higher rate is 40%.
As a result of a pay rise, Luke's **net** income for the year increases by €1500.
Find Luke's new **gross** income for the year.

Section 3F Compound Interest

If you save money in a bank, credit union or post office, your money will earn interest. Interest is the money added to an amount invested or borrowed over a certain period of time.

Compound interest on a sum invested is calculated so that, as time goes on, you get **interest on the interest** as well as on the original sum invested. The sum invested or borrowed is known as the **principal**.

Financial Maths

Example 1

David invests €1000 for two years. The compound interest rate is 8% per annum.

(i) Calculate how much David will have in the bank after 2 years.

(ii) What is the total amount of interest earned?

Solution

(i) Investment at the start of year 1 = €1000

Final amount at end of year 1 = €1000 × 1.08 = €1080

Investment at the start of year 2 = €1080

Final amount at end of year 2 = €1080 × 1.08 = €1166.40

Amount at end of 2 years = €1166.40

(ii) Interest earned = final amount – principal invested

= €1166.40 – €1000

= €166.40

In Example 1, we multiplied by 1.08 (108%) each year for the 2 years. So we could very quickly get the same result by multiplying €1000 by $(1.08)^2$. This would be written as $1000(1.08)^2$ = €1164.40.

This gives us a formula for compound interest:

Compound interest formula:

$F = P(1 + i)^t$

where F = final amount

P = principal

i = the annual interest rate (**as a decimal**)

t = time in years

(This formula is in the *Formulae and tables* booklet, page 30.)

Example 2

Michelle invested €3000 at a bank offering 3.5% interest, compounded annually. Find the amount of her investment after 3 years.

Solution

Using the formula:

$F = P(1 + i)^t$

$= 3000(1.035)^3$ … notice that 3.5% = 0.035 as a decimal

= €3326.15 to the nearest cent

Annual Percentage Rate (APR) and Annual Equivalent Rate (AER)

When dealing with **loan and credit agreement** calculations, we refer to the **Annual Percentage Rate (APR)**. This is the interest rate paid **to** the financial institution.

When dealing with **savings and investments**, we refer to the **Annual Equivalent Rate (AER)**. This is the interest rate paid **by** the financial institution.

Example 3

Maeve gets a loan of €9000 to buy a car. The interest rate available on this loan is 10.9% APR. She has arranged to pay back the loan as follows.

- Pay €2000 at end of year 1.
- Pay another €2000 at end of year 2.
- Pay the remainder at end of the 3rd year.

What amount will Maeve have to pay at the end of the 3rd year?

Solution

- Amount owed at end of year 1: €9000 × 1.109 = €9981
- Loan repayment at end of year 1: = €2000
- Total loan owed at start of 2nd year: €9981 – €2000 = €7981
- Amount owed at end of year 2: €7981 × 1.109 = €8850.93
- Loan repayment at end of year 2: = €2000
- Total loan owed at start of 3rd year: €8850.93 – €2000 = €6850.93
- Amount owed at end of year 3: €6850.93 × 1.109 = €7597.68

Example 4

Emily would like to invest €10,000 for two years. A bank is offering a rate of 2% for the first year and a higher rate for the second year if the money is retained in the account. Tax of 35% will be deducted each year from the interest earned.

(i) How much will the investment be worth at the end of one year after tax has been deducted?

(ii) Emily calculates that after tax has been deducted, her investment will be worth €10,294.61 at the end of the second year. Calculate the rate of interest for the second year.

Solution

(i)

Principal for 1st Year		€10,000
Interest for 1st Year @2%	+	€200
Less tax on interest @35%	–	€70
Amount after one year		€10,130

(ii) Amount after 2 years = €10,294.61

$\Rightarrow$ Interest for second year after tax = €10,294.61 – €10,130 = €164.61

$\Rightarrow$ €164.61 = 65% of the 2nd year interest before tax

$\Rightarrow €\frac{164.61}{65} = 1\%$

$\Rightarrow €\frac{164.61}{65} \times 100 = 100\%$ of the 2nd year interest before tax = €253.25

$\Rightarrow$ The interest rate for 2nd year $= \frac{253.25}{10\,130} \times 100 = 2.5\%$

Answer = 2.5%

Activity 3.7

1 Jimmy invested €15,000 for 3 years at a bank offering 4% interest, compounded annually. What is the total value of his investment after 3 years?

2 Kate borrows €2500 from a bank at 11% compound interest per year. She pays it off in a lump sum after 2 years. How much will she have to pay in total?

3 A company borrows €80,000 at 9% compound interest per annum. The loan is to be repaid in one instalment after 3 years. What is the cost of the loan to the nearest euro?

4 The table below details six different investments over a three-year period. Calculate the missing values in the table (rounding to the nearest cent).

	Investment amount	Interest rate	Value of investment after 3 years (€)	Interest earned after 3 years (€)
(i)	€6,000	4%		
(ii)	€8,400	6%		
(iii)	€20,000	8%		
(iv)	€45,000	7.5%		
(v)	€90,000	10%		
(vi)	€200,000	9%		

5 Calculate the final amount outstanding for each of the following loans if no repayments have been made.

	Principal amount	Interest rate	Time (years)
(i)	€10,100	5%	2
(ii)	€25,000	4%	3
(iii)	€20,000	8%	3
(iv)	€5,000	3%	2
(v)	€300	10%	3
(vi)	€2,000,000	9%	2

6 Joseph borrows €32,000 at 11% annual compound interest. He repays €8000 at the end of each of the first two years. How much does Joseph owe at the end of the third year?

7 Paul invested €1500 in a savings account that offers 3% compound interest per annum.

(i) How much will Paul have in his account at the end of the first year?

(ii) Calculate the compound interest earned over 3 years if Paul leaves his money in the account. (Round your answer to the nearest euro.)

(iii) If Paul withdrew €600 from his savings account at the end of the first year, how much money will Paul have in the account at the end of the third year?

8 Kevin, a band manager, gets a loan of €2000 to buy musical instruments. The interest rate available on this loan is 10%. Kevin has two payment options:

- Option A: Pay the full amount owed at the end of the second year.
- Option B: Pay €1000 at the end of year 1 and the remaining amount at the end of the year 2.

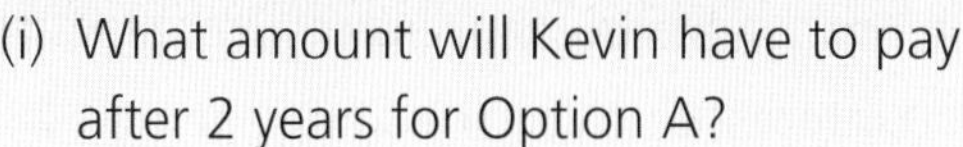

(i) What amount will Kevin have to pay after 2 years for Option A?

(ii) What is the amount that Kevin will have to pay in full for Option B?

(iii) Calculate the total amount of interest paid for Option A.

(iv) Calculate the total amount of interest paid for Option B.

(v) Which option represents the best 'value for money'?

9 €4000 was invested for 2 years at $r\%$ compound interest. A tax of 20% was deducted each year from the interest gained. At the end of the first year, the investment amounted to €4135, after tax was deducted.

(i) Calculate the rate of interest $r\%$.

(ii) Find the amount of the investment to the nearest % at the end of 2 years, after tax has been deducted.

10 Frank has €5000 and would like to invest it for two years. A special savings account is offering a rate of 3% for the first year and a higher rate for the second year, if the money is retained in the account. Deposit Interest Retention Tax (D.I.R.T.) of 35% will be deducted each year from the interest earned.

(i) How much will the investment be worth at the end of one year, after tax is deducted?

(ii) Frank calculates that, after tax has been deducted, his investment will be worth €5246.60 at the end of the second year. Calculate the rate of interest for the second year.

Give your answer as a percentage, correct to one decimal place.

Revision Activity 3

1 (a) What is profit (reference cost and selling price)?

(b) What is loss (reference cost and selling price)?

(c) How do you calculate % profit?

(d) How do you calculate % loss?

(e) What is the difference between mark-up and margin?

2 A shop buys a set of branded suitcases for €150. They resell the suitcases for €225. Calculate the:

(a) % profit

(b) Margin

(c) Mark-up

(d) What do you notice about the value of the margin compared with the mark-up? Can you explain why this is the case?

3 A retailer sells two litres of car engine antifreeze and coolant concentrate for €19.49. There is a 50% profit margin on this product.

(a) Calculate the actual cost price of the antifreeze and coolant concentrate, to the nearest cent.

(b) Calculate the mark-up on the antifreeze and coolant concentrate.

4 Oscar borrows €10,000 for three years at 6% per annum compound interest.

He repays €2700 at the end of each of the first two years.

(a) How much must he repay at the end of the third year to clear his loan?

He extends the duration of the loan to 5 years. Hence, he pays off the remainder of the loan in equal instalments at the end of

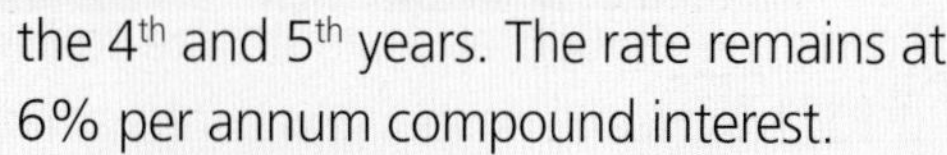

the 4th and 5th years. The rate remains at 6% per annum compound interest.

(b) How much would he need to repay, at the end of each year, to clear his loan at the end of 5 years? Give your answer correct to the nearest cent.

(c) What was the total amount of interest Oscar paid for this loan?

Hint

› Calculate the interest paid per year.

5 €12,000 was invested for 2 years. The interest rate for the first year was 4%.

(a) Calculate the amount of the investment at the end of the first year.

At the end of the second year the investment amounted to €13,228.80.

(b) Calculate the interest rate for the second year.

Exam-style Questions

1 Eleanor has a **gross** income of €38,500 for the year.

She has an annual tax credit of €3300.

The standard rate cut-off point is €33,800.

The standard rate of income tax is 20% and the higher rate is 40%.

(a) Find Eleanor's **net** income for the year (i.e. after tax is paid).

Eleanor receives a pay rise. As a result, her **net** income for the year is €34,780.

(b) Find Eleanor's new **gross** income for the year.

JCHL 2015

2 A sports shop buys t-shirts for €25 and sells them for €49.

(a) (i) Find the **mark-up** for the t-shirts (profit as a percentage of cost price).

(ii) Find the **margin** for the t-shirts (profit as a percentage of selling price). Give your answer correct to the nearest percent.

(b) The shop also sells runners, at a **mark-up** of 50%.

Find the **margin** for these runners. Give your answer correct to the nearest percent.

JCHL 2017

KEY WORDS AND PHRASES

- Selling price
- Cost price
- Profit
- Loss
- Percentage profit
- Percentage loss
- Mark-up
- Margin
- Gross pay/salary/ income
- Gross tax
- Tax credits
- Compound interest
- APR (Annual Percentage Rate)
- AER (Annual Equivalent Rate)
- Standard rate of tax
- Higher rate of tax
- Pay As You Earn (PAYE)
- Standard Rate Cut-Off Point (SRCOP)
- Tax payable/tax due
- Universal Social Charge (USC)
- Pay Related Social Insurance (PRSI)
- Statutory deductions
- Net income/pay or take-home pay

Chapter Summary 3

Profit and Loss

- The **percentage profit or loss** formulae are:

$$\% \text{ Profit} = \frac{\text{Profit amount}}{\text{Cost price}} \times 100\% \qquad \% \text{ Loss} = \frac{\text{Loss amount}}{\text{Cost price}} \times 100\%$$

Mark-up

Mark-up is the profit as a percentage (%) of the **cost price**.

$$\text{Mark-up} = \frac{\text{Profit}}{\text{Cost price}} \times 100\%$$

Margin

Margin is the profit as a percentage (%) of the **selling price**.

$$\text{Margin} = \frac{\text{Profit}}{\text{Selling Price}} \times 100\%$$

Compound Interest

- The compound interest formula states:
  $F = P(1 + i)^t$ …found on page 30 of the *Formulae and Tables* booklet

Income Tax

Gross pay is taxed at two different rates:

- **the 'standard rate' of 20%** which is applied to all earnings up to the standard rate cut-off point of €32,800; and
- **the 'higher rate' of 40%** applied to the balance of the gross pay.
- PRSI and USC are deducted from gross pay.

Chapter

4 Geometry 1

Learning Intentions

In this chapter, you will learn about:

- Pythagoras' theorem
- Using Pythagoras' theorem
- The fact that two right-angled triangles which have hypotenuse and another side equal, respectively, are congruent (RHS)
- Constructing a right-angled triangle given the length of the hypotenuse and one other side (Construction 13)
- Constructing a right-angled triangle given one side and one of the acute angles (Construction 14)
- Constructing a rectangle given the side lengths (Construction 15)
- Constructing a line perpendicular to a given line *l*, passing through a point on *l* (Construction 4)
- Constructing a line perpendicular to a given line *l*, passing through a point not on *l* (Construction 3)

LO: U.5, U.6, U.7–U.10, U.11–13, GT.3(a–e)

You will need...

- a pencil
- a ruler
- a geometry set

Why do we study triangles?

One type of building which uses equilateral triangles is the **geodesic dome**. This was patented in 1954 by a remarkable man from America named Buckminster Fuller.

The famous geodesic dome in Montreal, Canada.

He wanted to build houses as efficiently as possible. He discovered that if a structure with the shape of a sphere was created from triangles, it would have great strength.

One of the ways Buckminster Fuller (known as 'Bucky') described the differences in strength between a rectangle and a triangle is that a triangle withstands much greater pressure and is much more rigid – in fact the triangle is twice as strong.

Section 4A Review

Points and Lines

- A **plane** is an **infinite set of points**.
- This is the **line *BC***. A line has no beginning or end. We name a line by any two points that it passes through. We could also call this **line *CB***.

  We can also name a line by a single lower case letter (as in 'line *l*').

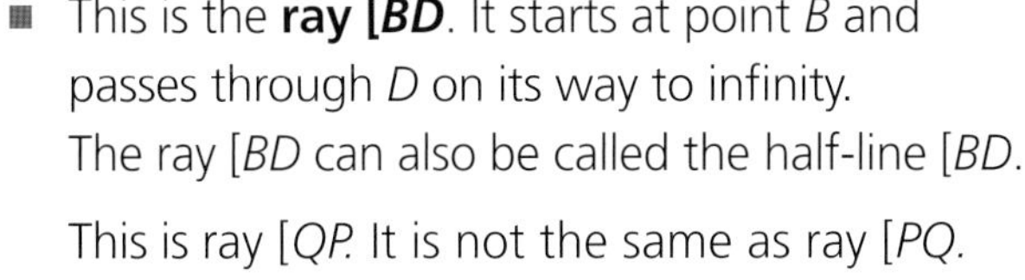

- Points on the same line are called **collinear points.**

  E, *G* and *F* are collinear points.

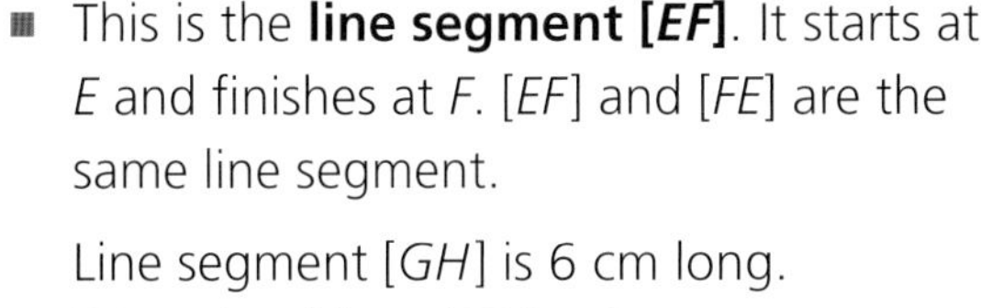

- This is the **ray [*BD***. It starts at point *B* and passes through *D* on its way to infinity. The ray [*BD* can also be called the half-line [*BD*.

  This is ray [*QP*. It is not the same as ray [*PQ*.

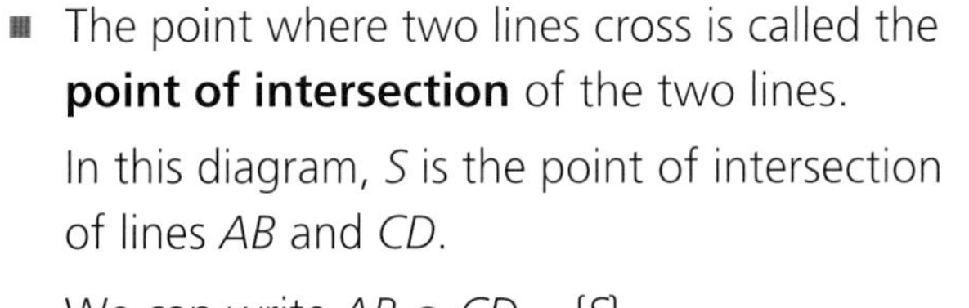

- This is the **line segment [*EF*]**. It starts at *E* and finishes at *F*. [*EF*] and [*FE*] are the same line segment.

  Line segment [*GH*] is 6 cm long. We write this as |*GH*| = 6 cm.

- The point where two lines cross is called the **point of intersection** of the two lines.

  In this diagram, *S* is the point of intersection of lines *AB* and *CD*.

  We can write $AB \cap CD = \{S\}$

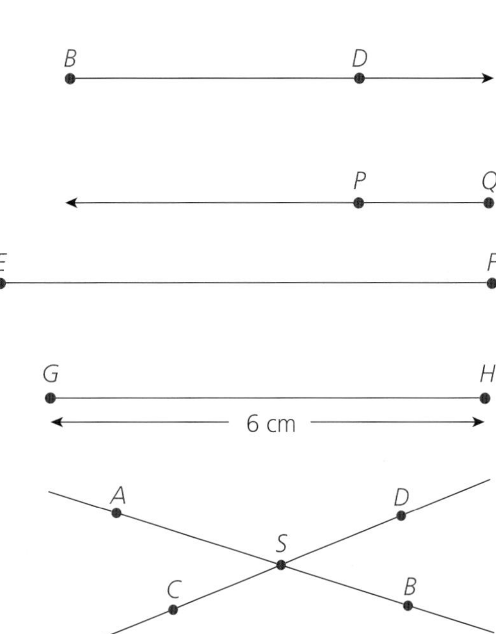

Angles

- Angles can be measured in degrees; $|\angle PQR|$ is between 0° and 360° where $\angle PQR$ is any angle.
- The following are the main types of angle. Notice that a right angle has a special symbol.

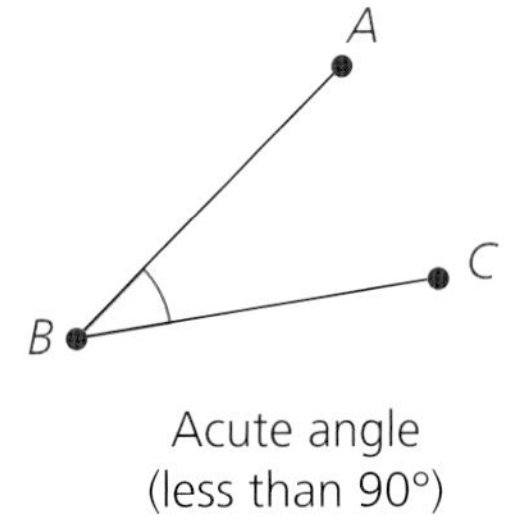

Acute angle
(less than 90°)

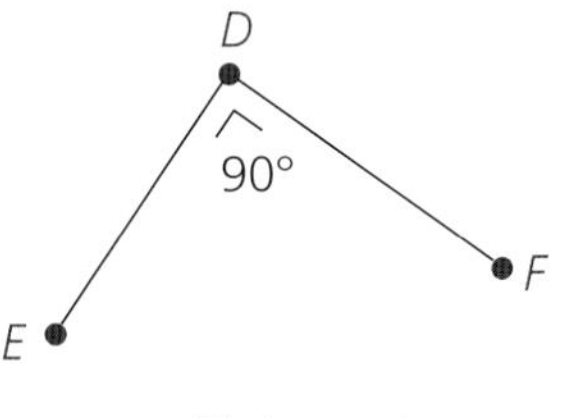

Right angle
(= 90°)

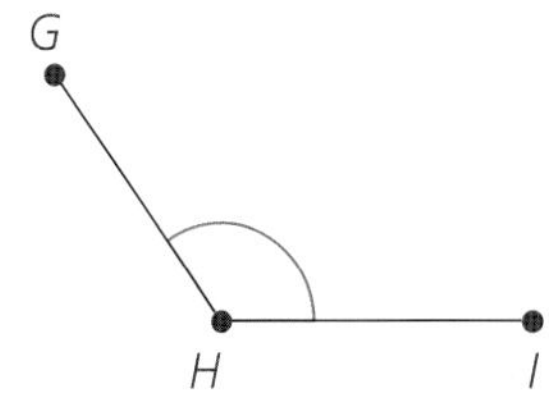

Obtuse angle
(more than 90°, less than 180°)

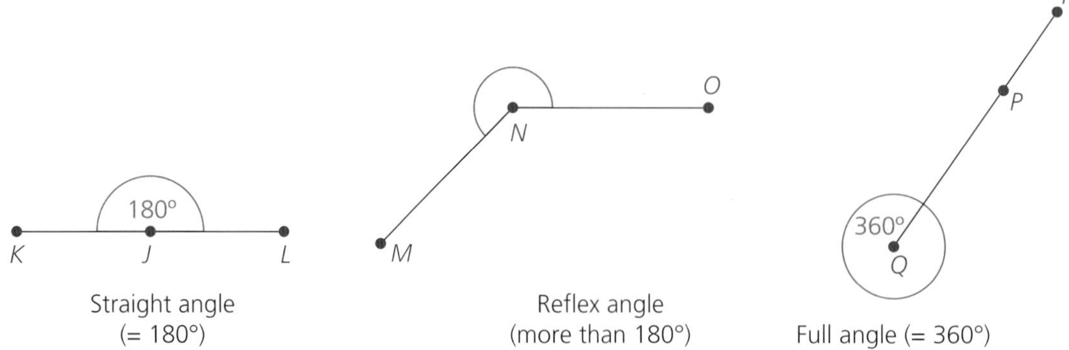

Straight angle (= 180°)

Reflex angle (more than 180°)

Full angle (= 360°)

We sometimes use the term '**ordinary angle**' to mean an angle which is less than 180°. So acute angles or obtuse angles could also be called ordinary angles.

- If $|\angle 1| + |\angle 2| = 180°$, then $\angle 1$ and $\angle 2$ are called **supplementary** angles.

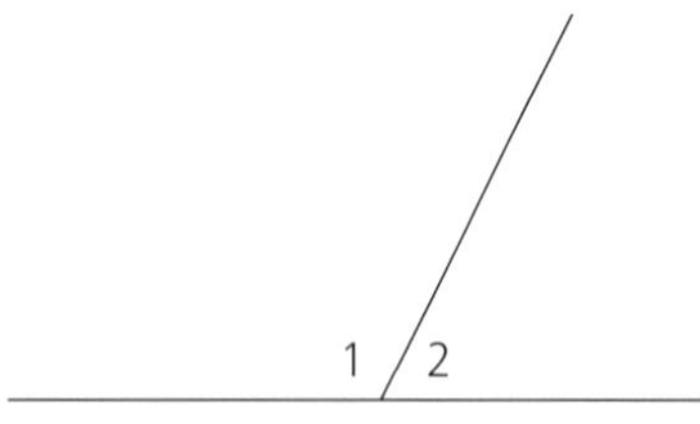

- The pairs of angles directly opposite each other when two lines intersect are called **vertically opposite angles**.

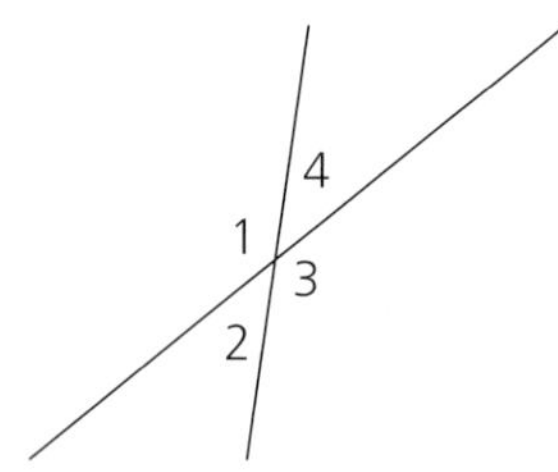

In the diagram there are two such pairs:

$\angle 1$ and $\angle 3$

$\angle 2$ and $\angle 4$

Parallel Lines and Transversals

A transversal is a line that cuts across two or more lines.

The two parallel lines l and m are both crossed by a transversal t.

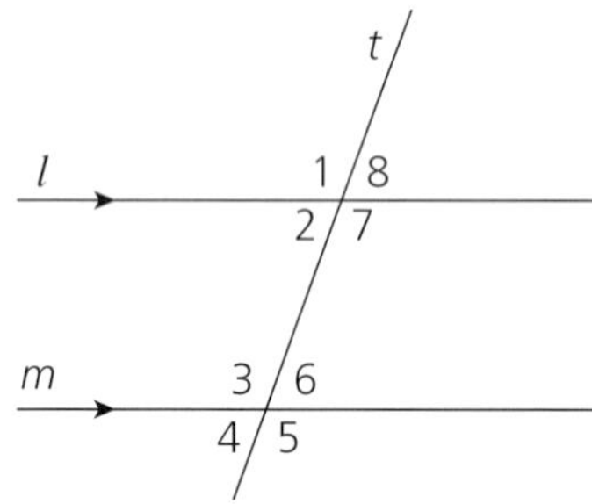

Interior angles

The angles 2, 7, 3 and 6 are between the parallel lines. We call these **interior** angles. There are two on each side of the transversal.

We found that the sum of two **interior angles** on the same side of the transversal is 180°, i.e. $|\angle 2| + |\angle 3| = 180°$ and $|\angle 7| + |\angle 6| = 180°$.

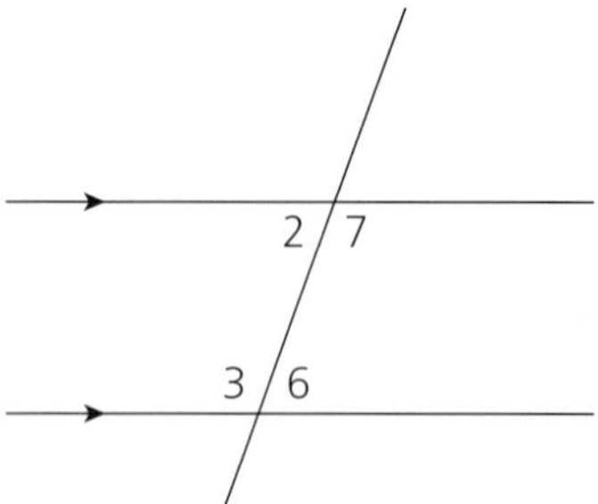

Corresponding angles

Here are all the corresponding angles from the diagram above.

When you see an 'F' shape formed, you have corresponding angles.

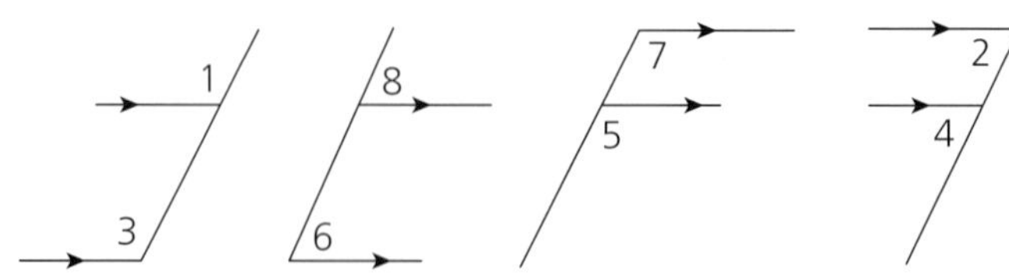

Alternate angles

When you see a 'Z' shape formed, you have alternate angles.

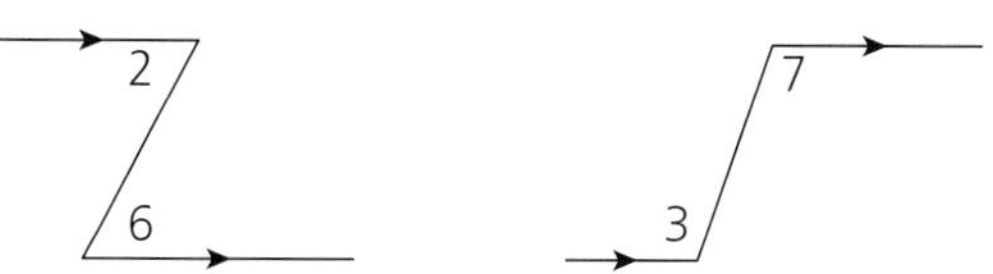

Key Point

Remember: Z shape – alternate angles
F shape – corresponding angles
X shape – vertically opposite angles.

Triangles

- Categories of triangle:
  1. By the number of equal sides:

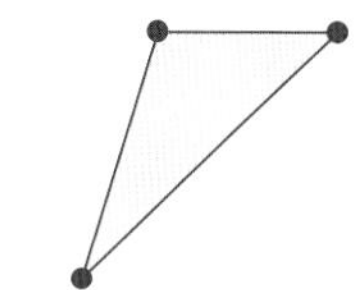
Scalene (no sides equal)

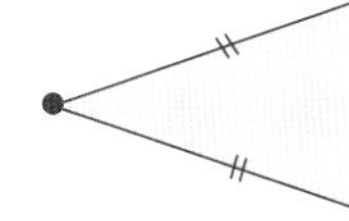
Isosceles (two sides equal)

Equilateral (three sides equal)

  2. By the size of the biggest angle:

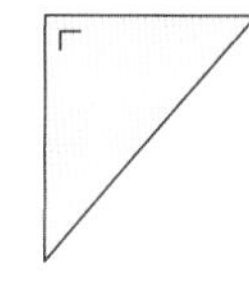
Right-angled

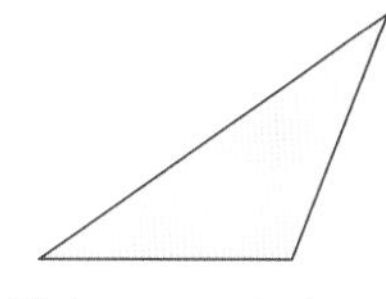
Obtuse-angled

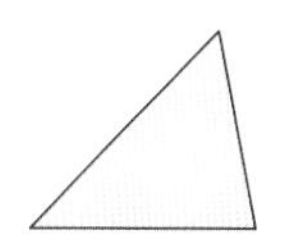
Acute-angled

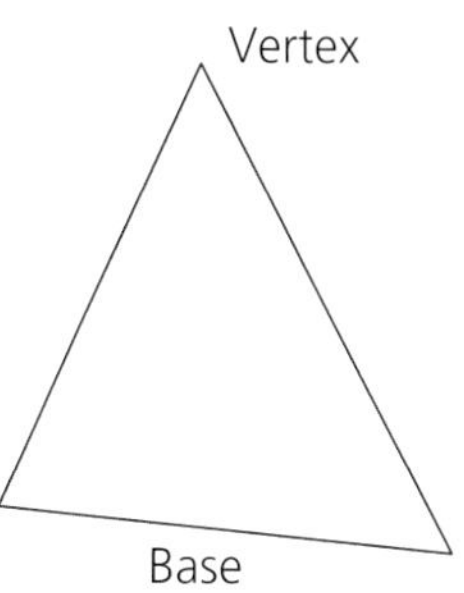

- The three sides and three angles of a triangle are called its **six parts**. Any one of the angular points of a triangle may be called a **vertex**, and the opposite side is then called the **base**.
- The angle between two sides of a triangle is referred to as the angle **included** by these two sides, or simply, **the included angle**.
- Two triangles which are equal in every respect are called **congruent triangles**.

Axioms

- An **axiom** is a mathematical statement which we accept to be true without proof. We need axioms in order to start proving other statements called **theorems**.
- We have five axioms on our course:
  - **Axiom 1 (two points axiom):** There is exactly one line through any two points.
  - **Axiom 2 (ruler axiom):**

(i) $|AB|$ is never negative

(ii) $|AB| = |BA|$

(iii) $|AC| + |CB| = |AB|$

- **Axiom 3 (protractor axiom)**:
  (i) A straight angle has 180°
  (ii) $|\angle a| = |\angle b| + |\angle c|$

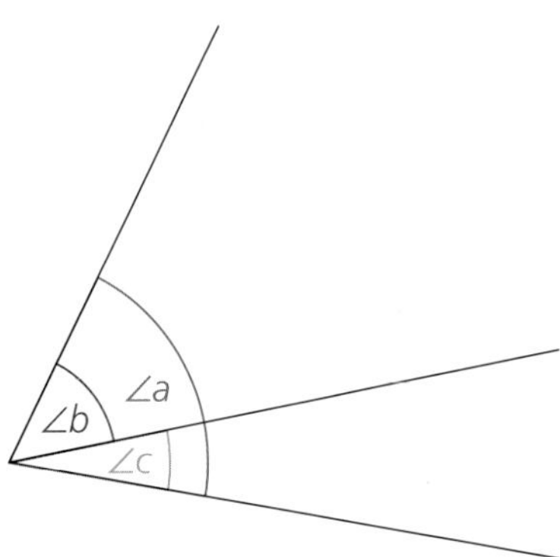

- **Axiom 4**:
  (i) Two triangles are congruent if the three sides of one triangle are equal to the three corresponding sides of the other (**SSS**).
  (ii) Two triangles are congruent if two sides and the included angle of one triangle are equal to the corresponding two sides and included angle of the other (**SAS**).
  (iii) Two triangles are congruent if two angles and the side between them are equal in size (**ASA**).
- **Axiom 5 (axiom of parallels)**: Given any line l and a point P, there is exactly one line through P that is parallel to l.

P Parallel line

l

Theorems

- A **theorem** is a statement obtained by logical argument from an axiom (or other theorem).

Theorem 1:

Vertically opposite angles are equal in measure.

Theorem 2:

(i) In an isosceles triangle, the angles opposite the equal sides are equal.
(ii) Conversely, if two angles in a triangle are equal, then the triangle is isosceles.

Theorem 3:

(i) If a transversal makes equal alternate angles on two lines, then the lines are parallel.
(ii) Conversely, if two lines are parallel, then any transversal will make equal alternate angles with them.

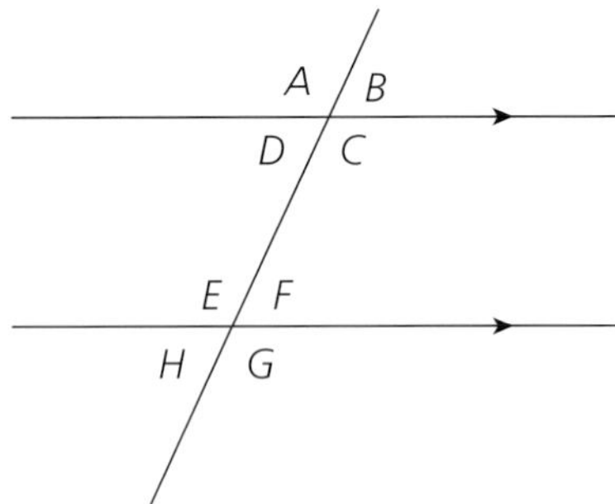

Theorem 4:

The angles in any triangle add to 180°.

Theorem 5:

Two lines are parallel if and only if for any transversal, corresponding angles are equal.

Theorem 6:

Each exterior angle of a triangle is equal to the sum of the two interior opposite angles.

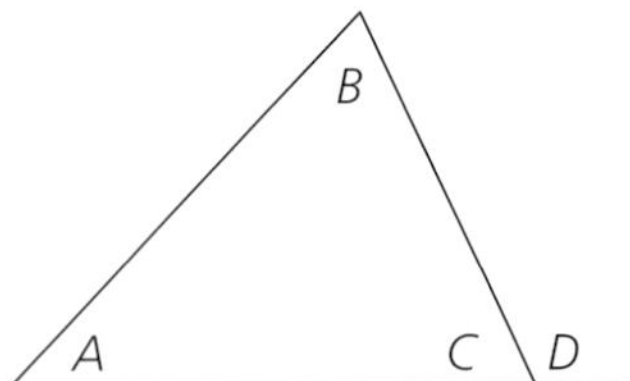

For this triangle, we say that $|\angle A| + |\angle B| = |\angle D|$, where $\angle D$ is the exterior angle and $\angle A$ and $\angle B$ are the interior opposite angles.

Constructions

Construction 1:

Use of a compass to bisect an angle

Construction 2:

Use of a compass to draw the perpendicular bisector of a line segment

Construction 4:

Line perpendicular to a given line l, passing through a given point on l (two methods: ruler and compass or ruler and set-square)

Construction 5:

Line parallel to a given line, through a given point

Construction 6:

Division of a line segment into two or three equal segments without measuring it

Construction 8:

Line segment of a given length on a given ray

Construction 9:

Angle of a given number of degrees with a given ray as one arm

Construction 10:

Triangle, given lengths of three sides

Construction 11:

Triangle, given SAS data

Construction 12:

Triangle, given ASA data

Transformations

- **Axial symmetry**

  Axial symmetry of an object is the reflection of that object through a line. It is also known as a mirror reflection.

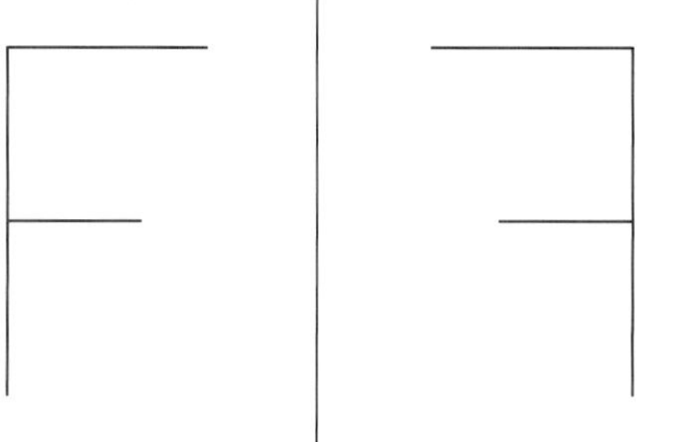

- **Axis of symmetry**

  The axis of symmetry of a shape is the line that divides the shape into two symmetrical parts such that each side is the mirror image of the other.

- **Translation**

  A translation moves every point of an object the same distance in the same direction.

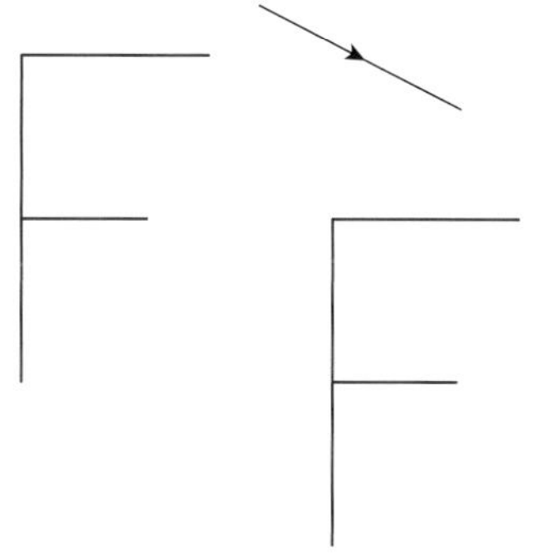

- **Central symmetry**

  Central symmetry is the reflection of an object through a point.

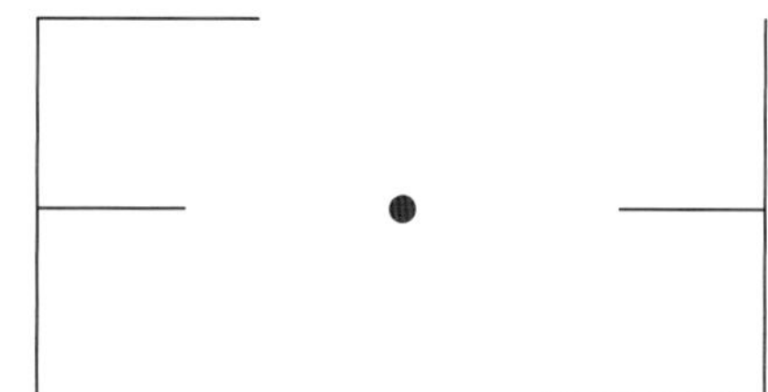

- **Centre of symmetry**

  Some shapes are mapped onto themselves under central symmetry in a point. The point P is called the centre of symmetry of the shape.

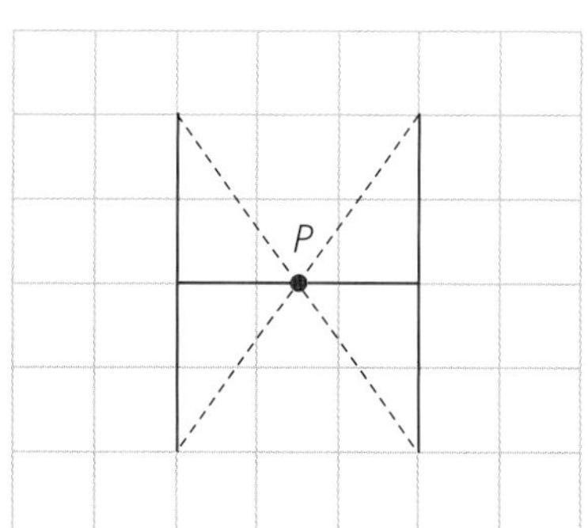

The **orientation** of an object after a transformation is the relative direction in which it is facing.

See how these three transformations change the orientation of an object:

Axial symmetry (back-to-front)	Central symmetry (upside down and back-to-front)	Translation (no change)

■ **Rotation**

To '**rotate**' means to move in a circle around (about) a point.

This diagram shows a triangle ABC and its image, $A'B'C'$, by an **anti-clockwise** rotation of **90°** about a **point *O***.

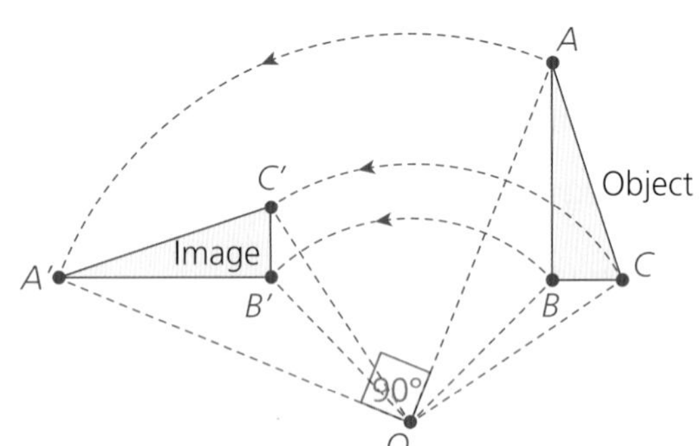

Every point of the triangle ABC turns through the same angle (90° in this case).

This means that $|\angle AOA'| = 90°$, $|\angle BOB'| = 90°$ and $|\angle COC'| = 90°$.

When we want to describe a rotation, we must name three things:

- The **centre of rotation**
- The **angle turned**
- The **direction** (clockwise or anti-clockwise).

All of the four transformations (axial symmetry, translation, central symmetry and rotation) preserve length, area and size of angle.

In the next activity, we will revise some of the main ideas we explored in *Connect With Maths: Introduction to Junior Cycle*.

Activity 4.1

1 (i) What is $|\angle\alpha| + |\angle\beta|$ in the diagram?

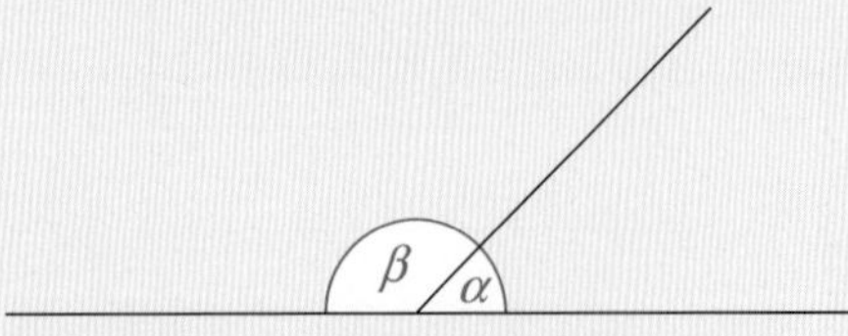

(ii) Copy and complete the following sentence:

'Angles α and β are known as ________________ angles.'

2 The diagram shows two intersecting lines.

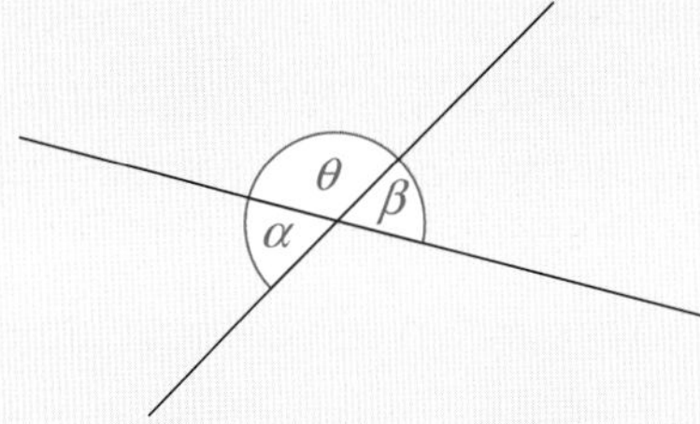

(i) Copy and complete the following sentence: 'Angles α and β are known as ____________________ angles.'

(ii) What is $|\angle\alpha| + |\angle\theta|$?

(iii) What is $|\angle\theta| + |\angle\beta|$?

(iv) Show that $|\angle\alpha| = |\angle\beta|$.

3 Show that $a + b + c = 360°$.

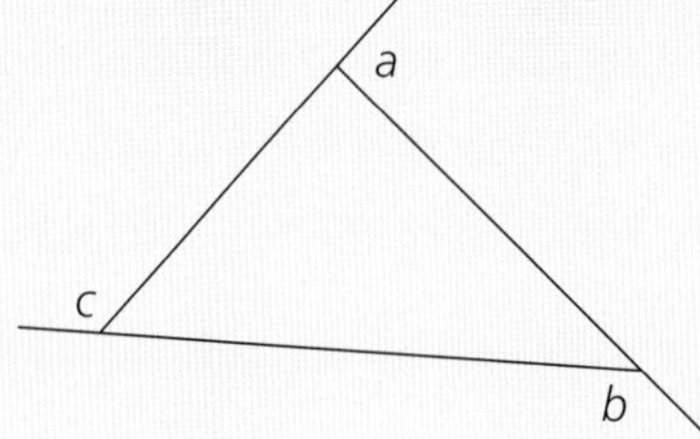

4 Draw separate diagrams to show a scalene triangle, an isosceles triangle and an equilateral triangle. Give a brief description of each.

5 (i) Draw a sketch of the triangle ABC where $|AB| = 6$ cm, $|BC| = 8$ cm and $|CA| = 7$ cm.

(ii) Construct the triangle ABC using a ruler and compass.

6 (i) Draw a sketch of the triangle TUV where $|\angle TUV| = 47°$, $|UV| = 8$ cm and $|\angle TVU| = 53°$.

(ii) Construct the triangle TUV using a ruler and protractor.

7 (i) Draw a sketch of the triangle PQR where $|PQ| = 8$ cm, $|\angle PQR| = 55°$ and $|QR| = 10$ cm.

(ii) Construct the triangle PQR using a ruler, compass and protractor.

8 (i) What are congruent triangles?

(ii) Name the three conditions where we can assume that two non-right-angled triangles are congruent.

(iii) Give a reason why each of the following pairs of triangles can be assumed to be congruent.

(a)

(b)

(c)

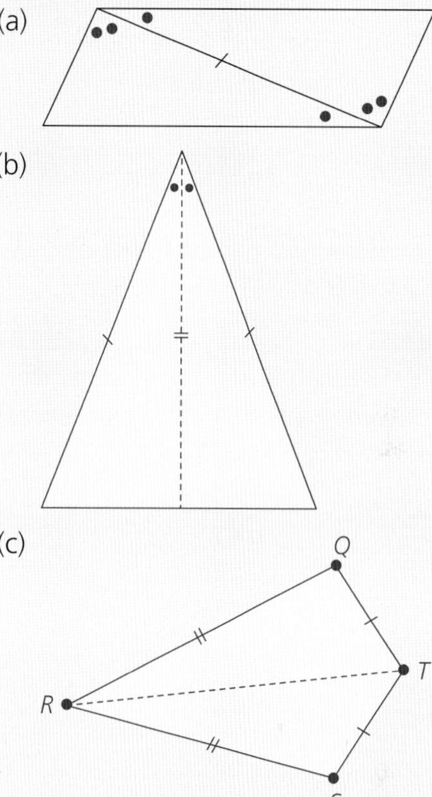

9 (i) Construct an angle ABC where $|\angle ABC| = 70°$ using a ruler and protractor.

(ii) Now construct the bisector of $\angle ABC$ using only a ruler and compass. Show all your construction marks.

10 ABC is an isosceles triangle with $|AB| = |BC|$.

BD is the bisector of $\angle ABC$.

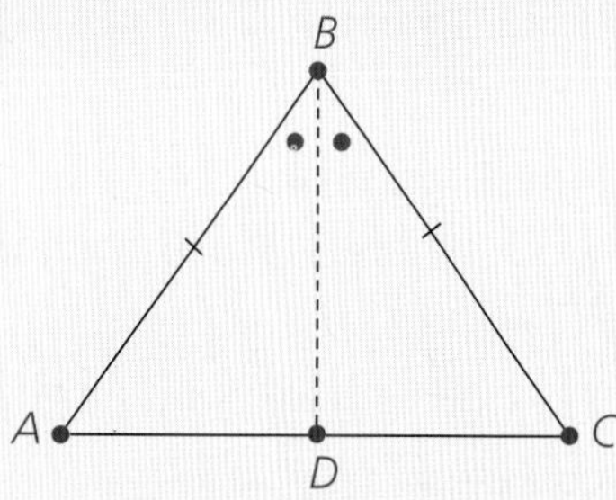

(i) Prove that the triangles *ABD* and *BDC* are congruent.

(ii) Hence, prove that $|\angle BAD| = |\angle BCD|$.

(iii) State, in your own words, what you have proved about the angles in an isosceles triangle.

(iv) What type of angles are $\angle ADB$ and $\angle CDB$? Explain your answer.

11 (i) Construct a line segment [*AB*] such that $|AB| = 6$ cm.

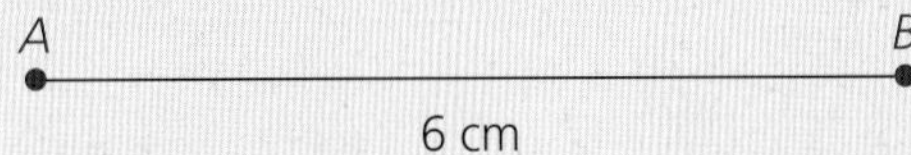

(ii) Construct the perpendicular bisector of [*AB*] using a ruler and compass only.

12 The diagram shows two parallel lines *m* and *n* with line *t* a transversal of them.

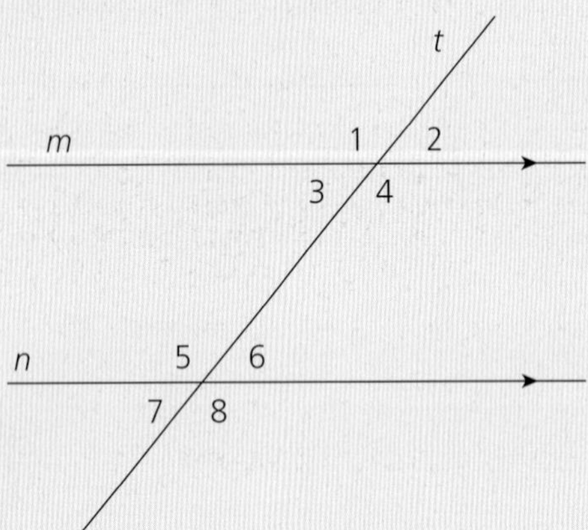

(i) Name two pairs of alternate angles.

(ii) What do you know about these alternate angles?

(iii) Name four pairs of corresponding angles.

(iv) What do you know about these corresponding angles?

(v) Name two pairs of interior angles.

(vi) Given that $|\angle 5| = 130°$, find the size of all the other angles.

13 (i) Draw a rough sketch of the rectangle *ABCD*, where $|AB| = 6$ cm and $|BC| = 8$ cm.

(ii) Construct the rectangle *ABCD* accurately.

14 (i) Draw the triangle with vertices *A*(0, 0), *B*(3, 5) and *C*(5, 4) in a co-ordinate plane.

(ii) Draw *A'B'C'*, the image of the triangle *ABC*, by a rotation of 90° anti-clockwise about *A*.

(iii) Write down the co-ordinates of *A'*, *B'* and *C'*.

(iv) Draw *A''B''C''*, the image of the triangle *ABC*, by a rotation of 180° about *A*.

(v) Write down the co-ordinates of *A''*, *B''* and *C''*.

15 Copy the diagram below into your copybook and construct the image of the '*T*' shape by:

(i) a rotation of 90° anti-clockwise

(ii) a rotation of 180°

(iii) a rotation of 270° anti-clockwise.

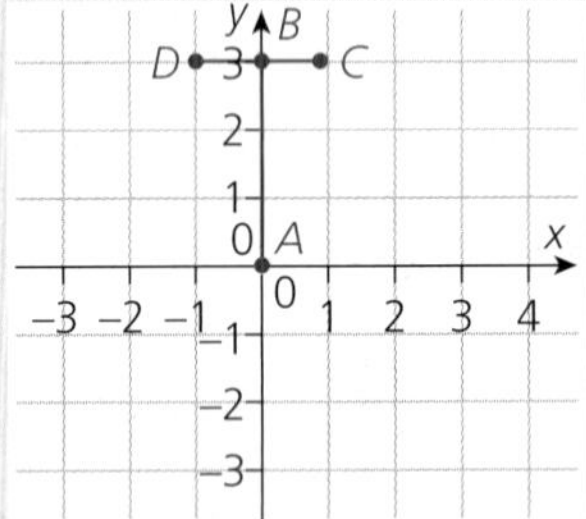

16 (i) Copy the diagram below into your copybook. Mark in the co-ordinates of *A*, *B* and *C*.

(ii) Draw *PQR*, the image of *ABC*, by axial symmetry in the *x*-axis.

(iii) Draw *XYZ*, the image of *ABC*, by central symmetry in the *y*-axis.

(iv) What other transformation would give *XYZ* as the image of *ABC*?

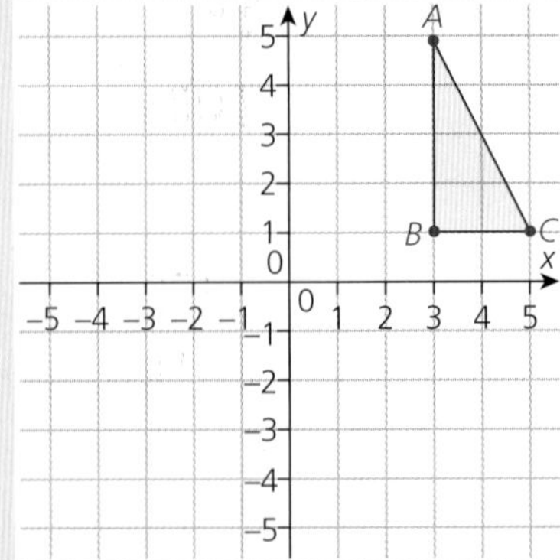

17 Each of the three hands labelled *A*, *B* and *C* shown below is an image of the hand shown in the box on the left under a transformation. For each of *A*, *B* and *C*, state what the transformation is (translation, central symmetry, axial symmetry or rotation) and in the case of a rotation, state the angle and direction.

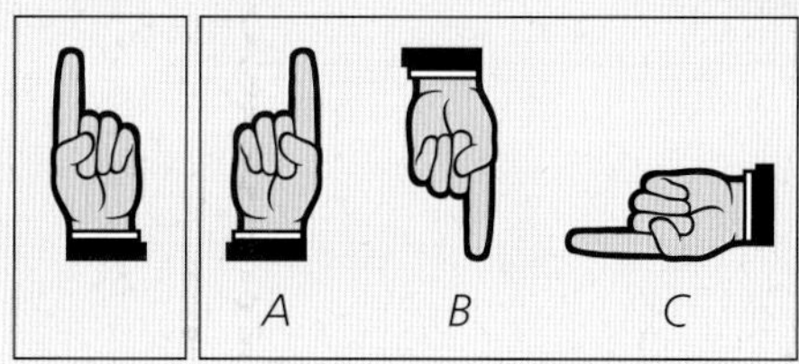

Section 4B Pythagoras' Theorem

Historical Background

In this section, we meet probably the most famous of all mathematical theorems, known as Pythagoras' theorem. It tells us a rather surprising thing about right-angled triangles, which you probably would not realise without being told.

Pythagoras was a Greek mathematician and philosopher who lived in the 6th century BC. He founded his society of disciples in Croton, which was a prosperous Greek city in southern Italy.

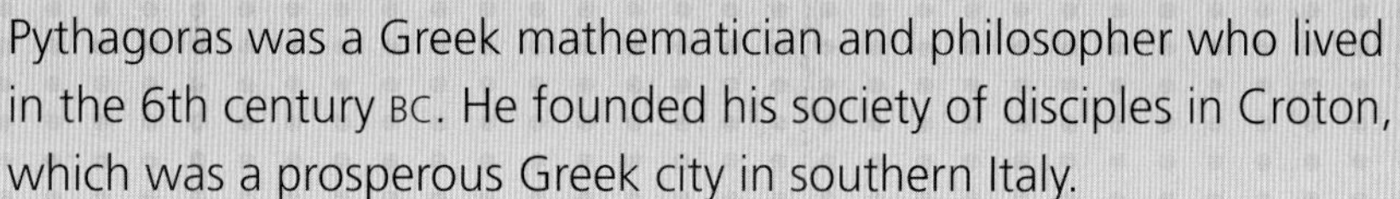

The longest side in a right-angled triangle is referred to as the **hypotenuse**.

The hypotenuse is the side opposite the right angle.

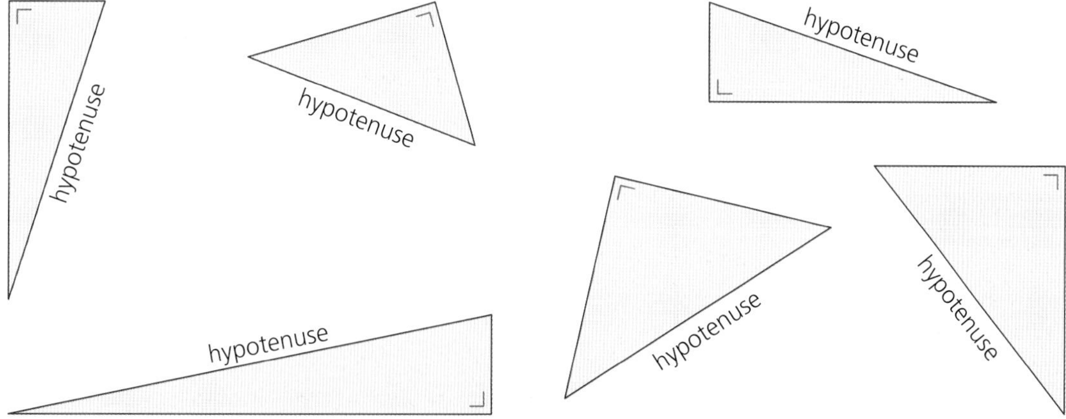

Frank and Ernest

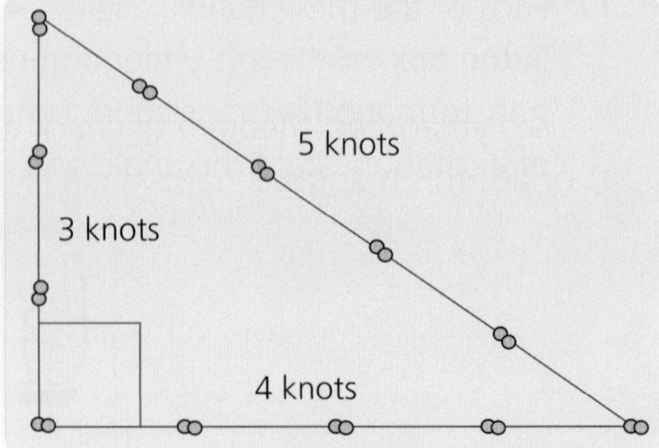

Ancient Egyptian square tool

THEOREM 14

Pythagoras' theorem

The square on the hypotenuse of a right-angled triangle is equal to the sum of the squares on the other two sides.

Conversely: If the square of one side of a triangle is equal to the sum of the squares of the other two sides, then the angle opposite the first side is a right angle.

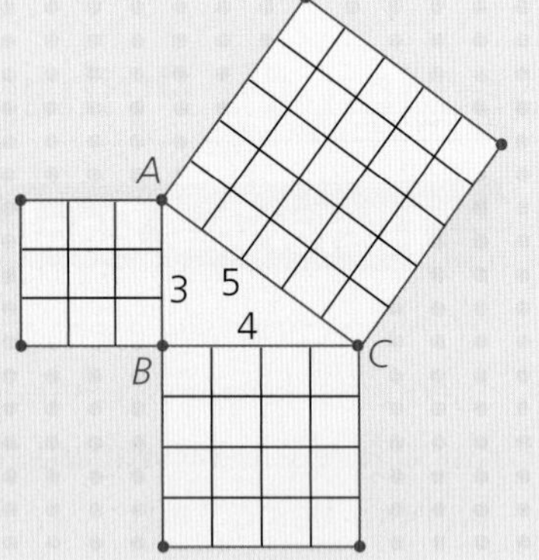

This is the way it appears in the *Formulae and tables* booklet:

$$c^2 = a^2 + b^2$$

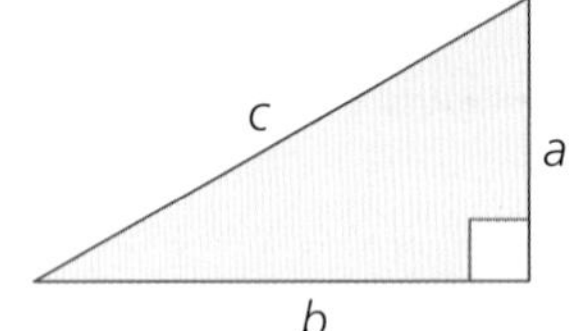

Note

A proof of Pythagoras' theorem is given in Chapter 20.

THEOREM 15: THE CONVERSE OF PYTHAGORAS' THEOREM

If the square of one side of a triangle is equal to the sum of the squares of the other two sides, then the angle opposite the first side is a right angle.

Example 1

Use Pythagoras' theorem to check whether or not this triangle is right-angled.

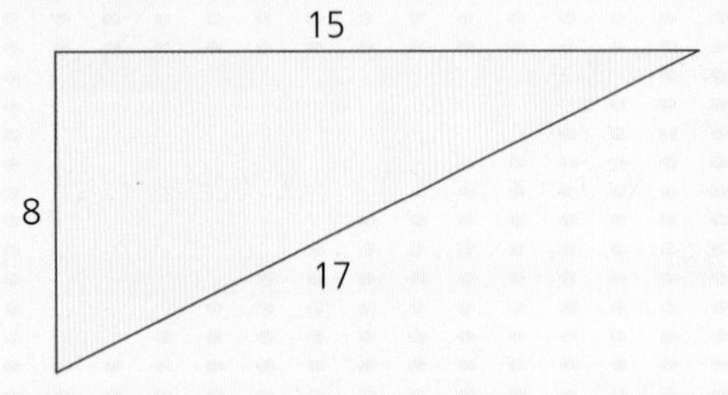

Solution

Look for the longest side: it is 17.

Check to see whether (longest side)^2 = sum of squares of the other two sides.

Is $17^2 = 8^2 + 15^2$?

$289 = 64 + 225$

$289 = 289$ ✓

$\Rightarrow$ It is a right-angled triangle.

Example 2

Use Pythagoras' theorem to check whether or not this triangle is right-angled.

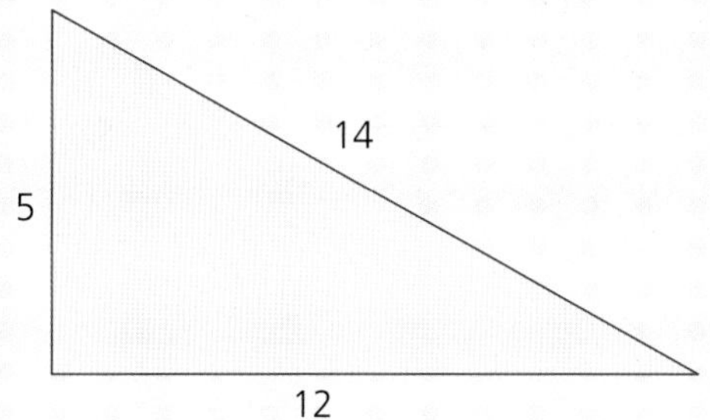

Solution

Look for the longest side: it is 14.

Check to see whether (longest side)^2 = sum of squares of the other two sides.

Is $14^2 = 5^2 + 12^2$?

$196 = 25 + 144$

$196 = 169$ ✗

$\Rightarrow$ It is not a right-angled triangle.

Connections

We can use our knowledge of algebraic equations to work with Pythagoras' theorem. We just need to remember how to solve quadratic equations.

When we are given two sides of a right-angled triangle and asked to find the third side, we use Pythagoras' theorem:

$$c^2 = a^2 + b^2$$

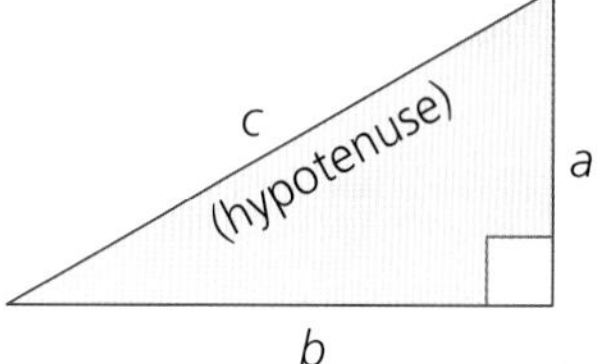

As you can see from the diagram, the hypotenuse is directly opposite the 90 degree angle and is represented by the letter c.

Example 3

Find the value of the missing side in each triangle. Give your answers correct to two decimal places if they are not integers.

(i)

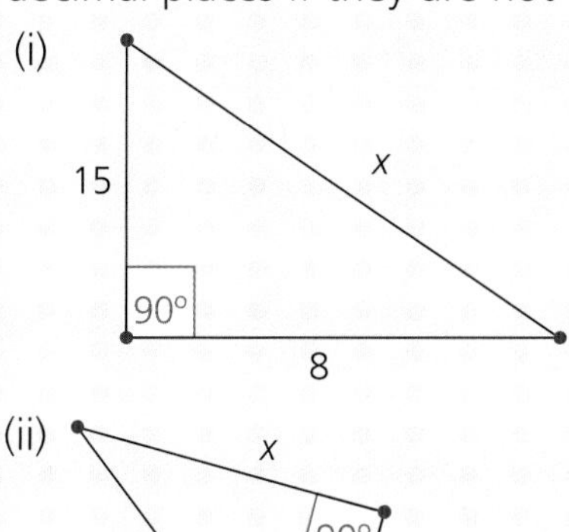

(ii)

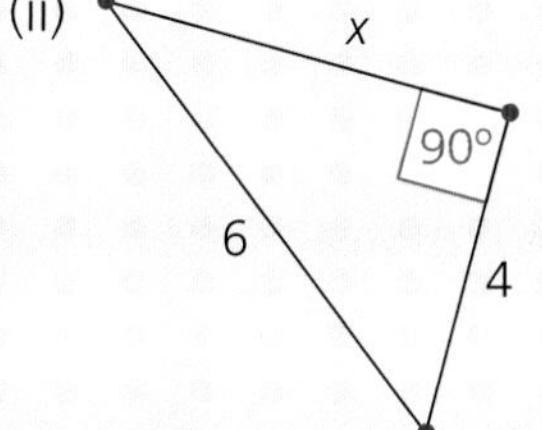

Solution

(i) We see from the diagram that x is the hypotenuse so

$x^2 = 15^2 + 8^2$

$x^2 = 225 + 64$

$x^2 = 289$

$x = \sqrt{289}$

$x = 17$

(ii) We see from the diagram that 6 is the hypotenuse so

$6^2 = x^2 + 4^2$

$36 = x^2 + 16$

$36 - 16 = x^2$

$20 = x^2$

$\sqrt{20} = x = 4.47$ (correct to 2 d.p.)

Example 4

Given any two integers p and q ($p > q$), it is possible to form three numbers a, b and c where:

$a = p^2 - q^2$, $\quad b = 2pq$, $\quad c = p^2 + q^2$

These three numbers a, b and c are then known as **Pythagorean triples**.

(i) For $p = 8$ and $q = 6$, calculate a, b and c.

(ii) If a, b and c are the lengths of a triangle, show that the triangle is right-angled.

Solution

(i) For $p = 8$ and $q = 6$:

$a = p^2 - q^2 = 8^2 - 6^2 = 64 - 36 = 28$

$b = 2pq = 2(8)(6) = 96$

$c = p^2 + q^2 = 8^2 + 6^2 = 64 + 36 = 100$

(ii) $c^2 = 100^2 = 10\,000$

$a^2 + b^2 = 28^2 + 96^2 = 784 + 9216$
$= 10\,000$

$\therefore c^2 = a^2 + b^2$

$\Rightarrow$ The triangle is right-angled.

Class Activity

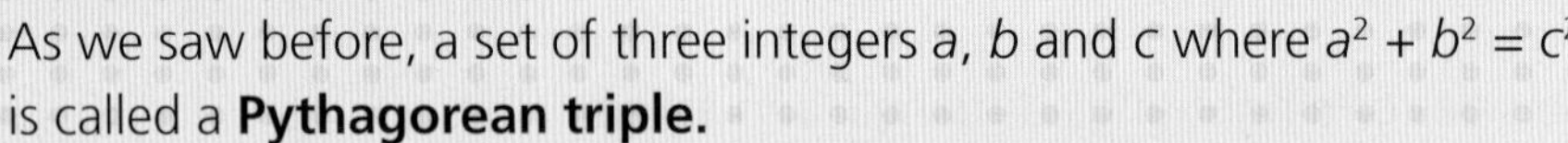

As we saw before, a set of three integers a, b and c where $a^2 + b^2 = c^2$ is called a **Pythagorean triple.**

For example, {3, 4, 5} is a Pythagorean triple, since $3^2 + 4^2 = 5^2$.

How many Pythagorean triples are there?

(i) Working in pairs, copy and complete this table.

	Triple	Is the longest² = sum of squares of other two?	Pythagorean triple?
Original	3, 4, 5	$3^2 + 4^2 = 5^2$ $9 + 16 = 25$ ✓	Yes
Multiply original by 2	6, 8, 10	$6^2 + 8^2 = 10^2$	
Multiply original by 3			
Multiply original by 4			
Multiply original by 5			
Multiply original by 6	18, 24, 30		
Multiply original by 7			

(ii) How many Pythagorean triples do you think there are?

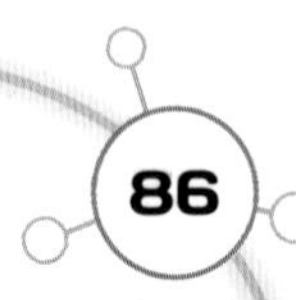

(iii) Copy this table and make up three new Pythagorean triples for each set below.

Original Pythagorean triple	Three new Pythagorean triples from these
5, 12, 13	
8, 15, 17	
7, 24, 25	

Historical Note

Pierre de Fermat (1601–65)

As you can see from the last activity, we can get many values for x, y and z which satisfy the equation $x^2 + y^2 = z^2$.

In 1637, Pierre de Fermat was looking for solutions to the equation $x^3 + y^3 = z^3$.

This equation differs from the previous equation only by the fact that each power of 2 has been replaced by a power of 3. However, Fermat could not find any solutions to this new equation.

In fact, amazingly, there are no values of x, y and z which satisfy the equation $x^3 + y^3 = z^3$.

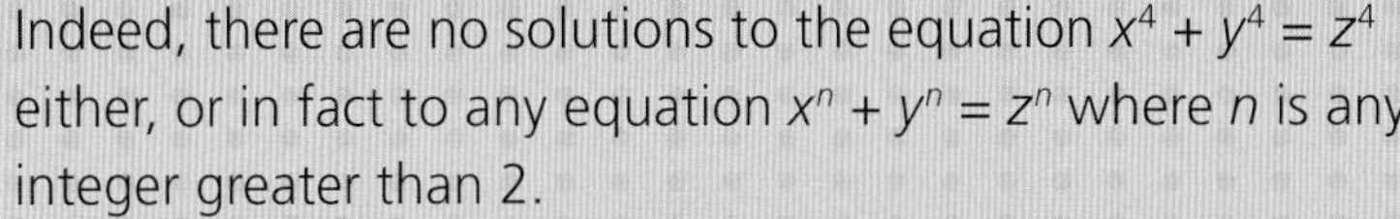

Indeed, there are no solutions to the equation $x^4 + y^4 = z^4$ either, or in fact to any equation $x^n + y^n = z^n$ where n is any integer greater than 2.

Fermat claimed to have proved this, but said that the margin of the page he was writing on was too narrow to write it in, and his proof was never found. Thus it became known as **Fermat's Last Theorem**.

For over 300 years mathematicians tried to prove or disprove Fermat's Last Theorem. It was finally proved to be true by Andrew Wiles, an English mathematician, in 1995. His proof is 400 pages long!

Andrew Wiles (born 1953)

Activity 4.2

1 State Pythagoras' theorem for each of these right-angled triangles.

(i)

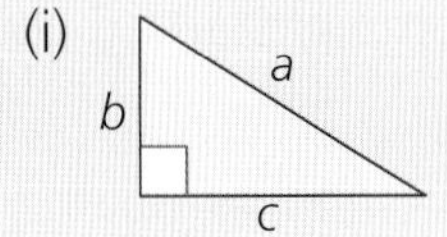

(ii)

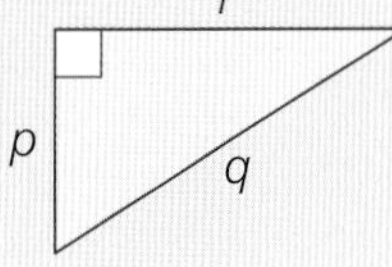

(iii)

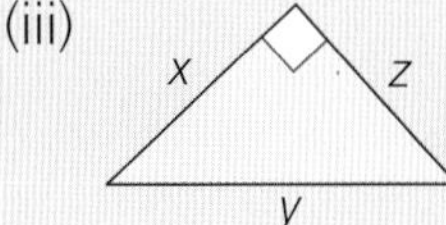

(iv)

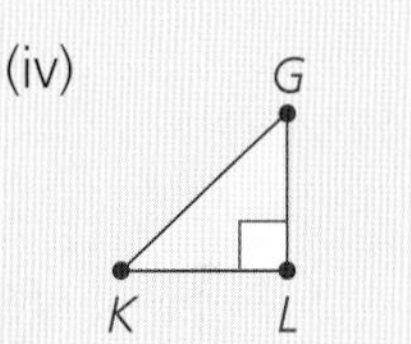

(v)

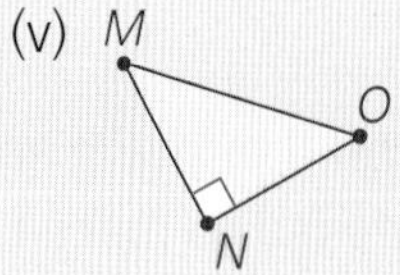

(vi)

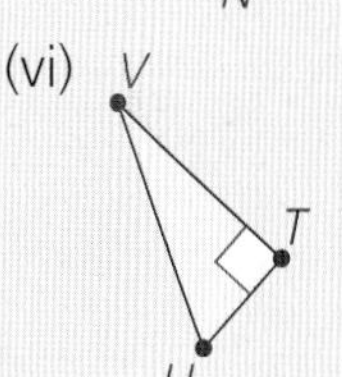

2 Find the value of x in each of the following right-angled triangles.

(i)

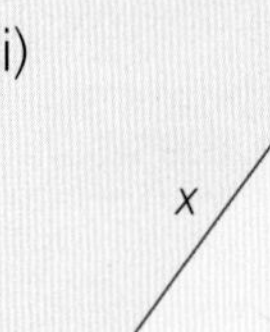
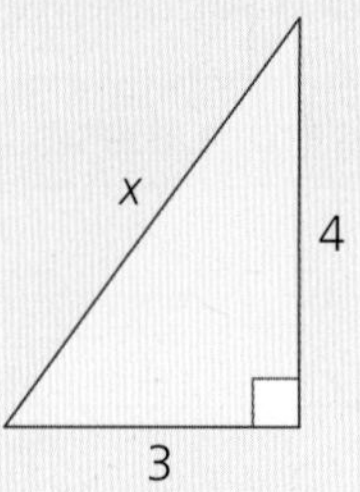

(iii)

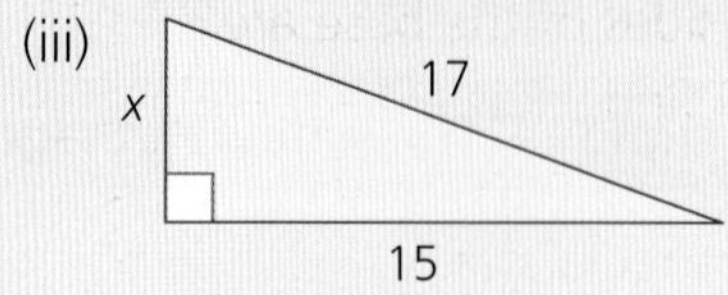

(v)

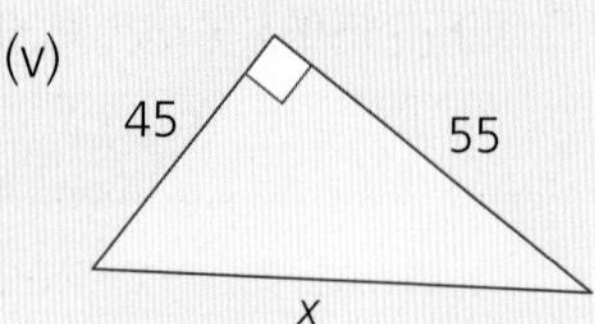

(ii)

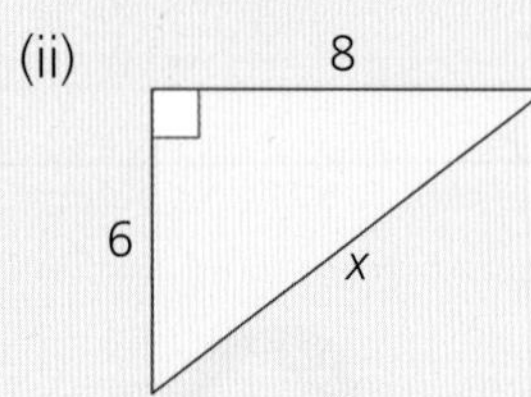

(iv)

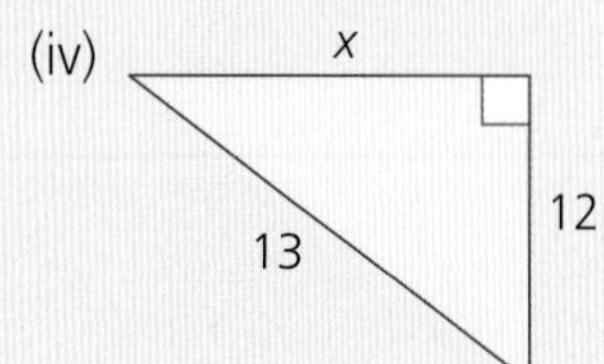

(vi)

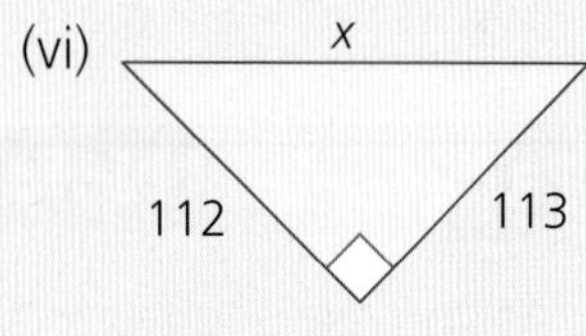

3 Use Pythagoras' theorem to show that the triangle with side lengths 7, 24 and 25 is right-angled.

4 Use Pythagoras' theorem to check whether or not the triangle with side lengths 9, 40 and 42 is right-angled.

5 Use Pythagoras' theorem to check whether or not the triangle with side lengths 33, 56 and 65 is right-angled.

6 Find the length of the missing side in each of the following right-angled triangles. Leave your answer in square root form if the answer is not an integer.

(i)

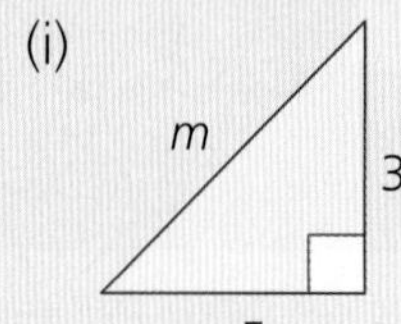

(ii)

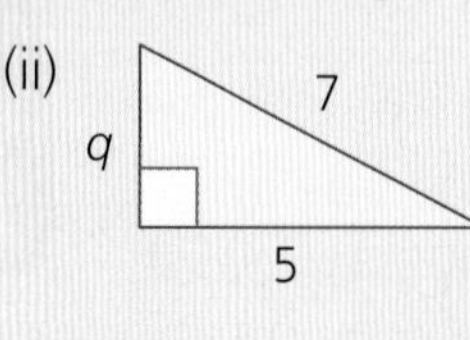

(iii)

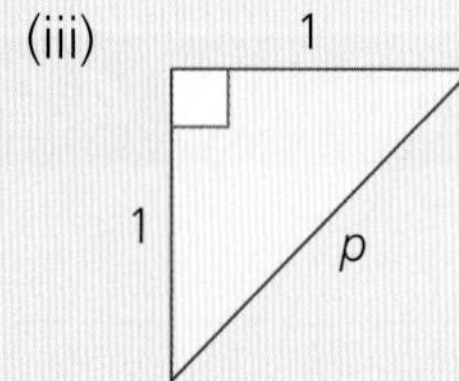

(iv)

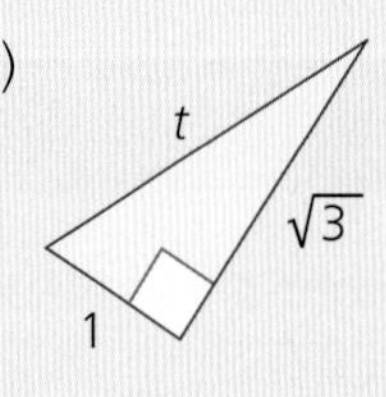

7 Find the total length of metal wire needed to make this outline shape.

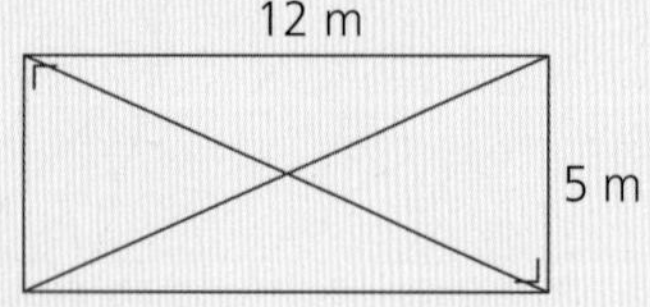

8 The sides of a triangle are 20, 99 and 101. Use Pythagoras' theorem to check whether or not it is right-angled.

9 The diagram below shows a section of a football and hurling pitch with goalposts (the H shape).

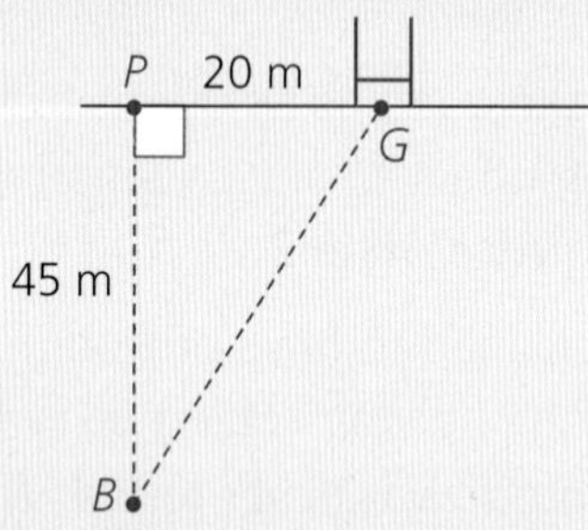

A ball is placed at B, which is 45 m from the end-line of the pitch. $|PG| = 20$ m.

Calculate $|BG|$, the distance from the ball to the goalposts. Give your answer correct to two decimal places.

10 Grace is walking in the country. Her path is shown in the diagram. She finishes 160 m north and 70 m east from her starting point.

How far is Grace from her starting point?

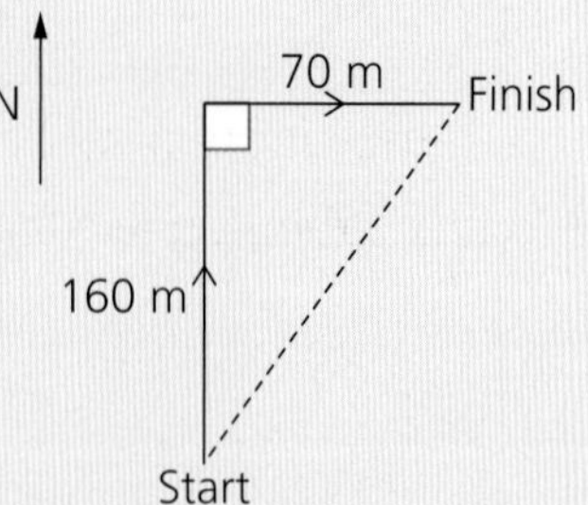

11 Colin is making a base for a garage. The base should be a rectangle. The sides of the base are to be 5 m and 4.5 m. Colin finds that a diagonal is 6.9 m. Use Pythagoras' theorem to decide whether or not the base is a rectangle.

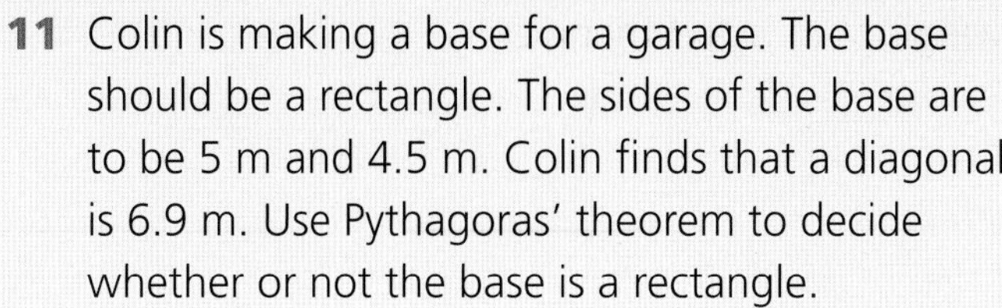

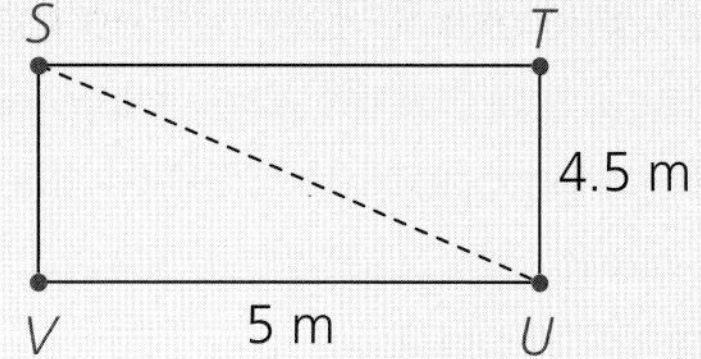

12 Aaron is using a ladder 4 m long against a wall.

He wonders if he moves the ladder 1 m closer to the wall, whether it will reach 1 m further up the wall.

The diagrams show the two positions of Aaron's ladder.

(1)

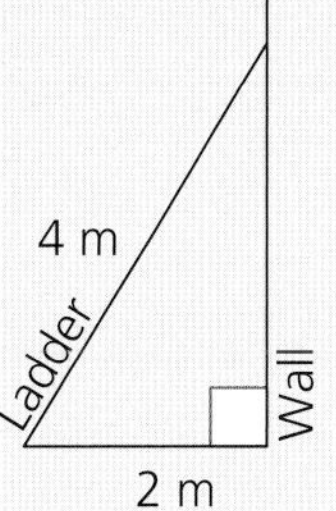

(2)

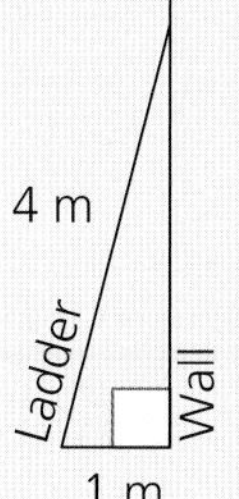

(i) Find the distance the ladder reaches up the wall in the two positions.

(ii) How much further up the wall is the ladder in the second position?

13 Find the values of p and q in each of the following diagrams:

(i)

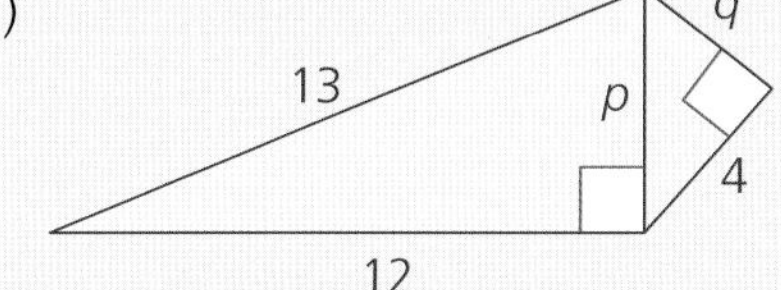

(iii)

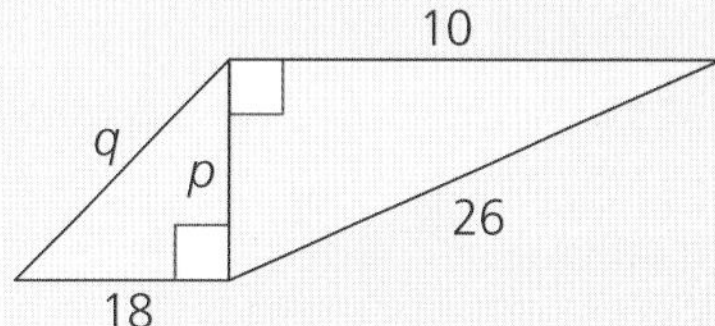

(ii)

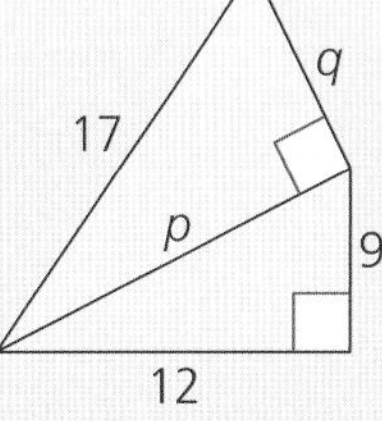

(iv)

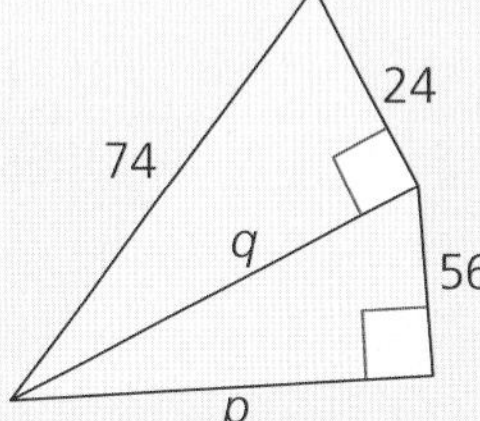

14 The diagram shows a ramp which is to be constructed over some steps.

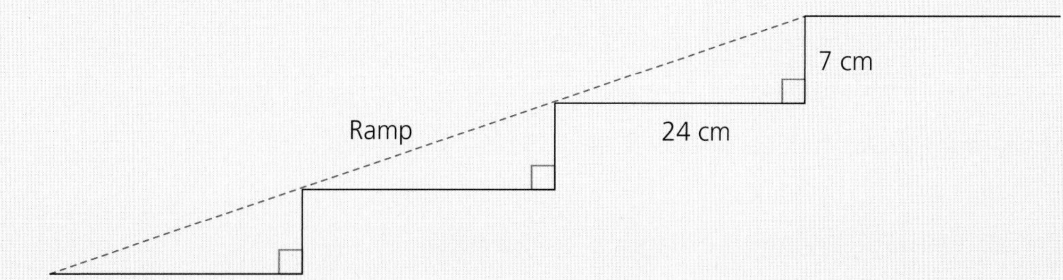

(i) Find the length of the ramp.

(ii) What is the slope of the ramp?

15 The pitch at Croke Park is 144.5 m long and 88 m wide. Find the distance between the corner flags on opposite sides of the pitch (i.e. the diagonal). Give your answer correct to one decimal place.

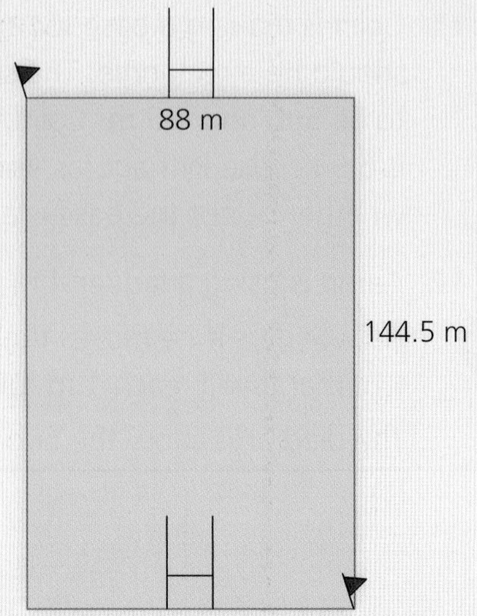

16 In the game of rugby, a player may be required to kick the ball from the ground over the bar between the goalposts (the 'H' shape in the diagram below).

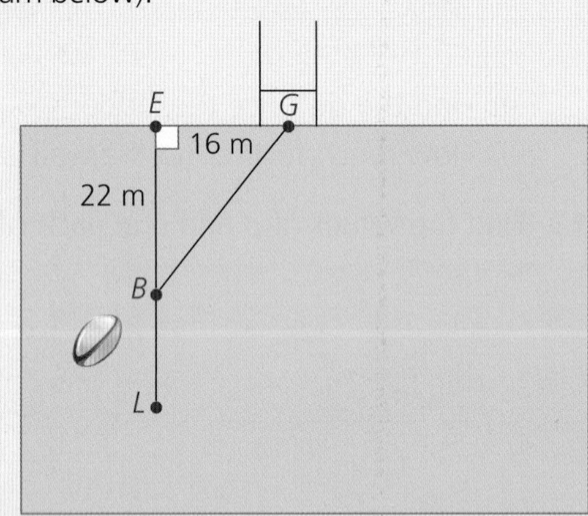

Jonathan is the team kicker and he aims to kick the ball over the bar and between the posts from the point B in the diagram. $|EG| = 16$ m, $|EB| = 22$ m and $|\angle GEB| = 90°$.

(i) How far is the ball from the goalposts (i.e. $|BG|$ in the diagram)?

(ii) The rules of the game indicate that, for certain kicks, you must choose a point along the line EL to kick the ball at the posts. If you were Jonathan, would you choose the point B? What measurements would help you in your decision?

(iii) To be sure to clear the bar of the goalposts, Jonathan must be able to kick the ball at least 10 metres beyond the posts. If his maximum length of kick is 55 metres, what is the maximum distance that he can be from the point E if the ball is on the line EL?

17 The diagram shows a cube of side 4 m.

(i) Calculate $|GC|$, a diagonal of the base of the cube.

(ii) Calculate $|EC|$, an internal diagonal of the cube.

Give your answers in surd form.

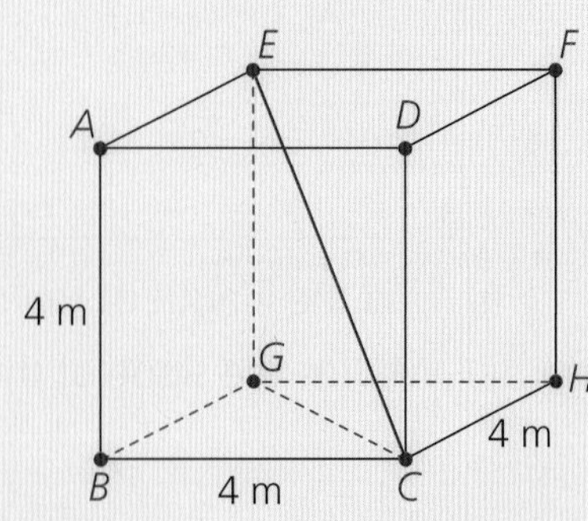

18 If $p^2 - q^2$, $2pq$ and $p^2 + q^2$ are the lengths of the sides of a triangle, show that the triangle is right-angled.

Section 4C Congruent Right-Angled Triangles

We already know from Axiom 4 that two triangles are congruent if we have SSS, SAS or ASA.

From Pythagoras' theorem, we can derive one more set of minimum conditions for congruent triangles. Since this comes from a theorem and we don't prove it, we call it a proposition.

Proposition: Two triangles are congruent if both are right-angled with the hypotenuse and one other side equal in each (RHS).

For example, we can assume that these pairs of triangles are congruent:

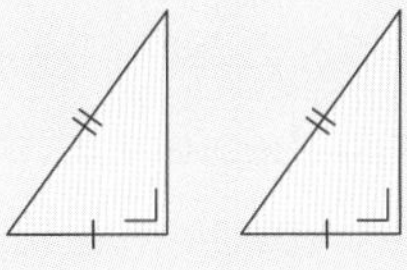

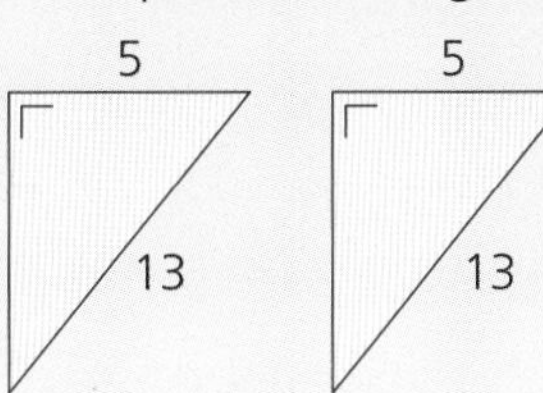

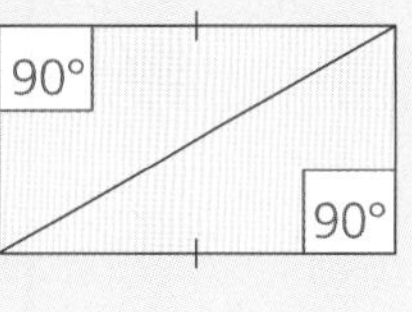

We now have four sets of minimum conditions for congruence of two triangles:

1. Two triangles are congruent if all three sides in each are equal (SSS).
2. Two triangles are congruent if two sides and the included angle in each are equal (SAS).
3. Two triangles are congruent if two angles and the side between them are equal in each (ASA).
4. Two triangles are congruent if both are right-angled with the hypotenuse and one other side equal in each (RHS).

Activity 4.3

1 *ABC* and *DEF* are two right-angled triangles. Equal sides are marked. Prove that these triangles are congruent.

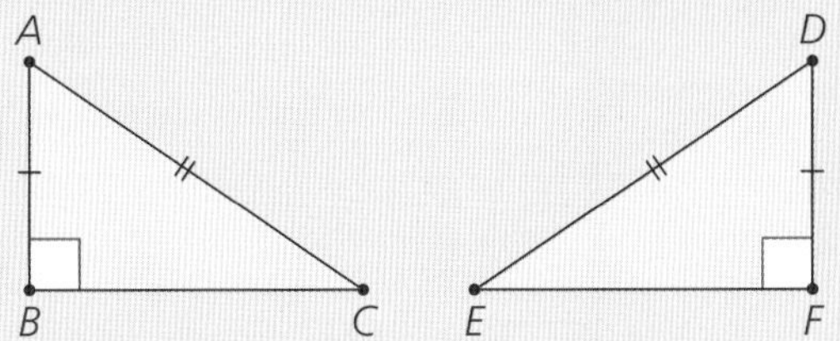

2 *PQR* and *SPR* are two right-angled triangles. |*PS*| = |*QR*|. Prove that these triangles are congruent.

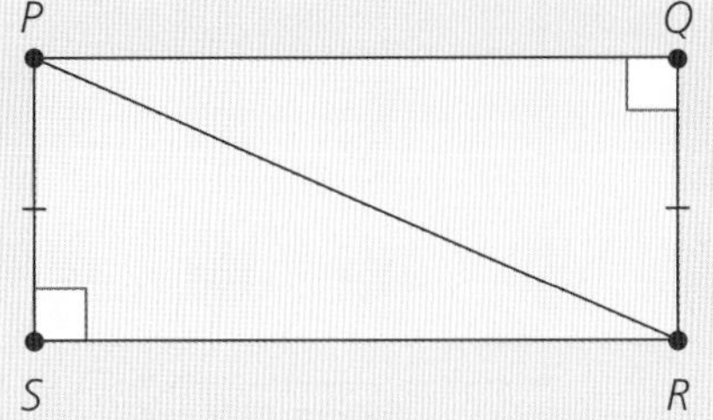

3 *ABCD* is a square.

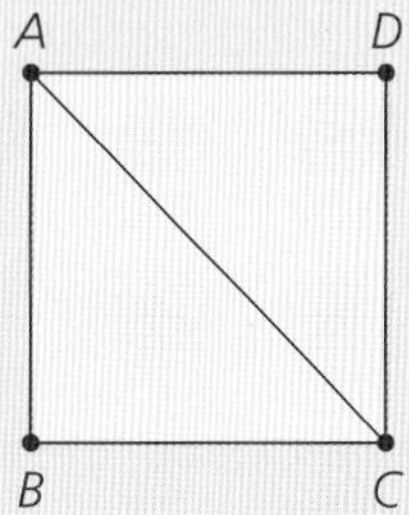

(i) Prove that the triangles *ADC* and *ABC* are congruent.

(ii) How many methods could you use to prove this (SSS, SAS, ASA, RHS)?

4 The diagram shows two poles [*PQ*] and [*RS*] of equal height. They are supported by two equal stay-wires [*PT*] and [*RT*].

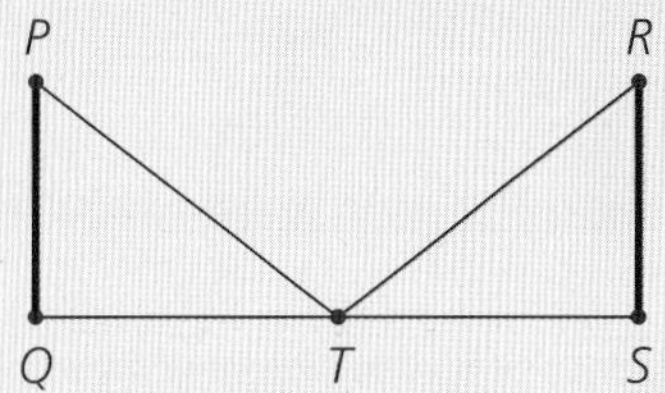

(i) Prove that the triangles *PQT* and *RTS* are congruent.

(ii) Hence, prove that |*QT*| = |*TS*|.

5 A vertical mast is held in place by two equal stay-wires as shown in the diagram. Find the length of each wire.

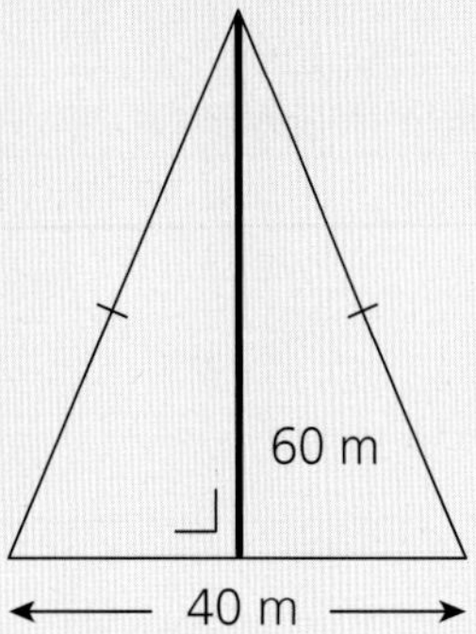

6 The diagram below shows a series of right-angled triangles.

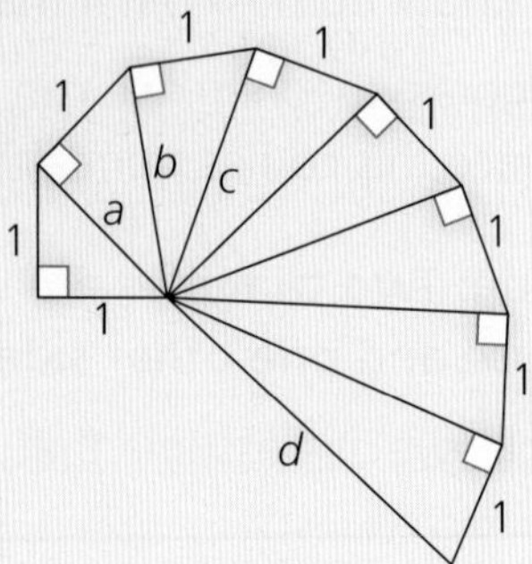

(i) Use Pythagoras' theorem to find a^2.

(ii) Use Pythagoras' theorem and your value of a^2 to find b^2 and c^2.

(iii) Use this pattern to find the value of *d*.

Section 4D Construction of Right-Angled Triangles

In this section, we learn how to construct right-angled triangles given information about different parts of the triangle.

Construction 13

Right-angled triangle given length of hypotenuse and one other side

Example: Construct the triangle *ABC* in which $|\angle ABC| = 90°$, $|AC| = 10$ cm and $|BC| = 8$ cm.

Step 1: Draw a rough sketch.

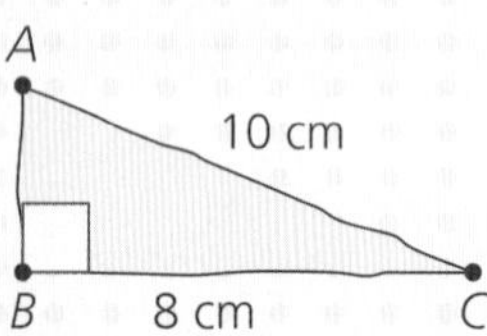

Step 2: Draw and label the base [*BC*] of length 8 cm.

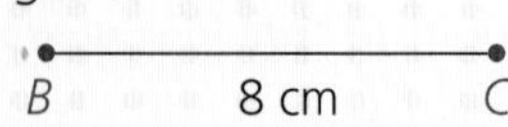

Step 3: Use a protractor to construct a right angle at *B*.

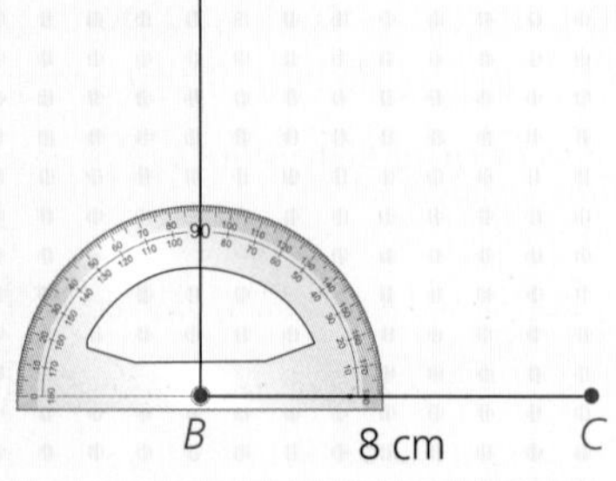

Step 4: With *C* as the centre, draw an arc of radius 10 cm to cut the vertical line. Mark this point *A*.

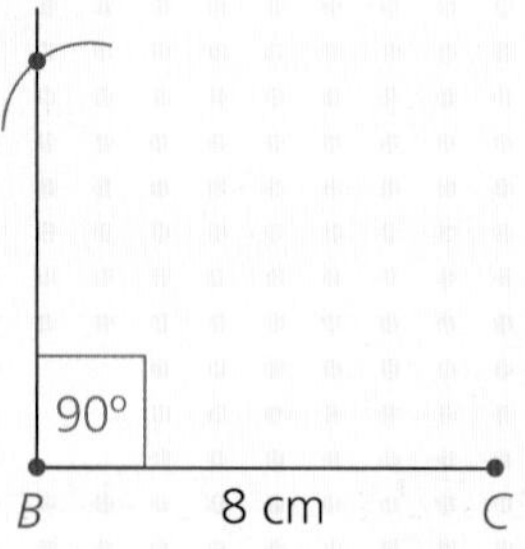

Step 5: Join *AC*. *ABC* is the required triangle.

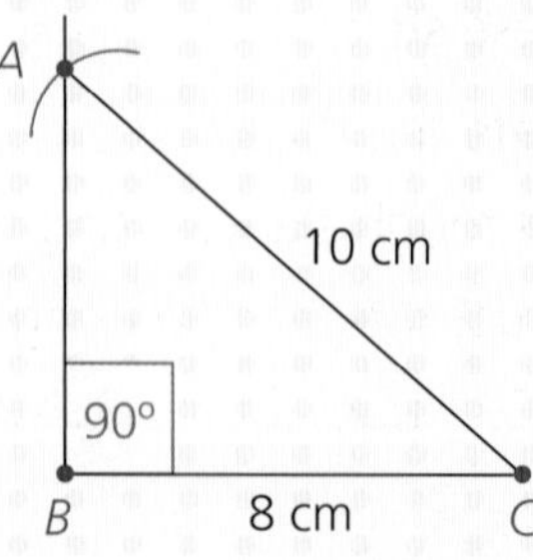

Activity 4.4

1 (i) Construct the triangle ABC where $|\angle ACB| = 90°$, $|BC| = 5$ cm and $|AB| = 12$ cm. Draw a rough sketch first. Show all your construction marks.

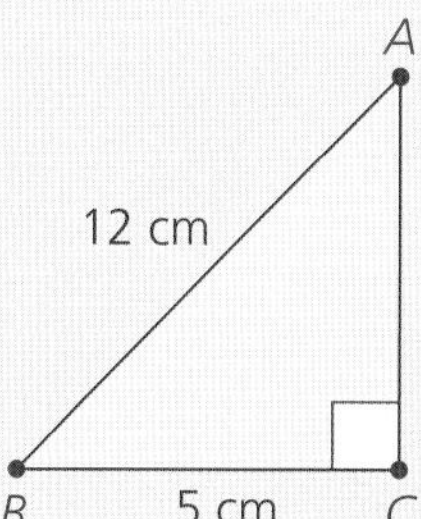

(ii) Measure the length of $[AC]$ on your construction. Check this length by using Pythagoras' theorem.

2 (i) Construct the triangle DEF where $|\angle DEF| = 90°$, $|EF| = 12$ cm and $|DF| = 13$ cm. Draw a rough sketch first. Show all your construction marks.

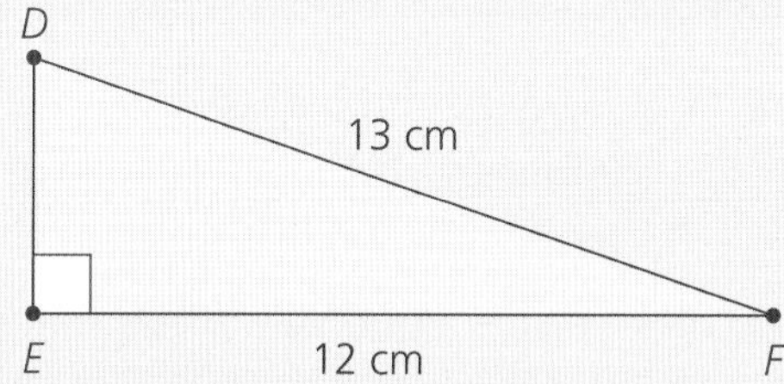

(ii) Measure the length of $[DE]$ on your construction. Check this length by using Pythagoras' theorem.

3 Construct the triangle PQR where $|\angle PQR| = 90°$, $|PR| = 10$ cm and $|QR| = 7$ cm. Draw a rough sketch first. Show all your construction marks.

4 Construct the triangle XYZ where $|\angle XYZ| = 90°$, $|XZ| = 5$ cm and $|YZ| = 4$ cm. Draw a rough sketch first. Show all your construction marks.

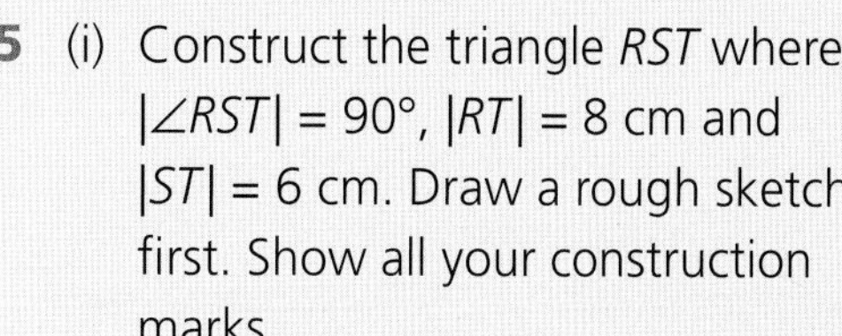

5 (i) Construct the triangle RST where $|\angle RST| = 90°$, $|RT| = 8$ cm and $|ST| = 6$ cm. Draw a rough sketch first. Show all your construction marks.

(ii) Measure the length of $[RS]$ on your construction. Check this length by using Pythagoras' theorem.

6 Construct the triangle MNR using the measurements as shown in the diagram.

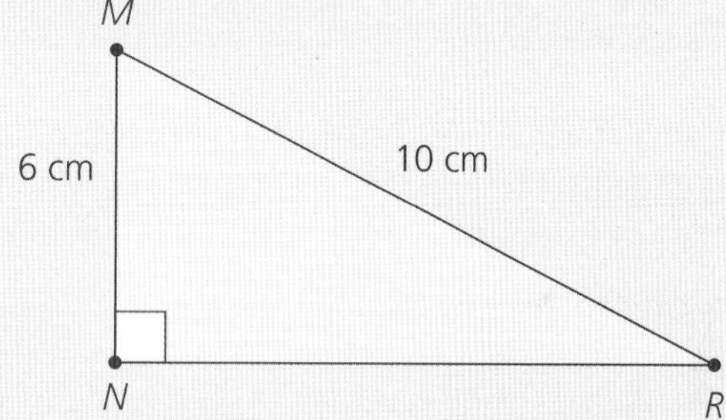

Construction 14

Right-angled triangle given one side and one of the acute angles

In this case, we are given two of the angles in the triangle, so we can calculate the third angle.

Follow these steps:

- Calculate the third angle.
- Draw a rough sketch using the given side as the base of the triangle.
- Construct the triangle using the method of Construction 12 (ASA).

Example: Construct the triangle ABC in which $|\angle ABC| = 90°$, $|AC| = 8$ cm and $|\angle BAC| = 30°$.

Step 1: Calculate the third angle: 60°.

Step 2: Draw a rough sketch with [AC] as the base of the triangle.

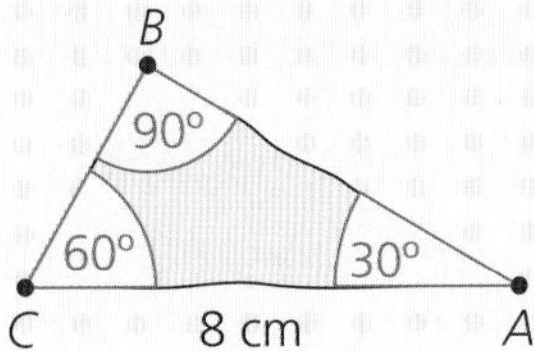

Step 3: Construct [CA] of length 8 cm.

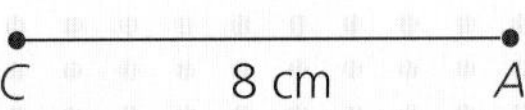

Step 4: Use a protractor to construct an angle of 60° at C.

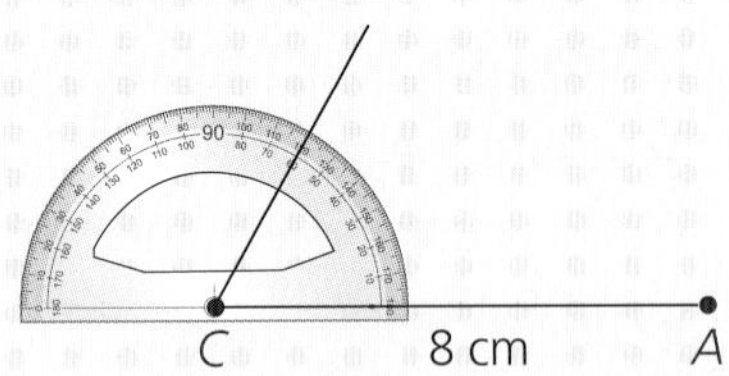

Step 5: Use a protractor to construct an angle of 30° at A. Mark the point B where the two construction lines meet.

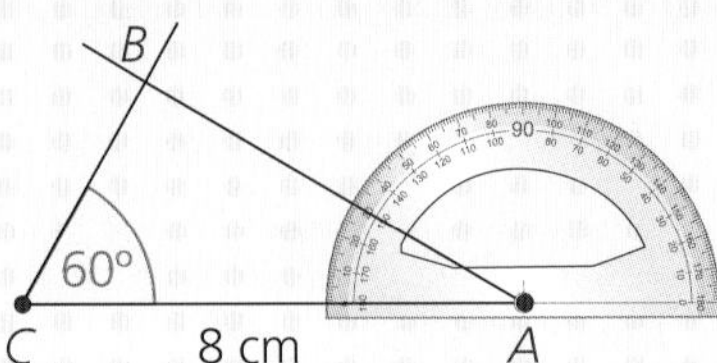

Step 6: The triangle ABC is complete.

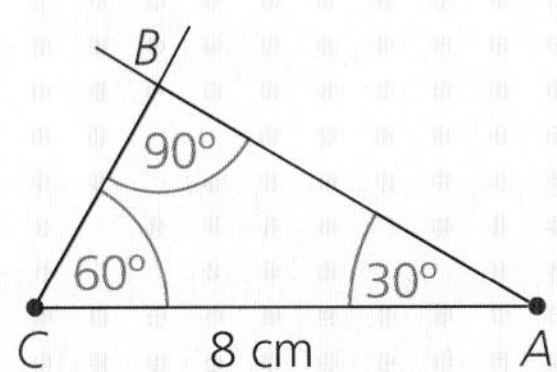

Activity 4.5

1 Construct the triangle *DEF* where $|\angle DFE| = 90°$, $|\angle DEF| = 40°$ and $|EF| = 5$ cm. Draw a rough sketch first. Show all your construction marks.

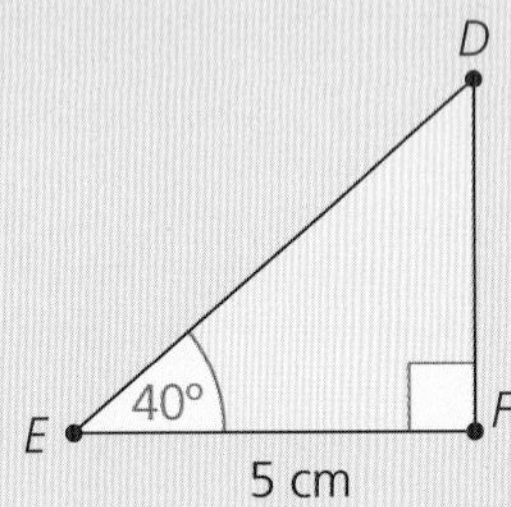

2 (i) Calculate the third angle in the triangle *PQR* in the diagram.

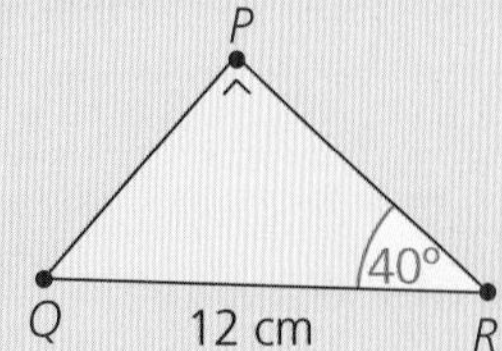

(ii) Construct the triangle *PQR* where $|\angle QPR| = 90°$, $|\angle PRQ| = 40°$ and $|QR| = 12$ cm.

Draw a rough sketch first. Show all your construction marks.

3 (i) Draw a sketch of the triangle *STV* where $|\angle STV| = 90°$, $|\angle TSV| = 35°$ and $|TV| = 7$ cm.

(ii) Calculate the size of the third angle in the triangle.

(iii) Construct the triangle *STV*, showing all your construction marks.

4 (i) Draw a sketch of the triangle *ABC* where $|\angle BAC| = 90°$, $|\angle ABC| = 55°$ and $|BC| = 10$ cm.

(ii) Calculate the size of the third angle in the triangle.

(iii) Construct the triangle *ABC*.

5 (i) Draw a sketch of the triangle *XYZ* where $|\angle XYZ| = 90°$, $|\angle XZY| = 25°$ and $|YZ| = 8$ cm.

(ii) Calculate the size of the third angle in the triangle.

(iii) Construct the triangle *XYZ* showing all construction marks.

6 Construct the triangle *PMN* where $|\angle PMN| = 90°$, $|\angle PNM| = 32°$ and $|PN| = 10$ cm. Draw a rough sketch first.

7 Construct the triangle *MNR* using the measurements as shown in the diagram.

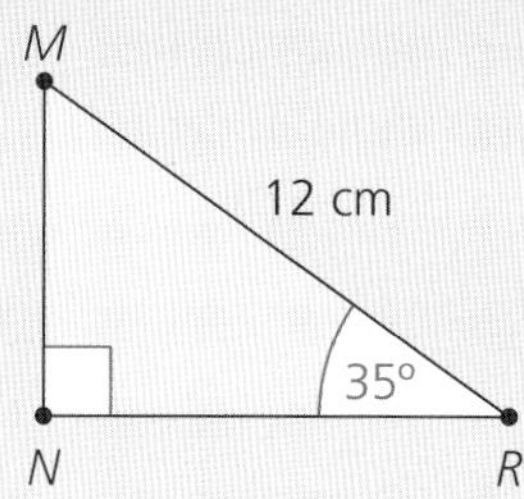

Section 4E Construction 15: A Rectangle Given the Side Lengths

A **rectangle** is a quadrilateral having right angles at all four vertices. The opposite sides of a rectangle are equal.

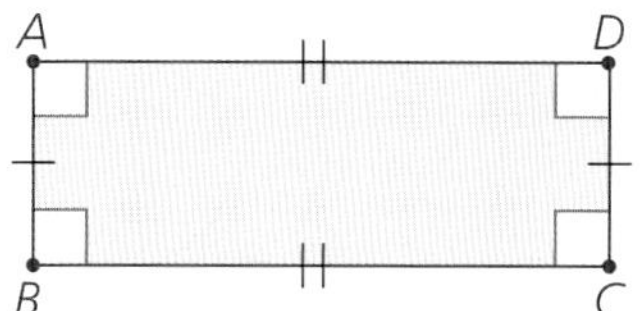

A **square** is a rectangle with all four sides equal.

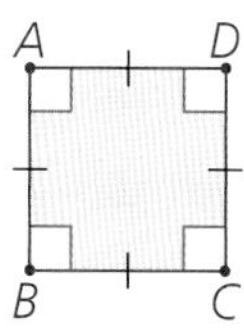

We need to be able to construct rectangles when given their side lengths.

Construction 15

Example: Construct the rectangle *PQRS* where $|PQ| = 5$ cm and $|QR| = 8$ cm.

Step 1: Draw a rough sketch.

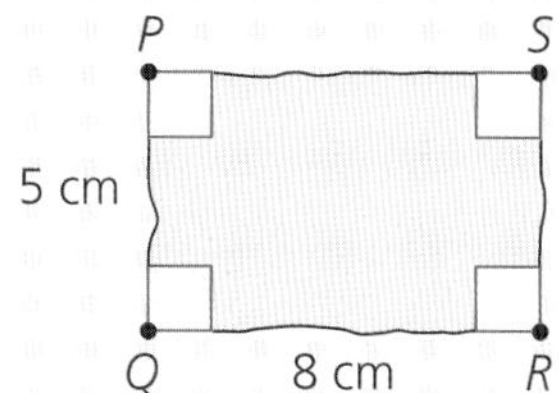

Step 2: Draw the line segment [*QR*] where $|QR| = 8$ cm.

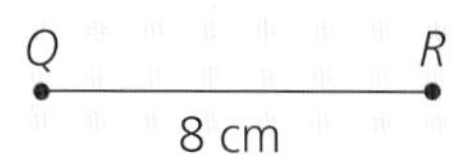

Step 3: Using a protractor, construct a right angle at point *Q*.

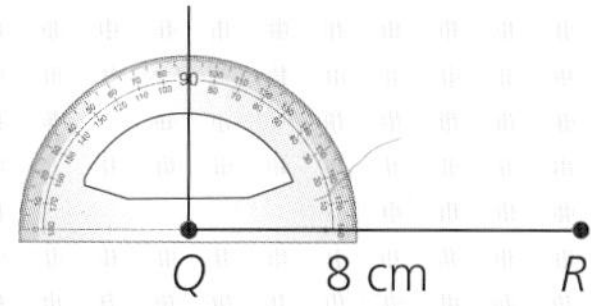

Step 4: Using a protractor, construct a right angle at point *R*.

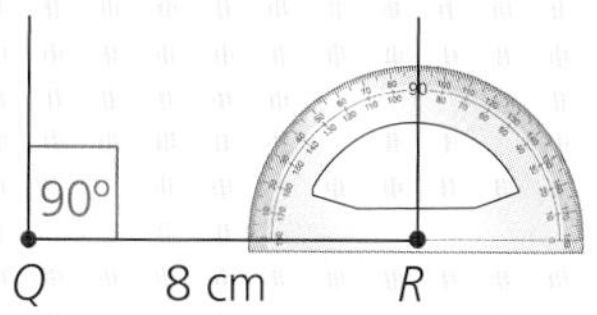

Step 5: Use your compass to mark off points *P* and *S* such that $|QP| = |RS| = 5$ cm.

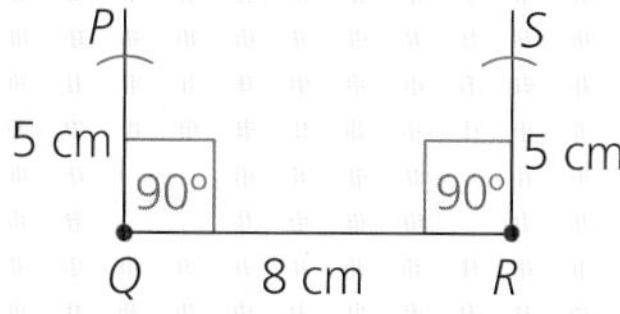

Step 6: Join *P* to *S*.

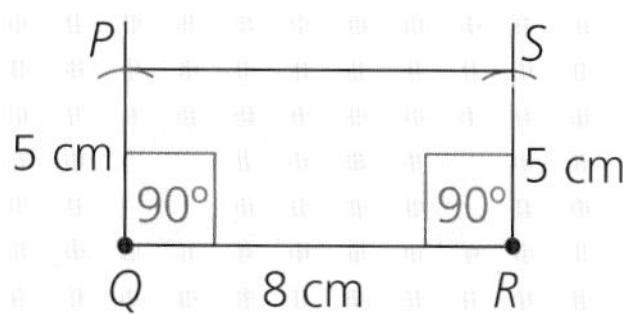

The rectangle *PQRS* is now complete.

Activity 4.6

In the following constructions, write in all your measurements on your diagram.

1 (i) Construct the rectangle *ABCD* where |*BC*| = 8 cm and |*AB*| = 6 cm. Draw a free-hand sketch first and remember to name the rectangle in cyclical order so that [*AC*] and [*BD*] are diagonals.

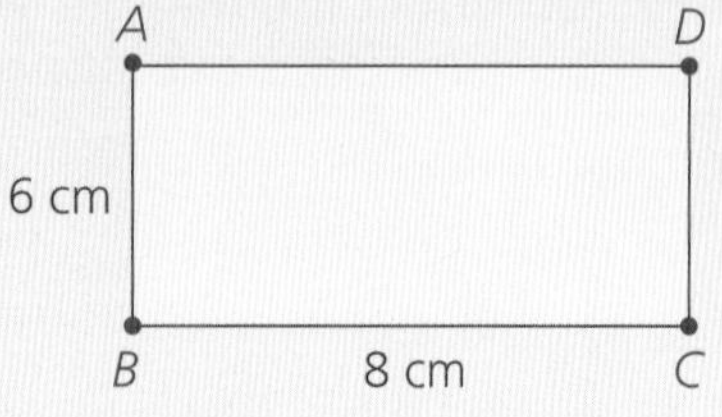

(ii) Draw in the diagonals. Measure |*AC*| and |*BD*| and mark these in on your construction.

(iii) Are these diagonals equal in length?

(iv) Use your protractor to measure the angles between the diagonals. Are the diagonals perpendicular?

2 (i) Construct the rectangle *PQRS* where |*QR*| = 12 cm and |*PQ*| = 5 cm. Draw a free-hand sketch first.

(ii) Draw in the diagonals. Measure |*PR*| and |*QS*|.

(iii) Are these diagonals equal in length? Do you think this would be true for all rectangles?

(iv) Are the diagonals perpendicular?

3 (i) Construct the rectangle *EFGH* where |*EF*| = 9 cm and |*FG*| = 3 cm. Draw a free-hand sketch first.

(ii) Draw in the diagonals [*EG*] and [*FH*] and measure them.

4 (i) Construct the rectangle *PQRS* where |*QR*| = 7 cm and |*PQ*| = 5 cm. Draw a free-hand sketch first.

(ii) Draw in the diagonals [*PR*] and [*QS*] and measure them.

(iii) Are the diagonals perpendicular?

5 (i) Construct the rectangle *ABCD* where |*BC*| = 5 cm and |*AB*| = 5 cm. Draw a free-hand sketch first.

(ii) Draw in the diagonals. Measure |*AC*| and |*BD*|.

(iii) Are the diagonals perpendicular?

6 From your observations in questions **1** to **5**, what conjecture would you make about the diagonals of a rectangle?

7 (i) Construct the rectangle *MPQR* where |*MP*| = 5 cm and |*PQ*| = 8 cm. Draw a free-hand sketch first and remember to name the rectangle in cyclical order so that [*MQ*] and [*PR*] are diagonals.

(ii) Draw in the diagonals. Measure |*MQ*| and |*PR*|.

(iii) Are these diagonals equal in length?

(iv) Compare the lengths of the diagonals with the side lengths of the rectangle.

8 (i) Construct the rectangle *ABCD* where |*BC*| = 10 cm and |*AB*| = 3 cm. Draw a free-hand sketch first.

(ii) Draw in the diagonals [*AC*] and [*BD*] and measure them.

(iii) Compare the lengths of the diagonals with the side lengths of the rectangle.

9 (i) Construct the rectangle *PQRS* where $|QR| = 6$ cm and $|PQ| = 5$ cm. Draw a free-hand sketch first.

(ii) Draw in the diagonals [*PR*] and [*QS*] and measure them.

(iii) Compare the lengths of the diagonals with the side lengths of the rectangle.

10 Jack is making a base for a garage. The base should be a rectangle. The sides of the base are 5 m and 4.5 m. What measurements should Jack make to ensure that the base is a rectangle?

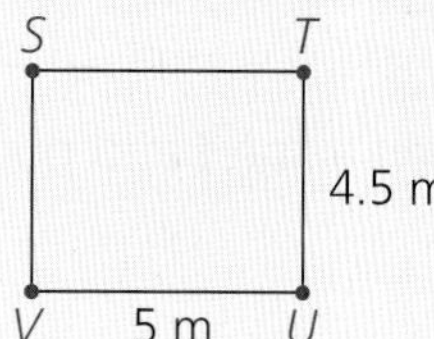

Section 4F Constructions 3 and 4

In this section, we look at how to construct a line perpendicular to a given line through a given point.

This construction was already shown in *Connect With Maths: Introduction to Junior Cycle*.

Construction 4

To construct a line perpendicular to a given line *l*, through a point **on** *l*.

Step 1: With *P* as centre and any radius, draw two arcs intersecting the line *l* at *X* and *Y*.

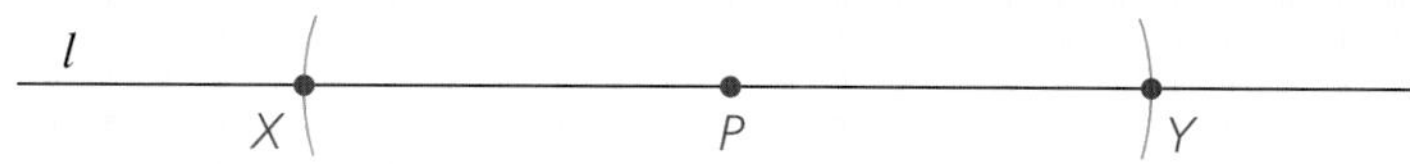

Step 2: Set your compass to draw an arc longer than $|PX|$.

Step 3: With *X* and *Y* as centres and the same radius, draw two more arcs intersecting at *Q* (above or below the line *l*).

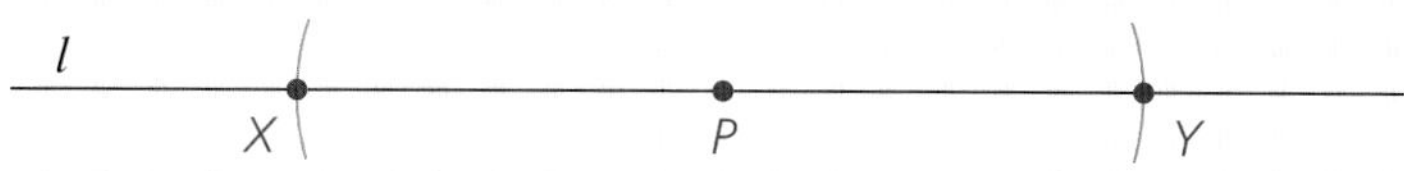

Step 4: Join *Q* to *P*. The line *QP* is perpendicular to *l*.

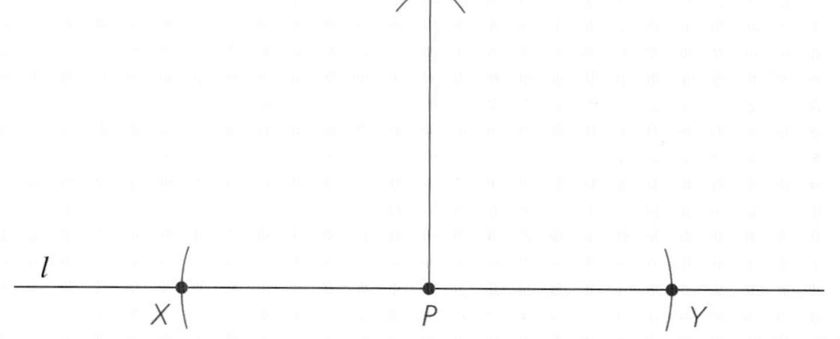

You can also use a set-square and straight-edge to perform Construction 4.

Construction 3

To construct a line perpendicular to a given line l, through a point **not on** l.

Method 1: Using a straight-edge and set-square

Step 1: Given a line l and point P not on l. (P could be above or below l.)

•P

l

Step 2: Place the straight-edge (or ruler) along line l and place the set-square on the straight-edge.

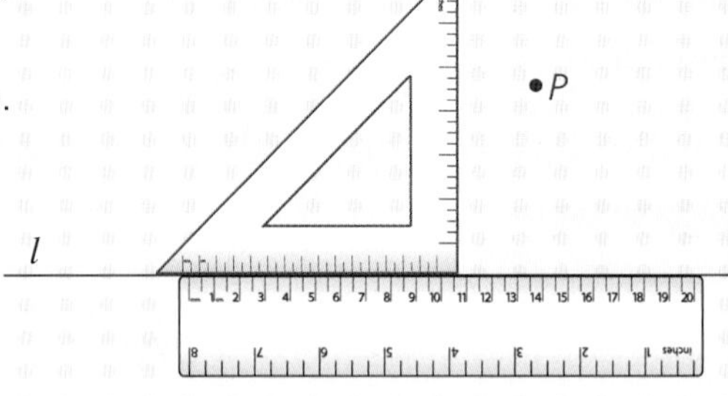

Step 3: Move the set-square along the straight-edge until it just reaches the point P. Draw the line m through P using the edge of the set-square.
m is the required line perpendicular to l through point P.

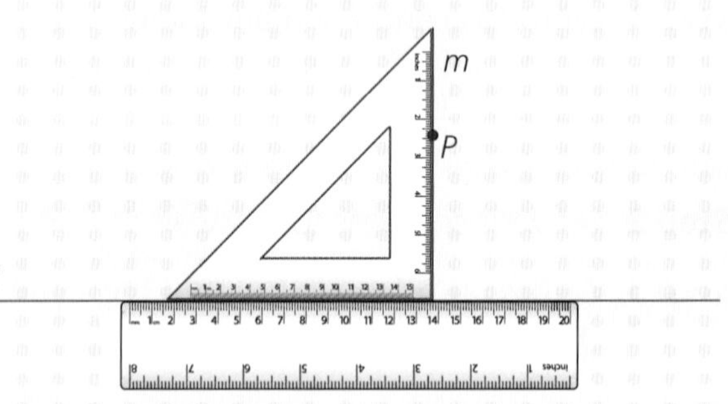

Method 2: Using a straight-edge and compass

Step 1: Given a line l and point P not on l. (P could be above or below l.)

P •

l

Step 2: Using P as centre and any radius, draw two arcs to cut l at R and S.

P •

l R S

Step 3: Using R as centre and the same radius, draw an arc on the opposite side of l to P. Using S as centre and the same radius, draw another arc to intersect the first arc at Q.

P

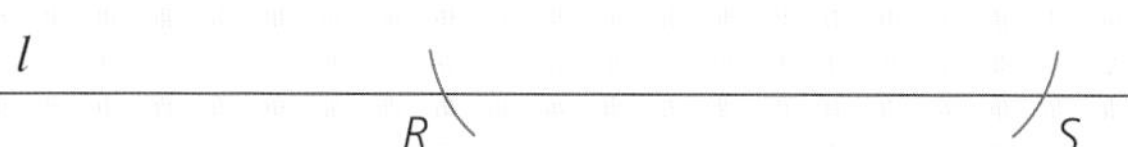

Step 4: Join PQ.

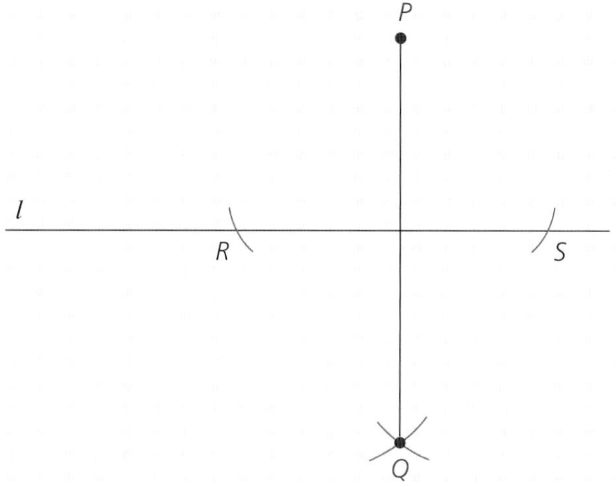

PQ is then the required perpendicular to l.

Activity 4.7

In questions **1–4**, copy the diagram into your copybook and construct the line segment $[PQ]$ perpendicular to AB using only a straight-edge and compass.

1

P

A B

2

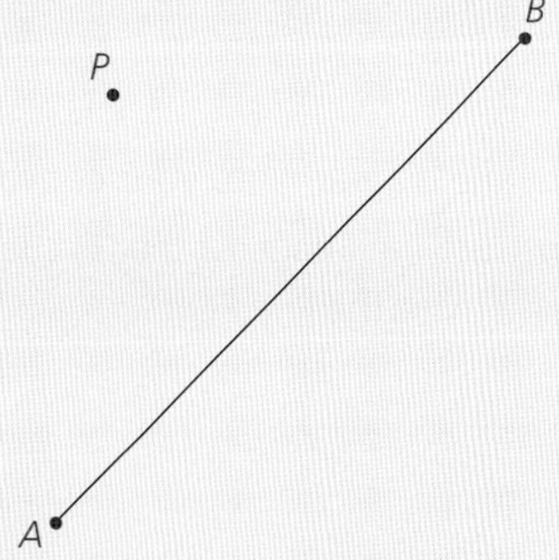

3

B

P

A

4

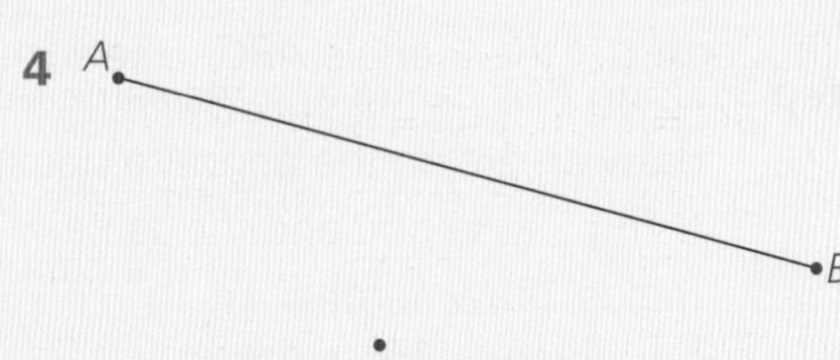

5 Repeat the constructions in questions **1–4** above, using a straight-edge and set-square.

6 The point $P \in AB$.

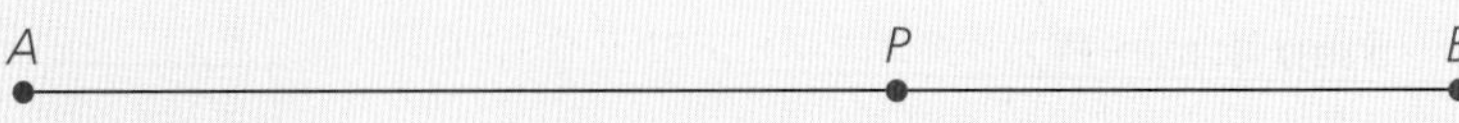

(i) Copy the diagram into your copybook.

(ii) Draw a line perpendicular to AB through P.

7 (i) Copy the diagram into your copybook.

(ii) Construct perpendiculars from the points D, C and E onto AB using a straight-edge and set-square.

(iii) Use the construction in part (ii) to construct the image of the triangle DEC by axial symmetry in the line AB.

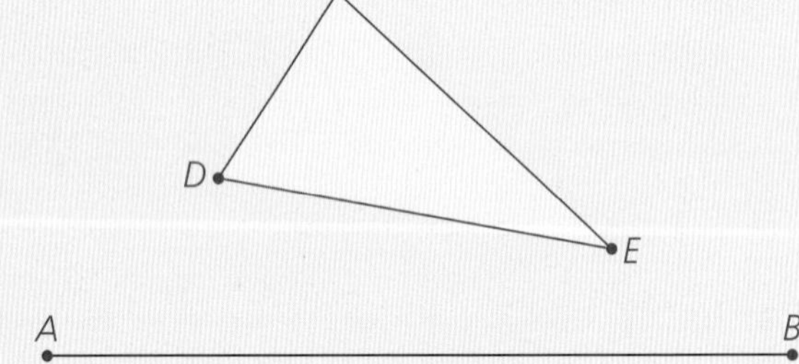

8 (i) Copy the diagram into your copybook.

(ii) Construct perpendiculars from the points D, C and E onto AB using a straight-edge and set-square.

(iii) Use the construction in part (ii) to construct the image of the triangle DEC by axial symmetry in the line AB.

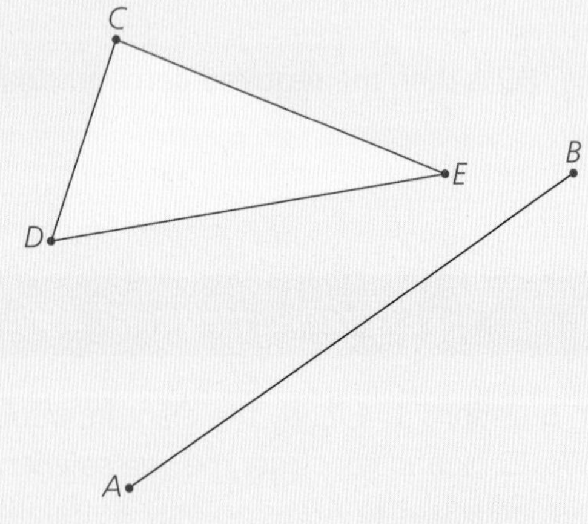

9 (i) Copy the diagram into your copybook.

(ii) Construct the image of the 'F' shape by axial symmetry in the line PQ.

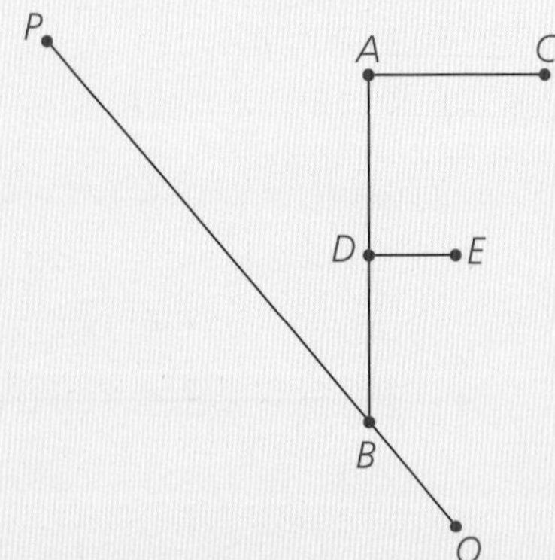

10 (i) Construct the triangle ABC, where $|AB| = 6$ cm, $|BC| = 7$ cm, $|AC| = 8$ cm.

(ii) Construct perpendiculars from each of the vertices of the triangle onto the opposite sides.

(iii) Your three perpendiculars should meet at one point. Label this point P. (P is called the **orthocentre** of the triangle.)

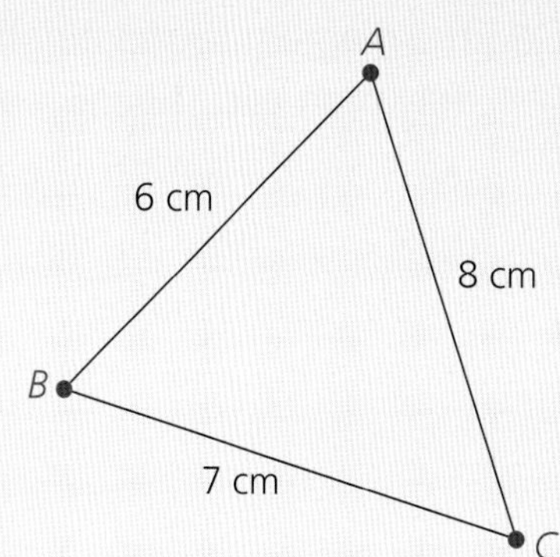

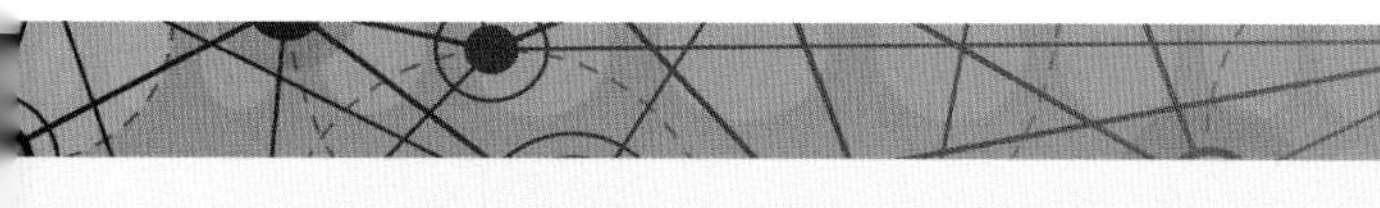

Revision Activity 4

1 Elizabeth and Rebecca are starting to construct an L-shaped building.

After putting pegs in the three main corners, they want to check that it is square before getting the rest of the profiles fixed.

They work out the length of the red dotted line to check for a right angle.

What length should the red dotted line be?

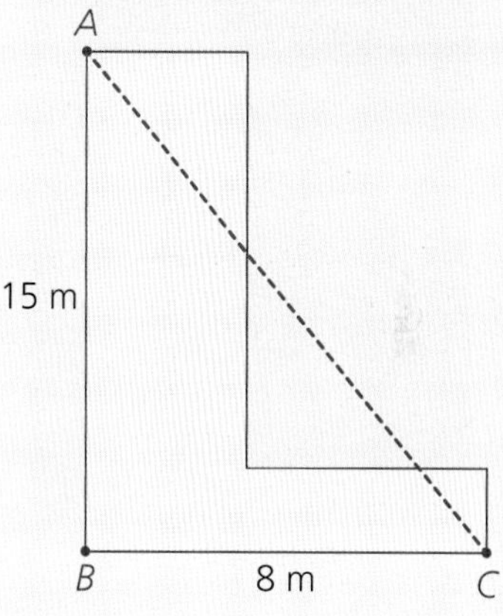

2 (a) Construct a triangle ABC where $|AB| = 6$ cm, $|AC| = 8$ cm and $|BC| = 10$ cm. Show all your construction marks clearly.

(b) What type of triangle is this? Mathematically show that this is so.

3 (a) Copy the table below and tick one box for each of the statements.

	Statement	Always true	Sometimes true	Never true
(i)	A triangle has two right angles.			
(ii)	A triangle has an obtuse angle.			
(iii)	If I know the size of two angles in a triangle, I can work out the size of the third angle.			
(iv)	A triangle has at least two acute angles.			
(v)	A right-angled triangle is also isosceles.			

(b) For each 'sometimes true' answer, explain your answer using a diagram.

4 The size of an A4 page is 210 mm × 297 mm.

(a) Describe how you would calculate the length of the longest line that could be drawn on an A4 page.

(b) Calculate the length of this longest line, correct to the nearest mm.

5 The diagram shows a right-angled triangle with a square drawn on each side. Each small box is 1 cm in length.

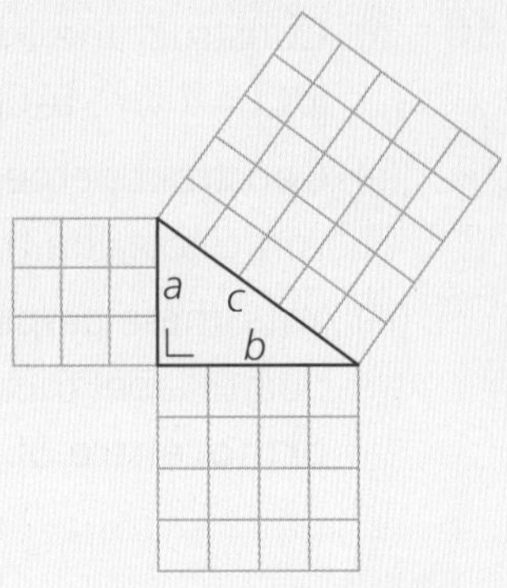

(a) State the length of each side of the triangle, a, b and c.

(b) Explain how the diagram can be used to demonstrate that Pythagoras' theorem can be applied to this triangle.

(c) Find the area of the triangle.

6 Windows are sometimes made with a pointed arch.

Mary is designing such an arched window.

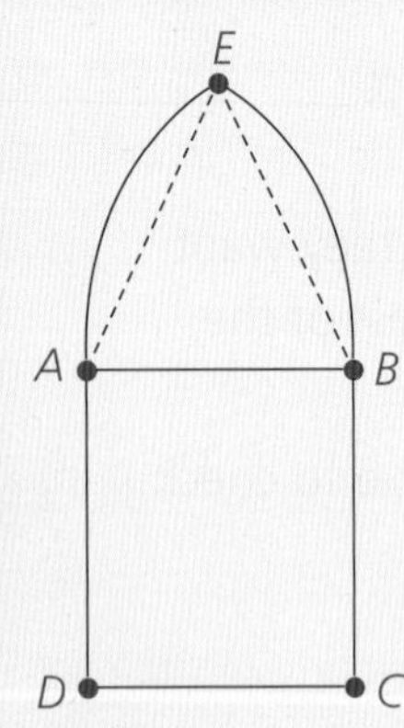

She has drawn an outline of the window as shown in the diagram.

$ABCD$ is a rectangle.

The centre for arc AE is B and the centre for arc EB is A.

$|AD| = 2.5$ m and $|DC| = 1.5$ m.

(a) Show that $|\angle EAB| = 60°$.

(b) Construct an accurate scale drawing of the outline of the window, using the scale 1 : 25. That is, 1 cm on your diagram should represent 25 cm in reality.

Exam-style Question

1 Given any two positive integers m and n ($n > m$), it is possible to form three numbers a, b and c where:

$$a = n^2 - m^2,\ b = 2nm,\ c = n^2 + m^2$$

These three numbers a, b and c are then known as a 'Pythagorean triple'.

(a) For $m = 3$ and $n = 5$, calculate a, b and c.

(b) If the values of a, b and c from part (a) are the lengths of the sides of a triangle, show that the triangle is right-angled.

(c) If $n^2 - m^2$, $2nm$ and $n^2 + m^2$ are the lengths of the sides of a triangle, show that the triangle is right-angled.

JCHL 2014 Sample Paper 1

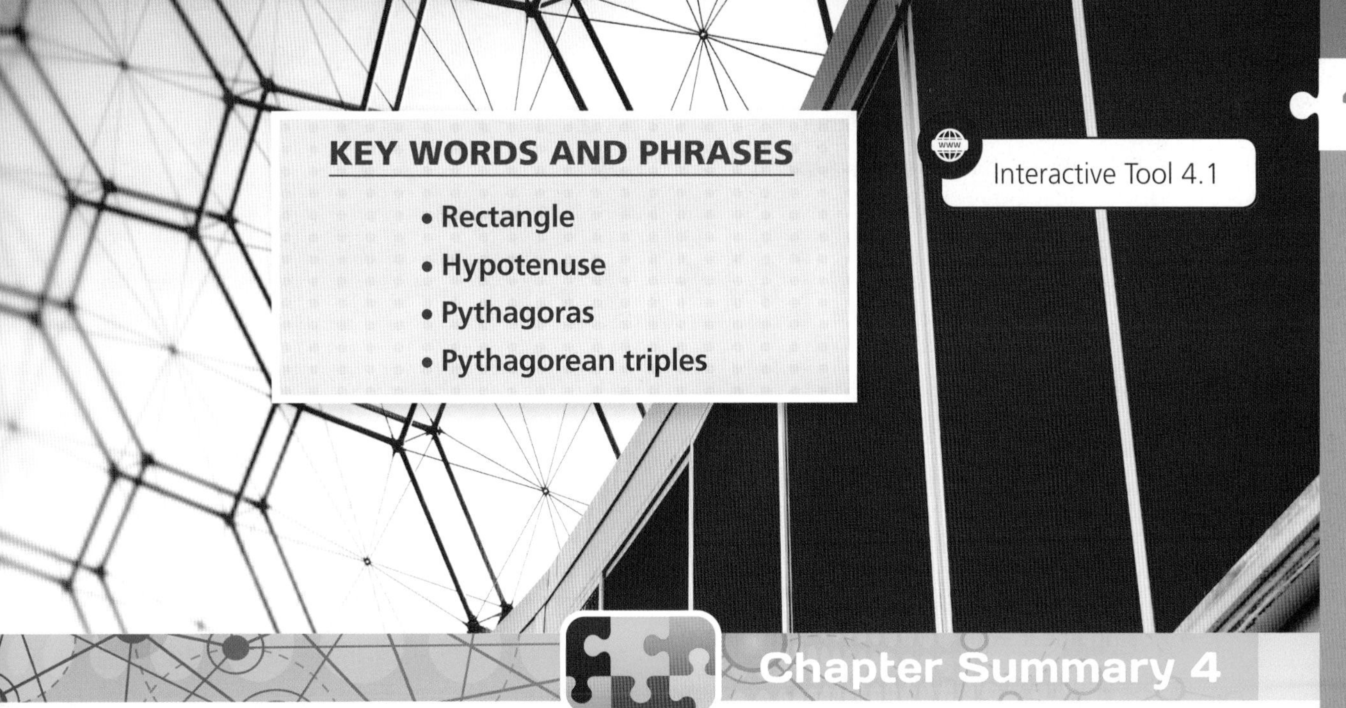

- **Pythagoras' theorem:** The square on the hypotenuse of a right-angled triangle is equal to the sum of the squares on the other two sides.

  This is the way it appears in the *Formulae and tables* booklet:

  $$c^2 = a^2 + b^2$$

  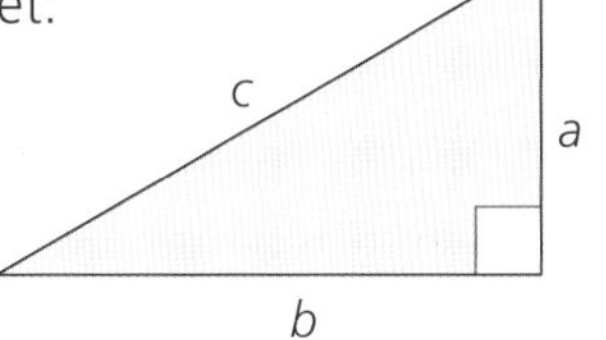

  Conversely: If the square of one side of a triangle is equal to the sum of the squares on the other two sides, then the angle opposite the first side is a right angle.

- Two **triangles** are **congruent** if both are right-angled with the hypotenuse and one other side equal in each (**RHS**).

  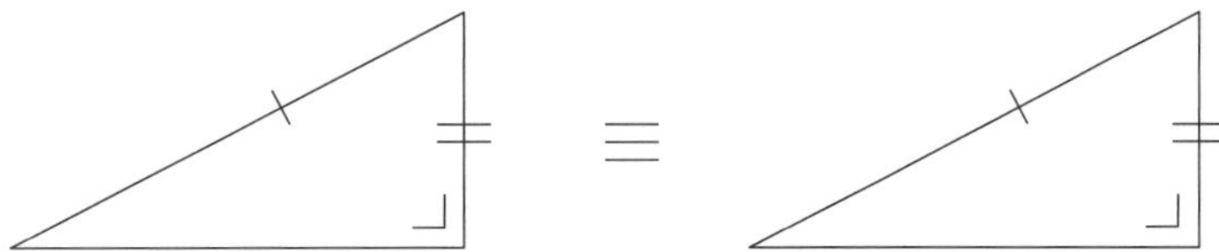

- Construction 13: Right-angled triangle given the length of hypotenuse and one other side.
- Construction 14: Right-angled triangle given one side and one of the acute angles.
- Construction 15: The construction of a rectangle given the lengths of sides.
- Diagonals of a rectangle are equal in length.

Chapter

5

Algebra 2

Learning Intentions

In this chapter, you will learn about:

- Solving linear equations with fractions
- Using linear equations to solve problems
- Solving linear inequalities in one variable

LO: U.3, U.5, U.6, AF.2(c), AF.4(a, d)

Section 5A Revision: Linear Equations

In an equation, a term or expression is equal (=) to another term or expression. We say that the equation is balanced.

On the scales here, the block weighing x units on the left side is balanced by five smaller blocks on the right side, each with a weight of 1 unit. It is because the scales are balanced that we can form the equation $x = 5$.

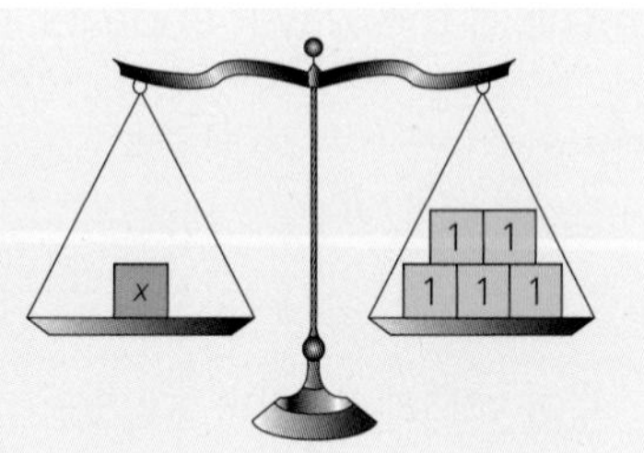

When we solve an equation, we find the value or values of the unknown variable or variables.

To keep an equation balanced, the same operation must be applied to both sides of the equation. This means that:

- If you add a number to one side of an equation, you must add the **same** number to the other side of the equation.
- If you subtract a number from one side of an equation, you must subtract the **same** number from the other side of the equation.
- If you multiply one side of an equation by a number, you must multiply the other side of the equation by the **same** number.
- If you divide one side of an equation by a number, you must divide the other side of the equation by the **same** number.

A linear equation is any equation of the form $ax + b = 0$ or $y = ax + b$ where $a, b \in \mathbb{R}$.

Example 1

Solve $36k - 13 = 149$.

Solution

$36k - 13 = 149$

$\Rightarrow \quad 36k = 149 + 13$ ... add 13 to both sides

$\Rightarrow \quad 36k = 162$

$k = \frac{162}{36}$ ... divide both sides by 36

$k = 4\frac{1}{2}$

Check answer by substituting $k = 4\frac{1}{2}$ into original equation:

$36k - 13 = 149$

$\Rightarrow 36\left(4\frac{1}{2}\right) - 13 = 149$

$\Rightarrow \quad 162 - 13 = 149$

$\Rightarrow \quad 149 = 149$ ✓

As LHS = RHS, the equation is balanced.

Example 2

Solve $3(n + 4) - 5(n - 1) = 9n + 28$.

Solution

$3(n + 4) - 5(n - 1) = 9n + 28$

$\Rightarrow 3n + 12 - 5n + 5 = 9n + 28$

$\Rightarrow \quad -2n + 17 = 9n + 28$

$\Rightarrow \quad 17 = 9n + 28 + 2n$ ... add $2n$ to both sides

$\Rightarrow \quad 17 - 28 = 11n$ ... subtract 28 from both sides

$\Rightarrow \quad -\frac{11}{11} = n$ ... divide both sides by 11

$\Rightarrow \quad -1 = n$

Check answer by substituting $n = -1$ into both sides of the original equation:

LHS: $3(n + 4) - 5(n - 1) = 3(-1 + 4) - 5(-1 - 1) = 3(3) - 5(-2) = 9 + 10 = 19$

RHS: $9n + 28 = 9(-1) + 28 = -9 + 28 = 19$ ✓ As LHS = RHS, the equation is balanced.

Example 3

Solve $\frac{2}{5}\left(4y - 7\right) = 8$.

Solution

$\frac{2}{5}\left(4y - 7\right) = 8$

$\Rightarrow \frac{2(4y - 7)}{5} = 8$

$\Rightarrow 2(4y - 7) = 5(8)$ ... multiply both sides by 5

$\Rightarrow \quad 8y - 14 = 40$

$\Rightarrow \quad 8y = 40 + 14$ ... add 14 to both sides

$\Rightarrow \quad \frac{8y}{8} = \frac{54}{8}$ ... divide both sides by 8

$\Rightarrow \quad y = 6\frac{3}{4}$

Check answer by substituting $y = 6\frac{3}{4}$ into the original equation:

$\frac{2}{5}\left[4\left(6\frac{3}{4}\right) - 7\right] = 8$

$\Rightarrow \frac{2}{5}\left(27 - 7\right) = 8$

$\Rightarrow \quad \frac{2}{5}\left(20\right) = 8$

$\Rightarrow \quad 8 = 8$ ✓

As LHS = RHS, the equation is balanced.

Activity 5.1

Solve the following equations and **verify** your answers.

1 $3x - 7 = 2$

2 $7y - 1 = 13$

3 $5a + 8 = -17$

4 $5x + 12 = 42$

5 $7g + 21 = -14$

6 $2h - 11 = 1 - h$

7 $4t + 3 = 7t + 39$

8 $12z - 1 = 7z + 49$

9 $\frac{x + 4}{2} = 3$

10 $\frac{4x + 13}{3} = 23$

11 $\frac{w + 5}{8} = -3$

12 $\frac{3y - 11}{4} = 16$

13 $\frac{11s - 2}{7} = -5$

14 $\frac{2}{3}(b + 3) = 8$

15 $3(5l - 2) = 9$

16 $7(-2m - 1) - 18 = 3$

17 $2(x - 3) = 3(4 - x)$

18 $4(p - 7) = 5(p + 1)$

19 $2(q + 3) - (q - 2) = 2q - 7$

20 $7(2 + n) - 2(3n + 1) = 10(n + 3)$

Section 5B More Linear Equations with Fractions

The examples below show how to solve linear equations where the coefficients of the variable and the solutions may be rational numbers (elements of $\mathbb{Q}$).

Example 1

Solve $\frac{7x}{3} = 6$ for x.

Solution

$$\frac{7x}{3} = 6$$

$\Rightarrow \quad 7x = 3(6)$ ... multiply both sides by 3

$\Rightarrow \quad 7x = 18$

$\Rightarrow \quad x = \frac{18}{7}$ ... divide both sides by 7

Check answer by substituting $x = \frac{18}{7}$ into the original equation:

$$\frac{7\left(\frac{18}{7}\right)}{3} = 6 \Rightarrow \frac{18}{3} = 6 \Rightarrow 6 = 6 ✓$$

As LHS = RHS, the equation is balanced.

Example 2

Solve $\frac{2p}{3} - \frac{5p}{4} = \frac{11}{6}$ for p.

Solution

$$\frac{2p}{3} - \frac{5p}{4} = \frac{11}{6}$$

$\Rightarrow \quad \frac{12(2p)}{3} - \frac{12(5p)}{4} = \frac{12(11)}{6}$

$\Rightarrow \quad 4(2p) - 3(5p) = 2(11)$ ... multiply all terms by the LCM of 3, 4 and 6, i.e. 12

$\Rightarrow \quad 8p - 15p = 22$

$\Rightarrow \quad -7p = 22$

$\Rightarrow \quad p = \frac{22}{-7}$ ... divide both sides by -7

Check answer by substituting $p = -\frac{22}{7}$ into the original equation:

$$\frac{2\left(-\frac{22}{7}\right)}{3} - \frac{5\left(-\frac{22}{7}\right)}{4} = \frac{11}{6} \Rightarrow \frac{-\frac{44}{7}}{3} + \frac{\frac{110}{7}}{4} = \frac{11}{6} \Rightarrow -\frac{44}{21} + \frac{110}{28} = \frac{11}{6} \Rightarrow \frac{11}{6} = \frac{11}{6} \checkmark$$

As LHS = RHS, the equation is balanced.

Activity 5.2

Solve the following equations.

1. $\frac{5h}{3} = 15$
2. $\frac{7d}{4} = -14$
3. $\frac{3n}{7} = 42$
4. $\frac{12y}{5} = -60$
5. $\frac{21m}{8} = 9$
6. $\frac{2}{3}x + 4 = 7$
7. $\frac{2c}{9} + 8 = 5$
8. $\frac{3}{5}p - 2 = 22$
9. $\frac{3}{4}v + 2 = 9$
10. $\frac{7}{9}z - 8 = 4$
11. $\frac{2x - 3}{7} = \frac{2}{3}$
12. $\frac{5h + 1}{3} = \frac{4}{5}$
13. $\frac{6m + 7}{8} = \frac{9}{2}$
14. $\frac{3d - 4}{7} = \frac{1}{8}$
15. $\frac{9k + 4}{5} = \frac{6}{11}$
16. $\frac{m + 1}{2} + \frac{2m + 3}{3} = 2$
17. $\frac{2l + 7}{4} + \frac{3l - 5}{2} = \frac{1}{8}$
18. $t - \frac{7t + 3}{9} = \frac{2}{3}$
19. $\frac{1}{5} + \frac{8a - 3}{7} = 3$
20. $\frac{5d - 2}{7} - \frac{9d}{2} = \frac{1}{7}$

Solve the following equations and verify your answers.

21. $\frac{b - 3}{5} - \frac{2b + 7}{2} = \frac{1}{10}$
22. $\frac{1}{3}(2g - 1) + \frac{2}{5}(3 - g) = \frac{2}{3}$
23. $\frac{1}{3}(6f + 1) + \frac{3f - 4}{2} = \frac{1}{6}$
24. $3(c - 2) - \frac{2}{5}(1 - c) = \frac{1}{3}$
25. $\frac{1}{5}(2k + 3) - \frac{7k - 4}{3} = 6$

Section 5C Solving Problems Using Linear Equations

Example 1

Conor collects 10 cent, 20 cent and 50 cent coins. He saves €13.50.

He saved twice as many 10 cent coins as 50 cent coins, and 4 times as many 20 cent coins as 50 cent coins.

(i) Write an equation in words to represent this information.
(ii) Write a linear equation to represent this information.
(iii) Solve the linear equation.
(iv) How many of each coin did he save?
(v) Check your answer by substituting the values back into the equation.

Solution

(i) Value of 10 cent coins + value of 20 cent coins + value of 50 cent coins = €13.50
= 1350 cent

(ii) Let n = number of 50c coins saved, i.e. $50n$ cent saved
$\Rightarrow 2n$ = number of 10c coins saved, i.e. $20n$ cent saved
$\Rightarrow 4n$ = number of 20c coins saved, i.e. $80n$ cent saved
Total $= 50n + 20n + 80n = 1350$

(iii) $50n + 20n + 80n = 1350$
$\Rightarrow \quad 150n = 1350$
$\Rightarrow \quad n = \dfrac{1350}{150} = 9$
So Conor saved nine 50 cent coins = €4.50

(iv) He saved twice as many 10 cent coins as 50 cent coins.
$2n = 2(9) = 18$ $\Rightarrow$ He saved eighteen 10 cent coins.
Value = 18(€0.10) = €1.80
He saved four times as many 20 cent coins as 50 cent coins.
$4n = 4(9) = 36$ $\Rightarrow$ He saved thirty-six 20 cent coins.
Value = 36(€0.20) = €7.20

(v) Total saved = €1.80 + €7.20 + €4.50 = €13.50
€13.50 = €13.50 ✓
As LHS = RHS, the equation is balanced.

Example 2

A triangle ABC of perimeter 18 cm has sides of length l cm, $(l + 2)$ cm and $(2l - 4)$ cm.

(i) Write an algebraic equation to represent this information.
(ii) Solve the equation.
(iii) What is the length of each side?
(iv) Substitute your answer to verify your solution.

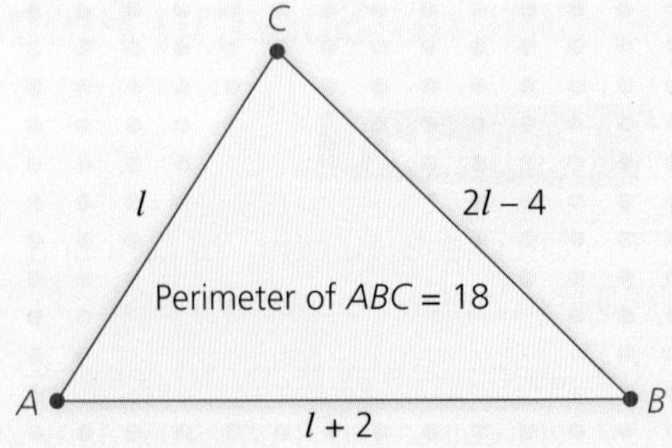

Solution

(i) Perimeter of the triangle =
$l + (l + 2) + (2l - 4) = 18$

(ii) $l + (l + 2) + (2l - 4) = 18$

$\Rightarrow \quad 4l - 2 = 18$

$\Rightarrow \quad 4l = 18 + 2$ ... add 2 to both sides

$\Rightarrow \quad l = \frac{20}{4} = 5$ ... divide both sides by 4

(iii) So the lengths of the sides of the triangle are:

$l = 5$ cm

$l + 2 = 5 + 2 = 7$ cm

$2l - 4 = 2(5) - 4 = 10 - 4 = 6$ cm

(iv) Check answer by substituting $l = 5$ into the original equation:

$l + (l + 2) + (2l - 4) = 18 \quad \Rightarrow 5 + (5 + 2) + (2(5) - 4) = 18$

$\Rightarrow \quad 5 + (7) + (10 - 4) = 18 \quad \Rightarrow 5 + (7) + (6) = 18$

$\Rightarrow \quad 18 = 18$ ✓

Activity 5.3

1 Write each statement as a linear equation and solve to find the unknown number.

(i) A number is doubled and 8 is added to the result. The answer is 32. Find the number.

(ii) If 8 is subtracted from five times a number, the answer is 112. Find the number.

(iii) A number decreased by 9 is 18. Find the number.

(iv) The sum of twice a number plus three times the number is 150. What is the number?

(v) When 14 is added to a number and the result is divided by 3, the answer is 7. What is the number?

(vi) When 10 is added to twice a number, the result is 40. What is the number?

2 The sum of three consecutive numbers is 126. Find the numbers.

3 The perimeter of the right-angled triangle shown is 12 cm. Find the value of k and the length of each side.

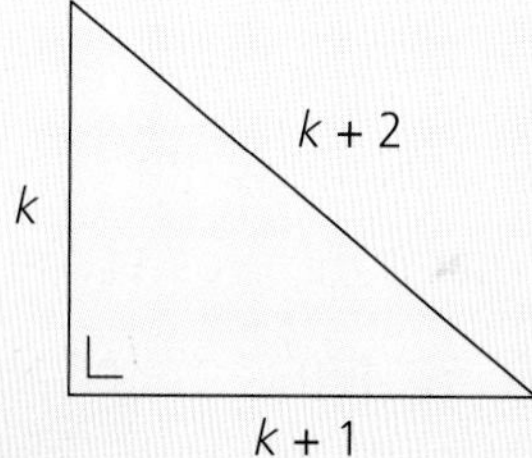

4 Jack and Josh ran a race. Jack ran twice as far as Josh in a set amount of time. If the total distance they ran was 12 km, how far did each run?

5 Seán and Sarah share €25 between them. If Sarah gets €5 more than Seán, how much money does each get?

6 I spent €x on a pair of shoes and €$(x - 15)$ on a pair of trousers. How much did I spend on each item if the total cost was €95?

7 If n is any even number, then n and $n + 2$ are consecutive even numbers (e.g. 2 and 4 are consecutive even numbers). Find two consecutive even numbers if their sum is 194.

8 The perimeter of a triangle is 122 m. The first side is 35 m long, the second side is x m long and the third side is twice as long as the second side. Find the length of the second and third sides.

9 The sum of half Harry's age plus one-third of his age is 50. Find out how old Harry is.

10 If the sum of two consecutive numbers is divided by 5, the answer is 5. Find both numbers.

11 The dimensions of a rectangle are shown in the diagram.

The perimeter of the rectangle is 32 units.

(i) Write a linear equation to represent this information.
(ii) Solve the linear equation.
(iii) What is the length of the rectangle?
(iv) What is the width of the rectangle?
(v) What is the area of the rectangle?

12 Peter is one-fifth of his father's age. Their combined age is 48.

(i) Write a linear equation to represent this information.
(ii) Solve the linear equation.
(iii) How old is Peter's father?
(iv) How old is Peter?

13 Joseph has saved a total of €210 made up from €1 and €2 coins. He has five times as many €1 coins as €2 coins.

(i) Write a linear equation to represent this information.
(ii) Solve the linear equation.
(iii) What is the value of the €1 coins that Joseph has saved?
(iv) What is the value of the €2 coins that Joseph has saved?
(v) Check your solution.

14 Mary went shopping and bought three times as many tins of beans as jars of jam. A tin of beans costs €0.69 and a jar of jam costs €1.50. The total bill was €7.14.

(i) Write a linear equation to represent this information.
(ii) Solve the linear equation.
(iii) Check your solution.
(iv) How many jars of jam did Mary buy?
(v) How many tins of beans did she buy?

15 Two angles are supplementary. The larger angle is 30° less than twice the smaller angle.

(i) What are supplementary angles?
(ii) Write a linear equation to represent this information.
(iii) Solve the linear equation.
(iv) Find the degree measure of the smaller angle.
(v) Find the degree measure of the larger angle.
(vi) Use the definition stated in part (i) to verify your solution.

Section 5D Introduction to Inequalities

The speed limit on a motorway is 120 km/h.

In mathematics we write this as:

speed ≤ 120 or $s \leq 120$.

This is an example of an **inequality**.

Inequalities are similar to equations, but instead of an "=" sign we have inequality symbols.

These are the four inequality signs which we use:

< *means* "less than"

≤ *means* "less than or equal to"

> *means* "greater than"

≥ *means* "greater than or equal to"

Key Points

Recall the number sets:

1. The natural numbers (ℕ): the positive whole numbers { 1, 2, 3, 4, 5,...}

   1 2 3 4 5

2. The integers (ℤ): the positive and negative whole numbers and including zero {...−3, −2, −1, 0, 1, 2, 3, ...}

   −3 −2 −1 0 1 2 3

3. The real numbers (ℝ): every number on the number line; they completely fill the number line

   −3 −2 −1 0 1 2 3

Example 1

Write the following inequalities in words.

(i) $10 > 6$ (ii) $-5 < 6$ (iii) $2x \geq 6, x \in \mathbb{N}$ (iv) $y \leq -1, y \in \mathbb{Z}$ (v) $w \geq -4, w \in \mathbb{R}$

Solution

Part	Inequality	Means
(i)	$10 > 6$	10 is greater than 6
(ii)	$-5 < 6$	−5 is less than 6
(iii)	$2x \geq 6, x \in \mathbb{N}$	$2x$ is greater than or equal to 6, where x is an element of the natural numbers.
(iv)	$y \leq -1, y \in \mathbb{Z}$	y is less than or equal to −1, where y is an element of the integers.
(v)	$w \geq -4, w \in \mathbb{R}$	w is greater than or equal to −4, where w is an element of the real numbers.

Example 2

For an Irish driving licence, there are restrictions on vehicle categories. Write down the meaning of the inequalities shown for the categories A1, A, B, C1, D1 and M, using the information in the box.

	A1 ≤ 125 c.c.
	A ≤ 25 kW
	B ≤ 3500 kg
	C1 ≤ 7500 kg
	D1 ≤ 1 + 16
	M ≤ 45 Km/h

Solution

Vehicle category	What does this inequality mean?
A1 ≤ 125 c.c.	A motorbike with an engine size less than or equal to 125 c.c.
A ≤ 25 kW	A motorbike with an engine size less than or equal to 25 kW.
B ≤ 3500 kg	A motor car with a weight less than or equal to 3500 kg.
C1 ≤ 7500 kg	A lorry with a weight less than or equal to 7500 kg.
D1 ≤ 1 + 16	A bus with 1 driver and less than or equal to 16 passengers.
M ≤ 45 Km/h	A moped restricted to speeds of less than or equal to 45 km per hour.

Class Discussion

Can you think of any other real-life situations when inequalities are used?

Section 5E Solving Inequalities

As there may be an infinite number of solutions to an inequality, each solution set is represented on a number line.

Example 1

Graph the following inequality on a number line: $x \leq 3$, where $x \in \mathbb{N}$.

Solution

x can be any **positive whole number** less than or equal to 3:

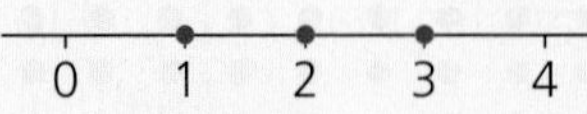

Example 2

Graph the following inequality on a number line: $x \leq 3$, where $x \in \mathbb{Z}$.

Solution

x can be any **whole number** (positive or negative) less than or equal to 3, including 0:

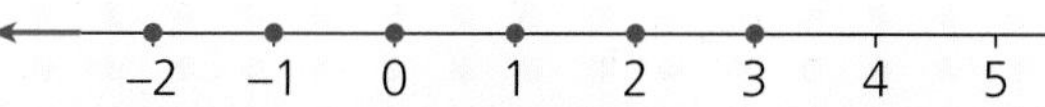

Note

Notice the difference between the answers to Examples 1 and 2 above.

Note

A linear inequality differs from a linear equation in that it may have an infinite number of solutions.

For example:

- $x = 3$ is a linear **equation** which has **one** solution.
- $x < 3$ is a linear **inequality** which may have **many** solutions.

Now spot the difference between the next two examples:

Example 3

Graph the following inequality on a number line: $x \leq 4$, where $x \in \mathbb{R}$.

Solution

x can be **any number** less than or equal to 4.

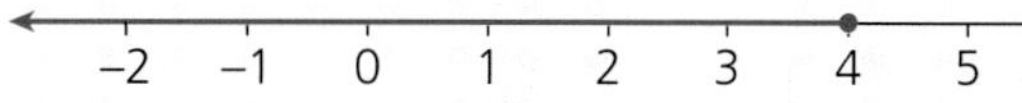

- Notice that there is a **filled** circle at 4 to indicate that 4 **is** included.

Example 4

Graph the following inequality on a number line: $x < 4$, where $x \in \mathbb{R}$.

Solution

x can be **any number** less than 4, but **not equal to** 4.

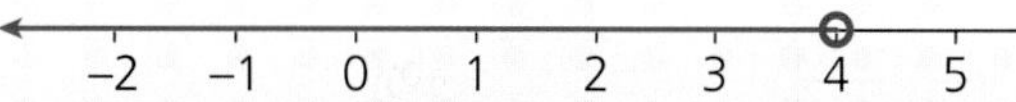

- Notice that there is a **hollow** circle at 4 to indicate that 4 is **not** included.

Note

An inequality in which $x \in \mathbb{N}$ or $x \in \mathbb{Z}$ looks like a row of ℕoℤes.

An inequality in which $x \in \mathbb{R}$ looks like a ℝoad.

Example 5

(i) Solve the inequality $x - 3 < 2$.

Hence, graph the solution sets to the following inequalities on a number line.

(ii) $x - 3 < 2, x \in \mathbb{N}$

(iii) $x - 3 < 2, x \in \mathbb{Z}$

(iv) $x - 3 < 2, x \in \mathbb{R}$

Solution

(i) $x - 3 < 2$

$\Rightarrow x < 2 + 3$ ← Add 3 to both sides. We did the same when we solved linear equations.

$\Rightarrow x < 5$

(ii) $x < 5, x \in \mathbb{N}$. Natural numbers are positive whole numbers excluding 0.

(iii) $x < 5, x \in \mathbb{Z}$. Integers are positive and negative whole numbers including 0.

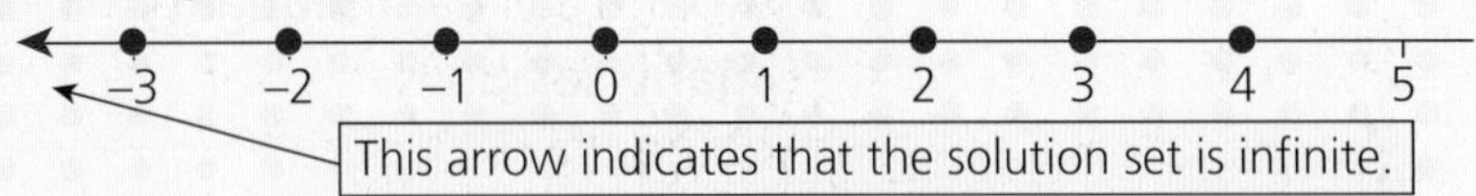

(iv) $x < 5, x \in \mathbb{R}$. The real numbers are all numbers (positive and negative whole numbers, fractions and decimals), so draw a heavy line along the number line.

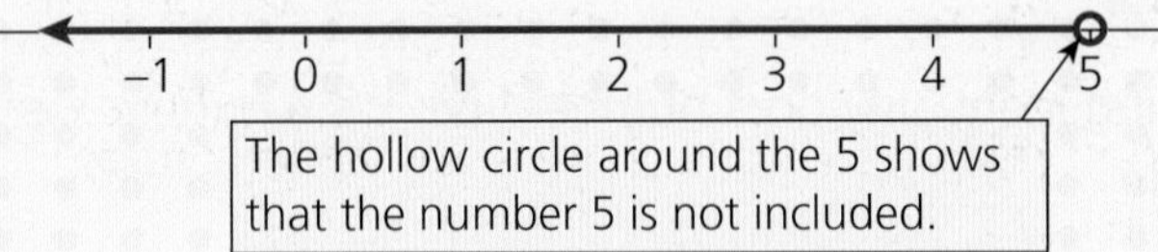

Example 6

(i) Solve the inequality $3x - 4 \geq -5$.

Hence, graph the solution sets to the following inequalities on a number line.

(ii) $3x - 4 \geq -5, x \in \mathbb{N}$ (iii) $3x - 4 \geq -5, x \in \mathbb{Z}$ (iv) $3x - 4 \geq -5, x \in \mathbb{R}$

Solution

(i) $3x - 4 \geq -5$

$3x - 4 + 4 \geq -5 + 4$ ← Add 4 to both sides.

$3x \geq -1$

$\frac{3x}{3} \geq -\frac{1}{3}$ ← Divide both sides by 3 to find x.

$x \geq -\frac{1}{3}$

(ii) $x \geq -\frac{1}{3}, x \in \mathbb{N}$. Natural numbers are positive whole numbers excluding 0.

–1 $-\frac{1}{3}$ 0 1 2 3 4 5

(iii) $x \geq -\frac{1}{3}$, $x \in \mathbb{Z}$. Integers are positive and negative whole numbers including 0.

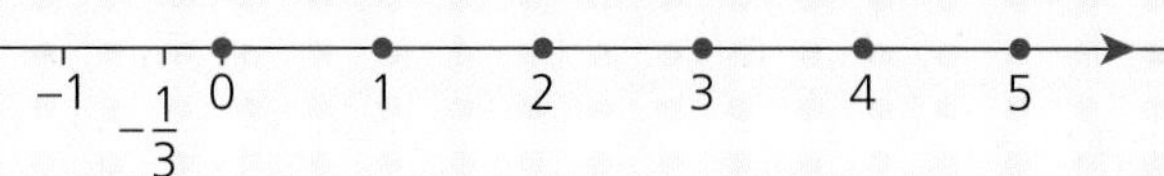

(iv) $x \geq -\frac{1}{3}$, $x \in \mathbb{R}$. The real numbers are all numbers (positive and negative whole numbers, fractions and decimals), so draw a heavy line along the number line.

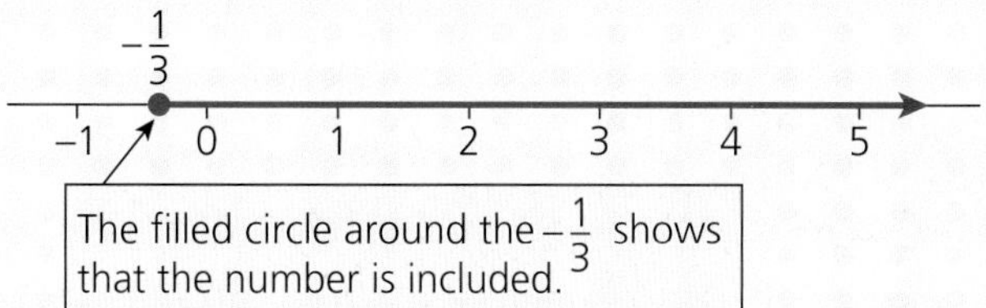

As you can see, solving inequalities is very similar to solving equations. Whatever we do to one side of an equation we must also do to the other side. But there is one important difference.

We can see that $2 < 3$. Multiply both sides by -1: we get $-2 < -3$ which is false. We must reverse the inequality sign to make a true statement: $-2 > -3$.

Key Point

If an inequality is multiplied or divided by the same **negative** number, the inequality sign must be reversed.

Example 7

Solve the inequality $-x + 2 > -3$, where $x \in \mathbb{N}$, and graph the solution set on a number line.

Solution

$-x + 2 > -3$

$\Rightarrow -x > -3 - 2$

$\Rightarrow -x > -5$

$\Rightarrow x < 5$ .... multiply both sides by -1, and **reverse the symbol**

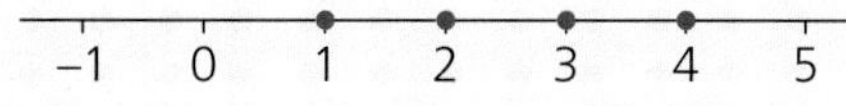

Activity 5.4

1 Graph each of the following inequalities on a number line. *Note*: x is an element of a different set ($\mathbb{N}$, $\mathbb{Z}$, or $\mathbb{R}$) in each case.

(i) $x < 4$, where $x \in \mathbb{N}$

(ii) $x < 4$, where $x \in \mathbb{Z}$

(iii) $x < 4$, where $x \in \mathbb{R}$

2 Graph the solution set for each of the following inequalities on a number line.

(i) $x < 3$, where $x \in \mathbb{N}$

(ii) $x \leq 3$, where $x \in \mathbb{N}$

(iii) List the elements of each solution set in parts (i) and (ii). What is the difference between the solution sets?

3 Graph the solution set for each of the following inequalities on a number line.

(i) $x < 3$, where $x \in \mathbb{Z}$

(ii) $x \leq 3$, where $x \in \mathbb{Z}$

4 Graph the solution set for each of the following inequalities on a number line.

(i) $x < 3$, where $x \in \mathbb{R}$

(ii) $x \leq 3$, where $x \in \mathbb{R}$

5 Write down the inequality graphed on each of the number lines.

(i) $x \in \mathbb{N}$

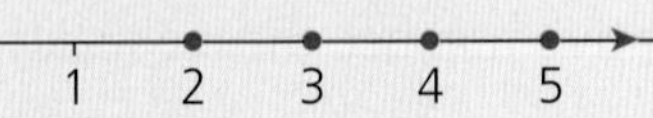

(ii) $x \in \mathbb{N}$

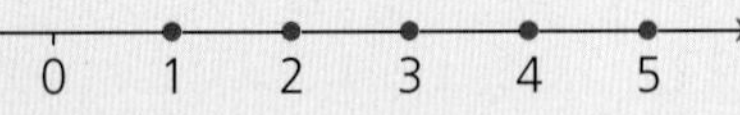

(iii) $x \in \mathbb{Z}$

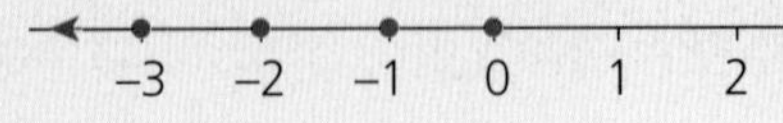

(iv) $x \in \mathbb{Z}$

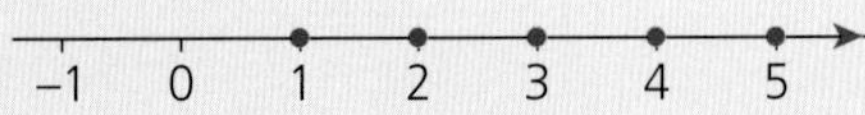

(v) $x \in \mathbb{R}$

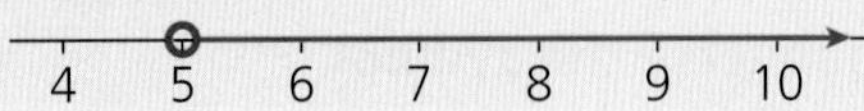

(vi) $x \in \mathbb{R}$

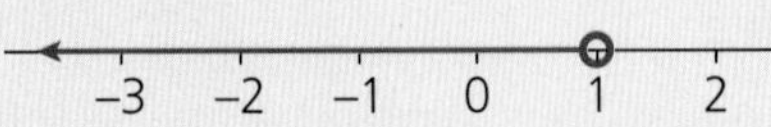

6 (i) Solve the inequality $x + 5 < 9$.

Hence, graph the following solution sets on a number line.

(ii) $x + 5 < 9, x \in \mathbb{N}$

(iii) $x + 5 < 9, x \in \mathbb{Z}$

(iv) $x + 5 < 9, x \in \mathbb{R}$

(v) List the elements of the solution set for the natural numbers.

7 (i) Solve the inequality $6l + 1 \geq 13$.

Hence, graph the following solution sets on a number line.

(ii) $6l + 1 \geq 13, l \in \mathbb{N}$

(iii) $6l + 1 \geq 13, l \in \mathbb{Z}$

(iv) $6l + 1 \geq 13, l \in \mathbb{R}$

8 (i) Solve the inequality $12n - 19 > 17$.

Hence, graph the following solution sets on a number line.

(ii) $12n - 19 > 17, n \in \mathbb{N}$

(iii) $12n - 19 > 17, n \in \mathbb{Z}$

(iv) $12n - 19 > 17, n \in \mathbb{R}$

9 (i) Solve the inequality $5f - 6 \leq 9$.

Hence, graph the following solution sets on a number line.

(ii) $5f - 6 \leq 9, f \in \mathbb{N}$

(iii) $5f - 6 \leq 9, f \in \mathbb{Z}$

(iv) $5f - 6 \leq 9, f \in \mathbb{R}$

(v) List the elements of the solution set for the natural numbers.

10 (i) Solve the inequality $-7x + 4 < -10$.

Hence, graph the following solution sets on a number line.

Hint

› Note the Key Point before Example 7.

(ii) $-7x + 4 < -10, x \in \mathbb{N}$

(iii) $-7x + 4 < -10, x \in \mathbb{R}$

11 (i) Solve the inequality $2t - 5 \geq 33$.

(ii) Hence, graph the solution set for $t \in \mathbb{R}$ on a number line.

12 (i) Solve the inequality $-8p + 5 \geq -14$.

Hence, graph the following solution sets on a number line.

(ii) $-8p + 5 \geq -14, p \in \mathbb{N}$

(iii) $-8p + 5 \geq -14, p \in \mathbb{Z}$

(iv) $-8p + 5 \geq -14, p \in \mathbb{R}$

(v) List the elements of the solution set for the natural numbers.

13 (i) Solve the inequality $11q + 12 \leq 36$.

Hence, graph the following solution sets on a number line.

(ii) $11q + 12 \leq 36, q \in \mathbb{N}$

(iii) $11q + 12 \leq 36, q \in \mathbb{Z}$

(iv) $11q + 12 \leq 36, q \in \mathbb{R}$

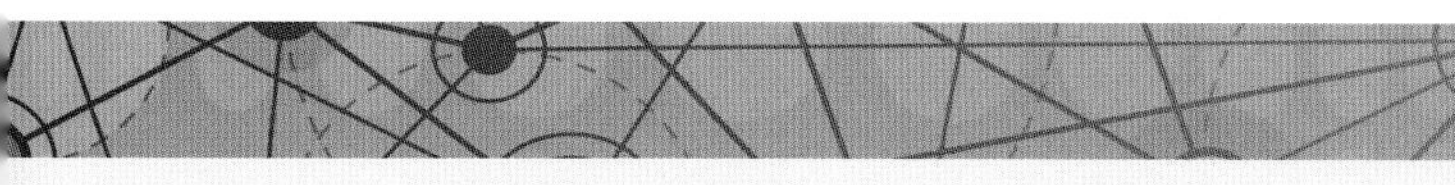

Revision Activity 5

1 (a) Solve the following linear equations and check your answers.

(i) $\frac{3}{17}(6c - 1) = 3$

(ii) $\frac{m - 2}{4} = \frac{2 - m}{6}$

(iii) $12 - 7y = -44$

(iv) $\frac{x - 3}{2} - \frac{x + 3}{5} = -\frac{10}{3}$

(b) The larger of two numbers is 14 greater than the smaller number. The smaller number is one-third of the larger number. Find both numbers.

2 Two numbers are consecutive. The sum of the smaller number minus two-thirds of the larger number is 34.

(a) Write two separate algebraic expressions for each number.

(b) Write a linear equation to represent this information.

(c) Solve the linear equation.

(d) Find the value of both numbers.

(e) Verify your answer.

3 For real numbers a, b and c, copy and complete the table below. Indicate whether each statement is always true, never true or sometimes true.

Statement	Always true	Never true	Sometimes true
If $a > b$ and $b > c$, then $a > c$			
If $-a < 4$ and $b < -4$, then $a < b$			
If $a > b$, then $-a > -b$			
If $a > b$ and $b < c$, then $a < c$			
If $3a + 1 > 2$, then $a > 0$			
If $2b - 4 < 3b - 8$, then $b > 4$			
If a and b are both positive and $a < b$, then $\frac{1}{a} < \frac{1}{b}$			

4 In a 20-question multiple-choice test, 5 marks were awarded for a correct answer and 2 marks were deducted for an incorrect answer. James got a total of 51 marks in the test. He attempted all the questions.

(a) Write a linear equation to represent this information.

(b) Solve the linear equation.

(c) How many questions did James get correct?

(d) How many questions did he get wrong?

(e) Verify your solution.

5 A taxi driver charges a €2 pick-up charge and €1.10 per km thereafter.

(a) If a customer is charged €20.70 for a journey of x km, write a linear equation to represent the situation.

(b) Solve the linear equation to find the number of kilometres the customer travelled.

(c) Using the linear equation from part (a), find the total taxi fare for the distances shown in the table below.

Distance travelled (km)	Linear equation	Total fare (€)
5		
10		
15		
20		
25		
30		
35		
40		

(d) Draw a graph to represent the information.

(e) Using your graph, if a customer travels 33 km, what is the total taxi fare?

6 A plumber charges €46 per hour and spends on average €18.50 per day on petrol. On a particular day, he earned €234.50 after deducting the cost of his petrol for the day.

(a) Write a linear equation to represent this information.

(b) Solve the linear equation to calculate how many hours he worked on this day.

(c) How much would he earn after deducting the cost of his petrol if he worked 7.5 hours?

(d) How much would he earn if he worked a total of 37 hours in 5 days, after he deducted the cost of his petrol?

7 Natalie saved €5, €10 and €20 notes during one year to pay for her annual family holiday. At the end of the year, she had saved a total of €2280.

She saved half as many €5 notes as €20 notes and three-fifths as many €10 notes as €20 notes.

(a) Write an equation in words to represent this information.

(b) Write a linear equation to represent this information.

(c) Solve the linear equation.

(d) How many of each note did she save?

(e) Check your answer by substituting the values back into the word equation.

8 Billy planted carrot seedlings in a 3 m by 1.2 m vegetable patch. After two days, one-quarter of the seedlings had been eaten by birds. A week later, one-third of the remaining seedlings had been eaten, leaving 432 seeds approximately (based on planting 6 seeds per 2.54 cm).

Let x = the number of seedlings Billy planted.

(a) Write an expression in x which represents the number of seedlings remaining after 2 days.
(b) Write an expression in x which represents the number of seedlings remaining a week later.
(c) Write a linear equation to represent the situation after 9 days.
(d) Solve the equation.
(e) How many seedlings had been eaten after two days?
(f) How many seedlings did Billy plant to begin with?

9 There are x cars available to carry a class of students to the cinema. If the students are shared 3 to a car, there is one student left over. If the students are shared 4 to a car, two cars get no students. Find the value of x and the number of students in the class.

Exam-style Questions

1 (a) If $n = 7$, find the value of $2n$ and also the value of $2n + 1$.

(b) (i) x represents an even number. Explain why $x + 2$ is also an even number.

(ii) If one-third of the smaller even number is subtracted from half of the larger even number the result is 8. Find the value of x.

JCHL 2013 Paper 1

2 Solve the following equation.

$$\frac{2x + 5}{3} - \frac{4x - 1}{2} = -\frac{1}{2}$$

JCHL 2012 Paper 1

KEY WORDS AND PHRASES

- **Linear equation**
- **Linear inequalities**
- **Algebraic fractions**
- **Infinite solutions**
- **Real numbers**
- **Number line**
- **Natural Numbers**
- **Integers**

Interactive Tool 5.1

Chapter Summary 5

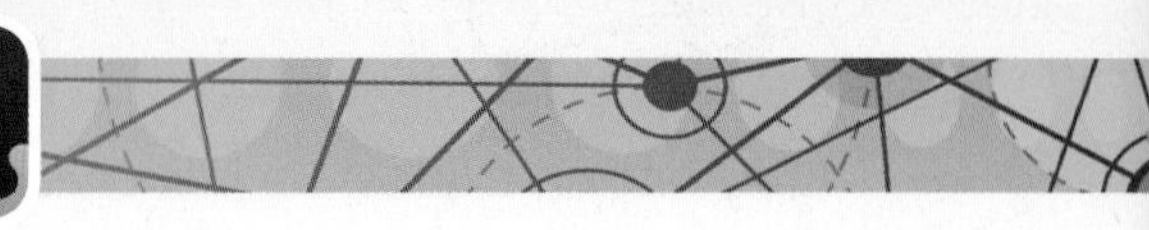

- We solve algebraic equations with fractions such as $\frac{x+4}{3} + \frac{5x+2}{4} = 5$ by multiplying both sides by the lowest common denominator.
- **Key symbols:**

  $<$ *means* "less than"

  $\leq$ *means* "less than or equal to"

  $>$ *means* "greater than"

  $\geq$ *means* "greater than or equal to"

  $\in$ *means* "is an element of the set"

  $\mathbb{N}$ Natural numbers: {1, 2, 3, 4, 5, …}

  $\mathbb{Z}$ Integers: {…, –5, –4, –3, –2, –1, 0, 1, 2, 3, 4, 5, …}

  $\mathbb{R}$ Real numbers: are all the numbers on the number line.
- We solve inequalities in much the same way that we solve equations. But if an inequality is multiplied or divided by the same **negative** number, the inequality sign must be reversed.
- When graphing the solution set to inequalities on a number line, we have to check the type of number we are using: natural numbers ($\mathbb{N}$), integers ($\mathbb{Z}$) or real numbers ($\mathbb{R}$).

Applied Measure

Chapter 6

Learning Intentions

In this chapter, you will learn about:

- Solving problems relating to the perimeter and area of squares, rectangles, triangles and figures made from a combination of these
- How the circumference and diameter of a circle are related
- Calculating the perimeter and area of circles
- The volume of rectangular solids and cylinders
- The nets of prisms and cylinders
- The surface area of triangular-based prisms and cylinders
- Solving problems relating to the curved surface area of rectangular solids, cylinders and spheres
- Calculations using formulae for the volume of rectangular solids, cylinders, triangular-based prisms, spheres and combinations of these

LO: U.5, U.6, GT.2(b–e)

Section 6A Area of a Triangle 1

In this section, we introduce the formulae for the area and perimeter of a triangle.

We have learned already that
the area of a rectangle = length × width.

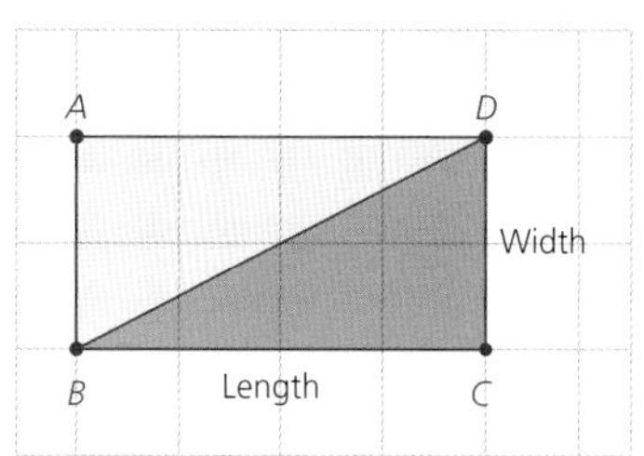

In the diagram on the right, it is clear that the area of triangle $BCD = \frac{1}{2} \times$ the area of rectangle $ABCD$.
In fact, you can probably see that the area of any triangle is **half** the area of the rectangle built around it, as in this diagram.

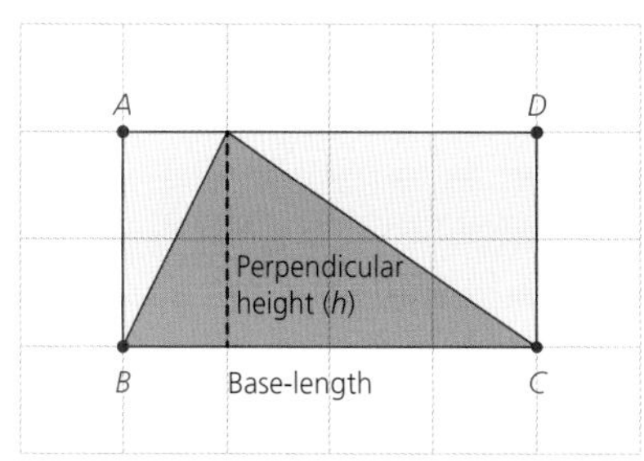

The triangle has a **base-length** and a (perpendicular) **height**.

Thus we have a formula for the area of a triangle:

$$\text{Area of a triangle} = \frac{1}{2} \times \text{base} \times \text{perpendicular height}$$

Key Points

1. Any one of the three sides of a triangle may be called the base. The perpendicular height is the distance from the third vertex (corner) to the base.

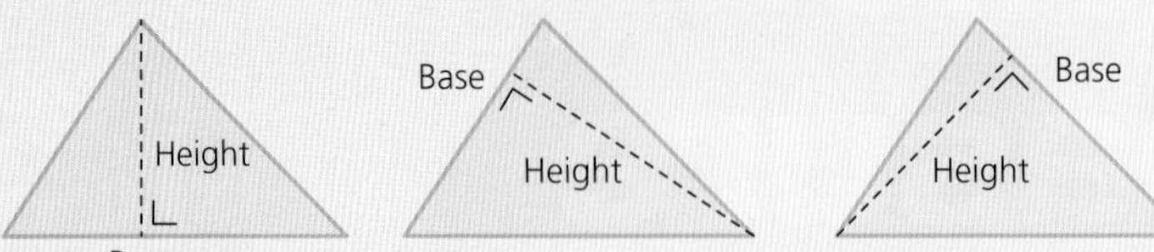

2. In the right-angled triangle on the right, $AB \perp BC$. Hence, the area of triangle ABC $= \frac{1}{2} \times |BC| \times |AB|$.

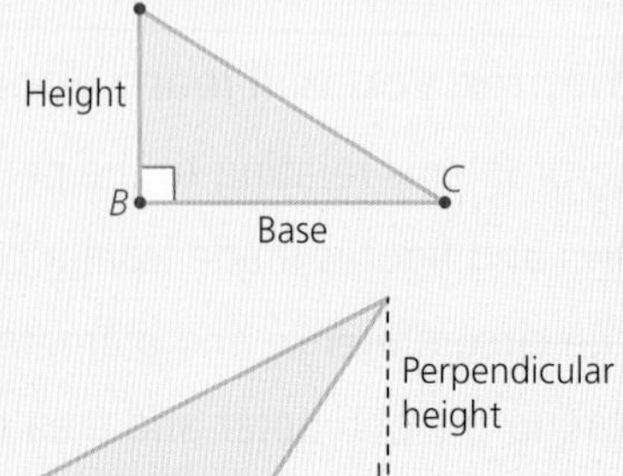

3. In the case of an obtuse-angled triangle, we may find that the perpendicular height is outside the triangle, as it is with the one shown on the right.

The formulae for the perimeter and area of various shapes are below.

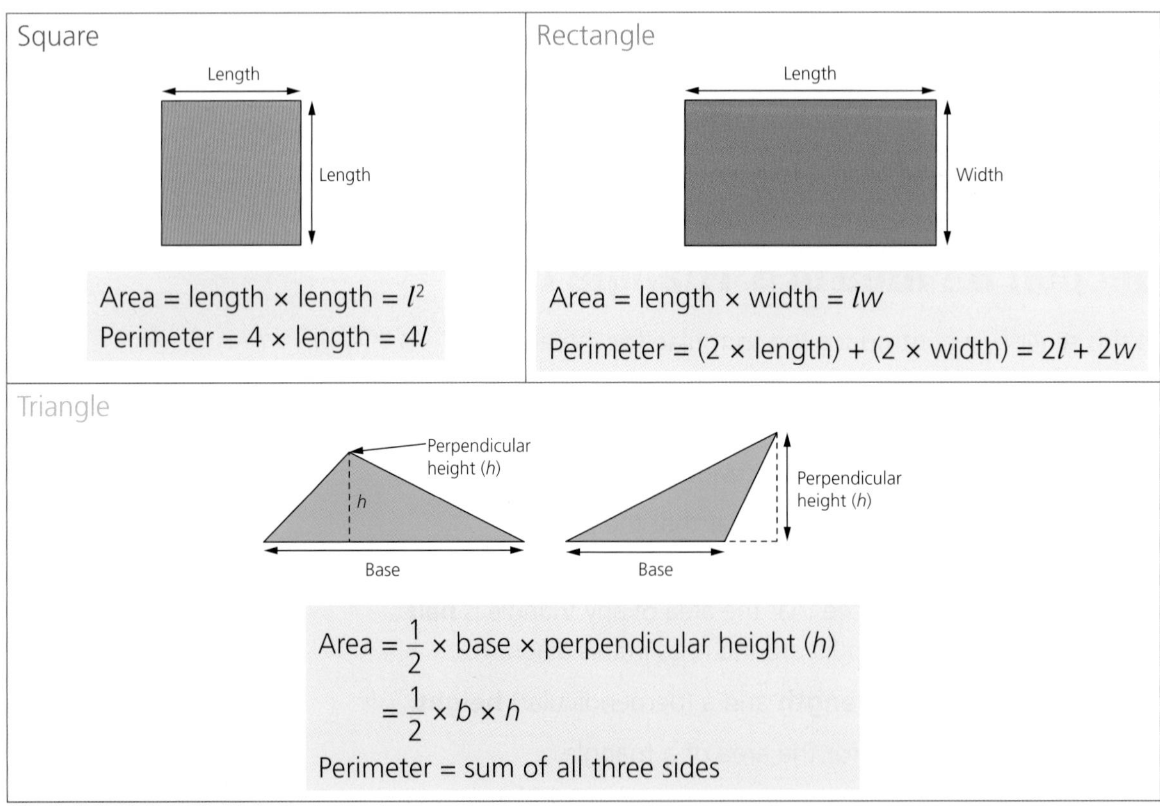

Square

Area = length × length = l^2

Perimeter = 4 × length = $4l$

Rectangle

Area = length × width = lw

Perimeter = (2 × length) + (2 × width) = $2l + 2w$

Triangle

Area $= \frac{1}{2} \times$ base × perpendicular height (h)

$= \frac{1}{2} \times b \times h$

Perimeter = sum of all three sides

The formula for the area of a triangle is on page 9 of the *Formulae and tables* booklet.

Example 1

Find the area of this triangle.

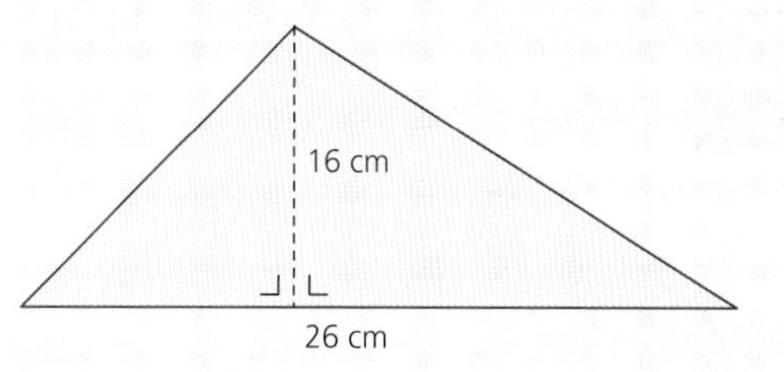

Solution

Area $= \frac{1}{2} \times$ base $\times$ perpendicular height

$= \frac{1}{2} \times (26) \times (16)$

$= 208$ cm^2

Example 2

Find the area and perimeter of this right-angled triangle.

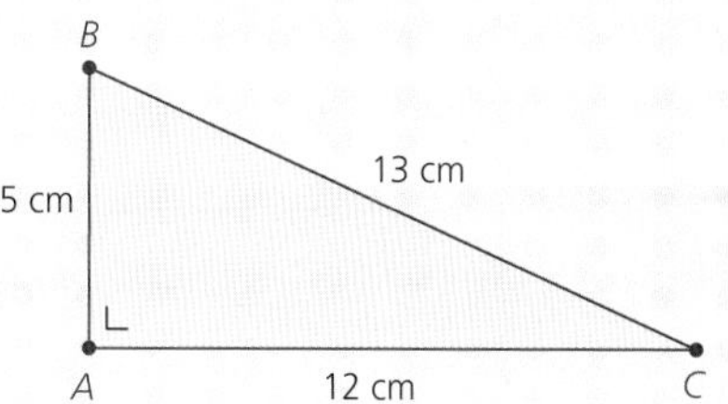

Solution

The triangle is right-angled, so if we use $[AC]$ as the base, $[AB]$ is the height.

Area $= \frac{1}{2} \times$ base $\times$ perpendicular height

$= \frac{1}{2} \times (12) \times (5)$

$= 30$ cm^2

The perimeter of the triangle is the sum of all three sides.

Perimeter = 12 + 5 + 13 = 30 cm

Example 3

Find the area of this obtuse-angled triangle.

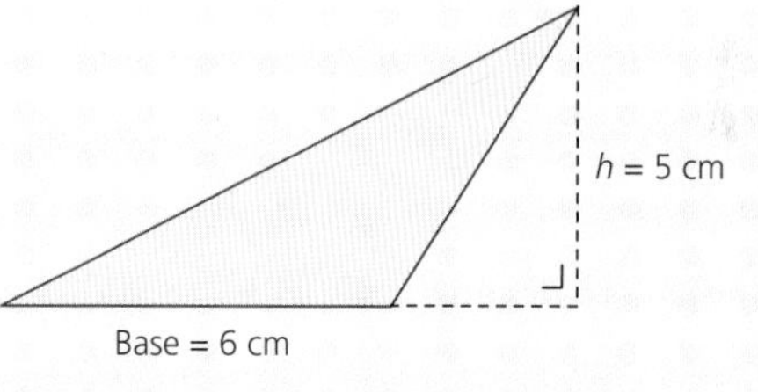

Solution

Area $= \frac{1}{2} \times$ base $\times$ perpendicular height

$= \frac{1}{2} \times (6) \times (5)$

$= 15$ cm^2

Example 4

Find the area of this shape.

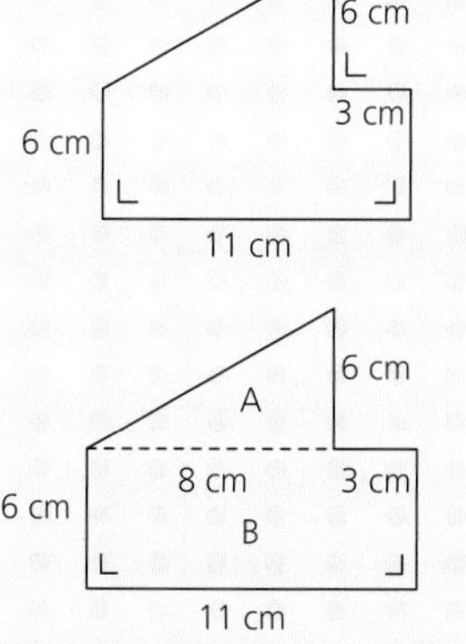

Solution

- Split the shape into two regular shapes.
- Find the area of each section and add the values together to find the total area.

  Shape A is a triangle. Area $= \frac{1}{2} \times b \times h = \frac{1}{2}(8)(6) = 24$ cm^2

  Shape B is a rectangle. Area $= (l)(h) = (11)(6) = 66$ cm^2
- Total area = 66 + 24 = 90 cm^2

Example 5

Find the length of the missing side in this triangle.

Solution

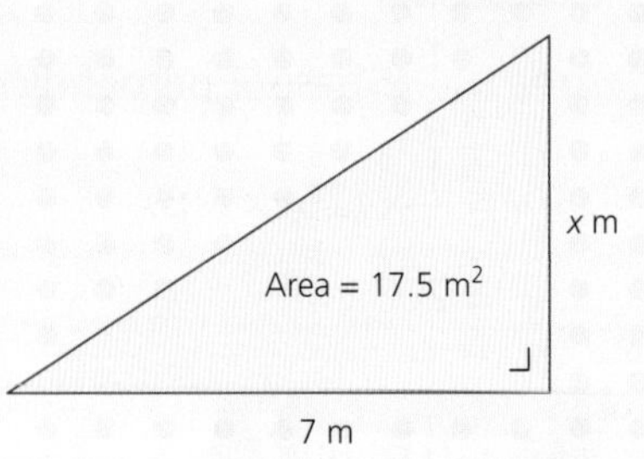

Area = $\frac{1}{2}$ × base × perpendicular height

$= 17.5 \text{ cm}^2$

$\Rightarrow \frac{1}{2} \times (7) \times (x) = 17.5$

$\Rightarrow 3.5x = 17.5$

$\Rightarrow x = \frac{17.5}{3.5}$ ... divide both sides by 3.5

$\Rightarrow x = 5 \text{ m}$

Activity 6.1

1 Find the area of each of these triangles:

(i) 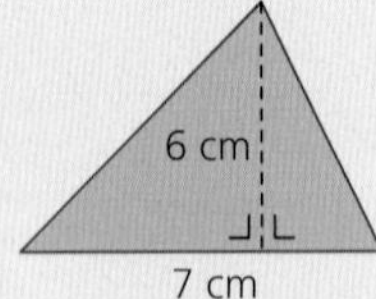

(ii) 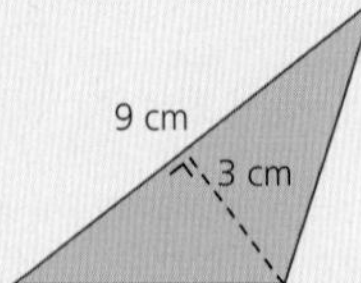

(iii) 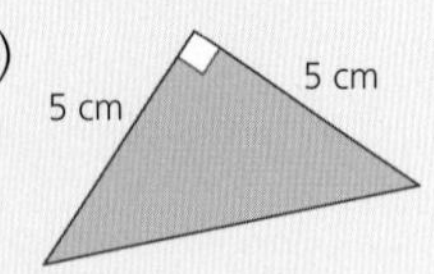

(iv) 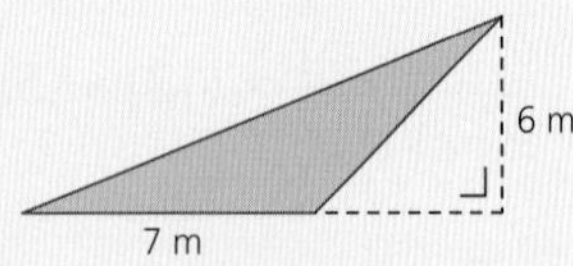

2 Find the area and perimeter of each of these triangles.

(i) 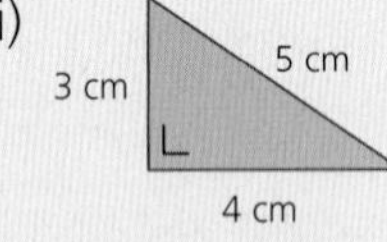

(ii) 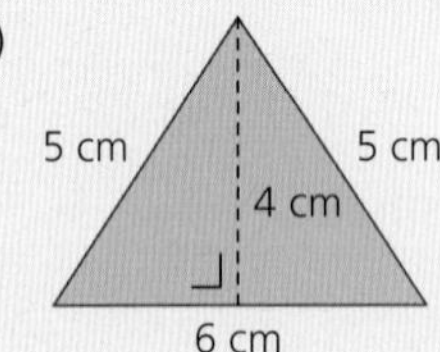

(iii) 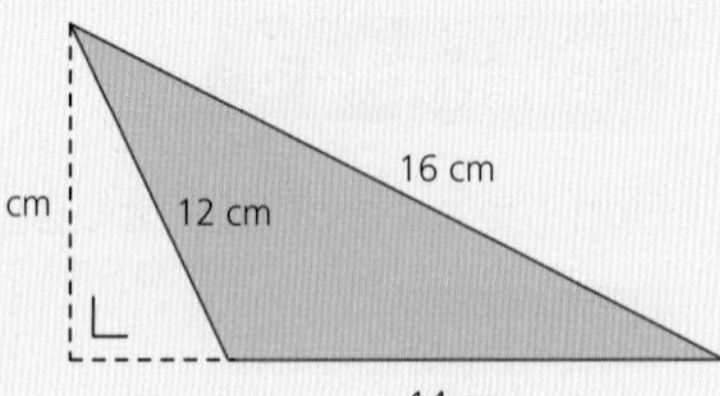

3 Find the area of each of the triangles below.

(i) 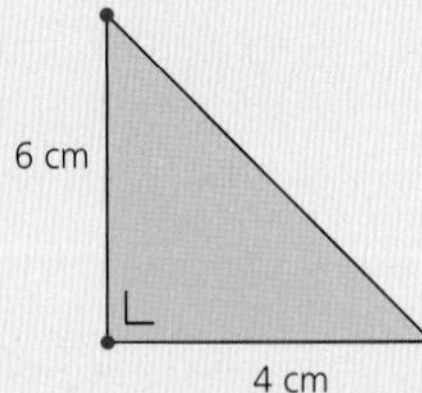

(ii) 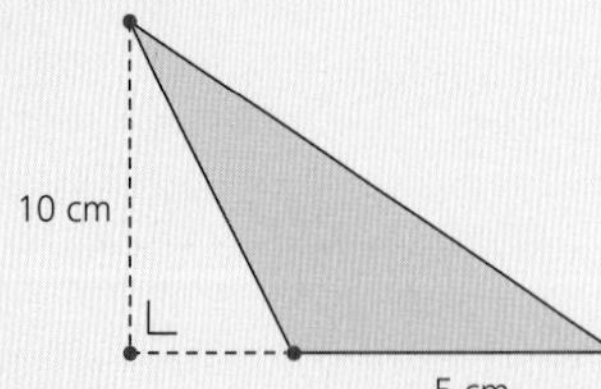

(iii) 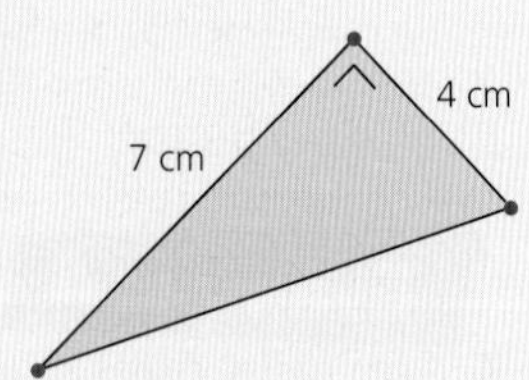

4 Find the area of each shape below.

(i) 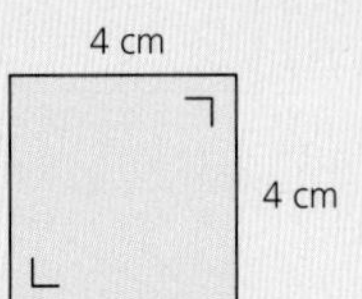

(iii) 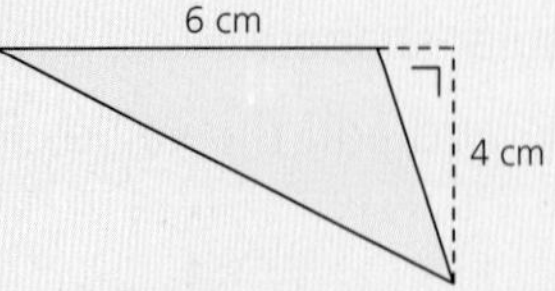

(v) 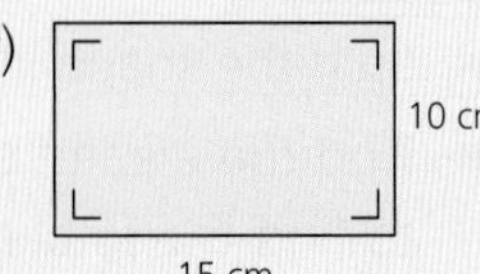

(ii) 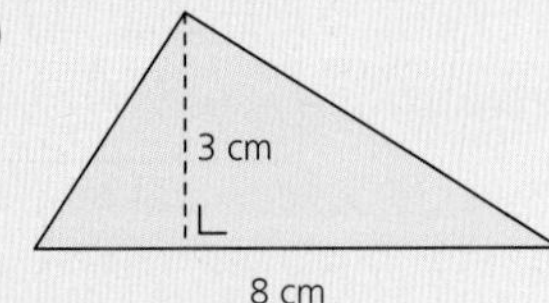

(iv) 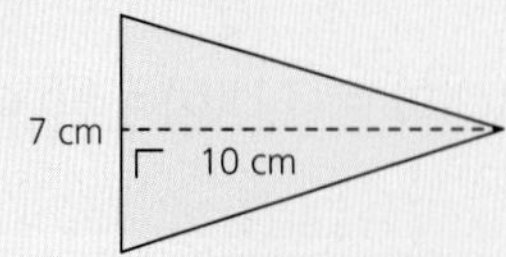

5 Find the area of each of the following shapes.

(i)

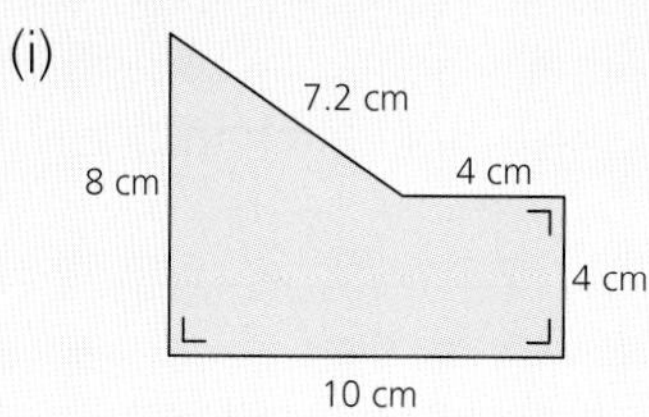

(ii)

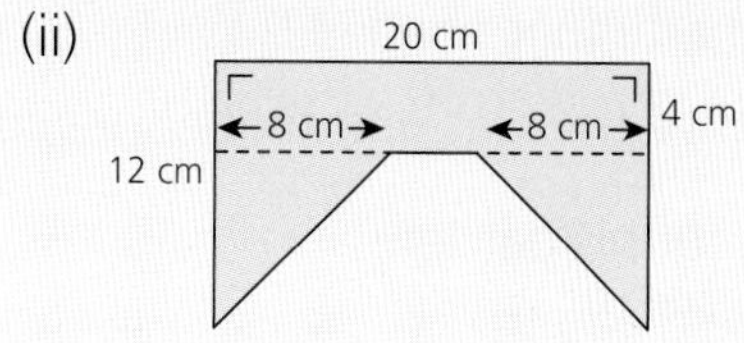

(iii)

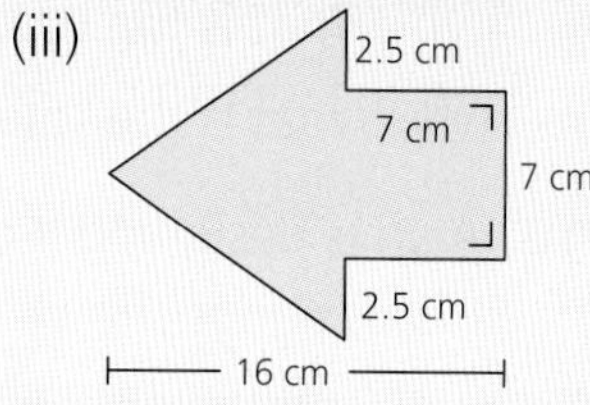

6 Find the values of the missing lengths in each of the following shapes.

(i)

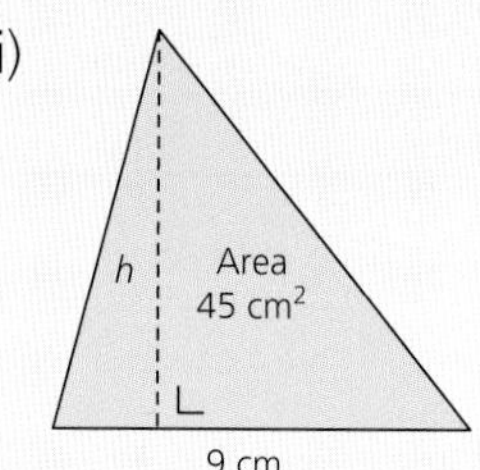

(ii)

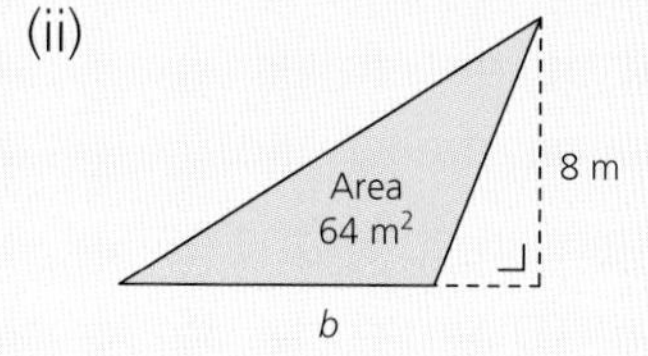

(iii)

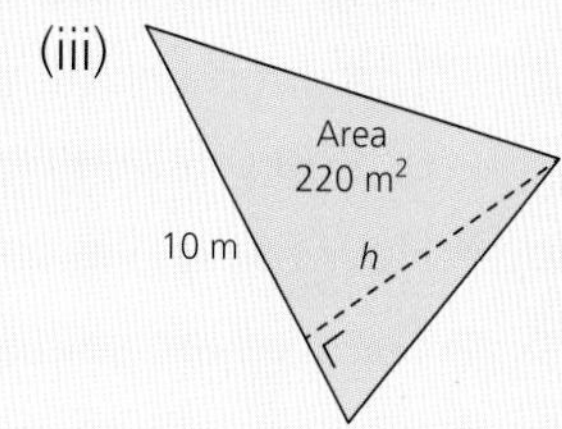

7 Find the area of each shape below.

(i)

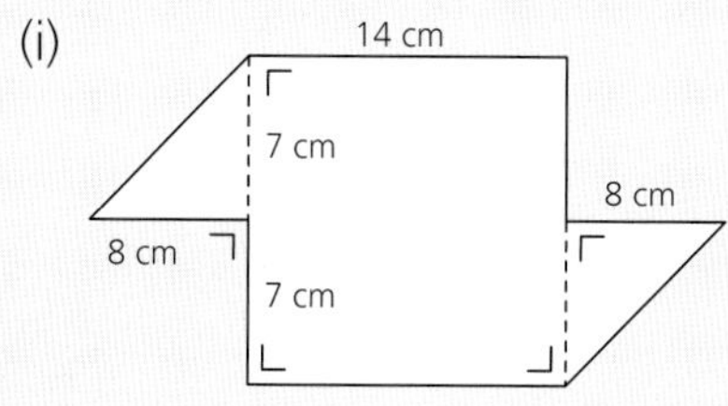

(ii)

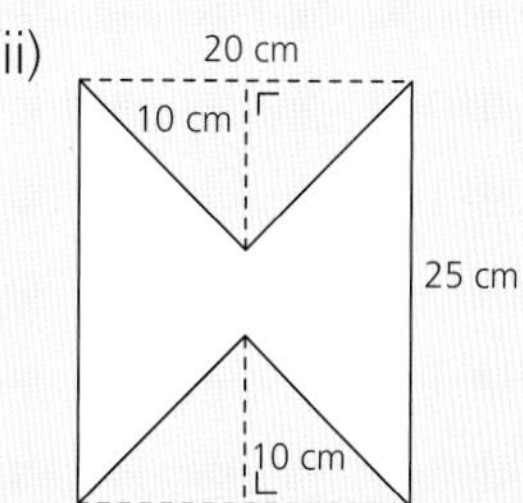

8 Find the area of the shaded region in each of the following shapes.

(i)

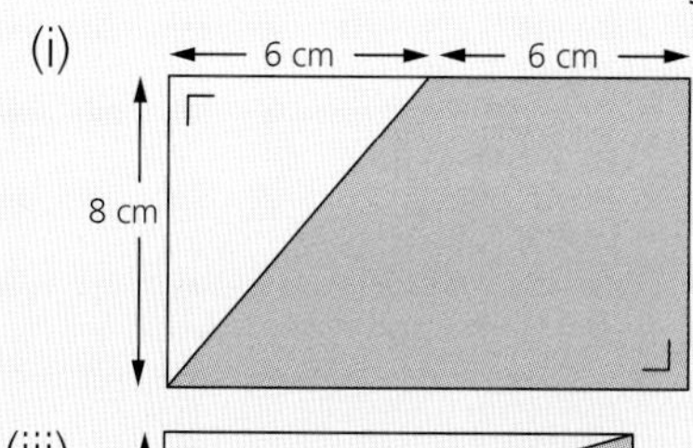

(ii)

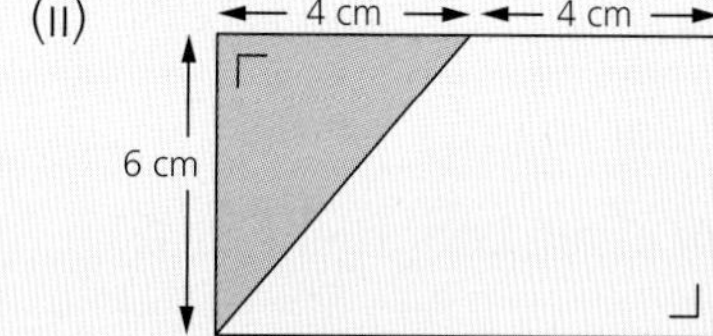

(iii)

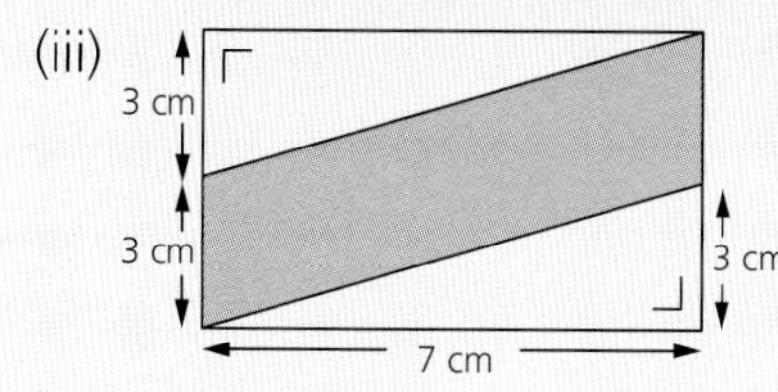

(iv)

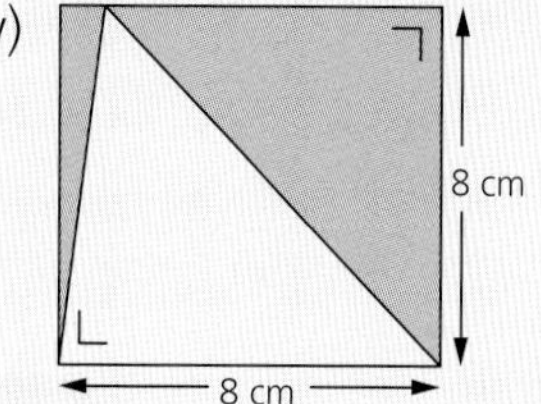

9 The floor layout of a kitchen is shown in the diagram.
One section of the floor is covered with tiles and the other section is covered with timber.

(i) What is the area of each section of floor?

The area of one tile is 0.25 m². The tiles cost €15 for a box of 10 tiles.

(ii) How many tiles are needed to cover the tiled floor area?

(iii) How many full boxes of tiles are needed?

(iv) What is the total cost of the tiles?

The timber needed is sold in 4 m lengths of width 20 cm.
The timber costs €25 for a box of 10 lengths.

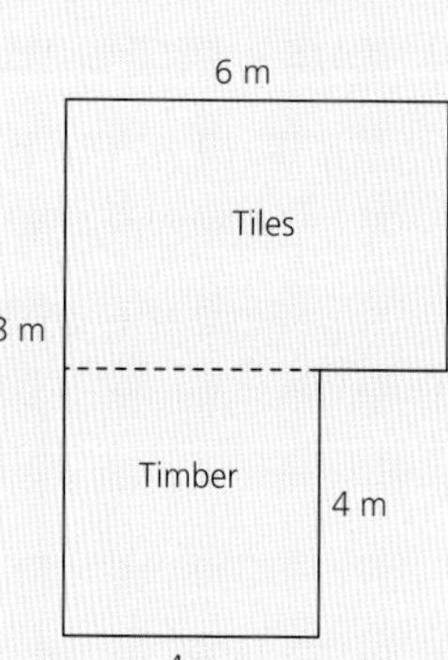

(v) How many lengths of timber will be needed?

(vi) What is the cost of the timber needed?

(vii) What is the total cost of the tiles and timber needed for the whole kitchen floor?

10 Alan is designing a patio for his garden. His design is shown in the diagram.

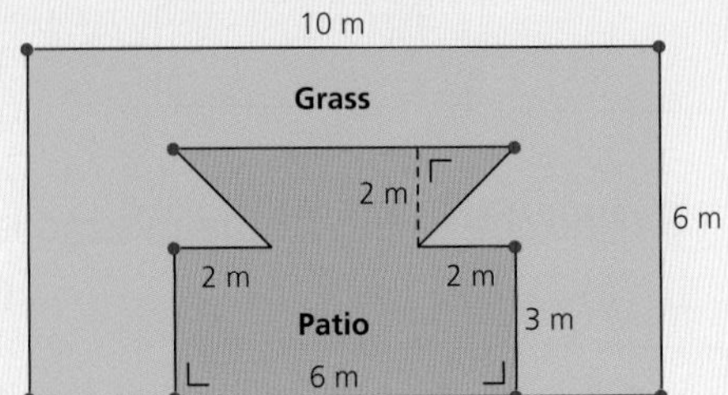

(i) Find the area of the patio.

(ii) What is the area of the grass?

(iii) The patio will be covered with square tiles of side 0.5 m. What is the area of each tile?

(iv) How many tiles will Alan need to cover the patio?

(v) The tiles are sold in packs of 10 and cost €35 per pack.

(a) How many packs of tiles are needed to cover the patio?

(b) What is the total cost of the tiles?

Section 6B Area of a Triangle 2

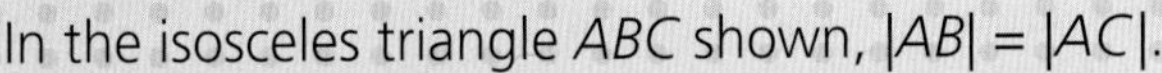

Connections

We need to use our knowledge of geometry theorems in this section, especially that which relates to congruent triangles.

In the isosceles triangle ABC shown, $|AB| = |AC|$.

$[AD]$ is drawn perpendicular to $[BC]$.

The triangles ABD and ADC are congruent (RHS).

Hence $|BD| = |DC|$.

We will use this information in the following examples.

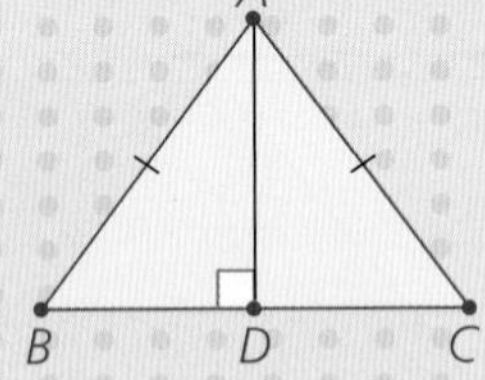

Example 1

ABC is an isosceles triangle with $|AB| = |AC| = 10$ cm and $|BC| = 12$ cm.

(i) Find h, the perpendicular height of the triangle ABC.

(ii) Find the area of ABC.

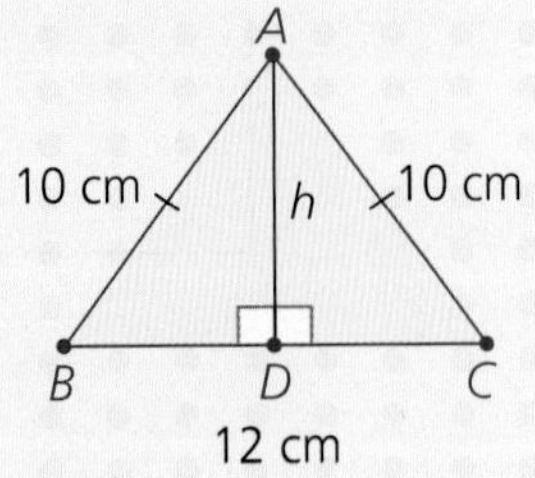

Solution

(i) The triangles ABD and ADC are congruent (RHS).

Hence $|BD| = |DC| = 6$ cm.

Using Pythagoras' theorem on triangle ADC, we have

$h^2 + 6^2 = 10^2$

$\Rightarrow h^2 = 10^2 - 6^2$

$\Rightarrow h^2 = 100 - 36 = 64$

$\Rightarrow h = \sqrt{64} = 8$ cm

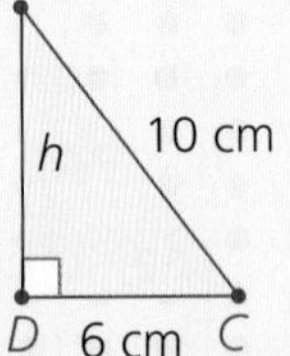

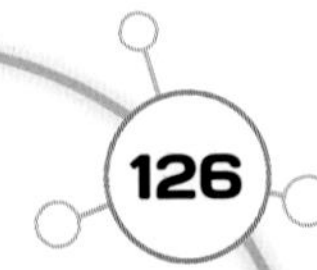

(ii) Area of triangle ABC

$= \frac{1}{2} \times \text{base} \times \text{perpendicular height}$

$= \frac{1}{2} \times 12 \times 8 = 48 \text{ cm}^2$

Example 2

ABC is an equilateral triangle of side length 8 cm.

Find the area of triangle ABC in surd form.

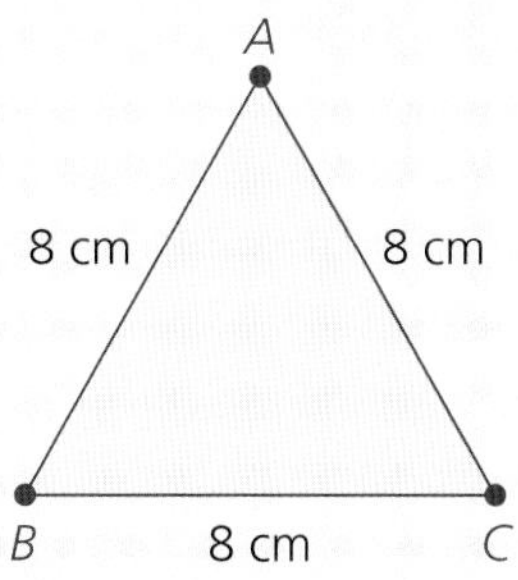

Solution

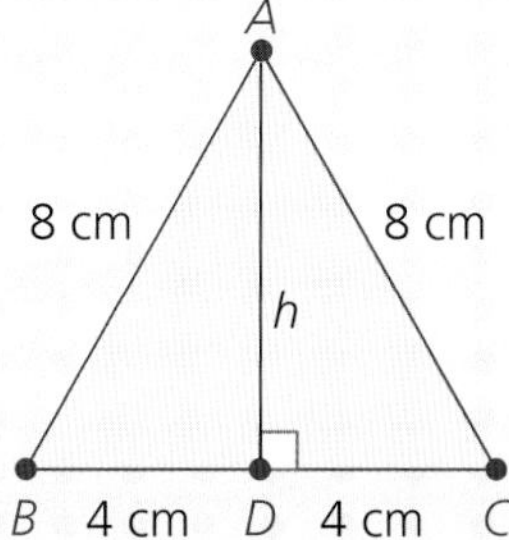

Draw $[AD] \perp [BC]$.

The triangles ABD and ADC are congruent (RHS).

Hence $|BD| = |DC| = 4$ cm.

Using Pythagoras' theorem on triangle ADC, we have

$h^2 + 4^2 = 8^2$

$\Rightarrow h^2 = 8^2 - 4^2$

$\Rightarrow h^2 = 64 - 16 = 48$

$\Rightarrow h = \sqrt{48} = 4\sqrt{3}$ cm

Area of triangle ABC

$= \frac{1}{2} \times \text{base} \times \text{perpendicular height}$

$= \frac{1}{2} \times 8 \times 4\sqrt{3} = 16\sqrt{3} \text{ cm}^2$

Activity 6.2

1 Find the area of each of the following isosceles triangles.

(i)

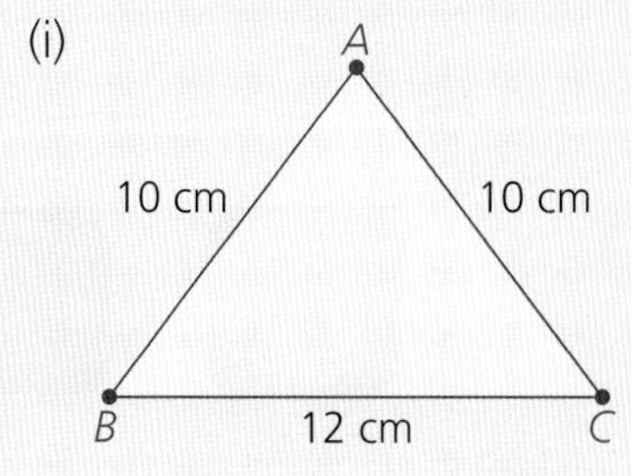

(ii)

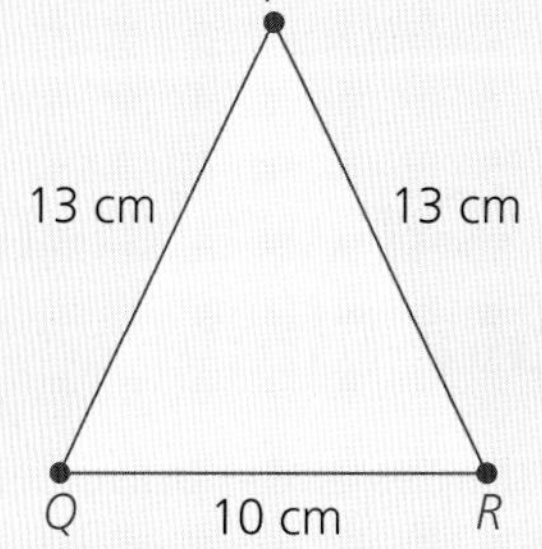

(iii)

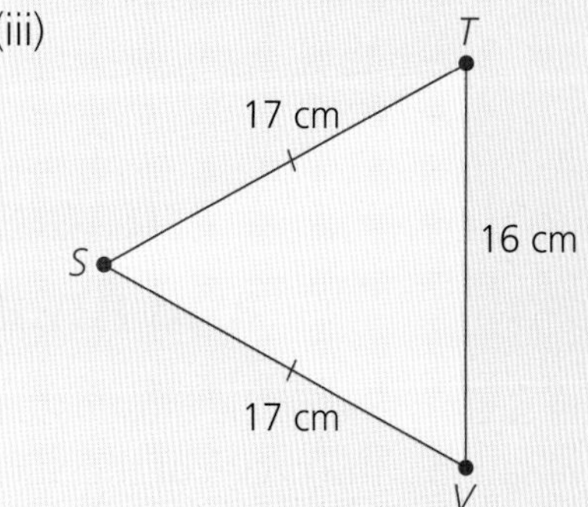

2 Find the area of the following equilateral triangles. Give your answers in surd (square root) form.

(i)

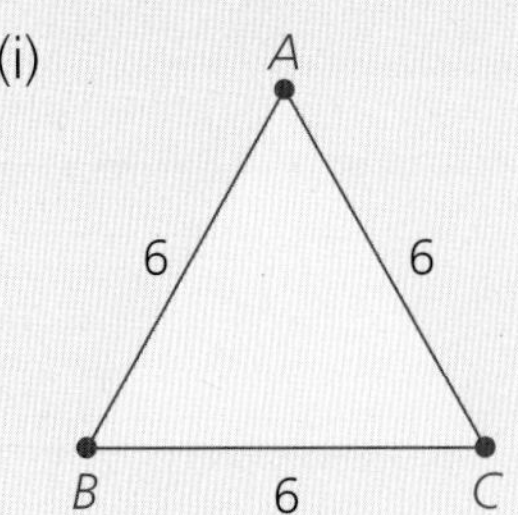

(ii)

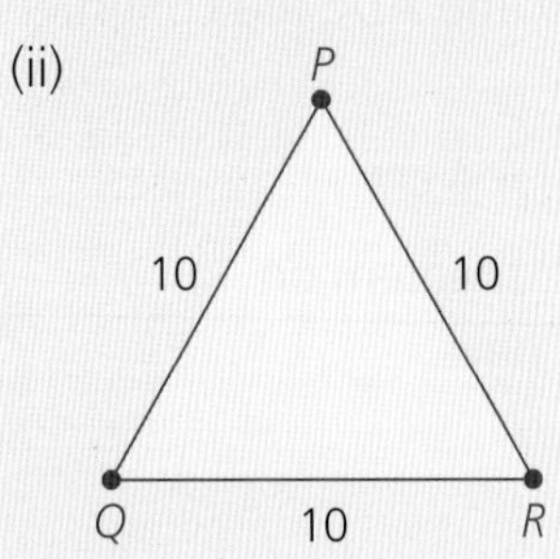

(iii)

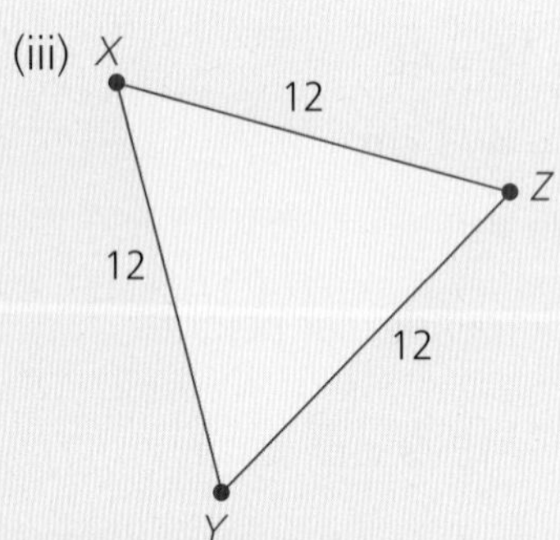

3 Find the area of the following right-angled triangles.

(i)

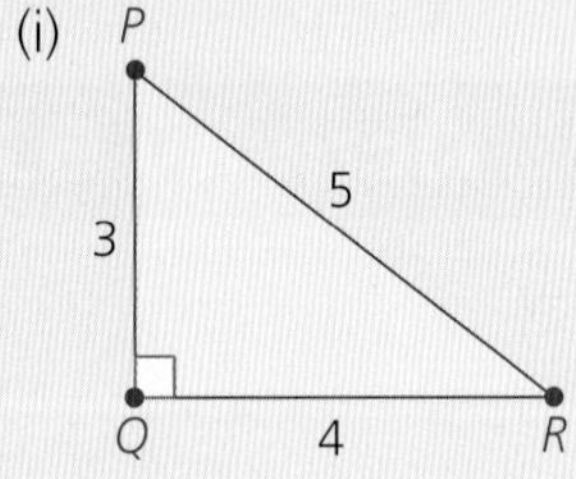

(ii)

(iii)

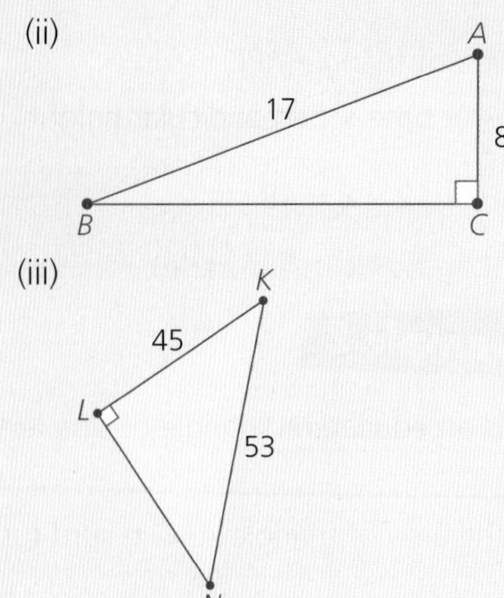

4 For each of the following triangles find:

(i) the area of the triangle to the nearest cm²

(ii) the perimeter of the triangle, to the nearest cm where appropriate.

(a)

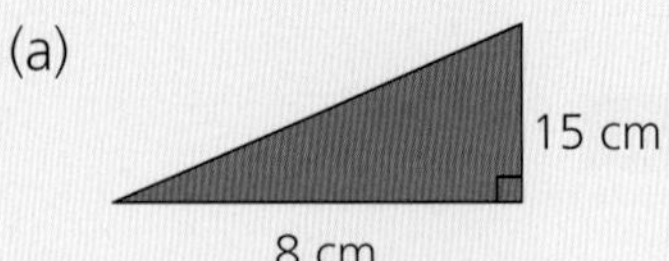

(b)

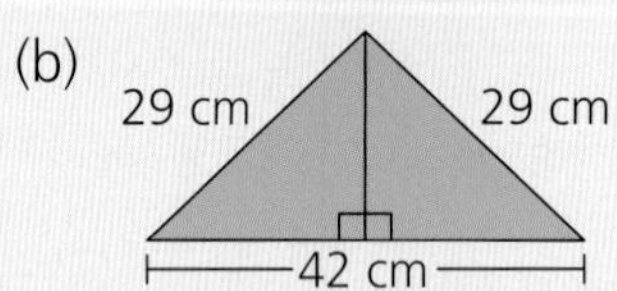

(c)

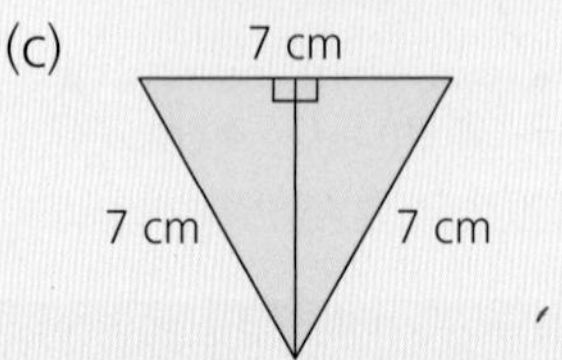

(d)

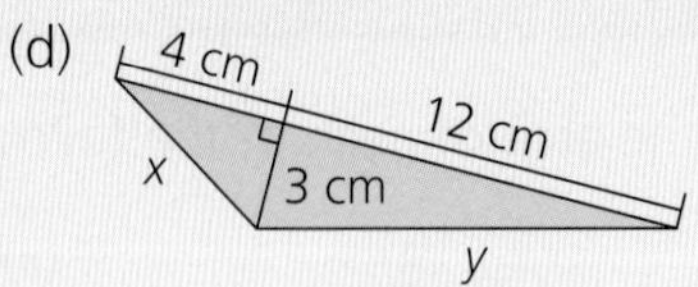

Section 6C Perimeter (Circumference) and Area of a Circle

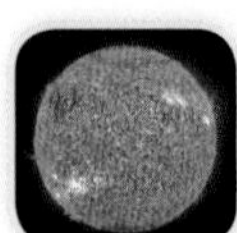

The Sun

The Moon

The circle is one of the most natural shapes in the universe. For ancient civilisations, the circles of the Sun and Moon were symbols of great power and mystery.

As far back as 5500 years ago, the inventors of the wheel showed their understanding of the circle shape and its application.

Depiction of a Sumerian battle cart, 2600 BC

Key Parts of a Circle

- A circle is the set of points at a given distance (its **radius**) from a fixed point (its **centre**).
- Each line segment joining the centre to a point on the circle is called a **radius** (plural **radii**).
- A **chord** is a line segment joining two points on a circle.
- A **diameter** is a chord through the centre. All diameters have length twice the radius. This length is also called the diameter of the circle.
- The length around the circle is called the **circumference**.
- A **semi-circle** is an arc (part) of a circle whose ends are the ends of a diameter.

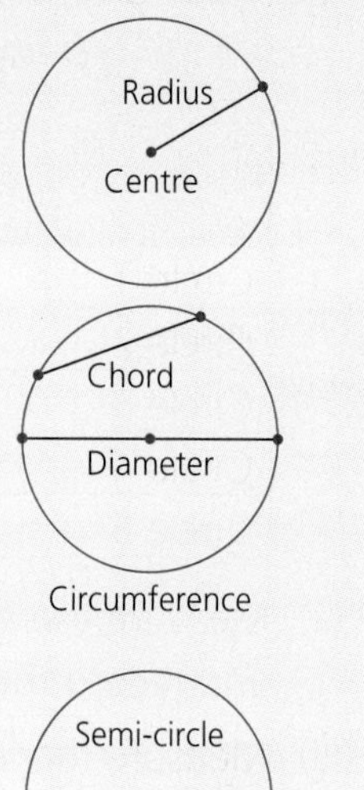

Class Activity

Investigate the relationship between the diameter and circumference of a circle.

You will need:

- a ruler and some string.

1

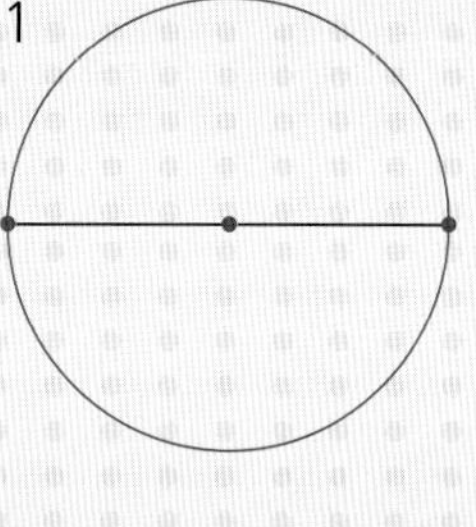

2

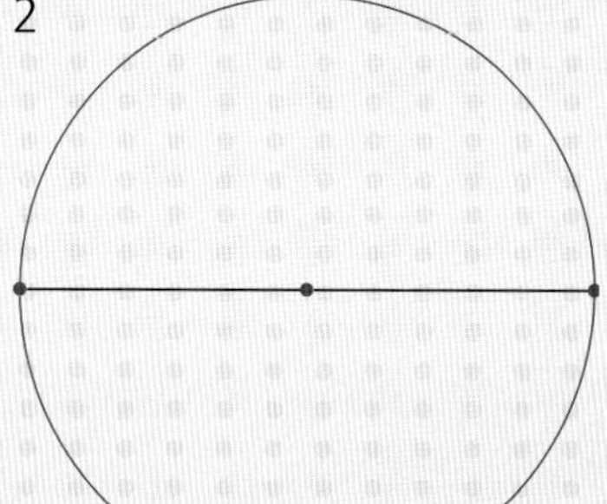

3

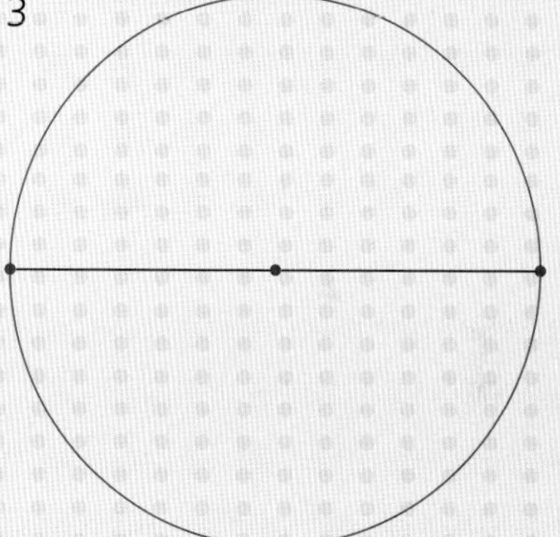

4

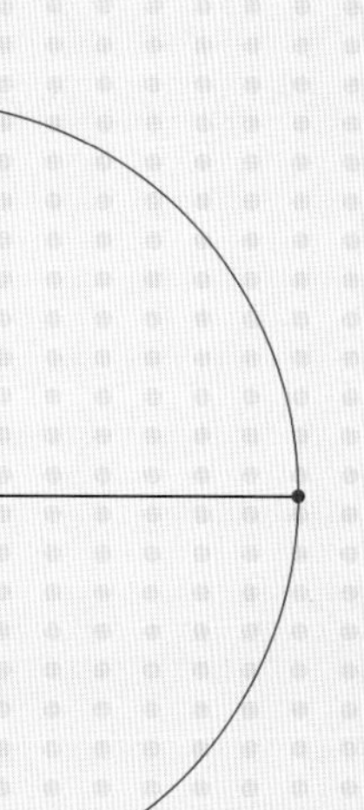

5

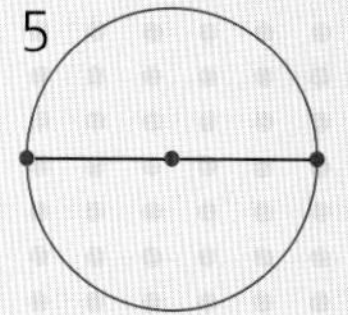

(i) Copy this table into your copybook.

	Diameter length	Circumference length (correct to one decimal place)	$\frac{\text{Circumference length}}{\text{Diameter length}}$ (correct to two decimal places)
Circle 1			
Circle 2			
Circle 3			
Circle 4			
Circle 5			

(ii) Measure the diameter of each of the five circles on the previous page using a ruler and record the measurements in your table.

(iii) Measure the length of the circumference of each circle by tracing each circle with the string. Record the measurements in your table (correct to one decimal place).

(iv) Using the values you recorded, calculate the ratio of the circumference length to the diameter length. Record the results in your table (correct to two decimal places).

(v) Make an observation about your results.

The Story of Pi (π)

From the Class Activity, you have seen that all the ratios are approximately 3.14. In fact, when you divide the circumference of any circle by its diameter you get the same number, no matter how big or small the circle is. This number is denoted by the Greek letter π (pi).

For any circle: $\pi = \frac{\text{circumference of the circle}}{\text{diameter of the circle}}$

The number π is one of the most important numbers in mathematics. You will see it in many formulae for area and volume.

People naturally wanted to find the exact value of π. However, it turns out that you cannot express the exact value of π in decimals because the decimals never end and never show a pattern. (A number such as this is called an **irrational number**.)

Just over 2000 years ago, the Greek mathematician Archimedes proved that π lies between two values: $\frac{223}{71} < \pi < \frac{22}{7}$. He did this by drawing polygons with 96 sides around and inside a circle.

The value of π correct to 30 decimal places is

3.141592653589793238462643383279

Archimedes (287–212 BC)

Connections

We can use geometry to get an approximate value for π, just as Archimedes did.

Draw a hexagon inside a circle as in the diagram on the right. Measure each side of the hexagon and find the total length. Divide this total by the diameter of the circle and you will get an answer close to π.

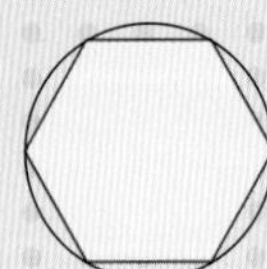

There are various ways to remember the digits of π. One way is to write a sentence where you replace each word with the number of its letters to get π.

Examples are: 'May I have a large container of coffee' and 'How I love a white Christmas'.

3. 1 4 1 5 9 2 6   3. 1 4 1 5 9

You may be able to compose some pi-etry of your own!

Using the Pi (π) Button on a Calculator

The π button on most calculators approximates π to nine decimal places.
To find the value of π on a Casio calculator, follow the steps below.

Press  then press $\times 10^x$ and π will appear.

Press = and 3.141592654 will appear.

Other approximations used for π are:

- $\pi = 3.14$
- $\pi = \frac{22}{7}$

The Circumference (Perimeter) and Area of a Circle

Now that we know about π, we can find the perimeter (circumference) and area of a circle using the formulae below:

- **Circumference of a circle** = $2\pi r$, which means $2 \times \pi \times r$, where r is the radius.
- **Area of a circle** = πr^2, which means $\pi \times r^2$

Key Point

If you are asked to give answers for the circumference and area of a circle in terms of π, this means that you must leave π in the answer.

These formulae are found on page 8 of the *Formulae and tables* booklet.

Example 1

A circle has radius = 8 cm. Using π = 3.14:

(i) Find the circumference of the circle, correct to two decimal places.

(ii) Find the area of the circle, correct to two decimal places.

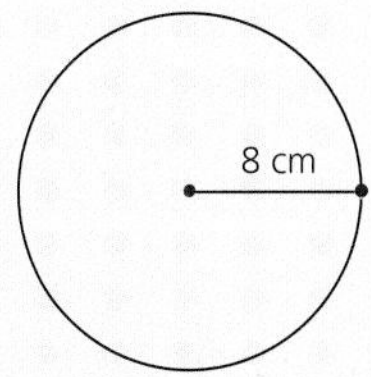

Solution

(i) Circumference $= 2\pi r$

$= 2(3.14)(8)$

$= 50.24$ cm (2 d.p.)

(ii) Area $= \pi r^2$

$= (3.14)(8)^2$

$= 200.96$ cm^2 (2 d.p.)

Example 2

The area of a circle is 5024 cm^2. Find the radius of the circle. (Let $\pi = 3.14$)

Solution

Area of a circle = πr^2

$$\pi r^2 = 5024$$

$$(3.14)r^2 = 5024$$

$$r^2 = \frac{5024}{3.14} \quad \text{... divide both sides by 3.14}$$

$$= 1600$$

$$r = \sqrt{1600} \quad \text{... square root both sides}$$

$$= 40 \text{ cm}$$

Example 3

The circumference of a circle is 56.52 cm. Find the diameter of the circle. (Let $\pi = 3.14$)

Solution

Circumference of a circle = $2\pi r$

$$2\pi r = 56.52$$

$$2(3.14)r = 56.52$$

$$2r = \frac{56.52}{3.14} \quad \text{... divide both sides by 3.14}$$

$$2r = 18$$

As the diameter = 2 × radius

diameter = 18 cm

Example 4

Find the area and circumference of this circle in terms of π.

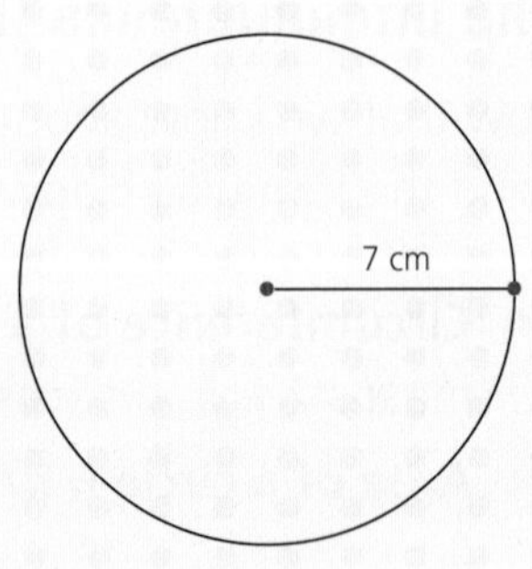

Solution

$$\text{Area} = \pi r^2$$

$$= \pi(7)^2$$

$$= 49\pi \text{ cm}^2$$

$$\text{Circumference} = 2\pi r$$

$$= 2\pi(7) = 14\pi \text{ cm}$$

Answer: Therefore, the area is 49π cm^2 and the circumference is 14π cm.

Activity 6.3

1 Using $\pi = 3.14$, calculate the circumference and area of each of the following circles.

(i)

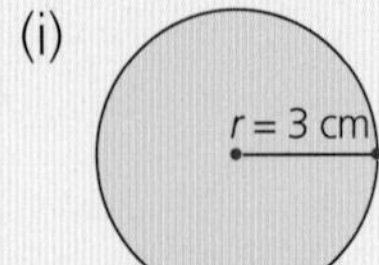

(iv)

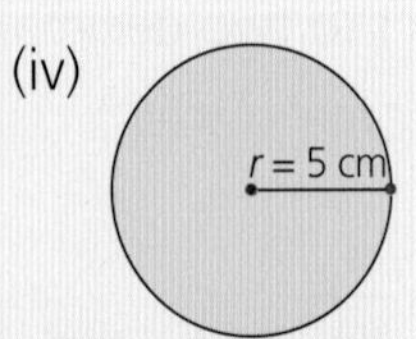

(ii)

r = 7 cm

(v)

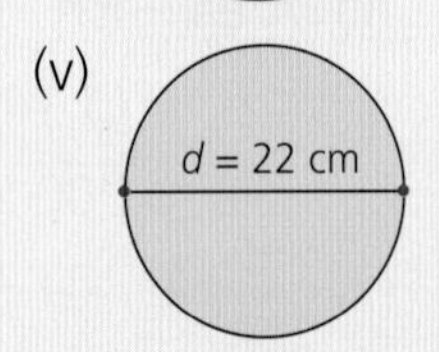

(iii)

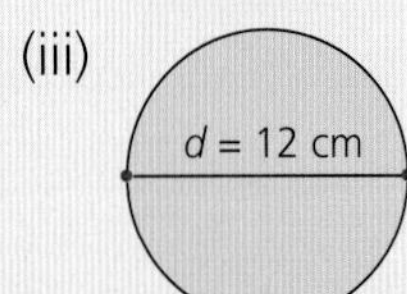

(vi)

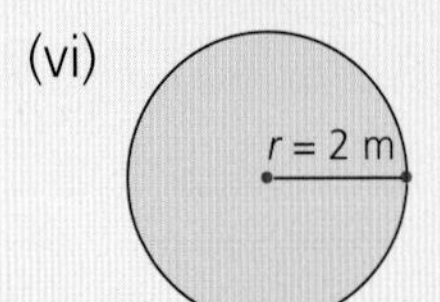

2 Using the π button on your calculator, find the circumference and area of circles with the following measurements. Give your answers correct to two decimal places.

(i) diameter = 16 cm

(ii) radius = 9 cm

(iii) diameter = 26 cm

(iv) radius = 4 cm

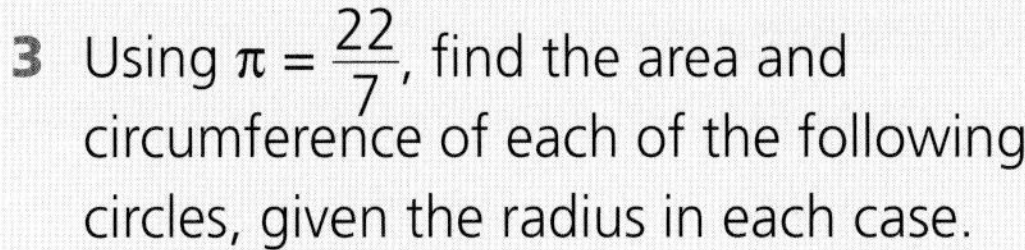

3 Using $\pi = \frac{22}{7}$, find the area and circumference of each of the following circles, given the radius in each case.

(i)

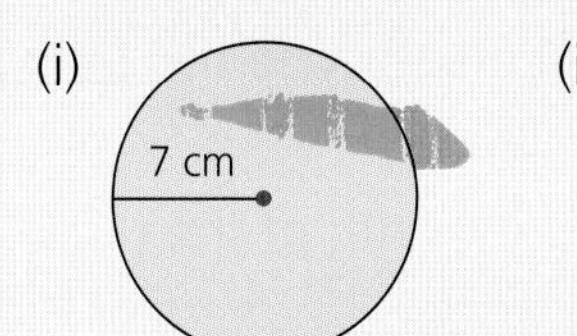

(ii)

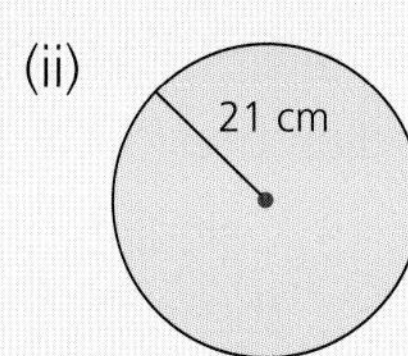

4 Calculate, in terms of π, the area and circumference of each of the following circles.

(i) radius = 5 cm (iii) radius = 3.5 m

(ii) radius = 8 cm (iv) radius = 65 mm

5 Given the circumference of each of the following circles, find the radius of each using $\pi = 3.14$.

(i) 50.24 cm (iii) 15.7 m

(ii) 87.92 cm (iv) 62.8 cm

6 Given the area of each of the following circles, find the radius of each, using $\pi = 3.14$.

(i) area = 314 cm^2

(ii) area = 113.04 cm^2

(iii) area = 706.5 cm^2

(iv) area = 28.26 cm^2

7 A cyclist travels 16.8 km. The circumference of each wheel of her bike is 1.4 m. How many times will the front wheel complete a full circle in the cyclist's journey?

8 (i) A wire of length 308 cm is bent into the shape of a circle. Find the diameter of the circle, using $\pi = \frac{22}{7}$.

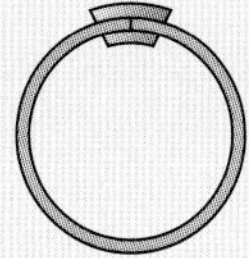

(ii) What length of wire is needed to make 20 circles of radius 14 cm? $\left(\text{Let } \pi = \frac{22}{7}\right)$

9 Find the area of each of the following shapes, using $\pi = 3.14$.

Give your answers correct to two decimal places.

(i)

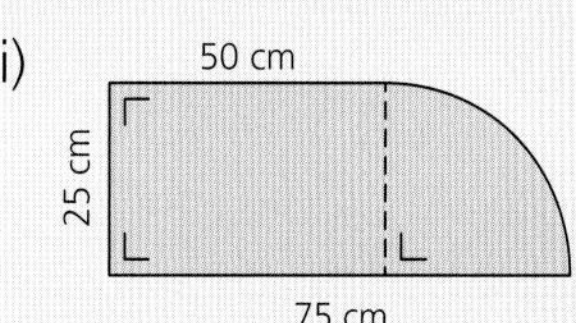

(ii)

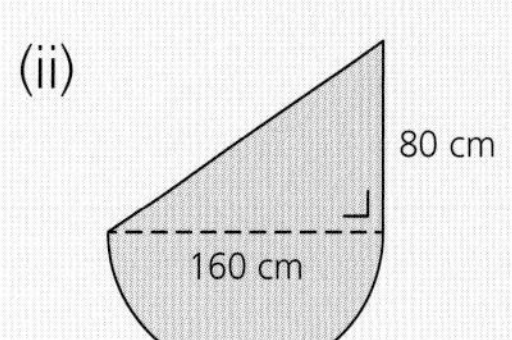

(iii)

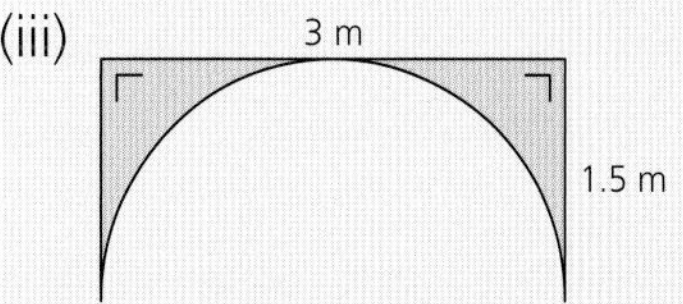

(iv)

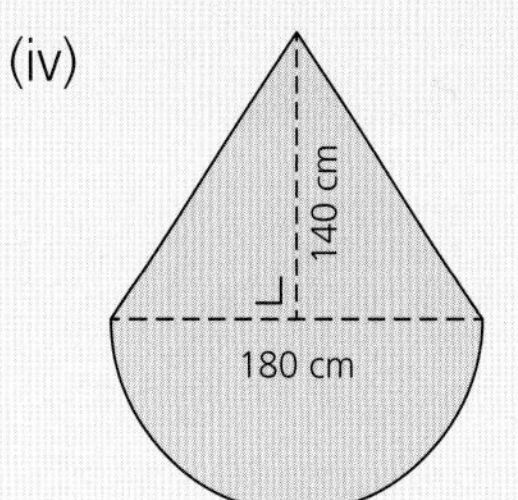

10 Find the area of the following shaded regions, correct to two decimal places, using $\pi = \frac{22}{7}$.

(i)

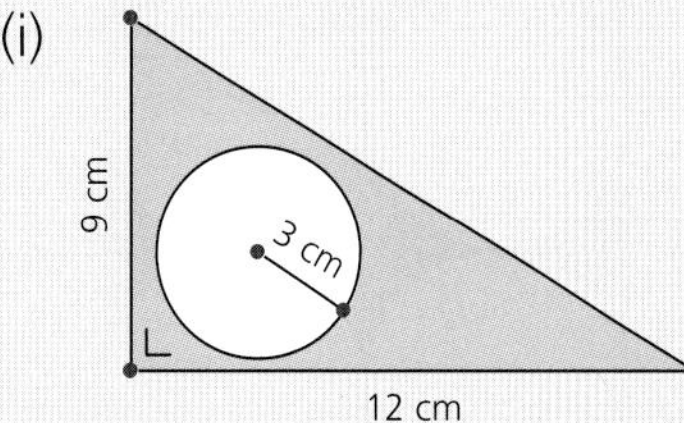

(ii)

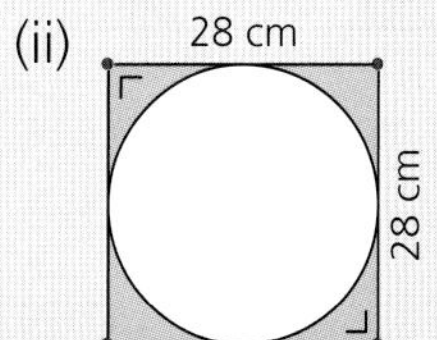

(iii)

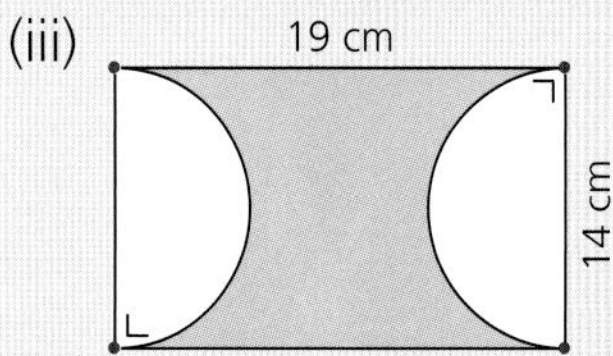

11 Find the area of the shaded region below, correct to two decimal places.

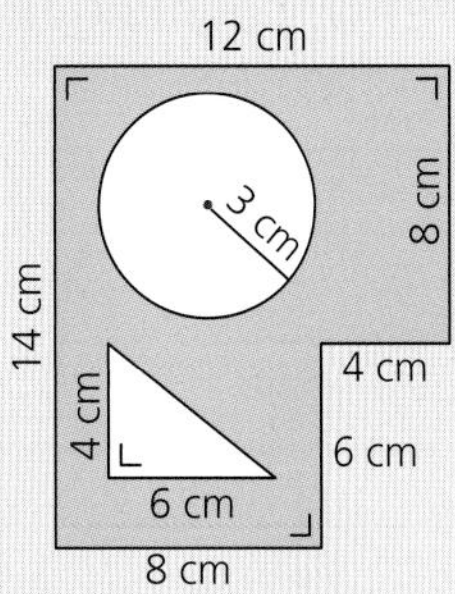

12 An athletics track is shown below.

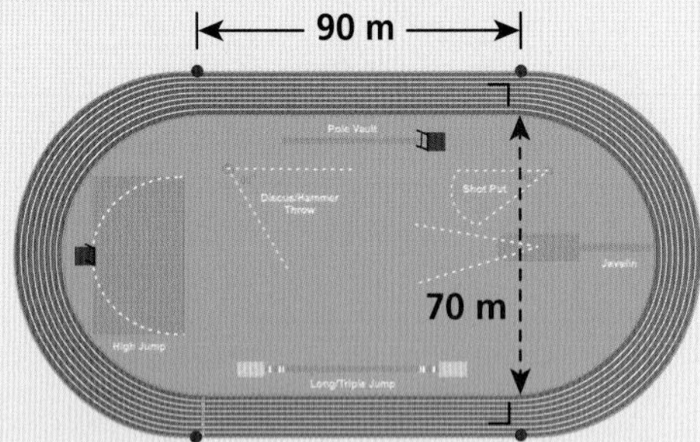

(i) Calculate the length of the track, using $\frac{22}{7}$ as a value for π.

(ii) How many laps will an athlete complete if she runs 10 km?

13 Four circular pieces are cut from a square piece of metal. Each circular piece has a radius of 5 cm.

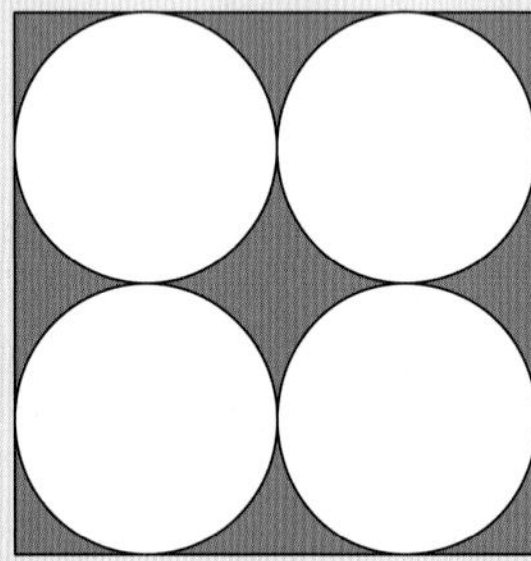

(i) Find, in cm² to two decimal places, the area of the remaining piece of metal.

(ii) What percentage of the metal was used to make the four circular pieces, to two decimal places?

14 The front wheel of a bicycle has a diameter of 56 cm.

(i) Calculate the length of the radius of the wheel, in cm.

(ii) Calculate the length of the circumference of the wheel, in cm. Take π as $\frac{22}{7}$.

(iii) How far does the bicycle travel when the wheel makes 250 complete turns? Give your answer in metres.

15 Pat designed the garden shown below for a pre-school.

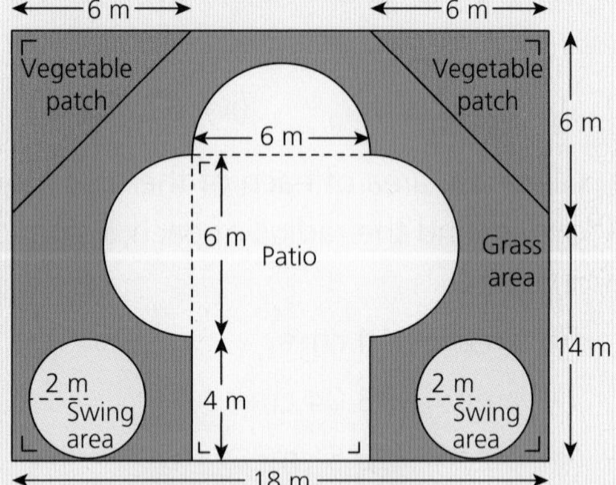

(i) What is the total area of the garden?

(ii) What is the total area of the two vegetable patches?

(iii) Find the area of the patio, correct to the nearest m².

(iv) What is the area of the grass region of the garden?

(v) What percentage of the garden is not grass? Give your answer to the nearest percentage.

Section 6D Volume of Rectangular Solids

The **volume** of an object is the amount of three-dimensional space it occupies.

Volume is measured in cubic units, usually cubic centimetres (cm^3).

Capacity is the volume of a liquid or gas and is measured in litres.

1 litre = 1000 cm^3 = 1000 ml

We regularly purchase products by volume, particularly when dealing with liquids.

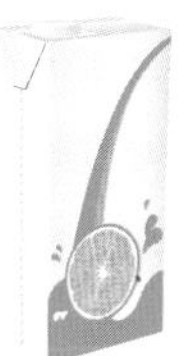

A rectangular object can be a solid such as a block or a container like a cardboard box. These are called **rectangular solids (cuboids)**.

The diagram below shows a cube of side 1 cm.

Its volume is 1 cm^3.

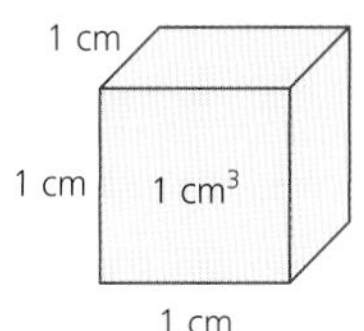

This is 1 unit of volume.

This cuboid is 5 cm long, 2 cm wide and 2 cm high. We can see by counting the small cubes that its volume is 20 cm^3.

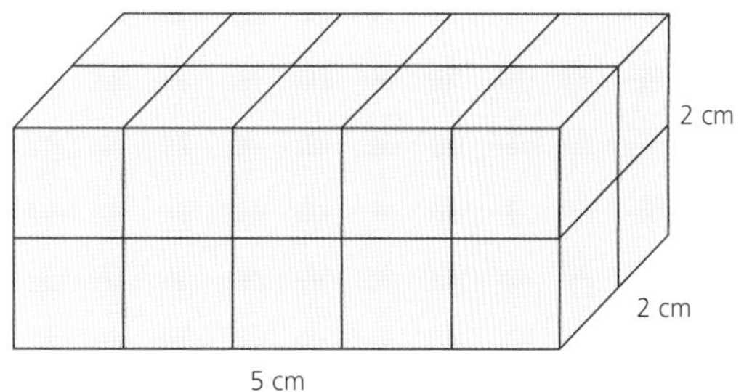

We could also get its volume by multiplication: $5 \times 2 \times 2 = 20$ cm^3.

Hence, the volume, V, of a rectangular solid can be calculated using the formula:

Volume = length × width × height

$$V = l \times w \times h$$

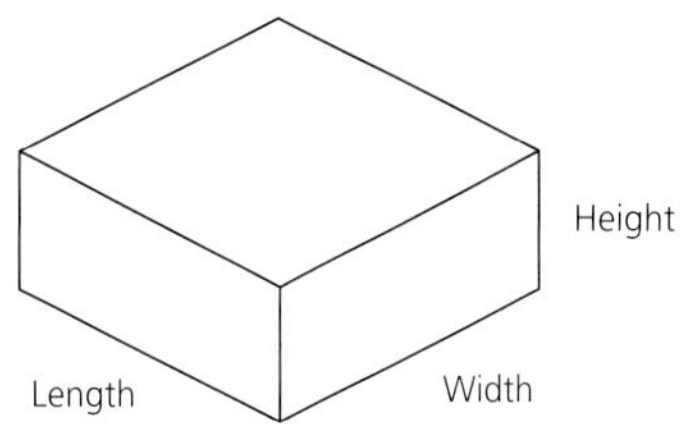

The cube below has sides of length 10 cm.
Its volume = $10 \times 10 \times 10 = 1000$ cm^3.

This is what **1 litre** looks like.

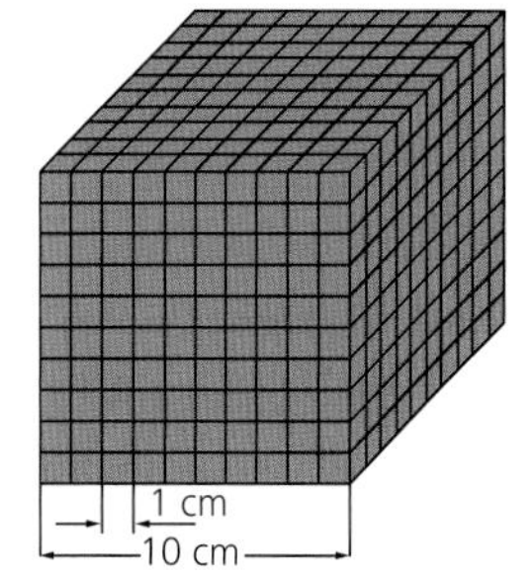

Example 1

Find the volume of each of the following rectangular solids:

(i)

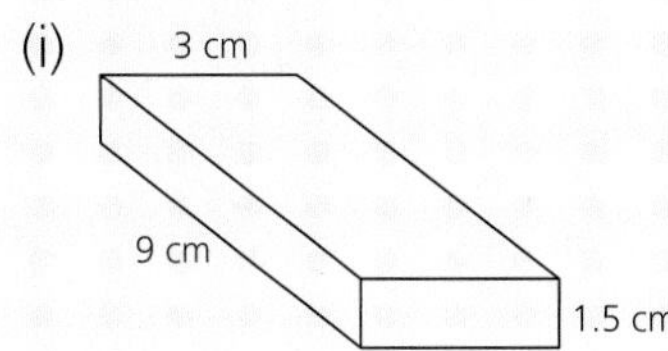

(ii)

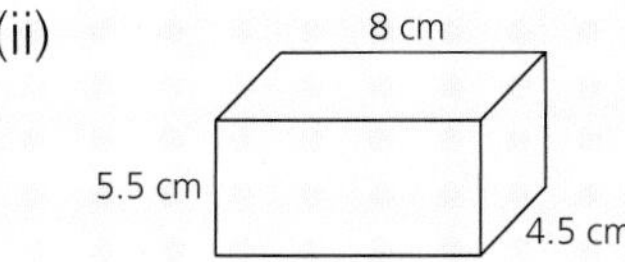

(iii)

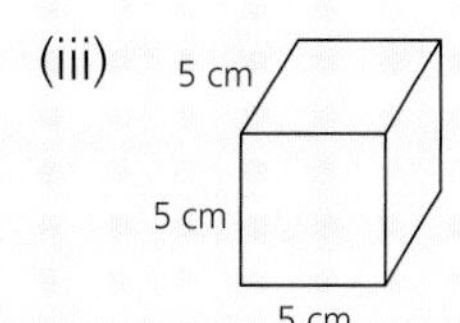

Solution

(i) Information given: length = 9 cm, width = 3 cm, height = 1.5 cm

Volume = $l \times w \times h$

Volume = $9 \times 3 \times 1.5 = 40.5 \text{ cm}^3$

(ii) Information given: length = 8 cm, width = 4.5 cm, height = 5.5 cm

Volume = $l \times w \times h$

Volume = $8 \times 4.5 \times 5.5 = 198 \text{ cm}^3$

(iii) Information given: length = 5 cm, width = 5 cm, height = 5 cm

Volume = $5 \times 5 \times 5 = 125 \text{ cm}^3$

Example 2

The volume of a rectangular solid is 150 cm³. Its length = 10 cm and its height = 5 cm. Find its width.

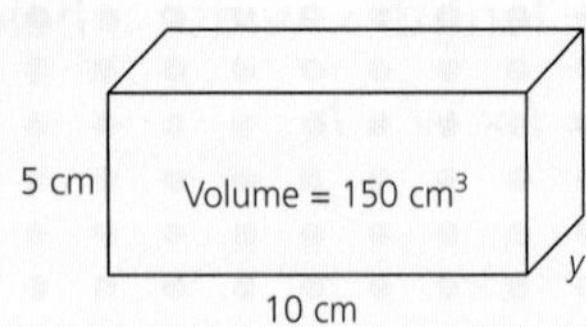

Solution

Let the width = y cm.

Volume = length × width × height

Volume of the cuboid = $(10)(y)(5) = 150$

$\Rightarrow (50)(y) = 150$

$\Rightarrow y = \frac{150}{50}$ ... divide both sides by 50

$= 3$ cm

Therefore, the width of the cuboid is 3 cm.

Activity 6.4

1 Find the volume of each of the following rectangular solids:

(i)

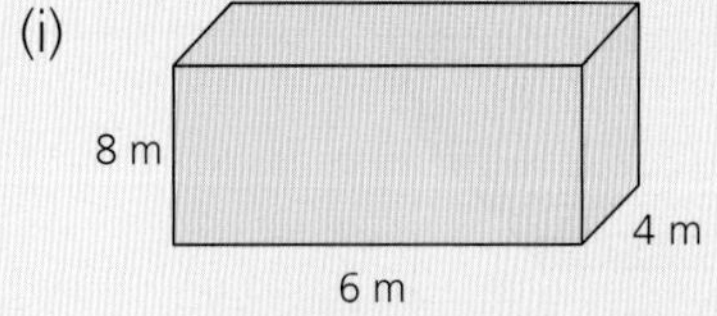

(ii)

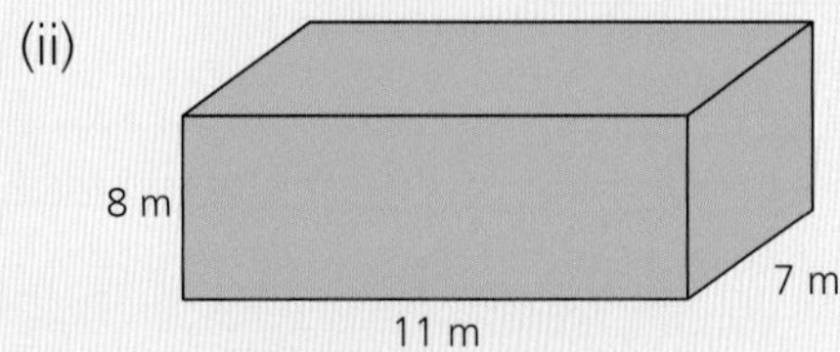

(iii)

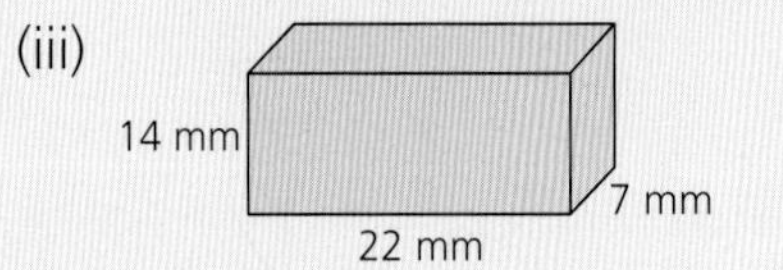

(iv)

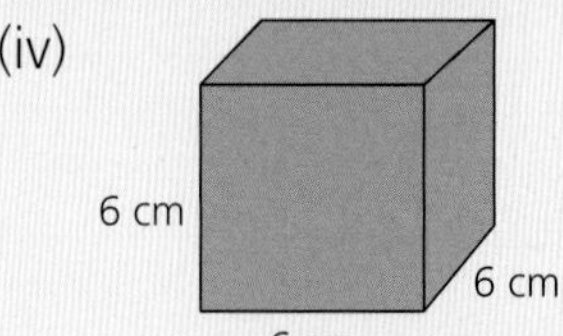

(v)

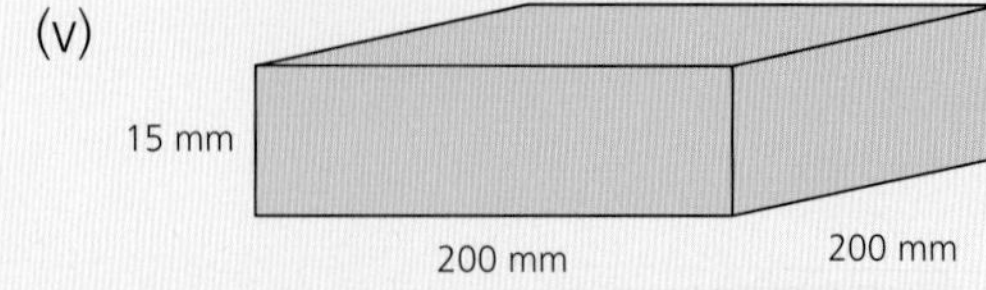

2 Find the volume in litres of each of the following cuboids.

(i)

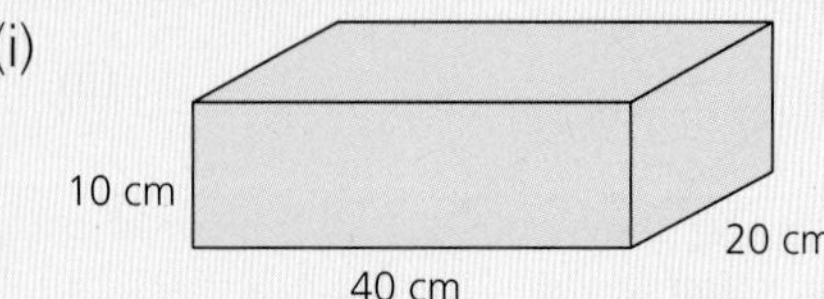

(ii)

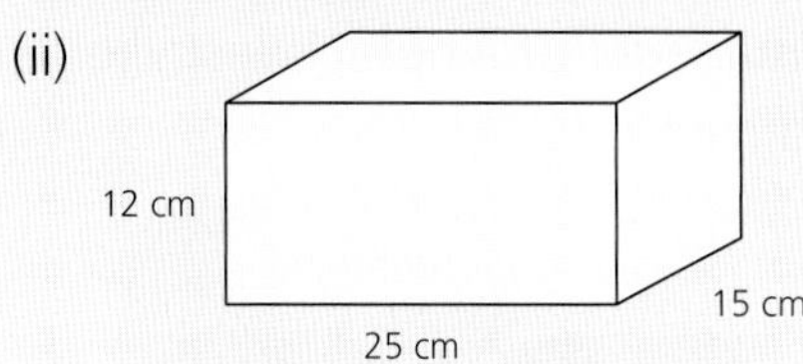

(iii)

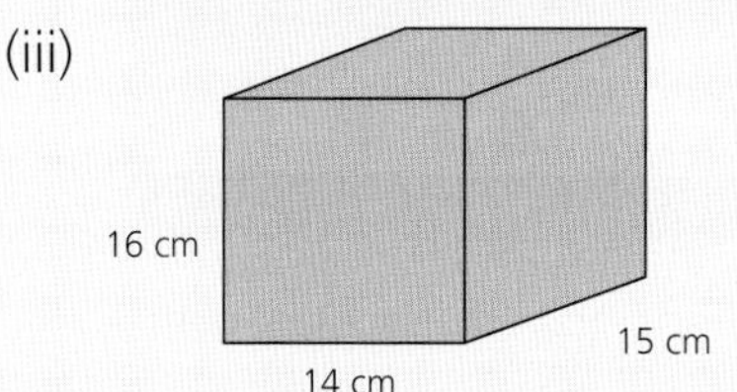

(iv)

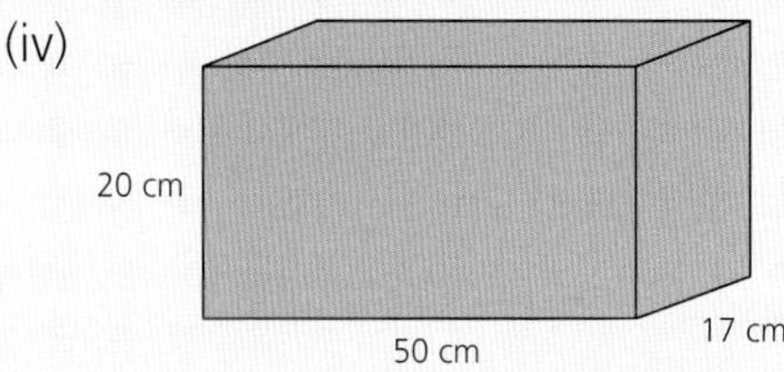

3 Find the value of the missing side of each of the following rectangular solids given the volume of each.

(i) Volume = 72 cm^3, height = x cm, length = 6 cm, width = 3 cm

(ii) Volume = 1080 cm^3, height = 8 cm, length = y cm, width = 9 cm

(iii) Volume = 36 cm^3, height = 3 cm, length = 6 cm, width = z cm

4 Sketch and label each cuboid below. Find the length of the missing side in each.

(i) Volume = 2040 cm^3, length = 17 cm, width = 15 cm and height = a cm

(ii) Volume = 9360 cm^3, length = 30 cm, width = w cm and height = 24 cm

(iii) Volume = 11.25 m^3, length = 2.5 m, width = 3 m and height = y m

(iv) Volume = 0.2475 m^3, length = d cm, width = 55 cm and height = 45 cm

5 A large rectangular box is shown below. How many cubes of side length 2 cm can fit in the box? (Diagrams not to scale.)

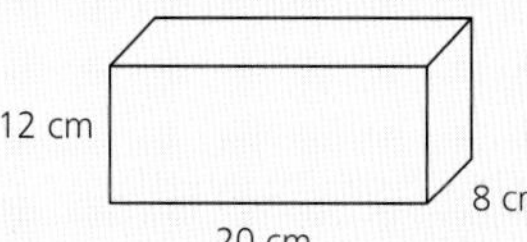

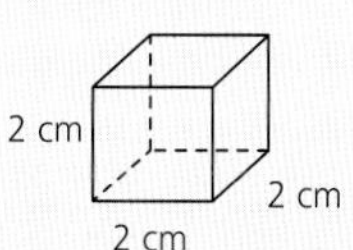

6 Alan is filling a large rectangular tank with water. He uses a small rectangular container to fill the tank.

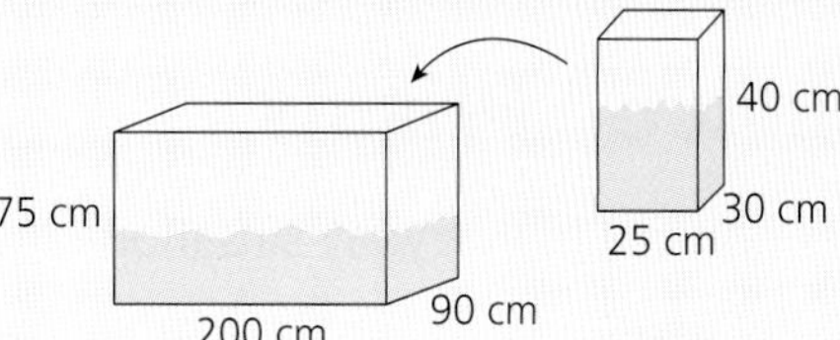

(i) Find the volume of the tank in litres.

(ii) Find the volume of the container in litres.

(iii) How many containers of water are needed to fill the tank?

7 A company manufactures plastic trays from flat shapes as shown below.

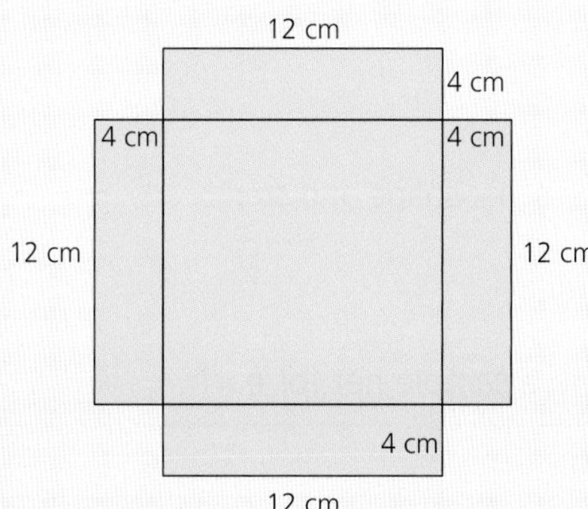

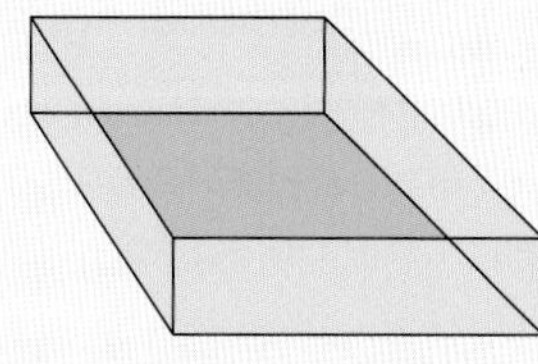

(i) Find the total surface area of one tray.

(ii) Find the volume of one tray.

The company buys plastic rectangular sheets of 1 m × 2 m to make the trays.

(iii) How many plastic sheets are needed to make 1000 trays?

8 The container shown is used to ship boxes.

(i) Calculate the volume of the container.

(ii) Calculate the volume in m³ of a box measuring 50 cm × 30 cm × 20 cm.

(iii) How many of these boxes can fit into the container?

(iv) The shipping company wants to ship 300 boxes with dimensions 100 cm × 50 cm × 50 cm. How many containers will be needed?

9 The manager of a hotel is installing a swimming pool.

The dimensions of the pool are:

- Length = 20 m, Width = 10 m, Depth = 2 m.

The swimming pool will be tiled with square tiles of side 0.5 m.

(i) What is the total surface area of the sides and bottom of the swimming pool?

(ii) How many tiles are needed to cover the total surface area of the pool?

Section 6E Prisms

We meet prisms in everyday situations. Here are some examples.

Key Points

A **prism** is a 3-dimensional figure where:

- the bases (or ends of the object) are the same shape and size
- the bases are parallel to one another
- the sides of the object form parallelograms.

The following is a range of prisms along with a sample net for each.

■ **Right-angled triangular-based prism**		
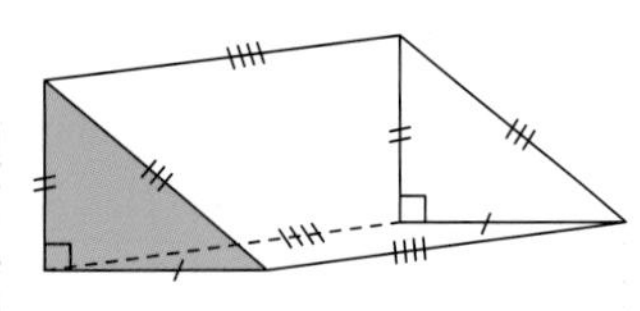	The cross-section or base of this prism is a right-angled triangle.	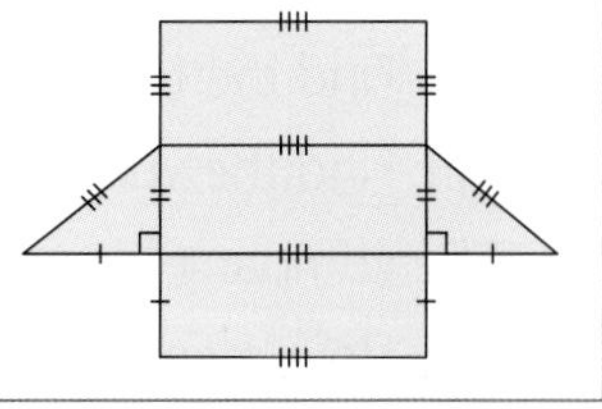

■ **Isosceles triangular-based prism**		
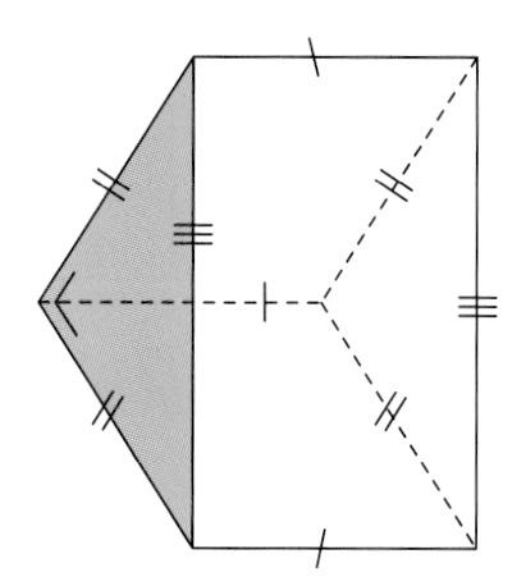	The cross-section or base of this prism is an isosceles triangle.	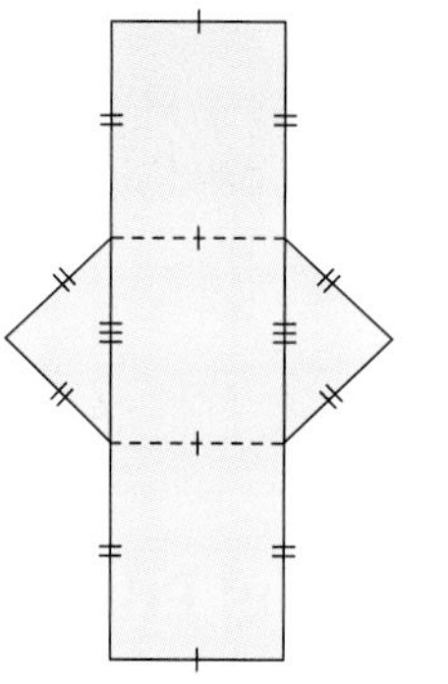
■ **Equilateral triangular-based prism**		
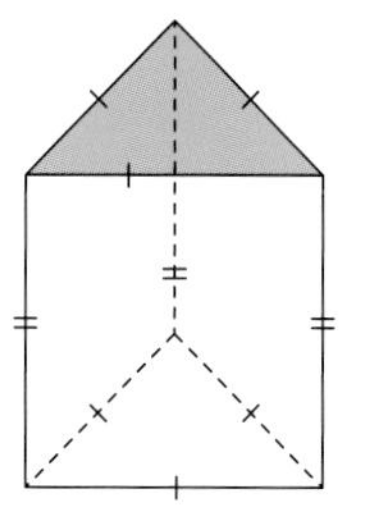	The cross-section or base of this prism is an equilateral triangle.	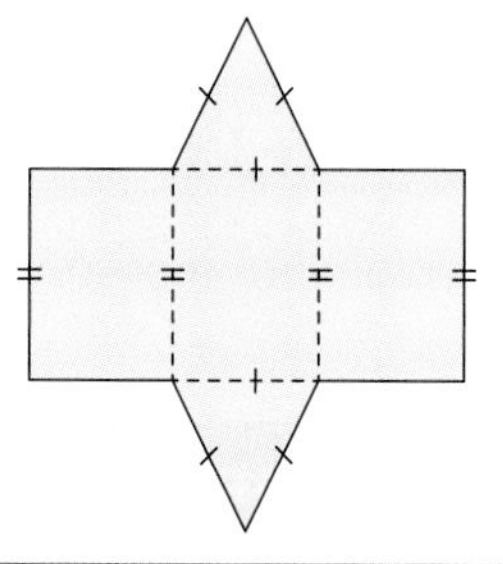
■ **Rectangular prism**		
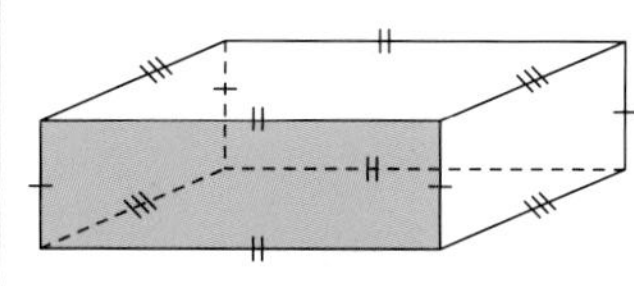	All six sides are flat, all angles are right angles and all of the faces are rectangles. It is also known as a **cuboid**.	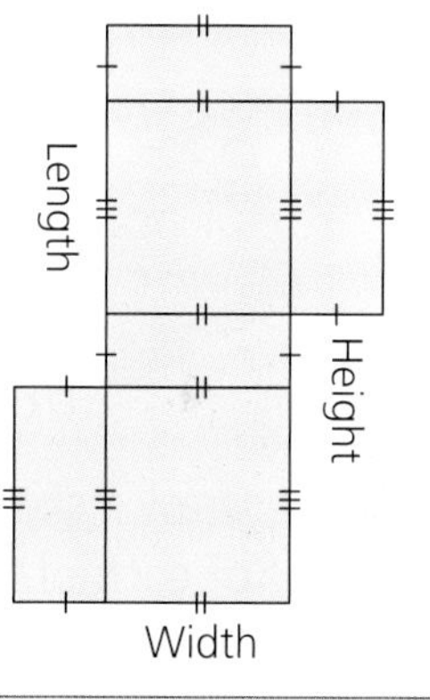
■ **Cube**		
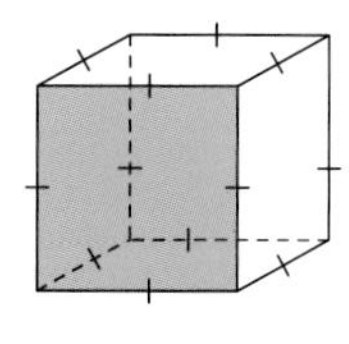	A cube has six identical square faces. It is also known as a **regular hexahedron**.	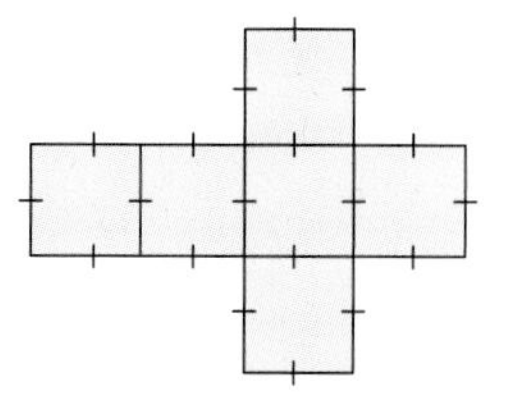
■ **Pentagonal prism**		
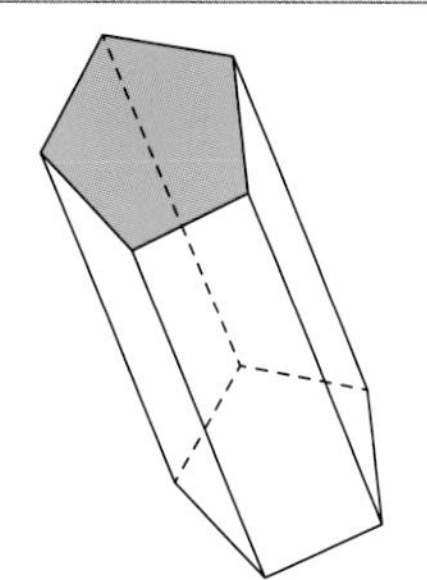	This prism has a pentagon-shaped cross-section. It has two pentagon bases and five rectangular sides.	

■ **Hexagonal prism**		
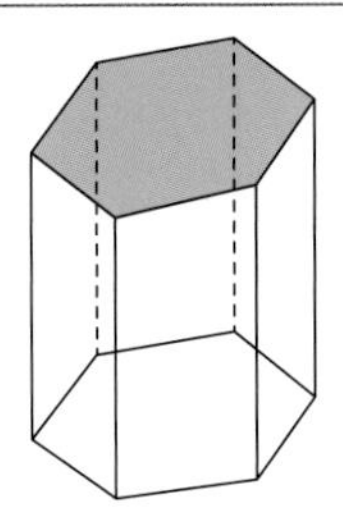	This prism has a hexagon cross-section. It has two hexagon bases and six rectangular sides.	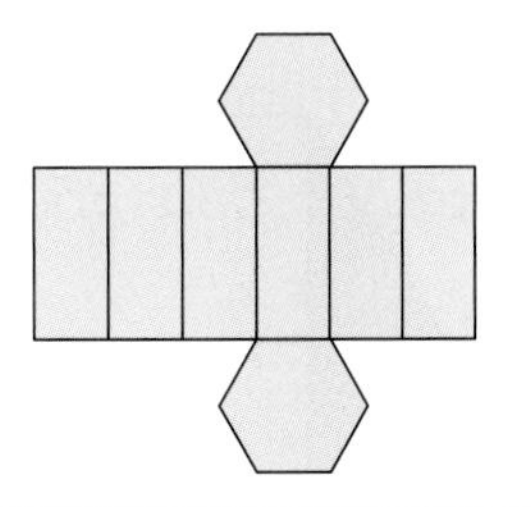

Volume of Prisms

To find the **volume** of any prism, we must find the area of the **cross-section** (or **base**) of the prism and multiply it by the height or depth of the prism.

Key Point

Volume of a prism = area of the cross-section × height/depth of the prism

Example 1

The images show (i) a regular prism and (ii) an irregular prism.

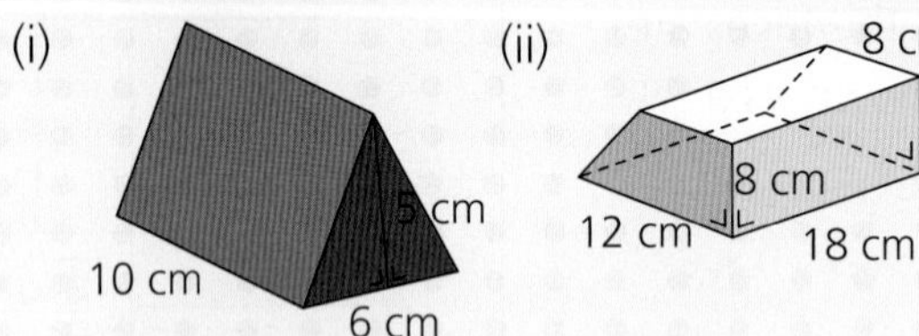

(a) Draw a sketch of the cross-section of each of the prisms above.

(b) Hence, find the volume of each prism.

Solution

(i) (a) Cross-section of the prism

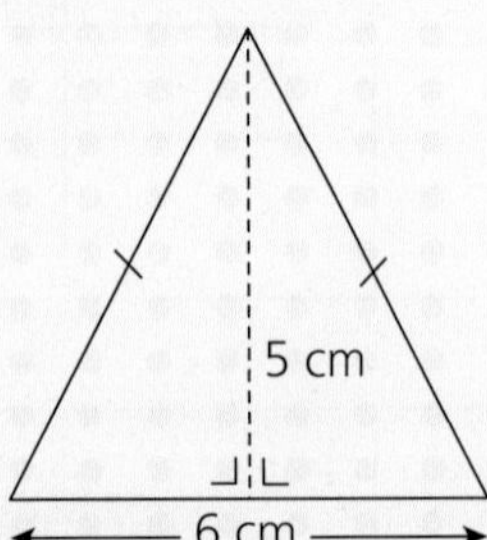

(b) Area of cross-section

= Area of a triangle

$= \frac{1}{2} \times b \times h$

$= \frac{1}{2} \times 6 \times 5 = 15 \text{ cm}^2$

Volume of the prism = area of the cross-section × depth of the prism

$= 15 \text{ cm}^2 \times 10 \text{ cm} = 150 \text{ cm}^3$

(ii) (a) Cross-section of the prism

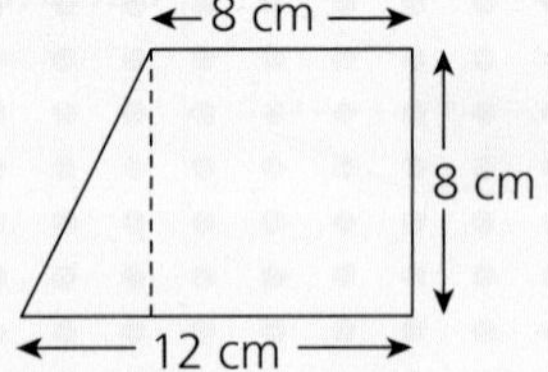

(b) Area of cross-section

= Area of triangle + Area of square

$= \left(\frac{1}{2} \times b \times h\right) + (l \times l)$

$= \left(\frac{1}{2} \times 4 \times 8\right) + (8 \times 8)$

$= 16 + 64 = 80 \text{ cm}^2$

Volume of the prism

= area of the cross-section × depth of the prism

$= 80 \text{ cm}^2 \times 18 \text{ cm}$

$= 1440 \text{ cm}^3$

Total Surface Area (TSA) of a Prism

We have already met the **total surface area** of rectangular solids. We used the net of a solid to assist in finding the total surface area of the solid.

The **total surface area** (TSA) of any prism can be found using the same method.

Key Point

The TSA of a prism is the sum of all the areas of the faces for a given prism.

Example 2

(i) Draw a net of the surface of this prism.

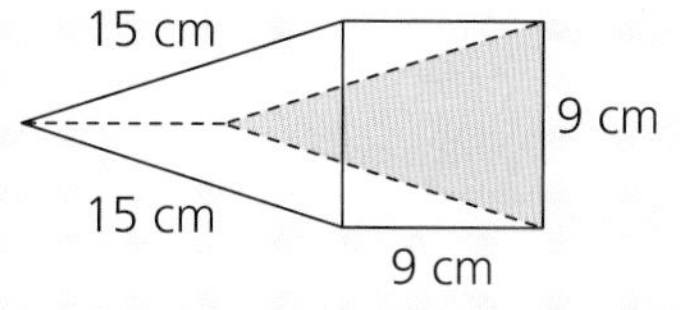

(ii) Find the total surface area of the prism, correct to one decimal place.

Solution

(i) Net for the prism

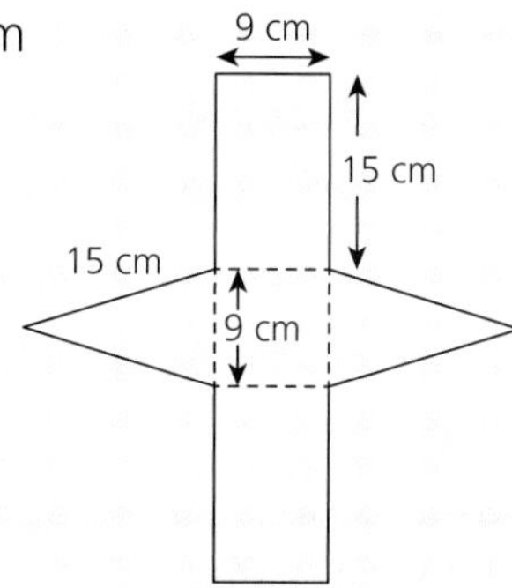

(ii) Form a right-angled triangle to find the perpendicular height of the prism base.

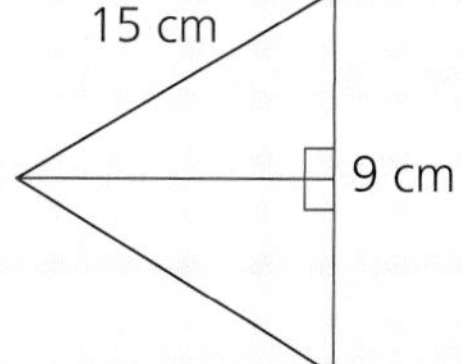

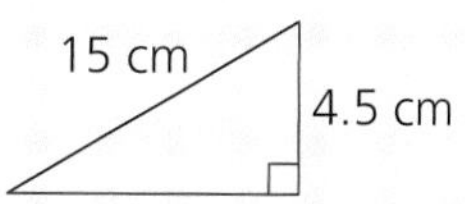

Pythagoras' Theorem:

b, c, a

$c^2 = a^2 + b^2$

$\Rightarrow 15^2 = 4.5^2 + b^2$

$\Rightarrow 225 = 20.25 + b^2$

$\Rightarrow 225 - 20.25 = b^2$ ... subtract 20.25 from both sides

$\Rightarrow 204.75 = b^2$

$\Rightarrow \sqrt{204.75} = b$ ... square root both sides

$\Rightarrow 14.309 ... = b$

$\Rightarrow b = 14.3$ cm (one decimal place)

Total surface area = 2(area of a triangular face) + 2(area of a rectangular face) + (area of the square face)

Total surface area

$= 2\left(\frac{1}{2} \times 14.3 \times 9\right) + 2(15 \times 9) + (9 \times 9)$

$= 128.7 + 270 + 81$

$= 479.7$ cm²

Activity 6.5

1 For the rectangular solid shown, find:

(i) the total surface area

(ii) the volume

(iii) the capacity in litres.

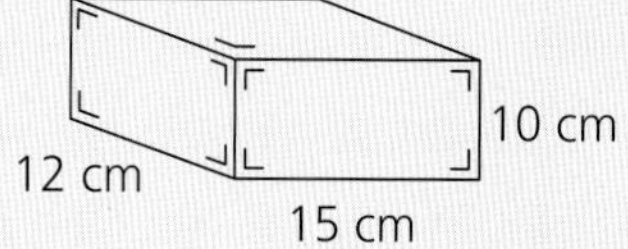

Hint

1000 cm³ = 1 litre

2 State which of the nets below (A, B, C or D) is a net for the rectangular solid shown. Explain your answer.

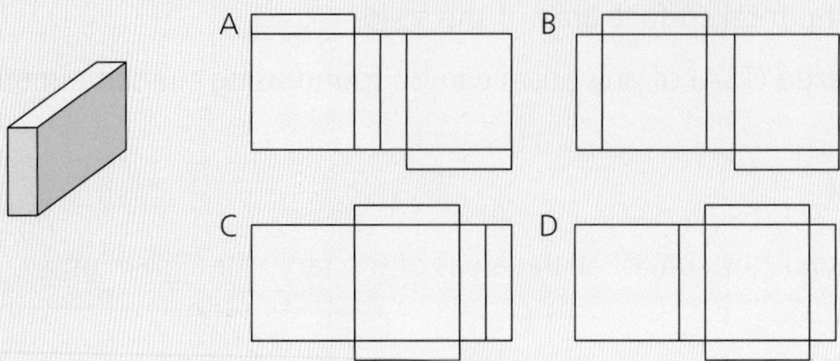

3 Copy and complete the table below, which relates to rectangular solids. Give your answers correct to three decimal places.

	Length (cm)	Width (cm)	Height (cm)	Volume (cm³)	Total surface area (cm²)
(i)	6	5.5	7		
(ii)	12.5	9	9		
(iii)	60	70	80		
(iv)	1.2	1.6	1.8		
(v)	$\frac{1}{2}$	$\frac{3}{4}$	$\frac{2}{3}$		
(vi)	15		17	4080	
(vii)		3.4	5.8	90.712	
(viii)	13	8		832	
(ix)	26		20		3662
(x)		22.6	11.7		2826.94

4 Find the capacity of each of the following rectangular water tanks. Give your answers in litres correct to two decimal places.

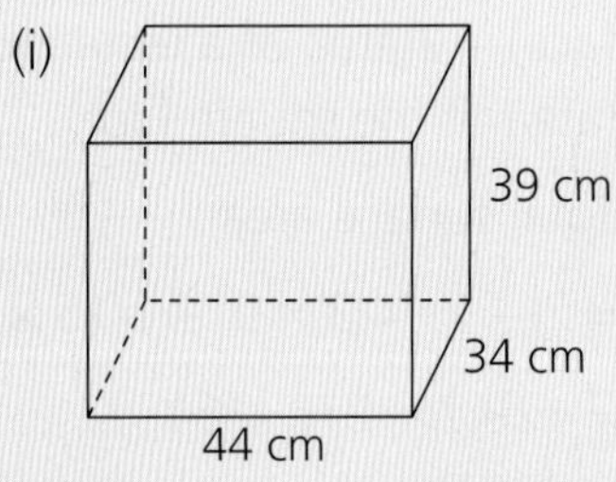

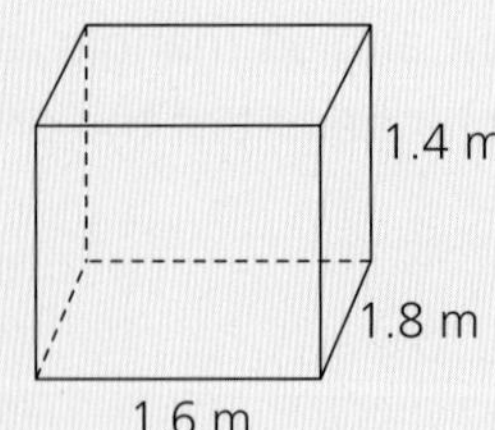

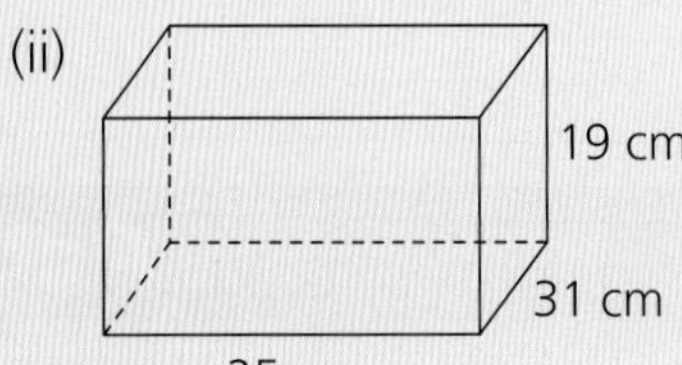

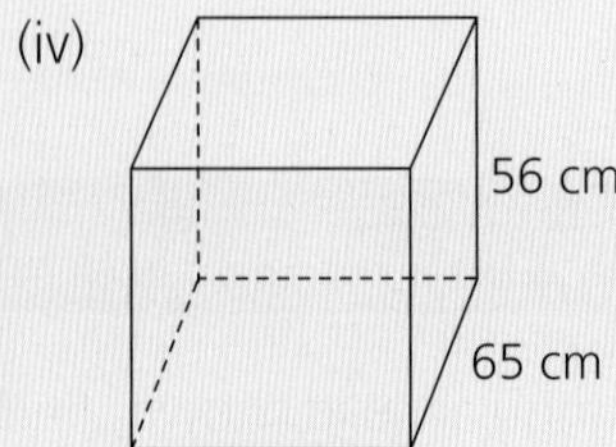

5 Find (a) the volume and (b) the surface area of each of these triangular-based prisms. Round your answers to two decimal places if required.

(i)

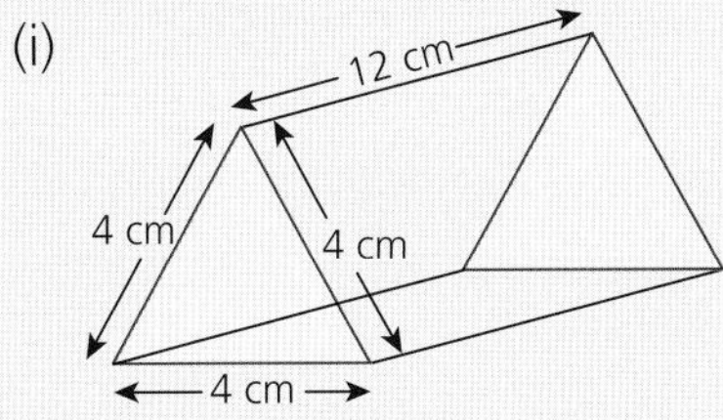

(ii)

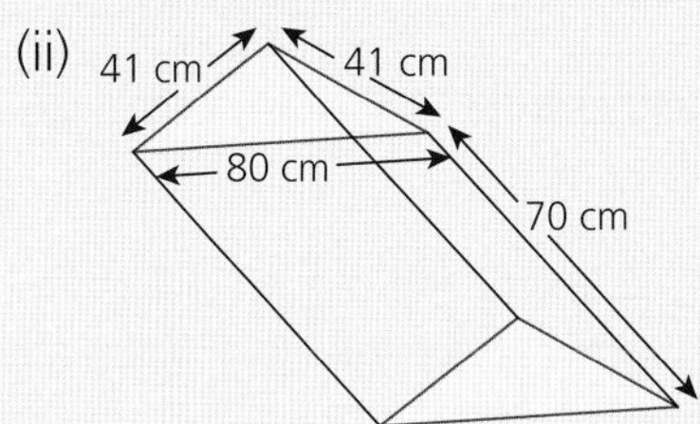

(iii)

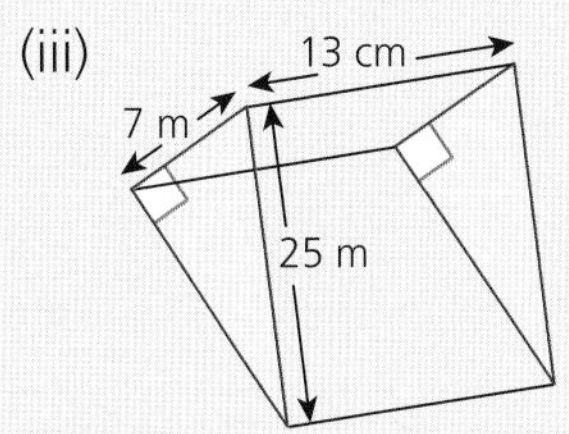

6 Find (a) the volume and (b) the surface area of each of these triangular-based prisms. Round your answers to two decimal places if required.

(i)

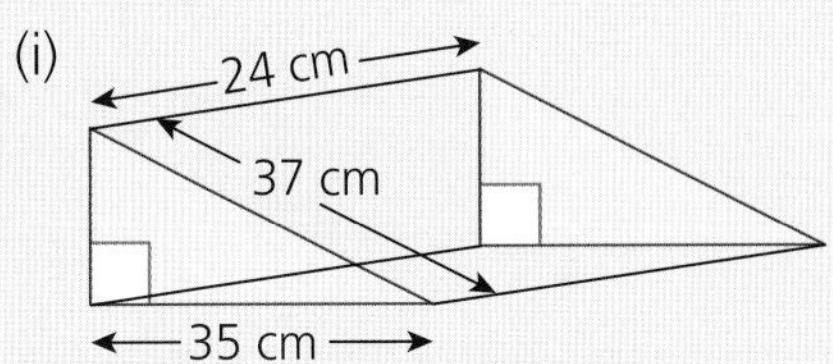

(ii)

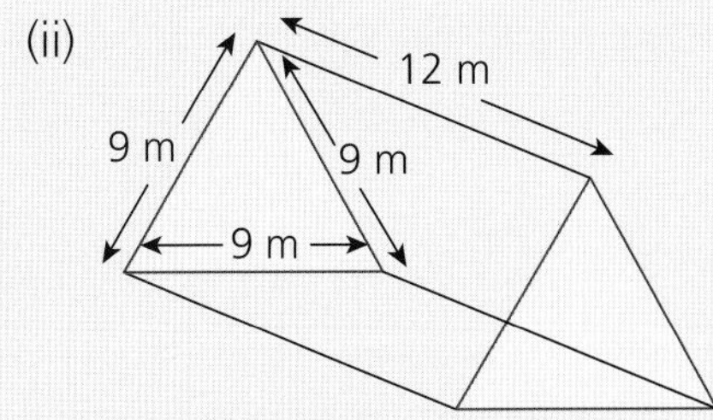

(iii)

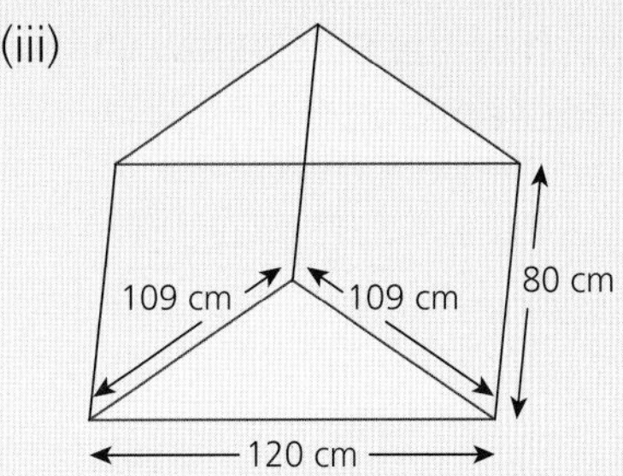

7 A 7-sided prism has the numbers 1, 2, 3, 4, 5, 6 and 7 written on each side. The diagram shows a net of this prism.

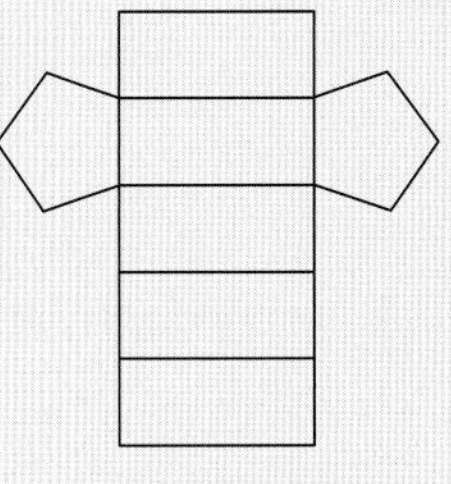

Draw a sketch of the net in your copybook and number each face such that no two consecutively numbered parallel faces touch when the net is formed into a prism.

8 When this net is formed into a polygonal prism, which sides are opposite each other?

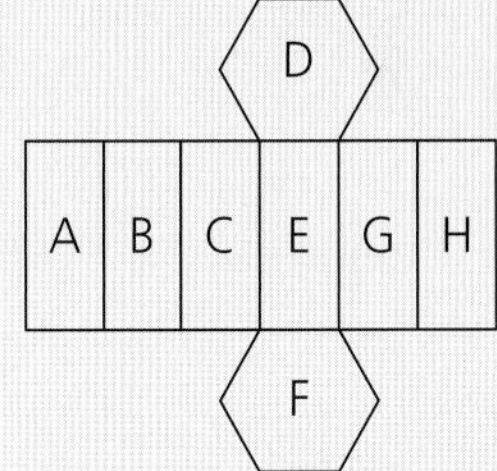

9 The diagram is a net for an 8-sided prism.

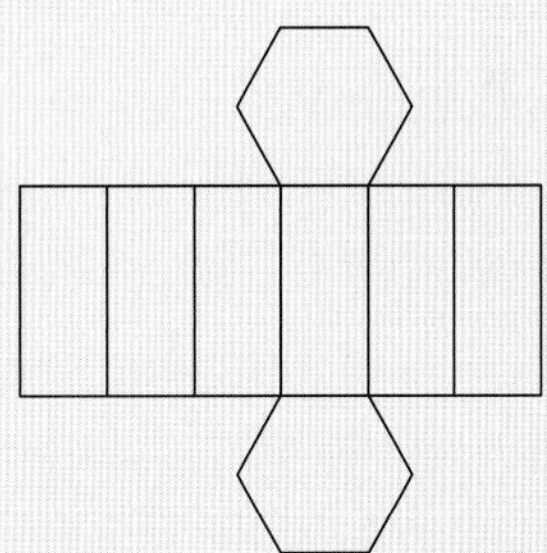

Draw a sketch of the net in your copybook and number each face from 1 to 8 such that no two consecutive parallel faces touch when the net is formed into a prism.

10 State which of the nets below (A, B, C or D) is an **incorrect** net for this object.

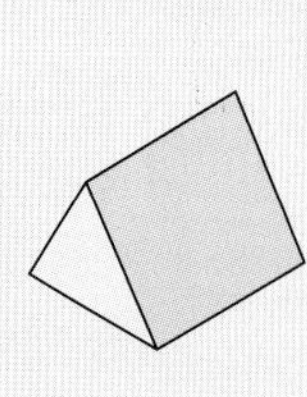

A

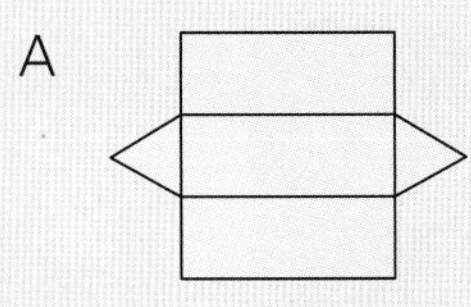

C

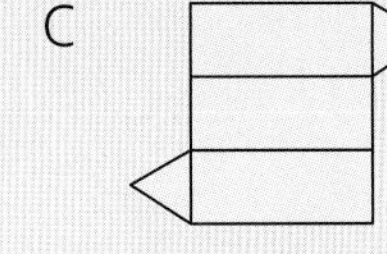

B

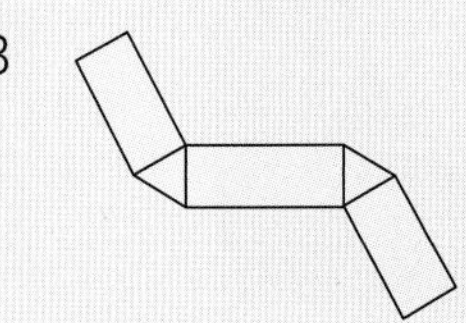

D

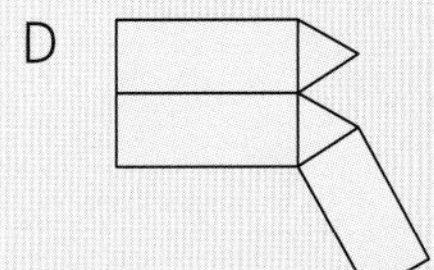

11 State which of the nets below (A, B, C or D) are the **correct** nets for this object.

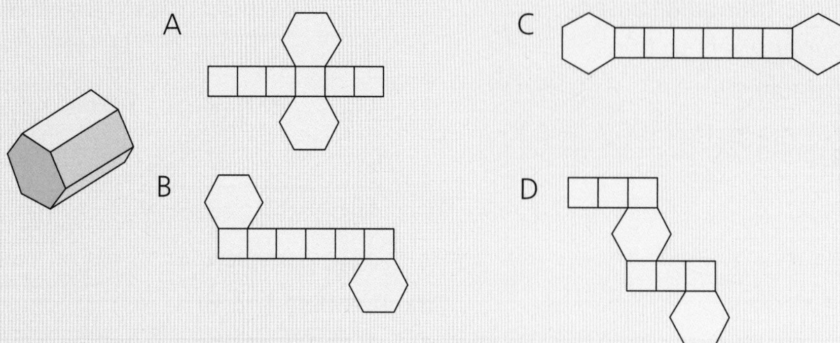

12 A company sells a range of fruit juices. One of the products is a rectangular carton of apple juice which has the dimensions 12 cm by 5 cm by 33 cm.

(i) Sketch a net of the apple juice carton.

(ii) Find the volume of apple juice in the carton, when filled to capacity.

The volume of one carton of apple juice is equivalent to five smaller cartons which have a square base of length 6 cm.

(iii) Find the volume of this smaller carton.

(iv) Find the height of this smaller carton.

13 The foundation of a new building is about to be poured. The shape of the foundation is shown.

The foundation is constructed by pouring concrete to a depth of 1 metre. Concrete is delivered to the site by cement lorries, which each have a capacity of 10 m³.

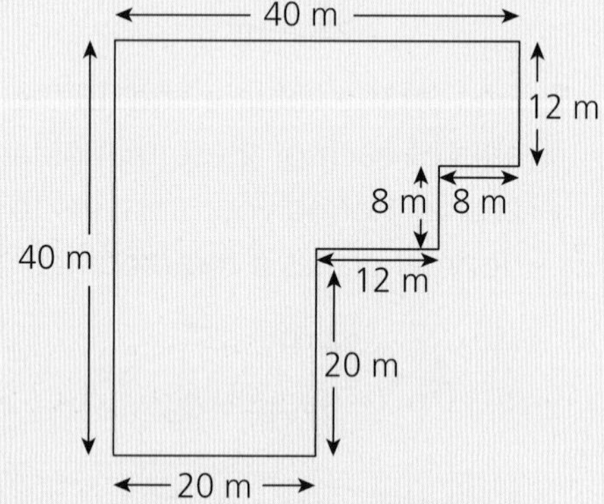

(i) What volume of concrete is required to lay the foundation for the new building? Give your answer to the nearest litre.

(ii) If the foundation was filled to a depth of 2 metres, what is the minimum number of trips each driver would have to make, assuming there are three drivers and they all do the same number of trips?

Section 6F Cylinders

The cylinder shape is seen in many different objects: pipes, oil storage tanks, medicine capsules, etc. Also, it is one of the most commonly used shapes for storing food products, typically in a tin can.

The volume of a cylinder is the area of the base (the bottom) multiplied by the height.

The base is a circle which has an area of πr^2.

Hence the volume of a cylinder $= \pi r^2 \times h$, where h = the height.

Volume of a cylinder $= \pi \times (\text{radius})^2 \times$ height of the cylinder $= \pi r^2 h$

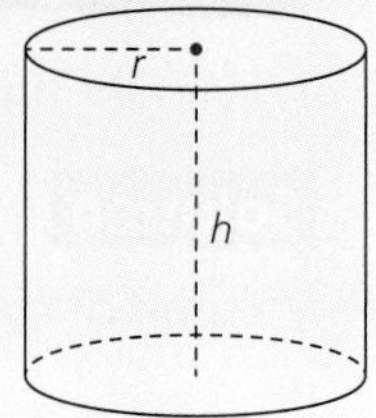

The formula for the volume of a cylinder is on page 10 of the *Formulae and tables* booklet.

Net of a Cylinder

- A cylinder has two congruent (equal) circles.
- The curved surface makes a rectangle when it is flattened out.
- The length of two of the sides of the rectangle is equal to the circumference of the circle formed at the top and bottom of the cylinder ($2\pi r$).
- The length of the other two sides in the rectangle is equal to the height of the cylinder (h).

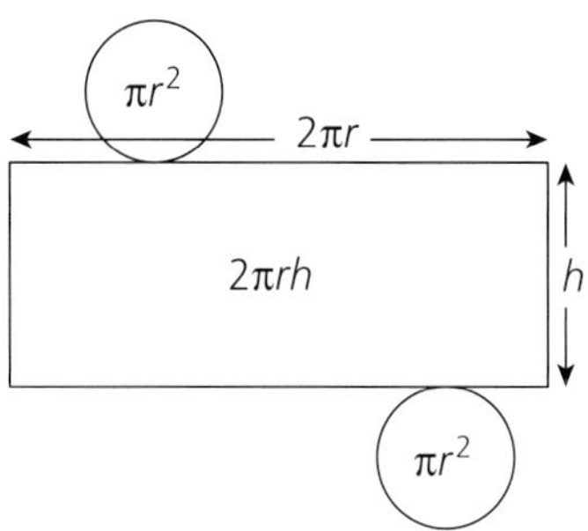

Surface Area of a Cylinder

The curved surface area is the area of the curved part of the cylinder. In the net it is the rectangular section, so to find its area we multiply length × width $= 2\pi r \times h = 2\pi rh$.

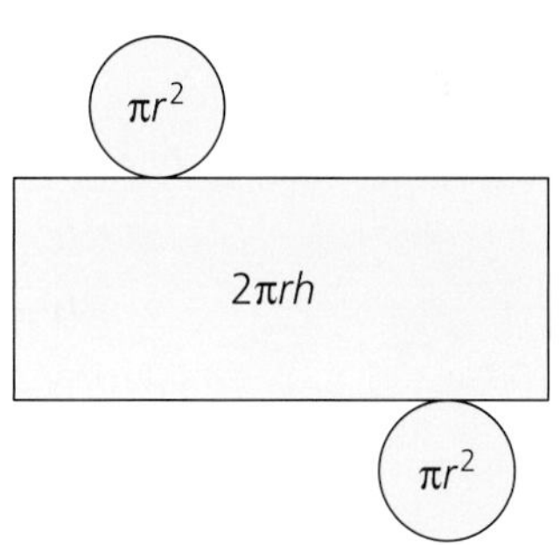

Curved surface area of a cylinder $= 2\pi rh$

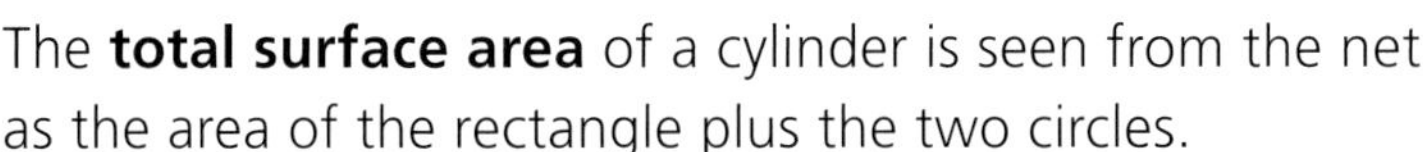

The **total surface area** of a cylinder is seen from the net as the area of the rectangle plus the two circles.

Total surface area of a cylinder $= 2\pi rh + 2\pi r^2$
$= 2\pi r(h + r)$

Example 1

Find the volume of this cylinder, using $\frac{22}{7}$ as an approximation for π.

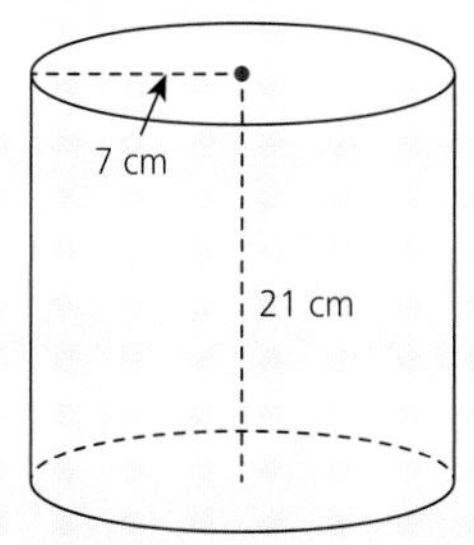

Solution

Volume of cylinder $= \pi r^2 h$

Volume $= \left(\frac{22}{7}\right)(7^2)(21)$

$= 3234 \text{ cm}^3$

Example 2

A cylinder has volume = $43\,750\pi$ cm^3 and radius = 25 cm. Find the height.

Solution

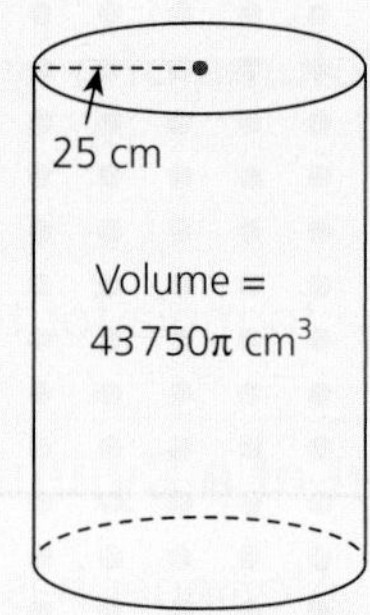

Volume of cylinder = $43\,750\pi$

$$\pi r^2h = 43\,750\pi$$

$$r^2h = 43\,750 \quad \text{... divide both sides by } \pi$$

$$(25)^2h = 43\,750$$

$$625h = 43\,750$$

$$h = \frac{43\,750}{625} \quad \text{... divide both sides by 625}$$

$$= 70 \text{ cm}$$

Therefore, height = 70 cm.

Example 3

A cylinder has volume = $32\,000\pi$ cm^3 and height = 80 cm. Find the radius.

Solution

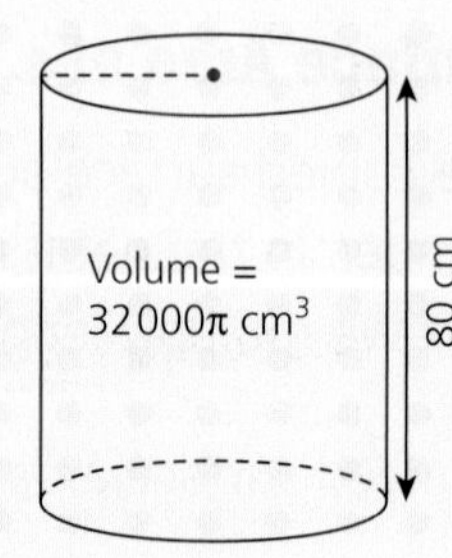

Volume of a cylinder = πr^2h

$$\pi r^2h = 32\,000\pi$$

$$r^2h = 32\,000 \quad \text{... divide both sides by } \pi$$

$$r^2(80) = 32\,000$$

$$r^2 = \frac{32\,000}{80} \quad \text{... divide both sides by 80}$$

$$= 400$$

$$r = \sqrt{400} \quad \text{... square root both sides}$$

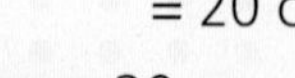

$$= 20 \text{ cm}$$

Therefore, radius = 20 cm.

Example 4

The diagram shows a cylinder of height 8 cm and base radius 3 cm.

3 cm

8 cm

(i) Find the volume of the cylinder, in terms of π.

(ii) Calculate the total surface area of the cylinder, using $\pi = 3.14$.

(iii) Find the dimensions of the smallest rectangular box that could contain this cylinder.

Solution

Given $r = 3$ cm, $h = 8$ cm

(i) Volume $= \pi \times r^2 \times h$

$= \pi \times 3^2 \times 8$

$= 72\pi$ cm^3

(ii) Total surface area (TSA) $= 2\pi rh + 2\pi r^2$

$= 2\pi(3)(8) + 2\pi(3)^2$

$= 48\pi + 18\pi$

$= 66\pi$ cm^2

$= 66\,(3.14)$

$= 207.24$ cm^2

(iii) ■ Smallest height of the box = height of cylinder
= 8 cm

■ Smallest width of the box = width of the cylinder
Width of the box = diameter of circle $\Rightarrow d = 2r$
$= 2(3) = 6$ cm

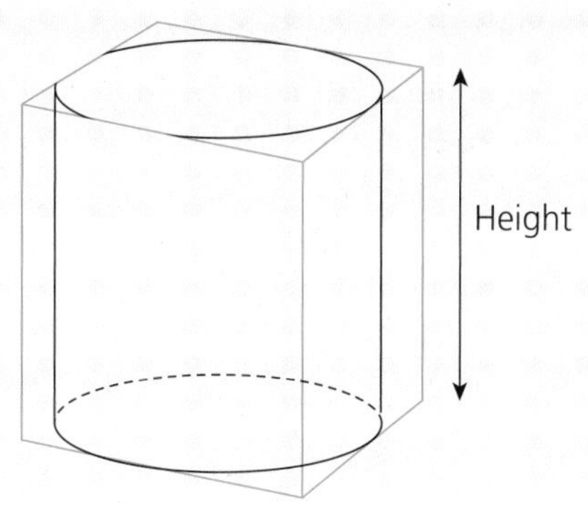

Example 5

The radii of two cylinders are in the ratio 2 : 1 and their heights are in the ratio 2 : 3. What is the ratio of the volumes of the two cylinders?

Solution

We are given the ratios that link both the radius and the height.

- Let x be a factor of the radii and let y be a factor of the height for both cylinders.
  - Radii ratio = 2 : 1, so $2x$ and x are the radii.
  - Height ratio = 2 : 3, so $2y$ and $3y$ are the heights.
- Draw a sketch of the two cylinders and label all known dimensions.

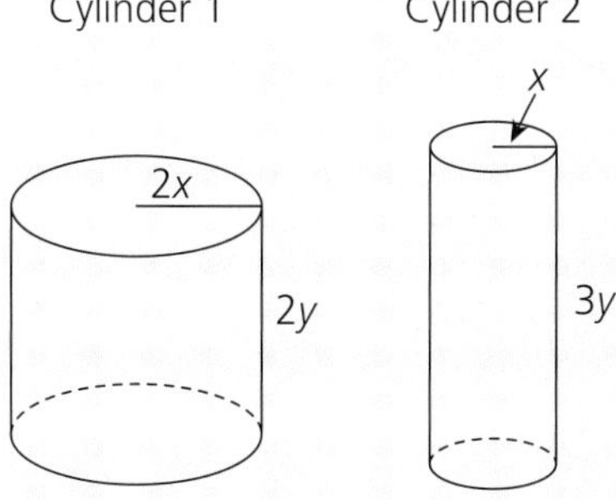

Volume of cylinder 1 $= \pi r^2 h = \pi(2x)^2(2y) = 8\pi x^2 y$

Volume of cylinder 2 $= \pi r^2 h = \pi(x)^2(3y) = 3\pi x^2 y$

Ratio

Volume of cylinder 1 : Volume of cylinder 2
$= 8\pi x^2 y : 3\pi x^2 y$ ... divide both parts of the ratio by $\pi x^2 y$
$= 8 : 3$

The ratio of the volumes is 8 : 3.

Activity 6.6

1 Find the volume of each of the following cylinders. Let $\pi = 3.14$ and give all your answers correct to two decimal places.

(i)

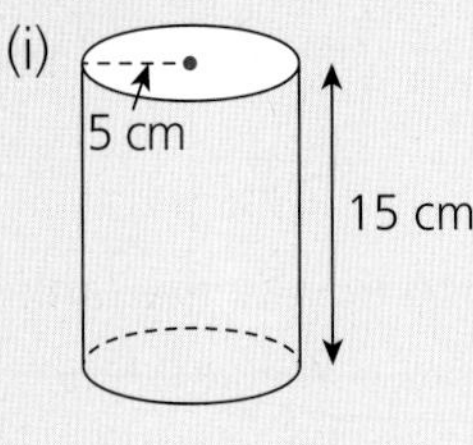

(ii)

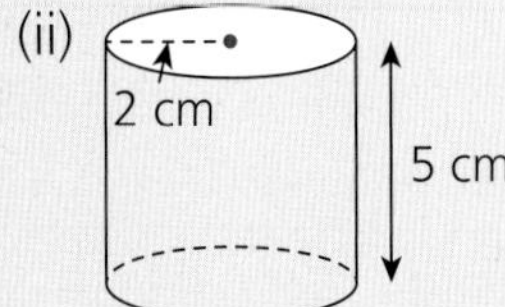

2 Find the volume in litres of each of the following cylinders, using $\pi = 3.14$. Give all answers to the nearest litre.

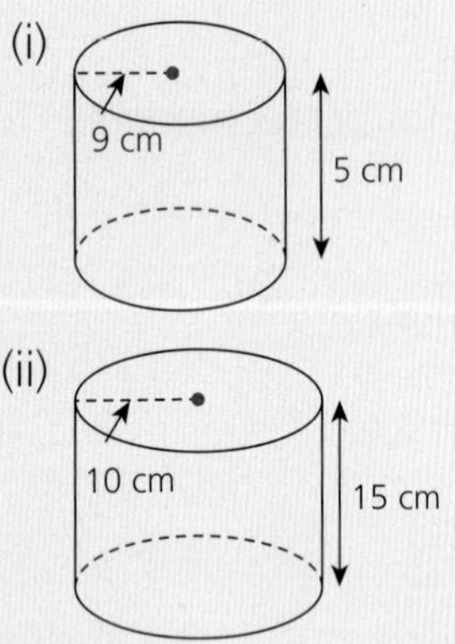

3 Find the height of each of the following cylinders.

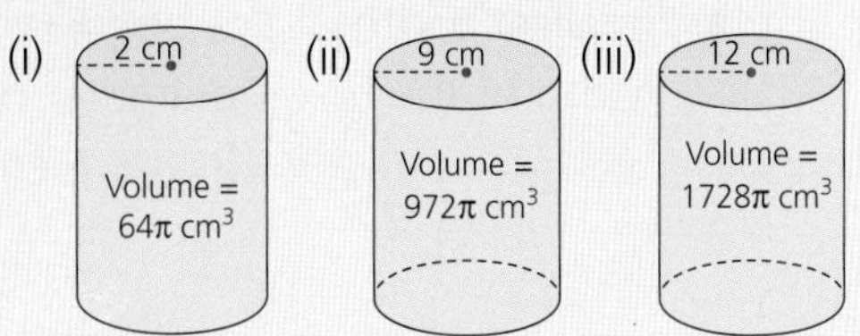

4 Find the radius of each of the following cylinders.

(i) cylinder 1: volume = 12π cm^3 and height = 3 cm

(ii) cylinder 2: volume = 540π cm^3 and height = 15 cm

(iii) cylinder 3: volume = 320π cm^3 and height = 20 cm

5 Barry is a farmer. He uses a cylindrical tank for storing water for his cattle. The tank is 2 m in height and has a diameter of 3 m.

2 m

3 m

Barry says, 'If I double the height of my tank and keep the same diameter, I will double the capacity.'
Is Barry correct? Justify your answer.

6 The table below gives some data relating to cylinders. Copy and complete the table. Give all answers correct to two decimal places.

	π	Height	Radius	Volume	Total surface area
(i)	3.14	6 cm	2 cm		
(ii)	π	5 m	5 m		
(iii)	$\frac{22}{7}$	28 cm	21 cm		
(iv)	$\frac{22}{7}$	7 cm		1985.5 cm^3	
(v)	π		8.4 m		368π m^2
(vi)	3.14	1.4 m		89.019 m^3	
(vii)	3.14		30 cm		6672.5 cm^2
(viii)	π		66 mm	$104\,544\pi$ mm^3	
(ix)	$\frac{22}{7}$		7 cm		748 cm^2
(x)	3.14		32 cm	176 844.8 cm^3	
(xi)	3.14		5.5 cm		500.83 cm^2
(xii)	3.14		35 cm	1099 cm^3	

7 How many cylindrical glasses can be filled from a full cylindrical jug, when they have the following measurements?

- Jug: radius 6 cm, height 30 cm
- Glass: radius 2 cm, height 5 cm

8 Draw a net of this cylinder, showing all dimensions clearly.

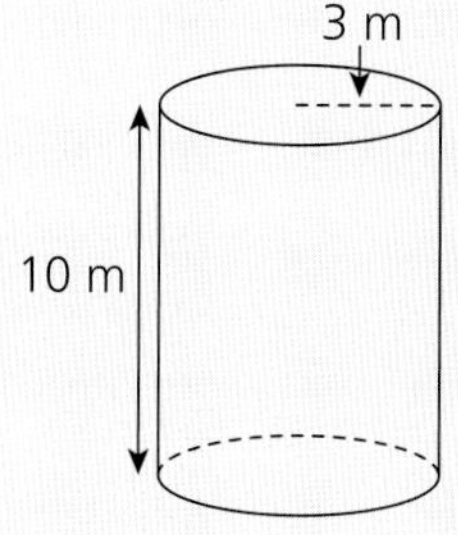

9 A company selling tinned fruit offers a 3-pack deal for tinned pineapples.

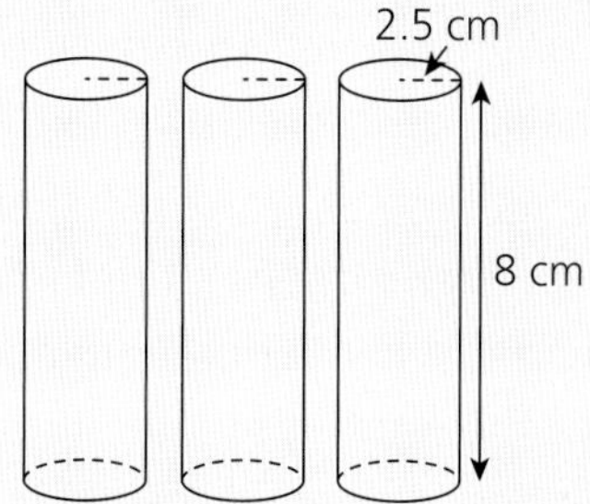

(i) If a new label is designed for the curved area of the tin, what size will each label be? Give your answer correct to one decimal place.

(ii) What is the capacity of one tin? Give your answer correct to two decimal places.

The company decides to package the three tins in a rectangular box.

(iii) What are the dimensions of the smallest box that can enclose the three tins? Give each dimension correct to one decimal place.

10 The table gives the ratio of radii and heights for different pairs of cylinders.

	Cylinders	Radii	Height
(i)	A and B	2 : 5	7 : 6
(ii)	C and D	3 : 8	7 : 3
(iii)	E and F	1 : 4	4 : 1
(iv)	G and H	11 : 15	17 : 13

For each pair of cylinders, find the ratio of their volumes.

11 The diagram shows a water-storage tank which a farmer uses in an outbuilding. It is a cylinder of diameter 2.7 m and height 1.8 m.

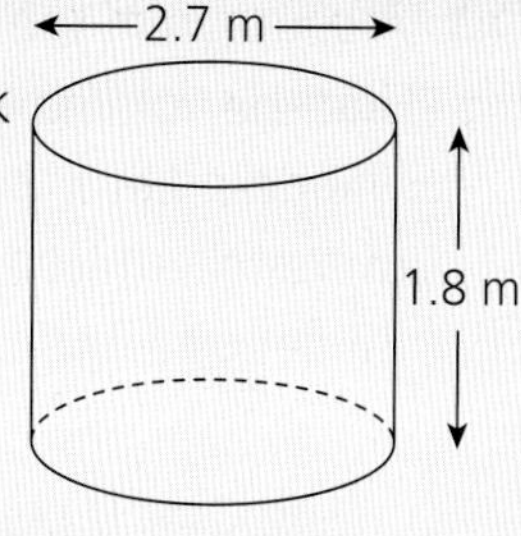

The farmer wants to buy a new tank to increase the volume of water he can store. He can either increase the diameter by 1 metre or increase the height by 1 metre.

(i) What is the difference, in litres, between the volume obtained by increasing the diameter by 1 m and the volume obtained by increasing the height by 1 m?

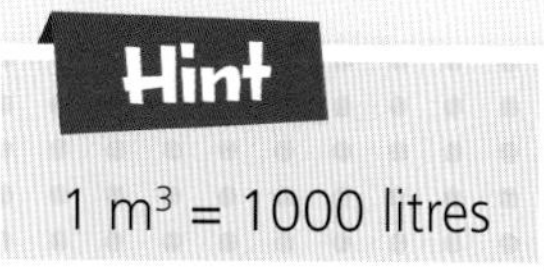

(ii) He chooses the tank that maximises the volume, and he wants to insulate the tank by wrapping insulation around the sides. The insulation comes in rolls 23.25 m long and 1.8 m wide. How many layers of insulation can he wrap around the new tank if he uses a complete roll?

12 A cylinder of height h having a base of radius $\sqrt{2}$ is placed inside another cylinder also of height h, as shown in the diagram.

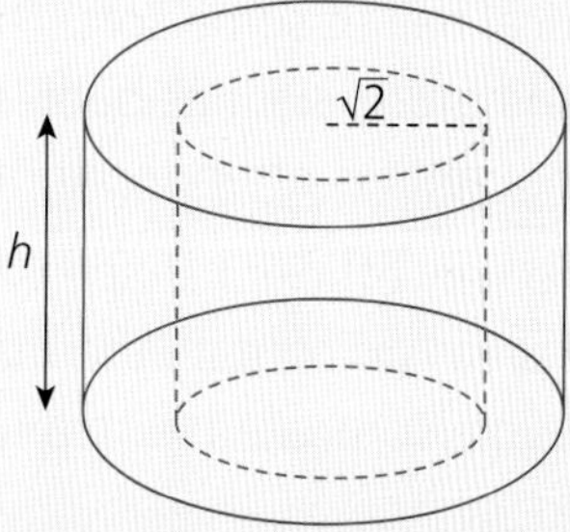

If the space between the two cylinders is to have a volume equal to the volume of the inner cylinder, calculate the radius of the base of the outer cylinder.

13 A soup tin in the form of a cylinder has a diameter of 7 cm and a height of 10 cm. The cylinder is constructed from pieces of metal cut from a thin sheet measuring 23 cm by 18 cm.

(i) Which one of the four diagrams, A, B, C or D could represent the sheet of metal from which the cylinder has been cut? Give a reason for your choice.

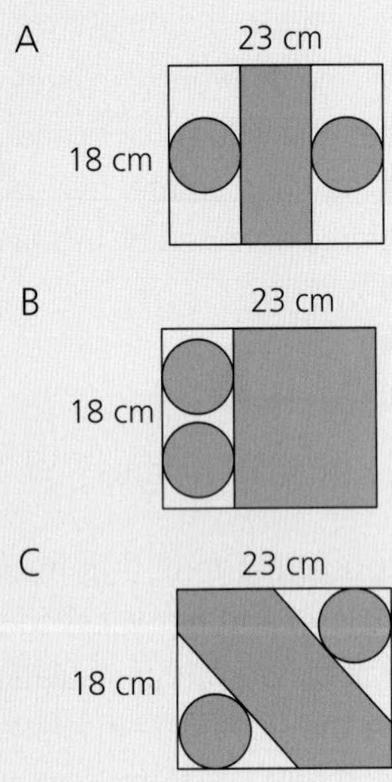

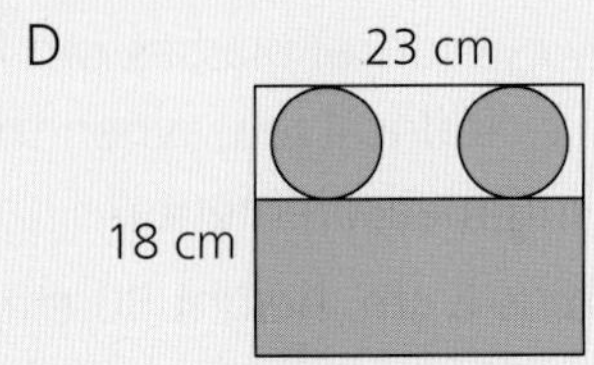

(ii) Find the area of metal which remains after the pieces have been cut out.

14 (i) A container in the shape of a cylinder has a capacity of 50 litres. The height of the cylinder is 0.7 m. Find the length of the diameter of the cylinder. Give your answer correct to the nearest whole number.

(ii) A rectangular tank has a length of 0.6 m, a width of 0.35 m and its height measures 15 cm. Find the capacity of the rectangular tank.

(iii) The rectangular tank is full of water. This water is then poured into the cylindrical container in (a) above. Find the depth of water in the cylinder. Give your answer correct to one decimal place.

Section 6G Spheres, Hemispheres and Combined Shapes

Spheres

The **sphere** shape is a very common shape as everyone who is interested in ball games will know. Many of the sports we play use a spherical ball of some sort. There are also many examples of spheres in nature, such as bubbles. The Earth is not quite a sphere, though it is often thought of as such.

A sphere is a very efficient shape when used as a container; the surface area can contain the maximum amount of volume possible compared with any other shape.

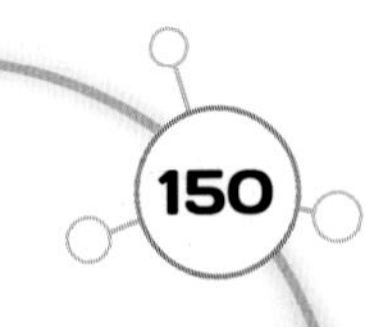

Key Points

A sphere will always have the following characteristics:

- All points on the surface are the same distance from the centre (radius).
- It is perfectly symmetrical.
- There are no edges or corners.
- The formula for calculating the surface area is:

  Surface area of a sphere = $4\pi r^2$

- The formula for calculating the volume is:

  Volume of a sphere = $\frac{4}{3}\pi r^3$

  These formulae are on page 10 of the *Formulae and tables* booklet.

Example 1

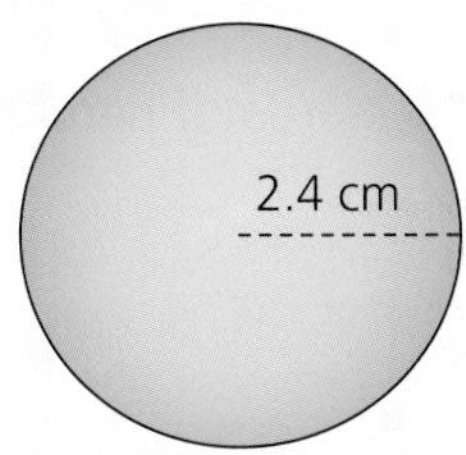

The diagram shows a sphere of radius 2.4 cm. Find:

(i) the surface area of the sphere

(ii) the volume of the sphere.

Give your answers in terms of π.

Solution

Given radius = 2.4 cm

(i) Surface area $= 4 \times \pi \times r^2$

$= 4 \times \pi \times (2.4)^2$

$= 4 \times \pi \times 5.76$

$= 23.04\pi$ cm²

(ii) Volume $= \frac{4}{3} \times \pi \times r^3$

$= \frac{4}{3} \times \pi \times (2.4)^3$

$= \frac{4}{3} \times \pi \times 13.824$

$= 18.432\pi$ cm³

Hemispheres

The hemisphere is the shape which is exactly half a sphere.

Our most common usage of the term hemisphere is when we make reference to the two hemispheres of the Earth: the Northern and Southern Hemispheres. The equator divides these two hemispheres.

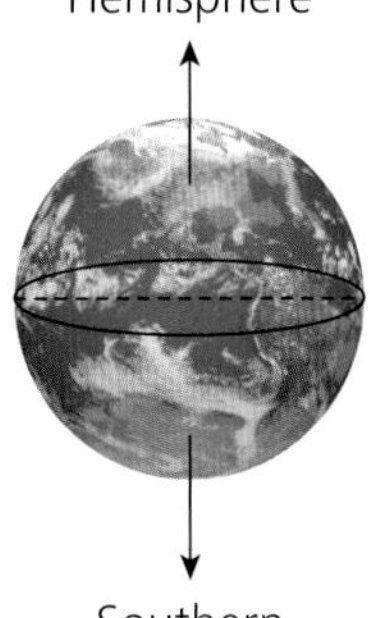

Key Points

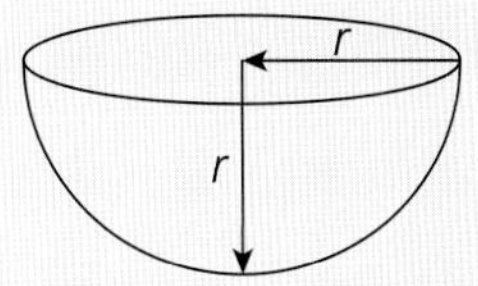

- The surface of a hemisphere has a curved part and a flat part in the shape of a circle.
- The formula for calculating the **volume** is:

  Volume of a hemisphere $= \frac{1}{2}\left(\frac{4}{3} \times \pi \times r^3\right) = \frac{2}{3}\pi r^3$

- The formula for calculating the **total surface area** is:

  Surface area of a hemisphere $= \frac{1}{2}(4\pi r^2) + \pi r^2 = 2(\pi r^2) + (\pi r^2) = 3\pi r^2$

- The volume and surface area of a hemisphere are **not** in the *Formulae and tables* booklet, but may be found by adapting the formulae for a sphere.

Example 2

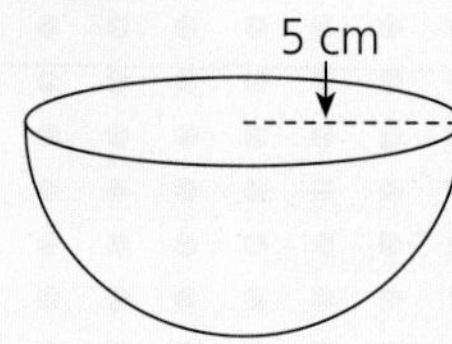

The diagram shows a hemisphere of radius 5 cm.

(i) Find the volume of the hemisphere correct to two decimal places.

(ii) Find the surface area of the hemisphere. Use $\pi = 3.14$.

Solution

(i) Volume of hemisphere $= \frac{2}{3} \times \pi \times r^3$

$= \frac{2}{3} \times (3.14) \times (5)^3$

$= 261.666666 \text{ cm}^3$

$= 261.67 \text{ cm}^3$ correct to two decimal places

(ii) Total surface area of hemisphere

$= 3 \times \pi \times r^2$

$= 3 \times (3.14) \times (5)^2$

$= 235.5 \text{ cm}^2$

Combined Shapes

Our next step in exploring applied measure is where we combine the solid shapes we have already encountered to make new shapes. A compound shape is composed of regular solid shapes.

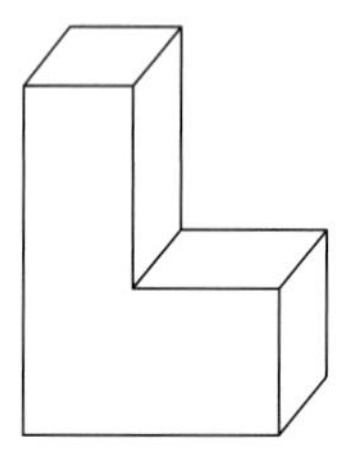

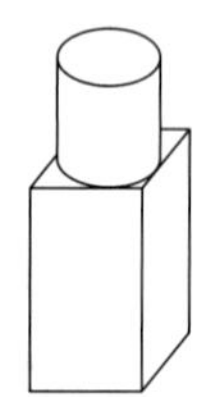

Example 3

A perfume bottle of height 21 cm is shown. It consists of a cylinder with radius 2 cm and height 5 cm and a rectangular portion with base 5 cm by 7 cm. Find the volume of the bottle, correct to the nearest cm³.

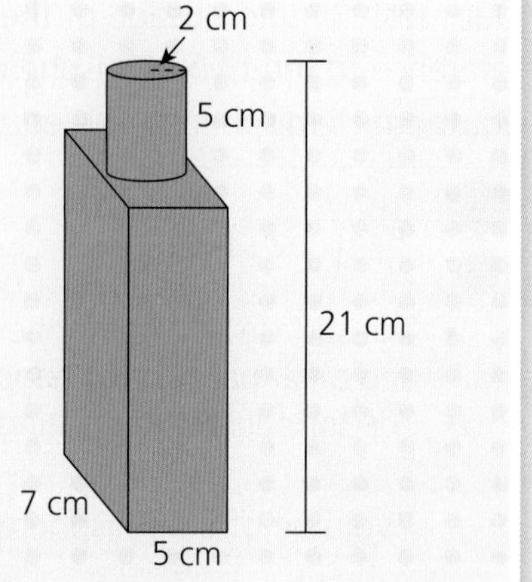

Solution

- Split the bottle into standard shapes.
- Cylinder portion:

  Volume $= \pi r^2 h$

  $= (3.14)(2)^2(5)$

  $= 62.8 \text{ cm}^3$

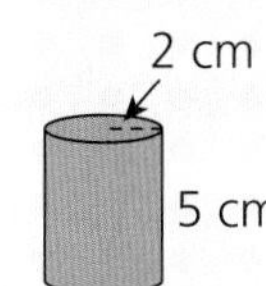

- Cuboid portion:

  Volume $= lwh$

  $= 5 \times 7 \times 16$

  $= 560 \text{ cm}^3$

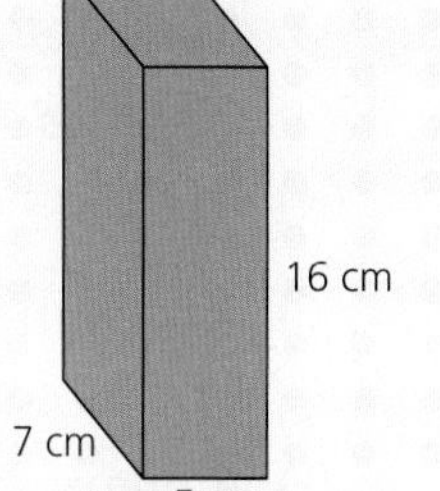

- Total volume of bottle

  $= 62.8 \text{ cm}^3 + 560 \text{ cm}^3 = 622.8 \text{ cm}^3$

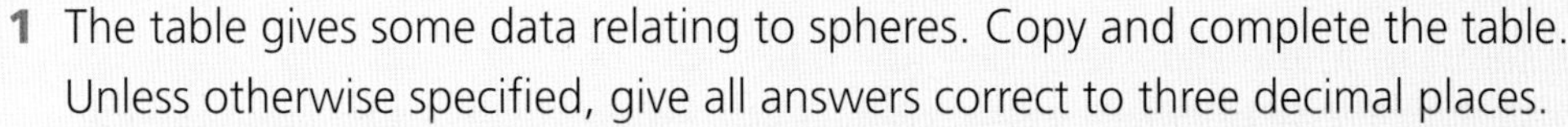

Activity 6.7

1 The table gives some data relating to spheres. Copy and complete the table.
Unless otherwise specified, give all answers correct to three decimal places.

	π	Radius	Volume	Curved surface area
(i)	3.14	7 m		
(ii)	$\frac{22}{7}$			25.872 cm^2
(iii)	3.14			383.328 m^2
(iv)	Use the calculator value for π	3.5 cm		
(v)	Use the calculator value for π	15 cm		
(vi)	$\frac{22}{7}$		21 214.286 cm^3	

2 A 'student of the year' award consists of a cylindrical base with a hemisphere on top.

The radius of the cylinder and hemisphere is 3 cm.

(i) Find the volume of the hemisphere, correct to two decimal places.

(ii) If the total volume of the award is 282.60 cm³, what is the height of the cylindrical portion of the award to the nearest cm?

(iii) What is the total height of the award?

3 A time capsule is constructed of a cylindrical section and two hemispherical ends.

The length of the cylindrical section is 85 cm and the radius is 28 cm.

(i) Find the surface area of the capsule in cm². Give your answer correct to two significant figures.

(ii) Find the volume of the capsule in m³. Give your answer correct to two decimal places.

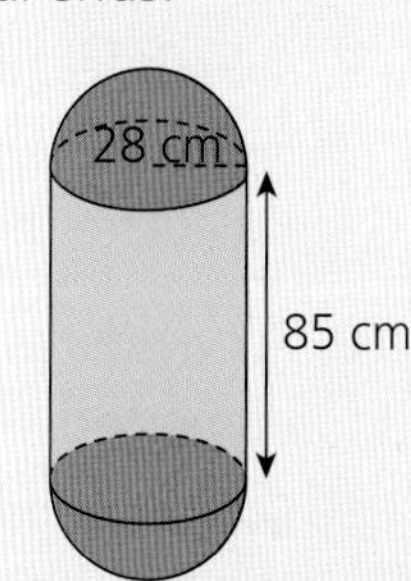

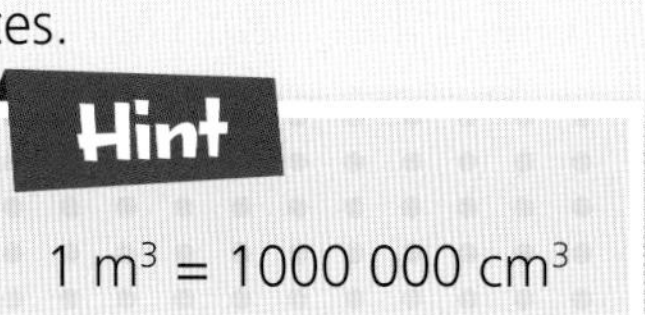

$1 \text{ m}^3 = 1000\,000 \text{ cm}^3$

4 A sculptor buys four wooden blocks with the dimensions shown.

(i) Find the volume of one of the wooden blocks.

(ii) The sculptor needs to turn the four blocks into the largest four spheres he can for a sculpture. What is the radius of the largest sphere the sculptor can make?

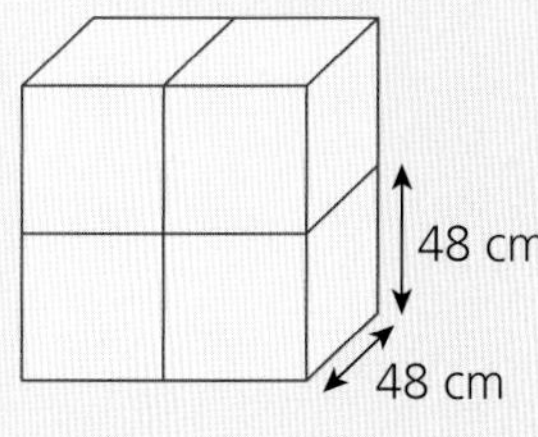

(iii) The volume of the sculpture must be under 160 000 cm³ to meet the requirements of the display. Will the sculpture meet the requirement?

(iv) By how much was the sculptor under or over the limit, in cm³?

5 (i) A solid metal cylinder has height 20 cm and diameter 14 cm. Find its curved surface area in terms of π.

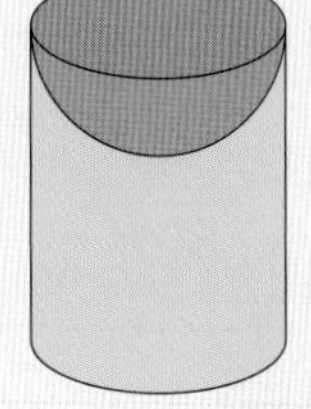

(ii) A hemisphere with diameter 14 cm is removed from the top of this cylinder, as shown.

Find the total surface area of the remaining solid in terms of π.

6 A golf club sells golf balls in packs of three. Each ball has radius 4.5 cm. The balls are packaged so that they fit exactly into a cylindrical tube, as shown.

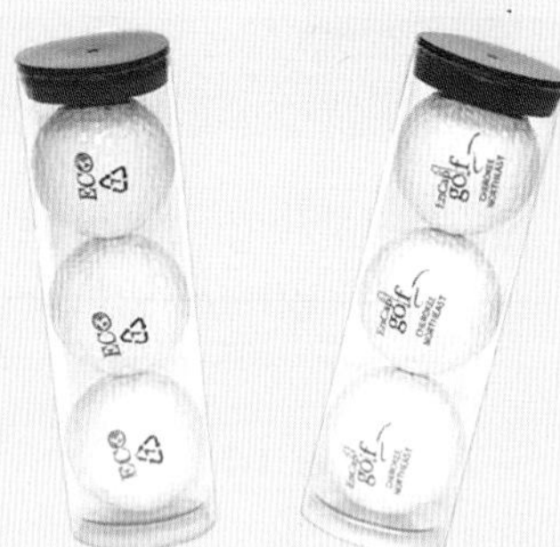

(i) Find, in terms of π, the volume of one golf ball.

(ii) Find, in terms of π, the volume of the air in the cylindrical tube.

7 An ornament is carved from a rectangular block of wood which has a square base and a height of 24 cm. The ornament consists of two identical spheres and two identical cubes as illustrated. The diameter of each sphere is equal to the length of the side of each cube. The ornament has the same width as the original block.

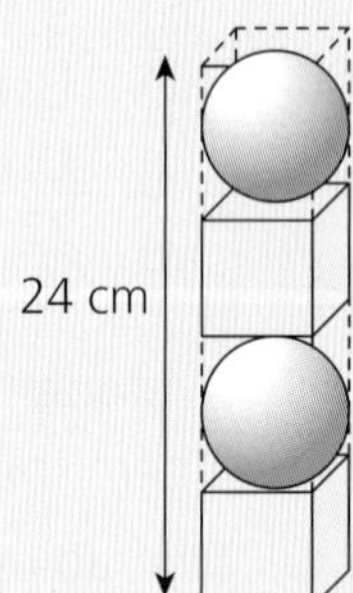

(i) Find the side length of each cube.

(ii) Find the volume of the ornament, correct to two decimal places.

(iii) To make the ornament, what percentage of the original block of wood is carved away?

8 A rectangular block of wax has dimensions $l = 1.6$ m, $w = 0.8$ m and $h = 1.2$ m. The block is melted down and turned into small cubes of side length 40 cm. How many cubes can be made from this block of wax?

9 A cylinder with radius 10 cm is partially filled with water. Six spheres of radius 3 cm are fully immersed in the water which causes the water to rise by H cm.

Calculate the increase in height correct to one decimal place.

10 A cylinder with radius 6 cm is filled with water and a sphere of radius 3 cm is fully immersed in the water. This sphere is then removed.

Calculate the drop in height, H cm, after the sphere has been removed.

1 The diagram shows the gable-end wall of a garage.

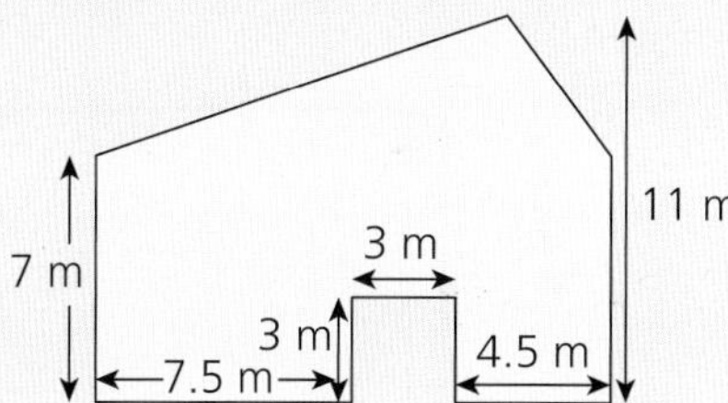

(a) Find the total area of the gable-end wall.

The cost of 5 litres of paint is €26.50. 5 litres of this paint will cover an area of 33 m².

(b) Find the cost of painting the gable-end wall with this paint.

2 Find (a) the volume and (b) the surface area of the triangular-based prism shown. Give your answers correct to two decimal places.

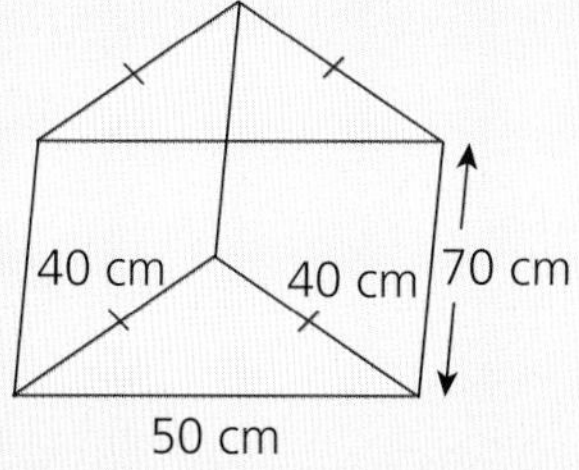

3 When this net is formed into a hexagonal prism, which sides are opposite each other?

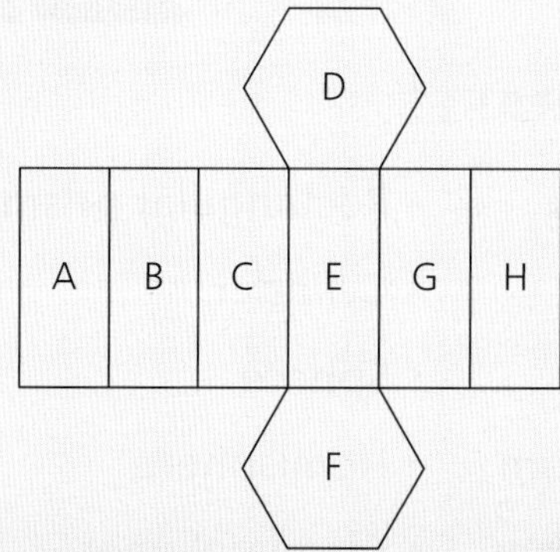

4 A cylinder with radius 10 cm is filled with water, then a sphere of radius 4.5 cm is fully immersed in the water.

Calculate the rise in height, H cm, after the sphere was added. Give your answer correct to two decimal places.

5 A rectangular container has length 36 cm and height 18 cm. The volume of the container is 15 552 cm³.

(a) Find the width of the rectangular container in cm.

(b) Find the total surface area of the closed container in cm².

This container is used to ship cube-shaped boxes of side 4 cm.

(c) How many of these cubes can fit into the rectangular container?

This container is also used to ship boxes containing spherical balls of radius 3 cm.

(d) How many of these balls can fit into the container?

6 A hot water tank is in the shape of a hemisphere on top of a cylinder as shown.

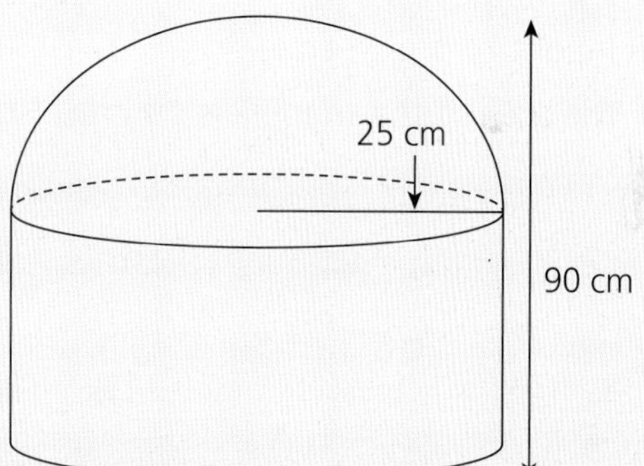

The hemisphere has a radius of 25 cm and the container has a height of 90 cm.

Find the volume of the container in litres, giving your answer correct to the nearest litre.

Exam-style Questions

1 Liam's garden is in the shape of a square. It has four equal right-angled triangular lawns and a smaller square patio in the centre, as shown.

(a) Find the length of the hypotenuse of one of the right-angled triangular lawns.

(b) Find the area of one of the triangular lawns.

(c) Find the area of the square patio in the middle.

(d) The patio is to be paved with rectangular flagstones of length 80 cm and width 50 cm. Calculate the number of flagstones Liam needs to buy to cover the patio, allowing an extra 20% for waste.

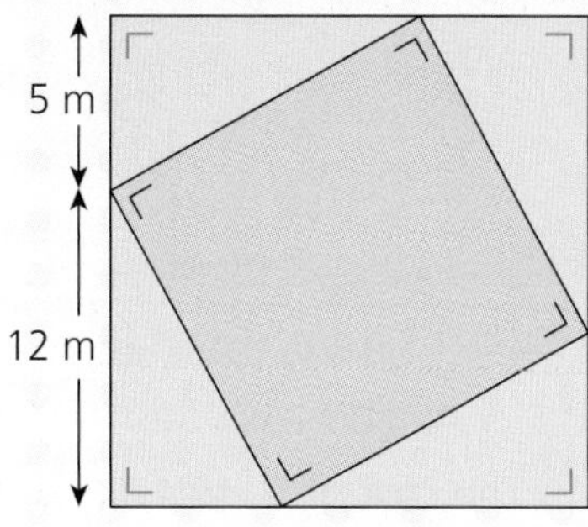

JCHL 2013 Phase 3

2 The dimensions of two solid cylinders are shown in the diagrams.

(a) Calculate the ratio of the curved surface area of the smaller cylinder to the curved surface area of the larger cylinder.

(b) Calculate the ratio of the volume of the smaller cylinder to the volume of the larger cylinder.

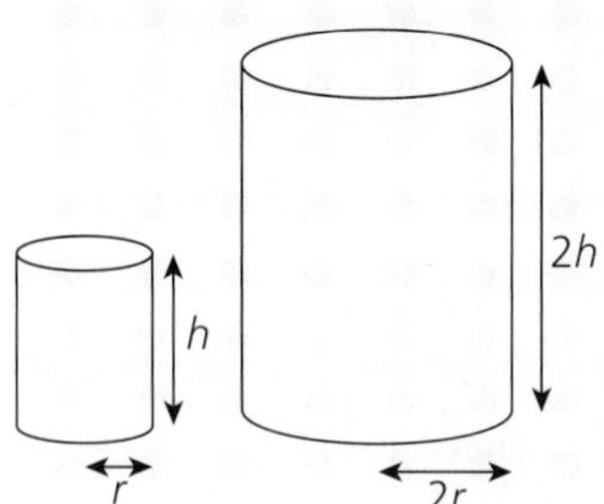

JCHL 2012

3 A triangle has a base length of $2x$ cm and a perpendicular height of $(x + 3)$ cm.

The area of the triangle is 10 cm^2. Find the distance x.

$x + 3$

$2x$

JCHL 2012

KEY WORDS AND PHRASES

- Rectangular solid
- Cube
- Capacity
- Volume
- Litre
- Curved surface area
- Total surface area
- Prism
- Cross-section of prism
- Triangular-based prism
- Rectangular prism
- Cylinder
- Sphere
- Hemisphere
- Equal volumes

Rectangular Solids

- Total surface area = $2(l \times w) + 2(l \times h) + 2(w \times h)$
- Volume = length (l) × width (w) × height (h)

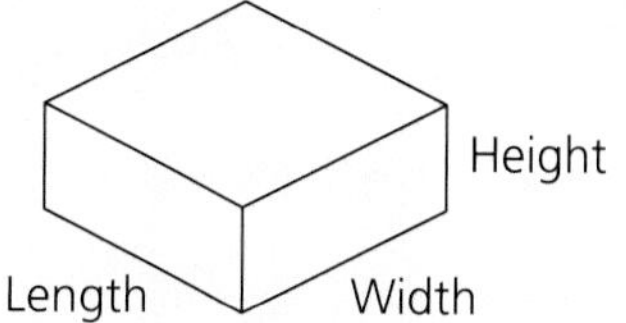

Prisms

- A prism is a 3-dimensional figure where:
  - the bases (or ends of the object) are the same shape and size
  - the bases are parallel to one another
  - the sides form parallelograms.

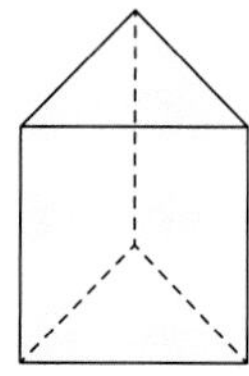

Triangular prism

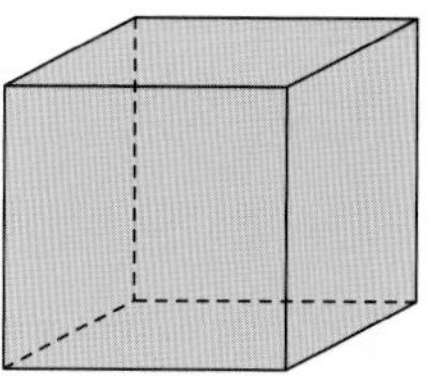

Cube

- Volume of a prism = area of the cross-section × height of the prism
- Total Surface Area (TSA) of a prism is the sum of the areas of all the faces of the prism.

Cylinder

- Volume = $\pi \times r^2 \times h$
- Curved surface area = $2\pi rh$
- Total surface area = $2\pi rh + 2\pi r^2$

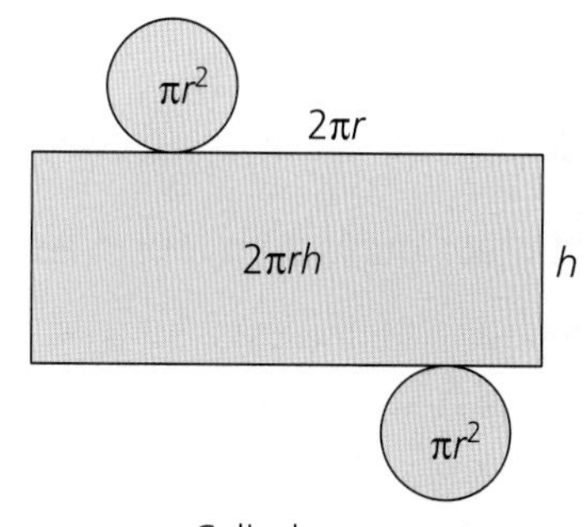

Cylinder net

Sphere and Hemisphere

- Surface area of a sphere = $4 \times \pi \times r^2$
- Volume of a sphere = $\frac{4}{3} \times \pi \times r^3$

- Volume of a hemisphere = $\frac{1}{2}\left(\frac{4}{3} \times \pi \times r^3\right) = \frac{2}{3} \times \pi \times r^3$
- Surface area of a hemisphere = $3\pi \times r^2$

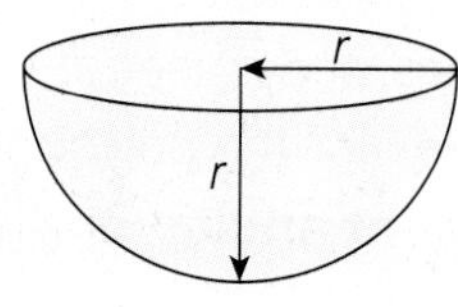

Chapter 7

Geometry 2

Learning Intentions

In this chapter, you will learn about:

LO: U.5, U.6, U.7–U.10, U.11–13, GT.3(a–e)

- The various types of quadrilateral
- Using the properties of triangles to work with quadrilaterals
- Parallelograms
- Theorem 9: The fact that opposite sides and angles of a parallelogram are equal
- Theorem 10: The fact that the diagonals of a parallelogram bisect each other
- Other properties of rectangles, squares and rhombuses

You will need...

- a pencil
- a ruler
- a geometry set

Section 7A Polygons

In this chapter, we will investigate shapes with more than three sides. We will look mostly at figures with four sides. These are called **quadrilaterals**.

It is important to have definitions, so that we know what the minimum requirements for each shape are.

- A **polygon** is a piece of the plane enclosed by a figure with many sides (a minimum of three, but it could be any number).

  Polygon:

- In any polygon, sides that meet are called **adjacent sides**; they meet at the **vertices** (singular, vertex) of the polygon. We also refer to **adjacent angles** which occur at the end of each side.

- A **regular polygon** has all its sides and angles equal.

  Regular polygon with 7 sides:

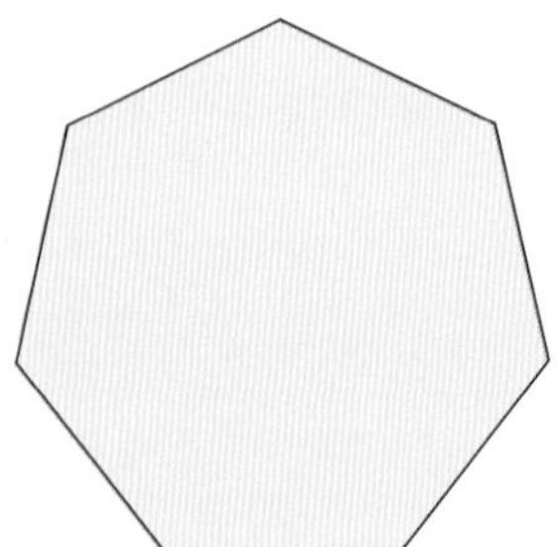

- A **quadrilateral** is a four-sided polygon. Two sides of a quadrilateral that are not adjacent are called **opposite sides**. Two angles of a quadrilateral that are not adjacent are called **opposite angles**.

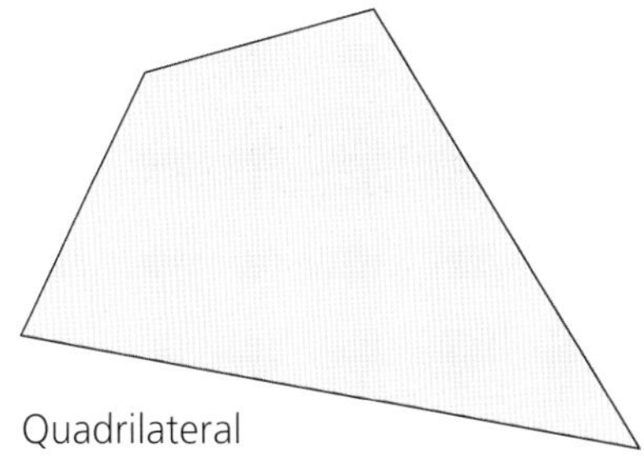
Quadrilateral

- A **rectangle** is a quadrilateral having right angles at all four vertices.

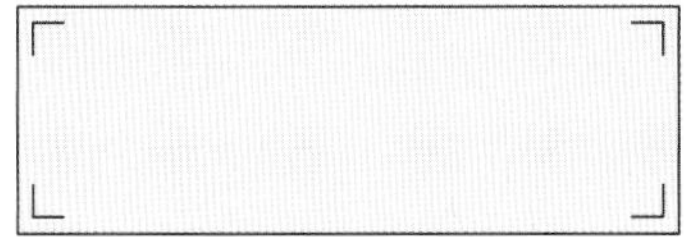
Rectangle

- A **rhombus** is a quadrilateral having all four sides equal.

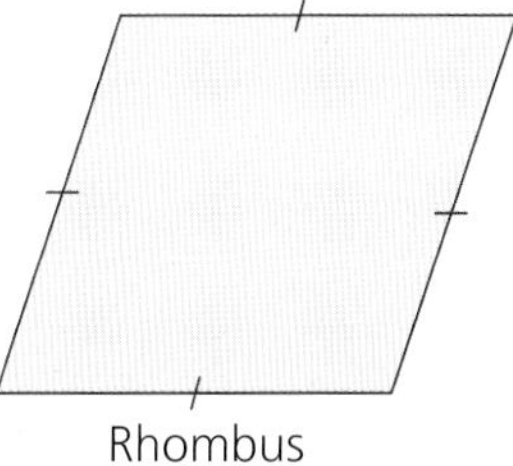
Rhombus

- A **square** is a rectangular rhombus.

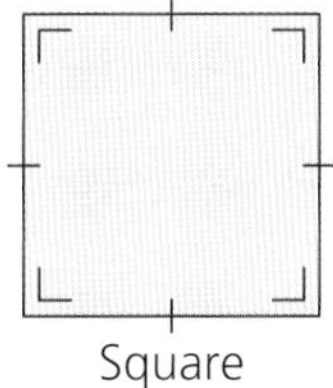
Square

- A **parallelogram** is a quadrilateral in which both pairs of opposite sides are parallel.

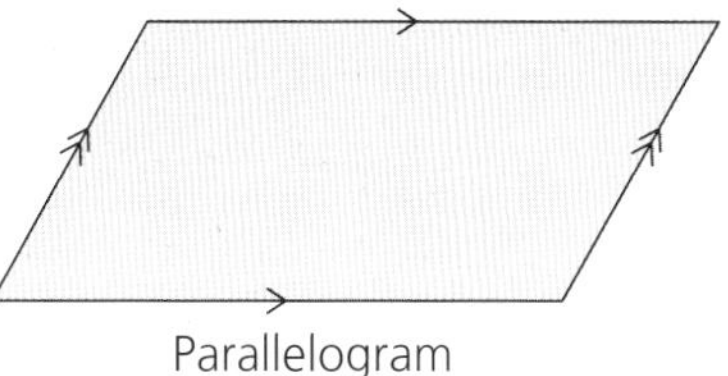
Parallelogram

- A **kite** is a quadrilateral that has two adjacent sides of equal length and the other two sides of equal length.

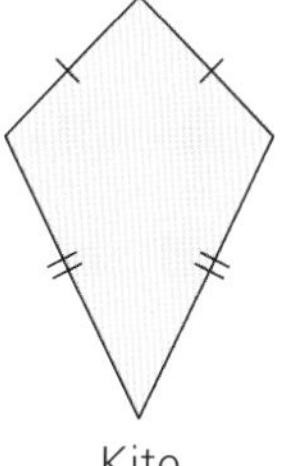
Kite

- A **trapezium** is a quadrilateral with two parallel sides.

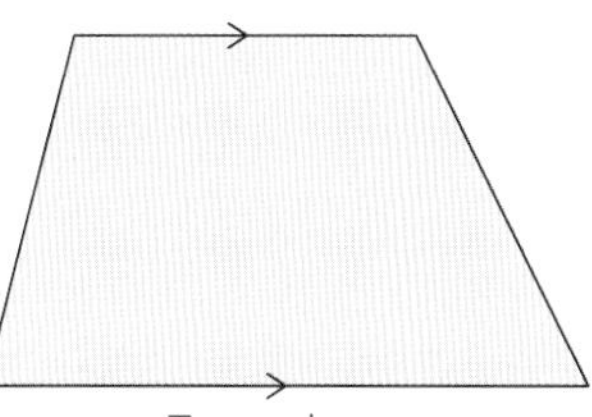
Trapezium

- Every quadrilateral has two **diagonals** which are lines from one vertex to the opposite vertex.

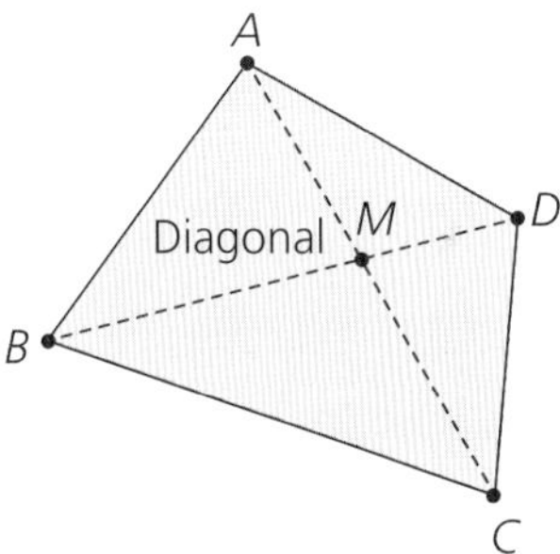

Hence, the quadrilateral is then divided into triangles. This gives us a way of using the properties of triangles to investigate quadrilateral properties.

Key Point

We name a quadrilateral by the letters of its four vertices in cyclical order, either clockwise or anti-clockwise. So the quadrilateral shown above could be called *ABCD* or *BCDA* or *ADCB*, etc.

Of course, there are shapes with more than four sides. For examples, a **pentagon** has five sides and a **hexagon** has six sides.

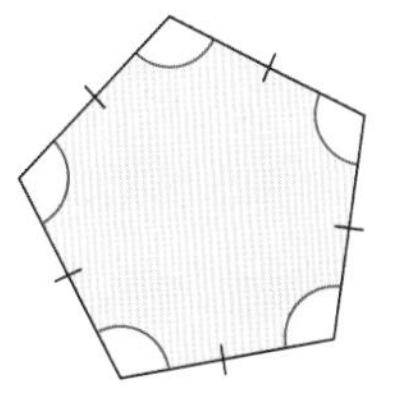
Regular pentagon

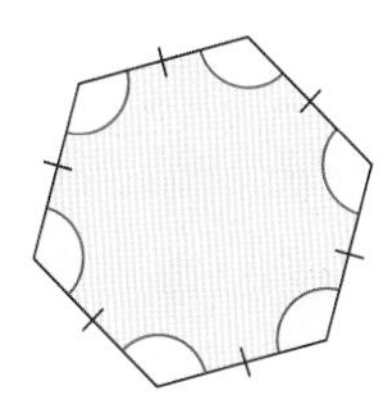
Regular hexagon

Activity 7.1

1 This quadrilateral has two diagonals drawn.

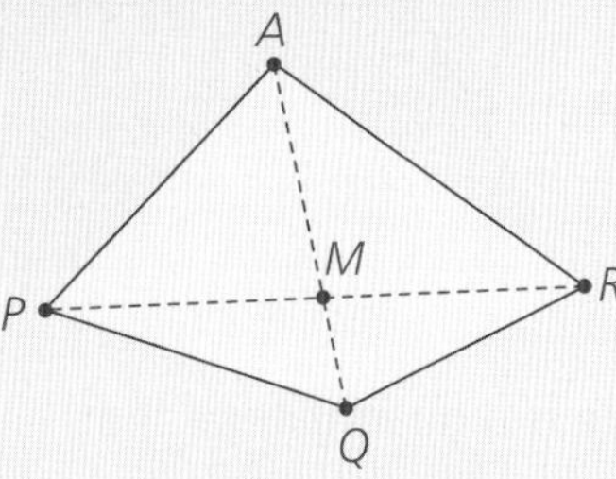

(i) Name the quadrilateral in four different ways, two clockwise and two anti-clockwise.

(ii) Name two pairs of opposite sides.

(iii) Name two pairs of opposite angles.

(iv) Name the two diagonals.

(v) Divide the quadrilateral into two triangles in two different ways. Draw a sketch of each triangle.

(vi) What is the sum of the angles in each triangle?

(vii) What is the sum of the four angles of the quadrilateral?

(viii) Name four smaller triangles that you can see inside the quadrilateral. Draw a sketch of each.

2 This quadrilateral has two diagonals drawn.

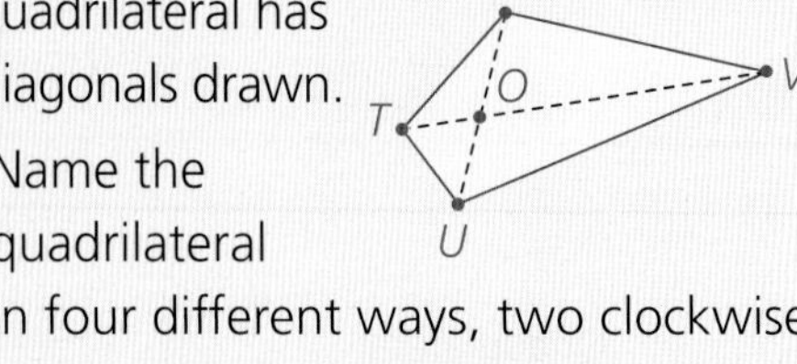

(i) Name the quadrilateral in four different ways, two clockwise and two anti-clockwise.

(ii) Name two pairs of opposite sides.

(iii) Name two pairs of opposite angles.

(iv) Name the two diagonals.

(v) Divide the quadrilateral into two triangles in two different ways. Draw a sketch of each triangle.

(vi) What is the sum of the four angles of the quadrilateral?

3 A pentagon is a five-sided figure.

(i) Draw a sketch of the pentagon on the right.

(ii) Draw lines dividing it into triangles which do not overlap.

(iii) What is the sum of all the angles in the pentagon?

E I F H G

4 Draw a hexagon. What is the sum of all the angles in a hexagon? Explain your answer.

5 Calculate the missing angles in the diagrams below.

(i)

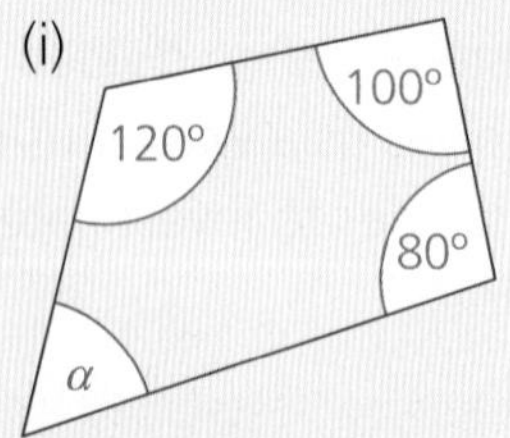

(ii)

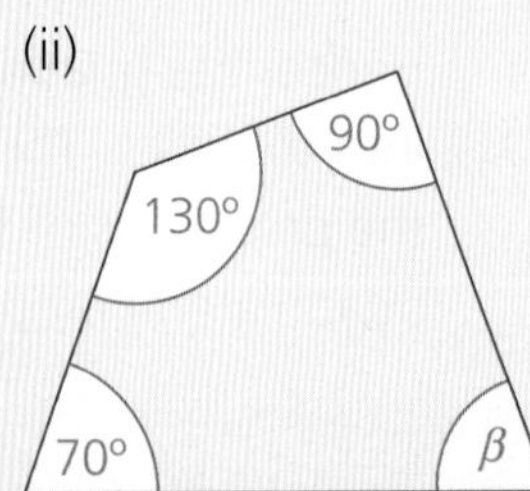

(iii)

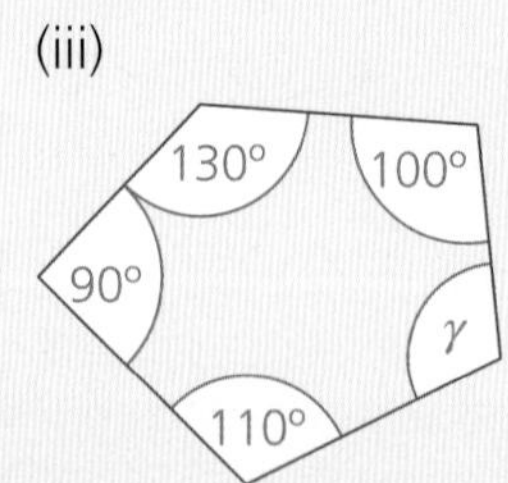

(iv)

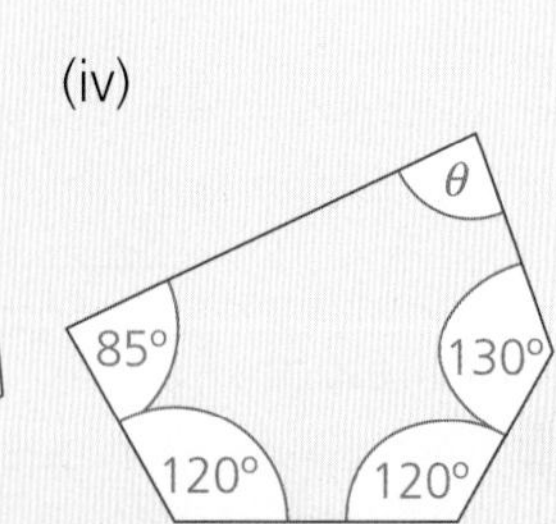

6 In the following figures, parallel lines are indicated by arrows. Calculate the missing angles in each.

(i)

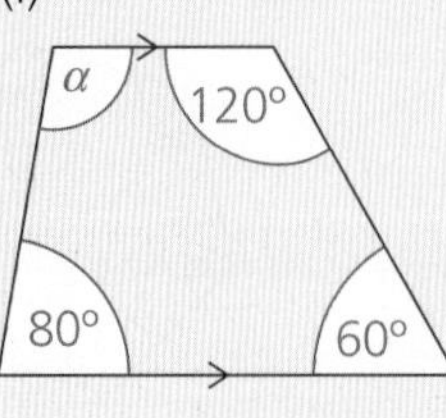

(ii)

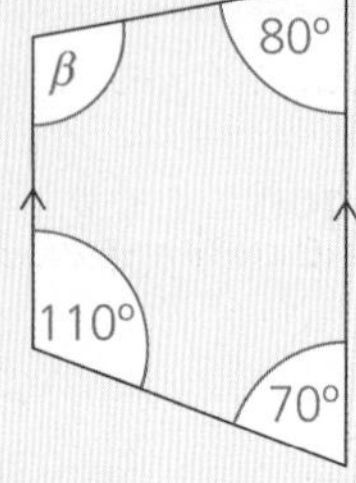

(iii)

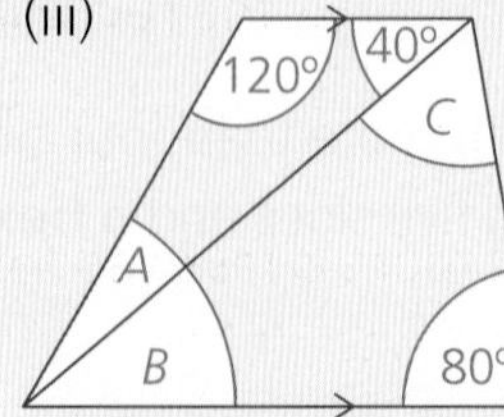

(iv)

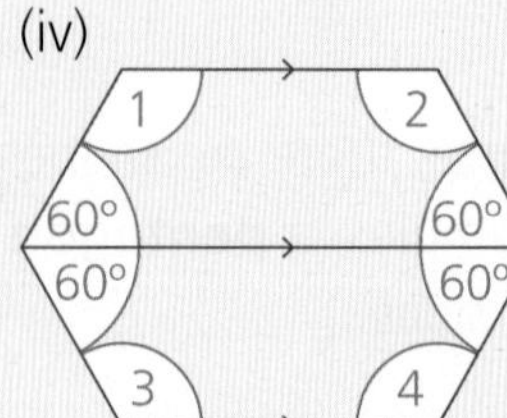

7 Calculate the values of the variable in each of the diagrams below:

(i) (ii) (iii) (iv)

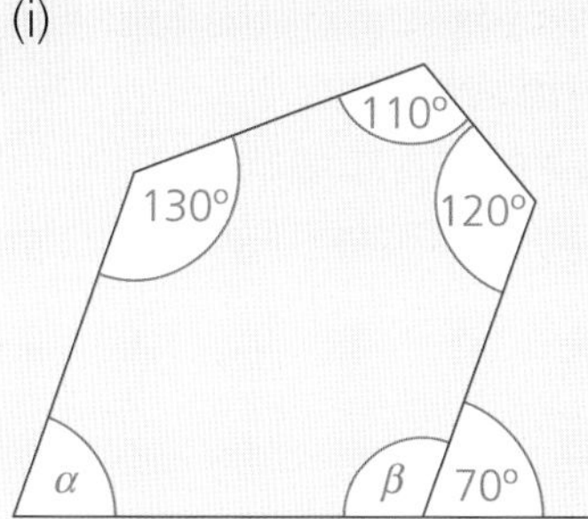

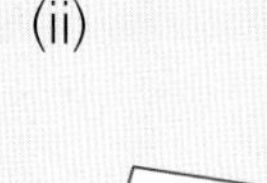

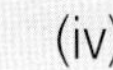

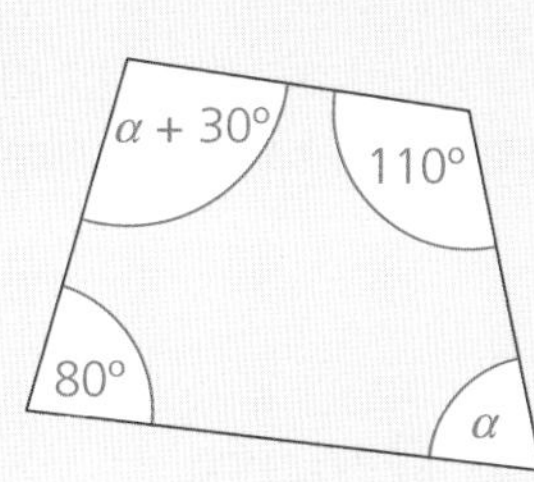

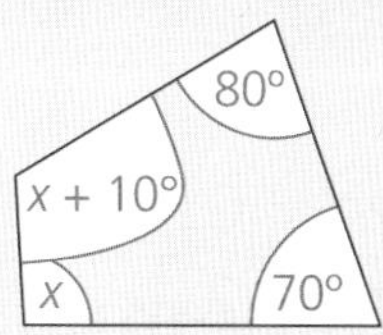

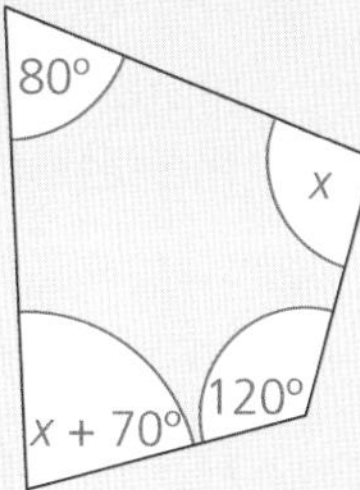

8 Calculate the values of the variables in the diagrams below.
Parallel lines are indicated by arrows.

(i) (ii) (iii) (iv)

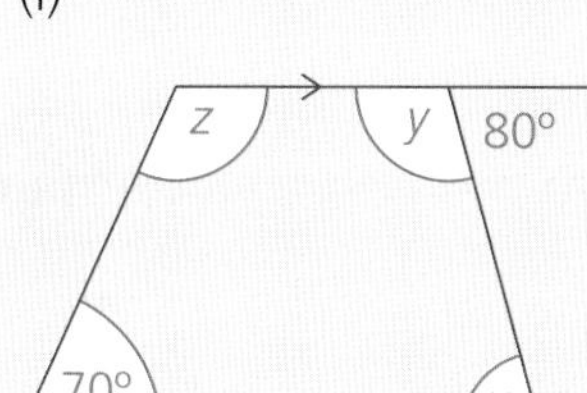

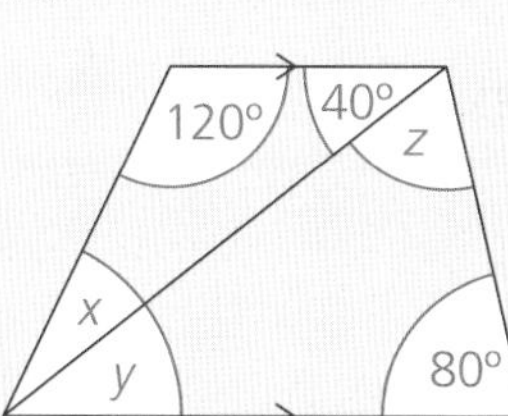

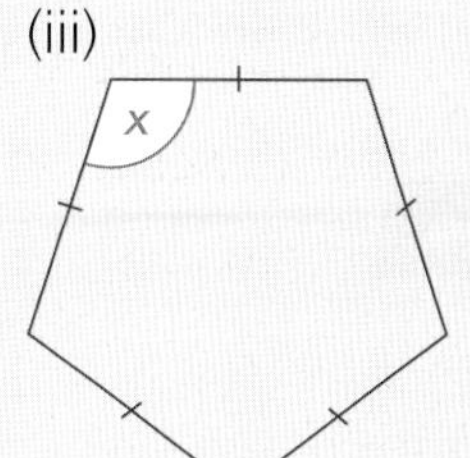

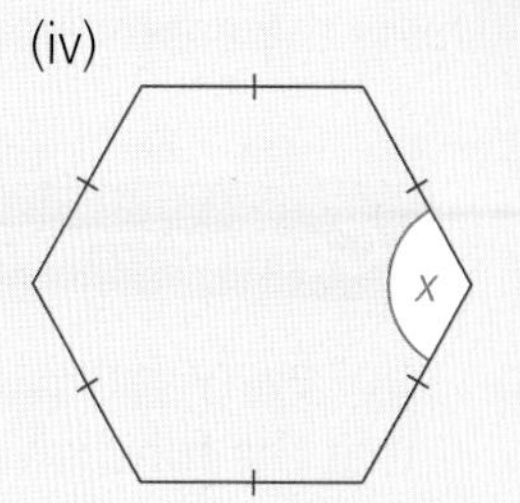

Section 7B The Quadrilateral Club

Look at this diagram. This is a plan of the 'Quadrilateral Club'. Only figures with **four sides** are allowed in the Quadrilateral Club. There are strict rules for admission. No triangles. No pentagons, hexagons or octagons. Definitely no circles.

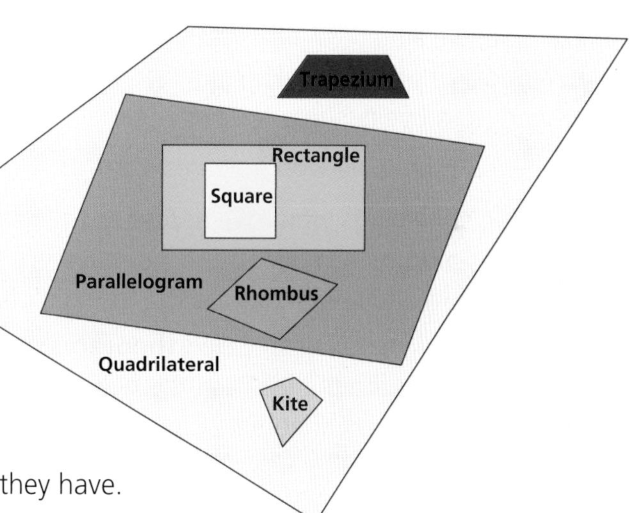

The main building has an odd irregular shape, because lots of quadrilaterals have odd shapes. But there are special members in the club and they occupy special sections inside the main building, depending on what extra features they have.

- The biggest inner building is in the shape of a **parallelogram**. Only those quadrilaterals with their opposite sides parallel are allowed in here. **Trapeziums** are not allowed – they have only one pair of parallel sides. Another rather special shape that does not qualify is the **kite**. It has two pairs of equal sides and has some special properties. But it has no parallel sides, so it is not a parallelogram.
- Inside the parallelogram section, there is another special room for those parallelograms which have four right angles. This is the **rectangle** section. That nice shape which is called a **rhombus** has to stay outside this area, even though it has four equal sides and some rhombuses are almost squares.
- Admission to the innermost room is reserved for the really special shape called a **square**. It really thinks it is the 'special one'. It has four equal sides and all its angles are right angles. It qualifies to be called a quadrilateral, a parallelogram and a rectangle as well, so it can move around anywhere it likes in the entire building.

Connections

- The 'Quadrilateral Club' diagram may remind you of sets and subsets represented by Venn diagrams. For example, the set of squares is a subset of the set of rectangles. You should be able to see several other examples.

Section 7C Mathematical Proofs

Mathematicians are always seeking to prove statements that they suspect are true. They form a **conjecture** (an opinion) and they are pretty sure that it is correct, but they need to **prove** it. This is the essence of mathematics.

Connections

Not every conjecture turns out to be true. In the Middle Ages, it was believed that the function $f(n) = n^2 + n + 41$ always gave a prime number result for every whole number n. However, there are values of n for which $n^2 + n + 41$ is not prime. Can you find the first one? (Try $n = 41$)

For example, we are pretty sure that the angles in any triangle add to 180° because we have measured lots of angles in triangles in the past. But we can never do this for every triangle, so we want to prove it is true for every triangle.

The following is how we work towards a **proof**.

1. We have statements which we accept as true, to get us started. These statements are known as **axioms**. On our course, we have five axioms. We also have some **definitions**. These axioms and definitions are the foundations of our 'geometry wall'.
2. We prove new statements, called **theorems**, one by one in order, starting with Theorem 1. These theorems are the bricks in the geometry wall. We use our **deductive logic** as the 'mortar' to bond the theorems together.

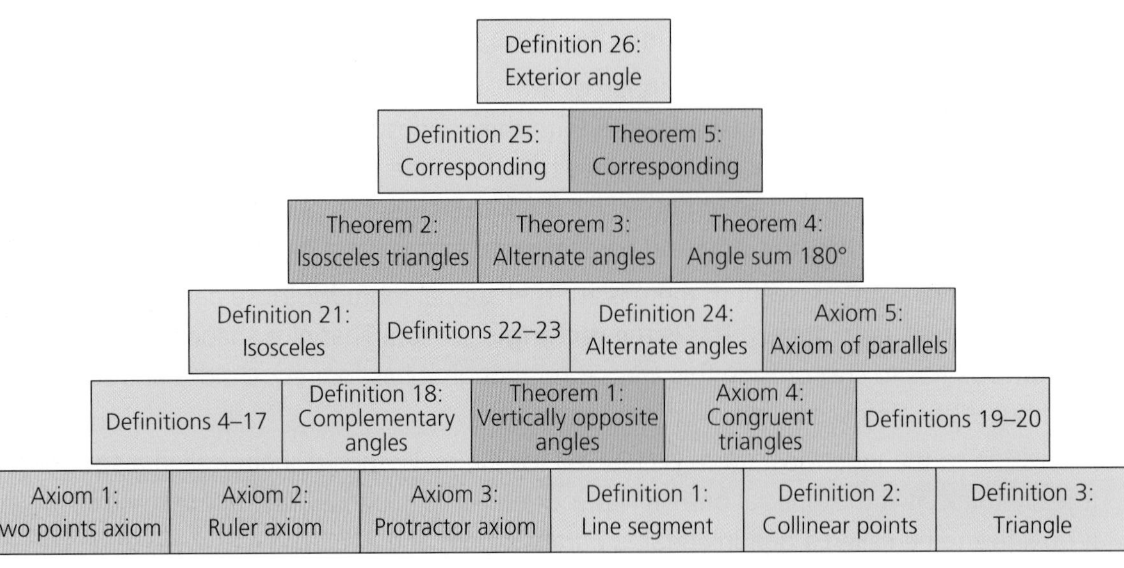

3. If one statement leads directly to another statement, we say that the first statement **implies** the second statement.
   E.g. The statement 'John is Mary's father' **implies** 'Mary is John's daughter'.
   We use the symbol '$\Rightarrow$' for the word 'implies'.
4. We continue to build up our knowledge using previous theorems.
5. Some theorems have **corollaries**, which are statements which come directly from the theorem, but which are not important enough to be called a theorem.
6. A theorem can have a **converse**, which is the statement read backwards.
   E.g. Theorem 2: In an isosceles triangle, the angles opposite the equal sides are equal.
   Converse of Theorem 2: If two angles are equal, then the triangle is isosceles.

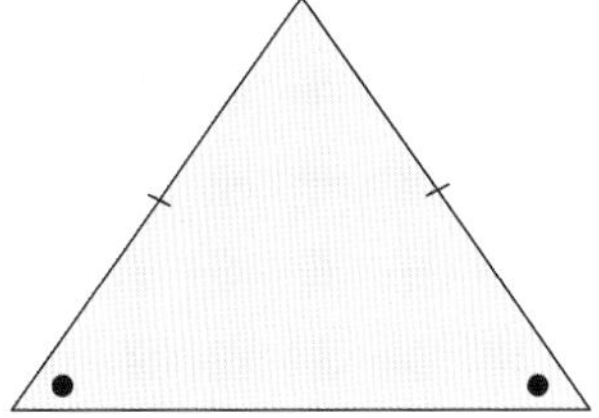

7. The converse of a mathematical statement is not always true. For example:

   Statement: If a triangle has sides 6, 6, and 7 cm long then it is an isosceles triangle (True)

   Converse: If a triangle is isosceles then its side lengths are 6, 6 and 7 cm (False)

The following is the formal proof of Theorem 4. Notice the steps required:

- The statement of the theorem
- Diagram
- Given (what you know about the situation)
- Required to prove
- Construction (if necessary)
- Proof.

THEOREM 4 (formal proof)

The angles in any triangle add to 180°.

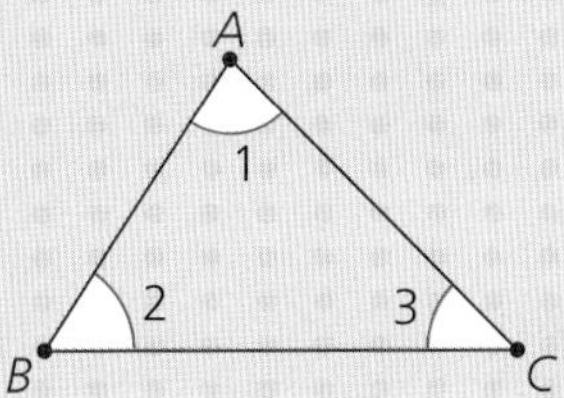

Given: Any triangle *ABC* with angles marked 1, 2 and 3.

Required to prove: $|\angle 1| + |\angle 2| + |\angle 3| = 180°$.

Construction: Draw the line $DE \parallel BC$ through vertex *A*.

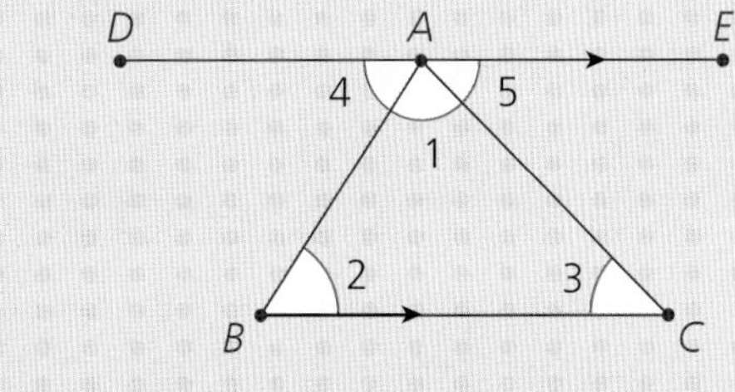

Proof: $|\angle 2| = |\angle 4|$ ... alternate angles

$|\angle 3| = |\angle 5|$ ... alternate angles

$\Rightarrow |\angle 2| + |\angle 3| = |\angle 4| + |\angle 5|$

$\Rightarrow |\angle 1| + |\angle 2| + |\angle 3| = |\angle 1| + |\angle 4| + |\angle 5|$

$= 180°$

$\Rightarrow |\angle 1| + |\angle 2| + |\angle 3| = 180°$ ... QED

Note: QED stands for the Latin words 'quod erat demonstrandum' which means 'which was required to be shown'. We put this at the end of a proof to signal that we have completed it.

As a further example, the formal proof of Theorem 6 follows and in the next section we have Theorem 9. You are not expected to be able to write these proofs out in an exam, but do try to understand how each statement leads to the next, until the proof is finished.

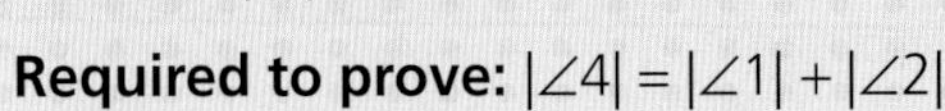

THEOREM 6 (formal proof)

Each exterior angle of a triangle equals the sum of the two interior opposite angles.

Given: Triangle ABC with $[BC]$ extended to D. The angles marked 1, 2, 3 and 4 are as shown in the diagram.

Required to prove: $|\angle 4| = |\angle 1| + |\angle 2|$

Proof: $|\angle 1| + |\angle 2| + |\angle 3| = 180°$ ... Theorem 4

$|\angle 4| + |\angle 3| = 180°$ ... supplementary angles

$\Rightarrow |\angle 1| + |\angle 2| + |\angle 3| = |\angle 4| + |\angle 3|$

$\Rightarrow |\angle 1| + |\angle 2| = |\angle 4|$ ... subtract $|\angle 3|$ from each side ... QED

Section 7D Parallelograms: Theorems 9 and 10

In the following activity, we investigate some properties of a parallelogram by dividing it into two triangles.

Class Discussion

The parallelogram $ABCD$ is shown below with diagonal $[BD]$. Some angles are numbered.

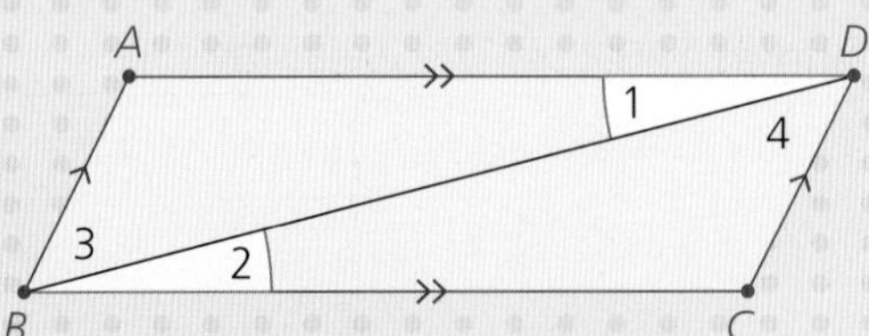

(i) Can you see these two Z shapes in the parallelogram?

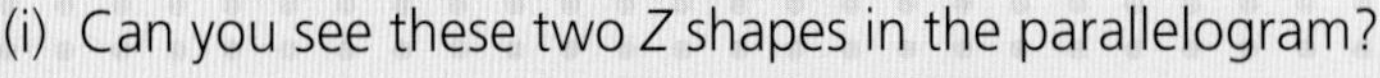

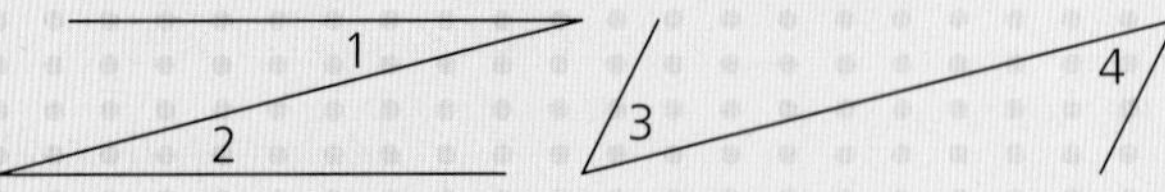

(ii) What do we call these pairs of angles and what can we say about them?

(iii) Draw out the two triangles ABD and BDC separately.

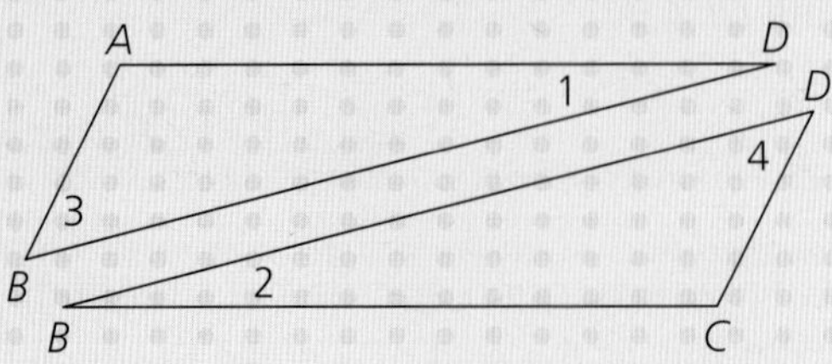

(iv) Mark in the parts of each that you know are equal with similar markings.

(v) Explain why (i.e. prove) that the triangles *ABD* and *BDC* are congruent.

(vi) Copy and complete the following statement:
'Because I know that the triangles *ABD* and *BDC* are congruent, I also know that the matching parts in each are equal, thus $|AD|$ = ____, $|DC|$ = ____ and $|\angle BAD|$ = ____.'

(vii) Peter said, 'This means that the opposite sides of the parallelogram *ABCD* are equal and we also have one pair of opposite angles equal as well.' Was he correct?

(viii) The angles *ADC* and *ABC* are the other pair of opposite angles of the parallelogram *ABCD*. They are broken up into angles 1, 2, 3 and 4. Use the information we have about these to prove that $|\angle ADC| = |\angle ABC|$.

The previous activity is in fact the proof of the following theorem.

THEOREM 9

In a parallelogram, opposite sides are equal and opposite angles are equal.

This is the formal proof.

THEOREM 9 (formal proof)

In a parallelogram, opposite sides are equal and opposite angles are equal.

Given: A parallelogram *ABCD*.

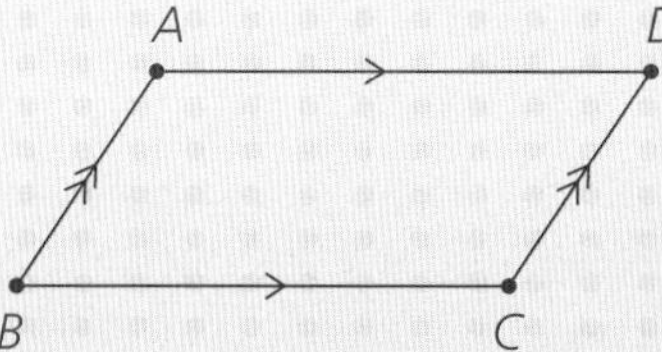

Required to prove: (i) $|AB| = |CD|$ and $|AD| = |BC|$

(ii) $|\angle ABC| = |\angle ADC|$ and $|\angle BAD| = |\angle BCD|$

Construction: Join *A* to *C*. Mark in angles 1, 2, 3 and 4.

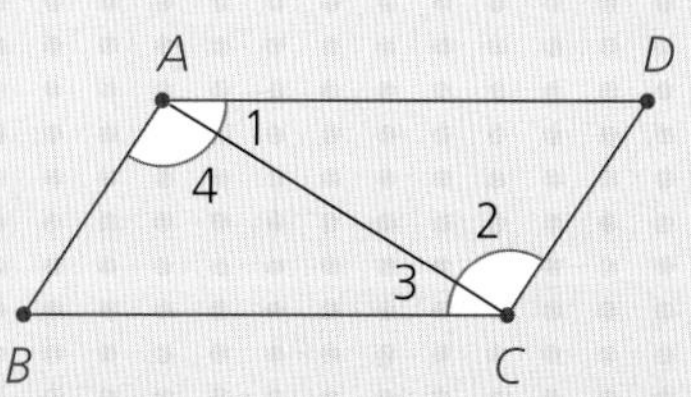

Proof: In the two triangles *ADC* and *ABC*

$|\angle 1| = |\angle 3|$ … alternate angles

$|AC| = |AC|$ … common side

$|\angle 2| = |\angle 4|$ … alternate angles

$\Rightarrow$ triangles *ADC* and *ABC* are congruent by ASA

$\Rightarrow |AB| = |CD|$ and $|AD| = |BC|$ and $|\angle ADC| = |\angle ABC|$

By adding equal angles, we also get $|\angle BAD| = |\angle BCD|$ … QED

COROLLARY TO THEOREM 9

A diagonal divides a parallelogram into two congruent triangles.

Proof: In the proof of the theorem we proved that triangles *ADC* and *ABC* are congruent by ASA. ... QED

THEOREM 9 (Converse)

(i) If the opposite angles of a convex quadrilateral are equal, then it is a parallelogram.

(ii) If the opposite sides of a convex quadrilateral are equal, then it is a parallelogram.

Activity 7.2

1 *PQRS* is a parallelogram.

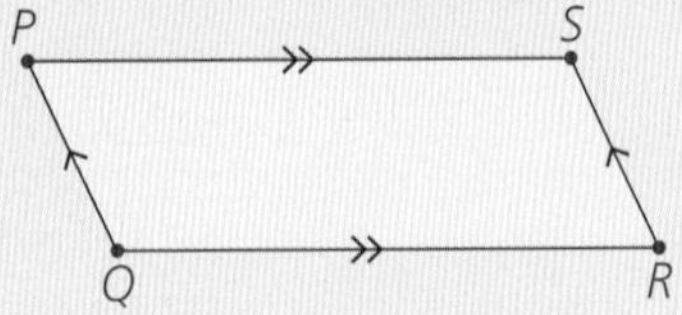

(i) Name two pairs of equal sides.

(ii) Name two pairs of equal angles.

2 *ABCD* is a parallelogram.

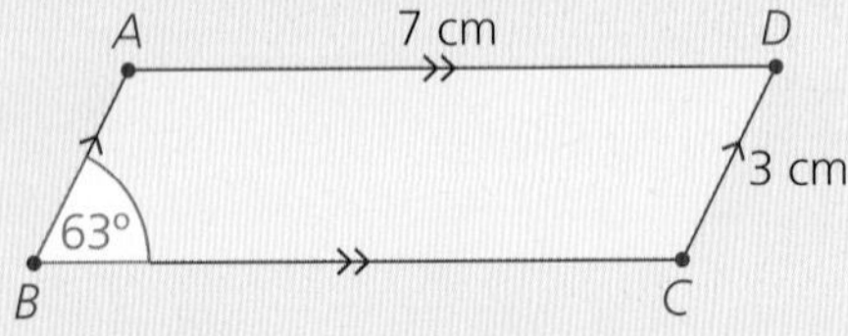

(i) What is $|AB|$? Explain your answer.

(ii) What is $|BC|$? Explain your answer.

(iii) What is $|\angle ADC|$? Explain your answer.

(iv) Calculate the other angles in the parallelogram.

(v) What is the sum of the adjacent angles in the parallelogram?

3 *EFGH* is a parallelogram.

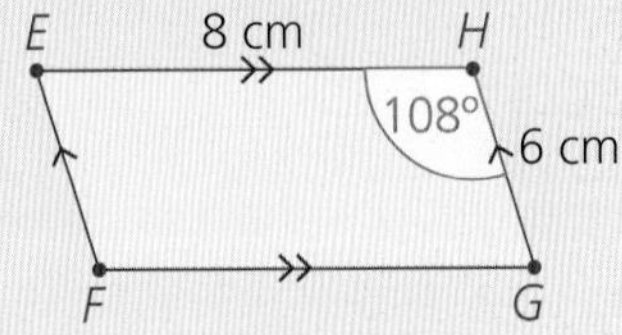

(i) Write down the lengths of [*EF*] and [*FG*].

(ii) Find the size of all the angles in the parallelogram.

(iii) What is the sum of the adjacent angles in the parallelogram?

4 The diagram shows two parallelograms. [*AF*] and [*EC*] are intersecting line segments.

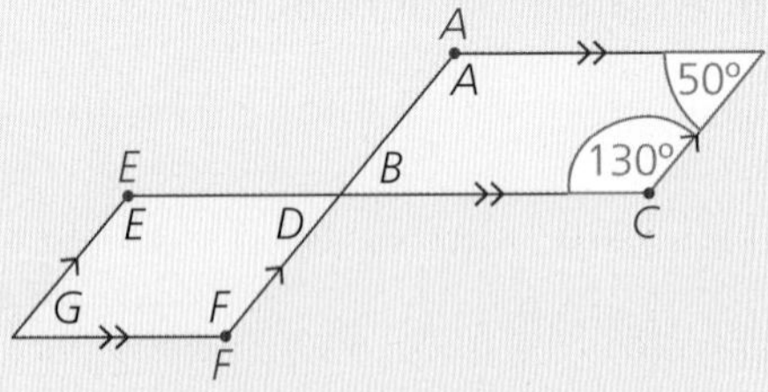

(i) Find the value of all the angles in the diagram.

(ii) What do you notice about the adjacent angles in each parallelogram?

5 The diagram shows a parallelogram with one side extended.

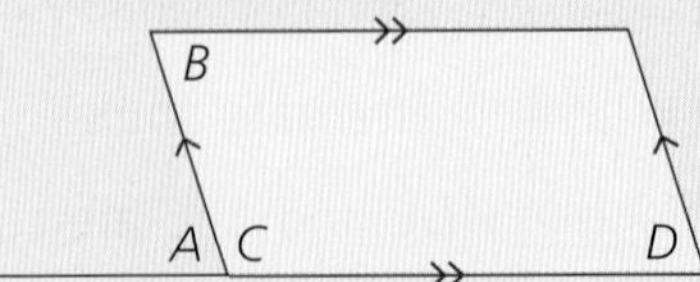

(i) From the diagram, write down the value of $|\angle A| + |\angle C|$.

(ii) Explain why $|\angle A| = |\angle B|$.

(iii) What can you conclude about $|\angle B| + |\angle C|$?

(iv) What is the value of $|\angle C| + |\angle D|$?

6 In each of the following diagrams, $ABCD$ is a parallelogram. Find the angles α, β and γ in each case.

(i)

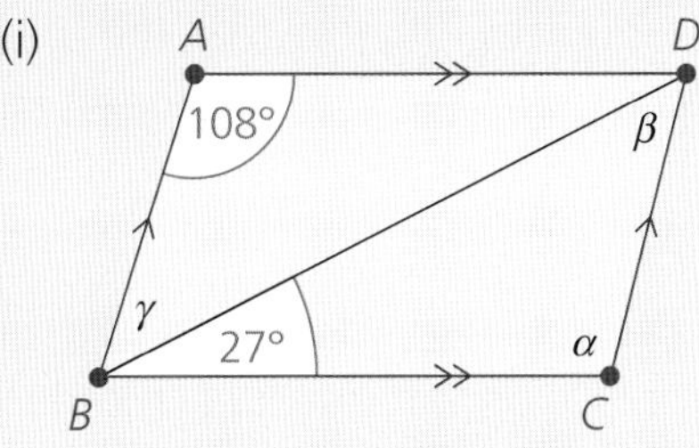

(ii)

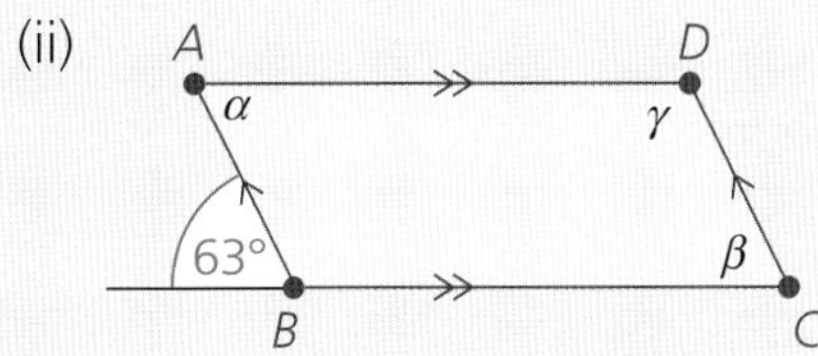

(iii)

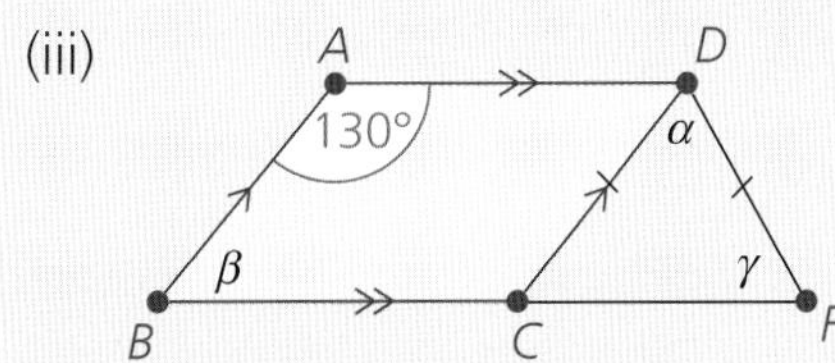

(iv)

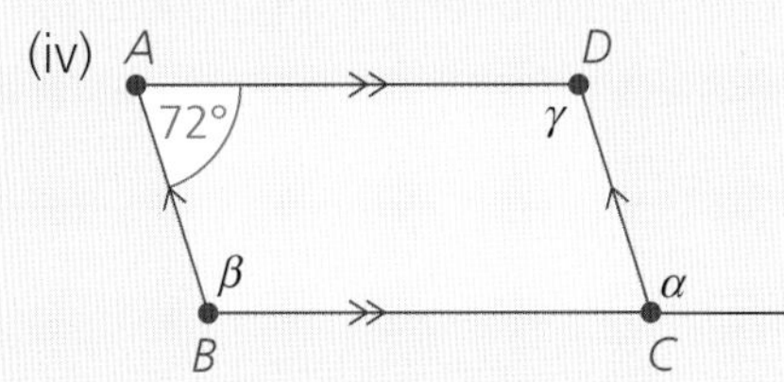

7 The diagram shows a parallelogram and one exterior angle. Find the value of x and the value of y.

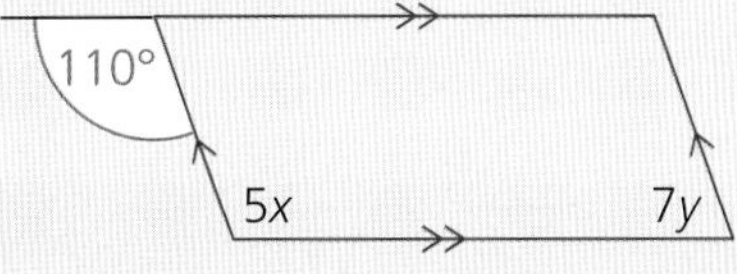

8 $STUV$ is a parallelogram where $|SV| = 2 \times |ST|$. M is the mid-point of $[TU]$. Angles 1 to 9 are marked.

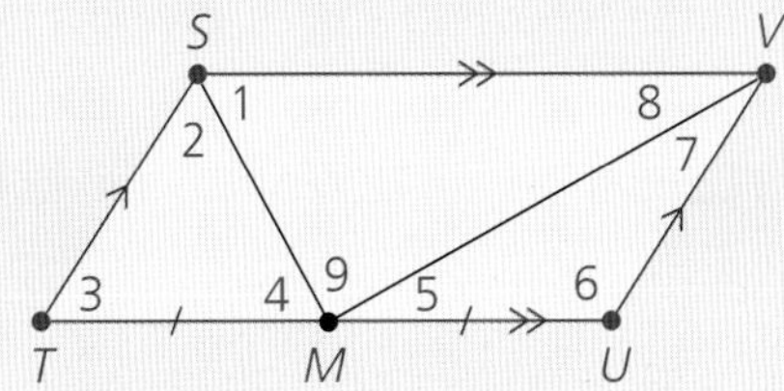

(i) Name another line segment which has length equal to $|SV|$.

(ii) Name three line segments which have length equal to $|ST|$.

(iii) Name two isosceles triangles in the diagram.

(iv) Name four pairs of equal angles, giving a reason in each case.

(v) Prove that SM bisects $\angle TSV$.

(vi) Does MV bisect $\angle SVU$? Give a reason for your answer.

(vii) Prove that $|\angle SMV| = 90°$.

9 (i) Explain the words axiom, theorem, converse and corollary.

(ii) The diagram shows a parallelogram $ABCD$ with diagonal $[AC]$.

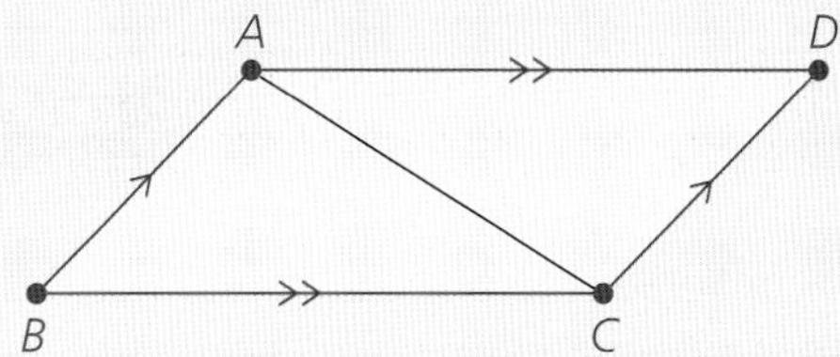

Prove that the diagonal divides the parallelogram into two congruent triangles.

(iii) Show by a diagram that the converse of the statement in part (ii) is not true, i.e. show that if a diagonal of a quadrilateral divides it into two congruent triangles, it does not mean that the quadrilateral has to be a parallelogram.

10 The diagram shows a quadrilateral with four sides of equal length. The mid-points of two of its sides are joined with a straight line.

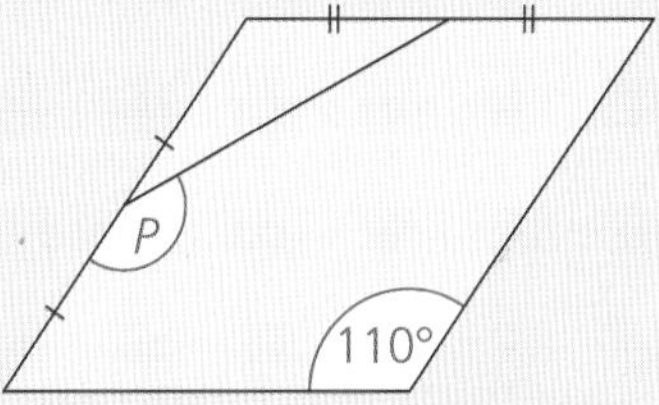

Calculate the size of angle P.
Show how you worked out your answer.

11 $ADBE$ is a rhombus. Prove that its diagonals are perpendicular.

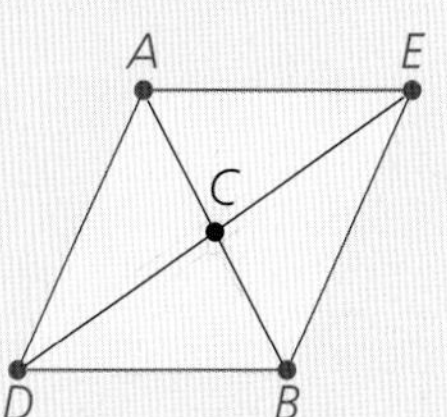

12 The diagram below shows a parallelogram *LMNP* which is not a rectangle or a rhombus. It has diagonals [*LN*] and [*PM*] intersecting at *R*.

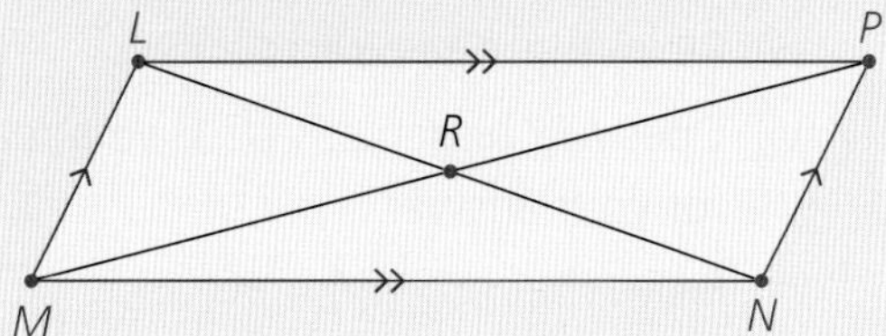

(i) Prove that the triangles *LPR* and *MNR* are congruent.

(ii) Copy and complete the following sentences: 'I know that the triangles *LPR* and *MNR* are congruent, so I also know that $|LR|$ = ________ and that $|RP|$ = ________.
Therefore, the diagonals of a parallelogram bisect each other.'

In question **12** of Activity 7.2 you proved the following theorem:

THEOREM 10

The diagonals of a parallelogram bisect each other.

The converse (the opposite statement) of Theorem 10 is also true.

THEOREM 10 (Converse)

If the diagonals of a quadrilateral bisect one another, then the quadrilateral is a parallelogram.

Key Points

We now have the following properties of all parallelograms:

- Opposite sides are parallel (the definition of a parallelogram).
- Opposite sides are equal.
- Opposite angles are equal.
- Adjacent angles add to 180°.
- The diagonals bisect each other.
- A diagonal divides the parallelogram into two congruent triangles.
- In the case of a square or a rhombus, the diagonals are perpendicular.

Activity 7.3

1 *ABCD* is a parallelogram. $|\angle ADC| = 60°$. $|AB| = 7$, $|BC| = 5$.

(i) Find $|\angle ABC|$. Give a reason for your answer.

(ii) Find $|\angle DAB|$. Explain your answer.

(iii) Find $|DC|$ and $|AD|$. Justify your answers.

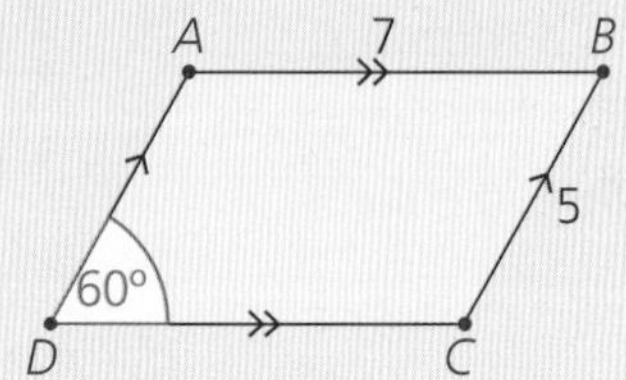

2 *PQRS* is a parallelogram. $|\angle PQR| = 50°$. [*QP*] has been extended to *T*.

Find the following angles, giving a reason for your answers.

(i) $|\angle PSR|$ (ii) $|\angle TPS|$ (iii) $|\angle QRS|$

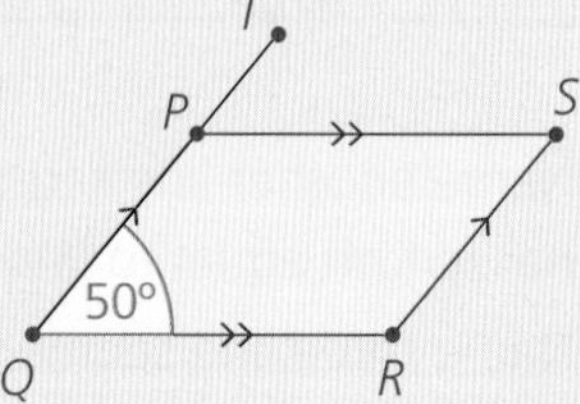

3 $ABCD$ is a parallelogram. $|\angle FCD| = 25°$, $|\angle BAD| = 70°$.

Find:

(i) $|\angle BCD|$

(ii) $|\angle BCF|$

(iii) $|\angle AEF|$

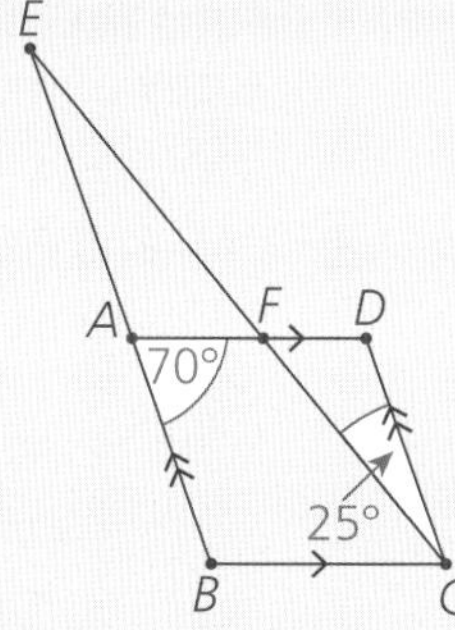

4 $DEFG$ is a parallelogram. The diagonals intersect at H. $|DF| = 6$ and $|HG| = 4$. $|DG| = 8$.

Find:

(i) $|EH|$ (iii) $|EG|$

(ii) $|DH|$ (iv) $|EF|$

Explain each of your answers.

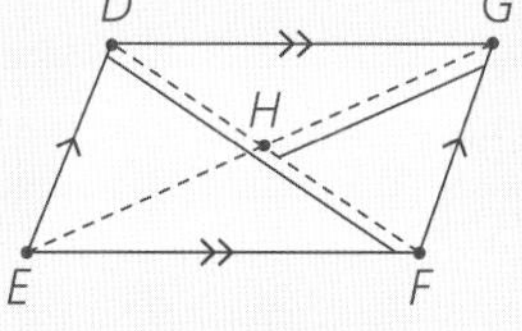

5 $STUV$ is a parallelogram. $|SR| = 4.5$, $|VR| = 3.5$, $|SV| = 5$ and $|VU| = 3.2$.

Find:

(i) $|SU|$

(ii) $|TV|$

(iii) $|TU|$

(iv) $|ST|$

6 $ABCD$ is a parallelogram which is not a rectangle or a rhombus.

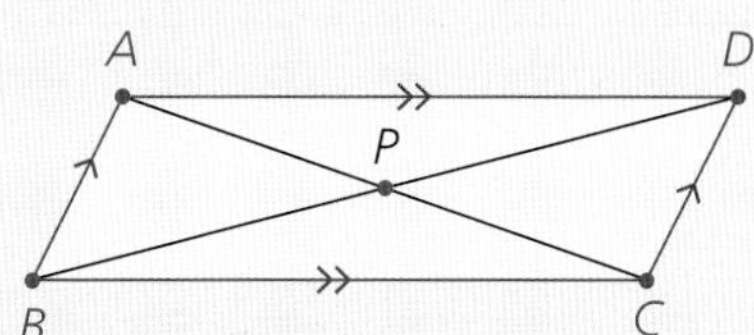

(i) Say whether the following statements are true or false:

(a) $|AP| = |PC|$ (c) $|AD| = |AB|$

(b) $|AP| = |BP|$ (d) $|\angle BAD| = |\angle BCD|$

(ii) Name four pairs of alternate angles.

(iii) Name a pair of congruent triangles in the diagram. Prove that they are congruent.

7 $WXYZ$ is a parallelogram. $|\angle WTX| = 90°$, $|WT| = 4$, $|TX| = 3$ and $|XY| = 6$.

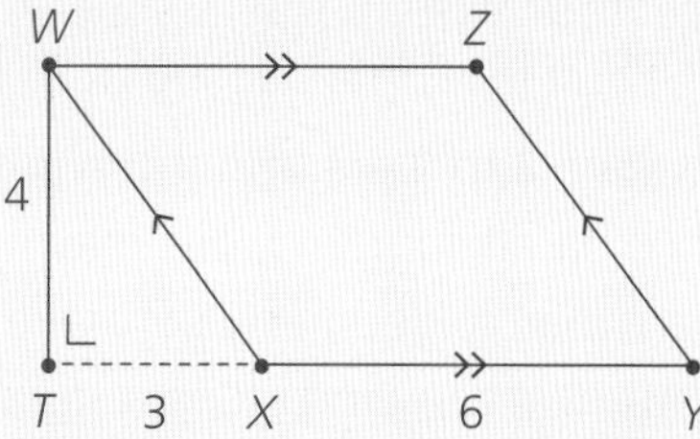

Find:

(i) $|WX|$ (ii) $|ZY|$ (iii) $|WZ|$

8 $ABCD$ and $EDGF$ are two parallelograms. D is the mid-point of $[AG]$ and also the mid-point of $[CE]$.

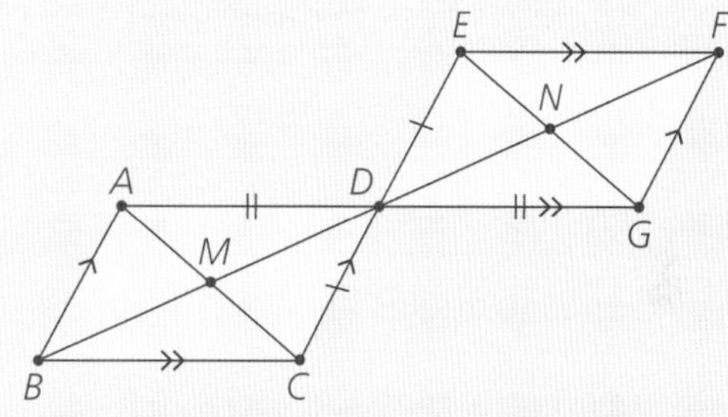

(i) Name three line segments equal in length to $[BC]$.

(ii) Name three angles equal to $|\angle EFG|$.

(iii) Name three angles equal to $|\angle EDF|$.

(iv) Name three line segments equal to $[NF]$.

9 $ABCE$ and $ACDE$ are parallelograms and $|\angle DFE| = 90°$, $|CD| = 7$, $|DF| = 4$ and $|EF| = 3$.

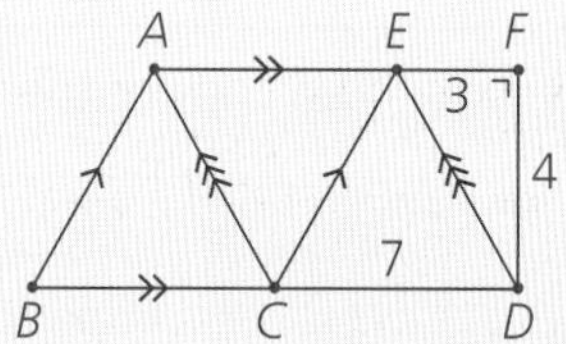

(i) Name two angles equal to $|\angle BAC|$.

(ii) Calculate the length of $[AC]$.

(iii) Explain why $[BC]$ and $[CD]$ are equal in length.

10 The diagram shows a parallelogram.

Calculate the value of d.

75°

40°

d

Revision Activity 7

1 Draw a mind-map using the theme of 'polygons'. Use the list of key words and phrases at the end of this chapter if it helps.

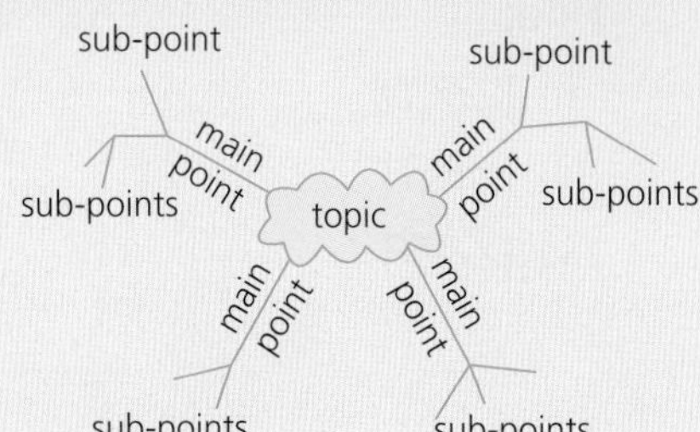

Questions **2** to **9** are about the properties that various parallelogram types may or may not have. Use a dynamic geometry software package or your own drawings to investigate the ones that you are not sure of.

2 Look at each statement in the following table. Copy the table and put a tick (✓) or a cross (×) in each box to show whether or not the statements are true.

	Square	Rectangle	Rhombus	Parallelogram (which is not one of these)
Opposite sides are parallel.				
Opposite sides are equal.				
All four sides are equal.				
Opposite angles are equal.				
Adjacent angles add to 180°.				
Four angles add to 360°.				
Diagonals bisect each other.				
Diagonals are perpendicular.				
It has a centre of symmetry.				
It has exactly four axes of symmetry.				

3 (a) In your own copy of the table below, tick one box for each of the following statements.

	Statement	Always true	Sometimes true	Never true
(i)	The four angles of any quadrilateral add to 360°.			
(ii)	A parallelogram has exactly two axes of symmetry.			
(iii)	The diagonals of a rectangle bisect each other.			
(iv)	A parallelogram has exactly two right angles.			
(v)	Adjacent angles in a rhombus add to 180°.			
(vi)	The diagonals of a parallelogram are perpendicular.			

(b) Explain each 'sometimes true' answer using diagrams.

4 Four shapes are shown.

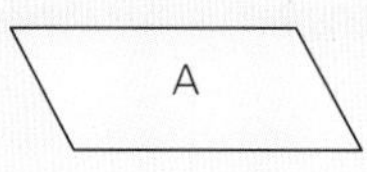

In a copy of the table below, put a tick in every box where the statement is **always true** for that shape.

	A	B	C	D
The diagonals bisect each other.				
Opposite sides are equal in length.				
The diagonals are equal in length.				
Opposite sides are parallel.				

5 (a) The diagram shows a parallelogram and its two diagonals. Some of the angles in the diagram are marked.

Write down the size of the angle K and the size of the angle L.

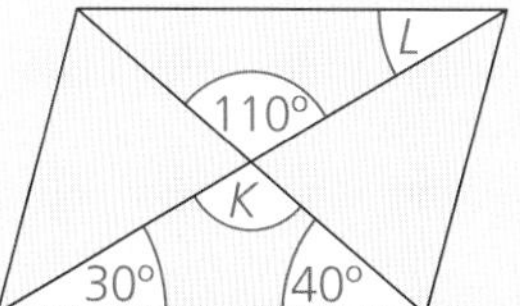

(b) There are four statements in the table below:

(i) In a copy of the table below, put a tick (✓) in the correct box on each line to show whether each statement is always true, sometimes true, or never true.

	Tick **one** box for each statement		
Statement	**Always true**	**Sometimes true**	**Never true**
In a rectangle, the opposite sides are equal.			
The sum of the four angles in a rectangle is 180°.			
A square has 4 axes of symmetry.			
Each of the angles in a parallelogram is 90°.			

(ii) **Justify** your answer to the following statement: 'The sum of the four angles in a rectangle is 180°.'

6 (a) On a copy of this table, tick one box for each of the statements.

	Statement	**Always true**	**Sometimes true**	**Never true**
(i)	In a triangle there is one angle which is bigger than the sum of the other two angles.			
(ii)	There is exactly one line through any two given points.			
(iii)	A parallelogram has a centre of symmetry.			
(iv)	Two triangles are congruent if two sides and an angle of one triangle are equal to two sides and an angle of the other.			
(v)	Given any line l and a point P, there is more than one line through P that is parallel to l.			
(vi)	A right-angled triangle is also isosceles.			

	Statement	Always true	Sometimes true	Never true
(vii)	A diagonal divides a parallelogram into two congruent triangles.			
(viii)	The diagonals of a rectangle which is not a square are perpendicular.			
(ix)	If the diagonals of a quadrilateral are perpendicular, then it is a square.			

(b) Explain each 'sometimes true' answer using diagrams.

7 If $l_1 \parallel l_2$ find the angles α, β and γ in the diagram.

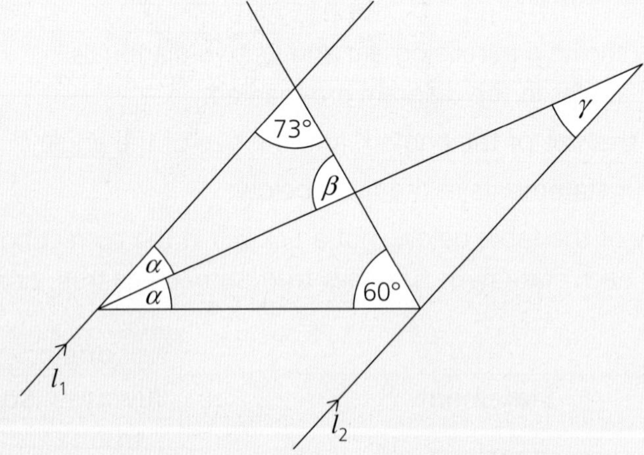

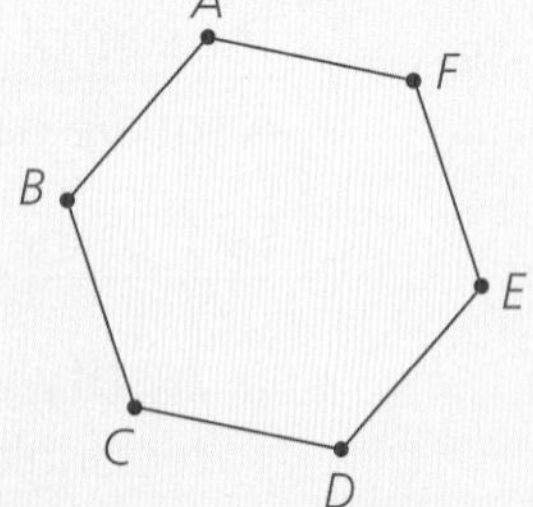

8 (a) The diagram shows a regular hexagon. Copy the diagram and draw in all its axes of symmetry.

(b) [BE] and [AD] intersect at O.

What is the measure of the angle of the rotation about O which maps E onto A?

(c) Describe two transformations which map [ED] onto [AB].

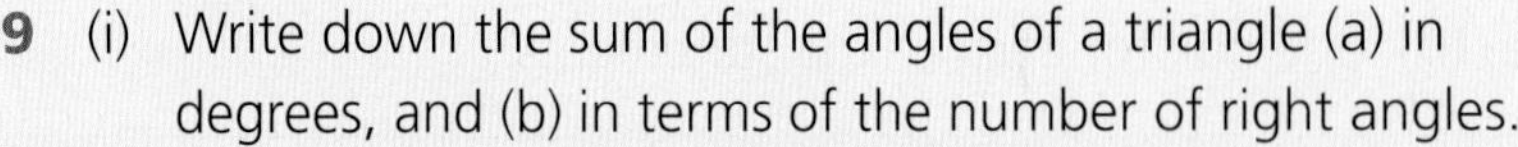

9 (i) Write down the sum of the angles of a triangle (a) in degrees, and (b) in terms of the number of right angles.

(ii) Write down the sum of the angles of a quadrilateral (a) in degrees, and (b) in terms of the number of right angles.

(iii) (a) Copy and complete this table, to show the sum of the angles of various polygons.

Name of polygon	Number of sides	Sum of angles in degrees	Sum of angles in terms of right angles
triangle	3	180°	2
quadrilateral	4		
pentagon	5		
hexagon	6		
heptagon	7		
octagon	8		

(b) Justify that there is a linear relationship between the number of sides of a polygon and the sum of its angles in terms of right angles.

(c) Draw a graph of this relationship on a copy of the grid.

(d) Derive a formula for the number of right angles in an n-sided polygon.

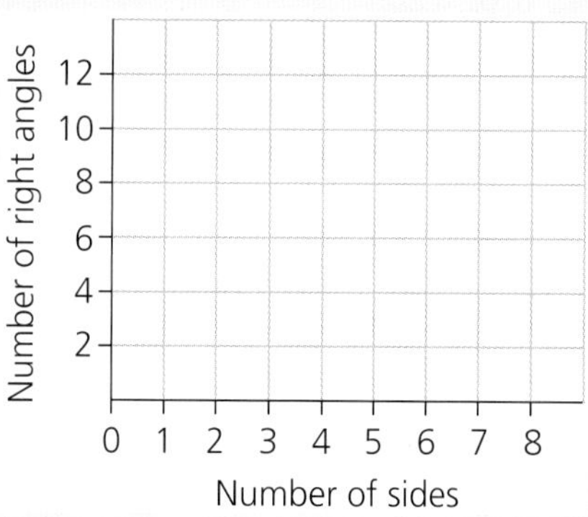

Interactive Tool 7.1

Exam-style Question

1 The diagram shows the rhombus $QRST$.

It is a parallelogram in which all four sides are equal in length.

The diagonals cross at the point K. Two of the angles are marked X and Y.

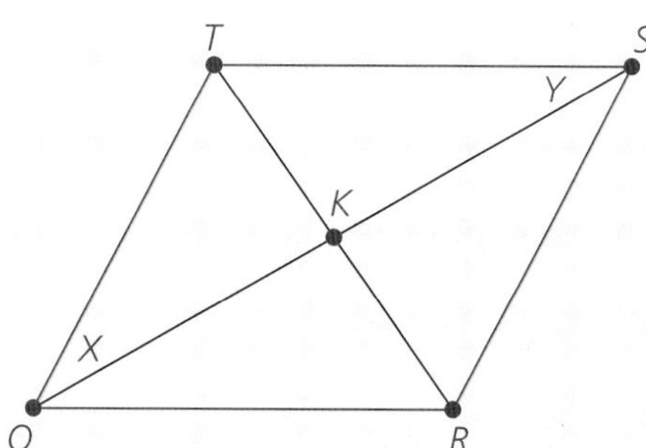

Sanjay is trying to prove that the triangles QKT and SKT are congruent.

Fill in the missing statements and reasons in a copy of the table below to complete Sanjay's proof correctly.

	Statement	**Reason**
1	$\lvert QT\rvert = \lvert TS\rvert$	$QRST$ is a rhombus
2	QST is an isosceles triangle	
3	$\lvert\angle X\rvert = \lvert\angle Y\rvert$	
4		The diagonals of a parallelogram bisect each other
5	QKT is congruent to SKT	

JCHL 2018

KEY WORDS AND PHRASES

- Polygon
- Regular polygon
- Adjacent sides
- Adjacent angles
- Opposite sides
- Opposite angles
- Vertices
- Quadrilateral
- Rectangle
- Rhombus
- Square
- Parallelogram
- Kite
- Trapezium
- Diagonal
- Pentagon
- Hexagon
- Conjecture
- Proof
- Theorem
- Converse of theorem

Chapter Summary 7

- A polygon is a piece of the plane enclosed by a figure with many sides.
- A quadrilateral is a four-sided polygon.
  - Rectangles, rhombuses, squares, parallelograms, kites and trapeziums are quadrilaterals.
- Theorem 9: In a parallelogram, opposite sides are equal and opposite angles are equal.
- Theorem 9 (converse):
  - If the opposite angles of a quadrilateral are equal, then it is a parallelogram.
  - If the opposite sides of a quadrilateral are equal, then it is a parallelogram.
- Theorem 10: The diagonals of a parallelogram bisect each other.
- Theorem 10 (converse): If the diagonals of a parallelogram bisect one another, then the quadrilateral is a parallelogram.

Algebra 3

Chapter 8

Learning Intentions

In this chapter, you will learn about:

- Solving quadratic equations using factors
- Finding a quadratic equation given its roots
- Solving quadratic equations using a formula
- Solving more problems with quadratic equations

LO: U.3, U.4, U.5, U.6, AF.4(b), AF.5, U.7–U.10

Section 8A Quadratic Equations

You may remember that **quadratic** means 'having a highest power of 2'.

In this section we want to solve equations such as $x^2 - x - 6 = 0$ or $x^2 - 5x = 0$.

These are called **quadratic equations**.

First, we need to discuss a very important idea.

Class Discussion

Think of two numbers which, when multiplied together, give 0 as the answer.
Think of five pairs of numbers which multiply together to give 0.
How many such pairs are there?
Can you think of two numbers which multiply together to give 0, but neither of them is 0?

In fact, there is no pair of non-zero numbers whose product is 0.

In other words, **if you multiply two numbers and the result is zero, then at least one of the numbers must be zero.**

It is this rule which will enable us to solve quadratic equations. It also means that we always get **two** solutions to a quadratic equation.

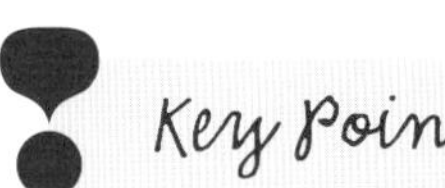

The zero rule for multiplication:

If $(a)(b) = 0$ then either $a = 0$ or $b = 0$.

Example 1

Solve the equation $(x - 2)(x + 5) = 0$.

Solution

- $(x - 2)(x + 5) = 0$

  $\Rightarrow$ either $(x - 2) = 0$ **or**

  $(x + 5) = 0$ ... the zero rule for multiplication

  $\Rightarrow x = 2$ or $x = -5$

  Answer: $x = 2$ or $x = -5$
- Check: $(x - 2)(x + 5) = 0$

  Substitute in $x = 2$:

  $\Rightarrow (0)(2 + 5) = 0(7) \Rightarrow 0 = 0$ ✓

  Substitute in $x = -5$:

  $\Rightarrow (-5 - 2)(0) = (-7)0 \Rightarrow 0 = 0$ ✓

Example 2

Solve the equation $y^2 - y = 0$.

Solution

- Factorise the left-hand side (Type 1 factor):

  $y^2 - y = 0$

  $(y)(y - 1) = 0$

  $\Rightarrow$ either $y = 0$ **or** $y - 1 = 0$

  $\Rightarrow y = 0$ or $y = 1$

  Answer: $y = 0$ or $y = 1$
- Check: $y^2 - y = 0$

  $y = 0 \Rightarrow 0^2 - 0 = 0 \Rightarrow 0 = 0$ ✓

  $y = 1 \Rightarrow 1^2 - 1 = 0 \Rightarrow 1 - 1 = 0$ ✓

Example 3

Solve $x^2 - x - 6 = 0$.

Solution

- Factorise the left-hand side (LHS):

  $x^2 - x - 6$ (Type 3 factor).

  Guide number = -6

  Write all the factors of -6: → $(-6)(1)$, $(6)(-1)$, $(-2)(3)$, $(2)(-3)$

  Only one pair of these factors will add to give the middle coefficient (-1).

  These are 2 and -3.

  So we write $-x$ as $(+2x - 3x)$:

  $\Rightarrow x^2 + 2x - 3x - 6$

  $\Rightarrow x(x + 2) - 3(x + 2)$

  $\Rightarrow (x + 2)(x - 3)$
- Solve the equation $(x + 2)(x - 3) = 0$.

  Either $(x + 2) = 0$ or $(x - 3) = 0$

  $\Rightarrow x = -2$ or $x = 3$

  Answer: $x = -2$ or $x = 3$
- Check: $x^2 - x - 6 = 0$

  $x = -2 \Rightarrow (-2)^2 - (-2) - 6 = 0$

  $\Rightarrow 4 + 2 - 6 = 0$ ✓

  $x = 3 \Rightarrow (3^2) - 3 - 6 = 0$

  $\Rightarrow 9 - 3 - 6 = 0$ ✓

Example 4

Solve the quadratic equation $9x^2 - 16 = 0$ for x.

Solution

$9x^2 - 16 = 0$

$\Rightarrow (3x)^2 - (4)^2 = 0$ … rewrite the LHS as the difference of two squares

$\Rightarrow (3x - 4)(3x + 4) = 0$ … factorise (difference of two squares)

Either $(3x - 4) = 0$ or $(3x + 4) = 0$ … zero rule for multiplication

$\Rightarrow 3x = 4$ or $3x = -4$

$\Rightarrow x = \frac{4}{3}$ or $x = -\frac{4}{3}$

Check answer by substituting $x = \frac{4}{3}$ and $x = -\frac{4}{3}$ into the original equation.

When $x = \frac{4}{3} \Rightarrow 9x^2 - 16 = 0 \Rightarrow 9\left(\frac{4}{3}\right)^2 - 16 = 0 \Rightarrow 0 = 0$ ✓

When $x = -\frac{4}{3} \Rightarrow 9x^2 - 16 = 0 \Rightarrow 9\left(-\frac{4}{3}\right)^2 - 16 = 0 \Rightarrow 0 = 0$ ✓

As LHS = RHS for both equations, both solutions are correct.

Example 5

Solve $x^2 + 3x = -2$.

Solution

- We must have 0 on one side of the equation, otherwise we can't use the zero rule.

  $x^2 + 3x = -2$

  $\Rightarrow x^2 + 3x + 2 = 0$ … add 2 to each side
- Factorise the left-hand side: $x^2 + 3x + 2$ (Type 3 factor).

  Guide number = +2

  Write all the factors of +2: ⟶ (2)(1) (−2)(−1)

  Only one pair of these factors will add to give the middle coefficient (+3).

  These are 2 and 1. So we write $3x$ as $(+2x + x)$:

  $\Rightarrow x^2 + 2x + x + 2 = 0$

  $\Rightarrow x(x + 2) + 1(x + 2) = 0$ … note the 1 outside the second bracket

  $\Rightarrow (x + 2)(x + 1) = 0$
- Solve the equation $(x + 2)(x + 1) = 0$.

  $\Rightarrow$ Either $x + 2 = 0$ or $x + 1 = 0$

  $\Rightarrow x = -2$ or $x = -1$

  Answer: $x = -2$ or $x = -1$
- Check: $x^2 + 3x = -2$

  $x = -2 \Rightarrow (-2)^2 + 3(-2) = -2$

  $\Rightarrow 4 - 6 = -2$ ✓

  $x = -1 \Rightarrow (-1)^2 + 3(-1) \Rightarrow 1 - 3 = -2$ ✓

Sometimes the two solutions are equal, as in the next example.

Example 6

Solve $x^2 - 4x + 4 = 0$.

Solution

$x^2 - 4x + 4 = 0$

$\Rightarrow x^2 - 2x - 2x + 4 = 0$

$\Rightarrow x(x - 2) - 2(x - 2) = 0$

$\Rightarrow (x - 2)(x - 2) = 0$

$\Rightarrow x = 2$ or $x = 2$

To factorise:
Guide number = +4
Factors of +4 are:
(1)(4)
(−1)(−4)
(2)(2)
(−2)(−2)

We have two equal solutions.

Answer: $x = 2$

Check: $x^2 - 4x + 4 = 0$

$x = 2 \Rightarrow (2)^2 - 4(2) + 4 = 0$

$\Rightarrow 4 - 8 + 4 = 0$ ✓

Example 7

(i) Solve the quadratic equation $x^2 - x - 6 = 0$.

(ii) Hence, solve the equation $(y - 2)^2 - (y - 2) - 6 = 0$.

Solution

(i) $x^2 - x - 6 = 0$

$\Rightarrow (x - 3)(x + 2) = 0$ ... factorise the left-hand side

$\Rightarrow$ either $x - 3 = 0$ or $x + 2 = 0$ ... zero rule for multiplication

$\Rightarrow$ $x = 3$ or $x = -2$

(ii) The equation $(y - 2)^2 - (y - 2) - 6 = 0$ is exactly the same as $x^2 - x - 6 = 0$ except that x has been replaced everywhere by $(y - 2)$.

We can therefore replace x by $(y - 2)$ in the answers.

$\therefore y - 2 = 3$ or $y - 2 = -2$

$\therefore$ $y = 5$ or $y = 0$

Activity 8.1

1 If you are given that $(a)(b) = 0$, where $a, b \in \mathbb{R}$, what can you conclude about a and b?

2 Write down the roots of these equations.

(i) $(x - 4)(x + 3) = 0$ (ii) $(x + 7)(x - 3) = 0$ (iii) $x(x - 7) = 0$ (iv) $(x - 5)(x + 5) = 0$

In questions **3–20**, solve the equation and verify your answers.

3 $x^2 + x - 6 = 0$

4 $x^2 + 8x + 7 = 0$

5 $x^2 + 4x = -3$

6 $x^2 - 6x = -5$

7 $x(x - 3) = 18$

8 $36x^2 - 81 = 0$

9 $225x^2 - 169 = 0$

10 $11x^2 - 22x = 0$

11 $(x+2)(x-3)=6$

12 $35x^2-7x=0$

13 $4x^2-25=0$

14 $9x^2-49=0$

15 $4x^2-8x=0$

16 $7x^2-x=0$

17 $5x^2+6x+1=0$

18 $7x^2+10x=-3$

19 $9x^2+10x+1=0$

20 $11x^2+15x+4=0$

---

21 (i) Solve the equation $x^2+5x-14=0$.
(ii) Hence, solve the equation $(k-2)^2+5(k-2)-14=0$.

22 (i) Solve the equation $3x^2+5x=2$.
(ii) Hence, solve the equation $3(m-3)^2+5(m-3)=2$.

23 (i) Solve the equation $3p^2+14p-5=0$.
(ii) Hence, solve the equation $3(a+1)^2+14(a+1)-5=0$.

Solve the following equations.

24 $13x^2-66x+5=0$

25 $3x^2-5x=-2$

26 $4x^2-7x+3=0$

27 $6x^2-7x+2=0$

28 $10x^2+11x-6=0$

29 $9x^2+9x-4=0$

30 $8x^2=5-3x$

31 $13x^2+10x-3=0$

32 $-4x^2-7x+2=0$

33 $-2x^2+7x+4=0$

34 $x^2+(x+1)^2=(x+2)^2$

Algebra 3

Section 8B Forming a Quadratic Equation Given the Roots

Example

(i) Form the quadratic equation with roots 2 and –5.
(ii) Verify your solution.

Solution

(i) Work backwards:

The roots are $x=2$ and $x=-5$

$\Rightarrow x-2=0$ and $x+5=0$

$\Rightarrow (x-2)(x+5)=0$

$\Rightarrow x^2+5x-2x-10=0$ … multiply out

$\Rightarrow x^2+3x-10=0$

(ii) Check answer by substituting $x=2$ and $x=-5$ into $x^2+3x-10=0$.

When $x=2 \Rightarrow (2)^2+3(2)-10=0$

$\Rightarrow 4+6-10=0 \Rightarrow 0=0$ ✓

When $x=-5 \Rightarrow (-5)^2+3(-5)-10=0$

$\Rightarrow 25-15-10=0 \Rightarrow 0=0$ ✓

Activity 8.2

In questions **1–10**, form quadratic equations with the given roots.

1 $x = -1$ and $x = 3$

2 $x = 2$ and $x = -3$

3 $x = -2$ and $x = 9$

4 $x = -5$ and $x = -4$

5 $x = 6$ and $x = 7$

6 $x = -4$ and $x = 3$

7 $x = 11$ and $x = -3$

8 $x = -8$ and $x = 10$

9 $x = -4$ and $x = 2$

10 $x = 3$ and $x = -5$

11 The roots of the quadratic equation $ax^2 + bx + c = 0$ are 5 and 9. Find the values of a, b and c.

12 The roots of the quadratic equation $ax^2 + bx + c = 0$ are -12 and 2. Find the values of a, b and c.

13 The roots of the quadratic equation $ax^2 + bx + c = 0$ are -7 and -1. Find the values of a, b and c.

14 The roots of the quadratic equation $x^2 + 6x + c = 0$ are the same. Find the value of c.

15 The roots of the quadratic equation $x^2 - 18x + c = 0$ are the same. Find the value of c.

Section 8C Solving a Quadratic Equation Using a Formula

We have solved quadratic equations which can be factorised. However, some quadratic equations cannot be factorised to give roots which are integers or rational numbers.

In such cases, we are often asked to find the roots in surd form or to a specific number of decimal places. In this situation, we use a formula to solve the quadratic equation.

Key Points

To use the formula for solving quadratic equations:

- The quadratic equation must be written in the form $ax^2 + bx + c = 0$.
- The values of a, b and c are substituted into the formula:

$$x = \frac{-b \pm \sqrt{b^2 - 4ac}}{2a}$$

Note that you can also use this formula in cases where factorising is possible. This formula is on page 20 of the *Formulae and tables* booklet.

Example 1

Solve $2x^2 + 10x + 7 = 0$, correct to two decimal places.

Solution

$2x^2 + 10x + 7 = 0$

Here $a = 2$, $b = 10$ and $c = 7$

$$\therefore\ x = \frac{-10 \pm \sqrt{10^2 - 4(2)(7)}}{2(2)}$$

$$= \frac{-10 \pm \sqrt{100 - 56}}{4}$$

$$= \frac{-10 \pm \sqrt{44}}{4}$$

$$= \frac{-10 \pm 6.633}{4}$$

$$= \frac{-10 + 6.633}{4} \quad \text{or} \quad \frac{-10 - 6.633}{4}$$

$$= \frac{-3.367}{4} \quad \text{or} \quad \frac{-16.633}{4}$$

$x = -0.84$ (2 d.p.) or $x = -4.16$ (2 d.p.)

Note

SURDS are numbers like $\sqrt{2}$, $\sqrt{5}$, $\sqrt{7}$, etc. which cannot be written as fractions. When we use the formula for solving quadratic equations, we often have to work with surds.

Example 2

Solve the equation $t^2 - 2t - 6 = 0$ and write the roots in the form $d \pm \sqrt{e}$ where $d, e \in \mathbb{Z}$.

Solution

$t^2 - 2t - 6$ cannot be factorised.

Solve the quadratic equation $t^2 - 2t - 6 = 0$ using the formula.

$t^2 - 2t - 6 = 0 \Rightarrow 1t^2 - 2t - 6 = 0$

$\therefore a = 1$, $b = -2$ and $c = -6$.

Substitute the values of a, b and c into the formula:

$$t = \frac{-b \pm \sqrt{b^2 - 4ac}}{2a}$$

$$\Rightarrow t = \frac{-(-2) \pm \sqrt{(-2)^2 - 4(1)(-6)}}{2(1)}$$

$$\Rightarrow t = \frac{2 \pm \sqrt{4 + 24}}{2}$$

$$\Rightarrow t = \frac{2 \pm \sqrt{28}}{2} = \frac{2 \pm 2\sqrt{7}}{2}$$ ... write the surd $\sqrt{28}$ as $2\sqrt{7}$

$$\Rightarrow t = \frac{2 + 2\sqrt{7}}{2} \quad \text{or} \quad t = \frac{2 - 2\sqrt{7}}{2}$$

$$\Rightarrow t = 1 + \sqrt{7} \quad \text{or} \quad t = 1 - \sqrt{7}$$

The roots of $t^2 - 2t - 6 = 0$ are $t = 1 \pm \sqrt{7}$.

Activity 8.3

1 (i) Solve the quadratic equation $4x^2 + 4x - 3 = 0$ using factors.
(ii) Solve the quadratic equation $4x^2 + 4x - 3 = 0$ by using the formula for solving quadratic equations.
(iii) Check your solutions.

2 (i) Solve the quadratic equation $2x^2 - 3x - 5 = 0$ using factors.
(ii) Solve the quadratic equation $2x^2 - 3x - 5 = 0$ using the formula for solving quadratic equations.
(iii) Check your solutions.

3 Solve the equation $2x^2 + 3x - 4 = 0$ correct to three decimal places using the formula for solving quadratic equations.

4 Find the roots of $x^2 + 6x + 3 = 0$ correct to two decimal places.

5 Find the roots of $x^2 - 4x - 2 = 0$ correct to two decimal places.

6 Find the roots of $4n^2 + 7n - 3 = 0$ correct to two decimal places.

7 Solve the equation $x^2 - 4x - 3 = 0$ and give your answers in surd form.

8 Find the roots of the following equations giving your answers in the form $a \pm \sqrt{b}$, where $a, b \in \mathbb{Z}$.
(i) $x^2 - 2x - 2 = 0$
(ii) $x^2 - 4x + 1 = 0$
(iii) $x^2 - 4x - 1 = 0$

9 Solve the equation $t^2 + 2t - 7 = 0$ and write the roots in surd form.

10 Solve the equation $p^2 - 5p - 2 = 0$ and write the roots in surd form.

11 Solve the equation $x^2 - 4x + 2 = 0$ correct to one decimal place.

12 (i) Solve the equation $x^2 - 6x + 4 = 0$ and give your answers in the form $a \pm \sqrt{b}$, where $a, b \in \mathbb{Z}$.
(ii) Hence, or otherwise, find two values of k for which $(3 + k)^2 - 6(3 + k) + 4 = 0$.
(iii) Show that the sum of the two values of k is zero.

13 (i) Solve the equation $x^2 - 4x + 2 = 0$.
Express your answer in the form $a \pm b\sqrt{2}$.
(ii) Use your answer to part (i) to find the two values of p for which $(p - 4)^2 - 4(p - 4) + 2 = 0$.

Section 8D Solving Quadratic Equations with Algebraic Fractions

A quadratic equation can have rational coefficients. Therefore, we need to be able to solve equations of this type.

Example 1

Solve the quadratic equation $\frac{x^2}{2} - \frac{7x}{2} - 9 = 0$. Verify your answer.

Solution

$\frac{x^2}{2} - \frac{7x}{2} - 9 = 0$ ... multiply both sides by 2 to clear the fractions

$\Rightarrow x^2 - 7x - 18 = 0$

$\Rightarrow (x + 2)(x - 9) = 0$

Either $x + 2 = 0$ or $x - 9 = 0$

$\Rightarrow x = -2$ or $x = 9$

Check answer by substituting $x = -2$ and $x = 9$ into $x^2 - 7x - 18 = 0$.

When $x = -2 \Rightarrow (-2)^2 - 7(-2) - 18 = 0 \quad \Rightarrow 4 + 14 - 18 = 0 \Rightarrow 0 = 0$ ✓

When $x = 9 \Rightarrow (9)^2 - 7(9) - 18 = 0 \quad \Rightarrow 81 - 63 - 18 = 0 \Rightarrow 0 = 0$ ✓

As LHS = RHS for both equations, both solutions are correct.

Example 2

Solve the equation $\frac{x^2}{3} + 2x - \frac{1}{2} = 0$ correct to two decimal places.

Solution

$\frac{x^2}{3} + 2x - \frac{1}{2} = 0$

$\Rightarrow 2x^2 + 12x - 3 = 0$ ... multiply both sides by 6 (LCM) to eliminate the fractions

Substitute the values $a = 2$, $b = 12$ and $c = -3$ into the formula:

$$x = \frac{-b \pm \sqrt{b^2 - 4ac}}{2a}$$

$$\Rightarrow x = \frac{-(12) \pm \sqrt{(12)^2 - 4(2)(-3)}}{2(2)}$$

$$\Rightarrow x = \frac{-12 \pm \sqrt{144 + 24}}{4}$$

$\Rightarrow x = 0.2404$ or $x = -6.2404$

$\Rightarrow x = 0.24$ or $x = -6.24$ ... write roots to two decimal places

Activity 8.4

Solve each of the quadratic equations below.

1 $\frac{x^2}{2} + 2x - \frac{21}{2} = 0$

2 $\frac{x^2}{6} + \frac{11x}{6} = 2$

3 $x^2 - \frac{15x}{2} = -9$

4 $\frac{x^2 + x}{2} - 2x - 1 = \frac{x}{4}$

5 $\frac{2x^2}{3} - \frac{x^2 + 1}{2} = \frac{3 - x - x^2}{6}$

6 $\frac{2x^2}{7} - \frac{x}{2} = 1$

7 $\frac{x^2}{10} - \frac{2x}{5} = -\frac{1}{5}$

8 $\frac{2x^2 + 3}{5} - \frac{x + 2}{3} = 2$

9 $\frac{6x^2 + x}{4} + \frac{8x}{2} = \frac{7}{2}$

10 $\frac{5x^2 - 1}{6} + \frac{x + 7x^2}{2} = \frac{1}{3}$

Section 8E Solving Problems Using Quadratic Equations

Example

The product of two consecutive natural numbers is 870.

(i) Write an equation in words to represent this information.

(ii) Represent this information algebraically and solve the equation.

(iii) Find the two consecutive numbers.

Solution

(i) The 1st natural number multiplied by the next natural number equals 870.

(ii) Let x = 1st natural number

$x + 1$ = 2nd natural number

$$\therefore x(x + 1) = 870$$

$$\Rightarrow x^2 + x - 870 = 0$$

$$\Rightarrow (x + 30)(x - 29) = 0$$

$$\Rightarrow (x + 30) = 0 \quad \text{or} \quad (x - 29) = 0$$

$$\Rightarrow x = -30 \quad \text{or} \quad x = 29$$

(iii) As the numbers both must be natural numbers, i.e. not negative, then $x = 29$.

$\therefore x = 29$ is the 1st natural number

$\therefore x + 1 = 29 + 1 = 30$ is the 2nd natural number.

Note: If you find it hard to factorise a quadratic expression, you can always use the formula if you prefer.

Activity 8.5

1 The product of two consecutive odd natural numbers is 255.

(i) Write an equation in words to represent this information.

(ii) Represent this information algebraically and solve the equation.

(iii) Find the two consecutive odd natural numbers.

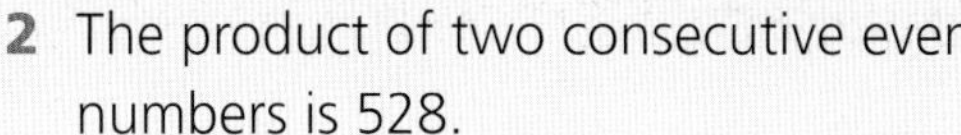

2 The product of two consecutive even numbers is 528.

(i) Write an equation in words to represent this information.

(ii) Represent this information algebraically and solve the equation.

(iii) Find all possible solutions for the two consecutive numbers.

3 The width of a rectangular flower bed is 0.5 m longer than half the length. The total area of the flower bed is 10 m^2.

(i) Draw a sketch of the flower bed, labelling the width and length.

(ii) Write a quadratic equation to represent this information.

(iii) Solve the quadratic equation.

(iv) Find the dimensions of the flower bed.

4 The height of a triangular window is 0.5 m shorter than its base. The total area of the window is 1.5 m^2.

(i) Write a quadratic equation to represent this information.

(ii) Solve the quadratic equation.

(iii) Find the dimensions of the triangular window.

(iv) Verify your answer.

5 The layout of a 300 m^2 suburban garden is shown below.

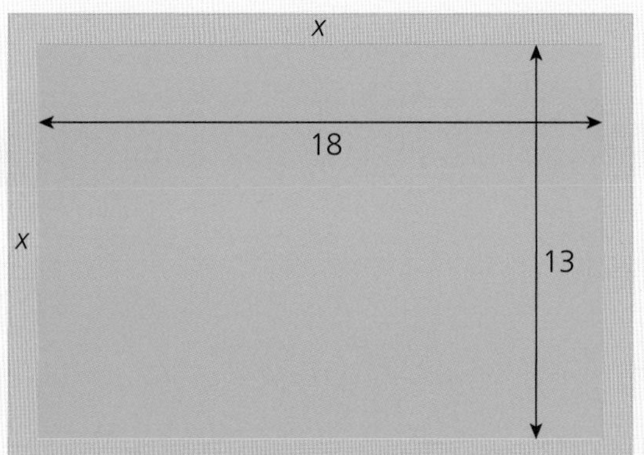

The inner area represents the lawn. The outer area represents the border which is x m wide.

(i) Write a quadratic equation to represent this information.

(ii) Solve the quadratic equation.

(iii) Find the width of the border.

(iv) Verify your answer.

6 Maria made a quilt that measures 1.5 m by 2 m. She wants to add a border using 4 m^2 of material. If she uses all the material and the border is the same width on all four sides:

(i) Draw a diagram to represent this information.

(ii) Write a quadratic equation to model this information.

(iii) Solve the quadratic equation.

(iv) Find the width of the border.

7 In a right-angled triangle ABC, the hypotenuse $[AB]$ is 8 cm longer than $[AC]$, and $[BC]$ is 7 cm longer than $[AC]$.

(i) Draw a sketch to represent this information.

(ii) Using Pythagoras' theorem, write a formula that represents this information and simplify to a quadratic equation.

(iii) Solve the quadratic equation.

(iv) Find the lengths of the three sides.

(v) Verify that the triangle is right-angled.

8 The volume of a box is 2250 cm^3. The box has a square bottom of length x cm and a height of 10 cm.

(i) Show that the volume (V) is represented by the equation $V = 10x^2$.

(ii) Find the width and length of the box.

(iii) Check your answer.

9 The volume of a cylindrical water storage tank is 1692.46 m^3.
The height of the tank is 11 m.

(i) Show that the volume (V) is represented by the equation $V = 11\pi r^2$.

(ii) Find the radius of the water tank, using 3.14 as the value of π.

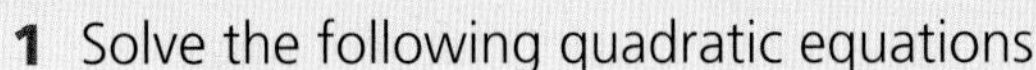

Revision Activity 8

1 Solve the following quadratic equations.

(a) $x^2 - 16x = 0$

(b) $3x^2 - 27x = 0$

(c) $2x^2 - 64x = 0$

(d) $4x^2 = 2x$

(e) $121x^2 - 49 = 0$

(f) $4x^2 - 144 = 0$

(g) $81x^2 = 64$

(h) $169x^2 = 196$

(i) $x^2 - 10x + 25 = 0$

(j) $x^2 - 13x + 36 = 0$

(k) $x^2 - 5x - 14 = 0$

(l) $x^2 + x - 56 = 0$

2 Factorise the following quadratic equations, then solve to find the solutions.

(a) $2x^2 + x - 15 = 0$

(b) $3x^2 - 11x + 6 = 0$

(c) $6x^2 + 7x + 2 = 0$

(d) $4x^2 + 11x + 7 = 0$

(e) $9x^2 - 9x - 4 = 0$

(f) $10x^2 - 51x - 22 = 0$

(g) $14x^2 + 47x - 7 = 0$

(h) $35x^2 - 8x - 3 = 0$

3 The roots of the quadratic equation $x^2 + 14x + c = 0$ are equal. Find the value of c.

4 Solve the following equation for y.

$$\frac{y}{10} - 1 = \frac{12}{5y}$$

5 The square of a number minus 12 equals four times the original number.

(a) Write a quadratic equation which represents this problem.

(b) Solve the quadratic equation.

(c) Find the value of the original number.

(d) Check your solution.

6 A garden measuring 13 m × 17 m has a pathway laid around it. When the pathway is laid, the total area including the pathway is 320 m^2.

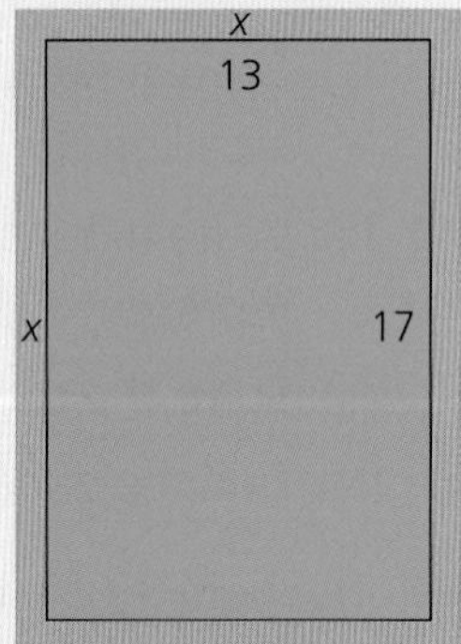

The diagram shows the layout of the garden. The inner area represents the lawn. The outer area represents the path which is x m wide.

(a) Write a quadratic equation to represent this information.

(b) Solve the quadratic equation.

(c) Find the width of the path.

(d) Check your answer.

Exam-style Questions

1 Solve for x: $3x^2 + 11x = 14$

JCHL 2013

2 Solve each of the following equations.

(a) $x^2 - 5x - 6 = 0$

(b) $8x^2 - 14x + 3 = 0$

(c) $\dfrac{2x+5}{3} - \dfrac{4x-1}{2} = -\dfrac{1}{2}$

(d) Find the roots of the equation $2x^2 - 7x - 6 = 0$. Give your answers correct to two decimal places.

JCHL 2012

KEY WORDS AND PHRASES

- **Roots**
- **Factors**
- **Quadratic formula**

Chapter Summary 8

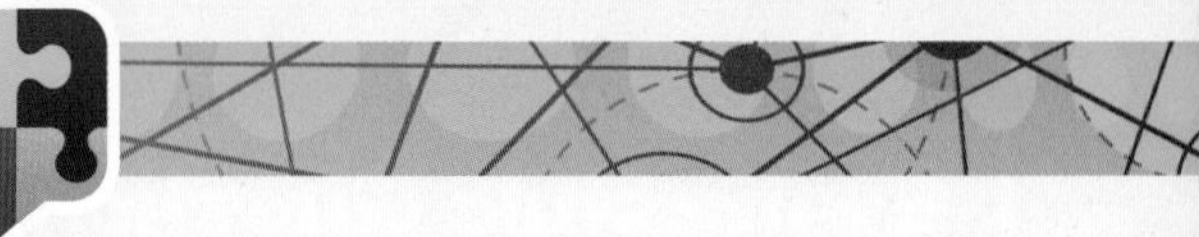

- The zero rule for multiplication: If $(a)(b) = 0$ then either $a = 0$ or $b = 0$.
- Solve equations of the form $ax^2 + bx + c = 0$ by
  - Factorising $ax^2 + bx + c$ if possible
  - Using the formula $x = \dfrac{-b \pm \sqrt{b^2 - 4ac}}{2a}$
- Get a quadratic equation from its roots by working backwards from the roots to the factors of $ax^2 + bx + c$.

Co-ordinate Geometry

Chapter 9

Learning Intentions

In this chapter, you will learn about:

LO: U.5, U.6, GT.5

- The length of a line segment (distance between two points)
- The mid-point between two given points
- The slopes of parallel lines and perpendicular lines
- The equation of a line, given the *y*-intercept and the slope
- The point of intersection of two lines

Historical Background

In mathematics, we seek connections between seemingly different topics. Geometry and algebra would appear to be very different parts of mathematics. However, in the early seventeenth century, two outstanding French mathematicians named René Descartes and Pierre de Fermat independently united the topics of geometry and algebra. This was a huge development and it is regarded as the birth of modern applied mathematics.

Pierre de Fermat

René Descartes

Co-ordinate geometry is where geometry and algebra come together.

Connections

- You will find a dynamic geometry software package particularly useful when working with co-ordinate geometry.

Section 9A Distance Between Two Points

We want to find the distance between two points on the co-ordinate plane. This is the same as finding the length of a line segment joining two points.

Remember:

- We write the length of line segment [*AB*] as $|AB|$.
- By Axiom 2, $|AB|$ is always positive. Length or distance is never negative.
- Length or distance is measured in mm, cm, m, km, etc. On the co-ordinate plane, we measure the distance in whatever the units are on the axes.

Example 1

Each of the line segments in the diagram is either horizontal or vertical. Find the length of each line segment (i) by using the grid and (ii) by using the co-ordinates.

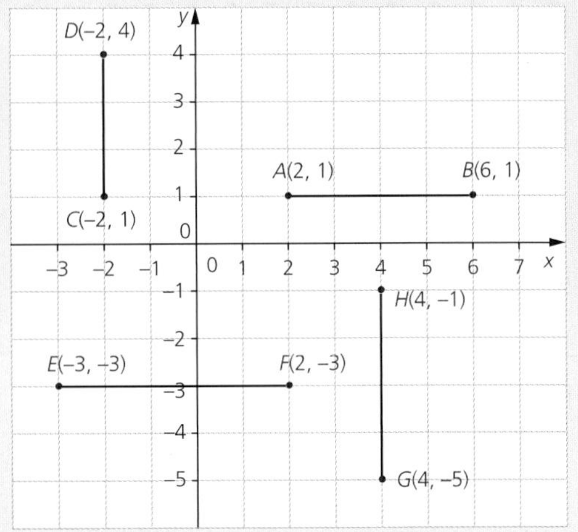

Solution

Line segment	Length using the grid	Length using co-ordinates
[AB]	Each square is 1 unit long 4 squares = 4 units	Horizontal line segment. Just subtract the x co-ordinates. $\lvert 6 - 2 \rvert = 4$ units Or $\lvert 2 - 6 \rvert = \lvert -4 \rvert = 4$ units
[CD]	3 squares = 3 units	Vertical line segment. Just subtract the y co-ordinates. $\lvert 4 - 1 \rvert = 3$ units Or $\lvert 1 - 4 \rvert = \lvert -3 \rvert = 3$ units
[EF]	5 squares = 5 units	Subtract the x co-ordinates. $\lvert -3 - 2 \rvert = \lvert -5 \rvert = 5$ units Or $\lvert 2 - (-3) \rvert = \lvert 2 + 3 \rvert = \lvert 5 \rvert = 5$ units
[GH]	4 squares = 4 units	Subtract the y co-ordinates. $\lvert -1 - (-5) \rvert = \lvert -1 + 5 \rvert = \lvert 4 \rvert = 4$ units Or $\lvert -5 - (-1) \rvert = \lvert -4 \rvert = 4$ units

Notice that we always take lengths to be positive, even when the answer is negative.

Summary

- To get the length of a line segment which is **horizontal**, **subtract the x co-ordinates** of the two points.
- To get the length of a line segment which is **vertical**, **subtract the y co-ordinates** of the two points.

Example 2

Each of the line segments in the diagram is either horizontal or vertical. Find the length of each line segment.

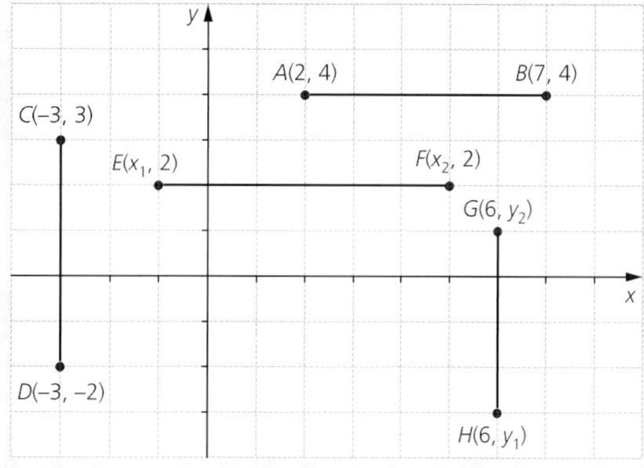

Solution

$|AB| = |7 - 2| = 5$ units ... subtract the x co-ordinates (either direction)

$|CD| = |3 - (-2)| = |3 + 2| = 5$ units ... subtract the y co-ordinates

$|EF| = |x_2 - x_1|$ units or $|x_1 - x_2|$ units ... subtract the x co-ordinates (either direction)

$|GH| = |y_2 - y_1|$ units or $|y_1 - y_2|$ units ... subtract the y co-ordinates

Key Point

In Example 2, we used variables for some of the co-ordinates. This is the way formulae have to be written so that they apply to any points in the plane.

Length of any Line Segment

Connections

- How do we find the distance between two points when the lines joining them are neither vertical nor horizontal?
- We will find Pythagoras' theorem very useful.

Example 3

Find the distance from $A(2, 1)$ to $B(6, 4)$.

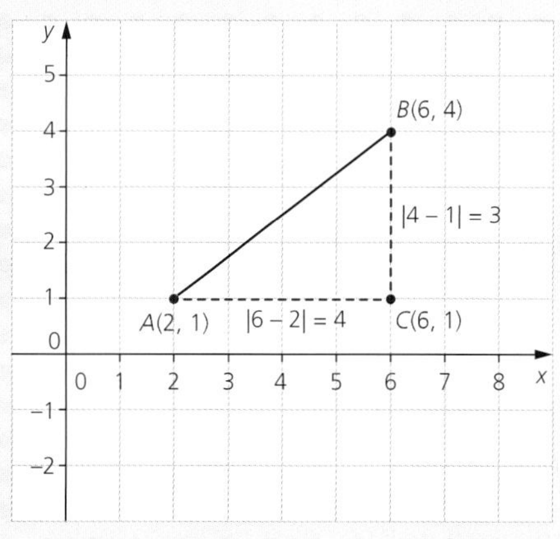

Solution

Draw $[AB]$. Then locate a point C so that ABC is a right-angled triangle.

BC is vertical, so subtract the y co-ordinates and $|BC| = |4 - 1| = 3$ units.

AC is horizontal, so subtract the x co-ordinates and $|AC| = |6 - 2| = 4$ units.

Now we can use Pythagoras' theorem to find $|AB|$.

$|AB|^2 = |AC|^2 + |BC|^2 = 3^2 + 4^2 = 25$

$\Rightarrow |AB| = \sqrt{25} = 5$ units

We can use this method for any two points. But we can also arrive at a formula using this method which will do it more quickly and efficiently. The formula must work for any pair of points. That is, the points must be **variable**, so we use variables for the co-ordinates. We usually let these points be called (x_1, y_1) and (x_2, y_2).

Example 4

Find the distance from $P(x_1, y_1)$ to $Q(x_2, y_2)$.

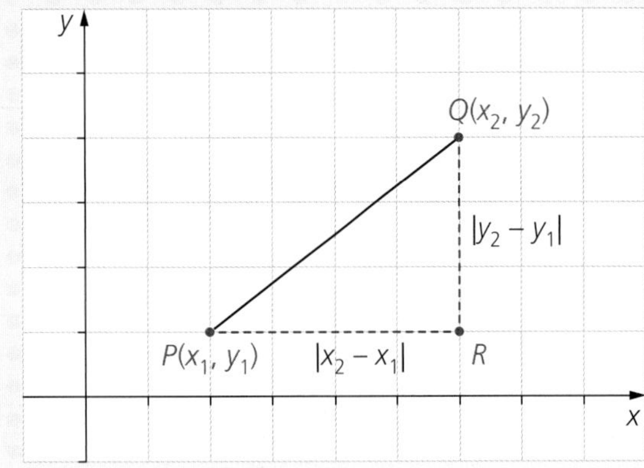

Solution

Draw [PQ]. Then locate a point R so that PQR is a right-angled triangle.

$|QR| = |y_2 - y_1|$ units

$|PR| = |x_2 - x_1|$ units

Now we can use Pythagoras' theorem to find $|PQ|$.

$|PQ|^2 = |PR|^2 + |QR|^2$

$= |x_2 - x_1|^2 + |y_2 - y_1|^2$

$\Rightarrow |PQ| = \sqrt{|x_2 - x_1|^2 + |y_2 - y_1|^2}$ units

Distance formula: The distance $|PQ|$ from $P(x_1, y_1)$ to $Q(x_2, y_2) = \sqrt{|x_2 - x_1|^2 + |y_2 - y_1|^2}$

This formula is given in the *Formulae and tables* booklet, page 18.

Using the formula in Example 3, the distance between $A(2, 1)$ and $B(6, 4)$ is:

$\sqrt{(x_2 - x_1)^2 + (y_2 - y_1)^2} = \sqrt{(6 - 2)^2 + (4 - 1)^2}$

$= \sqrt{(4)^2 + (3)^2} = \sqrt{16 + 9} = \sqrt{25} = 5$

Example 5

$A(0, -2)$, $B(4, 3)$ and $C(8, -2)$ are the vertices of a triangle.

Use the distance formula to verify that this is an isosceles triangle. You can leave your answers in surd (square root) form.

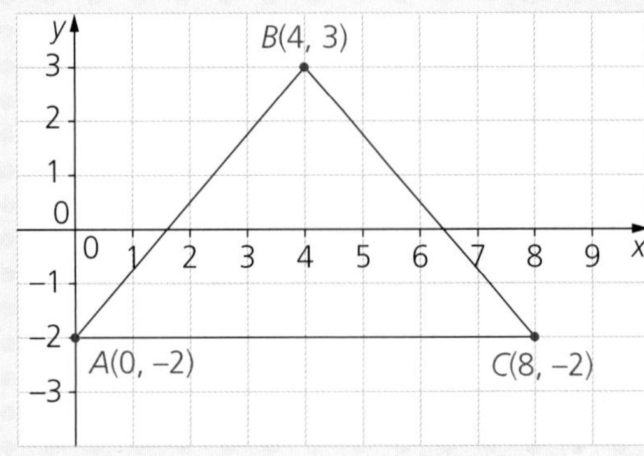

Solution

$|AB| = \sqrt{(x_2 - x_1)^2 + (y_2 - y_1)^2}$

$= \sqrt{(4 - 0)^2 + (3 + 2)^2}$

$= \sqrt{(4)^2 + (5)^2}$

$= \sqrt{16 + 25}$

$= \sqrt{41}$

$A(0, -2) = (x_1, y_1)$

$B(4, 3) = (x_2, y_2)$

$|BC| = \sqrt{(x_2 - x_1)^2 + (y_2 - y_1)^2}$

$= \sqrt{(4 - 8)^2 + (3 + 2)^2}$

$= \sqrt{(-4)^2 + (5)^2}$

$= \sqrt{16 + 25}$

$= \sqrt{41}$

$B(4, 3) = (x_2, y_2)$

$C(8, -2) = (x_1, y_1)$

Since $|AB| = |BC|$, this triangle is isosceles.

In this activity, you can leave your answers in square root (surd) form if the square root does not work out as a whole number.

1 Each of the line segments in the diagram is either horizontal or vertical. Find the length of each line segment (i) by using the grid and (ii) by using the co-ordinates. Copy and complete the table below.

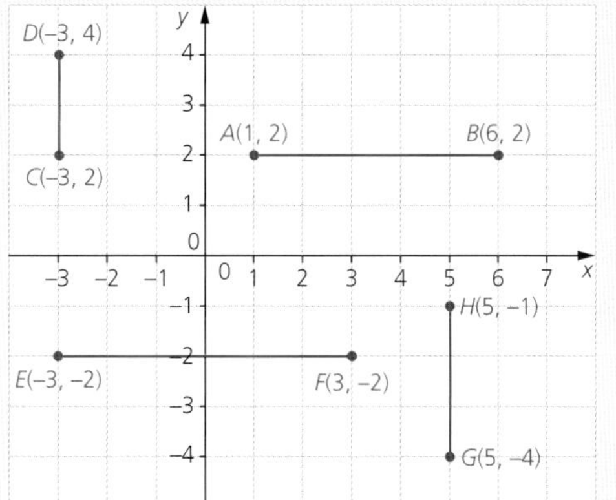

Line segment	Length using the grid	Length using co-ordinates
[*AB*]		
[*CD*]		
[*EF*]		
[*GH*]		

2 Find the length of each line segment (i) by using the grid and (ii) by using the co-ordinates.

Copy and complete the table below.

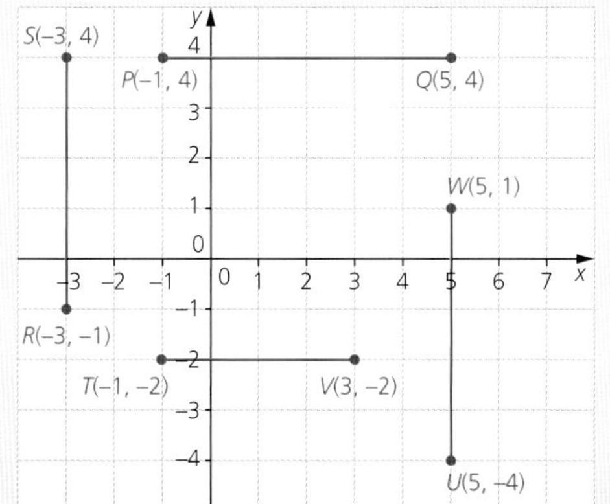

Line segment	Length using the grid	Length using co-ordinates
[*PQ*]		
[*RS*]		
[*TV*]		
[*UW*]		

3 Copy and complete the table below using the diagram.

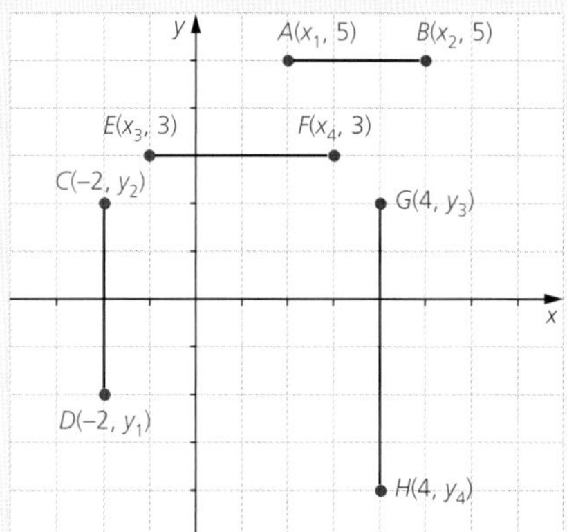

Line segment	Length using co-ordinates
[*AB*]	
[*CD*]	
[*EF*]	
[*GH*]	

4 Look carefully at the diagram.

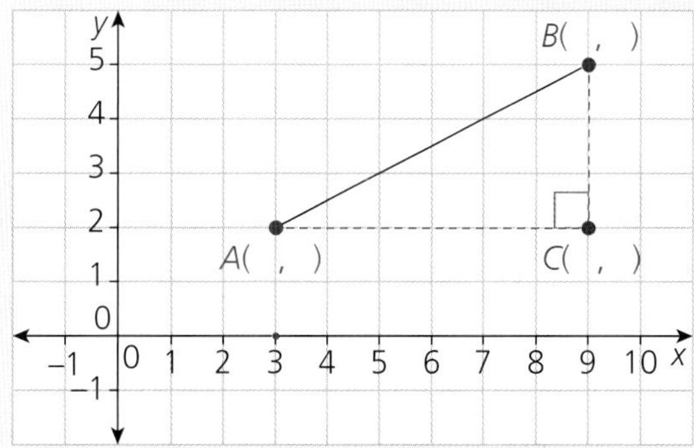

(i) Copy the diagram into your copybook. Fill in the co-ordinates of *A*, *B* and *C*.

(ii) Write down |*AC*| and |*BC*|.

(iii) Use Pythagoras' theorem to find the hypotenuse of the triangle *ABC*.

(iv) Use the distance formula to find |*AB*|.

5 For each of the following pairs of points:

(i) Draw them on a co-ordinate plane.

(ii) Find the distance between them.

(a) (0, 0) and (4, 5)

(b) (7, 4) and (1, 2)

(c) (4, 3) and (−3, 1)

(d) (1, 7) and (4, 5)

(e) (–5, –1) and (–2, 6)

(f) (–2, 3) and (–1, –1)

6 The triangle PQR has co-ordinates (–5, 3), (1, 6) and (4, 0) respectively.

(i) Show these points on a co-ordinate plane.

(ii) Use the distance formula to show that PQR is an isosceles triangle which is also right-angled.

7 $A(8, 1)$, $B(1, 6)$ and $C(-4, -1)$ are three points in the plane.

(i) Show these points on a co-ordinate plane.

(ii) Use the distance formula to find out if the triangle ABC is isosceles.

8 $P(0, 4)$, $Q(3, 2)$ and $R(9, -2)$ are three points.

(i) Show these points on a co-ordinate plane.

(ii) Use the distance formula to show that these points are collinear.

9 $A(-1, 5)$ and $B(-3, 2)$ are two points.

(i) Draw the line segment $[AB]$ on a co-ordinate plane.

(ii) Draw $[A'B']$, the image of $[AB]$ by reflection in the y-axis.

(iii) Find $|AB|$ and $|A'B'|$.

(iv) From your answer to part (iii), what observation can be made about reflection of this line segment in the y-axis?

10 $PQRS$ is a quadrilateral in the co-ordinate plane as shown below.

(i) Write down the co-ordinates of P, Q, R and S.

(ii) Work out whether the opposite sides of $PQRS$ are equal in length.

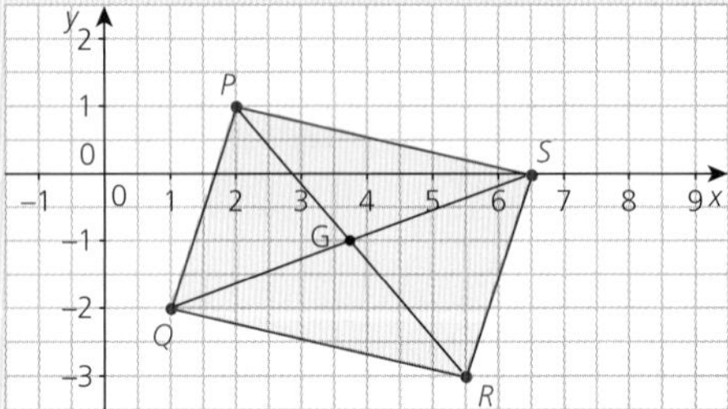

(iii) Is $PQRS$ a parallelogram? Justify your answer.

Section 9B Mid-point of a Line Segment

We now want to find the mid-point of a line segment $[AB]$ when we are given the co-ordinates of A and B.

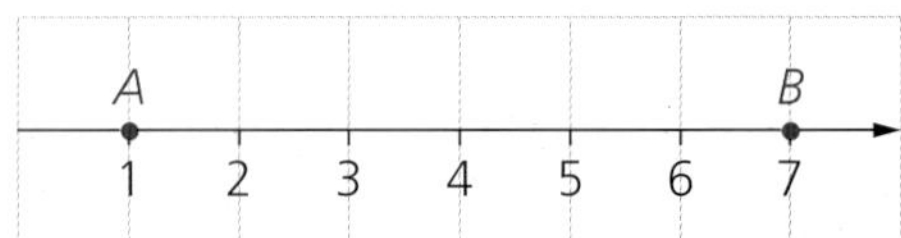

Look at this number line. Where is the mid-point between A and B?

It is obviously at the point 4, but can you think how you might calculate it from the numbers?

Connections

- This may remind you of the mean in statistics. How do you get the mean of 1 and 7?
- Add 1 and 7 and divide by 2 since there are two numbers. The answer is 4.

This is, in fact, how we get the mid-point between two points on the co-ordinate plane. Remember that co-ordinates are just numbers in pairs that we use to name points.

Example 1

Find the mid-point between $A(2, 1)$ and $B(6, 5)$.

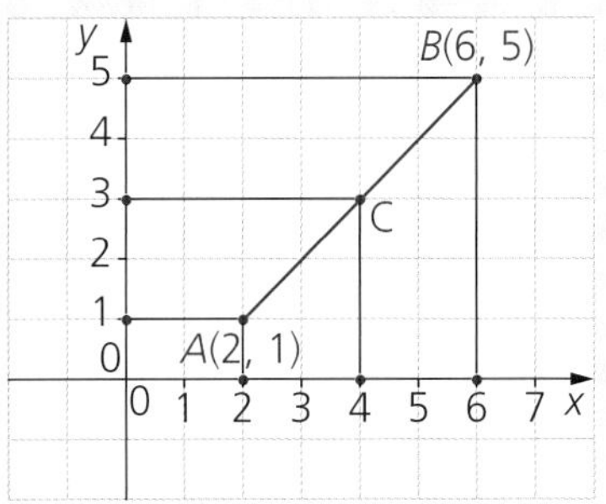

Solution

The x co-ordinates of the points are 2 and 6.

The mean of these is $\frac{(2 + 6)}{2} = 4$

The y co-ordinates are 1 and 5.

The mean of these is $\frac{(1 + 5)}{2} = 3$

Putting these together as a co-ordinate pair gives (4, 3), the mid-point of [AB].

We can put this into a neat formula:

The mid-point between $P(x_1, y_1)$ and $Q(x_2, y_2)$ is

$$\left(\frac{x_1 + x_2}{2}, \frac{y_1 + y_2}{2}\right)$$

This formula is given in the *Formulae and tables* booklet, page 18.

Note

You may find it easier to remember the mid-point as (the mean of the 'x's, the mean of the 'y's).

Example 2

Find the mid-point M between $A(-2, 5)$ and $B(4, -1)$.

Solution

$$M = \left(\frac{-2 + 4}{2}, \frac{5 - 1}{2}\right) = (1, 2)$$

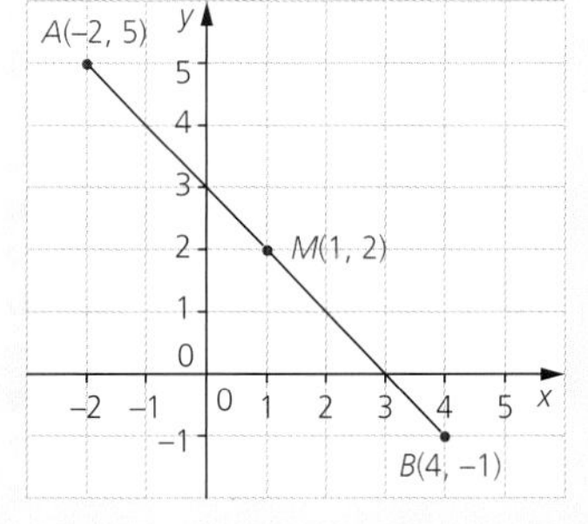

Activity 9.2

1 Draw each of the following pairs of points on a co-ordinate plane.

Find the co-ordinates of the mid-point between each pair.

(i) $A(2, 1)$ and $B(6, 7)$

(ii) $P(-4, 6)$ and $Q(4, 1)$

(iii) $O(0, 0)$ and $T(5, -2)$

(iv) $U(-4, -2)$ and $V(4, 2)$

(v) $C(1, 1)$ and $D(7, -3)$

(vi) $M(3, -3)$ and $N(7, 4)$

2 $P(-5, -4)$ and $Q(5, 4)$ are two points.

(i) Find S, the mid-point of [PQ].

(ii) Show that S is also the mid-point between $R(3, -7)$ and $T(-3, 7)$.

3 (i) Plot the following parallelogram $ABCD$ on a co-ordinate plane:

$A(-2, 4)$ $B(6, 4)$

$C(3, -2)$ $D(-5, -2)$

(ii) Find E and F, the respective mid-points of [AB] and [CD].

(iii) Show that the mid-points of the diagonals [AC] and [BD] are the same.

(iv) Find the mid-point of [EF].
What do you notice?

4 The following diagrams show end points of diameters on two circles.
Find the centre of each circle.

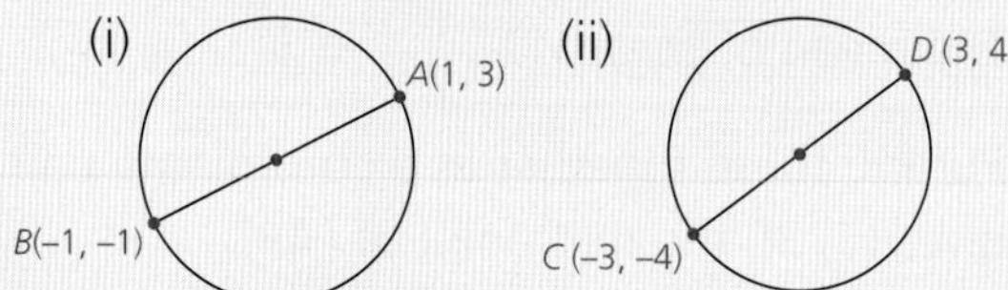

5 *ABCD* is a parallelogram.

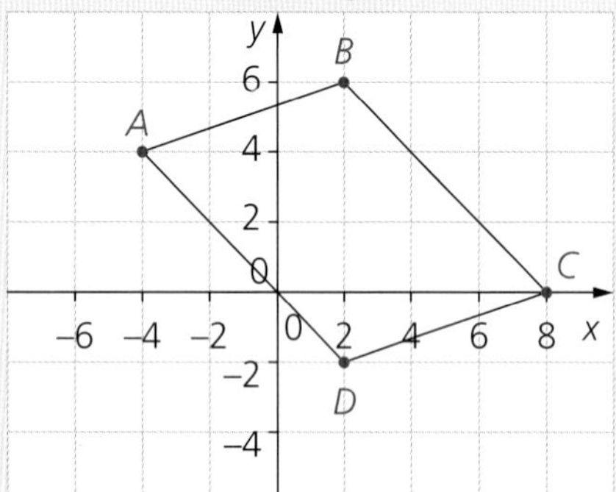

Show that the diagonals have the same mid-point.

6 (i) Find the mid-point *P* between *A*(–2, 5) and *B*(4, –7).

(ii) Verify your answer to part (i) by showing that |*AP*| = |*PB*|.

7 The map shows a ship at sea and a lighthouse situated at location (8,12).
Distances are measured (in kilometres) horizontally and vertically from the harbour and shown in co-ordinate form.

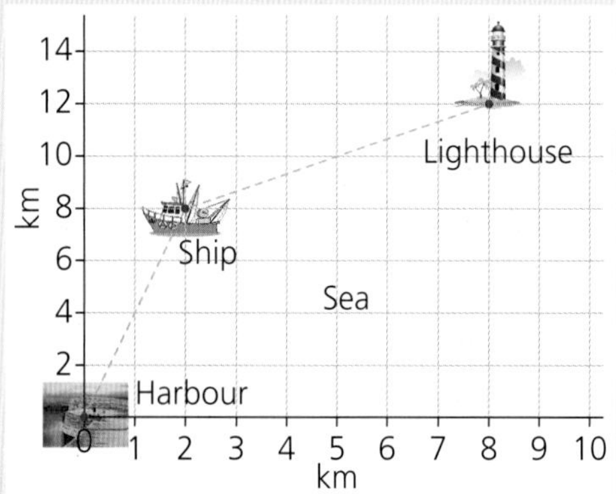

At 12.00 pm, the ship is at location (2, 8).

(i) How far is the ship from the harbour at 12.00 pm? Give your answer correct to one decimal place.

(ii) How far is the ship from the lighthouse at 12.00 pm? Give your answer correct to one decimal place.

(iii) Find the co-ordinates of the location *M*, which is half-way from the lighthouse to the ship.

(iv) Find the distance from the harbour to the lighthouse. Give your answer correct to one decimal place.

8 Copy the diagram into your copybook.

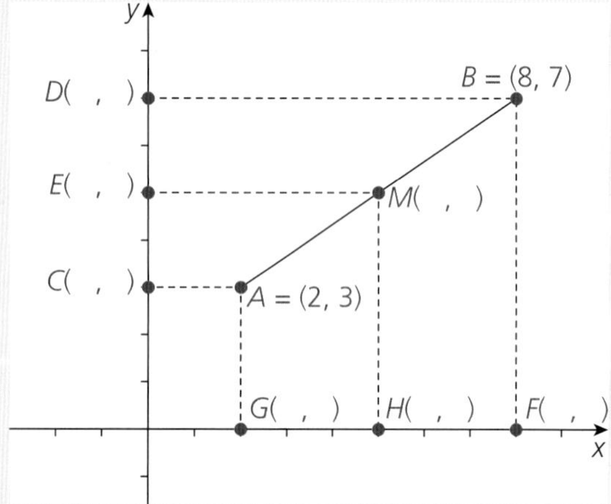

(i) Fill in the co-ordinates of points *D*, *C*, *G* and *F*.

(ii) *E* is the mid-point of [*DC*]. Fill in its co-ordinates on the diagram.

(iii) *H* is the mid-point of [*GF*]. Fill in its co-ordinates on the diagram.

(iv) Use the co-ordinates of *E* and *H* to fill in the co-ordinates of *M*, the mid-point of [*AB*].

(v) Write, in your own words, the formula for getting the co-ordinates of the mid-point between two points.

9 *A*(–2, 3) and *B*(5, 6) are two points.

(i) Show these points on a co-ordinate plane.

(ii) Calculate |*AB*|.

(iii) Find *M*, the mid-point of [*AB*].

(iv) Verify that *M* is the mid-point of [*AB*] by showing that |*AM*| = |*MB*|.

Section 9C The Slope of a Line

We have already worked with slopes in the Co-ordinate Geometry chapter of *Connect with Maths Introduction to Junior Cycle*.

- The slope of a line is measured as $\frac{\textbf{rise}}{\textbf{run}}$.

- **Positive** slopes go up from left to right:

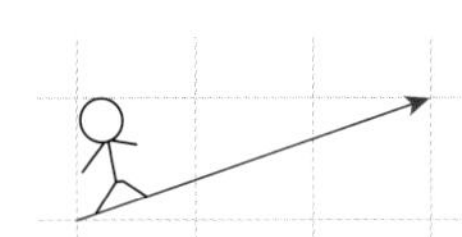

- **Negative** slopes go down from left to right:

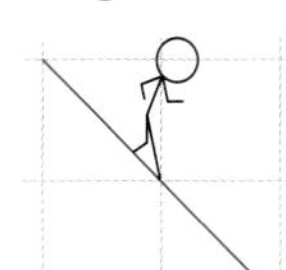

We can use a formula to calculate slope.

As with all formulae we use two points with variable co-ordinates: $P(x_1, y_1)$ and $Q(x_2, y_2)$.

On the diagram, we can see that the rise is the change in the y co-ordinates $= y_2 - y_1$ and the run is the change in the x co-ordinates $= x_2 - x_1$.

Put $\frac{\text{rise}}{\text{run}}$ to get this formula:

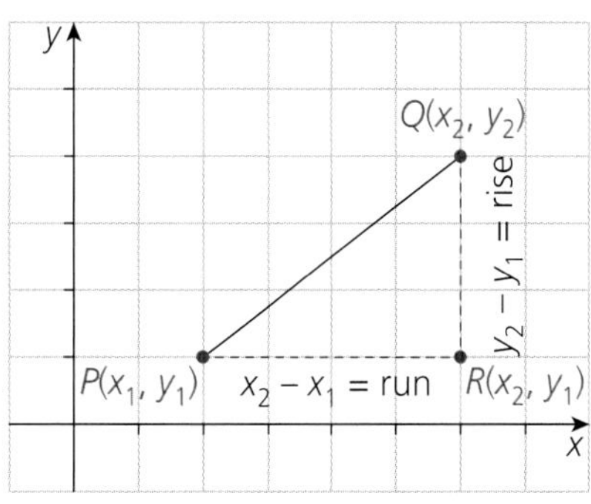

Slope formula

The slope of the line through $P(x_1, y_1)$ and $Q(x_2, y_2) = \frac{y_2 - y_1}{x_2 - x_1}$

This formula is given in the *Formulae and tables* booklet, page 18.
The letter m is used to denote the slope in formulae.

Example 1

Find the slope of the line which passes through $A(-3, -1)$ and $B(4, 5)$.

Solution

Let $A(-3, -1) = (x_1, y_1)$ and $B(4, 5) = (x_2, y_2)$

The slope of $AB = \frac{y_2 - y_1}{x_2 - x_1} = \frac{5 - (-1)}{4 - (-3)} = \frac{6}{7}$

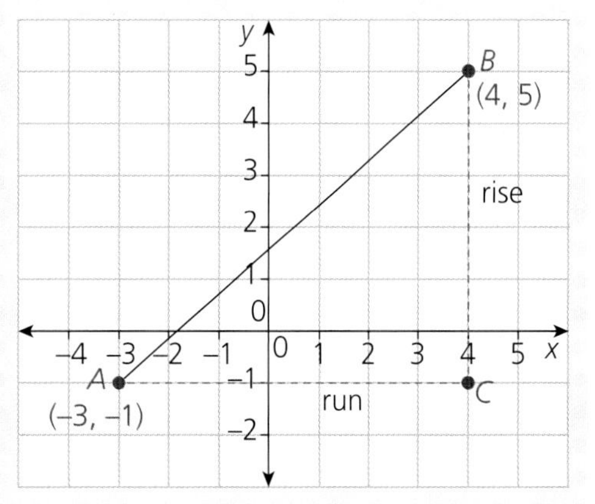

Parallel Lines

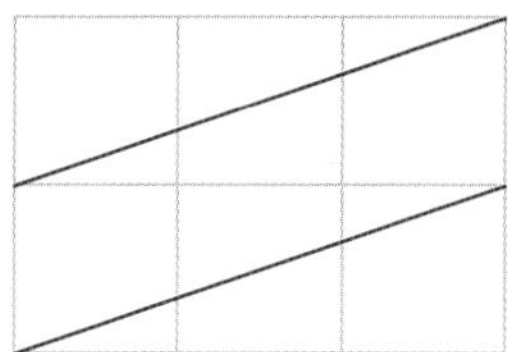

It is easy to see that two lines with equal slopes are parallel.

If l is a line with slope m_1 and p is a line with slope m_2, and l is parallel to p, then $m_1 = m_2$.

Key Point

$l \parallel p \Rightarrow m_1 = m_2$

The opposite is also true: if $m_1 = m_2$ then the lines are parallel, i.e. $l \parallel p$.

Perpendicular Lines

The relationship between the slopes of perpendicular lines is not obvious.

Look carefully at the example in the diagram.

$P(0, 0)$, $A(-3, 4)$ and $B(4, 3)$ are points.

The triangles ADP and BPE are congruent because each has a right angle included between sides 3 and 4 units long (SAS).

Thus the angles in each triangle are equal as marked on the diagram.

Thus, since $\alpha + \beta = 90°$, we have $|\angle APB| = 90°$ and so $AP \perp PB$.

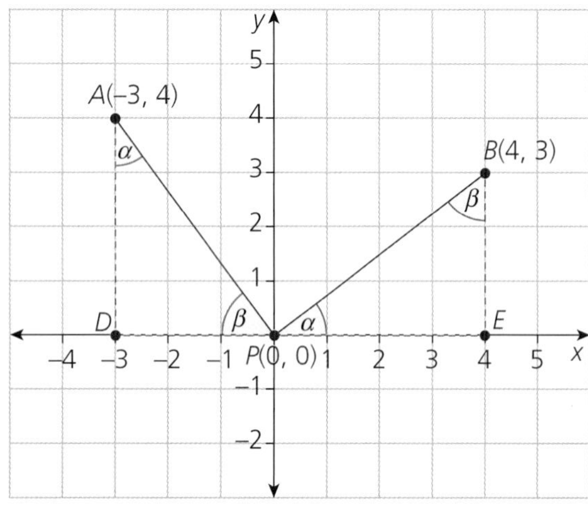

Now look at the slopes of AP and PB.

The slope of $PB = m_1 = \frac{3}{4}$

The slope of $AP = m_2 = -\frac{4}{3}$

If l is a line with slope m_1 and p is a line with slope m_2 and $l \perp p$, then $(m_1)(m_2) = -1$

To get a slope perpendicular to a given slope, turn the slope upside down and change the sign.

Key Point

$l \perp p \Rightarrow (m_1)(m_2) = -1$

The opposite is also true: If $(m_1)(m_2) = -1$, then the lines are perpendicular, i.e. $l \perp p$.

The slopes of all perpendicular lines behave like this.

Example 2

$A(1, 5)$ and $B(-3, 2)$ are two points in the plane.

(i) Find the slope of a line which is parallel to AB.

(ii) Find the slope of a line which is perpendicular to AB.

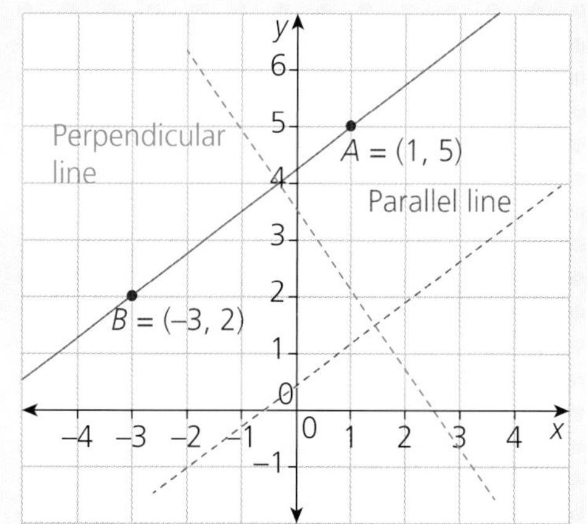

(i) Let $A(1, 5) = (x_1, y_1)$ and $B(-3, 2) = (x_2, y_2)$

Slope of $AB = \dfrac{y_2 - y_1}{x_2 - x_1} = \dfrac{2 - 5}{-3 - 1} = \dfrac{-3}{-4} = \dfrac{3}{4}$

Slope of any line parallel to $AB = \dfrac{3}{4}$

(ii) Slope of any line perpendicular to $AB = -\dfrac{4}{3}$

Note: We cannot measure the slope of a vertical line.

This is because the run = 0 for a vertical line. When we put $\dfrac{\text{rise}}{\text{run}}$, we would have to divide by zero, which we know we cannot do.

So we say that the slope of a vertical line is undefined.

Activity 9.3

1 Use the grid to find the slope of each line segment on the graph.

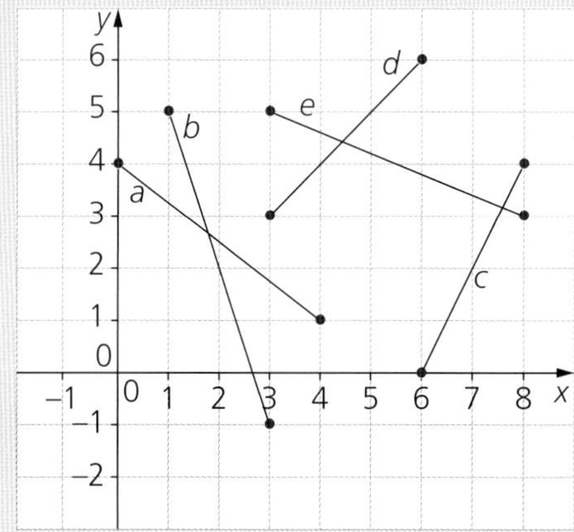

2 Find the slope of the line passing through these pairs of points:

(i) $(-1, 3)$ and $(4, 5)$

(ii) $(10, -4)$ and $(4, -7)$

(iii) $(3, -4)$ and $(0, 2)$

(iv) $(4, -5)$ and $(-1, 1)$

(v) $(2, -4)$ and $(-2, 6)$

(vi) $(-5, 12)$ and $(6, 8)$

(vii) $(0, -3)$ and $(-4, 2)$

(viii) $(-10, -1)$ and $(8, 5)$

3 On graph paper, draw lines with the following slopes:

(i) $-\dfrac{1}{2}$

(ii) 1

(iii) $\dfrac{3}{4}$

(iv) -2

4 Find the slope of each side of the quadrilateral *ABCD*. Show that its opposite sides are parallel.

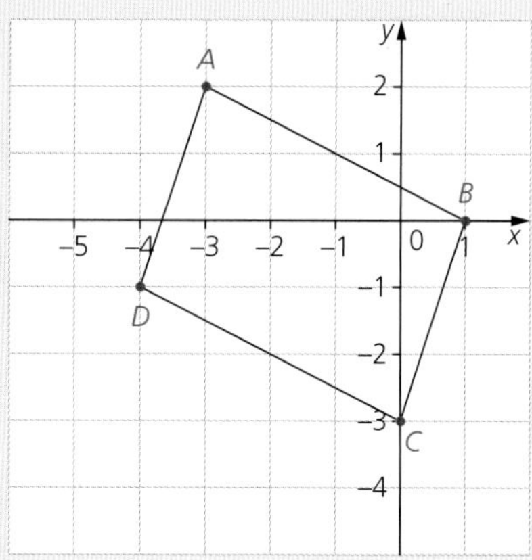

5 Copy and complete this table.

Slope of line k	Slope of line parallel to k	Slope of line perpendicular to k
$\frac{2}{3}$		
$\frac{5}{2}$		
$-\frac{3}{7}$		
$-\frac{1}{3}$		
4		
$-\frac{1}{6}$		
1		
−1		

6 *A*(−1, 2), *B*(3, 4) and *C*(4, −8) are three points.

(i) Plot these points on a co-ordinate plane.

(ii) Show that $AB \perp AC$.

7 *A*(1, −1), *B*(5, 3), *C*(1, 7) and *D*(−3, 3) are the vertices of a quadrilateral.

(i) Draw the quadrilateral on a co-ordinate plane.

(ii) Prove that opposite sides of the quadrilateral are parallel. What type of quadrilateral has this property?

(iii) Show that adjacent sides of *ABCD* are perpendicular. With this extra property, what type of quadrilateral is *ABCD*?

8 *FGHD* is a quadrilateral as shown.

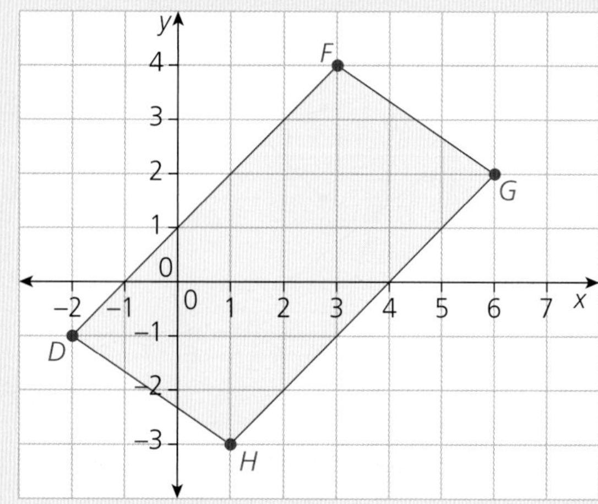

(i) Write down the co-ordinates of *F*, *G*, *H* and *D*.

(ii) Show that *FGHD* is a parallelogram.

9 The diagram shows a quadrilateral *ABCD*.

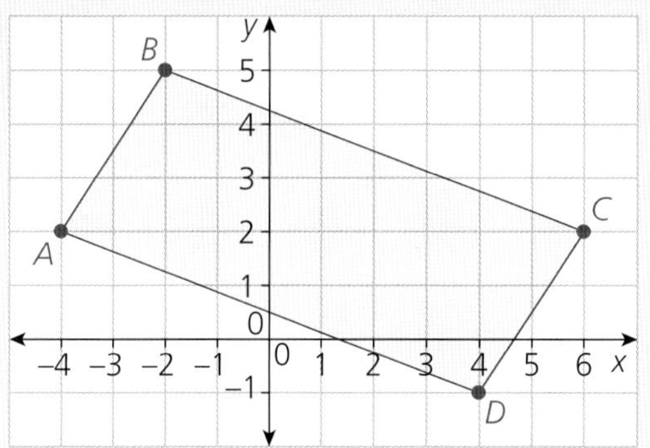

(i) Show that one pair of opposite sides are equal in length and are parallel.

(ii) Can you now conclude that *ABCD* is a parallelogram?

10 The picture shows a roadway sign (in Irish and English) on a road in Slane, Co. Meath. It indicates that the road will have a slope downwards of 10% for the next 500 metres.

(i) Express 10% as a fraction.

(ii) On squared paper, draw a line which has a slope of 10%.

(iii) Imagine a car or lorry driving down a road with the same slope. Why does the sign instruct drivers to use crawl gear?

Section 9D The Equation of a Line

The diagram shows a series of points all on the same straight line.

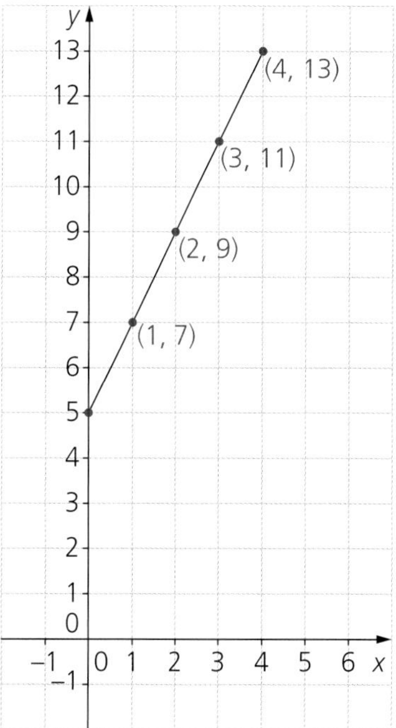

There is a **relationship** between the *x* co-ordinate and the *y* co-ordinate for each point, which is:

"Double the *x* co-ordinate and add 5 to get the *y* co-ordinate."

We can write this simply as: $y = 2x + 5$

Check this for each point. Every point on this line will follow this rule.

$y = 2x + 5$ is known as **the equation of the line**.

Key Point

The equation of a line is a rule which every point on the line obeys. This means that we can use the equation of a line to see if a particular point is on that line.

Notice that (0, 5) is where the line cuts the *y*-axis (called the ***y*-intercept**) and that the slope of the line is 2.

The equation $y = 2x + 5$ is said to be **in the form $y = mx + c$**.

The letter *m* is used to represent the slope.

Formula: The equation of the line *PQ* which passes through (0, *c*) and has slope *m* is $y = mx + c$.

This formula is given in the *Formula and tables* booklet, page 18.

Connections

The equation $y = 2x + 5$ could represent many situations.

Example: A plant has a height of 5 cm today (day 0). It grows at the rate of 2 cm per day. This is a linear pattern. Its height after d days is given by $h = 5 + 2d$ or $h = 2d + 5$.

On the graph on the previous page:

- (0, 5) is on the line: after 0 days, the height = 5 cm
- (1, 7) is on the line: after 1 day, the height = 7 cm
- (2, 9) is on the line: after 2 days, the height = 9 cm, etc.

The growth rate of the plant (2 cm per day) is shown by the slope of the graph.

Example 1

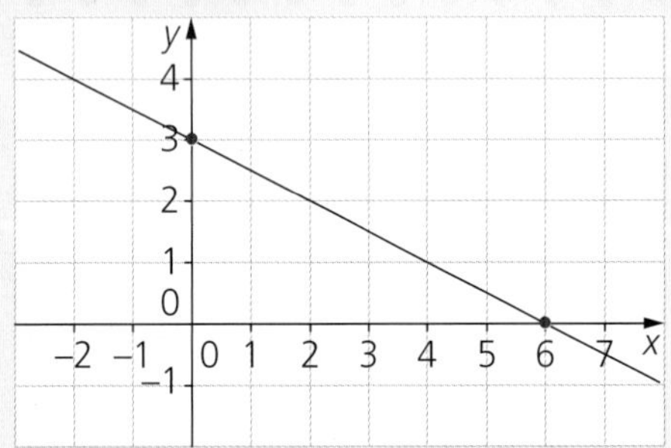

(i) Write down the co-ordinates of the y-intercept of the line shown.

(ii) Find the slope of the line.

(iii) Write the equation of the line.

Solution

(i) (0, 3) is the y-intercept. So $c = 3$

(ii) The slope of the line $= \frac{3-0}{0-6} = \frac{3}{-6}$

$= -\frac{1}{2} = m$

(iii) The equation of the line is $y = -\frac{1}{2}x + 3$

Example 2

A line passes through the point (0, −6) and has a slope = 2.

Find the equation of the line.

Solution

The formula is: $y = mx + c$

m = slope = 2

(0, −6) is (0, c) so $c = -6$

The equation of the line is $y = 2x - 6$

1 The line l passes through (0, 4) and has a slope = 2. Find the equation of l.

2 The line k passes through (0, –3) and has a slope = $\frac{1}{2}$. Find the equation of k.

3 The line n passes through (0, –1) and has a slope = 2. Find the equation of n.

4 The line q passes through (0, 5) and has a slope = $-\frac{1}{3}$. Find the equation of q.

5 The line r passes through (0, 2) and has a slope = $-\frac{1}{2}$. Find the equation of r.

6 Find the equations of the following lines.

	(y-intercept)	Slope of line
(i)	(0, 5)	–1
(ii)	(0, 3)	–2
(iii)	(0, –3)	–2
(iv)	(0, –2)	$\frac{1}{2}$
(v)	(0, 6)	$-\frac{1}{3}$
(vi)	(0, –2)	4
(vii)	(0, 50)	5
(viii)	(0, 30)	2

7 Write down the slope and y-intercept for each of these lines.

(i) $y = 4x + 3$
(ii) $y = -2x - 1$
(iii) $y = -x + 10$
(iv) $y = \frac{1}{2}x + 5$
(v) $y = -4x - 7$
(vi) $y = 10x - 100$

8 The table below gives the equations of four lines.

Line 1	$y = 2x + 3$
Line 2	$y = 5x + 4$
Line 3	$y = 2x - 1$
Line 4	$y = -x + 3$

Which two lines are parallel? Draw a sketch of these two lines on a co-ordinate plane.

9 The co-ordinate diagram below shows the lines n, p, r, and s.

The table shows the equation of each line.

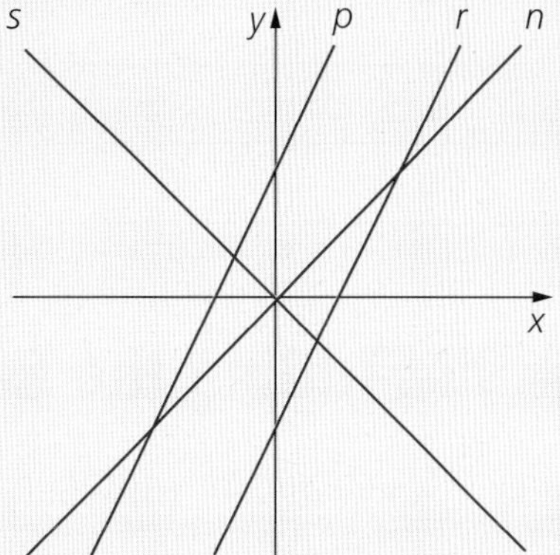

Equation	Line
$y = 2x - 4$	
$y = x$	
$y = -x$	
$y = 2x + 4$	

Copy the table and write the letters n, p, r and s into the table to match each line to its equation.

10 The table gives the equations of five lines.

Line 1	$y = 2x - 5$
Line 2	$y = -2x + 5$
Line 3	$y = 6x + 15$
Line 4	$y = 2x + 10$
Line 5	$y = \frac{1}{2}x - 5$

(i) Which lines are parallel? Give a reason for your answer. Draw a sketch of these two lines on a co-ordinate plane.

(ii) Which lines are perpendicular? Give a reason for your answer. Draw a sketch of these two lines on a co-ordinate plane.

(iii) The table shows some values of x and y for the equation of one of the lines. Which equation do they satisfy?

x	y
6	–2
8	–1
20	5

(iv) There is one value of x which will give the same value of y for Line 1 as it will for Line 3. Find, using algebra, this value of x and the corresponding value of y.

(v) Verify your answer to part (v) above.

Section 9E Finding the Equation of Any Line

The equation $y = 5 + 2x$ can be written in different ways:

$y - 2x = 5$ or $2x - y + 5 = 0$ are just two other ways.

- The following are examples of equations of lines:

$$3x + 5y = 6$$
$$2x - 7y + 8 = 0$$
$$x + y = 7$$
$$x = 5$$
$$y = -3$$

- Every line in the plane has an equation in the form $\boldsymbol{ax + by + c = 0}$.

The Equation of a Line in the Form $ax + by + c = 0$

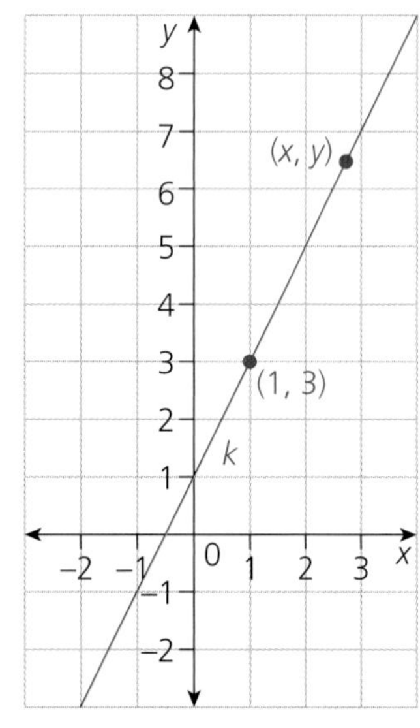

There is only one line which has a given slope and passes through a given point.

For example, there is **only one line** k in the plane that passes through (1, 3) and has a slope = 2.

The slope of a line is the same all along the line, so if we pick **any point** (x, y) on the line k, then the slope of the line $= \dfrac{y-3}{x-1}$.

The slope of this line also = 2

$\therefore$ we have the equation $\dfrac{y-3}{x-1} = 2$ which can be simplified:

$\Rightarrow \quad y - 3 = 2(x - 1)$

$\Rightarrow \quad y - 3 = 2x - 2$

$\Rightarrow \; 2x - y + 1 = 0$ … this is what the equation of a line often looks like.

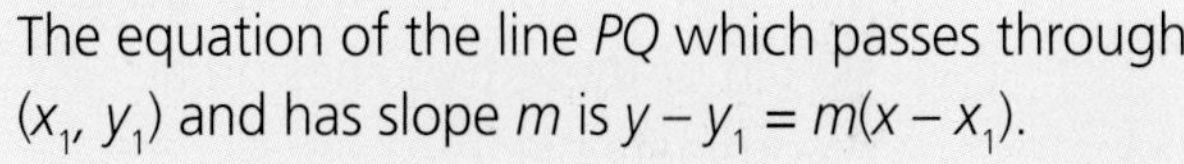

The equation of the line PQ which passes through (x_1, y_1) and has slope m is $y - y_1 = m(x - x_1)$.

This formula is given in the *Formulae and tables* booklet, page 18.

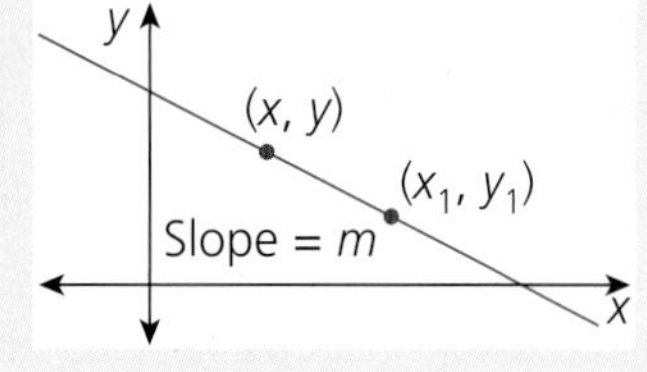

To use this formula, we need two pieces of information:

- one point on the line
- the slope of the line.

Example 1

A line l passes through the point $(-3, 2)$ and has a slope $= \frac{3}{4}$. Find the equation of the line.

Solution

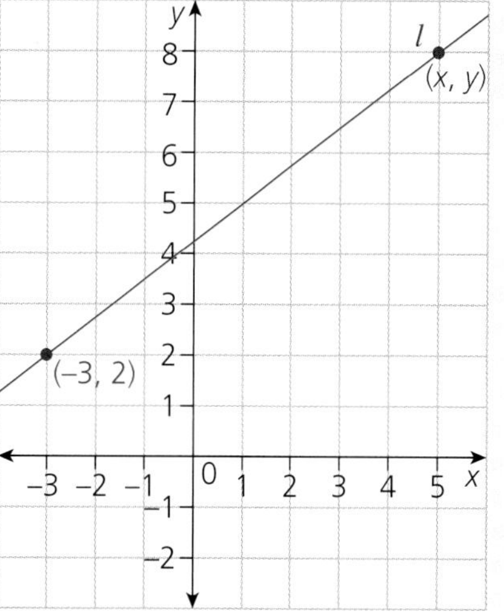

Use the formula $y - y_1 = m(x - x_1)$

The point (x_1, y_1) here is $(-3, 2)$, so $x_1 = -3$ and $y_1 = 2$.

$m = \frac{3}{4}$

Apply the formula:

$$y - 2 = \frac{3}{4}(x + 3)$$

$\Rightarrow \quad 4y - 8 = 3x + 9$ ... multiply both sides by 4

$\Rightarrow -3x + 4y - 8 - 9 = 0$

$\Rightarrow \quad -3x + 4y - 17 = 0 \quad$ or $\quad 3x - 4y + 17 = 0$

Equation of l is $3x - 4y + 17 = 0$.

Example 2

A line l passes through the points $(-2, 2)$ and $(1, -5)$. Find the equation of the line.

Solution

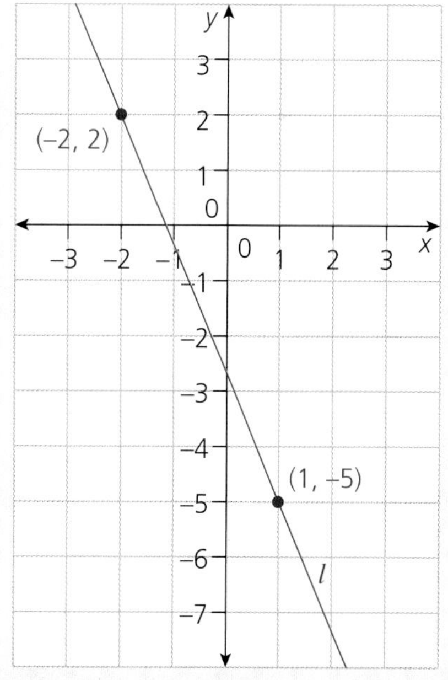

First we need to get the slope:

slope $= \frac{y_2 - y_1}{x_2 - x_1} = \frac{-5 - 2}{1 + 2} = -\frac{7}{3}$

Use the formula: $y - y_1 = m(x - x_1)$

We can use either of the points.

Use $(1, -5)$, so $x_1 = 1$ and $y_1 = -5$

$m = -\frac{7}{3}$

Apply the formula:

$$y + 5 = -\frac{7}{3}(x - 1)$$

$\Rightarrow \quad 3y + 15 = -7x + 7$ ... multiply both sides by 3

$\Rightarrow 7x + 3y + 15 - 7 = 0$

$\Rightarrow \quad 7x + 3y + 8 = 0$ is the equation of the line.

Key Point

Think of the equation of a line as a **rule** which every point on the line obeys; if a point is on the line, its co-ordinates will satisfy the equation of the line.

Key Point

When you are given the **equation** of a line, always try to imagine what its **graph** looks like.

Activity 9.5

1 Find the equations of the lines which have the following slopes and which contain the following points:

	Slope (m in the formula)	Point (x_1, y_1) in the formula
(i)	2	(1, 2)
(ii)	−3	(4, 2)
(iii)	1	(3, 1)
(iv)	−2	(1, 0)
(v)	4	(−1, 2)
(vi)	−5	(1, −2)
(vii)	3	(−1, 8)
(viii)	−1	(−1, −6)

2 Find the equations of the lines which have the following slopes and which contain the following points:

	Slope (m in the formula)	Point (x_1, y_1) in the formula
(i)	$\frac{1}{2}$	(1, −2)
(ii)	$-\frac{1}{3}$	(−4, 2)
(iii)	0	(−3, 1)
(iv)	$\frac{4}{3}$	(1, 0)
(v)	$\frac{4}{5}$	(1, −2)
(vi)	$-\frac{2}{5}$	(1, −2)
(vii)	3	(−1, 8)
(viii)	−4	(1, −6)

3 $C(0, 0)$ and $D(3, -2)$ are two points on a line. Find the equation of the line CD.

4 $P(-4, -4)$ is a point on a line which has a slope of $\frac{1}{3}$. Find the equation of the line.

5 $A(5, 0)$ and $B(3, 4)$ are two points.

(i) Find the equation of the line through A and B.

(ii) Investigate which of the following points are **not** on the line in part (i):
$C(4, 2)$ $D(1, 8)$ $E(3, 5)$ $F(-4, 7)$

6 Find the equation of the line which contains the point (0, 0) and has a slope of $\frac{3}{5}$.

7 The point M is the mid-point of the line segment $[BC]$. $B(3, 0)$ and $C(7, 6)$. 

Find the equation of:

(i) The line p that contains both points B and C.

(ii) The line containing point M, which has slope = 5.

(iii) The line containing the point (6, 6) and which is parallel to p.

Section 9F How to Draw a Line Given its Equation

To draw a line, we need two points on the line. **Any two points will do**, but we are often interested in the points where a line crosses the axes.

The points on the x-axis and the y-axis have special properties.

- Every point on the x-axis has a y co-ordinate = 0.

  Thus $y = 0$ is the equation of the x-axis.

- To find the point where a line crosses the x-axis, let $y = 0$ and find x.
  The point is $(x, 0)$.

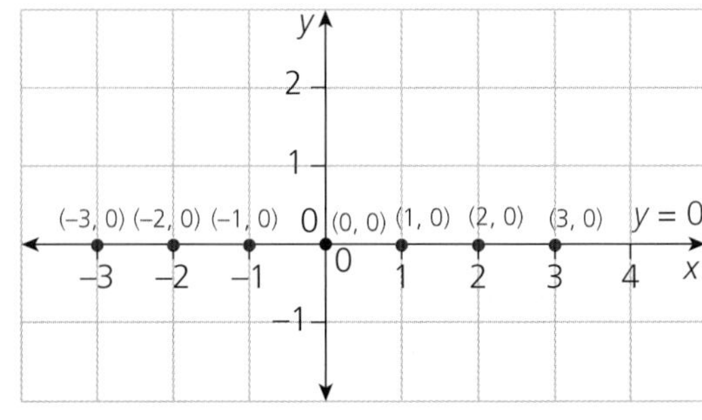

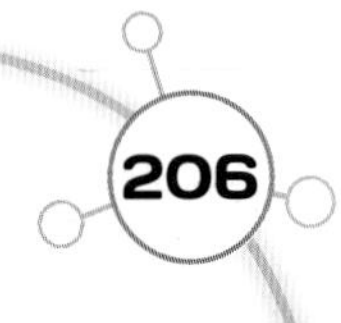

- Every point on the y-axis has an x co-ordinate = 0.

  Thus $x = 0$ is the equation of the y-axis.

- To find the point where a line crosses the y-axis, let $x = 0$ and find y. The point is $(0, y)$.

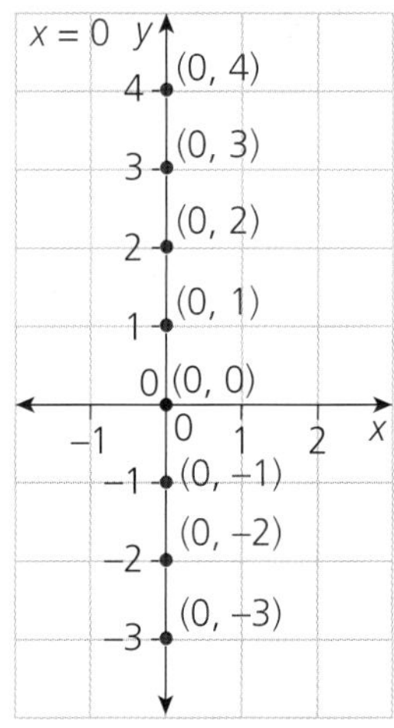

Example 1

(i) Find the points where the line $3x + 2y = 12$ cuts the x-axis and the y-axis.

(ii) Hence, sketch the line on a co-ordinate plane.

(iii) Is (2, 4) on this line?

Solution

(i) Let $y = 0$

$3x + 2(0) = 12$

$3x = 12$

$\therefore \quad x = 4$

Crosses x-axis at (4, 0)

Let $x = 0$

$3(0) + 2y = 12$

$2y = 12$

$\therefore \quad y = 6$

Crosses y-axis at (0, 6)

(ii)

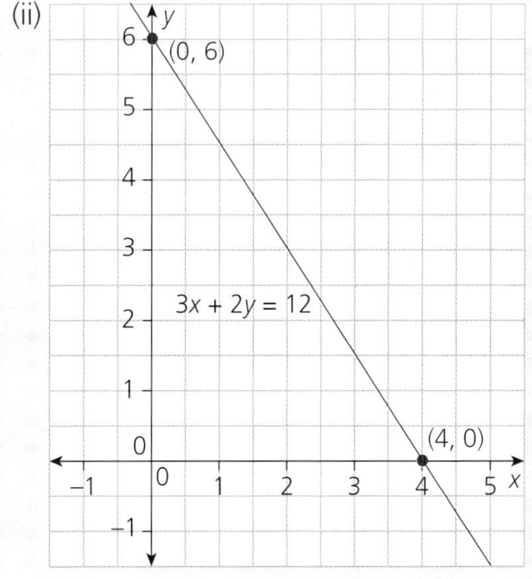

(iii) Substitute (2, 4) into the equation $3x + 2y = 12$

$3(2) + 2(4) = 6 + 8 = 14 \neq 12$

$\therefore$ (2, 4) is not on this line. (A look at the graph confirms this.)

Connections

In chapter 10, you will learn how to use algebra to find the point of intersection of two lines.

Example 2

Sketch the line $x = 2y$.

Solution

Find two points on the line:

Let $x = 0$

$\therefore \quad 0 = 2y$

$\therefore \quad y = 0$

$\therefore$ Point (0, 0) is on the line.

Let $x = 4$

$\therefore \quad 4 = 2y$

$\therefore \quad y = 2$

$\therefore$ Point (4, 2) is on the line.

This is the line:

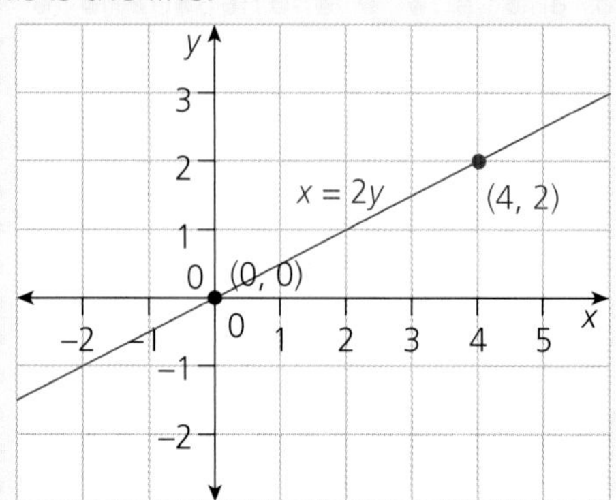

Every line with an equation of the form $y = mx$ passes through the origin. These lines have a slope $= m$.

Example 3

Sketch the line $y = -3$.

Solution

The line $y = -3$ is made up of all the points which have a y co-ordinate of -3.

For example: $(0, -3)$, $(1, -3)$, $(2, -3)$, $(-1, -3)$, $(-\frac{1}{4}, -3)$, etc.

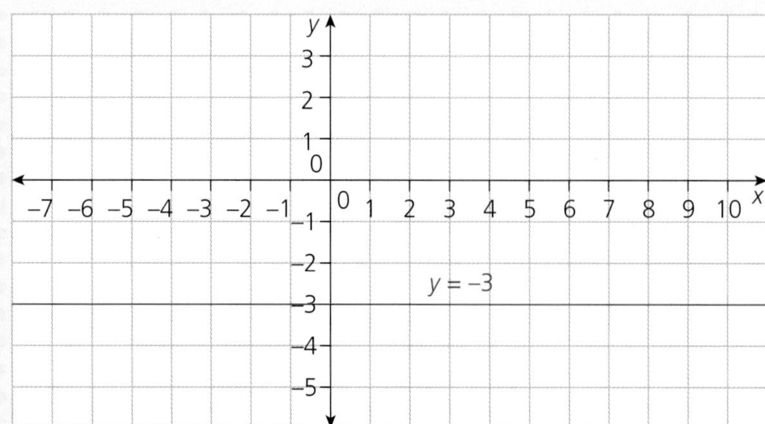

Every line with an equation of the form $y = b$ is parallel to the x-axis. These lines are horizontal and so each of them has a slope $= 0$.

Example 4

Sketch the line $x = 2$.

Solution

The line $x = 2$ is made up of all the points which have an x co-ordinate of 2.

For example: (2, 0), (2, 1), (2, 2), (2, −1), $\left(2, -\frac{1}{2}\right)$, etc.

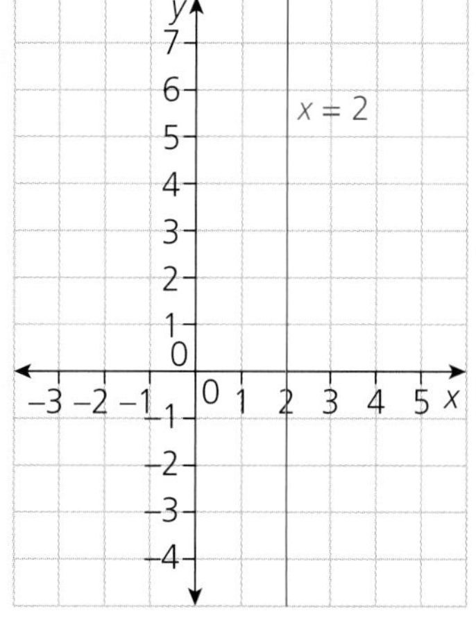

Every line of the form $x = a$ is parallel to the y-axis.
These lines are vertical and so have an undefined slope.

Activity 9.6

1 For each of the lines below:

(i) Find three points on the line.
(ii) Draw a graph of the line.
(iii) Find the slope of the line.

(a) $x + y = 5$ (c) $y - 3x = 9$
(b) $2x + y = 6$ (d) $4x + y = 8$

2 For each of the lines below:

(i) Find three points on the line.
(ii) Draw a graph of the line.
(iii) Find the slope of the line.

(a) $3x - y = 6$ (c) $x + 3y = 9$
(b) $x - 2y = 6$

3 Which of the following points is on the line $3x + 2y = 12$?

$A(4, 0)$, $B(2, 4)$, $C(2, 3)$, $D(6, -3)$, $E(1, 5)$

4 Which of the following points is on the line $4x - y = 8$?

$A(4, 8)$, $B(1, 4)$, $C(3, 4)$, $D(2, 0)$, $E(3, -4)$

5 (i) Plot the points (−1, 3), (0, 3), (2, 3), (3, 3), (4, 3), (5, 3).

(ii) Join the points. What type of line is this? What is the slope of this line?

(iii) Give a rule which all the points on this line obey (i.e. give the equation of the line).

6 (i) Plot the points (2, 3), (2, 2), (2, 1), (2, 0), (2, −1), (2, −2).

(ii) Join the points. What type of line is this?

(iii) The slope of this line is undefined. Explain why.

(iv) Give a rule which all the points on this line obey.

7 (i) Sketch the line $3x - 2y = 6$ in the Cartesian (co-ordinate) plane.

(ii) Is (2, −1) on the line?

8 (i) Sketch the line $4x + y = 2$ in the Cartesian (co-ordinate) plane.

(ii) Is (1, −2) on the line?

9 Sketch the line $x = y$ on a co-ordinate plane.

10 Plot these lines on the same co-ordinate plane (label each line):

$x = 3$, $y = 0$, $x = -4$, $y = -3$

Co-ordinate Geometry

Section 9G Finding the Slope of a Line From its Equation

You need to be able to read the slope of a line from its equation. This is easy if the equation is in the form $y = mx + c$. In this case, the slope is the coefficient of the x term.

When the equation is in the form $ax + by + c = 0$ (the standard form of the equation), we have to change it to the form $y = mx + c$.

Example 1

Find the slope of the line $3x + 2y + 6 = 0$.

Solution

$3x + 2y + 6 = 0$

$\Rightarrow \quad 2y = -3x - 6$

$\Rightarrow \quad y = -\frac{3}{2}x - 3$

$\Rightarrow$ slope $m = -\frac{3}{2}$ ... coefficient of x

Key Point

Notice that the slope of $3x + 2y + 6 = 0$ is $\frac{-3}{2}$ (the negative of the coefficient of the x term divided by the coefficient of the y term).
We can use this fact if the equation is in the form $ax + by + c = 0$:

The slope of $ax + by + c = 0$ is $\frac{-a}{b}$

Example 2

Find the slope of the line $5x - 3y + 7 = 0$.

Solution

Method 1

$5x - 3y + 7 = 0$

$\Rightarrow \quad -3y = -5x - 7$

$\Rightarrow \quad y = \frac{-5}{-3}x - \frac{7}{-3}$

$\Rightarrow \quad y = \frac{5}{3}x + \frac{7}{3}$

$\Rightarrow \quad$ slope $m = \frac{5}{3}$

Method 2

$5x - 3y + 7 = 0$ is of the form $ax + by + c = 0$

$a = 5$ and $b = -3$

slope $= \frac{-a}{b} = \frac{-5}{-3} = \frac{5}{3}$

Example 3

State whether the lines k: $3x - 4y + 6 = 0$ and p: $4x + 3y - 5 = 0$ are
(i) parallel (ii) perpendicular or (iii) neither parallel nor perpendicular.

Solution

Find the slopes of the lines k and p and compare them.

k: $3x - 4y + 6 = 0$ Slope of $k = m_1 = \frac{-a}{b} = \frac{-3}{-4} = \frac{3}{4}$

p: $4x + 3y - 5 = 0$ Slope of $p = m_2 = \frac{-a}{b} = -\frac{4}{3}$

$(m_1)(m_2) = \frac{3}{4} \times -\frac{4}{3} = -1 \Rightarrow$ the lines k and p are perpendicular.

Example 4

(i) Write down the equations of three lines which are parallel to the line:
k: $4x - y + 5 = 0$.

(ii) Write down the equations of three lines which are perpendicular to the line:
p: $2x + 5y - 6 = 0$.

Solution

(i) $4x - y + 5 = 0$ is **parallel** to any line with the same ratio of x coefficient to y coefficient.
Three such lines are: $4x - y + 3 = 0$; $4x - y + 10 = 0$; $4x - y + 50 = 0$.

(ii) $2x + 5y - 6 = 0$ is **perpendicular** to any line with the coefficients of the x and y terms switched and one sign changed.
Three such lines are: $5x - 2y + 3 = 0$; $5x - 2y + 6 = 0$; $-5x + 2y + 22 = 0$.

Activity 9.7

1 The line p has the equation $2x + 3y + 6 = 0$.
- (i) Write the equation in the form $y = mx + c$.
- (ii) Write down the slope of p.

2 Find the slopes of the following lines.
- (i) $y = 3x + 7$
- (ii) $y = \frac{1}{2}x - 20$
- (iii) $2x + y = 12$
- (iv) $3x - 2y + 4 = 0$
- (v) $x - 4y = 0$
- (vi) $y = 2$
- (vii) $2x - 7y = 15$
- (viii) $x = 3$
- (ix) $2x = 4y + 7$
- (x) $y + 3x - 2 = 0$

3 $3x - 2y + 12 = 0$ is the equation of a line k.
- (i) Find the slope of this line.
- (ii) Write down an equation of a line which is parallel to k.
- (iii) Write down an equation of a line which is perpendicular to k.

4 Write down the equations of three lines which are parallel to $2x - y + 3 = 0$.

5 Write down the equations of three lines which are perpendicular to $3x + 4y - 6 = 0$.

6 For each of the following pairs of lines, say whether they are (a) parallel, (b) perpendicular, (c) neither parallel nor perpendicular.

(i) $2x - 3y + 12 = 0$ and $3x - 2y + 11 = 0$

(ii) $2x - 5y + 10 = 0$ and $2x - 5y - 2 = 0$

(iii) $x - y + 3 = 0$ and $y + x - 1 = 0$

(iv) $x - 2 = 0$ and $x + 3 = 0$

(v) $y = 0$ and $y - 5 = 0$

(vi) $y = 0$ and $x = 0$

(vii) $5x - 2y + 12 = 0$ and $5x + 2y + 1 = 0$

7 In the diagram, the lines p, q and r are parallel to the x-axis and the line n is parallel to the y-axis.

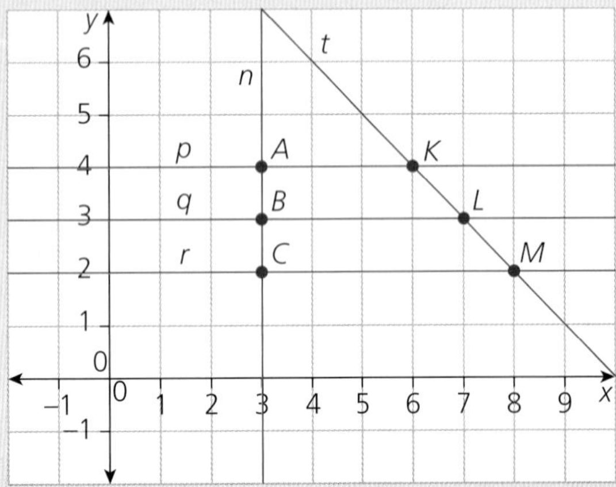

(i) Write down the equations of the lines p, q, r and n.

(ii) Write down the co-ordinates of A, B and C and verify that $|AB| = |BC|$.

The line t intersects the lines p, q and r at the points K, L and M respectively.

(iii) Use the distance formula to verify that $|KL| = |LM|$.

8 In the co-ordinate diagram shown, the lines p and q are parallel, and so are the lines m and n.

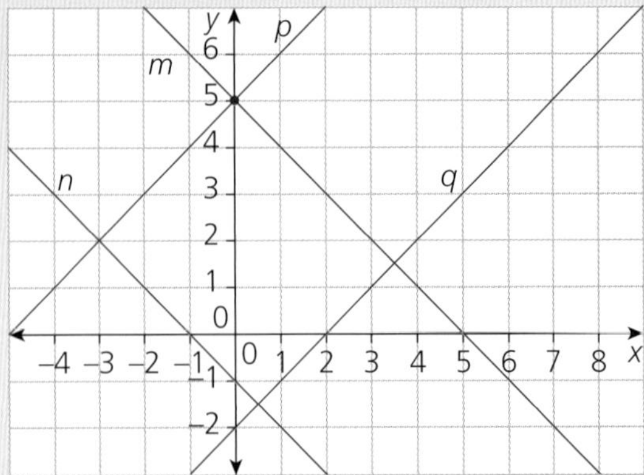

The equations of the four lines are given in the table.

Equation	Line
$x + y = -1$	
$x - y = -5$	
$x + y = 5$	
$x - y = 2$	

Copy and complete the table by matching the lines to their equations.

9 The equation of the line k is $5x - 2y = 6$.

(i) Find the slope of k.

(ii) Find the equation of the line p which is perpendicular to k and contains the point $(-2, 5)$. Give your answer in the form $ax + by + c = 0$.

10 Find the equation of the line which is parallel to $3x - 2y = 5$ and which contains the point $(3, -4)$.

11 Find the equation of the line which is perpendicular to the line $4x + y = 10$ and which contains the point $(-1, 2)$.

12 Find the equation of the line which is parallel to $x = 3y$ and which contains the point $(1, 0)$.

13 Find the equation of the line which is perpendicular to $3x - 2y = 5$ and which contains the point $(2, 2)$.

1 (a) Plot the following points on a co-ordinate plane.

A	B	C	D	E
(–2, 0)	(3, 0)	(6, –3)	(1, –3)	(0, 3)

(b) Calculate the mid-point of $[EC]$.

(c) Find the slope of BC.

(d) Write down the equation of BC in the form $y = mx + c$.

(e) Find the slope of AD.

(f) Write the equation of the line AD in the form $ax + by + c = 0$.

(g) What type of quadrilateral is $ABCD$? Justify your answer.

(h) Say whether the triangles ABC and ADC are congruent. Give a reason for your answer.

(i) What is the ratio of the area of the triangle ABC to the area of the quadrilateral $ABCD$? Justify your answer.

2 $A(3, -2)$ and $B(-4, 5)$ are two points.

(a) Find $|AB|$. Express your answer as a surd.

(b) Find the mid-point of $[AB]$.

(c) Find the slope of AB.

(d) Find the equation of AB.

3 (a) Find the equation of the line l which passes through $(3, -1)$ and has slope $= \frac{2}{3}$.

(b) Draw a sketch of l.

4 The equation of the line q is $3x - 2y = 6$.

(a) Find the slope of q.

(b) Find the equation of the line m which is perpendicular to q and contains the point $(1, -3)$. Give your answer in the form $ax + by + c = 0$.

5 The quadrilateral $ABCD$ is shown in the diagram.

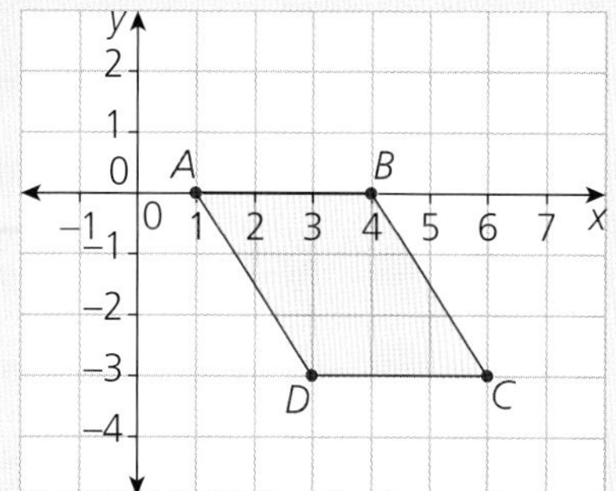

(a) Show that $ABCD$ is a parallelogram.

(b) Find the equations of the lines containing the two diagonals $[AC]$ and $[BD]$.

(c) Find the point of intersection of the diagonals.

6 (a) l is the line $3x + 2y + 18 = 0$. Find the slope of l.

(b) The line k is perpendicular to l and cuts the x-axis at the point $(7, 0)$. Find the equation of line k.

7 The map shows part of a town. Distances are measured (in kilometres) horizontally and vertically from the Train Station, at (0, 0), and shown in co-ordinate form.

(a) First Street and Second Street run from east to west. Write down the equations of First Street and Second Street.

(b) Fifth Avenue runs from north to south. Write down the equation of Fifth Avenue.

(c) Transverse Road runs through (0, 6) and (4, 0). Find its equation.

(d) Verify that $|TU| = |UV|$.

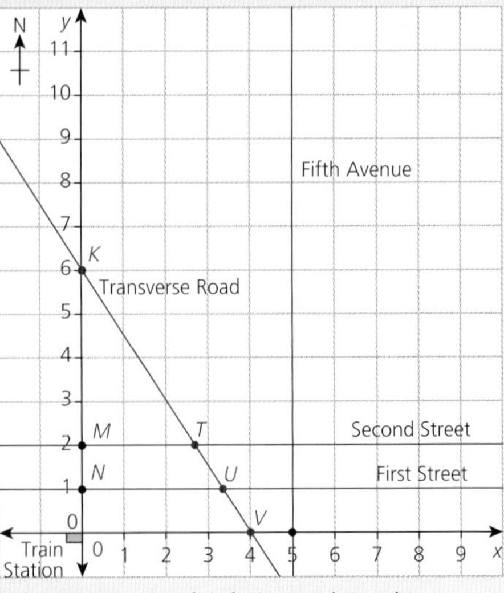

8 The diagram shows a ship's path. It has passed through location P which is 30 km due west of a lighthouse at L. It has also passed through location Q.

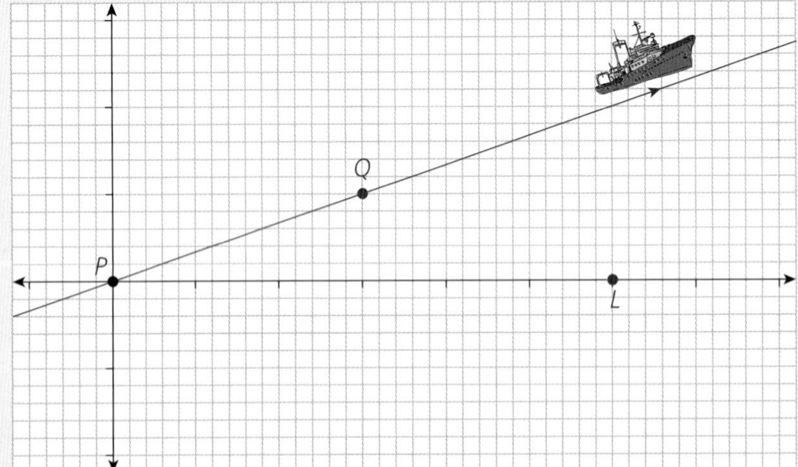

(a) Copy the diagram and draw in a set of co-ordinates that takes the point P as the origin, the line east–west through P as the x-axis, and kilometres as units.

(b) Fill in the co-ordinates of Q and L on your diagram.

(c) Find the distance from Q to the lighthouse correct to three decimal places.

(d) Find the equation of the line along which the ship is moving.

(e) Show by calculation that the ship also passes through location (36, 12).

(f) Construct accurately the point R on the ship's path which is closest to the lighthouse. Show all your construction lines clearly.

(g) Write in the co-ordinates of R as accurately as you can and find its distance from the lighthouse.

(h) Find the direction in which the ship is travelling.

Exam-style Question

1 The co-ordinate diagram below shows the lines q, r, s, and t.
q is parallel to s, and r is parallel to t.

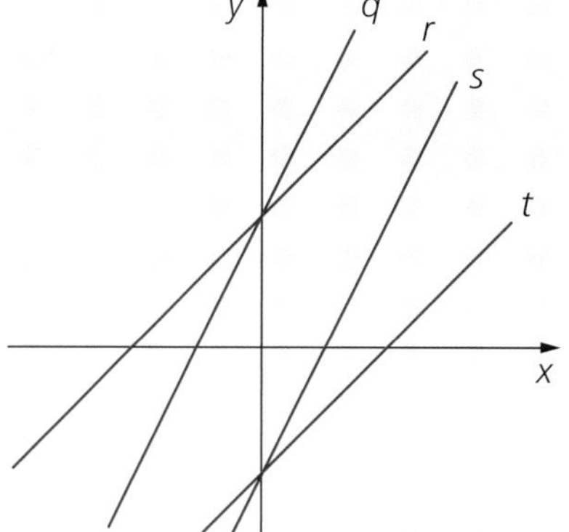

Line (q, r, s, or t)	Equation
	$y = x + 3$
	$y = x - 3$
	$y = 2x + 3$
s	

Complete the table above to show the equation of each line in the diagram.
Three equations and one line are already filled in.

JCHL 2018

KEY WORDS AND PHRASES

- Co-ordinate geometry
- Length of line segment
- Distance between points
- Mid-point
- Slope
- Equation of a line
- Intersection of lines

Chapter Summary 9

- Distance formula: The distance $|PQ|$ from $P(x_1, y_1)$ to $Q(x_2, y_2) = \sqrt{|x_2 - x_1|^2 + |y_2 - y_1|^2}$
- The mid-point between $P(x_1, y_1)$ and $Q(x_2, y_2)$ is $\left(\frac{x_1 + x_2}{2}, \frac{y_1 + y_2}{2}\right)$
- Slope formula: The slope of the line through $P(x_1, y_1)$ and $Q(x_2, y_2) = \frac{y_2 - y_1}{x_2 - x_1}$
- $l \parallel p \Rightarrow m_1 = m_2$
- $l \perp p \Rightarrow (m_1)(m_2) = -1$
- The slope of a horizontal line = 0.
- The slope of a vertical line is undefined.
- The equation of the line which passes through $(0, c)$ and has slope m is $y = mx + c$.
- The equation of the line which passes through (x_1, y_1) and has slope m is $y - y_1 = m(x - x_1)$.
- The slope of $ax + by + c = 0$ is $\frac{-a}{b}$.

Chapter 10 Algebra 4

Learning Intentions

In this chapter, you will learn about:

- How to use various methods to solve linear equations in two variables (simultaneous equations)
- How to use algebra to find the point of intersection of two lines given their equations
- Solving word problems using simultaneous equations

LO: U.3, U.4, U.5, U.6, AF.4(c)

Historical Background

It is not known exactly who invented simultaneous equations. However, we know that they were used in Samaria as far back as 2000 BC and by the Babylonians as far back as 1800 BC.

It was Gottfried Leibniz (1646–1716) and Carl Friedrich Gauss (1777–1855) who developed methods to solve simultaneous equations.

Leibniz

Gauss

Section 10A Solving Simultaneous Equations

Sometimes, we are looking for two unknown values (say x and y). To find these values, we need two equations. These two equations are known as **simultaneous equations** because they are two equations which are both true at the same time.

We can solve simultaneous equations using various methods.

Example 1

Solve the following simultaneous equations and verify your solutions:

$$x + y = 11$$
$$x - y = 1$$

Solution

Method 1

Using the **elimination** method:

- Label the equations (1) and (2).

$x + y = 11 \quad (1)$

$x - y = 1 \quad (2)$

- Add equations (1) and (2) to eliminate the y terms and solve for x.

$$\begin{aligned} x + y &= 11 \quad (1) \\ +(x - y &= 1) \quad (2) \\ \hline 2x &= 12 \\ \frac{2x}{2} &= \frac{12}{2} \quad \text{... divide both sides by 2} \\ x &= 6 \end{aligned}$$

- Substitute $x = 6$ into equation (1) to find the value of y.

$$\begin{aligned} x + y &= 11 \quad (1) \\ (6) + y &= 11 \\ y &= 11 - 6 \quad \text{... subtract 6 from both sides} \\ y &= 5 \quad \text{... simplify} \end{aligned}$$

- Verify the solution by substituting $x = 6$ and $y = 5$ into equation (2).

$$\begin{aligned} x - y &= 1 \quad (2) \\ 6 - 5 &= 1 \\ 1 &= 1 \checkmark \end{aligned}$$

As the LHS equals the RHS of the equation, then $x = 6$ and $y = 5$ is the correct solution.

Method 2

Using the **substitution** method

- Label the equations (1) and (2).

$$\begin{aligned} x + y &= 11 \quad (1) \\ x - y &= 1 \quad (2) \end{aligned}$$

- Rearrange equation (1) into the form '$x =$'.

$$\begin{aligned} x + y &= 11 \quad (1) \\ \Rightarrow x &= 11 - y \quad (3) \quad \text{... label as equation (3)} \end{aligned}$$

- Find the value of the y variable.

$$\begin{aligned} x - y &= 1 \quad (2) \\ (11 - y) - y &= 1 \quad \text{... substitute } (11 - y) \text{ for } x \text{ in equation (2)} \\ 11 - y - y &= 1 \quad \text{... expand} \\ 11 - 2y &= 1 \\ -2y &= 1 - 11 \quad \text{... subtract 11 from both sides} \\ -2y &= -10 \\ \frac{-2y}{-2} &= \frac{-10}{-2} \quad \text{... divide both sides by } -2 \\ y &= 5 \end{aligned}$$

- Substitute $y = 5$ into equation (3) to find the value of x.

$$\begin{aligned} x &= 11 - y \\ x &= 11 - 5 \\ x &= 6 \end{aligned}$$

- Verify the solution as before.

Example 2

Solve the following simultaneous equations using an algebraic method:

$$2x - y = 7$$
$$3x + 2y = 21$$

Solution

We will solve the simultaneous equations using the 'elimination method'.

- Label the equations (1) and (2).

$$2x - y = 7 \quad (1)$$
$$3x + 2y = 21 \quad (2)$$

- Multiply both sides of equation (1) by 2, and label as equation (3).

$$4x - 2y = 14 \quad (3)$$

- Add equations (2) and (3) to eliminate the y terms.

$$\begin{aligned} 3x + 2y &= 21 \quad (2) \\ + 4x - 2y &= 14 \quad (3) \\ \hline 7x \qquad &= 35 \end{aligned}$$

$$\frac{7x}{7} = \frac{35}{7} \quad \text{... divide both sides by 7}$$

$$x = 5$$

- Substitute $x = 5$ into equation (1) to find the value of y, or equation (2) if you wish.

$$2x - y = 7 \quad (1)$$
$$2(5) - y = 7$$
$$10 - y = 7$$
$$-y = 7 - 10 \quad \text{... subtract 10 from both sides}$$
$$-y = -3 \quad \text{... simplify}$$
$$\frac{-y}{-1} = \frac{-3}{-1} \quad \text{... divide both sides by } -1$$
$$y = 3$$

Answer: $x = 5$, $y = 3$

- Verify the solution by substituting $x = 5$ and $y = 3$ into equation (2).

$$3x + 2y = 21 \quad (2)$$
$$3(5) + 2(3) = 21$$
$$15 + 6 = 21$$
$$21 = 21 \checkmark$$

As the LHS equals the RHS of the equation, then $x = 5$ and $y = 3$.

(i) Solve the following simultaneous equations.

$$2x - \frac{y}{3} = -1$$

$$6x - 7y = -39$$

(ii) Verify your solutions algebraically.

Solution

(i) Label the equations (1) and (2):

$2x - \frac{y}{3} = -1$ (1)

$6x - 7y = -39$ (2)

- Multiply equation (1) by 3 to eliminate the fraction and label as equation (3):

  $6x - y = -3$ (3)

- Multiply equation (2) by −1 and label as equation (4):

  $-6x + 7y = 39$ (4)

- Add equations (3) and (4) to eliminate the x terms:

$$\begin{array}{rl} 6x - y = -3 & (3) \\ -6x + 7y = 39 & (4) \\ \hline 6y = 36 & \end{array}$$

$\Rightarrow y = \frac{36}{6}$ ... divide both sides by 6

$\Rightarrow y = 6$

- Substitute $y = 6$ into either equation (1) or (2) to find x:

  $6x - 7y = -39$ (2)

$\Rightarrow 6x - 7(6) = -39$ ... expand brackets

$\Rightarrow 6x = -39 + 42$ ... add 42 to both sides

$\Rightarrow x = \frac{3}{6}$ ... divide both sides by 6

$\Rightarrow x = \frac{1}{2}$

Answer: $x = \frac{1}{2}$ and $y = 6$

(ii) Substitute both values back into equation (1) as we did not use this equation to find the solutions originally.

$2x - \frac{y}{3} = -1$ (1)

$\Rightarrow 2\left(\frac{1}{2}\right) - \frac{6}{3} = -1$ ... substitute $x = \frac{1}{2}$ and $y = 6$ into equation (1)

$\Rightarrow 1 - 2 = -1$

$\Rightarrow -1 = -1$ ✓

As the LHS = the RHS, then $x = \frac{1}{2}$ and $y = 6$.

Activity 10.1

Solve the following simultaneous equations using an algebraic method.

1 $2m + n = -12$
$m - n = 6$

2 $s - t = -3$
$2s + t = 6$

3 $5c - d = 15$
$c + d = -3$

4 $p + q = 5$
$p - q = -1$

5 $3f - g = 15$
$4f + g = 6$

6 $3w + z = 7$
$-w - z = 5$

7 $3x - y = 6$
$2x + 5y = -13$

8 $2m - 3n = 5$
$3m + n = 2$

9 $2g - h = -7$
$g + 2h = 4$

10 $2p + q = 6$
$3p - 2q = 16$

11 $2v + 3w = 8$
$5v - 2w = 1$

12 $4x + y = 14$
$x + 5y = 13$

For questions **13** to **17**, solve the simultaneous equations algebraically and verify your answers using the substitution method.

13 $2a - 3b = -13$
$-a + 4b = 29$

14 $7d = 71 - c$
$2d + 7c - 27 = 0$

15 $p + 5q = 45$
$q - p = 3$

16 $9v = -2w + 93$
$8v + w = 85$

17 $2x = -17 + y$
$-2y = -23 - 3x$

For questions **18** to **25**,

(i) Solve the simultaneous equations algebraically.

(ii) Verify your solutions using a suitable method.

18 $a - 4b = 5$
$\frac{a}{2} + b = 1$

19 $3f + 5g = 23$
$5f + 3g = \frac{181}{5}$

20 $5m - 6n = -23$
$m - n = -\frac{19}{5}$

21 $3s + 4t = -6$
$2s - \frac{t}{2} = \frac{7}{3}$

22 $c + h = 5$
$\frac{4c}{3} - \frac{h}{2} = -8$

23 $l + 7m = 12$
$\frac{l}{2} + m = \frac{79}{14}$

24 $7r - s = \frac{29}{3}$
$-r + \frac{s}{2} = -\frac{19}{6}$

25 $\frac{3x - 1}{2} - \frac{y - 1}{2} = -\frac{3}{4}$
$\frac{x + 3}{3} + \frac{y + 4}{6} = \frac{13}{12}$

Section 10B Intersecting Lines

Connections

We can use the methods of solving simultaneous equations to find the point of intersection of two lines in co-ordinate geometry.

Example 1

(i) Sketch the lines l: $2x + y = 6$ and n: $x - 2y = -2$.

(ii) Find $l \cap n$, their point of intersection.

Solution

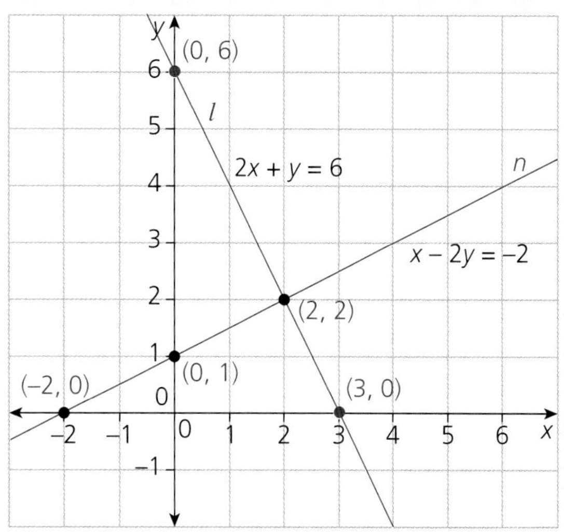

(i) To sketch the line l, we need two points on $2x + y = 6$

If $x = 0$, then $y = 6$ $\quad \therefore (0, 6) \in l$

If $y = 0$, then $2x = 6 \Rightarrow x = 3$ $\quad \therefore (3, 0) \in l$

To sketch the line n, we need two points on $x - 2y = -2$

If $x = 0$, then $-2y = -2$

$\Rightarrow y = 1$ $\quad \therefore (0, 1) \in n$

If $y = 0$, then $x = -2$ $\quad \therefore (-2, 0) \in n$

We can now sketch the two lines:

(ii) The graph suggests that (2, 2) is the point of intersection, but we must use algebra to be sure. We solve the simultaneous equations:

$2x + y = 6$

$x - 2y = -2$

We can use one of two methods:

Method 1

Elimination method

$2x + y = 6 \ \ldots (1)$

$x - 2y = -2 \ \ldots (2)$

$\Rightarrow 4x + 2y = 12 \ \ldots$ multiply (1) by 2

$\Rightarrow \quad 5x = 10 \ \ldots$ add to eliminate y

$\Rightarrow \quad x = 2$

Using equation (1) substitute 2 for x

$\Rightarrow 2(2) + y = 6$

$\Rightarrow \quad y = 6 - 4$

$\Rightarrow \quad y = 2$

$\Rightarrow$ (2, 2) is confirmed as the point of intersection.

Verify:

Substitute (2, 2) into $2x + y = 6$

$\Rightarrow 2(2) + 2 = 6$ ✓

Substitute (2, 2) into $x - 2y = -2$

$\Rightarrow 2 - 2(2) = -2$ ✓

Method 2

Substitution method

$2x + y = 6 \ \ldots (1)$

$x - 2y = -2 \ \ldots (2)$

Rewrite (1): $y = (6 - 2x)$

Substitute $(6 - 2x)$ into (2):

$\Rightarrow x - 2(6 - 2x) = -2$

$\Rightarrow \ x - 12 + 4x = -2$

$\Rightarrow \quad 5x = -2 + 12$

$\Rightarrow \quad 5x = 10$

$\Rightarrow \quad x = 2$

$y = (6 - 2x) \Rightarrow y = 6 - 4 \Rightarrow y = 2$

$\Rightarrow$ (2, 2) is confirmed as the point of intersection.

You will find the substitution method easier if one or both of the equations is in the form $y = mx + c$.

Example 2

(i) Find the point where the line $y = 2x + 1$ intersects the line $y = x + 3$.

(ii) Draw the lines in the co-ordinate plane.

Solution

(i) At the point of intersection,

$y = 2x + 1$ and $y = x + 3$ (simultaneously)

$\therefore$ at this point, $2x + 1 = x + 3$

$\Rightarrow \quad 2x - x = 3 - 1$

$\Rightarrow \quad x = 2$ … the x co-ordinate

Substitute $x = 2$ into one of the equations:

$y = x + 3$

$\Rightarrow y = 2 + 3 = 5$ … the y co-ordinate

The lines intersect at (2, 5).

(ii) 3 points on $y = 2x + 1$ are (0, 1), (1, 3) and (2, 5).

3 points on $y = x + 3$ are (0, 3), (1, 4) and (2, 5).

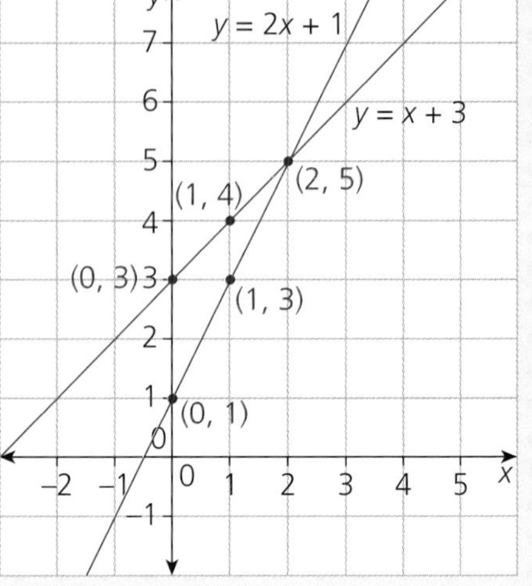

Example 3

Use algebra to find the point of intersection of the lines $y = x - 2$ and $2x - 4y = 5$.

Solution

$y = (x - 2)$

Substitute $(x - 2)$ for y in the second equation: $2x - 4y = 5$

$\Rightarrow 2x - 4(x - 2) = 5$

$\Rightarrow 2x - 4x + 8 = 5$

$\Rightarrow -2x = 5 - 8$

$\Rightarrow -2x = -3$

$\Rightarrow x = \frac{3}{2}$

$\Rightarrow y = \frac{3}{2} - 2 = -\frac{1}{2}$

Answer: $\left(\frac{3}{2}, -\frac{1}{2}\right)$

We can see this clearly if we graph the lines:

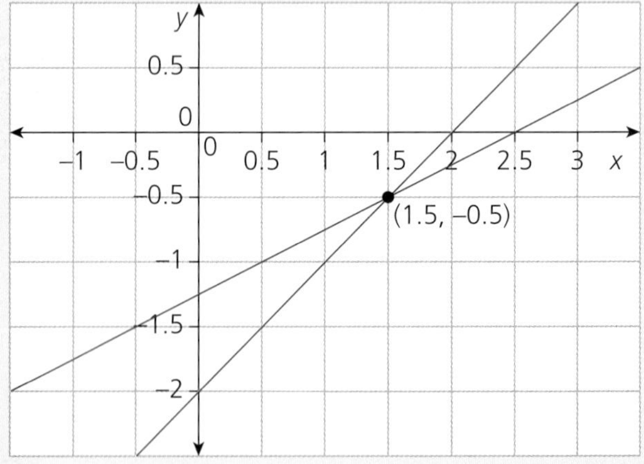

Activity 10.2

1 (i) Use algebra to find the point of intersection of the lines $y = x - 4$ and $4x + 2y = 7$.

(ii) Verify your answer by graphing the lines.

2 (i) Use algebra to find the point of intersection of the lines $y = x - 3$ and $y = 2x + 3$.

(ii) Verify your answer by graphing the lines.

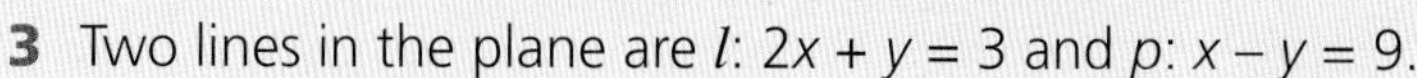

3 Two lines in the plane are l: $2x + y = 3$ and p: $x - y = 9$.
(i) Find two points on each line and draw the lines in the co-ordinate plane.
(ii) Find $l \cap p$ as accurately as you can from your graph.
(iii) Find $l \cap p$ algebraically.

4 Two lines in the plane are p: $3x + 2y = 6$ and q: $2x - 3y = 4$.
(i) Find two points on each line and draw the lines in the co-ordinate plane.
(ii) Find $p \cap q$ as accurately as you can from your graph.
(iii) Find $p \cap q$ algebraically.
(iv) What is the relationship between lines p and q?

In questions **5** to **9**, sketch each of the pairs of lines, p and q, and find their point of intersection by solving as simultaneous equations.

5 p: $x + y = 6$
q: $x - y = 2$

6 p: $x = 3$
q: $x + 3y = 9$

7 p: $x = y$
q: $3x - y = 9$

8 p: $x + y = 0$
q: $2x + y = -4$

9 p: $3x - 2y = 11$
q: $2x + 3y = 3$

10 The equations $2x + 2y - 7 = 0$ and $x + y + 3 = 0$ represent lines in the plane.
Explain what happens, through algebra and with a diagram, when you try to find the point of intersection of these two lines.

11 The equations $x + 2y + 3 = 0$ and $2x + 4y + 6 = 0$ represent lines in the plane.
Explain what happens, through algebra and with a diagram, when you try to find the point of intersection of these two lines.

Section 10C Problems Leading to Simultaneous Equations

Some real-life problems can be solved using simultaneous equations.

Example

If Sarah and Seán put their money together, they have €36.
If Seán's money were doubled and added to Sarah's money, they would have €42.
(i) Calculate how much money each person has using an algebraic method.
(ii) Verify the amounts of money obtained in part (i) graphically.

Solution

(i) Let €x = amount of money Sarah has
€y = amount of money Seán has

$x + y = 36$ ... equation (1)
$x + 2y = 42$ ... equation (2)

- Multiply equation (2) by -1

$-x - 2y = -42$ (3) ... label as equation (3)

- Add equations (1) and (3) to eliminate the x terms.

$$\begin{array}{rl} x + y = 36 & (1) \\ -x - 2y = -42 & (3) \\ \hline -y = -6 & \end{array}$$

$$\frac{-y}{-1} = \frac{-6}{-1} \quad \text{... divide both sides by } -1$$

$$y = 6$$

- Substitute $y = 6$ into equation (1) to find the value of x.

$$x + y = 36 \quad (1)$$

$$x + (6) = 36$$

$$x + 6 - 6 = 36 - 6 \quad \text{... subtract 6 from both sides}$$

$$x = 30$$

Answer: Therefore, Sarah has €30 and Seán has €6.

- Verify the solution is correct by substituting $x = 30$ and $y = 6$ into (2).
  $x + 2y = 42 \quad (2) \Rightarrow 30 + 2(6) = 42 \Rightarrow 30 + 12 = 42 \Rightarrow 42 = 42$ ✓
  As the LHS equals the RHS of the equation, then $x = 30$ and $y = 6$.

(ii) Verify the amounts of money obtained in part (i) graphically.

- Label both equations.

$$x + y = 36 \quad (1)$$

$$x + 2y = 42 \quad (2)$$

- Find two points for each linear equation.

Equation 1: $x + y = 36 \quad (1)$
When $x = 0, 0 + y = 36 \Rightarrow y = 36$ Point 1 is (0, 36)
When $y = 0, x + 0 = 36 \Rightarrow x = 36$ Point 2 is (36, 0)

Equation 2: $x + 2y = 42 \quad (2)$
When $x = 0, 0 + 2y = 42 \Rightarrow 2y = 42 \Rightarrow y = 21$ Point 1 is (0, 21)
When $y = 0, x + 2(0) = 42 \Rightarrow x = 42$ Point 2 is (42, 0)

- Plot the points and draw a graph for each linear equation, labelling each line.
- Find the point of intersection.
  We see from the graph that the two lines cross at the point (30, 6).
  So, as in part (i), Sarah has €30 and Seán has €6.

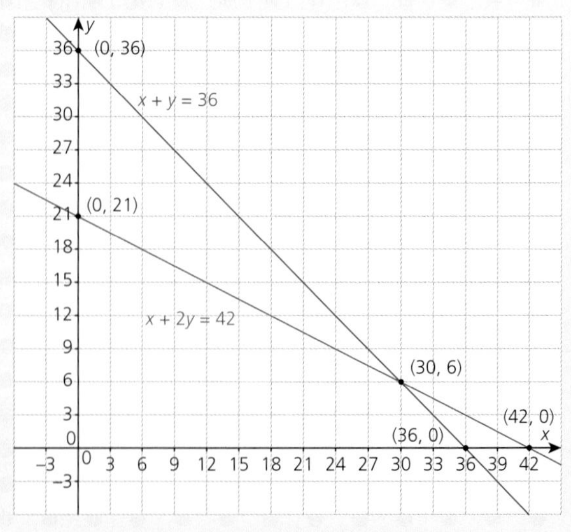

In the following questions, form two linear equations and solve them using an algebraic method.

1 The sum of two numbers is 52 and their difference is 8. Find the numbers.

2 If a father's age is added to his son's age, the sum is 70. If twice the son's age is added to the father's age, the sum is 90. Find the ages of the father and the son.

3 A bar of chocolate and three packets of crisps cost €3.00. Two bars of chocolate and one packet of crisps cost €2.50. Find the cost of a bar of chocolate and the cost of a packet of crisps.

Hint

› Change the prices into cent when writing the linear equations.

4 A school puts on a musical. Find the cost of an adult ticket and the cost of a student ticket if:

- The price for one adult and three students is €25.
- The price for two adults and four students is €40.

5 Joanne bought some phone credit and a sandwich at a cost of €14. Alanna bought the same amount of phone credit and three of the same sandwiches at a cost of €22.

(i) How much did the phone credit cost?

(ii) How much did a sandwich cost?

6 If I double a number and add three times a second number, the answer is 1. If I multiply the first number by 3 and take away twice the second number, the answer is 8. Find the numbers.

7 Two concert tickets plus the credit card charge costs €125. Five of the same tickets plus the credit card charge costs €305. How much is:

(i) a concert ticket

(ii) the credit card charge?

8 A shop sells four notebooks and two pens for €16. The same shop sells three identical notebooks and five pens for €19. How much does:

(i) a pen cost

(ii) a notebook cost?

9 The admission fee at a fair is €1.50 for children and €4.00 for adults. On Saturday, 2200 people came to the fair and a total of €5050 was collected. How many children and how many adults went to the fair?

10 (i) Write down two linear equations in x and y, using the information shown in the rectangle.

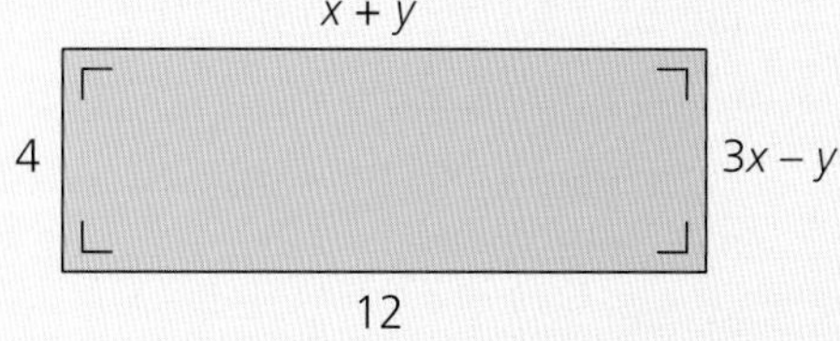

(ii) Hence, solve for x and y using an algebraic method.

11 (i) Write down two equations in a and b, using the information shown in the rectangle.

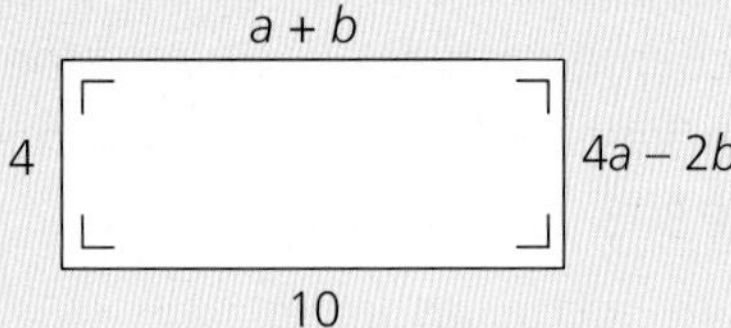

(ii) Hence, solve for a and b using an algebraic method.

12 The sum of two numbers is 40. The difference of the two numbers is 4.6.

(i) Write two linear equations to represent this information.

(ii) Solve the pair of simultaneous equations to find the values of both numbers.

(iii) Verify your answers.

13 If I double one number, then add a second number, the answer is 50. If I multiply the first number by 7 and subtract half the second number, the answer is 75.

(i) Write two linear equations to represent this information.

(ii) Solve the pair of simultaneous equations to find the values of both numbers.

(iii) Verify your answers.

14 If I multiply a number by 4 and subtract half of a second number, the answer is 6.5. If I add 3 to the first number and divide the answer by 2, then subtract one-third of the second number, the answer is 1.5.

(i) Write two linear equations to represent this information.

(ii) Solve the pair of simultaneous equations to find the values of the numbers.

(iii) Verify your answers.

15 A classical music concert is being held at the local Arts Centre.

- The price for 2 adults and 3 concession tickets is €47.50.
- The price for 1 adult and 2 concession tickets is €27.50.

(i) Write two linear equations to represent this information.

(ii) Solve the pair of simultaneous equations to find the price of each type of ticket.

(iii) Verify your answers.

16 A grocer sells apples and bananas at set prices, irrespective of weight.

- 1 banana and 4 apples cost €2.00
- 2 bananas and 3 apples cost €1.90

(i) Write two linear equations to represent this information.

(ii) Solve the pair of simultaneous equations to find the price of a banana and the price of an apple.

(iii) Verify your answers.

17

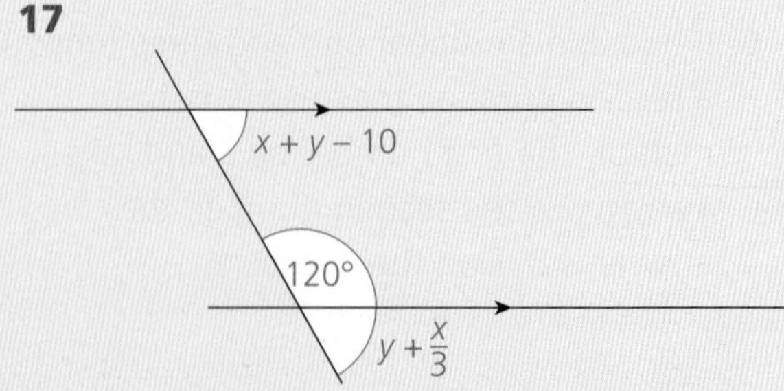

(i) What is the degree measure of the angles $(x + y - 10)°$ and $\left(y + \frac{x}{3}\right)°$? Explain your answer using any relevant theorems.

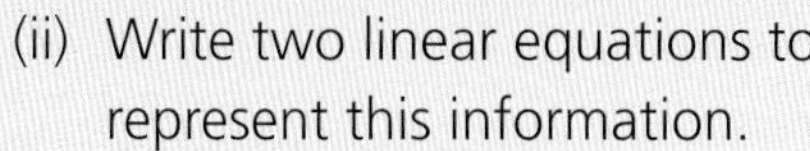

(ii) Write two linear equations to represent this information.

(iii) Solve the pair of simultaneous equations to find the value of x and the value of y.

(iv) Verify your answers for x and y.

18 The perimeter of a rectangle is 60 cm. The width of the rectangle is one quarter of its length.

(i) Write two linear equations to represent this information.

(ii) Solve the pair of simultaneous equations to find the length and the width of the rectangle.

(iii) Verify your answers.

(iv) Find the area of the rectangle.

19

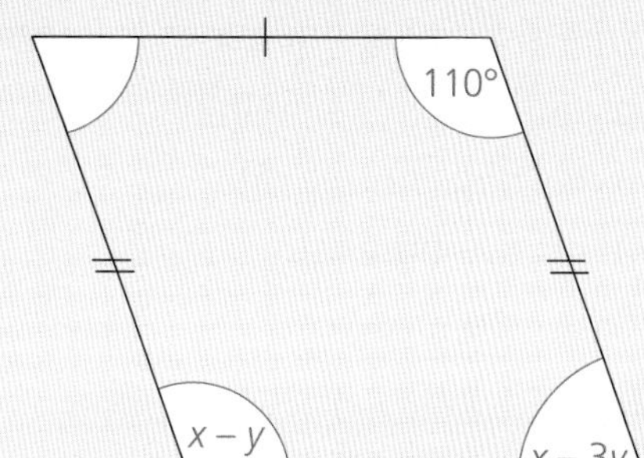

(i) What is the degree measure of the angle $(x - y)$? Explain your answer using any relevant theorems.

(ii) What is the degree measure of the angle $(x - 3y)$? Explain your answer using any relevant theorems.

(iii) Write two linear equations to represent this information.

(iv) Solve the pair of simultaneous equations to find the values of x and y.

(v) Verify your answers for x and y.

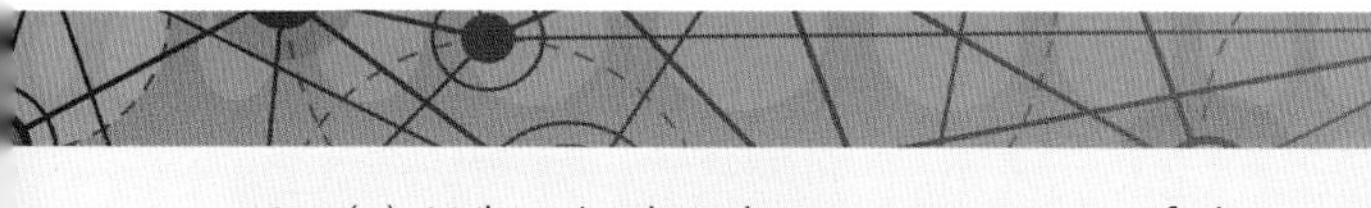

Revision Activity 10

1 (a) What is the degree measure of the angles $\left(\frac{x}{2} + 2y - 10\right)$ and $(x + y)$? Explain your answer using any relevant theorems.

70°

$x + y$ $\quad$ $\left(\frac{x}{2} + 2y - 10\right)$

(b) Write two linear equations to represent this information.

(c) Solve the pair of simultaneous equations to find the values of x and y.

(d) Verify your answers for x and y.

2 Julie pays €8.10 for two hamburgers and a glass of cola. Adam pays €18 for four hamburgers (of the same size) and four glasses of cola for his family.

(a) Write two linear equations to represent this information.

(b) Solve the simultaneous equations.

(c) What price is a glass of cola?

(d) What price is a hamburger?

3 Seán works in a local restaurant. He gets paid a basic rate of €x per hour for his contracted 37 hours per week. If he works overtime, he gets paid a higher rate of €y per hour.

- If Seán works 8 hours overtime, he gets paid €423.65
- If Seán works 11 hours overtime, he gets paid €462.50

(a) Write two linear equations to represent this information.

(b) Solve the pair of simultaneous equations to find:

(i) his basic hourly rate

(ii) his overtime rate.

(c) Verify your answers.

4 In the English Soccer Championship, no points are awarded for a loss. The table below shows the total number of points received for the teams at the top and the bottom of the league after each had played six games.

Team	Games played	Games won	Games drawn	Games lost	Total points
Top team	6	5	1	0	16
Bottom team	6	1	2	3	5

(a) If the number of points awarded for a win is x and the number of points awarded for a draw is y, write two linear equations to represent this information.

(b) Solve the pair of simultaneous equations.

(c) Find the number of points awarded for:

(i) a win

(ii) a draw.

(d) Verify your answers.

5 The perimeter of the top of a rectangular garden table is 8 m. The width of the garden table is one third of its length.

(a) Write two linear equations to represent this information.

(b) Solve the pair of simultaneous equations.

(c) Verify your answers algebraically.

(d) (i) Find the width of the table.

(ii) Find the length of the table.

(e) Find the area of the garden table.

6 A group of 30 students went to a local restaurant for a meal at the end of the school year. They had a choice of two set meals: Meal A costing €6 and Meal B costing €8. A certain number of students bought Meal A and the remainder chose Meal B. The total cost of the 30 meals was €216.

(a) Write two linear equations to represent this information.

(b) Solve the simultaneous equations.

(c) How many students chose Meal A?

(d) How many students chose Meal B?

7 Martin needs to hire a car for 5 days. He contacts two different car rental companies to get the best value. The tables below shows the rental charges for each company.

	Company A				
Number of days	1	2	3	4	5
Total cost (€)	100	115	130		

	Company B				
Number of days	1	2	3	4	5
Total cost (€)	40	80	120		

(a) Copy and complete the tables for both companies, assuming the patterns continue.

(b) Draw a graph to represent the information for both companies.

(c) After how many days is the cost of the car rental the same?

(d) Which company provides the best value for 5 days car rental?

Exam-style Questions

1 Use algebra to find the point of intersection of the lines k and l.

Line k: $y = x - 1$
Line l: $2x - 3y = 6$

JCHL 2018 Paper 2

2 A company employs two drivers, John and David. Each has use of a company car and a small van. The company buys €30 worth of Toll Tags for each driver. Each time a vehicle goes through the M50 Toll, a charge will be deducted from the Toll Tags.

John goes through the M50 Toll five times in his car and four times in his small van. He then has €7.90 remaining on his Toll Tags. David goes through the M50 Toll twice in his car and six times in his small van. He then has €8.40 left on his Toll Tags.

Calculate how much it costs for a car and for a small van to go through the M50 Toll.

JCHL 2013 Paper 1

3 Consideration is being given to changing the number of points a team gets for a win and also the number of points a team gets for a draw in a soccer league. No points will be awarded for a loss. The table below shows the standing of two teams after six games under the proposed new system.

Team	Played	Won	Drawn	Lost	Points (new system)
Team A	6	2	2	2	12
Team B	6	1	5	0	10

(a) Find the number of points which would be awarded for:
 (i) a win
 (ii) a draw under this proposed system.

(b) The current system awards 3 points for a win and 1 point for a draw. Suggest one reason why it might be preferable to change to the system proposed in part (a).

JCHL 2012 Paper 1

KEY WORDS AND PHRASES

- **Simultaneous equations**
- **Solve/verify**
- **Algebraic**
- **Graphical**

Chapter Summary 10

- A pair of simultaneous equations are two equations which are both true at the same time. The two equations can be solved to find the values of the two unknown variables.
- Simultaneous equations can be solved algebraically or graphically.
- We can find the point of intersection of two lines using simultaneous equations.

Speed, Distance, Time and Graphs

Chapter 11

Learning Intentions

In this chapter, you will learn about:

- Average speed, distance and time
- Graphs involving distance and time
- Graphs involving speed and time
- Constant flow-rate graphs

LO: U.4, U.5, U.6, U.7–U.10

You will need...

- a pencil
- a ruler
- a geometry set
- squared paper

Section 11A Connecting Slope and Speed

We are all familiar with the word 'speed' in everyday life, and everywhere we look, we see things moving at speed – people walking, cars and tractors on the roads, birds flying in the air, clouds moving slowly across the sky. So we all have some idea of what speed means.

A car travelling at 60 km/h will cover 60 kilometres in 1 hour.

In mathematics, we need to be very precise in what we mean by speed.

In this section, we will look at speed and what it means. We will see that slope is useful in calculating speed. Look at the following example:

Conor is walking in the country. He is walking at a steady speed. The table shows the distances that Conor walked and the times that it took him.

Time elapsed (hours)	Distance from the start (km)
0	0
1	5
2	10
3	15
4	20

Look carefully at the table.

- The time elapsed is going up by **1 hour** in every row.
- The distance travelled is going up by **5 km** in every row.

So **for every 1 hour** that passes, the **distance travelled** by Conor increases by 5 km.

We would say that Conor is travelling at a **steady speed** of 5 km per hour (5 km/h).

Time elapsed (hours)	Distance from the start (km)	Change in distance
0	0	
1	5	+5
2	10	+5
3	15	+5
4	20	+5

Key Point

Notice that **two** things are changing: the **distance** travelled and the **time** elapsed. Speed measures how much the distance travelled changes as the time changes. So we say that speed is the **rate of change** of distance **with respect to** time.

We can show Conor's journey on a graph.

- We put **time** from the start on the x-axis.
- We put **distance** from the start on the y-axis.
- This is known as a **distance–time graph**.
- (1, 5) means 'after 1 hour Conor has travelled 5 km'; (2, 10) means 'after 2 hours Conor has travelled 10 km', etc.
- The points are all in line (collinear).
- We can get the slope of this line by getting $\frac{\text{rise}}{\text{run}}$ between any two points:

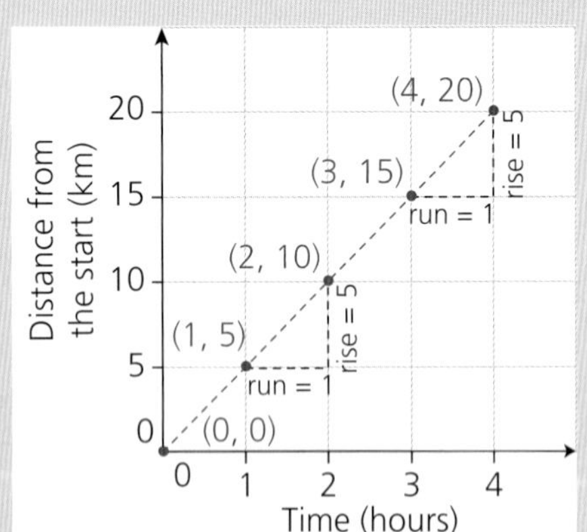

The slope = $\frac{5}{1}$ = 5 (the distance axis is in units of 5)

- The rise = the change in distance
- The run = the change in time
- So $\frac{\text{rise}}{\text{run}} = \frac{\text{change in distance}}{\text{change in time}}$ = speed

Key Point

This is how we can see Conor's speed in the graph. **The speed is the slope** of the graph.

- Note that Conor is travelling at a **steady speed**. If he had travelled at different speeds, we would talk about his **average speed** for the journey.

Average speed = $\frac{\text{change in distance}}{\text{change in time}}$

This can be remembered by this triangle:

D for (change in) distance,

S for (average) speed,

T for (change in) time.

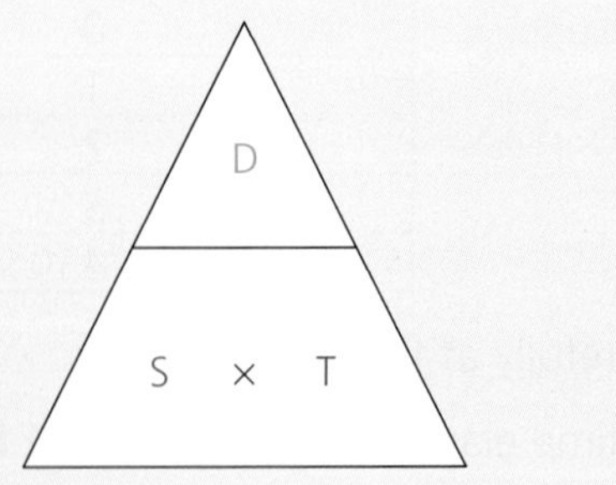

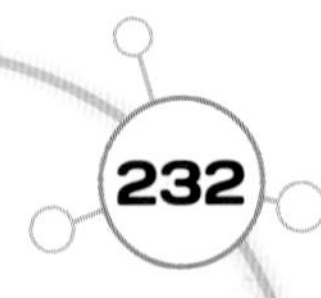

Example

The graph shows distance travelled by a cyclist over a period of time. Notice that the distance axis is in units of 5.

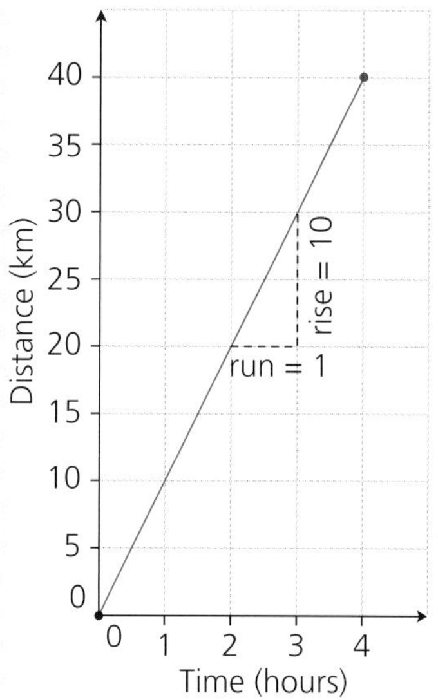

(i) Copy and complete this table.

Time elapsed (hours)	Distance from the start (km)	Change in distance
0	0	
1	10	+10
2		
3		
4		

(ii) What is the speed of the cyclist?

(iii) Where do you see her speed in the table?

(iv) Where do you see her speed in the graph?

Solution

(i)

Time elapsed (hours)	Distance from the start (km)	Change in distance
0	0	
1	10	+10
2	20	+10
3	30	+10
4	40	+10

(ii) The cyclist is travelling at a steady 10 km/h.

(iii) In the table, the distance travelled is increasing by 10 km for every 1 hour increase in time.

(iv) The graph is a **distance–time graph**. So the slope of the line gives the speed.

Slope $= \frac{\text{rise}}{\text{run}}$ between any two points

$= \frac{10}{1} = 10$ km/h.

Activity 11.1

1 Tom is travelling at a steady speed. The table shows his distance and time measurements.

Time elapsed (hours)	Distance from the start (km)	Change in distance travelled
0	0	
1	15	+15
2	30	+15
3	45	+15

(i) Draw a distance–time graph of Tom's journey.

(ii) What speed is Tom travelling at? Explain how you get your answer from the table and the graph.

2 The following table shows the distances travelled by a train and the times taken.

Time elapsed (hours)	Distance from the start (km)	Change in distance travelled
0	0	
1	40	+40
2	80	+40
3	120	+40

(i) Draw a distance–time graph of the train's journey.

(ii) Is the train travelling at a steady speed? Explain your answer.

(iii) What is the speed of the train? Explain how you get your answer from the table and the graph.

3 The graph shows the journey of an object over a period of time.

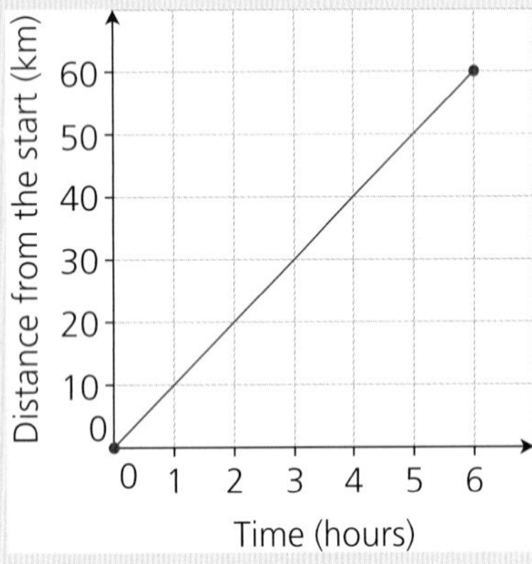

(i) Copy and complete this table of the journey:

Time elapsed (hours)	Distance from the start (km)	Change in distance
0	0	
1	10	+10
2		
3		
4		
5		
6		

(ii) Is the object travelling at a steady speed?

(iii) What is its speed?

(iv) Explain your answer using the table and the graph.

4 (i) Referring to the graph below, who is travelling faster, Mary or Sophie?

(ii) Explain your answer.

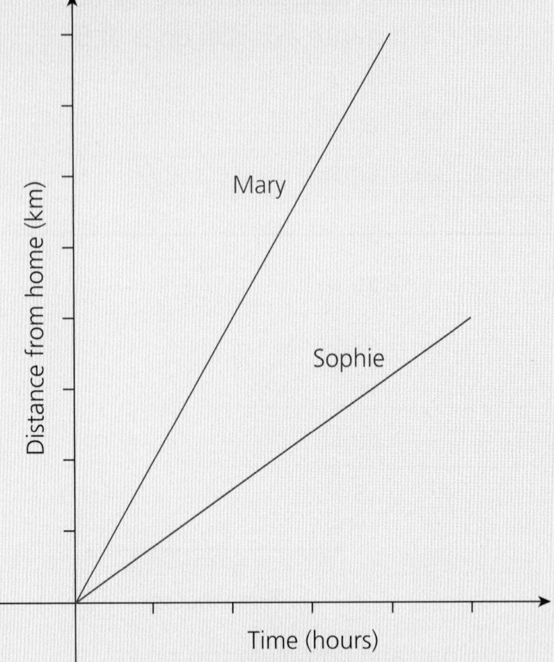

5 Find the speeds of the two cars in this graph.

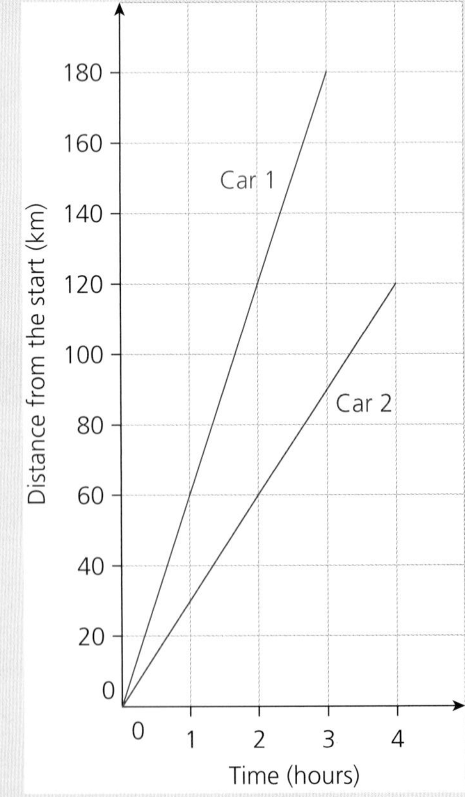

6 Calculate the speed of each car shown by the following distance–time graphs:

(i)

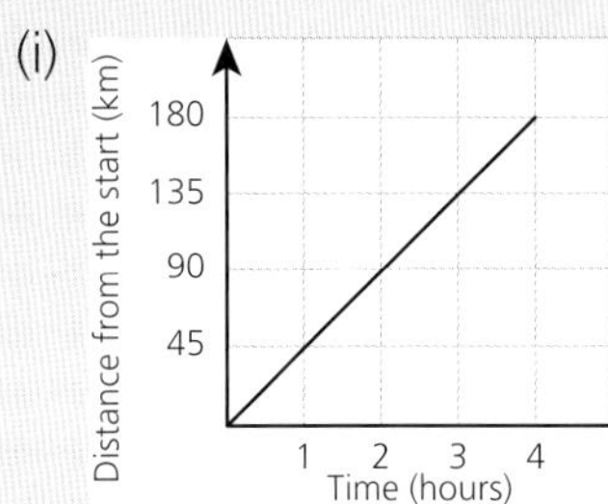

(iii)

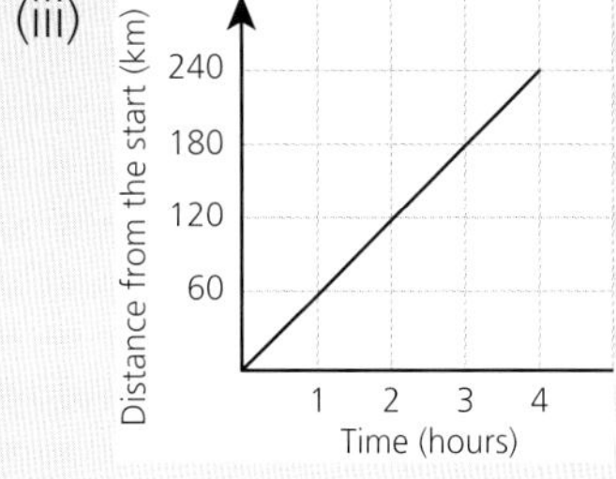

(ii)

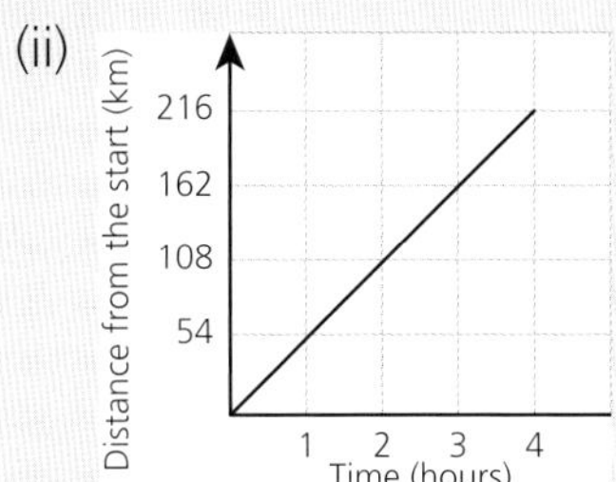

(iv)

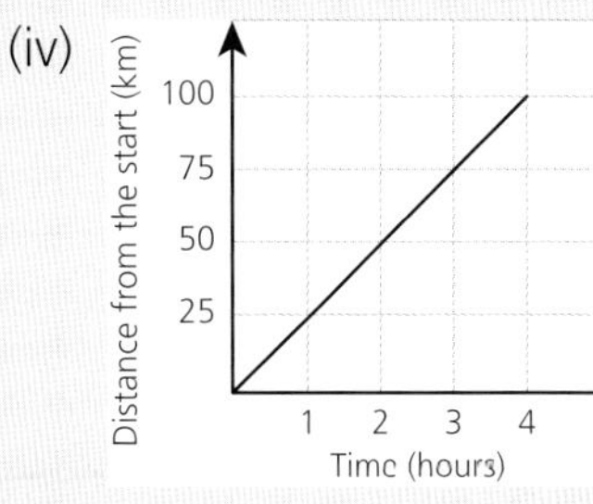

7 Bob and Cathy are walking in the country at steady speeds. The following graph shows their progress.

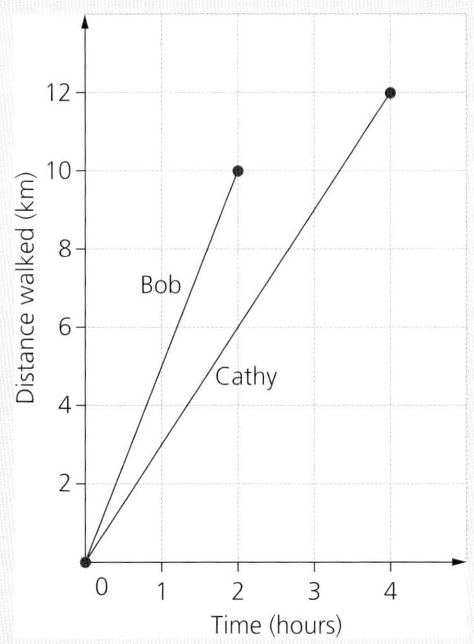

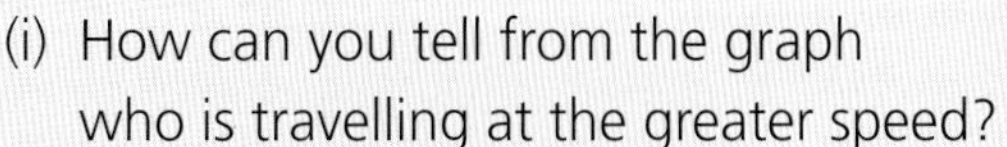

(i) How can you tell from the graph who is travelling at the greater speed?

(ii) Find their speeds from the graph.

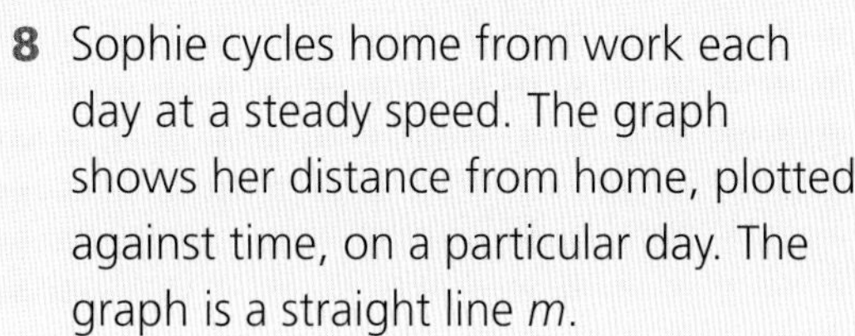

8 Sophie cycles home from work each day at a steady speed. The graph shows her distance from home, plotted against time, on a particular day. The graph is a straight line m.

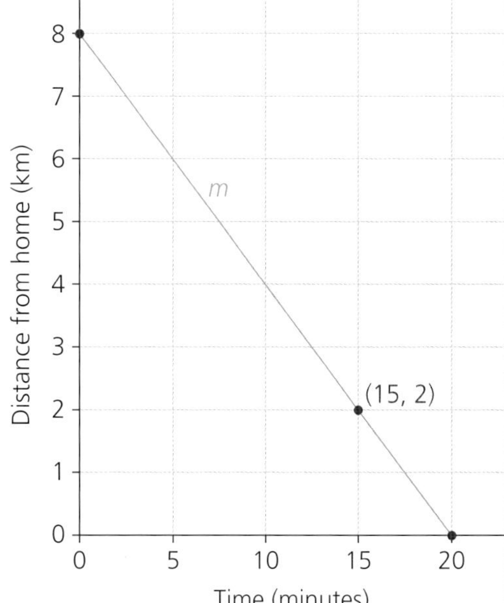

(i) How far from her work-place does Sophie live?

(ii) How long did it take her to cycle home from work that day?

(iii) The point (15, 2) is on the line m. Explain what this point means in the context of this journey.

(iv) Explain what the slope of m means in the context of this journey.

Section 11B Speed, Distance and Time

Example 1

A car travels at an average speed of 55 km/h.

(i) What distance will the car travel in $2\frac{1}{2}$ hours?

(ii) How long will it take the car to travel a distance of 275 km?

Solution

(i) Speed = 55 km/h

Time = $2\frac{1}{2}$ hours or 2.5 hours

Distance = ???

Distance = speed × time

= 55 × 2.5

= 137.5 km

(ii) Speed = 55 km/h

Distance = 275 km

Time = ???

$$\text{Time} = \frac{\text{distance}}{\text{speed}}$$

$$= \frac{275}{55} = 5 \text{ hours}$$

Key Point

In general we say,

$$\text{Average speed} = \frac{\text{change in the distance}}{\text{change in time}}$$

or we could just say for short,

$$\textbf{Average speed} = \frac{\textbf{distance}}{\textbf{time}}$$

Example 2

A truck travels a distance of 304 km in 4 hours and 45 minutes. Find its average speed in km/h.

Solution

Distance = 304 km

Time = 4 hours and 45 minutes or 4.75 hours

Speed = ???

$$\text{Speed} = \frac{\text{distance}}{\text{time}} = \frac{304}{4.75} = 64 \text{ km/h}$$

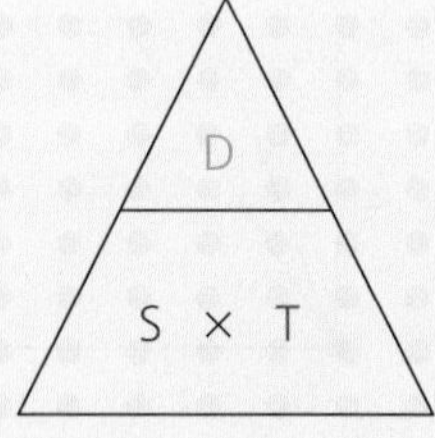

Key Points

When working with problems that involve time, we usually want to have time expressed as a decimal number. Thus, we often must convert time given in minutes to a decimal number of hours by dividing the number of minutes by 60.

For example:

$$1 \text{ hour } 45 \text{ minutes} = 1 \text{ hour} + \frac{45}{60} \text{ hours}$$

$$= 1 \text{ hour} + 0.75 \text{ hours}$$

$$= 1.75 \text{ hours}$$

Sometimes we want to convert time that is expressed as hours given in decimal form into hours and minutes, as this is more conversational. To do this, we multiply the decimal portion by 60.

For example:

2.35 hours = 2 hours + 0.35 hours

= 2 hours + (0.35)(60) minutes

= 2 hours 21 minutes

Changing Units

We have already seen some different units for speed, kilometres per hour (km/h) and metres per second (m/s). Example 3 illustrates how to convert from one of these units to the other.

Example 3

Convert 108 km/h to m/s.

Solution

Method 1

Unitary method

108 km in 1 hour

$\Rightarrow$ 108 000 m in (60 × 60) seconds

$\Rightarrow$ 108 000 m in 3600 seconds

$\Rightarrow \frac{108\,000}{3600}$ m in 1 second

$\Rightarrow$ 30 m in 1 second

i.e. 30 m/s

Method 2

- Convert 108 km to metres.

1 km = 1000 m

108 km = 108 × 1000 = 108 000 m

- Convert 1 hour to seconds.

1 hour = 60 minutes = 60 × 60 seconds

= 3600 seconds

$$\text{Speed} = \frac{\text{distance}}{\text{time}}$$

$$= \frac{108\,000}{3600}$$

$$= 30\text{ m/s}$$

Activity 11.2

1 Copy and complete the table by filling in the values for *x*.

Distance	Time	Average speed
100 km	2 hours	*x* km/h
20 km	20 minutes	*x* km/h
240 km	*x* hours	80 km/h
1600 m	*x* seconds	20 m/s
x km	15 minutes	10 m/s
x m	90 seconds	100 km/h

2 Find the time taken for each of the following journeys.

(i) A car travelled at an average speed of 60 km/h for a distance of 150 km.

(ii) A man jogs 10 km at an average speed of 8 km/h.

(iii) A bus travels 250 km at a steady speed of 100 km/h.

3 A train has an average speed of 70 km/h.

(i) How long will it take the train to travel 210 km?

(ii) How far will the train travel in 1 hour 45 min?

4 (i) Convert 54 km/h to m/s.

(ii) Convert 72 km/h to m/s.

(iii) Convert 36 km/h to m/s.

(iv) Convert 126 km/h to m/s.

5 Susan drives to work in her car every morning, a distance of 27 km. Susan normally takes 30 minutes to complete her journey.

(i) What is Susan's average speed?

(ii) If Susan was delayed in traffic by 15 minutes on her way to work, what was her average speed on that day?

6 John cycles to school every morning. He lives 1.8 km from the school. He leaves his house at 8.26 am and arrives at school at 8.50 am.

(i) How long does it take John to get to school?

(ii) What is John's average speed?

(iii) If John takes a shortcut home and travels at the same speed, the journey now takes him 18 min.
How much shorter in distance is this shortcut compared with his normal route?

7 Paul walks to his school every morning. The school is 2.4 km from Paul's house. Paul's walking speed is 6 km/h and his jogging speed is 8 km/h.

(i) How long does it take Paul to walk to school?

(ii) How much time can Paul save if he jogs to school?

8 The approximate distance between London and New York is 5600 km. An Airbus A380 plane has a cruising speed of 800 km/h.

(i) How long will the plane take to fly between London and New York?

(ii) If the prevailing wind reduces the speed of the plane by 100 km/h over the entire journey, what is the time delay in minutes?

Section 11C Average Speed for Two-Part Journeys

We now look at problems which involve calculations of speed, distance and time for journeys where different parts of the journey are travelled at different speeds.

Key Point

When a car travels at two different speeds for two different parts of a journey, we can calculate the average speed for the entire journey.
To do this, we must use the formula:

$$\text{Average speed} = \frac{\text{total distance travelled}}{\text{total time taken}}$$

The average speed **is not** found by finding the average of the two speeds.

Example 1

Jane commutes to work by car and train. It takes 15 minutes to drive to her local train station 10 km from her house. She then takes 30 minutes to travel 30 km to work by commuter train.

(i) What is the average speed in km/h of Jane's car journey?

(ii) What is the average speed in km/h of Jane's train journey?

(iii) What is the average speed in km/h of Jane's total journey to work?

Solution

(i) Average speed of Jane's car journey:

Distance travelled = 10 km

Time taken = 15 minutes = $\frac{15}{60}$ = 0.25 h

Using,

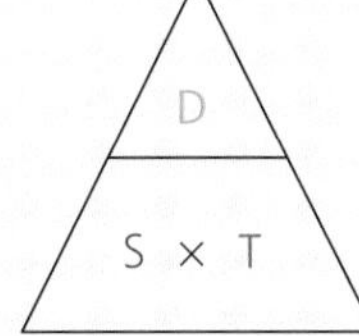

Average speed

$= \frac{\text{distance}}{\text{time}} = \frac{10}{0.25} = 40$ km/h

(ii) Average speed for the train journey:

Distance travelled = 30 km

Time taken = 30 minutes = 0.5 h

Average speed $= \frac{\text{distance}}{\text{time}}$

$= \frac{30}{0.5} = 60$ km/h

(iii) Average speed for whole journey

$= \frac{\text{total distance travelled}}{\text{total time taken}}$

$= \frac{10\text{ km} + 30\text{ km}}{0.25\text{ hr} + 0.5\text{ hr}}$

$= \frac{40}{0.75}$

$= 53\frac{1}{3}$ km/h

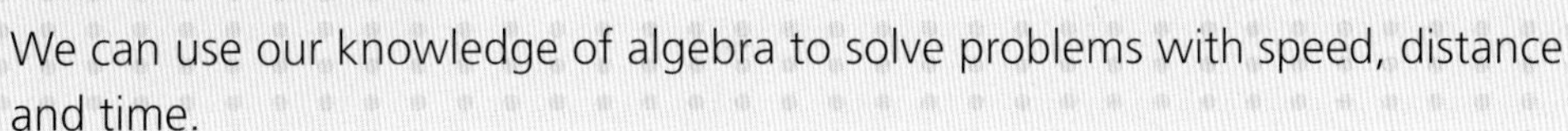

Connections

We can use our knowledge of algebra to solve problems with speed, distance and time.

Example 2

Mary drove from her home to the shop at a speed of 40 km/h. She drove back from the shop to her home at a speed of 60 km/h. What was her average speed for the whole journey to the shop and back?

Solution

Here we don't know the distance to the shop. Hence, we use a variable.

Let x be the distance from Mary's home to the shop.

- Journey from **home to the shop**:

  Distance travelled = x km

  Speed = 40 km/h

  Time taken = $\frac{x}{40}$ h

- Journey from the **shop back to home**:

  Distance travelled = x km

  Speed = 60 km/h

  Time taken = $\frac{x}{60}$ h

- Total time for **whole journey**

  $= \frac{x}{40} + \frac{x}{60}$

  $= \frac{3x + 2x}{120}$

  $= \frac{5x}{120} = \frac{x}{24}$ h

  Average speed for whole journey

  $= \frac{\text{total distance}}{\text{total time}} = \frac{2x}{\left(\frac{x}{24}\right)}$

  $= \frac{2x(24)}{x}$

  $= 48$ km/h

Activity 11.3

1 A man travels from Arklow to Blanchardstown, a distance of 90 km. He leaves Arklow at 09:25 and arrives in Blanchardstown at 10:55.

(i) Calculate his average speed for the journey.

He continues from Blanchardstown to Cootehill, a distance of 112 km. He increases his average speed by 4 km/h for this section of his journey.

(ii) At what time does he arrive in Cootehill?

2 Seán leaves his house at 7.15 am and travels by car to the train station 25 km away arriving at 7.45 am. He then catches the train to Dublin which takes 1 hour and 30 minutes to travel 120 kilometres.

(i) What is the average speed of Seán's car journey in km/h?

(ii) What is the average speed of Seán's train journey in km/h?

(iii) What is the average speed of Seán's complete journey in km/h?

3 A van travels an average speed of 65 km/h for 2 hours and then travels at an average speed of 70 km/h for half an hour. What is the average speed travelled over the $2\frac{1}{2}$ hours?

4 A car travelled a distance of 250 km in 4 hours 24 minutes. The average speed for the first 180 km was 60 km/h. What was the average speed for the remainder of the journey?

5 A man walks 2 km to a bus stop at an average speed of 2.5 km/h. He then takes a bus which takes 42 minutes to travel 49 km to his workplace.

(i) How long in hours did the man take to walk to the bus stop?

(ii) Find the average speed of the bus journey in km/h.

(iii) Find the average speed of the complete journey in km/h.

6 To get to a shopping centre, Grace walks 1 km to the bus station and then gets a bus to the shopping centre, which is 7 km from the bus stop. Grace's walking speed is 4 km/h and the average speed of the bus is 35 km/h.

(i) How long in hours was Grace walking?

(ii) How long was Grace on the bus?

(iii) What is the average speed over the full journey? Give your answer correct to two decimal places.

7 Tom cycled against a headwind from Ballyfore to Newtown at a speed of 20 km/h. He cycled back from Newtown to Ballyfore at a speed of 30 km/h. What was his average speed for the complete journey?

8 The distance from Allentown to Balyna is half the distance from Balyna to Courtown. The total distance from Allentown to Courtown, through Balyna, is 60 km.

A car travels at x km/h from Balyna to Courtown. The total time for the journey is 50 minutes. Find the value of x.

Section 11D Speed–Time Graphs

Another type of travel-graph is a **speed–time** graph. This may look like a distance–time graph but it is very different.

On a speed–time graph, we can read the speed directly from the values on the speed axis (the vertical axis). Look at the diagram and notice the differences between it and the distance–time graphs you met earlier.

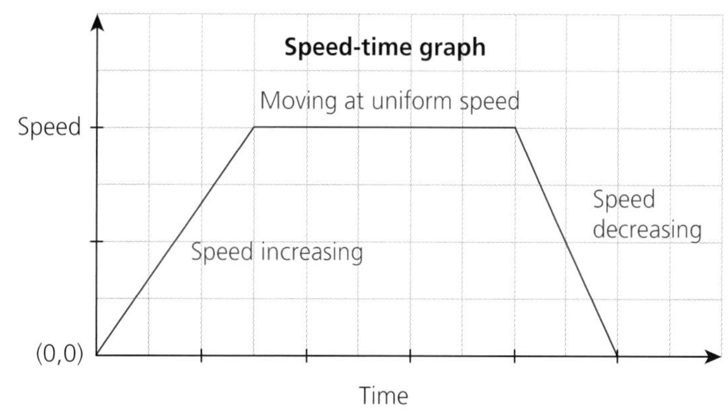

Remember: When looking at any graph, **always check what the variables are on the axes**.

Key Points

- On a linear **distance–time** graph, the constant speed is given by the slope of the graph.
- On a **speed–time** graph, we read the speed directly from the graph.

Example 1

The graph below shows some details of a train's journey as it travelled from one station to the next.

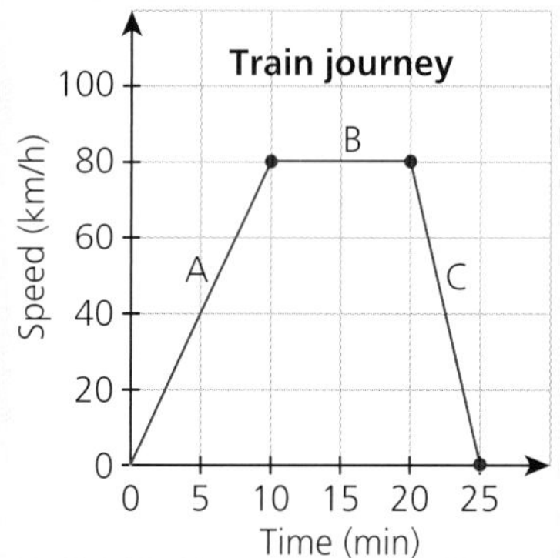

(i) Describe the progress of the train during the three stages A, B and C of the journey.

(ii) What was the train's highest speed during the journey?

(iii) How far did the train travel at the highest speed?

Solution

This is a **speed–time** graph, so we read the speed directly from the vertical axis.

(i) During stage A, the train is steadily increasing its speed from 0 km/h to 80 km/h over a period of 10 minutes.

During stage B, the train travels at a steady 80 km/h for 10 minutes $\left(\text{i.e. } \frac{1}{6} \text{ of an hour}\right)$

During stage C, the train is steadily decreasing its speed from 80 km/h to 0 km/h over a period of 5 minutes.

(ii) The train's highest speed was 80 km/h.

(iii) distance = speed × time

$$= 80 \times \frac{1}{6}$$

$$= 13\frac{1}{3} \text{ km}$$

The train travelled $13\frac{1}{3}$ km at the highest speed.

Example 2

The graph shows the speed of a car as it moves from a traffic light at A to a traffic light at D.

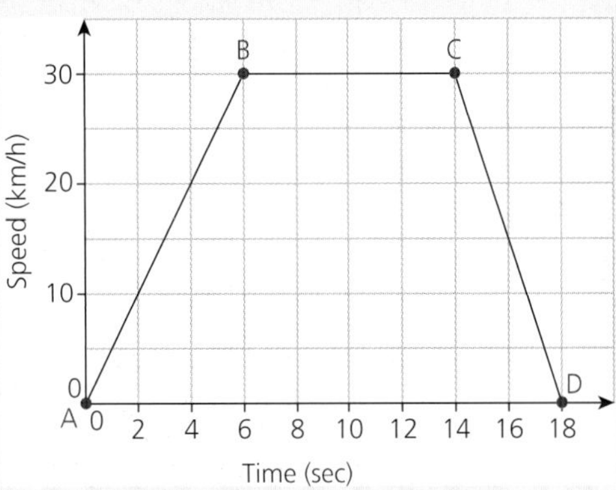

(i) At which part of the journey is the speed of the car increasing?

(ii) At which part of the journey is the speed of the car constant?

(iii) At which part of the journey is the speed of the car decreasing?

(iv) What is the maximum speed of the car?

(v) How long does it take the car to go from A to D?

Solution

(i) The speed of the car is increasing (the car is **accelerating**) between A and B. It goes from 0 km/h to 30 km/h in 6 seconds.

(ii) The speed of the car is constant between B and C.

(iii) The speed of the car is decreasing (the car is **decelerating**) between C and D. It goes from 30 km/h to 0 km/h in 2 seconds.

(iv) The maximum speed of the car is 30 km/h. It stays at this speed for 8 seconds.

(v) It takes 18 seconds to go from A to D.

Example 3

The diagram shows the **distance–time** graph of an object. Sketch the **speed–time** graph of the object. Explain your answer.

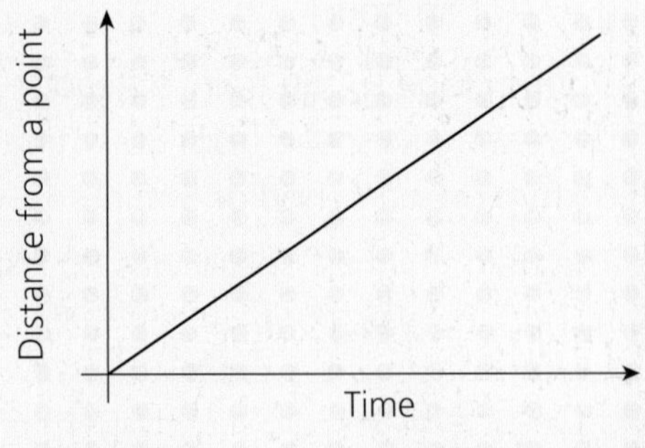

Solution

The rate of change of distance with time gives the speed. The distance–time graph is a straight line which means that the speed is constant.

Hence, the speed–time graph is a horizontal line.

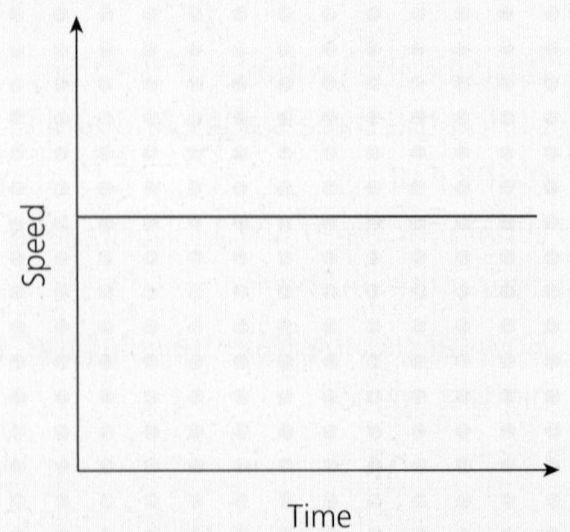

1 The graph below shows some details of a train journey.

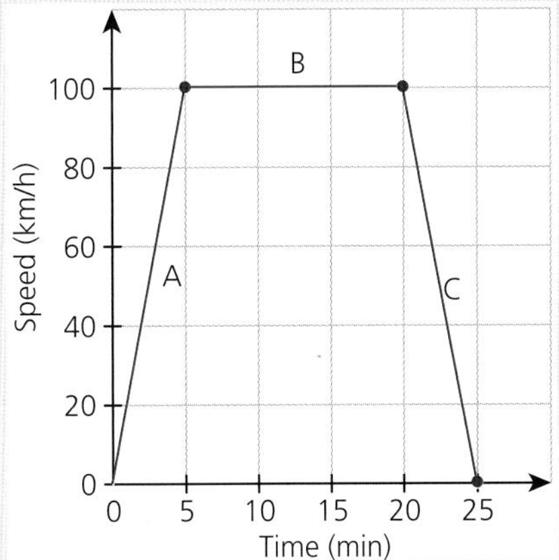

(i) Describe the progress of the train during the three stages A, B and C of the journey.

(ii) What was the train's highest speed during the journey?

(iii) How far did the train travel at the highest speed?

2 The graph below shows some details of a journey Peter made by car.

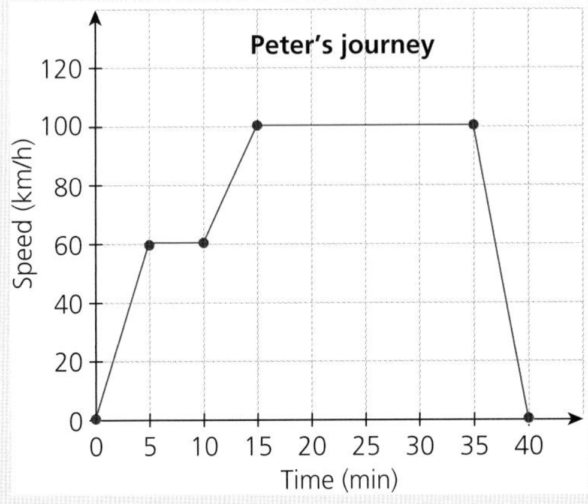

(i) At the start of the journey, Peter's speed went from 0 km/h to 60 km/h. What length of time did this take?

(ii) For how long was Peter travelling at 60 km/h?

(iii) What was Peter's highest speed during the journey?

(iv) For how long was Peter travelling at the highest speed?

(v) How far did Peter travel at the highest speed?

3 The graph below shows some details of Grace's cycle ride in the country.

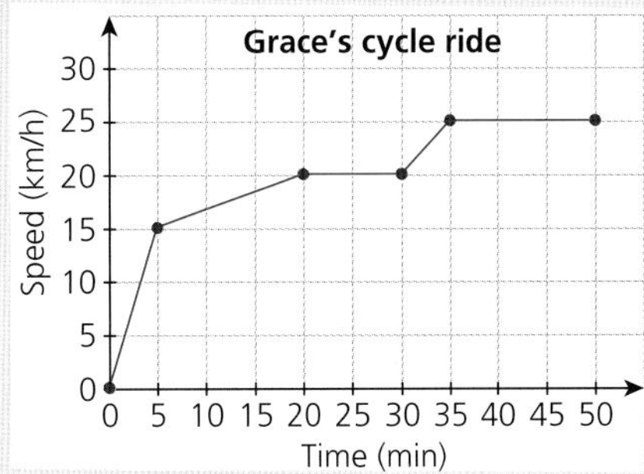

(i) Describe Grace's progress during the different parts of her journey.

(ii) What was Grace's highest speed during the journey?

(iii) For what length of time was Grace travelling at the highest speed?

(iv) How far did Grace travel at the highest speed?

4 The graph below shows some details of a car's journey as it travelled from one set of traffic lights to the next.

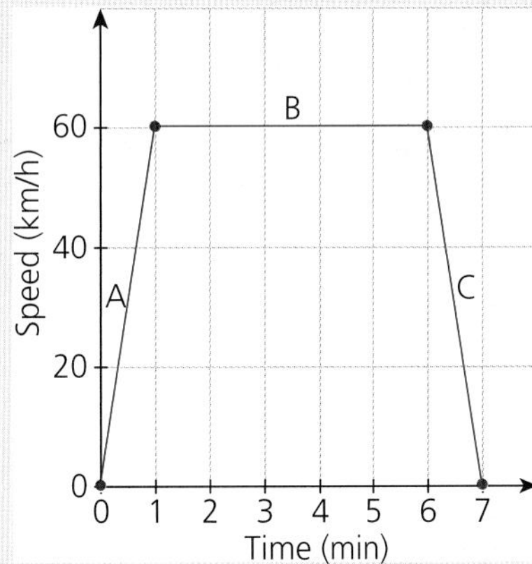

(i) Describe the progress of the car during the three stages A, B and C of the journey.

(ii) What was the car's highest speed during the journey?

(iii) How far did the car travel at the highest speed?

5 The graph below shows some details about a journey Alex made by bicycle.

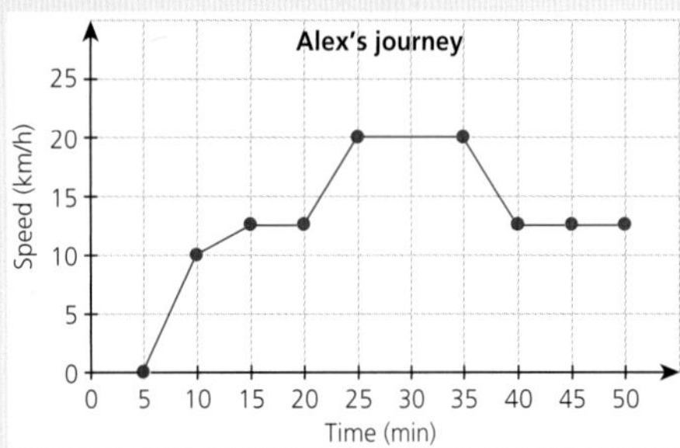

Alex waited for his friend before he set off on his journey.

(i) How long did he wait before setting out?

(ii) What was Alex's highest speed during the journey?

(iii) For what length of time was Alex travelling at the highest speed?

(iv) How far did Alex travel at the highest speed?

6 A train was at rest in a station. It then moved off, increasing its speed steadily up to 80 km/h over a period of 2 minutes. The train then travelled at this steady speed for 6 minutes. Finally, it steadily reduced its speed until it came to rest after a further 1 minute.

Show the details of this train's journey on a speed–time graph.

Hint

› Always note what the variables on each axis are.

7 What information is given by the following graphs?

(i)

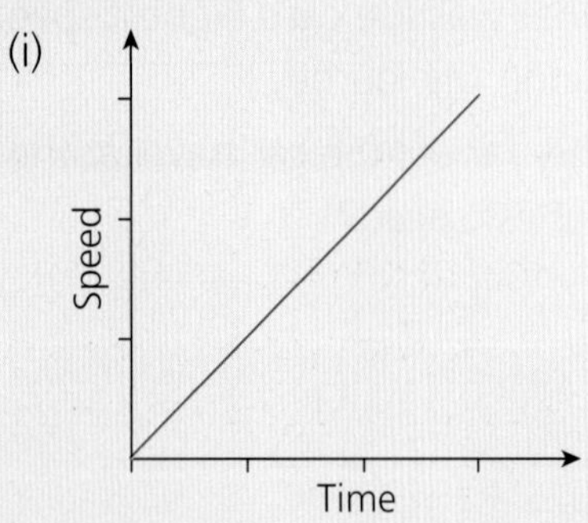

(ii)

(iii)

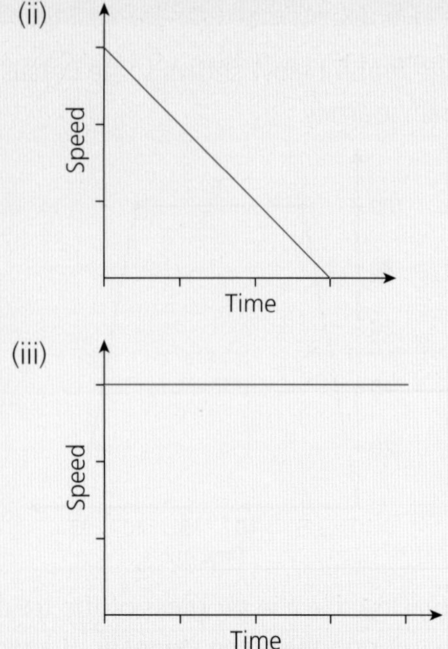

8 The graph shows how the speed of a car varied on a short journey.

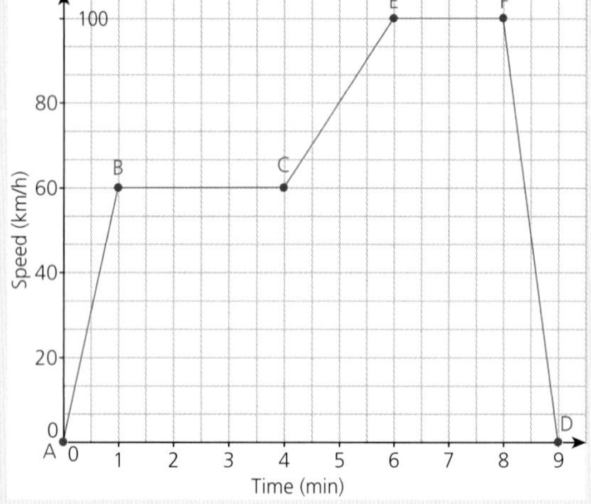

(i) What is the speed of the car after 3 minutes?

(ii) For how long is the speed of the car increasing?

(iii) What is the car's maximum speed?

(iv) Find the distance travelled by the car at its maximum speed.

(v) What is happening to the speed of the car between 8 and 9 minutes?

(vi) If the total distance travelled is $10\frac{1}{3}$ km, find the average speed of the car over the whole journey.

9 The graph shows the speed of a train during the first minute of its journey as it leaves a station.

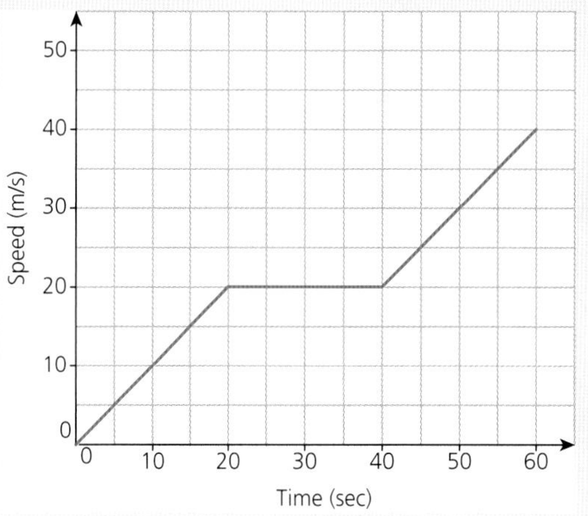

(i) Describe the train's progress during this minute.

(ii) What was the highest speed reached by the train in the first minute? Express this speed in km/h.

10 A car starts from rest at a traffic light and accelerates (increases its speed) uniformly at the rate of 3 m/s every second. As it starts, it is passed by a cyclist who is moving at a constant speed of 12 m/s.

Draw a speed–time graph to show this information and use it to see how long it will take the car to reach the same speed as the cyclist.

11 A tractor and a fast car are stopped at a traffic light. Sketch a speed–time graph to show the speeds of the two vehicles as they move away from the traffic light.

Section 11E Graphs in Real-life Contexts

Constant Flow Rate Graphs

Now we will look at some general graphs that represent the change in height of water for a given container versus the time taken to pour the water into the container.

In these questions, the water is always flowing at a constant rate. However, the graphs will vary due to the different-shaped containers being filled.

For example, let's consider these two cylinders. Which container do you think will fill faster?

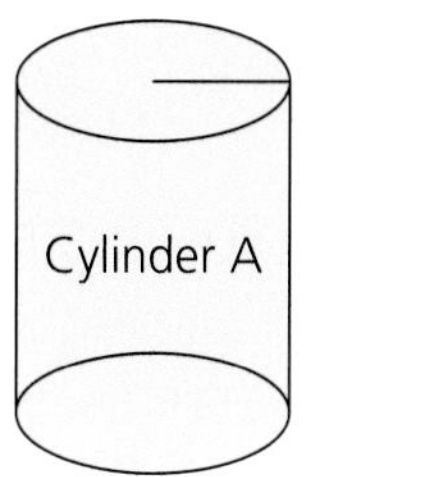

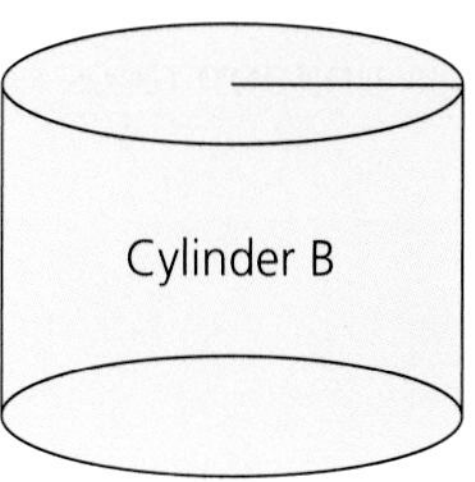

Water is poured into both cylinders at the same time and rate.

Let's look at the graphs that represent these cylinders.

Height (cm)

A

B

Time (sec)

From observation:

- As each cylinder fills up with water flowing at a constant rate, its graph is linear.
- Cylinder A fills faster as it has the smaller base (or radius) of the two cylinders. We can see this on the graph by the fact that the slope of the graph of A is greater than the slope of B.

Example 1

Below are four containers, labelled 1 to 4. Water is poured into each container at a constant rate, until it is full.

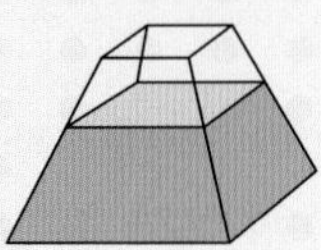
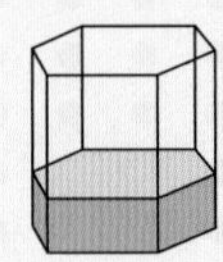
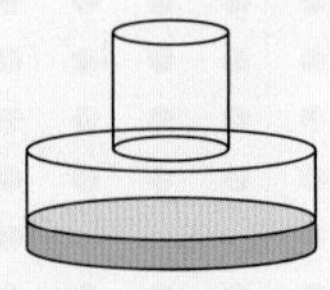
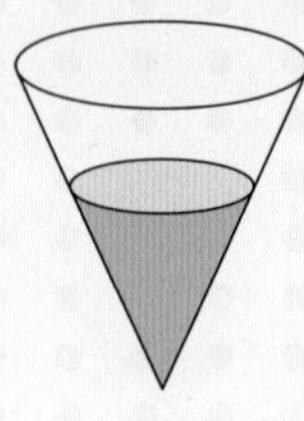

1 2 3 4

Draw a graph showing the height of the water, h, in each container after time t.

Solution

Container 1: Water rising slowing at first, then gradually rising faster; a curved graph:

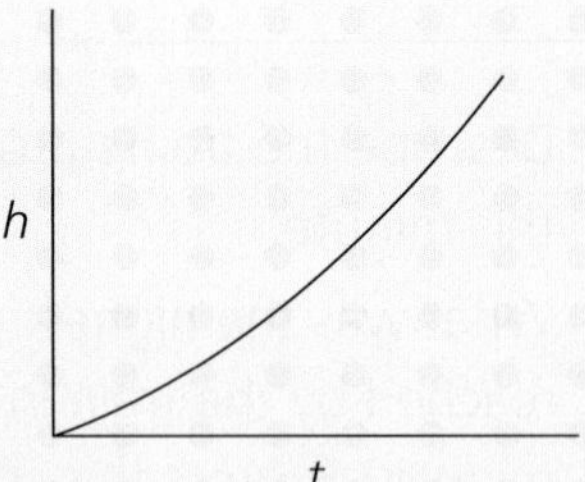

Container 2: Water rising at the same rate all the time; a straight-line graph:

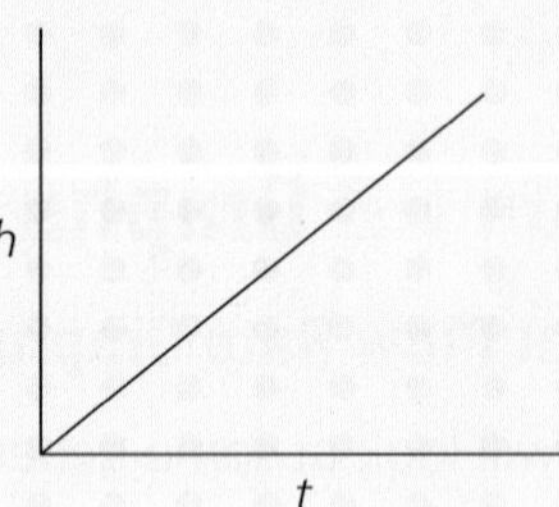

Container 3: Water rising at two different two uniform rates:

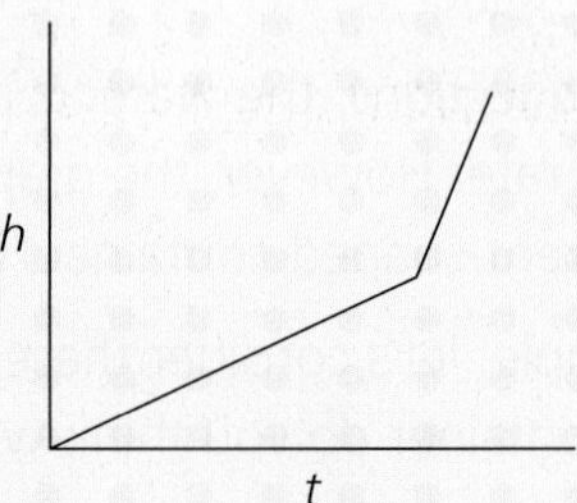

Container 4: Water rising fast at first, then gradually rising more slowly; a curved graph:

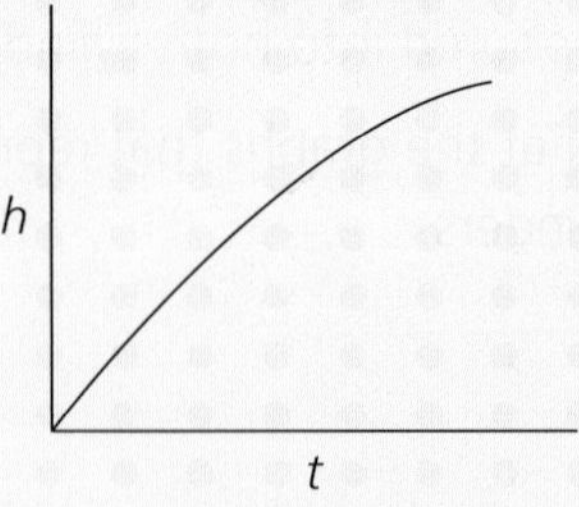

Distance–Time Graphs with Varying Speed

When a distance–time graph is linear, it means that the rate of change of the y-variable with respect to the x-variable is constant.

We will now look at distance–time graphs which are not linear.

Example 2

The table gives the approximate distances of a car from a point at different times.

Time (sec)	Distance from a point (m)
0	0
1	2
2	8
3	18
4	32
5	50

(i) What does the table tell you about the distance travelled per second by the car for each successive second?

(ii) Draw a distance–time graph for the car's journey in the first 5 seconds.

(iii) What does the graph reveal about the speed of the car?

Solution

(i) We can see from the table that with each successive second the distance travelled per second by the car is increasing. The car travels 2 m in the 1st second, 6 m in the 2nd second, 10 m in the 3rd second, 14 m in the 4th second and 18 m in the 5th second. Hence, the speed of the car is constantly increasing.

(ii)

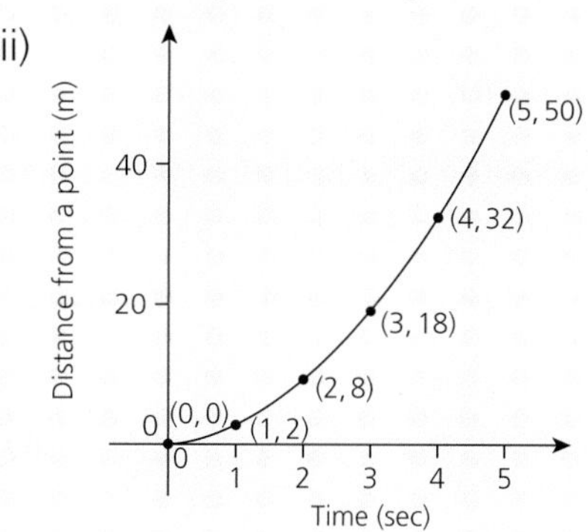

(iii) The slope is increasing all the time. Hence, the speed is increasing all the time.

Note: As the distance from the point is increasing, this means that the car is moving away from the point.

Activity 11.5

1 Robert cycled to the shop to get some groceries. He cycled along a particular route and returned by the same route. The graph shows the different stages of his journey.

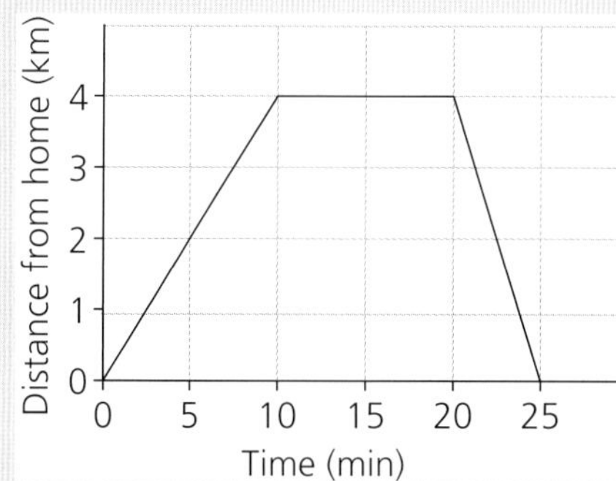

(i) How long did Robert stay in the shop?

(ii) How far from home is the shop?

(iii) Compare the speed of his trip to the shop with his speed on the way home.

(iv) Write a short paragraph to describe his journey.

2 Daniel went walking. He walked along a particular route and returned by the same route. The graph shows the different stages of his walk.

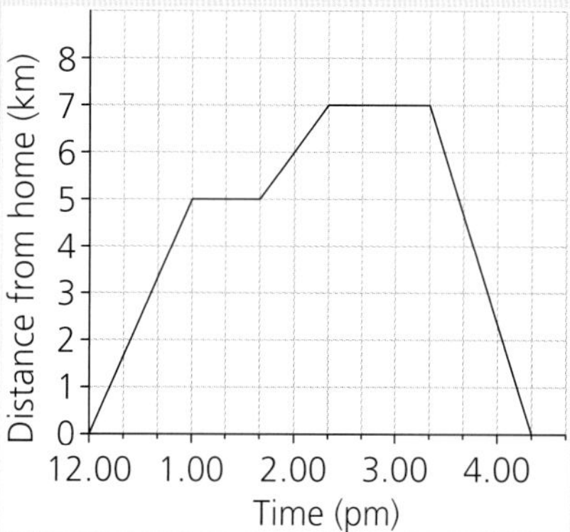

(i) At what time did Daniel leave home?

(ii) At what time did he return?

(iii) How far was he from home at 2.00 pm?

(iv) At approximately what two times was he 4 km from home?

(v) When was he travelling fastest?

(vi) When was he travelling slowest?

(vii) Write a short paragraph to describe his journey.

3 Kiera went on a scenic drive from Youghal to Cahir. She drove along a particular route and returned by the same route.

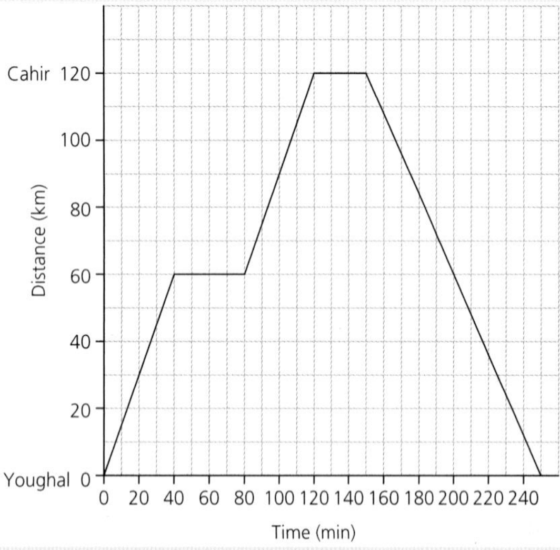

(i) For how long did she stop on the way?

(ii) Compare her speeds in the two sections when she was heading towards Cahir.

(iii) How long did she stay in Cahir?

(iv) Find her speed on the journey back by the slope of the graph on that section.

(v) Describe her trip in a short paragraph.

4 Lily was walking to the hairdressers. Having left the house, she suddenly remembered that she had forgotten her money. She returned to the house and got a lift to the hairdressers from a friend with a car.

The graph of this story is shown below.

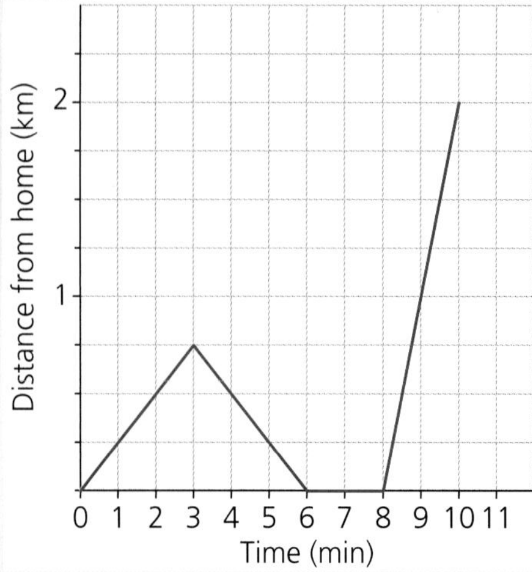

(i) How far from home was Lily when she turned back?

(ii) How long did she spend in the house before getting a lift?

(iii) How far is it from her house to the hairdressers?

(iv) Compare her walking speeds to the speed of the car.

5 The graph below maps distance from home against time.

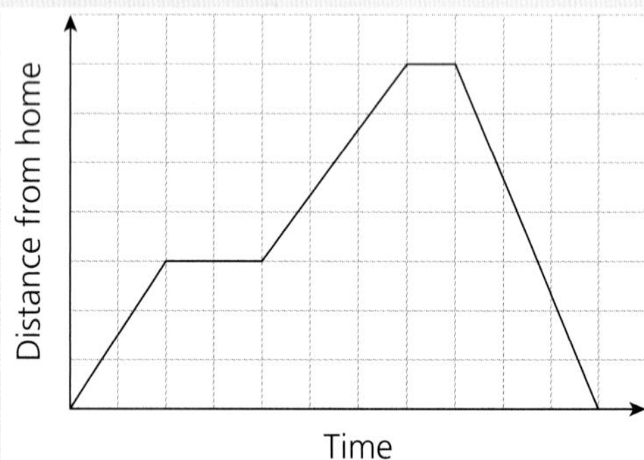

Write a story about speed which could be told by the graph. You should include:

- units on the axes
- references to the speed at various times
- total distances and times.

6 Do you remember the story of the hare and the tortoise? This graph tells the story.

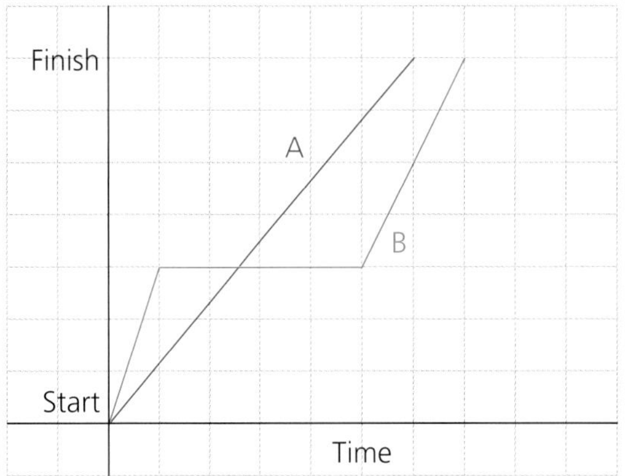

(i) Which is the hare and which is the tortoise?

(ii) Use the graph to re-tell the story in words.

7 Mary and John run against each other in a 200 metre race. Mary's time is 20 seconds and John's time is 25 seconds.

(i) Draw graphs to show their runs using just one set of scales and axes, assuming that they each ran at a steady speed throughout.

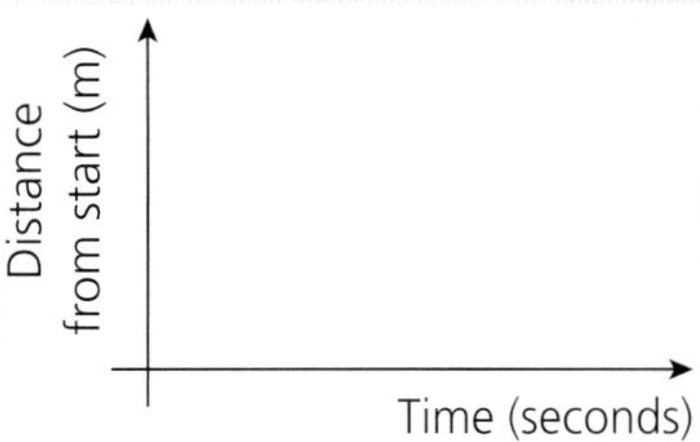

(ii) How do your graphs show that Mary ran faster than John?

(iii) Calculate the speeds of Mary and John. What units do you use?

8 This is a distance–time graph of Susan in her new car. What is happening?

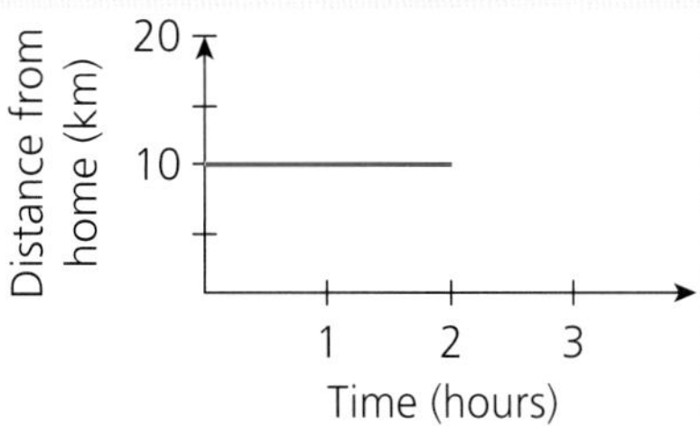

9 I started walking to school at a steady pace and then realised that I had left my books at home, so I hurried back to get them. Then my mother drove me to school so that I wouldn't be late.

Draw a graph of this story, with distance from home on the y-axis and time on the x-axis.

10 The graph shows a short section of a car's journey.

(i) Approximately how far did the car travel and how long did the car take to do it?

(ii) Approximately how far did the car travel in the first 10 seconds?

(iii) Approximately how far did it travel in the last 10 seconds?

(iv) Was the car travelling at a steady speed throughout? Justify your answer.

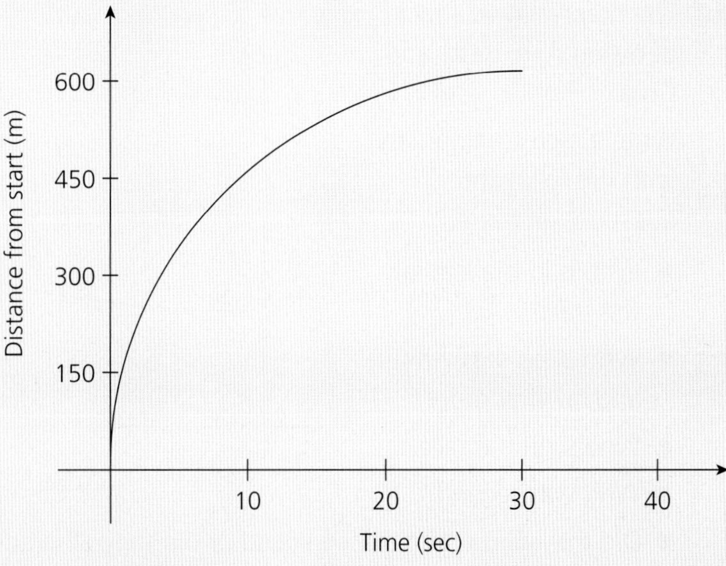

(v) Describe the speed of the car during this part of the journey.

11 Match each of these distance–time graphs with the situation which best fits it.

Situation	Graph
A. Moving at steady moderate pace	**1.** Distance / Time
B. Moving at a very fast pace then gradually moving to a slower pace	**2.** Distance / Time
C. Moving at a fast steady pace	**3.** Distance / Time
D. Moving fast, then slowing slightly, then going faster again	**4.** Distance / Time

12 The graph shows a race between Ann, Betty and Cora.

Write a race commentary, with the following questions answered:

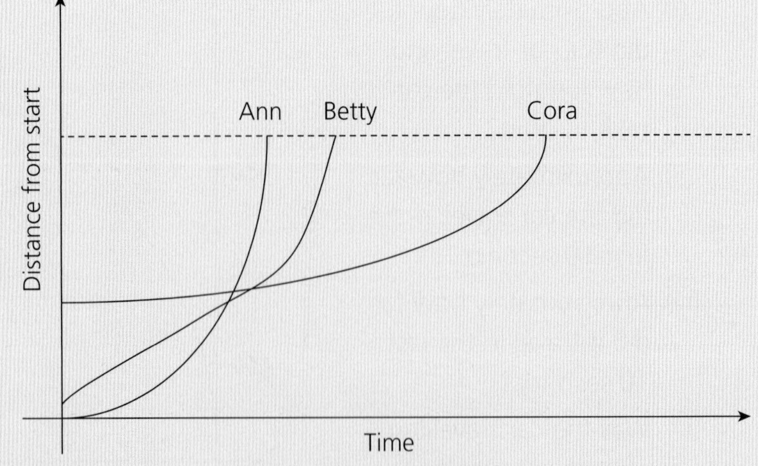

- Who is in the lead at the start?
- Who overtakes whom and in what order?
- Who won the race?
- Who was second?
- Did they all run at a steady speed or did they all gradually get quicker?

13 The graph shows the journey of three objects A, B and C.

Write a short paragraph to describe each journey.

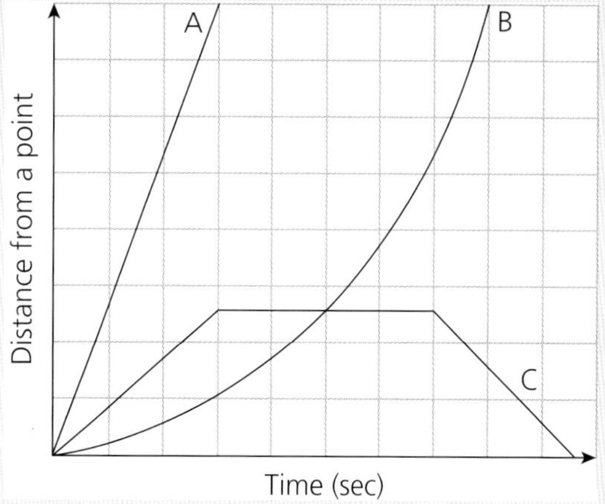

14 The following seven graphs show the change in the height of water in a bathtub with a rectangular cross-section, over time. Match each story with the correct graph.

Graph	Story
1. Height of water / Time	**A.** The height of the water is increasing at a constantly increasing rate as the tap is opened more and more.
2. Height of water / Time	**B.** The tap is open and the height of the water is increasing at a constant rate.
3. Height of water / Time	**C.** The bath plug is in, the tap is closed and the height of the water is constant.
4. Height of water / Time	**D.** The water is draining at a constant rate.
5. Height of water / Time	**E.** The height of the water is decreasing, slowly at first but then at a continuously increasing rate.

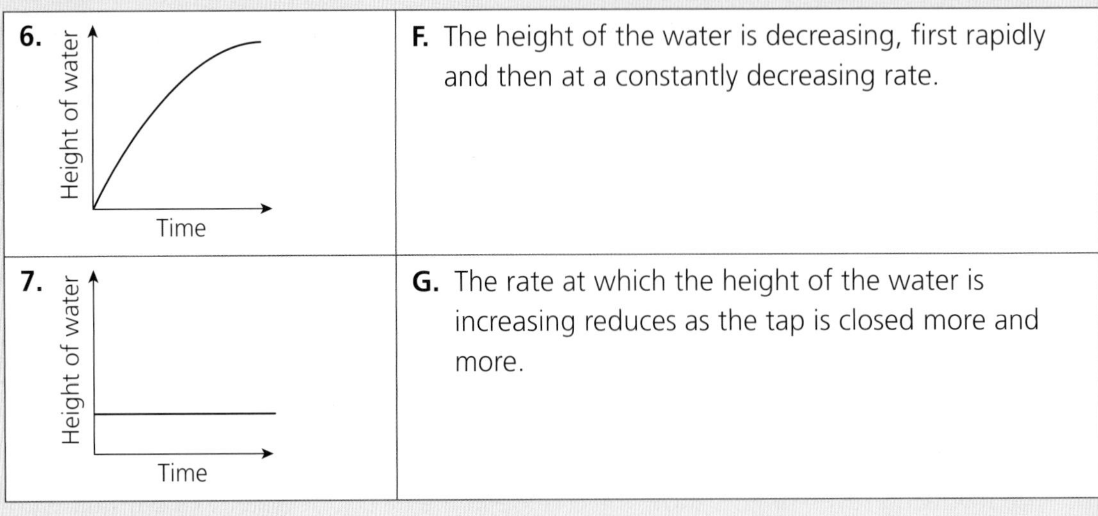

6. Height of water / Time	**F.** The height of the water is decreasing, first rapidly and then at a constantly decreasing rate.
7. Height of water / Time	**G.** The rate at which the height of the water is increasing reduces as the tap is closed more and more.

15 Match the following graphs with the correct statements.

1. 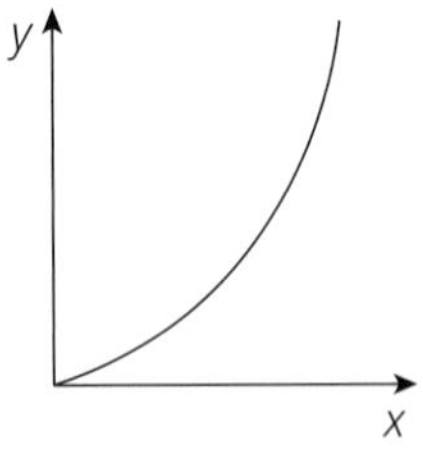 y, x	**A.** The rate of change of y with respect to x is not constant. The rate of change of y with respect to x is slow at first but increases continuously. The graph gets continuously steeper.
2. 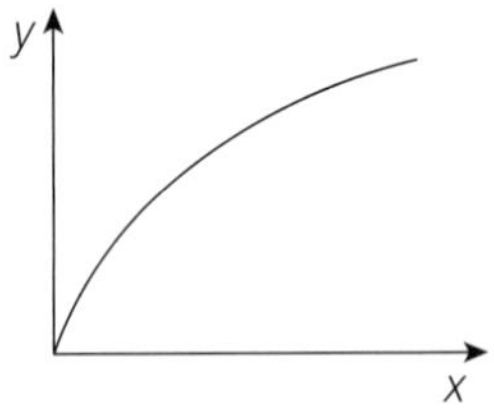 y, x	**B.** The rate of change of y with respect to x is not constant. The rate of change of y with respect to x is slow at first but gradually increases and then it gradually decreases again.
3. 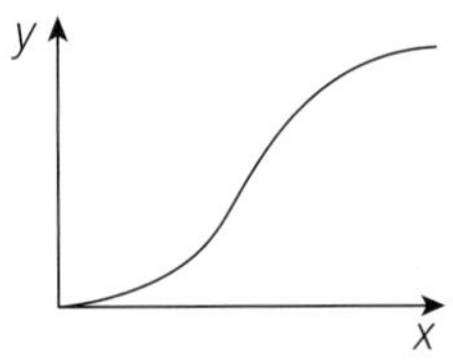 y, x	**C.** The rate of change of y with respect to x is not constant. The rate of change of y with respect to x is fast at first but gradually decreases and then it gradually increases again.
4. 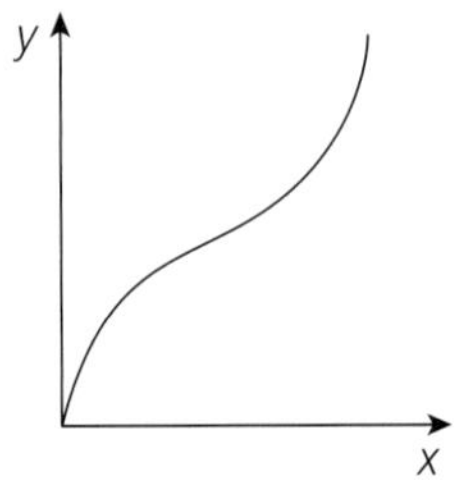 y, x	**D.** The rate of change of y with respect to x is not constant. The rate of change of y with respect to x is fast at first but decreases continuously. The graph continuously becomes less steep.

16 The table shows containers of various shapes which are being filled at a constant rate. Match each container to the graph which shows how the height of liquid in the container is varying with time.

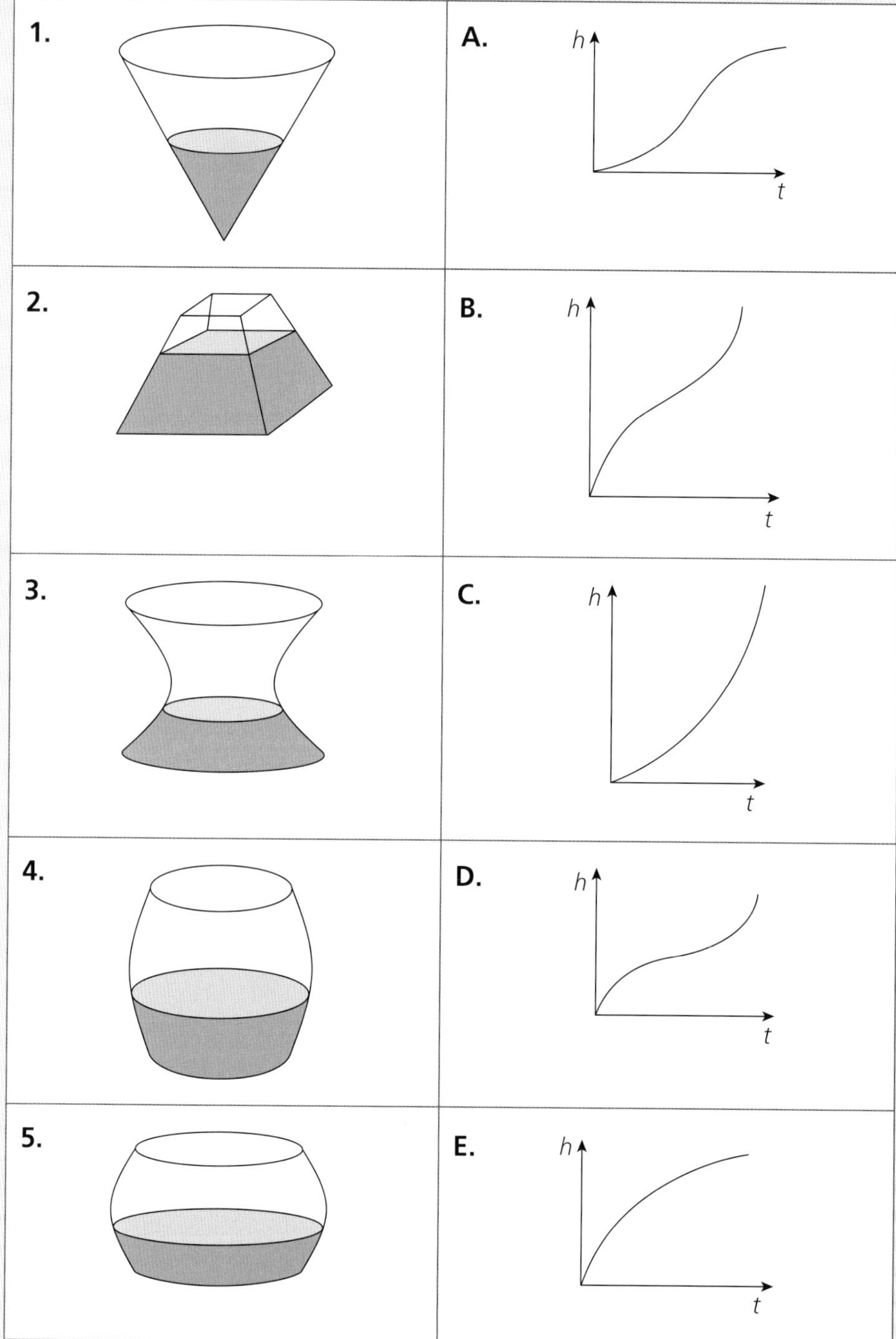

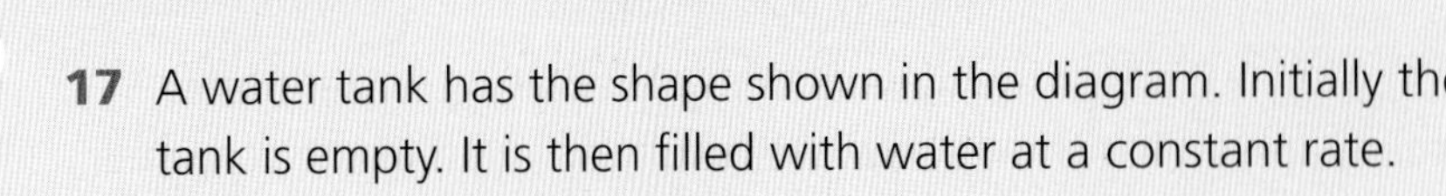

17 A water tank has the shape shown in the diagram. Initially the tank is empty. It is then filled with water at a constant rate.

Which of the following graphs shows how the height of the water surface in the tank changes over time?

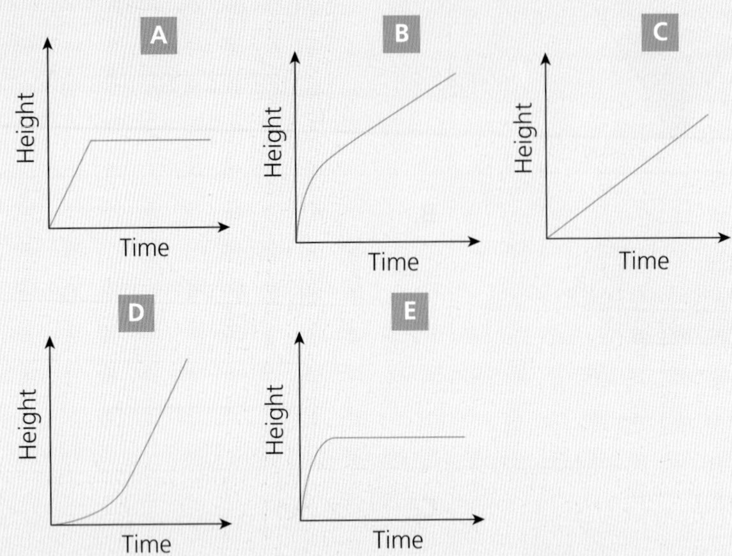

18 The containers shown are being filled with liquid at a constant rate.

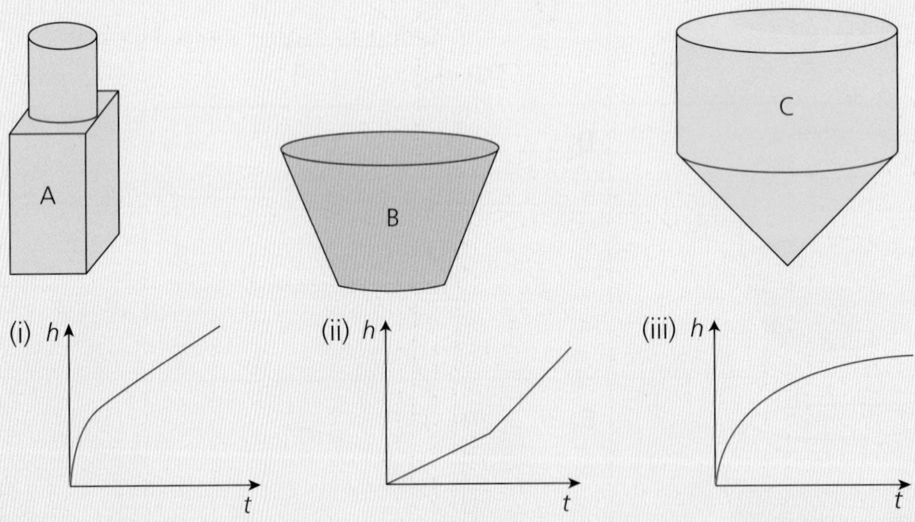

Match each of the containers to the correct graphical representation of the change in height of the level of liquid over time.

Revision Activity 11

1 The time taken by Jack to travel from Derry to Waterford, a distance of 378 km, is 6 hours. His return journey from Waterford to Derry, by the same route, takes an extra 45 minutes. By how many km/h is his average speed slower on the return journey?

2 The diagram shows a distance–time graph representing a practice cycle ride that Killian completed one evening.

(a) What is Killian's average speed between the points C and D?

(b) Between which points did Killian reach his highest speed and what was the highest speed?

(c) Between which two points did Killian travel at his slowest speed?

(d) What is Killian's overall average speed, correct to two decimal places?

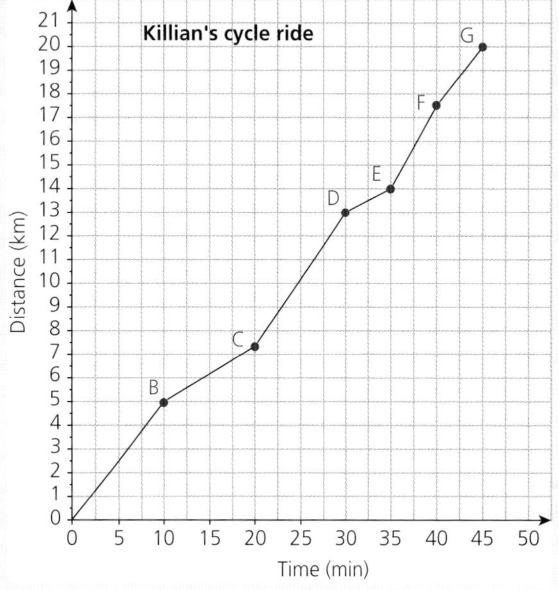

3 Represent the following journey on a distance–time graph and then calculate the overall average speed. Assume that each stage of the journey is travelled at steady speeds.

Tom travelled from his home to the bus station, a distance of 1 km, in 10 minutes. Tom arrived at the bus station and travelled by bus a distance of 5 km in 25 minutes to reach the city centre. Tom walked the last 500 m in 5 minutes.

4 Given that the speed of sound in air is 330 metres per second, express this speed in km/h.

5 This is the distance–time graph of a cyclist.

(a) How many stops did the cyclist make throughout the journey?

(b) How far did the cyclist travel between 12:45 and 1:45?

(c) At how many different speeds did the cyclist travel?

(d) What is the overall average speed of the cyclist, including the stops?

(e) What is the overall average speed of the cyclist excluding the time spent stopped?

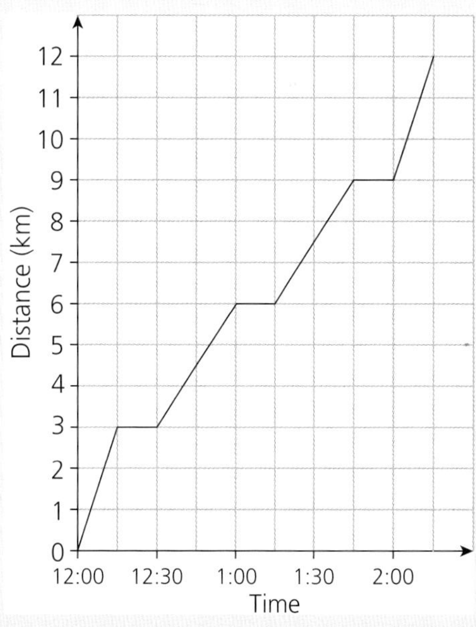

6 Draw the distance–time graph for the following journey.

Philip left his house to walk to the shop. He travelled 800 m in 10 minutes before stopping for 5 minutes to chat to a friend. Philip then walked 1200 m in 15 minutes to arrive at the shop. Philip spent 10 minutes in the shop. Philip left the shop and walked another 1000 m in 10 minutes to get to another friend's house, where he stayed for 20 minutes.

Philip was tired at this stage and decided to walk home, it took him 20 minutes to walk the 1000 m to get home.

Exam-style Questions

1 Angela leaves home (H) at 5 pm to go to football practice, which is 700 m away. The graph shows her journey, on foot, to football practice.

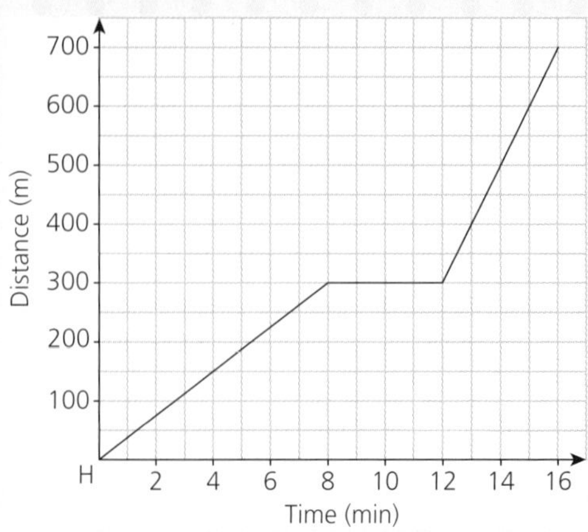

(a) Only one of the stories below matches Angela's journey. Which is the correct matching story?

A	Angela walks at a constant pace and stops at 5.08 for four minutes. She then walks at a slower pace and arrives at practice at 5.16.
B	Angela walks at a constant pace and stops at 5.12 for four minutes. She then walks at a faster pace and arrives at practice at 5.16.
C	Angela walks at a constant pace and stops at 5.08 for five minutes. She then walks at a faster pace and arrives at practice at 5.16.
D	Angela walks at a constant pace and stops at 5.08 for four minutes. She then walks at a faster pace and arrives at practice at 5.16.
E	Angela walks at a constant pace and stops at 5.08 for four minutes. She then walks at the same pace and arrives at practice at 5.16.

(b) Mary also lives 700 m from football practice, but cycles to practice. She leaves home five minutes after Angela. She cycles at a constant pace and arrives at practice two minutes before Angela.

Represent Mary's journey on the graph above.

JCHL 2013 Paper 1

2 Car A and car B set off from a starting point S at the same time. They travel the same route to destination D, which is 70 km away. Car A travels at an average speed of 50 km/h and car B travels at an average speed of 45 km/h.

How far will car B have travelled by the time car A arrives at destination D?

S ———————————————— D

JCHL 2013 Paper

KEY WORDS AND PHRASES

- **Average speed**
- **Distance–time graph**
- **Speed–time graph**

- **Average speed, distance and time**

Average speed = $\dfrac{\text{total distance travelled}}{\text{total time taken}}$

In two-speed problems, the average speed is not found by finding the average of the two speeds.

- When looking at any graph, always check what the variables are on both axes.

- In **distance–time** graphs:
  - the independent variable (on the x-axis) is time
  - the dependent variable (on the y-axis) is distance from a point.
  - When the rate of change of the distance from some point is constant, the distance–time graph is a straight line.

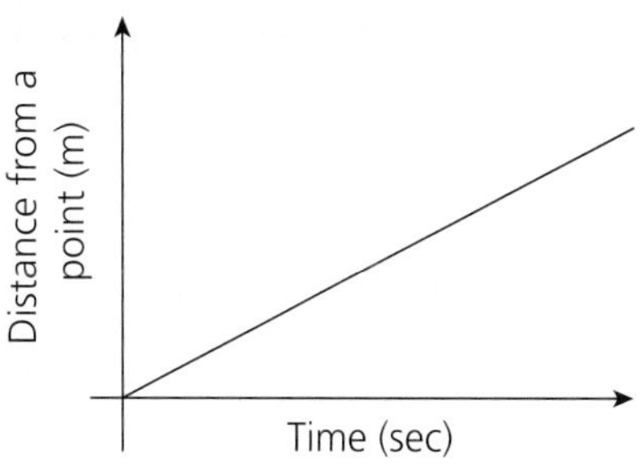

Slope = $\dfrac{\text{rise}}{\text{run}} = \dfrac{\text{metres}}{\text{seconds}}$ = speed in metres per second

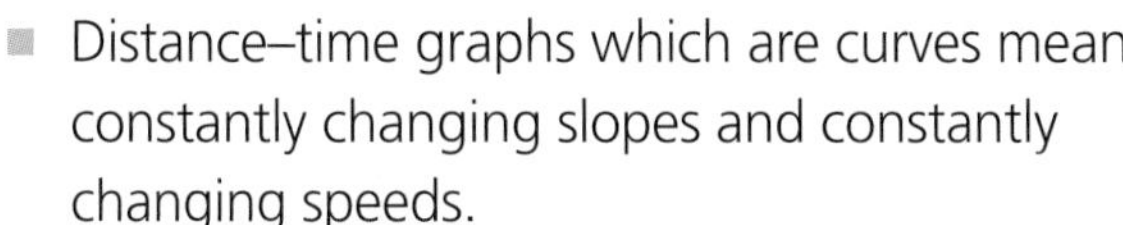

  - Distance–time graphs which are curves mean constantly changing slopes and constantly changing speeds.

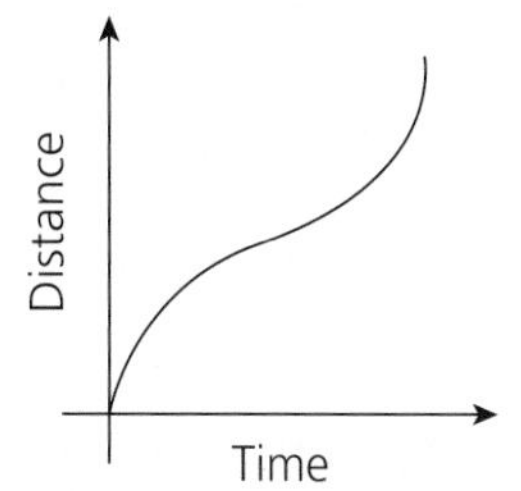

- In **speed–time** graphs:
  - the independent variable (on the x-axis) is time
  - the dependent variable (on the y-axis) is speed.

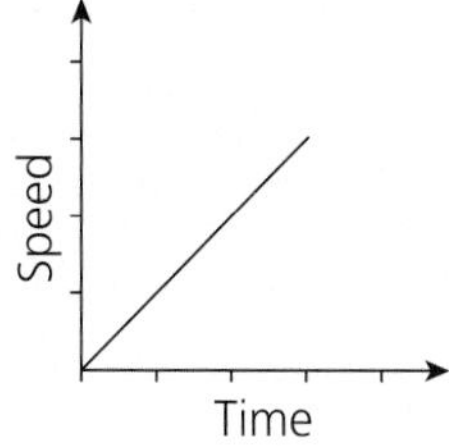

Chapter 12

Functions 1

Learning Intentions

In this chapter, you will learn about:

LO: U.5, U.6, AF.7

- Relations
- Ordered pairs (couples)
- Functions as special relations
- Functions as machines
- Representing functions using tables, mapping (arrow) diagrams, formulae and graphs
- The terminology of functions:
  - Inputs and Outputs
  - Domain, Codomain and Range
- Function notation

Historical Background

The idea of a function was developed in the 17th century by three mathematicians: René Descartes, Gottfried Wilhelm Leibniz and Leonhard Euler.

René Descartes (1596–1650) in his book *Geometry*, was the first to use the concept of a function.

Gottfried Wilhelm Leibniz (1646–1716) was the first person to use the term 'function', which he did nearly 50 years later.

Leonhard Euler (1707–1783) was the first person to use the notation $f(x)$ for a function.

Descartes

Leibniz

Euler

Section 12A Introduction to Relations and Functions

The word **relationship** means a connection or link.

In mathematics, a **relation** describes a **relationship** between two sets.

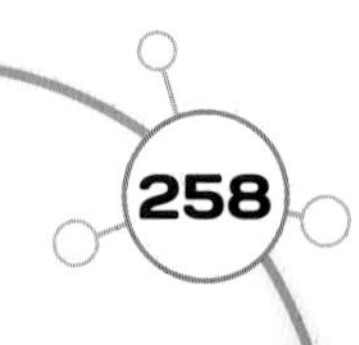

Example: Mary is saving €5 each week.

This table shows Mary's savings over a number of weeks:

Week number (x)	0	1	2	3	4
Amount of savings (€) (y)	5	10	15	20	25

There is a **relationship** between the week number (x) and her amount of savings (y).

We see that each week number has *exactly one* amount of savings associated with it.

This is a special type of relation called a **function**.

We say that the amount of Mary's savings (y) **is a function of** the number of weeks she has been saving (x) and we write this as $y = f(x)$.

As well as using a table, there are other ways of representing a function like this one:

- As the savings start at €5 and increase by €5 each week, we see that it is a **linear** relationship. We can describe it by its formula $y = 5x + 5$ where y is the amount of Mary's savings after x weeks.
- This function can be described as a set of **ordered pairs** (couples):

  $\{(0, 5), (1, 10), (2, 15), (3, 20), (4, 25)\}$
- We can also represent this relation on an **arrow diagram** (mapping diagram) from set A to set B like this:

  The set A contains the **inputs** and set B contains the **outputs**.

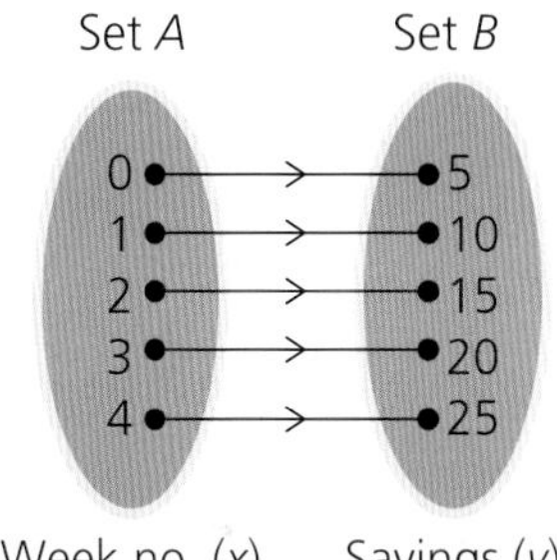

Notice that there is **exactly one arrow** coming out of each of the elements of set A. This is how we recognise a function from such a diagram.

- We also find it helpful to think of a function as an **input-output** machine where the output is somehow related to the input:

In the example of Mary's savings, the inputs are the week numbers and the outputs are the amount of savings for each week. For example, for an input of 2, the output is 15 and for an input of 4 the output is 25.

The concept of a function is important not only in mathematics, but in everyday life.

Simple examples are:

- Each person is given **one** Personal Public Service (PPS) number
- Each item in a shop is assigned a **unique** bar-code number
- Each home or business in the country is assigned a **unique** Eircode as part of their address

Every function has a set of inputs, a set of outputs and a relationship which links them.

A **function** must have:

1. A set, A, which contains the inputs.
2. A rule which works on **every** element of set A.
3. A set, B, which contains all the possible outputs when the rule is applied to set A.

In addition, a relation is a function if:

4. Every couple in the relation **has a different first co-ordinate**.
5. On an arrow diagram, **exactly one** arrow leaves each element of the input set A.

The following mapping diagrams explain the conditions above.

Mapping 1

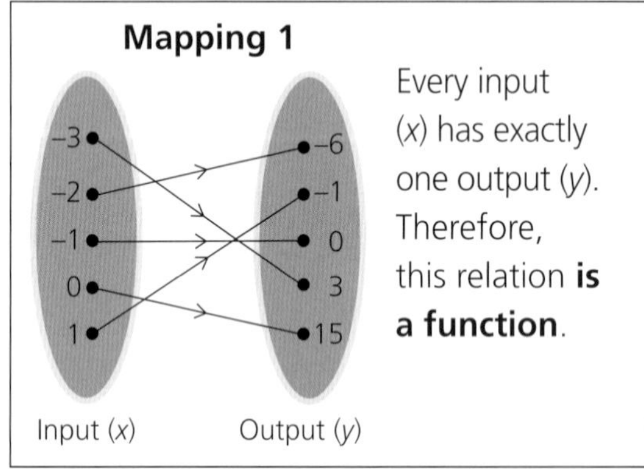

Every input (x) has exactly one output (y). Therefore, this relation **is a function**.

Mapping 2

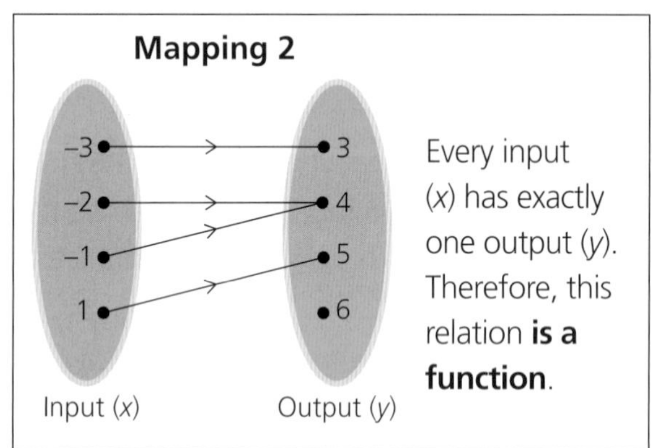

Every input (x) has exactly one output (y). Therefore, this relation **is a function**.

Note that in Mapping 2, the element 6 has no relationship, but that does not matter. The relation is still a function.

Mapping 3

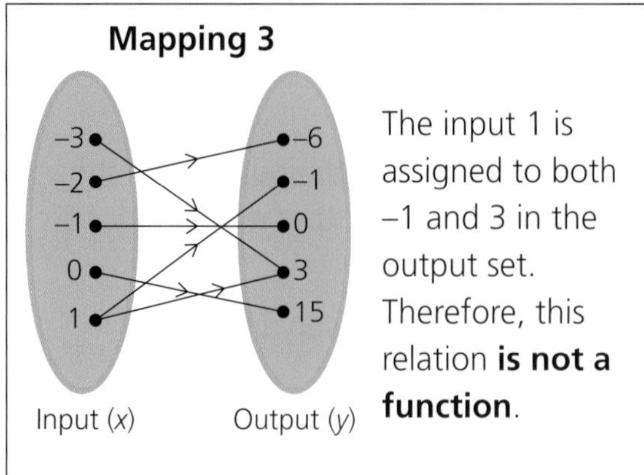

The input 1 is assigned to both −1 and 3 in the output set. Therefore, this relation **is not a function**.

Mapping 4

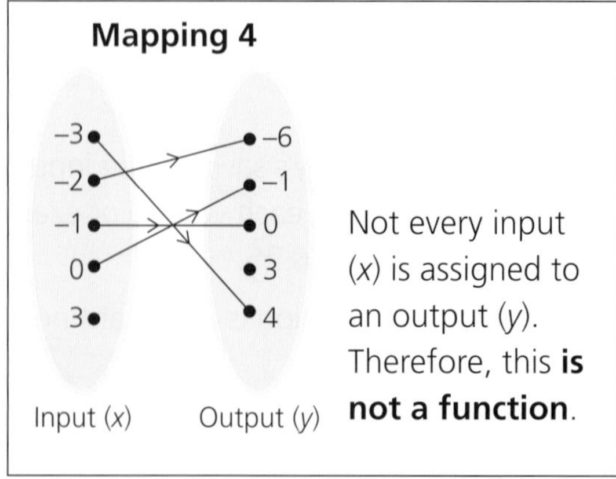

Not every input (x) is assigned to an output (y). Therefore, this **is not a function**.

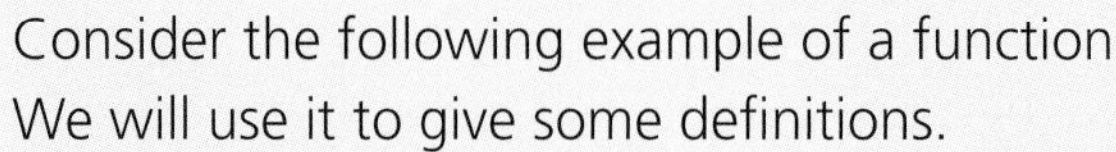

Consider the following example of a function.
We will use it to give some definitions.

A = {Mon, Tues, Wed, Fri}

B = {1, 2, 3, 4, 5, 6, 7}

The rule is 'the position of this day in the week is'.

- The **domain** of a function is the set which has all the inputs. In this example, the domain A = {Mon, Tues, Wed, Fri}
- The **codomain** is the set B which contains all the **possible outputs**. In this example, the codomain B = {1, 2, 3, 4, 5, 6, 7}.

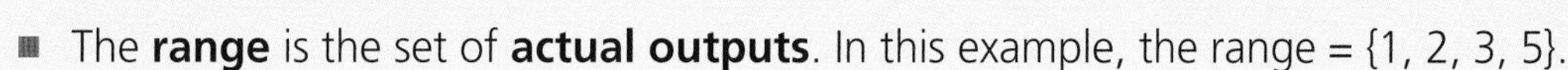

- The **range** is the set of **actual outputs**. In this example, the range = {1, 2, 3, 5}.

To summarise:

A **function** is a special relation in which no two couples have the same first element.

On an arrow diagram, we have a function if **exactly one** arrow leaves each element of the input set A.

Example 1

(i) Say why the relation represented by the arrow diagram below is a function.

(ii) Work out a rule for the function.

(iii) List the elements of the:

(a) domain

(b) codomain

(c) range.

(iv) What do you notice about the elements in the codomain and the range?

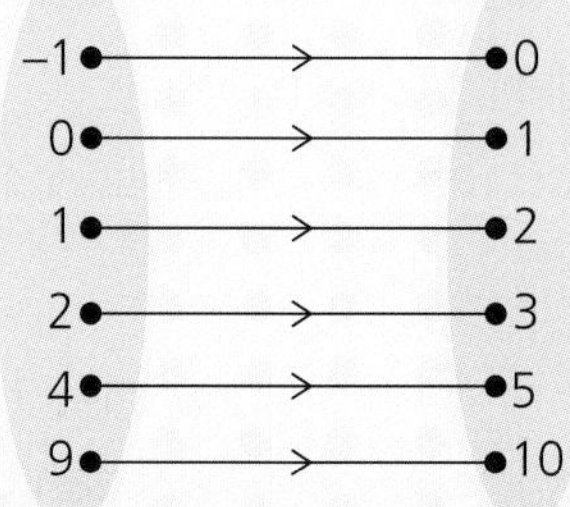

Solution

(i) This relation is a function because:

Exactly one arrow leaves each element of the input set.

(ii) From the input-output table below, we see that the output value is 1 more than the input value. So the function rule is:

Output = input + 1

Input (x)	Rule: add 1 to the input: $y = x + 1$	Output (y)
–1	–1 + 1	0
0	0 + 1	1
1	1 + 1	2
2	2 + 1	3
4	4 + 1	5
9	9 + 1	10

(iii) (a) Domain = {–1, 0, 1, 2, 4, 9}.

(b) Codomain = {0, 1, 2, 3, 5, 10}.

(c) Range = {0, 1, 2, 3, 5, 10}.

(iv) The elements in the codomain and the range are the same, as all the possible outputs have an input.

Example 2

A relation is given by these ordered pairs: {(2, 6), (1, 4), (2, 4), (0, 0), (1, 6), (–3, 0)}

(i) Represent the relation on an arrow diagram.

(ii) Can you think of a rule which describes this relation?

(iii) Is this relation a function? Explain your answer.

Solution

(i)

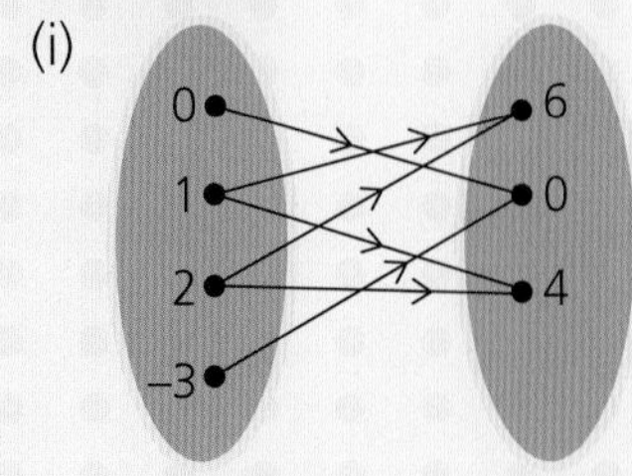

(ii) One possible rule is 'the input is less than or equal to the output'.

(iii) This is **not** a function. There are two couples with 1 as the first co-ordinate. There are also two couples with 2 as the first co-ordinate.

Example 3

(i) Write down the ordered couples of the function shown in the mapping diagram.

(ii) List the elements of the:

(a) domain

(b) codomain

(c) range.

(iii) What do you notice about the elements in the codomain and the range?

(iv) Work out the rule for the function.

(v) Show the function on a co-ordinate plane.

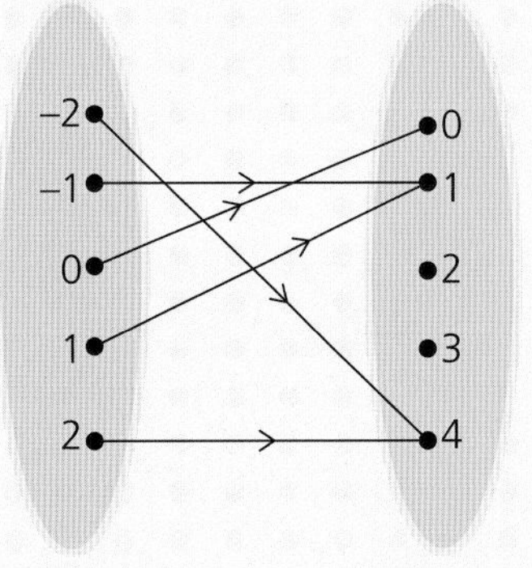

Solution

(i) The ordered couples are:
{(–2, 4), (–1, 1), (0, 0), (1, 1), (2, 4)}.

(ii) (a) Domain = {–2, –1, 0, 1, 2}.

(b) Codomain = {0, 1, 2, 3, 4}.

(c) Range = {0, 1, 4}.

(iii) The elements in the codomain and the range are different. This is because not all of the possible outputs are mapped onto.

(iv) From the input-output table below, we see that the function rule is:
output = (input)^2

or $y = x^2$

Input (x)	Rule: square the input	Output (y)
–2	$(-2)^2$	4
–1	$(-1)^2$	1
0	$(0)^2$	0
1	$(1)^2$	1
2	$(2)^2$	4

(v) Graph:

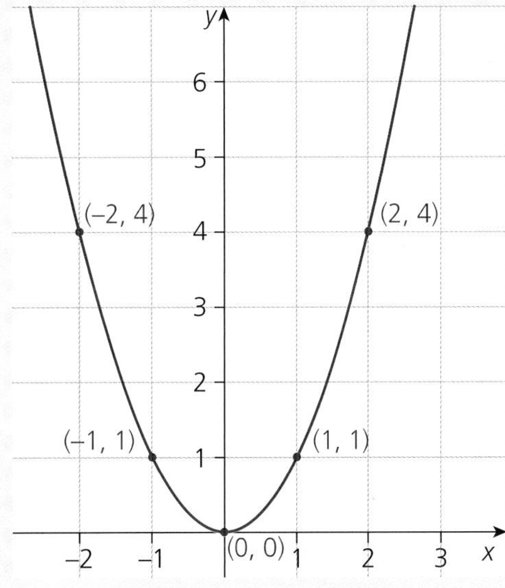

Key Point

Note that the shape of an x^2 graph is U-shaped. 

Activity 12.1

1 For each of the following relations:

(i) Represent it on an arrow diagram.

(ii) State whether or not it is a function, giving a reason.

(iii) Give a rule for each relation.

(a) {(4, 6), (6, 8), (5, 7), (0, 2)}

(b) {(2, 3), (2, 4), (4, 5) (4, 4), (2, 2)}

(c) {(9, 18), (8, 16), (7, 14), (6, 12)}

(d) {(1, 1), (2, 4), (–1, 1), (–2, 4), (3, 9), (–3, 9)}

(e) {(10, 10), (10, 9), (8, 8), (8, 7), (7, 7), (7, 6)}

2 Given the following relation:

{(9, 3), (9, –3), (4, 2), (4, –2), (1, 1), (1, –1)}

(i) Represent it on an arrow diagram.

(ii) Give a rule for the relation.

(iii) State whether or not it is a function, giving a reason.

3 There are ten houses on Clarkemount Avenue, numbered 1 to 10. In one week, the number of letters delivered to the houses were: 1, 4, 3, 2, 16, 6, 7, 4, 6, 5.

The relation is mapped below:

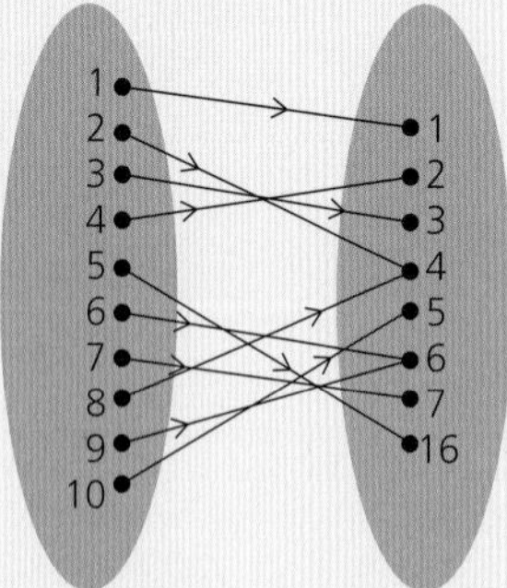

House Number of letters

(i) Write the relation as a set of ordered couples.

(ii) Explain why it is a function.

(iii) Write down the domain.

(iv) List the elements of the codomain.

(v) List the elements of the range.

4 The function mapped below gives the percentages achieved by five students in a mathematics test.

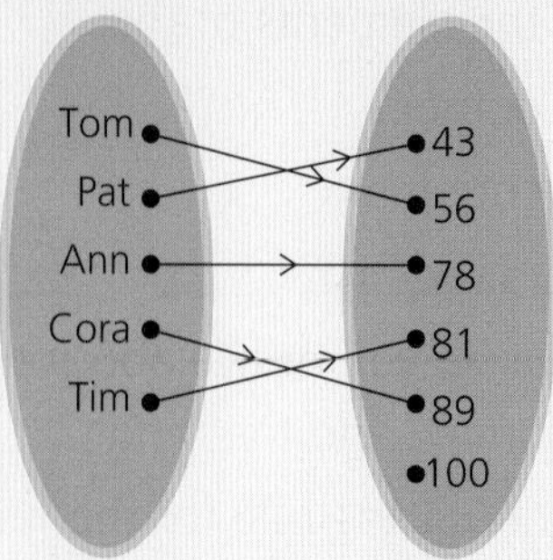

(i) Write the function as a set of ordered couples.

(ii) Explain why it is a function.

(iii) Write down the domain.

(iv) List the elements of the codomain.

(v) List the elements of the range.

5 The pattern of John's savings is shown below, where each pair means (week number, money saved):
{(0, 10), (1, 15), (2, 20), (3, 25)}.

(i) Describe, in words, the pattern of John's savings.

(ii) State whether or not this relation is a function, giving a reason.

Each mapping in Questions 6–11 shows a relation.

(i) Decide which mappings are functions and which ones are not. Give a reason for each answer.

(ii) For each function you have identified, use an input-output table to work out a rule which connects the inputs to the outputs.

(iii) Find the domain, codomain and range for each function you have identified.

6

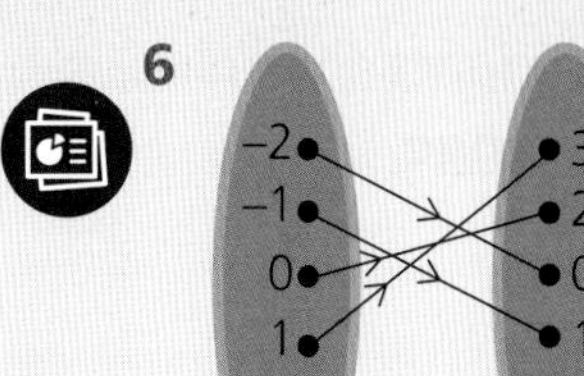

7

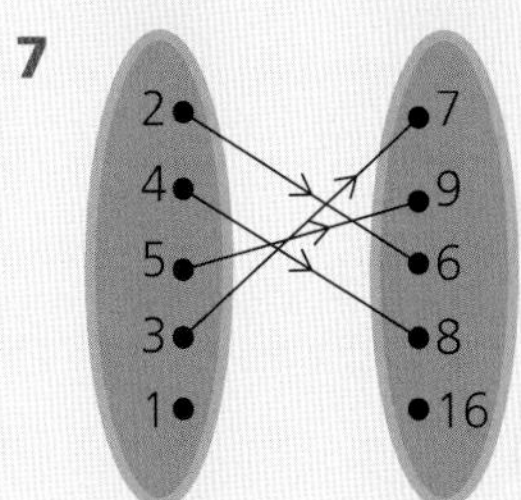

8

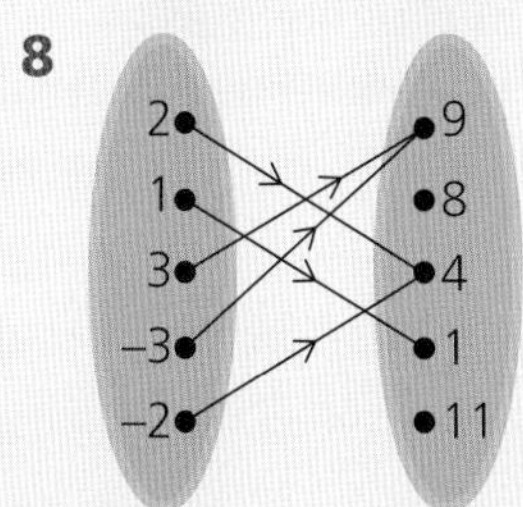

9

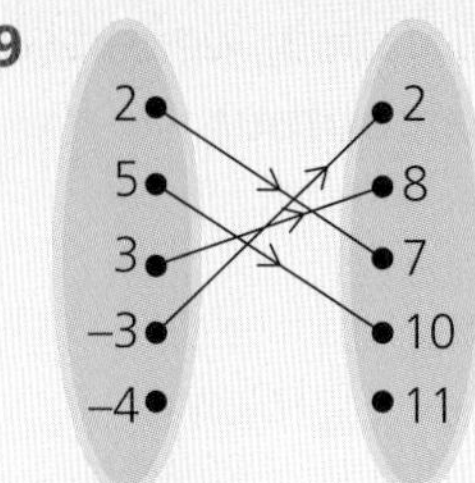

10

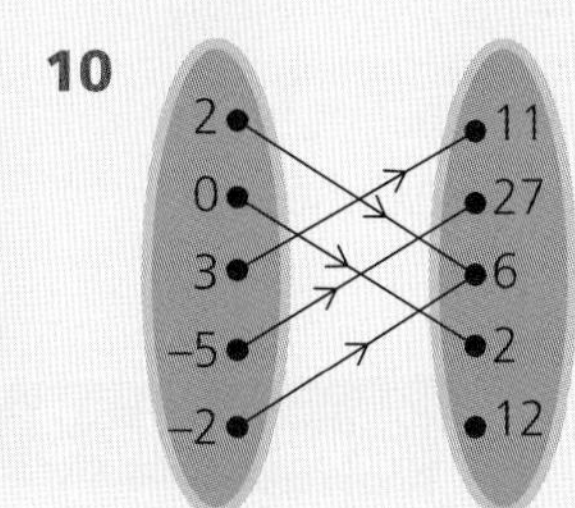

11

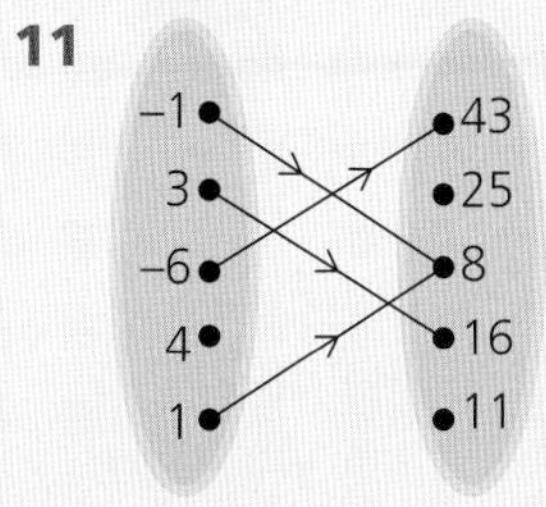

12 The area of a circle changes with the radius. The approximate area of the circle is given by the rule: 'the area of the circle is 3 times the radius squared'.

(i) Find the area of circles of radii: {2 cm, 3 cm, 4 cm, 5 cm}.

(ii) Write as a set of couples the function whose domain is the set in (i).

13 The area of a square is given by the rule: 'the area of the square is the length squared'.

(i) Find the area of squares of length: {2 cm, 4 cm, 6 cm, 8 cm}.

(ii) Write, as a set of couples, the function whose domain is the set in (i).

14 The area of a triangle is given by the rule 'the area of the triangle is half the base times the perpendicular height'.

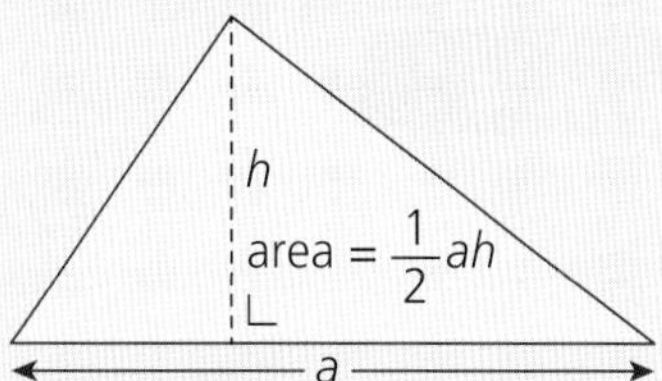

(i) Find the area of each of these four triangles if the perpendicular height is a constant 5 cm and the base lengths are: {2 cm, 4 cm, 6 cm, 8 cm}.

(ii) Write as a set of couples the function whose domain is the set in (i).

Section 12B Function Notation

We generally label functions using letters. As the word 'function' begins with the letter f, that letter is commonly used to refer to functions. However, if we have more than one function in a question, then we also use other letters, e.g. g, h, k, etc. Words are also used to name functions.

Functions can be referred to using the following notations:

$f(x) =$ OR $f: x \rightarrow$ OR $y =$

So the function: $f(x) = 2x^2 - 3x + 6$ can be also written as:

$$f: x \rightarrow 2x^2 - 3x + 6 \quad \text{OR} \quad y = 2x^2 - 3x + 6$$

So, if we think of a function f in terms of this new notation, we can say that a function applies a rule to every **input** (x) in the **domain** to produce an **output** $y = f(x)$ in the **range**.

Function: applies a rule to the input

We can look at this process in terms of this function machine.

Example 1

Given the linear function $f(x) = 2x + 4$, find the value of:

(i) $f(0)$
(ii) $f(2)$
(iii) $f(-2)$
(iv) $f(2) - f(0)$
(v) $f(-2) - f(0)$

Solution

(i) $f(0)$ means the output of the function $f(x)$ obtained by substituting 0 for x.

$f(x) = 2x + 4$

$\Rightarrow f(0) = 2(0) + 4$ … note brackets

$= 0 + 4$

$= 4$

(ii) $f(2) = 2(2) + 4$

$= 8$

(iii) $f(-2) = 2(-2) + 4$

$= -4 + 4$

$= 0$

(iv) $f(2) - f(0)$

$= 8 - 4$

$= 4$

(v) $f(-2) - f(0)$

$= 0 - 4$

$= -4$

Example 2

A quadratic function is defined as $f(x) = 2x^2 - 3x + 6$.

Find the value of:

(i) $f(2)$
(ii) $f(-2)$
(iii) $f(2) - 2f(-2)$

Solution

(i) $f(2)$ means the output of the function $f(x)$ obtained by substituting 2 for x.

$f(x) = 2x^2 - 3x + 6$

$\Rightarrow f(2) = 2(2)^2 - 3(2) + 6$

$= 2(4) - 6 + 6$

$= 8 - 6 + 6$

$= 8$

(ii) $f(-2) = 2(-2)^2 - 3(-2) + 6$

$= 2(4) - (-6) + 6$

$= 8 + 6 + 6$

$= 20$

(iii) We know $f(2) = 8$ and $f(-2) = 20$ from (i) and (ii)

$\Rightarrow f(2) - 2f(-2) = 8 - 2(20)$

$= 8 - 40$

$= -32$

Example 3

(i) Use an input-output table to find the range of the function $f(x) = x^2 + 5x + 6$ in the domain {–2, –1, 0, 1, 2}.

(ii) List the set of couples $(x, f(x))$.

Solution

(i)

Input (x)	Rule: $f(x) = x^2 + 5x + 6$	Output f(x)
–2	$(-2)^2 + 5(-2) + 6$	0
–1	$(-1)^2 + 5(-1) + 6$	2
0	$(0)^2 + 5(0) + 6$	6
1	$(1)^2 + 5(1) + 6$	12
2	$(2)^2 + 5(2) + 6$	20

The range = {0, 2, 6, 12, 20}

(ii) Couples: {(–2, 0), (–1, 2), (0, 6), (1, 12), (2, 20)}

Example 4

(i) Use an input-output table to find the range of the function $f(x) = x^2 + 4x + 3$ in the domain {–4, –3, –2, –1, 0}.

(ii) Show the set of couples $(x, f(x))$ on an arrow diagram.

Solution

(i)

Input (x)	Rule: $f(x) = x^2 + 4x + 3$	Output f(x)
–4	$(-4)^2 + 4(-4) + 3$	3
–3	$(-3)^2 + 4(-3) + 3$	0
–2	$(-2)^2 + 4(-2) + 3$	–1
–1	$(-1)^2 + 4(-1) + 3$	0
0	$(0)^2 + 4(0) + 3$	3

The range = {–1, 0, 3}

(ii) Arrow diagram for the function:

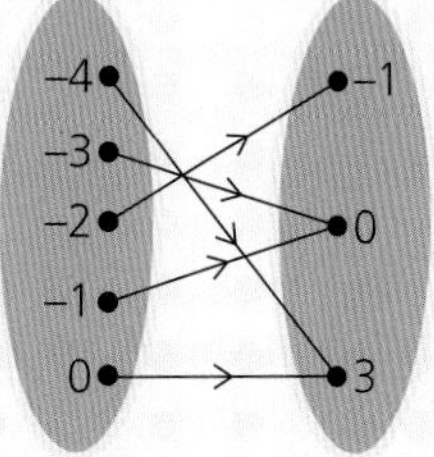

The couples of $f(x)$ are {(–4, 3), (–3, 0), (–2, –1), (–1, 0), (0, 3)}.

Activity 12.2

1 Given the function $f(x) = 4x - 1$, find:

(i) $f(-1)$ (ii) $f(2)$ (iii) $f(1)$ (iv) $f(-1) + f(2)$ (v) $f(-1) - f(1)$

2 A function $P(x)$ connects the pay received by an employee and the number of hours worked (x). The pay rate is €8 per hour. If $P(x) = 8x$:

(i) Explain what $P(5)$ means in this context.

(ii) Find the pay received by an employee if she works 10, 20, 30 or 40 hours.

3 If a function is: $g(x) = x^2 - 4$, evaluate:

(i) $g(0)$
(ii) $g(-2)$
(iii) $g(1)$
(iv) $g(-1) + g(2)$
(v) $g(-1) - g(1)$

4 The function $m: x \longrightarrow x + 6$ is defined on the domain {−2, 1, 4, 7}. Write out the elements of the range.

5 Draw an arrow diagram for the functions below.

(i) $f(x) = 3x - 2$ in the domain {−2, 1, 0, 1, 2}
(ii) $g(x) = -x + 8$ in the domain {−4, −3, −2, −1, 0, 1}

6 A function is $f: x \rightarrow x^2 - 4x + 3$. Evaluate:

(i) $f(-1)$
(ii) $f(2)$
(iii) $f(-3)$
(iv) $f(2) + f(-1)$
(v) $3f(-1) - f(-3)$

7 State three different ways that you can write (notate) a function.

8 Write out the following rules using function notation.

(i) Add 5 to the input.
(ii) Double the input and add 9.
(iii) Treble the input and subtract 7.
(iv) Square the input and subtract 2.
(v) Square the input, then subtract twice the input and add 3.

9 The function $v(t) = 5 + 10t$ connects the final speed v m/s and the time t in seconds of an object. Find:

(i) $v(0)$
(ii) Explain what $v(0)$ means in this context.
(iii) $v(2)$
(iv) Explain what $v(2)$ means in this context.
(v) $v(5)$
(vi) $v(8)$
(vii) $v(10)$

10 (i) Use an input-output table to find the range of the function $f(x) = x^2 - 6x + 7$ in the domain {−2, −1, 0, 1, 2}.

(ii) Show the set of couples $(x, f(x))$ on an arrow diagram.

11 (i) Use an input-output table to find the range of the function $f(x) = 2x^2 - 5x + 7$ in the domain {−1, 0, 1, 2, 3}.

(ii) Show the set of couples $(x, f(x))$ on an arrow diagram.

12 (i) Use an input-output table to find the range of the function $f(x) = x^2 + 5x + 5$ in the domain {−5, −4, −3, −2, −1, 0, 1}.

(ii) Show the set of couples $(x, f(x))$ on an arrow diagram.

Revision Activity 12

1 If $a = 4$ and $b = 5$, find the value of:

(a) $2a + b$ (b) $ab - 3$

2 If $f(x) = 4x - 5$, find:

(a) $f(3)$ (b) $f(-2)$

3 If $x = 3$, find:

(a) $4x + 5$ (b) $2x^2 - 11$

4 If $a = 4$, find the value of:

(a) $3a + 6$ (b) $3a^2 - 20$

5 If $d = 5$, find the value of:

(a) $4d + 1$ (b) $d^2 - 3d + 6$

6 $P = \{(1, a), (2, a), (3, b), (4, c)\}$.

(a) Draw a mapping diagram to represent this relation.
(b) Write out the domain of P.
(c) Write out the range of P.
(d) Is this relation a function? Explain your answer.

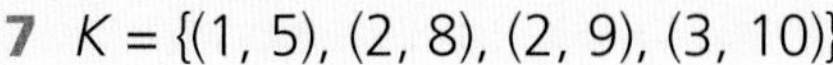
7 $K = \{(1, 5), (2, 8), (2, 9), (3, 10)\}$

(a) Draw a mapping diagram to represent this relation.
(b) Write out the domain of K.
(c) Write out the range of K.
(d) Is this relation a function? Explain your answer.

8 $M = \{(1, 3), (4, 6), (5, 8), (7, 9)\}$

(a) Draw a mapping diagram to represent this relation.
(b) Write out the domain of M.
(c) Write out the range of M.
(d) Is this relation a function? Explain your answer.

9 To convert square metres into square inches, you 'multiply the number of square metres by 1550'.

(a) Draw an input-output table to find the number of square inches for each of the following square metres: $\{2, 3, 4, 5\}$.
(b) Is this relation a function? Explain your answer.

10 To convert pints into gallons, you 'divide the number of pints by 8'.

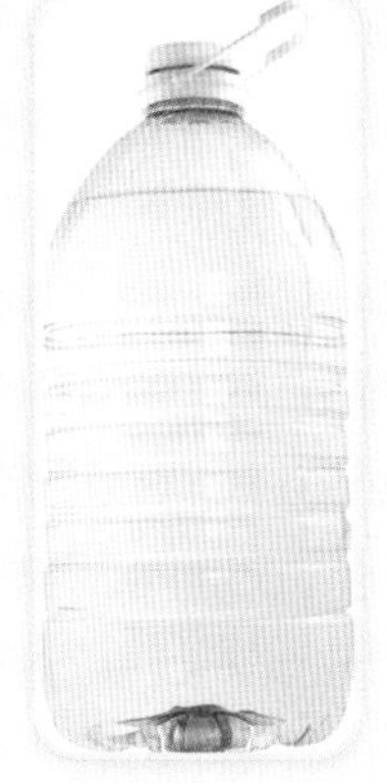
1 gallon

1 pint

(a) Using an input-output table, find the number of gallons for each of the following numbers of pints: $\{32, 48, 64, 120\}$.
(b) Represent the inputs and outputs graphically.
(c) Is this relation a function? Explain your answer.

Exam-style Question

1 Let g be the function $g : x \mapsto 2^{x-3}$.

(a) Find the value of $g(3)$.
(b) Let h be the function $h : x \mapsto x^2 - 3x$.
  (i) Express $h(t)$ and $h(2t + 1)$ in terms of t.
  (ii) Hence, find the values of t for which $h(t) = h(2t + 1)$.

JCHL 2012

KEY WORDS AND PHRASES

- **Relation**
- **Function**
- **Ordered couples**
- **Input**
- **Output**
- **Domain**
- **Range**
- **Codomain**
- **Relationship**

Interactive Tool 12.1

Chapter Summary 12

- A function is a special relation where:
  - Every input (x) must have an output (y).
  - Every input (x) must have only one output (y).
- In terms of an arrow diagram, for a relation to be a function there must be exactly one arrow coming from each input.
- The **domain** of the function f is the set of all **possible** inputs (x values) in the relation.
- The **codomain** is the set of all possible outputs.
- The **range** of the function f is the set of all **actual** outputs ($f(x) = y$ values) in the relation.
- Functions can be referred to using the following notation:

  $f(x) =$

  or $f : x \rightarrow$

  or $y =$

  pronounced 'f of x', 'f onto x' or 'y equals' respectively.
- The function $f(x) = 2x^2 - 3x + 6$ can be also written as:

  $f : x \rightarrow 2x^2 - 3x + 6$ or

  $y = 2x^2 - 3x + 6$

Functions 2

Chapter 13

Learning Intentions

In this chapter, you will learn about:

- Graphing linear functions
- Graphing quadratic functions
- Applications of linear and quadratic functions
- Exponential functions and their applications
- Transformations of functions

LO: U.5, U.6, AF.7

You will need...

- a pencil
- a ruler
- a geometry set

This chapter looks at how to graph linear, quadratic and exponential functions on the co-ordinate plane.

Recall:

Note

- ℕ is the set of natural numbers {1, 2, 3, ...}
- ℤ is the set of integers {..., −3, −2, −1, 0, 1, 2, 3, ...}
- ℝ is the set of real numbers, i.e. any number on the number line.
- On the co-ordinate plane:
  - the y-intercept is found when $x = 0$
  - the x-intercept is found when $y = 0$.
- Functions of the form $f(x) = ax + b$ are **linear functions**.
- Functions of the form $f(x) = ax^2 + bx + c$ are **quadratic functions**.

Key Points

When drawing the graph of a function, you must:

1. Use graph paper or squared paper.
2. Use a pencil to draw the graph.
3. Make the graph as big as possible by choosing suitable scales.
4. Label the x-axis and the y-axis (include required units).
5. Plot each point clearly.
6. For linear functions, use a ruler and a pencil to join up all the points, as graphs of linear functions are always straight lines.
7. For quadratic or exponential functions, use a pencil to join the points freehand, as these graphs are always curves.
8. Label each function clearly.

Section 13A Graphing Linear Functions

Example 1

Draw the graph of the linear function $f(x) \to -x + 3$, in the domain $-1 \leq x \leq 4$, $x \in \mathbb{R}$.

Solution

- As the function is linear, we need to plot only two points to draw the graph of the straight line. To ensure we don't make a mistake in our calculations, we always plot three points. We usually plot the points for the smallest and largest values in the domain, and another value somewhere in the middle.
- To graph the function, we find the couples for the x values -1, 2 and 4.

x	$-x + 3$	$f(x)$	Couple
-1	$-(-1) + 3$	4	$(-1, 4)$
2	$-(2) + 3$	1	$(2, 1)$
4	$-(4) + 3$	-1	$(4, -1)$

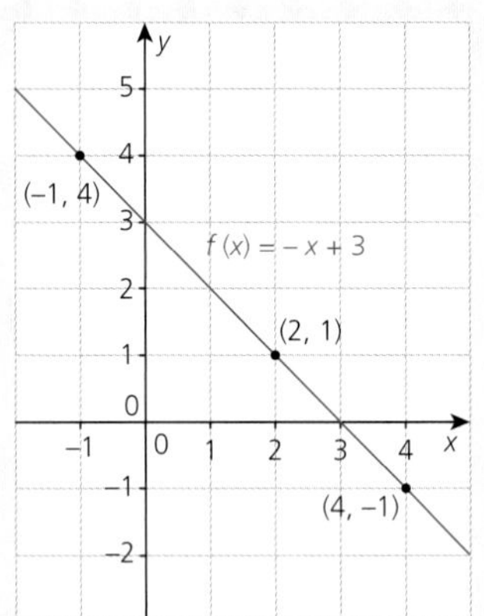

- Verify these answers using a calculator.
- Plot the couples and use a ruler and a pencil to join all the points.

When we draw graphs of functions, there are a number of values that we can find from the graphs. We can find:

- The root(s) of functions. These are found when $y = 0$. This is also called the x-intercept.
- The y-intercept of the function. This is found when $x = 0$.
- The value of the function $f(x)$ for given values of x.
- The value of x for a given value of $f(x)$.

Example 2

From the graph of the linear function $f(x) = 2x + 5$:

(i) Find the root of the equation $f(x) = 0$.

(ii) Find the value of $f(0)$.

(iii) Find the value of $f(-1)$.

(iv) Solve for $f(x) = 1$.

(v) Solve for $f(x) = -1$.

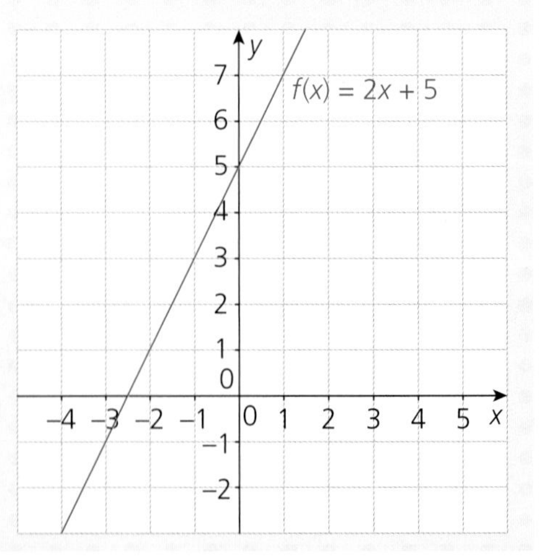

Solution

From the graph of the linear function:

(i) The root is $x = -2.5$, as this is the point on the line when $y = 0$.

(ii) The y-intercept is 5, from the y co-ordinate of the couple (0, 5).

(iii) $f(-1) = 3$. (The y co-ordinate of the couple (–1, 3) on the graph.)

(iv) The value of x when $f(x) = 1$ is found when $x = -2$. (The x co-ordinate of the couple (–2, 1) on the graph.)

(v) The value of x when $f(x) = -1$ is found when $x = -3$.

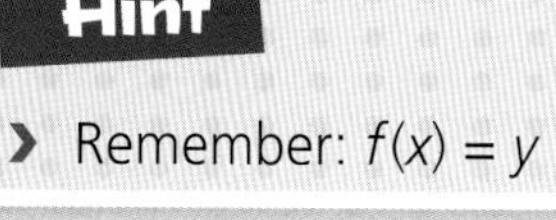

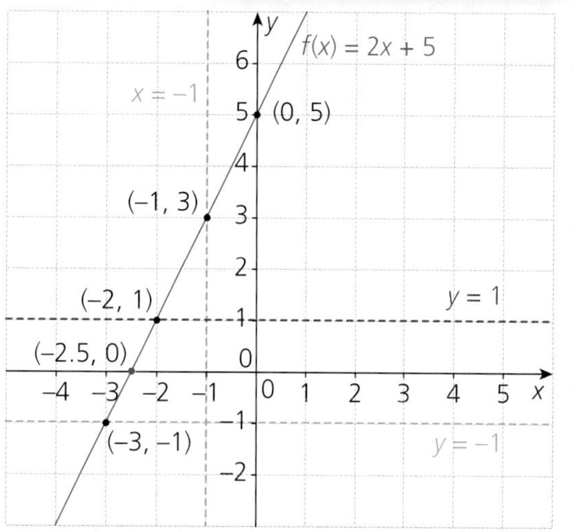

Finding Approximate Solutions to Equations

We can use the graphs of functions to solve equations such as $f(x) = g(x)$, where $f(x)$ and $g(x)$ are linear and/or quadratic functions.

Example 3

On the same co-ordinate plane, graph the functions $f(x) = -x + 6$ and $g(x) = 2x + 3$ in the domain $-2 \leq x \leq 3$, $x \in \mathbb{R}$.

Hence, find the value of x for which $f(x) = g(x)$.

Solution

- Find three couples for the function $f(x) = -x + 6$ in the domain $-2 \leq x \leq 3$, $x \in \mathbb{R}$.

x	$-x + 6$	y	Couple
–2	–(–2) + 6	8	(–2, 8)
0	–(0) + 6	6	(0, 6)
3	–(3) + 6	3	(3, 3)

- Find three couples for the function $g(x) = 2x + 3$ in the domain $-2 \leq x \leq 3$, $x \in \mathbb{R}$.

x	$2x + 3$	y	Couple
–2	2(–2) + 3	–1	(–2, –1)
0	2(0) + 3	3	(0, 3)
3	2(3) + 3	9	(3, 9)

- Graph both functions on the same co-ordinate plane. Then mark the point of intersection.

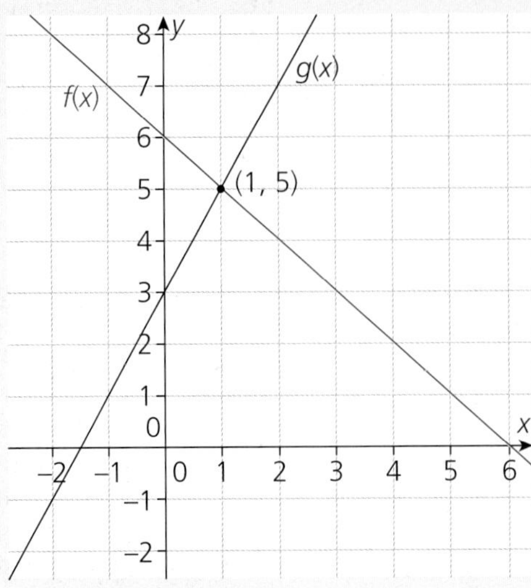

- From the graph, the point of intersection is the couple (1, 5).

  So, the value of x for which $g(x) = f(x)$ is 1.

Activity 13.1

1 (i) Copy and complete the table for the function $y = x + 2$ in the domain $-1 \leq x \leq 4, x \in \mathbb{R}$.

x	$x + 2$	y	Couple
−1			
0			
1			
2			
3			
4			

(ii) Verify that the graph of the function is linear by calculating the differences in the y values.

(iii) Plot the graph of the function using suitable scales.

2 (i) Copy and complete the table for the function $f: x \rightarrow -x + 2$ in the domain $-1 \leq x \leq 4, x \in \mathbb{R}$.

x	$-x + 2$	$y = f(x)$	Couple
−1			
0			
1			
2			
3			
4			

(ii) Verify that the graph of the function is linear by calculating the differences in the y values.

(iii) Plot the graph of the function using suitable scales.

3 Consider the function $f: x \rightarrow 5x + 2$ in the domain $-1 \leq x \leq 2, x \in \mathbb{R}$.

Draw the graph representing this function.

4 Consider the function $f: x \rightarrow -6x + 1$ in the domain $-2 \leq x \leq 2, x \in \mathbb{R}$.

Draw the graph representing this function.

5 (i) Draw the graphs of the functions $f(x) = x$ and $h(x) = 2x$ in the domain $-2 \leq x \leq 2$, $x \in \mathbb{R}$, using suitable scales on the same co-ordinate plane.
(ii) Write down the slopes of these graphs.
(iii) What do you notice about the y-intercepts of these graphs?
(iv) Predict the shape of the graph of the function $k(x) = 3x$ in the domain $-2 \leq x \leq 2$, $x \in \mathbb{R}$. Sketch the graph of the function $k(x)$ on the same co-ordinate plane.

For questions **6** and **7**:
(i) Draw an input–output table.
(ii) Draw the graph of the functions on the same co-ordinate plane.
(iii) Hence, find the value(s) of x for which $f(x) = g(x)$.

6 $f(x) = x - 2$ and $g(x) = 2x + 3$ in the domain $-8 \leq x \leq 0$, $x \in \mathbb{R}$.

7 $f(x) = 2x + 4$ and $g(x) = 3x + 2$ in the domain $-3 \leq x \leq 3$, $x \in \mathbb{R}$.

8 Here is part of the graph of the linear function $g(x) = 2x + 3$:

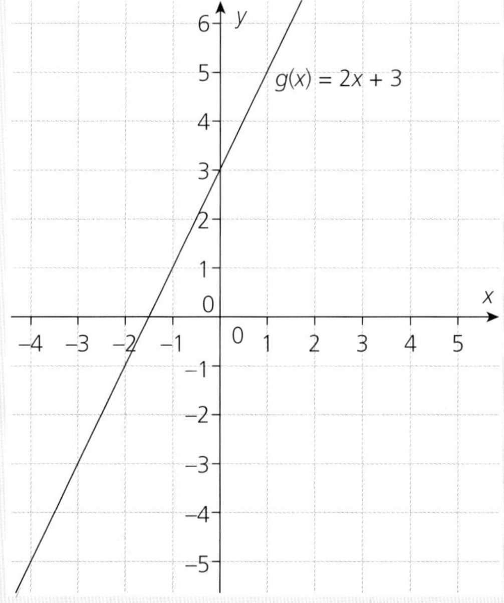

(i) Find the root of $g(x) = 0$.
(ii) Find the value of $g(0)$.
(iii) Find the value of $g(-1)$.
(iv) Find the value of $g(1)$.
(v) Solve $g(x) = -1$.

9 Draw the graph of $k(x) = -x + 6$ in the domain $-2 \leq x \leq 7$, $x \in \mathbb{R}$.
Use the graph to:
(i) Find the root of $k(x) = 0$.
(ii) Find the value of $k(0)$.
(iii) Find the value of $k(4)$.
(iv) Find the value of $k(1.5)$.
(v) Solve $k(x) - 4$.

10 Draw the graph of the linear function $m(x) = 2x - 7$ in the domain $0 \leq x \leq 5$, $x \in \mathbb{R}$.
Use the graph to:
(i) Find the root of $m(x) = 0$.
(ii) Find the value of $m(0)$.
(iii) Find the value of $m(1)$.
(iv) Find the value of x for which $m(x) = -2$.
(v) Solve $m(x) = -3$.

11 Draw the graph of the linear function $n(x) = 3x$ in the domain $-2 \leq x \leq 3$, $x \in \mathbb{R}$.
Use the graph to:
(i) Find the root of $n(x) = 0$.
(ii) Find the value of $n(0)$.
(iii) Find the value of $n(1)$.
(iv) Find the value of $n(-1)$.
(v) Solve $n(x) = 2$.

Section 13B Graphing Quadratic Functions

In Example 1, we look at the function $f(x) = x^2$, which is the simplest quadratic function.

Example 1

(i) Graph the function $f: x \to x^2$ in the domain $-3 \leq x \leq 3, x \in \mathbb{R}$.

(ii) Find the range of values of x for which $f(x)$ is increasing.

(iii) Find the range of values of x for which $f(x)$ is decreasing.

(iv) Find the minimum point of the graph.

(v) Find the minimum value of $y = f(x)$.

(vi) Write down the equation of the axis of symmetry of the graph.

Solution

(i) Make an input/output table.

Input: x	Output: $y = f(x)$	Couples
−3	$(-3)^2 = 9$	(−3, 9)
−2	$(-2)^2 = 4$	(−2, 4)
−1	$(-1)^2 = 1$	(−1, 1)
0	$(0)^2 = 0$	(0, 0)
1	$(1)^2 = 1$	(1, 1)
2	$(2)^2 = 4$	(2, 4)
3	$(3)^2 = 9$	(3, 9)

Draw the graph.

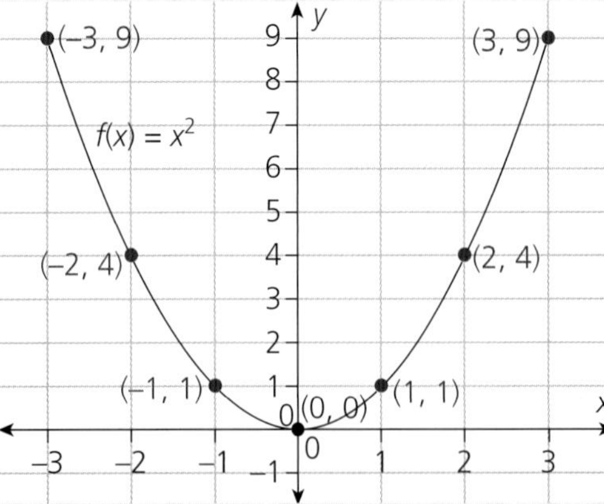

(ii) The function (y-value) is increasing if the graph (y-value) is rising as you read from **left to right**. The function is increasing for $x > 0$.

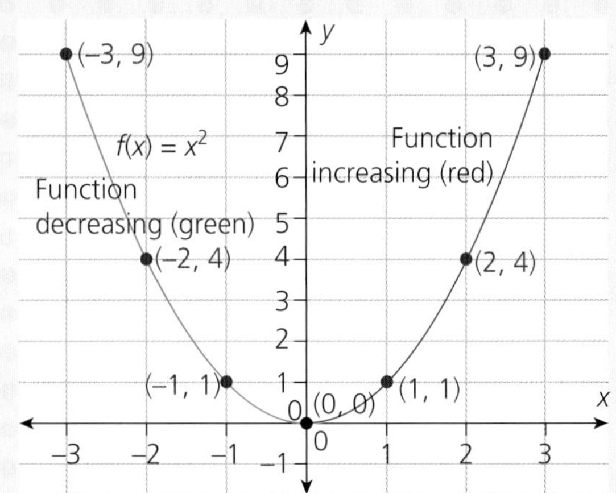

(iii) The function (y-value) is decreasing if the graph is 'falling' as you read from **left to right**.

The function $f(x)$ is decreasing for $x < 0$.

(iv) The minimum point on the graph is (0, 0).

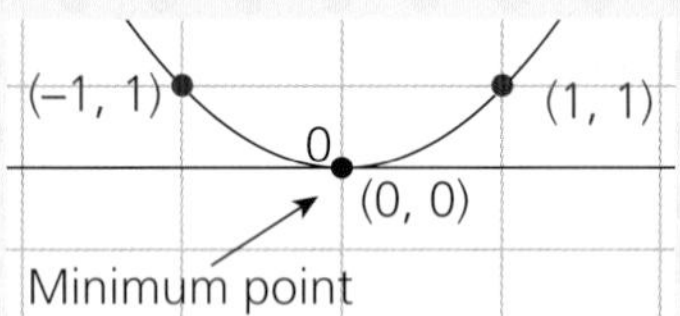

(v) The minimum value of $y = f(x) = 0$.

(vi) To find the axis of symmetry, draw a vertical line through the minimum point of the graph.

The axis of symmetry for $f(x) = x^2$ is the y-axis, i.e. the line $x = 0$.

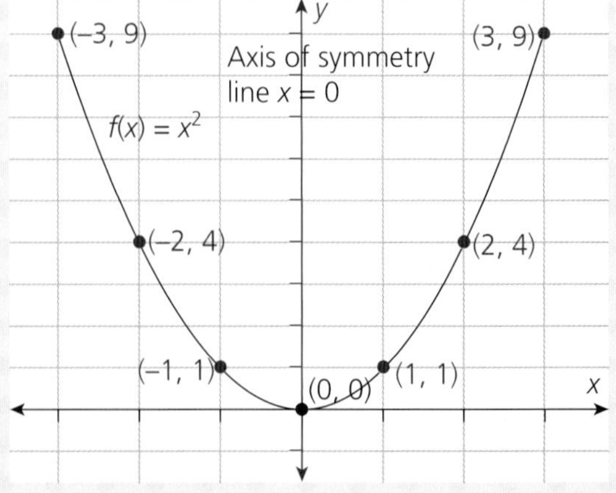

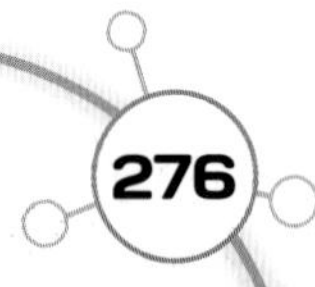

The shape of this graph is known as a **parabola**. Parabolas are seen in many everyday objects such as the reflectors of car headlights, satellite dishes, etc.

Example 2

(i) Graph the function $g: x \to -x^2$ in the domain $-3 \leq x \leq 3, x \in \mathbb{R}$.
(ii) Compare and contrast this graph with the graph of $f(x) = x^2$.
(iii) Find the maximum point of the graph.
(iv) Find the maximum value of the function (i.e. the maximum y-value).
(v) Find the range of values of x for which $f(x)$ is increasing.
(vi) Find the range of values of x for which $f(x)$ is decreasing.
(vii) Write down the equation of the axis of symmetry of the graph.

Solution

(i) Make an input/output table.

Input: x	Output: $y = g(x)$	Couples
-3	$-(-3)^2 = -9$	$(-3, -9)$
-2	$-(-2)^2 = -4$	$(-2, -4)$
-1	$-(-1)^2 = -1$	$(-1, -1)$
0	$(0)^2 = 0$	$(0, 0)$
1	$-(1)^2 = -1$	$(1, -1)$
2	$-(2)^2 = -4$	$(2, -4)$
3	$-(3)^2 = -9$	$(3, -9)$

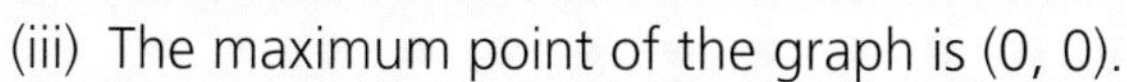

Draw the graph.

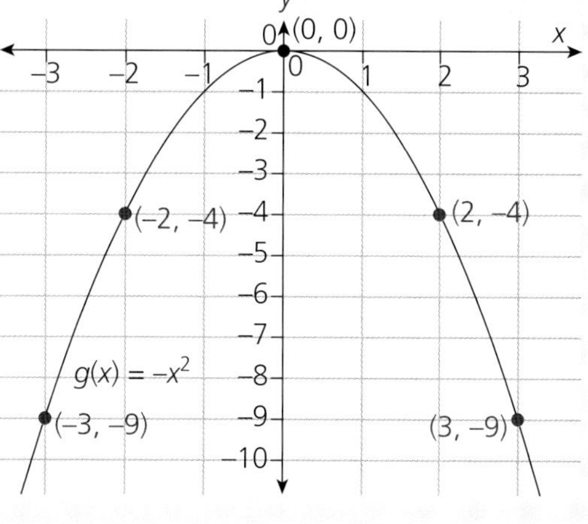

(ii) This graph of $g(x) = -x^2$ is the image of the graph of $f(x) = x^2$ by axial symmetry in the x-axis. It is also a parabola. It has a maximum point.
(iii) The maximum point of the graph is $(0, 0)$.
(iv) The maximum value of the function (maximum y-value) is 0.
(v) The function $g(x)$ is increasing for $x < 0$.
(vi) The function $g(x)$ is decreasing for $x > 0$.
(vii) The axis of symmetry for $g(x) = -x^2$ is the y-axis. i.e. the line $x = 0$.

Note from Examples 1 and 2 how the coefficient of x^2 determines the shape of the graph.

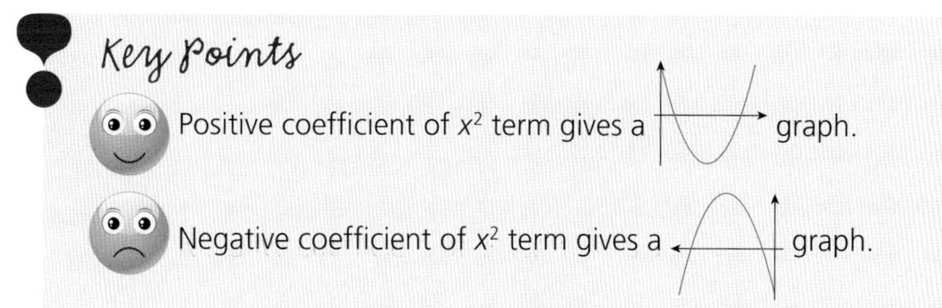

Example 3

(i) Graph the function $h: x \rightarrow 4 + 3x - 2x^2$ in the domain $-2 \leq x \leq 4$, $x \in \mathbb{R}$.

Use your graph to estimate:

(ii) $h(3.5)$

(iii) the values of x for which $h(x) = -3$

(iv) the roots of the equation $4 + 3x - 2x^2 = 0$

(v) the range of values of x for which $h(x) > 0$.

Solution

(i) Make an input/output table.

Input: x	Function: $4 + 3x - 2x^2$	Output: $y = h(x)$	Couples
−2	$4 + 3(-2) - 2(-2)^2$	−10	(−2, −10)
−1	$4 + 3(-1) - 2(-1)^2$	−1	(−1, −1)
0	$4 + 3(0) - 2(0)^2$	4	(0, 4)
1	$4 + 3(1) - 2(1)^2$	5	(1, 5)
2	$4 + 3(2) - 2(2)^2$	2	(2, 2)
3	$4 + 3(3) - 2(3)^2$	−5	(3, −5)
4	$4 + 3(4) - 2(4)^2$	−16	(4, −16)

Draw the graph.

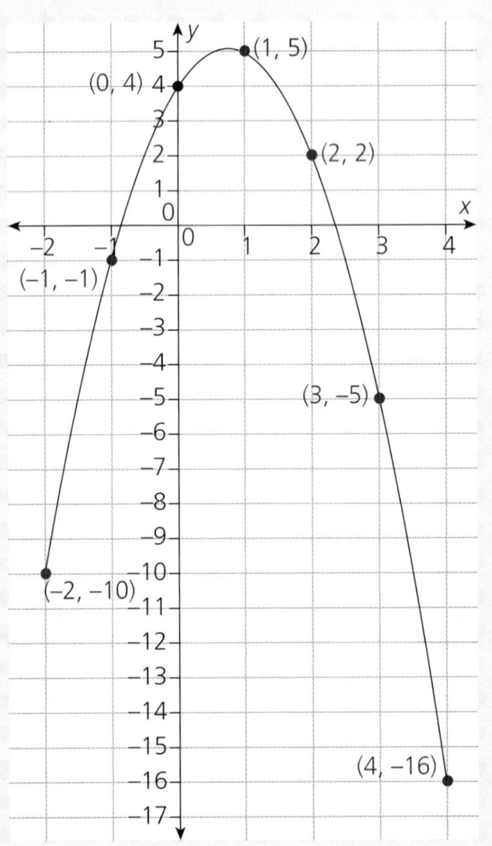

(ii) $h(3.5)$ = the **value of y** when $x = 3.5$.

- Go to 3.5 on the x-axis.
- Draw a vertical line to meet the graph.
- Follow horizontally to meet the y-axis.

$h(3.5) = -10$

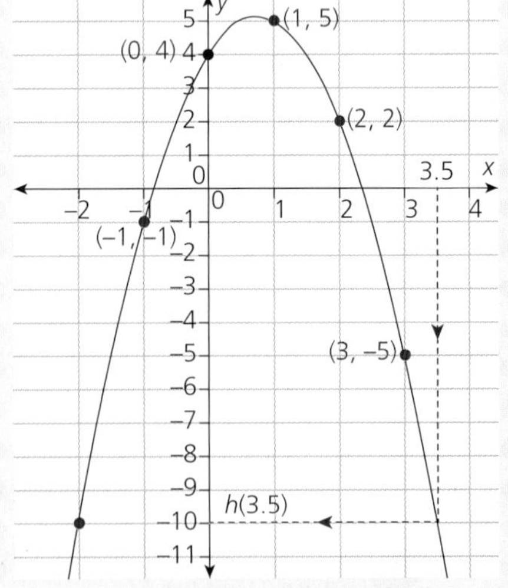

(iii) $h(x) = -3$ means that $y = -3$.

We are looking for the **values of x** which give a y-value of -3.

- Find the points where the line $y = -3$ meets the graph.
- Draw vertical lines on each side to meet the x-axis.
- Read the x values.

$h(x) = -3$ for $x = -1.25$ and 2.8 approximately.

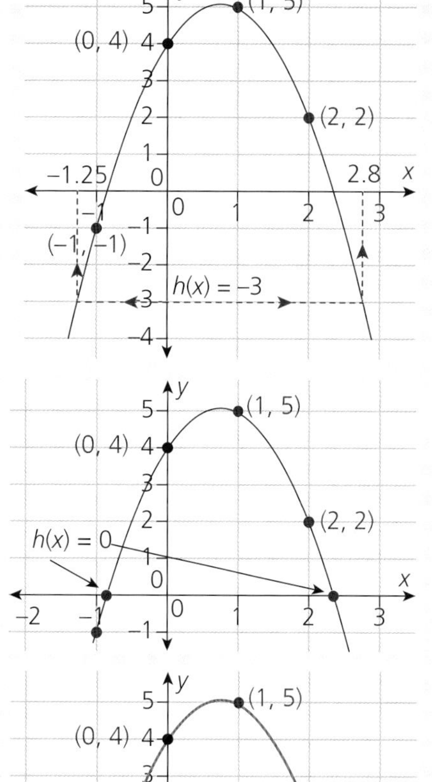

(iv) The x-values that give a y-value of zero are the 'roots' of the equation.

The roots of the equation

$h(x) = 4 + 3x - 2x^2 = 0$ are found where the graph intersects the x-axis.

The roots are -0.9 and 2.4 approximately.

(v) We are looking for the values of x which make the y-values greater than zero (i.e. > 0).

$h(x) > 0$ when the graph is above the x-axis (red section).

The range of values of x is $-0.9 < x < 2.4$.

Example 4

(i) Using the same axes and scales, draw the graphs of:

$f: x \rightarrow 2x^2 - 2x - 3$

$g: x \rightarrow 2 - 3x$

in the domain $-2 \leq x \leq 3$, $x \in \mathbb{R}$.

(ii) Use your graphs to estimate the values of x for which $f(x) = g(x)$.

Solution

(i) Make input/output tables.

Input: x	$f(x) = 2x^2 - 2x - 3$	Output: $y = f(x)$
-2	$2(-2)^2 - 2(-2) - 3$	9
-1	$2(-1)^2 - 2(-1) - 3$	1
0	$2(0)^2 - 2(0) - 3$	-3
1	$2(1)^2 - 2(1) - 3$	-3
2	$2(2)^2 - 2(2) - 3$	1
3	$2(3)^2 - 2(3) - 3$	9

Input: x	$g(x)$: $2 - 3x$	Output: $y = g(x)$
-2	$2 - 3(-2)$	8
0	$2 - 3(0)$	2
3	$2 - 3(3)$	-7

Draw the graphs.

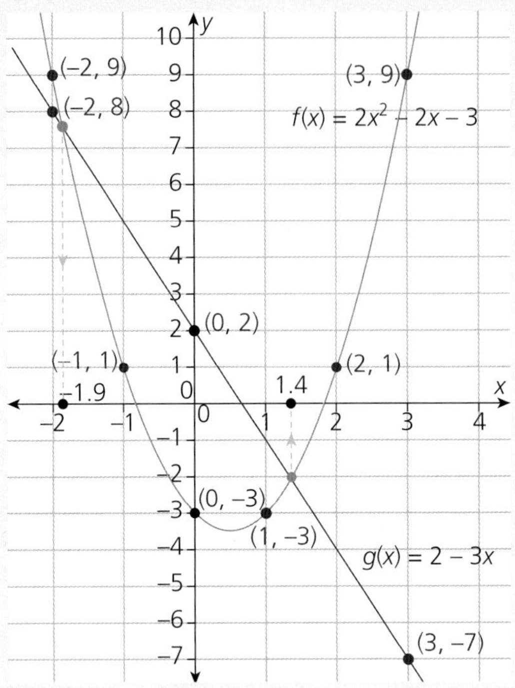

(ii) We want the values of x which give the same y-value for each function. $f(x) = g(x)$ at the points where the graphs intersect. The x-values are -1.9 and 1.4 approximately.

Example 5

Part of the quadratic function $y = x^2 + ax + b$ where $a, b \in \mathbb{Z}$ is shown.

The points $P(4, 6)$ and $Q(2, -2)$ are on the curve.

(i) Use the given points to form two equations in a and b.

(ii) Solve your equations to find the value of a and the value of b.

(iii) Write down the co-ordinates of the points where the curve crosses the y-axis.

(iv) Find the points where the curve crosses the x-axis. Give your answers correct to one decimal place.

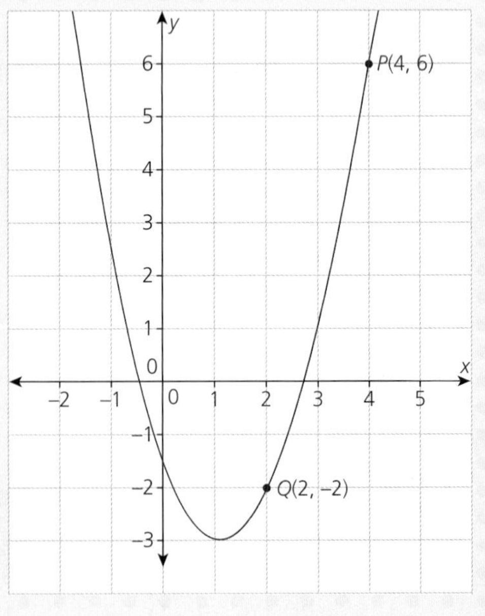

Solution

(i) $y = x^2 + ax + b$

(4, 6) is on the curve

$\Rightarrow \quad 6 = (4)^2 + 4a + b$

$\Rightarrow \quad 6 = 16 + 4a + b$

$\Rightarrow 4a + b = -10$ … equation 1

(2, −2) is on the curve

$\Rightarrow \quad -2 = (2)^2 + 2a + b$

$\Rightarrow \quad -2 = 4 + 2a + b$

$\Rightarrow -2a - b = 6$ … equation 2

(ii) Solve:

$4a + b = -10$

$-2a - b = 6$

Add $\Rightarrow 2a = -4$

$\Rightarrow \quad a = -2$

Substitute into equation 1:

$4a + b = -10$

$\Rightarrow 4(-2) + b = -10$

$\Rightarrow \quad b = -10 + 8$

$\Rightarrow \quad b = -2$

Thus the function is $y = x^2 - 2x - 2$.

(iii) The curve crosses the y-axis where $x = 0$

$\Rightarrow y = 0 - 0 - 2 = -2$

i.e. at the point (0, −2)

(iv) The curve crosses the x-axis where $y = 0$

$\Rightarrow x^2 - 2x - 2 = 0$

Use the formula $x = \dfrac{-b \pm \sqrt{b^2 - 4ac}}{2a}$

$\Rightarrow x = \dfrac{+2 \pm \sqrt{(-2)^2 - 4(1)(-2)}}{2}$

$\Rightarrow x = \dfrac{+2 \pm \sqrt{4 + 8}}{2}$

$\Rightarrow x = \dfrac{+2 \pm \sqrt{12}}{2}$

$x = 2.73$ or -0.73 correct to two decimal places

$\Rightarrow$ the co-ordinates are (2.73, 0) and (−0.73, 0)

Activity 13.2

1 Let f be the function $f: x \rightarrow x^2 + 2x$.

(i) Find the value of $f(5)$.

(ii) Find the value of $f(2) - f(-2)$.

(iii) Express $f(t)$ and $f(t + 1)$ in terms of t.

(iv) Find the value of t for which $f(t) = f(t + 1)$.

2 $f: x \rightarrow 3x + k$ and $g: x \rightarrow 4x^2 - k$ are two functions defined on $\mathbb{R}$, where $k \in \mathbb{Z}$.

(i) If $f(2) = 4$, find the value of k.

(ii) Find the two values of x for which $f(x) + g(x) = 0$.

3 (i) Graph the function $f: x \rightarrow 10 + 2x - 2x^2$ in the domain $-3 \leq x \leq 3$, $x \in \mathbb{R}$.

(ii) Find the maximum point of the graph.

(iii) Find the range of values of x for which $f(x)$ is increasing.

(iv) Find the range of values of x for which $f(x)$ is decreasing.

(v) Draw in the axis of symmetry of the graph and write down its equation.

4 (i) Graph the function $f: x \rightarrow -2x^2 + 7x - 1$ in the domain $-2 \leq x \leq 4$, $x \in \mathbb{R}$.

Use your graph to estimate:

(ii) $f(2.5)$

(iii) the values of x for which $f(x) = 2.5$

(iv) the roots of the equation $-2x^2 + 7x - 1 = 0$

(v) the range of values of x for which $f(x) > 0$.

5 Part of the graph of the quadratic function $y = x^2 + bx + c$ where b and $c \in \mathbb{Z}$, is shown.

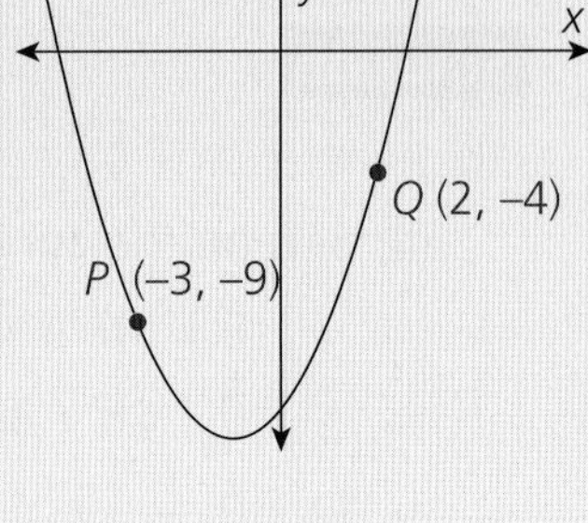

The points $P(-3, -9)$ and $Q(2, -4)$ are on the curve.

(i) Use the given points to form two equations in b and c.

(ii) Solve your equations to find the value of b and the value of c.

(iii) Write down the co-ordinates of the point where the curve intersects the y-axis.

(iv) Find the points where the curve crosses the x-axis. Give your answers correct to one place of decimals.

6 Part of the graph of the quadratic function $y = ax^2 + bx + c$ where a, b and $c \in \mathbb{Z}$, is shown.

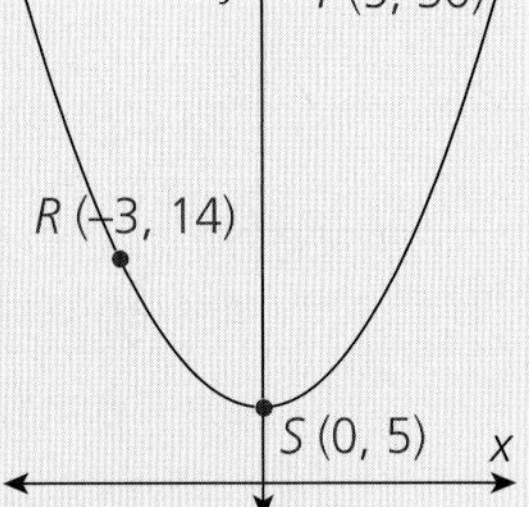

The points $R(-3, 14)$, $S(0, 5)$, $T(5, 30)$ are on the curve.

(i) What is the value of c in the equation of the function?

(ii) Form two equations in a and b.

(iii) Solve your equations to find the value of a and the value of b.

7 The following couples belong to a function:
$\{(-4, -4), (-3, -9), (-2, -12), (-1, -13), (0, -12), (1, -9), (2, -4), (3, 3), (4, 12)\}$.

(i) Using patterns of first and second differences, show that these couples satisfy the equation of a quadratic function $f(x)$.

(ii) What is the value of c in the equation $f(x) = ax^2 + bx + c$?

(iii) Find the equation of the function.

8 (i) Three functions $f(x)$, $g(x)$ and $h(x)$ are defined as follows:

$f(x) = 2x^2 + 5x - 3, \quad g(x) = x^2 - 4x + 4, \quad h(x) = x^2 - 3x.$

(a) Solve $f(x) = 0$. (b) Solve $g(x) = 0$. (c) Solve $h(x) = 0$.

(ii) The table shows the sketches of six different functions. Three of the sketches belong to the three functions from part (i).

Decide which of the graphs belong to functions $f(x)$, $g(x)$ and $h(x)$.

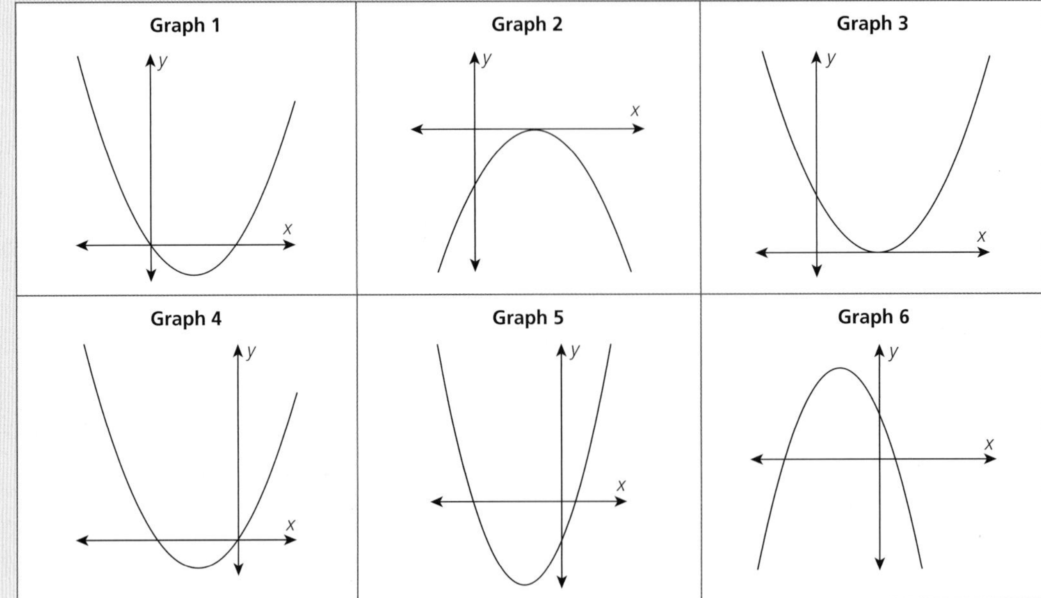

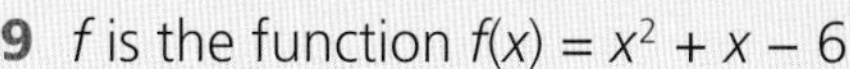

9 f is the function $f(x) = x^2 + x - 6$.

(i) Draw the graph of the function $f(x)$ in the domain $-4 \leq x \leq 4$, $x \in \mathbb{R}$.

(ii) The graph of another function $g(x)$ is linear. $g(-2) = 10$ and $g(3) = 0$.

Using the same axes, draw the graph of the function g.

(iii) Use the graphs to find the values of x for which $f(x) = g(x)$.

10 (i) Using the same axes, draw the graphs of

$f: x \to 5 - 3x - 2x^2$

$g: x \to -2x - 1$

in the domain $-3 \leq x \leq 2$, $x \in \mathbb{R}$.

(ii) Use your graphs to estimate:

(a) the maximum value of $f(x)$

(b) the values of x for which $f(x) = g(x)$

(c) the range of values of x for which $f(x) \geq g(x)$.

11 The picture shows the top section of the Spanish Arch in Galway city. George wants to see if the arch can be described by a function. He puts a co-ordinate grid over the arch as shown.

(i) Copy and complete the table to estimate the value of y for each of the given values of x.

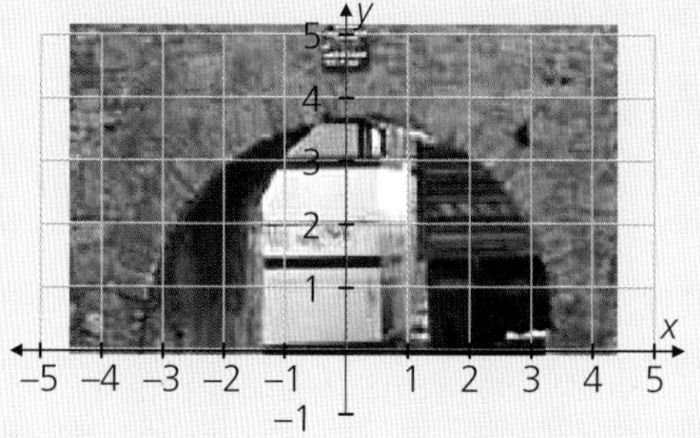

x	y
–3	
–2	
–1	
0	
1	
2	
3	

(ii) Is it possible to represent this section of the Spanish Arch by a quadratic function? Give a reason for your answer.

Section 13C Applications of Linear and Quadratic Functions

Functions can be used to model many real-life applications. We can use models to make predictions and for optimisation. The points where a graph intercepts the axes and maximum and minimum points are very important in applications.

Example 1

A farmer wishes to use 100 metres of fencing to enclose a rectangular field. What is the biggest area that she can enclose?

Class Discussion

What problem-solving strategy could you use here?

Before reading the solution, try 'guess and test'. Try out different possible lengths for the sides of the rectangle and see what you come up with.

Solution

The farmer can try different lengths for the rectangle and she will get different areas each time.

Thus the area enclosed depends on the length of the rectangle.

We say that **the area is a function of the length**.

Let x be the length of the rectangle.

Let y be the width of the rectangle.

Then the perimeter $= 2x + 2y = 100$

$$\Rightarrow \quad x + y = 50$$

$$\Rightarrow \quad y = 50 - x$$

Thus, the area (A) of the rectangle = length × width

$$= x(50 - x)$$

$$= 50x - x^2$$

Now we have the area (A) as a function of the length (x).

We can write this in function notation as $\mathbf{A(x) = 50x - x^2}$.

We can draw the graph of this function and use it to estimate the value which will give the farmer the maximum area.

Make an input/output table.

Input: x (metres)	$A(x) = 50x - x^2$	Output: $y = A(x)$ (m^2)
0	$50(0) - 0^2$	0
10	$50(10) - 10^2$	400
20	$50(20) - 20^2$	600
30	$50(30) - 30^2$	600
40	$50(40) - 40^2$	400
50	$50(50) - 50^2$	0

Draw the graph.

The graph has a maximum point at (25, 625) … this point is estimated from the graph.

The greatest area is 625 m^2 which is obtained when the length is 25 m.

That is, the rectangle with the greatest area is actually a square.

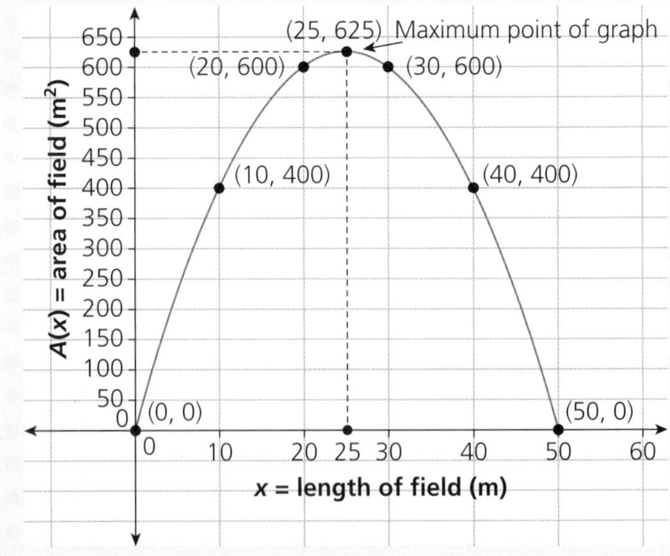

Alternatively: The roots of the equation $f(x) = 0$ are $x = 0$ and $x = 50$. Therefore the axis of symmetry of the graph is the line $x = 25$. This line passes through the maximum point of the graph.

Substituting $x = 25$ into the equation $y = 50x - x^2$ gives $y = 625$.

Example 2

The height, y metres, of a golf ball above ground level x seconds after it is hit, is represented by the function $f: x \to 6x - x^2$.

(i) Draw the graph of f for $0 \leq x \leq 6$, $x \in \mathbb{R}$.

Use your graph:

(ii) to find the maximum height reached by the golf ball

(iii) to estimate the number of seconds the golf ball was more than 3 metres above the ground.

Solution

(i) Draw an input/output table:

Input (x)	Output ($6x - x^2$)	Couples
0	$6(0) - (0)^2 = 0$	(0, 0)
1	$6(1) - (1)^2 = 5$	(1, 5)
2	$6(2) - (2)^2 = 8$	(2, 8)
3	$6(3) - (3)^2 = 9$	(3, 9)
4	$6(4) - (4)^2 = 8$	(4, 8)
5	$6(5) - (5)^2 = 5$	(5, 5)
6	$6(6) - (6)^2 = 0$	(6, 0)

Graph:

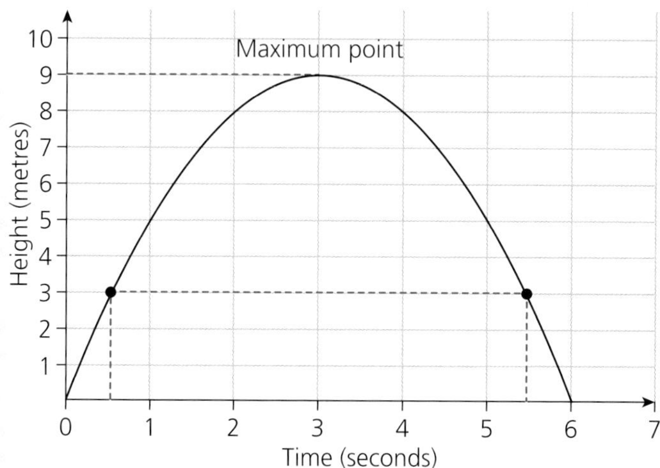

(ii) From the graph, the maximum height reached = 9 m.

(iii) The ball was more than 3 metres above the ground from approximately 0.5 seconds to 5.5 seconds; in other words, for about 5 seconds.

Activity 13.3

1 A rectangular site, with one side facing the road, is to be fenced off.

The side facing the road, which does not require fencing, is l m in length.

The sides perpendicular to the road are x m in length.

The length of fencing that will be used to enclose the site is 140 m.

(i) Write an expression in terms of x, for the length (l) of the side facing the road.

(ii) (a) Show that the area of the site, in m^2, is $-2x^2 + 140x$.

(b) Let f be the function $f: x \rightarrow -2x^2 + 140x$.

Evaluate $f(x)$ when $x = 0, 10, 20, 30, 40, 50, 60$ and 70.

Hence, draw the graph of f for $0 \leq x \leq 70$, $x \in \mathbb{R}$.

(iii) Use your graph from part (ii) to estimate:

(a) the maximum possible area of the site

(b) the area of the site when the road frontage (l) is 30 m long.

2 The formula for the height, y metres, of a ball above ground level, x seconds after it is fired vertically into the air, is given by:

$f(x) = y = 35x - 5x^2$.

(i) Draw the graph of f for $0 \leq x \leq 7$, $x \in \mathbb{R}$.

(ii) Use your graph to estimate:

(a) the maximum height reached by the ball

(b) the height of the ball after 5.5 seconds

(c) the two times that the ball is 20 metres above the ground.

3 A company manufactures rectangular wooden frames for framing photographs. One particular frame has inside dimensions of 10 cm by 15 cm.

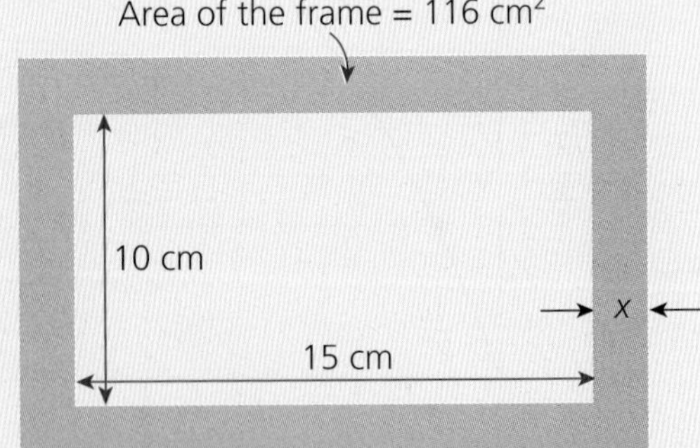

(i) Find the width, x cm, of wood in the frame which will make the area of the frame itself equal to 116 cm^2.

(ii) Explain how the value of x could be estimated from a graph.

(iii) Estimate the value of x using a graph.

4 A coin is dropped from a height of 50 m. Its height above the ground varies with time. The function representing how its height, in metres, changes with time is $h = f(t) = 50 - 5t^2$ where t is measured in seconds.

(i) Use a table to show the height above the ground for the first four seconds after the coin is dropped.

(ii) Estimate from the table when the coin hits the ground.

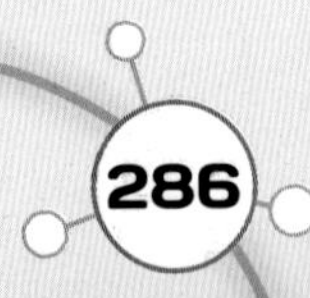

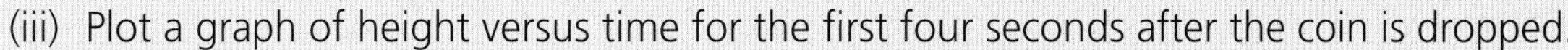

(iii) Plot a graph of height versus time for the first four seconds after the coin is dropped.

(iv) Estimate from the graph when the coin hits the ground.

(v) Use the formula for height to verify your estimates of when the coin hits the ground. Give your answer correct to two decimal places.

(vi) If you wanted the coin to hit the ground after three seconds, from what height would it need to be dropped?

(vii) If the coin was dropped from the top of the Eiffel Tower, which is approximately 300 metres high, the function representing how height changes with time would be $h = g(t) = 300 - 5t^2$. How long would it take the coin to fall to the ground when dropped from the top of the Eiffel Tower? Give your answer correct to two decimal places.

5 The height of a rocket t seconds after it has been launched is given by $h = f(t) = -5t^2 + 90t$.

(i) What is the height of the rocket above ground when it is launched?

(ii) Copy and complete the following table for the height of the rocket above ground from the time it is launched.

Time elapsed since launch (s)	Height above ground (m)
0	
2	
4	
6	
8	
10	
12	
14	
16	
18	

(iii) How long after the launch does it take the rocket to fall back to the ground?

(iv) Draw a graph of the height versus time since launch.

(v) Using the graph, estimate the time at which the rocket is at its greatest height.

(vi) Calculate the greatest height reached by the rocket.

6 The diagram shows a rectangular garden of perimeter 36 m.

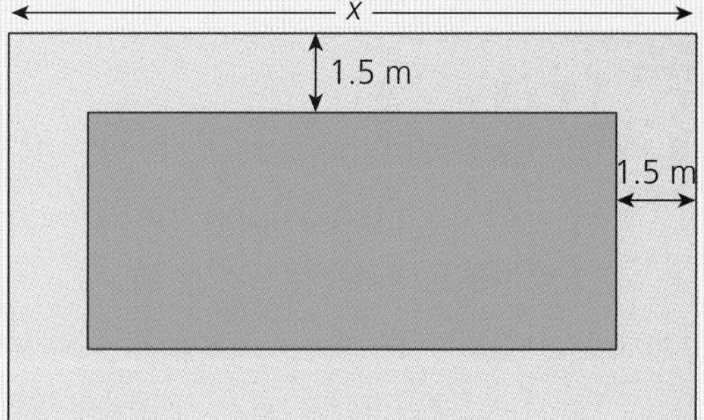

The length of the garden is x m.

(i) Write down an expression in x for the width of the garden.

A path 1.5 m wide is built around the garden's edge as in the diagram.

(ii) Write expressions in x for the length and width of the inner section.

(iii) Show that the area, in m^2, of the inner section is $-x^2 + 18x - 45$.

The area of the inner section is represented by the function:

$f: x \to -x^2 + 18x - 45$.

(iv) Draw the graph of f for $3 \leq x \leq 15$, $x \in \mathbb{R}$.

(v) Find the maximum possible area of the inner section.

7 The price for a tour decreases by €20 for every additional person who buys a ticket to go on the tour. The price per ticket is €520 before anyone signs up.

Let n be the number of tickets sold.

(i) What is the cost of a ticket if five people sign up to go on the tour?

(ii) What is the cost of a ticket if n people sign up to go on the tour?

(iii) Revenue equals the number of tickets sold multiplied by the price per ticket.
If n people sign up to go on the tour, write in terms of n, the total revenue collected by the tour company.

(iv) Copy and complete the following table showing the relationship between the number of people n, and the revenue, R.

n	R (€)
0	
5	
10	
15	
20	
25	
30	

(v) What does the negative answer mean in the table for $n = 30$?

(vi) Draw a graph for the revenue function $R(n)$ using the table in part (iv).

(vii) For what numbers of people signing up for the tour will the revenue be zero? Estimate from the graph first and then find the answer algebraically.

(viii) Using the graph, find the value of n which will maximise the value of R.

(ix) What is the maximum revenue possible under the given conditions?

8 Two identical cylindrical tanks, A and B, each have a height of 100 cm. At a particular instant, the water in tank A is 15 cm high and the height of water is increasing at a steady rate of 10 cm every 5 seconds. At the same time the height of water in tank B is 100 cm and the height of water is decreasing at 10 cm every 5 seconds.

(i) Draw up a table showing the height of water in each tank at 5 second intervals, until tank A is almost full and tank B is empty.

(ii) Based on your table, is the relationship between time and height a linear relationship? Justify your answer.

(iii) Calculate the rate of change of height with time for the water in each tank.

(iv) For each tank, using the same axes and scales, draw the graph to represent the height of water in the tank.

(v) Explain what the co-ordinates (50, 0) for tank B mean in the context of the question.

(vi) For each tank, write down a formula which gives the height of water in the tank at any given time. State clearly the meaning of any letters used in your formulae.

(vii) Estimate, from your graphs, when the height of water is the same in both tanks and what that height is.

(viii) Verify your answer to part (vii) using your formulae from part (vi).

9 A stadium has seating capacity for 13 000 spectators. Tickets for an event must be purchased in advance. When the ticket price for a regular event is €25, the expected attendance at the event is 8500 people. Market research suggests that for every €1 that the ticket price is reduced, the expected attendance would increase by 500 people.

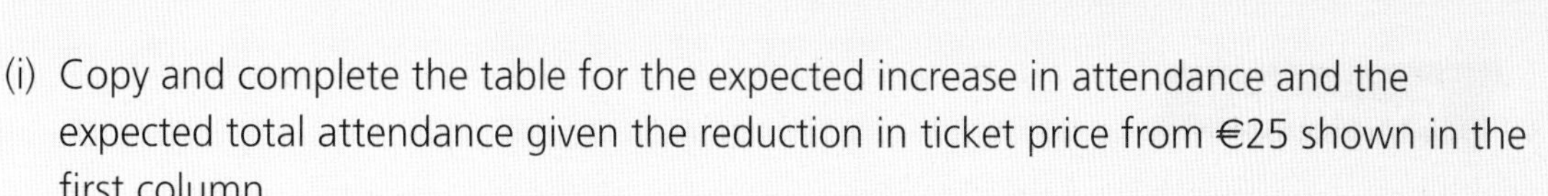

(i) Copy and complete the table for the expected increase in attendance and the expected total attendance given the reduction in ticket price from €25 shown in the first column.

Ticket price (€)	Expected increase in attendance	Expected total attendance (n)
24	(1)(500)	8500 + (1)(500) = 9000
23		
22		
21		
20		
...	...	...
x		

(ii) If n people attend the event, what is the total income generated from ticket sales, given that each ticket costs €x? Write this equation in terms of x.

(iii) What ticket prices would yield zero income?

(iv) Sketch the graph of the relationship between ticket price and income.

(v) What ticket price would yield maximum income? Calculate this income.

(vi) What would the ticket price be if the organisers wished to fill the stadium?

(vii) What is the difference between the income generated using the answer to part (v) and the income generated at a ticket price which would fill the stadium?

(viii) Could the organisers charge €10 per ticket given the expected attendance and the effect of reducing the ticket price? Explain.

Section 13D Exponential Functions

Katie was asking for pocket money. She said, 'For pocket money, I would like just 3 cent right now, 6 cent tomorrow, 12 cent the next day, 24 cent the next day and so on, doubling each day for the 31 days of the month. Surely that's not too much to ask.'

Is this a good deal for Katie or is it a good deal for her parents?

Katie is asking for the following amounts in cent:

$3 + 3(2) + 3(2)(2) + 3(2)(2)(2) + \dots$ for thirty-one days

$= 3 + 3(2) + 3(2)^2 + 3(2)^3 + 3(2)^4 + \dots + 3(2)^{30}$

This relationship between the number of days and the amount of pocket money is an example of an **exponential function**.

In this example, the function $f(x) = 3(2^x)$ gives the amount of pocket money each day where x is the number of days that have passed since the first day (day 0).

Key Point

In an exponential function, **the variable is in the exponent** (index).

Example 1 will tell us whether this is a good idea for Katie or for her parents.

Example 1

(i) Make a table of values for the function $f(x) = 3(2^x)$ for $0 \leq x \leq 5, x \in \mathbb{Z}$.

(ii) How can you tell from the table that the graph of f is not a straight line?

(iii) Use these values to plot the graph of $f(x) = 3(2^x)$.

(iv) Where does the curve intercept the y-axis?

(v) As x increases, is y increasing or decreasing?

(vi) Evaluate $3(2^x)$ for $x = 10$, 20 and 30 using your calculator.

Solution

(i)

x	$f(x) = 3(2^x)$	Couples
0	$(3)2^0 = 3$	(0, 3)
1	$(3)2^1 = 6$	(1, 6)
2	$(3)2^2 = 12$	(2, 12)
3	$(3)2^3 = 24$	(3, 24)
4	$(3)2^4 = 48$	(4, 48)
5	$(3)2^5 = 96$	(5, 96)

(ii) The differences in the output values for consecutive values of x are not constant, so the graph is not a straight line.

(iii)

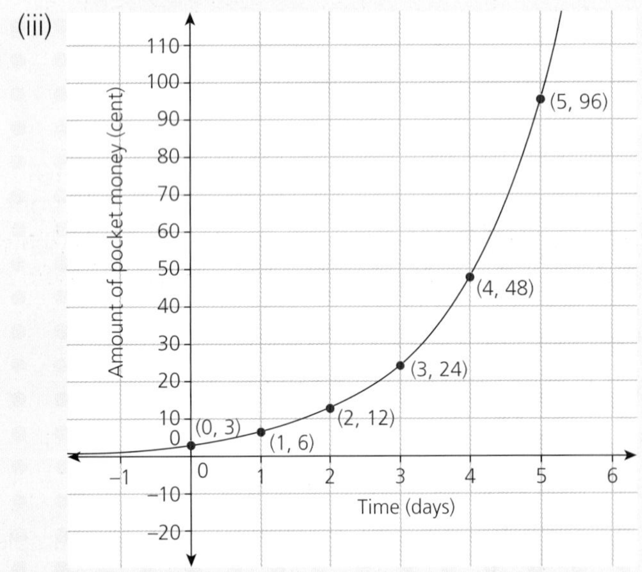

(iv) The y-intercept = 3, i.e. the curve crosses the y-axis at (0, 3).

(v) As x increases, y is increasing very quickly.

(vi) $3(2^{10}) = 3072$

$3(2^{20}) = 3\,145\,728$

$3(2^{30}) = 3\,221\,225\,472$

- You can see that the graph in Example 1 'zooms' upwards. This is what all **exponential** graphs look like.
- The graph in Example 1 shows what Katie's pocket money would be for the first five days because $3(2^x)$ is the graph of a 'doubling' function.
- The point (5, 96) on the graph indicates that Katie would get 96 cent on the 5th day. This seems reasonable enough.
- Now see what she would get on the 10th, 20th and 30th days, from part (vi).

Katie would have to be given

- 3072 cent = €30.72 on the 10th day
- 3 145 728 cent = €31,457.28 on the 20th day
- 3 221 225 472 cent = €32,212,254.72 on the 30th day!

You can see what people mean when they say that something is **growing exponentially**.

2^x is just one example of an exponential function; other examples are 3^x, 4^x or a^x, where $a \in \mathbb{R}$.

Example 2

For $f(x) = 2^x$:

(i) What is the base?
(ii) What is the exponent (index)?
(iii) What is varying in the function?
(iv) What is constant in the function?
(v) What is the domain (the possible inputs for x)?
(vi) For what values of x is 2^x negative?
(vii) What is the range of f?
(viii) What happens to the output as x decreases?
(ix) Is an output of 0 possible?

Solution

(i) The base = 2
(ii) The exponent = x
(iii) x is varying.
(iv) 2 (the base) is constant.
(v) The domain is $\mathbb{R}$, the set of real numbers.
(vi) There are no values of x for which 2^x is negative.
(vii) The range is the set of positive real numbers.
(viii) As x decreases, the output (y-values) gets smaller and smaller.
(ix) An output of 0 is impossible. There is no value of x which will make $2^x = 0$.

Activity 13.4

1 (i) Make a table of values for the function $f(x) = 3^x$ for $0 \leq x \leq 4$, $x \in \mathbb{Z}$.
(ii) How can you tell from your table that the graph of f is not a straight line?
(iii) Use these values to plot the graph of $f(x) = 3^x$.
(iv) What is the y-intercept of the graph?
(v) As x increases, is y increasing or decreasing?
(vi) Evaluate 3^x for $x = 10$, 20 and 30 using your calculator. Why does the calculator show the value of 3^{30} differently?

2 For $f(x) = 3^x$:
(i) What is the base?
(ii) What is the exponent (index)?
(iii) What is varying in the function?
(iv) What is constant in the function?
(v) What is the domain (the possible inputs for x)?
(vi) For what values of x is 3^x negative?
(vii) What is the range of f?
(viii) What happens to the output as x decreases?
(ix) Is an output of 0 possible?

3 (i) Make a table of values for the function $f(x) = 2(3^x)$ for $0 \leq x \leq 3$.

(ii) Use these values to plot the graph of $f(x) = 2(3^x)$.

(iii) Where does the curve intercept the y-axis?

(iv) Evaluate $2(3^x)$ for $x = 10$ and 20 using your calculator.

4 (i) Draw the graphs of $f(x) = x^2$ and $g(x) = 2^x$, $0 \leq x \leq 3$, $x \in \mathbb{R}$, using the same axes.

(ii) Use your graphs to solve the equation $x^2 = 2^x$.

5 A cell divides itself into two every day. The number of cells C after D days is given by the function $C = 2^D$.

(i) Draw a graph of the function for $0 \leq D \leq 6$.

(ii) Use your calculator to find the number of cells after 18 days.

6 In an experiment, the number of bacteria B found in a sample after m minutes is given by the formula:

$B = 50(3)^{0.04m}$.

(i) Find the number of bacteria in the sample at the start of the experiment.

(ii) Find the number of bacteria in the sample after 3 hours.

7 Part of the graph of $f(x) = ka^x$ is shown.

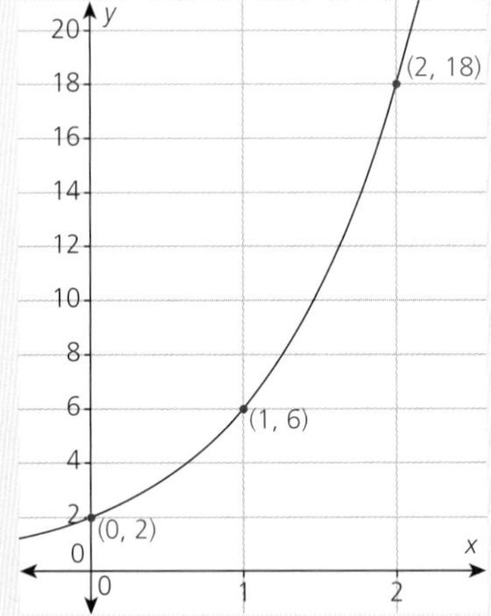

(i) Find the value of k and the value of a.

(ii) Hence, find $f(7)$.

8 The graphs of four functions are shown below. The graphs are labelled A, B, C and D. The four functions are listed in the table. Match the graphs to the functions, by putting the correct letter beside each one in a copy of the table.

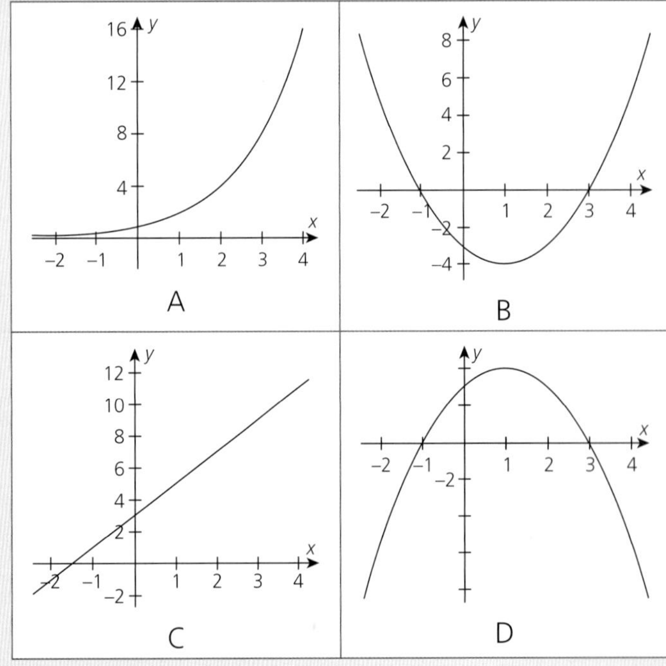

Function	Graph
$f(x) = 2x + 3$	
$g(x) = (x - 3)(x + 1)$	
$h(x) = 2^x$	
$j(x) = 3 + 2x - x^2$	

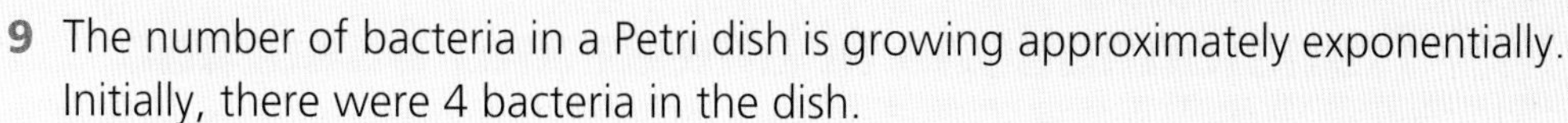

9 The number of bacteria in a Petri dish is growing approximately exponentially. Initially, there were 4 bacteria in the dish.

The table shows the approximate number of bacteria in the dish from the time when counting started, at the end of each hour for a period of 4 hours.

Time elapsed *t* (hours)	0	1	2	3	4
Number of bacteria *N* = *f*(*t*)	4	12	36	108	324

(i) Using the function $f(t) = ab^t$ to model the growth of the bacteria, what are the values of a and b?

(ii) How many bacteria will be in the dish after 24 hours?

(iii) Write the answer to part (ii) correct to two significant figures.

(iv) Write the answer to part (iii) in words.

(v) Use your calculator to help you to estimate how long in hours it would take for the number of bacteria to reach 250 000. Give your answer correct to three decimal places.

(vi) Why might the exponential growth of an organism not continue indefinitely?

10 Two functions f and g are defined for $x \in \mathbb{R}$ as follows:

$$f \mapsto 3^x$$

$$g \mapsto -4x^2 + 20x + 5$$

(i) Use your calculator to copy and complete the table below. Use your table to draw the graphs of f and g for $0 \leq x \leq 4$.

x	**0**	**0.5**	**1**	**1.5**	**2**	**2.5**	**3**	**3.5**	**4**
$f(x)$									
$g(x)$									

(ii) Use the graphs to estimate the value of x for which $f(x) = g(x)$.

(iii) Let k be a number such that $(3^k) = 8$.

Use your graph to estimate the value of k. Use your calculator to estimate the value of k to two decimal places.

(iv) Estimate $g(k)$ from the graph.

Section 13E Transformations of Linear and Quadratic Functions

Linear Functions

Example 1 looks at graphs of functions of the form $f(x) = ax$, where $a \in \mathbb{Z}$, $x \in \mathbb{R}$.

Example 1

(i) Draw the graphs of the functions $f(x) = 1x$, $g(x) = 2x$ and $h(x) = 3x$, in the domain $-3 \le x \le 3$, using the same axes.

(ii) Compare and contrast the three graphs you have plotted.

(iii) The graphs are of the form $f(x) = ax$. What effect does varying a have on the graphs?

(iv) What would you expect $p(x) = 7x$ to look like?

Solution

(i) Make an input/output table for each graph.

x	$f(x) = x$
−3	3
0	0
3	3

x	$g(x) = 2x$
−3	−6
0	0
3	6

x	$h(x) = 3x$
−3	−9
0	0
3	9

Draw the graphs.

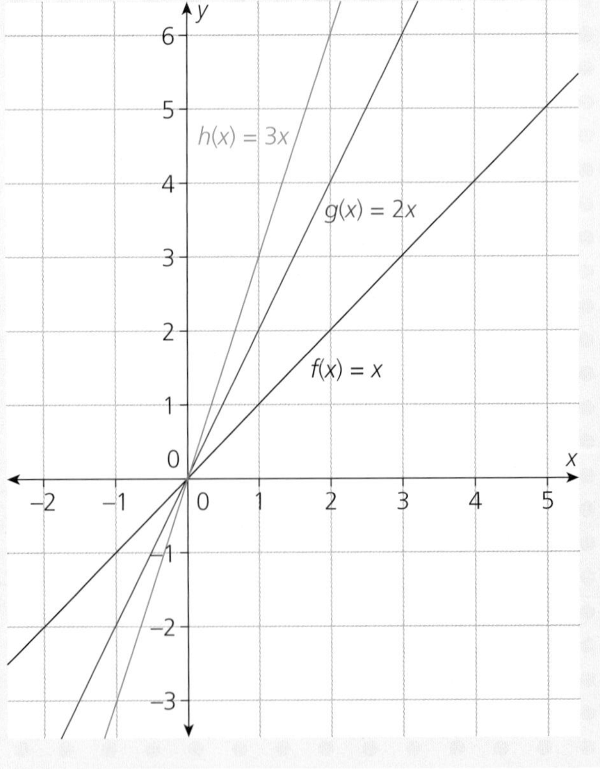

(ii) All three graphs:

- are lines of the form $y = mx$, where m = the slope
- have **positive** slopes
- pass through the point (0, 0) and therefore represent proportional relationships.

The graphs differ in that $g(x) = 2x$ has a slope twice that of $f(x) = x$, and $h(x) = 3x$ has a slope three times that of $f(x) = x$.

(iii) Since a is the slope of each graph, as a increases, the slope (rate of change) increases.

(iv) The graph of $p(x) = 7x$ will be a line through the point (0, 0) with a slope = 7.

Example 2 looks at graphs of functions of the form $f(x) = ax + b$, where $a, b \in \mathbb{Z}$, $x \in \mathbb{R}$.

Example 2

(i) Draw the graphs of the functions $g(x) = x$, $h(x) = x + 1$, $k(x) = x + 3$ and $l(x) = x - 2$, in the domain $-3 \leq x \leq 3$, using the same axes.

(ii) Compare and contrast the four graphs you have plotted.

(iii) The graphs are of the form $f(x) = ax + b$. What effect does varying b have on the graphs?

(iv) Where do the graphs cut the y-axis?

(v) What would you expect $f(x) = x + 6$ to look like?

Solution

(i) Make an input/output table for each graph.

x	$g(x) = x$
−3	−3
0	0
3	3

x	$h(x) = x + 1$
−3	−2
0	1
3	4

x	$k(x) = x + 3$
−3	0
0	3
3	6

x	$l(x) = x - 2$
−3	−5
0	−2
3	1

Draw the graphs.

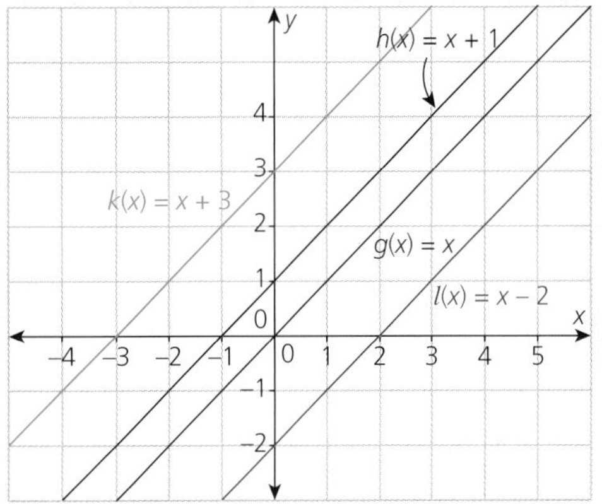

(ii) The graphs are lines which are parallel with positive slope.

- The graph of $h(x) = x + 1$ is the image of the graph of $g(x)$ by a translation of 1 unit up the y-axis.
- The graph of $k(x) = x + 3$ is the image of the graph of $g(x)$ by a translation of 3 units up the y-axis.
- The graph of $l(x) = x - 2$ is the image of the graph of $g(x)$ by a translation of 2 units down the y-axis.

(iii) Varying b has the effect of translating the line.

(iv) The graphs all cut the y-axis at the point b, i.e. $(0, b)$.

(v) The graph of the function $f(x) = x + 6$ is a line parallel to $g(x)$, intercepting the y-axis at $(0, 6)$.

Quadratic Functions

Example 3 looks at graphs of functions of the form $f(x) = ax^2$, where $a \in \mathbb{N}$, $x \in \mathbb{R}$.

Example 3

(i) Graph the functions $g(x) = x^2$, $h(x) = 2x^2$, $k(x) = 3x^2$, in the domain $-3 \le x \le 3$, using the same axes.

(ii) Compare and contrast the three graphs you have plotted.

(iii) The graphs are of the form $f(x) = ax^2$. What effect does varying a have on the shape of the graphs?

(iv) What would you expect $l(x) = 7x^2$ to look like?

Solution

(i) Draw an input/output table for each function.

x	$g(x) = x^2$
−3	9
−2	4
−1	1
0	0
1	1
2	4
3	9

x	$h(x) = 2x^2$
−3	18
−2	8
−1	2
0	0
1	2
2	8
3	18

x	$k(x) = 3x^2$
−3	27
−2	12
−1	3
0	0
1	3
2	12
3	27

Draw the graphs.

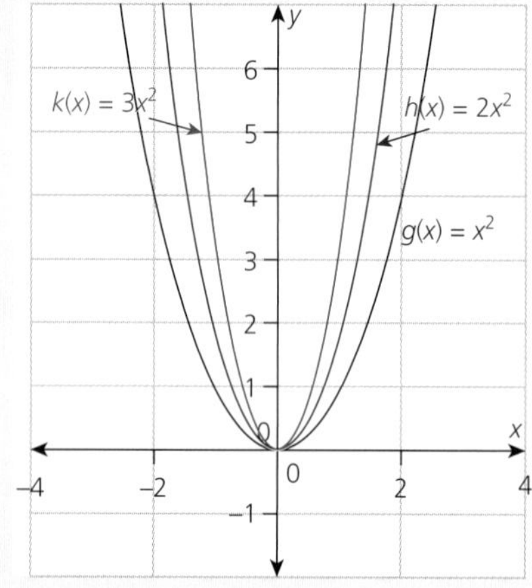

(ii) Each graph is a parabola, all are symmetrical about the y-axis, have $y > 0$ for all $x \in \mathbb{R}$, and all have the same minimum point (0, 0).

The rate of change of $y = 3x^2$ is greater than the rate of change of $y = 2x^2$ which is greater than the rate of change of $y = x^2$.

(iii) Varying a varies the rate of change of the function. For $a > 0$, the bigger the value of a the 'narrower' the graph of the function.

(iv) $l(x) = 7x^2$ is a parabola, symmetrical about the y-axis, has $y > 0$ for all $x \in \mathbb{R}$, and has a minimum point of (0, 0). The rate of change of y with respect to x for $y = 7x^2$ is seven times greater than the rate of change of y with respect to x for $y = x^2$. Hence, the graph of $y = 7x^2$ is 'narrower' than the graph of $y = x^2$.

Example 4 looks at graphs of functions of the form $f(x) = x^2 + c$, where $c \in \mathbb{Z}$, $x \in \mathbb{R}$.

Example 4

(i) Graph the functions $g(x) = x^2$, $h(x) = x^2 + 3$, $k(x) = x^2 - 2$, in the domain $-3 \leq x \leq 3$, using the same axes.

(ii) Compare and contrast the three graphs you have plotted.

(iii) The graphs are of the form $f(x) = x^2 + c$. What effect does varying c have on the shape of the graphs?

(iv) What would you expect $f(x) = x^2 + 8$ to look like?

(v) What would you expect $n(x) = x^2 - 3$ to look like?

Solution

(i) Draw an input/output table for each function.

x	g(x) = x²
−3	9
−2	4
−1	1
0	0
1	1
2	4
3	9

x	h(x) = x² + 3
−3	12
−2	7
−1	4
0	3
1	4
2	7
3	12

x	k(x) = x² − 2
−3	7
−2	2
−1	−1
0	−2
1	−1
2	2
3	7

Draw the graphs.

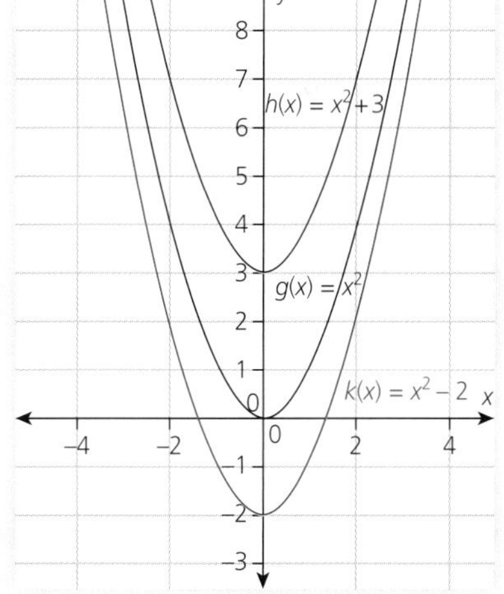

(ii) Each graph is a parabola, all are symmetrical about the y-axis, and have **the same rate of change** at each x value.

The minimum point of each graph is different.

(iii) Varying c shifts the graph of $y = x^2$ vertically. In other words, the graph of $y = x^2 + c$ is translated c units vertically with respect to the graph of $y = x^2$.

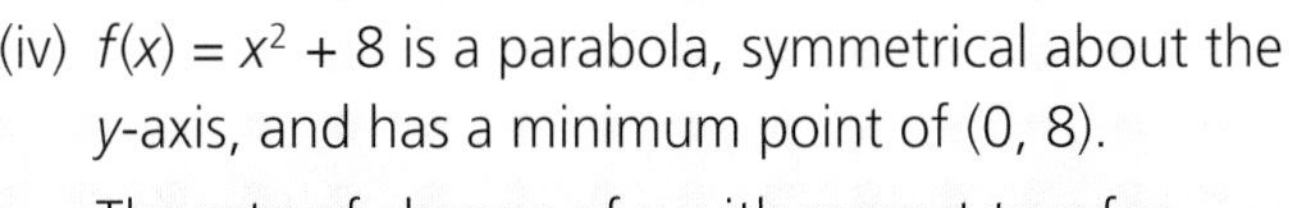
(iv) $f(x) = x^2 + 8$ is a parabola, symmetrical about the y-axis, and has a minimum point of (0, 8).

The rate of change of y with respect to x for $y = x^2 + 8$ is the same as the rate of change of y with respect to x for $y = x^2$.

The graph of $y = x^2 + 8$ is the image of the graph of $y = x^2$ by a vertical translation of 8 units upwards.

(v) $n(x) = x^2 - 3$ is a parabola, symmetrical about the y-axis, and has a minimum point of (0, −3).

The rate of change of y with respect to x for $y = x^2 - 3$ is the same as the rate of change of y with respect to x for $y = x^2$.

The graph of $y = x^2 - 3$ is the image of the graph of $y = x^2$ by a vertical translation of 3 units downwards.

Examples 5 and 6 look at graphs of functions of the form $f(x) = (x + a)^2 + b$.

Example 5

(i) Graph the functions $g(x) = x^2$, $h(x) = (x - 2)^2$, $k(x) = (x + 3)^2$ in the domain $-5 \leq x \leq 5$, using the same axes.

(ii) Compare and contrast the three graphs you have plotted.

(iii) Copy and complete this table.

Function	Minimum point of the graph	Equation of the axis of symmetry
$g(x) = x^2$	(0, 0)	$x = 0$ (y-axis)
$h(x) = (x - 2)^2$		
$k(x) = (x + 3)^2$		

(iv) What would you expect $l(x) = (x - 5)^2$ to look like?

Solution

(i) Draw an input/output table for each function.

x	$g(x) = x^2$
−5	25
−4	16
−3	9
−2	4
−1	1
0	0
1	1
2	4
3	9
4	16
5	25

x	$h(x) = (x - 2)^2$
−5	49
−4	36
−3	25
−2	16
−1	9
0	4
1	1
2	0
3	1
4	4
5	9

x	$k(x) = (x + 3)^2$
−5	4
−4	1
−3	0
−2	1
−1	4
0	9
1	16
2	25
3	36
4	49
5	64

Draw the graphs.

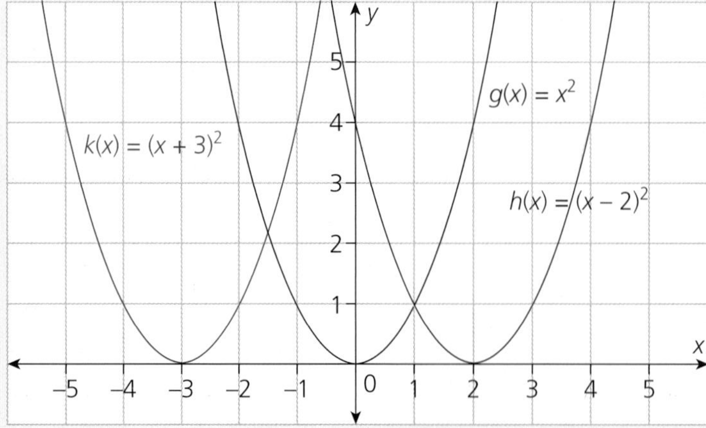

(ii) The graph of $h(x) = (x - 2)^2$ is the image of $g(x) = x^2$ by a translation of 2 units to the right.

The graph of $k(x) = (x + 3)^2$ is the image of $g(x) = x^2$ by a translation of 3 units to the left.

(iii)

Function	Minimum point of the graph	Equation of the axis of symmetry
$g(x) = x^2$	(0, 0)	$x = 0$ (y-axis)
$h(x) = (x - 2)^2$	(2, 0)	$x = 2$
$k(x) = (x + 3)^2$	(−3, 0)	$x = -3$

(iv) The graph of $h(x) = (x - 5)^2$ is a parabola which is the image of $g(x) = x^2$ by a translation of 5 units to the right. Its minimum point is (5, 0) and its axis of symmetry is the line $x = 5$.

Example 6

(i) Graph the functions $g(x) = x^2$, $h(x) = (x - 2)^2$, $k(x) = (x - 2)^2 + 3$ in the domain $-3 \leq x \leq 6$, using the same axes.

(ii) Compare and contrast the three graphs you have plotted.

(iii) Copy and complete this table.

Function	Minimum point of the graph	Equation of the axis of symmetry
$g(x) = x^2$	(0, 0)	$x = 0$ (y-axis)
$h(x) = (x - 2)^2$		
$k(x) = (x - 2)^2 + 3$		

(iv) What would you expect $l(x) = (x - 3)^2 - 5$ to look like?

Solution

(i) Draw an input/output table for each function.

x	$g(x) = x^2$
−3	9
−2	4
−1	1
0	0
1	1
2	4
3	9
4	16
5	25
6	36

x	$h(x) = (x - 2)^2$
−3	25
−2	16
−1	9
0	4
1	1
2	0
3	1
4	4
5	9
6	16

x	$k(x) = (x - 2)^2 + 3$
−3	28
−2	19
−1	12
0	7
1	4
2	3
3	4
4	7
5	12
6	19

Draw the graphs.

(ii) The graph of $h(x) = (x - 2)^2$ is the image of $g(x) = x^2$ by a translation of 2 units to the right.

The graph of $k(x) = (x - 2)^2 + 3$ is the image of $h(x)$ by a translation of 3 units vertically upwards.

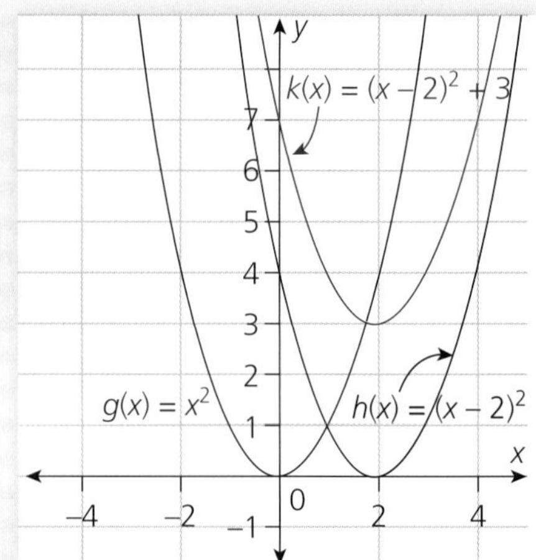

(iii)

Function	Minimum point of the graph	Equation of the axis of symmetry
$g(x) = x^2$	(0, 0)	$x = 0$ (y-axis)
$h(x) = (x - 2)^2$	(2, 0)	$x = 2$
$k(x) = (x - 2)^2 + 3$	(2, 3)	$x = 2$

(iv) The graph of $l(x) = (x - 3)^2 - 5$ is the image of $g(x) = x^2$ by a translation of 3 units to the right followed by a translation of 5 units vertically downwards. Its minimum point is (3, –5) and its axis of symmetry is the line $x = 3$.

Activity 13.5

1 The following functions are of the form $f(x) = ax$, where $a \in \mathbb{Z}$, $x \in \mathbb{R}$:

$p(x) = -1x$, $q(x) = -2x$ and $r(x) = -3x$.

(i) Graph each function in the domain $-3 \leq x \leq 3$, using the same axes.

(ii) Compare and contrast the three graphs you have plotted.

(iii) What would you expect $t(x) = -7x$ to look like?

2 The following functions are of the form $f(x) = ax + b$, where $a, b \in \mathbb{Z}$, $x \in \mathbb{R}$:

$g(x) = -2x$, $h(x) = -2x - 2$, $k(x) = -2x - 4$ and $l(x) = -2x - 5$.

(i) Graph each function in the domain $-3 \leq x \leq 3$, using the same axes.

(ii) Compare and contrast the four graphs you have plotted.

(iii) Where do the graphs cut the y-axis (when $x = 0$)?

(iv) What would you expect $f(x) = -2x + 2$ to look like?

3 The following functions are of the form $f(x) = ax^2$, where $a \in \mathbb{N}$, $x \in \mathbb{R}$.

(i) Graph the functions $g(x) = x^2$, $h(x) = 3x^2$, $k(x) = 4x^2$ in the domain $-3 \leq x \leq 3$, using the same axes.

(ii) Compare and contrast the three graphs you have plotted.

(iii) What effect does varying a have on the shape of the graphs?

(iv) What would you expect $p(x) = 5x^2$ to look like?

4 The following functions are of the form $f(x) = x^2 + c$, where $c \in \mathbb{Z}$, $x \in \mathbb{R}$.

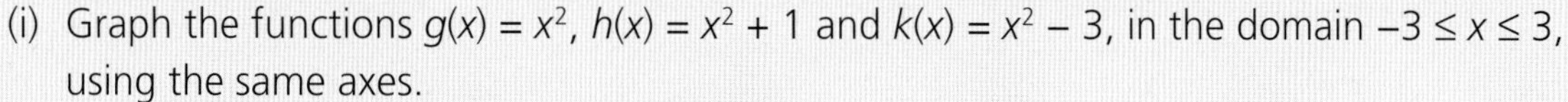

(i) Graph the functions $g(x) = x^2$, $h(x) = x^2 + 1$ and $k(x) = x^2 - 3$, in the domain $-3 \leq x \leq 3$, using the same axes.

(ii) Compare and contrast the three graphs you have plotted.

(iii) What effect does varying c have on the shape of the graphs?

(iv) What would you expect $p(x) = x^2 + 5$ to look like?

(v) What would you expect $n(x) = x^2 - 5$ to look like?

5 (i) Graph the functions $g(x) = x^2$, $h(x) = (x - 1)^2$, $k(x) = (x + 2)^2$ in the domain $-5 \leq x \leq 5$, using the same axes.

(ii) Compare and contrast the three graphs you have plotted.

(iii) Copy and complete this table.

Function	Minimum point of the graph	Equation of the axis of symmetry
$g(x) = x^2$	(0, 0)	$x = 0$ (y-axis)
$h(x) = (x - 1)^2$		
$k(x) = (x + 2)^2$		

(iv) What would you expect $l(x) = (x - 4)^2$ to look like?

6 (i) Graph the functions $g(x) = x^2$, $h(x) = (x + 1)^2$ and $k(x) = (x + 1)^2 + 2$ in the domain $-3 \leq x \leq 6$, using the same axes.

(ii) Compare and contrast the three graphs you have plotted.

(iii) Copy and complete this table.

Function	Minimum point of the graph	Equation of the axis of symmetry
$g(x) = x^2$	(0, 0)	$x = 0$ (y-axis)
$h(x) = (x + 1)^2$		
$k(x) = (x + 1)^2 + 2$		

(iv) What would you expect $l(x) = (x + 1)^2 - 4$ to look like?

7 Use the patterns emerging from your work so far to copy and complete this table.

Function	Minimum point of the graph	Equation of the axis of symmetry
$g(x) = x^2$	(0, 0)	$x = 0$ (y-axis)
$h(x) = (x + 2)^2$		
$k(x) = (x + 2)^2 + 2$		
$p(x) = (x - 5)^2$		
$q(x) = (x - 5)^2 + 4$		
$r(x) = (x - 1)^2 - 6$		
$t(x) = (x + 3)^2 + 2$		

8 The graphs of two functions f and g are shown below.

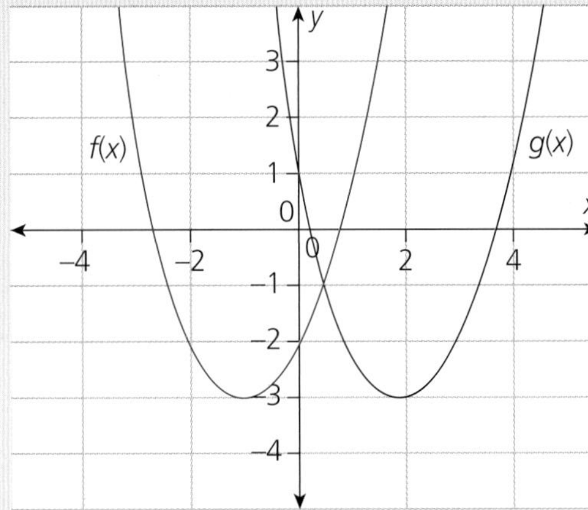

The functions are $(x - 2)^2 - 3$ and $(x + 1)^2 - 3$. Identify clearly which is f and which is g.

9 (i) If $(x - k)^2 - 4 = x^2 - 6x + 5$ for all x and $k \in \mathbb{N}$, find the value of k.

(ii) Hence, write down:

(a) the co-ordinates of the minimum point

(b) the equation of the axis of symmetry of the function $f: x \to x^2 - 6x + 5$.

10 (i) If $(x + h)^2 + 3 = x^2 + 4x + 7$ for all x and $h \in \mathbb{N}$, find the value of h.

(ii) Hence, write down:

(a) the co-ordinates of the minimum point

(b) the equation of the axis of symmetry of the function $f: x \to x^2 + 4x + 7$.

Revision Activity 13

1 Let f be the function $f: x \to x^2 + bx + c$, $x \in \mathbb{R}$, and $b, c \in \mathbb{Z}$.

The graph of f cuts the x-axis at the points where $x = -3$ and $x = 2$.

(a) Find the value of b and the value of c.

(b) Find the value of x for which $f(x) = f(x + 2)$.

2 The graphs of six functions are shown. The graphs are labelled A to F.

The six functions are listed in the table following the graphs.

(a) Match the graphs to the functions.

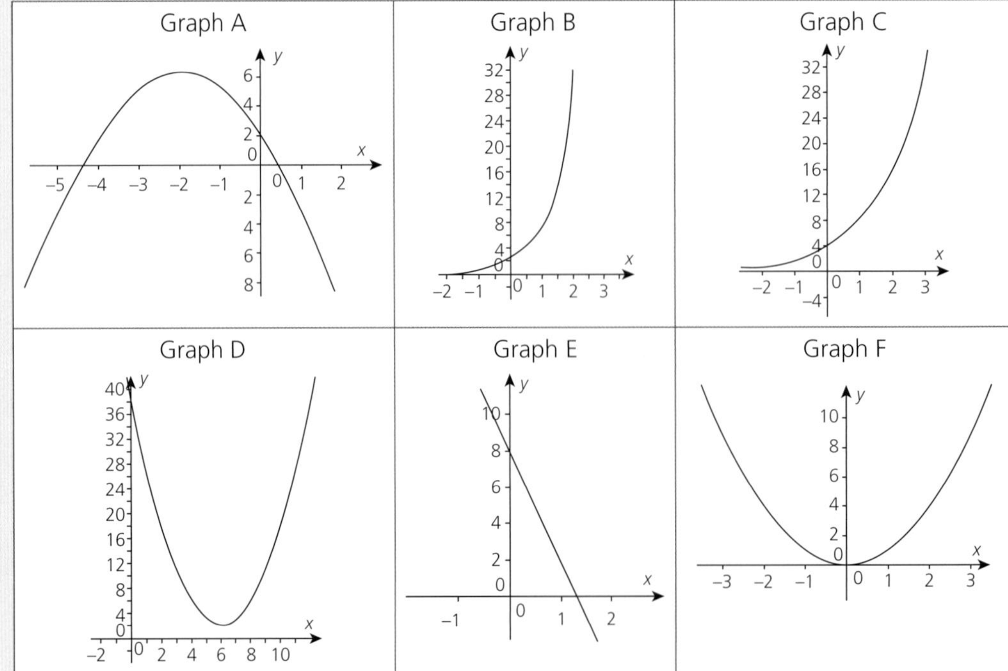

Function	Graph
$f(x) = 4(2^x)$	
$g(x) = 2(4^x)$	
$k(x) = -(x + 2)^2 + 6$	
$m(x) = (x - 6)^2 + 2$	
$n(x) = x^2$	
$p(x) = -6x + 8$	

(b) Explain how you decided on your answers.

3 Two functions f and g are defined for $x \in \mathbb{R}$ as follows.

$$f : x \mapsto 2(3^x)$$

$$g : x \mapsto -5x^2 + 20x - 4$$

(a) Copy and complete the table and use it to draw the graphs of f and g for $0 \leq x \leq 4$.

x	0	0.5	1	1.5	2	2.5	3	3.5	4
$f(x)$									
$g(x)$									

(b) Use your graphs to estimate the values of x for which $f(x) = g(x)$.

(c) Let k be a number such that $2(3^k) = 8$.

Use your graph to estimate the value of k. Use your calculator to find the value of k to two decimals places.

(d) Estimate $g(k)$ from the graph.

4 Fruit flies can multiply very fast. Starting with 20 fruit flies in a large jar with lots of food, the number of fruit flies in the jar was counted every three days for a number of weeks. The table shows the results.

Time (days)	0	3	6	9	12	15	18	21	24	27	30
Number of fruit flies	20	23	28	34	40	48	57	67	80	95	113

(a) Verify that the relationship between time and the number of fruit flies in the jar is (i) not linear, (ii) not quadratic but is approximately exponential.

(b) If this pattern continued, how many fruit flies would be in the jar after (i) 36 days, (ii) 72 days?

(c) Could this pattern of growth continue indefinitely? Explain your answer.

5 A manufacturing company models its total cost in euro for producing x items using the cost function $C(x) = 500 + 90x$. It models the total revenue in euro from the sales of the x items using the revenue function $R(x) = 150x - x^2$. The company expects to sell all the items it produces.

(a) The company produced 50 items on one day. Find the production cost and total revenue for the 50 items.

(b) What do the answers to part (a) tell you about the profit on the day in question?

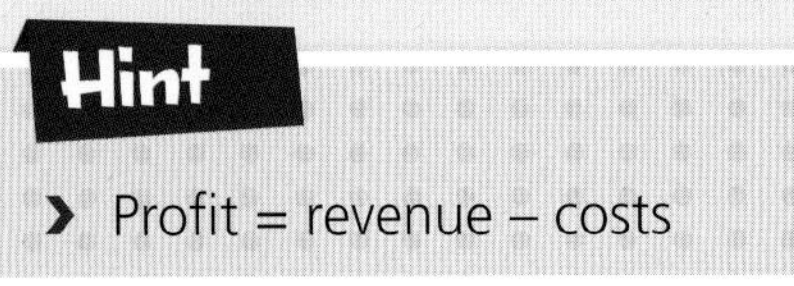

Hint

› Profit = revenue – costs

(c) Write a general expression for the profit made by the company when it produces x items.

(d) What is the situation regarding profit if the company produces no items?

(e) What number of items produced will yield zero profit?

(f) Sketch a graph of the profit function.

(g) What number of items should be produced to give maximum profit?

Hint

› Use the axis of symmetry of the graph.

(h) What is the maximum profit?

6 A tennis ball is thrown upwards from the top of a 10 m high building.
Its height in metres above the ground t seconds after it is thrown up is given by:
$h = f(t) = -5t^2 + 20t + 10$.

(a) Copy and complete the table for the height of the tennis ball above the ground.

Time (seconds)	Height above the ground (metres)
0	
1	
2	
3	
4	
5	

(b) From the table, estimate the time it takes to fall back to ground level.

(c) Verify your answer to part (b) and find a more accurate answer using algebra.

(d) Draw a graph of the height of the tennis ball versus time.

(e) Estimate the time at which the tennis ball is at its maximum height.

(f) At what time will the ball be at the same height as the building from which it was thrown, as it travels downward on its way to the ground?

(g) What is a realistic domain for the function for this context?

(h) What is the range of the function for this context?

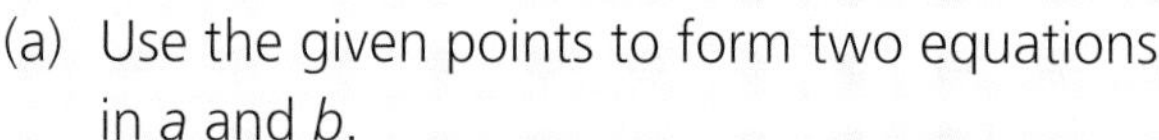

Exam-style Questions

1 Part of the quadratic function $y = x^2 + ax + b$ where $a, b \in \mathbb{Z}$ is shown.

The points $R(2, 3)$ and $S(-5, -4)$ are on the curve.

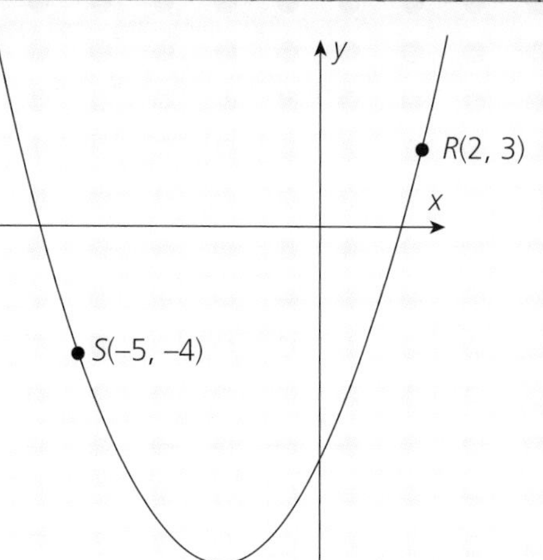

(a) Use the given points to form two equations in a and b.

(b) Solve your equations to find the value of a and the value of b.

(c) Write down the co-ordinates of the point where the curve crosses the y-axis.

(d) Find the points where the curve crosses the x-axis. Give your answers correct to 1 decimal place.

JCHL 2013 Sample Paper 1

2 Let f be the function $f: x \mapsto x^2 - 3x + 12$. Let g be the function $g: x \mapsto 2^{x-1}$. Show that $f(4) = g(5)$.

JCHL 2013 Sample Paper 1

3 Portions of the graphs of two functions f and g are shown on the grid. The functions are:

$f(x) = (x + 2)^2 - 4$

$g(x) = (x - 3)^2 - 4$

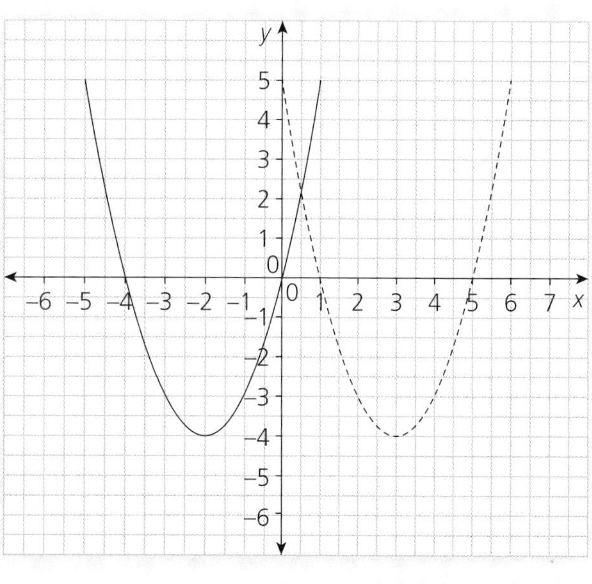

(a) Match the graphs to the functions by putting $f(x)$ or $g(x)$ beside the corresponding graphs on a copy of the grid.

(b) Write down the roots of $f(x)$ and the roots of $g(x)$.

(c) Sketch the graph of $h: x \mapsto (x - 1)^2 - 4$ on your grid.

(d) If $(x - h)^2 - 2 = x^2 - 10x + 23$, $h \in \mathbb{N}$, find the value of h.

(e) Write down the equation of the axis of symmetry of the graph of the function $f: x \mapsto x^2 - 10x + 23$.

JCHL 2013 Sample Paper 1

4 (a) Three functions, $f(x)$, $g(x)$ and $h(x)$, are defined as follows:

$f(x) = 2x^2 + x - 6$, $g(x) = x^2 - 6x + 9$ and $h(x) = x^2 - 2x$.

Solve $f(x) = 0$. Solve $g(x) = 0$. Solve $h(x) = 0$.

(b) Sketches of six different functions are shown. Three of the sketches belong to the three functions from part (a).

Match each of $f(x)$, $g(x)$, $h(x)$ with the correct sketch.

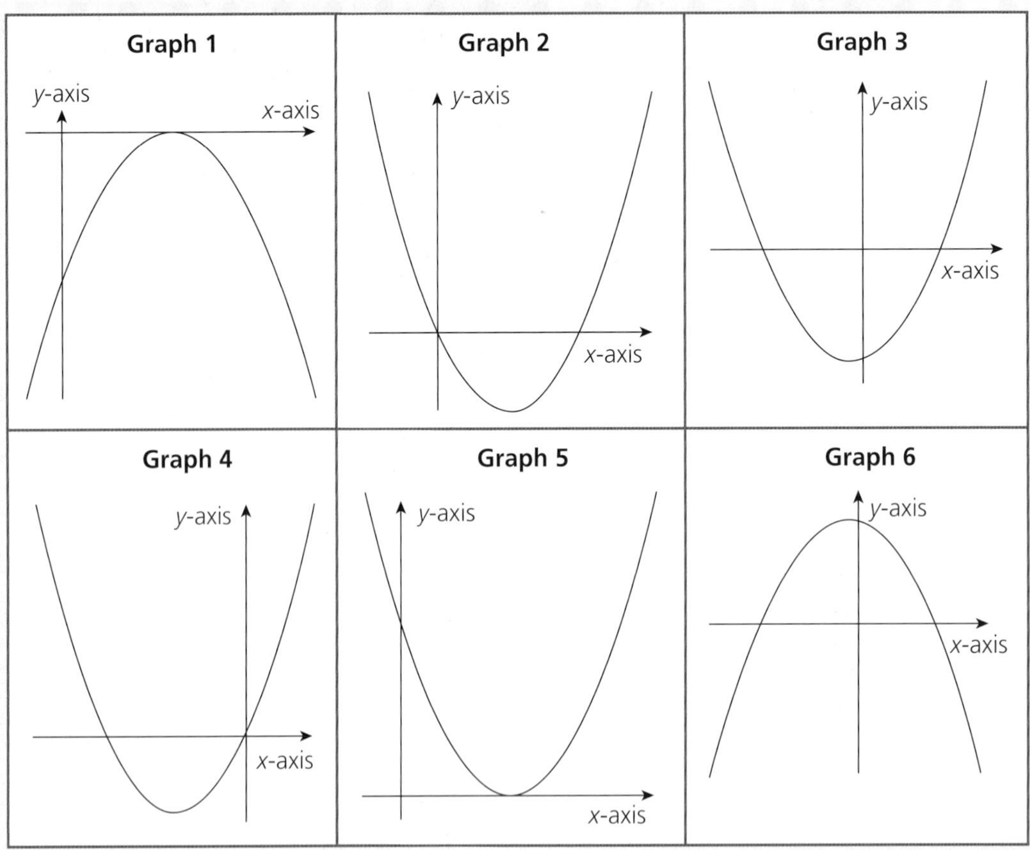

JCHL 2013 Paper 2

KEY WORDS AND PHRASES

- **Linear function** • **Quadratic function** • **Exponential function**

- Graphs of quadratic functions:
  - Positive coefficient of x^2 term gives a ∪ shaped graph:

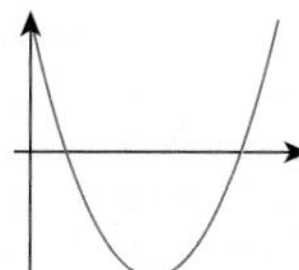

  - Negative coefficient of x^2 term gives a ∩ shaped graph:

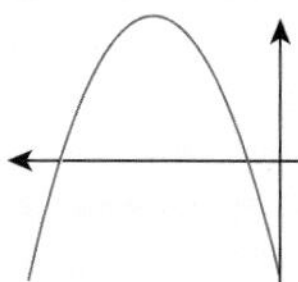

- Graphs of exponential functions 'zoom' to infinity.

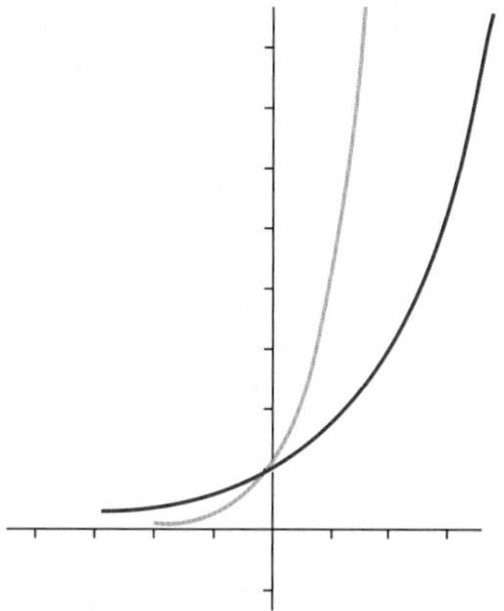

- Transformations of functions (examples):
  - The graph of $g(x) = 2x$ has a slope twice that of $f(x) = x$, and the graph of $h(x) = 3x$ has a slope three times that of $f(x) = x$.
  - The graph of $k(x) = x + 3$ is the image of the graph of $f(x) = x$ by a vertical translation of 3 units upwards.
    The graph of $l(x) = x - 2$ is the image of the graph of $f(x) = x$ by a vertical translation of 2 units downwards.
  - The rate of change of y with respect to x for $y = 7x^2$ is seven times greater than the rate of change of y with respect to x for $y = x^2$. Hence the graph of $y = 7x^2$ is 'narrower' than the graph of $y = x^2$.
  - The rate of change of y with respect to x for $y = x^2 + 8$ is the same as the rate of change of y with respect to x for $y = x^2$ when plotted on the same axes and scales. The graph of $y = x^2 + 8$ is the image of the graph of $y = x^2$ by a vertical translation of 8 units upwards.

Chapter 14

Linear, Quadratic and Exponential Patterns and Relationships

Learning Intentions

In this chapter, you will learn about:

- More linear relationships and patterns
- Directly proportional relationships
- How to distinguish proportional from non-proportional relationships
- The nature of quadratic relationships
- Distinguishing quadratic relationships from linear relationships
- Exponential relationships – doubling and trebling

LO: U.5, U.6, N.4

You will need...

- a pencil
- a ruler
- a geometry set

Section 14A Solving Problems with Patterns

In *Connect With Maths Introduction to Junior Cycle* we met linear patterns and sequences. This chapter looks further into linear relationships and also non-linear relationships.

Remember:
A sequence where a constant (the **same** number) is added each time to get the next term is called a **linear sequence** (also called an arithmetic sequence).
The number added each time is called the **common difference** or **first difference**.
Any term T_n in a linear sequence = (common difference) × n ± some number

We will now use graphs of patterns and sequences to solve problems.

Example 1

Mary bought a sunflower in her local nursery. It was 10 cm tall when she bought it. She recorded its height on 7 successive days and noted that it grew at an average rate of 2 cm per day.

(i) Copy and complete this table for the progress of the sunflower for the first seven days. Take day 0 to be the day she bought the sunflower.

Time in days	Sunflower Height (cm)	Pattern	Difference (cm)
At day 0	10	10	
After day 1	12	10 + 2	+2
After day 2	14	10 + 2(2)	+2
After day 3			
After day 4			
After day 5			
After day 6			
After day 7			

(ii) Write in words the growth pattern of the sunflower.

(iii) What do you notice about the changes in height each day? What sort of a relationship is this?

(iv) Draw a graph to represent the growth of the sunflower over the seven days.

(v) Find the slope of the line. Explain what the slope means in this context.

(vi) Express in words the relationship between the growth of the sunflower and the number of days since it was bought.

(vii) Express using symbols the relationship between the growth of the sunflower and the number of days since it was bought.

(viii) Predict when the sunflower will be 24 cm tall if this growth pattern continues.

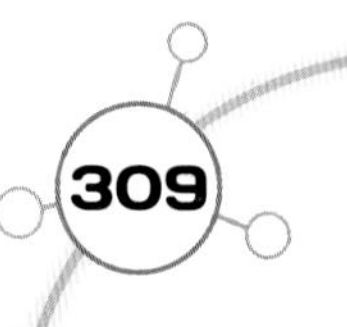

Solution

(i)

Time in days	Sunflower Height (cm)	Pattern	Difference (cm)
At day 0	10	10 + 2(0)	
After day 1	12	10 + 2(1)	+2
After day 2	14	10 + 2(2)	+2
After day 3	16	10 + 2(3)	+2
After day 4	18	10 + 2(4)	+2
After day 5	20	10 + 2(5)	+2
After day 6	22	10 + 2(6)	+2
After day 7	24	10 + 2(7)	+2

(ii) The sunflower is growing at a rate of 2 cm per day.

(iii) The change in height each day is a constant 2 cm. This is a linear relationship.

(iv) The graph represents the growth of the sunflower over the seven days.

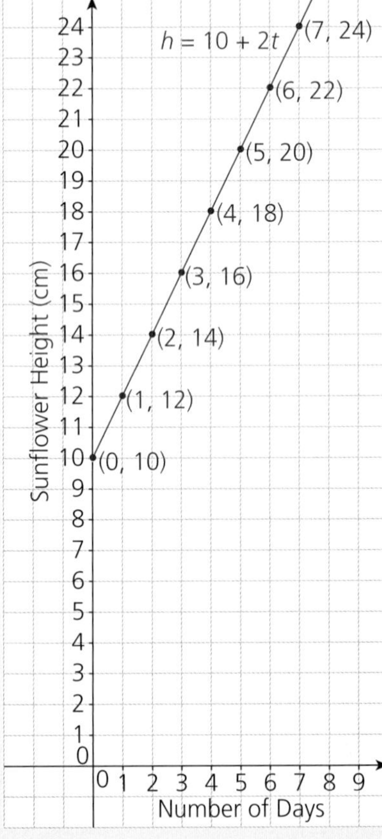

(v) The slope of the line $= \frac{rise}{run} = \frac{y_2 - y_1}{x_2 - x_1} = \frac{14 - 12}{2 - 1} = \frac{2}{1} = 2.$

The slope means the rate of growth of the sunflower per day is 2 cm.

(vi) The height of the sunflower in centimetres is '10 plus 2 times the number of days'.

(vii) The relationship between the growth of the sunflower and the number of days since it was bought, is: "$h = 10 + 2(t)$".

(viii) From the formula:

$h = 10 + 2(t) \Rightarrow 24 = 10 + 2t \Rightarrow 14 = 2t \Rightarrow t = 7$

The sunflower will be 24 cm tall after 7 days, if this growth pattern continues.

Note:

- As the rate of growth of the sunflower is constant, we say that there is a **constant rate of change** – the sunflower is growing by the same amount for each successive day.
- We can see that **the rate of change is constant** because the **difference = +2** for each successive day.
- We can see the rate of growth in the **slope** of the dotted line.
  - A *rise* of 2 occurs for every *run* of 1 week, so the slope = $\frac{rise}{run} = \frac{2}{1} = 2$.
  - This is the rate of growth in the sunflower.

Connections

Can you see the connection between $h = 2t + 10$ in the above example and the formula $y = mx + c$ which we met in Chapter 9 Co-ordinate Geometry? They are really the same!

Example 2

John makes a sequence where each stage is made up of a certain number of **X**s arranged in a pattern. The first three stages of John's sequence are shown below:

The sequence starts at **stage 0**.

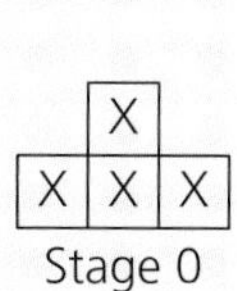

Stage 0

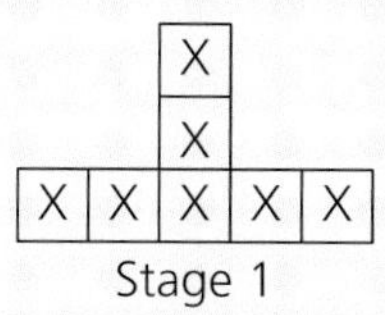

Stage 1

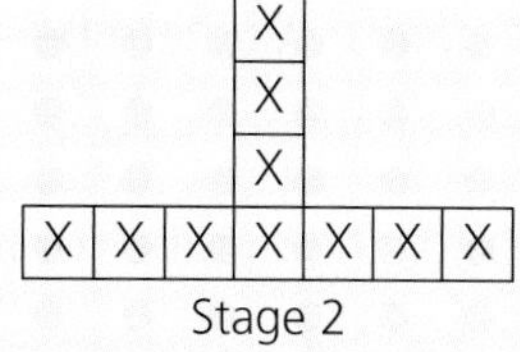

Stage 2

(i) Draw the next stage of John's sequence.

(ii) Using a table, a graph, or otherwise, write a **formula** to express N in terms of S, where N is the number of **X**s in stage S of John's sequence.

Solution

(i) **Stage 3:**

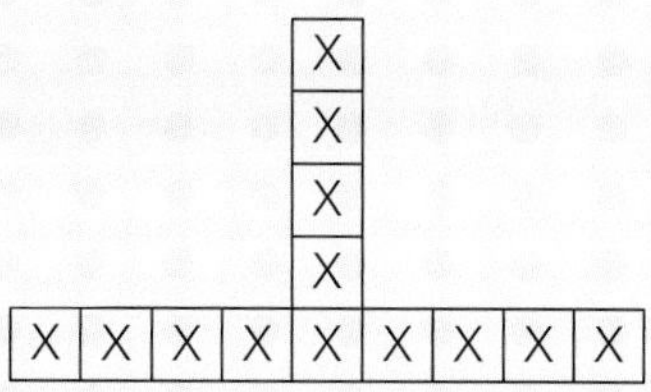

(ii)

Stage (S)	Number (N)
0	4 + 0(3)
1	4 + 1(3)
2	4 + 2(3)
3	4 + 3(3)
.	.
.	.
S	4 + 3(S)

$N = 4 + 3S$

Activity 14.1

1 The first four numbers in a pattern are:

Position	First	Second	Third	Fourth
Term	2	4	6	8

(i) Show that the relationship between the position and the number is linear.
(ii) Describe the pattern in words.
(iii) What is the 5th number in the pattern?
(iv) What is the 10th number in the pattern?
(v) Write down the relationship between the position number and the term value in each stage of the pattern.

2 The first four numbers in a pattern are:

Position	First	Second	Third	Fourth
Term	4	7	10	13

(i) Show that the relationship between the position and the number is linear.
(ii) Describe the pattern in words.
(iii) What is the 7th number in the pattern?
(iv) Write down the relationship between the position number and the term value in each stage of the pattern.
(v) In what position will the number 37 be?

3 (i) Fill in the next three terms of this sequence: 5, 8, 11, 14, ...
(ii) Write in words the pattern of the sequence.
(iii) Work out T_n, the nth term of the sequence.

4 The following patterns are made of matchsticks and beads.

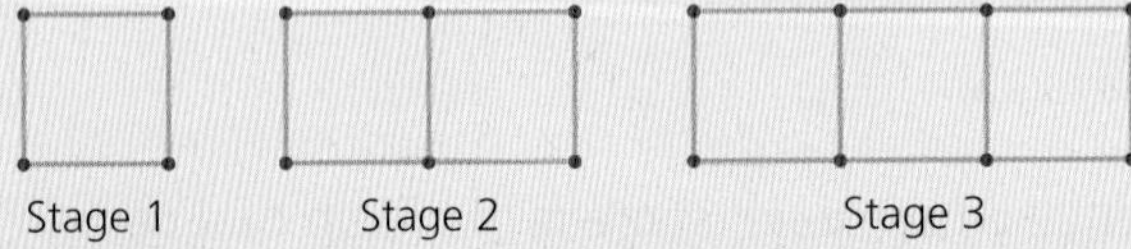

Stage 1 Stage 2 Stage 3

(i) Draw stage 4 of the pattern.
(ii) Give a rule for the number of beads if you are given any pattern number.
(iii) How many beads will there be in stage 100?
(iv) Tom used 34 beads to make a pattern. Find the stage number.

5 Write a formula for the number of matchsticks in any stage of the pattern in question **4**.

6 The first three stages of a pattern of yellow squares and blue squares are shown below.

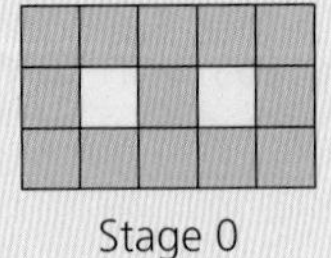

Stage 0

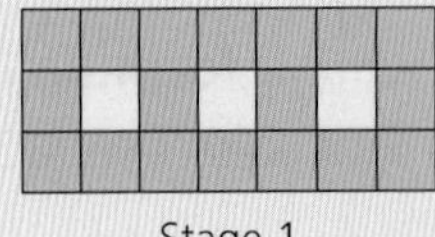

Stage 1

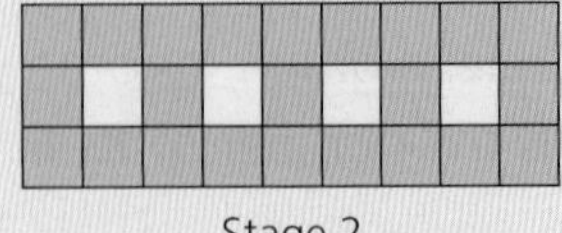

Stage 2

(i) Draw stage 3
(ii) Complete the table below:

Stage number	Number of yellow squares	Number of blue squares
0		
1		
2		
3		
4		
5		

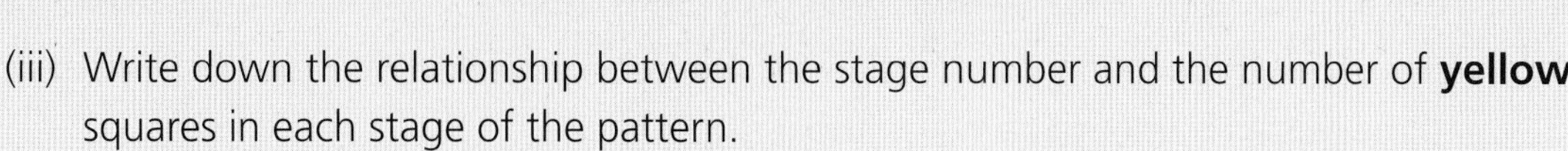

(iii) Write down the relationship between the stage number and the number of **yellow** squares in each stage of the pattern.

(iv) Write down the relationship between the stage number and the number of **blue** squares in each stage of the pattern.

(v) Write down the relationship between the stage number and the **total** number of squares in each stage of the pattern.

7 Peter has €10 in his money box today. He plans to save €2 every week.

(i) Copy and complete this table to represent this situation for the first five weeks.

Time in weeks (input variable)	Money in the box (€) (output variable)	Difference in money saved each week (€)
At week 0	10	
After week 1	12	**+2**
After week 2		
After week 3		
After week 4		
After week 5		

(ii) What feature of the table tells you that the pattern is linear?

(iii) Draw a graph to represent this situation for the first five weeks.

(iv) Find the slope of the line. Explain what the slope means in this context.

(v) Copy and complete this sentence: "The amount of money saved in euro at any time is €10 plus 2 times the number of ________ that have passed".

(vi) Using symbols, express the relationship between the money saved and the number of weeks of saving.

(vii) Predict what will be in Peter's money box after 20 weeks.

8 Marie has €50 in the Credit Union now. She plans to save €10 every week.

(i) Copy and complete this table to represent this situation for the first six weeks.

Time in weeks (input variable)	Money in the Credit Union (€) (output variable)	Difference in money saved for each week (€)
At week 0	50	
After week 1	60	**+10**
After week 2		
After week 3		
After week 4		
After week 5		
After week 6		

(ii) Represent this situation on a graph for the first six weeks. Put number of weeks on the *x*-axis and amount saved on the *y*-axis.

(iii) The point (0, 50) is on the graph. Explain what these co-ordinates mean in this context.

(iv) Find the slope of the line. Explain what the slope means in this context.

(v) Express in words the relationship between the money saved and the number of weeks of saving.

(vi) Using symbols, express the relationship between the money saved and the number of weeks of saving.

(vii) If Marie saved for two years, how much would she have in her account?

9 The following table shows the measured heights of two different sunflowers on a particular day and the amount they grew each day afterwards:

Sunflower	A	B
Start height (cm)	6	10
Growth per day (cm)	3	3

(i) Copy and complete these tables for the progress of the sunflowers for the first five days. Take Day 0 to be the day of the starting heights.

Time in days	Sunflower A		Diff. (cm)
	Height (cm)	Pattern	
At day 0	6	6	
After day 1	9	6 + 3	+3
After day 2			

Time in days	Sunflower B		Diff. (cm)
	Height (cm)	Pattern	
At day 0	10	10	
After day 1	13	10 + 3	+3
After day 2			

(ii) Draw two graphs on the same axes to represent the growth of the sunflowers over the five days. Join the points in each and label each graph Sunflower A and Sunflower B, respectively.

(iii) Using symbols, express the relationship between the growth of the sunflowers and the number of days since they were bought. Choose your own variable names.

(iv) Find the slope of each line. Explain what the slopes mean in this context. What can you say about these lines?

(v) If growth continues at the same rate, will the sunflowers ever be the same height? Explain your reasoning.

Section 14B Proportional and Non-proportional Relationships

Example

A courier company charges for its services in two ways:

Plan A: A registration fee of €10 and €2 per kg for delivering a package within the city.

Plan B: A flat rate of €4 per kg.

(i) Draw tables to represent the cost to the customer of these charges.

(ii) Draw graphs of the two relationships.

(iii) Compare the two plans.

Solution

(i) **Plan A:**

Number of kg (x) (input variable)	Cost (y) in Euro (output variable)	Pattern in output variable (y)	Output (y)	Difference
0	10	10	10	
1	10 + 2	10 + 2(1)	12	+2
2	10 + 2 + 2	10 + 2(2)	14	+2
3	10 + 2 + 2 + 2	10 + 2(3)	16	+2
4	10 + 2 + 2 + 2 + 2	10 + 2(4)	18	+2
5	10 + 2 + 2 + 2 + 2 + 2	10 + 2(5)	20	+2
6	10 + 2 + 2 + 2 + 2 + 2 + 2	10 + 2(6)	22	+2
x		10 + 2(x)		

This is a linear pattern as the differences in the outputs are constant for consecutive inputs.

The formula is $y = 10 + 2x$ where x is the weight in kg and y is the cost in euro.

Plan B:

Number of kg (x) (input variable)	Cost (y) in Euro (output variable)	Pattern in output variable (y)	Output (y)	Difference
0	0	0	0	
1	4	4(1)	4	+4
2	4 + 4	4(2)	8	+4
3	4 + 4 + 4	4(3)	12	+4
4	4 + 4 + 4 + 4	4(4)	16	+4
5	4 + 4 + 4 + 4 + 4	4(5)	20	+4
6	4 + 4 + 4 + 4 + 4 + 4	4(6)	24	+4
x		4x		

This is also a linear pattern as the changes are constant.

The formula is $y = 4x$.

(ii)

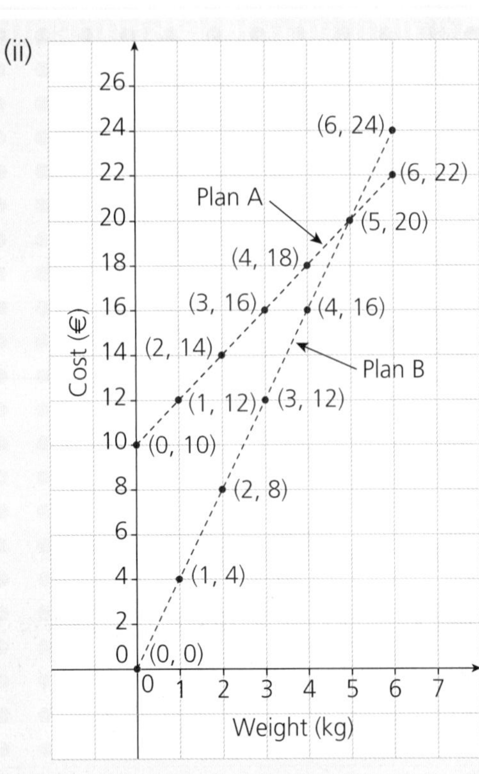

(iii) From the graph, we can see the comparison between the two plans:

- For packages up to 5 kg, plan B is cheaper.
- For a package of 5 kg, the plans cost the same.
- For packages over 5 kg, Plan A is cheaper.

Plan B is an example of a **directly proportional relationship**.

This means that:

- If you double the number of kg, you double the cost.
- If you triple the number of kg, you triple the cost, etc.
- The starting value is 0.

Key Points

The **graph of a proportional relationship**:

- Is a **straight line**.
- **Passes through (0, 0)**.
- If one variable is doubled, the other variable is doubled.

The **formula** of a proportional relationship is $\boldsymbol{y = mx}$ where m is the slope.

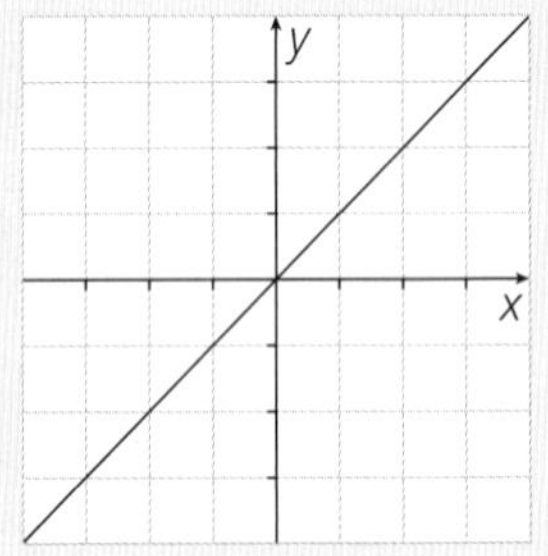

Plan A in the Example is **not a proportional relationship**. Its graph does not go through the origin.

Key Points

The **graph of a non-proportional relationship**:

- Does not pass through (0, 0).
- If one variable is doubled, the other variable is not doubled.

The **formula** of a non-proportional relationship is $\boldsymbol{y = mx + c}$ where m is the slope and **$(0, c)$** is the **y-intercept**.
A non-proportional relationship has a starting value. c is the starting value.

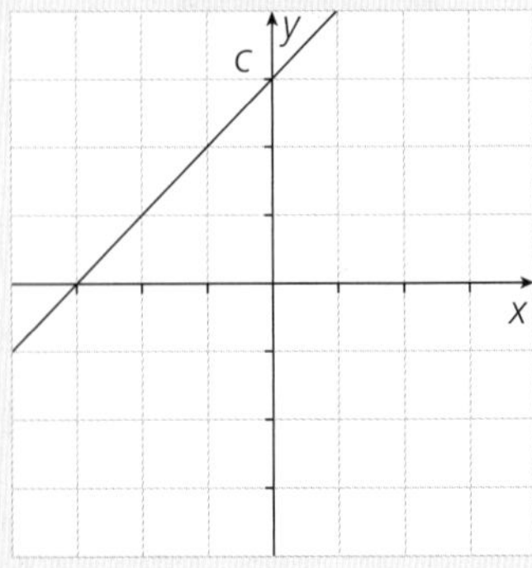

Examples of **directly proportional relationships** include:

- Changing euro to dollars. If you have no euro, you have no dollars. If you double the number of euro, you double the number of dollars, etc.
- Changing miles to kilometres.
- If you get paid by the hour, the more hours you work the more money you get paid. If you work zero hours, you get zero pay.

Examples of **non-proportional relationships** include:

- You start with €40. You save €5 per week. The amount you have in your account is not proportional to the number of weeks of saving. If you double the number of weeks, the amount saved does not double.
- When you pay your electricity bill, you pay a fixed standing charge plus a fixed amount per unit of electricity used.

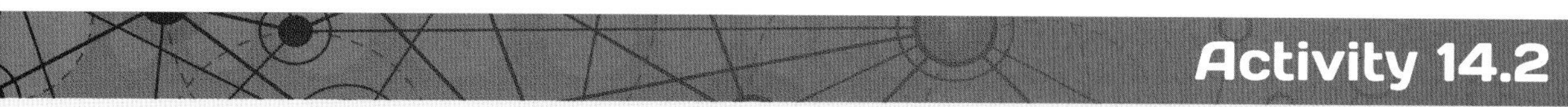

Activity 14.2

1 Oisin has €15 in a bank account. He puts €6 into the account each week for 10 weeks.

(i) Copy and complete the table to show how much he will have saved at the end of each week.

Week number	0	1	2	3	4	5	6	7	8	9	10
Amount saved (€)	15	21									

(ii) Draw a graph to show the relationship between the week number and the amount saved.

(iii) Write down, in words, how you would find the amount in the account at the end of any given week.

(iv) Write a formula for the amount of Oisin's savings for n weeks.

(v) If the number of weeks is doubled, is the amount of money doubled?

(vi) Is the amount of money saved proportional to the number of weeks?

(vii) How much will Oisin have in the account at the end of 10 weeks?

2 Emily is on a particular plan for her electricity. She pays a standing charge of €20 each month even if no electricity is used. She also pays a rate per unit used. The table shows the cost, including the standing charge, of using different numbers of units, in a month.

Units used	0	100	200	300	400	500	600	700
Cost (€)	20	38	56	74	92	110	128	146

(i) Use the data in the table to show that the relationship between the number of units used and the cost is linear.

(ii) Draw a graph to show the relationship between the number of units used and the cost of electricity.

(iii) If the number of units used is doubled, does the cost of electricity also double?

(iv) Explain why the number of units used is not proportional to the cost of electricity.

3 Lucy has saved €50. She gets €8 a week for babysitting and spends €3 of this. She saves the rest.

(i) How much has she saved at the end of week 1?

(ii) Copy and complete the table to show how her savings grow in the first six weeks.

Week number	0	1	2	3	4	5	6
Amount saved (€)	50		60				

(iii) Write down how you would show that the relationship between the week number and the amount saved is linear.

(iv) Draw a graph to show the relationship between the week number and the amount saved.

(v) Write down a formula (in words) and in variables to represent the amount she has saved at the end of each week.

(vi) Lucy is saving for an outfit which costs €150. Use your formula to find out how many weeks she needs to save to have enough money to buy the outfit.

(vii) After 6 weeks, Lucy decides to save all her earnings. She thinks that she can get the outfit 6 weeks earlier with the extra savings. Do you agree with Lucy? Explain your answer.

4 The graph here shows Aaron's and Julia's savings over a number of weeks.

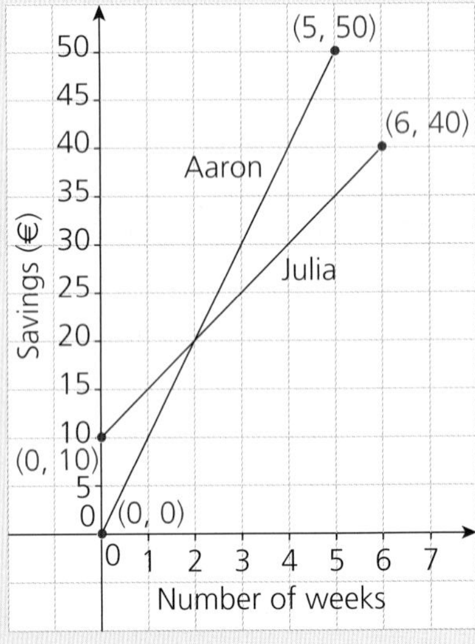

(i) Who is saving more each week? How can you tell from the graph?

(ii) Write down a formula (in words or symbols) to represent the amount of Julia's savings at the end of each week.

(iii) Write down a formula (in words or symbols) to represent the amount of Aaron's savings at the end of each week.

(iv) After how many weeks are Julia's savings equal to Aaron's?

(v) Which line represents a directly proportional relationship between savings and the number of weeks?

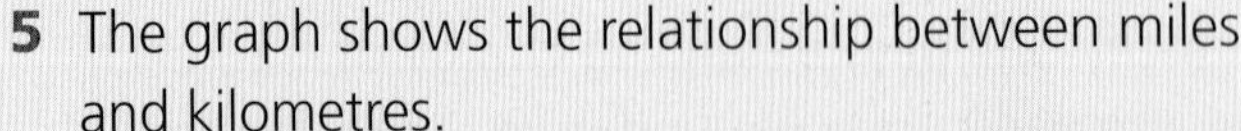

5 The graph shows the relationship between miles and kilometres.

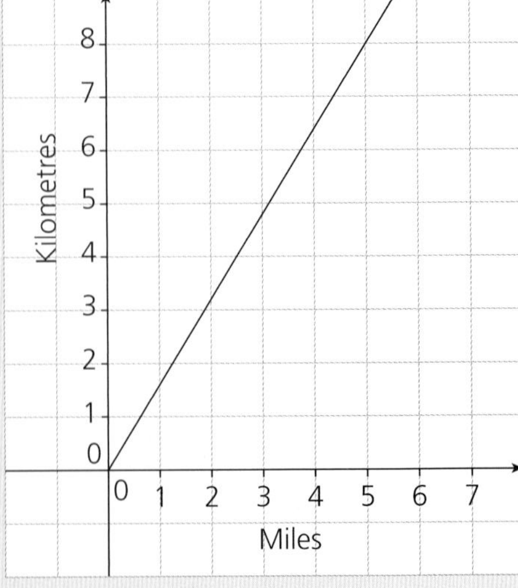

(i) Name two features of the graph that tell you that it represents a directly proportional relationship.

(ii) Use the graph to convert 5 miles to kilometres (give your answer to the nearest kilometre).

(iii) Approximately how many miles are there in 5 kilometres?

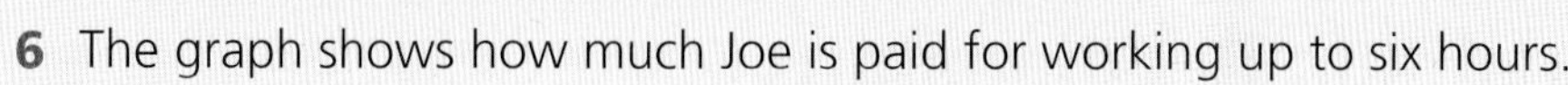

6 The graph shows how much Joe is paid for working up to six hours.

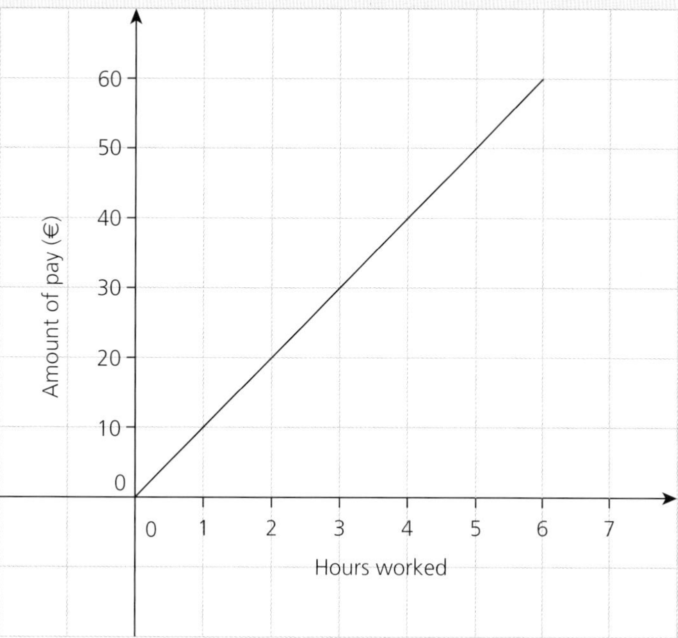

(i) How much does Joe get paid for 1 hour's work?

(ii) If the number of hours worked is doubled, does Joe's pay double?

(iii) If the number of hours worked is trebled, does Joe's pay treble?

(iv) Copy and complete this sentence: 'The amount that Joe gets paid is directly proportional to ____________________.'

7 Two trains, A and B, are travelling in the same direction on parallel tracks. They pass a house beside the tracks. At a particular time train A has gone 80 m beyond the house and its speed is 10 m/s. At the same instant, train B has gone 40 m beyond the house and its speed is 20 m/s.

(i) Copy and complete the table below to show the distance between train A and the house and train B and the house during the next 8 seconds.

Time (seconds)	0	1	2	3	4	5	6	7	8
Train A distance (m)	80	90							
Train B distance (m)	40	60							

(ii) After how many seconds will both trains be the same distance from the house?

(iii) After 8 seconds, which train is furthest away from the house and how far ahead of the other train is it?

(iv) Draw a graph of the distance between train A and the house and train B and the house over the 8 seconds, on the same co-ordinate plane.

(v) Write down a formula to represent the distance between train A and the house for any given time. State clearly the meaning of any letters used in your formula.

(vi) Write down a formula to represent the distance between train B and the house for any given time.

(vii) Use your formulae from parts (v) and (vi) to verify the answer you gave to part (ii).

Section 14C Quadratic Relationships

So far, we have looked at relationships where the graphs were straight lines.

In this section, we will deal with relationships where the graphs are not straight lines.

The sequence of squares in this pattern is 1, 4, 9, 16, ...
These are the square numbers:
$1^2, 2^2, 3^2, 4^2, ...$
$T_n = n^2$
Sequences that have an nth term with n^2 as the highest power of n are called **quadratic sequences**.
If we look for the differences in this sequence we find that the first differences are not constant but the second differences are:

	1		4		9		16		25		36		49
First differences:		3		5		7		9		11		13	
Second differences:			2		2		2		2		2		

The second differences are all = 2

Key Point

In a quadratic sequence the **second difference** between the terms is **always constant**.

Example 1

The nth term T_n of a sequence is given by $T_n = n^2 + n$.
(i) Write out the first five terms of the sequence.
(ii) Find the second difference between these terms and show that they are constant.

Solution

(i) $T_1 = (1)^2 + (1) = 1 + 1 = 2$
$T_2 = (2)^2 + (2) = 4 + 2 = 6$
$T_3 = (3)^2 + (3) = 9 + 3 = 12$
$T_4 = (4)^2 + (4) = 16 + 4 = 20$
$T_5 = (5)^2 + (5) = 25 + 5 = 30$

(ii)

	2		6		12		20		30
First differences:		4		6		8		10	
Second differences:			2		2		2		

The second differences are constant.

Write out three different quadratic sequences whose first two terms are 1 and 4.

Solution

The first differences must increase by the same number each time.

1, 4, 8, 13, 19, … … differences increasing by 1 each time

1, 4, 9, 16, 25, … … differences increasing by 2 each time

1, 4, 10, 19, 31, … … differences increasing by 3 each time

Example 3

The first three stages of a pattern of squares are shown below.

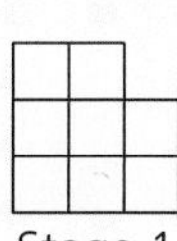
Stage 1

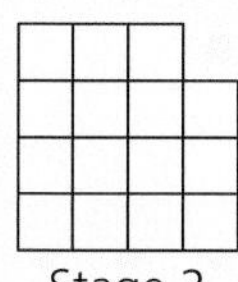
Stage 2

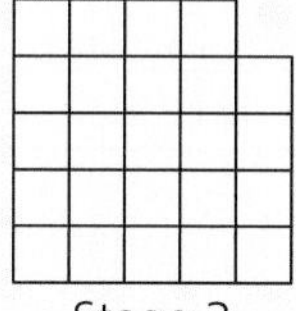
Stage 3

(i) Draw the fourth stage.

(ii) Complete the table below:

Stage number	Number of squares	First difference	Second difference
1			
2			
3			
4			
5			
6			

(iii) Show that there is a quadratic relationship between the stage number and the number of squares in each stage of the pattern.

Solution

(i) The fourth stage.

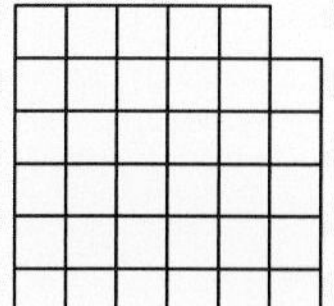

(ii)

Stage number	Number of squares	First difference	Second difference
1	8		
2	15	+7	
3	24	+9	+2
4	35	+11	+2
5	48	+13	+2
6	63	+15	+2

(iii) This is a quadratic relationship because the second differences are constant.

Example 4

The following table represents a relationship between *x* and *y*.

Input variable (*x*)	0	1	2	3	4	5
Output variable (*y*)	0	4	6	6	4	0

(i) Show that it is a quadratic relationship.

(ii) Draw a graph of the relationship.

Solution

(i) (You can use a vertical or horizontal table, as you wish.)

Input variable (*x*)	Output variable (*y*)	First difference	Second difference
0	0		
1	4	+4	
2	6	+2	–2
3	6	0	–2
4	4	–2	–2
5	0	–4	–2

The **second differences are constant**. This means that it is a quadratic relationship.

(ii) The graph:

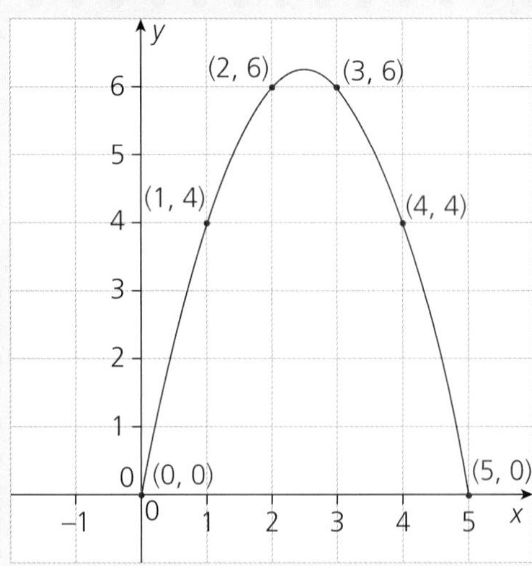

1 The nth term T_n of a sequence is given by $T_n = 2n^2 + 1$.

(i) How can you tell that this is a quadratic sequence?

(ii) Write out the first five terms of the sequence.

(iii) Find the second differences between these terms and show that they are constant.

2 For each of these sequences, write the next three terms to make them quadratic:

(i) 1, 3, 7,

(ii) 1, 5, 11,

(iii) 2, 4, 10,

(iv) 3, 6, 12,

(v) 4, 9, 16,

3 The following table represents a relationship between x and y.

Input variable (x)	0	1	2	3	4	5	6	7
Output variable (y)	0	6	10	12	12	10	6	0
First differences		+6	+4	+2				
Second differences			−2					

(i) Copy and complete the table showing the first and second differences.

(ii) Show that it is a quadratic relationship.

4 The first three stages of a pattern of coloured tiles are shown below.

(i) Draw the fourth stage.

(ii) Copy and complete the table below.

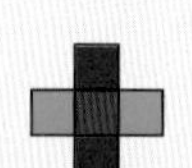
Stage 1

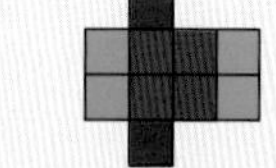
Stage 2

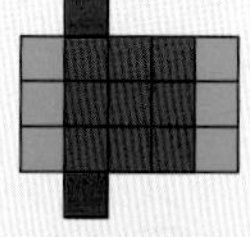
Stage 3

Stage number	Number of red tiles	Number of green tiles	Number of blue tiles	Total number of tiles	First difference (of total tiles)	Second difference (of total tiles)
1				5		
2						
3						
4						
5						
6						

(iii) Show that there is a quadratic relationship between the stage number and the **total** number of squares in each stage of the pattern.

(iv) How many red tiles are in the nth stage of the pattern?

(v) Write down the relationship between the stage number and the number of **green** tiles.

(vi) Write down the relationship between the stage number and the number of **blue** tiles.

(vii) Write down the relationship between the stage number and the **total** number of tiles (red + green + blue).

5 The following table represents a relationship between x and y.

Input variable (x)	−4	−3	−2	−1	0	1
Output variable (y)	4	0	−2	−2	0	4

(i) Show that it is a quadratic relationship. (ii) Draw a graph of the relationship.

6 The first three stages of a pattern of coloured tiles are shown here.

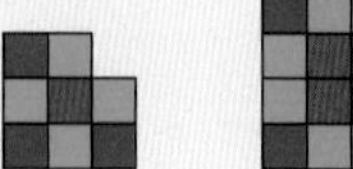
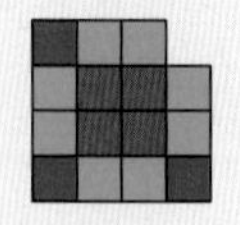

Stage 1 Stage 2 Stage 3

(i) Draw the fourth stage.

(ii) Copy and complete the table below.

Stage number	Number of red tiles	Number of green tiles	Number of blue tiles	Total number of tiles	First difference (of total tiles)	Second difference (of total tiles)
1						
2						
3						
4						
5						
6						

(iii) Show that there is a quadratic relationship between the stage number and the **total** number of squares in each stage of the pattern.

(iv) How many red tiles are in the nth stage of the pattern?

(v) Write down the relationship between the stage number and the number of **green** tiles.

(vi) Write down the relationship between the stage number and the number of **blue** tiles.

(vii) Write down the relationship between the stage number and the **total** number of tiles (red + green + blue).

7 The following table represents a relationship between x and y.

Input variable (x)	0	1	2	3	4	5	6
Output variable (y)	0	5	8	9	8	5	0
First differences		+5	+3	+1			
Second differences			−2				

(i) Copy and complete the table showing the first and second differences.

(ii) Say why you know that the relationship is not linear.

(iii) Show that it is a quadratic relationship.

Finding the *n*th Term of a Quadratic Sequence

To find the *n*th term of a quadratic sequence we note the following:

- The T_n of a quadratic sequence will be of the form $an^2 + bn + c$
- The second difference = $2a$ always, so we can always get the value of a first
- The rest of T_n is $(bn + c)$ which is linear and which we know already how to find.

Example 5

Find the *n*th term T_n of the sequence beginning

5, 11, 19, 29, …

Solution

- First get the differences:

5, 11, 19, 29, …

First differences: 6 8 10

Second differences: 2 2

So $2a = 2$

$\Rightarrow a = 1$

$\Rightarrow T_n = 1n^2 + bn + c$

- To get the sequence $bn + c$ we can use this table:

n	1	2	3	4
T_n	5	11	19	29
Subtract n^2	1	4	9	16
$bn + c$	4	7	10	13

- $bn + c$ 4, 7, 10, 13, …

First differences 3 3 3

We can see that the *n*th term of this linear sequence is $3n + 1$

So $\Rightarrow T_n = n^2 + 3n + 1$.

Example 6

Find the *n*th term T_n of the sequence beginning

4, 13, 26, 43, …

Solution

- First get the differences:

4, 13, 26, 43, …

First differences: 9 13 17

Second differences: 4 4

So $2a = 4$

$\Rightarrow a = 2$

$\Rightarrow T_n = 2n^2 + bn + c$

- To get the sequence $bn + c$ we can use this table:

n	1	2	3	4
T_n	4	13	26	43
Subtract $2n^2$	2	8	18	32
$bn + c$	2	5	8	11

- $bn + c$ 2, 5, 8, 11, ...

  First differences 3 3 3

  We can see that the nth term of this linear sequence is $3n - 1$

  So $\Rightarrow T_n = 2n^2 + 3n - 1$.

Activity 14.4

1 (i) Show that each of the following sequences is quadratic.

(ii) Find T_n, the nth term of each sequence.

(a) 2, 6, 12, 20, ...

(b) 5, 10, 17, 26, ...

(c) 6, 12, 20, 30, ...

(d) 3, 10, 21, 36, ...

2 The first three stages of a pattern of orange squares are shown below.

Stage 1

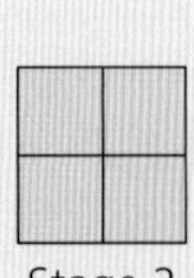
Stage 2

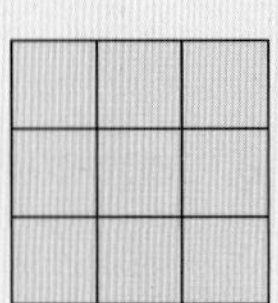
Stage 3

(i) Draw the fourth and fifth stages.

(ii) Complete the table below:

Stage number	Number of squares
1	
2	
3	
4	
5	
6	

(iii) Write a formula which gives the relationship between the stage number and the number of squares in each stage of the pattern.

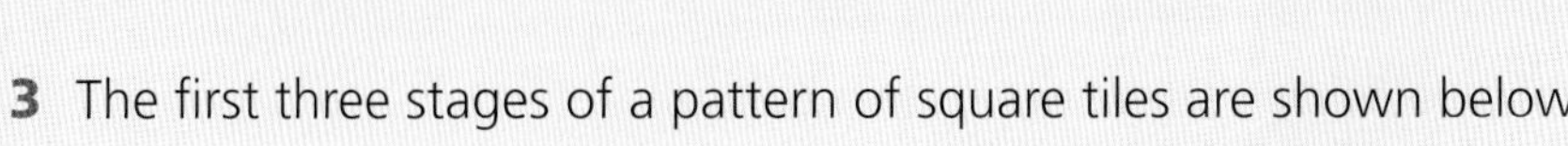

3 The first three stages of a pattern of square tiles are shown below

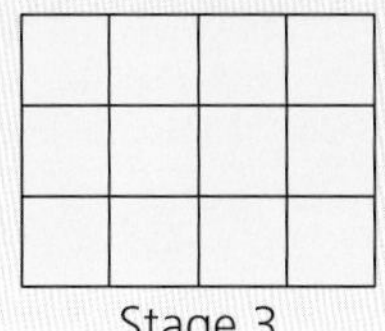

Stage 1 Stage 2 Stage 3

(i) Draw the fourth and fifth stages.

(ii) Complete the table below:

Stage number	Number of tiles	First Differences	Second Differences
1			
2			
3			
4			
5			

(iii) Write a formula which gives the relationship between the stage number and the number of tiles in each stage of the pattern.

(iv) How many tiles are there in the 8th stage of the pattern?

4 The first three stages of a pattern of squares are shown below

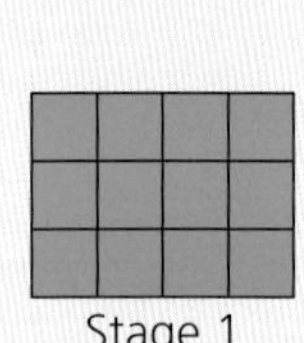

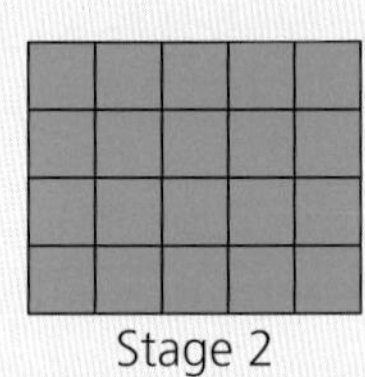

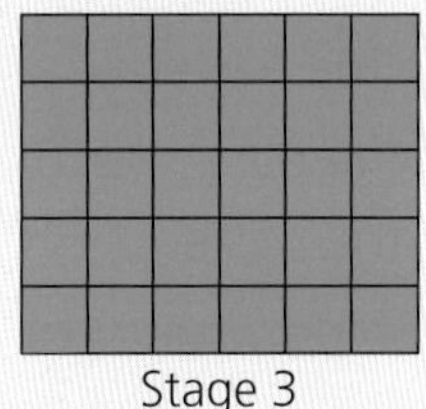

Stage 1 Stage 2 Stage 3

(i) Draw the fourth and fifth stages

(ii) Complete the table below:

Stage number	Number of squares	First Differences	Second Differences
1			
2			
3			
4			
5			

(iii) Write a formula which gives the relationship between the stage number and the number of tiles in each stage of the pattern.

(iv) How many squares are there in the 10th stage of the pattern?

5 The first three stages of a growing pattern are shown below.
Each stage of the pattern is made up of small squares.
Each small square has an area of one square unit.
Write down a general formula for the area of Stage n of the growing pattern below, where $n \in \mathbb{N}$.

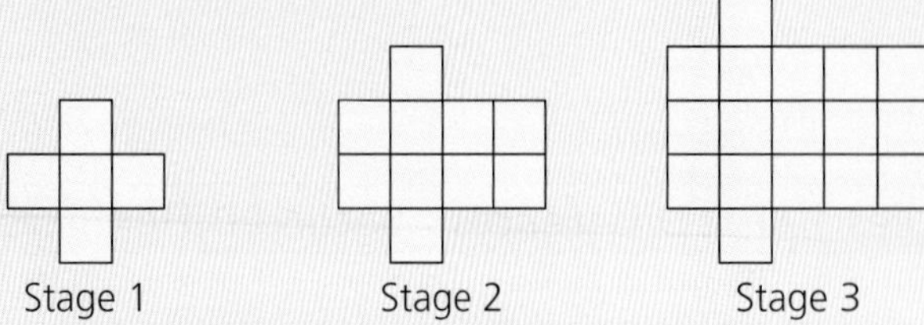

Stage 1 Stage 2 Stage 3

6 The first three stages of a growing pattern are shown below.
Each stage of the pattern is made up of small squares.
Each small square has an area of one square unit.

Pattern 1

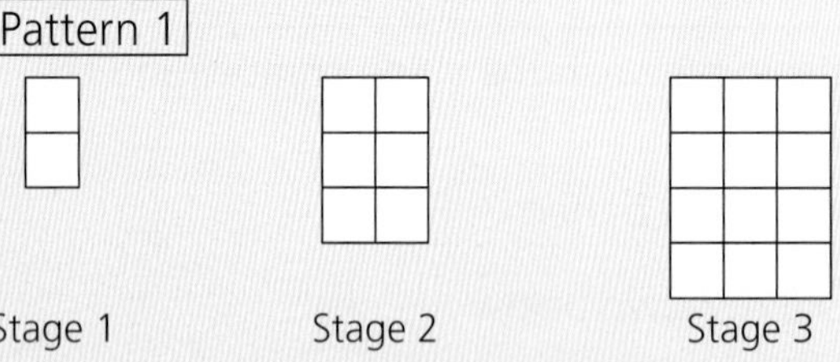

Stage 1 Stage 2 Stage 3

(i) Draw the next two stages of the pattern.

(ii) The perimeter of Stage 1 of the pattern is 6 units.
The perimeter of Stage 2 of the pattern is 10 units.
Find a general formula for the **perimeter** of Stage n of the pattern, where $n \in \mathbb{N}$.

(iii) Find a general formula for the **area** of Stage n of the pattern, where $n \in \mathbb{N}$.

(iv) Compare the area and perimeter of Stage n of Pattern 2 below to the area and perimeter of Stage n of Pattern 1 above.

Pattern 2

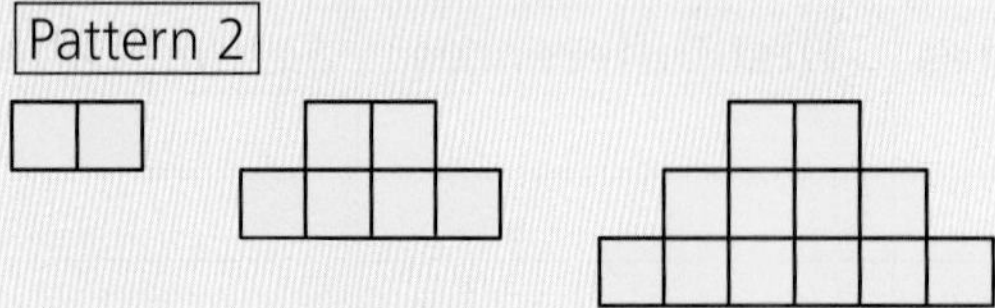

7 The following is an example of a growing pattern for which the first three stages are shown.
Each stage of the pattern is made up of small squares.
Each small square has an area of one square unit.

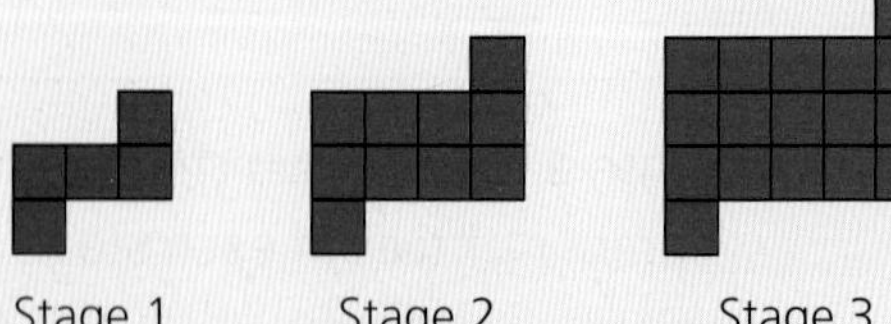

Stage 1 Stage 2 Stage 3

(i) Draw the next two stages of the pattern.

(ii) The perimeter of Stage 1 of the pattern is 12 units.
The perimeter of Stage 2 of the pattern is 16 units.
Find a general formula for the **perimeter** of Stage n of the pattern, where $n \in \mathbb{N}$.

(iii) Find a general formula for the **area** of Stage n of the pattern, where $n \in \mathbb{N}$.

Section 14D Doubling and Trebling: Exponential Relationships

Another type of relationship is called an **exponential relationship**. In an exponential relationship, we multiply each term by the same number to get the next term.

We will be looking only at doubling and trebling.

Doubling and trebling make numbers get large very quickly. This is what people mean when they say that something is **growing 'exponentially'**. We can see this clearly when we graph these relationships.

Drawing the Graph of 2^x

Example

(i) Copy and complete this table of powers of 2.

Input variable (x)	1	2	3	4	5
Output variable (2^x)	2^1	2^2			
Value	2	4			

(ii) From the table, say why the relationship is not linear and not quadratic.

(iii) Draw a graph of the relationship.

Solution

(i)

Input variable (x)	1	2	3	4	5
Output variable (2^x)	2^1	2^2	2^3	2^4	2^5
Value (y)	2	4	8	16	32
First differences		2	4	8	16
Second differences			2	4	8

(ii) The first differences (for successive inputs) are not constant, so the relationship is not linear.

The second differences are not constant, so the relationship is not quadratic.

We can also recognise that the **output values are in the same ratio**

$\left(\text{e.g. } \frac{4}{2} = \frac{8}{4} = \frac{16}{8} \text{ etc.}\right)$.

(iii) The graph of 2^x (doubling) looks like this:

You can see that the graph 'zooms' upwards. This is what all exponential graphs look like. This is the graph of a 'doubling' relationship.

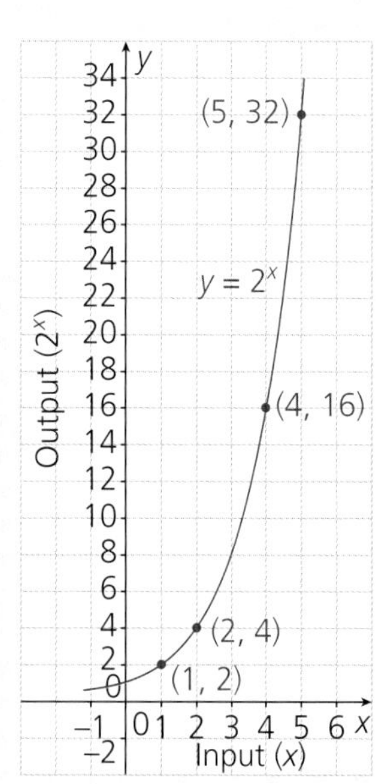

Activity 14.5

1 The table below shows the values when 2 is raised to various powers.

Copy and complete the table.

Power of 2	Expanded power of 2	Answer
2^1	2	2
2^2	2×2	4
2^3	$2 \times 2 \times 2$	8
2^4		
2^5		
2^6		
2^7		
2^8		
2^9		
2^{10}		

2 You have seen in question **1** that the values of the powers of 2 increase very quickly. The following table has more powers of 2 with the powers going up in 5s.

(i) Copy and complete the table using your calculator.

Power of 2	Answer
2^1	2
2^5	32
2^{10}	
2^{15}	
2^{20}	
2^{25}	
2^{30}	
2^{35}	
2^{40}	

(ii) Why did the calculator give you answers for the last two values in a different way?
What do you call this notation?

(iii) Write out the values of the last two rows in figures without powers.

3 The table below shows the values when 3 is raised to various powers.

Copy and complete the table.

Power of 3	Expanded power of 3	Answer
3^1	3	3
3^2	3×3	9
3^3		27
3^4		
3^5		
3^6		
3^7		
3^8		
3^9		
3^{10}		

4 (i) Copy and complete the following table.

Input variable (x)	1	2	3	4
Output variable (2^x)	2^1	2^2		
Values (y)	2	4		

(ii) Explain how you know that this is not a linear or quadratic relationship.

(iii) Draw the graph of the relationship from the table.

5 (i) Copy and complete the following table.

Input variable (x)	1	2	3	4
Output variable (3^x)	3^1	3^2		
Values (y)	3			

(ii) Explain how you know that this is not a linear or quadratic relationship.

(iii) Draw the graph of the relationship from the table.

6 The diagram shows the graphs of two relationships.

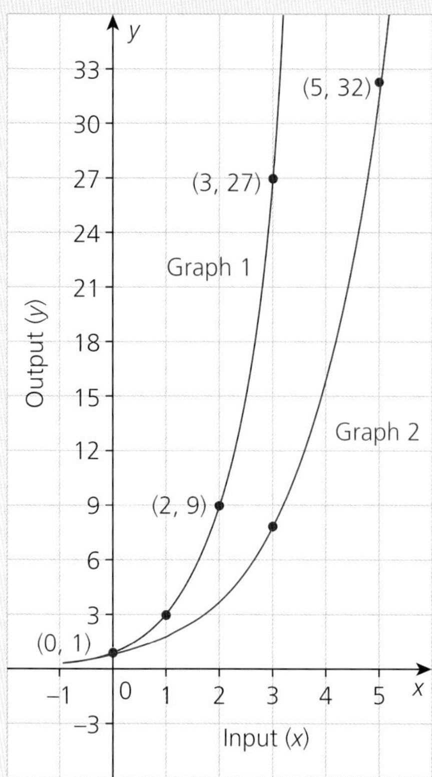

(i) The graphs are of the relationships $y = 2^x$ (doubling) and $y = 3^x$ (trebling). Identify which graph is which.

(ii) Explain what (3, 27) means on Graph 1.

(iii) (1, a) is also on Graph 1. What is the value of a?

(iv) Explain what (5, 32) means on Graph 2.

(v) (3, b) is also on Graph 2. What is the value of b?

7 Three experiments on temperature are done in a science lab. Students record and plot the temperature of each experiment each hour, for 5 hours.

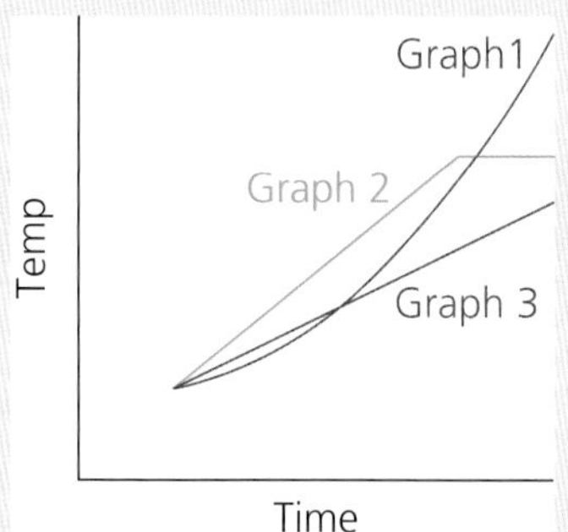

In experiment A, the temperature doubles every hour.

In experiment B, the temperature increases by 2° every hour.

In experiment C, the temperature increases by 3° each hour for three hours and then remains constant.

Identify each experiment by its number.

8 Claire and Nicola are each given €2 on day 1.

On each of the next 3 days, Claire gets an extra €2 added to her amount and Nicola gets double the money she had the previous day.

(i) Draw tables to show the amount of money that each gets over the four days.

(ii) Draw the graphs of each relationship on the same axes.

(iii) What is the difference in the amounts after 4 days?

9 There are 64 squares on a chessboard. Imagine that you put 2 cent on the first square, 4 cent on the second square, 8 cent on the third square, 16 cent on the fourth square and so on, doubling each amount to get the next one.

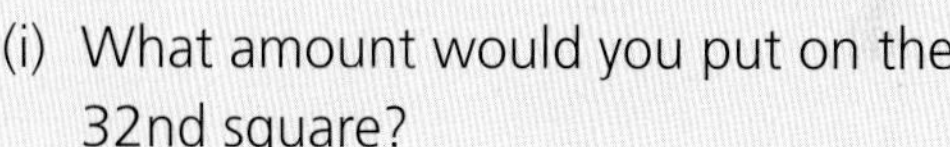

(i) What amount would you put on the 32nd square?

(ii) What amount would you put on the 64th square?

(iii) Write out the answer to part (ii) in figures. How much is this in euro?

Revision Activity 14

1 Kevin has saved €20. He gets €7 a week for doing jobs at home. He spends €2 on sweets and saves the rest in a piggybank.

(a) How much money has he saved at the end of week 1?

	Week 1	Week 2	Week 3	Week 4	Week 5
€20		€30			

(b) Copy and complete the table to show how his savings grow in the first five weeks.

(c) Write down a formula to represent the amount he has saved at the end of each week.

(d) Kevin would like to buy a mobile phone costing €100. Use your formula to find out how many weeks he has to save to have enough money to buy the phone.

(e) Kevin stops buying sweets after 5 weeks. How much can he save each week after that?

(f) Kevin thinks he can buy the phone 3 weeks earlier with the extra savings. Do you agree with Kevin? Explain your answer.

2 James worked for five hours at €10 per hour.

(a) Copy and complete this table showing the total amount earned by James at the end of each hour.

Hours worked	0	1	2	3	4	5
Total amount earned (€)			20			

(b) Draw a graph of the relationship.

(c) Say why the relationship between the hours worked and the total money earned at the end of each hour is linear.

(d) Say why this is a directly proportional relationship.

3 (a) A pattern of rectangles is shown in the diagram below.

(i) Draw the next two rectangles in the pattern. Under each rectangle, write its dimensions (e.g. 3×1, 4×2, etc.).

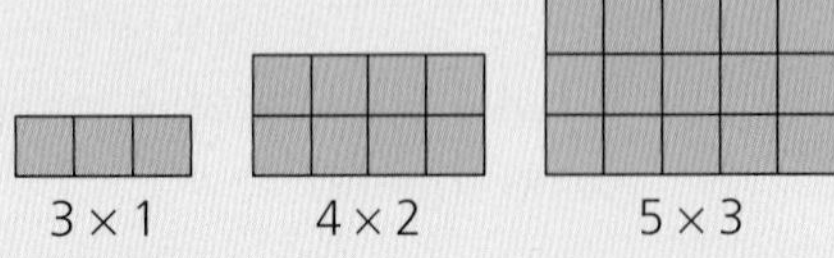

(ii) Complete the table below.

Height of rectangle	No. of small squares in the rectangle
1	3
2	8
3	
4	
5	

(b) The number of small squares in each rectangle in part (a) can be calculated by using one of the following three expressions, where h is the height of the rectangle.

$h^2 + h$ $\quad$ $h^2 + 2$ $\quad$ $h^2 + 2h$

Which expression always gives the correct number of small squares? Give a reason for your answer.

4 Match up the stories to the graphs and formulae.

Story	Formula	Graph
S1 Tom has €5 in his piggy bank. He saves €4 a day from his wages.	**F1** $y = 15000 - 5000x$	**G1** 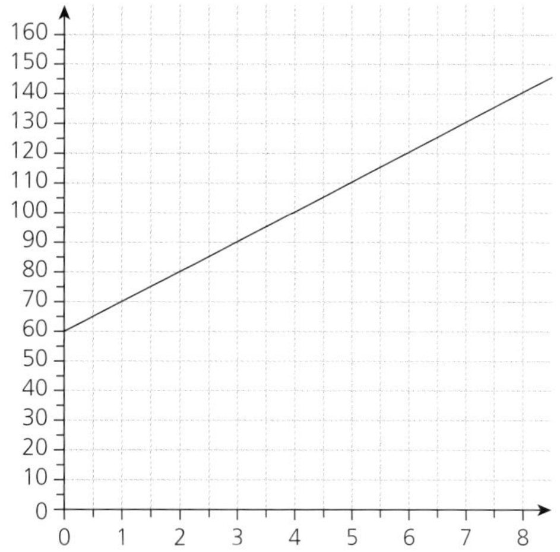
S2 Catherine has €600 in her savings account. She spends €40 every month from this account. She does not save any additional money.	**F2** $y = 60 + 10x$	**G2** 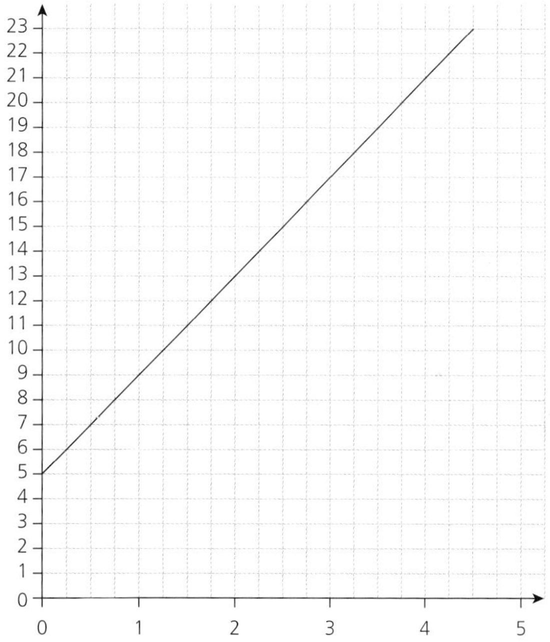
S3 A soccer team is holding a car wash to raise money. They charge a flat rate of €10.00 for each car that gets washed.	**F3** $y = 5 + 4x$	**G3** 

Story	Formula	Graph
S4 A car was bought for €15,000 and depreciates at a constant rate of €5000 per year for a number of years.	**F4** $y = 600 - 40x$	**G4** 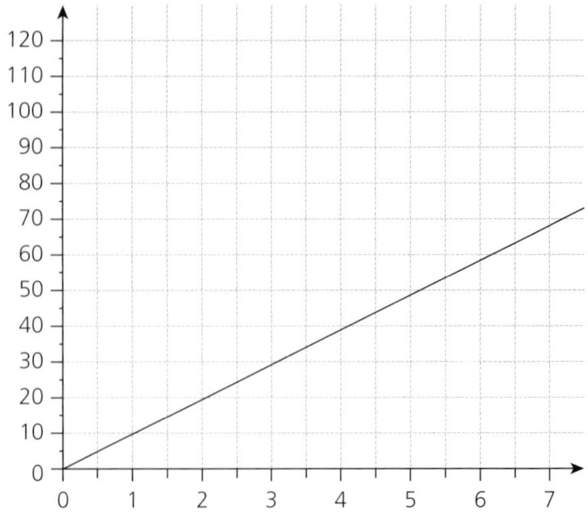
S5 A painter charges €60 to come to your house plus €10 per square metre painted.	**F5** $y = 10x$	**G5** 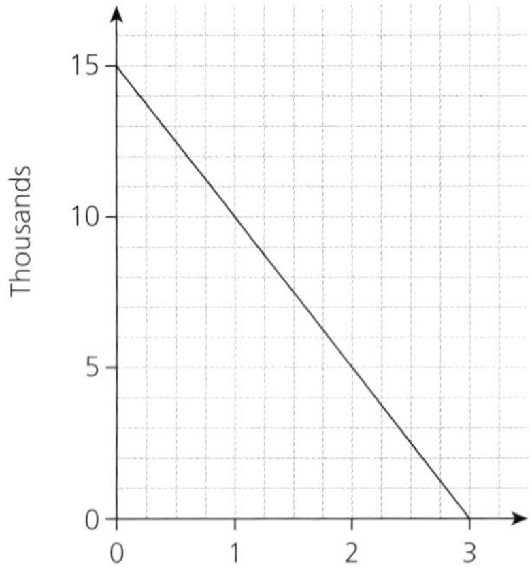

5 Maria is interested in the pattern below for her patio. How many tiles will be needed in total if the patio area needs 36 green tiles in the centre?

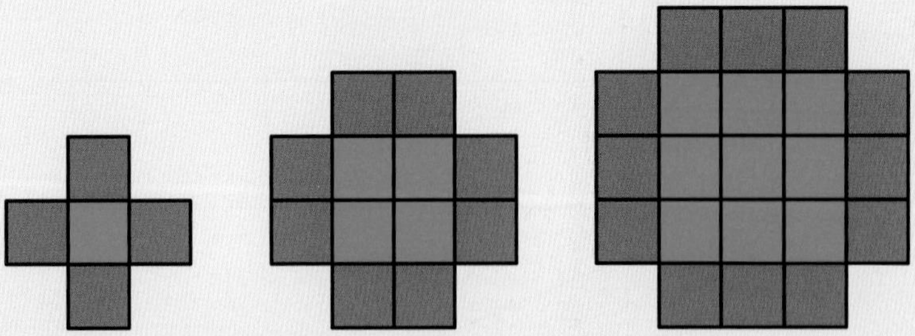

Exam-style Question

1 The first three stages of a pattern are shown below.

Each stage of the pattern is made up of small squares.

Each small square has an area of one square unit.

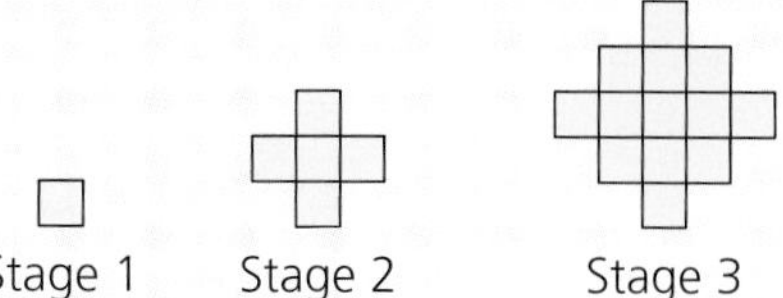

Stage 1 Stage 2 Stage 3

(a) Draw the next two stages of the pattern.

(b) The perimeter of Stage 1 of the pattern is 4 units.

The perimeter of Stage 2 of the pattern is 12 units.

Find a general formula for the **perimeter** of Stage n of the pattern, where $n \in \mathbb{N}$.

(c) Find a general formula for the **area** of Stage n of the pattern, where $n \in \mathbb{N}$.

(d) What kind of sequence (linear, quadratic, exponential, or none of these) do the **areas** follow? Justify your answer.

JCHL Sample Paper 2015

KEY WORDS AND PHRASES

- **Linear relationships**
- **Linear functions**
- **Directly proportional**
- **Proportional relationships**
- **Quadratic**
- **Quadratic relationships**
- **Quadratic functions**
- **Doubling**
- **Trebling**
- **Exponential relationships**

Chapter Summary 14

- The **graph of a proportional relationship:**
  - Is a **straight line**.
  - **Passes through (0, 0)**.
  - If one variable is doubled, the other variable is doubled.
- The formula for a proportional relationship is $\boldsymbol{y = mx}$ where m is the slope.
- In a **quadratic** relationship, for successive inputs, the **second differences of the outputs are constant**.
- Another type of relationship is called an **exponential** relationship. This is where we multiply each term by the same number each time to get the next term. We deal only with doubling and trebling ($y = 2^x$ and $y = 3^x$).
- The formula for a non-proportional relationship is $y = mx + c$ where m is the slope and c is the y-intercept.

Chapter

15 Sets

Learning Intentions

In this chapter, you will learn about:

LO: U.4, U.5, U.6, U.7–U.10, N.5

- Set builder notation
- Union and intersection as commutative operators on two sets
- Set difference and complement of sets
- The operations of intersection, union, set difference and complement for three sets
- The associative property of sets in relation to intersection, union and difference
- The distributive property of union over intersection and intersection over union in sets
- Using three sets to solve word problems

Section 15A Revision of Sets

What is a Set?

A **set** is a collection of things, objects or symbols that are **well defined**. The objects that make up a set are called the **elements** or **members** of the set.

For example, set $A = \{1, 3, 5, 7, 9\}$ has five elements.

If we want to say '5 is an element of set A', we write $\mathbf{5 \in A}$.

or

If we want to say '6 is **not** an element of set A', we write $\mathbf{6 \notin A}$.

Cardinal number (#) of a set

The **cardinal number** of a set is the number of elements or members in the given set.

For example, the cardinal number of the set A above is 5. We write $\#(A) = 5$.

Null set

The **null set** is the set that contains no elements or members.

The symbols for the null set are **{ }** or $\varnothing$.

For example, the set of the days of the week beginning with the letter X is { }.

Equal sets

Two sets are equal if they have the same elements. For example, if $A = \{2, 4, 6, 8\}$ and B = the set of even natural numbers less than 10, then A and B are equal sets. We write $A = B$. If A and B are not equal we write $A \neq B$.

Subsets

B is a **subset** of A if every element of set B is also in set A.

For example, if set A = { , , , , } and set B = { , }

we can write $\boldsymbol{B \subset A}$.

Venn Diagrams

We often use Venn diagrams to represent sets.

Intersection of two sets

A intersection B ($A \cap B$) is the set of all common elements which are in set A and in set B.

As $A \cap B = B \cap A$, for all sets A and B, we can say that the intersection of two sets is a **commutative operation**.

$A \cap B$

Union of two sets

A union B ($A \cup B$) is the set of elements which are in A or in B or in both.

As $A \cup B = B \cup A$, for all sets A and B, we can say that the union of two sets is a **commutative operation**.

$A \cup B$

The universal set

The **universal set** is the set that contains all the elements in a given question or problem.
The symbol U is used for the universal set.

Describing a Set

We have met two ways of describing a set:

- The **written method**

  For example: C is the set of odd numbers greater that 5 but less than 20.
- The **list method**

  For example: $C = \{7, 9, 11, 13, 15, 17, 19\}$

We have another way to describe sets using symbols:

- The **rule method** (also known as **set builder notation**)

  For example: $C = \{x \mid x$ is the set of odd numbers greater than 5 and less than 20$\}$

  How to read the rule method:

$C =$ \{	x	|	x is an odd number greater than 5 and less than 20\}
C is the set	of all x	such that	x is an odd number greater than 5 and less than 20.

Example

Describe each of the following sets in two different ways.

(i) *A* is the set of vowels in the English alphabet.

(ii) *B* is the set of the odd numbers between 10 and 20.

Solution

(i) Method 1 – the **list method**

$A = \{a, e, i, o, u\}$

Method 2 – the **rule method**

$A = \{ x \mid x$ is a vowel in the English alphabet$\}$

(ii) Method 1 – the **list method**

$B = \{11, 13, 15, 17, 19\}$

Method 2 – the **rule method**

$B = \{ x \mid x$ is an odd number between 10 and 20$\}$

Activity 15.1

1 *A* is the set of even numbers greater than 20 and less than 30.

(i) Write the set *A* using the list method.

(ii) What is the cardinal number of set *A*?

(iii) List all the subsets of set *A* that have three elements.

2 B = {the letters in the word 'HAPPY'}

(i) Write the set *B* using the list method.

(ii) What is the cardinal number of set *B*?

(iii) List all the subsets of set *B* that have one element.

3 List the elements of each of these sets.

(i) $A = \{x \mid x$ is an odd number greater than 50 and less than 70$\}$

(ii) $B = \{x \mid x$ is a day of the weekend$\}$

(iii) $C = \{x \mid x$ is a primary colour$\}$

(iv) $D = \{x \mid x$ is a colour on the Irish flag$\}$

(v) $E = \{x \mid x$ is a letter in the word 'PARALLELOGRAM'$\}$

4 Write down the cardinal number of each of the sets in question **3**.

5 Describe each of the following sets using the rule method (set builder notation).

(i) X = the set of divisors of 12

(ii) P = the set of letters in the word 'SURPRISE'

(iii) S = the set of multiples of 5 which are less that 50

(iv) Y = the set of even numbers less than 15

6 Describe each of the following sets in words.

(i) { }

(ii) {1, 2, 3, 4, 5, 6, 7, 8, 9, 10}

(iii) {Adam, Alan, Andrew, Aaron}

(iv) {English, Irish, French, Spanish, German}

7

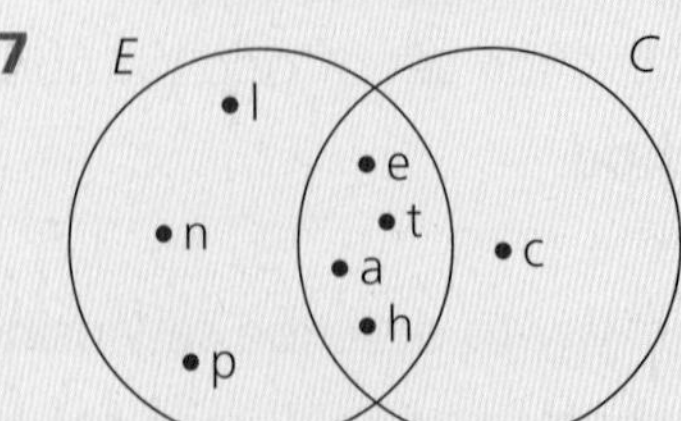

From the Venn diagram above, list the elements of each of the following.

(i) E (ii) C (iii) $E \cup C$ (iv) $E \cap C$

8

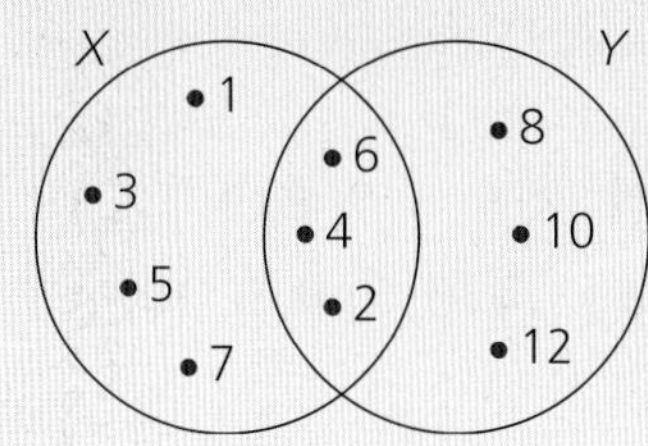

(i) List the elements of:

(a) $X \cup Y$ (b) $X \cap Y$

(ii) Find the values of:

(a) $\#X$ (c) $\#(X \cup Y)$

(b) $\#Y$ (d) $\#(X \cap Y)$

9 (i) Represent the following sets on a Venn diagram.

$U = \{10, 11, 12, 13, ..., 25\}$
$S = \{10, 12, 14, 16, 18, 20, 22, 24\}$
$T = \{10, 15, 20, 25\}$

(ii) Write down the elements of each of the following.

(a) $S \cup T$ (b) $S \cap T$

Section 15B Set Difference and the Complement of a Set

Set Difference

$A \backslash B$ (called 'A less B') is the set of elements which are **in A but not in B**.

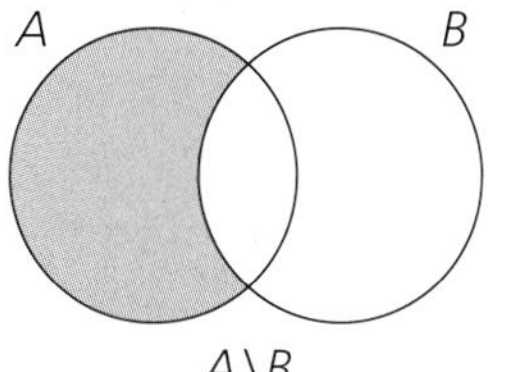

$A \backslash B$

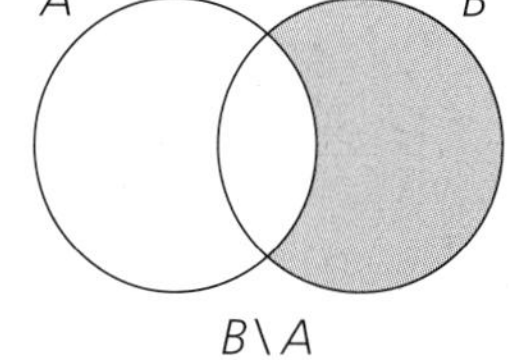

$B \backslash A$

As you can see, $A \backslash B$ is not the same as $B \backslash A$.

So we can say that **set difference is not a commutative operation**.

Complement of a Set

B' (called 'B complement' or 'B dashed') is the set of all the elements in the universal set that are **not in B**. That is $B' = U \backslash B$

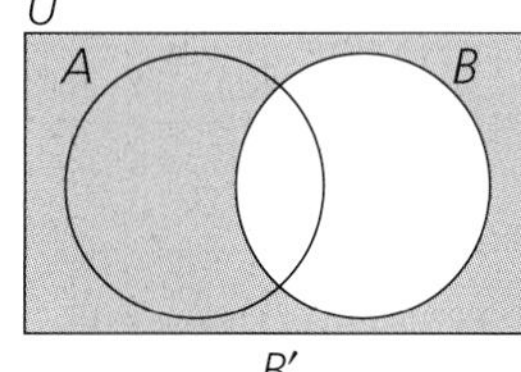

B'

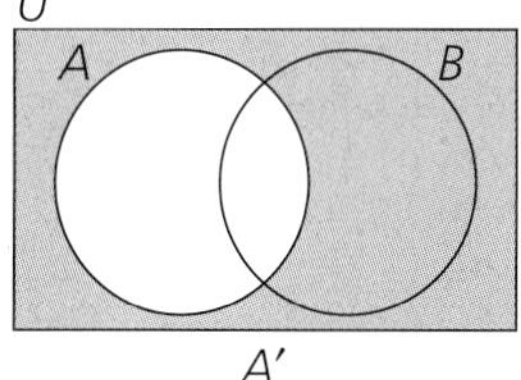

A'

Example

(i) Represent the following sets on a Venn diagram.

$U = \{1, 2, 3, ..., 10\}$, $A = \{1, 3, 5, 7, 9\}$, $B = \{1, 2, 3, 4, 5\}$

(ii) List the elements of the following.

(a) A' (b) B' (c) $A \backslash B$ (d) $(B \backslash A)'$ (e) $(A \cap B)'$

Solution

(i) Always start by filling in the intersection and working outwards.

- $A \cap B = \{1, 3, 5\}$ (elements that are common to set A and set B)
- Only A = set $A - A \cap B$
  $= \{1, 3, 5, 7, 9\} - \{1, 3, 5\}$
  $= \{7, 9\}$
- Only B = set $B - A \cap B$
  $= \{1, 2, 3, 4, 5\} - \{1, 3, 5\}$
  $= \{2, 4\}$
- Only U = set $U - A \cup B$
  $= \{1, ..., 10\} - \{1, 2, 3, 4, 5, 7, 9\}$
  $= \{6, 8, 10\}$

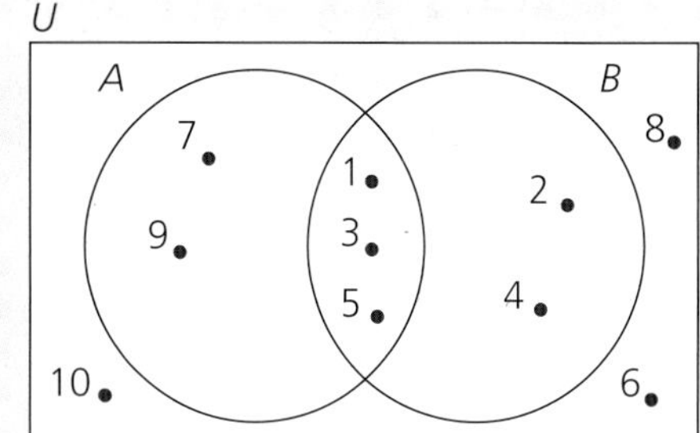

(ii) From observation we can see the following.

(a) $A' = \{2, 4, 6, 8, 10\}$

(b) $B' = \{6, 7, 8, 9, 10\}$

(c) $A \backslash B = \{7, 9\}$

(d) $(B \backslash A)' = \{1, 3, 5, 6, 7, 8, 9, 10\}$

(e) $(A \cap B)' = \{2, 4, 6, 7, 8, 9, 10\}$

Activity 15.2

1 (i) Represent the following sets on a Venn diagram.

$U = \{1, 2, 3, 4, 5, 6, 7, 8, 9, 10\}$ and $A = \{1, 2, 5, 6, 10\}$

(ii) What are the elements of A'?

2 List the elements of each of the following.

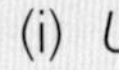

(i) U

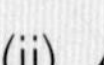

(ii) A

(iii) $U \backslash A$

(iv) A'

U

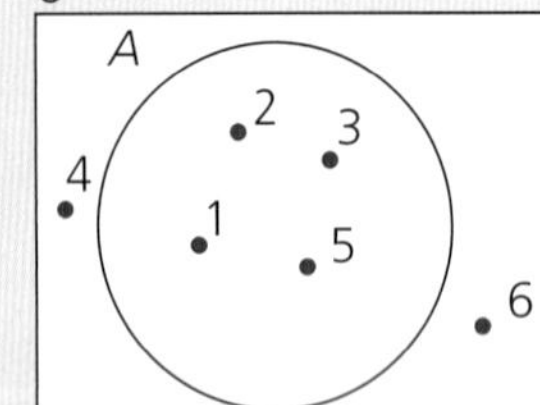

3

U

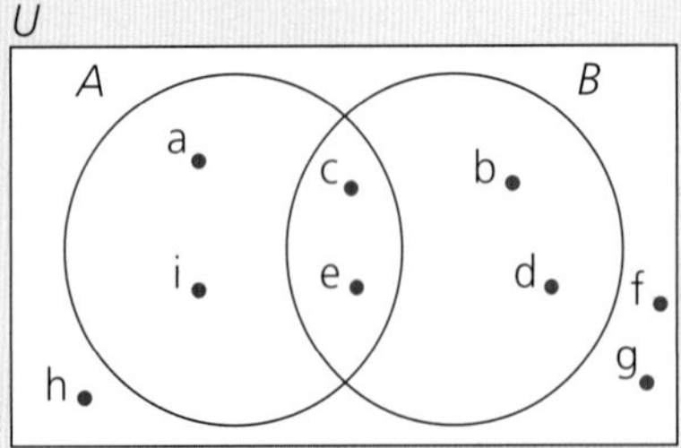

List the elements of:

(i) A'

(ii) B'

(iii) $(A \cup B)'$

(iv) $A \backslash B$

4 (i) Represent the following sets on a Venn diagram.

$U = \{1, \ldots, 10\}$, $P = \{2, 4, 6, 8, 10\}$ and $Q = \{3, 6, 9\}$

(ii) Write down the elements of each of the following.

(a) $P \cup Q$

(b) $P \cap Q$

(c) P'

(d) Q'

(e) $(P \cup Q)'$

(f) $(P \cap Q)'$

(g) $P \backslash Q$

(h) $Q \backslash P$

(iii) Find the value of:

(a) $\#(P \cup Q)$

(b) $\#(P \cap Q)'$

5 (i) Represent the following sets on a Venn diagram.

$U = \{a, b, c, d, e, f, g, h\}$, $X = \{b, d, f, h\}$ and $Y = \{a, b, c, d\}$

(ii) Write down the elements of each of the following.

(a) $X \cup Y$

(b) $X \cap Y$

(c) X'

(d) Y'

(e) $(X \cup Y)'$

(f) $(X \cap Y)'$

(g) $X \backslash Y$

(h) $Y \backslash X$

(i) $(X \backslash Y)'$

(j) $(Y \backslash X)'$

6

U

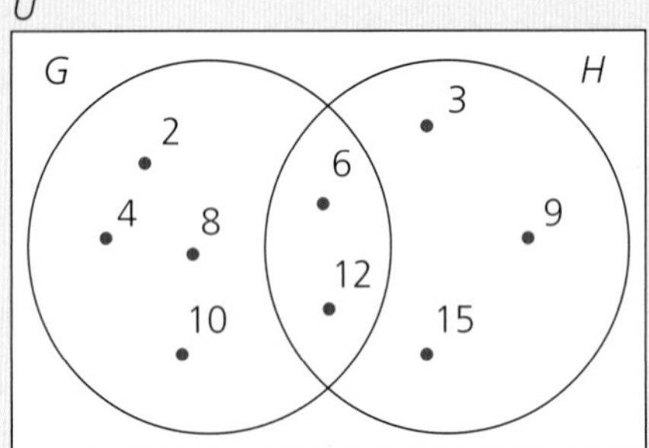

(i) Using the Venn diagram, list the elements in each of the following.

(a) G

(b) H

(c) $G \cup H$

(d) $(G \cap H)'$

(e) $G \backslash H$

(ii) Using the Venn diagram, pick the correct symbol to fill in the blank space to make each statement true.

$\in \quad \notin \quad \cup \quad \cap \quad \subset \quad \not\subset \quad \backslash$

(a) G __ $H = \{6, 12\}$

(b) 6 __ H

(c) G __ $H = \{2, 4, 8, 10\}$

(d) G __ $H = \{2, 3, 4, 6, 8, 9, 10, 12, 15\}$

(e) 3 __ G

(f) $\{3, 9, 15\}$ __ H

7 (i) Draw a Venn diagram to represent the following information.

$U = \{1, 2, 3, 4, ..., 15\}$

L = {the prime numbers from 1 to 15}

N = {the odd numbers from 1 to 15}

(ii) Use your Venn diagram to find the elements of each of the following.

(a) L' (b) $L \cap N$ (c) $(L \cup N)'$ (d) $N \backslash L$ (e) $L \backslash N$

8 Copy the Venn diagram six times and shade in the following sets.

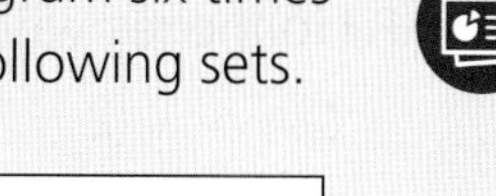

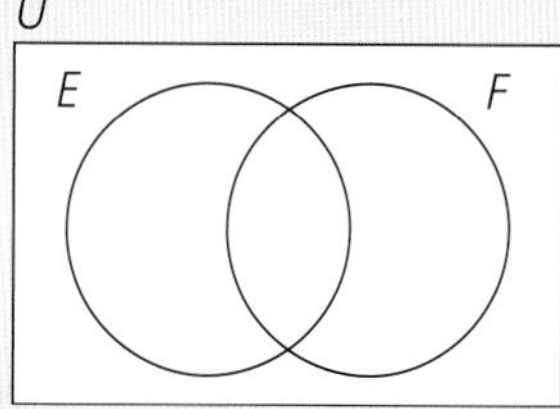

(i) $E \backslash F$ (ii) E' (iii) F' (iv) $F \backslash E$ (v) $(E \cap F)'$ (vi) $(E \backslash F)'$

Section 15C Problem-Solving with Two Sets

Drawing a diagram is a very useful problem-solving strategy in many areas of mathematics. Venn diagrams are just another example of this.

Key Point

When dealing with problems involving sets, we use the **cardinal number** of each set in Venn diagrams. This is indicated by square [ ] brackets.

Example 1

A group of 75 people were asked how they travel to work. 43 said they use a car, 60 said they use public transport and 30 said they use both.

(i) Draw a Venn diagram to represent the information.

(ii) Find:

(a) The number of people who don't use cars or public transport to get to work.

(b) The number of people who use either cars or public transport but not both.

Solution

Identify all the information given in the question:

- U = group of 75 people that are the universal set.
- 43 people travel by car; they are the set 'Car'.
- 60 people travel by public transport; they are the set 'Public transport'.
- 30 people travel by both modes of transport; they are the set 'Car $\cap$ Public transport'.

(i)

- Fill in the intersection (Car $\cap$ Public transport) = 30

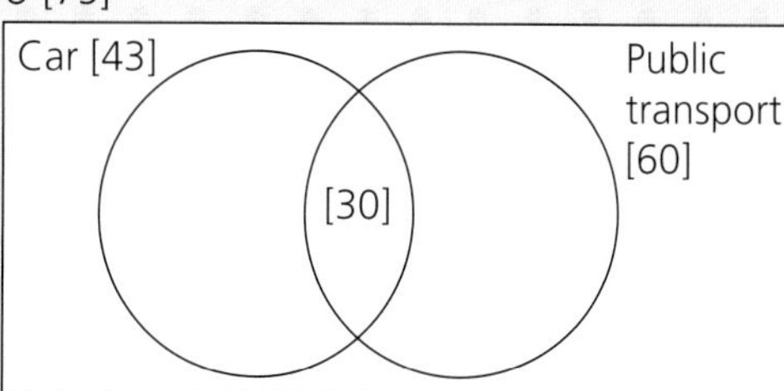

- Fill in the remainder of the sets given.

  'Car only' = (people who travel by car) − (Car ∩ Public transport)
  = 43 − 30
  = 13 people

  'Public transport only' = (people who travel by Public transport) − (Car ∩ Public transport)
  = 60 − 30
  = 30 people

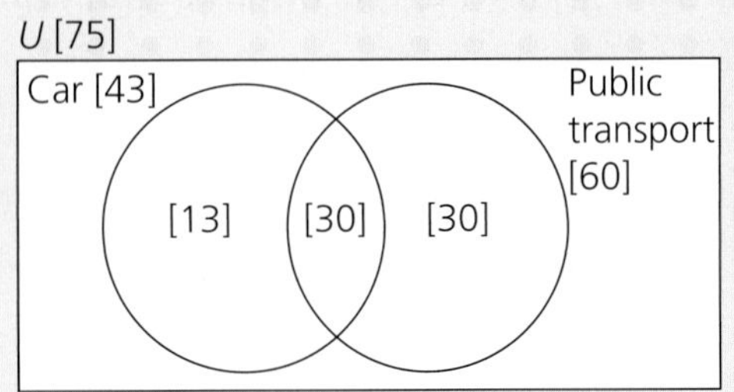

- Now fill in the remainder for U.

  Remainder for $U = U$ − (Car ∪ Public transport)
  = 75 − (13 + 30 + 30)
  = 75 − 73
  = 2 people

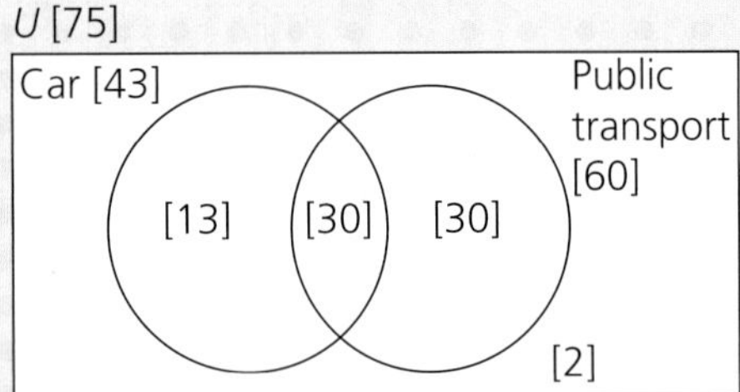

(ii) From observation we can see that:

(a) Two people don't use either mode of transport to get to work.

(b) The number of people who use only one mode of transport is 13 + 30 = 43 people.

Example 2

Use a Venn diagram to solve the following.

Given that $\#S = 15$, $\#R = 11$, and $\#(S \cup R) = 20$, find the value of $\#(S \cap R)$.

Solution

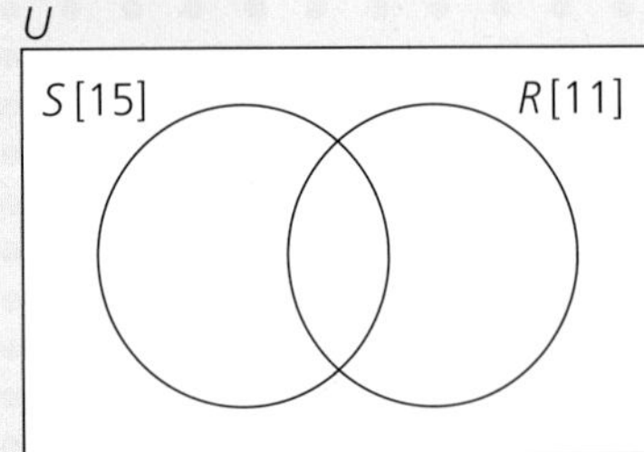

$\#(S \cup R) = 20$

But $\#S + \#R = 15 + 11 = 26$

The difference between them is 26 − 20 = 6.

So 6 elements are being counted twice.

Therefore, $\#(S \cap R) = 6$.

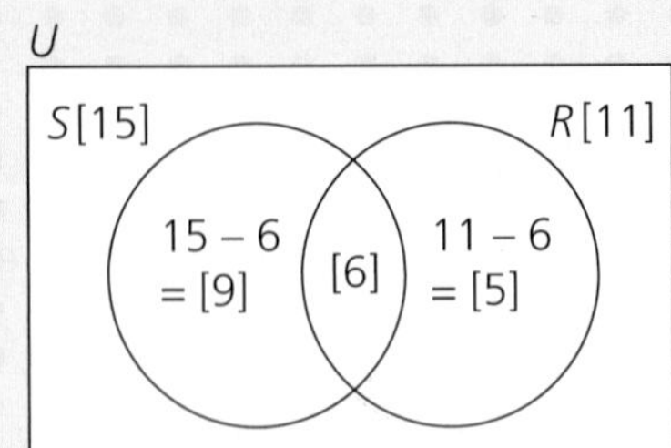

1 In a class of 30 students, 12 students study Art, 16 study History and 5 don't study either subject.

(i) Draw a Venn diagram to represent this information.

(ii) How many students study only History?

2 In a Junior Infants class, there are 25 students. 14 students can tell the time and 15 can sing the alphabet. Every student can do at least one of these.

(i) Copy the Venn diagram and fill in this information.

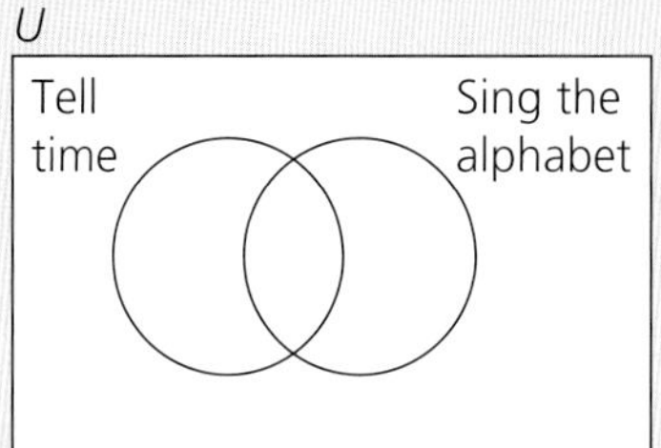

(ii) How many students can tell the time and sing the alphabet?

3 A tennis club has 59 members. A tournament was held. 26 people played in the singles tournament, 32 members played in the doubles tournament and 10 members didn't take part at all.

(i) Copy the Venn diagram and fill in this information.

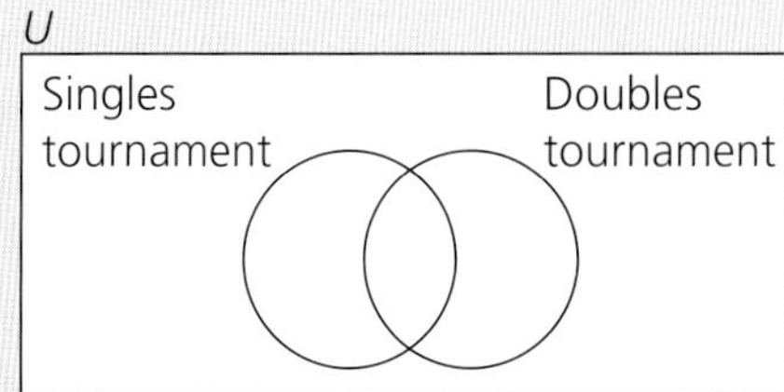

(ii) How many members took part in both the singles and doubles tournaments?

4 48 boy scouts went camping. They were asked if they liked hot dogs (H) or burgers (B). The Venn diagram represents the responses from all of the boy scouts.

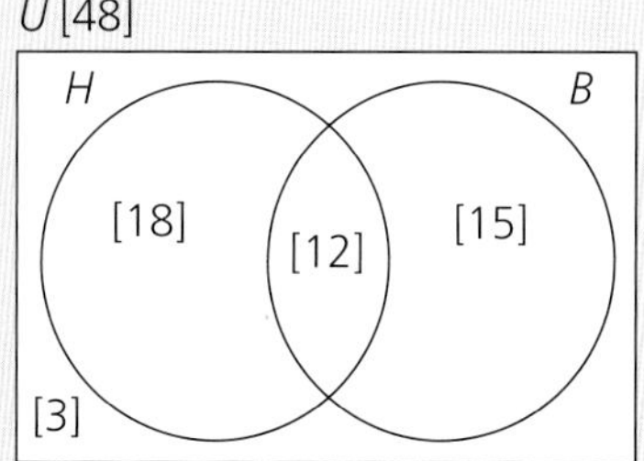

(i) How many boy scouts said that they liked hot dogs?

(ii) How many boy scouts said that they didn't like burgers?

(iii) How many boy scouts liked only one option?

5 A survey was completed by 50 people. They were asked which food they liked, Italian food and/or Chinese food.
32 people said Italian food, 24 people said Chinese food and 4 said neither.

(i) Represent the information on a Venn diagram.

(ii) How many people said that they liked both types of food?

6 W = {the students in the class who have blue eyes}

Y = {the students in the class who wear glasses}

Describe, in your own words, the members of the following sets.

(i) $W \cup Y$

(ii) $W \cap Y$

(iii) $(W \cup Y)'$

7 Draw a Venn diagram and fill in the following information.

$\#U = 15$, $\#Q = 6$, $\#P = 5$ and $\#(P \cap Q) = 4$.

Find the value of $\#(P \cup Q)$.

8 The Venn diagram below represents the responses given by a youth group of 42 members who were asked whether they could sing or dance.

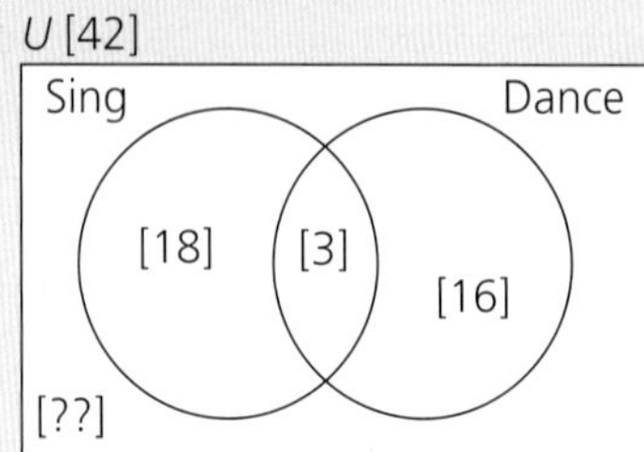

(i) How many members can sing but not dance?

(ii) How many members can do neither?

9 24 students were asked if they had ever baked a lemon cake or a fudge cake. 17 students had baked a lemon cake and 13 students had made a fudge cake. Every student had baked at least one of these.

(i) Represent this information on a Venn diagram.

(ii) How many students had baked both types of cake?

10 X and Y are two sets. $\#X = 25$, $\#Y = 16$, and $\#(X \cup Y) = 34$.

Represent this on a Venn diagram.
Find the value of $\#(X \cap Y)$.

11 S and T are two sets. $\#S = 19$, $\#(S \cap T) = 3$ and $\#(S \cup T) = 31$.

Represent this on a Venn diagram.
Find the value of $\#T$.

12 U is the universal set, M and N are two subsets of U.

$\#U = 125$, $\#M = 83$, $\#N = 69$

(i) Find the minimum value of $\#(M \cap N)$. Use a Venn diagram to illustrate your answer.

(ii) Find the maximum value of $\#(M \cap N)$. Use a Venn diagram to illustrate your answer.

13 U is the universal set; J and K are two subsets of U.

$\#U = 82$, $\#J = 47$ and $\#K = 27$.

(i) Find the minimum value of $\#(J \cup K)'$. Use a Venn diagram to illustrate your answer.

(ii) Find the maximum value of $\#(J \cup K)'$. Use a Venn diagram to illustrate your answer.

14 Below are four statements about three **non-empty** sets P, Q, and R in a universal set U.

(i) In your own copy of this table, put a tick (✓) in the correct box in each case to show whether each statement is **always true**, **sometimes true**, or **never true**.

Note: P' is the complement of the set P.

		Tick **one** box only in each case		
	Statement	**Always true**	**Sometimes true**	**Never true**
1	$\#(P \cup Q) = \#(P) + \#(Q)$	☐	☐	☐
2	$P \backslash Q = P \cap Q$	☐	☐	☐
3	$(P \cap Q)' = P' \cup Q'$	☐	☐	☐
4	$P \cup (Q \cap R) = (P \cup Q) \cap (P \cup R)$	☐	☐	☐

(ii) In the case of **Statement 1** in the table, justify your answer.

Section 15D Venn Diagrams with Three Sets

We will now work with Venn diagrams involving three sets. Study the following Venn diagram carefully. It has eight regions.

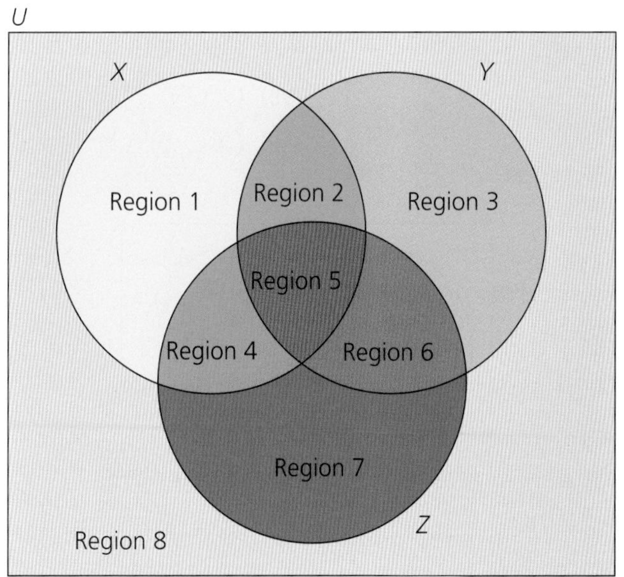

Region	Symbol	Meaning
1	$X \backslash (Y \cup Z)$	X less (Y union Z): Elements in X but not in Y or Z
2	$(X \cap Y) \backslash Z$	(X intersection Y) less Z: Elements common to X and Y less the elements in Z
3	$Y \backslash (X \cup Z)$	Y less (X union Z): Elements in Y but not in X or Z
4	$(X \cap Z) \backslash Y$	(X intersection Z) less Y: Elements common to X and Z less the elements in Y
5	$X \cap Y \cap Z$	X intersection Y intersection Z: Elements common to X, Y and Z
6	$(Y \cap Z) \backslash X$	(Y intersection Z) less X: Elements common to Y and Z less the elements in X
7	$Z \backslash (X \cup Y)$	Z less (X union Y): Elements in Z but not in X or Y
8	$(X \cup Y \cup Z)'$ or $U \backslash (X \cup Y \cup Z)$	(X union Y union Z) complement ■ Elements in the universal set that are **not in** (X union Y union Z) ■ Universal set less (X union Y union Z) ■ Elements in the universal set less the elements in (X union Y union Z)

Example 1

Given the Venn diagram below, list the elements of each of the following.

(i) $X \cup Z$

(ii) $(X \cup Y \cup Z)'$

(iii) $Y \backslash Z$

(iv) $(X \cap Y \cap Z)'$

(v) $X \backslash (Y \cap Z)$

(vi) $(X \cap Y) \cup Z$

(vii) $(X \backslash Z)'$

(viii) $(X \cup Z)' \backslash Y$

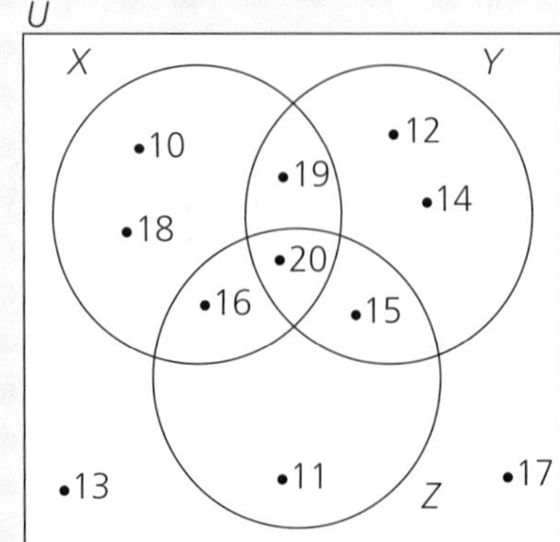

Solution

(i) $X \cup Z$

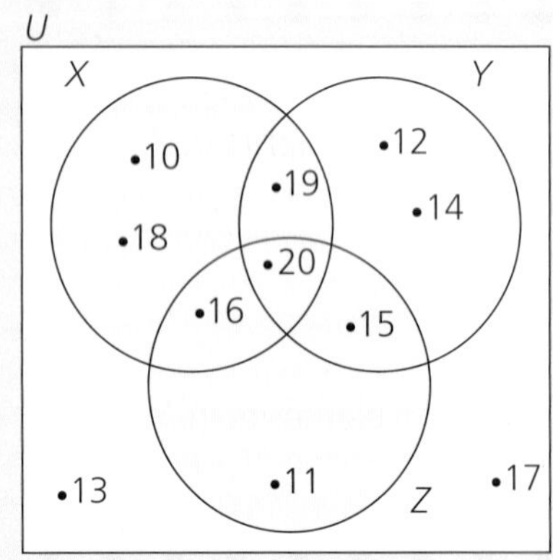

$X \cup Z = \{10, 11, 15, 16, 18, 19, 20\}$

(ii) $(X \cup Y \cup Z)'$

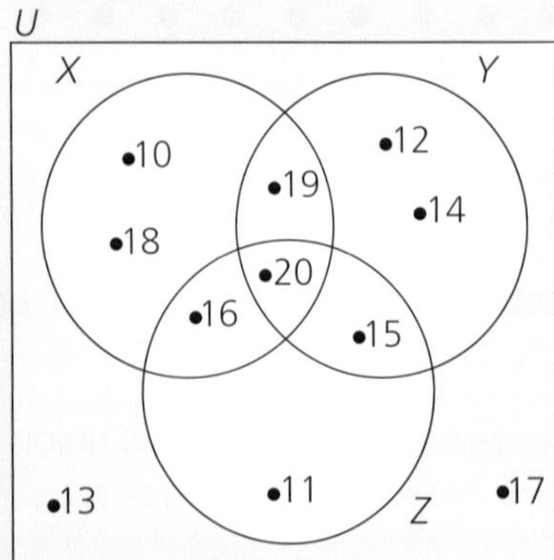

$(X \cup Y \cup Z)' = \{13, 17\}$

(iii) $Y \backslash Z$

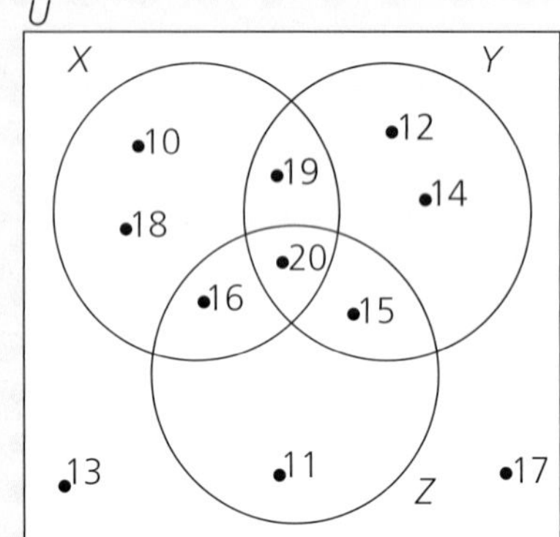

$Y \backslash Z = \{12, 14, 19\}$

(iv) $(X \cap Y \cap Z)'$

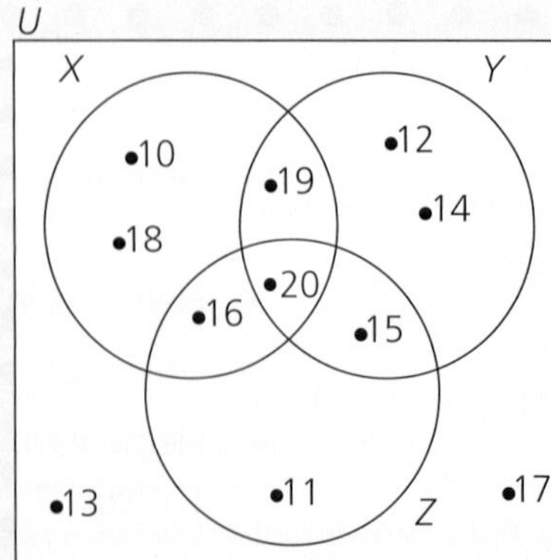

$(X \cap Y \cap Z)' = \{10, 11, 12, 13, 14, 15, 16, 17, 18, 19\}$

(v) $X\backslash(Y \cap Z)$

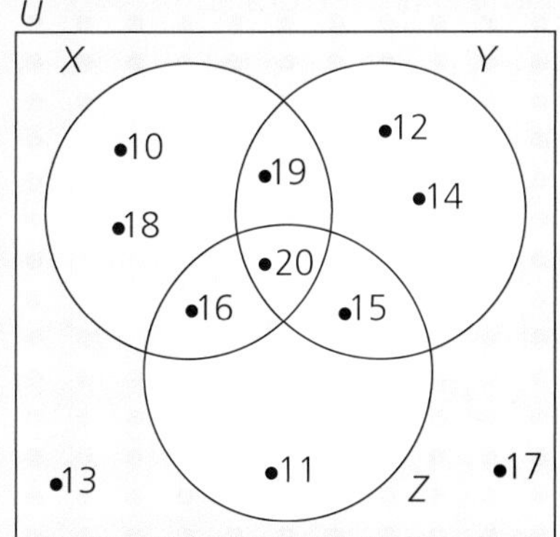

$X\backslash(Y \cap Z) = \{10, 16, 18, 19\}$

(vi) $(X \cap Y) \cup Z$

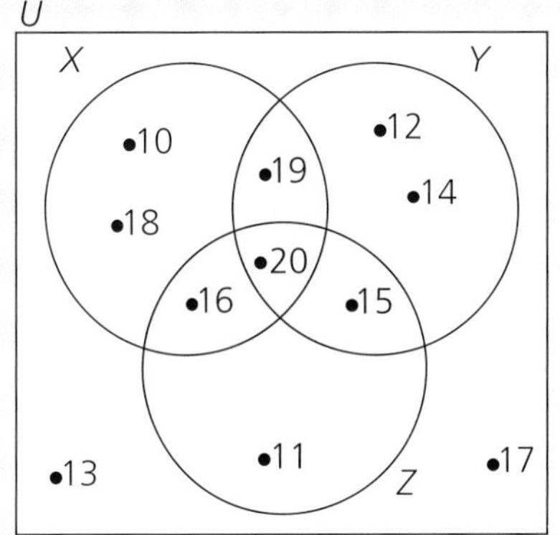

$(X \cap Y) \cup Z = \{11, 15, 16, 19, 20\}$

(vii) $(X\backslash Z)'$

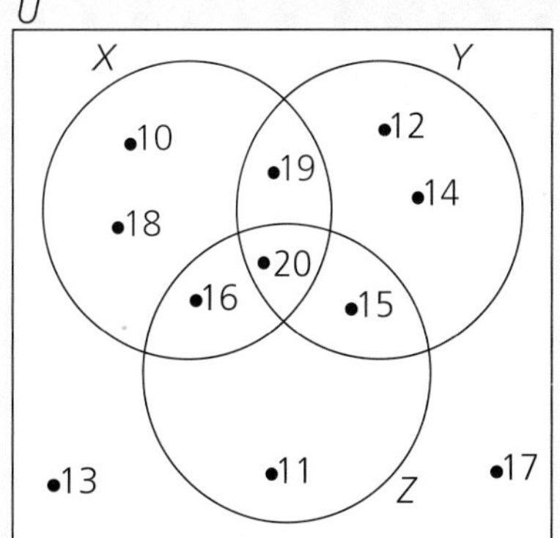

$(X\backslash Z)' = \{11, 12, 13, 14, 15, 16, 17, 20\}$

(viii) $(X \cup Z)' \backslash Y$

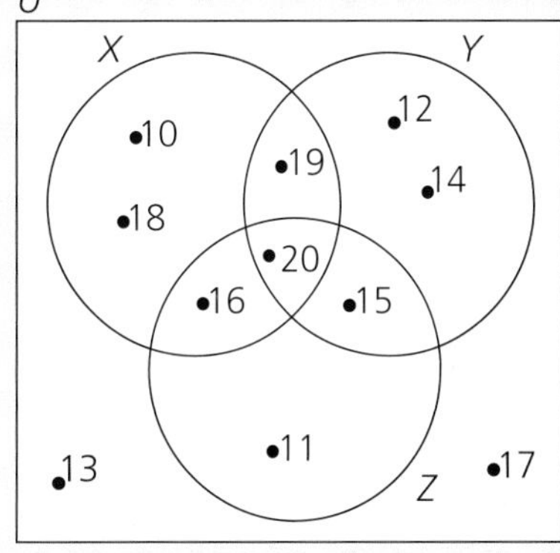

$(X \cup Z)' \backslash Y = \{13, 17\}$

Example 2

$U = \{1, 2, 3, 4, 5, 6, 7, 8, 9, 10, 11, 12\}$

$A = \{2, 3, 4, 5, 7, 9\}$

$B = \{2, 4, 8, 10, 12\}$

$C = \{2, 3, 6, 12\}$

(i) Draw a Venn diagram to represent the information given.

(ii) List the elements of:

(a) C'

(b) $(A \cup B)'$

(c) $(A \cap B) \cup C$

(d) $(A\backslash B)\backslash C$

Solution

(i) **Step 1:** Fill in the elements that are common to all three sets.

- $A \cap B \cap C = \{2\}$

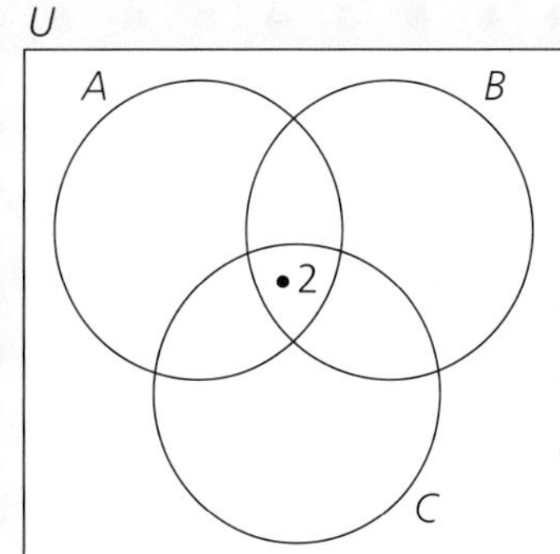

Step 2: Fill in the elements that are common to two sets.

- $(A \cap B)\backslash C = \{4\}$
- $(A \cap C)\backslash B = \{3\}$
- $(B \cap C)\backslash A = \{12\}$

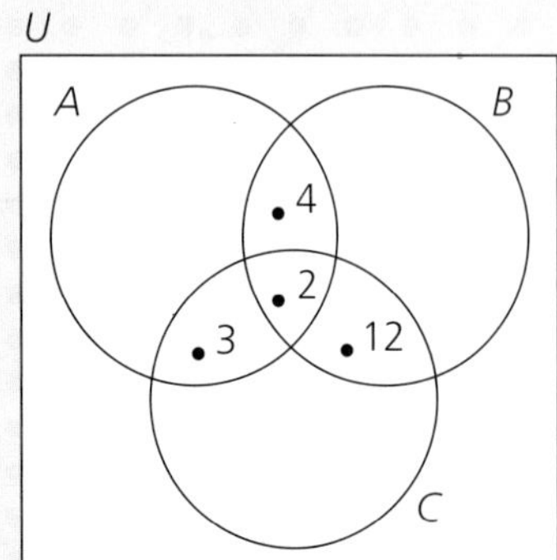

Step 3: Fill in the elements unique to each set.

- $A\backslash(B \cup C) = \{5, 7, 9\}$
- $B\backslash A \cup C) = \{8, 10\}$
- $C\backslash(A \cup B) = \{6\}$

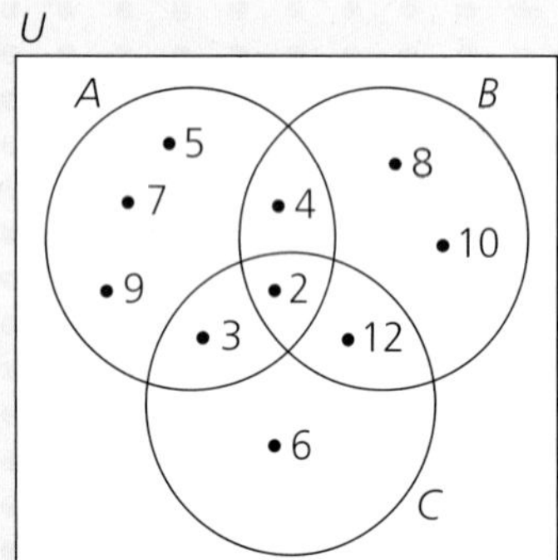

Step 4: Fill in any remaining elements listed in the universal set.

- $(A \cup B \cup C)' = \{1, 11\}$

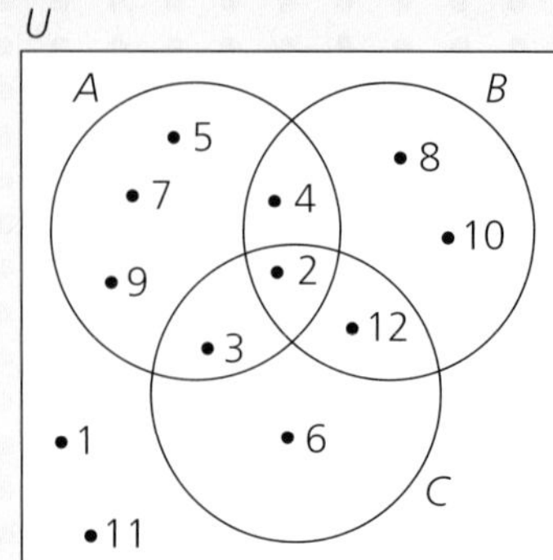

(ii) From observation, we can see that:

(a) $C' = \{1, 4, 5, 7, 8, 9, 10, 11\}$

(b) $(A \cup B)' = \{1, 6, 11\}$

(c) $(A \cap B) \cup C = \{2, 3, 4, 6, 12\}$

(d) $(A\backslash B)\backslash C = \{5, 7, 9\}$

Activity 15.4

1 Use the Venn diagram to list the elements of:

(i) $A \cup B$

(ii) C

(iii) $(B \cap C)\backslash A$

(iv) $(B \cap C) \cup A$

(v) $A\backslash C$

(vi) $A \cap B \cap C$

(vii) $(A\backslash B)\backslash C$

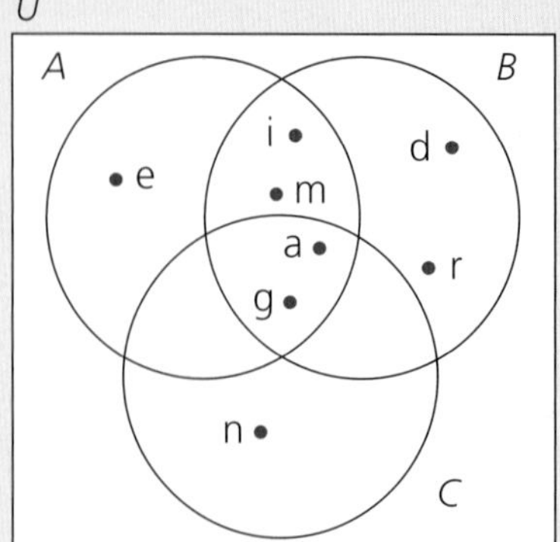

2 Use the Venn diagram below to list the elements of:

(i) J
(ii) K
(iii) L
(iv) $J \cup L$
(v) $(J \cap K) \setminus L$
(vi) $(J \cup K)'$
(vii) $J \setminus (K \cup L)$
(viii) $(L \cup J) \cap K$
(ix) $(K \cap L) \setminus J$

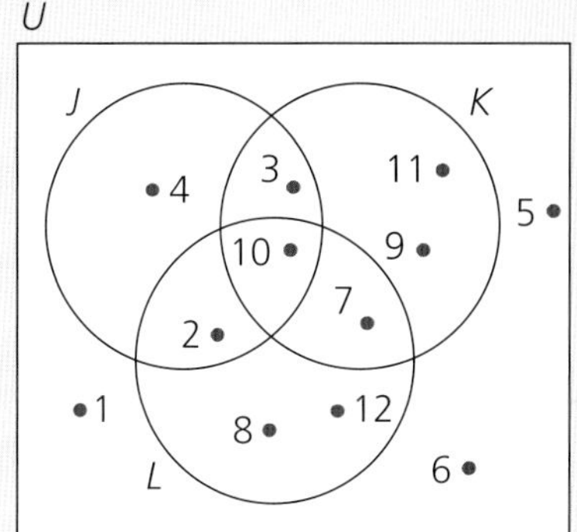

3 $U = \{1, 2, 3, 4, 5, 6\}$
$P = \{1, 2, 3, 4\}$
$Q = \{2, 3, 5\}$
$R = \{1, 3, 4, 5, 6\}$
List the elements in each of the following.

(i) $(P \cup Q) \cap (R \setminus Q)$
(ii) $(P \setminus Q) \cup (R \setminus P)$
(iii) $(R') \cap (P \setminus Q)$

4

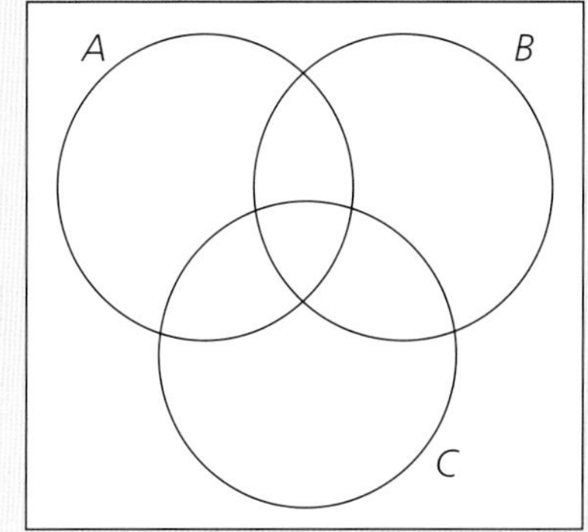

Copy the Venn diagram above four times and shade in the following regions.

(i) $(A \cap B) \cup C$
(ii) $(A \setminus B) \setminus C$
(iii) $(A \cup C) \setminus B$
(iv) $(A \setminus B) \cap (C \setminus B)$

5 $U = \{x \mid x$ is a letter of the alphabet from a to n inclusive$\}$
$B = \{x \mid x$ is a letter in the word 'beamed'$\}$
$D = \{x \mid x$ is a letter in the word 'defined'$\}$
$L = \{x \mid x$ is a letter in the word 'cable'$\}$

(i) Represent this information on a Venn diagram.
(ii) List the elements of:
(a) B'
(b) $(B \cup D)'$
(c) $B \setminus (D \cap L)$
(d) $(D \cap L) \cup B$
(e) $(B \setminus D) \setminus L$
(iii) Find the value of:
(a) $\#(B \cap D \cap L)$
(b) $\#((B \cup D) \cap L)$
(c) $\#(B \cap L)'$

6 $U = \{2, 3, 4, 5, ..., 30\}$, $A = \{$multiples of 2$\}$, $B = \{$multiples of 3$\}$, $C = \{$multiples of 5$\}$.

(i) Find $\#(A \cup B \cup C)'$, the number of elements in the complement of the set $A \cup B \cup C$.
(ii) How many divisors does each of the numbers in $(A \cup B \cup C)'$ have?
(iii) What name is given to numbers that have this many divisors?

7 $U = \{1, 2, 3, ..., 20\}$
$Q = \{x \mid x$ is a factor of 20$\}$
$R = \{x \mid x$ is a multiple of 2$\}$
$S = \{x \mid x$ is a prime number between 1 and 20$\}$

(i) Draw a Venn diagram to represent sets U, Q, R and S.
(ii) Find the value of each of the following.
(a) $\#Q$
(b) $\#R$
(c) $\#(Q \setminus R) \setminus S$
(d) $\#(Q \cup R)'$
(e) $\#((Q \cup R) \setminus (S \cap R))$
(f) $\#((Q \cap R) \cup (S \cap R) \cup (Q \cap S))$

8 $U = \{x \mid x \text{ is a letter in the word 'numerically'}\}$
$N = \{x \mid x \text{ is a letter in the word 'name'}\}$
$M = \{x \mid x \text{ is a letter in the word 'miracle'}\}$
$R = \{x \mid x \text{ is a letter in the word 'rally'}\}$
(i) Represent the sets above on a Venn diagram.
(ii) List the elements of the following.
(a) U
(b) M
(c) R
(d) R'
(e) $(N \cup R) \cap M$
(f) $(R \cap N)'$
(g) $(N \backslash M) \backslash R$
(h) $U \backslash (R \cup N)'$

9 U = {the students in a class}
M = {the students in the class who are afraid of mice}

S = {the students in the class who are afraid of spiders}
W = {the students in the class who are afraid of wasps}
Describe, in your own words, the members of the following sets.
(i) $(M \cup S)$
(ii) $(M \cap W)$
(iii) $W \backslash S$
(iv) $(M \cap S) \backslash W$
(v) $(M \cup S \cup W)'$

10 U = {the people who live in Ireland}
A = {the people living in Ireland who own a pet}

B = {the people living in Ireland who like dogs}
C = {the people living in Ireland who have pet insurance}
Describe, in your own words, the members of the following sets.
(i) $(A \cup B) \backslash C$
(ii) $(A \cap B \cap C)$
(iii) $C \backslash (A \cap B)$
(iv) $(A \cup B \cup C)'$

11 U is the universal set and D, E and F are three subsets of U.
$\#U = 154$
$\#(D \cap E \cap F) = x$
$\#(D \backslash (E \cup F)) = 21$
$\#((D \cap E) \backslash F) = 18 - x$
$\#(F \backslash (D \cup E)) = 5x$
$\#(D \cup E \cup F)' = 3\ \#(D \cap E \cap F)$
$\#(E \backslash (D \cup F)) = 10 + x$
$\#(E \cap F) = 23$
$\#((D \cap F) \backslash E) = 10$
(i) Draw a Venn diagram to represent the information above.
(ii) Find the value of x.
(iii) Find the value of:
(a) $\#D$
(b) $\#E$
(c) $\#F$
(d) $\#((D \cap F) \cup E)$

Section 15E Operations on Sets

From our previous working with two sets, we know that:

- Union of sets is commutative, i.e. $A \cup B = B \cup A$ where A and B are any sets.
- Intersection of sets is commutative, i.e. $A \cap B = B \cap A$ where A and B are any sets.
- Set difference is not commutative, i.e. $A \backslash B \neq B \backslash A$ where A and B are any sets.

When working with numbers, we found that:

- Addition of numbers is associative, i.e. $(a + b) + c = a + (b + c)$ where a, b and c are any three numbers.
- Multiplication of numbers is associative, i.e. $(a \times b) \times c = a \times (b \times c)$ where a, b and c are any three numbers.
- Division of numbers is not associative.
- Subtraction of numbers is not associative.

We will now investigate some operations on three sets.

Example 1

Let $A = \{a, n, t\}$, $B = \{c, a, t\}$, and $C = \{m, a, t\}$.

(i) Show that $(A \cup B) \cup C = A \cup (B \cup C)$.

(ii) Show that $(A \cap B) \cap C = A \cap (B \cap C)$.

(iii) Show that $(A \backslash B) \backslash C \neq A \backslash (B \backslash C)$.

Solution

(i) LHS $= (A \cup B) \cup C$

$(A \cup B) = \{a, n, t\} \cup \{c, a, t\} = \{a, c, n, t\}$

$(A \cup B) \cup C = \{a, c, n, t\} \cup \{m, a, t\}$
$= \{a, c, m, n, t\}$

RHS $= A \cup (B \cup C)$

$(B \cup C) = \{c, a, t\} \cup \{m, a, t\} = \{a, c, m, t\}$

$A \cup (B \cup C) = \{a, n, t\} \cup \{a, c, m, t\}$
$= \{a, c, m, n, t\}$

$\therefore (A \cup B) \cup C = A \cup (B \cup C)$

(ii) LHS $= (A \cap B) \cap C$

$(A \cap B) = \{a, n, t\} \cap \{c, a, t\} = \{a, t\}$

$(A \cap B) \cap C = \{a, t\} \cap \{m, a, t\} = \{a, t\}$

RHS $= A \cap (B \cap C)$

$(B \cap C) = \{c, a, t\} \cap \{m, a, t\} = \{a, t\}$

$A \cap (B \cap C) = \{a, n, t\} \cap \{a, t\} = \{a, t\}$

$\therefore (A \cap B) \cap C = A \cap (B \cap C)$.

(iii) We need to show that LHS $\neq$ RHS.

LHS $= (A \backslash B) \backslash C$

$(A \backslash B) = \{a, n, t\} \backslash \{c, a, t\} = \{n\}$

$(A \backslash B) \backslash C = \{n\} \backslash \{m, a, t\} = \{n\}$

RHS $= A \backslash (B \backslash C)$

$(B \backslash C) = \{c, a, t\} \backslash \{m, a, t\} = \{c\}$

$A \backslash (B \backslash C) = \{a, n, t\} \backslash \{c\} = \{a, n, t\}$

$\therefore (A \backslash B) \backslash C \neq A \backslash (B \backslash C)$

Key Points

- **The Associative Property for Union** of sets states that the order in which the sets are grouped does not change the result.
  $(A \cup B) \cup C = A \cup (B \cup C)$
- **The Associative Property for Intersection** of sets states that the order in which the sets are grouped does not change the result.
  $(A \cap B) \cap C = A \cap (B \cap C)$
- Set difference is not associative.
  $(A \backslash B) \backslash C \neq A \backslash (B \backslash C)$

When working with numbers, we found that:

- Multiplication is **distributive over addition**, i.e. $a(b + c) = ab + ac$ where a, b and c are any three numbers.

We will now investigate whether or not we can operate like this on sets.

Example 2

Let $A = \{1, 2, 3, 4\}$, $B = \{2, 3, 5, 7\}$, and $C = \{2, 4, 6\}$.

(i) Show that $A \cup (B \cap C) = (A \cup B) \cap (A \cup C)$

(ii) Show that $A \cap (B \cup C) = (A \cap B) \cup (A \cap C)$

(iii) Show that $A \backslash (B \cup C) \neq (A \backslash B) \cup (A \backslash C)$

(iv) Show that $A \backslash (B \cap C) \neq (A \backslash B) \cap (A \backslash C)$

Solution

(i) LHS $= A \cup (B \cap C)$

$(B \cap C) = \{2, 3, 5, 7\} \cap \{2, 4, 6\}$
$= \{2\}$

$A \cup (B \cap C) = \{1, 2, 3, 4\} \cup \{2\}$
$= \{1, 2, 3, 4\}$

RHS $= (A \cup B) \cap (A \cup C)$

$(A \cup B) = \{1, 2, 3, 4\} \cup \{2, 3, 5, 7\}$
$= \{1, 2, 3, 4, 5, 7\}$

$(A \cup C) = \{1, 2, 3, 4\} \cup \{2, 4, 6\}$
$= \{1, 2, 3, 4, 6\}$

$(A \cup B) \cap (A \cup C) = \{1, 2, 3, 4\}$

$\therefore A \cup (B \cap C) = (A \cup B) \cap (A \cup C)$

(ii) LHS $= A \cap (B \cup C)$

$(B \cup C) = \{2, 3, 5, 7\} \cup \{2, 4, 6\}$
$= \{2, 3, 4, 5, 6, 7\}$

$A \cap (B \cup C) = \{2, 3, 4\}$

RHS $= (A \cap B) \cup (A \cap C)$

$(A \cap B) = \{1, 2, 3, 4\} \cap \{2, 3, 5, 7\}$
$= \{2, 3\}$

$(A \cap C) = \{1, 2, 3, 4\} \cap \{2, 4, 6\} = \{2, 4\}$

$(A \cap B) \cup (A \cap C) = \{2, 3, 4\}$

$\therefore A \cap (B \cup C) = (A \cap B) \cup (A \cap C)$

(iii) LHS $= A \backslash (B \cup C)$

$(B \cup C) = \{2, 3, 4, 5, 6, 7\}$

$A \backslash (B \cup C) = \{1, 2, 3, 4\} \backslash \{2, 3, 4, 5, 6, 7\}$
$= \{1\}$

RHS $= (A \backslash B) \cup (A \backslash C)$

$(A \backslash B) = \{1, 2, 3, 4\} \backslash \{2, 3, 5, 7\} = \{1, 4\}$

$(A \backslash C) = \{1, 2, 3, 4\} \backslash \{2, 4, 6\} = \{1, 3\}$

$(A \backslash B) \cup (A \backslash C) = \{1, 3, 4\}$

$\therefore A \backslash (B \cup C) \neq (A \backslash B) \cup (A \backslash C)$

(iv) LHS $= A \backslash (B \cap C)$

$(B \cap C) = \{2\}$

$A \backslash (B \cap C) = \{1, 2, 3, 4\} \backslash \{2\} = \{1, 3, 4\}$

RHS $= (A \backslash B) \cap (A \backslash C)$

$(A \backslash B) = \{1, 4\}$

$(A \backslash C) = \{1, 3\}$

$(A \backslash B) \cap (A \backslash C) = \{1, 4\} \cap \{1, 3\} = \{1\}$

$\therefore A \backslash (B \cap C) \neq (A \backslash B) \cap (A \backslash C)$

Key Points

- Distributive Property of **Union over Intersection**
  $A \cup (B \cap C) = (A \cup B) \cap (A \cup C)$
- Distributive Property of **Intersection over Union**
  $A \cap (B \cup C) = (A \cap B) \cup (A \cap C)$
- Set difference is not distributive over union.
  $A \backslash (B \cup C) \neq (A \backslash B) \cup (A \backslash C)$
- Set difference is not distributive over intersection.
  $A \backslash (B \cap C) \neq (A \backslash B) \cap (A \backslash C)$

1 U

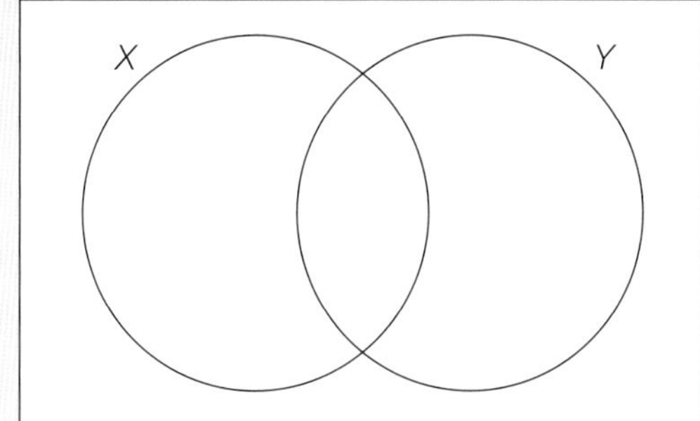

(i) Copy the Venn diagram four times and shade in:

(a) X'

(b) Y'

(c) $X' \cap Y'$

(d) $(X \cup Y)'$

(ii) Is $X' \cap Y' = (X \cup Y)'$? Explain your answer.

2 $U = \{10, 11, 12, 13, 14, 15, \ldots, 20\}$

$A = \{10, 11, 12, 13, 14\}$

$B = \{10, 12, 14, 16, 18, 20\}$

$C = \{10, 13, 17, 20\}$

(i) Draw a Venn diagram to represent these sets.

(ii) Show that $A \cup (B \cap C) = (A \cup B) \cap (A \cup C)$.

(iii) Show that $(A \cap B) \cap C = A \cap (B \cap C)$.

(iv) Show that $A \setminus (B \cap C) \neq (A \setminus B) \cap (A \setminus C)$.

3 $U = \{x \mid x$ is a natural number between 24 and 36$\}$

$C = \{x \mid x$ is an odd natural number between 24 and 36$\}$

$D = \{x \mid x$ is a prime number between 24 and 36$\}$

$E = \{x \mid x$ is a multiple of 3 between 24 and 36$\}$

(i) Draw a Venn diagram to represent these sets.

(ii) Show that $(C \cup D) \cup E = C \cup (D \cup E)$.

(iii) Show that $C \cup (D \cap E) = (C \cup D) \cap (C \cup E)$.

(iv) Show that $C \setminus (D \cup E) \neq (C \setminus D) \cup (C \setminus E)$.

(v) Investigate whether or not $(C \setminus D) \setminus E = C \setminus (D \setminus E)$.

4 Identify the property of sets illustrated in each of the following statements and draw Venn diagrams to show each property.

(i) $X \cup (Y \cap Z) = (X \cup Y) \cap (X \cup Z)$

(ii) $X \cap Y = Y \cap X$

(iii) $(X \cap Y) \cap Z = X \cap (Y \cap Z)$

(iv) $X \cap (Y \cup Z) = (X \cap Y) \cup (X \cap Z)$

(v) $Y \cup Z = Z \cup Y$

(vi) $(X \cup Y) \cup Z = X \cup (Y \cup Z)$

5 $U = \{$all people who live in Ireland$\}$

$B = \{$all people who own their own home$\}$

$C = \{$all people who own a car$\}$

$D = \{$all people who are married$\}$

Describe in words:

(i) $B \cup (C \cap D)$

(ii) $(B \cap C) \cup (B \cap D)$

(iii) $(B \cup C) \cup D$

6 (i) From the Venn diagram below, list the elements of:

(a) $P \cup Q$

(b) $Q \cap R$

(c) $P \cup (Q \cap R)$

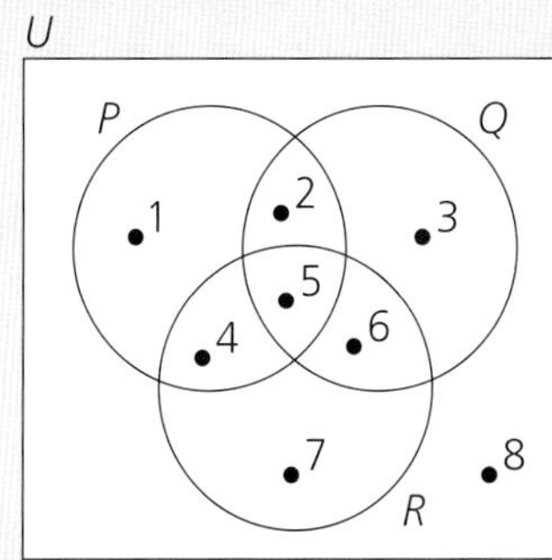

(ii) Miriam says, 'For all sets, union is distributive over intersection.' Name a set that you would use along with $P \cup (Q \cap R)$ to show that Miriam's claim is true for the sets P, Q and R in the Venn diagram.

Section 15F Problems Involving Three Sets

Example 1

A group of Transition Year students were surveyed and asked whether they watch TV, read or sketch to relax. The results are displayed in the Venn diagram.

(i) Find the number of students who participated in the survey.

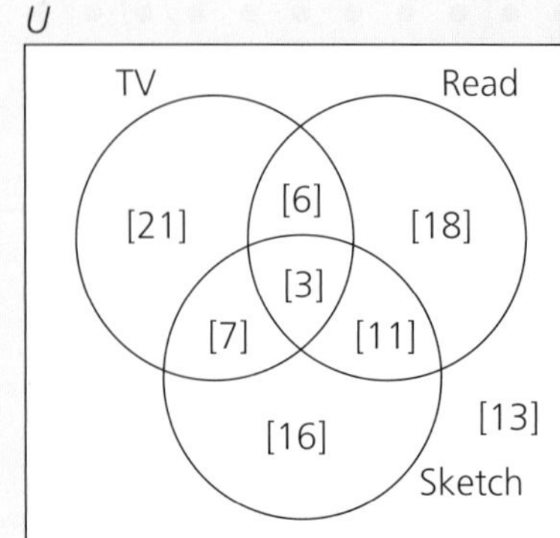

Using the Venn diagram, find the number of students who relax by:

(ii) reading

(iii) sketching

(iv) watching TV

(v) only one option

(vi) two options only.

Solution

(i) The number of students who participated in the survey is:

$21 + 6 + 18 + 7 + 3 + 11 + 16 + 13 = 95$ students.

(ii) The number of students who read is:

$3 + 6 + 11 + 18 = 38$ students.

(iii) The number of students who sketch is:

$7 + 3 + 11 + 16 = 37$ students.

(iv) The number of students who watch TV is:

$21 + 6 + 3 + 7 = 37$ students.

(v) The number of students who relax using only one option:

$21 + 18 + 16 = 55$ students.

(vi) The number of students who relax using only two options:

$7 + 6 + 11 = 24$ students.

Drawing a Venn Diagram Involving Three Sets

To solve these types of problems, we generally use the following steps.

Step 1: Fill in the cardinal number for members that are common to all three sets in the question. So fill in $\#(A \cap B \cap C)$ first.

Step 2: Fill in the cardinal numbers for members that are common to two sets only.

Step 3: Fill in the cardinal numbers for members that are in one set only.

Step 4: Finally, fill in the cardinal number for any remaining members listed in the universal set.

Example 2

A school PE department have to decide on the colours for their new school tracksuit. The school colours are blue, white and red and the tracksuit must have at least one of these colours or a combination of them. The PE department survey the students and the results are as follows.

- 142 students wanted all three colours
- 231 students wanted blue and red
- 205 students wanted blue and white
- 41 students wanted white and red only
- 321 students wanted blue
- 256 students wanted white
- 52 students wanted red only.

Based on this information:

(i) Draw a Venn diagram to represent this information.

(ii) How many students want only one colour on the tracksuit?

(iii) How many students are in the school?

Solution

(i) **Step 1:** Fill in the cardinal number for members that are common to all three sets in the given question. So fill in:

$\#(\text{blue} \cap \text{white} \cap \text{red}) = 142$ students

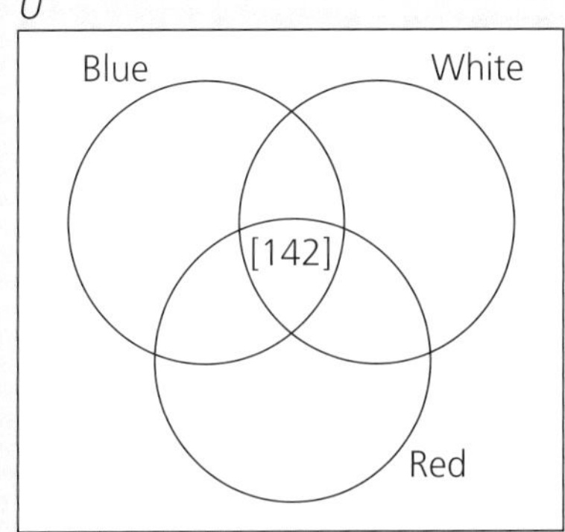

Step 2: Fill in the cardinal numbers for members that are common to two sets only.

- $\#(\text{blue} \cap \text{white}) - 142$
  $= 205 - 142$
  $= 63$ students
- $\#(\text{blue} \cap \text{red}) - 142$
  $= 231 - 142$
  $= 89$ students
- $\#(\text{white} \cap \text{red}) = 41$ students

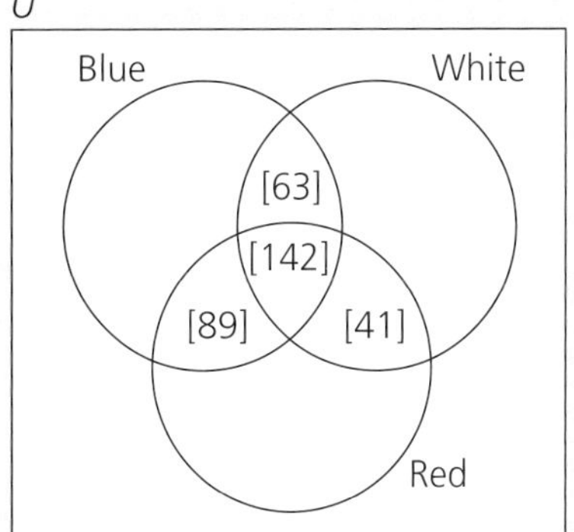

Step 3: Fill in the cardinal numbers for members that are in one set only.

- $\#(\text{blue only}) = 321 - (63 + 142 + 89)$
  $= 27$ students
- $\#(\text{white only}) = 256 - (63 + 142 + 41)$
  $= 10$ students
- $\#(\text{red only}) = 52$ students

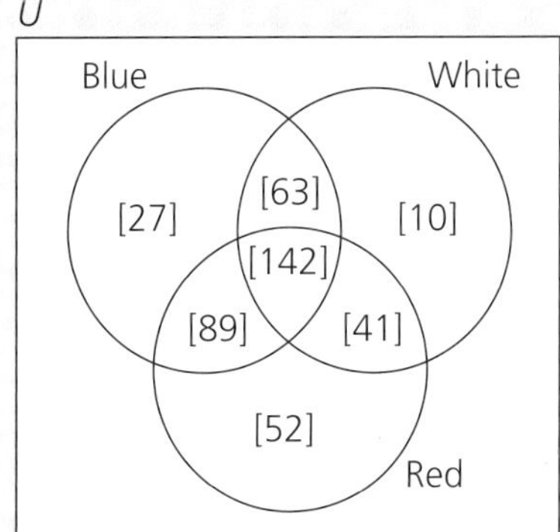

(ii) $(27 + 52 + 10) = 89$ students want only one colour on the tracksuit.

(iii) Add all values included on the Venn diagram:

$27 + 63 + 89 + 142 + 10 + 41 + 52$
$= 424$ students

Example 3

A survey carried out on 200 First Year Art students at a university showed that:

- 76 study English
- 62 study History
- 81 study Maths
- 18 don't study English, History or Maths
- 11 study Maths and History
- 16 study History and English
- 18 study Maths and English
- x study all three subjects.

(i) Draw a Venn diagram to represent this information.

(ii) How many students study all three subjects?

Solution

(i) **Step 1:** Let H = History, E = English and M = Maths.

Fill in the cardinal number for members that are common to all three sets.

$\#(H \cap E \cap M) = [x]$

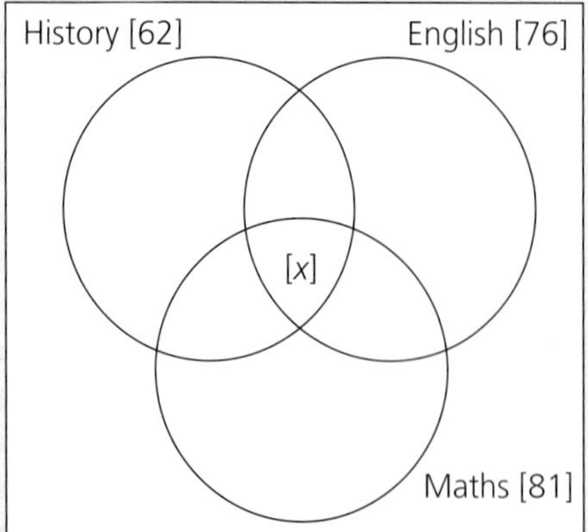

Step 2: Fill in the cardinal numbers for members that are common to two sets. Make sure to subtract $\#(H \cap E \cap M)$ each time.

- $\#(H \cap E) - \#(H \cap E \cap M) = [16 - x]$
- $\#(H \cap M) - \#(H \cap E \cap M) = [11 - x]$
- $\#(E \cap M) - \#(H \cap E \cap M) = [18 - x]$

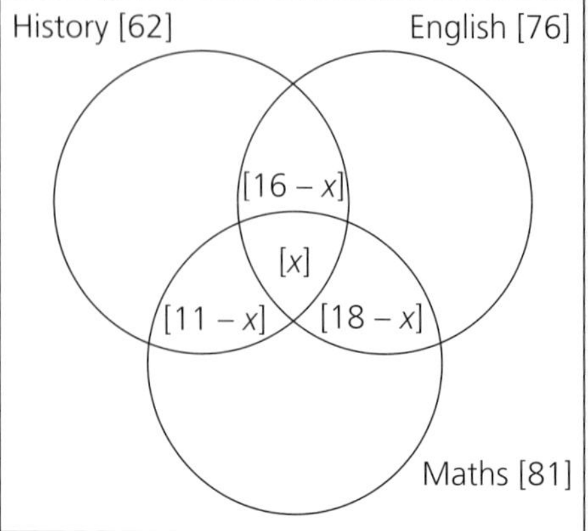

Step 3: Fill in the cardinal numbers for members that are in one set only.

- $\#H \text{ only} = 62 - (16 - x + x + 11 - x)$
  $= 62 - (27 - x)$
  $= 62 - 27 + x = 35 + x$
- $\#E \text{ only} = 76 - (16 - x + x + 18 - x)$
  $= 76 - (34 - x)$
  $= 76 - 34 + x = 42 + x$
- $\#M \text{ only} = 81 - (11 - x + x + 18 - x)$
  $= 81 - (29 - x)$
  $= 81 - 29 + x = 52 + x$

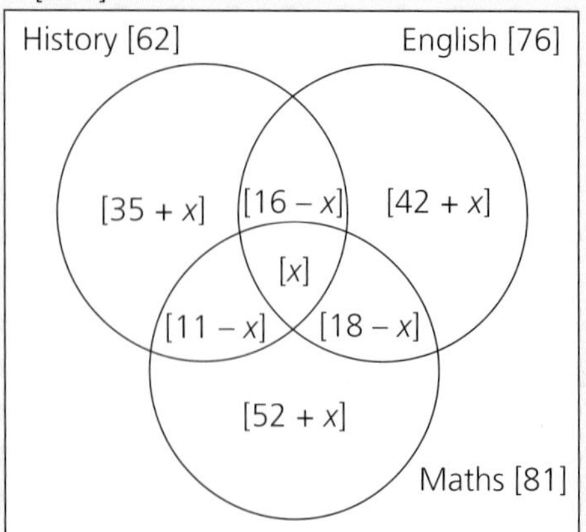

Step 4: Finally, fill in the cardinal number that represents the members of the universal set that are not in any of the sets given.

$\#(H \cup E \cup M)' = 18$

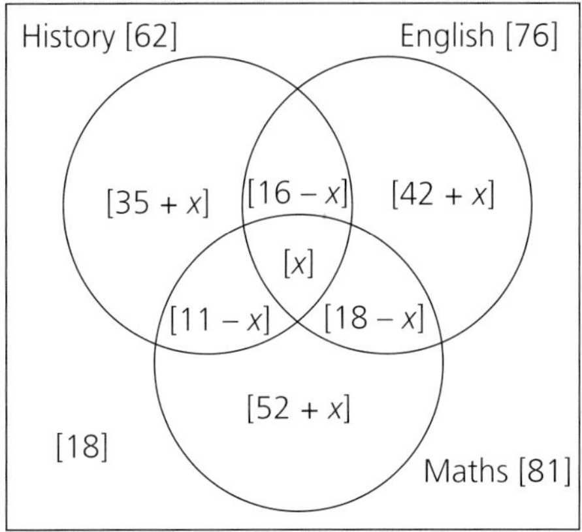

(ii) $\#U = 200$, the total number of students who did the survey.

Form an equation in x:

$$(35 + x) + (16 - x) + (42 + x) + x + (11 - x) + (18 - x) + (52 + x) + 18 = 200$$

$\Rightarrow\ 192 + x = 200$ (subtract 192 from both sides)

$\Rightarrow\ x = 200 - 192$

$= 8$

Therefore, 8 students study all three subjects.

Activity 15.6

1 280 shoppers were surveyed as they entered a shopping centre. The survey asked which of the following facilities in the shopping centre could be improved upon:

A: Public toilets
B: Child care
C: Lifts

The results were as follows.

- 73 people said all of the facilities mentioned
- 106 people said the public toilets and the child care facilities
- 31 people said public toilets only
- 82 people said the public toilets and the lift facilities
- 127 people said the lifts and the child care facilities
- 212 people said the child care facilities
- 162 people said the lift facilities.

(i) Represent the above information on a Venn diagram.

(ii) How many people choose more than one facility to improve upon?

(iii) How many people said none of the facilities needed improvement?

2 A Maths teacher gave a revision test to her class of 32 students.

The test had three questions:

Q1 – Algebra
Q2 – Statistics
Q3 – Probability

The results from the test were as follows:

- 17 answered question 1 correctly
- 21 answered question 2 correctly
- 18 answered question 3 correctly
- 12 answered both questions 1 and 2 correctly
- 8 answered both questions 1 and 3 correctly
- 13 answered both questions 2 and 3 correctly
- 7 answered all three questions correctly.

(i) Draw a Venn diagram using the following notation:

Set A = Students who got Q1 correct

Set B = Students who got Q2 correct

Set C = Students who got Q3 correct.

(ii) How many students didn't get any of the questions correct?

(iii) How many students got exactly two questions correct?

3 The Venn diagram below represents the results of a survey carried out on 149 people at a train station. They were asked what mode of transport they used to get from the train station to their homes. They were given three options: walk, cycle or car.

(i) Find the value of x.

Based on the results, how many:

(ii) Walk and cycle

(iii) Walk

(iv) Use a car

(v) Don't use any of these

(vi) Use just two different modes of transport

(vii) Only use one mode of transport

(viii) Use all three forms of transport?

4 70 teenagers responded to a survey based on holiday destinations. 30 had travelled to France, 26 had travelled to Spain and 28 had travelled to Italy. 12 had travelled to both France and Spain, 8 had travelled to both Spain and Italy, while x had travelled to both France and Italy only. 4 teenagers had travelled to all three countries. Twice as many teenagers had never travelled abroad as had travelled to France and Italy only.

(i) Represent the above information on a Venn diagram.

(ii) Find the value of x.

(iii) Find the number of teenagers who had travelled to France only.

5 In a survey, 250 people were asked if they like plums, kiwi or grapefruit. The results were as follows.

- 124 said that they like plums
- 101 said they like grapefruit
- 147 said they like kiwi
- 72 said they like kiwi and plums
- 38 said they like grapefruit and plums
- 21 said they like grapefruit and kiwi
- x said they like all three fruits
- $2x$ said they didn't like any of the fruits.

(i) Represent the information above on a Venn diagram.

(ii) How many people like all three fruits?

6 272 students were asked if they had an account on any of these three different social networking sites: Facebook (FB), Twitter (TW) or Instagram (IN). The results were as follows.

- 183 have a Facebook account
- 127 have a Twitter account

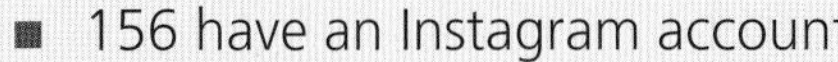

- 156 have an Instagram account
- 89 have both Twitter and Facebook accounts
- $5x$ have a Twitter and Instagram account but not a Facebook account
- 48 have an Instagram and a Facebook account
- x have all three accounts
- 18 stated that they did not have any of these accounts.

(i) Draw a Venn diagram to represent the information given.
(ii) Use the Venn diagram to solve for x.
(iii) Hence, calculate the number of students who only have one of these accounts.

7 A survey of 109 students was carried out to find how many students owned an MP3 player, an iPod or a smartphone. The results were as follows.

- 18 own an MP3 player and an iPod
- 16 students own none of these
- x students own all three
- 15 own an iPod only
- 24 own an MP3 player only
- 39 own a smartphone
- $3x$ own an MP3 player and a smartphone but not an iPod
- 25 own an iPod and a smartphone.

(i) Construct a Venn diagram and solve for x.
(ii) Hence, calculate the number of students who own one item only.

8 A sports club wants to improve the facilities at their centre. They ask all 336 members which of the following equipment they should invest in: new rowing machines, treadmills or abdominal crunch machines. The results are as follows.

- 174 said new rowing machines
- 210 said new treadmills
- 91 said new abdominal crunch machines
- 35 said they should get all three different machines
- 19 members said that no new equipment was needed
- x said they should invest in rowing machines and treadmills but not abdominal crunch machines
- 53 said they should invest in abdominal crunch machines and rowing machines
- $6x$ said they should get treadmills and abdominal crunch machines.

(i) Construct a Venn diagram and solve for x.
(ii) Hence, calculate the number of members who think that the club should get two different machines.

9 A GAA club surveyed 143 junior members to find out which of the following sports they have played at the club:
Hurling (H), Basketball (B) or Gaelic football (G).

- 65 members have played hurling
- 49 have played basketball
- 47 have played Gaelic football
- 20 have not played any of these sports.

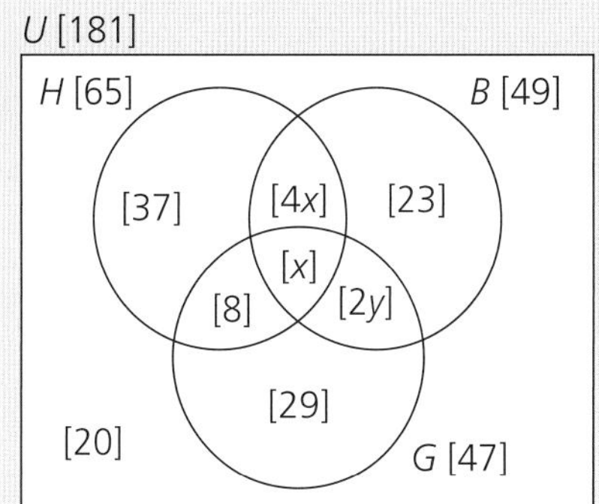

Based on the information given and the Venn diagram, answer the following questions.

(i) Find the value of x and the value of y.

(ii) How many members have played only two of these sports?

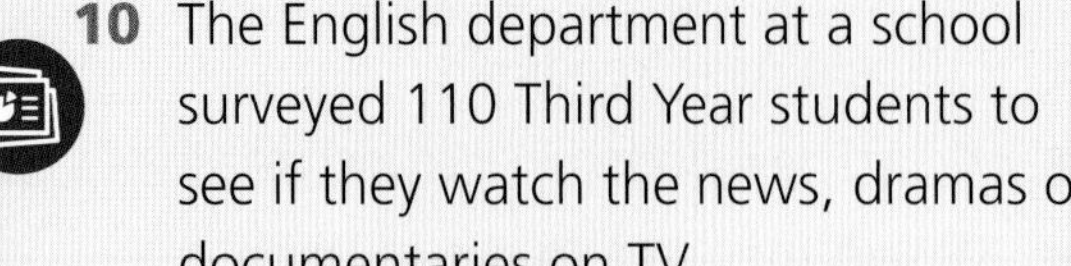

10 The English department at a school surveyed 110 Third Year students to see if they watch the news, dramas or documentaries on TV.

- 32 watch the news
- 50 watch dramas
- 55 watch documentaries
- 11 watch both news and dramas.

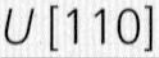

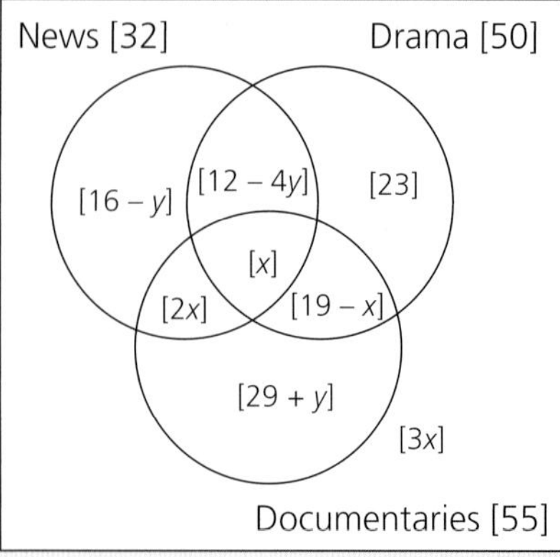

Based on the information given above and the Venn diagram, answer the following questions.

(i) Solve for x and y.

(ii) Verify your answers for x and y.

(iii) How many students watch more than one type of programme?

Revision Activity 15

1 Set A and set B are shown in the Venn diagram.

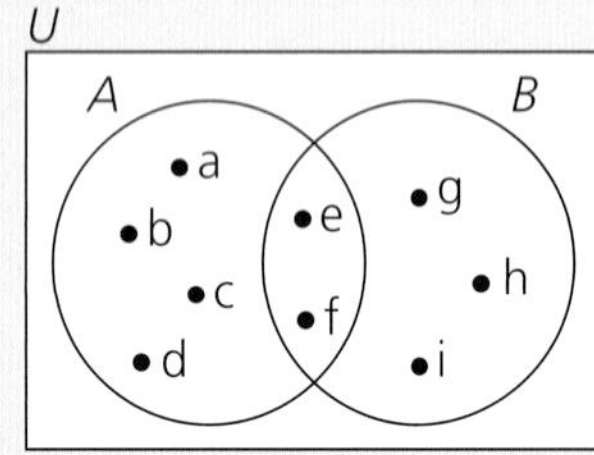

(a) List the elements of:

(i) A (iii) $A \cup B$ (v) $(A \setminus B)$

(ii) B (iv) $A \cap B$

(b) Write down the cardinal number of each set in part (a).

2 A leisure centre has 650 members. The gym (G) is used by 459 members and the swimming pool (S) is used by 532 members. 29 members do not use either of these facilities.

(a) Draw a Venn diagram to represent this information.

(b) Find the number of members who use the gym and the pool.

3 A and B are two sets and U is the universal set.

$\#U = 60$, $\#A = 34$, $\#(A \cap B) = 7$ and $\#(A \cup B) = 56$.

Find the value of:

(a) $\#B$ (b) $\#(A \setminus B)$ (c) $\#(B \setminus A)$

4 U is the universal set and P and Q are two subsets of U.

$\#U = u$ $\#(P \cap Q) = c$

$\#P = p$ $\#(U \setminus (P \cup Q)) = d$

$\#Q = q$

(a) Represent the information given on a Venn diagram.

(b) Hence, express u in terms of p, q, c and d.

(c) Show that if $p > q$, then the minimum possible value of u is $d + p$.

5 (a) Draw a Venn diagram to represent the following information.

$U = \{a, b, \ldots, l\}$

$V = \{a, b, c, d, e, f\}$

$W = \{a, d, g, j\}$

$X = \{e, g, i, k\}$

(b) List the elements for each of the following.

(i) $V \backslash W$ (iv) $X \cup (W \cap V)$

(ii) W' (v) $(V \cup X)'$

(iii) $V \cup W \cup X$ (vi) $U \backslash (V \cup X)$

(c) Show that $W \cap (V \cup X) = (W \cap V) \cup (W \cap X)$.

(d) Which property is being illustrated in part (c)?

6

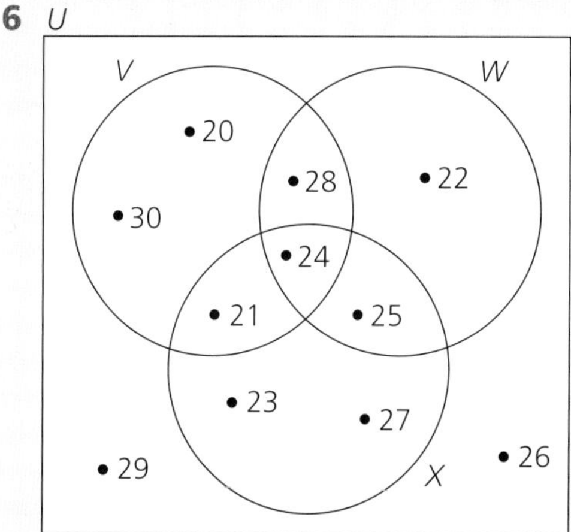

Using the Venn diagram, decide if each of the following is true or false.

(a) $\{21, 24, 30\} \subset V$

(b) $\#W = 7$

(c) $X \cup W = \{21, 22, 23, 24, 25, 28\}$

(d) $V' = \{22, 23, 24, 25, 26, 27, 29\}$

(e) $X \backslash V = \{23, 25, 27\}$

(f) $\#X = \#V$

(g) $\{\} \subset W$

(h) $V' = (W \cup X)'$

(i) $X \backslash (V \cup W) = \{23, 27\}$

(j) $(W \cap X) \backslash V = \{25\}$

(k) $\#U = 10$

(l) $\{29, 30\} \subset (V \cup W \cup X)$

7

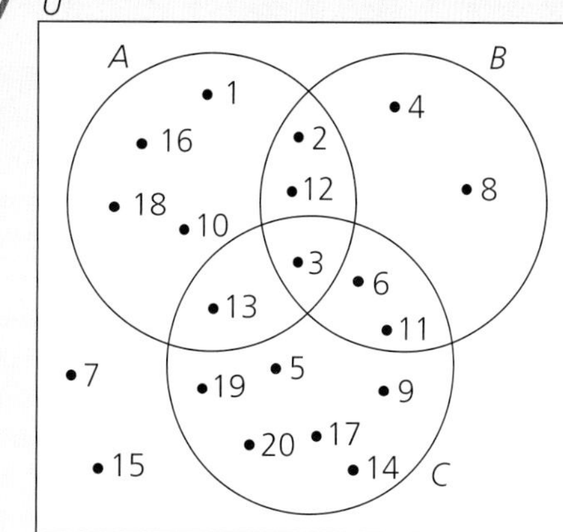

Using the Venn diagram, list the elements of each of the following.

(a) $A \cup B \cup C$ (f) $(C \cup B) \cap A$

(b) $(A \cup B)'$ (g) $A \cap B \cap C$

(c) $B \backslash C$ (h) $(A \backslash C) \cap B$

(d) $(A \cap C)$ (i) $C \backslash (A \cap B)$

(e) $(A \backslash B) \backslash C$ (j) $(A \cap B \cap C)'$

8 U = {all the students in a given class}

A = {the students in a class that have been to America}

S = {the students in a class that have been to Spain}

F = (the students in a class that have been to France}

Describe, in your own words, the members of the following.

(a) $(A \cup S)$ (c) $S \backslash F$

(b) $(A \cap S \cap F)'$ (d) $(A \backslash F) \cap S$

9 A group of 50 students were asked which of the following they liked: ice cream, chocolate or crisps. 28 said they like ice cream. 26 said they like chocolate while 26 said they like crisps. 8 said they like all three. 17 said they like chocolate and crisps. 11 said they like crisps and ice cream. 5 said they do not like any of these. Let x represent those students who like ice cream and chocolate but not crisps.

(a) Represent the above information on a Venn diagram.

(b) Calculate the value of x.

(c) Calculate the percentage of students who like one choice only.

Interactive Tool 15.1

Exam-style Questions

1 $U = \{1, 2, 3, ..., 12\}$. P is the set of prime numbers less than 12. E is the set of even numbers less than 12. O is the set of odd numbers less than 12.

(a) Represent these sets on a Venn diagram.

(b) Name any set on your diagram (after part (a) has been completed) that is a null set.

(c) If a number is drawn at random from set P, what is the probability that it is even?

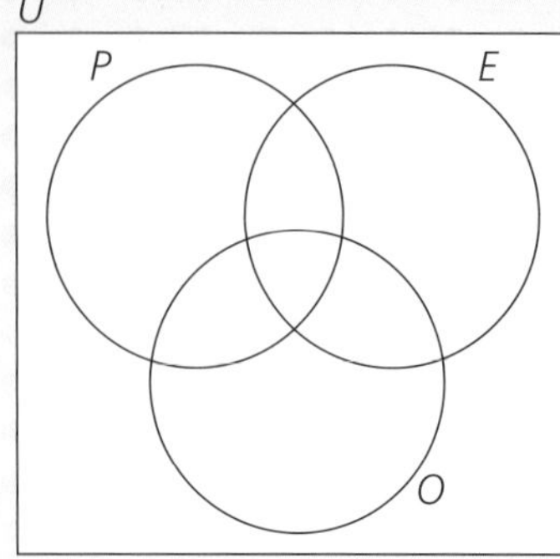

JCHL 2013 Paper 1

2 (a) Copy the diagrams (i) and (ii) below, and shade in the named region.

(i) 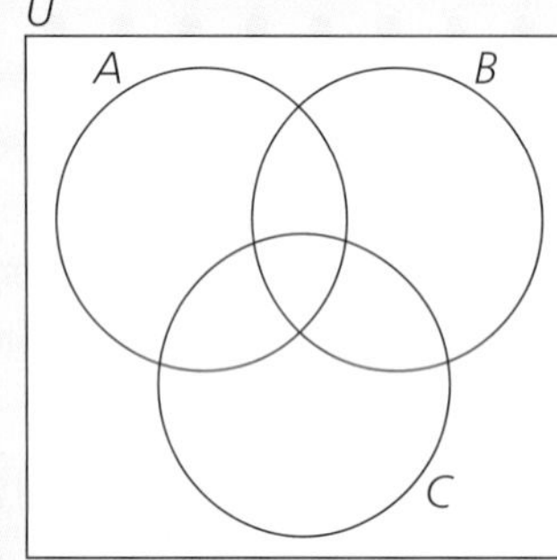

$A \cap B \cap C$

(ii) 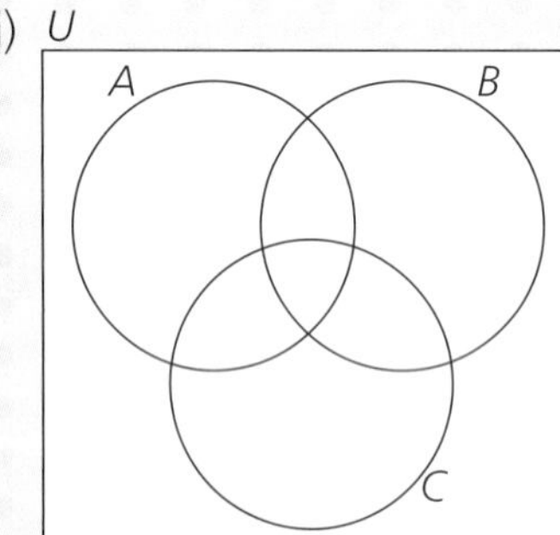

$(A \cap B) \setminus C$

(b) The box contains six statements (**note**: P' is the complement of set P). A number of the statements are incorrect. Write down one incorrect statement.

Statements

(i) $(A \cup B) = (B \cup A)$

(ii) $(A \cup B) \cup C = A \cup (B \cup C)$

(iii) $(A \setminus B) \setminus C = A \setminus (B \setminus C)$

(iv) $(A \cap B)' = U \setminus (A \cap B)$

(v) $A \setminus B = B \setminus A$

(vi) $B \setminus (A \cup C) = (B \cup C) \setminus A \setminus C$

(c) A group of 38 students were asked if they had ever been to France or Spain. The number who had been to Spain only was 3 more than the number who had been to both countries. Twice as many had been to France as Spain. 4 students had not been to either country. Find how many had been to both countries.

JCHL 2013

KEY WORDS AND PHRASES

- **Associative property**
- **Distributive property**

- To represent three sets on a Venn diagram:

  Step 1: Fill in the elements that are common to all three sets in the given question.

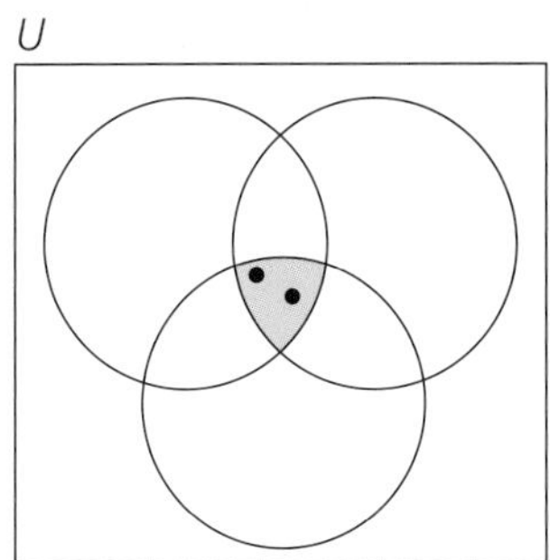

Step 2: Fill in the elements that are common to two sets.

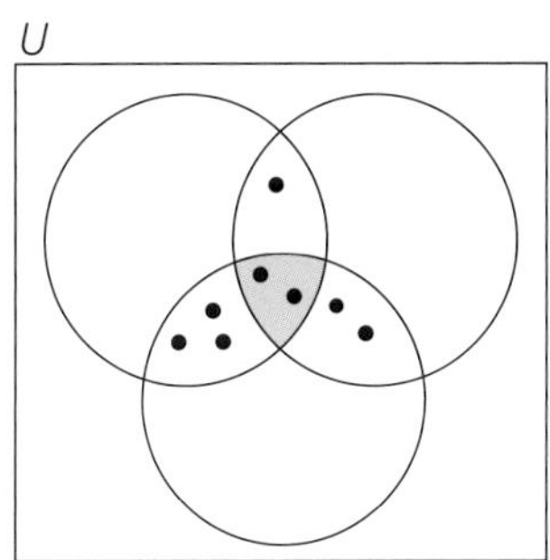

Step 3: Fill in the elements that are unique to each set.

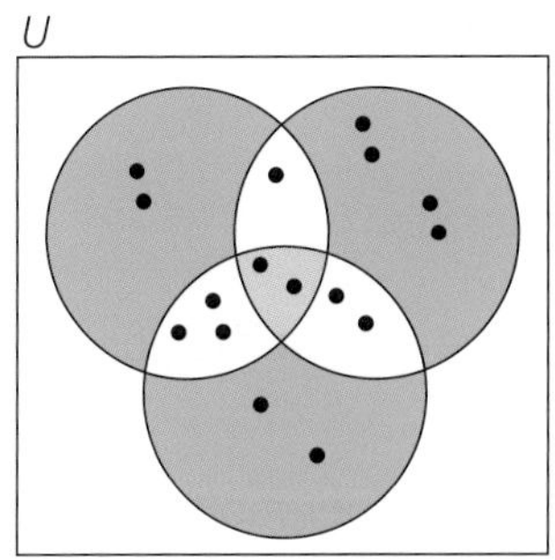

Step 4: Fill in any remaining elements listed in the universal set.

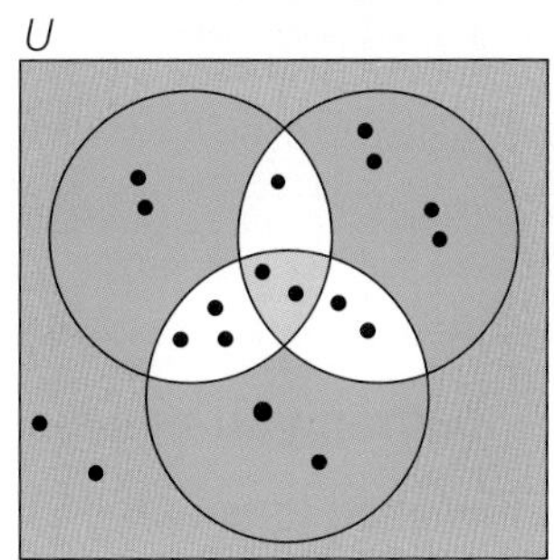

- To fill in a Venn diagram for word problems involving three sets:

  Step 1: Fill in the cardinal number for members that are common to all three sets in the given question.

  Step 2: Fill in the cardinal numbers for members that are common to two sets.

  Step 3: Fill in the cardinal numbers for members that are unique to each set.

  Step 4: Finally, fill in the cardinal number for any remaining members listed in the universal set.

Chapter 16 Algebra 5

Learning Intentions

In this chapter, you will learn about:

- Manipulating formulae
- Solving problems using manipulation

LO: AF.6

Section 16A Manipulating Formulae

A **formula** is a statement which connects variables, usually as an equation.

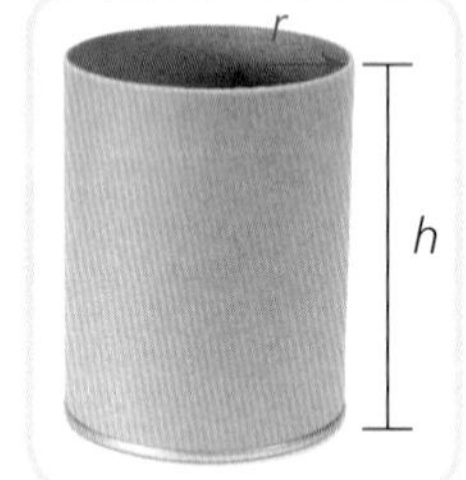

For example, $\boldsymbol{V = \pi r^2 h}$ is a formula which we know very well.
It gives the volume of a cylinder, V, in terms of r, the radius of its base and h, its height.

This formula holds true for every cylinder and may be used in this form to calculate V when given values for r and h.

V is called the **subject** of the formula, since it is on its own on one side of the equation.

We may want to change the subject of this formula. This means getting one of the other variables on its own on one side. We do this by using the rules of equations that we know very well already:

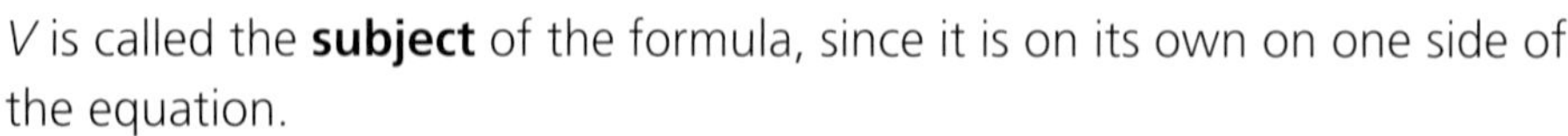

What we do to one side of an equation, we must do to the other side.

In practice, we do this by moving terms, or parts of terms, from one side of the equation to the other by performing opposite operations.

Example 1 shows how we use multiplication and division as opposite operations to change the subject of very simple equations.

Example 1

Make a the subject of each of the following equations.

(i) $4a = n$ (iii) $\frac{a}{2} = p$

(ii) $ma = n$ (iv) $\frac{a}{m} = p$

Solution

Multiplication and division are opposite operations. We want a on its own on one side only.

(i) $4a = n$ ... a is being multiplied by 4

$\Rightarrow a = \frac{n}{4}$ ... divide both sides by 4

(ii) $ma = n$ ... a is being multiplied by m

$\Rightarrow a = \frac{n}{m}$ ... divide both sides by m

(iii) $\frac{a}{2} = p$ ... a is being divided by 2

$\Rightarrow a = 2p$ ... multiply both sides by 2

(iv) $\frac{a}{m} = p$ ... a is being divided by m

$\Rightarrow a = mp$ ... multiply both sides by m

The next example shows how we use addition and subtraction as opposite operations to change the subject of equations.

Example 2

Make x the subject of the following equations.

(i) $x + m = p$

(ii) $x - h = k$

Solution

Addition and subtraction are opposite operations. We want x on its own on one side only.

(i) $x + m = p$ ... m is being added to x

$\Rightarrow x = p - m$ ... subtract m from both sides

(ii) $x - h = k$ ... h is being subtracted from x

$\Rightarrow x = k + h$ ... add h to both sides

Example 3

Make a the subject of the formula $v = u + at$.

Solution

We want a on its own on one side only.

$v = u + at$ ... u is being added to the term containing a

$\Rightarrow v - u = at$ ... subtract u from both sides. Now a is being multiplied by t

$\Rightarrow \frac{v-u}{t} = a$ ... divide both sides by t

$\Rightarrow a = \frac{v-u}{t}$ ... rearrange with a on the left side

In Example 4, the variable required is in more than one term.

Example 4

Make k the subject of the following formula.

$akb - 2ck = 7mn$

Solution

We want k on its own on one side only.

$akb - 2ck = 7mn$ ... both terms on the left-hand side contain k

$\Rightarrow k(ab - 2c) = 7mn$ ... factorise k out. Now k is being multiplied by $(ab - 2c)$

$\Rightarrow k = \dfrac{7mn}{ab - 2c}$ ... divide both sides by $(ab - 2c)$

Example 5

Express P as the subject of the formula $A = \dfrac{P - S}{t}$

Solution

We want P on its own on one side only.

$A = \dfrac{P - S}{t}$ ... the term containing P is being divided by t

$\Rightarrow At = P - S$ ... multiply both sides by t. Now S is being subtracted from P

$\Rightarrow At + S = P$ ... add S to both sides

So $P = At + S$

Example 6

Make v the subject of the formula $s = \left(\dfrac{u + v}{2}\right)t$

Solution

We want v on its own on one side only.

$s = \left(\dfrac{u + v}{2}\right)t$ ... the bracket containing v is being multiplied by t

$\Rightarrow \dfrac{s}{t} = \left(\dfrac{u + v}{2}\right)$ ... divide both sides by t. Now the expression containing v is being divided by 2

$\Rightarrow \dfrac{2s}{t} = u + v$ ... multiply both sides by 2. Now u is being added to v

$\Rightarrow \dfrac{2s}{t} - u = v$ ... subtract u from both sides

So $v = \dfrac{2s}{t} - u$

Taking the square root of a number is the opposite of squaring the number, i.e. $\sqrt{a^2} = a$ and $(\sqrt{a})^2 = a$. We will use this in the next example.

Example 7

(i) Make b the subject of the formula $\sqrt{a + 4b} = 5c$.

(ii) Make r the subject of the formula $V = \pi r^2$.

Solution

(i) We want b on its own on one side only.

$\sqrt{a + 4b} = 5c$ ... the term with b is under the square root sign

$\Rightarrow \left(\sqrt{a + 4b}\right)^2 = (5c)^2$ ... square both sides to eliminate the root

$\Rightarrow a + 4b = 25c^2$ ... now a is being added to the term with b

$\Rightarrow 4b = 25c^2 - a$ ... subtract a from both sides. Now b is being multiplied by 4

$\Rightarrow b = \dfrac{25c^2 - a}{4}$ ... divide both sides by 4

(ii) We want r on its own on one side only.

$V = \pi r^2$ ... r^2 is being multiplied by π

$\Rightarrow \dfrac{V}{\pi} = r^2$ ... divide both sides by π. Now r is squared

$\Rightarrow \sqrt{\dfrac{V}{\pi}} = r$ ... take the square root of both sides

So $r = \sqrt{\dfrac{V}{\pi}}$

Example 8

Make L the subject of the formula $T = 2\pi\sqrt{\dfrac{L}{g}}$

Solution

We want L on its own on one side only.

$T = 2\pi\sqrt{\dfrac{L}{g}}$ ... the term containing L is being multiplied by 2π

$\Rightarrow \dfrac{T}{2\pi} = \sqrt{\dfrac{L}{g}}$ ... divide both sides by 2π. Now L is under a square root sign

$\Rightarrow \left(\dfrac{T}{2\pi}\right)^2 = \dfrac{L}{g}$ ... square both sides. Now L is being divided by g

$\Rightarrow g \times \left(\dfrac{T}{2\pi}\right)^2 = L$ ... multiply both sides by g

So $L = g \times \left(\dfrac{T}{2\pi}\right)^2$

Activity 16.1

1 Rearrange the following equations to make t the subject of the equation.

(i) $a + t = 2s$

(ii) $p - t = 5q$

(iii) $wt = x$

(iv) $\dfrac{t}{k} = r$

(v) $\dfrac{f}{t} = gh$

(vi) $w(t - d) = y$

2 Rearrange the following formulae to make the variable in the brackets the subject of the formula.

(i) $A = l \times w$ (w)

(ii) $F = ma$ (a)

(iii) $T = Fd$ (d)

(iv) $P = \frac{F}{A}$ (F)

(v) $W = mg$ (m)

(vi) $P = \frac{W}{t}$ (t)

3 Rearrange the following equations to make x the subject of the equation.

(i) $x^2 = \frac{a}{b}$

(ii) $\frac{(d - x)}{e} = s - q$

(iii) $\sqrt{(x + g)} = a$

(iv) $\frac{x}{2} - d = p$

(v) $rx^2 + qs^2 = y$

(vi) $\frac{w}{x^2} + t = s - u$

4 Rearrange the following formulae to make the variable in the brackets the subject of the formula.

(i) $E = mgh$ (h)

(ii) $E = mc^2$ (m)

(iii) $v^2 = u^2 + 2as$ (a)

(iv) $T^2 = \frac{4\pi^2R^3}{GM}$ (M)

(v) $s = ut + \frac{1}{2}at^2$ (u)

(vi) $A = \pi r^2$ (r)

(vii) $F = \frac{Gm_1m_2}{d^2}$ (d)

(viii) $V = \frac{1}{3}\pi r^2h$ (r)

(ix) $T = 2\pi\sqrt{\frac{l}{g}}$ (g)

5 Rearrange the following equations to make b the subject of the equation.

(i) $ab - c = bp$

(ii) $u(2 - b) = sb$

(iii) $\frac{(b + y)}{c} = 3b$

(iv) $k = \frac{(b - w)}{b}$

(v) $\sqrt{\frac{b + e}{b}} = c^2$

6 Make l the subject of each of the following equations.

(i) $\frac{yl}{q} = w$

(ii) $p - \frac{u}{l} = s$

7 Rearrange the following formulae.

(i) $A = l^2$, to make l the subject

(ii) $T^2 = \frac{4\pi^2R^3}{GM}$, to make R the subject

8 Make w the subject of each of the following equations.

(i) $2(w - 2) = p - w$

(ii) $\frac{5w - p}{w} = bu$

Section 16B Working with Everyday Formulae

This section looks at real-life applications where it is necessary to rearrange a given formula to make another variable the subject.

Example 1

This is the formula used to calculate the **curved surface area** (A) of a cylinder:

$$A = 2\pi rh$$

(i) Rearrange the formula to make r the subject.

(ii) If the curved surface area (A) is 376.8 cm² and the height (h) is 10 cm, find the radius (r) of the cylinder. (Take $\pi = 3.14$)

(iii) Verify your solution.

Solution

(i) We want r on its own on one side.

$A = 2\pi rh$ ... r is being multiplied by $2\pi h$

$\Rightarrow \frac{A}{2\pi h} = r$ ... divide both sides by $2\pi h$

(ii) Substitute $A = 376.8$ cm² and $h = 10$ cm into the rearranged formula.

$r = \frac{A}{2\pi h}$

$\Rightarrow r = \frac{376.8}{2(3.14)(10)}$

$\Rightarrow r = 6$ cm

(iii) Check:

$A = 2\pi rh = 2(3.14)(6)(10) = 376.8$ cm²

The solution is correct.

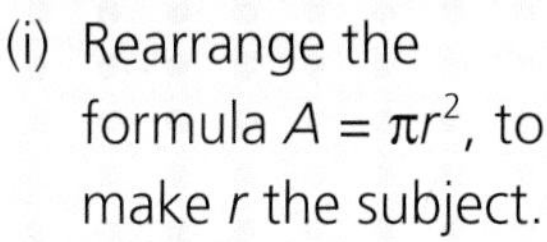

Example 2

The area of a circular flowerbed is 38.5 m².

(i) Rearrange the formula $A = \pi r^2$, to make r the subject.

If $\pi = \frac{22}{7}$ and $A = 38.5$ m²:

(ii) Find the radius of the flower bed.

(iii) Verify your solution.

Solution

(i) $A = \pi r^2$

$\Rightarrow \frac{A}{\pi} = r^2$ ... divide both sides by π

$\Rightarrow \sqrt{\frac{A}{\pi}} = r$ ... square root both sides

(ii) Substitute $\pi = \frac{22}{7}$ and $A = 38.5$ m² into the formula found in part (i).

$r = \sqrt{\frac{A}{\pi}}$

$\Rightarrow r = \sqrt{\frac{38.5}{\left(\frac{22}{7}\right)}}$

$\Rightarrow r = 3.5$ m

(iii) Check:

$A = \pi r^2 = \left(\frac{22}{7}\right)(3.5)^2 = 38.5$ m²

The solution is correct.

Activity 16.2

1 The formula $K = C + 273.15$ is used to calculate degrees Kelvin (°K) where

C = temperature in degrees Celsius

K = temperature in degrees Kelvin.

(i) If C is 37°C, calculate the value of K.

(ii) Rearrange the formula to make C the subject.

(iii) If K is 306.15°K, calculate the value of C.

(iv) Check your solution.

2 The area of a parallelogram is

$A = ah$

where

a = base length

h = perpendicular height.

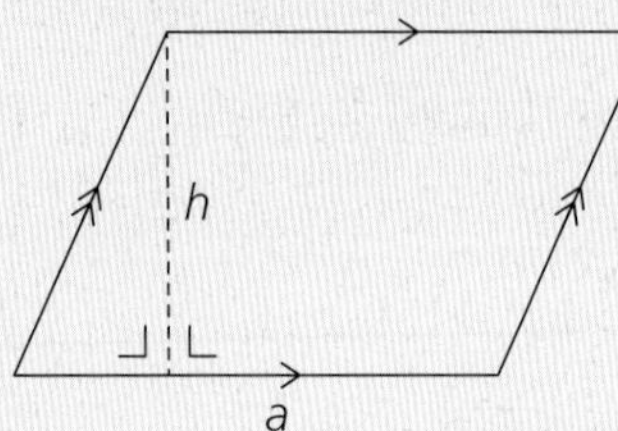

(i) Rearrange the formula to make h the subject.

(ii) Rearrange the formula to make a the subject.

If A is 378 cm^2 and h is 21 cm,

(iii) Find the base length (a) of the parallelogram.

(iv) Check your solution.

3 The area of a triangular window on an A-frame building is given by the formula:

$A = \frac{1}{2}ah$

where

A = area of triangle

a = base length

h = perpendicular height.

(i) Make a the subject of the formula.

(ii) Find the base length (a) of the triangular window if the perpendicular height (h) is 11 m and the area is 55 m^2.

4 (i)

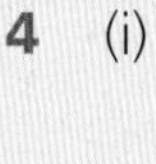

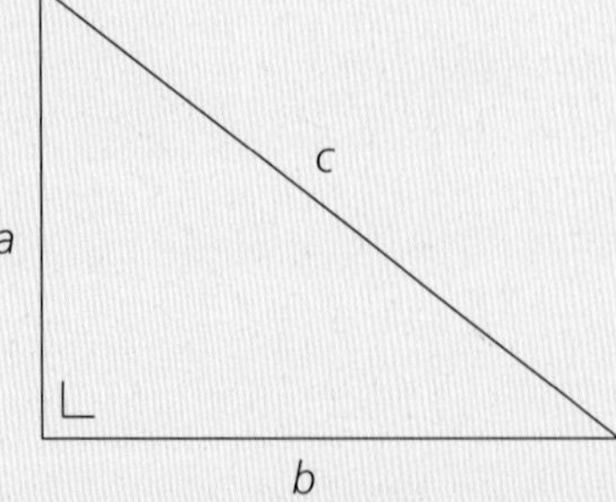

Rearrange Pythagoras' theorem: $c^2 = a^2 + b^2$, to make b the subject.

(ii) In the right-angled triangle shown, find the length of the side b when $a = 3$ and $c = 5$.

(iii) Check your solution.

5 If an object is dropped from a height, the formula

$v = u + at$

gives the velocity after t seconds where

v = the final speed

u = the initial speed

and a = the acceleration due to gravity.

(i) Rearrange the formula to make u the subject.

(ii) If v is 35.48 m/s, a is 9.8 m/s^2 and t is 2.6 s, find the value of u, the initial speed in m/s.

(iii) Check your solution.

6 The force (F) required to move a car is given by the formula

$F = ma$

where

m is the mass of the car

and a is the acceleration of the car.

(i) Rearrange the formula to make m the subject.

If a Formula 1 car speeds down a track with an acceleration of 0.05 m/s^2:

(ii) Find the value of m if $F = 35$ N. (Ignore units.)

(iii) Check your solution.

7 The volume of a sphere is given by the formula

$$V = \frac{4}{3}\pi r^3$$

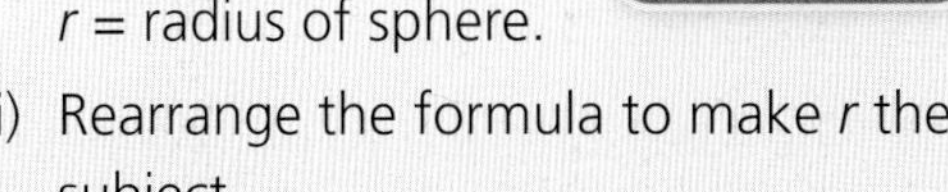

where

V = volume of sphere

r = radius of sphere.

(i) Rearrange the formula to make r the subject.

(ii) The volume of a Premiership size 5 soccer football is 1843.71 cm^3. Assuming the ball is perfectly spherical, find the radius of the ball to one decimal place. (Take $\pi = 3.14$)

(iii) Check your solution.

8 The formula used to calculate the voltage in an electrical circuit is

$$V = IR$$

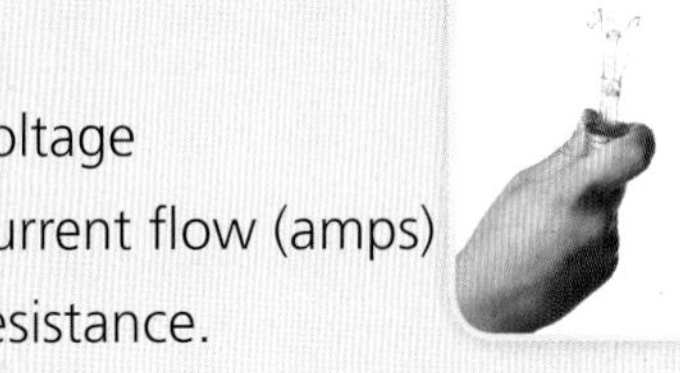

where

V = voltage

I = current flow (amps)

R = resistance.

(i) Rearrange the formula to make R the subject.

(ii) If a 12 volt (V) battery causes 2 amps (I) of current to flow through a light bulb, calculate the resistance (R) of the bulb in ohms.

(iii) Verify your solution.

9 The volume of an ice cream cone is 314 cm^3. The volume of a cone is

$$V = \frac{1}{3}\pi r^2 h$$

where

V = volume of a cone

h = perpendicular height

r = radius.

(i) Rearrange the formula to make r the subject.

(ii) Find the radius of the cone if the height (h) of the cone is 12 cm. (Take $\pi = 3.14$)

(iii) Verify your solution.

10 To convert degrees Celsius (°C) to degrees Fahrenheit (°F), we use the formula

$$C = \frac{5}{9}(F - 32)$$

where

C = degrees Celsius (°C)

F = degrees Fahrenheit (°F).

(i) Rearrange the formula to make F the subject.

(ii) If C is 29°C, calculate the value of F.

(iii) Check your solution.

11 The formula used to calculate density is

$$\rho = \frac{m}{V}$$

where

ρ = density

m = mass

V = volume.

(i) Rearrange the formula to make m the subject.

(ii) Calculate the mass (m) of water if the density of water (ρ) is 1 g/cm^3 and the volume of water (V) in a container is 3000 cm^3.

(iii) Check your solution.

Revision Activity 16

1 Rearrange the following formulae to make the variable in the brackets the subject.

(a) $P = \frac{F}{A}$ (A)

(b) $W = mg$ (g)

(c) $P = \frac{W}{t}$ (W)

(d) $F = \frac{Gm_1m_2}{d^2}$ (m_2)

(e) $E = mgh$ (h)

(f) $E = mc^2$ (c)

(g) $v^2 = u^2 + 2as$ (u)

(h) $s = ut + \frac{1}{2}at^2$ (a)

(i) $T^2 = \frac{4\pi^2R^3}{GM}$ (R)

(j) $T = 2\pi\sqrt{\frac{l}{g}}$ (l)

2 This is the formula used to calculate the volume of a sphere:

$$V = \frac{4}{3}\pi r^3$$

where

V = volume of sphere

r = radius of sphere.

(a) Rearrange the formula to make r the subject.

The volume of the planet Venus is 9.28×10^{11} km³.

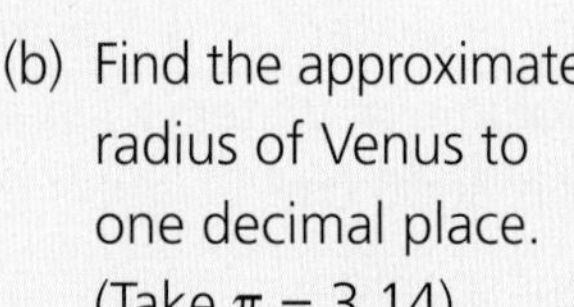

(b) Find the approximate radius of Venus to one decimal place. (Take $\pi = 3.14$)

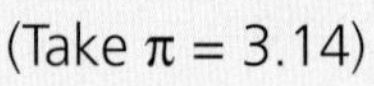

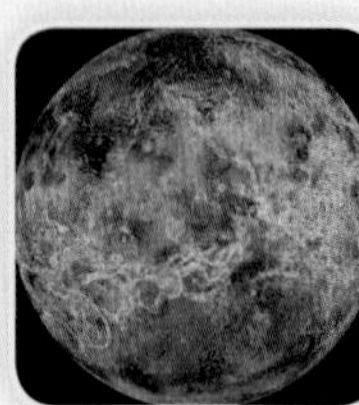

3 Kinetic energy is the energy associated with the movement of an object. The formula for kinetic energy is:

$$E = \frac{1}{2}mv^2$$

where

E = kinetic energy

m = mass

v = velocity.

(a) Rearrange the formula to make v the subject.

(b) If m is 5 kg and E is 10 joules, calculate the velocity in m/s.

(c) Check your solution.

4 The total surface area (A) of a baked bean tin is 98π cm².

(a) Rearrange the formula $A = 2\pi r(h + r)$ to make h the subject.

(b) If the radius (r) of the tin is 3.5 cm, find the height (h) of the tin.

(c) Check your solution.

5 A capacitor is a device which stores electricity. The formula for the amount of energy stored in a capacitor is:

$$W = \frac{1}{2}CV^2$$

where

W = energy stored

C = the capacitance

V = the potential difference.

(a) Rearrange the formula to make V the subject.

(b) Find the potential difference (V) in volts of the capacitor if the capacitance (C) is 10×10^{-6} farads and the energy stored (W) is 0.26 joules.

(c) Check your solution.

Exam-style Questions

1 The 'Multiplier' is a variable used by economists to measure the effect of an increase in spending in an economy. One version of the Multiplier is $M = \frac{1}{S+P}$ where M is the Multiplier, S relates to savings and P relates to imports.

(a) Calculate the value of M, the Multiplier, if $S = 0.2$ and $P = 0.1$.

(b) Explain the effect on the size of M if the value of P increases.

(c) Sometimes the above formula is used to calculate P. Rearrange the formula to make P its subject.

JCHL 2013

2 A capacitor is a device which stores electricity. The formula $W = \frac{1}{2}CV^2$ gives the energy stored in the capacitor, where W is the energy, C is the capacitance and V is the voltage, and standard units are used throughout.

(a) Find the amount of energy stored in a capacitor when $C = 2500$ and $V = 32$.

(b) Write V in terms of W and C.

JCHL 2012

KEY WORDS AND PHRASES

- **Manipulate formula**
- **'Opposite' operation**

Chapter Summary 16

When manipulating formulae or equations, there are two general rules to follow:

- When you perform an operation on one side of an equation, you must perform the same operation on the other side in order for the equation to remain true.
- To move or cancel a variable on one side of the equation, you must carry out the 'opposite' operation on both sides of the equation.

When solving a problem where the subject appears on both sides of the equation:

- Rearrange the equation to bring the subject variable to the left-hand side and all other variables to the right-hand side.
- Take out the common factor (i.e. the subject variable).
- Continue rearranging the formula as normal.

Chapter 17 Number

Learning Intentions

In this chapter, you will learn about:

LO: U.5, U.6, N.1

- Fractions, decimals and percentages (review)
- Division involving zero
- Indices
- Equations in which the unknown is an index
- Reciprocals
- Recurring decimals
- Irrational numbers
- Some properties of even, odd and prime numbers

Historical Background

Leonhard Euler, from Switzerland, is often regarded as the greatest mathematician of all time. We have already learned that he was the first to put forward the notion of a mathematical function. But a lot of people know him for his formula which contains the five most important numbers in mathematics:

$$e^{i\pi} + 1 = 0$$

This is considered to be one of the most beautiful formulae in all of mathematics.

Leonhard Euler (1707–1783)

You are familiar with three of these numbers: 0, 1 and π. You will meet the other two numbers, e and i later in your studies.

Section 17A Review of Fractions, Decimals and Percentages

In mathematics, we have different categories of numbers.

1. The set of **natural numbers** $\mathbb{N} = \{1, 2, 3, 4, 5, \ldots\}$
   We can think of them as the numbers we use to count natural things: 1 dog, 2 mountains, etc.
   We can show these on a number line:

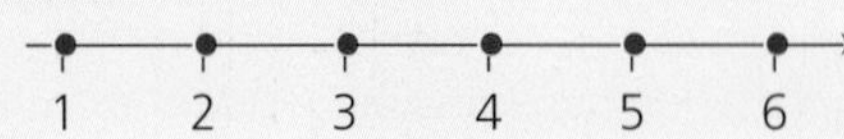

If we add two natural numbers, we always get a natural number and if we multiply two natural numbers, we always get a natural number.

However, we cannot always subtract or divide natural numbers and get an element of $\mathbb{N}$ as an answer. For example, if we subtract 3 from 2, or divide 3 by 2, we don't get a natural number.

So we need more numbers.

2. The set of **integers** $\mathbb{Z} = \{\ldots, -3, -2, -1, 0, 1, 2, 3, \ldots\}$

   The integers include all the natural numbers, along with 0 and the negative whole numbers.

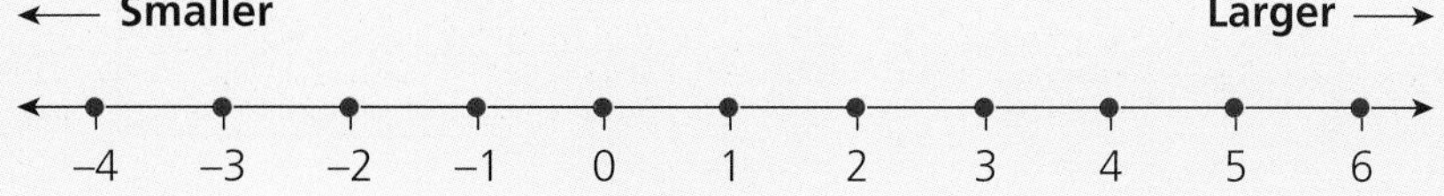

These allow us to **add**, **subtract** and **multiply** always.

However, we cannot always divide and get an element of $\mathbb{Z}$ as an answer.

This is where fractions (rational numbers) are needed.

3. The **rational numbers** $\mathbb{Q}$ = the set of all numbers which can be written in the form $\frac{p}{q}$ where p and $q \in \mathbb{Z}$ and $q \neq 0$.

   This means that a rational number is any number which can be written as a fraction with whole numbers as numerator and denominator.

Of course, the sets $\mathbb{N}$ and $\mathbb{Z}$ are included in $\mathbb{Q}$, since any whole number can be written as a fraction with 1 as the denominator.

We cannot show all the rational numbers on the number line, but this diagram shows a small selection of them:

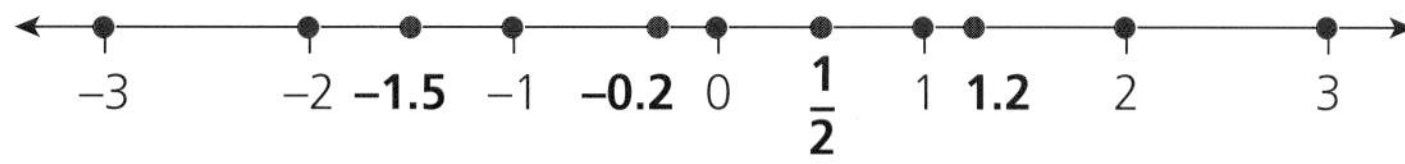

$\mathbb{N} \subset \mathbb{Z} \subset \mathbb{Q}$, and we can represent these sets of numbers on a diagram like this:

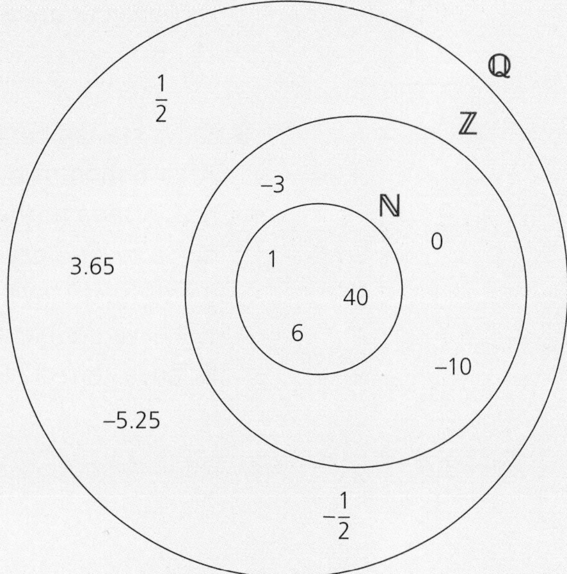

Note: The definition of a rational number $\frac{p}{q}$ above says that q must $\neq 0$. We will discuss why this is in the next section.

Activity 17.1

1 (i) Write down a fraction between $\frac{1}{3}$ and $\frac{1}{4}$.

(ii) Can you list two fractions between $\frac{1}{3}$ and $\frac{1}{4}$?

2

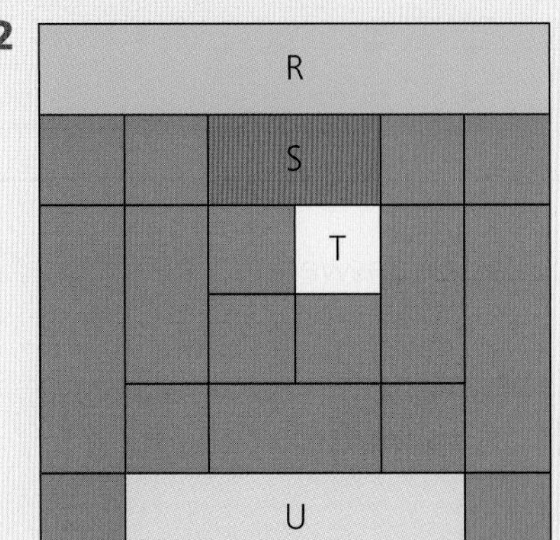

(i) What fraction of the whole square is R?

(ii) What fraction of the whole square is S?

(iii) What fraction of the whole square is T?

(iv) What fraction of the whole square is U?

3 Calculate:

(i) 30% of €26

(ii) 125% of €12

(iii) 40% of 80% of €25

(iv) $\frac{1}{3}$ of $\frac{1}{3}$ of $\frac{1}{3}$ of 81

4 Which of these rectangles has $\frac{3}{4}$ shaded in?

(i)

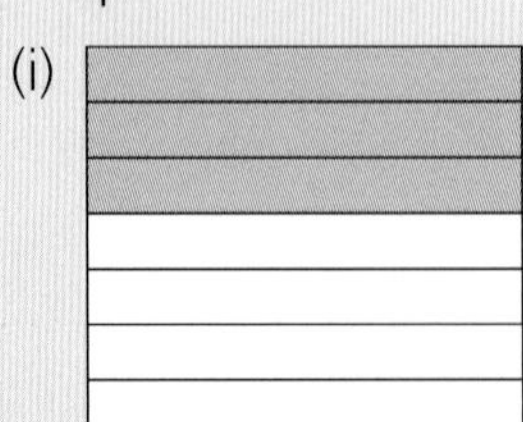

(ii)

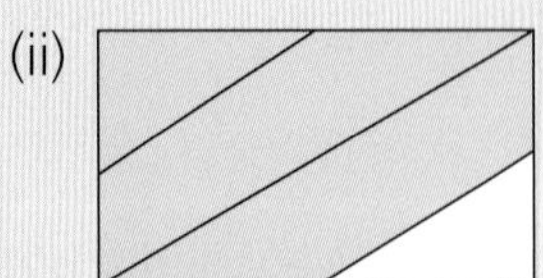

(iii)

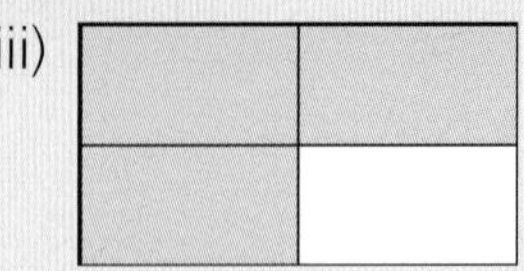

(iv)

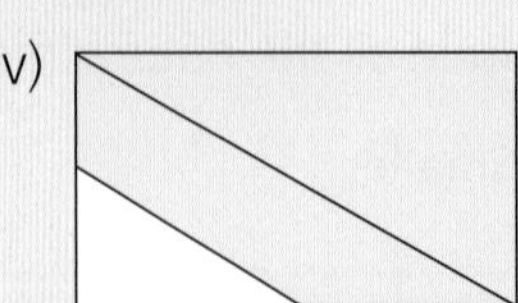

5 Kate gave $\frac{1}{5}$ of her pocket money to charity. Joe gave $\frac{1}{5}$ of his pocket money to another charity. Joe said that he gave more money to charity than Kate did. Explain how Joe could be right.

6 (i) Decrease €16 by 20%.

(ii) Increase €8 by 70%.

(iii) Decrease 50% of €3.60 by $\frac{1}{6}$.

7 Students were asked to explain why $\frac{5}{6}$ is greater than $\frac{4}{5}$. Which of the following explanations is the correct one?

- Because 5 is greater than 4
- Because 6 is greater than 5
- Because 5 + 6 is greater than 4 + 5
- Because $\frac{5}{6}$ is closer to 1 than $\frac{4}{5}$

8 Which of these fractions is smallest? Explain your answer.

(i) $\frac{3}{7}$ (ii) $\frac{1}{4}$ (iii) $\frac{2}{5}$ (iv) $\frac{1}{2}$

9 Tanya started her new job as a trainee. After 6 months she is to get a 50% pay rise. After a further 6 months she will be due a second pay rise of 50%. 'This is great', said Tanya, 'One year from now I will have double my present pay.'
Is Tanya correct? Explain your reasoning.

10 Here are three number lines all of which are the same length.

This number line shows $\frac{2}{3}$ shaded.

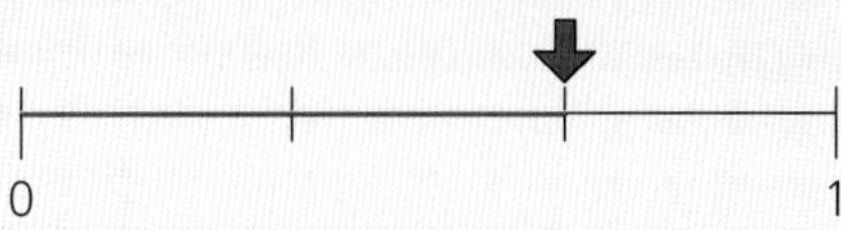

(i) What fraction of this number line is shaded?

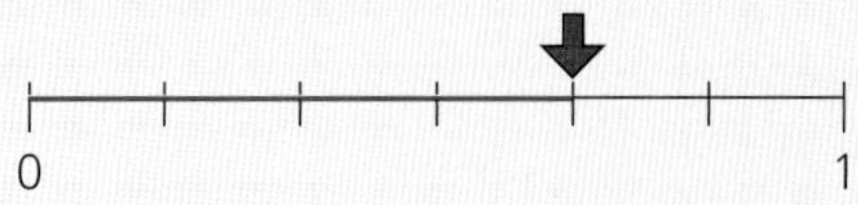

(ii) What fraction of this number line is shaded?

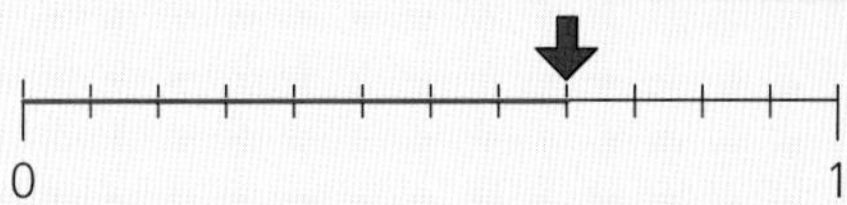

(iii) What do these three fractions have in common?

11 The diagrams show two circles of the same size.

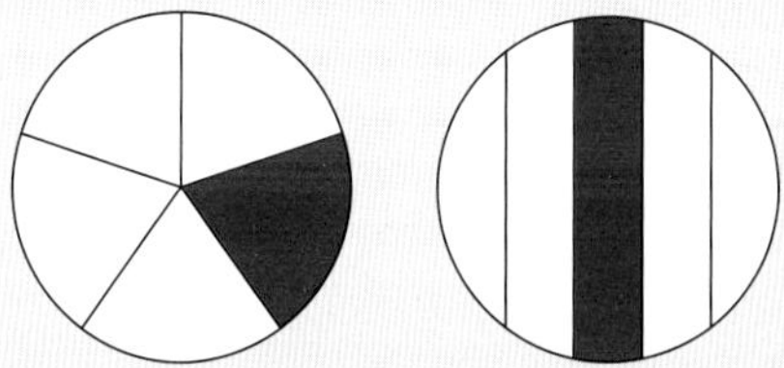

Are the shaded portions in each circle the same size? Explain your answer.

12 The diagram shows $\frac{2}{3}$ of a garden.

(i) Copy the diagram into your copybook.

(ii) Modify the diagram to show the whole garden.

13

(i) If the shaded portion represents $2\frac{3}{4}$, how many small squares make 1 unit?

(ii) Using the same unit, what would 6 small squares represent?

(iii) If 3 shaded squares represent 1 unit, what number would be represented by the total number of shaded squares?

(iv) On a copy of the table, list some other numbers that the shaded portion could represent and give the unit in each case.

Number of squares in one unit	Number represented by the shaded rectangles

14

The shaded part of this diagram could represent the numbers

A: 5 B: $2\frac{1}{2}$ C: $\frac{5}{8}$ D: $1\frac{1}{4}$

Identify the unit in each case.

15 Tony tiled $\frac{4}{5}$ of a bathroom wall. The next day he grouted $\frac{7}{8}$ of the tiled section. What fraction of the bathroom wall had grouted tiles?

16 Sheila buys $\frac{5}{6}$ kg of cheese. She keeps $\frac{3}{4}$ of it and gives $\frac{1}{4}$ to her sister.

What is the weight of:

(i) the cheese that Sheila keeps

(ii) the cheese that Sheila gives to her sister?

17 A shop's sales of ice cream in August was €700. In September, their sales went down to €500.

(i) What fraction is this of August's sales?

(ii) By what fraction must €500 be multiplied to get back to August's sales figures of €700?

18 (i) The diagram shows $\frac{3}{5}$ of a rectangle. Copy the grid and complete the rectangle.

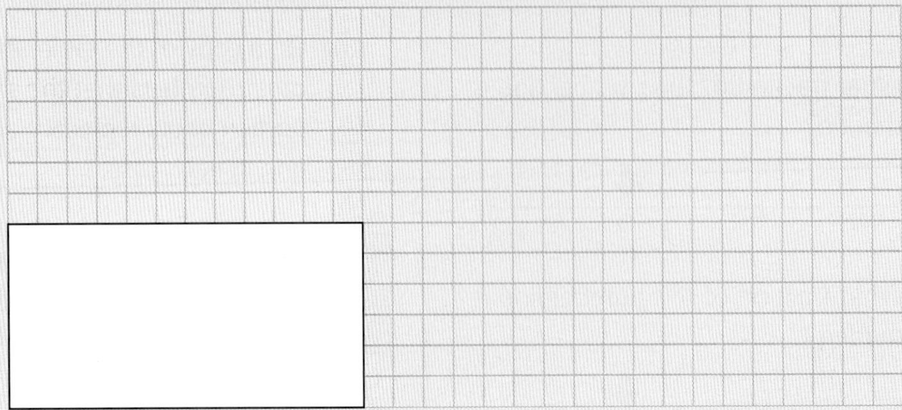

(ii) Copy the diagram below and by shading appropriate sections of the strips below, show that:

$$\frac{1}{3} + \frac{2}{6} \neq \frac{3}{9}$$

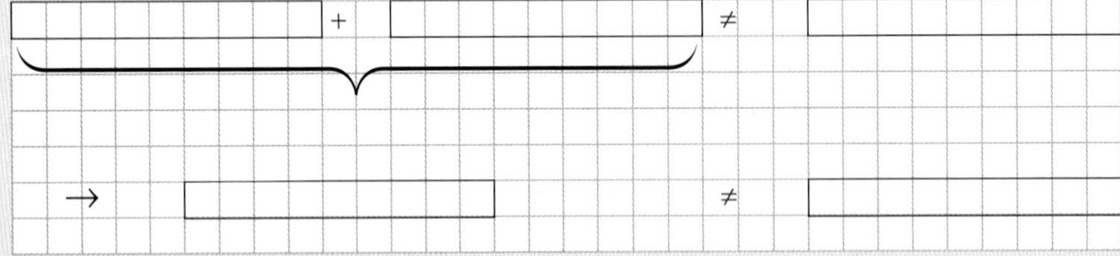

Section 17B Division Involving Zero

Division involving zero needs to be looked at carefully.

1. **Zero as the numerator**

   What does $\frac{0}{3}$ mean? It could mean that we are dividing €0 among 3 people.

   Each gets €0. So $\frac{0}{3} = 0$.

   Thus, if a fraction has zero as numerator, its value = 0.
   Rule:

   If $\frac{a}{b} = 0$ then $a = 0$ If $a = 0$ then $\frac{a}{b} = 0$ (provided that $b \neq 0$)

2. **Zero as the denominator**

   What does $\frac{2}{0}$ mean? Key this into your calculator. You get 'math error'. Why is this?
   Put in simple terms, **we cannot divide by zero!**
   The next activity explains why.

Class Activity

Why can't we divide by zero?

In this activity, we will see if we can get a value when dividing a number divided by 0. We will use the number 5 for this example, but we could have chosen any number at all.

Step 1 Draw a number line showing –3, –2, –1, 0, 1, 2 and 3. You will use this number line in the steps which follow.

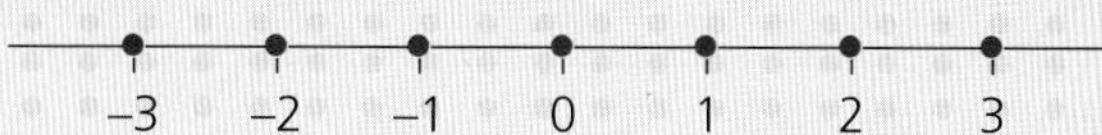

Step 2 Now we pick a number **close to 0**. Let's choose 1. (You can see that it is right next to 0 on the number line.) Now find the value of $\frac{5}{1}$. The answer is 5. Since 0 is close to 1, we could say that $\frac{5}{0}$ is close to $\frac{5}{1}$ which = 5.

Step 3 Now let's pick a number **closer to 0**. Let's choose 0.5. Mark it on your number line. You can see that it is very close to 0. Now find the value of $\frac{5}{0.5}$.
Write down its value.
Is this close to the value of $\frac{5}{0}$?

Step 4 Now take another number which is **closer still to 0**. Let's choose 0.1. Mark it on your number line. It is really close to 0. So now find the value of $\frac{5}{0.1}$.
Write down its value.
Is this close to the value of $\frac{5}{0}$?

Step 5 Now take another number which is **closer still to 0**. Let's choose 0.01. Mark it on your number line if you can. It is really very close to 0. Find the value of $\frac{5}{0.01}$.
Write down its value.
Are we close to the value of $\frac{5}{0}$?

Step 6 One more time, take another number which is **really close to 0**. Let's choose 0.001. Point to where it is on your number line if you can (you won't have space to mark it). You can imagine that it is really very close to 0. Now find the value of $\frac{5}{0.001}$.
Write down its value.
Surely the value of $\frac{5}{0.001}$ is near to the value of $\frac{5}{0}$?

Number

Number

Step 7 In order to clearly see the pattern, copy and complete this table using your answers from steps 2 to 6 and a calculator.

Value of a	$\frac{5}{a}$	Value of $\frac{5}{a}$
1	$\frac{5}{1}$	5
0.1	$\frac{5}{0.1}$	50
0.01		
0.001		
0.0001		
0.00001		

Step 8 We have divided 5 by numbers which are very close to 0. When do we get to 0? What then is the value of $\frac{5}{0}$?

We cannot get a value for $\frac{a}{0}$ where a is any number, so we say that $\frac{a}{0}$ is **undefined**.

Note: You might ask 'what about $\frac{0}{0}$?'

Now this is really complicated. Mathematicians call this 'an indeterminate form'. We won't deal with this here!

Section 17C Indices

We know already that 2^4 (we say '2 to the power of 4') is a short way of writing $2 \times 2 \times 2 \times 2$.

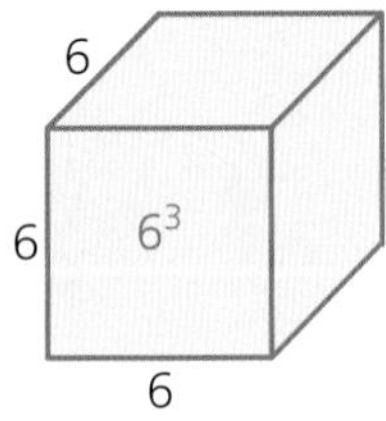

The number 4 is called the **exponent** or **index** (plural indices).

The number 2 is called the **base**.

The expression 6^2 is pronounced 'six to the power of two' or 'six squared'.

The expression 6^3 is pronounced 'six to the power of three' or 'six cubed'.

*n*th Roots

Since $6^2 = 36$, we also say that $\sqrt{36} = 6$.

Since $2^3 = 8$, we also say that $\sqrt[3]{8} = 2$.

Since $3^4 = 81$, we also say that $\sqrt[4]{81} = 3$.

Since $2^5 = 32$, we also say that $\sqrt[5]{32} = 2$.

Note: $\sqrt{9}$ stands for the **non-negative** square root of 9, so $\sqrt{9} = 3$.

We have learned some rules of indices which we will now extend to include negative powers and fractional powers.

Rules of Indices

Rules of indices	Examples
Rule 1: $a^m \times a^n = a^{m+n}$	$5^3 \times 5^6 = 5^{3+6} = 5^9$
Rule 2: $\frac{a^m}{a^n} = a^{m-n}$	$\frac{3^7}{3^5} = 3^{7-5} = 3^2$
Rule 3: $a^0 = 1$	$27^0 = 1$
Rule 4: $(a^m)^n = a^{mn}$	$(3^2)^4 = 3^8$
Rule 5: $a^{-m} = \frac{1}{a^m}$	$5^{-3} = \frac{1}{5^3}$
Rule 6: $a^{\frac{1}{q}} = \sqrt[q]{a}$	$8^{\frac{1}{2}} = \sqrt{8}$
Rule 7: $a^{\frac{p}{q}} = (\sqrt[q]{a})^p$	$27^{\frac{2}{3}} = (\sqrt[3]{27})^2 = 3^2 = 9$
Rule 8: $(ab)^m = a^m b^m$	$(3\sqrt{2})^2 = 3^2 \times (\sqrt{2})^2 = 9 \times 2 = 18$
Rule 9: $\left(\frac{a}{b}\right)^m = \frac{a^m}{b^m}$	$\left(\frac{2}{3}\right)^3 = \frac{2^3}{3^3} = \frac{8}{27}$

These rules are on page 21 of the *Formulae and tables* booklet.

Example

Write as rational numbers: (i) 2^{-3} (ii) $27^{\frac{1}{3}}$ (iii) $(32)^{\frac{3}{5}}$ (iv) $\left(\frac{4}{9}\right)^{-\frac{3}{2}}$

Solution

(i) 2^{-3}

$= \frac{1}{2^3}$ ...Rule 5

$= \frac{1}{8}$

(ii) $27^{\frac{1}{3}}$

$= \sqrt[3]{27}$ ...Rule 6

$= 3$

(iii) $(32)^{\frac{3}{5}}$

$= (32^{\frac{1}{5}})^3$ ...Rule 4

$= (\sqrt[5]{32})^3$ ...Rule 6

$= (2)^3$

$= 8$

(iv) $\left(\frac{4}{9}\right)^{-\frac{3}{2}}$

$= \frac{4^{-\frac{3}{2}}}{9^{-\frac{3}{2}}}$ ...Rule 9

$= \frac{9^{\frac{3}{2}}}{4^{\frac{3}{2}}}$ ...Rule 5

$= \frac{(9^{\frac{1}{2}})^3}{(4^{\frac{1}{2}})^3}$ ...Rule 4

$= \frac{(3)^3}{(2)^3}$ ...Rule 6

$= \frac{27}{8}$

Activity 17.2

1 Simplify: (i) $a^4 \times a^5$ (ii) $\frac{a^6}{a^2}$ (iii) $\frac{a^3 \times a^7}{a^8}$ (iv) $(a^3)^4$ (v) $(a^3b^2)^3$ (vi) $(ab^4)^5$

2 Complete the following by filling in values for ?: $a^0 = \frac{a^0 \times a^7}{a^7} = \frac{?}{a^7} = ?$

3 Complete the following by filling in values for ?: $a^{-5} = \frac{a^{-5} \times a^5}{a^5} = \frac{?}{a^5} = \frac{?}{a^5}$

Evaluate the following.

4 $25^{\frac{1}{2}}$

5 6^{-2}

6 77^{0}

7 $16^{\frac{1}{2}}$

8 5^{-1}

9 $9^{\frac{1}{2}}$

10 $9^{-\frac{1}{2}}$

11 $100^{\frac{1}{2}}$

12 $100^{-\frac{1}{2}}$

13 $1000^{\frac{1}{3}}$

14 $16^{\frac{1}{4}}$

15 $\left(\frac{4}{9}\right)^{\frac{1}{2}}$

16 $8^{\frac{2}{3}}$

17 $27^{\frac{1}{3}}$

18 $9^{\frac{3}{2}}$

19 $32^{\frac{3}{5}}$

20 $\left(\frac{1}{1000}\right)^{\frac{1}{3}}$

21 $\left(\frac{8}{9}\right)^{0}$

22 $216^{\frac{1}{3}}$

23 $81^{\frac{1}{4}}$

24 $243^{\frac{1}{5}}$

25 $243^{-\frac{1}{5}}$

26 $125^{\frac{1}{3}}$

27 $125^{\frac{2}{3}}$

28 $\left(\frac{16}{81}\right)^{\frac{1}{2}}$

29 $\left(\frac{16}{81}\right)^{\frac{3}{2}}$

30 $\left(\frac{27}{64}\right)^{\frac{1}{3}}$

31 $\left(\frac{27}{64}\right)^{\frac{4}{3}}$

32 $\left(\frac{16}{81}\right)^{\frac{1}{4}}$

33 $\left(\frac{16}{81}\right)^{\frac{3}{4}}$

34 $\left(\frac{81}{16}\right)^{-\frac{3}{4}}$

35 $\left(\frac{169}{25}\right)^{\frac{1}{2}}$

36 $\left(\frac{8}{125}\right)^{\frac{1}{3}}$

37 $\left(\frac{8}{125}\right)^{\frac{2}{3}}$

38 $\left(\frac{8}{125}\right)^{\frac{4}{3}}$

39 $\left(\frac{27}{64}\right)^{-\frac{2}{3}}$

40 $\left(1\frac{24}{25}\right)^{\frac{3}{2}}$

41 $\left(3\frac{1}{16}\right)^{-\frac{3}{2}}$

42 Write each of these in the form x^m, where $m \in \mathbb{Q}$.

(i) $\sqrt{x}$ (iii) $\frac{x^2}{\sqrt{x}}$ (v) $(\sqrt{x})(\sqrt[3]{x})$

(ii) $x\sqrt{x}$ (iv) $\sqrt[4]{x}$

43 Answer true or false to these statements. Explain your answers.

(i) $3^2 + 2^2 = 5^2$

(ii) $5^8 \times 5^{-6} = 5^2$

(iii) $(4^2)^3 = 4^5$

(iv) $(4^2)(3^3) = 12^5$

(v) $5^{-1} = -5$

(vi) $4^{\frac{1}{2}} + 9^{\frac{1}{2}} = 13^{\frac{1}{2}}$

(vii) $36^{\frac{1}{2}} - 25^{\frac{1}{2}} = 11^{\frac{1}{2}}$

44 Write $4\sqrt{2}$ in the form 2^n where $n \in \mathbb{Q}$.

45 Write $\frac{27\sqrt{3}}{3^{-2}}$ in the form 3^n where $n \in \mathbb{Q}$.

46 Write $\frac{125^{\frac{2}{3}} \times \sqrt{5}}{25^{\frac{1}{2}}}$ in the form 5^n where $n \in \mathbb{Q}$.

Section 17D Equations in Which the Unknown is an Index

In an equation such as $3^x = 81$, the unknown variable (x) is an index.

To solve such equations, we use the following rule:

If $a^x = a^y$ then $x = y$.

To solve such equations:

- Write all numbers as powers of the same number
- Use the rules of indices to write each side of the equation as a power of the same number
- Equate the indices and solve.

Example 1

Solve for x the equation $3^x = 81$.

Solution

$3^x = 81$

$\Rightarrow 3^x = 3^4$ ... write 81 as a power of 3

$\Rightarrow x = 4$ ... equate the indices.

Example 2

Find the value of x for which $4^{x-1} = 32$.

Solution

$4^{x-1} = 32$

$\Rightarrow (2^2)^{x-1} = 2^5$ ... write 4 and 32 as powers of 2

$\Rightarrow 2^{2x-2} = 2^5$ ... rule 4 of indices

$\Rightarrow 2x - 2 = 5$ ... equate the powers

$\Rightarrow 2x = 5 + 2$

$\Rightarrow 2x = 7$

$\Rightarrow x = \frac{7}{2}$

Example 3

Solve for x the equation $4^{x+2} = 8^{1-x}$.

Solution

$4^{x+2} = 8^{1-x}$

$\Rightarrow (2^2)^{x+2} = (2^3)^{1-x}$ ... write all numbers as powers of 2

$\Rightarrow 2^{2x+4} = 2^{3-3x}$ .... rule 4 of indices

$\Rightarrow 2x + 4 = 3 - 3x$ ... equate the indices

$\Rightarrow 2x + 3x = 3 - 4$

$\Rightarrow 5x = -1$

$\Rightarrow x = -\frac{1}{5}$

Example 4

If $\frac{5^2 \times 125^{\frac{1}{3}}}{25^{\frac{5}{2}} \times 5^3} = 5^n$, find n, where $n \in \mathbb{Z}$.

Solution

$\frac{5^2 \times 125^{\frac{1}{3}}}{25^{\frac{5}{2}} \times 5^3} = 5^n$

$\Rightarrow \frac{5^2 \times (5^3)^{\frac{1}{3}}}{(5^2)^{\frac{5}{2}} \times 5^3} = 5^n$ ... write all numbers as powers of 5

$\Rightarrow \frac{5^2 \times 5^{3\times\frac{1}{3}}}{5^{2\times\frac{5}{2}} \times 5^3} = 5^n$ ... rule 4 of indices

$\Rightarrow \frac{5^2 \times 5^1}{5^5 \times 5^3} = 5^n$

$\Rightarrow \frac{5^3}{5^8} = 5^n$ ... rule 1

$\Rightarrow 5^{3-8} = 5^n$ ... rule 2

$\Rightarrow 5^{-5} = 5^n$

$\Rightarrow -5 = n$

i.e $n = -5$

Activity 17.3

1 Solve each of the following equations:

(i) $3^x = 27$

(ii) $2^x = 64$

(iii) $5^x = 125$

(iv) $10^x = 1000$

(v) $5^{3x} = 5^{15}$

(vi) $7^{x+2} = 7^3$

(vii) $3^{x-2} = 3^5$

(viii) $2^x = 256$

2 Solve each of the following equations:

(i) $2^x = 8^2$

(ii) $3^{3x} = 9^6$

(iii) $4^{2x} = 8^2$

(iv) $10^{2x} = 100^2$

(v) $5^{2x} = 25^8$

(vi) $7^{x+5} = 49^3$

(vii) $3^{x+2} = 27^5$

(viii) $2^{4x} = 8^{x+1}$

3 Find the value of x for which $2^{x+5} = 4^x$.

4 Find the value of x for which $25^x = 5^{9-x}$.

5 Find the value of x for which $\frac{5^x}{2} = \frac{5^6}{50}$.

6 (i) Find the value of 3^6.

(ii) Write 81 in the form 3^k, where $k \in \mathbb{N}$.

(iii) Solve for x the equation

$81 \times 3^x = \frac{1}{729}$.

7 (i) Evaluate $8^{\frac{1}{3}}$.

(ii) Express $4^{\frac{1}{4}}$ in the form 2^k, $k \in \mathbb{Q}$.

(iii) Find the value of x for which

$\left(8^{\frac{1}{3}}\right)\left(4^{\frac{1}{4}}\right) = 2^{4-x}$.

8 (i) Write as a power of 2:

(a) 8 (b) $8^{\frac{2}{3}}$.

(ii) Solve for x the equation $8^{\frac{2}{3}} = \frac{2^{3x-4}}{8}$.

9 (i) Write as a power of 3:

(a) 243 (b) $\sqrt{27}$

(ii) Solve for x the equation $3^x = \left(\frac{243}{\sqrt{27}}\right)^2$.

10 (i) Write $2^6 - 2^5$ in the form 2^k, where $k \in \mathbb{N}$.

(ii) Solve for x the equation:

$2^{3x-4} = 2^6 - 2^5$.

11 (i) Write $\sqrt{125}$ as a power of 5.

(ii) Solve for x the equation

$\frac{5^{2x+1}}{5} = \left(\frac{1}{\sqrt{125}}\right)^2$.

12 Solve for p the equation $9^p = \frac{1}{\sqrt{3}}$.

13 If $\frac{5^2 \times 25^{\frac{1}{2}}}{125^{\frac{2}{3}} \times 5^3} = 5^n$, find n, where $n \in \mathbb{Z}$.

14 Solve the equation $\frac{\sqrt[3]{27} \times 3}{9^{\frac{1}{2}} \times 3^4} = 3^n$,

where $n \in \mathbb{Z}$.

Section 17E Recurring Decimals

Divide 10 by 3. You get 3.33333333333333…

On the calculator, you see $3.\dot{3}$. The dot on top of the second 3 indicates that the 3s go on indefinitely.

Similarly, 3.456745674567… is written as $3.\dot{4}56\dot{7}$.

These are examples of **recurring decimals**.

Other examples:

Recurring decimal	Written as
3.65656565…	$3.\dot{6}\dot{5}$
5.494494494…	$5.\dot{4}9\dot{4}$
6.12341234…	$6.\dot{1}23\dot{4}$

Despite the fact that the decimals never end, we can still write these numbers as fractions.

Example 1

Express 0.3333333… as a rational number.

Solution

Let $x = 0.3333333\ldots$

$\Rightarrow 10x = 3.3333333\ldots$

$\Rightarrow 9x = 3.3333333\ldots - 0.3333333\ldots$

$\Rightarrow 9x = 3$

$\Rightarrow x = \frac{3}{9} = \frac{1}{3}$

Example 2

Express 0.246246246… as a rational number.

Solution

Let $x = 0.246246246\ldots$

$\Rightarrow 1000x = 246.246246246\ldots$

$\Rightarrow 999x = 246.246246246\ldots - 0.246246246\ldots$

$\Rightarrow 999x = 246$

$\Rightarrow x = \frac{246}{999}$

We can see that even though there is no limit to the number of decimal places, we can write the number as a fraction **provided the decimals repeat at some stage**. In the next section, we deal with numbers where this does not happen.

Activity 17.4

1 Express 0.22222222… as a rational number.

2 Express 0.66666… as a fraction.

3 Express 0.4545454545… as a rational number.

4 Express 0.237892378923789… as a rational number.

5 Express $5.\dot{4}9\dot{4}$ in the form $\frac{a}{b}$ where $a, b \in \mathbb{Z}$.

6 Express $0.\dot{3}2\dot{3}$ in the form $\frac{a}{b}$ where $a, b \in \mathbb{Z}$.

7 Express 1.444444… as a rational number.

8 Can you express 1.414213562… as a rational number? Why? Why is this number different from the previous ones in this activity?

9 The following are the first 60 digits of a very familiar number which you have been using for some time. What number is it?

3.14159265358979323846264338327950288419716939937510582097494…

Why can't it be written as a rational number?

Section 17F Irrational Numbers

Remember what 'square root' means. When we say that $\sqrt{25} = 5$, we are getting a number which when multiplied by itself gives 25.

We can write a few of the natural numbers in a table and see their squares.

Natural numbers	1	2	3	4	5	6	7	…
Squares	1	4	9	16	25	36	49	…

Only the natural numbers that appear on the bottom line of this table have a square root which is a natural number. They are known as **perfect squares**.

The square roots of all other numbers are not natural numbers. Examples are $\sqrt{2}, \sqrt{3}, \sqrt{5}$, etc. In fact, these numbers cannot be written as fractions either. They are known as **irrational numbers** for this reason. Irrational numbers like these are also called **surds**.

One of the most famous irrational numbers is $\sqrt{2}$. When we insert $\sqrt{2}$ on a calculator which has a 10-digit display, we get 1.414213562. But these digits are only the start of a never-ending sequence of digits which never shows a pattern.

(Remember that we were able to express numbers with an infinite number of decimal places as fractions **if they had a repeating pattern**. Irrational numbers show no pattern.)

Connections

We find $\sqrt{2}$ appearing in geometry constructions quite often.

Take a square of side 1 unit, for example.
Using Pythagoras' theorem, we get:

$1^2 + 1^2 = 1 + 1 = 2$

$\therefore$ the diagonal is $\sqrt{2}$ units long.

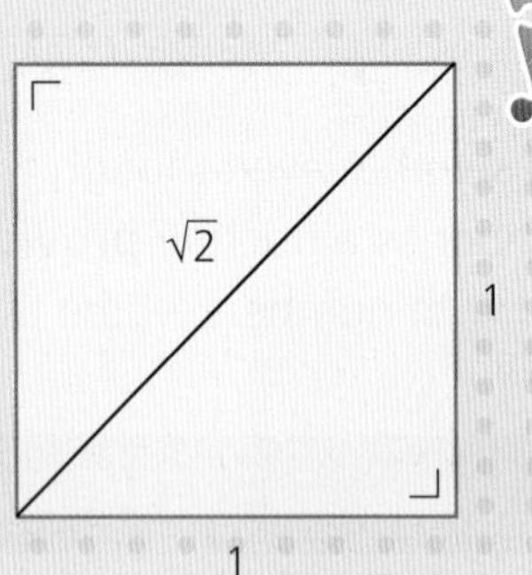

Connections

Locating $\sqrt{2}$ on the Number Line

Even though we cannot write $\sqrt{2}$ precisely, we can still find its location on the number line by using Pythagoras' theorem and our geometry constructions.

- On the number line at number 1, construct a perpendicular line segment of length 1 unit.

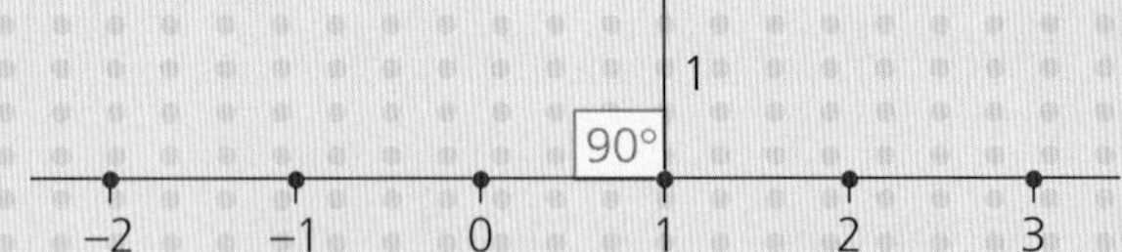

- Complete the right-angled triangle as shown. By our work above with Pythagoras' Theorem, the hypotenuse = $\sqrt{2}$ units.

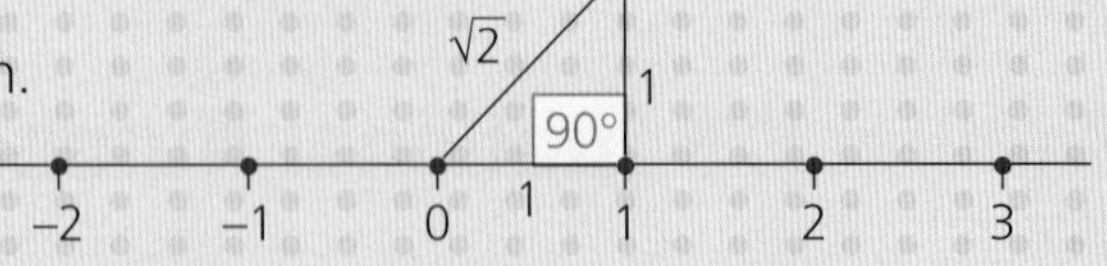

- Using a compass, draw an arc with centre at point 0 and radius = the hypotenuse, to meet the number line. This point is the location of $\sqrt{2}$ on the number line.

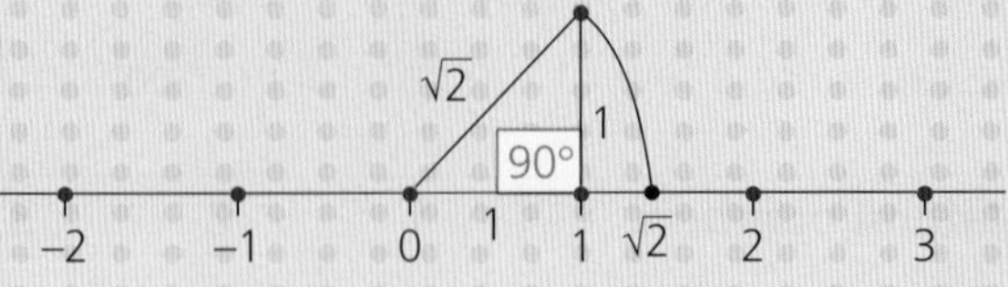

Historical Background

The number π is another famous irrational number. You will recall that π is the number you get when you divide the circumference of any circle by its diameter. Even though this number was known for many hundreds of years, it was not until 1767 that it was proved to be irrational by Swiss mathematician Johann Heinrich Lambert.

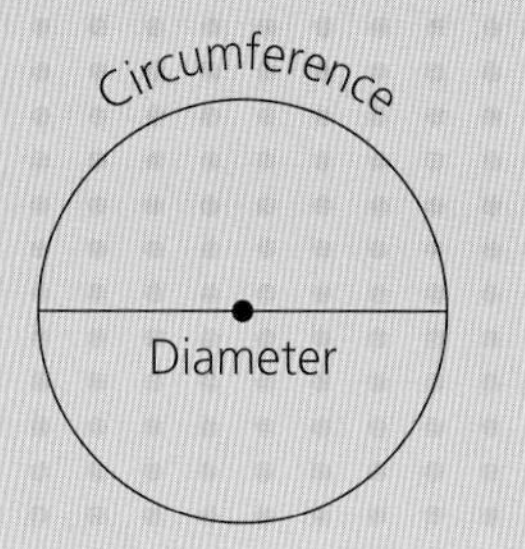

Real Numbers $\mathbb{R}$

When we put the rational numbers together with the irrational numbers, we get the set of real numbers $\mathbb{R}$. The **real numbers** completely 'fill up' the number line:

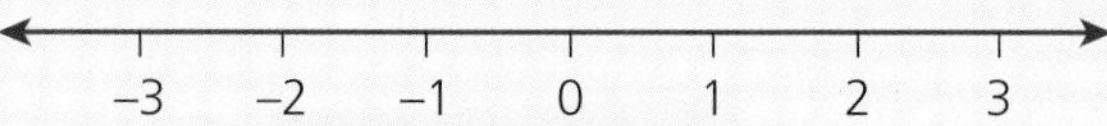

The irrational numbers are thus often referred to as $\mathbb{R}\backslash\mathbb{Q}$.

Now we have all the sets of numbers up to the real numbers: $\mathbb{N}$, $\mathbb{Z}$, $\mathbb{Q}$ and $\mathbb{R}$.

We can represent them on a Venn diagram like this:

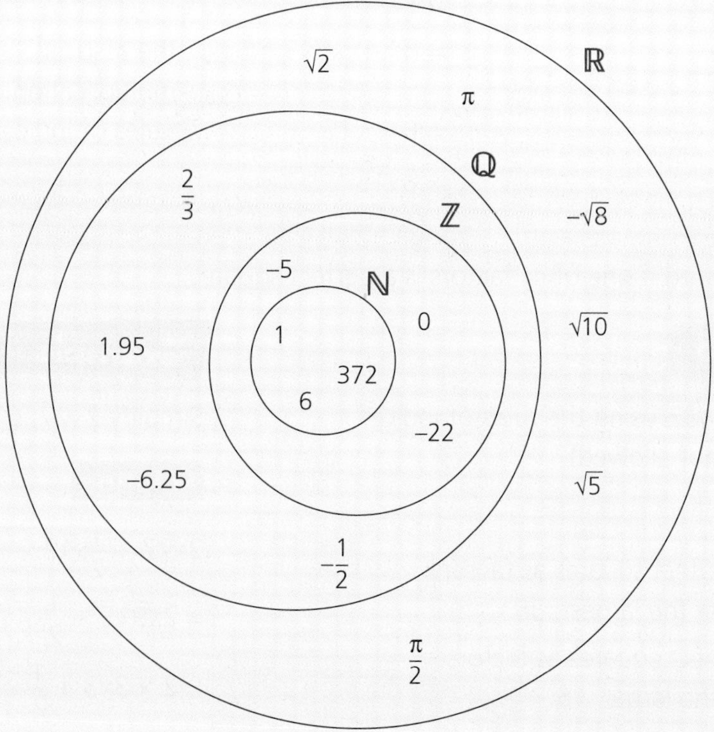

These are just a very small selection of the numbers in these sets.

We can see that $\mathbb{N} \subset \mathbb{Z} \subset \mathbb{Q} \subset \mathbb{R}$.

Working with Surds

Remember that $\sqrt{a} = a^{\frac{1}{2}}$, so when we work with surds we are really working with indices, and the same rules apply.

Rules	Examples
$\sqrt{a}\sqrt{a} = a^{\frac{1}{2}} \times a^{\frac{1}{2}} = a^1 = a$	$\sqrt{6}\sqrt{6} = 6^{\frac{1}{2}} \times 6^{\frac{1}{2}} = 6^1 = 6$ $2\sqrt{5} \times 3\sqrt{5} = (2 \times 3) \times 5^{\frac{1}{2}} \times 5^{\frac{1}{2}} = 6 \times 5^1 = 30$
$\sqrt{a}\sqrt{b} = a^{\frac{1}{2}} \times b^{\frac{1}{2}} = (ab)^{\frac{1}{2}} = \sqrt{ab}$	$\sqrt{3}\sqrt{5} = 3^{\frac{1}{2}} \times 5^{\frac{1}{2}} = (3 \times 5)^{\frac{1}{2}} = 15^{\frac{1}{2}} = \sqrt{15}$
$\frac{\sqrt{a}}{\sqrt{b}} = \frac{a^{\frac{1}{2}}}{b^{\frac{1}{2}}} = \left(\frac{a}{b}\right)^{\frac{1}{2}} = \sqrt{\frac{a}{b}}$	$\frac{\sqrt{15}}{\sqrt{5}} = \sqrt{\frac{15}{5}} = \sqrt{3}$
Like terms can be added.	$4\sqrt{2} + 5\sqrt{2} - 6\sqrt{2} = 9\sqrt{2} - 6\sqrt{2} = 3\sqrt{2}$
Unlike terms cannot be added, so $\sqrt{a} + \sqrt{b}$ cannot be simplified, $\sqrt{a} - \sqrt{b}$ cannot be simplified.	$\sqrt{16} + \sqrt{9} \neq \sqrt{25}$ $\sqrt{25} - \sqrt{16} \neq \sqrt{9}$

Example 1

Simplify $3\sqrt{5} + 4\sqrt{5} - 2\sqrt{5}$.

Solution

$3\sqrt{5} + 4\sqrt{5} - 2\sqrt{5}$

$= 7\sqrt{5} - 2\sqrt{5}$

$= 5\sqrt{5}$

Example 2

Simplify $(2\sqrt{3}) \times (4\sqrt{5})$.

Solution

$(2\sqrt{3}) \times (4\sqrt{5})$

$= (2)(4) \times (\sqrt{3})(\sqrt{5})$ ... the associative law for multiplication

$= 8 \times \sqrt{15}$ .... rules of indices

$= 8\sqrt{15}$

We can simplify a surd if one of its factors is a perfect square.

Example 3

Simplify $\sqrt{72} + \sqrt{32}$ using the rules of indices (i.e. calculator not allowed).

Solution

72 has three perfect squares as factors: 4, 9 and 36. Use the largest: 36.

32 has two perfect squares as factors: 4 and 16. Use the larger: 16.

$\Rightarrow \sqrt{72} + \sqrt{32}$

$= \sqrt{2 \times 36} + \sqrt{2 \times 16}$

$= \sqrt{2} \times \sqrt{36} + \sqrt{2} \times \sqrt{16}$

$= 6\sqrt{2} + 4\sqrt{2}$

$= 10\sqrt{2}$

Example 4

Simplify $2\sqrt{27} + \frac{1}{2}\sqrt{12} - \sqrt{75}$.

Solution

$2\sqrt{27} + \frac{1}{2}\sqrt{12} - \sqrt{75}$

$= 2\sqrt{9}\sqrt{3} + \frac{1}{2}\sqrt{4}\sqrt{3} - \sqrt{25}\sqrt{3}$

$= 2 \times 3\sqrt{3} + \frac{1}{2} \times 2\sqrt{3} - 5\sqrt{3}$

$= 6\sqrt{3} + \sqrt{3} - 5\sqrt{3}$

$= 2\sqrt{3}$

Example 5

Simplify $(3 + \sqrt{5})(4 - 2\sqrt{5})$.

Solution

$(3 + \sqrt{5})(4 - 2\sqrt{5})$

$= 3(4 - 2\sqrt{5}) + \sqrt{5}(4 - 2\sqrt{5})$

$= 12 - 6\sqrt{5} + 4\sqrt{5} - 2(5)$

$= 2 - 2\sqrt{5}$

Example 6

Simplify $\dfrac{-7 + \sqrt{98}}{7}$.

Solution

$\dfrac{-7 + \sqrt{98}}{7}$

$= \dfrac{-7 + \sqrt{49 \times 2}}{7}$

$= \dfrac{-7 + 7\sqrt{2}}{7}$

$= -1 + \sqrt{2}$

Example 7

(i) Write $\dfrac{1}{\sqrt{3}}$ in the form $a\sqrt{3}$, where $a \in \mathbb{Q}$.

Solution

(i) $\dfrac{1}{\sqrt{3}} = \dfrac{1}{\sqrt{3}} \times \dfrac{\sqrt{3}}{\sqrt{3}}$

$= \dfrac{\sqrt{3}}{3}$

$= \dfrac{1}{3}\sqrt{3}$

(ii) Write $\dfrac{2}{\sqrt{5}}$ in the form $a\sqrt{5}$, where $a \in \mathbb{Q}$.

Solution

(ii) $\dfrac{2}{\sqrt{5}} = \dfrac{2}{\sqrt{5}} \times \dfrac{\sqrt{5}}{\sqrt{5}}$

$= \dfrac{2\sqrt{5}}{5}$

$= \dfrac{2}{5}\sqrt{5}$

Example 8

Write $\dfrac{4 + \sqrt{3}}{\sqrt{2}}$ in the form $a\sqrt{b} + c\sqrt{d}$,

where $a, c \in \mathbb{Q}$ and $b, d \in \mathbb{N}$.

Solution

$\dfrac{4 + \sqrt{3}}{\sqrt{2}} = \dfrac{4 + \sqrt{3}}{\sqrt{2}} \times \dfrac{\sqrt{2}}{\sqrt{2}}$

$= \dfrac{4\sqrt{2} + \sqrt{6}}{2}$

$= 2\sqrt{2} + \dfrac{1}{2}\sqrt{6}$

Activity 17.5

1 (i) Give two reasons why $-\dfrac{3}{4}$ is not a natural number.

The diagram represents the sets: natural numbers $\mathbb{N}$, integers $\mathbb{Z}$, rational numbers $\mathbb{Q}$ and real numbers $\mathbb{R}$.

(ii) Copy the diagram into your copybook.

(iii) Insert each of the following numbers in the correct place on the diagram.

$-5, 0, \dfrac{1}{2}, 7, \sqrt{5}, -5.6, 5^{-1}, \pi, \sqrt{2}, \sqrt{9}$

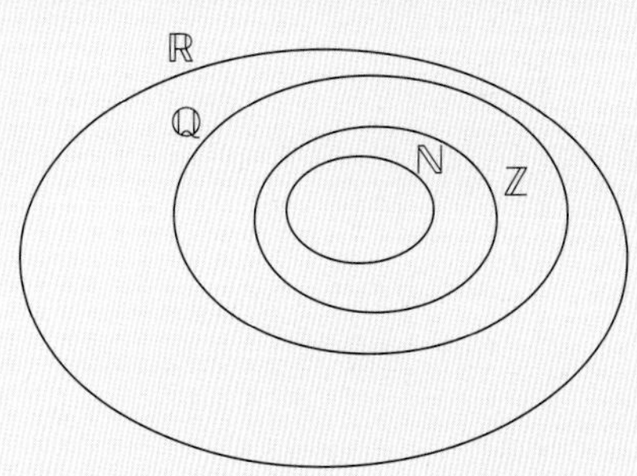

Number

2 The table shows a column of numbers and five sets that each number could be an element of. Copy the table into your copybook and tick each box where the number is an element of that set.

Number	Natural numbers $\mathbb{N}$	Integers $\mathbb{Z}$	Rational numbers $\mathbb{Q}$	$\mathbb{R}\backslash\mathbb{Q}$	Real numbers $\mathbb{R}$
4					
–77					
–1.6					
$2\frac{1}{5}$					
$\sqrt{4}$					
$\frac{\pi}{2}$					
$\sqrt{5}$					

3 Simplify:

(i) $2\sqrt{5} + 7\sqrt{5}$

(ii) $3\sqrt{7} + 7\sqrt{3} + 5\sqrt{7} - 2\sqrt{3}$

(iii) $2\sqrt{3} \times 5\sqrt{3}$

(iv) $(-4\sqrt{5})(\sqrt{5})$

(v) $4\sqrt{7} \times 3\sqrt{2}$

(vi) $(5\sqrt{2})(-3\sqrt{2})$

4 Simplify:

(i) $3\sqrt{2} + 10\sqrt{2}$

(ii) $4\sqrt{6} + 2\sqrt{13} + 5\sqrt{13} - 3\sqrt{6}$

(iii) $4\sqrt{6} \times 5\sqrt{6}$

(iv) $(3\sqrt{2})(-\sqrt{5})$

(v) $-3\sqrt{17} \times 4\sqrt{2}$

(vi) $(7\sqrt{3})(-5\sqrt{3})$

5 Simplify these surds as far as possible.

(i) $\sqrt{45}$ (iii) $\sqrt{63}$ (v) $\sqrt{72}$

(ii) $\sqrt{24}$ (iv) $\sqrt{200}$ (vi) $\sqrt{8}$

6 Simplify:

(i) $\sqrt{\frac{9}{16}}$ (iv) $2\sqrt{5} + 3\sqrt{5}$

(ii) $4\sqrt{32}$ (v) $5\sqrt{7} - 2\sqrt{7}$

(iii) $\sqrt{80}$

7 Simplify each of the following as far as possible.

(i) $\sqrt{75} + \sqrt{48} - \sqrt{12}$

(ii) $\sqrt{45} + \sqrt{20} - \sqrt{5}$

(iii) $\sqrt{50} + \sqrt{32} - \sqrt{8}$

(iv) $\sqrt{28} + \sqrt{63} - \sqrt{7}$

8 In each of the following, find the value of p.

(i) $\sqrt{48} + \sqrt{75} = p\sqrt{3}$

(ii) $\sqrt{125} - \sqrt{45} = p\sqrt{5}$

(iii) $3\sqrt{108} - \sqrt{12} = p\sqrt{3}$

(iv) $\sqrt{112} - \sqrt{28} = p\sqrt{7}$

9 Simplify each of the following as far as possible.

(i) $\sqrt{8} \times 6\sqrt{2}$

(ii) $(-4\sqrt{18})(\sqrt{2})$

(iii) $3\sqrt{28} \times 3\sqrt{2}$

(iv) $(3\sqrt{27})(-4\sqrt{12})$

(v) $(3\sqrt{5})(2\sqrt{7})$

10 Show that $(3\sqrt{5} - 2)(3\sqrt{5} + 2)$ simplifies to a natural number.

11 Multiply out and simplify as far as possible:

(i) $(3 + \sqrt{2})(3 - \sqrt{2})$

(ii) $(7 + \sqrt{5})(7 - \sqrt{5})$

(iii) $(\sqrt{7} + \sqrt{6})(\sqrt{7} - \sqrt{6})$

(iv) $(5 + \sqrt{2})^2$

12 The rectangle and square below have the same area. The dimensions of both are in cm. The diagrams are not drawn to scale.

$6 - \sqrt{11}$

$6 + \sqrt{11}$

(i) Find the area of the rectangle.

(ii) Find the length of one side of the square.

13 Simplify $\sqrt{5}(\sqrt{2} + \sqrt{5}) - \sqrt{8}(\sqrt{2} - \sqrt{5})$ without using a calculator. Express your answer in the form $p + q\sqrt{r}$, where $p, q, r \in \mathbb{N}$.

14 Write $\dfrac{\sqrt{3} \times 81}{3^3}$ in the form 3^n where $n \in \mathbb{Q}$.

15 Let $a = \sqrt{5}$.

(i) Copy the table below into your copybook. For each of the numbers in the table, tick (✓) the correct box to say whether it is rational or irrational. Show all your calculations.

Number	Rational	Irrational
a		
a^{-2}		
$(-a)^2$		
$(a^{-1})^2$		
$a^2 - 7$		

(ii) Mark the numbers in your table on a number line and label each number clearly.

16 Simplify $\sqrt{3}(2\sqrt{6} - 4\sqrt{3}) - \sqrt{10}(3\sqrt{5} - 2\sqrt{10})$ without using a calculator. Express your answer in the form $a + b\sqrt{2}$, where $a, b \in \mathbb{Z}$.

17 Write $\dfrac{1}{\sqrt{2}}$ in the form $a\sqrt{2}$, where $a \in \mathbb{Q}$.

18 Write $\dfrac{2}{\sqrt{3}}$ in the form $a\sqrt{3}$, where $a \in \mathbb{Q}$.

19 Write each of the following in the form $a\sqrt{b} + c\sqrt{d}$, where $a, c \in \mathbb{Q}$ and $b, d \in \mathbb{N}$.

(i) $\dfrac{3 + \sqrt{2}}{\sqrt{3}}$ (ii) $\dfrac{\sqrt{5} - 1}{\sqrt{2}}$ (iii) $\dfrac{5 - \sqrt{3}}{\sqrt{5}}$

Section 17G Scientific Notation

Scientific notation is a special way of writing extremely large or small numbers.

It is commonly used in Astronomy, Science and Engineering.

Numbers in scientific notation are written in the form $a \times 10^n$, where $1 \leq a < 10$ and $n \in \mathbb{Z}$.

For example,

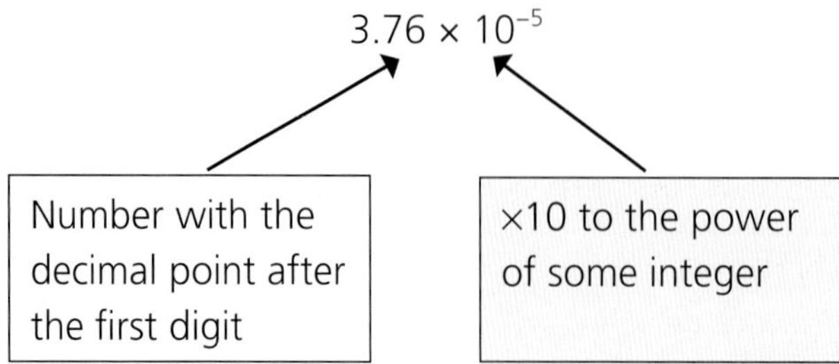

Example 1

Some tortoises have been known to live more than 150 years, or about 4 730 000 000 seconds. Express this number of seconds in scientific notation.

Solution

4 730 000 000 = 4.73×10^9 seconds, since 4.73 would have to be **multiplied** by 10 nine times to get 4 730 000 000.

Example 2

Hair on the human body can grow as fast as 0.000 000 004 3 metres per second.

Express this rate in scientific notation.

Solution

0.000 000 004 3 = 4.3×10^{-9} m/s, since 4.3 would have to be **divided** by 10 nine times to get 0.000 000 004 3.

Example 3

Write the reciprocal of 10 000 in the form 1×10^n, where $n \in \mathbb{Z}$.

Solution

The reciprocal of 10 000 $= \dfrac{1}{10\,000}$

$= 0.0001$

$= 1 \times 10^{-4}$

Example 4

Calculate $(4.6 \times 10^8) \times (3.1 \times 10^{-3})$ and give your answer in scientific notation.

Solution

$(4.6 \times 10^8) \times (3.1 \times 10^{-3}) = (4.6)(3.1) \times (10^8)(10^{-3})$ ...associative law for multiplication

$= 14.26 \times 10^5$

$= 1.426 \times 10^6$ ...we must have $1 \leq a < 10$.

Alternatively, using a calculator:

Type 

1426000 will appear on the screen.

Change to scientific notation: 1.426×10^6

Example 5

Calculate $(9.5 \times 10^{-3}) + (2.8 \times 10^{-4})$.

Solution

- Write the numbers in decimal (ordinary) form and add.

  0.0095 + 0.000 28

  = 0.009 78

  Write the answer in scientific notation: 9.78×10^{-3}
- Using a calculator:

  Type 9 · 5 $\times 10^x$ − 3 + 2 · 8 $\times 10^x$ − 4 =

  9.78×10^{-3} will appear on the screen.

Activity 17.6

1 The longest human life recorded was more than 122 years, or about 3 850 000 000 seconds. Express this number of seconds in scientific notation.

2 Write each of the following values in scientific notation.

(i) 760

(ii) 4620

(iii) 25 000 000

(iv) 315 000

(v) 1 075 000 000

(vi) 63 000 000 000 000

3 The mass of one electron is 9.11×10^{-28} grams. A uranium atom contains 92 electrons. Find the total mass of the electrons in a uranium atom. Express your answer in scientific notation.

4 Write each of the following values in the form $a \times 10^n$, where $1 \le a < 10$, $n \in \mathbb{Z}$.

(i) 0.00086
(ii) 0.00462
(iii) 27 000 000
(iv) 0.000 000 326
(v) 1 077 000 000
(vi) 0.000 000 078

5 Given that 1 billion is a thousand million, find the sum of €4.7 billion and €600 million.

6 Express each of these as a decimal number.

(i) 6.3×10^5
(ii) 9.2×10^{-5}
(iii) 3.45×10^6
(iv) 2.9×10^{-4}
(v) 8.23×10^8
(vi) 3.3×10^{-6}
(vii) 1×10^{-3}

7 The amount of gold in the Earth's crust is about 120 000 000 000 000 kilograms. Express this amount in the form $a \times 10^n$, where $1 \le a < 10$, $n \in \mathbb{Z}$.

8 Write the reciprocal of 100 000 in the form 1×10^n, where $n \in \mathbb{Z}$.

9 Write the reciprocal of 400 000 in the form $a \times 10^n$, where $1 \le a < 10$, $n \in \mathbb{Z}$.

10 Calculate each of the following and give your answers in scientific notation.

(i) $8.1 \times 10^3 + 3.2 \times 10^2$
(ii) $1.8 \times 10^4 - 4.5 \times 10^3$
(iii) $6.5 \times 10^2 + 3.2 \times 10^2$
(iv) $(2.2 \times 10^{-2}) - (5 \times 10^{-3})$
(v) $(3 \times 10^{-3}) + (9 \times 10^{-4})$
(vi) $(5 \times 10^{-2}) - (7 \times 10^{-6})$

11 Our nearest star (other than the sun) is Alpha Centauri.

(i) Alpha Centauri is 41 600 000 000 000 000 metres from our sun. Express this distance in kilometres in scientific notation.
(ii) Alpha Centauri is actually a double star. The two stars that comprise it are 3 500 000 000 metres apart. Express this distance in kilometres in scientific notation.

12 Write the reciprocal of 500 000 in the form 2×10^n, where $n \in \mathbb{Z}$.

13 Calculate each of the following and give your answers in the form $a \times 10^n$, where $1 \le a < 10$, $n \in \mathbb{Z}$.

(i) $(4.3 \times 10^3) \times (2 \times 10^4)$
(ii) $(9 \times 10^{-3}) \times (3 \times 10^1)$
(iii) $(5.2 \times 10^{-3}) \times (4 \times 10^4)$
(iv) $(3.3 \times 10^4) \times (3 \times 10^{-4})$

14 Calculate each of the following and give your answers in scientific notation.

(i) $\dfrac{5 \times 10^5}{2.5 \times 10^2}$
(ii) $\dfrac{7.4 \times 10^4}{2 \times 10^{-4}}$
(iii) $\dfrac{8.8 \times 10^{-3}}{1.1 \times 10^{-5}}$
(iv) $\dfrac{28 \times 10^5}{2 \times 10^{-1}}$

15 Calculate each of the following and express your answers in scientific notation.

(i) $\dfrac{(2 \times 10^4) + (6 \times 10^5)}{(2 \times 10^3)}$
(ii) $\dfrac{(3.5 \times 10^6) - (20 \times 10^4)}{(3 \times 10^4)}$
(iii) $\dfrac{(6.1 \times 10^{-3}) \times (4 \times 10^4)}{(2 \times 10^3)}$

16 Add 1.8×10^6 and 3.5 million.
Give your answer in the form $a \times 10^n$, where $1 \le a < 10$, $n \in \mathbb{Z}$.

17 The diameters of Venus and Saturn are 1.21×10^4 km and 1.21×10^5 km respectively.
What is the difference between the diameters of the two planets?
Give your answer in the form $a \times 10^n$, where $1 \le a < 10$, $n \in \mathbb{Z}$.

18 Given that $x = 2 \times 10^{-4}$ and $y = 7 \times 10^{-3}$, evaluate $x + 5y$.
Express your answer in the form $a \times 10^n$, where $1 \le a < 10$, $n \in \mathbb{Z}$.

19 Light travels at a speed of approximately (2.9×10^5) km/s. How many kilometres will light travel in 7 seconds?
Express your answer in the form $a \times 10^n$, where $1 \le a < 10$, $n \in \mathbb{Z}$.

Section 17H Exploring Even, Odd and Prime Numbers

An **even** number is a number which can be divided by 2 without remainder.
The set of even numbers = {2, 4, 6, 8, 10, ...}
Thus, every even number = 2 × some number.
If we let n = any number, then every even number is of the form $2n$.

An **odd** number is a number which cannot be divided by 2 without remainder.
The set of odd numbers = {1, 3, 5, 7, 9, ...}
Thus, every odd number = (2 × some number) – 1.
If we let n = any number, then every odd number is of the form $(2n - 1)$.
A number of the form $(2n + 1)$ is also odd.

A **prime number** is a number that is divisible only by itself and 1.
Thus, the prime numbers = {2, 3, 5, 7, 11, 13, 17, 19, 23, ...}

The square of every number is never negative. For example:
$(3)^2 = +9$, and
$(-3)^2 = +9$

Connections

Connection to Algebra

Remember that algebra is just generalised arithmetic. We can explore number theory through algebra.

Example 1

Show that $(3x - 2)^2 + 12x$ is positive for all values of $x \in \mathbb{R}$.

Solution

$(3x - 2)^2 + 12x$

$= 9x^2 - 12x + 4 + 12x$

$= 9x^2 + 4$

But x^2 is positive, so $9x^2$ is positive and $9x^2 + 4$ is positive QED.

Example 2

Prove that the sum of any two even numbers is even.

Solution

Let $2m$ be one even number and let $2n$ be the other even number, where m and n are any two natural numbers.

Then the sum of these two numbers $= 2m + 2n$

$= 2(m + n)$

which is a multiple of 2 and thus is even.

Example 3

Prove that the sum of any odd number and any even number is odd.

Solution

Let $2m$ be the even number, where m is any natural number.

Let $(2n - 1)$ be the odd number, where n is any natural number.

Then the sum of these numbers $= 2m + (2n - 1)$

$= 2m + 2n - 1$

$= 2(m + n) - 1$

= an odd number

Activity 17.7

1 List all the prime numbers less than 50.

2 Find the prime factors of 72.

3 It is thought that all even numbers greater than 4 can be written as the sum of two odd prime numbers.

(i) Write down the even numbers from 6 to 16 as the sum of two odd prime numbers (e.g. $6 = 3 + 3$).

(ii) Can you do this for 86?

4 A pair of consecutive prime numbers which differ by 2 are known as 'twin primes'. For example, 3 and 5 are twin primes and so are 5 and 7. Can you list all the twin primes less than 100?

5 List any five **even** natural numbers. Verify that each is of the form $2m$, where m is any whole number.

6 List any five **odd** natural numbers. Verify that each is of the form $2m - 1$, where m is any natural number.

7 Take any two even natural numbers and add them. Is your result even or odd? Try this for five other pairs of even natural numbers. Are the results always even, always odd, or sometimes even and sometimes odd?

8 Prove your answer to question **7**.

Hint

› Let $2m$ be one even number and $2n$ be the other even number.

9 Take any two odd whole numbers and add them. Is your result even or odd? Try this for five other pairs of odd whole numbers. Are the results always even, always odd, or sometimes even and sometimes odd?

10 Prove your answer to question **9**.

11 Take any two whole numbers, one even the other odd. Add them. Is your result even or odd? Try this for five other pairs of whole numbers, one even and one odd. Are the results always even, always odd, or sometimes even and sometimes odd?

12 Prove your answer to question **11**.

13 Now do questions **7**, **9** and **11** again, but this time replace the word 'add' with the word 'subtract'. Summarise your findings.

14 Take any two even whole numbers and multiply them. Are the results always even, always odd, or sometimes even and sometimes odd? Can you prove this?

15 Take any two odd whole numbers and multiply them. Are the results always even, always odd, or sometimes even and sometimes odd? Can you prove this?

16 Show by examples that if a is odd, then a^2 is odd. Can you prove this?

17 Take any two natural numbers, one even the other odd. Multiply them. Is your result even or odd? Try this for five other pairs of natural numbers, one even and one odd. Are the results always even, always odd, or sometimes even and sometimes odd? Can you prove this?

18 Find two even whole numbers where one is a multiple of the other. Divide the smaller into the bigger. Is the result even or odd? Are the results always the same?

19 Show, by factorising, that $x^2 - 4x + 4$ is positive for all values of $x \in \mathbb{R}$.

Revision Activity 17

1 (a) The mean distance from the Earth to the sun is 149 597 871 km. Write this number in the form $a \times 10^n$, where $1 \leq a < 10$ and $n \in \mathbb{Z}$, correct to two significant figures.

(b) (i) Write each of the numbers below as a decimal correct to two decimal places.

	A	B	C	D	E	F
Number	3.4	$\sqrt{3}$	$\frac{187}{63}$	tan 58°	$\frac{\pi}{2}$	350%
Decimal number						

(ii) Mark the numbers in the table on a number line and label each number clearly.

2 (a) Find $\sqrt[3]{139.6}$ correct to three decimal places.

(b) Find the exact value of $\frac{1}{(0.5)^3} - (1.2)^2$.

(c) Write down the whole number closest to $\sqrt{50} + \tan 72°$.

3 (a) Write 7^{-2} and $81^{\frac{1}{2}}$ without using indices.

(b) Express 2^{24} in the form $a \times 10^n$, where $1 \leq a < 10$ and $n \in \mathbb{Z}$, correct to three significant figures.

(c) Show that $\frac{(a\sqrt{a})^3}{a^4}$ simplifies to $\sqrt{a}$.

4 Write $\dfrac{\sqrt{3} \times 81}{3^2}$ in the form 3^n where $n \in \mathbb{Q}$.

5 Simplify $\dfrac{2^8 \times 8^{\frac{2}{3}}}{64^{\frac{1}{2}} \times 4^3}$.

Give your answer in the form 2^n, where $n \in \mathbb{Z}$.

6 Simplify $(\sqrt{6} - 3\sqrt{3})(4\sqrt{3} - 2\sqrt{6})$ without the use of a calculator.

Express your answer in the form $p\sqrt{2} + q$, where $p, q \in \mathbb{Z}$.

7 Simplify (a) $64^{\frac{3}{2}}$ (b) $64^{\frac{2}{3}}$

8 Solve the equation $\dfrac{2^5 \times 8^{\frac{2}{3}}}{64^{\frac{1}{2}} \times 4^2} = 2^n$, where $n \in \mathbb{N}$.

9 (a) Express $(2^3)(2^3)(2^3)(2^3)$ in the form 2^p, where $p \in \mathbb{N}$.

(b) Express $2^3 + 2^3 + 2^3 + 2^3$ in the form 2^p, where $p \in \mathbb{N}$.

10 Express $3^{\frac{1}{2}} + 3^{\frac{1}{2}} + 3^{\frac{1}{2}}$ in the form 3^p, where $p \in \mathbb{Q}$.

Exam-style Questions

1 (a) (i) The columns in the table below represent the following sets of numbers: natural numbers ($\mathbb{N}$), integers ($\mathbb{Z}$), rational numbers ($\mathbb{Q}$), irrational numbers ($\mathbb{R}\backslash\mathbb{Q}$) and real numbers ($\mathbb{R}$).

Copy and complete the table by writing **Yes** into each box whenever the number is an element of that set.

	$\mathbb{N}$	$\mathbb{Z}$	$\mathbb{Q}$	$\mathbb{R}\backslash\mathbb{Q}$	$\mathbb{R}$
$\sqrt{5}$					
8					
–4					
$3\frac{1}{2}$					
$\frac{3\pi}{4}$					

(ii) In the case of $\sqrt{5}$, explain your choice in relation to the set of irrational numbers ($\mathbb{R}\backslash\mathbb{Q}$).

(b) Use the properties of surds to show that $\sqrt{98} - \sqrt{18} + \sqrt{2}$ simplifies to $5\sqrt{2}$.

JCHL 2013 Paper 1

2 (a) Give two reasons why –7.3 is not a natural number.

(b) The diagram represents the sets:

Natural Numbers $\mathbb{N}$

Integers $\mathbb{Z}$

Rational Numbers $\mathbb{Q}$

Real Numbers $\mathbb{R}$

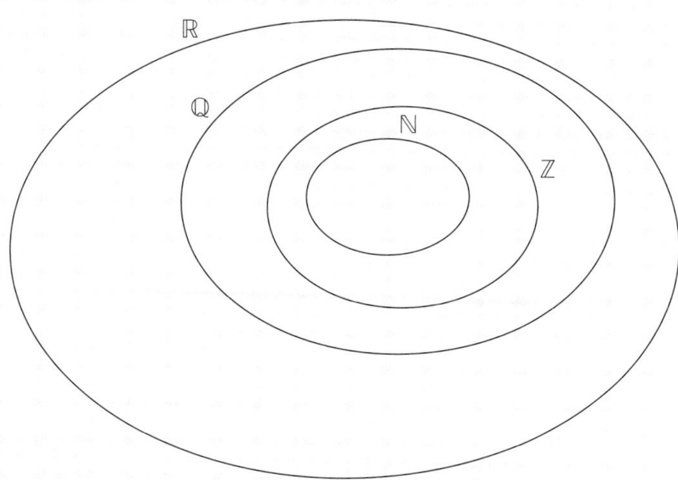

Insert each of the following numbers in the correct place on the diagram.

$-8, \pi, \frac{1}{3}, 6, \sqrt{2}, -4.5$ and 7^{-1}.

JCHL 2012 Paper 1

KEY WORDS AND PHRASES

- **Natural number**
- **Integer**
- **Rational number**
- **Irrational number**
- **Surd**
- **Real number**
- **Recurring decimal**

Chapter Summary 17

- The set of **natural numbers** $\mathbb{N} = \{1, 2, 3, 4, 5, \ldots\}$

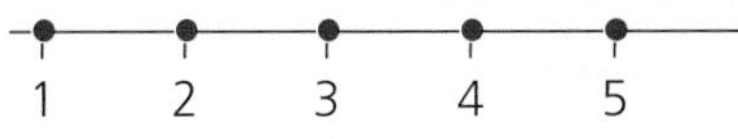

- The set of **integers** $\mathbb{Z} = \{\ldots, -3, -2, -1, 0, 1, 2, 3, \ldots\}$

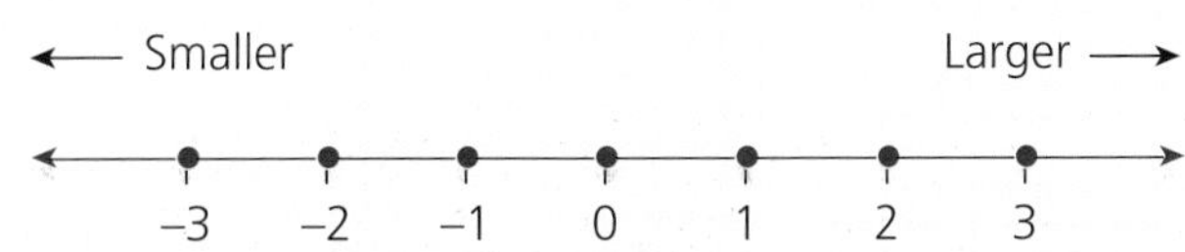

Number

- The **rational numbers** $\mathbb{Q}$ = the set of all numbers which can be written in the form $\frac{p}{q}$ where p and $q \in \mathbb{Z}$ and $q \neq 0$.
- The set of irrational numbers $\mathbb{R}\backslash\mathbb{Q}$ = the set of all numbers which cannot be written in the form $\frac{p}{q}$, e.g. π, $\sqrt{2}$, $\sqrt{5}$ etc.
- **Real numbers** $\mathbb{R}$

  When we put the rational numbers together with the irrational numbers, we get the set of real numbers $\mathbb{R}$. The real numbers 'fill up' the number line completely.
- We cannot divide by zero.
- **Rules of indices**

Rules of indices	Examples
Rule 1: $a^m \times a^n = a^{m+n}$	$5^3 \times 5^6 = 5^{3+6} = 5^9$
Rule 2: $\frac{a^m}{a^n} = a^{m-n}$	$\frac{3^7}{3^5} = 3^{7-5} = 3^2$
Rule 3: $a^0 = 1$	$27^0 = 1$
Rule 4: $(a^m)^n = a^{mn}$	$(3^2)^4 = 3^8$
Rule 5: $a^{-m} = \frac{1}{a^m}$	$5^{-3} = \frac{1}{5^3}$
Rule 6: $a^{\frac{1}{q}} = \sqrt[q]{a}$	$8^{\frac{1}{2}} = \sqrt{8}$
Rule 7: $a^{\frac{p}{q}} = (\sqrt[q]{a})^p$	$27^{\frac{2}{3}} = (\sqrt[3]{27})^2 = 3^2 = 9$
Rule 8: $(ab)^m = a^m b^m$	$(3\sqrt{2})^2 = 3^2 \times (\sqrt{2})^2 = 9 \times 2 = 18$
Rule 9: $\left(\frac{a}{b}\right)^m = \frac{a^m}{b^m}$	$\left(\frac{2}{3}\right)^3 = \frac{2^3}{3^3} = \frac{8}{27}$

- **Operations on surds**

Rules	Examples
$\sqrt{a}\sqrt{a} = a^{\frac{1}{2}} \times a^{\frac{1}{2}} = a^1 = a$	$\sqrt{6}\sqrt{6} = 6^{\frac{1}{2}} \times 6^{\frac{1}{2}} = 6^1 = 6$ $2\sqrt{5} \times 3\sqrt{5} = (2 \times 3) \times 5^{\frac{1}{2}} \times 5^{\frac{1}{2}} = 6 \times 5^1 = 30$
$\sqrt{a}\sqrt{b} = a^{\frac{1}{2}} \times b^{\frac{1}{2}} = (ab)^{\frac{1}{2}} = \sqrt{ab}$	$\sqrt{3}\sqrt{5} = 3^{\frac{1}{2}} \times 5^{\frac{1}{2}} = (3 \times 5)^{\frac{1}{2}} = 15^{\frac{1}{2}} = \sqrt{15}$
$\frac{\sqrt{a}}{\sqrt{b}} = \frac{a^{\frac{1}{2}}}{b^{\frac{1}{2}}} = \left(\frac{a}{b}\right)^{\frac{1}{2}} = \sqrt{\frac{a}{b}}$	$\frac{\sqrt{15}}{\sqrt{5}} = \sqrt{\frac{15}{5}} = \sqrt{3}$
Like terms can be added.	$4\sqrt{2} + 5\sqrt{2} - 6\sqrt{2} = 9\sqrt{2} - 6\sqrt{2} = 3\sqrt{2}$
Unlike terms cannot be added, so $\sqrt{a} + \sqrt{b}$ cannot be simplified, $\sqrt{a} - \sqrt{b}$ cannot be simplified.	$\sqrt{16} + \sqrt{9} \neq \sqrt{25}$ $\sqrt{25} - \sqrt{16} \neq \sqrt{9}$

Probability

Chapter 18

Learning Intentions

In this chapter, you will learn about:

LO: U.5, U.6, SP.1, SP.2

- Counting and probability (review)
- Using binary/counting methods to solve problems involving successive random events where only two possible outcomes apply to each event
- The use of set theory to discuss outcomes and experiments

The Birthday Paradox

Imagine that there are 365 people in a room. It is possible that each one of them has a different birthday. Now if there were just 23 people in a room, what do you think the chances are that at least two of them have the same birthday?

You might be surprised to learn that there is a 50–50 chance of this happening with just 23 people in a room. Furthermore, if you have 47 people in a room there is a 95% chance that at least two of them will have the same birthday. This is known as the **Birthday Paradox** and is just one example of how working with probabilities can sometimes give surprising results.

Section 18A Review of Probability

These are some of the important ideas that we have learned previously.

1. The Fundamental Principle of Counting:
   If one event has m possible outcomes and a second event has n possible outcomes, then the total number of outcomes is $m \times n$.
2. Probability deals with uncertainty and measures the likelihood of an event.

3. The probability scale goes from 0 to 1.

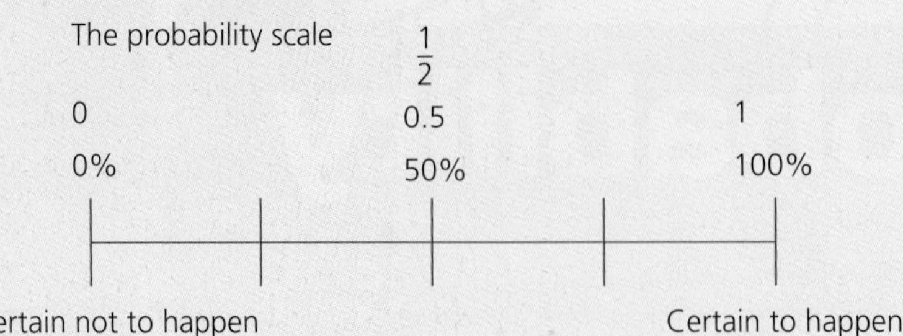

4. **Relative frequency** = $\dfrac{\text{number of times an event occurs in a trial}}{\text{total number of trials}}$
5. As the number of trials increases, the relative frequency leads to better estimates of the probability of an event. In other words, theoretical probability is relative frequency over a very large number of trials.
6. For **equally likely** outcomes:

   Probability of an event $[P(E)] = \dfrac{\text{number of favourable outcomes}}{\text{total number of possible outcomes}}$
7. Expected frequency = probability × the number of trials.
8. Probability of an event **not** happening = 1 – probability that it will happen.

Key Points

- The probability P of any event must satisfy the inequality $0 \leq P \leq 1$. Any probability answer less than 0 or greater than 1 must be incorrect.
- The sum of the probabilities of all the outcomes of an experiment is 1.

The following worked examples will help to revise these topics.

Example 1

(i) When you roll a die, which number is most likely to come up?

(ii) If you roll a die 720 times, how many fives would you expect to get?

Solution

(i) All numbers are equally likely.

(ii) You would expect to get a five in about $\frac{1}{6}$ of the rolls.

Expected frequency = probability × the number of trials

$= 720 \times \frac{1}{6}$

$= 120$ fives

Example 2

The probability that Tom scores a goal in a match is $\frac{2}{3}$. What is the probability that Tom does not score?

Solution

Either Tom scores a goal or he does not score,

so $P(\text{score}) + P(\text{no score}) = 1$

$\Rightarrow \quad P(\text{no score}) = 1 - P(\text{score})$

$= 1 - \frac{2}{3}$

$= \frac{1}{3}$

Example 3

Joe tossed a coin 300 times and threw 164 heads. Anna tossed the same coin 400 times and threw 235 heads. Joe and Anna think that this coin may be biased.

(i) Give a reason why they think that the coin may be biased.

(ii) Isabella used all the above data and calculated that an estimate of the probability of throwing a head with this coin is 0.57. Show how Isabella might have calculated this probability.

Solution

(i) The probability of throwing a head with a fair coin = $\frac{1}{2}$.

Therefore in 300 tosses of a coin we expect $\left(300 \times \frac{1}{2}\right) = 150$ heads.

In 400 tosses, the expected number of heads = 200.

In each of Joe and Anna's experiments, the number of heads was greater than the expected number and the number of trials was quite large, so the coin might be biased. We would need a larger number of trials to say this with more confidence.

(ii) Isabella's calculations:

Total number of trials = 300 + 400 = 700

Total number of heads = 164 + 235 = 399

Relative frequency of getting a head

$= \frac{399}{700} = 0.57$

Using Relative Frequency to Estimate Probabilities

We have learned that we can use relative frequency to estimate the probability of an event. Example 4, which follows, has more searching questions.

Example 4

The colours of 500 cars that pass a particular set of traffic lights during a two-hour period are recorded by a group of students.

Colour	Frequency	Relative frequency	Daily frequency (see part (v))
Red	70		
Blue	100		
Yellow	45		
White	55		
Black			
Silver	140		
Total	500		

(i) Calculate the number of black cars and write it into the table.

(ii) Calculate the relative frequency of each colour and write these into the table.

(iii) Suggest a method to check that your relative frequency calculations are correct. Perform this check.

(iv) What is the probability that the next car to pass the lights is red?

(v) Use the information to estimate the frequency of each colour if 2400 cars pass the lights in a full day. Write this information into the table.

(vi) The data collected by the students is not a random sample of the cars passing throughout the day. Do you think that this makes your estimates in part (v) unreliable? Give a reason for your answer.

Solution

(i) $500 - (70 + 100 + 45 + 55 + 140) = 500 - 410$

$= 90$ black cars

(ii)

Colour	Frequency	Relative frequency	Daily frequency (see part (v))
Red	70	$\frac{70}{500} = 0.14$	336
Blue	100	$\frac{100}{500} = 0.2$	480
Yellow	45	$\frac{45}{500} = 0.09$	216
White	55	$\frac{55}{500} = 0.11$	264
Black	90	$\frac{90}{500} = 0.18$	432
Silver	140	$\frac{140}{500} = 0.28$	672
Total	500	$\frac{500}{500} = 1$	2400

(iii) The sum of the relative frequencies should be 1
or The percentages should sum to 100%.
Check: $0.14 + 0.2 + 0.09 + 0.11 + 0.18 + 0.28 = 1$ ✓

(iv) $\frac{70}{500} = 0.14 = 14\%$

(v) Frequency of each colour:

Red: $\frac{70}{500} \times 2400 = 336$

Blue: $\frac{100}{500} \times 2400 = 480$

Yellow: $\frac{45}{500} \times 2400 = 216$

White: $\frac{55}{500} \times 2400 = 264$

Black: $\frac{90}{500} \times 2400 = 432$

Silver: $\frac{140}{500} \times 2400 = 672$

(vi) No. A test is reliable if repeated runs of the test would give the same results. There is no reason to say that if this test was run again it would be different because of the sample not being random. The colour of a vehicle is random and running the test at different times of the day or on different days would not necessarily make the test any more reliable.

Using Relative Frequency to Check for Fairness

Sometimes we wish to see if a coin or a die or a spinner is fair (unbiased).

Example 5

Isla wants to see if this spinner is fair.

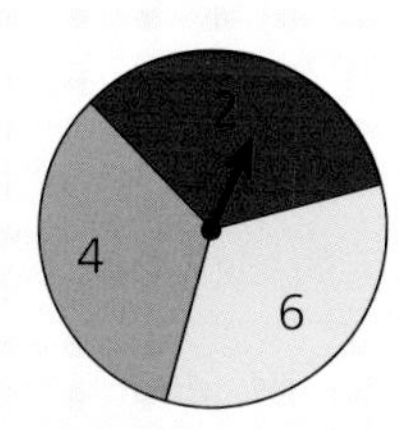

She suspects that the outcome is more likely to be 6 than the other two outcomes.

Describe how she could find the probability of getting a six with this spinner.

Solution

Spin the spinner lots of times and count how many sixes you get. The fraction of the time you get a six (i.e. the **relative frequency**) is the best estimate of the probability.

For example, if you spin the spinner 100 times and you get 50 sixes, then you would say the probability of getting a six is $\frac{50}{100} = \frac{1}{2}$. This would indicate that the spinner is biased.

Example 6

Isla spun the spinner 300 times in Example 5.

The following table shows the results.

Outcome	2	4	6
Frequency	40	92	168
Relative frequency	$\frac{40}{300}$	$\frac{92}{300}$	$\frac{168}{300}$

Is the spinner unfair (biased)?

Solution

If the spinner is fair, the probability of each number on the spinner is $\frac{1}{3}$.

The expected frequency of each number is $(300)\left(\frac{1}{3}\right) = 100$.

So we expect each outcome 2, 4 or 6 to occur about 100 times.

The number of times that a six occurred is a lot more than this and the number of twos is very low.

Thus, we can say that this spinner **appears to be** biased in favour of six. More trials would be needed in order to say this with more confidence.

Activity 18.1

1 (i) Use one of the following to describe each one of the statements below.

Certain; Very likely; Likely;
Even chance; Unlikely;
Very unlikely; Impossible

A: I will win the Lotto this week.

B: I will be in school on the next school day after tomorrow.

C: It will rain on at least one day in November.

D: The next baby born in Ireland will be a boy.

E: The next time I roll a die, a seven will be the outcome.

(ii) Show each of the above on a probability scale.

2 If you toss a coin 1000 times, how many times would you expect it to land:

(i) heads up

(ii) tails up

(iii) on its edge?

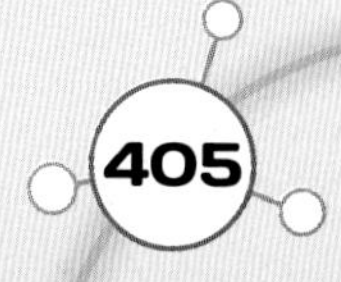

3 Find the probability that it will not rain tomorrow, if the probability that it will rain tomorrow is:

(i) $\frac{1}{2}$

(ii) $\frac{3}{4}$

(iii) 0.7

(iv) 20%

4 Grace plays chess with her friends. Based on previous matches, the probability that Grace beats Linda is 0.6 and the probability that she beats Michael is 0.4.

(i) What is the probability that Linda beats Grace?

(ii) What is the probability that Michael beats Grace?

5 Emer has a three-course lunch at a restaurant. She selects a starter, a main course and a dessert from the menu below.

Starter	**Main course**	**Dessert**
Soup	Roast chicken	Fruit salad
Melon	Baked cod	Apple crumble
Smoked salmon	Roast beef	Ice cream
Green salad	Vegetarian lasagne	Cheesecake
	Hamburger	

(i) Write one three-course lunch that Emer could select.

(ii) How many different selections for a three-course lunch can Emer make?

Assuming that each selection is equally likely, find the probability that she selects:

(iii) soup for her starter

(iv) a green salad, roast beef and fruit salad for her three-course lunch.

6 (i) (a) What is the probability of an event that will never happen?

(b) What is the probability of an event that is certain to happen?

(c) What is the probability of an event that has an even chance of happening?

(ii) In an experiment, a standard fair die is tossed. In the context of that experiment, give one example of each of the following.

(a) an event that has an even chance of happening

(b) an event that will never happen

(c) an event that is certain to happen.

7 (i) What is the (theoretical) probability of getting a Head from a single toss of a coin?

Around 1900, a famous English statistician named Karl Pearson tossed a coin **24 000** times as an experiment. The following table shows the result:

Outcome	**Head**	**Tail**
Frequency	12 012	11 988
Relative frequency (in decimals)		

(ii) Calculate the relative frequencies as decimals.

(iii) Use the results of Pearson's experiment to estimate the probability of getting a Head from a single toss of a coin.

(This activity is designed to show you that probability is obtained from relative frequency in the long term – the very long term!)

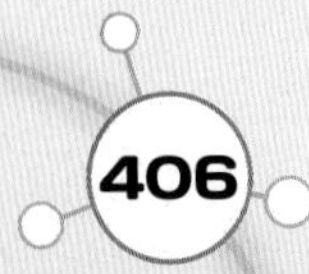

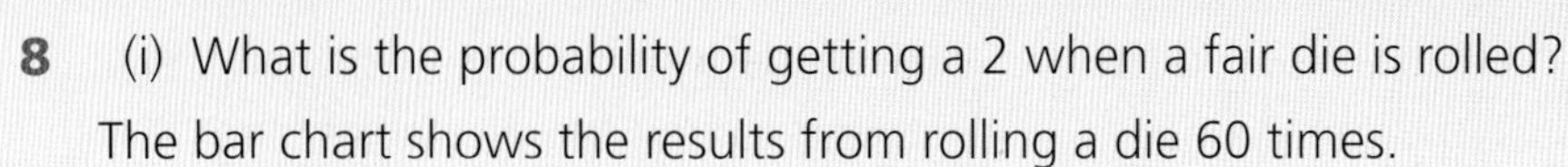

8 (i) What is the probability of getting a 2 when a fair die is rolled?

The bar chart shows the results from rolling a die 60 times.

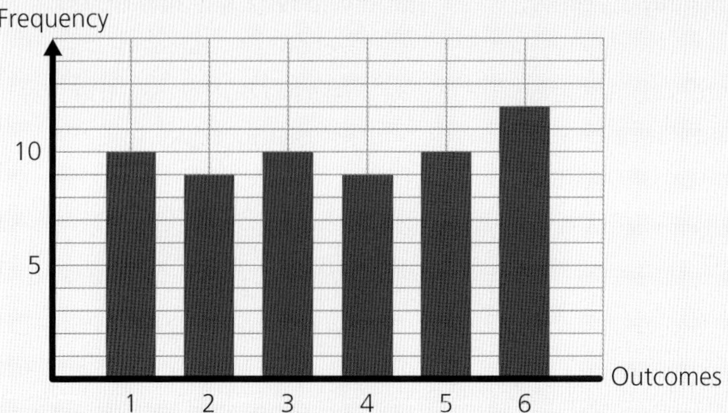

(ii) Copy and complete the table below showing the results and the relative frequencies.

Number on die	**1**	**2**	**3**	**4**	**5**	**6**
Frequency						
Relative frequency						

(iii) Do you think this die is fair? Explain your answer.

9 The diagram shows a 9 × 9 square target in a computerised dart game.

The target contains a 'T' shape within it as shown.

The dart always lands inside one of the squares in the 9 × 9 target.

A dart is thrown at the target and lands at random on one of the squares.

Find the probability that the dart lands in the 'T' shape.

10 Paul has some boxes containing different-coloured counters. Box A has 8 blue counters, Box B has 1 blue and 5 yellow counters, and Box C has 3 red, 2 yellow and 1 blue counter.

Paul takes one counter from each box without looking.

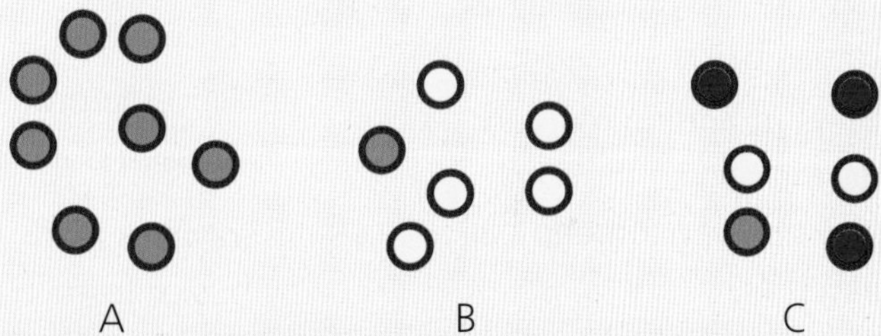

(i) There is a 50 : 50 chance of picking a red counter from Box _______. Explain.

(ii) State 'a 50 : 50 chance' in two other ways.

(iii) The probability of picking a green counter from these boxes is _______.

(iv) It is more than likely that a yellow counter will be chosen from Box ______. Explain.

(v) It is impossible to pick a yellow counter from Box _______.

(vi) What changes could be made to the counters in Box C so that there is an even chance of picking a yellow counter?

(vii) How many red counters could be put into Box A so that Paul would be more likely to choose a red than a blue counter? Is the answer just one number? Explain.

(viii) There are only two colours in Box B. Eva says that because there are only two colours in Box B, Paul is just as likely to choose a yellow as a blue. Is she correct? Explain.

(ix) Paul has another box of counters containing 75 counters which are either blue or red. There is a 60% chance of him choosing a red counter out of this box without looking. How many of each colour counter must be in the box?

11 A bag contains 2 green balls, 3 red balls and 1 blue ball.

(i) What is the probability of drawing a green ball from the bag?

(ii) How many green balls must be added to the bag so that the probability of drawing a green ball from the bag is $\frac{1}{2}$?

(iii) If the number of green balls in the bag stayed the same, how many balls of another colour would need to be in the bag so that the probability of drawing a green ball is $\frac{1}{5}$?

(iv) Give two ways of adding red and blue balls to the bag so that the probability of drawing a green ball from the bag is $\frac{1}{5}$.

12 A plastic toy is in the shape of a hemisphere. When it falls on the ground, there are two possible outcomes: it can land with the flat side facing down or with the flat side facing up. Two groups of students (Group X and Group Y) are trying to find the probability that it will land with the flat side down.

(i) Explain why, even though there are just two outcomes, the answer is not necessarily equal to $\frac{1}{2}$.

(ii) In their experiment, Group X dropped the toy 50 times. From this, they estimated the probability that the toy lands flat side down is 0.68. Group Y dropped the toy 300 times and estimated that it lands flat side down with probability 0.74.

(a) Which group's estimate is likely to be better, and why?

(b) How many times did the toy land flat side up for Group Y?

(c) Using the data from the two groups, what is the best estimate of the probability that the toy lands flat side down?

13 A bag contains 32 beads of which 12 are red, 15 are blue and 5 are white.

A bead is taken at random from the bag.

Find the probability that the colour of the bead is:

(i) blue

(ii) red or white.

14 One letter is chosen at random from the letters of the word MISSISSIPPI.

(i) Find the probability that the letter chosen is S.

(ii) Find the probability that the letter chosen is a consonant.

15 To travel to work, Jack can walk or travel by bus or travel by car with a friend. To return home, he can walk or travel by bus.

(i) In how many different ways can Jack travel to and from work on any one day?

(ii) List all the different ways.

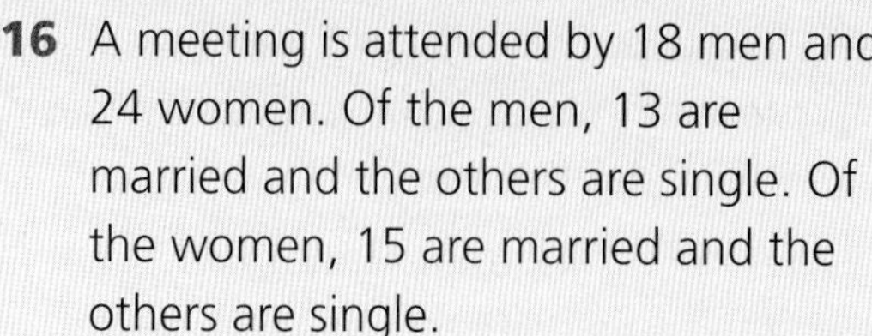

16 A meeting is attended by 18 men and 24 women. Of the men, 13 are married and the others are single. Of the women, 15 are married and the others are single.

(i) A person is picked at random. What is the probability that this person is a man?

(ii) A person is picked at random. What is the probability that this person is married?

(iii) A man is picked at random. What is the probability that he is single?

(iv) A woman is picked at random. What is the probability that she is married?

17 Anete writes down the date as 09082019. She then selects one of the digits at random.

(i) What is the probability that Anete selects the 8?

(ii) What is the probability that Anete selects a prime number?

18 A letter is picked at random from the words on the front page of a newspaper. The table shows the probabilities of choosing the vowels.

Vowel	A	E	I	O	U
Probability	0.05	0.14	0.06	0.09	0.02

What is the probability that a vowel is not picked?

19 Three cards, numbered 2, 3 and 4 respectively, are shuffled and placed in a row with the numbers visible.

(i) Write down all the possible arrangements of the digits.

(ii) Find the probability that the numbers shown are in the order 2, 4, 3.

(iii) Find the probability that the middle digit is 3.

20 Eight teams take part in a basketball competition. The teams are divided into two pools. Teams A, B, C and D are in Pool 1, while teams P, Q, R and S are in Pool 2.

In the final, the winning team from Pool 1 plays the winning team from Pool 2. Each team is equally likely to be the winner from its pool.

(i) How many different team pairings are possible for the final?

(ii) What is the probability that team D plays team R in the final?

(iii) What is the probability that team A plays in the final?

(iv) What is the probability that team C does not play in the final?

21 In Tom's bookcase there are 96 books. He categorises them as fiction or general and they are either hardback or paperback.

	Hardback	**Paperback**
Fiction	17	37
General	30	12

Tom picks one book at random from the bookcase.

Find the probability that the book selected is:

(i) a hardback book of fiction

(ii) a hardback book

(iii) a general paperback

(iv) not a paperback book of fiction.

22 Primrose Hill Post-Primary School has 760 students: 410 girls and 350 boys. The school has a Junior Cycle and a Senior Cycle.

(i) Copy and complete the following table to show the numbers of boys and girls at each level in the school.

	Girls	**Boys**
Junior Cycle	220	
Senior Cycle		155

(ii) What is the probability that a student picked at random is a boy?

(iii) What is the probability that a student picked at random is in Junior Cycle?

(iv) A Senior Cycle student is picked at random. What is the probability that the student is a boy?

(v) A girl is picked at random. What is the probability that she is in Senior Cycle?

23 (i) What is the probability of getting a 6 when a fair die is tossed?

A fair die is tossed 1000 times. The results are partially recorded in the table.

Number on die	1	2	3	4	5	6
Frequency	166	159	180		165	151
Relative frequency						

(ii) Copy the table and calculate the number of times a 4 appeared.

(iii) Calculate the relative frequency of each outcome and write it into the table.

(iv) Give a possible reason for the difference in value between the relative frequency for 6 in the table and your answer to part (i).

24 A spinner has four unequal sections: blue, yellow, white and brown.

The probability that the spinner will land on blue = 0.3.

The probability that the spinner will land on yellow = 0.2.

The probability that the spinner will land on white is the same as the probability that it will land on brown.

(i) Calculate the probability that the spinner will land on brown. Justify your answer.

(ii) Construct this spinner accurately, showing all angle sizes clearly.

25 A spinner has four unequal sections: red, black, pink and grey.

The probability that the spinner will land on red is 0.1 [P(red) = 0.1].

The probability that the spinner will land on black is 0.15 [P(black) = 0.15].

The probability that the spinner will land on pink is the same as the probability that it will land on grey.

Calculate the probability that the spinner will land on grey. Justify your answer.

Section 18B Using Two-way Tables and Tree Diagrams

When you toss two coins, how many possible outcomes are there?
What is the probability of getting two heads?

In 1754, a French mathematician named d'Alembert got this wrong. He thought that there were just three possibilities: two heads, two tails or a head and a tail.

So he figured that the probability of getting two heads from tossing two coins was $\frac{1}{3}$.

To see why he was wrong, we can use a tree diagram or a two-way table.

Jean le Rond d'Alembert

Example 1: Using a tree diagram to show the possible outcomes from two coin tosses.

- We start our tree with two branches to show the two possible outcomes:

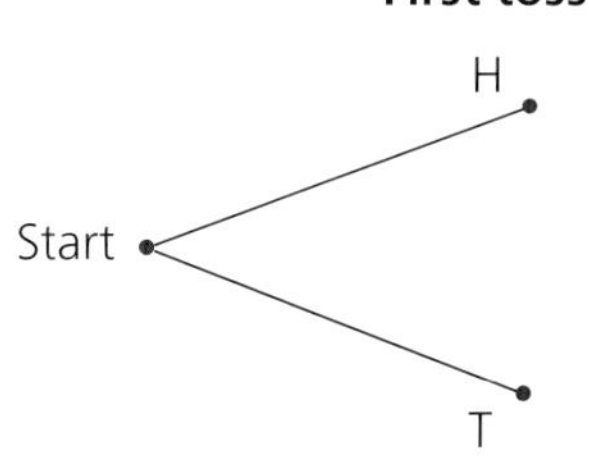

This shows that when we toss the first coin, we can get either a head or a tail (H or T).

- Then we put four more branches on our tree for the second toss of the coin:

First toss | Second toss | Outcome

Start → H → H: Head, Head
Start → H → T: Head, Tail
Start → T → H: Tail, Head
Start → T → T: Tail, Tail

There are four possible outcomes: (H, H), (H, T), (T, H) and (T, T).

Just one of these has two heads, (H, H).

So the probability of getting two heads = $\frac{1}{4}$.

Example 2: Using a two-way diagram to show the possible outcomes from two coin tosses, we can see the 4 possible outcomes in the table.

Just one of these has (H, H).

Hence, the probability of getting two heads = $\frac{1}{4}$.

		Second coin	
		Head (H)	**Tail (T)**
First coin	**Head (H)**	H, H	H, T
	Tail (T)	T, H	T, T

Mutually Exclusive Events

Two events are **mutually exclusive** if the two events cannot happen at the same time.

For example, when tossing a coin, the events 'heads' and 'tails' are mutually exclusive because they cannot both happen at the same time.

Example 1

State whether or not the following pairs of events are mutually exclusive.

(i) *E*: a die is rolled and shows a 4.
F: a die is rolled and shows an odd number.

(ii) *G*: picking a student from a class who plays hurling.
H: picking a student from a class who plays soccer.

Solution

(i) It is not possible to show a 4 and an odd number at the same time, so these are mutually exclusive events.

(ii) It is possible for a student to play hurling and soccer, so these events are not mutually exclusive.

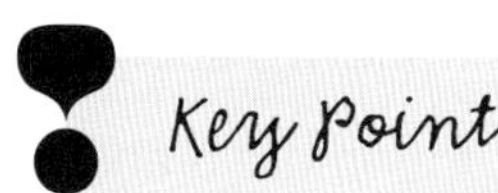

Key Point

If E and F are **mutually exclusive** events then $\mathbf{P(E \text{ or } F) = P(E) + P(F)}$.

Example 2

A card is picked at random from a pack of playing cards. Find the probability that the card is a Heart or the Jack of Clubs.

Solution

E = the event that a Heart card is picked

$P(E) = \frac{13}{52} = \frac{1}{4}$

F = the event that the Jack of Clubs is picked

$P(F) = \frac{1}{52}$

E and F are mutually exclusive events as a card cannot be a Heart and be the Jack of Clubs at the same time.

$$\therefore P(E \text{ or } F) = P(E) + P(F)$$
$$= \frac{1}{4} + \frac{1}{52}$$
$$= \frac{13}{52} + \frac{1}{52}$$
$$= \frac{14}{52}$$
$$= \frac{7}{26}$$

Independent Events

Two events are **independent** if one event happening has no effect on the probability of the other happening.

For example: E = event of getting a 6 in one roll of a fair die

F = event of getting a head in one toss of a fair coin

These are independent events as one event happening has no effect on the other.

Note that $P(E) = \frac{1}{6}$ and $P(F) = \frac{1}{2}$.

If we use a two-way diagram, we can see the 12 possible outcomes of rolling a die and tossing a coin.

		Die					
		1	**2**	**3**	**4**	**5**	**6**
Coin	**Head**	(H, 1)	(H, 2)	(H, 3)	(H, 4)	(H, 5)	(H, 6)
	Tail	(T, 1)	(T, 2)	(T, 3)	(T, 4)	(T, 5)	(T, 6)

Thus $P(E \text{ and } F) = \frac{1}{12}$ which is the same as $\frac{1}{6} \times \frac{1}{2}$.

We can see that $P(E \text{ and } F) = P(E) \times P(F)$.

Key Point

The multiplication rule for independent events:
If E and F are **independent** events then $\mathbf{P(E \text{ and } F) = P(E) \times P(F)}$.

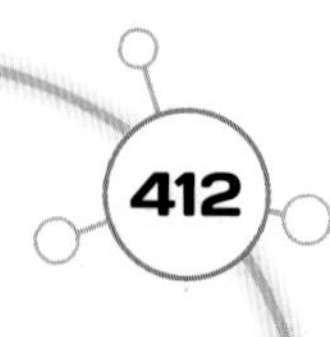

Example 3

A coin is tossed twice.

(i) If event E is the first toss shows a head and event F is the second toss shows a tail, are these events independent?

(ii) Find $P(E$ **and** $F)$.

Solution

(i) These are independent events as the outcome of the first toss has no effect on the outcome of the second.

(ii) $P(E) = \frac{1}{2}$ **and** $P(F) = \frac{1}{2}$

$\Rightarrow P(E \text{ and } F) = P(E) \times P(F)$

$= \frac{1}{2} \times \frac{1}{2} = \frac{1}{4}$

Finding Probabilities With Tree Diagrams

Tree diagrams can be used to find the probabilities for two independent events, even when the outcomes are not equally likely.

Example 4

The probability that Michelle is late for school on any day is 0.2.

Find the probability that on two consecutive days she is:

(i) not late either day (ii) late just once.

Solution

The probability that Michelle is late for school on any day is 0.2

$\therefore$ the probability that Michelle is not late on any day = 1 – 0.2 = 0.8.

Use a tree diagram:

(i) The probability that Michelle is not late is on the bottom set of branches:

$P(\text{not late, not late}) = 0.8 \times 0.8$
$= 0.64$

(ii) The probability that Michelle is late just once is found from the two middle sets of branches.

We add these probabilities:

$P(\text{late, not late}) + P(\text{not late, late})$
$= 0.16 + 0.16 = 0.32$

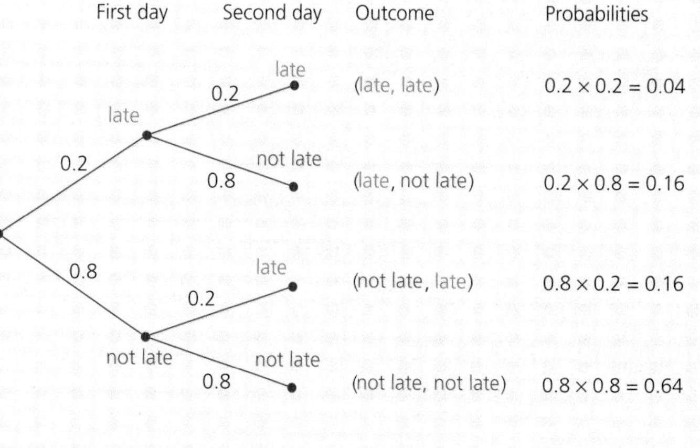

Key Point

When using tree diagrams, we always **multiply along the branches** to get the probabilities of combined events.

Activity 18.2

1 (i) Use each of the following methods to show all the possible outcomes when two fair coins are tossed.

(a) Systematic listing of all the possible outcomes

(b) A two-way diagram

(c) A tree diagram

(ii) Two fair coins are tossed. What is the probability of getting two heads?

(iii) Two fair coins are tossed 800 times. How often would you expect to get two heads?

(iv) In a class exercise, two coins are tossed 30 times. Two heads are recorded on 18 of these occasions. If this exercise was repeated, is it likely that two heads would again be recorded 18 times? Explain your reasoning.

(v) Lucy tosses a coin repeatedly. She records eight heads in successive throws. How likely is it that the next toss will be a head? Choose from the following answers, giving your reason:

Extremely unlikely; Fairly unlikely; 50–50 chance; Fairly likely; Almost certain.

2 Sarah and Callum are playing a game with two dice. The dice are rolled and the scores are added together.

(i) Copy and complete the two-way table below showing all the possible outcomes.

		First die					
		1	2	3	4	5	6
Second die	1	2					
	2			5			
	3						
	4				8		
	5						
	6						12

(ii) What is the total number of possible outcomes?

(iii) Are all outcomes equally likely?

(iv) In the game, Sarah wins if the outcome is 5, 6, 7, 8 or 9. Callum wins if the outcome is 2, 3, 4, 10, 11 or 12.

(a) Is this a fair game?

(b) What is the probability that Sarah wins?

(c) What is the probability that Callum wins?

(v) Change the rules of the game to make it fair.

3 Doug is buying a ticket to the theatre. He can choose a ticket in the Balcony (B) or the Stalls (S). He can go on Monday (M), Wednesday (W) or Friday (F).

You may assume that all choices are **equally likely**.

(i) What is the probability that he chooses a balcony seat?

(ii) What is the probability that he chooses a Wednesday?

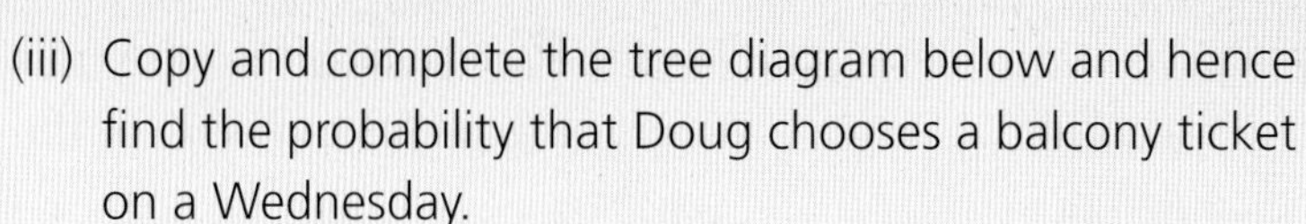
(iii) Copy and complete the tree diagram below and hence find the probability that Doug chooses a balcony ticket on a Wednesday.

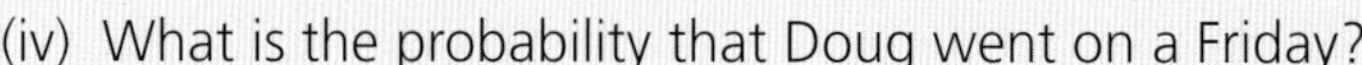
(iv) What is the probability that Doug went on a Friday?

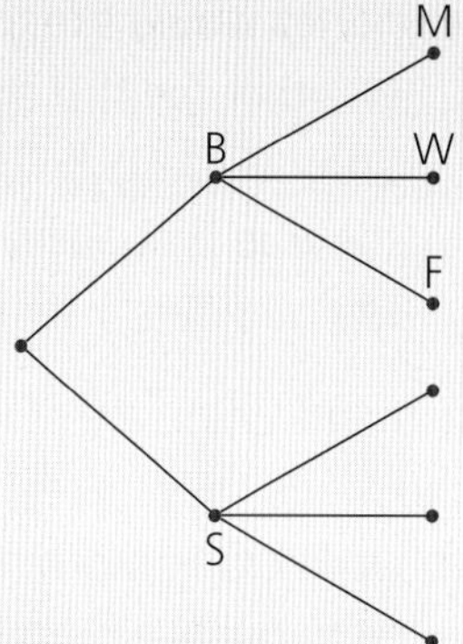

4 The 2016 Census of Ireland shows that the number of males (M) living in Ireland is about the same as the number of females (F).

(i) If a person in Ireland is selected at random, write down the probability that the person is male.

(ii) Three people are chosen at random. We are interested in whether they are male or female. Copy and complete the tree diagram to show the eight equally likely outcomes.

(iii) Hence, copy and complete the table of probabilities below.

First person | Second person | Third person | Outcome

M, M, M — MMM

F, M, F

Three males	Two males, one female	One male, two females	Three females
$\frac{1}{8}$			

(iv) Examine this statement carefully: 'If you pick three people at random, it's **more likely than not** that you'll get two males and one female.' Is this statement correct? Justify your answer using your results in part (iii).

5 A game is played by spinning two unbiased spinners and adding the numbers. Each spinner is divided into equal sections. Players get a prize if they get a total of 7.

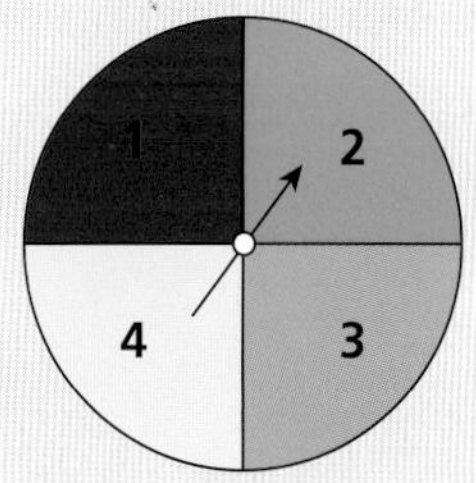

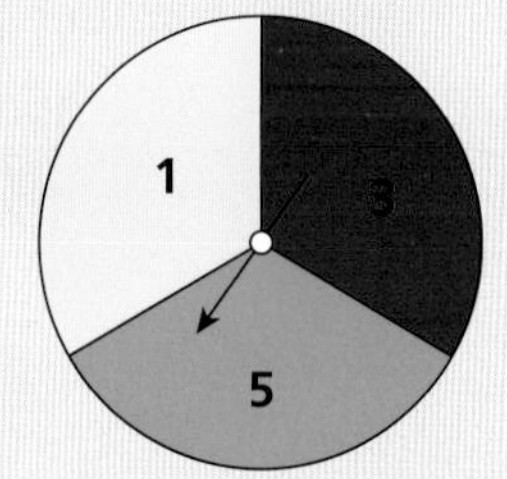

(i) Draw a two-way table to show all the possible outcomes.

(ii) James plays the game once. Find the probability that he will get a score of 3.

(iii) Find the probability that James wins a prize.

(iv) Which of the following best describes James's chances of winning a prize?
Extremely unlikely; Not very likely; Even chance; Very likely; Certain.

(v) James would like to investigate whether the first spinner is really fair after all. Describe how he could find the true probability of getting each of the numbers 1 to 4 with that spinner.

6 Zach and Chloe are students at a large school and they are experimenting with probability. One morning before class, they decide to guess whether each of the next three students to arrive will be a boy or a girl.

(i) Zach says that these outcomes are equally likely. Chloe says they are not. What information about the students in the school would you need to decide which of them is correct?

(ii) Use a tree diagram to write out the sample space (i.e. the set of all possible outcomes). For example, in your diagram, use BGB to stand for the outcome Boy, Girl, Boy.

(iii) If the outcomes are equally likely, what is the probability that the three students will be two boys followed by a girl?

(iv) Chloe bets that there will be at least one girl among the next three students. What is the probability that Chloe is correct, assuming all outcomes are equally likely?

(v) Zach bets that the next three students will be either two girls and a boy or three girls. What is the probability that Zach is correct, assuming all outcomes are equally likely?

7 An unbiased spinner has five equal sectors: two coloured yellow and three coloured blue.

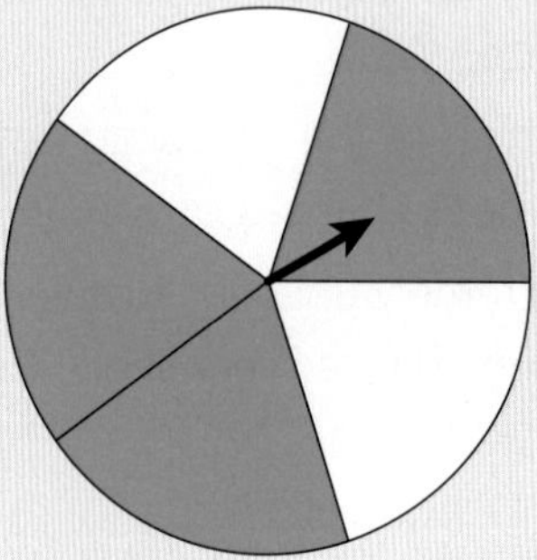

(i) Find the probability that the pointer stops on blue for one spin of the spinner.

(ii) Use a tree diagram to list all the possible outcomes of three successive spins of the spinner.

8 Three coins are tossed. Each coin gives either a head (H) or a tail (T).

(i) Use a tree diagram to write out the sample space (i.e. list all the possible outcomes).

(ii) Find the probability that the result is three heads.

(iii) Find the probability that the result includes at most one head.

(iv) Find the probability that the number of heads is two or more.

9 Two spinners, each with four equal segments numbered 1 to 4, are spun.

(i) Using a list, table, tree diagram, or otherwise, show all the possible outcomes.

(ii) If the spinner is fair, what is the probability of getting two threes?

(iii) Vesna thinks that one of the spinners is not fair. Describe an experiment that she could perform to find out whether or not the spinner is fair.

10 A calculator is set up to show the numbers **1** and **7** at random.

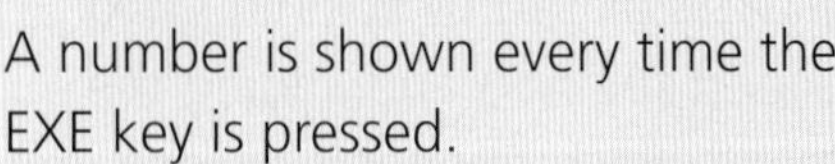

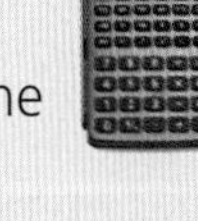

A number is shown every time the EXE key is pressed.

The EXE key is pressed 3 times.

Find the probability that:

(i) the number **1** is shown each time

(ii) the same number is shown each time.

11 Aaron and Billy are running in a 800 m race followed later by a 1500 m race.

Based on previous performances, the probabilities of each of them winning each race are given in the table. The probability that neither of them wins the 800 m race is also given.

	Aaron	Billy	Neither
800 m race	$\frac{1}{5}$	$\frac{2}{5}$	$\frac{2}{5}$
1500 m race	$\frac{1}{4}$	$\frac{1}{3}$	

(i) Copy and complete the table.

(ii) Copy the tree diagram below. Complete the list of possible outcomes. For example, (A, A) represents the outcome that Aaron wins the first race and the second race. Write in the probability of each outcome.

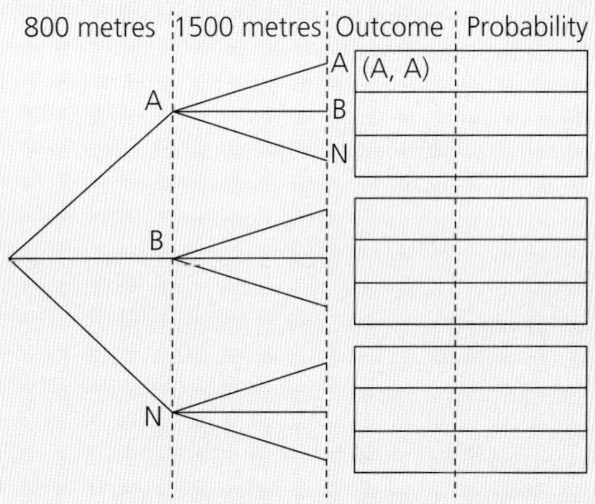

(iii) What is the probability that Aaron and Billy win a race each?

12 The diagram shows two spinners. The first spinner has four equal segments numbered 1, 2, 3 and 4. The second spinner has three equal segments labelled A, B and C.

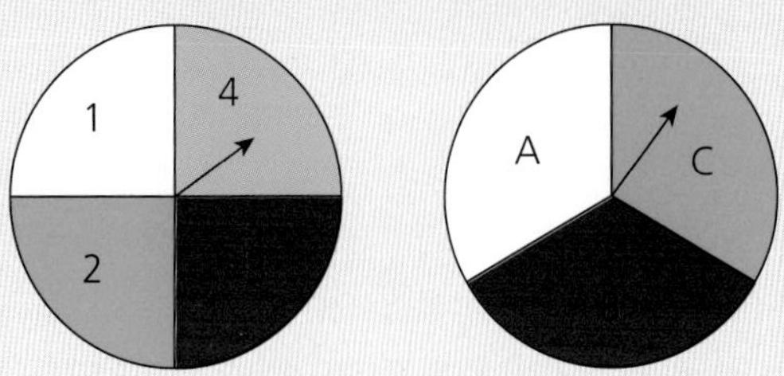

A game consists of spinning the two spinners and noting the result on each. For example, the outcome shown is (4, C).

(i) List all the possible outcomes.

(ii) Find the probability that the outcome is (3, B).

(iii) Find the probability that the outcome is an even number with the letter A.

(iv) Find the probability that C is in the outcome.

13 These two spinners are part of a game. A player gets to spin each spinner once. A prize is won only if both spinners point to blue after each has been spun once.

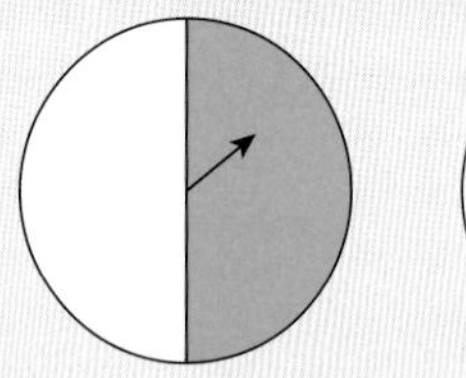 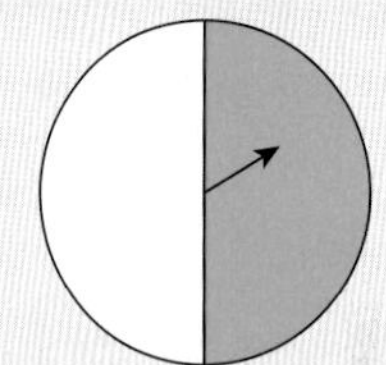

Ben thinks that he has a 50–50 chance of winning.

Chloe thinks that the probability of her winning is $\frac{1}{3}$, since, she says, 'There are three outcomes: (yellow, yellow), (blue, blue) and (yellow, blue).'

(i) Is Ben correct?

(ii) Is Chloe correct?

Explain your reasoning with diagrams.

14 Ava and Ryan are taking part in a quiz. They are asked a particular question and are unsure of the answer.

The probability that Ava will get the answer correct = 0.8.

The probability that Ryan will get the answer correct = 0.7.

(i) Construct a probability tree diagram to show all the possible outcomes.

(ii) What is the probability that at least one of them answers correctly?

(iii) What is the probability that neither of them answers correctly?

15 Suppose that every child that is born has an equal chance of being a boy or a girl.

(i) Write out the sample space for the situation where a mother has two children.

(ii) What is the probability that a randomly chosen mother of two children would have two girls?

(iii) What is the probability that this mother of two children would have two boys?

(iv) What is the probability that this mother of two children would have one boy and one girl?

Section 18C Connecting Probability with Sets

We can use sets to represent a situation and make it easier to work out the probability of an event.

Example

100 students were surveyed to find out whether they drank tea (T), coffee (C) or a soft drink (D) at any time in the previous week.

24 had not drunk any of the three drinks.

51 drank tea or coffee but not a soft drink.

41 drank tea.

20 drank at least two of the three.

8 drank tea and a soft drink but not coffee.

9 drank a soft drink and coffee.

4 drank all three.

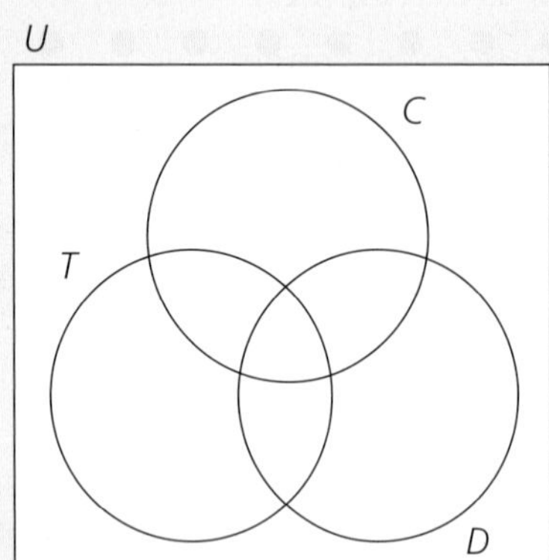

(i) Copy and represent the above information on the Venn diagram.

(ii) Find the probability that a student chosen at random from the group had drunk tea or coffee.

(iii) Find the probability that a student chosen at random from the group had drunk tea and coffee but not a soft drink.

Solution

(i) U [100]

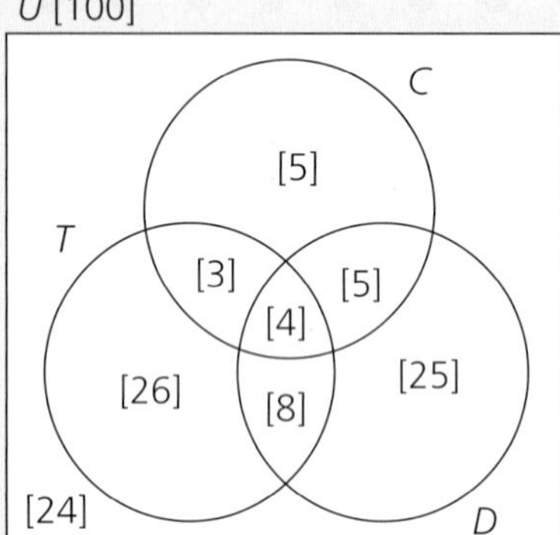

(ii) Number who had drunk tea or coffee
$= 26 + 3 + 5 + 8 + 4 + 5 = 51$

Total number of students = 100

Probability $= \frac{51}{100}$

(iii) Number who had drunk tea and coffee but not a soft drink = 3

Total number of students = 100

Probability $= \frac{3}{100}$

1 The sets in the Venn diagram represent the students in a class of 28 students who study Spanish and French.

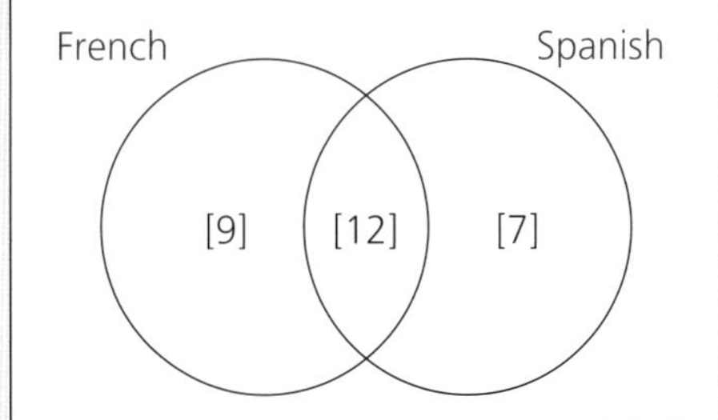

(i) How many students study both Spanish and French?

A student is picked at random from the class.

(ii) Find the probability that the student studies both Spanish and French.

(iii) Find the probability that the student studies Spanish but not French.

2 In this Venn diagram, the universal set is a normal deck of 52 playing cards. The two sets shown represent Spades and picture cards (Kings, Queens and Jacks).

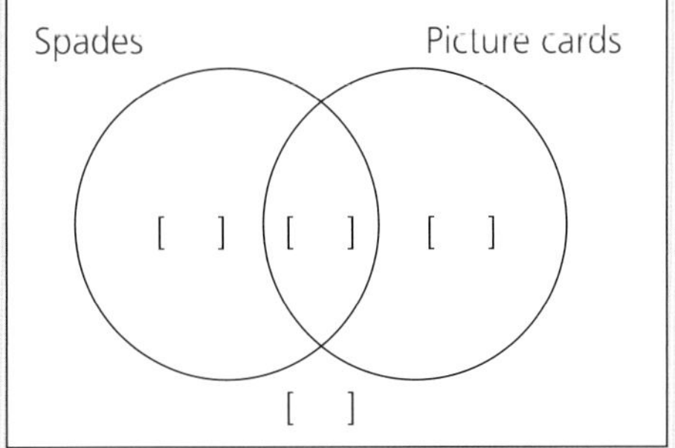

(i) Copy the Venn diagram and show the number of elements in each region.

(ii) (a) A card is drawn at random from a pack of 52 cards. Find the probability that the card drawn is a Spade that is not a picture card.

(b) A card is drawn at random from a pack of 52 cards. Find the probability that the card drawn is a Spade or a picture card.

(c) A card is drawn at random from a pack of 52 cards. It is not replaced. A second card is drawn at random. Find the probability that neither card drawn is a Spade or a picture card.

3 80 Third Year students responded to a survey about their travels in Europe.

30 had been to France.

26 had been to Spain.

28 had been to Germany.

12 had been to both France and Spain.

8 had been to both Germany and Spain.

x had been to France and Germany only.
4 students had been to all three countries.

Twice as many had never been to any of these destinations as had been to France and Germany only.

(i) Represent this information on a Venn diagram.

(ii) Find the value of x.

(iii) If a student is picked at random from the whole group, what is the probability that the student had been to all three countries?

(iv) If a student is picked at random from the whole group, what is the probability that the student had been to France only?

4 Two events A and B are such that $P(A) = 0.6$, $P(B) = 0.4$ and $P(A \cap B) = 0.2$.

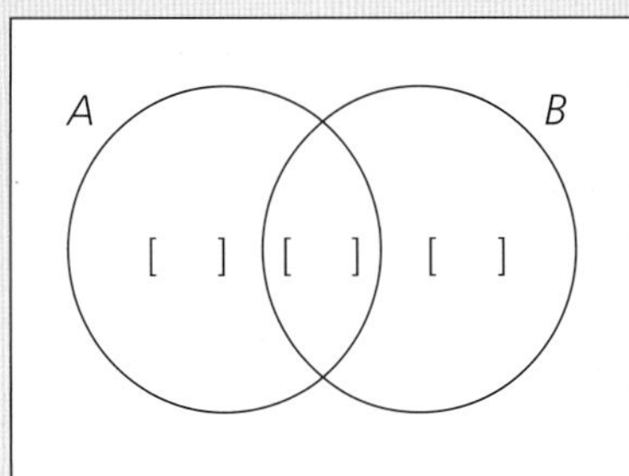

(i) Copy and complete this Venn diagram for the above probabilities.

(ii) Use your diagram to find $P(A \cup B)$.

5 In a survey, 54 people were asked which political party they had voted for in the last three elections. The results were:

30 had voted for the Conservatives.

22 had voted for the Liberals.

22 had voted for the Republicans.

12 had voted for the Conservatives and the Liberals.

9 had voted for the Liberals and the Republicans.

8 had voted for the Conservatives and the Republicans.

5 had voted for all three parties.

(i) Represent this information on a Venn diagram.

(ii) If one person is chosen at random, what is the probability that the person chosen did not vote in any of the three elections?

(iii) If one person is chosen at random, what is the probability that the person chosen voted for at least two different parties?

(iv) If one person is chosen at random, what is the probability that the person chosen voted for the same party in all three elections?

Revision Activity 18

1 A, B, C, D and E represent the probabilities of certain events occurring.

(a) Write the probability of each of the events listed in a copy of the table below.

Event		Probability
A Club is randomly selected from a pack of playing cards	A	
A tossed fair coin shows a tail on landing	B	
The sun will rise in the east tomorrow	C	
May will follow directly after June	D	
A randomly selected person was born on a Thursday	E	

(b) Place each of the letters A, B, C, D and E at its correct position on a copy of the probability scale below.

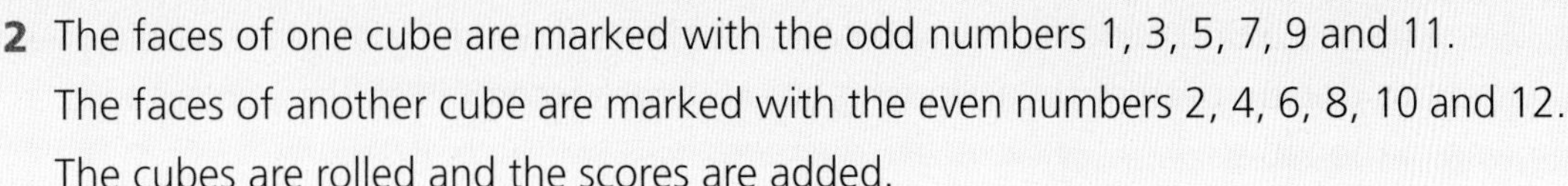

2 The faces of one cube are marked with the odd numbers 1, 3, 5, 7, 9 and 11.
The faces of another cube are marked with the even numbers 2, 4, 6, 8, 10 and 12.
The cubes are rolled and the scores are added.

(a) Copy and complete the following table to show all the possible scores.

		First cube					
		1	**3**	**5**	**7**	**9**	**11**
Second cube	**2**	3					
	4						
	6				13		
	8		11				
	10						
	12						23

(b) What is the highest possible score?
(c) What is the probability of getting the highest score?
(d) What is the probability of getting an even-numbered score?

3 There are four main blood groups: group O, group A, group B and group AB. The blood in each group is further classed as either rhesus positive (+) or rhesus negative (–).
The percentage of a population having each blood group is given in the table below.

Blood group	O		A		B		AB	
Rhesus positive (+) or rhesus negative (–)	O^-	O^+	A^-	A^+	B^-	B^+	AB^-	AB^+
Percentage	8	47	5	26	2	9	1	2

(a) (i) Find the percentage of the population in blood group O.
(ii) Find the percentage of the population with rhesus negative blood.

(b) The table below has statements about a person's blood group. A person is picked at random from the population. In each case, find the probability that the statement is true for that person.

Statement	**Probability**
Is in blood group A^-	
Is in blood group AB	
Is in blood group A or B	
Has blood which is rhesus positive	
Is not in blood group O	

(c) Over a period, 8000 people donate blood at a clinic. How many of these would you expect to donate each of the following blood types, according to the percentages given in the table?

(i) type AB blood

(ii) rhesus positive blood

(iii) rhesus negative blood.

4 In a class of students, there are 12 boys and 16 girls. Three of the boys wear glasses and four of the girls wear glasses.

A student is picked at random from the class.

(a) What is the probability that the student is a boy?

(b) What is the probability that the student wears glasses?

(c) What is the probability that the student is a boy who wears glasses?

A girl is picked at random from the class.

(d) What is the probability that she wears glasses?

5 Lily and David were both born in the same week (Monday to Sunday inclusive). Assuming that a baby is equally likely to be born on any day of the week, find the probability that:

(a) Lily was born on Saturday

(b) Lily was born on Saturday and David was born on Tuesday

(c) Lily and David were both born on Sunday.

6 Tickets for a raffle are placed in a box. The box contains 15 blue tickets and 10 red tickets. Tickets are drawn at random from the box and they are not replaced.

Find the probability that:

(a) the first ticket drawn is red

(b) the first ticket drawn and the second ticket drawn are both red

(c) the first ticket drawn is red and the second ticket drawn is blue.

7 A fair circular spinner consists of three equal sectors. Two are coloured blue and one is coloured white.

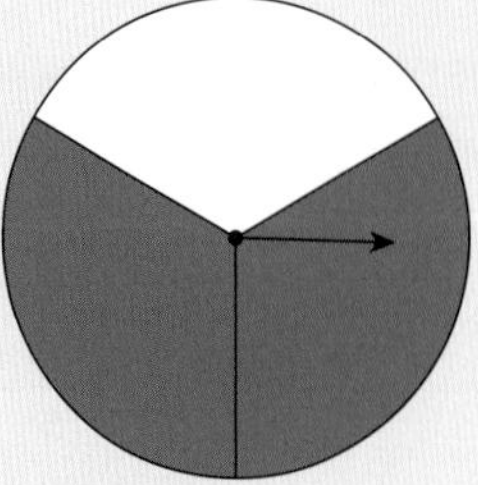

The spinner is spun and a fair coin is tossed.

(a) What is the probability of the spinner landing on a blue sector?

(b) Find the probability of getting white on the spinner and a head on the coin toss.

(c) Find the probability of getting blue on the spinner and a tail on the coin toss.

Exam-style Questions

1 The arrows on the diagram below represent the routes that a skier can take when skiing down a mountain. The circles represent different points on the routes.

(a) When leaving any particular point on the mountain, a skier is equally likely to choose any of the available routes from that point. Fill in the boxes in the diagram which represent the probability that the skier will take that route.

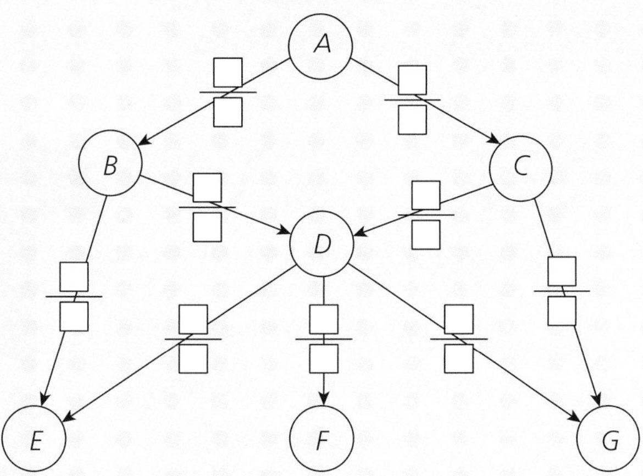

(b) (i) If the skier starts at point A, in how many different ways can the skier reach the point E?

(ii) If the skier starts at point A, find the probability that the skier will reach the point E.

JCHL 2013 Paper 2

2 The percentage distribution of blood groups in the Irish population is given in the table below. The table also gives information about which types of blood can be safely used when people need to be given blood during an operation.

Blood group	Percentage in Irish population	Blood groups to which transfusions can be safely given	Blood groups from which transfusions can be safely received
O^-	8	All	O^-
O^+	47	O^+, AB^+, A^+, B^+	O^+ and O^-
A^-	5	A^-, A^+, AB^+, AB^-	A^- and O^-
A^+	26	A^+ and AB^+	A^+, O^-, O^+, A^-
B^-	2	B^-, B^+, AB^-, AB^+	B^- and O^-
B^+	9	B^+ and AB^+	B^+, B^-, O^-, O^+
AB^-	1	AB^- and AB^+	AB^-, O^-, A^-, B^-
AB^+	2	AB^+	All

Source: Irish Blood Transfusion Service

Interactive Tool 18.1 and 18.2

(a) If an Irish person is chosen at random, what is the probability that this person will have blood group AB^-?

(b) Mary has blood group B^-. If a person is chosen at random from the population, what is the probability that Mary could safely receive blood from that person?

(c) Aaron has blood group O^+ and donates blood. What is the probability that his blood can be given to a person randomly chosen from the population?

(d) The Irish Blood Transfusion Service recently asked that people with blood group O^- should give blood as regularly as possible. Give a reason why this might be.

JCHL 2011 Paper 2

KEY WORDS AND PHRASES

- **Mutually exclusive events**
- **Independent events**
- **Tree diagram**
- **Systematic list**

Chapter Summary 18

- For equally likely outcomes:

  $$\text{Probability of an event } [P(E)] = \frac{\text{number of favourable outcomes}}{\text{total number of possible outcomes}}$$

- Expected frequency = probability × the number of trials
- Probability of an event not happening = 1 – probability that it will happen.
- We can identify the set of all the possible outcomes (the sample space):
  - by systematic listing
  - using a two-way table
  - using a tree diagram.
- Two events are mutually exclusive if the two events cannot happen at the same time.
  - If E and F are mutually exclusive events then $P(E \text{ or } F) = P(E) + P(F)$.
- Two events are independent if one event happening has no effect on the probability of the other happening.
  - If E and F are independent events, $P(E \text{ and } F) = P(E) \times P(F)$.
- When using tree diagrams, we always multiply along the branches to get the probabilities of combined events.
- We can use sets to represent a situation and make it easier to work out the probability of an event.

Chapter 19

Statistics

Learning Intentions

In this chapter, you will learn about:

- Avoiding bias in statistics
- Finding the mean from a frequency table
- Some misuses of statistics
- Using pie charts to represent categorical data
- Histograms with equal class intervals for numerical continuous data
- Comparing samples

LO: U.5, U.6, SP.3

Historical Background

One of the most famous statisticians was Karl Pearson. He has been attributed with forming the discipline of mathematical statistics. Pearson developed many of the ideas that we use today, like the mode and the histogram, which we will learn about in this chapter.

Karl Pearson (1857–1936)

Section 19A Revision of Statistics

- **Statistics** is all about **variation** (differences in people and things).
- There are four stages in a statistical investigation (the **data handling cycle**):
  - Pose a question
  - Collect the data
  - Analyse the data
  - Interpret the data and answer the question or refine the question.

Pose a question → Collect data → Analyse the data → Interpret the results

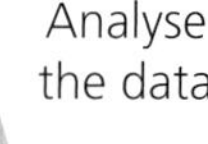

- A **population** is an entire set of objects that we want to find out about.
- A **sample** is a subset of the population.
- A sample should be a **representative sample** if it is to give us meaningful information about the population.
- Data which we collect ourselves are **primary data**.
- Data which we get from books, journals and the Internet are **secondary data**.
- A **spreadsheet** is a rectangular array (table) of cells with data.
- In a spreadsheet: rows represent individuals; columns are what we ask people (**variables**).
- Types of data:

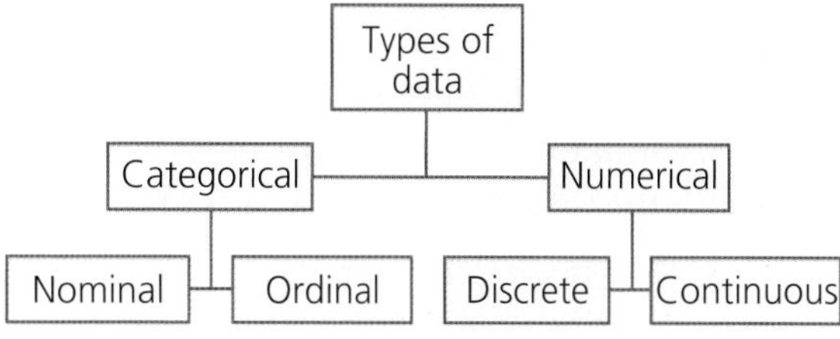

- We can use **bar charts** for categorical data: frequency bar charts or relative frequency.

You have met the following types of graphical analysis of data.

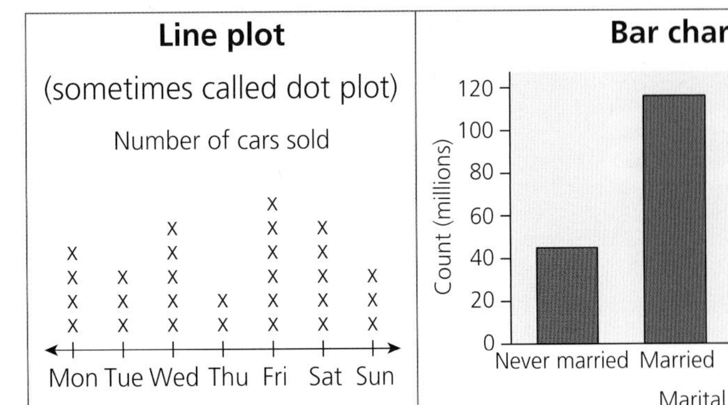

Stem-and-leaf plot

Ages of people at a meeting

1	9
2	2 5 6 7 8 9
3	0 4 6 7
4	2 3 4 6 8 8 9
5	2 3 5 7 8
6	2

Key: 1 | 9 means 19 years

- We can use **bar charts** for categorical data: frequency bar charts or relative frequency bar charts.
- We can use a **stem-and-leaf plot** to show discrete numerical data.
- We can use a **line plot** to show categorical data and discrete numerical data.
- There are three types of average:
  - The **mode** is the item of data which occurs most often.
  - The **mean** is the fair share: the sum of the values divided by the number of values.
  - The **median** is the middle value in a complete list of all the data arranged from smallest to largest.
- The **range** of the data = maximum value – minimum value.
- A **frequency table** shows each data item and its frequency – the **frequency distribution**.

The following activities will help you to recall these main ideas.

Activity 19.1

1 A questionnaire contained the question:

'When going out on sunny days in the summer, do you use sun cream?'

Always ☐ Sometimes ☐ Never ☐

Below is a sample of data for this question.

Sun cream use				
sometimes	sometimes	never	sometimes	never
never	sometimes	always	sometimes	sometimes
sometimes	sometimes	always	always	sometimes
sometimes	sometimes	always	always	sometimes
always	sometimes	never	always	always
never	never	always	sometimes	sometimes

(i) How many people took part in this sample?

(ii) Make a tally chart for how often these people said they used sun cream and find the frequency for each category.

(iii) Represent the data using a bar chart.

(iv) Write a brief summary of what the bar chart tells you about the usage of sun cream by these people (include the mode in your answer).

(v) If a person is picked at random from this group, what is the probability that the person **always** uses sun cream?

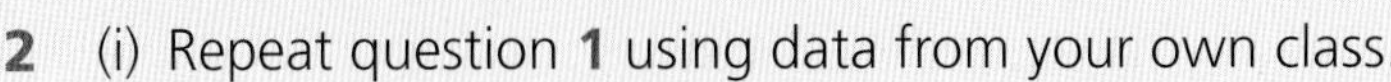

2 (i) Repeat question **1** using data from your own class.
(ii) Write a brief summary comparing the results with the data given in question **1**.

3 The students in a Junior Cycle class decided to investigate their heights. Each student's height was measured, in centimetres, and the results were as follows:

190 182 173 165 150 149 133 100 187
171 165 150 170 167 158 176 164 153 178

(i) Construct a stem-and-leaf plot of the data.
(ii) Find the range of the data.
(iii) Find the mean height of these students.
(iv) Find the median height.

4 All the families in a certain street were surveyed to find how many children are in each family. The results of the survey are shown in the frequency table below. For example, 3 families have 1 child each.

Number of children per family	1	2	3	4	5	6
Number of families	3	5	7	9	4	2

(i) Using squared paper, draw a line plot to show the information.
(ii) How many families live in the street?
(iii) Write down the modal number of children per family.
(iv) What percentage of families in the street have more than 4 children?
(v) If a family is picked at random from these families, what is the probability that it has more than 4 children?

5 Here is a stem-and-leaf plot of the heights of a group of students, in centimetres.

Stem	Leaf					
13	3					
13	5	6				
14	0	0	1			
14	6	6	7	8		
15	0	1	2	2	3	3
15	5	5	6	7		

Key: 13 | 3 means 133 cm.

(i) How many students are in the group?
(ii) What is the range of heights in the group?
(iii) What percentage of the students are between 145 cm and 154 cm in height?
(iv) If a student is picked at random from this group of students, what is the probability that he/she is between 145 cm and 154 cm in height?

6 The following list gives the number of bedrooms in each of 20 homes.

3 1 4 2 5
4 5 2 3 4
2 1 3 2 3
5 2 4 3 2

(i) Copy and complete the following frequency table:

Number of bedrooms per home	1	2	3	4	5
Number of homes					

(ii) Draw a bar chart to show this information.
(iii) Draw a line plot to show this information.
(iv) Which diagram do you think is better at displaying the data? Explain your answer.

7 A survey contained the question:
'On a school day, do you eat breakfast?' This bar chart shows the percentage of students by gender and year who said that they do **not** eat breakfast.

(i) Compare the percentages of girls to the percentages of boys who do not eat breakfast.

(ii) Use the chart to write a brief summary of the results of the survey.

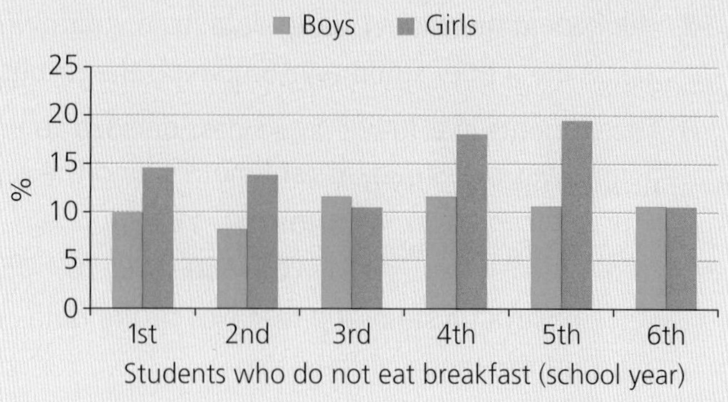

Section 19B Collecting Data: Sampling

A **population** is the entire group, of size N, of people, animals or objects about which we want information.

A **unit** is any individual member of the population.

A **census** occurs when every member of the population has data collected about them.

A **sample** of size n is a subset of a population from which we actually collect information. When $n = N$, we have a **census**.

A sample should be **representative of the population** it is chosen from, i.e. it should have approximately the same variations we would see in the population.

Sample data are collected and summarised in order to give us insights into the population.

Sampling is carried out in situations where a census would be too expensive, would take too long or would be impractical. For example, one cannot test the lifetimes of all batteries produced. In similar cases, where measurement destroys the units being tested, a census is not feasible.

How big should a sample be? There is no magic number which tells us how large a sample should be to allow us to make inferences about the population. A large random sample will include a lot of people with lots of variation, whereas a small sample will not have the same degree of variation. For political polls, 1000 people is considered to be a big enough sample size regardless of the population size.

In **market research**, people's opinions are sampled in order to get an idea of the views of the whole population.

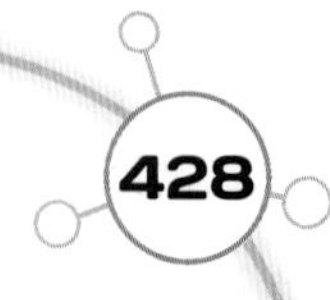

Simple Random Sampling

To enable us to make generalisations about a population from a sample, sampling should be **random**. Random sampling does not mean that we can just pick anyone for the sample.

In a **random sample**, each unit in the population has an equal chance of being selected.

In **simple random sampling**, each unit of the population has an equal chance of being selected and each sample of a particular size has an equal chance of being chosen.

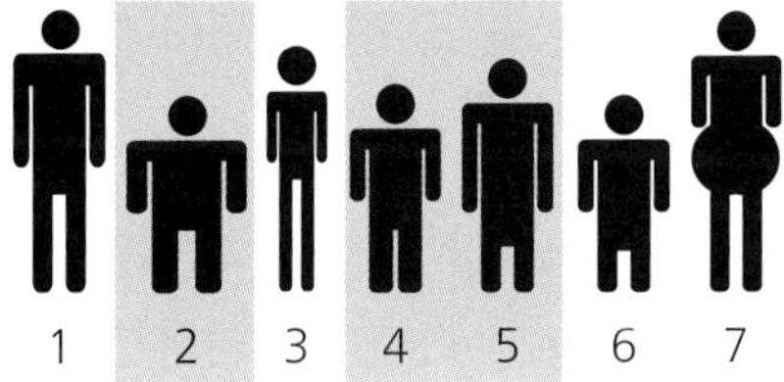

- Assign numbers
- Generate random selections

To produce a simple random sample, you need two things:

- a list of the units in the population
- a source of random numbers.

Example

Select a simple random sample from a class of 30 students.

Solution

The **population** is the class of 30 students.

Let's decide on a sample of size 5.

(We chose this size as it is convenient for calculating several values of the mean and we have limited time.)

Method 1

RanInt#(1,30)

- Assign a number from 1 to 30 to each student.
- Use a calculator to generate five different random integers from 1 to 30.
- The students who have been assigned those randomly generated integers form the sample.

Method 2

- Put the numbers 1 to 30 into a container, mix them up, and choose five different random numbers in succession.
- Each time we choose a number, we should replace it in the container.
- The students with those integers assigned to them in the list make up the random sample.

When we use a large sample size, **random sampling** will approximate a representative sample.

A Random Sample which is not a Simple Random Sample

If, in a school which has an equal number of male and female students, we decide to flip a coin to decide whether a sample will be from the males or the females, then every student has an equal chance of selection. If the coin comes up heads, we select 20 male students at random and if it comes up tails, we select 20 female students at random. Even though every student has an equal chance of being selected, every sample of 20 has not an equal chance of selection as the sample consists of one gender only.

Statistics

Bias in Sampling

Whenever a sample overestimates or underestimates whatever we are trying to measure for the population, then that sample is **biased**.

Bias in sampling occurs when a particular group is **excluded**, **under-represented** or **over-represented** in the sample.

For example:

- If a sample survey about a whole-school issue is completed only by First Year students, the sample is biased because all other class groups are excluded.
- Self-selection of sample members, i.e. volunteers, can cause those with strong opinions about the survey issues to be over-represented, e.g. when asking people to phone in their opinions on a particular subject to a radio show, people who are free to ring in at that time of day, those with a particular interest in the topic and those who are not shy about speaking in public will be over-represented.
- Low response rates, e.g. people who do not fill in responses to questionnaires sent through the post, can cause a sample to be biased.

Other examples of bias are:

- Dishonest answers to survey questions, e.g. sometimes people are dishonest when asked their age or how much they earn.
- Wording of survey questions, the order in which questions are asked, the type of options offered and whether or not the question is open to misinterpretation, e.g. Are you tall?
- The sample size is too small, e.g. a sample of 10 people from the population of a country is asked which brand of dog food they prefer for their dog.

Questionnaires

There are a few points to remember when writing a questionnaire.

Questionnaires should:

1. Be as brief as possible.
2. Start with simple questions to encourage the person who is filling it in.
3. Be clear as to where the answers should be recorded.
4. Have some tick boxes to make it easy to answer and to use as data afterwards.
5. Never have leading questions which will influence the answer.
6. Never ask embarrassing questions.

If you want to conduct a survey of your own, the following questionnaire could be used to get you started. You can adapt it to the needs of your survey.

Questionnaire

Please answer all the questions by ticking the relevant box or entering a number.

1. Gender Male ☐ Female ☐
2. How did you get to school today? (tick one box only)

   Cycle ☐ Walk ☐ Car ☐ Bus ☐

   Other (please specify) ____________________
3. Do you live in an urban ☐ or ☐ rural area?
4. How far from school do you live? (nearest km) ______________
5. How much did you spend on your last haircut (to the nearest euro)? ______________
6. In a typical week, how often would you exercise for 20 minutes or more?

   Never ☐ Several times ☐

   Once or twice ☐ Every day ☐
7. How concerned are you about environmental issues?

   Not at all ☐ A little concerned ☐ Fairly concerned ☐ Very concerned ☐

Being a Statistically Aware Consumer

When evaluating information from a survey or opinion poll carried out by someone else, consider:

- Who carried out the survey?
- What is the population?
- How was the sample selected?
- How large was the sample?
- What was the response rate?
- How were the subjects contacted?
- When was the survey conducted?
- What were the exact questions asked?

We also need to consider variation (apart from natural variation) which is due to measurement error and input error, i.e. data being recorded incorrectly.

Always question the logic, the numbers, the sources and the procedures used to generate the statistics when evaluating statistical claims.

Misleading Statistics

We have to be aware of occasionally being misled by the wrong use of statistics either in error or deliberately. The following are examples.

- **Misleading graphs and diagrams**

  Example: the following bar chart was drawn to compare the price of a pair of shoes in 2008 and 2018.

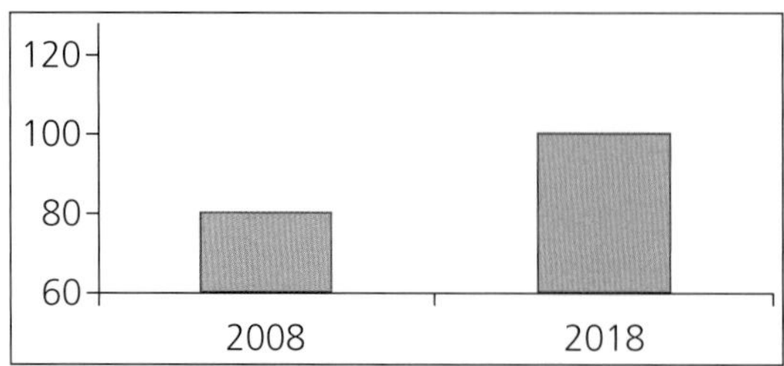

  The sizes of the bars suggest that the price doubled in that time. This is because the vertical axis does not start at 0. When redrawn with a different scale we get a different impression:

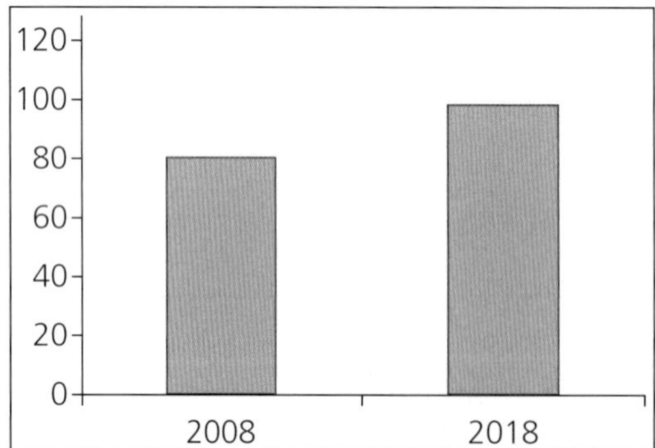

  Here the vertical axis starts at 0 and we see thing very differently.
  The actual increase was only 25%.

- Advertising with questionable statistics:

  Example: '9 out of 10 dog owners who expressed a preference said that they prefer Chappie.'

  This actually does not tell us much at all. This statement would actually be true if 990 people out of 1000 surveyed said they didn't have a preference and 9 out of the remaining 10 preferred Chappie!

  The advertisement also did not give a sample size or indicate if it was random sample.

- When using **small samples**, it is possible to conduct a survey repeatedly until the results are favourable and then report just that sample result.

The following example shows how we have to be careful when listening to people who use statistics to make claims.

There are five houses on a cul-de-sac. The annual incomes of the people living in these houses are: €30,000 €30,000 €40,000 €60,000 €140,000.

An auctioneer who is valuing one of the houses says that the average income is €60,000.

The residents are looking for improvements in services from the local authority.
They say that the average income is only €40,000.

Who is telling the truth?

In fact, both parties are telling the truth.

The auctioneer is using the **mean** as his average:

$$\frac{30000 + 30000 + 40000 + 60000 + 140000}{5} = \frac{300000}{5}$$
$$= €60,000$$

The residents are using the **median** as their average: €40,000.

The mean is affected by one very high figure.
The median is not.

In this case, the median is probably the better figure to use as the income of a typical householder on the cul-de-sac. However, it would be better to mention the one very high figure (€140,000) which is very different from the others. This figure would be referred to as an **outlier** by statisticians.

So when you hear the word **average** used by people quoting statistics, always ask 'Which average?'

Activity 19.2

1 Your teacher has asked you to carry out a statistical investigation.
- (i) What are the main steps in carrying out a statistical investigation?
- (ii) Describe a statistical investigation you could carry out using these steps.

2 There are 80 people at a meeting. Describe how you would take a simple random sample of 20 people from this group.

3 (i) What is meant by the term 'bias' as applied to sampling?
- (ii) Which of the following sampling methods is most likely to produce bias?

  1: A simple random sample of size $n = 50$

  2: A volunteer sample of size $n = 500$

  Explain your answer.

4 (i) Copy and fill in the questionnaire in Section 19B.
- (ii) Give the types of data which come from each question.

5 Indicate where there might be bias in these situations:
- (i) Students measure their heights with their shoes on.
- (ii) Students want to do a survey of student attitudes to politics. They give a questionnaire to 12 First Year girls.
- (iii) The government wants to find out what people think of the Gardaí. They make out a questionnaire. The survey is conducted by the Gardaí.
- (iv) A survey is done on the reliability of cars. Only cars less than three years old are included in the survey.
- (v) A manufacturer of cars is surveyed on 'Which cars do you think are the most popular?'

6 Why are the following sampling methods poor and how could they be improved?
- (i) A survey to find out how many people buy a newspaper is conducted outside a newsagent's shop.
- (ii) A survey on people's attitude to religion is carried out by telephone on a Sunday morning.
- (iii) A survey is designed to find out how long students spend on social networking sites in a typical week. The survey is conducted on the first day back after mid-term break.
- (iv) A survey is carried out to find out how people feel about a certain political party. The survey is done in a wealthy part of a town.

7 A survey is carried out to find out how people feel about the importance of education in Ireland. The survey is conducted by telephone on a sample of 12 people. Numbers are randomly chosen from the Dublin telephone directory.

The calls are made in the evening from 6 pm to 8 pm.

What problems are there with this survey that would make the results of the investigation unreliable?

8 List eight questions you should ask when evaluating a survey or opinion poll done by somebody else.

9 A question asked in a survey is shown below. Name two faults with this question.

Questionnaire

"How much do you pay each month on your mortgage ☐ ?"

Under €800   €800–1200   €1200–1600

10 Explain what is wrong with each of the following survey questions:

(i) How old are you?

(ii) Would you agree that Premier League players are paid too much?

(iii) Have you ever taken illegal drugs?

(iv) There have been many accidents in your housing estate. Do you agree that traffic ramps should be installed?

11 The diagram below has been drawn to show the increase in car sales over a two-year period. Explain why this diagram is misleading.

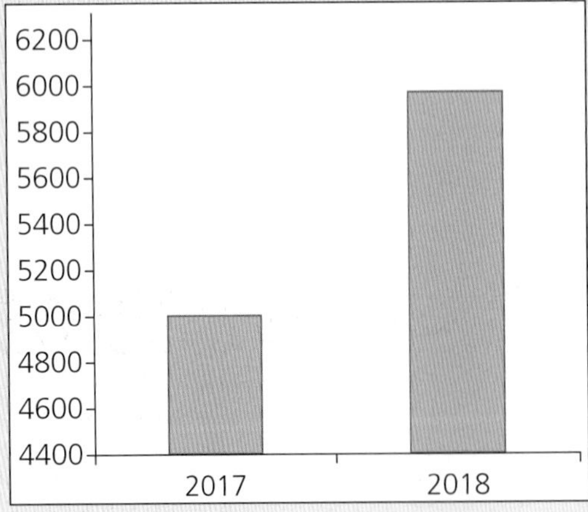

Section 19C Numerical Analysis of Data

Numbers calculated from data that are used to summarise the data are referred to as **summary statistics** or **descriptive statistics**.

The two most useful questions to ask to help you to summarise a set of data are:

(i) What is a typical or average value, i.e. a **measure of central tendency**?

(ii) How widely '**spread**' are the numbers?

Measures of Central Tendency

The **mode** is the most frequent value or category. The centre of a **categorical data set** is always described by the mode.

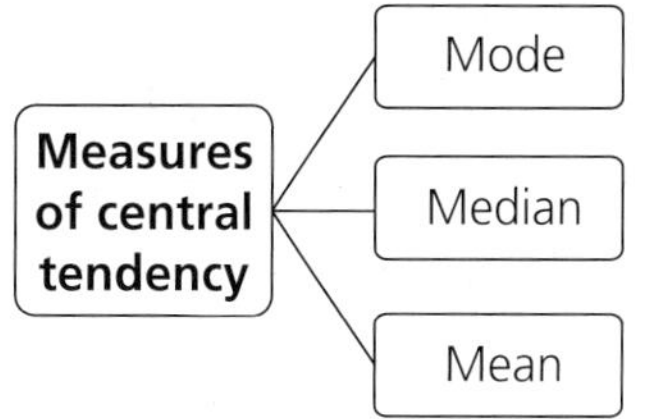

The modal women's shoe size is the size worn by the most women.

The **median** is the number that divides the **ordered** data in half.

Before finding the **median**, the data must be put in order from the smallest to the largest value. The median is the middle value. 50% of the ordered data lies below the median and the other 50% lies above it. The median is not affected by unusually large or unusually small data values.

The **mean** is the sum of all the values divided by the total number of values in the data set. It represents the '**fair share**' value of the data.

The median and mean are used with **numerical data** only.

One quick way to summarise data is to give a **three-number summary**:

the minimum, the median and the maximum.

Minimum — Median — Maximum

50% of the data | 50% of the data

These three figures give a basic indication of the **centre** and **spread** of the data.

Calculating the Mean of Larger Data Sets

If we want to calculate the mean of a lot of numbers, it can be tedious and time-consuming, so we look for a shorter way.

Example 1

Find the mean of the 12 numbers:

3, 4, 4, 5, 3, 4, 5, 3, 4, 5, 4, 4

Solution

$$\text{The mean} = \frac{3+4+4+5+3+4+5+3+4+5+4+4}{12} = \frac{48}{12} = 4$$

We are adding the same numbers several times.

If we rearrange the 12 numbers to put them in order, we get:

3, 3, 3, 4, 4, 4, 4, 4, 4, 5, 5, 5

Now multiplication is a quick way of adding, so we have:

$$\text{The mean} = \frac{3(3)+6(4)+3(5)}{12} = \frac{48}{12} = 4$$

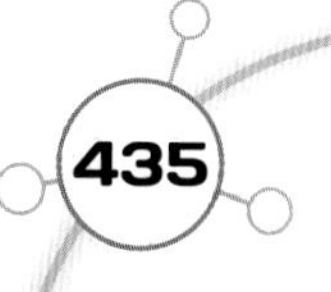

We display repeating numbers using a frequency table:

Number	3	4	5
Frequency	3	6	3

In order to find the mean from a frequency table:

- Multiply each number by its frequency
- Add up the answers
- Divide the result by the sum of the frequencies.

Example 2

The heights of ten students (in cm) are as follows:
166, 166, 154, 171, 154, 171, 154, 154, 166, 179

(i) Find the mean of the unsorted data.

(ii) Find the mean by making a frequency table.

Solution

(i) $\text{Mean} = \frac{166 + 166 + 154 + 171 + 154 + 171 + 154 + 154 + 166 + 179}{10} = \frac{1635}{10}$

$= 163.5 \text{ cm}$

(ii) Frequency table:

Height (cm)	154	166	171	179
Frequency	4	3	2	1

$\text{Mean} = \frac{4(154) + 3(166) + 2(171) + 1(179)}{4 + 3 + 2 + 1} = \frac{616 + 498 + 342 + 179}{10} = \frac{1635}{10}$

$= 163.5 \text{ cm}$

Activity 19.3

1 The number of sports played by twelve boys and girls were as follows:

1 3 3 2 2 2
3 4 1 3 1 3

(i) Find the mean of the data given (correct to two decimal places).

(ii) Complete a copy of this table and use it to find the mean.

Number of sports	1	2	3	4
Frequency				

2 When asked, 'How many people are in your household?', a group of students gave the following responses:

7 6 3 4 6 5 6 4 3 6 5 4
3 4 5 4 4 4 4 4 5 6 4 4

(i) Copy and complete the following table and use it to find the mean:

Number in household	3	4	5	6	7
Number of students					

(ii) Is your answer a natural number? Comment on this.

3 A questionnaire contained the question 'How many cars are there in your household?' The following are the responses of a sample of Irish students:

2 7 2 2 2 2 2 1 8 2 4 2
4 2 2 2 2 1 2 1 0 3 2 1

(i) Draw a frequency table to represent these data.

(ii) Calculate the mean number of cars per household for this sample of students.

(iii) Find the mode.

(iv) Find the median.

(v) How many cars does a typical household from this sample have?

4 The mean age of six students is 14. What is the sum of their ages?

5 Jack works for an average of 7 hours per day for 5 days one week. How many hours did Jack work that week?

6 The mean age of four students in a room is 12 years. A teacher joins the group. The mean age is now 16.
What age is the teacher?

7 The mean height of five people is 160 cm. One person leaves. The mean height is now 158 cm. What was the height of the person who left?

8 There are 12 houses on Cherrymount Avenue. In one week, the number of letters delivered to the houses were:

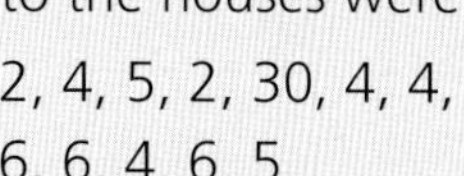

2, 4, 5, 2, 30, 4, 4, 6, 6, 4, 6, 5.

(i) Calculate the range of the data.

(ii) Calculate the mean number of letters.

(iii) Calculate the median number of letters.

(iv) Calculate the mode.

(v) Which of these averages is the best measure of the number of letters delivered to a typical house on Cherrymount Avenue?

9 The marks that Oscar got in his English tests for a term are listed in the table.

Test	Test 1	Test 2	Test 3	Test 4	Test 5
Mark	86	90	76	45	83

(i) Calculate the range of Oscar's marks.

(ii) What is Oscar's median mark for the term?

(iii) Calculate Oscar's mean mark for the term.

(iv) Which one of Oscar's marks is out of line with the others?

(v) Which do you think is a fairer summary of Oscar's work for the term: the median or the mean? Give a reason for your answer.

10 Michelle's maths teacher gives tests that are marked out of 20.
Michelle got the following results in five tests: 14, 10, 12, 20, 14.

(i) Find Michelle's mean mark for the five tests.

(ii) Fiachra got the following results in the same tests: 16, 10, –, 14, 14.
He was absent for the third test.
Is Fiachra better than Michelle at maths? Or is Michelle better? Give a reason for your answer.

11 Emily has six cards, each of which has a positive whole number printed on it. Four of the cards have the number 9 on them.
Without knowing the numbers on the other two cards, give the value of:

(i) the median

(ii) the mode

(iii) the range.

12 What types of data do we need to use (i) mean (ii) median (iii) mode?

Mean of a Grouped Frequency Distribution

When we have continuous data, we often group the data into **intervals**. We need to be able to find the mean of such a grouped frequency distribution.

Example 3

The weights in kg of a sample of 19 male university students are as follows.

62, 64, 70, 80, 62, 64, 70, 64, 71, 112, 70, 66, 71, 75, 65, 73, 66, 70, 72

(i) Calculate the mean of the data.

(ii) Fill in the grouped frequency table.

Weights (kg)	60–65	65–70	70–75	75–80	80–85	85–90
Frequency						

Weights (kg)	90–95	95–100	100–105	105–110	110–115
Frequency					

60–65 means: 60 kg ≤ weight < 65 kg

(iii) Using the **mid-interval value**, calculate the mean of the grouped frequency distribution.

> The mid-interval value is the mean of the two extreme values of the interval.
> The mid-interval value for the interval 60–65 = (60 + 65) ÷ 2 = 62.5.

(iv) Why is the mean of the grouped frequency distribution not equal to the mean of the raw data?

(v) In which interval of the grouped frequency distribution does the median lie?

(vi) Use the values in the table to estimate the median weight, as accurately as you can.

Solution

(i) Mean = (62 + 64 + 70 + 80 + 62 + 64 + 70 + 64 + 71 + 112 + 70 + 66 + 71 + 75 + 65 + 73 + 66 + 70 + 72) ÷ 19 = 70.9 kg

(ii)

Weights (kg)	60–65	65–70	70–75	75–80	80–85	85–90
Frequency	5	3	8	1	1	0

Weights (kg)	90–95	95–100	100–105	105–110	110–115
Frequency	0	0	0	0	1

(iii) $\text{Mean} = \dfrac{(62.5)(5) + (67.5)(3) + (72.5)(8) + (77.5)(1) + (82.5)(1) + (112.5)(1)}{19} = 71.97 \text{ kg}$

(iv) The mean of a grouped frequency distribution assumes that each value in an interval is equal to the mid-interval value, which is not the case.

(v) The median is the 10th data item which lies in the interval 70–75 kg.

(vi) The median = 10th value

The 9th and 10th items are in the 70–75 kg class so we would estimate that the median is 2/8 of the way into the class interval, i.e. estimated median = 71 kg

1 The following table refers to the ages of 70 guests at a wedding.

Age (in years)	0–20	20–40	40–60	60–80
Number of guests	5	18	21	26

40–60 years means: 40 years ≤ age < 60 years

(i) Using mid-interval values, estimate the mean age of the guests to the nearest year.
(ii) What percentage of the guests were over 40 years old?
(iii) What is the greatest number of guests who could have been over 65?
(iv) What is the smallest number of guests who could have been over 65? Explain.

2 The heights in centimetres of 60 randomly selected female students aged 16 years are given in the table.

Height (cm)	150–155	155–160	160–165	165–170	170–175	175–180
Frequency	2	9	14	20	11	4

150–155 cm means: 150 cm ≤ height < 155 cm

(i) What is the modal interval?
(ii) In which interval does the median lie?
(iii) Calculate the mean height to the nearest centimetre using the mid-interval values.
(iv) Under what circumstances could this be exactly equal to the actual mean of the raw data?

3 The grouped frequency table below refers to the marks obtained by 80 students in a test. Note that in this case the intervals are not equal.

Marks	0–40	40–55	55–70	70–100
Number of students	12	20	25	23

40–55 marks means: 40 ≤ mark < 55

(i) What percentage of students obtained 55 marks or higher?
(ii) In what interval does the median lie? Estimate the median mark.
(iii) Using mid-interval values, estimate the mean mark for the class to the nearest integer.

4 Below is a list of the ages in years of 44 people who signed up for an aerobics class.

27	17	21	34	42	19	40	39	22	45	29	22	30	39
60	24	25	38	29	30	28	21	53	58	24	61	28	31
35	18	22	27	47	30	34	62	48	54	19	20	23	24
52	49												

(i) Use the data to copy and complete the grouped frequency table.

Age in years	15–20	20–25	25–30	30–35	35–40	40–45	45–50	50–55	55–60	60–65
Tally										
Frequency										
Relative frequency (%)										

15–20 means 15 years or more but less than 20 years

(ii) What is the modal interval?

(iii) What percentage of the participants are over 60 years of age?

(iv) Calculate the mean using (a) the raw data, (b) the mid-interval values.

5 The salaries, in €, of the different employees working in a call centre are listed below.

22 000	16 500	38 000	26 500	15 000	21 000	15 500	46 000
42 000	9500	32 000	27 000	33 000	36 000	24 000	37 000
65 000	37 000	24 500	23 500	28 000	52 000	33 000	25 000
23 000	16 500	35 000	25 000	33 000	20 000	19 500	16 000

(i) Use this data to copy and complete the grouped frequency table below.

Salary (€1000)	0–10	10–20	20–30	30–40	40–50	50–60	60–70
No. of employees							

10–20 means €10 000 or more but less than €20 000

(ii) Using mid-interval values, find the mean salary of the employees.

(iii) (a) Outline another method which could have been used to calculate the mean salary.

(b) Which method is more accurate? Explain your answer.

6 Twenty people enrolled in a weight loss programme. Their weights in kilograms before the programme were:
129, 153, 86, 77, 94, 124, 103, 76, 89, 83, 98, 86, 107, 128, 78, 82, 94, 79, 115, 104.

(i) Order the data from smallest to largest.

(ii) Fill in a grouped frequency table for the data starting at 75 kg using intervals of 10 kg.

(iii) Estimate the mean of the data, correct to the nearest kilogram, using mid-interval values from the grouped frequency table in part (ii).

(iv) If each person on the programme lost 4 kg after six weeks, what would the mean weight of the group be after the six weeks? Guess first and then verify your answer.

(v) If each person on the programme lost y kg after six weeks, what would the mean weight of the group be after the six weeks?

7 The following table shows the distribution of the amounts spent by a number of people in a restaurant.

Amount spent (€)	0–16	16–32	32–48	48–64	64–80
Number of customers	2	9	x	11	5

€32–€48 means: €32 ≤ amount spent < €48

(i) Taking the mid-interval values, the estimate of the mean amount spent by the customers was €43.20. How many people spent between €32 and €48?

(ii) What percentage of the customers spent less than €64?

(iii) If each of the customers had spent €2 more, use the mean estimated in part (i) to find the estimate of the new mean amount spent by the customers. Use two methods.

Section 19D Graphical Analysis of Data

A pie chart is a good way of representing data when you want to show how something is shared or divided, i.e. **parts of a whole**.

Example 1

The data in the table below came from a survey of males and females. Represent this data on a pie chart.

Males	Females	Total
17	13	30

Solution

To calculate the angles:

$$\text{Angle} = \frac{\text{no. of each gender}}{\text{total no. of students}} \times 360°$$

Male: $\frac{17}{30} \times 360° = 204°$

Female: $\frac{13}{30} \times 360° = 156°$

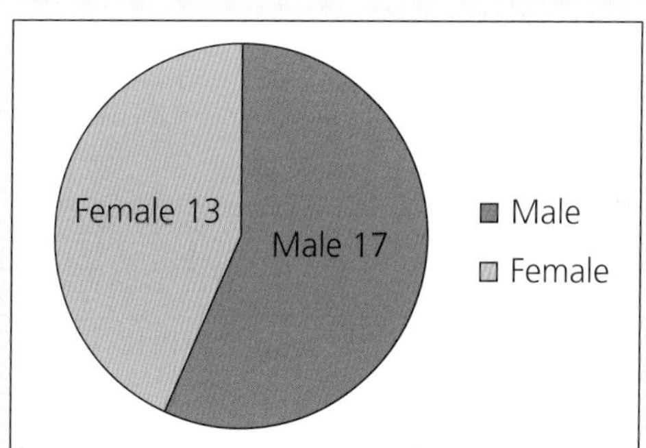

The pie chart shows the proportion of males to females clearly.

Example 2

Saoirse asked the members of her class the question 'How often do you watch reality TV?'

The following data were collected:

A lot	Sometimes	Rarely	Never
6	13	8	3

(i) How many students were surveyed?
(ii) Represent the data on a pie chart, showing the percentages clearly.
(iii) Explain what the table and the chart tell you about the data.
(iv) If a student was picked at random from this group, what would be the probability that he/she never watches reality TV?

Solution

(i) 6 + 13 + 8 + 3 = 30 students

(ii) To calculate the angles:

$$\text{Angle} = \frac{\text{no. for a category}}{\text{total no. of students}} \times 360°$$

a lot: $\frac{6}{30} \times 360° = 72°$

sometimes: $\frac{13}{30} \times 360° = 156°$

rarely: $\frac{8}{30} \times 360° = 96°$

never: $\frac{3}{30} \times 360° = 36°$

This pie chart shows the values and the percentages. The percentages are good for comparison purposes.

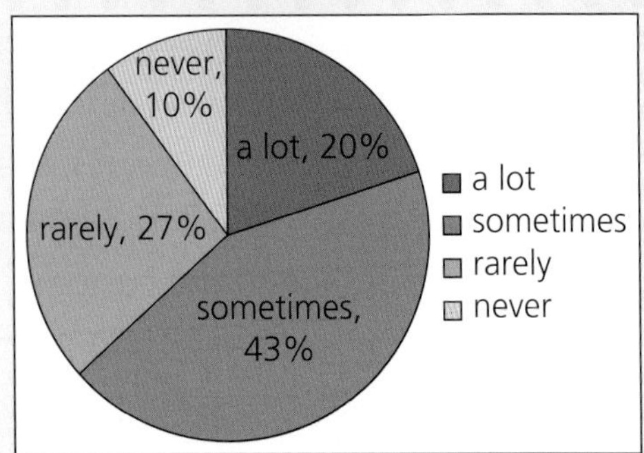

(iii) 43% of these students watch reality TV sometimes. Nearly a third (37%) watch it rarely or never.

1 in 5 of these students watch reality TV a lot.

(iv) 3 students never watch reality TV.

Total number of students = 30

Probability $= \frac{3}{30} = \frac{1}{10} = 10\%$

Example 3

The number of dog licences issued by Wicklow County Council from 1999 to 2009 is shown in the pie chart and in the bar chart below.

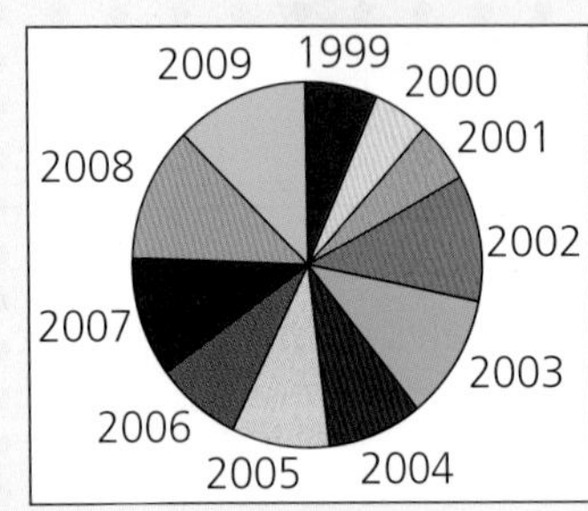

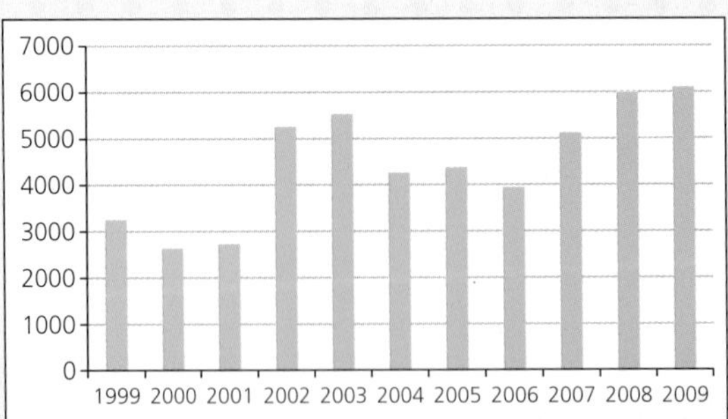

Give two reasons why the bar chart is a better way of showing the data than the pie chart.

Solution

Two possible reasons:

- With the large number of categories, the trends, changes and patterns are easier to see on a bar chart.
- The bar chart clearly shows all the data for each year and how the number in each year **compares** with the others.

1 This pie chart shows the favourite sport of 24 students. Basketball is the favourite sport of how many students?

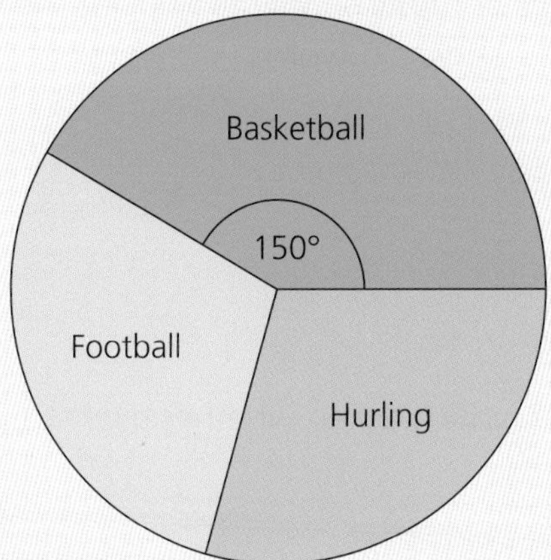

2 This pie chart shows how a household budget of €180 was spent.

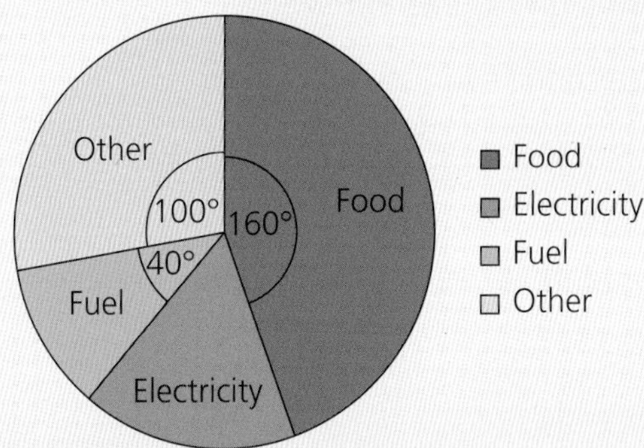

(i) Find the missing angle on the chart.

(ii) Work out how the budget was shared out for each category.

3 Some students were asked 'Do you live in an urban or rural area?' Their replies are given in this table:

Urban	Rural
21	9

(i) How many students were surveyed?

(ii) Draw a pie chart to display the data.

(iii) Write a brief summary of what the table and the chart tell you about the data.

(iv) If a student is picked at random from this group of students, what is the probability that the student lives in an urban area?

4 Repeat question **3** using data from your own class (primary data).

5 A class survey was performed to find out how students get to school. The results are given in this table:

Cycle	Walk	Car	Bus	Other
1	16	10	2	1

(i) Draw a pie chart to display the data.

(ii) Explain what the table and the chart tell you about the data.

6 Repeat question **5** using data from your own class.

7 A transition year class was asked 'In a typical week, how often do you exercise for 20 minutes or more?' Their replies are given in this table:

Never	Once or twice	Several times	Every day
2	6	7	9

(i) Draw a pie chart to display the data.

(ii) Write a brief summary of what the table and the chart tell you about the data.

(iii) If a student was picked at random from this class, what is the probability that the student exercises every day? Give your answer as a decimal, a fraction and a percentage.

8 Repeat question **7** using data from your own class.

9 A group of 30 students were asked 'How concerned are you about environmental issues?' Their replies are represented on this pie chart:

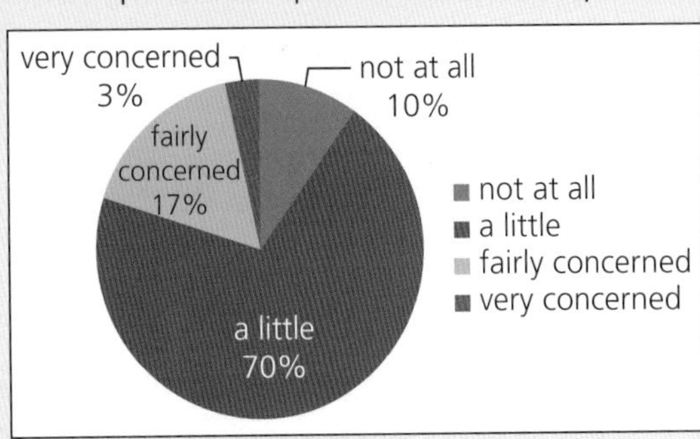

(i) Calculate the numbers in each category.

(ii) Summarise the findings of the survey in words.

10 Repeat question **9** using data from your own class.

11 Thirty students responded to a question in a survey which asked whether they would like to support proposed changes to the school timetable.

Their answers are summarised in the table below.

Answer	Yes	No	No opinion
Number of Students	6	15	9

Draw a pie chart to show the proportion of students giving each answer.

12 The table shows the results of a school survey regarding favourite types of music.

Music Type	Pop	Rock	Classical	Other
Number of Students	40	30	5	15

Draw a pie chart to illustrate this information, showing clearly how you calculate the size of each angle.

13 An exit-poll was taken on election day to find out which of the political parties, A, B or C, people had voted for.

(i) Calculate the third angle in the diagram.

480 had voted for party B.

(ii) How many people took part in the poll?

(iii) How many of these voted for party C?

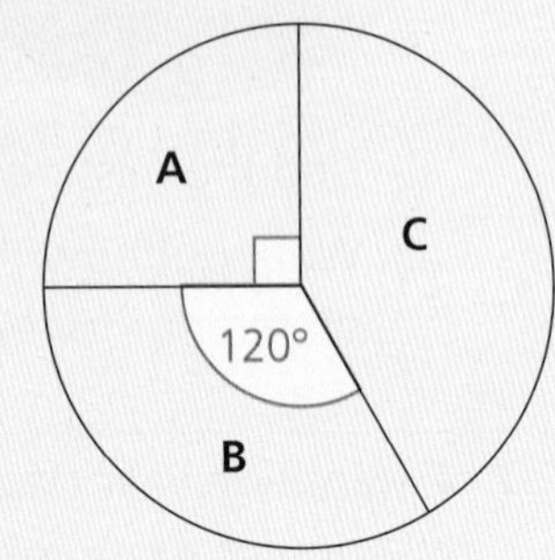

Representing Continuous Data

When we have a lot of data, it can be hard to 'see the wood for the trees'.

For example, here are the heights (in cm) of thirty students from one class:

143	153	164	162	172	140	165	153	175	154
169	158	175	180	172	163	150	165	165	150
165	163	190	140	160	180	166	160	175	160

There are a lot of figures here. To help us to make sense of all these figures, we need to sort them into groups or **classes**. We make a **grouped frequency table**:

Height (cm)	140–150	150–160	160–170	170–180	180–190
No. of students	3	6	13	5	3

[Note: 140–150 means 140 cm or more, but less than 150 cm, etc.]

Now we can see a lot more information than before.

For example, we can now see that nearly half of these students (13) are between 160 and 170 cm in height. We wouldn't have noticed that from the raw data.

People say that 'a picture paints a thousand words'. Therefore, we will draw a diagram to make this even clearer.

Histograms

A diagram that is used to represent continuous data is a **histogram**.

A histogram is very similar to a bar chart, but the bars are joined **without gaps** to show that the data are continuous.

The student height data is represented in the histogram below.

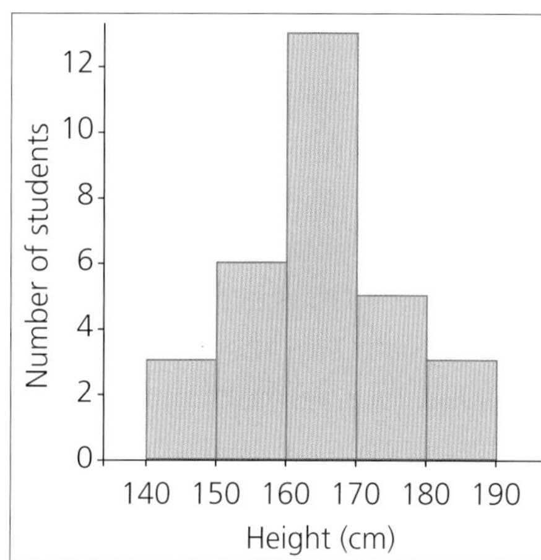

From the table and the histogram, we can see that:

- The modal class height is 160–170 cm. This is the interval with the largest number of students.
- The range of heights is from 140 cm to 190 cm.

People who study statistics are also very interested in the **shape** of histograms.

This histogram of students' heights is quite **symmetrical** in shape. It is often referred to as being bell-shaped.

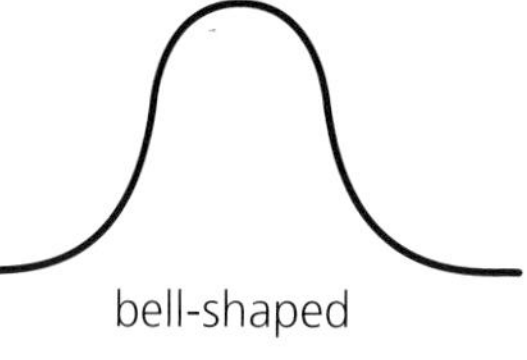

Height is just one feature of a person. In fact, the data about all adult human and animal characteristics take on this symmetrical shape. So look out for it in histograms. Younger people grow at different rates, so their data might look different.

The following example is quite different from this.

Example 4

The English Premier League is a soccer tournament which is run over a complete season. 1066 goals were scored in one season. A soccer match runs for 90 minutes in two halves of 45 minutes. The times when goals were scored in matches for the season are given in percentages in this table:

Time in match	0–15 min	15–30 min	30–45 min (including added time)	45–60 min	60–75 min	75–90 min (including added time)
Percentage of goals scored (to the nearest percent)	13%	14%	17%	16%	18%	22%

[Note: 0–15 is from 0 minutes to just before 15 minutes, etc.]

(i) Draw a histogram of the data.

(ii) Write a summary of what the table and the graph tell you about the data.

(iii) Based on the data, what is the probability of scoring a goal in the last fifteen minutes of a match in the Premier League this season?

Solution

(i)

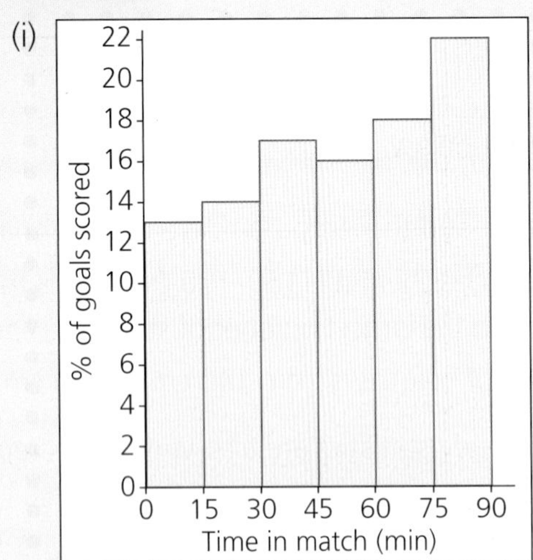

(ii)
- The least number of goals were scored in the first fifteen minutes. This is probably due to the teams getting settled into the match.
- The **modal class** is 75–90 min. This means that most goals were scored in the last 15 minutes.
- 40% of the goals came in the last half-hour.
- As each half progresses, the number of goals increases. Defenders need to be on their guard in the last fifteen minutes of each half!
- 56% of goals were scored in the second half, and 44% were scored in the first half.

(iii) 22% of goals came in the last 15 minutes of the 1066 matches in the season. This is the relative frequency as a percentage. Therefore, if the rules of the league stay the same, we would estimate that there is a 22% $\left(\frac{22}{100}\right)$ probability of a goal coming in the last fifteen minutes of a match this season.

You can see that the **shape** of the soccer histogram is quite different from that of the histogram of the students' heights.

The soccer histogram is highest on the right and lowest on the left. These data are said to be **left-skewed**. A set of data could also be **right-skewed**.

The shapes of histograms are usually described as being one of these:

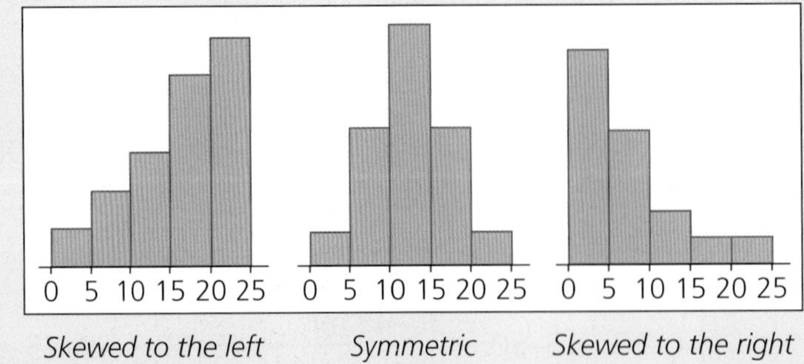

Skewed to the left *Symmetric* *Skewed to the right*

In a histogram, the area of each bar represent the frequency, but we will be working only with histograms with equal class intervals.

Key Points

It is important to note that:
- Bar charts are for discrete data.
- Histograms are for continuous data.

1 A group of 32 students were asked 'How long does it take you to get to school?' The following histogram represents the data.
[Note: This is an example of a histogram which is **right-skewed** in shape.]

(i) Use the data from the histogram to complete a copy of the frequency table below.

No. of minutes	No. of students
0–5	
5–10	9
10–15	
15–20	
20–25	
25–30	
30–35	
35–40	
40–45	

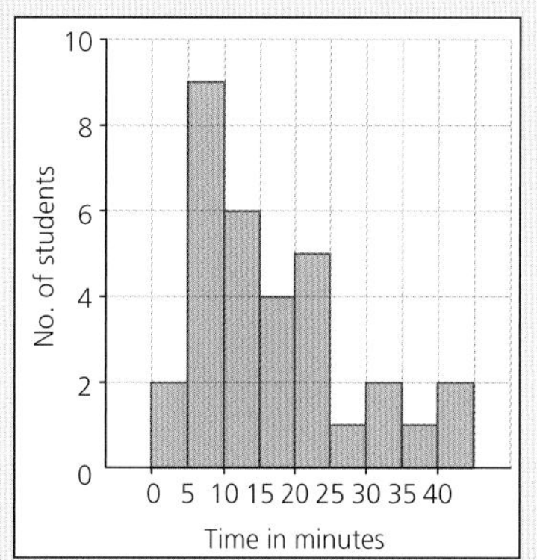

[Note: 5–10 means 5 minutes or more but less than 10 minutes, etc.]

(ii) What is the modal interval? Explain, in words, what the mode means in this context.

(iii) How many of these students take less than 10 minutes to get to school?

(iv) If a student is selected at random from this group, what is the probability that it takes him/her less than 10 minutes to get to school? Give your answer as a fraction, a decimal and a percentage. Show your answer on a number line.

2 (i) A questionnaire contained the question 'Approximately how long do you spend on social networking sites each week?' The histogram illustrates the answers given by 100 students, randomly selected from those who completed the survey.

Use the data from the histogram to complete a copy of the frequency table below.

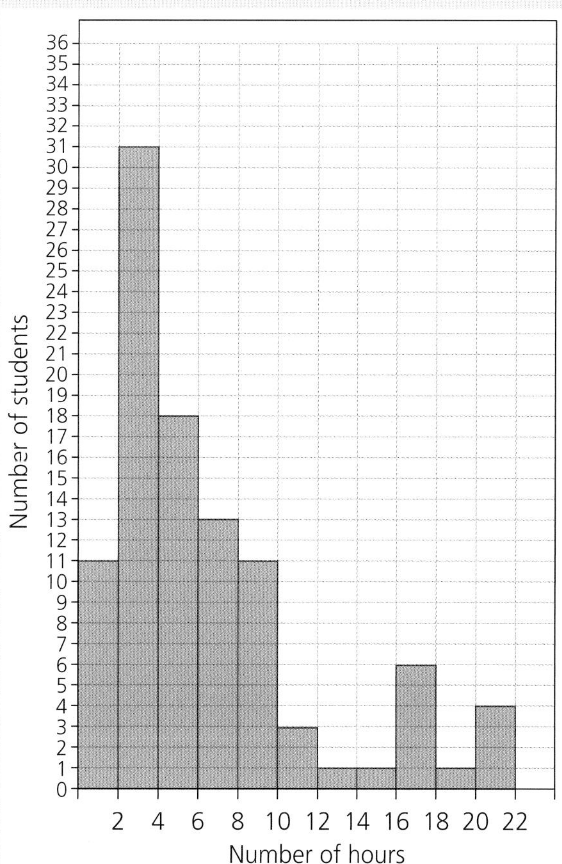

No. of hours	No. of students
0–2	
2–4	
4–6	
6–8	
8–10	
10–12	
12–14	
14–16	
16–18	
18–20	
20–22	

[Note: 2–4 means 2 hours or more but less than 4 hours, etc.]

(ii) What is the modal class?

(iii) Describe the shape of the histogram. Your answer should include the word 'skewed'.

(iv) How many of these students spend more than 12 hours per week on social networking sites?

(v) If a student is chosen at random from this group, what is the probability that he/she spends more than 12 hours per week on social networking sites?

3 A class of students were asked 'How much did you spend on your last haircut?' The histograms below show the responses of the girls and boys separately.

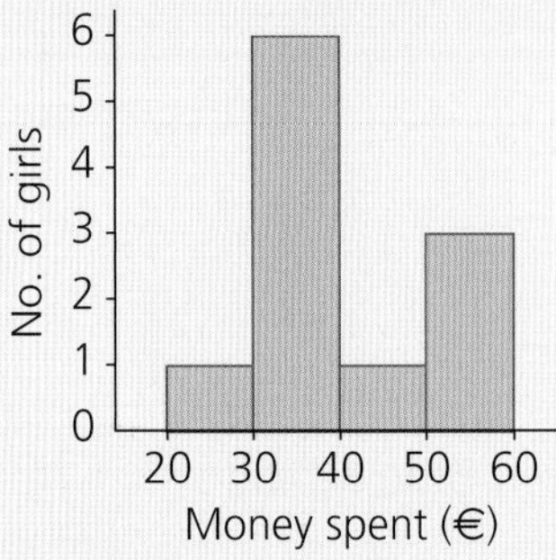

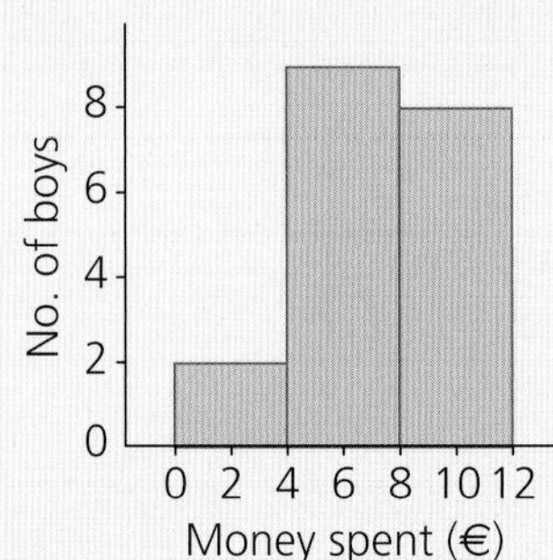

(i) What is the modal class for the boys?

(ii) What is the range of the boys' data?

(iii) Find the modal class for the girls.

(iv) Find the range of the girls' data.

(v) Write a brief summary comparing the data for the boys and the girls.

4 The table below shows the data from a students' survey question which asked 'What is your right foot length?'

Length (cm)	20–23	23–26	26–29	29–32
No. of students	5	17	3	5

[Note: 20–23 means 20 cm or more but less than 23 cm, etc.]

(i) Draw a histogram to represent the data.

(ii) What is the range of the data?

(iii) What is the modal interval? Explain, in words, what the mode means in this context.

(iv) How many of these students have a foot length in the range 29–32 cm?

(v) If a student is taken at random from this group, what is the probability that his/her foot length is in the range 29–32 cm?

5 A question on a survey asks 'What is your height (in cm)?' The following are data randomly selected from 24 Irish **boys** aged 14 and 15 who completed the survey:

Height (cm)	160–165	165–170	170–175	175–180	180–185
Number of students	4	2	5	9	4

[Note: 160–165 means 160 cm or taller but less than 165 cm, etc.]

(i) Draw a histogram to represent the data. What type of data are these?

(ii) What is the range of the data?

(iii) What is the modal height?

(iv) How many of these boys are 170 cm or more in height?

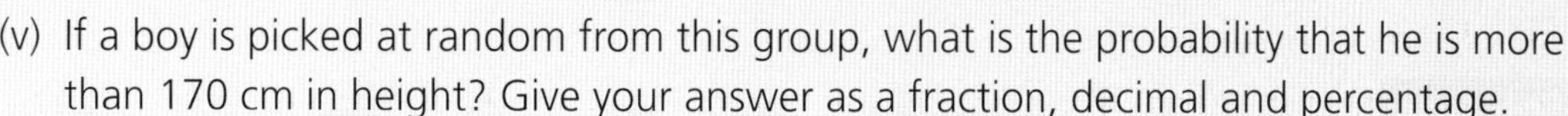

(v) If a boy is picked at random from this group, what is the probability that he is more than 170 cm in height? Give your answer as a fraction, decimal and percentage.

(vi) Can we say from this sample that most Irish boys aged 14 and 15 are taller than 170 cm?

6 A question on a survey asks 'What is your height (in cm)?'
The following are data randomly selected from 24 Irish **girls** aged 14 and 15 who completed the survey:

Height (cm)	140–145	145–150	150–155	155–160	160–165	165–170	170–175
Number of students	2	0	1	2	6	7	6

[Note: 160–165 means 160 cm or taller but less than 165 cm, etc.]

(i) Draw a histogram to represent the data.

(ii) What is the range of the data?

(iii) What is the modal interval for height?

(iv) How many of these girls are 170 cm or more in height?

(v) If a girl is picked at random from this group, what is the probability that she is more than 170 cm in height?

7 Look at the tables and the histograms that you drew for questions **5** and **6**.
Would you say that these boys are taller than these girls? Give reasons for your answer.

Back-to-back Stem-and-Leaf Plots

Stem-and-leaf plots are a good way to **compare** two related data sets.
The way we do this is to place the stem-and-leaf plots **back-to-back**.

Example 5

The pulse rates in beats per minute (bpm) of a group of participants in an aerobics class are taken before and after exercise.

Rate before (bpm)	53	61	79	72	50	58	64	67	59	66	60	52	67	76	66
Rate after (bpm)	64	82	67	84	72	59	92	62	71	68	74	71	74	89	78

(i) Draw a back-to-back stem-and-leaf plot to display the data before and after exercise.

(ii) Looking at the stem-and-leaf plots, how do the pulse rates compare before and after exercise?

(iii) Describe the shape of the distributions before and after exercise.

(iv) Find the maximum, minimum and range of the data before and after exercise.

(v) Use the back-to-back stem-and-leaf plot to compare the medians before and after exercise.

(vi) Do you think it is reasonable to say that pulse rates were greater after exercise compared to before exercise? Justify your answer.

Solution

(i)

Leaves ordered		
Pulse rate before exercise		Pulse rate after exercise
9 8 3 2 0	5	9
7 7 6 6 4 1 0	6	2 4 7 8
9 6 2	7	1 1 2 4 4 8
	8	2 4 9
	9	2
Key:	8	2 means 82 bpm
2	7	means 72 bpm

(ii) The pulse rates have shifted upwards after exercise. They were clustered between 50 and 80 bpm before exercise and now they are clustered between 60 and 90 bpm. They are also more spread out after exercise than before exercise.

(iii) Before exercise, the values are clustered towards the lower values with a slight tail in the positive direction, i.e. towards the higher values. After exercise, the shape is approximately symmetrical and bell-shaped.

(iv) Before exercise: minimum = 50 bpm; maximum = 79 bpm; range = 29 bpm
After exercise: minimum = 59 bpm; maximum = 92 bpm; range = 33 bpm

(v) Median before exercise = value of the 8th data point = 64 bpm
Median after exercise = value of the 8th data point = 72 bpm

(vi) Yes, in general pulse rates were greater after exercise compared to before exercise. Both the maxima and minima rates are greater after exercise.
The median is greater after exercise. The mean before exercise = 63 bpm and the mean after exercise is 74 bpm, which is greater.

Activity 19.7

1 A teacher records the marks from the same test for two different class groups, class A and class B.

Class A	58	62	65	70	71	75	75	75	78	78	80	80	82	84	85	91	96	98	99
Class B	61	53	54	75	99	98	98	96	78	57	90	75	93	51	75	96	99	59	95

(i) Compare the modes, medians and means for both class groups.

(ii) Given the measures of central tendency only without the raw data, what conclusion might you draw about the two distributions?

(iii) Draw a back-to-back stem-and-leaf plot to compare the two classes' test marks.

(iv) Compare the two classes based on the graphical representations for each class.

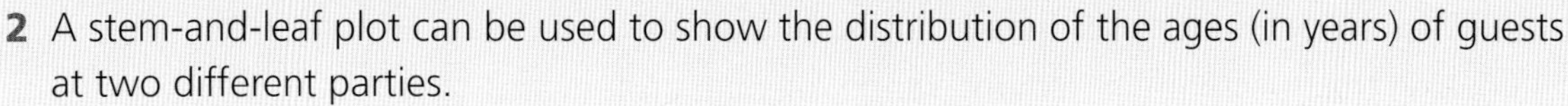

2 A stem-and-leaf plot can be used to show the distribution of the ages (in years) of guests at two different parties.

John's party		Saoirse's party
	0	0 0 1 5 7
	1	2 2 3
9 9 9 8 8	2	5 7 7 8
5 4 3 3 1 1	3	3 4 4 4 5 5 6 7 8
0	4	0
	5	3 5 5 6 7 8 8 8 9
	6	5 6 6
	7	2 3
	8	5 5
	9	2
Key:	7	2 means 72 years

(i) Write one sentence to compare the distribution of the ages of people at each party using initial impressions of the plot.

(ii) How many people attended each party?

(iii) Write down the minimum age, maximum age and range of ages for both parties.

(iv) Make a suggestion as to what people were celebrating for each party.

(v) Describe the shape of both distributions of ages.

(vi) Find the measures of central tendency, mode, median and mean, of those attending both parties.

3 A full class of students is given a test in Statistics. Following the test (**Test 1**), the teacher revises the test material with the students. She then gives them another test which is similar to the first test to see if the students have improved their marks based on the revision.

The test results for the second test (**Test 2**) are given in this table.

83	86	79	43	58	38	69	58	57	100
86	35	62	97	82	78	46	77	77	100
98	98	83	37	58	45	68	49	59	100

(i) Copy and complete the back-to-back stem-and-leaf plot showing the results for Test 2.

Test 2		Test 1
	0	5 7
	1	8
	2	2 3 6
	3	4 7 8
	4	4
	5	1 1 2 3 5 8
	6	2 4 4
	7	1 8 8 9
	8	2 3 8 8 9
	9	4 6
	10	0
Key:	9	4 means 94 marks

(ii) Was anyone absent for the second test? Explain.
(iii) Find the maximum, minimum, range, median and mean.
(iv) Do the results indicate that marks have improved in Test 2 from Test 1? Justify your answer.
(v) The teacher wonders what proportion of the students improved in the second test. Can she find this using the stem-and-leaf plot?

4 Students measured the heights in metres of two different churches in their town using a clinometer. The following data was collected.

Church A: estimated heights (m)

53	65	87	35	39
40	53	60	59	42
46	55	57	78	57
65	74	65	82	48
48				

Church B: estimated heights (m)

49	38	84	58	52
40	47	49	48	48
40	50	54	56	52
39	58	56	55	39
43	48			

When they measured the height of church A, it was their first time using the clinometer and they measured the height of church B on the next day.

(i) How many students were in the class on the first and second days?
(ii) Draw a back-to-back stem-and-leaf plot to compare the distributions of the two data sets.
(iii) Looking at the stem-and-leaf plot, how would you describe the height of 84 m as an estimate for the height of church B?
(iv) State one difference between the two distributions.
(v) Compare the range of the estimated heights for both churches.
(vi) Do the answers to part (v) indicate to you that students have improved, in general, in their use of the clinometer?

5 The weights in kg of babies born on each day of the week in a certain hospital to mothers who smoke and mothers who do not smoke are given in the table.

	Monday	Tuesday	Wednesday	Thursday	Friday	Saturday	Sunday
Smoker	2.5 2.7 3	1.9 3.1 3.7	2.9 2.8	4.3 3.4	3.7 2.5	2.3 2.8	3.4 3.2
Non-smoker	2.4	2.9 3.2	3.3 4.2 4.1	3.7 3.1 5	3.8 2.9	3.6 4.1 2.3	3.4 3.6

(i) Use a back-to-back stem-and-leaf plot to display the data.

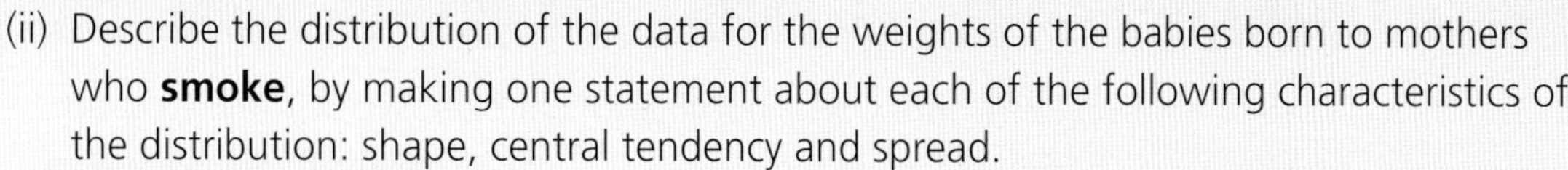

(ii) Describe the distribution of the data for the weights of the babies born to mothers who **smoke**, by making one statement about each of the following characteristics of the distribution: shape, central tendency and spread.

(iii) Describe the distribution of the data for the weights of the babies born to mothers who **do not smoke**, by making one statement about each of the following characteristics of the distribution: shape, central tendency and spread.

6 A quality controller arranged to have a random sample of walnuts measured and then tasted. The tasters were asked to classify the walnuts as either sweet or sour.

The lengths of the walnuts which were classified as **sour** are given below in mm:

65, 67, 75, 73, 71, 83, 55, 82, 87, 74, 69, 88, 75, 63

The lengths of the walnuts which were classified as **sweet** are given below in mm:

32, 56, 76, 73, 59, 75, 67, 68, 85, 63, 63, 46, 101, 70, 73, 72, 82

(i) Draw a suitable graphical representation to compare the distribution of lengths of this sample of sweet and sour walnuts.

(ii) Find the median length for each of the sets of data.

(iii) What appears to be similar and what appears to be different about the lengths of sweet and sour walnuts based on this sample?

7 The ages of the Academy Award winners for best male actor and best female actor (at the time they won the award) from 1992 to 2011 are as follows.

Male actor	54	52	37	38	32	45	60	46	40	36	47	29	43	37	38	45	50	48	60	50
Female actor	42	29	33	36	45	49	39	26	25	33	35	35	28	30	29	61	32	33	45	29

(i) Represent the data on a back-to-back stem-and-leaf plot. Be sure to include a key.

Male actors		Female actors
	2	
	3	
	4	
	5	
	6	
		Key:

(ii) State one similarity and one difference that can be observed between the ages of the male and female winners.

(iii) Mary says, 'The female winners were younger than the male winners.' Investigate this statement in relation to:

(a) the mean age of the male winners and mean age of the female winners

(b) the median age of the male winners and the median age of the female winners.

1 The runtimes of the 1980s' best film Oscar nominations are shown in the histogram.

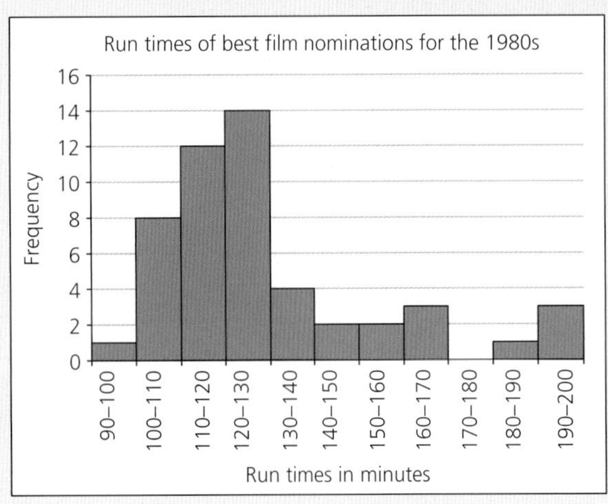

(a) How many films were nominated for best film as shown in the histogram for this period?

(b) What are the minimum and maximum runtime intervals?

(c) Describe the shape of the distribution. Explain your answer.

(d) Using the histogram, make a table showing the frequency for each runtime interval.

(e) What is the modal runtime interval?

(f) Estimate the mean runtime using mid-interval values.

(g) Which interval contains the median runtime interval?

(h) Describe what the histogram tells you about the runtimes of these films.

2 The table shows the results of a school survey regarding favourite types of music.

Music type	Pop	Rock	Classical	Other
Number of students	50	25	4	16

(a) Draw a pie chart to illustrate this information, showing clearly how you calculate the size of each angle.

(b) What other graphical representations could you use to display this data?

(c) Use one of the graphical representations you suggested in part (b) to display the data.

(d) Comment on the usefulness of both graphical representations in this case. Under what circumstances would one of them be better than the other?

3 The number of students attending primary and post-primary level schools in Ireland in 2010 is illustrated in the pie charts below.

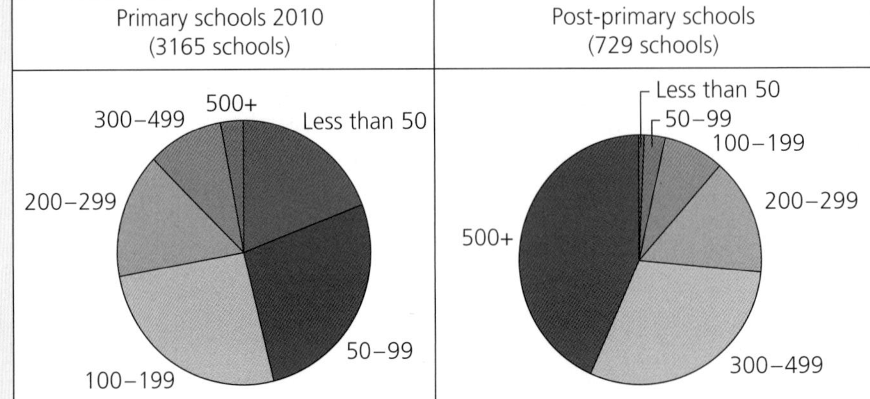

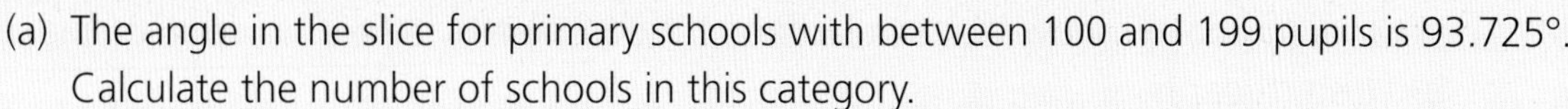

(a) The angle in the slice for primary schools with between 100 and 199 pupils is 93.725°. Calculate the number of schools in this category.

(b) Mary claims that the charts show that there is roughly the same number of post-primary schools as primary shools in the 200–299 range. Do you agree with Mary? Give a reason for your answer based on the data in the charts.

4 Data on the type of broadband connection used by enterprises in Ireland for 2008 and 2009 is contained in the table below.

	2008	**2009**
	%	%
Broadband connection	84	84
By type of connection		
DSL [< 2Mb/s]	31	29
DSL [> 2Mb/s]	41	45
Other fixed connection	31	20
Mobile broadband	24	27

Source: Central Statistical Office

(a) Display the data in a way that allows you to compare the data for the two years.

(b) Identify any trends that you think are shown by the data.

5 Thirty randomly selected students were surveyed to find the number of times they had bought lunch in the school canteen during the previous week.

The following results were obtained.

2	3	1	2	2	3	2	1	2	3
4	4	5	5	4	3	3	2	2	2
3	2	3	4	4	4	4	2	3	3

(a) Organise the data using a frequency table.

(b) Construct a pie chart, bar chart and line plot to display the data.

(c) Comment on whether or not you think one of the graphical displays is better than the others at presenting the data in a helpful way.

(d) What does the data tell you about the eating habits of the students in the sample?

(e) Can you apply the conclusions to the population of students in the school?

6 The following three questions are taken from *CensusAtSchool* questionnaires.

Q1. 'How important do you think the census is to education?'
(The students answered using a sliding scale from 1 to 1000.)

Q2. 'How tall are you without shoes?' (Answer in centimetres)

Q3. 'What is your best time on the interactive question?'
(This was a 'reaction-time' type of question.)

The histograms below show the distribution of the responses from a random sample of 100 Irish students.

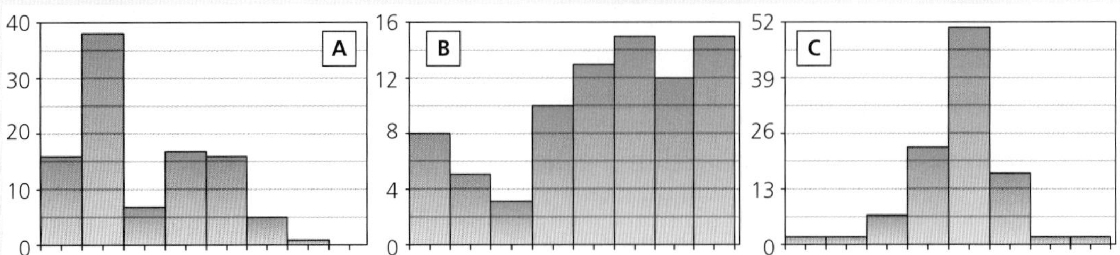

(a) Match each histogram to either of Q1, Q2 or Q3. Explain your choice.

(b) Describe the shape of each histogram.

7 Ten students submitted their Design portfolios which were marked out of 40. The marks they obtained were:

37 34 34 34 29 27 27 10 4 28

(a) For these marks find

(i) the mode (ii) the median (iii) the mean.

(b) Comment on your results.

(c) An external moderator reduced all the marks by 3. Find the mode, median and mean of the moderated marks.

8 A clerk entering salary data into a company spreadsheet accidentally put an extra '0' in the boss's salary, listing it as €2,000,000 instead of €200,000. Explain how this error will affect the following measures of central tendency for the company payroll: (a) the median, (b) the mean.

9 The following back-to-back stem-and-leaf plot shows the ages of all the Oscar winners for best supporting actress and best supporting actor over a given period of time.

Ages of best supporting actors		Ages of best supporting actresses
	1	0 1
	1	6
0	2	3 4 4 4
9 8 7	2	5 7 8 8 8 8 9 9 9
4 3 2 1	3	0 0 0 0 0 1 2 3 3 3 3 3 4 4 4 4
9 9 8 8 7 7 6 6 5	3	5 5 5 5 5 8 9 9 9 9 9
4 4 4 4 3 3 2 1 1 0 0 0	4	0 1 1 1 2 2 3 4 4 4 4 5 5 5 5 5
9 9 8 7 7 7 7 6 6 6 6 6 6 6 5 5	4	6 6 7 8
4 4 3 3 2 1	5	0 3
9 7 7 6 6 5	5	6 6 9
4 3 3 3 3 1	6	1 2 4
7 7 6 1	6	5 5
3 2 1 0 0	7	0 1 2
9 7 7	7	7
2 0	8	
	8	

Key: 3 | 6 = 36 years

(a) Describe the shape of the distribution of the ages of (i) the actors, (ii) the actresses.

(b) How many actors and actresses are shown in the back-to-back stem-and-leaf plot?

(c) What is the range of ages shown in the plot for (i) the actors, (ii) the actresses?

(d) What is the median age for the actors?

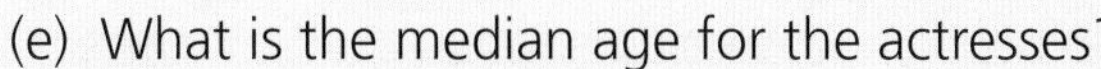

(e) What is the median age for the actresses?

(f) Would you agree that the age at which best supporting actors win an Oscar tends to be older than the age at which best supporting actresses tend to win an Oscar? Justify your answer.

10 The phase 9 *CensusAtSchool* questionnaire contained the question 'Approximately how long do you spend on social networking sites each week?' The histogram below illustrates the answers given by 100 students, randomly selected from those who completed the survey.

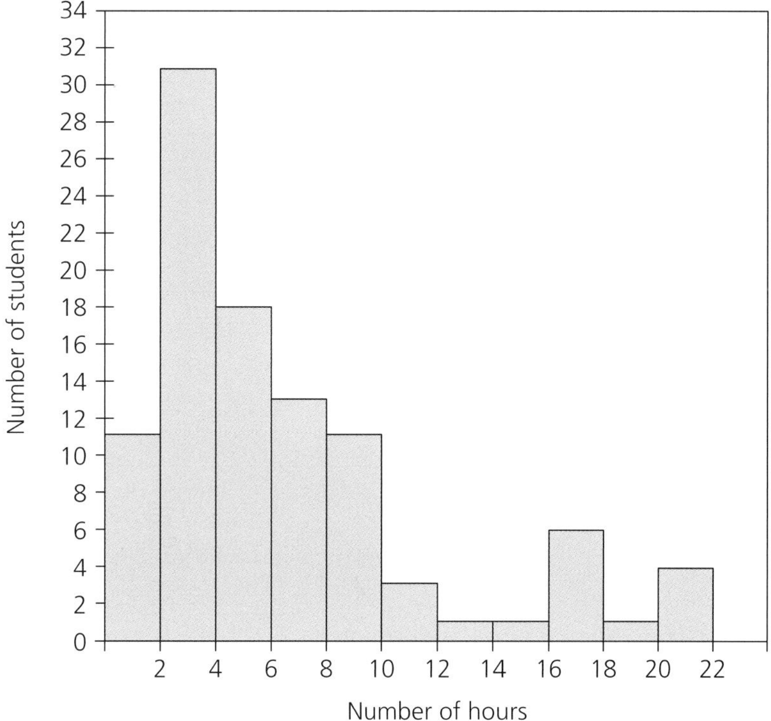

(a) Use the data from the histogram to complete a copy of the frequency table below.

No. of hours	0–2	2–4	4–6	6–8	8–10	10–12	12–14	14–16	16–18	18–20	20–22
No. of students											

[Note: 2–4 means 2 hours or more but less than 4 hours, etc.]

(b) What is the modal interval?

(c) Taking mid-interval values, find the mean amount of time spent on social networking sites.

(d) John is conducting a survey on computer usage by students at his school. His questionnaire asks the same question. He plans to carry out his survey by asking the question to twenty First Year boys on the Monday after the mid-term break. Give two reasons why the results from John's survey might not be as representative as those in the histogram.

Exam-style Questions

1 The ages of the 30 people who took part in an aerobics class are as follows:

18	24	32	37	9	13	22	41	51	49
15	42	37	58	48	53	27	54	42	24
33	48	56	17	61	37	63	45	20	39

The ages of the 30 people who took part in a swimming class are as follows:

16	22	29	7	36	45	12	38	52	13
33	41	24	35	51	8	47	22	14	24
42	62	15	24	23	31	53	36	48	18

(a) Represent this data on a back-to-back stem-and-leaf plot.

(b) Use your plot to identify the median in each case.

(c) What other measure of central tendancy could have been used when examining this data?

(d) Based on the data, make one observation about the ages of the two groups.

Aerobics class		Swimming class
	0	
	1	
	2	
	3	
	4	
	5	
	6	
		Key:

JCHL 2013 Paper 2

2 In total, 7150 second level school students from 216 schools completed the 2011/2012 phase 11 *CensusAtSchool* questionnaire. The questionnaire contained a question relating to where students keep their mobile phones while sleeping.

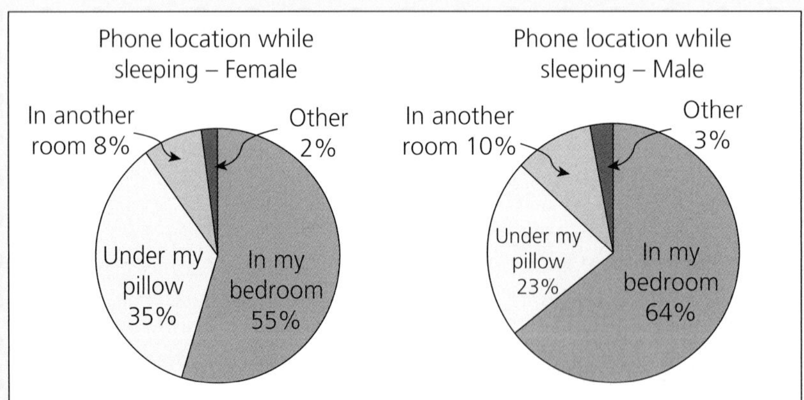

(a) Given that this question was answered by 4171 girls and 2979 boys, calculate how many female students kept their mobile phones under their pillow.

(b) Calculate the overall percentage of students who kept their mobile phones under their pillow.

(c) A new pie chart is to be drawn showing the mobile phone location for all students. Calculate the measure of the angle that would represent the students who kept their mobile phones under their pillow.

JCHL 2013 Paper 2

KEY WORDS AND PHRASES

- Average
- Bar chart
- Bias
- Categorical data
- Class interval
- Clustered data
- Data
- Data handling cycle
- Data set
- Descriptive statistics (summary statistics)
- Distribution
- Five-number summary
- Frequency
- Frequency table
- Histogram
- Mean
- Measure of central tendency
- Measure of spread
- Median
- Mode
- Line plot (dot plot)
- Numerical data
- Normal distribution
- Pie chart
- Population
- Random sample
- Range
- Sample
- Sample size
- Simple random sample
- Skewed positively (right)
- Skewed negatively (left)
- stem-and-leaf plot

Chapter Summary 19

- Statistics is about **variation**. The **data handling cycle** shows how we proceed in solving problems using data.
- A **census** is when we collect data on the entire population.
- We often make **inferences** about the population based on **random samples**.
- Samples must be **representative** of the population in order to be useful.
- **Biased samples** over or underestimate what we are trying to measure for the population.

- The **type of data** we collect determines the type of analysis we can perform on it.

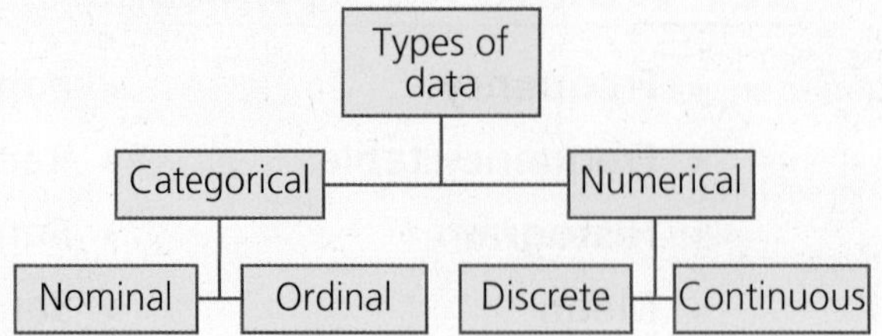

- We can perform **numerical** and **graphical analysis** of data.
- Numerical analysis involves
  - **Measures of central tendency**, i.e. mode (for categorical and numerical data), median and mean (for numerical data only)
  - **Measures of spread**, i.e. the range is for numerical data only.
- The type of graphical analysis and the types of data suited to each type of graph are summarised in the table:

Type of data	Line plot	Bar chart	Frequency table	Histogram	Pie chart	Stem plot
Categorical	✓	✓	✓		✓	
Discrete numerical	✓	✓	✓		✓	✓
Continuous numerical	✓		✓	✓		✓

- Histograms and stem-and-leaf plots involve grouped data.
- If we wish to compare data sets graphically, we can use back-to-back stem-and-leaf plots.

Geometry 3

Chapter 20

Learning Intentions

In this chapter, you will learn about:

LO: U.5, U.6, GT.3, U.11–13

- Similar triangles
- The difference between similar triangles and congruent triangles
- Theorem 13: The properties of similar triangles
- Theorem 11: The properties of parallel lines and transversals
- Theorem 12: Parallel lines and triangle ratios
- Some properties of circles
- Theorem 19: The properties of angles in circles

You will need...

- a pencil
- a ruler
- a geometry set

Section 20A Similar Triangles

Look at these two cars. They are similar. In what way are they similar? In what way are they different?

They are similar in that they have the **same shape**. They are different in size. One is just a bigger version of the other.

This section deals with triangles which have exactly the same shape but not always the same size.

They are known as **similar triangles**.

Class Discussion

Look carefully at these two triangles.
In what way are they similar?
In what way are they different?

Are these triangles congruent?

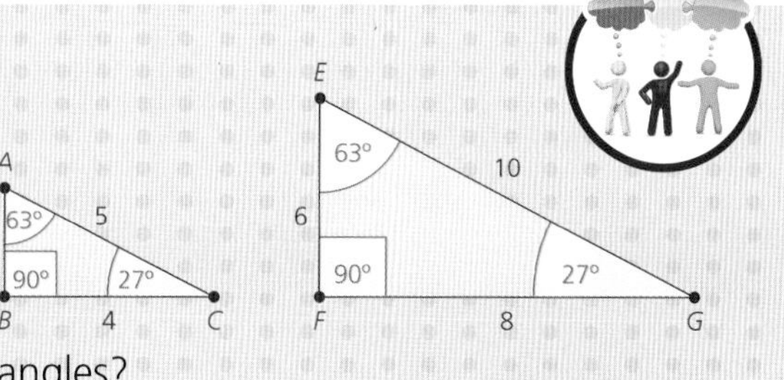

What about the lengths of the sides of the triangles?

Corresponding sides are the sides which match in each triangle.
For example, in the triangles on the previous page, [*AB*] matches [*EF*] so we say that [*AB*] and [*EF*] are corresponding sides.

These triangles are called **equiangular** triangles or **similar** triangles.

These triangles have a special property:
their sides are proportional, in order.

This means that for these similar triangles:

$$\frac{|PQ|}{|ST|} = \frac{|PR|}{|SV|} = \frac{|QR|}{|TV|}$$

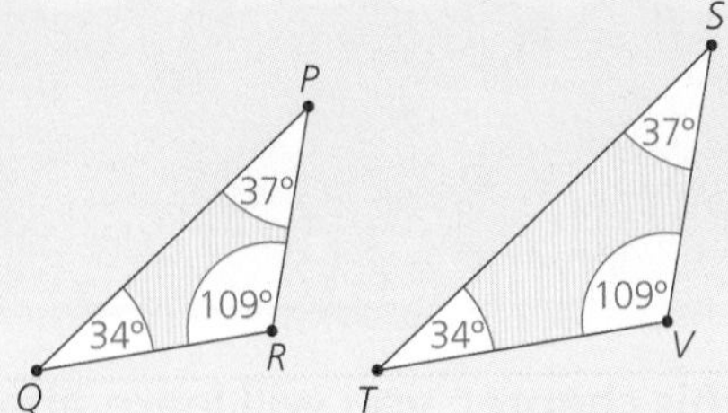

THEOREM 13

If two triangles are similar, their sides are proportional, in order.

The converse (opposite statement) of Theorem 13 also applies:

If the sides of two triangles are proportional (in order), the two triangles are similar.

It is very important to understand the difference between **congruent** triangles and **similar** triangles.

Congruent triangles are equal in **every way**. The three angles and the three sides are equal in each:

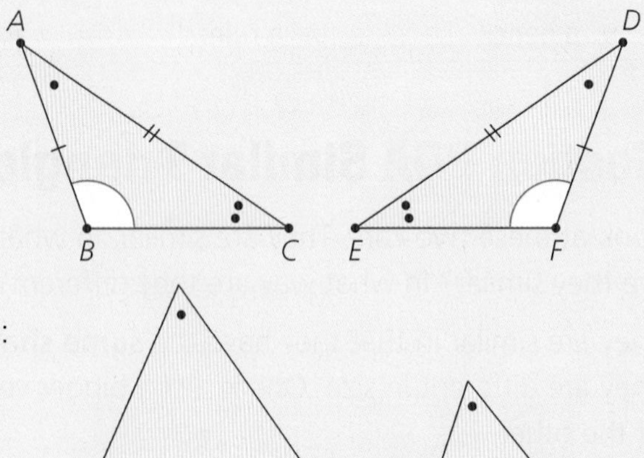

Similar triangles just have **equal angles** (AAA):

Example 1

Find the length of the side marked *x* in this pair of similar triangles.

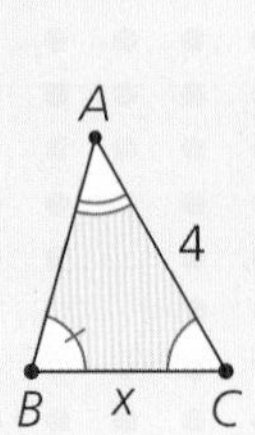

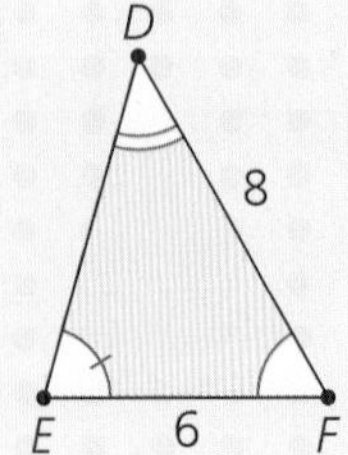

Solution

First, identify the corresponding sides. The corresponding sides are opposite the equal angles.

Hence:

- [*BC*] in ΔABC corresponds to [*EF*] in ΔDEF
- [*AC*] in ΔABC corresponds to [*DF*] in ΔDEF

Method 1

Start with the side marked x:

$\frac{|BC|}{|EF|} = \frac{|AC|}{|DF|}$ ... this is what the theorem says for these triangles.

$\Rightarrow \frac{x}{6} = \frac{4}{8}$

Multiply both sides by 24 (LCM of 6 and 8)

$\Rightarrow \frac{24}{1} \times \frac{x}{6} = \frac{24}{1} \times \frac{4}{8}$

$\Rightarrow \quad 4x = 12$

$\Rightarrow \quad x = 3$

Method 2

$[AC]$ in ΔABC corresponds to $[DF]$ in ΔDEF.

$|AC| = \frac{1}{2}|DF|$

Since the triangles are similar, then each side of ΔABC is half the corresponding side in ΔDEF.

$\Rightarrow x = \frac{1}{2}(6) = 3$

Example 2

Find the value of y in this pair of similar triangles.

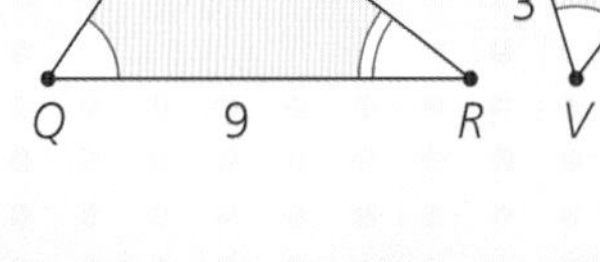

Solution

First identify the corresponding sides.
The corresponding sides are opposite the equal angles.

Hence:

- $[PQ]$ in ΔPQR corresponds to $[SV]$ in ΔSTV
- $[QR]$ in ΔPQR corresponds to $[VT]$ in ΔSTV

Method 1

Start with the side marked y:

$\frac{|PQ|}{|SV|} = \frac{|QR|}{|VT|}$ ... this is what the theorem says for these triangles.

$\Rightarrow \frac{y}{3} = \frac{9}{6}$

Multiply both sides by 6 (LCM of 6 and 3)

$\Rightarrow \frac{6}{1} \times \frac{y}{3} = \frac{6}{1} \times \frac{9}{6}$

$\Rightarrow 2y = 9$

$\Rightarrow y = 4.5$

Method 2

$[QR]$ in ΔPQR corresponds to $[VT]$ in ΔSTV.

$|QR| = 1.5 \times |VT|$

$\Rightarrow$ The sides in ΔPQR are 1.5 times the sides of ΔTSV

$\Rightarrow y = 1.5 \times 3$

$y = 4.5$

Example 3

Grace is standing beside a building on a sunny day. She is 1.5 metres tall. Her shadow is 0.7 metres in length. The building casts a shadow which is 7.5 metres long.

(i) Draw two triangles to show this.

(ii) Explain how this information can be used to find the height of the building.

(iii) Find the height of the building correct to one decimal place.

Solution

(i)

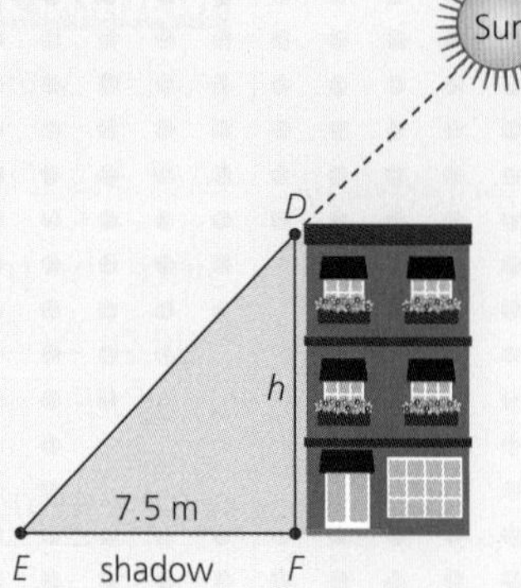

(ii) These are similar triangles, so we can use the fact that the corresponding sides are in proportion.

(iii) First, identify the corresponding sides.

- [AC] in ΔABC corresponds to [DF] in ΔDEF (the two heights)
- [BC] in ΔABC corresponds to [EF] in ΔDEF (the two shadows)

Start with the side marked h:

$\frac{|DF|}{|AC|} = \frac{|EF|}{|BC|}$ ... this is what the theorem says for these triangles.

$\frac{h}{1.5} = \frac{7.5}{0.7}$

Multiply both sides by 1.5:

$\frac{1.5}{1} \times \frac{h}{1.5} = \frac{1.5}{1} \times \frac{7.5}{0.7}$

$\Rightarrow h = 16.07142 = 16.1$ m, correct to one decimal place.

Example 4

In the triangle ABC, $|\angle BAC| = 90°$ and $AD \perp BC$.

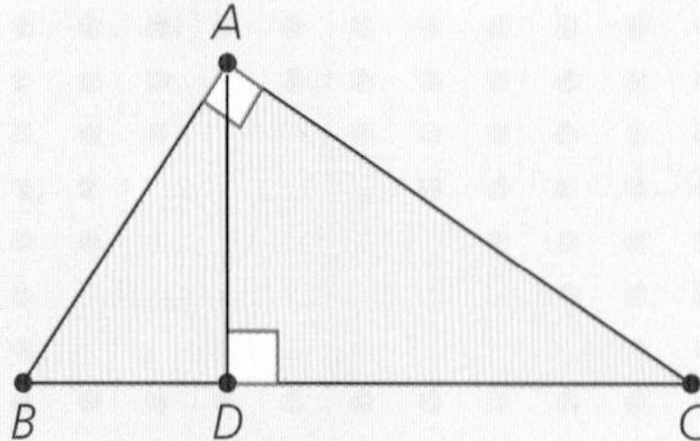

(i) Prove that triangles ABC and ADC are similar.

(ii) Hence prove that $|BC| \times |DC| = |AC|^2$.

Solution

(i) Draw the two triangles ABC and ADC separately.

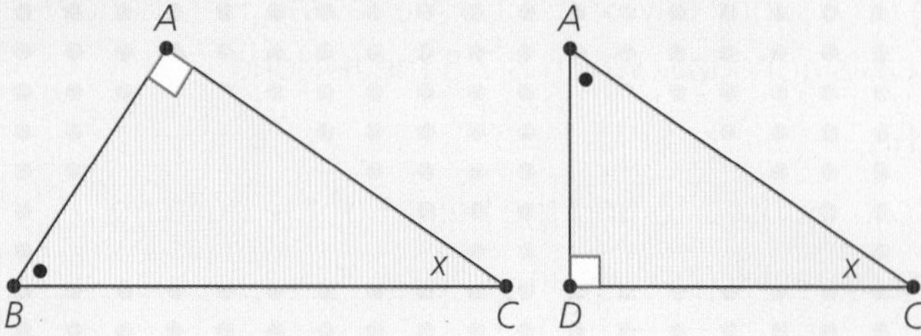

Both the triangles ADC and ABC have a right angle and $\angle C$.

$\therefore$ the 3rd angles in each triangle are equal … Theorem 4

$\therefore$ ADC and ABC are similar triangles.

(ii) $\therefore \dfrac{|AC|}{|DC|} = \dfrac{|BC|}{|AC|}$ … Theorem 13

$\Rightarrow |AC|^2 = |BC|.|DC|$ … cross-multiply … QED

Activity 20.1

1 Two similar triangles PQR and STV are shown.

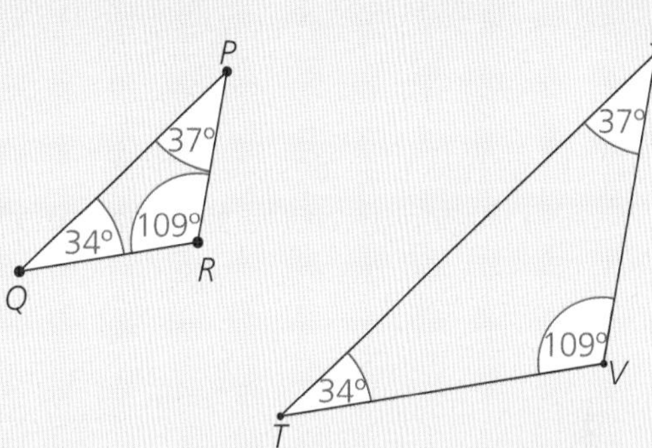

(i) Pick out the sides in triangle PQR which correspond to the sides in triangle STV.

Copy and complete this sentence:

'[PQ] corresponds to [ST], [QR] corresponds to __________ and [PR] corresponds to ____________.'

(ii) Measure the lengths of all six side lengths. Be as accurate as you can.

(iii) Copy and complete this table, giving lengths in mm.

(iv) Compare the values of the ratios. Write down what you found.

Triangle PQR	$\lvert PQ\rvert =$	$\lvert QR\rvert =$	$\lvert PR\rvert =$
Triangle STV	$\lvert ST\rvert =$	$\lvert TV\rvert =$	$\lvert SV\rvert =$
Ratio	$\dfrac{\lvert PQ\rvert}{\lvert ST\rvert} =$	$\dfrac{\lvert QR\rvert}{\lvert TV\rvert} =$	$\dfrac{\lvert PR\rvert}{\lvert SV\rvert} =$
Value of ratio			

2

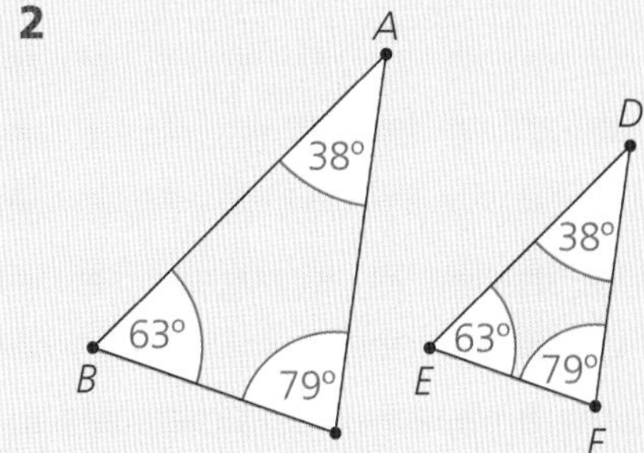

Pick out the sides in triangle ABC which correspond to the sides in triangle DEF.

Copy and complete this sentence:

'[AB] matches with [DE], [BC] matches with __________ and [AC] matches with ____________.'

3 Identify the pairs of corresponding sides in each of the following pairs of similar triangles.

(i)

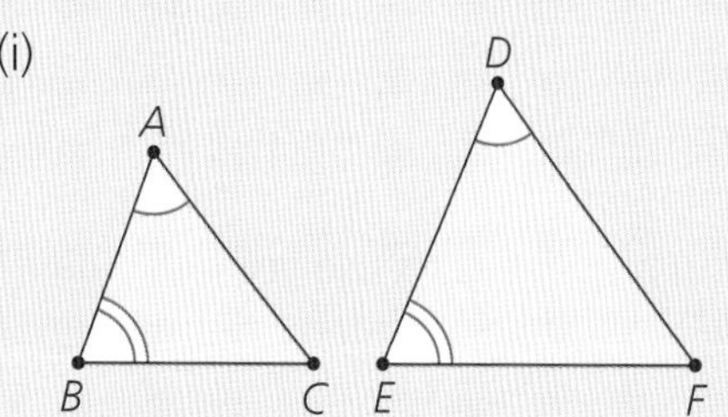

(ii)

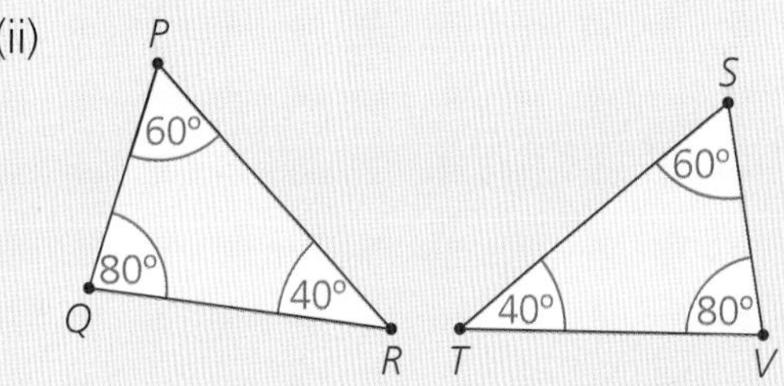

(iii)

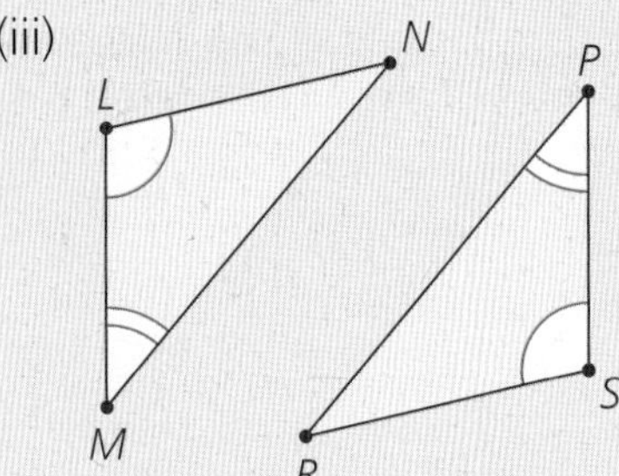

(iv)

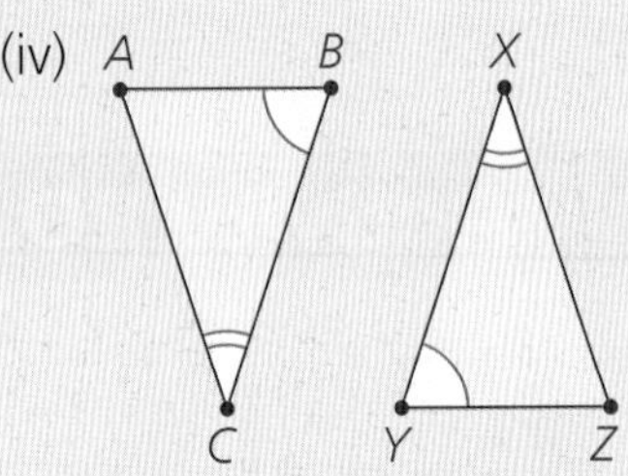

4 These two triangles are similar.
Find the length of the side marked x.

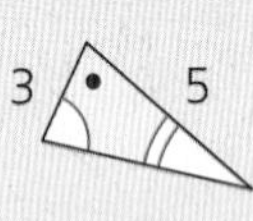

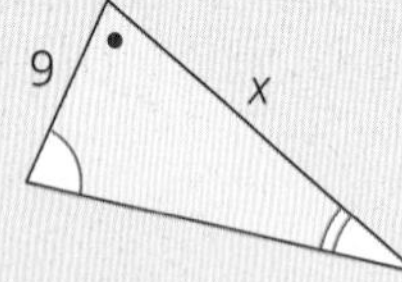

5 These two triangles are similar.

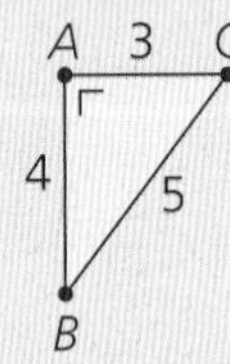

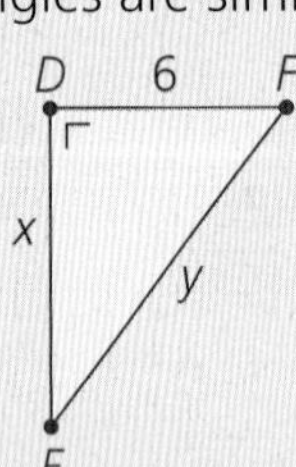

(i) Copy and complete this statement:
'Each side of ΔDEF is __ times the corresponding side in ΔABC.'

(ii) Find the values of x and y.

6 Find the value of x in each of the following pairs of similar triangles. You may need to use your calculator.

(i)

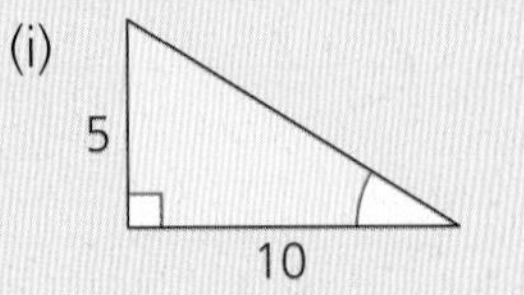

(ii)

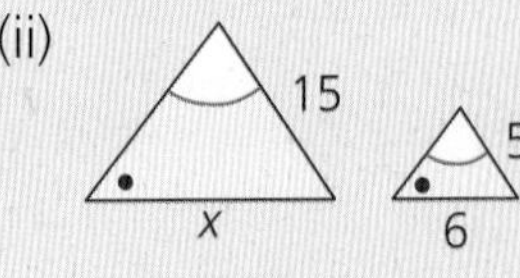

(iii)

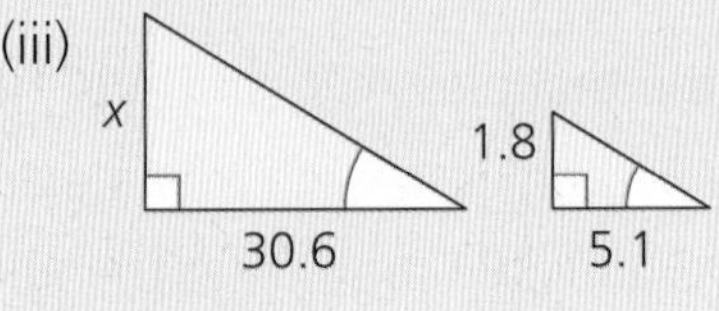

(iv)

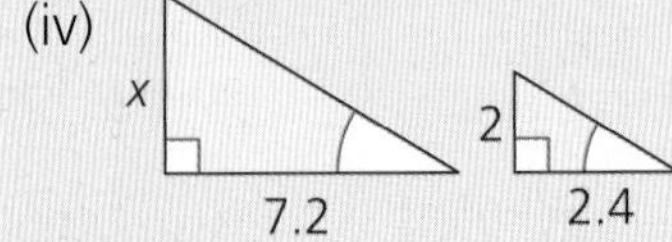

7 Michael is standing beside a building on a sunny day. He is 1.9 m tall. His shadow is 1.1 m in length. The building casts a shadow which is 7 m long.

(i) Draw two triangles to show this.

(ii) Explain how this information can be used to find the height of the building.

(iii) Find the height of the building correct to two decimal places.

8 Tom and Mary wanted to measure the height of a tree. They erected a pole 5 metres high.

In sunshine, the shadow of the pole was 3 metres long, while the tree cast a shadow 10 metres long.

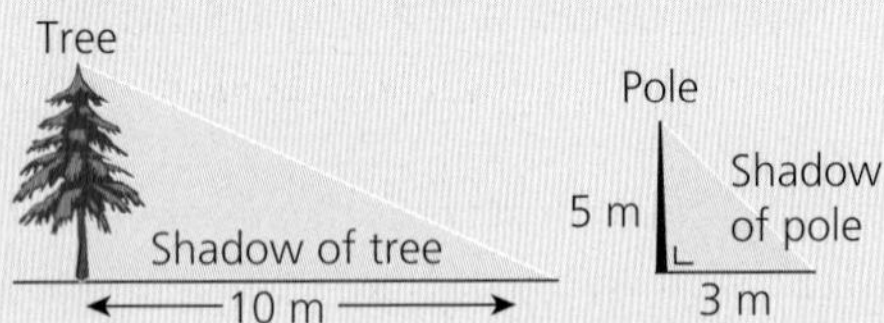

Find the height of the tree.

9 On a sunny day, Adi stands with her back to the sun. She is 150 cm tall and her shadow is 180 cm long.

At the same time, a vertical pole casts a shadow 540 cm long.

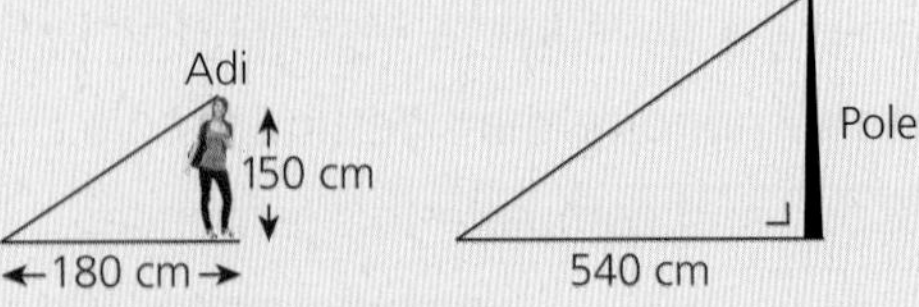

What is the height of the pole?
Show all your work.

10 A group of students are working outdoors to find the height of a tree in the school grounds.

They choose a sunny day and measure the length of the shadow cast by the tree. They find it to be 14.2 m.

Michael, one of the students, stands near the tree. The students measure his shadow and find it to be 2.9 m. Michael has already had his height measured and knows that it is 171 cm.

(i) Draw two triangles to illustrate the measurements given and show all the data clearly.

(ii) Calculate the height of the tree correct to two decimal places.

11 CF and BE intersect at A.

(i) Is ΔAEF similar to ΔACB?

Give a reason for your answer.

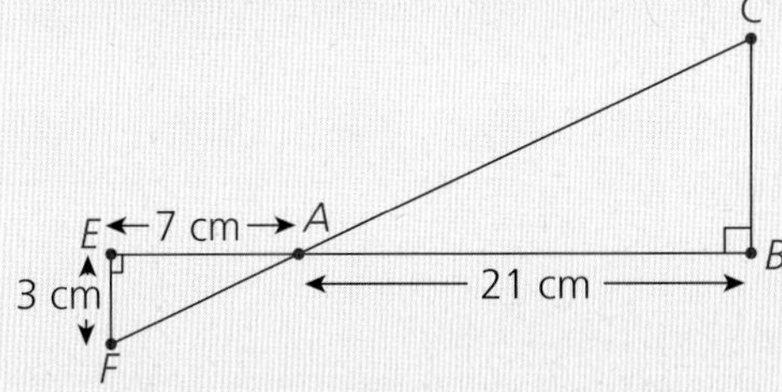

(ii) Calculate the lengths AF, AC and CB.

12 In the diagram below, triangles DFE and GHE are right-angled triangles.

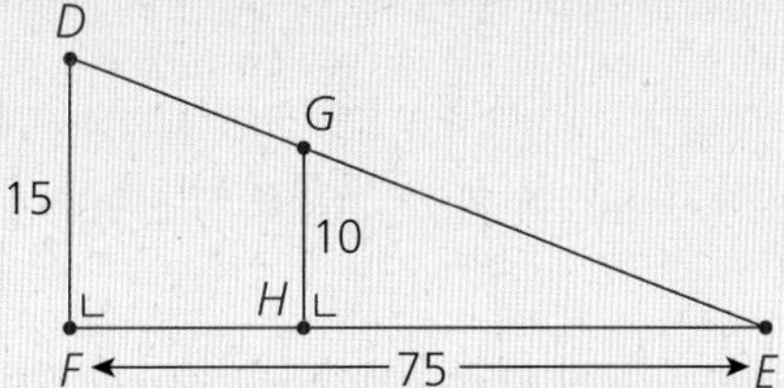

(i) Draw the two triangles DFE and GHE separately in your copybook. Mark in the dimensions given.

(ii) Explain why triangles DFE and GHE are similar.

(iii) Find $|HE|$.

13 Find the value of x for the following pairs of similar triangles, correct to two decimal places.

(i)

(ii)

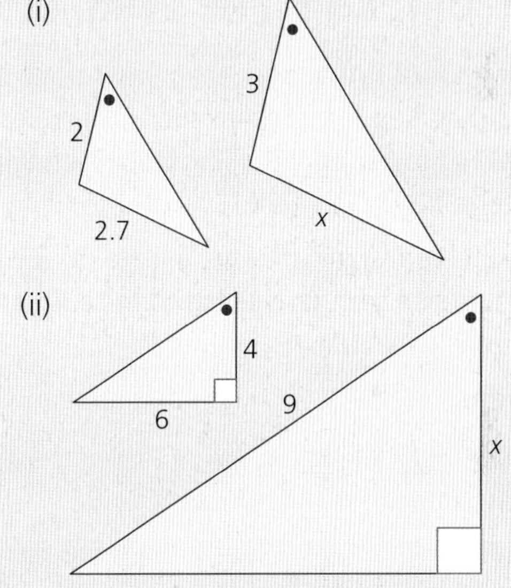

14 In this diagram, DC is parallel to AB. AC and BD intersect at E.

(i) Prove that triangles DEC and AEB are similar.

(ii) Hence, prove that $|DC| \times |EB| = |AB| \times |DE|$.

$|DC| = 3$ cm, $|AE| = 6$ cm and $|AB| = 8$ cm.

(iii) Find $|EC|$ correct to one decimal place.

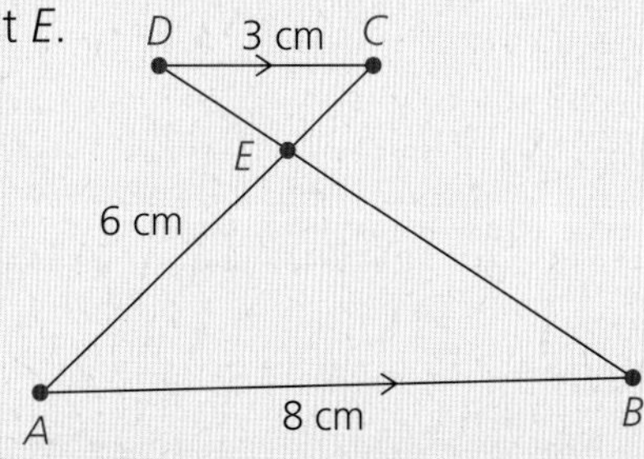

15 In the triangle ABC, $|\angle BAC| = 90°$ and $AD \perp BC$.

Using similar triangles, prove that $|BD| \times |BC| = |BA|^2$.

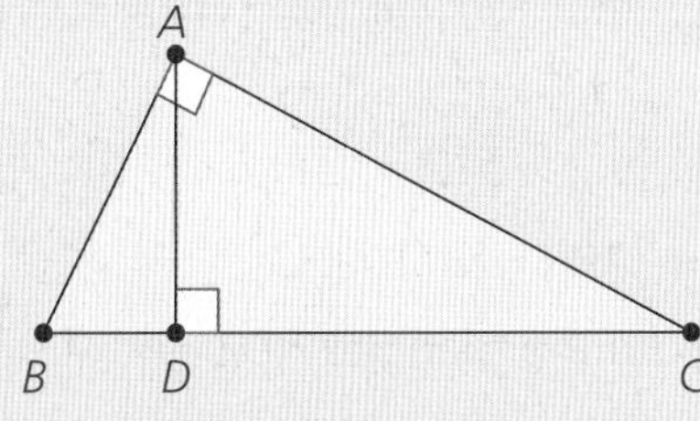

Hint

› In question 15, draw the triangles out separately and mark in all the equal angles.

16 In the triangle ABC, $|\angle BAC| = 90°$ and $AD \perp BC$.

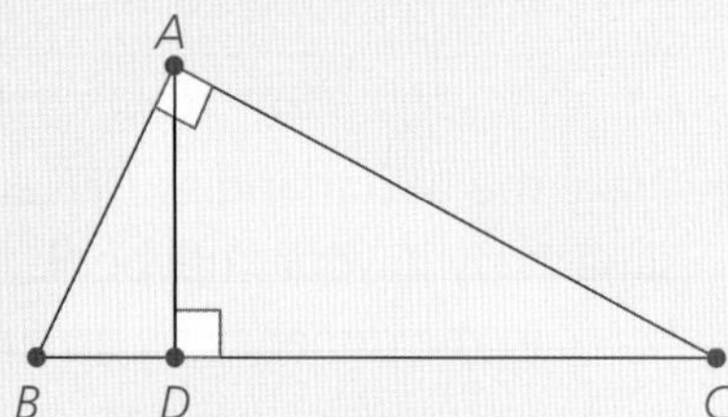

(i) Prove that the triangles ADC and ABC are similar.

(ii) Write down one ratio equal to $\frac{|AC|}{|AB|}$.

(iii) If $|AC| = 2 \times |AB|$ and $|AD| = 4$, find the value of $|DC|$.

Section 20B The Proof of Pythagoras' Theorem

The proof of Pythagoras' theorem is done by dividing a right-angled triangle into similar triangles. You are not expected to learn the full proof, but a general idea of how the proof is shown here.

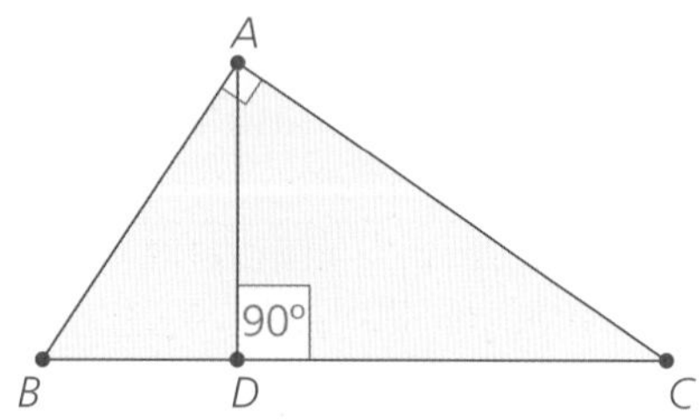

The theorem states that the square on the hypotenuse of a right-angled triangle is equal to the sum of the squares on the other two sides.

Given: Right-angled triangle ABC with $|\angle BAC| = 90°$.

Required to prove: $|BC|^2 = |AB|^2 + |AC|^2$

Construction: Draw $AD \perp BC$.

Proof: Draw the three triangles in the diagram separately.

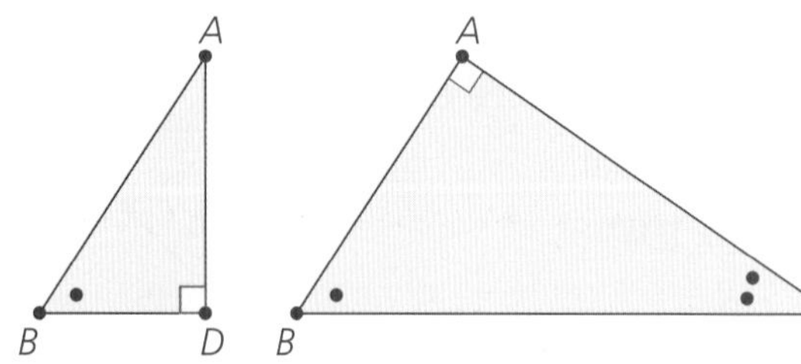

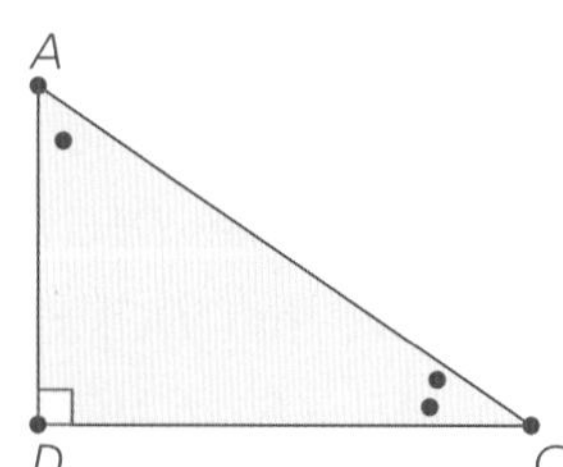

Both the triangles ABD and ABC have a right angle and $\angle B$.

$\therefore$ the 3rd angles in each triangle are equal ... Theorem 4

$\therefore$ ABD and ABC are similar triangles.

$\therefore \frac{|AB|}{|BC|} = \frac{|BD|}{|AB|}$ ... Theorem 13

$\Rightarrow |AB|^2 = |BC| \times |BD|$ ... equation (1)

Both the triangles ADC and ABC have a right angle and $\angle C$.

$\therefore$ the 3rd angles in each triangle are equal ... Theorem 4

$\therefore$ *ADC* and *ABC* are similar triangles.

$$\therefore \frac{|AC|}{|BC|} = \frac{|DC|}{|AC|}$$

$\Rightarrow |AC|^2 = |BC| \times |DC|$ ... equation (2)

Adding equations (1) and (2), we get

$$\begin{aligned} |AB|^2 + |AC|^2 &= |BC| \times |BD| + |BC| \times |DC| \\ &= |BC|(|BD| + |DC|) \\ &= |BC| \times |BC| \\ &= |BC|^2 \quad \text{... QED} \end{aligned}$$

Section 20C Theorems 11 and 12 and Construction 7

THEOREM 11

If three parallel lines cut off equal segments on some transversal line, then they will cut off equal segments on any other transversal.

Example 1

The diagram shows three parallel lines *a*, *b* and *c*. *ZV* is a transversal of them such that $|ZW| = |WV|$. *SU* is another transversal. Name a line segment equal to $|ST|$.

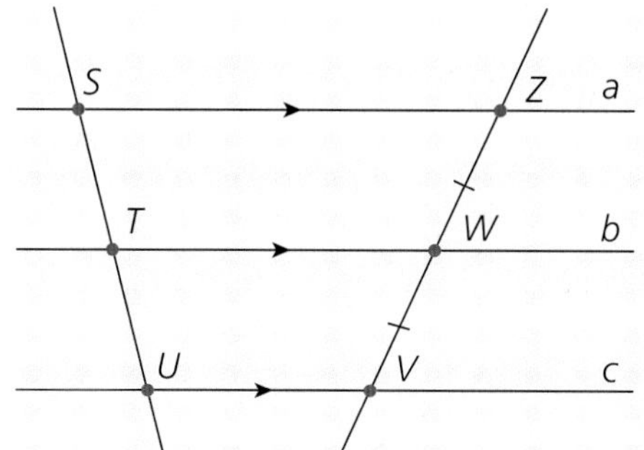

Solution

The three parallel lines *a*, *b* and *c* cut off equal intercepts on transversal *ZV*.

$\therefore$ they cut equal intercepts off the transversal *SU*.

$\therefore |ST| = |TU|$

THEOREM 12

Let *ABC* be a triangle. If a line *DE* is parallel to *BC* and cuts [*AB*] in the ratio $m:n$, then it also cuts [*AC*] in the same ratio.

i.e. $|AD|:|DB| = |AE|:|EC|$

We can write this as $\frac{|AD|}{|DB|} = \frac{|AE|}{|EC|}$ i.e. $\frac{\text{Top}}{\text{Bottom}} = \frac{\text{Top}}{\text{Bottom}}$.

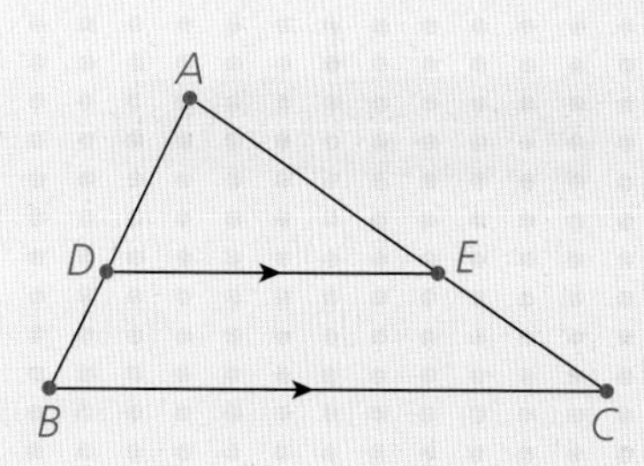

Key Points

In the previous diagram, it is also true that:

- $\frac{|AD|}{|AB|} = \frac{|AE|}{|AC|}$ i.e $\frac{\text{Top}}{\text{Whole}} = \frac{\text{Top}}{\text{Whole}}$
- $\frac{|AB|}{|DB|} = \frac{|AC|}{|EC|}$ i.e $\frac{\text{Whole}}{\text{Bottom}} = \frac{\text{Whole}}{\text{Bottom}}$

Example 2

In the diagram, $DE \parallel BC$. Find x.

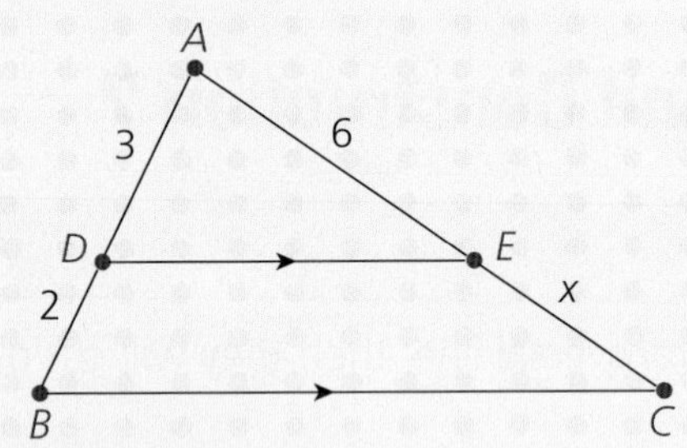

Solution

$\frac{|AD|}{|DB|} = \frac{|AE|}{|EC|}$ ... Theorem 12

$\Rightarrow \quad \frac{3}{2} = \frac{6}{x}$

$\Rightarrow 3(x) = 6(2)$

$\Rightarrow \quad 3x = 12$

$\Rightarrow \quad x = 4$

Example 3

In the diagram, $ST \parallel QR$. Find x.

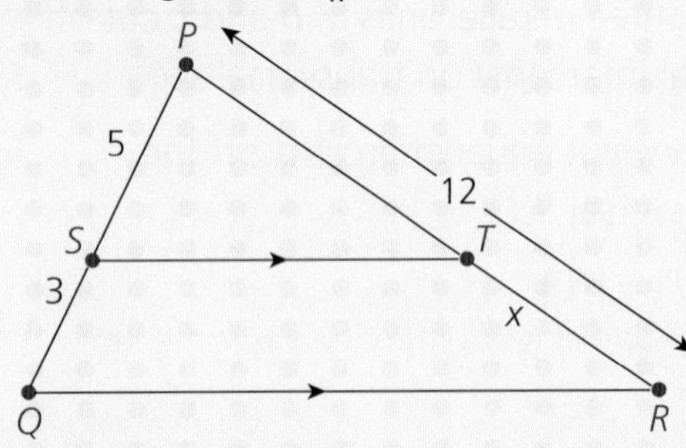

Solution

$\frac{|PR|}{|TR|} = \frac{|PQ|}{|SQ|}$ ... Theorem 12

$\Rightarrow \frac{12}{x} = \frac{5+3}{3}$

$\Rightarrow \quad 8(x) = 12(3)$

$\Rightarrow \quad 8x = 36$

$\Rightarrow \quad x = \frac{36}{8} = \frac{9}{2}$

THEOREM 12 (CONVERSE)

Let ABC be a triangle. If a line l cuts the sides AB and AC in the same ratio, then it is parallel to BC.

The results of Theorem 7 allow us to perform Construction 7 which is our last construction.

Construction 7

Division of a line segment into any number of equal segments, without measuring.

E.g. to divide a line into four equal segments, without measuring.

Method

Step 1: Draw a line segment $[AB]$.

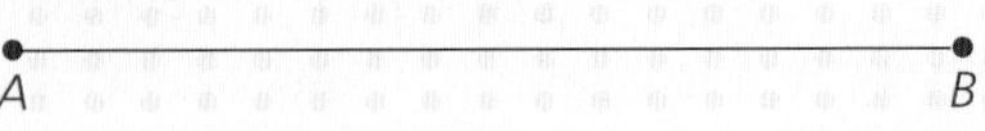

Step 2: Draw a ray from the point A, making an acute angle with $[AB]$.

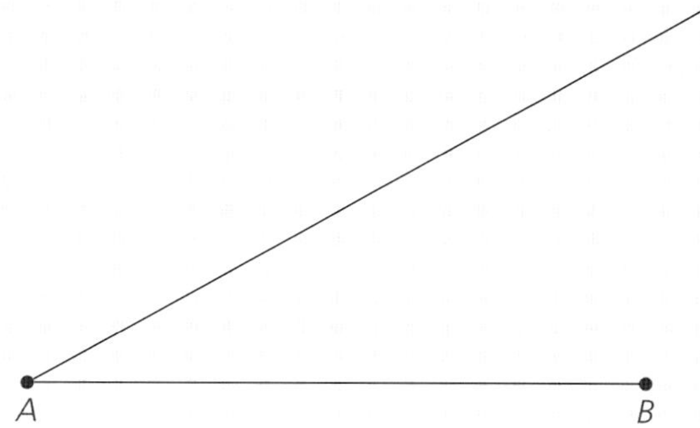

Step 3: With A as centre and any radius, draw an arc crossing the ray at P.

With P as centre and the same radius, draw a second arc crossing the ray at Q.

With Q as centre and the same radius, draw a third arc crossing the ray at R.

With R as centre and the same radius, draw a fourth arc crossing the ray at S.

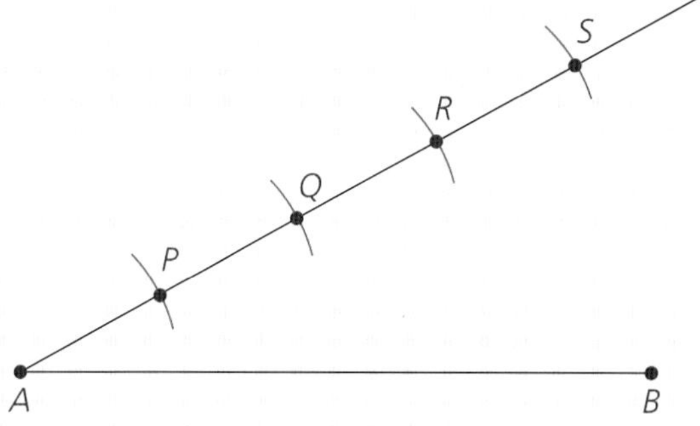

Step 4: Join B to S.

Use a set-square and ruler to draw $[RK]$, $[QL]$ and $[PM]$ parallel to SB.

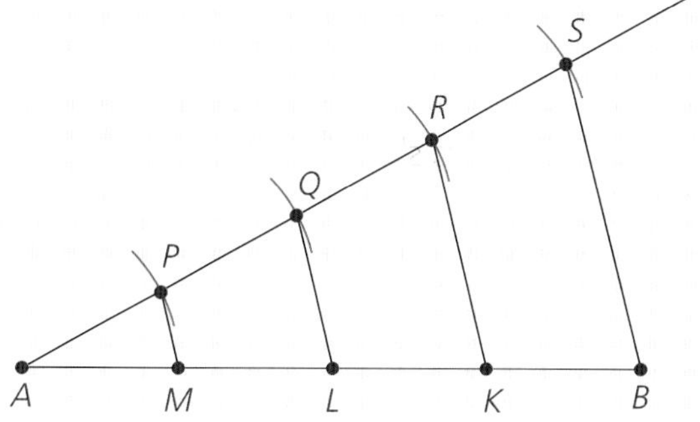

$[AB]$ is now divided into four equal parts.

Activity 20.2

1 In each of these diagrams, lines a, b and c are parallel.

Find the value of x in each. Explain your answers.

(i)

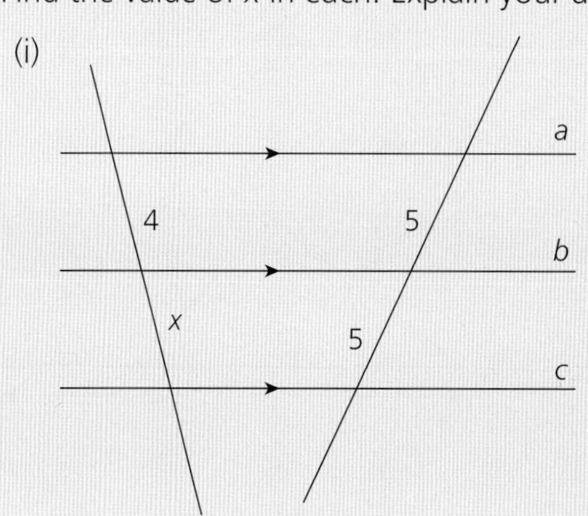

(ii)

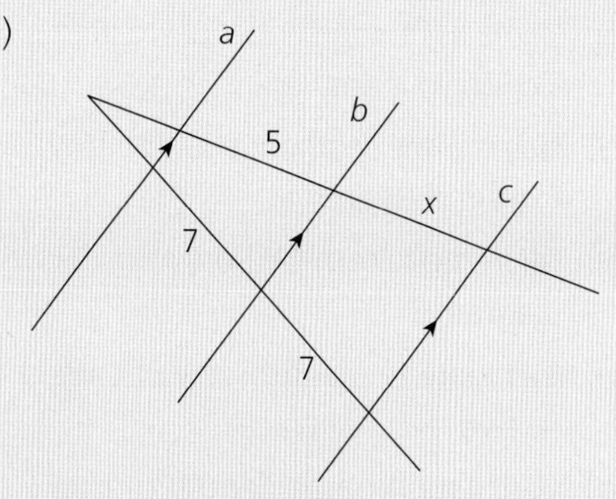

2 The diagram shows a street map. Russell Street, Farrell Street and Elizabeth Street are all parallel to each other. How far is it from Elizabeth Street to Russell Street? Explain your answer.

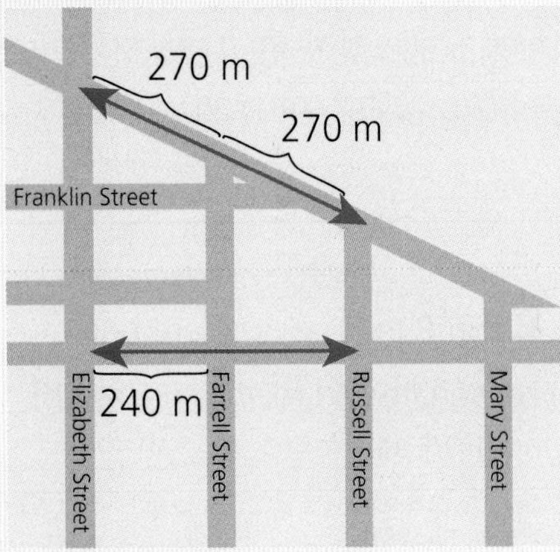

3 Peter is designing a new iron gate and has drawn this sketch of it. The gate is to be 2 metres wide and 1.8 metres high. The horizontal bars are to be an equal distance apart.

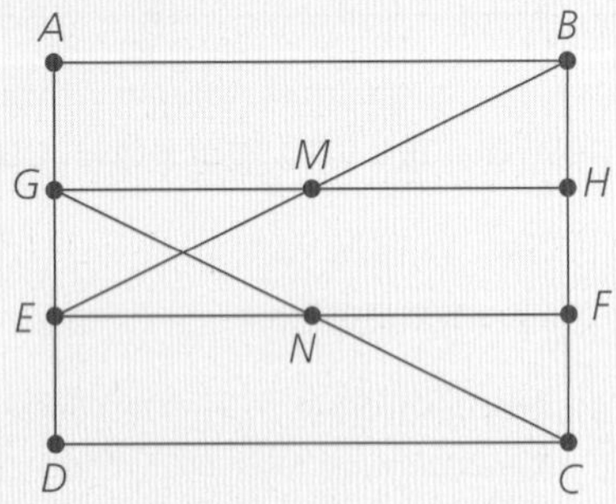

(i) Copy the diagram into your copybook and mark in the dimensions.

(ii) Name five line segments equal to $|AG|$.

(iii) Name a line segment equal to $|BM|$. Explain your answer.

(iv) Name a line segment equal to $|GN|$. Explain your answer.

(v) Fill in the length $|AE|$ on your diagram.

(vi) Calculate the length of $[EB]$ correct to two decimal places.

(vii) Calculate the total length of iron needed to make the gate.

4 Find the value of x in each of these diagrams.

(i)

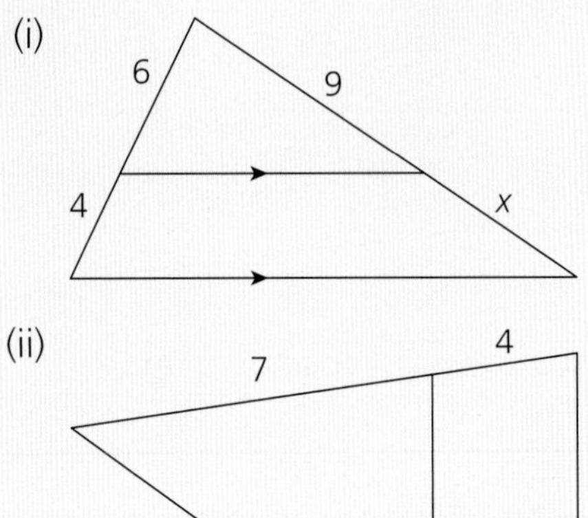

(ii)

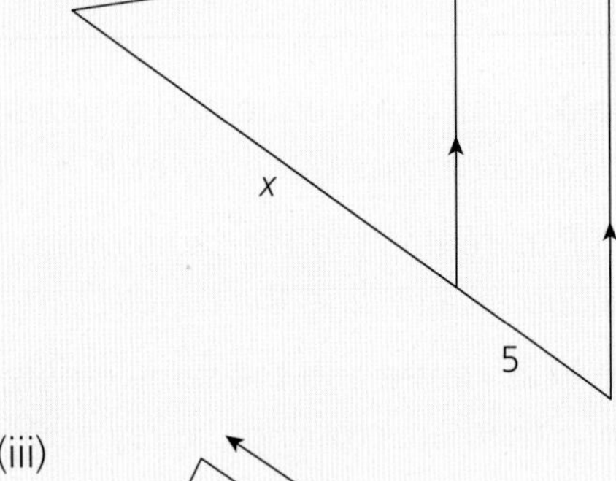

(iii)

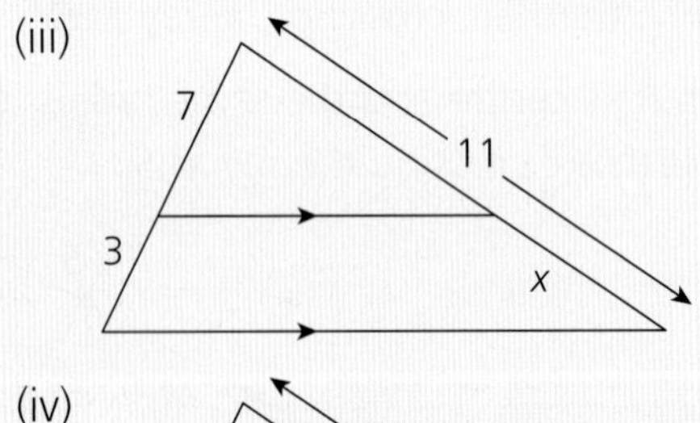

(iv)

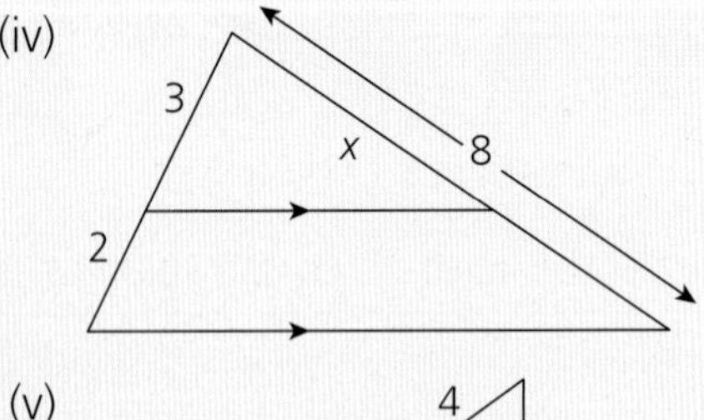

(v)

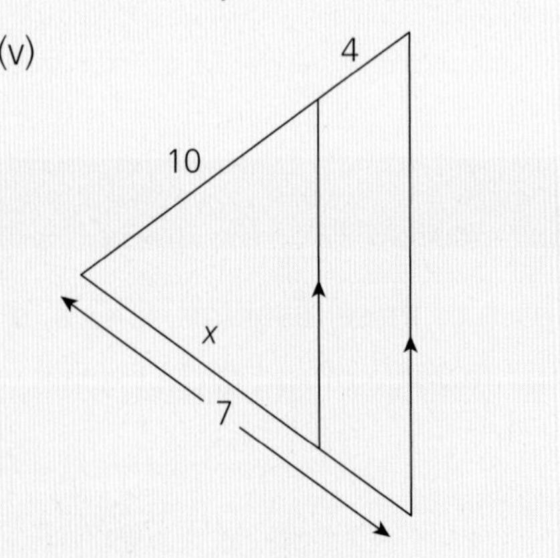

(vi)

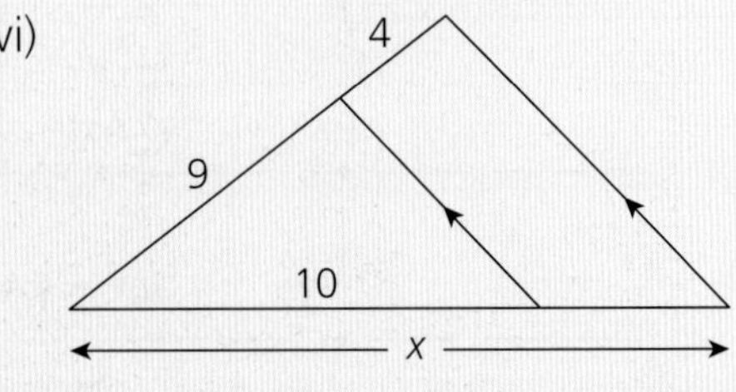

5 In the diagram, $ST \parallel QR$.
$|PS|:|SQ| = 5:3$.

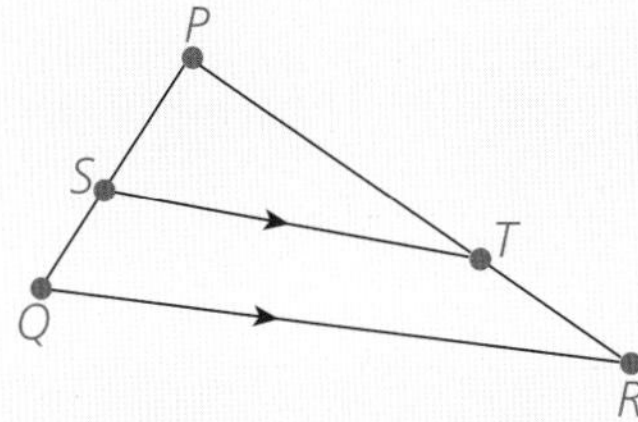

Write down the following ratios.

(i) $|PT|:|TR|$

(ii) $|PQ|:|PS|$

(iii) $|TR|:|PR|$

6 In the diagram, $MN \parallel BC$.

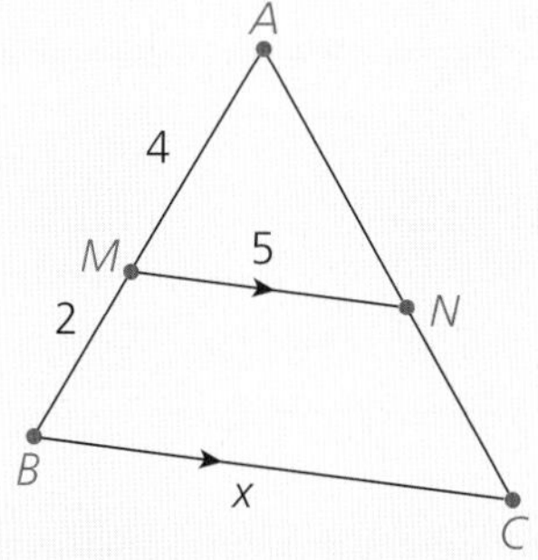

(i) Show that the triangles AMN and ABC are similar.

(ii) Use this fact to find x.

7 Find the value of x and the value of y in this diagram.

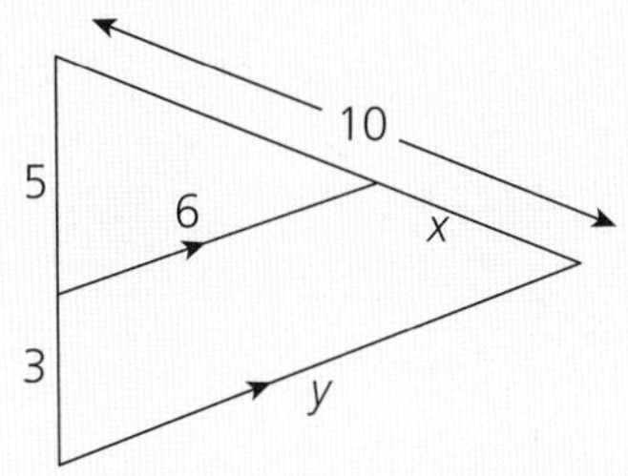

8 Calculate w in this picture.

9 In the diagram, $HM \parallel GB$ and $MN \parallel BC$.

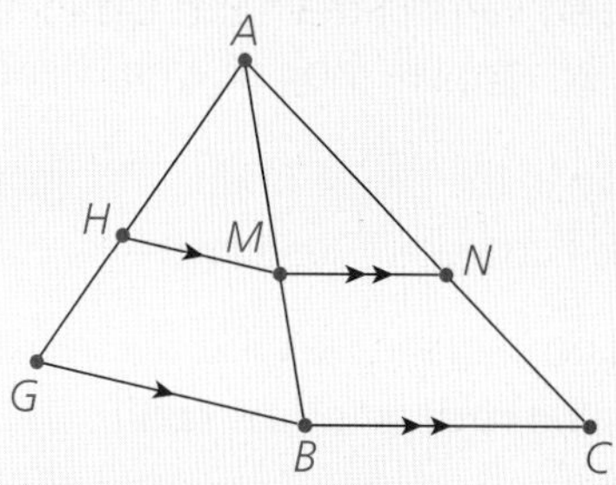

Prove that $HN \parallel GC$.

10 In the diagram, the three lines a, b and c are parallel. Also $KW \parallel LM$, $KW \parallel TV$, and $|KL| = |LN|$.

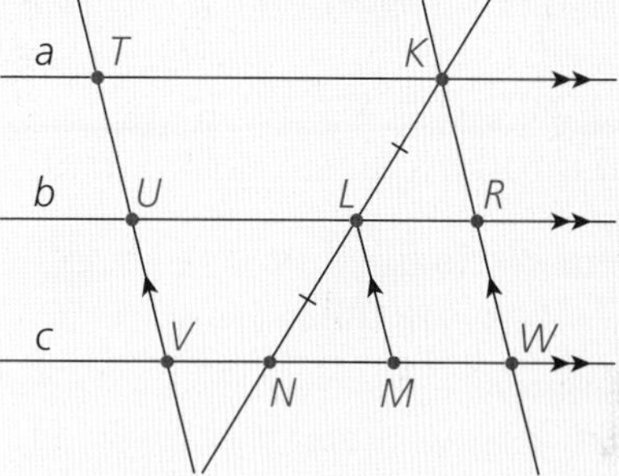

(i) State the theorem that tells you that $|TU| = |UV|$.

(ii) Name three line segments equal to $|KR|$. Explain your answers.

(iii) Prove that the triangles KLR and LMN are congruent.

11 ABC is a triangle and DE is parallel to BC. $|AD| = 2$, $|DB| = 3$ and $|AE| = 3$.

(i) Find $|EC|$.

(ii) Given that $|\angle BAC| = 90°$, show that area of ΔADE : area of $BDEC = 4:21$.

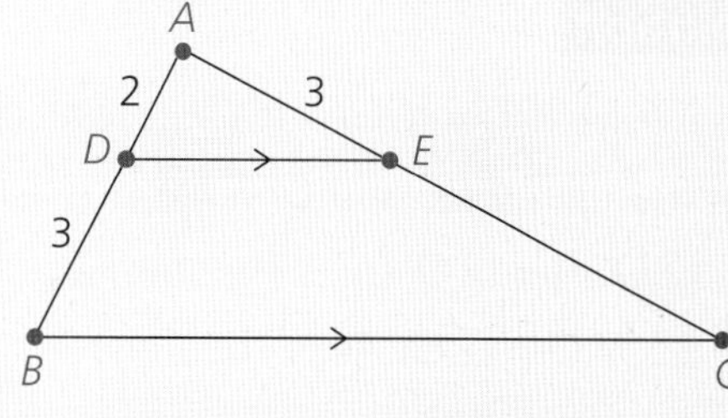

Section 20D Circles, Angles and Triangles

In this section, we look at what happens when angles and triangles are drawn inside circles.

A **circle** is the set of points at a given distance (its **radius**) from a fixed point (its **centre**).

Each line segment joining the centre to a point on the circle is called a **radius** (plural **radii**).

A **chord** is a line segment joining two points on a circle.

A **diameter** is a chord through the centre. All diameters have a length that is twice the radius. This length is also called the diameter of the circle.

The perimeter of the circle is called the **circumference**.

Two points *A* and *B* on a circle cut it into two pieces called **arcs**.

A **semi-circle** is an arc of a circle whose ends are the ends of a diameter.

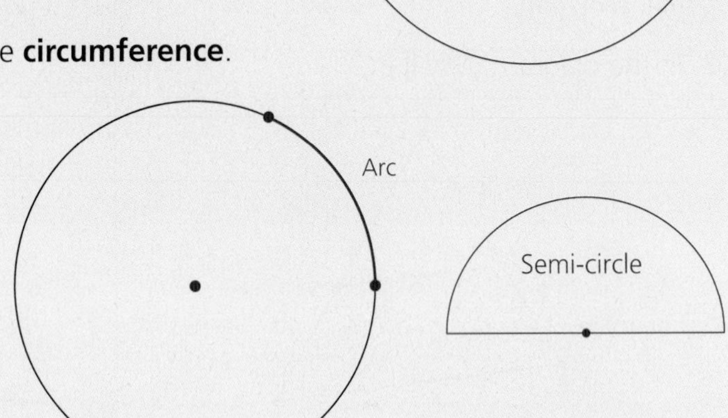

Example 1

The diagram shows a circle of centre O.

(i) Name four equal line segments in the diagram. Explain your answer.

(ii) Name two isosceles triangles in the diagram.

(iii) Name an angle that is equal to $|\angle OFG|$.

(iv) Name another pair of equal angles.

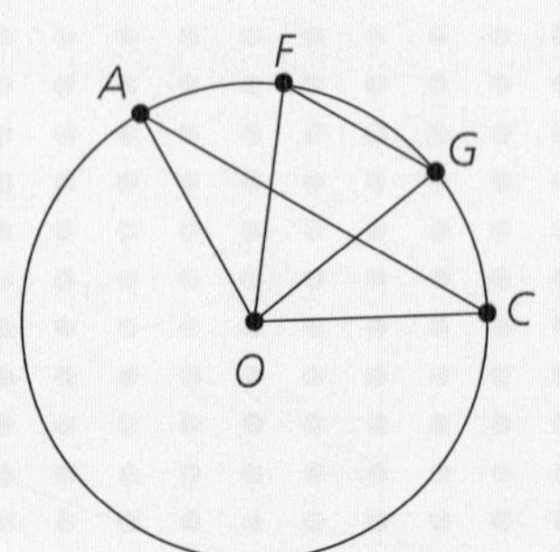

Solution

(i) $|OA| = |OF| = |OG| = |OC|$ ... radii of the same circle

(ii) Triangles OAC and OFG are isosceles.

(iii) $|\angle OGF| = |\angle OFG|$ ... Theorem 2

(iv) $|\angle OAC| = |\angle OCA|$ ... Theorem 2

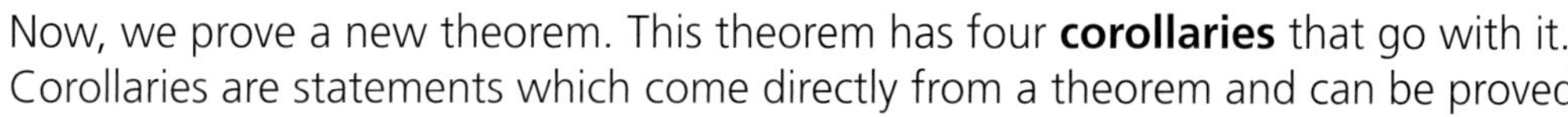

Now, we prove a new theorem. This theorem has four **corollaries** that go with it. Corollaries are statements which come directly from a theorem and can be proved.

THEOREM 19 (formal proof)

The angle at the centre of a circle standing on a given arc is twice the angle at any point of the circle standing on the same arc.

Given: $\angle CAD$ at the centre and $\angle CBD$ at the circumference standing on the same arc CD of a circle.

Required to prove: $|\angle CAD| = 2|\angle CBD|$

Construction: Join B to A and extend to E. Label angles as shown.

Proof: $[AB]$ and $[AC]$ are radii of the circle

$\Rightarrow |AB| = |AC|$

$\Rightarrow$ triangle ACB is isosceles

$\Rightarrow \quad |\angle 2| = |\angle 3|$ ... Theorem 2

$\Rightarrow |\angle 2| + |\angle 3| = 2|\angle 3|$

Also, exterior angle $|\angle 1| = |\angle 2| + |\angle 3|$ ... Theorem 6

$\Rightarrow |\angle 1| = 2|\angle 3|$

Similarly, $|\angle 4| = 2|\angle 5|$

$\Rightarrow |\angle 1| + |\angle 4| = 2|\angle 3| + 2|\angle 5|$ ... by addition

i.e. $|\angle 1| + |\angle 4| = 2[\, |\angle 3| + |\angle 5|\,]$

i.e. $|\angle CAD| = 2|\angle CBD|$ ... QED

COROLLARY 1 OF THEOREM 19

All angles at points of a circle standing on the same arc are equal.

Given: $\angle ABC$ and $\angle ADC$ at a circle standing on the same arc AC of the circle.

Required to prove: $|\angle 1| = |\angle 2|$

Proof:

$|\angle 3| = 2|\angle 1|$

$|\angle 3| = 2|\angle 2|$

$\Rightarrow |\angle 1| = |\angle 2|$ ... QED

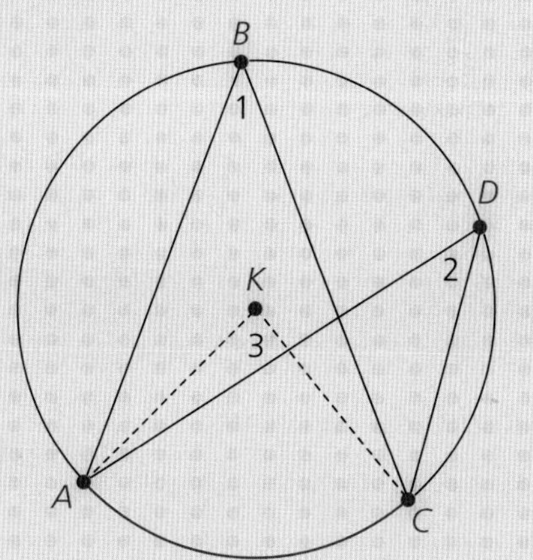

COROLLARY 2 OF THEOREM 19

Each angle in a semi-circle is a right angle.

Required to prove: $|\angle PQR| = 90°$

Proof:

Let PR be a diameter of circle with centre O.

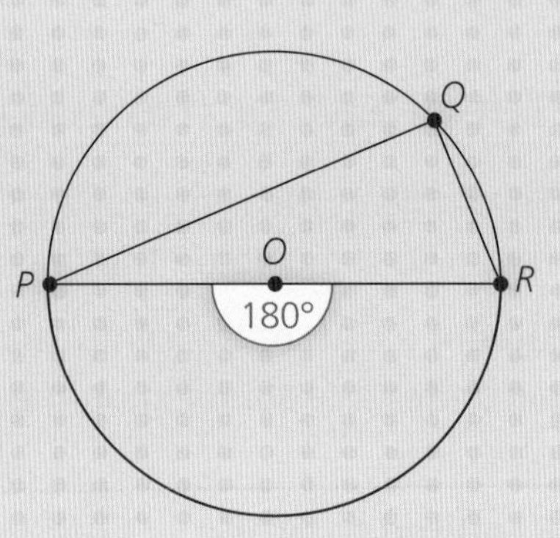

$\|\angle POR\| = 180°$	... straight angle
$\|\angle POR\| = 2\|\angle PQR\|$	... Theorem 19
$\Rightarrow \|\angle PQR\| = 90°$	... QED

COROLLARY 3 OF THEOREM 19

If the angle standing on a chord $[PR]$ at some point of the circle is a right angle, then $[PR]$ is a diameter.

Given: Right angle $\angle PQR$ standing on a chord $[PR]$ of a circle of centre O.

Required to prove: $[PR]$ is a diameter of the circle.

Proof:

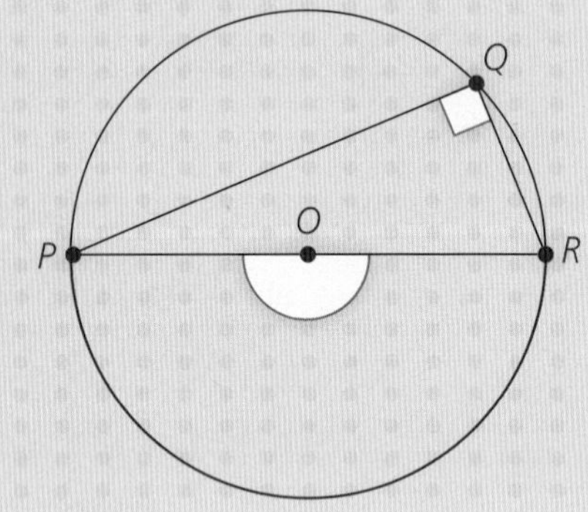

$\|\angle PQR\| = 90°$	... given
$\Rightarrow \|\angle POR\| = 180°$	
$\Rightarrow \angle POR$ is a straight angle	
$\Rightarrow [PR]$ is a diameter	... QED

A **cyclic quadrilateral** is a quadrilateral whose four vertices are on a circle. Both of the quadrilaterals in these diagrams are cyclic quadrilaterals.

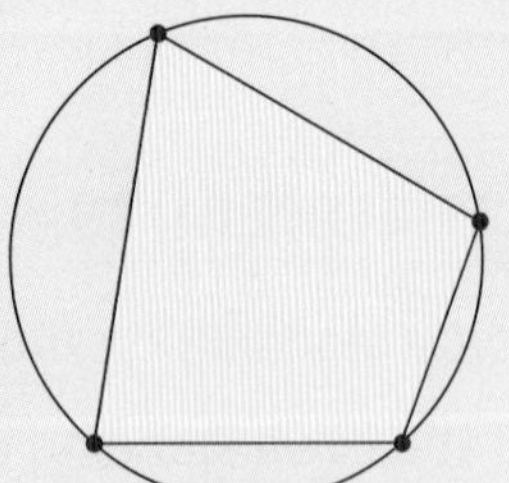

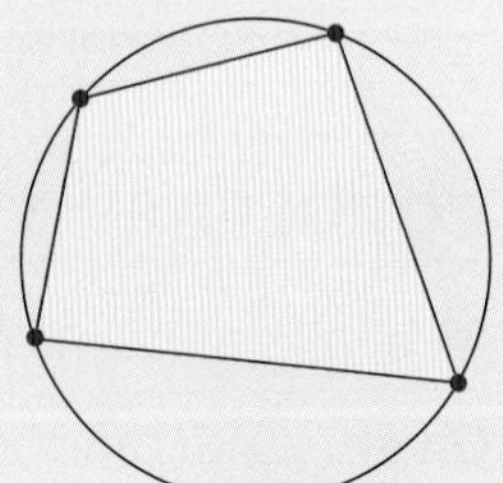

COROLLARY 4 OF THEOREM 19

If $ABCD$ is a cyclic quadrilateral, then opposite angles sum to 180°.

Given: Cyclic quadrilateral $ABCD$ in a circle of centre K.

Required to prove:

$|\angle ABC| + |\angle ADC| = 180°$

$|\angle BAD| + |\angle BCD| = 180°$

Proof:

$|\angle AKC| = 2|\angle 1|$ ... Theorem 19

Also, reflex $|\angle AKC| = 2|\angle 2|$ ... Theorem 19

But $|\angle AKC|$ + reflex $|\angle AKC| = 360°$ ... full revolution

$\Rightarrow |\angle 1| + |\angle 2| = 180°$

Similarly, it may be shown that

$|\angle BAD| + |\angle BCD| = 180°$ ... QED

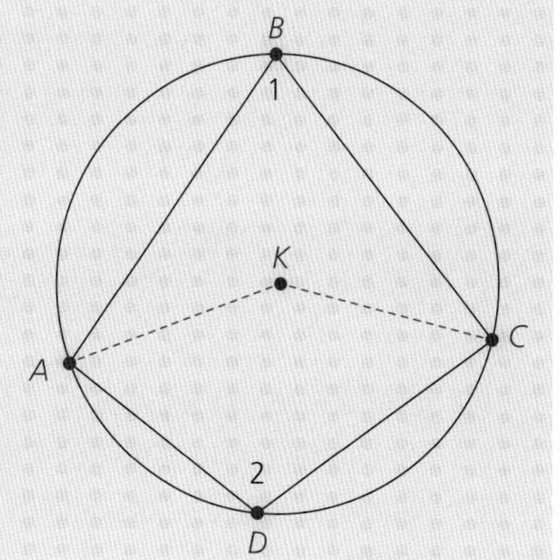

Example 2

(i) What type of quadrilateral is *BDEF*?

(ii) Find the value of α.

(iii) Write down the value of β.

(iv) Write down the value of angle θ.

(v) What is the value of $\alpha + \theta$?

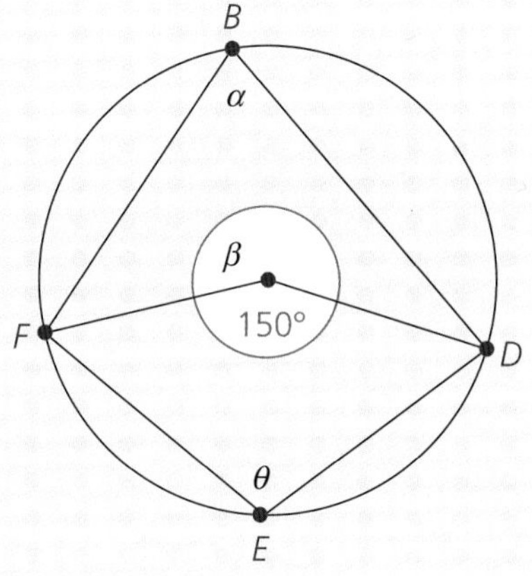

Solution

(i) *BDEF* is a cyclic quadrilateral.

(ii) $\alpha = \frac{1}{2}(150) = 75°$

(iii) $\beta = 360 - 150 = 210°$

(iv) $\beta = 2(\theta)$

$\Rightarrow 210 = 2(\theta)$

$\Rightarrow \theta = 105°$

(v) $\alpha + \theta = 180°$ ...cyclic quadrilateral.

Activity 20.3

1 (i) Construct a circle of radius 5 cm. Label the centre *O*.

(ii) Draw in a diameter [*CD*].

(iii) Draw a radius [*OP*].

(iv) Draw another radius [*OQ*].

(v) Draw a chord [*MN*].

Geometry 3

2 (i) In this circle, name three line segments equal to $[OA]$. Explain your answer.

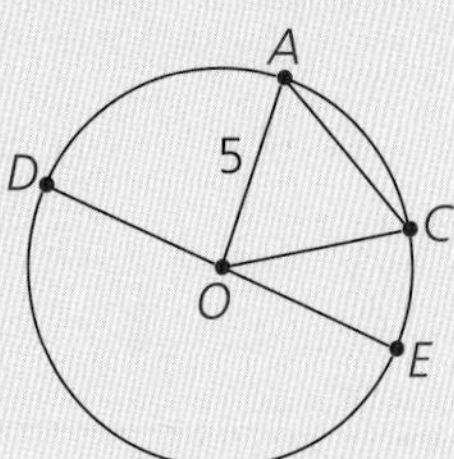

(ii) $|OA| = 5$. What is $|DE|$? Explain how you got your answer.

(iii) Name an isosceles triangle in the figure.

(iv) What two line segments could be added to the diagram to make two more isosceles triangles?

(v) Calculate the area of this circle correct to two decimal places.

3 The diagram shows a circle of centre O.

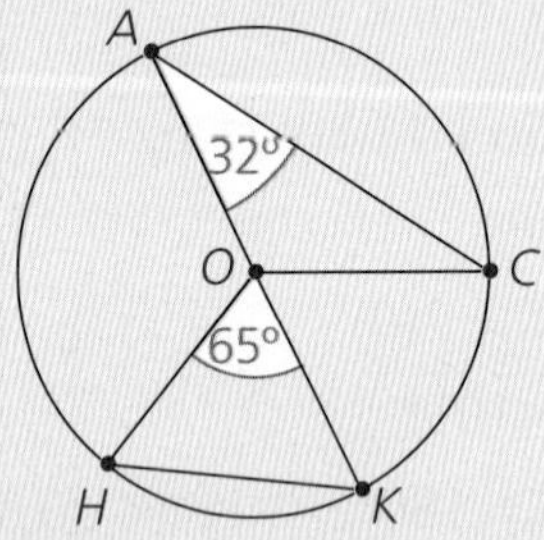

(i) Name four equal line segments in the diagram. Explain your answer.

(ii) Name two isosceles triangles.

(iii) Name an angle equal to $|\angle OAC|$.

(iv) Name another pair of equal angles.

4 Find the angle α in each of the following diagrams. The centre of each circle is C.

(i)

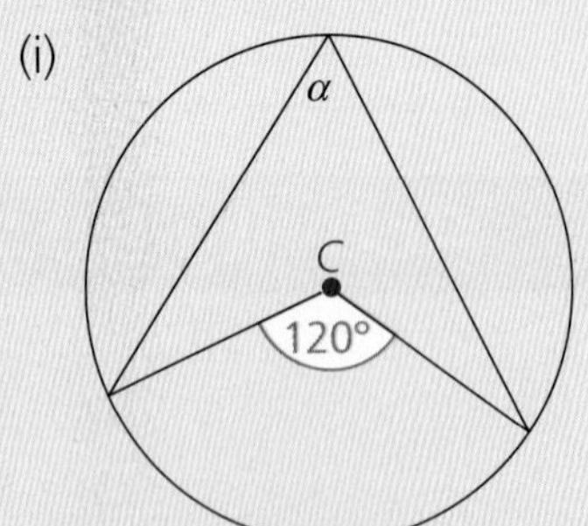

(ii)

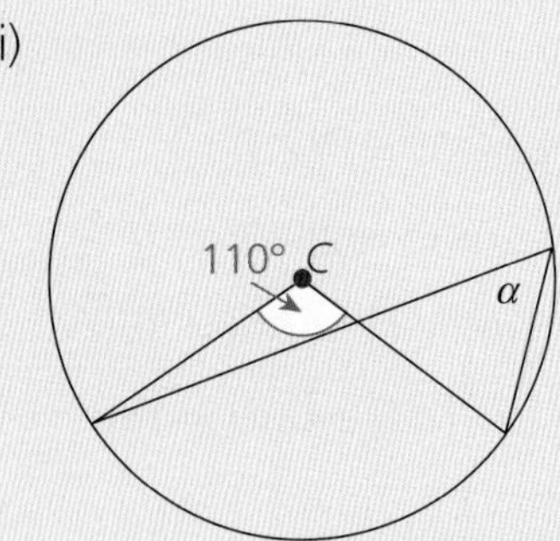

(iii)

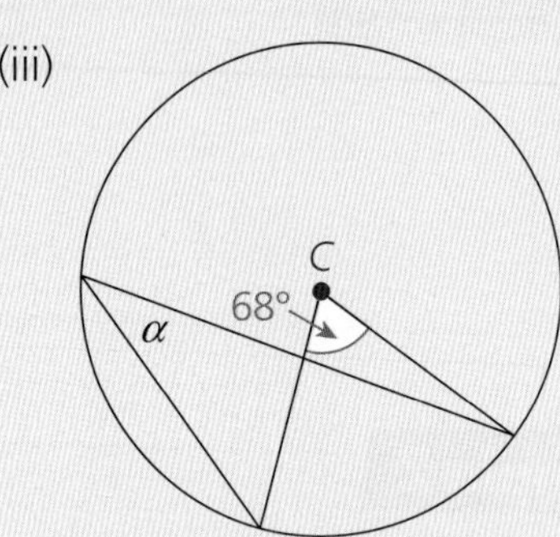

(iv)

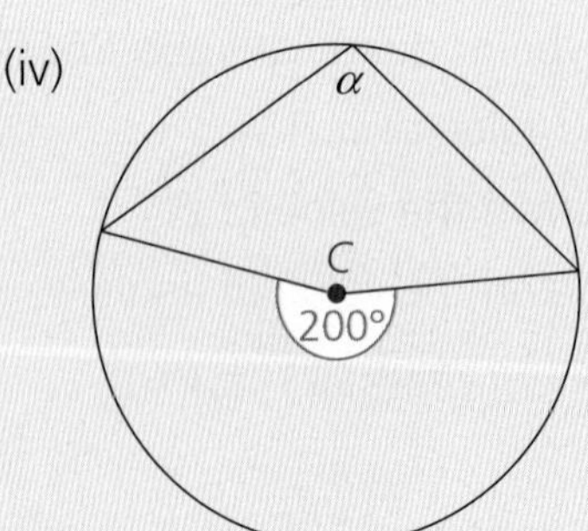

(v)

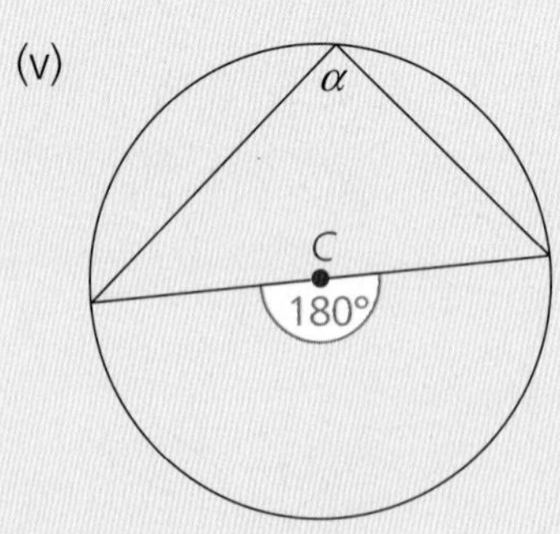

(vi)

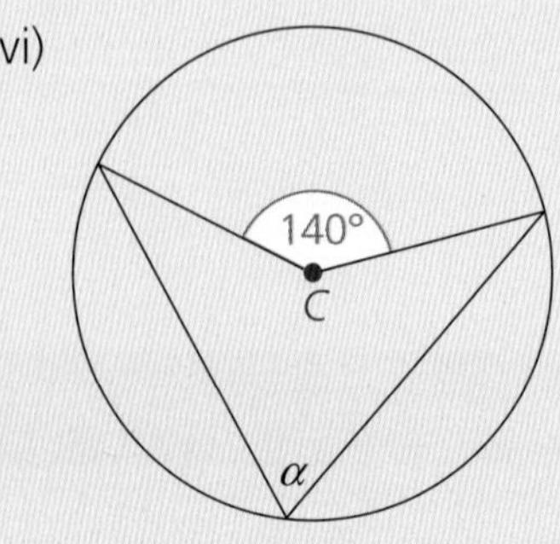

(vii)

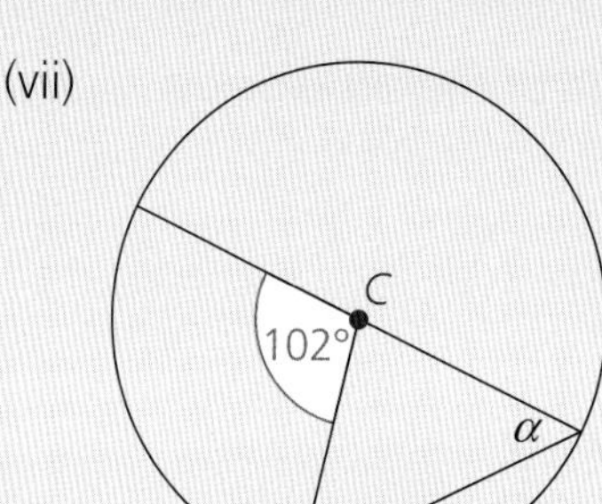

(viii)

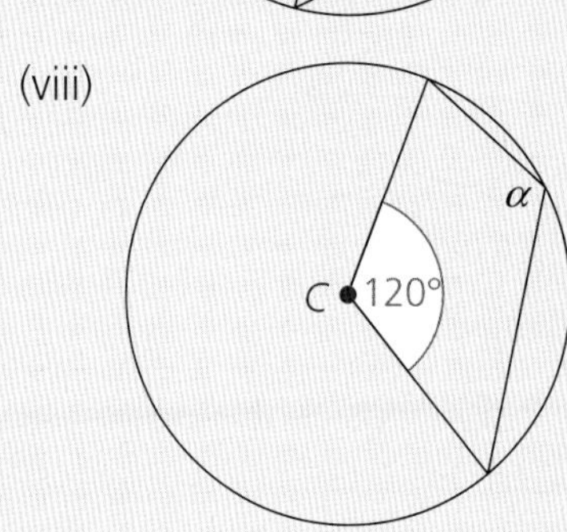

5 The circle in the diagram below has A as its centre.

(i) Write down the value of α.

(ii) Write down the value of β.

(iii) What can you conclude about α and β?

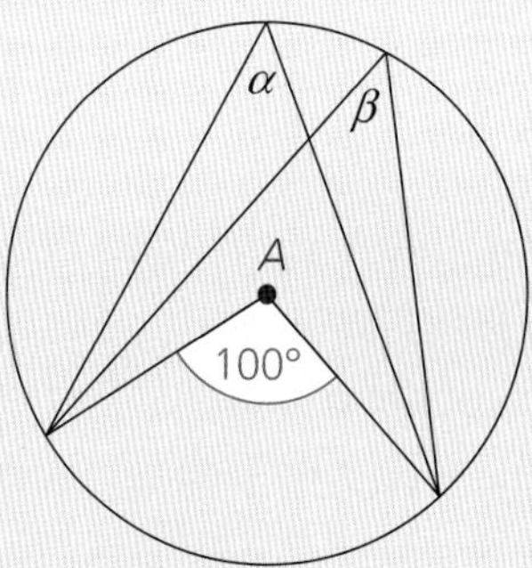

6 Find the value of θ in each of the following diagrams. The centre of each circle is C.

(i)

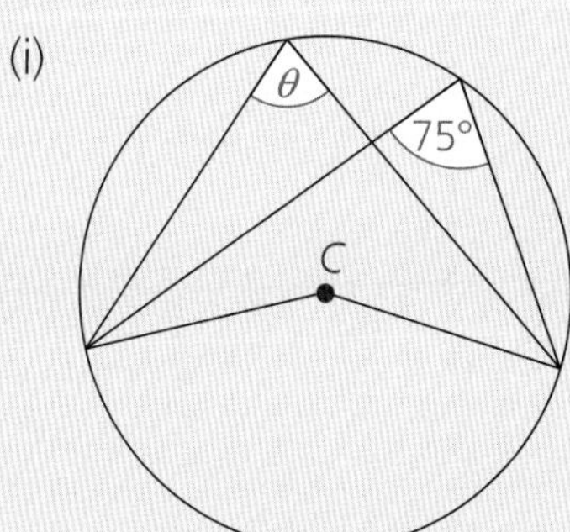

(ii)

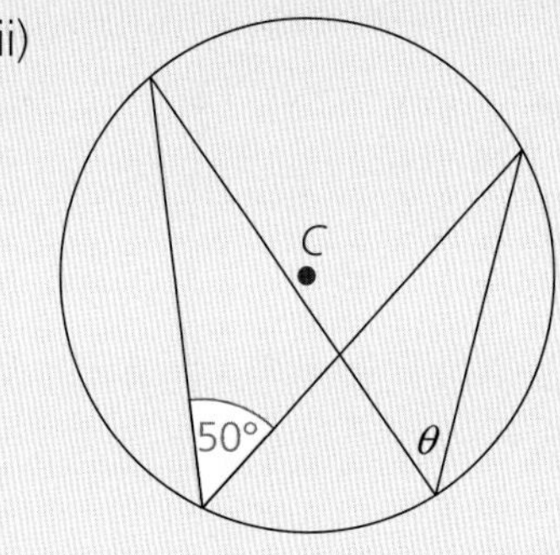

(iii)

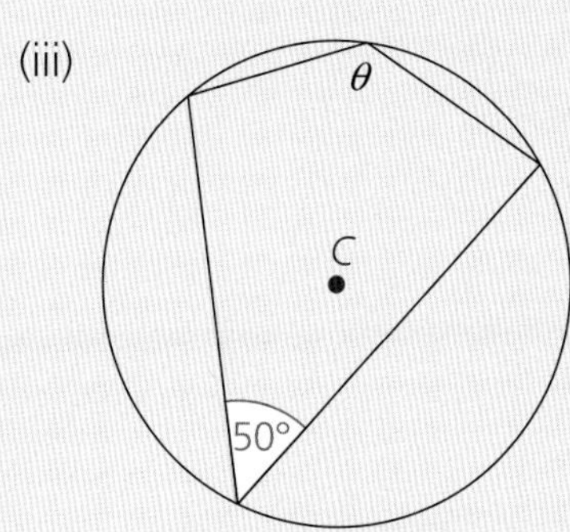

(iv)

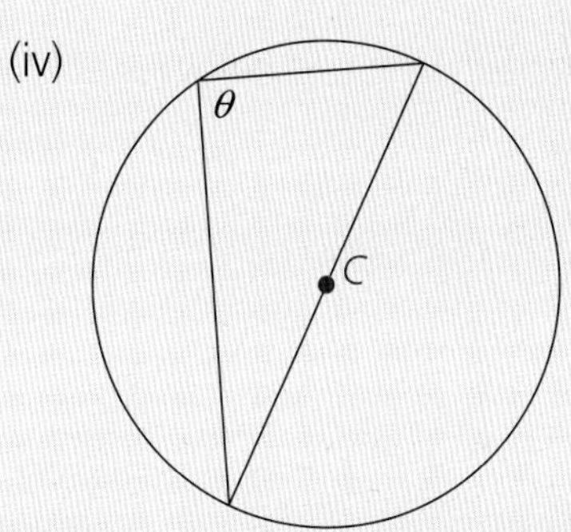

(v)

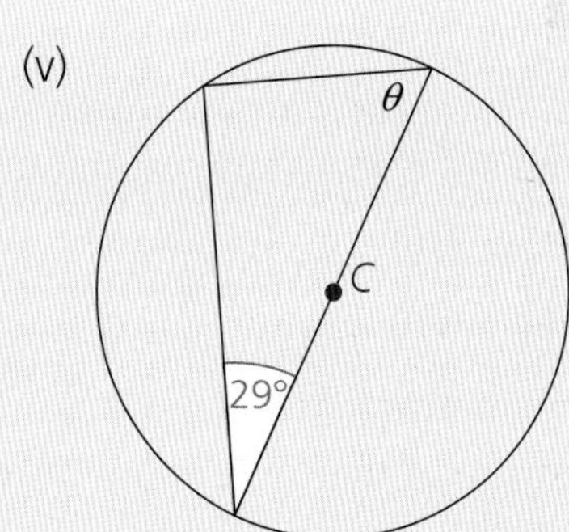

(vi)

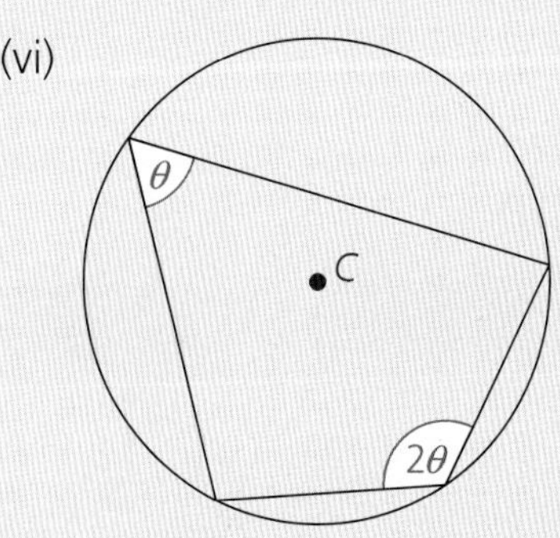

(vii)

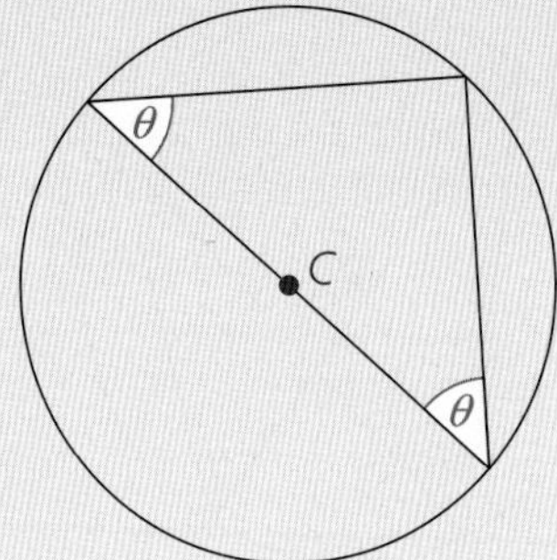

(viii)

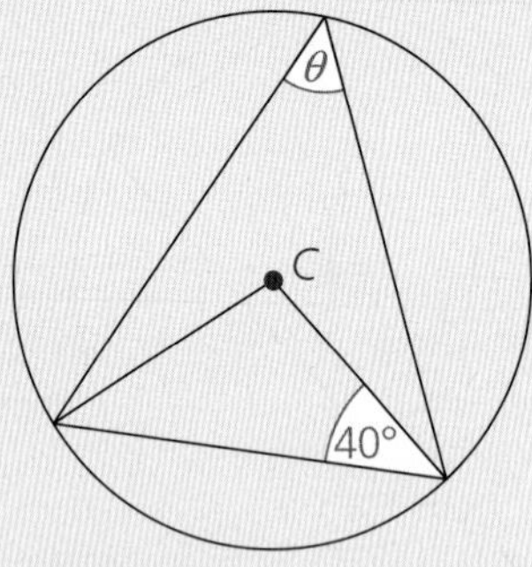

7 The centre of the circle below is O.

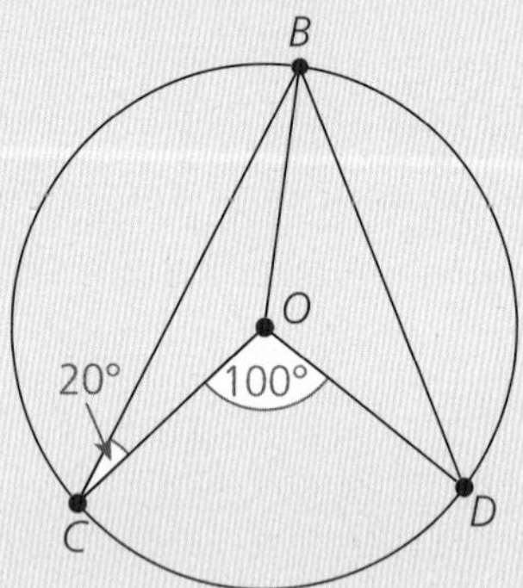

(i) Find $|\angle COB|$.

(ii) Find $|\angle ODB|$.

8 The centre of the circle below is O.

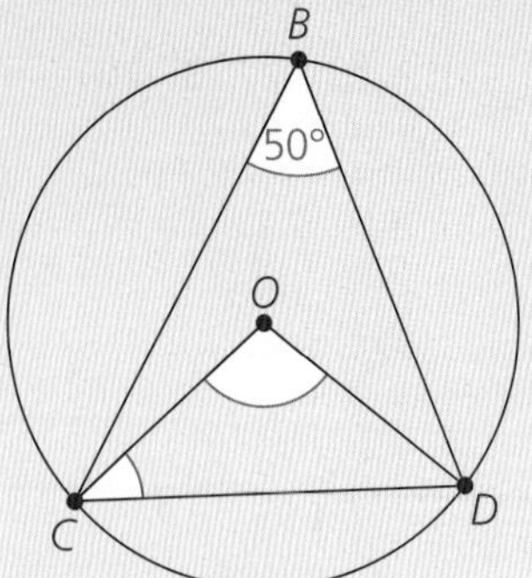

(i) Find $|\angle COD|$.

(ii) Find $|\angle OCD|$.

9 The circle below has centre E and a chord $[GH]$. $EP \perp GH$.

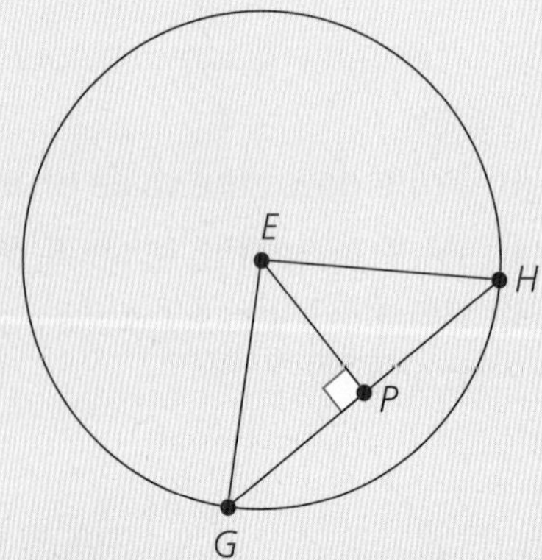

(i) Prove that the triangles EGP and EPH are congruent.

(ii) Hence, prove that $|GP| = |HP|$.

(iii) State in words what you have proved.

10 K is the centre of the circle and $|PM| = |MN|$. $|\angle PQN| = 70°$.

Find:

(i) $|\angle QPN|$

(ii) $|\angle QPM|$

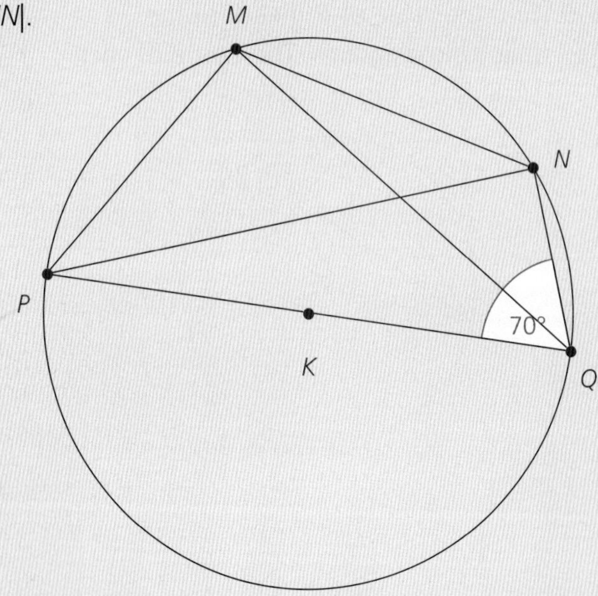

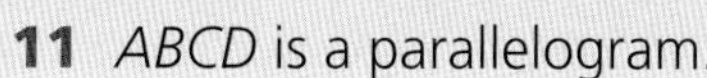

11 *ABCD* is a parallelogram.

The points *A*, *B* and *C* lie on the circle which cuts [*AD*] at *P*. The line *CP* meets the line *BA* at *Q*.

Prove that $|CD| = |CP|$.

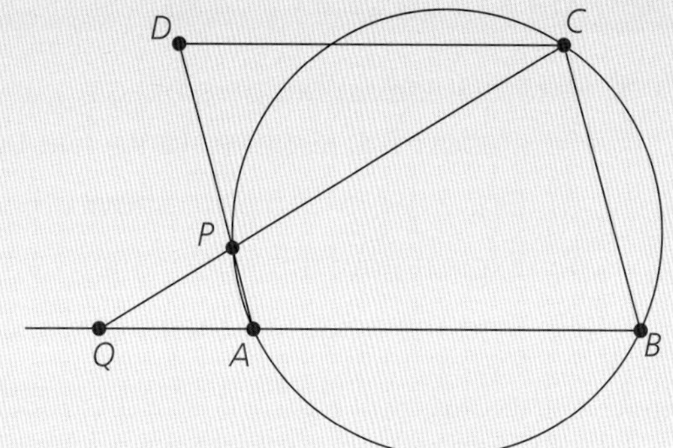

12 (i) Prove that the two triangles *STP* and *QTR* are similar.

(ii) Prove that $|ST| \times |TR| = |QT| \times |TP|$.

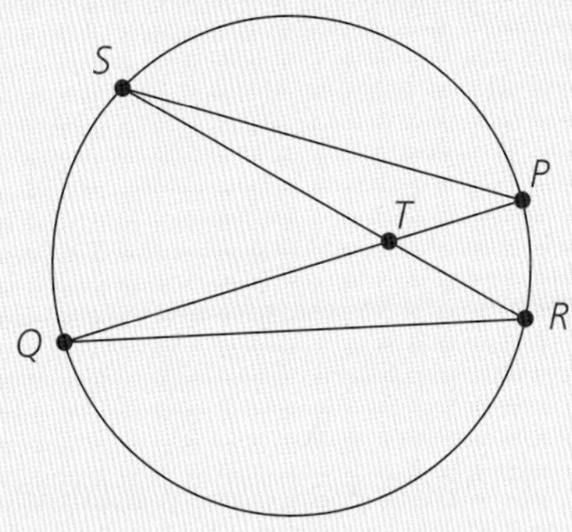

13 The angles indicated in the diagram are equal.

Prove that [*KN*] is a diameter of the circle.

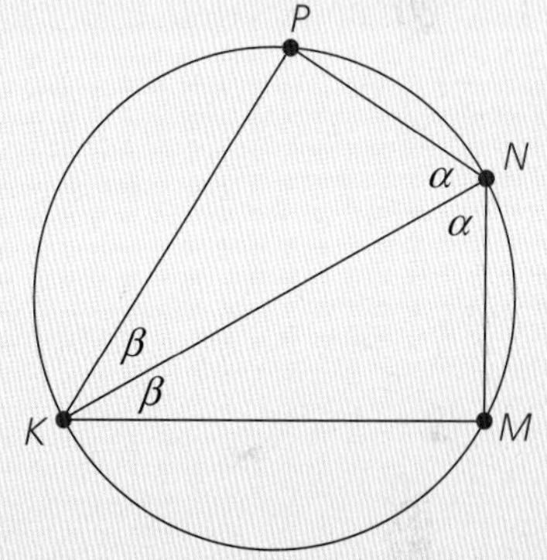

14 *ACBD* is a quadrilateral. $|AC| = |AB| = |AD|$.

$|\angle CAD| = 121°$.

Calculate $|\angle CBD|$ and explain your reasoning.

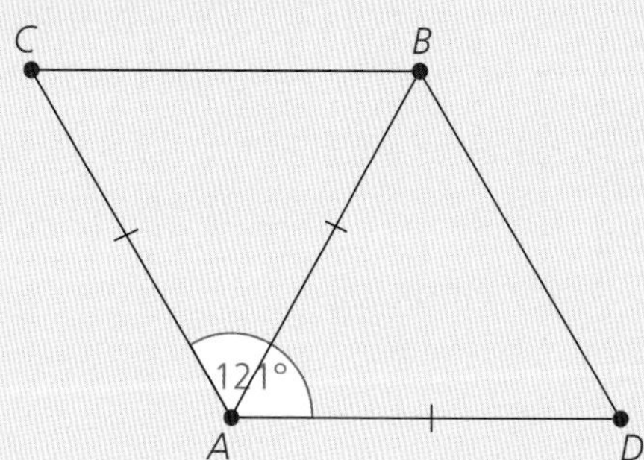

Revision Activity 20

1 Ryan is standing beside a building on a sunny day. He is 1.83 metres tall. His shadow is 0.9 metres long. The building casts a shadow which is 6.5 m long.

(i) Draw two triangles to show this.

(ii) Explain how this information can be used to find the height of the building.

(iii) Find the height of the building, correct to one decimal place.

2 In the diagram, $ABCD$ is a cyclic quadrilateral and $ABCF$ is a parallelogram.

Show that $DEFG$ is a cyclic quadrilateral.

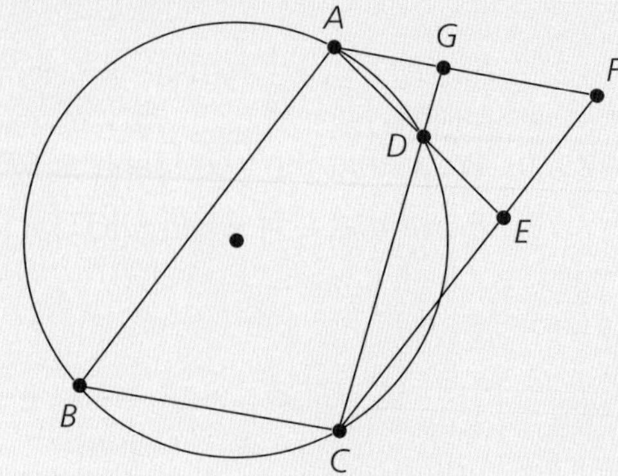

3 $ABCD$ is a cyclic quadrilateral. The opposite sides, when extended, meet at P and Q, as shown. The angles α, β, and γ are as shown.

Prove that $\beta + \gamma = 180° - 2\alpha$.

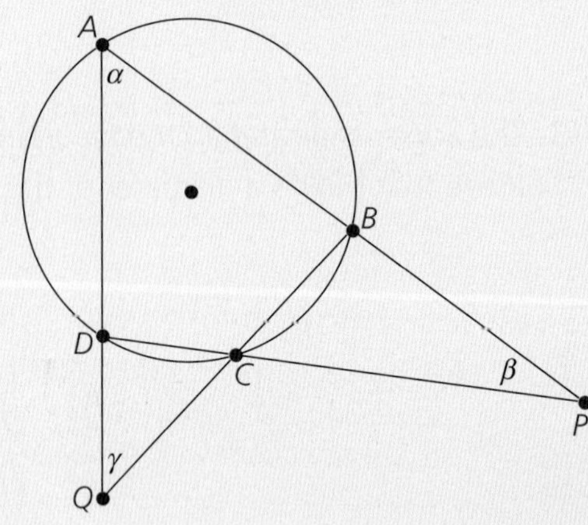

4 ABC is a right-angled triangle. E is the mid-point of $[BC]$. DE is perpendicular to BC. $|DE| = 3$ and $|DC| = 5$.

(a) Find $|EC|$.

(b) Prove that $|\angle ABC| = |\angle EDC|$.

(c) Find $|AB|$.

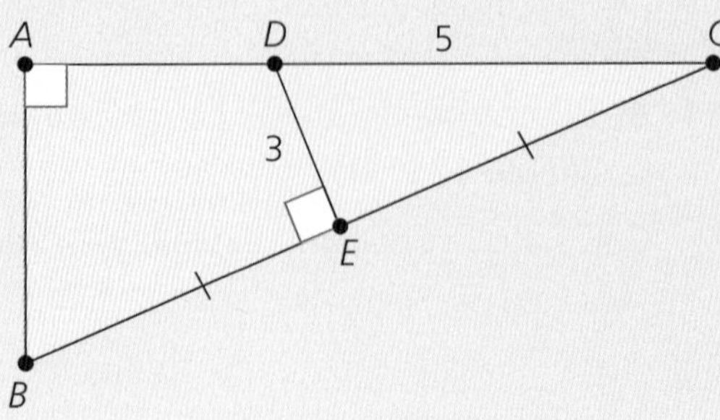

Exam-style Questions

1 The diagram here shows a circle with centre O. The five points A, B, C, D, and E are on the circle. $[AB]$ and $[DE]$ are diameters of the circle, and $|\angle BOE| = 40°$. The angles α, β, and γ are labelled.

(a) Write down the size of the angle α.

(b) Work out the size of the angle β.

(c) Work out the size of the angle γ.

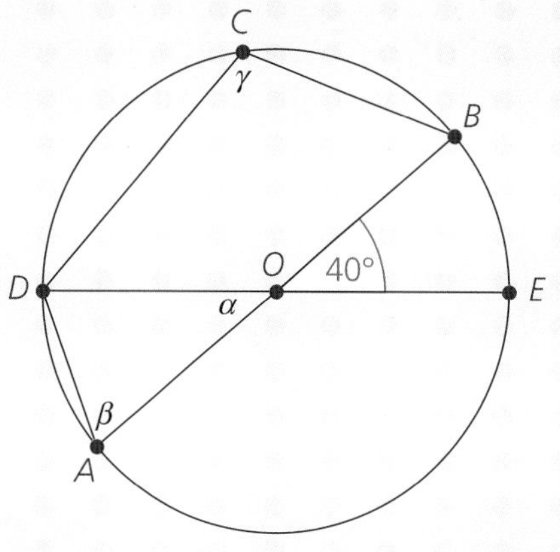

JCHL 2018

2 A, B, C and D are four points on a circle as shown. $[AD]$ bisects $\angle BAC$.

P is the point of intersection of AD and BC.

(a) Show that ΔADB and ΔAPC are similar.

(b) Show that $|AC| \times |BD| = |AD| \times |PC|$.

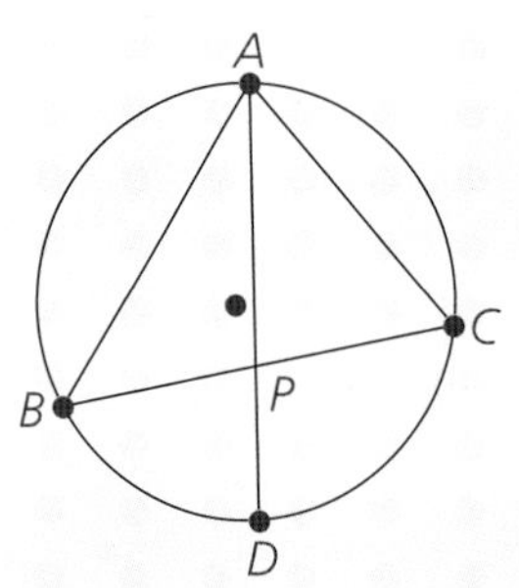

JCHL 2014 Sample Paper 2

KEY WORDS AND PHRASES

- **Similar triangles**
- **Equilateral triangles**
- **Proportional**
- **Corresponding sides**
- **Circle**
- **Radius, radii**
- **Centre of circle**
- **Chord**
- **Diameter**
- **Circumference**
- **Arc**
- **Semi-circle**
- **Cyclic quadrilateral**

Interactive Tool 20.1

- **Theorem 11**

  If three parallel lines cut off equal segments on some transversal line, then they will cut off equal segments on any other transversal.

- **Theorem 12**

  Let *ABC* be a triangle. If a line *l* is parallel to *BC* and cuts [*AB*] in the ratio $m:n$, then it also cuts [*AC*] in the same ratio.

- **Construction 7:** Division of a line segment into any number of equal segments, without measuring.
- Triangles *ABC* and *DEF* are similar triangles if each of the angles of ΔABC is equal to a corresponding angle in ΔDEF.
- Similar triangles have the same shape.

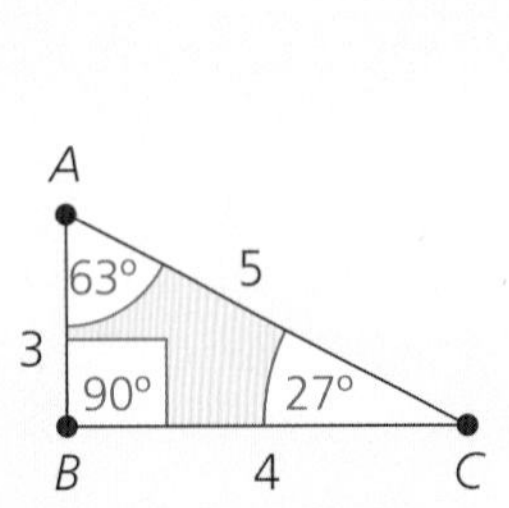

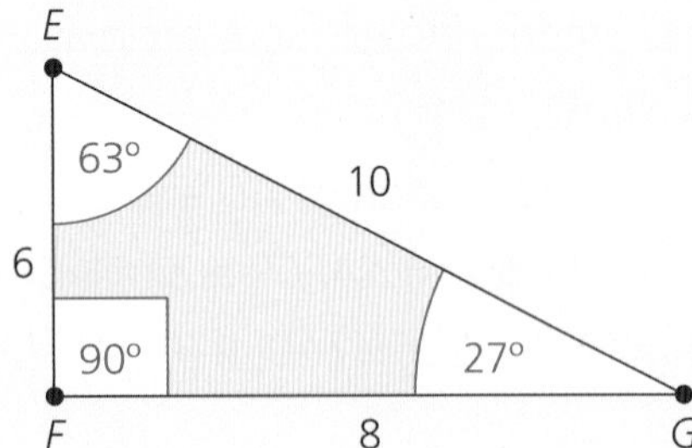

- **Theorem 13:** If two triangles are similar, their sides are proportional, in order.
- If the sides of two triangles are proportional (in order), the two triangles are similar.
- We can use similar triangles to find the height of objects from the length of their shadows.
- **Theorem 19**

  The angle at the centre of a circle standing on a given arc is twice the angle at any point of the circle standing on the same arc.

- **Corollary 1 of Theorem 19**

  All angles at points of a circle standing on the same arc are equal.

- **Corollary 2 of Theorem 19**

  Each angle in a semi-circle is a right angle.

- **Corollary 3 of Theorem 19**

  If the angle standing on a chord [*PR*] at some point of the circle is a right angle, then [*PR*] is a diameter.

- **Corollary 4 of Theorem 19**

  If *ABCD* is a cyclic quadrilateral, then opposite angles sum to 180°.

Trigonometry

Chapter 21

Learning Intentions

In this chapter, you will learn about:

LO: U.5, U.6, GT.4

- The relationship between the angles and sides of a right-angled triangle
- The trigonometric ratios sine, cosine and tangent
- Using trigonometry to solve problems involving right-angled triangles
- Angles of elevation and depression
- Using a clinometer to measure the height of tall objects

Imagine that you are an engineer in charge of constructing a tunnel under a mountain. You want two teams of workers to start at different ends and to meet somewhere under the mountain.

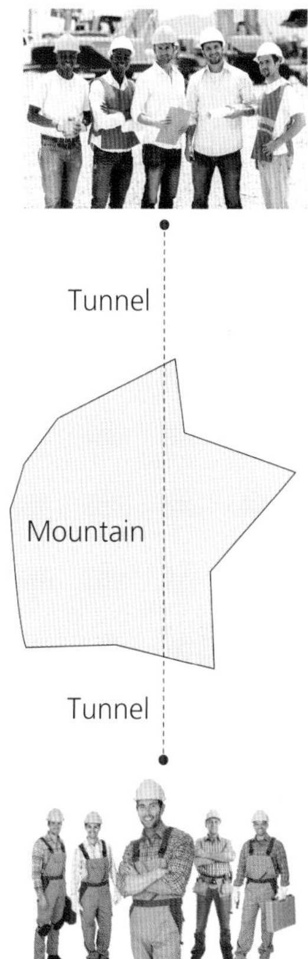

The teams cannot see each other. How do you ensure that the teams meet?

This problem was solved by Heron, a Greek mathematician who lived around 50 AD. His solution shows the power of simple geometry and trigonometry.

We will see how this problem is solved later in the chapter.

Section 21A Sides and Angles in a Right-Angled Triangle

In this chapter we are going to look at the relationships between the side lengths and angle sizes in a right-angled triangle. First, here are two important words to learn:

- The word **adjacent** means **beside**, as in 'Sam's tent is **adjacent** to Leah's tent.'

- The word **opposite** means **across from**, as in 'Tom was on the **opposite** side of the road from me.'

We label the sides of a right-angled triangle in this way:

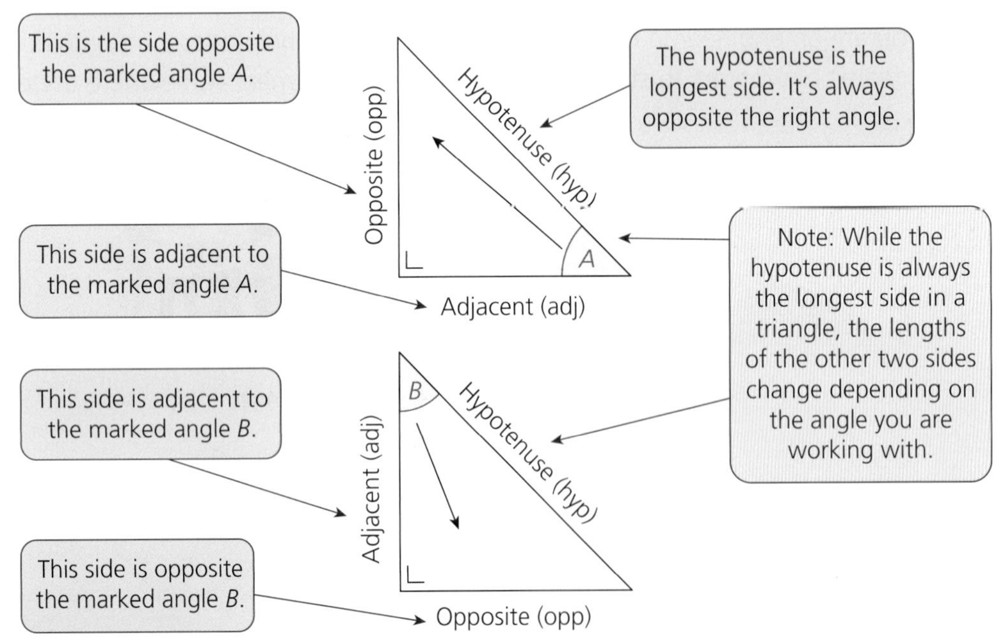

Example

Name the side which is:

(i) The hypotenuse

(ii) Opposite angle A

(iii) Adjacent to angle A

(iv) Opposite angle B

(v) Adjacent to angle B.

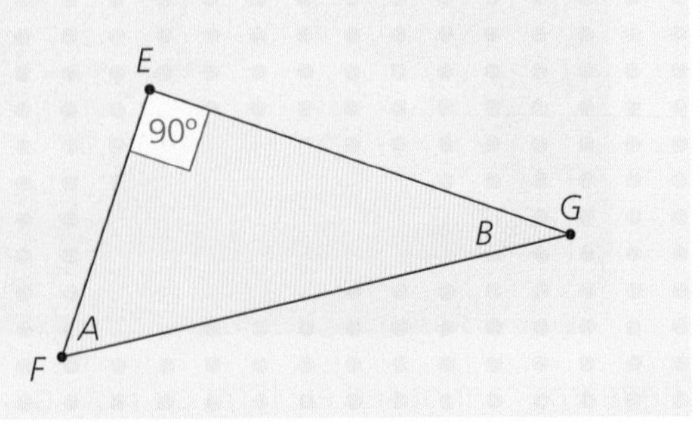

Solution

(i) The hypotenuse = [*FG*]

(ii) Side opposite angle A = [*EG*]

(iii) Side adjacent to angle A = [*EF*]

(iv) Side opposite angle B = [*EF*]

(v) Side adjacent to angle B = [*EG*]

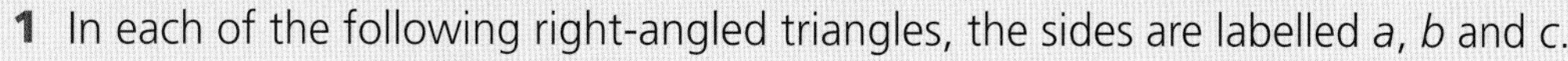

Activity 21.1

1 In each of the following right-angled triangles, the sides are labelled a, b and c.
Name: (i) The hypotenuse
(ii) The side opposite the angle θ
(iii) The side adjacent to the angle θ.

(a)

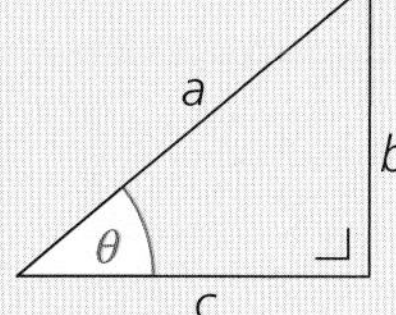

(b)

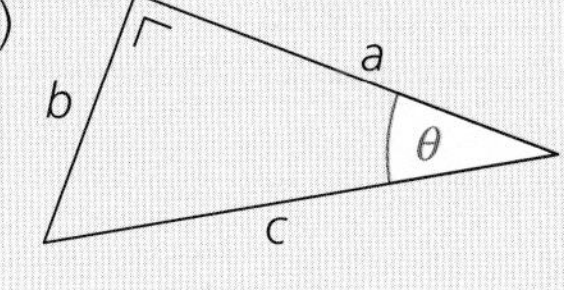

(c)

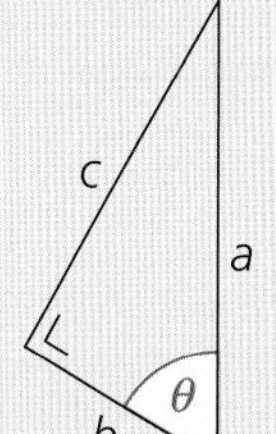

(d)

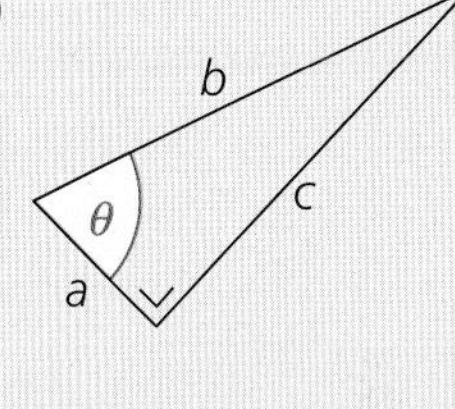

2 In this triangle, name the side that is:

(i) The hypotenuse

(ii) The side adjacent to angle α

(iii) The side opposite angle α

(iv) The side adjacent to angle β

(v) The side opposite angle β.

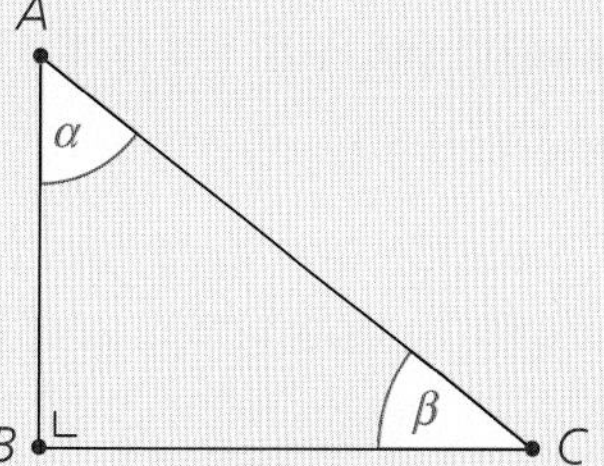

3 In each triangle, name the sides in relation to angle θ.

(i)

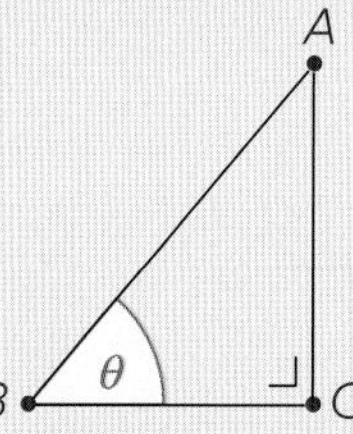

(ii)

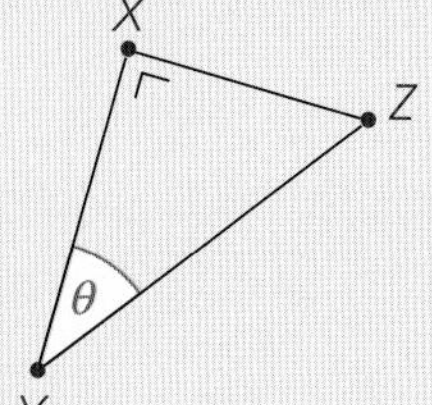

(iii)

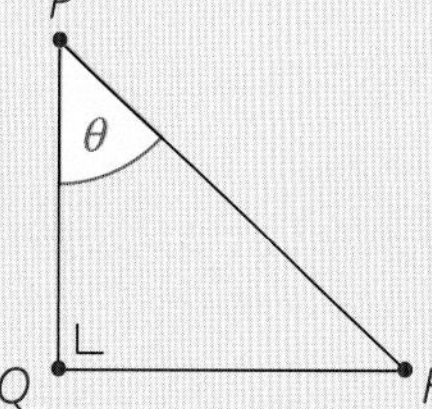

4 In each of the following right-angled triangles, calculate the length of the missing side and write down the length of:

(i) The side adjacent to angle α

(ii) The side opposite angle α

(iii) The hypotenuse.

(a)

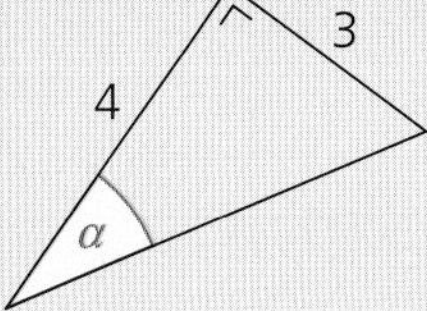

(b)

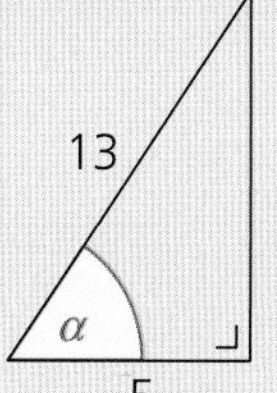

(c)

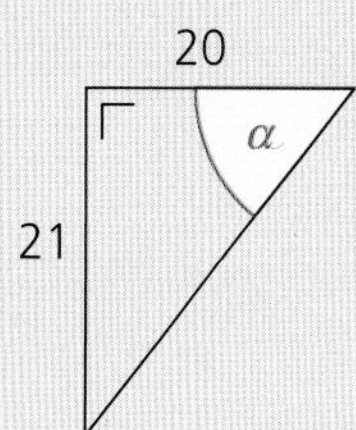

5 Look at the following diagrams carefully. Each triangle is right-angled with another angle of **30°**. So they are similar triangles.

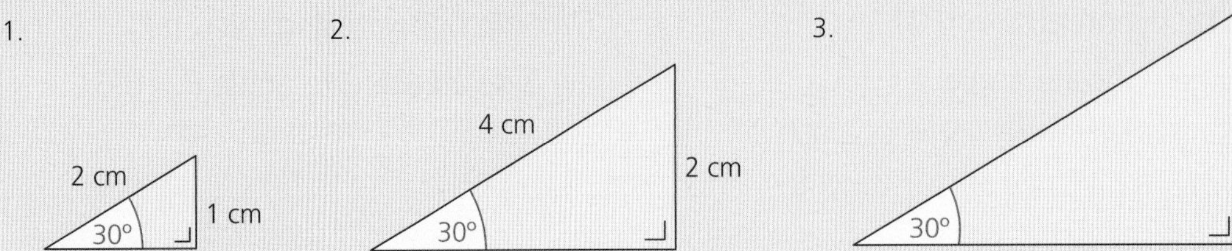

(i) Copy the table below into your copybook. Fill in the measurements for triangles 1 and 2, and calculate the ratios in columns 5, 6 and 7 on your calculator in decimal form.

(ii) Measure the sides in triangle 3 as accurately as possible and fill these into your table.

Column 1	2	3	4	5	6	7
				Ratios (decimals)		
Angle of 30°	**Opp**	**Adj**	**Hyp**	**Opp/Hyp**	**Adj/Hyp**	**Opp/Adj**
Triangle 1						
Triangle 2						
Triangle 3						
Mean value of the ratios						

(iii) Did you find that the ratios in column 5 were all approximately equal?

(iv) Did you find that the ratios in column 6 were all approximately equal?

(v) Did you find that the ratios in column 7 were all approximately equal?

(vi) Find the mean values for columns 5, 6 and 7 and fill them into the table.

6 Look at these diagrams carefully. This is similar to question **5**, but here, each triangle is right-angled with another angle of **50°**.

(i) Copy the table below into your copybook.

(ii) Measure the sides of triangles 1, 2 and 3 as accurately as possible and fill these into your table.

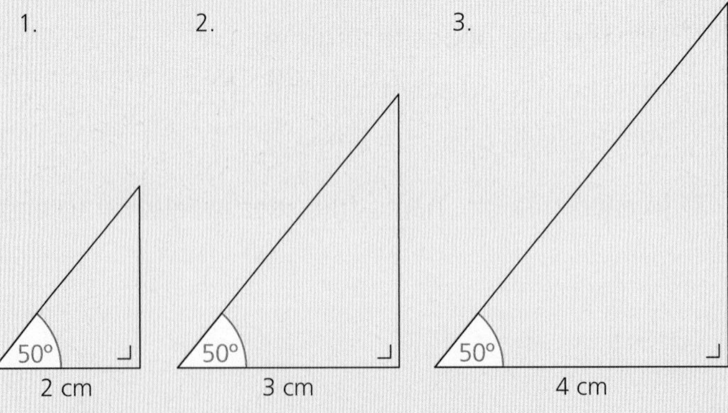

(iii) Calculate the ratios in columns 5, 6 and 7 on your calculator in decimal form.

Column 1	2	3	4	5	6	7
				Ratios (decimals)		
Angle of 50°	**Opp**	**Adj**	**Hyp**	**Opp/Hyp**	**Adj/Hyp**	**Opp/Adj**
Triangle 1						
Triangle 2						
Triangle 3						
Mean value of the ratios						

(iv) Did you find that the ratios in column 5 were all approximately equal?

(v) Did you find that the ratios in column 6 were all approximately equal?

(vi) Did you find that the ratios in column 7 were all approximately equal?

(vii) Find the mean values for columns 5, 6 and 7 and fill them into the table.

Section 21B Introduction to Sine, Cosine and Tangent

In questions 5 and 6 of Activity 21.1 you worked out the three ratios (fractions):

$\frac{\text{Opp}}{\text{Hyp}}, \frac{\text{Adj}}{\text{Hyp}}, \frac{\text{Opp}}{\text{Adj}}$, with respect to the angle involved.

These ratios have special names which come from Greek words:

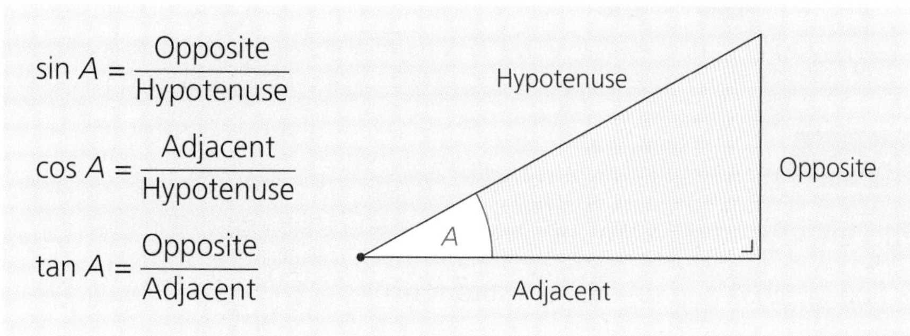

$$\sin A = \frac{\text{Opposite}}{\text{Hypotenuse}}$$

$$\cos A = \frac{\text{Adjacent}}{\text{Hypotenuse}}$$

$$\tan A = \frac{\text{Opposite}}{\text{Adjacent}}$$

'sin' is short for 'sine' (and is pronounced 'sine'), 'cos' is short for 'cosine' and 'tan' is short for 'tangent'. For example: we write sin 30°, tan 63°, cos 48°, etc.

Never write 'sin' or 'cos' or 'tan' without the angle name or value. These ratios have no meaning unless the angle is specified.

You will find these ratios on page 16 of the *Formulae and tables* booklet, but it is better to learn them yourself. Many students remember them by saying 'SOH-CAH-TOA'.

Note

You will find sin, cos and tan buttons on your calculator. Angles can be measured in different units, such as degrees, radians and gradians. For this course you must **make sure that your calculator is in DEGREE mode** (usually denoted by a D at the top of the screen).

Connections

Just as there are 60 minutes in an hour and 60 seconds in a minute, there are 60 minutes in a degree and 60 seconds in a minute.

You can use the °’’’ button on a calculator to add units of time or angles.

Example 1

(i) Use your calculator to evaluate sin 55°, cos 64° and tan 32° correct to 4 decimal places.

(ii) From the triangle shown, write the following ratios as fractions:

sin A, cos A, tan A,

sin B, cos B, tan B.

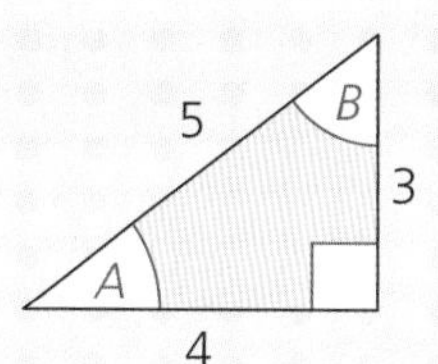

Solution

(i) Using a calculator: sin 55 =

sin 55° = 0.8192

Using a calculator: cos 64 =

cos 64° = 0.4384

Using a calculator: tan 32 =

tan 32° = 0.6249

(ii) $\sin A = \frac{3}{5}$ $\cos A = \frac{4}{5}$ $\tan A = \frac{3}{4}$

$\sin B = \frac{4}{5}$ $\cos B = \frac{3}{5}$ $\tan B = \frac{4}{3}$

Example 2

(i) Construct an angle A such that $\tan A = \frac{4}{5}$.

(ii) Hence, find (a) $\sin A$ and (b) $\cos A$ in surd form.

Solution

(i) $\tan A = \frac{\text{opposite}}{\text{adjacent}}$

Construct a right-angled triangle with base 5 units and height 4 units.

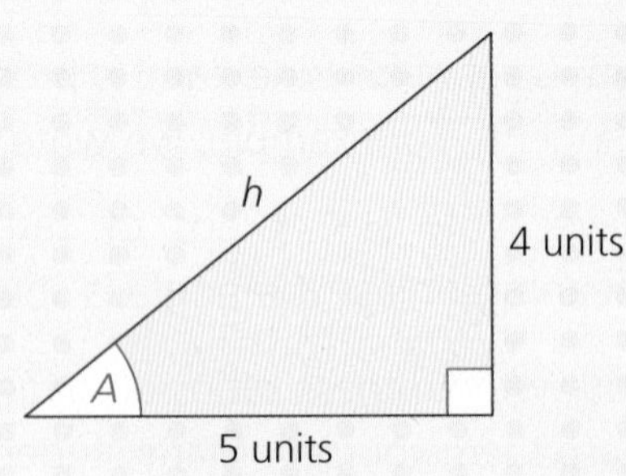

(ii) Find the hypotenuse h:

$h^2 = 4^2 + 5^2$

$\Rightarrow h^2 = 41$

$\Rightarrow h = \sqrt{41}$

$\Rightarrow$ (a) $\sin A = \frac{\text{Opp}}{\text{Hyp}} = \frac{4}{\sqrt{41}}$

(b) $\cos A = \frac{\text{Adj}}{\text{Hyp}} = \frac{5}{\sqrt{41}}$

Activity 21.2

1 Use the diagram to write the following ratios as fractions.

(i) $\sin X$ (iii) $\tan X$ (v) $\cos Y$

(ii) $\cos X$ (iv) $\sin Y$ (vi) $\tan Y$

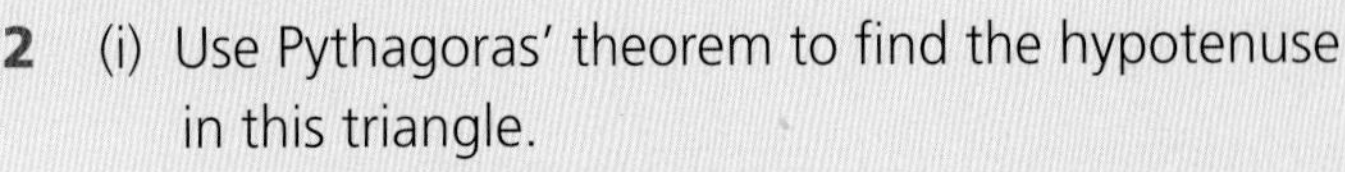

2 (i) Use Pythagoras' theorem to find the hypotenuse in this triangle.

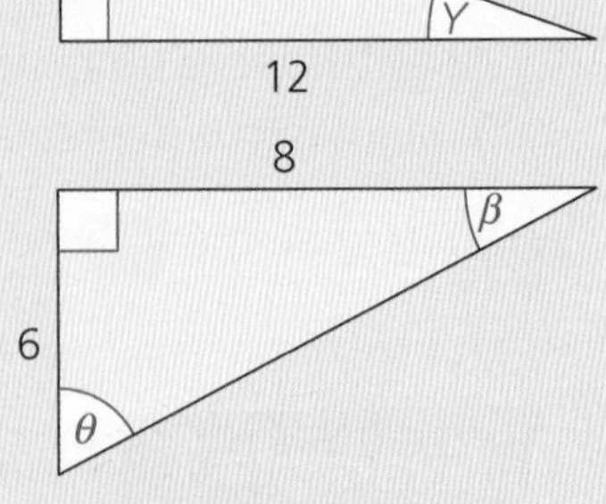

(ii) Use the diagram to write the following ratios.

(a) $\sin \beta$ (c) $\tan \beta$ (e) $\cos \theta$

(b) $\cos \beta$ (d) $\sin \theta$ (f) $\tan \theta$

3 (i) Use Pythagoras' theorem to find the hypotenuse in this triangle.

(ii) Use the diagram to write the following ratios.

(a) $\sin \beta$ (c) $\tan \beta$ (e) $\cos \alpha$

(b) $\cos \beta$ (d) $\sin \alpha$ (f) $\tan \alpha$

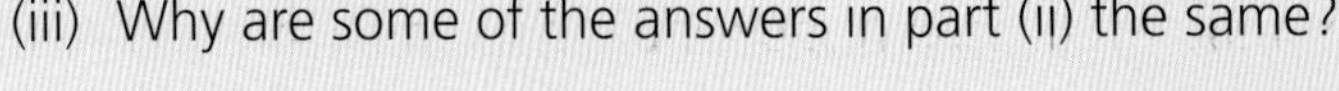

(iii) Why are some of the answers in part (ii) the same?

4 Use your calculator to evaluate the following ratios correct to four decimal places.

(i) $\cos 42°$ (iii) $\cos 10°$ (v) $\tan 72°$

(ii) $\cos 63°$ (iv) $\sin 72°$ (vi) $\cos 72°$

Hint

Make sure your calculator is in DEGREE mode.

5 Use your calculator to check whether the following statements are true or false.

(i) $\sin 40° + \sin 30° = \sin 70°$ (iii) $2(\sin 30°) = \sin 60°$

(ii) $\cos 60° - \cos 40° = \cos 20°$ (iv) $3(\tan 15°) = \tan 45°$

6 (i) Use Pythagoras' theorem to find the hypotenuse in this triangle.

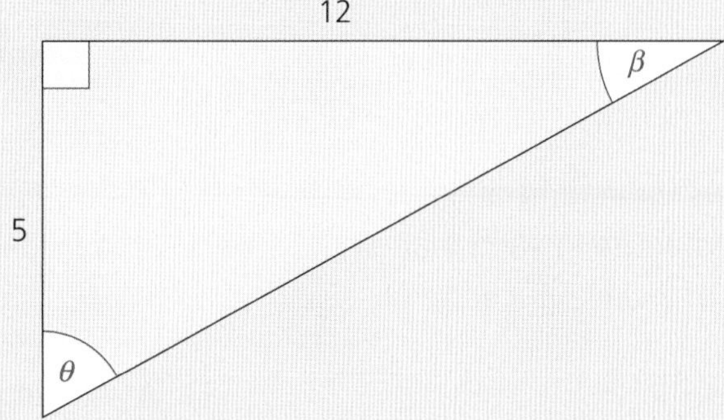

(ii) Use the diagram to write the following ratios.

(a) $\sin \beta$ (b) $\cos \beta$ (c) $\tan \beta$ (d) $\sin \theta$ (e) $\cos \theta$ (f) $\tan \theta$

(iii) Explain why some of the answers in part (ii) are the same.

7 (i) Find the following ratios from this right-angled triangle.

(a) $\sin A$

(b) $\cos B$

(c) $\sin B$

(d) $\cos A$

(ii) Write down the ratios for $\tan A$ and $\tan B$. How are they related?

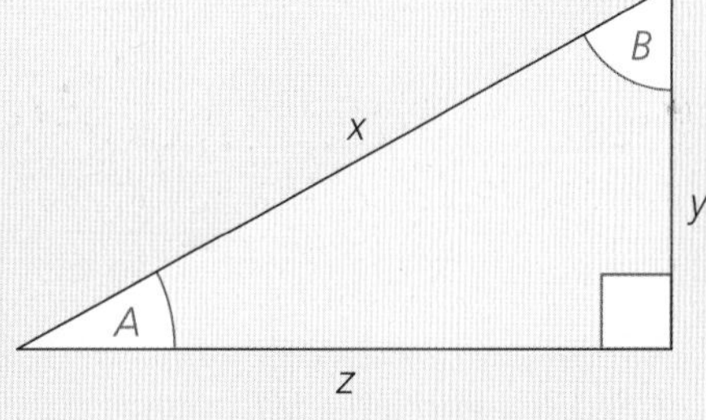

8 Which of the following equals $|AC|$?

(i) $6 \sin 30°$

(ii) $6 \tan 30°$

(iii) $6 \cos 30°$

(iv) $\tan 30°$

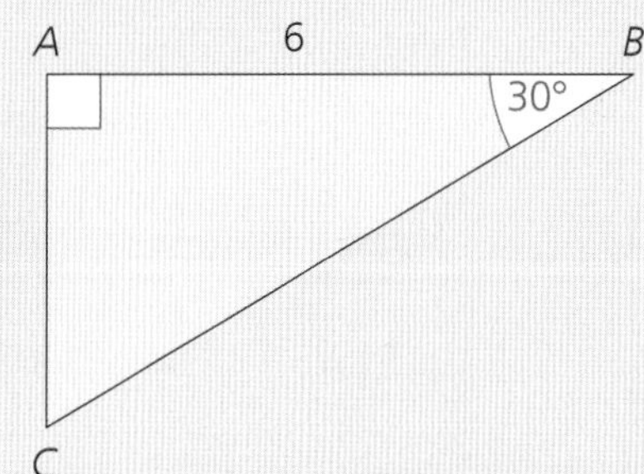

9 (i) Construct a right-angled triangle containing an angle A such that $\sin A = 0.7$

(ii) From your triangle, find $\cos A$ in surd form.

10 Construct a right-angled triangle containing an angle B where $\tan B = \frac{4}{5}$.

11 Which of the statements below are correct for this right-angled triangle?

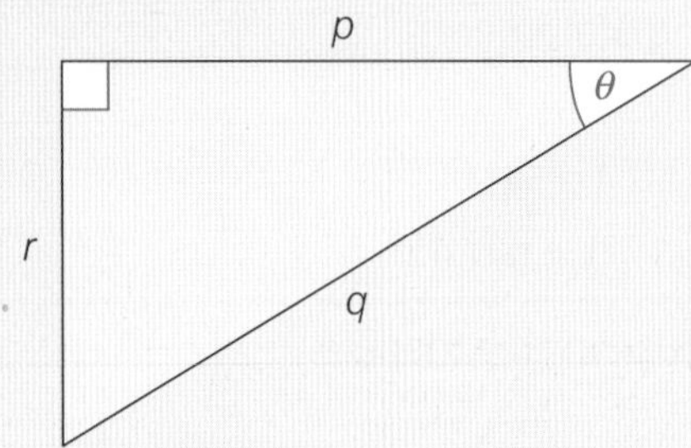

(i) $r = p \cos \theta$

(ii) $r = p \tan \theta$

(iii) $q = p \sin \theta$

(iv) $p = q \cos \theta$

12 The diagram shows three right-angled triangles. The hypotenuse in each triangle equals the radius of a circle of centre O.

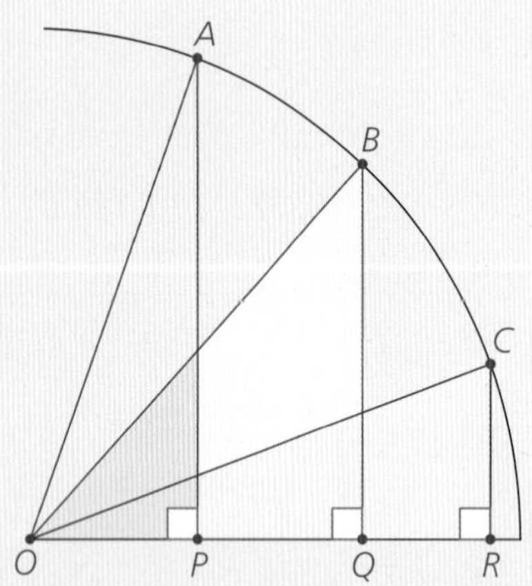

(i) Find the length of the hypotenuse of each triangle with your ruler.

(ii) Find $|CR|$, $|BQ|$ and $|AP|$ with your ruler.

(iii) Copy and fill in the table below.

Hypotenuse =	
$\lvert CR\rvert =$	$\sin \angle COR = \frac{\lvert CR\rvert}{\lvert OC\rvert} =$
$\lvert BQ\rvert =$	$\sin \angle BOQ =$
$\lvert AP\rvert =$	$\sin \angle AOP =$

(iv) What can you conclude about the value of the sine of an angle as the angle gets bigger?

(v) Can the value of the sine of an angle ever be bigger than 1?

13 Refer back to the diagram in question **12**. This question is about the cosine function.

(i) Find $|OR|$, $|OQ|$ and $|OP|$ with your ruler.

(ii) Copy and fill in the table below.

Hypotenuse =	
$\lvert OR\rvert =$	$\cos \angle COR = \frac{\lvert OR\rvert}{\lvert OC\rvert} =$
$\lvert OQ\rvert =$	$\cos \angle BOQ =$
$\lvert OP\rvert =$	$\cos \angle AOP =$

(iii) What can you conclude about the cosine of an angle as the angle gets bigger?

(iv) Can the cosine of an angle ever be bigger than 1?

14 Refer again to the diagram in question **12**. This question is about the tangent function.

(i) Copy and fill in the table below.

Side lengths	**tan values**
$\lvert CR\rvert =$ $\lvert OR\rvert =$	$\tan \angle COR = \frac{\lvert CR\rvert}{\lvert OR\rvert} =$
$\lvert BQ\rvert =$ $\lvert OQ\rvert =$	$\tan \angle BOQ =$
$\lvert AP\rvert =$ $\lvert OP\rvert =$	$\tan \angle AOP =$

(ii) What can you conclude about the value of the tangent of an angle as the angle gets bigger?

(iii) Can the tangent of an angle ever be bigger than 1?

Section 21C Solving Right-Angled Triangles – To Find a Side

In this section, we look at finding a missing side of a right-angled triangle when we know one side and one other angle.

Example 1

Find the side marked x in this triangle.

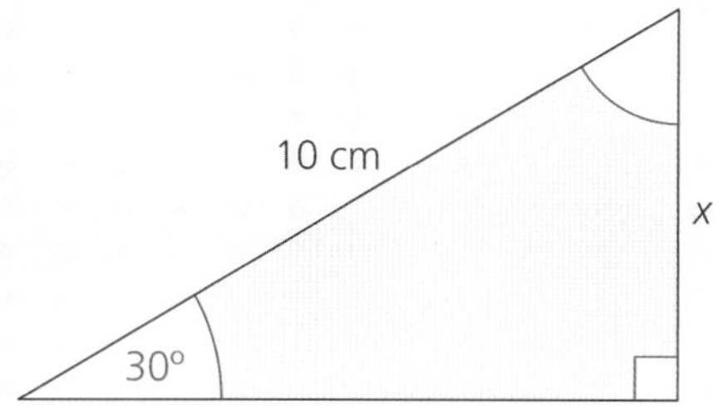

Discussion

What's new in this problem?
Could we use Pythagoras' theorem?
Could we use similar triangles?

Solution

Always start by identifying the angle concerned.

The angle concerned is 30°.

x is opposite this angle.

The other side (10 cm) is the hypotenuse.

The ratio that has Opp and Hyp is sine, so we use this.

$$\Rightarrow \sin 30° = \frac{\text{Opp}}{\text{Hyp}}$$

$$\Rightarrow \sin 30° = \frac{x}{10}$$

$$\Rightarrow 10 \sin 30° = x$$ ... multiply both sides by 10

$$\Rightarrow 10(0.5) = x$$

$$\Rightarrow \quad 5 = x$$

So $x = 5$ cm.

Example 2

Find $[BC]$ in the diagram, correct to two decimal places.

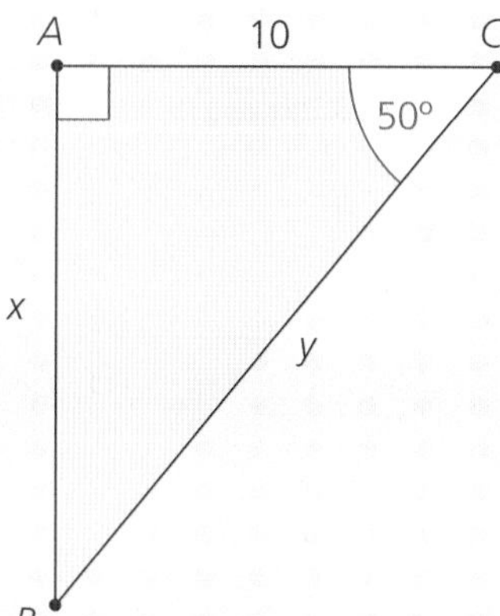

Solution

Method 1

Let $|BC| = y$

Angle concerned = 50°

10 = adjacent (Adj)

y = hypotenuse (Hyp)

The ratio that uses Adj and Hyp is cos.

$$\cos 50° = \frac{10}{y}$$

$\Rightarrow y \cos 50° = 10$ ... multiply both sides by y

$\Rightarrow \quad y = \frac{10}{\cos 50°}$ ... divide both sides by cos 50°

$\Rightarrow \quad y = 15.5572$

$= 15.56$ ... to 2 decimal places

Method 2

First find $|AB|$, then use it to find $|BC|$.

Let $|AB| = x$

x = Opp, 10 = Adj

$\Rightarrow \quad \tan 50° = \frac{x}{10}$

$\Rightarrow 10 \tan 50° = x$

$\Rightarrow \quad x = 11.92$ ... to 2 decimal places

Now use Pythagoras' theorem:

$y^2 = 10^2 + 11.92^2 = 100 + 142.0864$

$= 242.0864$

$\Rightarrow y = 15.56$ ... to 2 decimal places

Activity 21.3

In questions **1–6**, find the side marked with a letter. Give all answers correct to three decimal places.

1

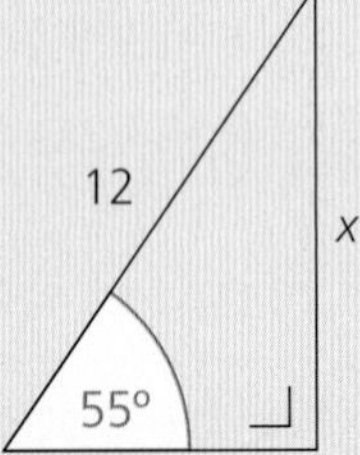

2

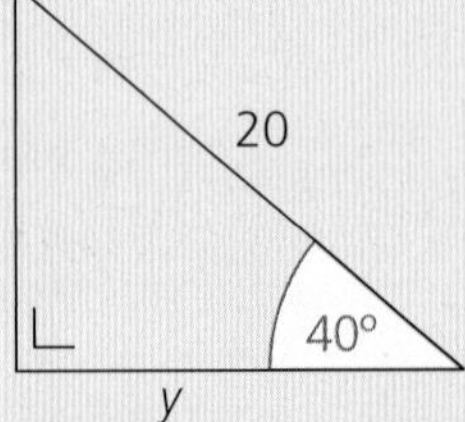

3

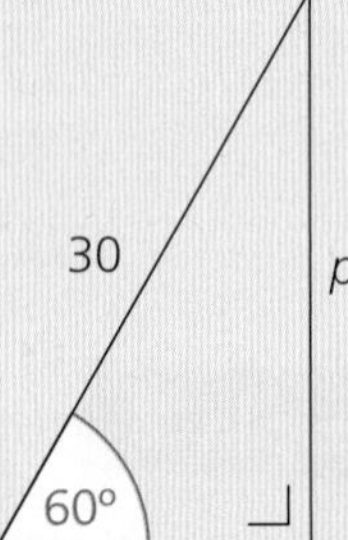

4

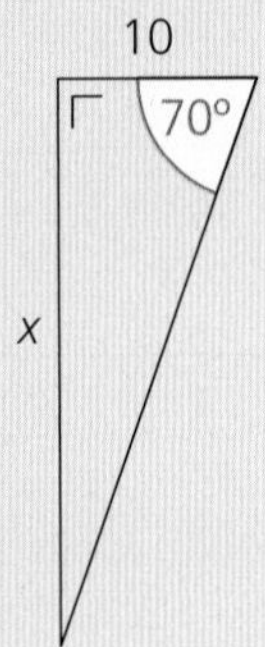

5

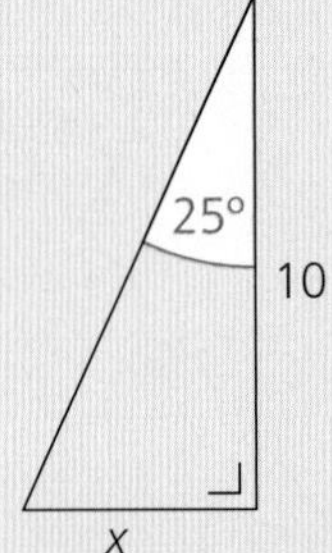

6

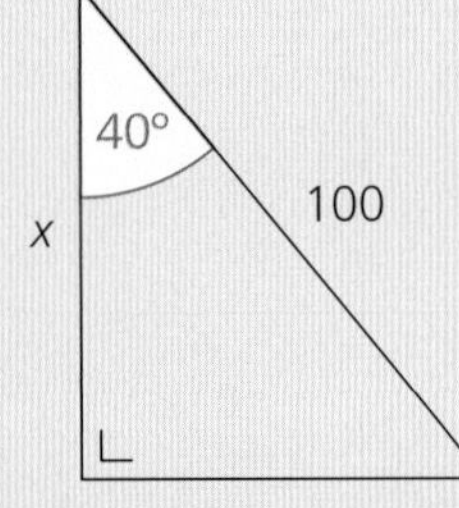

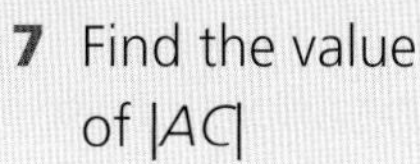

7 Find the value of $|AC|$
   (i) by finding $|BC|$ first
   (ii) by using $\sin 50°$.

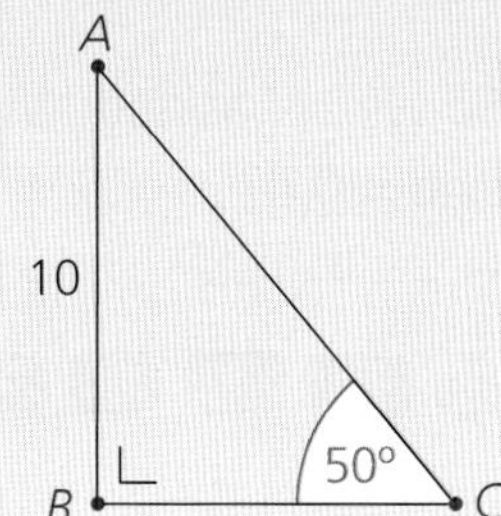

8 Find $|PQ|$ and $|QR|$ in this triangle.

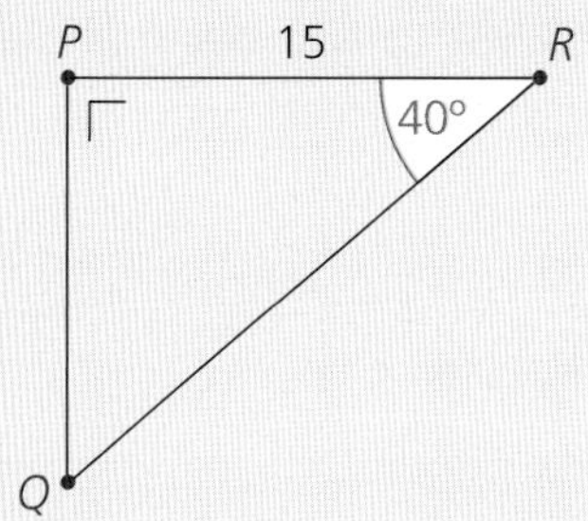

9 Find the value of x in these triangles.

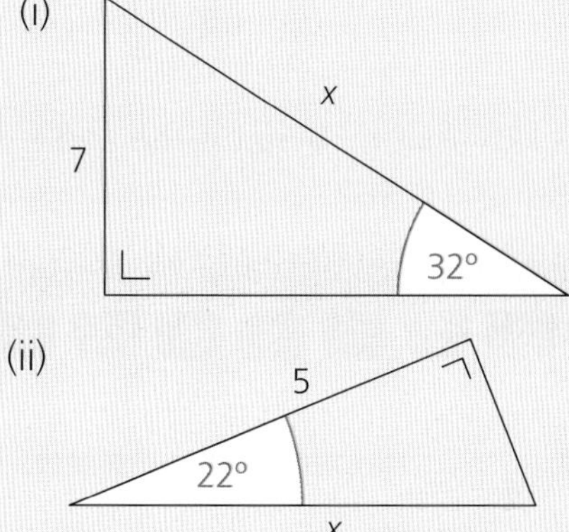

10 (i) In the triangle below, find the value of x by working with ΔACD.
   (ii) Use your value of x to find $|BC|$.

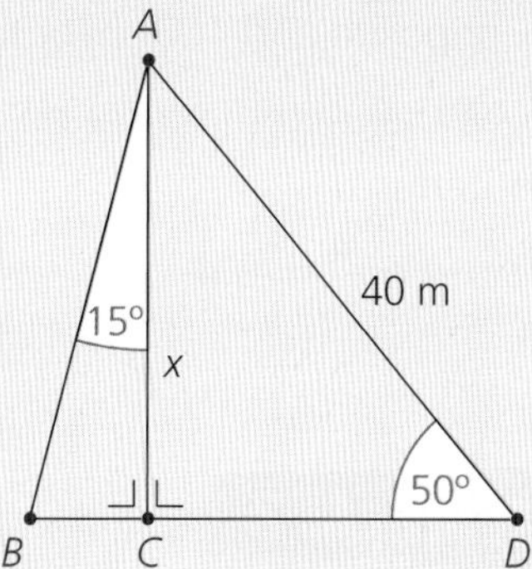

11 (i) Find $|PR|$.
   (ii) Find $|RS|$.

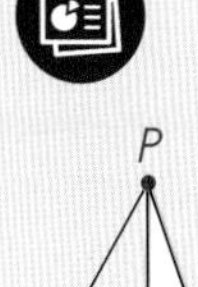

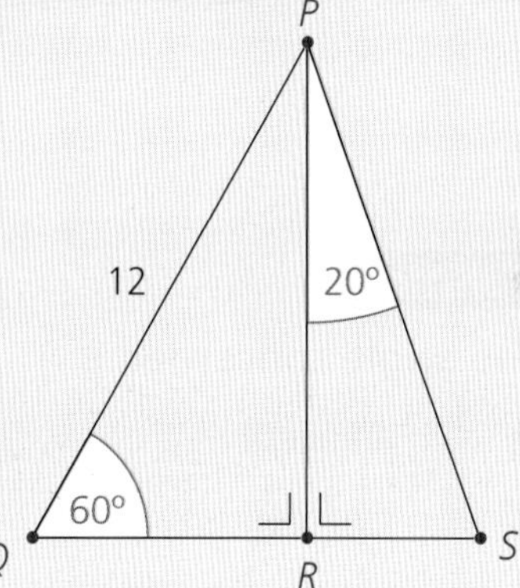

Section 21D Solving Right-Angled Triangles – To Find an Angle

We often need to find a missing angle in a triangle.

Example 1

Find the angle α in this triangle, correct to two decimal places.

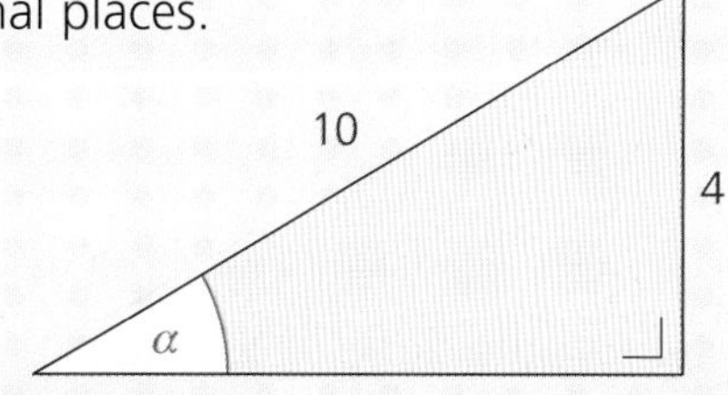

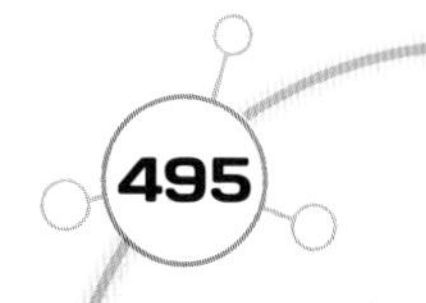

Solution

The angle concerned is α.

4 = opposite and 10 = hypotenuse

Sine is the ratio that uses opposite and hypotenuse.

So $\sin \alpha = \frac{4}{10} = 0.4$

So we are asking: 'What is the angle whose sine = 0.4?'

This is found on the calculator by pressing:

sin⁻¹(0.4) 23.57817848 appears on the screen.

So $\alpha = 23.58°$ to two decimal places.

Example 2

Find the angle A in this triangle, correct to two decimal places.

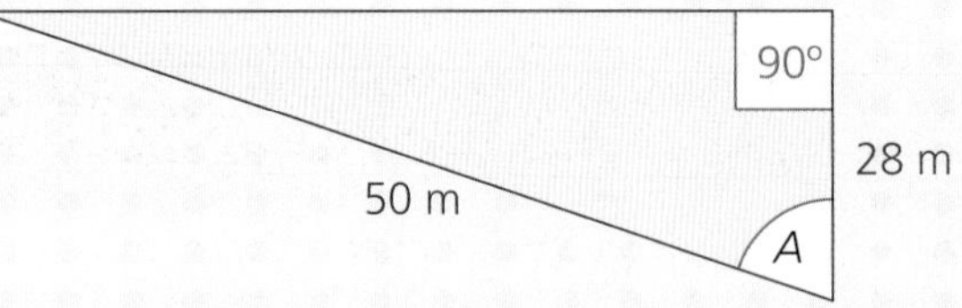

Solution

The angle concerned is A.

28 m = adjacent

50 m = hypotenuse

Cosine is the ratio that uses Adj and Hyp.

$\cos A = \frac{28}{50} = 0.56$

So, this is like asking: 'What is the angle whose cosine = 0.56?'

This is found on the calculator by pressing:

cos⁻¹(0.56) 55.94420226 appears on the screen.

So $A = 55.94°$ to two decimal places.

Connections

Connection to Co-ordinate geometry:

The slope of a line $= \frac{\text{rise}}{\text{run}}$.

In the diagram, the line makes an angle θ with the positive x-axis.

Hence $\tan \theta = \frac{\text{opposite}}{\text{adjacent}} = \frac{\text{rise}}{\text{run}}$

i.e. $\tan \theta =$ the slope of the line.

Hence, we have the following rule:

The slope of a line = $\tan \theta$ where θ is the angle which the line makes with the positive x-axis.

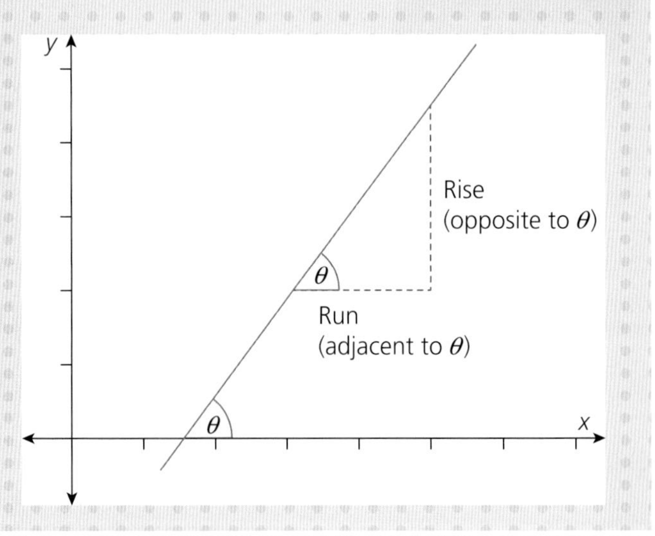

Example 3

Find the slope of the line AB in this diagram.

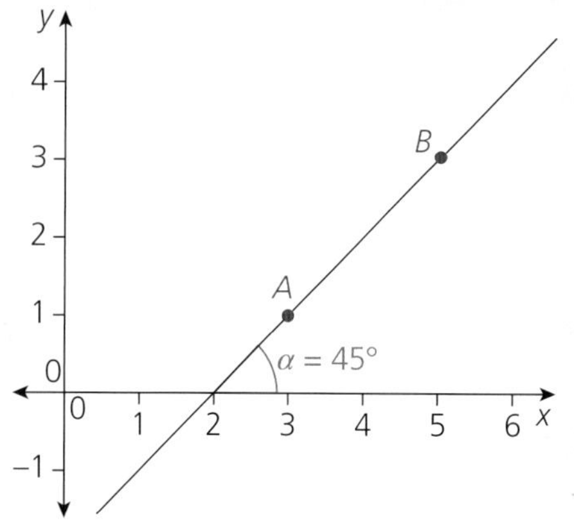

Solution

AB makes an angle of 45° with the positive x-axis.

⇒ the slope = tan 45° = 1

Activity 21.4

1 Use your calculator to find the following angles to the nearest degree.

(i) $\sin A = 0.1736$ (iv) $\tan \theta = 1.7321$ (vii) $\tan \alpha = 1$

(ii) $\cos \alpha = 0.1736$ (v) $\sin \beta = 0.7071$ (viii) $\sin \beta = 0.5$

(iii) $\tan \beta = 0.5773$ (vi) $\cos B = 0.7071$ (ix) $\cos \beta = 0.5$

2 Use your calculator to find the following angles to the nearest degree.

(i) $\cos \alpha = 0.9455$ (v) $\cos \beta = 0.9848$ (ix) $\cos \beta = \frac{\sqrt{3}}{2}$

(ii) $\sin \beta = 0.9782$ (vi) $\sin \beta = 0.9848$ (x) $\tan \alpha = \frac{1}{\sqrt{3}}$

(iii) $\tan \theta = 0.4245$ (vii) $\tan \alpha = 2$

(iv) $\tan \alpha = 1.4826$ (viii) $\tan \beta = \frac{1}{2}$

3 Find the missing angles (to the nearest degree) and the missing sides in these triangles.

(i)

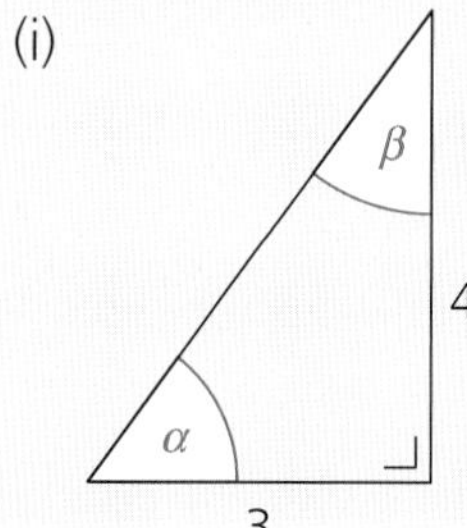

(ii)

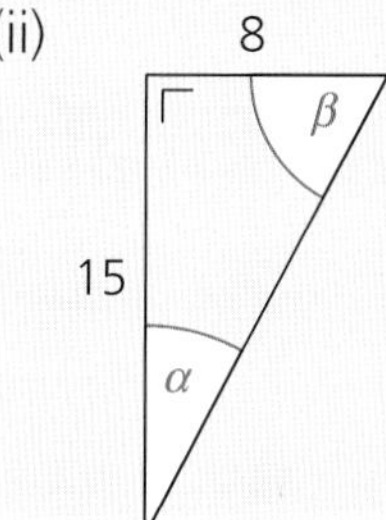

(iii)

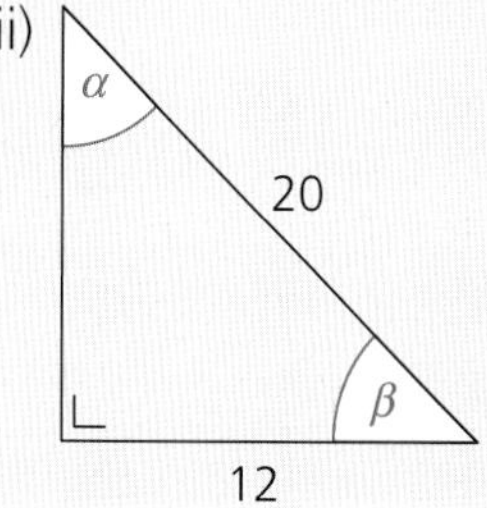

4 Find angle A in this triangle in three ways:

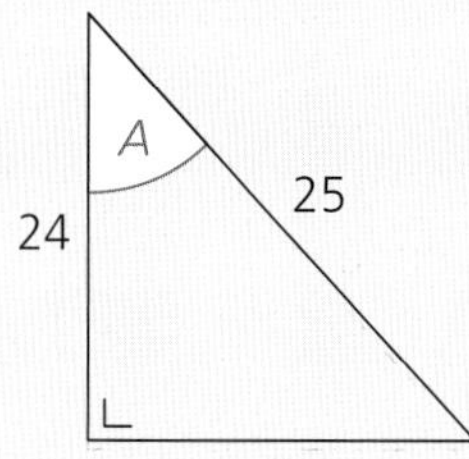

(i) using $\sin^{-1} A$

(ii) using $\cos^{-1} A$

(iii) using $\tan^{-1} A$.

5 (i) Use Pythagoras' theorem to show that this triangle is right-angled.

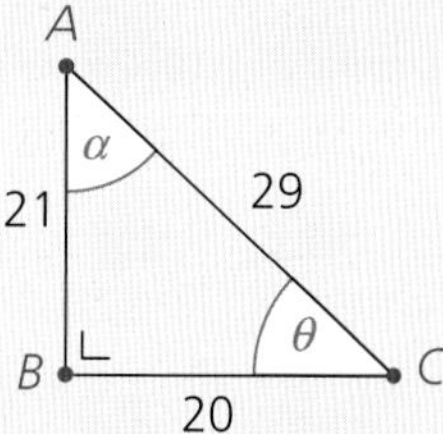

(ii) Find the size of angles α and θ.

6 (i) Find the size of angle A in each of these triangles.

(a)

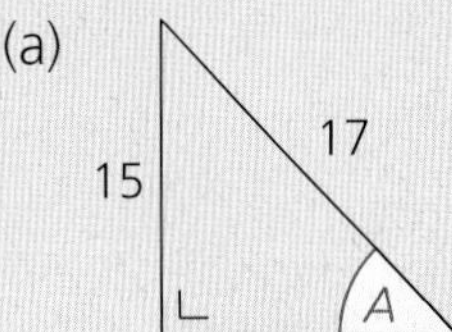

(b)

(c)

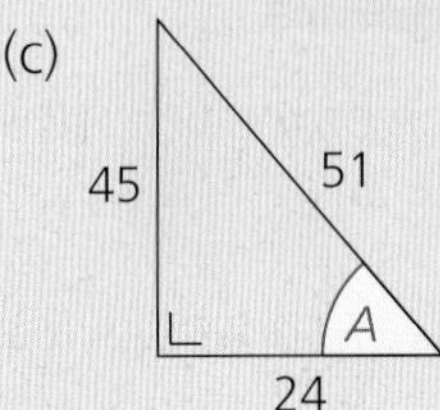

(ii) What do you notice? Can you explain this?

In questions **7–12**, find the missing angles to the nearest degree and the missing sides correct to two decimal places.

7

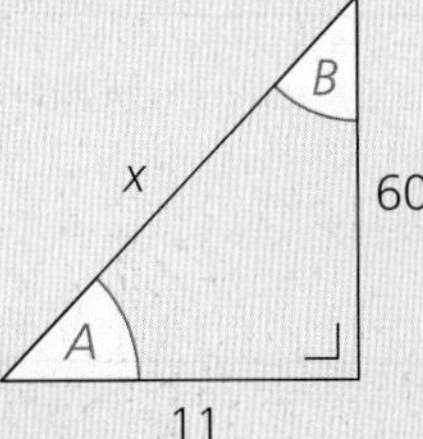

9

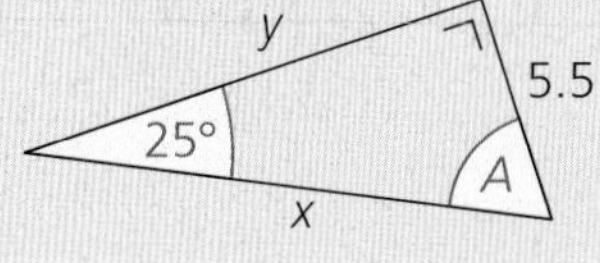

11

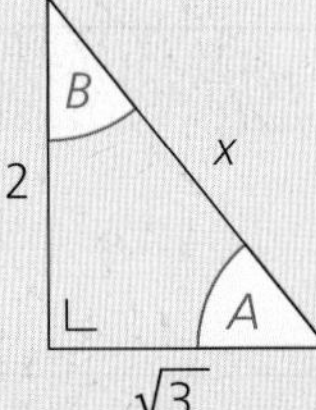

8

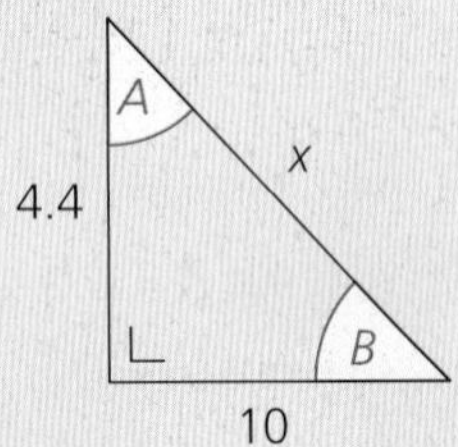

10

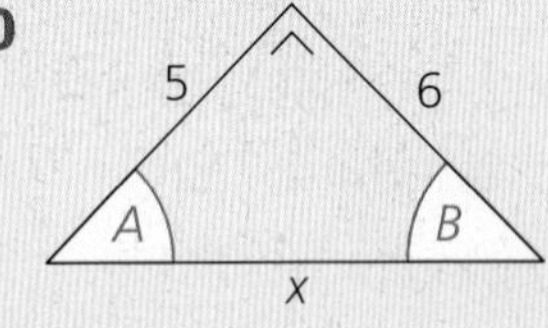

12

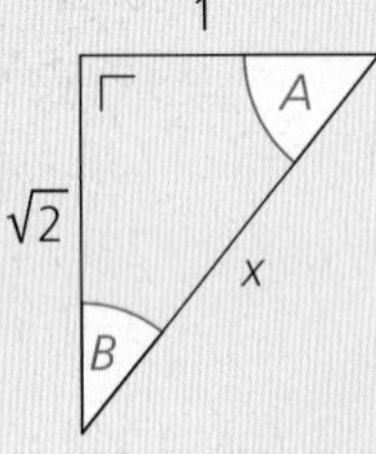

13 Find the slope of line k in surd form. Hence, write down the equation of line k in the form $y = mx + c$.

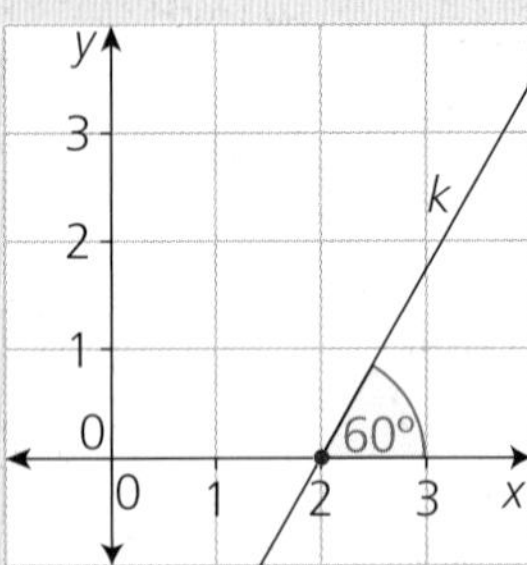

Section 21E Angles of Elevation and Depression

- The diagram shows a person looking up at an object.

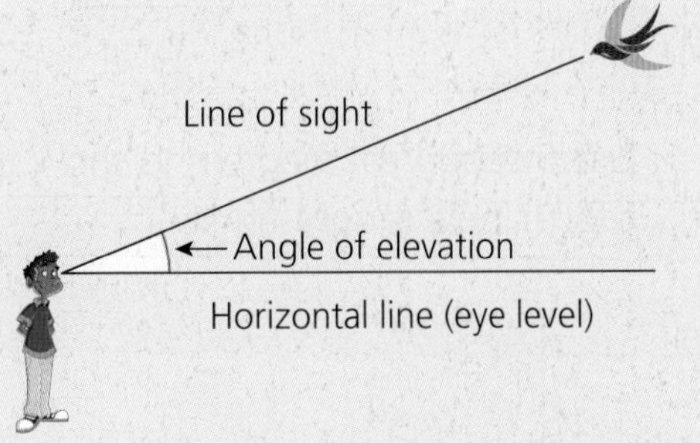

The angle between his line of sight and the horizontal line is called the **angle of elevation**.

- In this diagram, a person is looking down at an object.

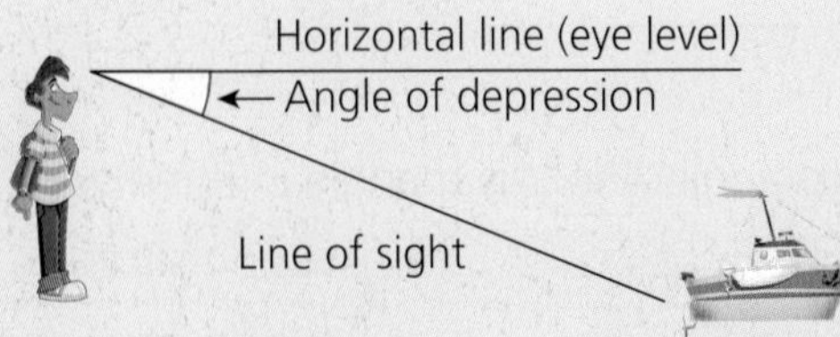

The angle between his line of sight and the horizontal line is called the **angle of depression**.

A **clinometer** or **theodolite** is used to measure angles of elevation and depression. You can make a simple clinometer using a protractor, a pen tube, some string and a small weight.

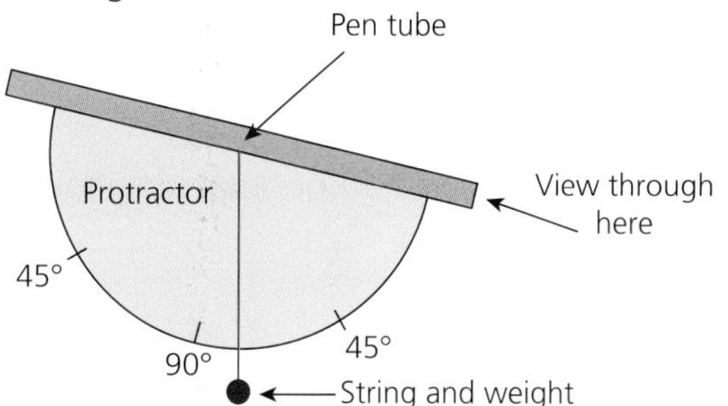

To measure distance, you can use a long measuring tape or a **trundle wheel**.

Example 1

On a sunny day, a pole 6 m in height casts a shadow 7.2 m long on the ground.

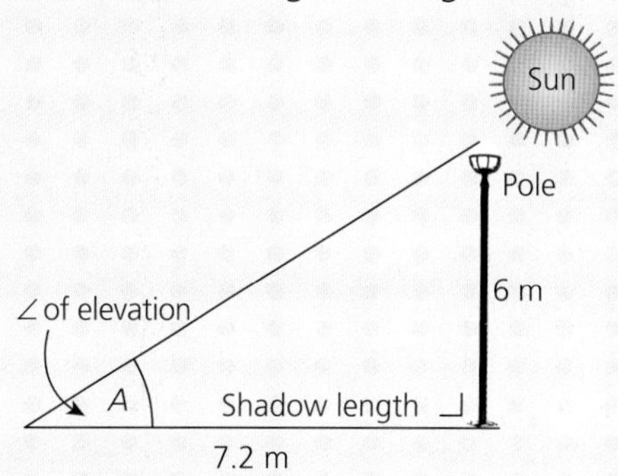

To the nearest degree, what is the angle of elevation of the sun?

Solution

6 m = Opp

7.2 m = Adj

The ratio that uses Opp and Adj is tan.

$\Rightarrow \tan A = \dfrac{\text{Opp}}{\text{Adj}} = \dfrac{6}{7.2}$

$\Rightarrow \tan A = 0.8333$

$\Rightarrow \quad A = \tan^{-1}(0.8333)$

$\Rightarrow \quad A = 39.81° = 40°$ to the nearest degree.

Example 2

Two students wanted to find the height of a tall building in the school grounds.

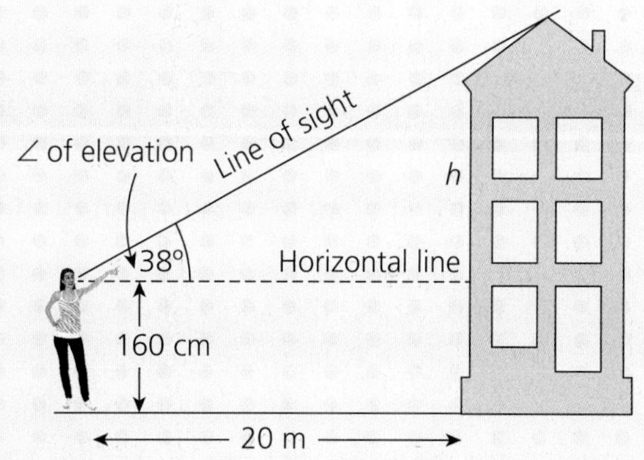

Kiera, who is 160 cm tall, stood at a point on level ground 20 m from the base of the building. Kiera pointed the clinometer at the top of the building and Michael measured the angle of elevation as 38°. To two decimal places, what is the height of the building?

Solution

h = Opposite

20 m = Adjacent

The ratio that uses Opposite and Adjacent is tan.

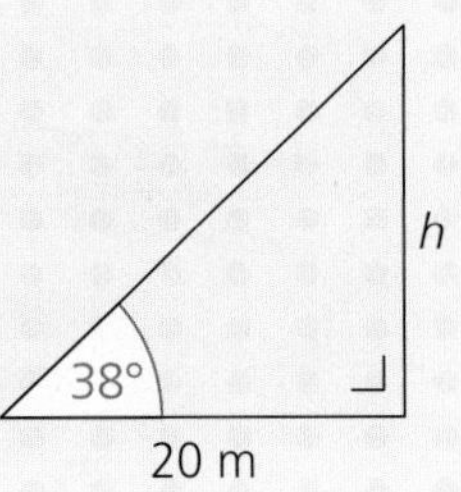

$\Rightarrow \quad \tan 38° = \dfrac{h}{20}$

$\Rightarrow$ 20 tan 38° = h

$\Rightarrow$ 20 (0.7813) = h

$\Rightarrow \quad h$ = 15.626 m

We must add Kiera's height (1.6 m),
so h = 15.626 + 1.6 m
= 17.226 m
= 17.23 m to two decimal places.

Example 3

From the seventh floor of a building (point P), Peter sights an object on level ground (point O). The object is 45 m from G, the base of the building. Peter measures the angle of depression to be 14°.

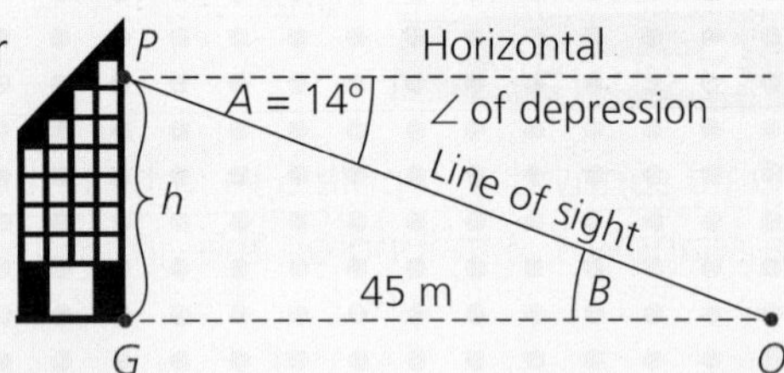

Find the height of P above ground level (correct to two decimal places).

Solution

In the diagram, we see that $\angle A$ and $\angle B$ are equal alternate angles.

$\Rightarrow |\angle B| = 14°$

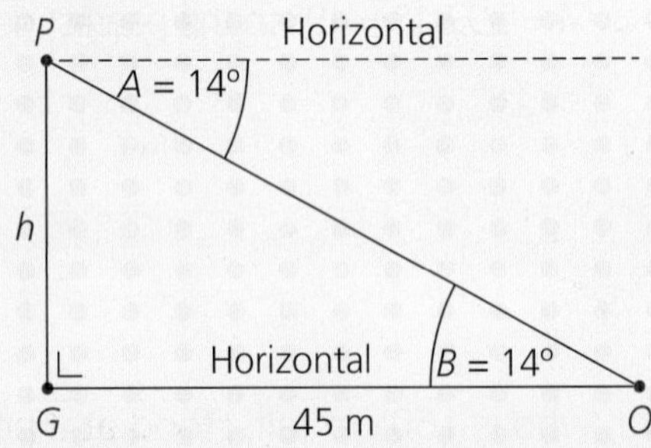

In ΔPGO: $\begin{cases} h = \text{Opp} \\ 45 \text{ m} = \text{Adj} \end{cases}$

$\Rightarrow \quad \tan 14° = \dfrac{h}{45}$

$\Rightarrow$ 45 tan 14° = h

$\Rightarrow$ 45 (0.2493) = h

$\Rightarrow \quad h$ = 11.2197
= 11.22 m to two decimal places.

Activity 21.5

1 Peter is at position P in the diagram, at a distance of 15 m from the base of a building. He sights a point Q on the side of the building.

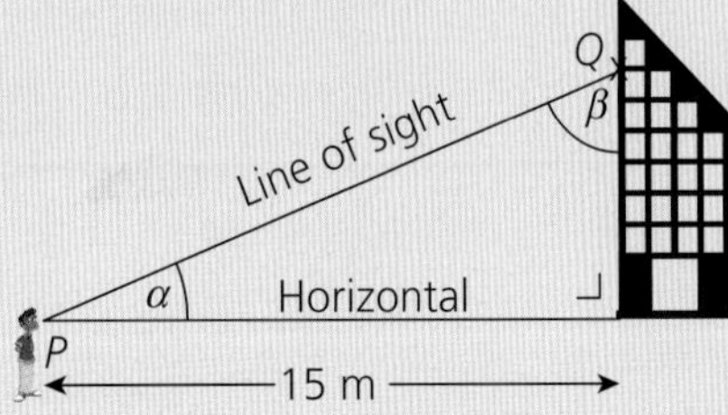

(i) Name the angle of elevation of the point Q.

(ii) How would the angle of elevation change if Peter were looking at the top of the building instead of point Q?

(iii) He measures the angle α to be 52°. Find the height of Q above the horizontal line.

2 Paul is a lifeguard who is sitting in an observation tower. He spots an aeroplane in the sky and a shark's fin in the water.

Make a sketch of the situation and mark in:

(i) The angle of elevation of the aeroplane

(ii) The angle of depression of the shark's fin.

3 A tree casts a shadow of 8 m when the angle of elevation of the sun is 52°. Calculate the height of the tree to the nearest metre.

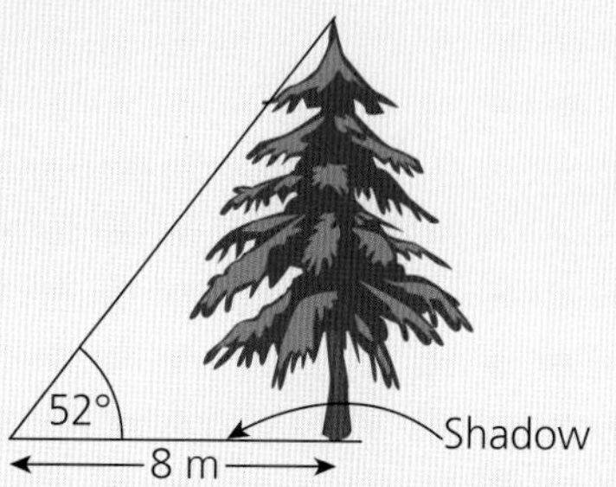

4 A vertical cliff is 49 m in height. From the top, the angle of depression of a boat at sea is 27°.

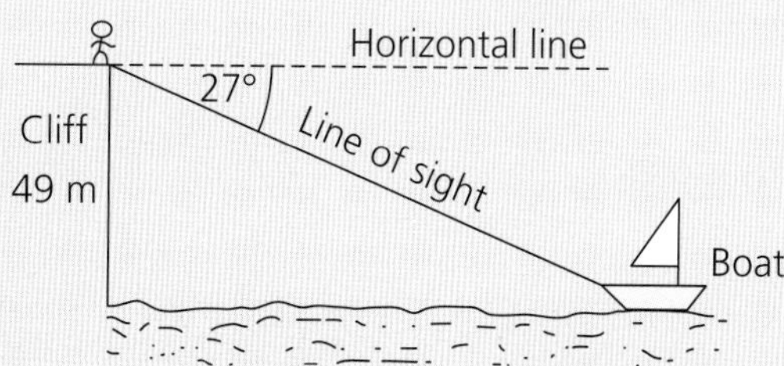

Find the distance from the foot of the cliff to the boat.

5 A person stands on level ground when the sun's elevation is 49°. The person casts a shadow of length 1.6 m.

(i) Draw a diagram to represent this situation.

(ii) Find the height of the person in cm, correct to the nearest cm.

6 A helicopter pilot sights Anna's house as shown in the diagram below. The helicopter is 50 m above the ground.

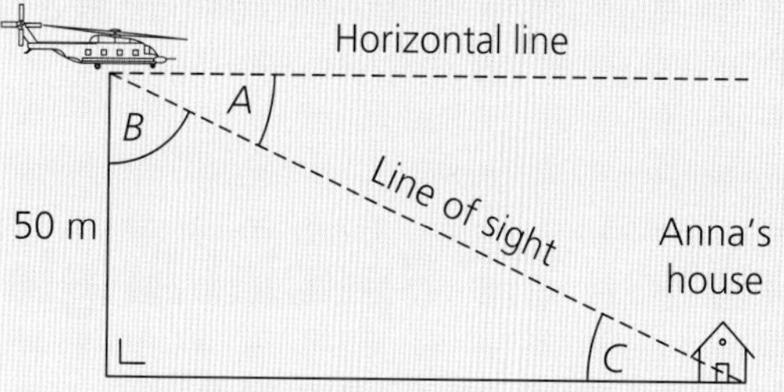

(i) Identify the angle of depression of Anna's house from the helicopter.

(ii) Name a pair of alternate angles in the above diagram.

(iii) If $|\angle A| = 35°$, find $|\angle B|$ and $|\angle C|$.

(iv) Find the shortest distance from the helicopter to Anna's house.

7 In question **6**, what is the angle of elevation of the helicopter from Anna's house?

8 The helicopter in question **6** moves to the right, at the same height, as shown in the diagram below.

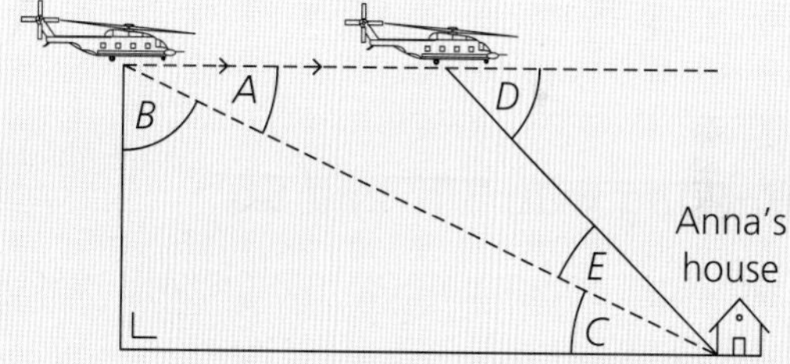

(i) As a result of this, how has the angle of depression of Anna's house from the helicopter changed?

(ii) What geometry theorem can you use to justify your answer?

(iii) $|\angle D| = \square + \square$

Copy the statement above and fill in the two boxes above in two different ways using angles from the diagram.

9 Aaron wants to know the height of a tall building near his house.

He is 175 cm tall. Using a clinometer, he measures the angle of elevation of the top of the building to be 51° at a distance of 50 m from the building. Find the height of the building.

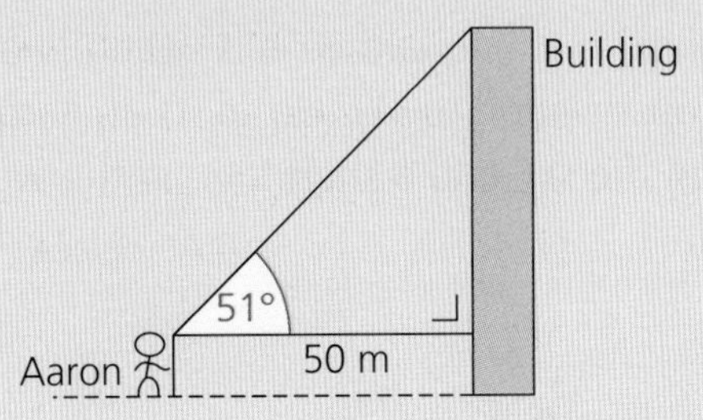

Section 21F Special Angles: 30°, 45° and 60°

Working with an Angle of 45°

If we construct a right-angled triangle with two sides equal to 1 unit, then we can calculate the hypotenuse:

$x^2 = 1^2 + 1^2$

$\Rightarrow x^2 = 2$

$\Rightarrow x = \sqrt{2}$

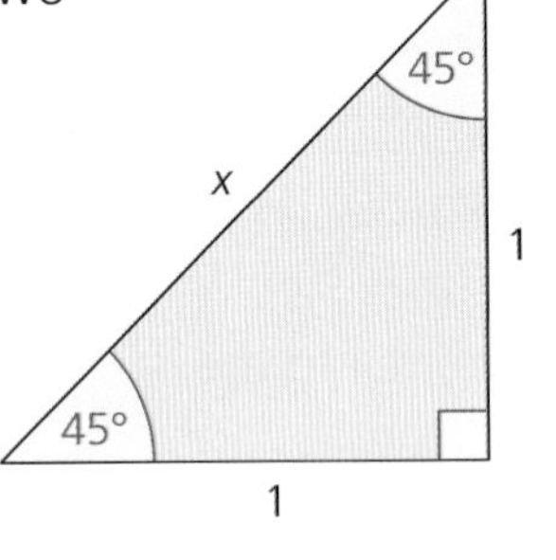

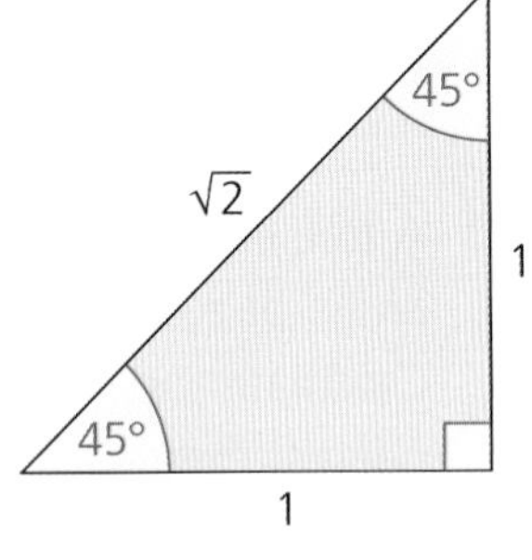

The triangle has two angles = 45°.

Thus, we have the following values:

$$\sin 45° = \frac{1}{\sqrt{2}}$$

$$\cos 45° = \frac{1}{\sqrt{2}}$$

$$\tan 45° = \frac{1}{1} = 1$$

Working with 30° and 60°

Construct an equilateral triangle with each side equal to 2 units.

Each angle of the triangle = 60°.

If we bisect the top angle, we get two congruent triangles (by SAS) which are right-angled.

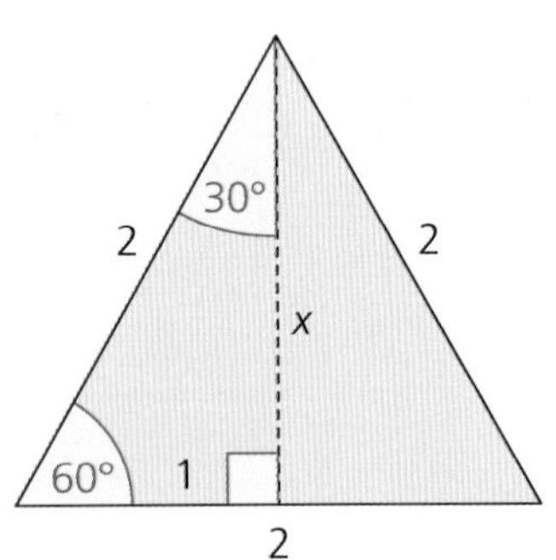

$x^2 + 1^2 = 2^2$

$\Rightarrow \quad x^2 = 2^2 - 1^2$

$\Rightarrow \quad x^2 = 3$

$\Rightarrow \quad x = \sqrt{3}$

Thus, we get these ratios:

$\sin 30° = \frac{1}{2}$	$\sin 60° = \frac{\sqrt{3}}{2}$
$\cos 30° = \frac{\sqrt{3}}{2}$	$\cos 60° = \frac{1}{2}$
$\tan 30° = \frac{1}{\sqrt{3}}$	$\tan 60° = \frac{\sqrt{3}}{1} = \sqrt{3}$

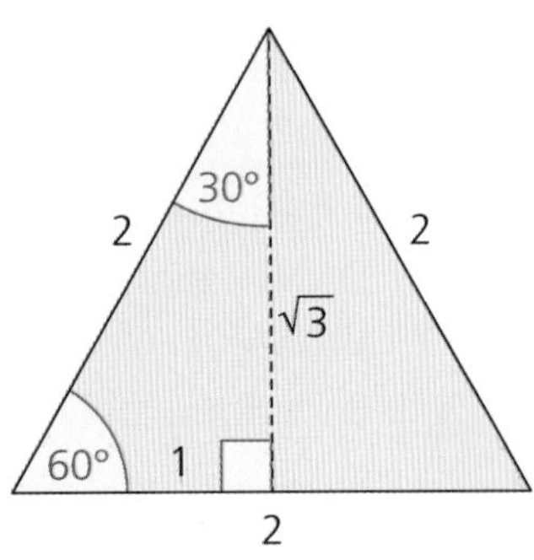

You can find these values in the *Formulae and tables* booklet on page 13.

The ratios for these special angles are given in surd form. Surds are irrational numbers and cannot be written precisely in decimal form. Thus, it is often better to write these ratios in this way.

Example 1

Find the value of x in this diagram.
Give your answer in the form $a\sqrt{b}$.

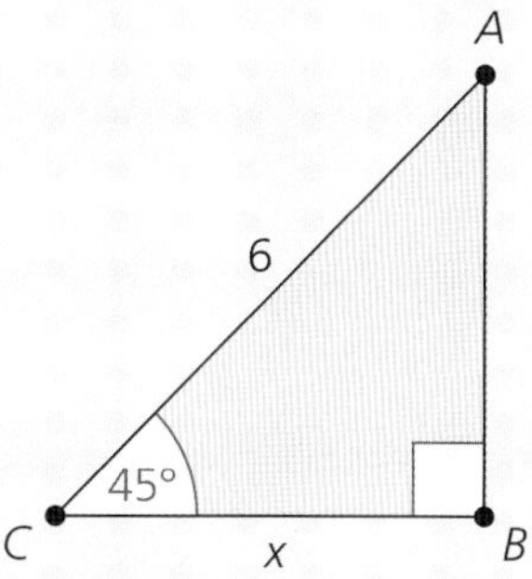

Solution

$\cos 45° = \dfrac{\text{adjacent}}{\text{hypotenuse}} = \dfrac{x}{6}$

$\Rightarrow \quad \dfrac{1}{\sqrt{2}} = \dfrac{x}{6}$

$\Rightarrow \sqrt{2}(x) = 6$

$\Rightarrow \quad x = \dfrac{6}{\sqrt{2}}$

$x = \dfrac{6}{\sqrt{2}} = \dfrac{6}{\sqrt{2}} \times \dfrac{\sqrt{2}}{\sqrt{2}} = \dfrac{6\sqrt{2}}{2} = 3\sqrt{2}$ units

Example 2

Find the value of
$\cos^2 (45°) + \sin^2 (60°) + \tan^2 (30°)$.

Hint

$\cos^2 (45°)$ is the same as $(\cos 45°)^2$.

Solution

$\cos^2 (45°) + \sin^2 (60°) + \tan^2 (30°)$

$= \left(\dfrac{1}{\sqrt{2}}\right)^2 + \left(\dfrac{\sqrt{3}}{2}\right)^2 + \left(\dfrac{1}{\sqrt{3}}\right)^2$

$= \dfrac{1}{2} + \dfrac{3}{4} + \dfrac{1}{3}$

$= \dfrac{19}{12}$ or $1\dfrac{7}{12}$

Activity 21.6

1 (i) Construct the following triangle. You may use any unit of length.

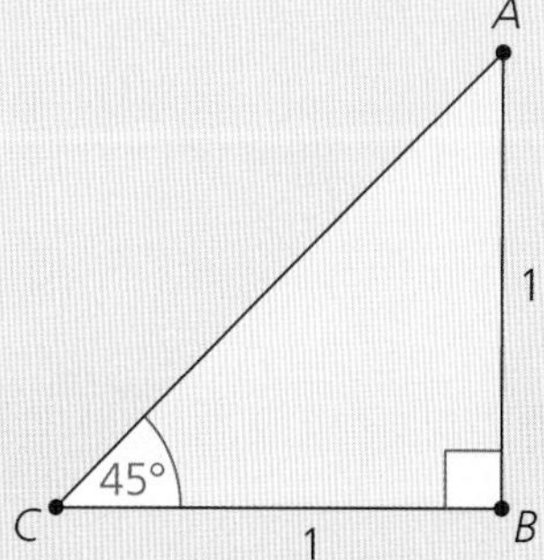

(ii) Calculate $|AC|$ and give your answer in surd form.

(iii) Copy this table and use your work in parts (i) and (ii) to complete it. All entries should be integers or in surd form.

A	45°
sin A	
cos A	
tan A	

Trigonometry

2 (i) Construct the following triangle and the perpendicular from E onto FG. You may use any unit of length.

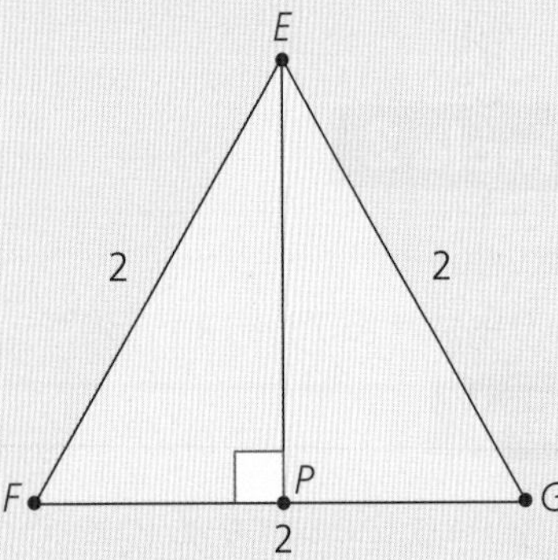

(ii) Prove that the triangles EFP and EPG are congruent.

(iii) Calculate $|EP|$ and fill in the missing angles.

(iv) Copy and complete this table. All entries should be fractions or in surd form.

A	30°	60°
$\sin A$		
$\cos A$		
$\tan A$		

3 Find the value of x in each of the following triangles. Give your answers in the form $a\sqrt{b}$.

(i)

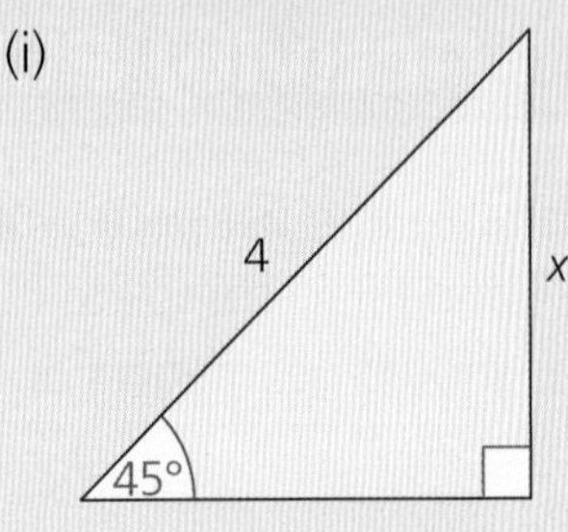

(ii)

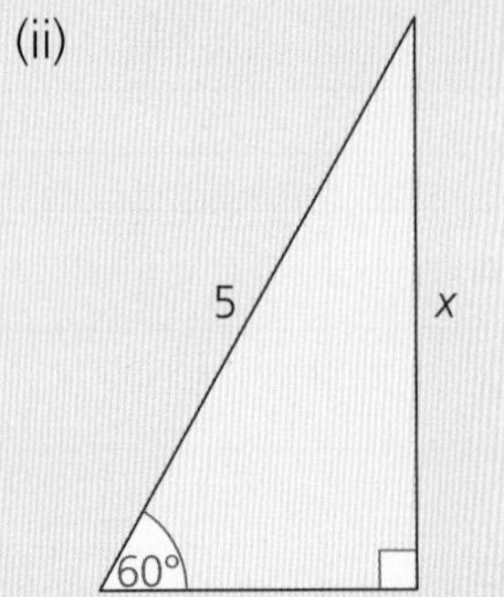

(iii)

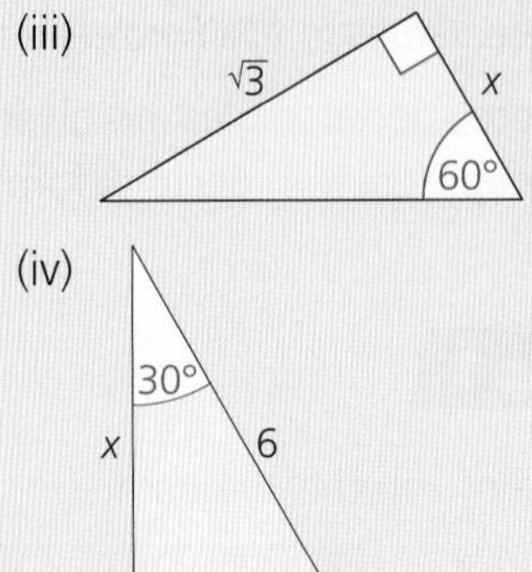

4 Find the lengths a and b and the angle θ in the diagram.

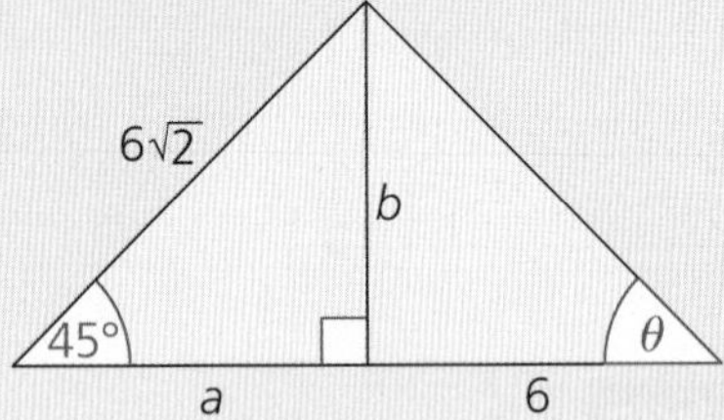

5 If $A = 45°$, verify that $\frac{\sin A}{\cos A} = \tan A$.

6 Find the value of x in the diagram.

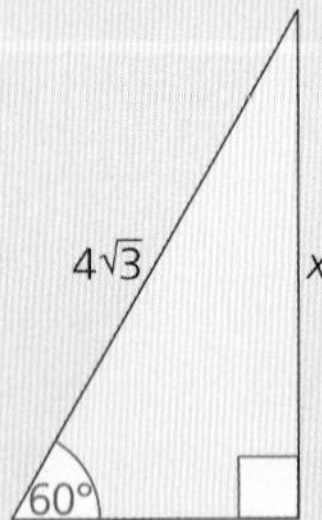

7 The diagram shows a circle of centre O. $[DC]$ is a diameter of the circle.

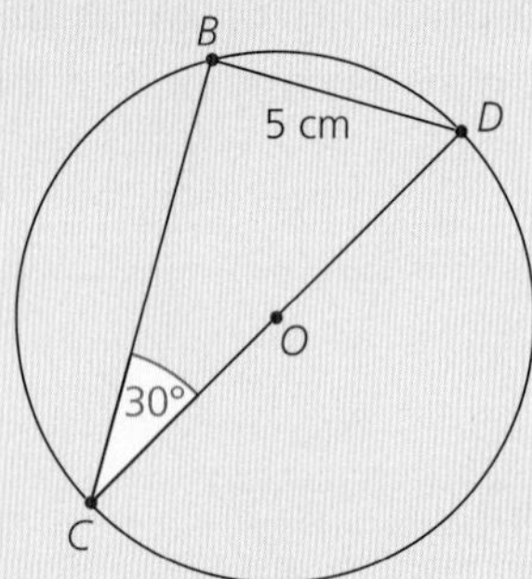

(i) Name a right angle and give a reason for your answer.

(ii) Find the radius of the circle.

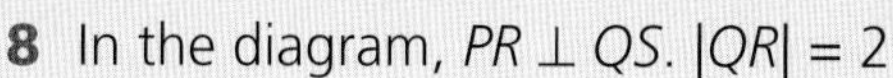

8 In the diagram, $PR \perp QS$. $|QR| = 2$.

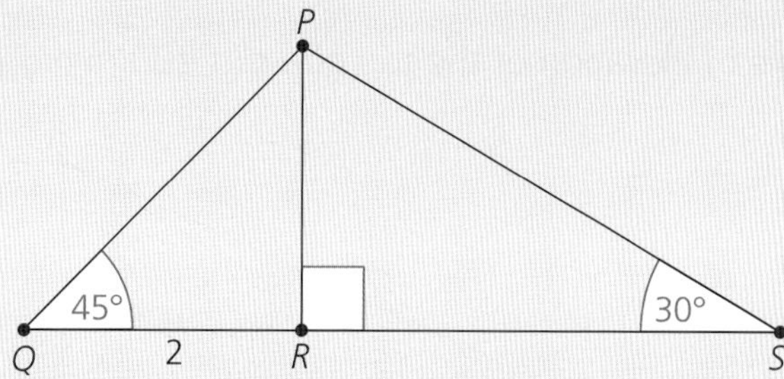

Find $|RS|$. Give your answer in surd form.

9 If $A = 60°$, verify that $\sin^2 A + \cos^2 A = 1$.

10 (i) If $A = 30°$, find $\sin 2A$ and $2 \sin A$.

(ii) Is $\sin 2A = 2 \sin A$?

11 (i) Find $(\sin 60°)(\cos 30°) + (\cos 60°)(\sin 30°)$.

(ii) Find $\sin (60° + 30°)$.

Section 21G Problem Solving

Example 1 below shows how Heron used simple trigonometry and geometry to solve the problem mentioned at the beginning of this chapter.

Example 1

You are an engineer in charge of constructing a tunnel under a mountain. You want two teams of workers to start at different ends and to meet somewhere under the mountain.

The teams cannot see each other. How do you ensure that the teams meet?

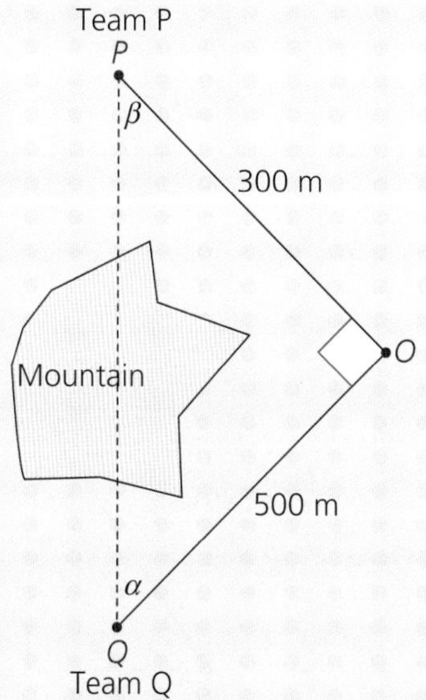

Solution

One team starts from P and the other team starts from Q so that both teams are visible from a point O. The point O is such that $|\angle POQ| = 90°$.

Measure the distances $|PO|$ and $|OQ|$.

Say $|PO| = 300$ m and $|QO| = 500$ m.

Find $\angle PQO$:

$|\angle PQO| = \tan^{-1}\left(\frac{300}{500}\right) = 30° \, 58'$

Team Q have to dig along a line making this angle with OQ.

The angle for team P is $(90° - 30° \, 58') = 59° \, 2'$. Team P have to dig along a line making this angle with OP.

The two teams then must meet in the middle.

In the 21st century, we would use satellites and GPS systems to sight the teams, but the maths involved is similar.

Example 2

Mary observes the angle of elevation of the top of a cliff 200 m high to be 24°.

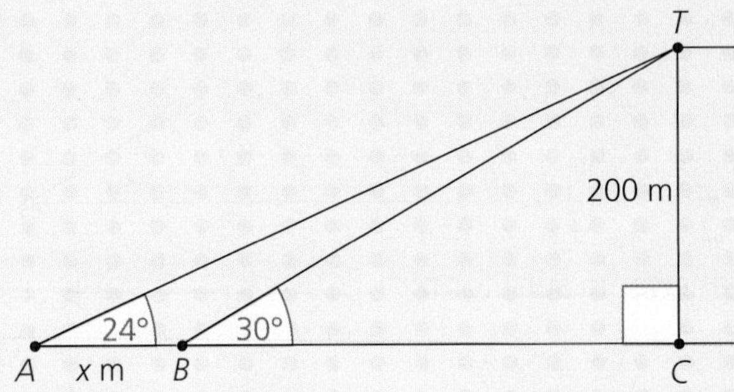

When she moves closer to the cliff by a distance of x metres the angle increases to 30°. How far did she travel towards the cliff? Give your answer correct to one decimal place.

Solution

In triangle ATC: $\tan 24° = \dfrac{200}{|AC|}$

$\Rightarrow \quad |AC| \times \tan 24° = 200$

$\Rightarrow \quad |AC| = \dfrac{200}{\tan 24°} = 449.21$ m

In triangle BTC: $\tan 30° = \dfrac{200}{|BC|}$

$\Rightarrow \quad |BC| \times \tan 30° = 200$

$\Rightarrow \quad |BC| - \dfrac{200}{\tan 30°} = 346.41$ m

$\therefore$ Mary travelled 449.21 – 346.41 = 102.8 metres.

Activity 21.7

1 The roof of this house has a pitch of 14°. Find the height h of the apex of the roof above the ground. Give your answer to two decimal places.

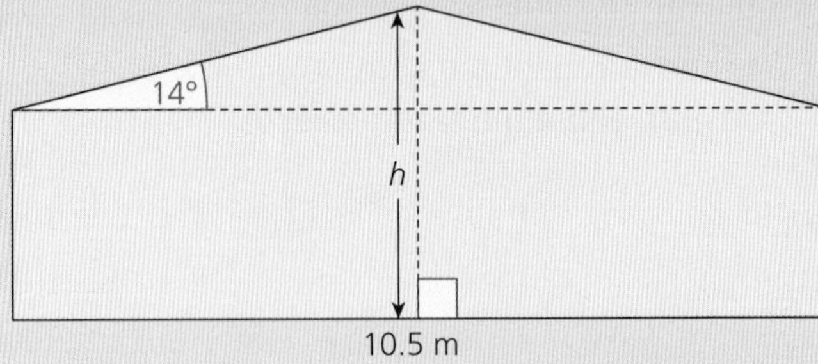

2 Robert used a tree on one bank of a river to mark a point R directly across from it. He then walked 70 m along the bank until he reached point S. Using a theodolite, he measured the angle TSR to be 56° 18′.

Find the width of the river, to two decimal places.

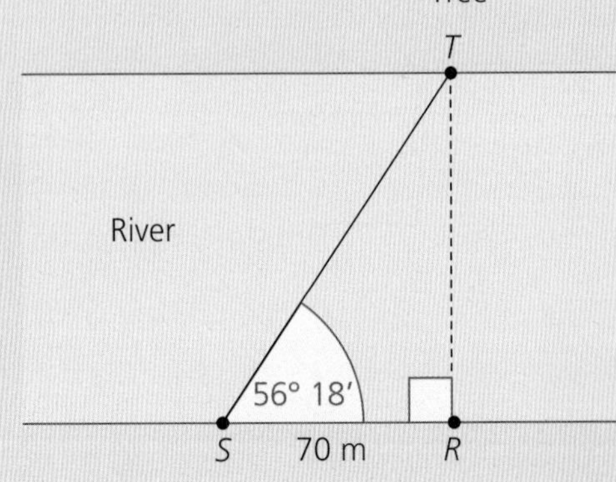

3 A swimming pool is 25 m long. At the shallow end, it is 1.4 m deep and the floor is inclined at 3° 15′ to the horizontal. The diagram shows a cross-section of the pool.

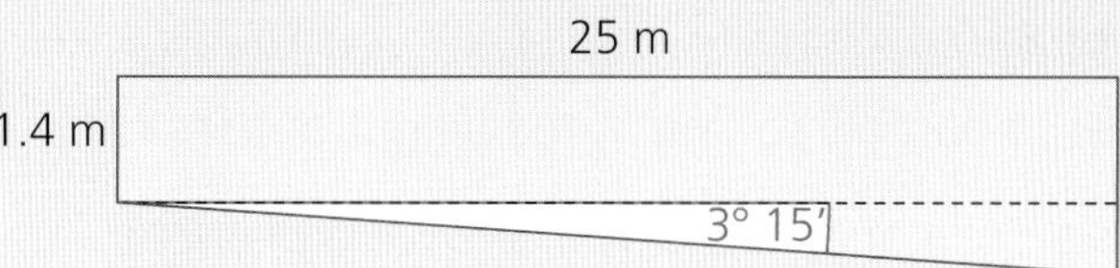

Find the depth of water at the deep end.

4 From a rooftop on one side of a street, Charlie observes the angle of elevation of the top of a building to be 21° 48′.

From the same position, the angle of depression of the bottom of the building is 50° 11′.

The bases of the buildings are 25 m apart.

Find the height of the building correct to two decimal places.

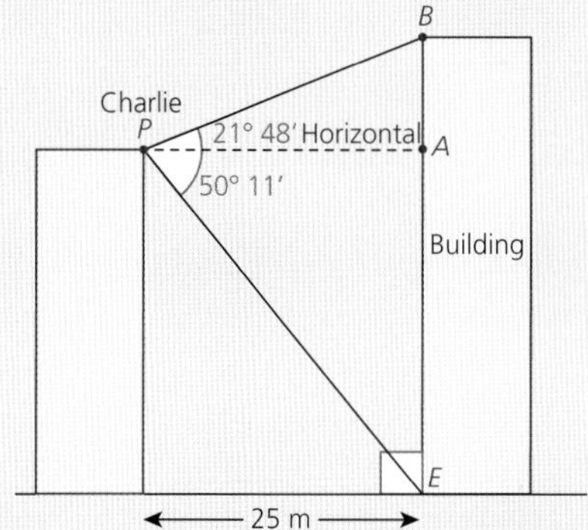

5 A boat is 500 m from the base of a cliff. From the top of the cliff, the angle of depression of the boat is 34°.

(i) Draw a diagram to represent this situation.

(ii) Find the height of the cliff.

6 A building is 15 m high.

Tom observes the angle of elevation of the top of the building to be 26°.

When he moves x metres closer to the building, the angle increases to 44°.

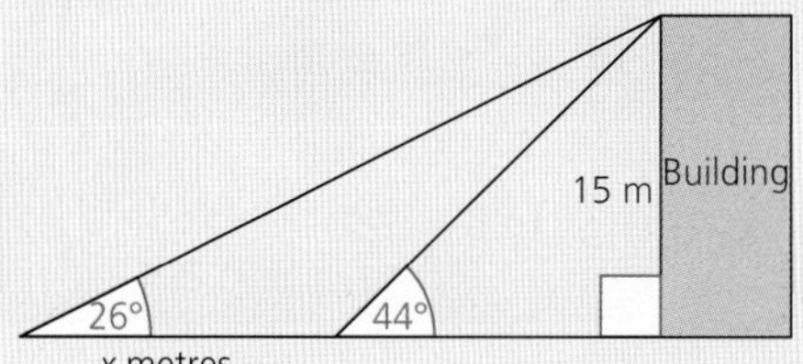

How far did Tom travel, correct to one decimal place?

7 A ladder is 13 m long. It is put against a wall so that it reaches a point on the wall 12.1 metres above the ground.

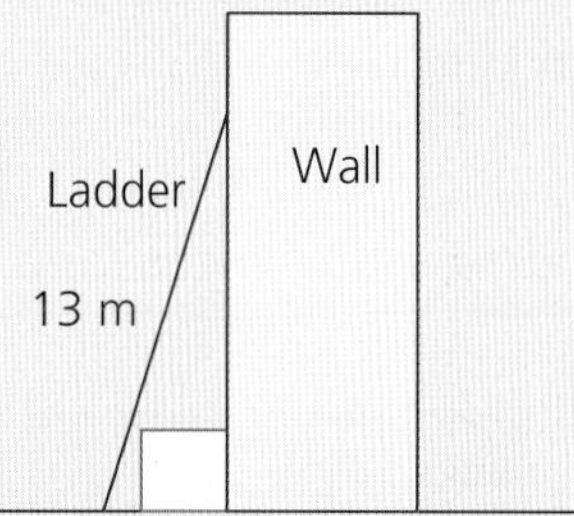

(i) What angle does the ladder make with the ground?

(ii) If the ladder were to reach a point 12.6 m high, what angle would the ladder make with the ground?

(iii) The correct angle for a ladder is 75°. How high will the ladder reach up the wall at this angle?

8 A road sign says that the slope of the road at that point is 10%.

What angle does the road make with the horizontal?

9 A vertical pole $[AB]$ is supported by two stay-wires $[AC]$ and $[AD]$. Points C and D are 20 m apart and in line with the pole. From C, the angle of elevation of the top of the pole is 60°. From D, the angle of elevation of the top of the pole is 30°. Let $x = |CB|$.

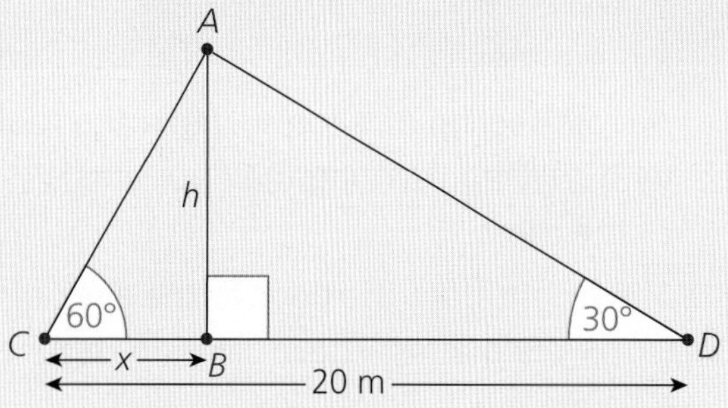

Trigonometry

(i) Use triangle ABC to write h in terms of x.
(ii) Use triangle ABD to write h in terms of x.
(iii) Find the value of x.
(iv) Use your answer to part (iii) to find h, the height of the pole.

10 The diagram shows a circle of centre O with $[PQ]$ as a diameter.

(i) Name three equal line segments in the diagram. Give a reason for your answer.
(ii) Name a right angle in the diagram. Explain your answer.
(iii) Calculate x and express your answer in surd form.

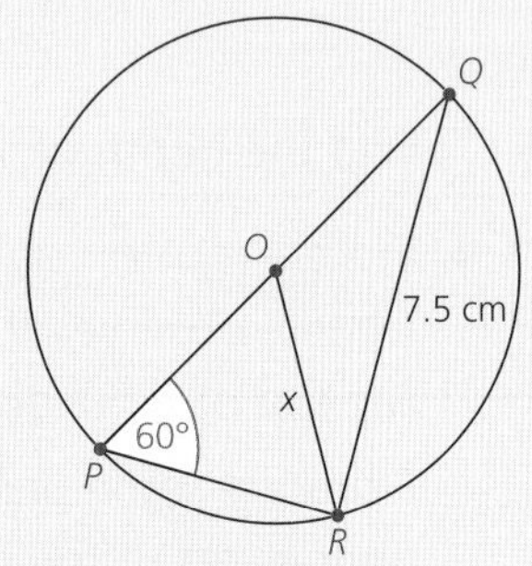

11 Two students want to find the height of a church spire in their locality. They have a clinometer (for measuring angles of elevation) and a 100 metre tape measure. The ground is level and they can get access to the interior of the church.

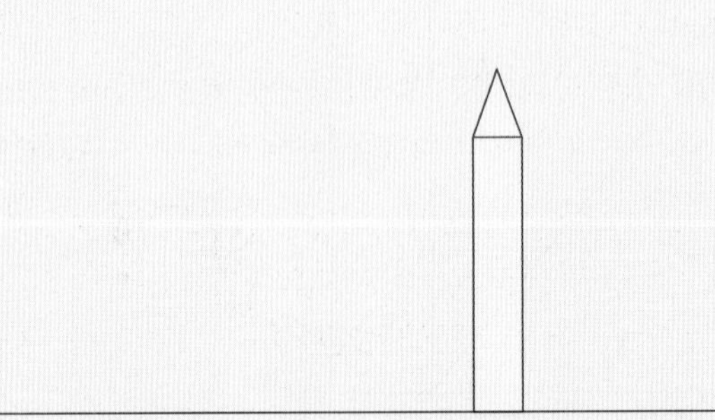

(i) Explain how they could find the height of the church. Your answer should be illustrated on a diagram like the one shown.
(ii) Show the point(s) where you think they should take measurements and write down what measurements they should take.
(iii) Outline briefly how these can be used to find the height of the church.

12 A mansard roof is a four-sided roof having a double slope, with the lower slope much steeper than the upper. Its shape allows it to be used to maximise living space in a house if necessary.

The following figure $ABCDE$ represents the outline of such a roof which a builder wishes to construct to replace an existing roof.

It is symmetrical about a vertical line through C.

A cross-section of a room within the roof is shaded, with $[TH]$ representing the floor and $[VW]$ the ceiling of the room.

The height from the floor to the apex of the roof is 4 metres. $|AE| = 6$ metres and $|AT| = 0.9$ metres. The inclination of AB is 22° from the vertical as in the diagram.

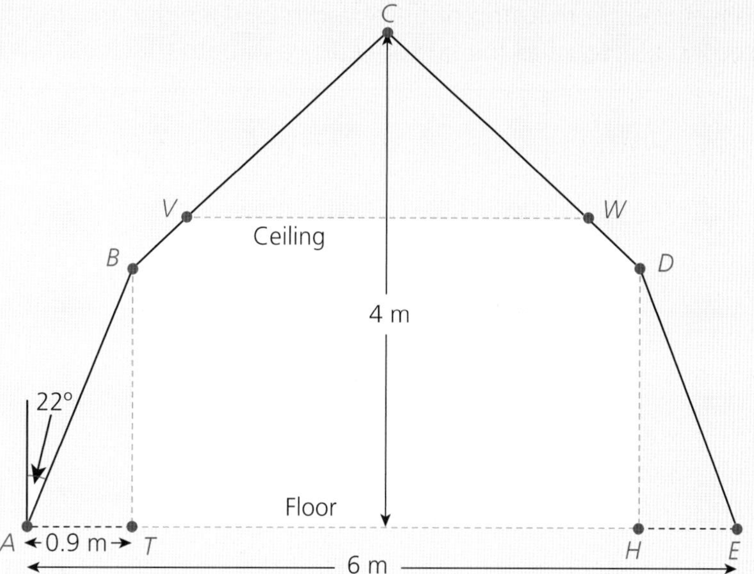

(i) Find $|AB|$.

(ii) Find the total length of the outline *ABCDE* of the roof correct to two decimal places.

(iii) In order to accommodate the largest possible windows, the floor to ceiling height is to be at least 2.4 metres. Find the maximum length of $[VW]$.

(iv) Make an accurate scale drawing of the outline of the roof, using the scale 1 : 60. In other words, 1 cm on your diagram should represent 60 cm in reality.

13 The diagram below represents a simplified model of a bridge known as a cable-stayed bridge where *PQ* is the supporting tower and *AF* is the carriageway for traffic.

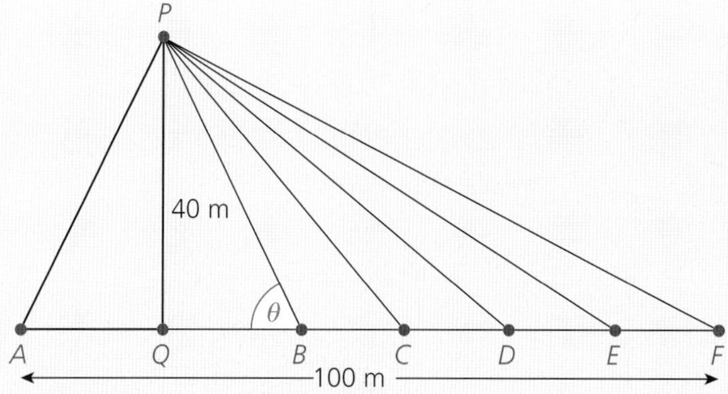

In this particular model, $|\angle APF| = 90°$, $|PQ| = 40$ m and $|AF| = 100$ m.

(i) If *Q* is to be nearer to *A* than *F*, use your knowledge of geometry to explain why there is only one location along *AF* for the tower *PQ* in this model.

(ii) Let $|AQ| = x$. Express $|QF|$ in terms of x.

(iii) Prove that the triangles *APQ* and *PQF* are similar.

(iv) Hence, find x.

(v) The five cables emanating from *P* meet *AF* at equal intervals of y metres at the points *B*, *C*, *D*, *E* and *F*. If $\tan \theta = 2$, where θ is the angle which the shortest cable $[PB]$ makes with *AF*, find the value of y.

14 Two discs are cut out from a strip of tin of width $2k$. One disc touches the top edge of the strip, the second disc touches the bottom edge and both touch each other, as shown.

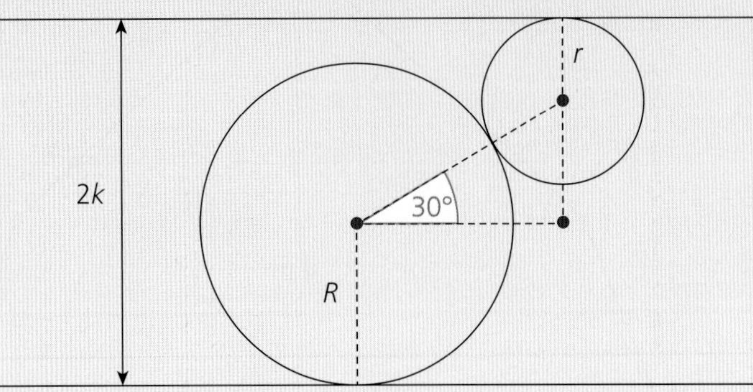

If the line joining the centres of the discs remains at the angle of 30° to the edge of the strip, show that $3(R + r) = 4k$.

Revision Activity 21

1 Find the lengths marked with letters in each of these triangles.

(a)

A
12 m
x
36° 52′
B
C

(b)

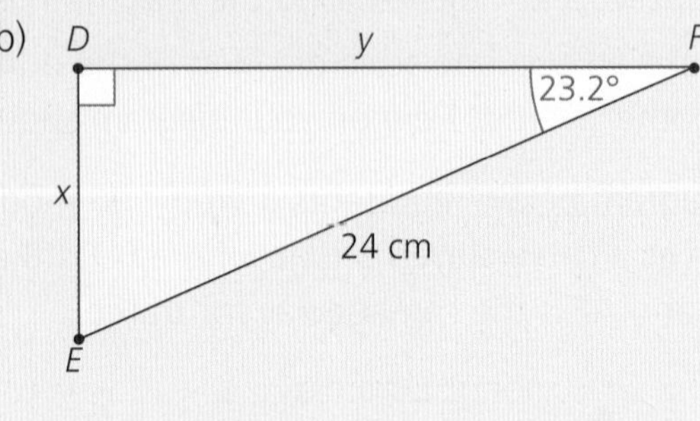

2 If $A = 30°$, verify that $\frac{\sin A}{\cos A} = \tan A$.

3 Find the angles marked with letters in each of these triangles.

(a)

A
5
x
B
$5\sqrt{3}$
C

(b)

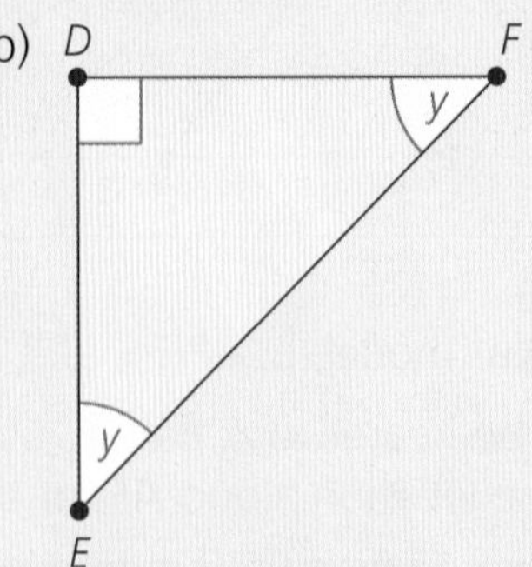

4 If $A = 30°$, verify that $\sin^2 A + \cos^2 A = 1$.

5 Two vertical poles A and B, each of height h, are standing on opposite sides of a level road. They are 24 m apart. The point P, on the road directly between the two poles, is a distance x from pole A. The angle of elevation from P to the top of pole A is 60°.

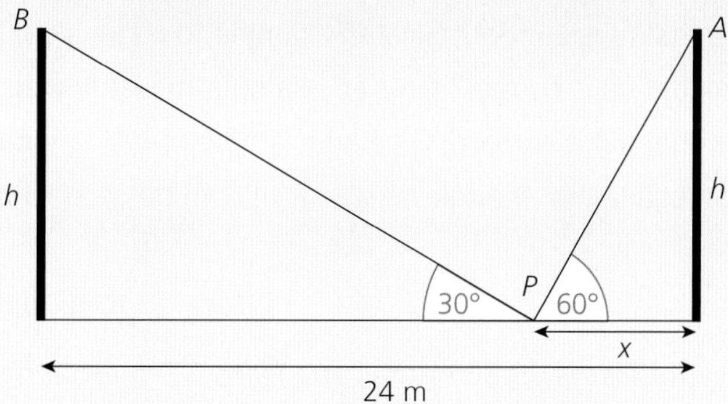

(a) Write h in terms of x.

(b) From P, the angle of elevation to the top of pole B is 30°. Find h, the height of the two poles.

6 A group of students wish to calculate the height of the Millennium Spire in Dublin. The spire stands on level ground. Maria, who is 1.72 m tall, looks to the top of the spire using a clinometer and records an angle of elevation of 60°. Her feet are 70 m from the spire's base. The circumference of the base of the spire is 7.07 m.

(a) Explain how the measurement of the circumference will be used in the calculation of the height of the spire.

(b) Draw a suitable diagram and calculate the height of the spire, to the nearest metre, using the measurements obtained by the students.

Exam-style Questions

1 During a trigonometry lesson, a group of students wrote down some statements about what they expected to happen when they looked at the values of trigonometric functions of some angles. Here are some of the things they wrote down.

(i) The value from any of these trigonometric functions will **always** be less than 1.

(ii) If the size of the angle is doubled, then the value from these trigonometric functions will not double.

(iii) The value from all of the trigonometric functions will increase if the size of the angle is increased.

(iv) I do not need to use a calculator to find sin 60°. I can find it by drawing an equilateral triangle. The answer will be in surd form.

The students then found the sin, cos and tan of some angles, correct to three decimal places, to test their ideas.

(a) Do you think that (i) is correct? Give an example to justify your answer.

(b) Do you think that (ii) is correct? Give an example to justify your answer.

(c) Do you think that (iii) is correct? Give an example to justify your answer.

(d) Show how an equilateral triangle of side 2 cm can be used to find sin 60° in surd form.

JCHL 2014 Sample Paper 2

2 The Leaning Tower of Pisa is 55.863 m tall and leans 3.9 m from the perpendicular, as shown below. The tower of the Suurhusen Church in north-western Germany is 27.37 m tall and leans 2.47 m from the perpendicular.

By providing diagrams and suitable calculations and explanations, decide which tower should enter the *Guinness Book of Records* as the **Most Tilted Tower in the World**.

JCHL 2014 Sample Paper 2

KEY WORDS AND PHRASES

- **Pythagoras' theorem**
- **Right-angled triangle**
- **Hypotenuse**
- **Opposite side**
- **Adjacent side**
- **Ratio**
- **Trigonometric ratio**
- **sin *A***
- **cos *A***
- **tan *A***
- **Angle of elevation**
- **Angle of depression**

- Three trigonometric ratios, sine, cosine and tangent:

$\sin A = \dfrac{\text{Opposite}}{\text{Hypotenuse}}$

$\cos A = \dfrac{\text{Adjacent}}{\text{Hypotenuse}}$

$\tan A = \dfrac{\text{Opposite}}{\text{Adjacent}}$

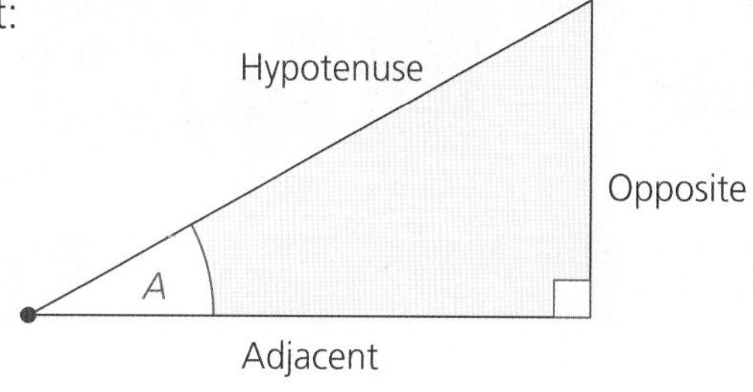

- When looking up at an object, the angle between the line of sight and the horizontal line is called the **angle of elevation**.

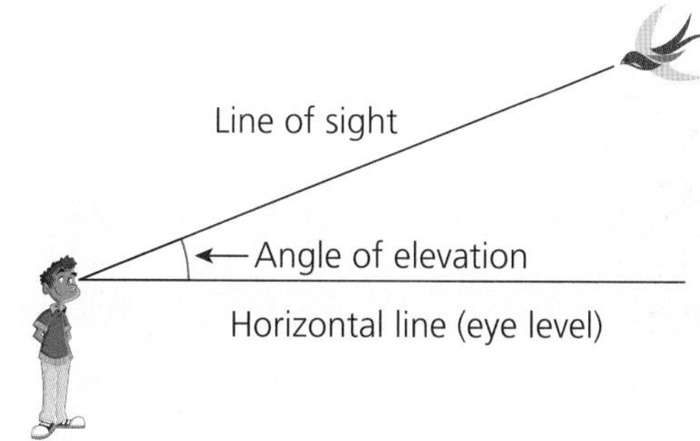

- When looking down at an object, the angle between the line of sight and the horizontal line is called the **angle of depression**.

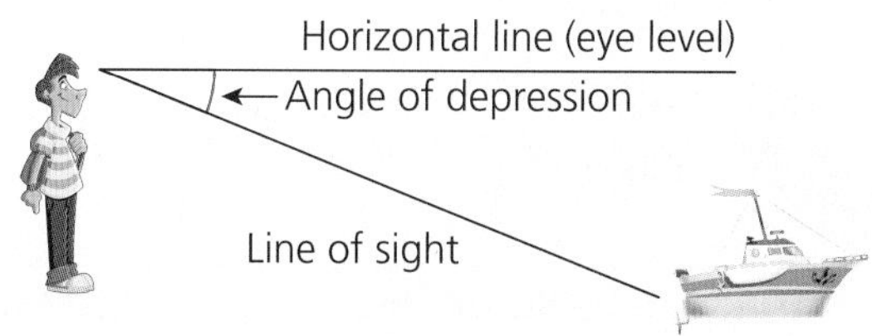

- Special angles:

$\sin 45° = \dfrac{1}{\sqrt{2}}$

$\cos 45° = \dfrac{1}{\sqrt{2}}$

$\tan 45° = \dfrac{1}{1} = 1$

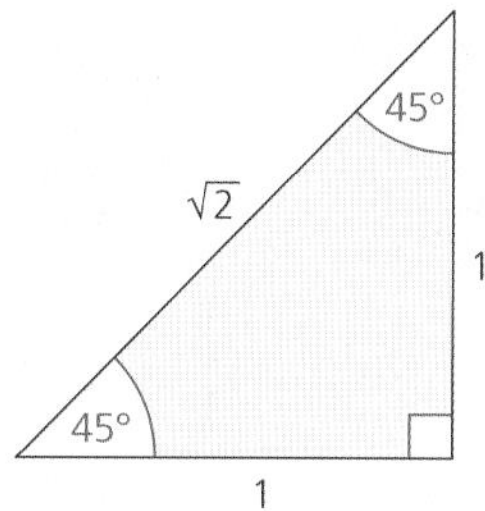

$\sin 30° = \dfrac{1}{2}$

$\cos 30° = \dfrac{\sqrt{3}}{2}$

$\tan 30° = \dfrac{1}{\sqrt{3}}$

$\sin 60° = \dfrac{\sqrt{3}}{2}$

$\cos 60° = \dfrac{1}{2}$

$\tan 60° = \dfrac{\sqrt{3}}{1} = \sqrt{3}$

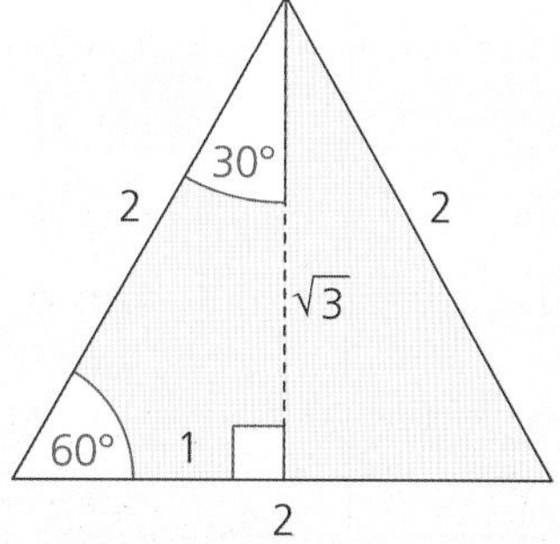

Appendix Problem Solving

Many mathematicians say that the main purpose of mathematics is to solve problems. All successful engineers, scientists, lawyers, accountants, business managers, etc. have to be good problem solvers.

Of course, they meet very different types of problems in their different types of work. But there are common strategies that can help everyone to be better at problem solving. You may be familiar with some of these already. This poster shows some of the strategies we can use to solve problems.

Problem-solving Strategies

Guess and test	Draw a diagram	Use algebra
Look for a pattern	Make a table or list	Solve a simpler problem
Act it out	Work backwards	Use direct reasoning

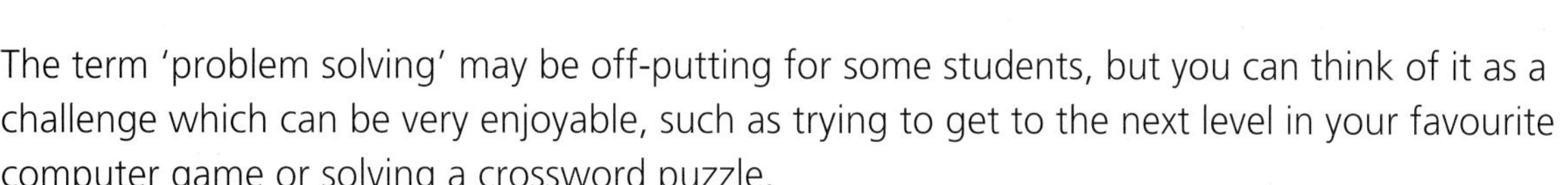

The term 'problem solving' may be off-putting for some students, but you can think of it as a challenge which can be very enjoyable, such as trying to get to the next level in your favourite computer game or solving a crossword puzzle.

Some of the benefits of practising problem solving are:

- It is a way to learn new mathematics
- It is a way to practise your mathematical skills
- It gives you an insight into the work of mathematicians
- It builds confidence
- It encourages you to work with other students
- It is enjoyable!

The first thing that we should all learn about problem solving is that being 'stuck' is no disgrace and is in fact an honourable state to be in! We all learn by getting stuck, and it is an essential part of learning to improve our thinking.

We learn more by doing harder problems which require a lot of reflection. However, to get the most out of being stuck, you must not just give up after a few minutes. Try every possible way. Discuss the problem with a friend if you need to. Your friend may see things somewhat differently from you.

A famous mathematician, **George Polya**, devoted much of his time to helping students become better problem solvers. He outlined four steps for solving problems:

Step 1: Understand the problem

- Read the question carefully – every word may be important.
- Do you understand all the words?
- Do you know what is given?
- Do you know what the goal is?
- Is there enough information?
- Is there information that is not needed?
- Have I met a similar problem before?

Step 2: Devise a plan

Which of these strategies could you use? See the poster on the previous page.

- Trial and error (guess and test)
- Draw a diagram
- Use an equation
- Look for a pattern
- Make up a table
- Solve a simpler problem
- Act it out
- Work backwards
- Eliminate possible solutions.

Problem Solving

Step 3: Carry out the plan

- Use the strategy you have chosen until the problem is solved or you see that a different course of action is better.
- Give yourself a reasonable amount of time, even days or more. You may get that flash of inspiration just as you are getting on a bus or putting on your jacket. The 'Aha' experience!

  This is how William Rowan Hamilton discovered quaternions.
- Get some hints from friends if you need to – they may know more than you think!
- Don't be afraid to start all over again.

Step 4: Look back

- Have you solved the problem correctly? Does the answer make sense?
- Does your answer satisfy the statement of the problem?
- Have you shown your working?
- Can you see an easier solution?
- Compare your answer to the way other people did it.
- Can you extend your solution to a general case?
- What did you learn from doing the problem?

Learning to use Polya's four steps will be a big help in becoming a good problem solver. In the following sections we will meet methods for tackling problems. We call these 'problem-solving strategies'.

Problem-solving Strategies

Strategy 1: Guess and Test ('Trial and Error')

Example 1

Place the digits 1, 2, 3, 4, 5 and 6 in the circles so that the sum of the three numbers on each side of the triangle is 12.

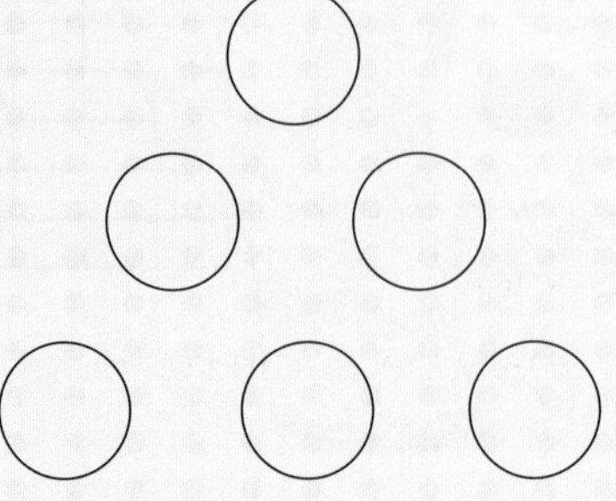

TRY this now before you read on.

Solution

Step 1: Understand the problem

Each number must be used once only; I must get 12 when I add the digits on each side of the triangle.

Step 2: Devise a plan

There are several approaches:

- Try combinations of these six numbers until one works.

- Keep rearranging the numbers until the solution appears.
- Eliminate some possible answers. I think that the corner circles are important because each of them is on two sides of the triangle. I will try each number in a corner.

Step 3: Carry out the plan

- Try 1 in a corner: then I need two pairs to go with 1 to make 12. 5, 6 is one pair, but I don't have a second pair. ∴ 1 cannot go in a corner.
- Try 2 in a corner: then I need two pairs to go with 2 to make 12. 4, 6 is one pair, but I don't have a second pair. ∴ 2 cannot go in a corner.
- Try 3 in a corner: then I need two pairs to go with 3 to make 12. 4, 5 is one pair, but I don't have a second pair. ∴ 3 cannot go in a corner.
- This means that 4, 5 and 6 are in the corners and I have the solution:

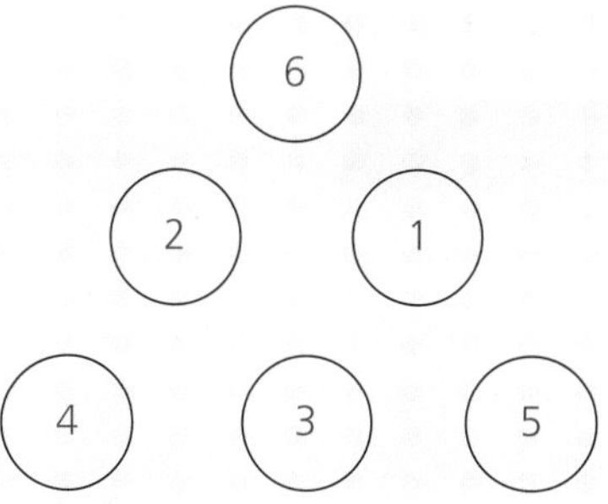

Step 4: Look back

- We have solved the problem; checking this is easy.
- A general method for doing larger triangles is not apparent.

The 'Trial and Error' strategy may be suitable when:

- There is a reasonably small number of possibilities
- You have a good idea of what the solution is
- You want to understand the problem better
- You can't think of other ways
- Your choice has been narrowed down by using other strategies.

Strategy 2: Draw a Diagram

Example 2

Cut a pizza into 7 pieces with three straight cuts.

TRY this now before you read on.

Solution

Step 1: Understand the problem
Do all the pieces have to be the same size and shape?

Step 2: Devise a plan
I tried to slice it the usual way but only got 6 pieces.

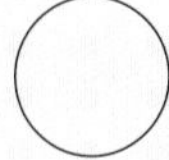
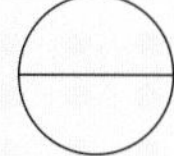
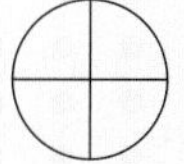
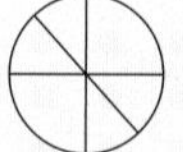

I will try to cut it differently.

Step 3: Carry out the plan

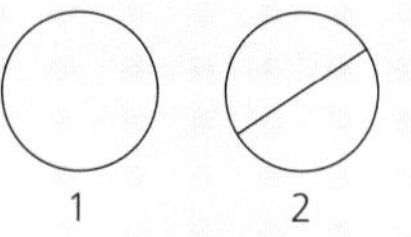

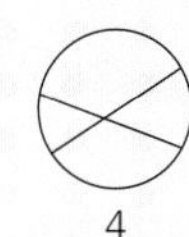

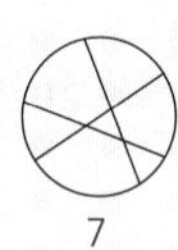

Step 4: Look back

- We have solved the problem satisfactorily.
- How many pieces can you get with 4 straight cuts?
- How many pieces can you get with 5 straight cuts?

The 'Draw a Diagram' strategy may be suitable when:

- Geometrical shapes or physical situations are involved
- You want to gain a better understanding of the problem
- A diagram is possible.

Strategy 3: Use Algebra

Example 3

The largest angle of a triangle is five times the smallest angle. The third angle equals the difference between the smallest and largest. What are the angles of the triangle?

TRY this now before you read on.

Solution

Step 1: Understand the problem

The three angles add to 180°; I need to use this with the values given.

Step 2: Devise a plan

I could use trial and error, but there seems to be a large number of possibilities.

Let x stand for the smallest angle; that will mean that the largest angle is $5x$.

(If I let x be the largest angle, it will involve division of x).

The third angle = $5x - x = 4x$

Step 3: Carry out the plan

Make an equation:

The three angles add to 180° so

$x + 5x + 4x = 180$

$\Rightarrow \quad 10x = 180$

$\Rightarrow \quad x = 18$

Therefore, the angles are 18°, 72° and 90°.

Step 4: Look back

- We have solved the problem satisfactorily.
- I could use this method for any such situation.

The 'Use Algebra' strategy may be suitable when:

- You see a phrase like 'for any number'
- The words 'is equal to' or 'equals' appear in a problem
- A proof or general solution is asked for
- A problem involves consecutive, even or odd whole numbers
- There is a large number of cases involved
- You want to develop a general formula.

Strategy 4: Look for a Pattern

Example 4

Find the units digit in 2^{39}.

TRY this now before you read on.

Solution

Step 1: Understand the problem

2^{39} means 2 multiplied by itself 39 times. Using a calculator, we get $5.497\,558\,139 \times 10^{11}$.

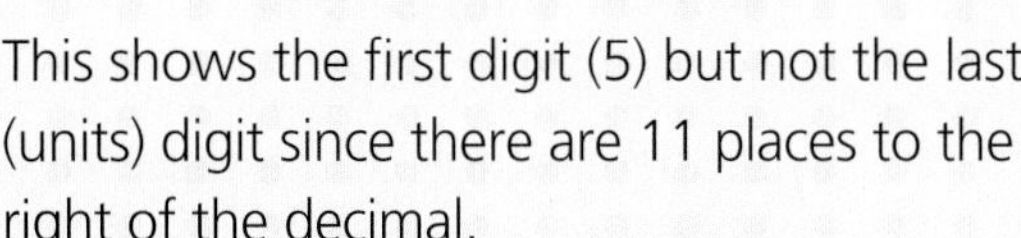

This shows the first digit (5) but not the last (units) digit since there are 11 places to the right of the decimal.

Step 2: Devise a plan

Try powers of 2 to see if there is any pattern forming which might lead to a solution.

i.e. try 2^1, 2^2, 2^3, 2^4, etc.

Step 3: Carry out the plan

$2^1 = 2$	$2^5 = 32$	$2^9 = 512$
$2^2 = 4$	$2^6 = 64$	
$2^3 = 8$	$2^7 = 128$	
$2^4 = 16$	$2^8 = 256$	

In fact, a pattern is emerging in the units digits: 2, 4, 8, 6, 2, 4, 8, 6, 2, …

Whenever the exponent (power) of the 2 is a multiple of 4, the units digit = 6

$\therefore$ 2^{40} has a units digit of 6, since 40 is a multiple of 4. The units digit of 2^{39} must be 8, since 8 precedes 6 in the pattern and 2^{39} precedes 2^{40}.

Step 4: Look back

The units digits of other numbers involving powers might be found in the same way.

The 'Look for a Pattern' strategy may be suitable when:

- A list of data is given
- A sequence of numbers is involved
- Listing special cases helps you deal with hard problems
- You can make a table in order to see the information more clearly.

Activity A.1

Use any of the four problem-solving strategies above (or your own) to solve these problems.

1 Read this question **carefully**:

'As I was going to St. Ives
I met a man with seven wives.
Each wife had seven sacks,
Each sack had seven cats,
Each cat had seven kittens.
Kittens, cats, sacks and wives,
How many were going to St. Ives?'

2 Place the digits 1 to 9 in the circles so that the sum of the numbers on each side of the triangle is 17.

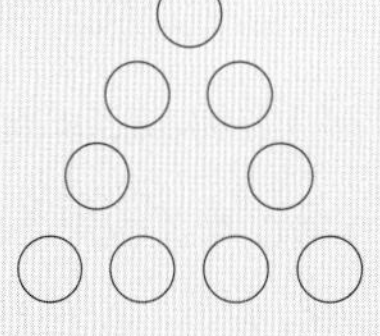

3 Divide a pizza into 11 pieces with just five straight cuts.

4 This puzzle is an example of a cryptarithm, where each letter represents a different digit. The digits in this example are 0, 1, 2, 3, 6, 7 and 9. Work out what digit each letter represents.

```
  S U N
+ F U N
S W I M
```

5 Think of a number. Add 20. Multiply by 3. Add 120. Divide by 3. Subtract your original number. Your result is 60. Why? Explain why this would work for any number.

6 Mary opened her book and said that the product of the two facing pages was 2077. Without doing any calculations, say why Mary was incorrect.

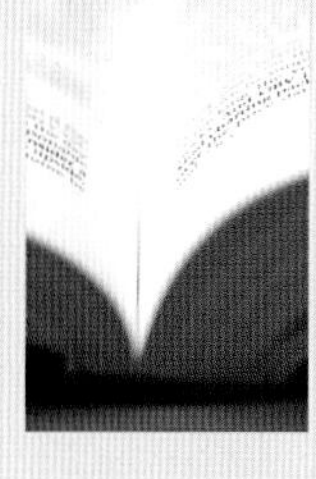

7 Find the units digit in 3^{47}.

8 There are only two rectangles whose sides are whole numbers and whose area and perimeter are the same numbers. What are they?

9 A farmer has a square field of side length 50 m. He has a choice of using one large irrigation system or four smaller ones, as shown.

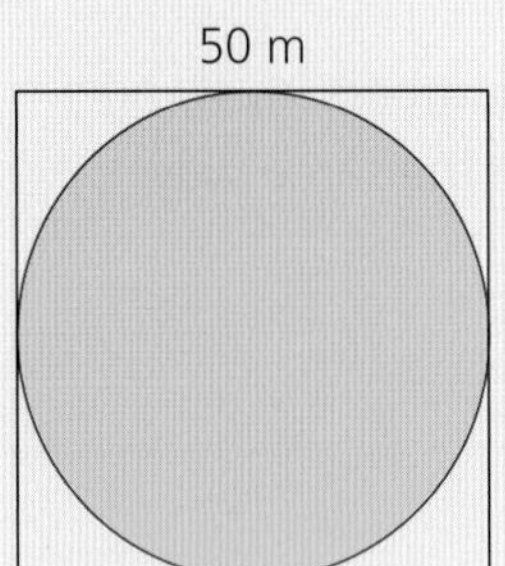

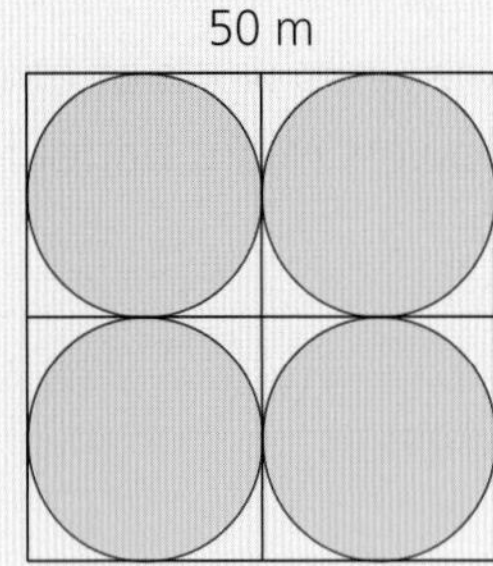

(i) What percentage of the field will the larger system irrigate?

(ii) What percentage of the field will the smaller system irrigate?

(iii) Which system will irrigate more land?

(iv) Can you make a general statement as a result?

10 There are 1000 households in a housing estate. A certain number of the households have one car. Of the other households in the estate, 50% have two cars and the other 50% have no car. How many cars are in the housing estate in total?

More Problem-solving Strategies; Combining Strategies

Strategy 5: Make a Table or List

Example 1

In how many ways can 20 be expressed as the sum of eight odd numbers?

TRY this now before you read on.

Solution

Step 1: Understand the problem

The odd numbers are 1, 3, 5, … We need to add 8 of these to get 20.

Step 2: Devise a plan

Make a list of all the possible odd numbers. The biggest possible odd number in the list is 13. Start with 13 and work down.

Step 3: Carry out the plan

$20 = 13 + 1 + 1 + 1 + 1 + 1 + 1 + 1$

$20 = 11 + 3 + 1 + 1 + 1 + 1 + 1 + 1$

$20 = 9 + 5 + 1 + 1 + 1 + 1 + 1 + 1$

$20 = 9 + 3 + 3 + 1 + 1 + 1 + 1 + 1$

$20 = 7 + 7 + 1 + 1 + 1 + 1 + 1 + 1$

$20 = 7 + 5 + 3 + 1 + 1 + 1 + 1 + 1$

$20 = 7 + 3 + 3 + 3 + 1 + 1 + 1 + 1$

$20 = 5 + 5 + 5 + 1 + 1 + 1 + 1 + 1$

$20 = 5 + 5 + 3 + 3 + 1 + 1 + 1 + 1$

$20 = 5 + 3 + 3 + 3 + 3 + 1 + 1 + 1$

$20 = 3 + 3 + 3 + 3 + 3 + 3 + 1 + 1$

= 11 ways in total

Step 4: Look back

We have solved the problem satisfactorily.

The 'Make a List or Table' strategy may be suitable when:

- You are asked 'in how many ways' something can be done
- Information is easily organised
- You are asked to list the results.

The 'Make a List or Table' strategy is often used with the 'Look for a Pattern' strategy.

Strategy 6: Solve a Simpler Problem

This is a very important strategy for many students.

Example 2

10 people take part in a chess competition. If each person plays each of the other people once, how many games take place?

TRY this now before you read on.

Solution

Step 1: Understand the problem

Person A plays once against B, C, D, … etc. So each person plays 9 games.

If this is the case, do I simply multiply 10 by 9 to get the number of games? This sounds too easy!

Step 2: Devise a plan

Solve for a smaller number of people and look for a pattern. See how many games there would be if there were just 2 people, then 3 people, then 4 people, …

Step 3: Carry out the plan

The 'Make a List or Table' and 'Look for a Pattern' strategies will also be useful.

Number of people	Games	Number of games	Pattern
2 (A and B)	A v B	1	The game A v B is the same as the game B v A The number is half of 2 × 1
3 (A, B, C)	A v B A v C B v C	3	This is half of 3 × 2
4 (A, B, C, D)	A v B A v C A v D B v C B v D C v D	6	This is half of 4 × 3

Now I see that, although all 10 people play 9 games each, I must multiply 10 × 9 and then divide by 2, since the game A v B is the same as the game B v A.

$(10 \times 9) \div 2 = 45$

Thus 45 games are played.

Step 4: Look back

We have solved the problem satisfactorily using a number of strategies together.

The 'Solve a Simpler Problem' strategy may be suitable when:

- The problem has very large or very small numbers
- You want to understand the problem better.

Strategy 7: Act it Out

Example 3

On a long corridor, there is a row of 100 closed lockers numbered 1 to 100.

A student goes down the corridor and opens every locker.

Then a second student goes down the corridor closing every second locker, starting at locker number 2.

A third student goes down the corridor and, starting at locker 3, she opens every third locker that she finds closed and closes every third locker that she finds open.

This continues until a total of 100 students have gone down the corridor opening and closing lockers.

How many lockers are open when the all the students are finished?

TRY this now before you read on.

Solution

Step 1: Understand the problem

Student number 4 will start at locker number 4 and visit every 4th locker. Student number 5 will start at locker number 5 and visit every 5th locker.

Step 2: Devise a plan

We will use the Solve a Simpler Problem strategy first, then Act it Out. Let's imagine that there were just 10 lockers and 10 students. Then act it out to see what happens as each student passes down the corridor.

Step 3: Carry out the plan

Use 10 sheets of paper to represent 10 lockers. Number the 'lockers' from 1 to 10 on both sides. Write 'open' on one side and 'closed' on the other side of each page. Now act out the opening and closing of these 10 lockers as the 10 students pass down the corridor. The 'Look for a Pattern' strategy is of great value here.

(We don't want to spoil this for you, so the final solution is not given here; but you **can** do it!)

Step 4: Look back

- Have you answered the question satisfactorily?
- Can you explain the solution?
- What is special about the numbers on these lockers?
- What is the link to factors and divisors of natural numbers?

The 'Act it Out' strategy may be suitable when:

- The 'Solve a Simpler Problem' strategy is used
- You want to get a better understanding of the problem.

Strategy 8: Work Backwards

Example 4

Patrick has a box of €1 coins. He has three students. Feeling generous, he gives half of his coins plus one to his eldest student. He then gives half of the remaining coins plus one to his next student and half of the remaining coins plus one to his youngest student. He now has one coin left.

How many coins did he have at the start?

TRY this now before you read on.

Solution

Step 1: Understand the problem

Patrick has one coin at the end. I need to know how many coins he had before giving money to his three students.

Step 2: Devise a plan

The only quantity I have is the €1 coin which Patrick has left at the end, so we could start from there and work backwards.

Step 3: Carry out the plan

Last step	Patrick has 1 coin left
Previous step (youngest student)	Patrick gave away half plus 1, so he must have had $(1 + 1) \times 2 = 4$ coins before this step.
Previous step (middle student)	Patrick gave away half plus 1, so he must have had $(4 + 1) \times 2 = 10$ coins before this step.
Previous step (eldest student)	Patrick gave away half plus 1, so he must have had $(10 + 1) \times 2 = 22$ coins before this step.

Patrick had 22 coins at the start.

Step 4: Look back

We have solved the question satisfactorily.

The 'Work Backwards' strategy may be suitable when:

- The last part of the problem is clear and you need the starting point
- A direct approach involves complicated algebra
- The problem involves a sequence of actions which are reversible.

Strategy 9: Use Direct Reasoning

Example 5

You have a jug of water which contains exactly 8 litres. You also have two empty jugs, one of which can hold 3 litres and the other 5 litres. How can you pour the water so that two of the jugs contain 4 litres?

TRY this now before you read on.

Solution

Step 1: Understand the problem

Only the 8-litre jug contains water at the beginning. I have to pour water into the other empty jugs.

Step 2: Devise a plan

Think through the problem in a logical way.

- Only the 8-litre and 5-litre jugs are big enough to contain 4 litres.
- This means that, at the end, I need to have 4 litres in each of the bigger jugs and zero litres in the 3-litre jug.
- There will have to be water in the 3-litre jug just before the end to achieve this.
- I can get 4 litres by 3 + 1 or 5 – 1.

Step 3: Carry out the plan

The steps:

Steps	Litres in 8-litre jug	Litres in 5-litre jug	Litres in 3-litre jug
Start	8	0	0
1	5	0	3
2	0	5	3
3	3	5	0
4	3	2	3
5	6	2	0
6	6	0	2
7	1	5	2
8	1	4	3
9	4	4	0

Step 4: Look back

This looks good. Is there a shorter way? Can you do it in fewer steps?

The 'Use Direct Reasoning' strategy may be suitable when:

- A proof is required
- You wish to imply a statement from a collection of given conditions.

Activity A.2

1 See the locker problem in Example 3 above.

(i) If there are 1000 lockers and 1000 students, which lockers remain open after the 1000th student has passed?

(ii) Which students touched both lockers 36 and 48?

(iii) Which lockers were touched by only two students? How do you know?

(iv) Which lockers were touched by only three students? How do you know?

(v) Which lockers were switched the most times?

2 There is exactly one three digit positive whole number (so a number between 100 and 999) with the following properties:

If you subtract 11 from it, the answer is divisible by 11;

If you subtract 10 from it, the answer is divisible by 10;

If you subtract 9 from it, the answer is divisible by 9.

What is the number?

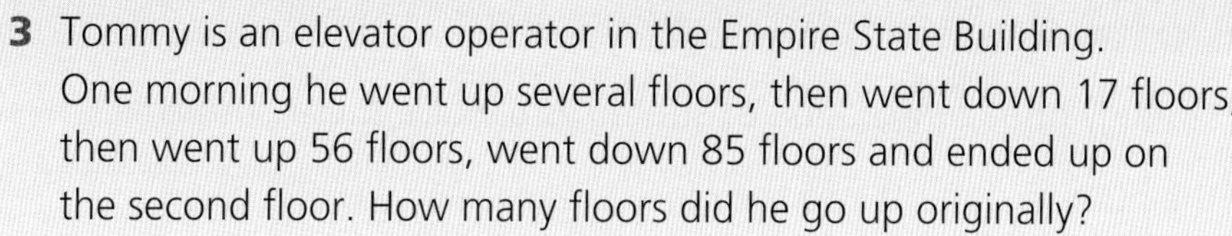

3 Tommy is an elevator operator in the Empire State Building. One morning he went up several floors, then went down 17 floors, then went up 56 floors, went down 85 floors and ended up on the second floor. How many floors did he go up originally?

4 Multiply a number by 4. Then add 12. Divide by 2. Subtract 18. Then divide by 4. If the answer is 6, what was your original number?

5 The last digit of a positive whole number is the digit in the 'ones' position, farthest to the right. For example, the last digit of 156 753 is 3.

What is the last digit of $2004^{1\,000\,000} + 2005^{1\,000\,000}$?

You should not need to work out the actual number!

6 The number 6 has the following property:

If you subtract 2 from it, you get 4 which is a perfect square,

$6 - 2 = 4 = (2 \times 2) = 2^2$

and if you add 2 to it, you get 8 which is a perfect cube,

$6 + 2 = 8 = (2 \times 2 \times 2) = 2^3$.

What is the next whole number, bigger than 6, with this property?
(This means that when you subtract 2 from it, you get a perfect square and when you add 2 to it, you get a perfect cube.)

7 A number like 27 472 or 5665 is called a palindrome because it reads the same backwards as forwards.

How many four-digit palindromes are there?

8 All four-digit palindromes are divisible by some number. Can you find it?

9 There is only one integer such that one less than it is a perfect square and one more than it is a perfect cube. What is the number?

10 Cross out all of the nine dots in the figure using only four straight lines and without lifting your pencil off the paper.

Revision Activity A

Problem Solving

Use any problem-solving strategy or a combination of strategies to solve these problems.

1 Magic Square: Place the numbers 1 to 9 into the nine cells of the three-by-three square so that:

- The sum of the entries in each row = 15
- The sum of the entries in each column = 15
- The sum of the entries in each of the two diagonals = 15.

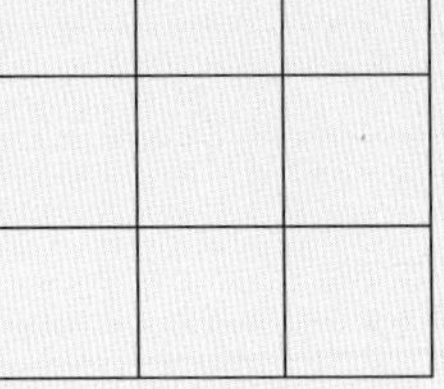

2 A multiple of 11 I be,
Not odd, but even, you see.
My digits, a pair,
When multiplied there,
Make a cube and a square
Out of me. Who am I?

3 When the famous mathematician Gauss was a boy in his first arithmetic class, he was asked by his teacher to do the following problem. He solved it very quickly. Can you work out a quick method to solve it?

Find the sum of all the natural numbers from 1 to 100, i.e. find the sum $S = 1 + 2 + 3 + 4 + 5 + \dots + 100$.

4 (a) Express 11 as the sum of two consecutive numbers.

(b) Express 13 as the sum of two consecutive numbers.

(c) Can every odd number be expressed as the sum of two consecutive numbers? Explain your answer.

5 If it is possible, find an odd number that can be expressed as the sum of four consecutive natural numbers. If it is impossible, explain why.

6 Luke and Isla are playing chess. Luke says, 'There are 64 equal squares on the chessboard. But I wonder how many of every size there are.' Isla says that she has read that there are in fact 204 squares on a chessboard. Can you justify Isla's claim?

7 Using the symbols +, −, ×, ÷, fill in the following three spaces to make a true equation (you may use a symbol more than once).

5___5___5___5 = 11

8 Mary has a square vineyard. She always plants her grapevines in square arrays like those in the diagram. Each year, she plants more vines but always keeps the vineyard square. This year, she planted 41 vines. How many vines does she have in the vineyard now?

```
              •  •  •
      •  •    •  •  •
 •    •  •    •  •  •
 1      4       9
```

9 If the diagonals of a rectangle are drawn in, how many triangles of all sizes are there in the shape?

10 A, B and C run a 100 m race, each running at a steady speed throughout. A beats B by 10 metres and B beats C by 10 metres. By how much does A beat C?

11 It takes 64 small cubes to completely fill a large cubic container with no top. How many cubes are not touching a side or the bottom?

12 Imagine that the Earth is a sphere with a circumference of 40 075 km and that a rope is tied tautly around the Equator. The rope will be 40 075 km long.

(a) You want to extend the rope so that it will have 1 metre clearance all round the Earth. How much longer will the rope have to be?

(b) If the Earth were replaced in part (a) by a football with a diameter of 22 cm, how much longer would the rope have to be?

13 In a sale, you get a discount of 30% off a washing machine, but you must pay 23% VAT. Which would you prefer to have applied first, the discount or the tax? Explain your answer.

14 A bag contains 28 red, 31 green, 36 black, 29 orange and 27 yellow wine gums. Michael has been blindfolded so that he cannot see into the bag. What is the smallest number of wine gums that Michael must choose from the bag to guarantee that he has chosen at least two of the same colour?

15 The total cost of a box of chocolates is €11. This includes the cost of the chocolates and the cost of the box.
If the box costs €7 less than the chocolates, how much do the chocolates cost?

16 There are ten teams in a football league. Each team plays every other team twice, once at home and once away. How many matches are played in total during the season? (Be careful that you do not count the same match twice!)

17 Julie and Brendan both have some money and each of them wants to buy a chocolate bar. However, Julie is 2 cent short of the price of the bar while Brendan is 18 cent short (of the price of the same bar). They decide to pool their resources and find that even when they combine their money, they still do not have enough money for the bar.
How much does the chocolate bar cost?
(Remember, both of them have **some** money so that each of them has at least one cent.)

18 You have two squares. The lengths of their sides are whole numbers of cm. The total area of the two squares is 34 cm^2. If you made a rectangle using two sides from one square and two sides from the other, what would its area be?

Problem Solving

19 A teacher picks two consecutive whole numbers between 6 and 10. She tells Rashid what one of the numbers is and tells Sheila the other one. Rashid and Sheila then have the following conversation:

Rashid: 'I do not know your number.'

After considering what Rashid said,

Sheila then said, 'I do not know your number.'

What number was given to Sheila?

20 There are 70 students in a year group, 36 girls and 34 boys. At the end of the school year, the students have a choice of two places to go on their school trip: either Galway or Cork. All of the students go on the trip, with 25 students going to Galway and the other 45 going to Cork. How many more girls went to Cork than boys went to Galway?

(You are asked for the difference between the number of girls who went to Cork and the number of boys who went to Galway.)

21 Shuffle a pack of 52 playing cards and then deal out 30 cards to form a pile. Let n be the number of red cards in the pile. Let m be the number of black cards in the reduced deck. What is the value of $n - m$?

Answers

Chapter 1

Activity 1.1

1. 12 **2.** 144 **3.** (i) 1 : 11 (ii) 1 : 5 : 10 (iii) 3 : 1 (iv) 5 : 1 : 10 (v) 1 : 4 : 2 (vi) 4 : 5 : 6 (vii) 1 : 8 : 10 (viii) 1 : 5 : 20 (ix) 1 : 6 : 3 (x) 1 : 5 : 15 **4.** (i) 5 : 2 (ii) 4 : 1 (iii) 2 : 1 (iv) 1 : 7 (v) 15 : 12 : 10 (vi) 11 : 19 (vii) 1 : 6 (viii) 10 : 21 (ix) 11 : 4 (x) 20 : 18 : 15 **5.** (i) 1 : 10 (ii) 7 : 12 (iii) 10 : 13 (iv) 1 : 6 (v) 1 : 5 (vi) 27 : 28 (vii) 1 : 7 (viii) 13 : 25 **6.** (i) €279, €186 (ii) \$212, \$371 (iii) 2905 g, 3486 g (iv) 76 min, 304 min (v) €3395, €1455 (vi) 49 m, 98 m, 245 m (vii) 58 kg, 203 kg, 261 kg (viii) £3205, £1923, £1282 (ix) 96 c, 72 c, 48 c (x) 972 cm, 3888 cm, 4860 cm **7.** (i) 20 (ii) 33 (iii) 27 (iv) 36 (v) 4 (vi) 2 (vii) 10 (viii) 3 (ix) 6 (x) 15 **8.** Susan 3, Maeve 9, Aoife 12 **9.** (i) 60 (ii) 105 **10.** (i) 1 : 8 (ii) 1 : 26 **11.** €35 **12.** (i) 153 m^2 (ii) 408 m^2 **13.** They are proportional **14.** The amount of cookies are not proportional **15.** Potatoes 12 m^2, Carrots 36 m^2 **16.** (ii) 450 **17.** (ii) 344.5 km

Activity 1.2

1. (iii) €2400 (iv) €1200 **2.** (i) 6 (ii) 30 days (iii) 15 days **3.** (i) 5 hours (ii) 10 chefs **4.** (i) €12 (ii) €60 (iii) 9 metres **5.** (i) 2 days (ii) 6 painters **6.** €256.25 **7.** (iii) €5.77 (iv) 24 **8.** 180 minutes **9.** €8.75 **10.** (i) 6 people paid €4 each. (ii) €3 (iv) €24

Activity 1.3

1. 200 cm **2.** (i) 240 metres (ii) 2.4 km (iii) 8.4 km (iv) 540 metres **3.** (i) 6.75 m (ii) 2.625 m (iii) 11.25 m (iv) 11.25 m **4.** (i) 3.5 m (ii) 3.6 m **5.** (i) 3 m × 4.95 m (ii) 11.7 m^2 (iii) 47.1 m **6.** (ii) Actual length = 23.5 m, Actual width = 11 m **7.** 16 m = height, length from head to toe = 22 metres **9.** (i) 90 km (ii) 90 km (iii) 52 km (iv) 127 km **10.** (i) 180 km (ii) 240 km (iii) 2.8 cm

Revision Activity 1

1. (a) 0.7 km, 0.8 km (b) €572.73, €286.36, €190.91 (c) 100 min, 200 min (d) €750, €250, €500 (e) 40, 60, 100 (f) 28.6 cm, 11.4 cm **2.** (i) 3 : 17 (ii) 1.7 litres **3.** (i) 1 : 8 (ii) 1 litre concentrate + 8 litres water = 9 litres of drink (iii) 750 ml **4.** (i) 120 kg (ii) 14 hours (iii) 67

Exam-style Question

1. (i) 6 litres (ii) 11 : 9

Chapter 2

Activity 2.1

1. (i) 5 (ii) 6 **2.** (i) Coefficient of x^2 is 3; coefficient of x is −4. (ii) −7 **3.** (i) a, b and c (ii) Coefficient of ab is 3; coefficient of ac is −5. (iii) −6 **4.** (ii) $(3m^2 - 6m + 2)$ is the most compact. **5.** $15x + 10y$ **6.** $-6a + 2b$ **7.** $21 - 14q - 7r$ **8.** $15a^2 - 10ab$ **9.** $-x + 2y$ **10.** $-10x + 29$ **11.** $-a - 9$ **12.** $5x^2 - 19xy$ **13.** $15ab - 7ac - 3bc$ **14.** $x^5 - x^4 - x^3 - 2x^2$ **15.** $2p + 11q - 20$ **16.** $2x^2 + 3x + 5$ **17.** $x^5 - x^4 - 3x^3 + 6x^2 - 3x$ **18.** (i) $8x^2 + 1$ (ii) $4a^3 + 2a^2 - 7a$ (iii) $-6x^2 - 16x + 2$ (iv) $-10x^2 - 11x - 8$ **19.** (i) $2x^2 + x + 4$ (ii) $-5x - 4$ (iii) $3x^2 - 16x - 8$ (iv) $7x^2 - 4x + 8$ **20.** (i) a^4 (ii) $2a$ (iii) $5ab^2$ (iv) $\frac{2x^2}{3y}$ (v) $\frac{4xy^2}{3}$ (vi) a^2 (vii) $\frac{x}{2}$ (viii) $6x^4y^7$ **21.** $-x + 7$ **22.** $-27a$

Activity 2.2

1. (i) $10x^2 - 11x - 6$ (ii) $-20x^2 - 16x + 4$ (iii) $-9a^2 + 9$ (iv) $-2p^2 + 16p - 30$ **2.** $x^2 + 7x + 10$ **3.** $a^2 + 10a + 24$ **4.** $y^2 - 6y + 5$ **5.** $3x^2 + 10x - 8$ **6.** $6x^2 - 23x + 20$ **7.** $10p^2 + 17p + 3$ **8.** $15x^2 + xy - 2y^2$ **9.** $21x^2 + 4xy - y^2$ **10.** $25a^2 - 4b^2$ **11.** $2x^3 - x^2 - 16x + 15$ **12.** $x^3 - 3xy^2 - 2y^3$ **13.** $5x^3 - 19x^2 + 12x$ **14.** $x^3 + 3x^2 - 5x - 4$ **15.** $6x^3 + x^2 - 13x + 4$ **16.** $a = -1$ **17.** $a = -2$ **18.** $(x + 4)$ **19.** $6x^2 - 5x - 4$ **20.** (i) $x^2 + 2xy + y^2$ (ii) $x^2 - 2xy + y^2$ **21.** (i) $x^2 + 4x + 4$ (ii) $x^2 - 6x + 9$ (iii) $a^2 + 8a + 16$ (iv) $a^2 - 10a + 25$ (v) $p^2 - 12p + 36$ (vi) $x^2 + 14x + 49$ **22.** (i) $a^2x^2 + 2abx + b^2$ (ii) $a^2x^2 - 2abx + b^2$ **23.** (i) $9x^2 + 12x + 4$ (ii) $16x^2 - 8x + 1$ (iii) $4a^2 - 20a + 25$ (iv) $16m^2 + 24m + 9$ (v) $4p^2 - 24p + 36$ (vi) $4x^2 + 4x + 1$

Activity 2.3

1. (i) 27 (ii) 0 (iii) −72 (iv) −66 (v) −18 (vi) 0 (vii) 30 **2.** (i) −60 (ii) 33 (iii) −4 (iv) −9 **3.** (i) −24 (ii) −4 (iii) 33 (iv) −7 (v) $\frac{1}{2}$ (vi) $\frac{7}{3}$ **4.** (i) 15 (ii) −45 (iii) −223 (iv) −98 (v) 1 (vi) −152 **5.** (i) −11 (ii) −8 (iii) 14 (iv) 4 (v) 108 (vi) 14 **6.** (i) 60 (ii) −94 (iii) −181 (iv) 101 **7.** 3 **8.** 1 **9.** 3 **10.** $5t$ **11.** $\frac{-1}{12}$ **12.** 4 **13.** $\frac{-6}{5}$

Activity 2.4

1. $4(x + 2y)$ **2.** $5(a + 3b)$ **3.** $6(2p + 3q)$ **4.** $7(2a + 3b)$ **5.** $3(4a - 5b)$ **6.** $10(3x - 5y)$ **7.** $x(3 + y)$ **8.** $p(p - q)$ **9.** $5x(2x - 1)$ **10.** $5xy(3 - 2y)$ **11.** $5a(2a - 3b)$ **12.** $7x(2x - 3y)$ **13.** $6a(2b - 3c)$ **14.** $15p(3p - 2q)$ **15.** $p^2(p + 1)$ **16.** $25x(y - 5p)$ **17.** $5(x - 3y + 4z)$ **18.** $x^2(x^2 + x - 1)$ **19.** $3(x + 2)$ **20.** $2(p + 5)$ **21.** $3(b - 3)$ **22.** $6(x - 6)$ **23.** $4(3y + 2)$ **24.** $12(2x + 3)$ **25.** $9(3x - 2)$ **26.** $6(3 - p)$ **27.** $5(3k + 7)$ **28.** $9(1 - 3q)$ **29.** $3(a + b + c)$ **30.** $4(p + q + 1)$ **31.** $2p(3p + 4q)$ **32.** $6p(4p + 5q)$ **33.** $8t^2(2 - 3t)$ **34.** $6x^2(x - 3)$ **35.** $3j^2(3j + 1)$ **36.** $5x(x^2 + 2x - 3)$ **37.** $4x(x^2 + 2x - 2)$ **38.** $3p(1 - p - 2p^2)$ **39.** $4a(2 - 3a - 5a^2)$ **40.** $5p(3 - q - 4q^2)$ **41.** $3a(a + b + ab)$ **42.** $4(a^3 - b^2 - b)$ **43.** $7p^2d^2(p - 2d)$ **44.** $ab(a - b)$ **45.** $mn(4n - 9m)$ **46.** $3a(3a - 4 + a^2)$ **47.** $2ab(a + 4 - 6b)$ **48.** $7xy(3x + 1 - 2xy)$ **49.** $p(p^2 + 1)$ **50.** $x^3(x^2 - x - 1)$ **51.** (i) $(a + 3)$ (ii) $(x + 1)$ (iii) $(5x + 6)$ (iv) $(2x^2 + x + 1)$ **52.** (i) $y(a + b)$ (ii) $(a + b)(y + 1)$ **53.** (i) $x(3 + a)$ (ii) $(3 + a)(x + 2)$ **54.** (i) $d(a + b)$ (ii) $(a + b)(d - 4)$ **55.** (i) $x(p - q)$ (ii) $(p - q)(x + 7)$

Activity 2.5

1. $-5x - 5y$ **2.** $-6a - 2b$ **3.** $-12a + 8$ **4.** $-10x^2 + 10x - 10$ **5.** $-2(x + y)$ **6.** $-4(3a + b)$ **7.** $-5(x - 2y)$ **8.** $-1(a + b)$ **9.** $-6(2x - 1)$ **10.** $-4(2m + n)$ **11.** $(m + n)(x + y)$ **12.** $(p + q)(a + b)$ **13.** $(5 + p)(a + b)$ **14.** $(w + 7)(a + b)$ **15.** $(c + b)(a + 5)$ **16.** $(m + 7)(x + y)$ **17.** $(a + 4)(m + n)$ **18.** $(p + 2)(p + y)$ **19.** $(x + y)(x + 2)$ **20.** $(p + t)(m + 3n)$ **21.** $(p + 4q)(p - 1)$ **22.** $(x + m)(a - b)$ **23.** $(x + p)(ax - b)$ **24.** $(y + 7)(x - y)$ **25.** $(7 + m)(m - 3n)$ **26.** $(4x + 3)(5x - 4y)$ **27.** $(x - y)(x + 1)$ **28.** $(4x - 3y)(2a + b)$ **29.** $(x - y)(c - d)$ **30.** $(px - q)(p - 2)$ **31.** $(p - 8)(q + s)$ **32.** $(ax + 6p)(3 - 2x)$ **33.** $(3 - x)(a - b)$ **34.** $(x - 5a)(3 - b)$ **35.** $(2c - d)(2c + 3)$ **36.** $(a + 3)(x - 1)$ **37.** $(2 - k)(x - y)$ **38.** $(3a - b)(1 + b)$ **39.** $(3y - 10)(x + b)$ **40.** $(x - 2y)(5x + 1)$ **41.** $(a - 2b)(6p + 2)$ **42.** $(x - b)(x + a)$

Activity 2.6

1. $(x + 9)(x + 2)$ **2.** $(p - 9)(p - 2)$ **3.** $(m + 10)(m + 1)$ **4.** $(a + 8)(a + 3)$ **5.** $(a - 9)(a - 9)$ **6.** $(a + 25)(a + 4)$ **7.** $(x - 4)(x + 3)$ **8.** $(x + 4)(x - 3)$ **9.** $(x - 6)(x + 2)$

10. $(x + 6)(x - 2)$ **11.** $(p + 9)(p - 2)$ **12.** $(a + 15)(a - 2)$
13. $(x - 6)(x + 1)$ **14.** $(x + 6)(x - 1)$ **15.** $(p - 2)(p + 1)$
16. $(p + 2)(p - 1)$ **17.** $(a - 10)(a + 7)$ **18.** $(x + 15)(x - 4)$
19. $(a - 8)(a - 7)$ **20.** $(x - 4)(x + 4)$ **21.** $(a + 3)(a + 2)$
22. $(x - 3)(x + 2)$ **23.** $(a - 11)(a + 8)$ **24.** $(m + 14)(m - 3)$
25. $(x + 11)(x - 6)$ **26.** $(a - 11)(a + 6)$ **27.** $(5x - 1)(x - 1)$
28. $(3x - 2)(x + 1)$ **29.** $(5x - 2)(2x + 3)$ **30.** $(4x - 5)(3x - 2)$
31. $(3x - 7)(2x + 5)$ **32.** $(11x - 2)(x + 7)$ **33.** $(6x - 5)(x + 2)$
34. $(3m - 4)(3m - 4)$ **35.** $(5x - 3)(5x - 3)$ **36.** $(6x + 5)(4x - 3)$
37. $(9x - 4)(4x + 1)$ **38.** $(5x + 4)(2x - 5)$ **39.** $(4x - 5)(3x + 1)$
40. $(3x - 10)(4x - 7)$ **41.** $(13x + 4)(x - 3)$ **42.** $(5x - 2)(x + 3)$
43. $(4x - 3)(3x - 2)$ **44.** $(6x - 11)(x + 2)$ **45.** $(4x + 1)(x - 16)$

Activity 2.8

1. $(x + y)(x - y)$ **2.** $(a + b)(a - b)$ **3.** $(m + n)(m - n)$
4. $(p + q)(p - q)$ **5.** $(x + 5)(x - 5)$ **6.** $(a + 6)(a - 6)$
7. $(x + 9)(x - 9)$ **8.** $(a + 11)(a - 11)$ **9.** $(m + 14)(m - 14)$
10. $(b + 20)(b - 20)$ **11.** $(16 + y)(16 - y)$ **12.** $(12 + a)(12 - a)$
13. $(a + 100)(a - 100)$ **14.** $(5x + 6)(5x - 6)$ **15.** $(7x + 1)(7x - 1)$
16. $(3x + 10)(3x - 10)$ **17.** $(3x + 4)(3x - 4)$
18. $(4a)^2$, $(4a + 3)(4a - 3)$ **19.** $(5x + 2)(5x - 2)$
20. $(7x + 6y)(7x - 6y)$ **21.** (i) 200 (ii) 400 (iii) −320
(iv) 82 (v) 72 (vi) 6.8 **22.** $(5x + 6y)(5x - 6y)$
23. $(7a + 4b)(7a - 4b)$ **24.** $(12x + 3y)(12x - 3y)$
25. $(13p + 12)(13p - 12)$ **26.** $(m + 100)(m - 100)$
27. $(x + y + z)(x + y - z)$ **28.** $(a + b + 1)(a + b - 1)$
29. $2(x + 3)(x - 3)$ **30.** $(x - 2 + 6y)(x - 2 - 6y)$ **31.** $(5x)(x + 2)$

Activity 2.9

1. $(x + 5)(x - 5)$ **2.** $(x + 7)(x - 7)$ **3.** $(a + m)(b - 2x)$
4. $(12 + y)(12 - y)$ **5.** $(x - 5)(x + 4)$ **6.** $(2 + c)(x - y)$
7. $d(5c + 7)$ **8.** $7(a + 2)(a - 2)$ **9.** $(a + 4)(x + 3y)$
10. $2(a + 3)(a - 3)$ **15.** 100 **16.** $k = 9$ **17.** $6x - 9x^2$
18. $12(2x^2 + 1)$ **19.** $\frac{4x}{2x - 3}$ **20.** $(2x - 3)$
21. $2(2x + 3y)(2x - 3y)$ **22.** (i) $y(17 - 5y)$ (ii) $(3a - 2)(2a - 5)$
23. $(3a - 2)(a)$ **24.** (a) $4(x - 3)$ and $3(x - 3)$
(c) not proportional

Activity 2.10

1. $\frac{11x}{9}$ **2.** $-\frac{a}{8}$ **3.** $\frac{3y}{14}$ **4.** $\frac{22b}{15}$ **5.** $-\frac{c}{20}$ **6.** $\frac{58x}{15}$
7. $\frac{103y}{42}$ **8.** $\frac{193x}{84}$ **9.** $\frac{167x}{26}$ **10.** $-\frac{11x}{20}$ **11.** $\frac{3x + 8}{4}$
12. $\frac{15x + 5}{2}$ **13.** $\frac{15x - 41}{10}$ **14.** $\frac{41x + 19}{15}$ **15.** $\frac{7x + 4}{4}$
16. $\frac{-18x - 33}{8}$ **17.** $\frac{x + 13}{6}$ **18.** $\frac{27x - 43}{10}$
19. $\frac{34x + 3}{12}$ **20.** $\frac{102p - 9}{14}$ **21.** $\frac{13k - 3}{12}$ **22.** $\frac{5}{2x}$ **23.** $\frac{19}{15k}$
24. $\frac{13x + 5}{2x^2 + x}$ **25.** $\frac{28x + 3}{(3x - 2)(2x + 3)}$ **26.** $\frac{3x - 13}{(3x + 1)(2x - 4)}$
27. $\frac{-13p + 27}{(3p - 5)(p + 1)}$ **28.** $\frac{3x - 18}{(3x + 2)(3x - 2)}$ **29.** $p = 3$
30. $k = 29$ **31.** (ii) $\frac{1}{x - 2}$ **32.** $\frac{2}{x - 3}$ **33.** $\frac{-4}{x - 4}$
34. $\frac{5x + 20}{(2x + 5)(x + 5)}$ **35.** $k = 17$

Activity 2.11

1. (i) $(3x^2)(4x^2) = 12x^4$ (ii) $\frac{16x^2}{4x} = 4x$ (iii) $\frac{25x^2}{5x} = 5x$
(iv) $(5x^2)(2x^3) = 10x^5$ (v) $(4y)(3x) = 12xy$ (vi) $\frac{20xy}{4x} = 5y$
(vii) $\frac{2a}{a} = 2$ (viii) $\frac{4ab}{2a} = 2b$ (ix) $\frac{8xyz}{4xy} = 2z$ (x) $\frac{25m^2n}{5mn} = 5m$
(xi) $\frac{20a^2b^2}{4ab} = 5ab$ (xii) $\frac{5ab}{ab} = 5$ **2.** (i) $\frac{8x^2}{4} = 2x^2$ (ii) $\frac{24y^3}{3} = 8y^3$
(iii) $\frac{27x^2}{9} = 3x^2$ (iv) $\frac{18a^2}{3} = 6a^2$ (v) $\frac{12x^2}{4x} = 3x$ (vi) $\frac{20x^3}{4x^2} = 5x$
(vii) $\frac{10x^2y}{5y} = 2x^2$ (viii) $\frac{16x^3}{8x^2} = 2x$ (ix) $\frac{25x^2y^3}{5xy} = 5xy^2$
(x) $\frac{16x^2y^3z^2}{8xy^2z} = 2xyz$ **3.** (i) $(x - 1)$ (ii) $(a + 5)$ (iii) $(3x - 4)$

4. $(x - 15)$ m **5.** (ii) $(3x + 2)$ **6.** $2x + 5$ **7.** $3x - 5$
8. (i) $x + 2$ (ii) $3a + 2$ (iii) $3x + 4$ (iv) $3p + 1$ (v) $3x + 2$
(vi) $x + 8$ (vii) $4x + 5y$ (viii) $3 + 2x$ **9.** $x^2 - 5x - 9$
10. $2x^2 + x - 5$ **11.** $a^2 - 5a - 17$ **12.** $2a^2 - a - 7$
13. $2p^2 + 3p + 4$ **14.** $3k^2 - 4k + 1$ **15.** $x^2 - 2x - 1$
16. $x + 4$ **17.** $3k^2 + 6k + 8$ **18.** $a = 3, b = -4, c = -5$
19. (i) $x^2 - 3x$ (ii) $x^2 - 3x$ **20.** $x^2 + 2x + 4$ **21.** $3 - 5x - 2x^2$

Revision Activity 2

1. (a) $4x(5y - x)$ (b) $(5x + 1)(x - 2)$ (c) $6(x + 2y)(x - 2y)$
2. $\frac{31}{12}$ **3.** $6x^3 + 7x^2 - 26x + 8$ **4.** (a) $(x - b)(x + a)$
(b) $2(2x + 3y)(2x - 3y)$ **5.** (a) $15x^3 - x^2 - 32x + 12$ (b) 28
6. (a) $3x(3x - 5)$ (b) $(3x - 5)(3x - 3)$ (c) $(y - x)(3 - 4x)$
7. $\frac{2x - 1}{(x - 3)(x - 2)}$ **8.** $2p + 10$ **9.** $\frac{-x + 43}{20}$ **10.** (a) $-\frac{1}{20}$
(b) $\frac{5}{8}$ (c) $-\frac{1}{20}$ (d) $\frac{65}{59}$

Exam-style Questions

1. (a) $\frac{x}{20}$ (b) $2x^2 - 5x + 2$ **2.** (a) $5x^2(x - 2)$
(b) $(2x + 9y)(2x - 9y)$ (c) $(a - b)(a + 3)$

Chapter 3

Activity 3.1

1. (i) £215 (ii) €517.44 **2.** (i) €60 (ii) $12.75
3. (i) 22 750 kronor (ii) €350 **4.** €156.25 **5.** (i) €28.04
(ii) 42 cent **6.** €1 = 8.34 Chinese yuan **7.** (i) €3200
(ii) €558.14 (iii) €1697.85 **8.** (i) €5429.13
(ii) 19 395 Rand (iii) €400 **9.** (i) €55.92 (ii) €52.70
10. $375.82

Activity 3.2

1. Car A % profit = 4%, Car B % profit = 7%, Car C % loss = 10%, Car D % loss = 7%, Car E % profit = 15% **2.** Waffle iron €43.20, TV €216, Oven €396, Coffee table €199.50, Suite of furniture €1293.75, Bookcase €331.20 **3.** (i) 20% loss (ii) €69 (iii) 2.5% loss **4.** (i) 75% (ii) €200 **5.** €600
6. (i) (a) €200 (b) €250 (c) €310 (d) €350 (ii) €655.20
7. (i) Small €67.50, Medium €100, Large €120 (ii) 35%
8. Leather jacket €120, Skirt €38, Blouse €29, Shoes €60, Jeans €31

Activity 3.3

1. (i) (a) Profit = €2.50 (b) Mark-up = 25% (c) Margin = 20% (ii) (a) Profit = €1.20 (b) Mark-up = 20% (c) Margin = 16.67% (iii) (a) Profit = €18.00 (b) Mark-up = 40% (c) Margin = 28.57% **2.** (i) Cost price = €13.99 (ii) Cost price = €32.49 (iii) Cost price = €60
3. (i) Selling price of shirt = €13.80 (ii) Selling price of jumper = €18 (iii) Selling price of jeans = €63.70 **4.** (i) Selling price = €522.06 (ii) Margin = 15% **5.** (i) Cost price of the television = €521.99 (ii) The mark-up for the television is 72.42%
6. (i) Cost price of the tablet = €249.91 (ii) Mark-up on the tablet = 144% **7.** (i) Profit = €0.86 (ii) Mark-up = 253% (iii) Margin = 72% **8.** (i) Cost price of car = €17,757 (ii) Cost price of car = €16,522 **9.** (i) €11 per kilogram (ii) Mark-up = 275% (iii) Margin = 73%
10. (i) Selling price = €281.40 (ii) Selling price = €318.18
11. (i) Selling price of bike = €97.28 (ii) Selling price of the bike = €105.56 **12.** 16.67% **13.** 37.5%

Activity 3.4

1. (i) €134.07 (ii) €424.35 (iii) €354.24 (iv) €30.75
(v) €82.41 **2.** €193.48 **3.** (i) €1.08 (ii) €2270 (iii) €9.99
4. (i) €420 (ii) €96.60 **5.** (i) €22 (ii) €32.46 (iii) €58
6. (i) €582 (ii) €34 (iii) €65 (iv) €200 (v) €86
7. Table 1: Bill including VAT = €74.12; Table 2: Bill excluding VAT = €142; Table 3: Bill excluding VAT = €186, Bill including VAT = €202.74; Table 4: Bill excluding VAT = €121, Bill including VAT = €131.89; Table 5: Bill excluding VAT = €265, Bill including VAT = €288.85 **8.** 25%

Activity 3.5

1. (i) €787.50 (ii) €158.40 (iii) €218.50 (iv) €434 (v) €1125 **2.** (i) 8% (ii) 5% (iii) 6% (iv) 12% (v) 3% **3.** (i) €9.60 (ii) €6.80 (iii) €13.20 (iv) €3.04 (v) €5.20 **4.** (i) €13.20 (ii) €278.40 **5.** (i) A €0.70, B €0.65, C €0.50 (ii) C (iii) A 12.5%, B 18.75%, C 37.5% **6.** (i) Package A €53, Package B €48, (ii) Package A €35, Package B €23.75 (iii) B **7.** (i) €1.20, €1.10 (ii) 4 kg for €4.40 (iii) €1.40, €1.36 (iv) 6 kg for €8.16 **8.** (i) (A) 52 c, (B) 50 c, (C) 49 c (ii) C **9.** Purple dress **10.** (i) Regular 12, Large 30 (ii) The large box is the better value **11.** A 178 minutes, B 26 texts, C €2.08, D €16.28 **12.** A 947, B €160.99, C €187.63, D €25.33

Activity 3.6

1. (i) €2900 (ii) €25,600 **2.** (i) €7000 (ii) €32,100 **3.** (i) €327.60 (ii) €264.14 (iii) €1185.86 (iv) €14,230.32 **4.** Scenario A: (i) €28,340 (ii) €25,040 (iii) €67,960 Scenario B: (i) €9940 (ii) €6140 (iii) €40,860 Scenario C: (i) €14,680 (ii) €11,380 (iii) €60,620 **5.** Scenario A: (i) €114 (ii) €82.27 (iii) €487.73; Scenario B: (i) €781.68 (ii) €506.68 (iii) €3293.32; Scenario C: (i) €1219.34 (ii) €669.34 (iii) €5320.66 **6.** (i) Income charged at 40% is €3975 (ii) Gross Income = €39,275 **7.** (i) Income charged at 40% is €13,600 (ii) Gross Income = €48,900 **8.** (i) Net Income = €31,900 (ii) Gross Income = €42,316.67 **9.** (i) Tax Credits = €1650 (ii) Gross Income = €43,787.50 (iii) Net Income = €34,982.50 **10.** (i) Net Tax = €20,490 (ii) Net Income = €54,510 (iii) Kathy's new gross income = €79,823.33 **11.** (i) (a) €0 (b) €179.82 (ii) (a) €307.84 (b) €492.27 (iii) (a) €1627.84 (b) €1977.97 (iv) (a) €2747.84 (b) €3832.97 **12.** (i) Gross Tax = €15,080 (ii) Tax Payable = €13,430 (iii) PRSI due = €1561.84 (iv) €1903.72 (v) Total deductions = €16,895.56 (vi) Net Income = €40,454.44 **13.** €52,500

Activity 3.7

1. €16,872.96 **2.** €3080.25 **3.** €103,602 **4.** (i) Value = €6749.18; interest = €749.18 (ii) Value = €10,004.53; interest = €1604.53 (iii) Value = €25,194.24; interest = €5194.24 (iv) Value = €55,903.36; interest = €10,903.36 (v) Value = €119,790; interest = €29,790 (vi) Value = €259,005.80; interest = €59,005.80 **5.** (i) €11,135.25 (ii) €28,121.60 (iii) €25,194.24 (iv) €5304.50 (v) €399.30 (vi) €2,376,200 **6.** €25,027.39 **7.** (i) €1545 (ii) €139.09 (iii) €1002.55 **8.** (i) €2420 (ii) €2320 (iii) €420 (iv) €320 (v) Option B **9.** (i) 4.2% (ii) €4273.94 **10.** (i) €5097.50 (ii) Interest rate 4.5%

Revision Activity 3

1. (a) Selling Price – Cost Price (b) Cost Price – Selling Price (c) $\frac{\text{Profit amount}}{\text{Cost price}} \times 100\%$ (d) $\frac{\text{Loss amount}}{\text{Cost price}} \times 100\%$ **2.** (a) 50% (b) 33.33% (c) 50% **3.** (a) €9.75 (b) 100% **4.** (a) He must repay €6014.44 at the end of year 3 to repay his loan. (b) He would need to repay €3280.50 at the end of year 4 and 5 in order to clear his loan. (c) Total interest paid = €1961 **5.** (a) €12,480 (b) 6%

Exam-style Questions

1. (a) €33,160 (b) €41,200 **2.** (a) (i) 96% (ii) 49% (b) 33%

Chapter 4

Activity 4.1

1. (i) 180° (ii) Angles α and β are known as supplementary angles. **2.** (i) Angles α and β are known as vertically opposite angles. (ii) 180° (iii) 180° **8.** (ii) SSS, SAS and ASA. (iii) (a) ASA (b) SAS (c) SSS **12.** (i) ∠3 and ∠6; ∠4 and ∠5 (ii) These alternate angles are equal. (iii) ∠1 and ∠5; ∠7 and ∠3; ∠2 and ∠6; ∠8 and ∠4 (iv) These corresponding angles are equal. (v) ∠3 and ∠5; ∠4 and ∠6 (vi) 130° = |∠8| = |∠4| = |∠1|; 50° = |7| = |∠6| = |∠2| = |∠3| **16.** (iv) A rotation of 180° about the origin. **17.** A: axial symmetry; B: central symmetry; C: rotation 90 degrees anticlockwise

Activity 4.2

1. (i) $a^2 = b^2 + c^2$ (ii) $q^2 = p^2 + r^2$ (iii) $y^2 = x^2 + z^2$ (iv) $|GK|^2 = |GL|^2 + |KL|^2$ (v) $|MO|^2 = |MN|^2 + |ON|^2$ (vi) $|VU|^2 = |VT|^2 + |TU|^2$ **2.** (i) 5 (ii) 10 (iii) 8 (iv) 5 (v) 71.06 (vi) 159.10 **3.** It is a right-angled triangle **4.** It is not a right-angled triangle **5.** It is a right-angled triangle **6.** (i) $\sqrt{34}$ (ii) $\sqrt{24}$ (iii) $\sqrt{2}$ (iv) 2 **7.** 60 m **8.** It is a right-angled triangle **9.** 49.24 m **10.** 174.64 m **11.** Not a rectangle **12.** (i) 3.46 m, 3.87 m (ii) 41 cm **13.** (i) $p = 5$, $q = 3$ (ii) $p = 15$, $q = 8$ (iii) $p = 24$, $q = 30$ (iv) $q = 70$, $p = 42$ **14.** (i) 75 cm (ii) $\frac{7}{24}$ **15.** $d = 169.2$ m **16.** (i) 27.2 m (iii) 42.1 m **17.** (i) $4\sqrt{2}$ m (ii) $4\sqrt{3}$ m

Activity 4.3

3. (ii) SSS, SAS and RHS **5.** 63.25 m **6.** (i) $a^2 = 2$ (ii) $b^2 = 3$; $c^2 = 4$ (iii) 3

Activity 4.4

1. (ii) $|AC| = 10.9$ cm (approx) **2.** (ii) $|DE| = 5$ cm **5.** (ii) $|RS| = 5.3$ cm (approx)

Activity 4.5

2. (i) 50° **3.** (ii) 55° **4.** (ii) 35° **5.** (ii) 65°

Activity 4.6

1. (ii) $|AC| = |BD| = 10$ cm (iii) Yes, the diagonals are equal (iv) No **2.** (ii) $|PR| = |QS| = 13$ cm (iii) Yes, they are equal (iv) The diagonals are not perpendicular **3.** (ii) $|EG| = |FH| =$ 9.5 cm (approx) **4.** (ii) $|PR| = |QS| = 8.6$ cm (approx) (iii) The diagonals are not perpendicular **5.** (ii) $|AC| = |BD| =$ 7.1 cm (approx) (iii) The diagonals are perpendicular **7.** (ii) $|MP| = |PR| = 9.4$ cm (approx) (iii) Yes (iv) The diagonals are longer than the sides **8.** (ii) $|AC| = |BD| = 10.4$ cm (approx) (iii) The diagonals are longer than the sides **9.** (ii) $|PR| = |QS| =$ 7.8 cm (approx) (iii) The diagonals are longer than the sides

Revision Activity 4

1. 17 m **2.** (b) This is a right-angled triangle **3.** (a) (i) Never true (ii) Sometimes true (iii) Always true (iv) Always true (v) Sometimes true **4.** (b) 364 mm **5.** (a) $|a| = 3$ cm, $|b| = 4$ cm, $|c| = 5$ cm (c) 6 cm²

Exam-style Question

1. (a) $a = 16$; $b = 30$; $c = 34$

Chapter 5

Activity 5.1

1. $x = 3$ **2.** $y = 2$ **3.** $a = -5$ **4.** $x = 6$ **5.** $g = -5$ **6.** $h = 4$ **7.** $t = -12$ **8.** $z = 10$ **9.** $x = 2$ **10.** $x = 14$ **11.** $w = -29$ **12.** $y = 25$ **13.** $s = -3$ **14.** $b = 9$ **15.** $l = 1$ **16.** $m = -2$ **17.** $x = \frac{18}{5}$ **18.** $p = -33$ **19.** $q = 15$ **20.** $n = -2$

Activity 5.2

1. $h = 9$ **2.** $d = -8$ **3.** $n = 98$ **4.** $y = -25$ **5.** $m = \frac{72}{21} = \frac{24}{7}$ **6.** $x = \frac{9}{2}$ **7.** $c = -\frac{27}{2}$ **8.** $p = 40$ **9.** $v = \frac{28}{3}$ **10.** $z = \frac{108}{7}$ **11.** $x = \frac{23}{6}$ **12.** $h = \frac{7}{25}$ **13.** $m = \frac{29}{6}$ **14.** $d = \frac{39}{24} = \frac{13}{8}$ **15.** $k = -\frac{14}{99}$ **16.** $m = \frac{3}{7}$ **17.** $l = \frac{7}{16}$ **18.** $t = \frac{3}{2}$ **19.** $a = \frac{113}{40}$ **20.** $d = -\frac{6}{53}$ **21.** $b = -\frac{21}{4}$ **22.** $g = -\frac{3}{4}$ **23.** $f = \frac{11}{21}$ **24.** $c = \frac{101}{51}$ **25.** $k = -\frac{61}{29}$

Activity 5.3

1. (i) 12 (ii) 24 (iii) 27 (iv) 30 (v) 7 (vi) 15 **2.** The first number = 41, the second number = 42, the third number = 43 **3.** $k = 3$, the lengths of each side are: 3 cm, 4 cm, 5 cm **4.** Josh ran 4 km, Jack ran 8 km **5.** Sean gets €10, Sarah gets €15 **6.** Shoes cost: €55, trousers cost: €40 **7.** 96 and 98 **8.** The second side is 29 m, the third side is 58 m **9.** Harry is 60 years old **10.** 12 and 13 **11.** (i) $2(5x + 1) = 32$ (ii) $x = 3$ (iii) 11 units (iv) 5 units (iv) 55 units^2
12. (i) $x + \frac{x}{5} = 48$ (ii) $x = 40$ (iii) 40 years old (iv) 8 years old
13. (i) $5x + 2x = 210$ (ii) $x = 30$ (iii) €150 (iv) €60
14. (i) $3x(0.69) + x(1.50) = 7.14$ (ii) $x = \frac{7.14}{3.57} = 2$ (iv) 2 (v) 6
15. (ii) $A + (2A - 30) = 180$ (iii) $A = 70$ (iv) 70° (v) 110°

Activity 5.4

2. (iii) $x = \{1, 2\}$, for $x < 3, x \in \mathbb{N}$, $x = \{1, 2, 3\}$, for $x \leq 3, x \in \mathbb{N}$
5. (i) $x \geq 2, x \in \mathbb{N}$ (ii) $x \geq 1, x \in \mathbb{N}$ (iii) $x \leq 0, x \in \mathbb{Z}$ (iv) $x > 0, x \in \mathbb{Z}$ (v) $x > 5, x \in \mathbb{R}$ (vi) $x < 1, x \in \mathbb{R}$ **6.** (i) $x < 4$ (v) $x = \{1, 2, 3\}, x \in \mathbb{N}$ **7.** (i) $l \geq 2$ **8.** (i) $n > 3$ **9.** (i) $f \leq 3$ (v) $f = \{1, 2, 3\}, f \in \mathbb{N}$ **10.** (i) $x > 2$ **11.** (i) $t \geq 19$
12. (i) $p \leq \frac{19}{8}$ (v) {1, 2} **13.** (i) $q \leq \frac{24}{11}$

Revision Activity 5

1. (a) (i) $c = 3$ (ii) $m = 2$ (iii) $y = 8$ (iv) $x = -\frac{37}{9}$ (b) Smaller number = 7, larger number = 21 **2.** (a) The first number = x, the second number = $x + 1$ (b) $x - \frac{2}{3}(x + 1) = 34$ (c) $x = 104$ (d) The first number = 104, the second number = 105
4. (a) $5x - 2(20 - x) = 51$ (b) $x = 13$ (c) 13 (d) 7
5. (a) $2 + 1.1x = 20.70$ (b) 17 km (e) €38.30
6. (a) $46x - 18.50 = 234.50$ (b) 5.5 hours (c) €326.50 (d) €1609.50 **7.** (b) $\frac{x}{2}(5) + \frac{3x}{5}(10) + x(20) = 2280$ (c) $x = 80$ (d) Number of €20 notes = 80, number of €10 notes = 48, number of €5 notes = 40 **8.** (a) $\frac{3x}{4}$ (b) $\frac{x}{2}$ (c) $\frac{x}{2} = 432$ (d) $x = 864$ (e) 216 (f) 864 **9.** 9 cars; 28 students

Exam-style Questions

1. (a) $2n = 14$; $2n + 1 = 15$ (b)(ii) $x = 42$ **2.** $x = 2$

Chapter 6

Activity 6.1

1. (i) 21 cm^2 (ii) 13.5 cm^2 (iii) 12.5 cm^2 (iv) 21 m^2
2. (i) Area = 6 cm^2, Perimeter = 12 cm (ii) Area = 12 cm^2, Perimeter = 16 cm (iii) Area = 70 cm^2, Perimeter = 42 cm
3. (i) 12 cm^2 (ii) 25 cm^2 (iii) 14 cm^2 **4.** (i) 16 cm^2 (ii) 12 cm^2 (iii) 12 cm^2 (iv) 35 cm^2 (v) 150 cm^2 **5.** (i) 52 cm^2 (ii) 144 cm^2 (iii) 103 cm^2 **6.** (i) $h = 10$ cm (ii) $b = 16$ m (iii) $h = 44$ m **7.** (i) 252 cm^2 (ii) 300 cm^2 **8.** (i) 72 cm^2 (ii) 36 cm^2 (iii) 21 cm^2 (iv) 32 cm^2 **9.** (i) Area of tiles = 24 m^2, Area of timber = 16 m^2 (ii) 96 (iii) 10 (iv) €150 (v) 20 (vi) €50 (vii) €200 **10.** (i) 26 m^2 (ii) 34 m^2 (iii) 0.25 m^2 (iv) 104 (v) (a) 11 (b) €385

Activity 6.2

1. (i) 48 cm^2 (ii) 60 cm^2 (iii) 120 cm^2 **2.** (i) $9\sqrt{3}$ units^2 (ii) $25\sqrt{3}$ units^2 (iii) $36\sqrt{3}$ units^2 **3.** (i) 6 units^2 (ii) 60 units^2 (iii) 630 units^2 **4.** (a) (i) 60 cm^2 (ii) 40 cm (b) (i) 420 cm^2 (ii) 100 cm (c) (i) 21 cm^2 (ii) 21 cm (d) (i) 24 cm^2 (ii) 33 cm

Activity 6.3

1. (i) Circumference = 18.84 cm; Area = 28.26 cm^2
(ii) Circumference = 43.96 cm; Area = 153.86 cm^2
(iii) Circumference = 37.68 cm; Area = 113.04 cm^2
(iv) Circumference = 31.4 cm; Area = 78.5 cm^2
(v) Circumference = 69.08 cm; Area = 379.94 cm^2
(vi) Circumference = 12.56 m; Area = 12.56 m^2
2. (i) Circumference = 50.27 cm; Area = 201.06 cm^2
(ii) Circumference = 56.55 cm; Area = 254.47 cm^2
(iii) Circumference = 81.68 cm; Area = 530.93 cm^2
(iv) Circumference = 25.13 cm; Area = 50.27 cm^2
3. (i) Area = 154 cm^2; Circumference = 44 cm
(ii) Area = 1386 cm^2; Circumference = 132 cm
4. (i) Circumference = 10π cm; Area = 25π cm^2
(ii) Circumference = 16π cm; Area = 64π cm^2
(iii) Circumference = 7π m; Area = 12.25π m^2
(iv) Circumference = 130π mm; Area = 4225π mm^2 **5.** (i) 8 cm (ii) 14 cm (iii) 2.5 m (iv) 10 cm **6.** (i) 10 cm (ii) 6 cm (iii) 15 cm (iv) 3 cm **7.** 12 000 **8.** (i) 98 cm (ii) 1760 cm **9.** (i) 1740.63 cm^2 (ii) 16 448 cm^2 (iii) 0.97 m^2 (iv) 25 317 cm^2 **10.** (i) 25.71 cm^2 (ii) 168 cm^2 (iii) 112 cm^2 **11.** 103.74 cm^2 **12.** (i) 400 m (ii) 25 **13.** (i) 85.84 cm^2 (ii) 78.54% **14.** (i) 28 cm (ii) 176 cm (iii) 440 m **15.** (i) 360 m^2 (ii) 36 m^2 (iii) 102 m^2 (iv) 197 m^2 (v) 45%

Activity 6.4

1. (i) 192 m^3 (ii) 616 m^3 (iii) 2156 mm^3 (iv) 216 cm^3 (v) 600 000 mm^3 **2.** (i) 8 litres (ii) 4.5 litres (iii) 3.36 litres (iv) 17 litres **3.** (i) 4 cm (ii) 15 cm (iii) 2 cm **4.** (i) 8 cm (ii) 13 cm (iii) 1.5 m (iv) 100 cm **5.** 240 **6.** (i) 1350 litres (ii) 30 litres (iii) 45 **7.** (i) 336 cm^2 (ii) 576 cm^3 (iii) 20 sheets **8.** (i) 22.5 m^3 (ii) 0.03 m^3 (iii) 750 (iv) 4 **9.** (i) 320 m^2 (ii) 1280

Activity 6.5

1. (i) 900 cm^2 (ii) 1800 cm^3 (iii) 1.8 litres **2.** B, D
3. (i) Volume = 231; Total surface area = 227
(ii) Volume = 1012.5; Total surface area = 612
(iii) Volume = 336 000; Total surface area = 29 200
(iv) Volume = 3.456; Total surface area = 13.92
(v) Volume = 0.25; Total surface area = 2.417 (vi) Width = 16; Total surface area = 1534 (vii) Length = 4.6; Total surface area = 124.08 (viii) Height = 8; Total surface area = 544 (ix) Width = 28.5; Volume = 14 820; (x) Length = 33.5; Volume = 8858.07 **4.** (i) 58.34 litres (ii) 14.73 litres (iii) 4032 litres (iv) 174.72 litres **5.** (i) (a) 83.14 cm^3 (b) 157.86 cm^2 (ii) (a) 25 200 cm^3 (b) 12 060 cm^2 (iii) (a) 1092 cm^3 (b) 896 cm^2 **6.** (i) (a) 5040 cm^3 (b) 2436 cm^2 (ii) (a) 210.44 m^3 (b) 394.15 m^2 (iii) (a) 436 800 cm^3 (b) 37 960 cm^2 **8.** E is opposite A, C is opposite H, B is opposite G, D is opposite F **10.** D **11.** A, B, D **12.** (ii) 1980 cm^3 (iii)396 cm^3 (iv) 11 cm **13.** (i) 1136 m^3 (ii) 76 trips

Activity 6.6

1. (i) 1177.5 cm^3 (ii) 62.8 cm^3 **2.** (i) 1 (ii) 5 **3.** (i) 16 cm (ii) 12 cm (iii) 12 cm **4.** (i) 2 cm (ii) 6 cm (iii) 4 cm
5. Barry is correct **6.** (i) Volume = 75.36 cm^2; Total surface area = 100.48 cm^2
(ii) Volume = 125π m^3; Total surface area = 100π m^2
(iii) Volume = 38 808 cm^2; Total surface area = 6468 cm^2
(iv) Radius = 9.5 cm; Total surface area = 985.29 cm^2
(v) Height = 13.5 m; Volume = 952.56π m^3 (vi) Radius = 4.5 m; Total surface area = 166.73 m^2 (vii) Height = 5.42 cm; Volume = 15 316.92 cm^3 (viii) Height = 24 mm; Total surface area = 11880π mm^2 (ix) Height = 10 cm; Volume = 1540 cm^3 (x) Height = 55 cm; Total surface area = 17 483.52 cm^2 (xi) Height = 9 cm; Volume = 854.87 cm^3 (xii) Height = 0.29 cm; Total surface area = 7756.74 cm^2
7. 54 glasses **9.** (i) 125.7 cm^2 (ii) 157.08 cm^3 (iii) Length = 15 cm, Width = 5 cm Height = 8 cm
10. (i) 14 : 75 (ii) 21 : 64 (iii) 1 : 4 (iv) 2057 : 2925
11. (i) 3322.23 litres (ii) He can wrap the new tank with 2 layers of insulation. **12.** $r = 2$ **13.** (i) D (ii) 117.1 cm^2
14. (i) 30 cm (ii) 31 500 cm^3 (3.15 L) (iii) 44.6 cm

Activity 6.7

1. (i) Volume = 1436.027 m^3; Curved surface area = 615.44 m^2
(ii) Radius = 1.435 cm; Volume = 12.383 cm^3

(iii) Radius = 5.524 m; Volume = 705.715 m^3
(iv) Volume = 179.594 cm^3; Curved surface area = 153.938 cm^2
(v) Volume = 14 137.167 cm^3; Curved surface area = 2827.433 cm^2
(vi) Radius = 17.171 cm; Curved surface area = 3706.601 cm^2
2. (i) 56.55 cm^3 (ii) h = 8 cm to the nearest cm (iii) 11 cm
3. (i) 24 806.02 cm^2 (ii) 0.30 m^3 **4.** (i) 110 592 cm^3 (ii) 24 cm
(iii) The sculptor will not meet the requirement.
(iv) 71 623.34 cm^3 **5.** (i) $280\pi\ cm^2$ (ii) $476\pi\ cm^2$
6. (i) $121.5\pi\ cm^3$ (ii) $182.25\pi\ cm^3$ **7.** (i) 6 cm (ii) 658.19 cm^3
(iii) 23.82% **8.** 24 **9.** 2.2 cm **10.** 1 cm

Revision Activity 6

1. (a) 126 m^2 (b) €106 **2.** (a) 54 643.73 cm^3
(b) 10661.25 cm^2 **3.** D is opposite F, C is opposite H, B is opposite G, A is opposite E **4.** 1.22 cm **5.** (a) 24 cm
(b) 3888 cm^2 (c) 216 boxes (d) 72 balls **6.** 160 litres

Exam-style Questions

1. (a) 13 m (b) 30 m^2 (c) 169 m^2 (d) 507 flagstones
2. (a) 1 : 4 (b) 1 : 8 **3.** 2 cm

Chapter 7

Activity 7.1

1. (ii) [AR] and [PQ], [AP] and [QR] (iii) $\angle PAR$ and $\angle PQR$, $\angle APQ$ and $\angle ARQ$ (iv) [PR] and [AQ] (v) $\Delta APR + \Delta PRQ$, $\Delta APQ + \Delta AQR$ (vi) 180° (vii) 360° **2.** (ii) [SV] and [TU], [TS] and [UV] (iii) $\angle TSV$ and $\angle TUV$, $\angle UTS$ and $\angle SVU$
(iv) [TV] and [SU] (vi) 360° **3.** (iii) 540° **4.** 720°
5. (i) 60° (ii) 70° (iii) 110° (iv) 85° **6.** (i) 100° (ii) 100°
(iii) A = 20°, B = 40°, C = 60° (iv) 1 = 2 = 3 = 4 = 120°
7. (i) β = 110°, α = 70° (ii) 70° (iii) 100° (iv) 45°
8. (i) y = 100°, x = 80°, z = 110° (ii) y = 40°, x = 20°, z = 60°
(iii) 108° (iv) 120°

Activity 7.2

1. (i) $|PS| = |QR|$ and $|PQ| = |SR|$ (ii) $|\angle QPS| = |\angle QRS|$, $|\angle PSR| = |\angle PQR|$ **2.** (i) 3 cm (ii) 7 cm (iii) 63°
(iv) $|\angle BAD| = |\angle BCD|$ = 117° (v) 180° **3.** (i) $|EF|$ = 6 cm, $|FG|$ = 8 cm (ii) $|\angle F|$ = 108°, $|\angle E| = |\angle G|$ = 72° (iii) 180°
4. (i) B = 50°, $A = C$ =130°, D = 50°, G = 50°, $E = F$ = 130° (ii) 180°
5. (i) 180° (ii) alternate angles (iii) 180° (iv) 180°
6. (i) α = 108°; β = 45°; γ = 45° (ii) β = 63°; α = 63°; γ = 117°
(iii) β = 50°; γ = 50°; α = 80° (iv) α = 108°; γ = 108°; β = 108°
7. x = 22°; y = 10° **8.** (i) $|TU|$ (ii) $|TM| = |MU| = |VU|$
(iii) STM and MUV (iv) $|\angle 1| = |\angle 4|$ (alternate angles); $|\angle 8| = |\angle 5|$ (alternate angles); $|\angle 2| = |\angle 4|$ (equal angles of isosceles triangle); $|\angle 7| = |\angle 5|$ (equal angles of isosceles triangle) **10.** 145° **12.** (ii) I know that the triangles LPR and MNR are congruent, so I also know that $|LR| = |RN|$ and $|PR| = |RM|$. Therefore the diagonals of a parallelogram bisect each other.

Activity 7.3

1. (i) 60° (ii) 120° (iii) $|DC|$ = 7 and $|AD|$ = 5 **2.** (i) 50°
(ii) 50° (iii) 130° **3.** (i) 70° (ii) 45° (iii) 25° **4.** (i) 4
(ii) 3 (iii) 8 (iv) 8 **5.** (i) 9 (ii) 7 (iii) 5 (iv) 3.2
6. (i) (a) true (b) false (c) false (d) true (ii) $\angle DAP$ and $\angle PCB$, $\angle ADP$ and $\angle PBC$, $\angle BAC$ and $\angle ACD$, $\angle ABD$ and $\angle BDC$
(iii) ABP and PDC **7.** (i) 5 (ii) 5 (iii) 6
8. (i) $|BC| = |AD| = |DG| = |EF|$ (ii) $|\angle EFG| = |\angle EDG| = |\angle ADC| = |\angle ABC|$ (iii) $|\angle EDF| = |\angle DFG| = |\angle BDC| = |\angle ABD|$
(iv) $|NF| = |DN| = |MD| = |BM|$ **9.** (i) $|\angle BAC| = |\angle ACE| = |\angle CED|$
(ii) 5 **10.** 65°

Revision Activity 7

7. α = 23.5; β = 83.5; γ = 23.5 **8.** (b) 120° anti-clockwise or 240° clockwise. (c) 180° rotation about O. Axial symmetry about [FC]. **9.** (i) (a) 180° (b) 2 (ii) (a) 360° (b) 4
(iii) (d) $N = -4 + 2x$ where x is the number of sides in the polygon and N is the sum of the angles in terms of right-angles.

Exam-style Question

1. Reason 2: $|QT| = |ST|$ **Reason 3:** angles opposite equal sides in an isosceles triangle are equal **Statement 4:** $|QK| = |SK|$
Reason 5: SAS (Side Angle Side)

Chapter 8

Activity 8.1

1. Either $a = 0$ or $b = 0$ **2.** (i) $x = 4$ or $x = -3$
(ii) $x = -7$ or $x = 3$ (iii) $x = 0$ or $x = 7$ (iv) $x = 5$ or $x = -5$
3. $x = -3$ or $x = 2$ **4.** $x = -7$ or $x = -1$
5. $x = -3$ or $x = -1$ **6.** $x = 5$ or $x = 1$ **7.** $x = 6$ or $x = -3$
8. $x = \frac{3}{2}$ or $x = -\frac{3}{2}$ **9.** $x = \frac{13}{15}$ or $x = -\frac{13}{15}$ **10.** $x = 0$ or $x = 2$
11. $x = 4$ or $x = -3$ **12.** $x = 0$ or $x = \frac{1}{5}$ **13.** $x = \frac{5}{2}$ or $x = -\frac{5}{2}$
14. $x = \frac{7}{3}$ or $x = -\frac{7}{3}$ **15.** $x = 0$ or $x = 2$ **16.** $x = 0$ or $x = \frac{1}{7}$
17. $x = -1$ or $x = -\frac{1}{5}$ **18.** $x = -\frac{3}{7}$ or $x = -1$ **19.** $x = -\frac{1}{9}$ or $x = -1$
20. $x = -\frac{4}{11}$ or $x = -1$ **21.** (i) $x = -7$ or $x = 2$ (ii) $k = -5$ or $k = 4$
22. (i) $x = \frac{1}{3}$ or $x = -2$ (ii) $m = \frac{10}{3}$ or $m = 1$ **23.** (i) $p = -5$ or $p = \frac{1}{3}$ (ii) $a = -6$ or $a = -\frac{2}{3}$ **24.** $x = \frac{1}{13}$ or $x = 5$
25. $x = \frac{2}{3}$ or $x = 1$ **26.** $x = \frac{3}{4}$ or $x = 1$ **27.** $x = \frac{2}{3}$ or $x = \frac{1}{2}$
28. $x = \frac{2}{5}$ or $x = -\frac{3}{2}$ **29.** $x = -\frac{4}{3}$ or $x = \frac{1}{3}$
30. $x = \frac{5}{8}$ or $x = -1$ **31.** $x = \frac{3}{13}$ or $x = -1$
32. $x = \frac{1}{4}$ or $x = -2$ **33.** $x = -\frac{1}{2}$ or $x = 4$ **34.** $x = 3$ or $x = -1$

Activity 8.2

1. $x^2 - 2x - 3 = 0$ **2.** $x^2 + x - 6 = 0$ **3.** $x^2 - 7x - 18 = 0$
4. $x^2 + 9x + 20 = 0$ **5.** $x^2 - 13x + 42 = 0$ **6.** $x^2 + x - 12 = 0$
7. $x^2 - 8x - 33 = 0$ **8.** $x^2 - 2x - 80 = 0$ **9.** $x^2 + 2x - 8 = 0$
10. $x^2 + 2x - 15 = 0$ **11.** $a = 1$, $b = -14$ and $c = 45$
12. $a = 1$, $b = 10$ and $c = -24$ **13.** $a = 1$, $b = 8$ and $c = 7$
14. 9 **15.** $c = 81$

Activity 8.3

1. (i) $x = -\frac{3}{2}$ or $x = \frac{1}{2}$ (ii) $x = \frac{1}{2}$, $x = -\frac{3}{2}$ **2.** (i) $x = \frac{5}{2}$, $x = -1$
(ii) $x = \frac{5}{2}$, $x = -1$ **3.** $x = 0.851$, $x = -2.351$ **4.** $x = -0.55$, $x = -5.45$ **5.** $x = 4.45$, $x = -0.45$ **6.** $n = 0.36$, $n = -2.11$
7. $x = 2 \pm \sqrt{7}$ **8.** (i) $x = 1 \pm \sqrt{3}$ (ii) $x = 2 \pm \sqrt{3}$ (iii) $x = 2 \pm \sqrt{5}$
9. $t = -1 \pm \sqrt{8}$ **10.** $p = \frac{5 + \sqrt{33}}{2}$, $p = \frac{5 - \sqrt{33}}{2}$ **11.** 3.4 or 0.6
12. (i) $x = 3 \pm \sqrt{5}$ (ii) $k = \sqrt{5}$, $k = -\sqrt{5}$ **13.** (i) $x = 2 \pm \sqrt{2}$
(ii) $p = 6 + \sqrt{2}$, $p = 6 - \sqrt{2}$

Activity 8.4

1. $x = -7$ or $x = 3$ **2.** $x = -12$ or $x = 1$ **3.** $x = \frac{3}{2}$ or $x = 6$
4. $x = -\frac{1}{2}$ or $x = 4$ **5.** $x = \frac{3}{2}$ or $x = -2$ **6.** $x = \frac{-7 \pm \sqrt{273}}{8}$
7. $2 \pm \sqrt{2}$ **8.** $x = \frac{5 \pm \sqrt{769}}{12}$ **9.** $x = \frac{2}{3}$, $x = -\frac{7}{2}$
10. $x = \frac{-3 \pm \sqrt{321}}{52}$

Activity 8.5

1. (ii) $x = 15$ (iii) 15 and 17 **2.** (ii) $x = -24$ or $x = 22$
(iii) −24 and −22; 22 and 24 **3.** (ii) $L^2 + L - 20 = 0$
(iii) L = 4 m (iv) 4 m, 2.5 m **4.** (i) $2x^2 - x - 6 = 0$ (ii) $x = 2$
(iii) Base = 2 m Perpendicular Height = 1.5 m (iv) 1.5 m^2
5. (i) $2x^2 + 31x - 33 = 0$ (ii) $x = 1$ (iii) 1 m **6.** (ii) $4x^2 + 7x - 4 = 0$
(iii) $x = 0.4537$ (iv) Width of border = 0.45 m
7. (ii) $x^2 - 2x - 15 = 0$ (iii) $x = 5$ (iv) 5 cm, 12 cm, 13 cm
8. (ii) 15 cm **9.** (ii) 7 m

Revision Activity 8

1. (a) $x = 0$ or $x = 16$ (b) $x = 0$ or $x = 9$ (c) $x = 0$ or $x = 32$ (d) $x = 0$ or $x = \frac{1}{2}$ (e) $x = \frac{7}{11}$ or $x = -\frac{7}{11}$ (f) $x = 6$ or $x = -6$ (g) $x = \frac{8}{9}$ or $x = -\frac{8}{9}$ (h) $x = \frac{14}{13}$ or $x = -\frac{14}{13}$ (i) $x = 5$ (j) $x = 9$ or $x = 4$ (k) $x = 7$ or $x = -2$ (l) $x = -8$ or $x = 7$ **2.** (a) $x = \frac{5}{2}$ or $x = -3$ (b) $x = \frac{2}{3}$ or $x = 3$ (c) $x = -\frac{2}{3}$ or $x = -\frac{1}{2}$ (d) $x = -\frac{7}{4}$ or $x = -1$ (e) $x = \frac{4}{3}$ or $x = -\frac{1}{3}$ (f) $x = -\frac{2}{5}$ or $x = \frac{11}{2}$ (g) $x = -\frac{7}{2}$ or $x = \frac{1}{7}$ (h) $x = \frac{3}{7}$ or $x = -\frac{1}{5}$ **3.** $c = 49$ **4.** $y = 12$ or $y = -2$ **5.** (a) $x^2 - 4x - 12 = 0$ (b) $x = 6$ or $x = -2$ (c) -2 or 6 **6.** (a) $4x^2 + 60x - 99 = 0$ (b) $x = \frac{3}{2}$ (c) 1.5 m

Exam-style Questions

1. $x = -\frac{14}{3}$ or $x = 1$ **2.** (a) $x = 6$ or $x = -1$ (b) $x = \frac{1}{4}$ or $x = \frac{3}{2}$ (c) $x = \frac{-16}{-8} = 2$ (d) $x = 4.21$ or $x = -0.71$

Chapter 9

Activity 9.1

4. (ii) $|AC| = 6, |BC| = 3$ (iii) $\sqrt{45}$ units (iv) $\sqrt{45}$ units **5.** (a) $\sqrt{41}$ units (b) $\sqrt{40}$ units (c) $\sqrt{53}$ units (d) $\sqrt{13}$ units (e) $\sqrt{58}$ units (f) $\sqrt{17}$ units **9.** (iii) $|AB| = |A'B'| = \sqrt{13}$ units

Activity 9.2

1. (i) $(4, 4)$ (ii) $\left(0, 3\frac{1}{2}\right)$ (iii) $\left(2\frac{1}{2}, -1\right)$ (iv) $(0, 0)$ (v) $(4, -1)$ (vi) $\left(5, \frac{1}{2}\right)$ **2.** (i) $(0, 0)$ **3.** (ii) $E(2, 4)$, $F(-1, -2)$ (iv) $\left(\frac{1}{2}, 1\right)$ **4.** (i) $(0, 1)$ (ii) $(0, 0)$ **6.** (i) $P(1, -1)$ **7.** (i) 8.2 km (ii) 7.2 km (iii) $(5, 10)$ (iv) 14.4 km **8.** (v) The mid-point between two points = (average of the x coordinates, average of the y coordinates) **9.** (ii) $\sqrt{58}$ units (iii) $\left(1\frac{1}{2}, 4\frac{1}{2}\right)$ (iv) $\sqrt{14.5}$ units

Activity 9.3

1. $a = -\frac{3}{4}$, $b = -\frac{6}{2} = -3$, $c = \frac{4}{2} = 2$, $d = \frac{3}{3} = 1$, $e = -\frac{2}{5}$ **2.** (i) $\frac{2}{5}$ (ii) $\frac{1}{2}$ (iii) -2 (iv) $-\frac{6}{5}$ (v) $-\frac{5}{2}$ (vi) $-\frac{4}{11}$ (vii) $-\frac{5}{4}$ (viii) $\frac{1}{3}$ **4.** Slope $AB = -\frac{1}{2}$, Slope $DC = -\frac{1}{2}$, Slope $AD = 3$, Slope $BC = 3$ **6.** (ii) -1 **10.** (i) $\frac{1}{10}$

Activity 9.4

1. $y = 2x + 4$ **2.** $y = \frac{1}{2}x - 3$ **3.** $y = 2x - 1$ **4.** $y = -\frac{1}{3}x + 5$ **5.** $y = -\frac{1}{2}x + 2$ **6.** (i) $y = -x + 5$ (ii) $y = -2x + 3$ (iii) $y = -2x - 3$ (iv) $y = \frac{1}{2}x - 2$ (v) $y = -\frac{1}{3}x + 6$ (vi) $y = 4x - 2$ (vii) $y = 5x + 50$ (viii) $y = 2x + 30$

7. (i) slope = 4, y-intercept = $(0, 3)$ (ii) slope = -2, y-intercept = $(0, -1)$ (iii) slope = -1, y-intercept = $(0, 10)$ (iv) slope = 0.5, y-intercept = $(0, 5)$ (v) slope = -4, y-intercept = $(0, -7)$ (vi) slope = 10, y-intercept = $(0, -100)$ **8.** Lines 1 and 3 are parallel because they both have slope = 2. **9.** r, n, s, p resp. **10.** (i) Lines 1 and 4 (ii) Lines 2 and 5 (iii) Line 5 (iv) $x = -5$, $y = -15$

Activity 9.5

1. (i) $y - 2 = 2(x - 1)$ (ii) $y - 2 = -3(x - 4)$ (iii) $y - 1 = 1(x - 3)$ (iv) $y = -2(x - 1)$ (v) $y - 2 = 4(x + 1)$ (vi) $y + 2 = -5(x - 1)$ (vii) $y - 8 = 3(x + 1)$ (viii) $y + 6 = -1(x + 1)$ **2.** (i) $y + 2 = \frac{1}{2}(x - 1)$ (ii) $y - 2 = -\frac{1}{3}(x + 4)$ (iii) $y - 1 = 0(x + 3) \Rightarrow y = 1$ (iv) $y = \frac{4}{3}(x - 1)$ (v) $y + 2 = \frac{4}{5}(x - 1)$ (vi) $y + 2 = -\frac{2}{5}(x - 1)$ (vii) $y - 8 = 3(x + 1)$ (viii) $y + 6 = -4(x - 1)$ **3.** $y - 0 = -\frac{2}{3}(x - 0)$ [or $y + 2 = -\frac{2}{3}(x - 3)$] **4.** $y + 4 = \frac{1}{3}(x + 4)$ **5.** (i) $y = -2x + 10$ (ii) $E(3, 5)$, $F(-4, 7)$ **6.** $y = \frac{3}{5}x$ **7.** (i) $y = \frac{3}{2}(x - 3)$ (ii) $y - 3 = 5(x - 5)$ (iii) $y - 6 = \frac{3}{2}(x - 6)$

Activity 9.6

1. (a) $m = -1$ (b) $m = -2$ (c) $m = 3$ (d) $m = -4$ **2.** (a) $m = 3$ (b) $m = \frac{1}{2}$ (c) $m = -\frac{1}{3}$ **3.** $A(4, 0)$, $C(2, 3)$, $D(6, -3)$ **4.** $A(4, 8)$, $C(3, 4)$, $D(2, 0)$ **5.** (ii) This is a horizontal line. The slope of the line is zero. (iii) $y = 3$ is the equation of the line **6.** (ii) This is a vertical line (iv) $x = 2$ for all points

Activity 9.7

1. (i) $y = -\frac{2}{3}x - 2$ (ii) $-\frac{2}{3}$ **2.** (i) Slope = 3 (ii) Slope = $\frac{1}{2}$ (iii) Slope = -2 (iv) Slope = $\frac{3}{2}$ (v) Slope = $\frac{1}{4}$ (vi) Slope = 0 (vii) Slope = $\frac{2}{7}$ (viii) Slope is undefined (ix) Slope = $\frac{1}{2}$ (x) Slope = -3 **6.** (i) (c) (ii) (a) (iii) (b) (iv) (a) (v) (a) (vi) (b) (vii) (c) **7.** (i) The equation of line p is $y = 4$, the equation of line q is $y = 3$, the equation of line r is $y = 2$, the equation of line n is $x = 3$ (ii) $A(3, 4)$, $B(3, 3)$, $C(3, 2)$ **9.** (i) $\frac{5}{2}$ (ii) $5y + 2x - 21 = 0$ **10.** $3x - 2y - 17 = 0$ **11.** (i) -4 (ii) $x - 4y + 9 = 0$ **12.** $x - 3y - 1 = 0$ **13.** $2x + 3y - 10 = 0$

Revision Activity 9

1. (b) $B(3, 0)$ (c) -1 (d) $y = -x + 3$ (e) -1 (f) $x + y + 2 = 0$ (g) $ABCD$ is a parallelogram **2.** (a) $\sqrt{98}$ units (b) $\left(-\frac{1}{2}, \frac{3}{2}\right)$ (c) -1 (d) $x + y - 1 = 0$ **3.** (a) $2x - 3y = 9$ **4.** (a) $\frac{3}{2}$ (b) $2x + 3y + 7 = 0$ **5.** (b) $3x - y - 12 = 0$ and $3x + 5y - 3 = 0$ (c) $\left(\frac{7}{2}, -\frac{3}{2}\right)$ **6.** (a) $-\frac{3}{2}$ (b) $2x - 3y = 14$ **7.** (a) The equation of First Street is $y = 1$, The equation of Second Street is $y = 2$. (b) The equation of Fifth Avenue is $x = 5$ (c) $3x + 2y = 12$ **8.** (c) 15.81 km (d) $3y = x$ (g) 9.487 km (h) The ship is travelling in a direction East 18.43° North

Exam-style Question

1. (a) r, t, q, $y = 2x - 3$

Chapter 10

Activity 10.1

1. $m = -2$, $n = -8$ **2.** $s = 1$, $t = 4$ **3.** $c = 2$, $d = -5$ **4.** $p = 2$, $q = 3$ **5.** $f = 3$, $g = -6$ **6.** $w = 6$, $z = -11$ **7.** $x = 1$, $y = -3$ **8.** $m = 1$, $n = -1$ **9.** $g = -2$, $h = 3$ **10.** $p = 4$, $q = -2$ **11.** $v = 1$, $w = 2$ **12.** $x = 3$, $y = 2$ **13.** $b = 9$, $c = 7$ **14.** $d = 10$, $c = 1$ **15.** $p = 5$, $q = 8$ **16.** $v = 11$, $w = -3$ **17.** $x = -11$, $y = -5$ **18.** $a = 3$, $b = -\frac{1}{2}$ **19.** $f = 7$, $g = \frac{2}{5}$ **20.** $m = \frac{1}{5}$, $n = 4$ **21.** $s = \frac{2}{3}$, $t = -2$ **22.** $c = -3$, $h = 8$ **23.** $l = 11$, $m = \frac{1}{7}$ **24.** $r = \frac{2}{3}$, $s = -5$ **25.** $x = -1$, $y = -\frac{3}{2}$

Activity 10.2

1. $x = 2\frac{1}{2}, y = -1\frac{1}{2}$ **2.** $x = -6, y = -9$ **3.** (ii) (4, –5) (iii) (4, –5) **4.** (ii) (2, 0) (iii) (2, 0) (iv) perpendicular lines **5.** (4, 2) **6.** (3, 2) **7.** $\left(4\frac{1}{2}, 4\frac{1}{2}\right)$ **8.** (–4, 4) **9.** (3, –1)

Activity 10.3

1. Numbers are 22 and 30. **2.** Son's age = 20, Father's age = 50 **3.** Bar of chocolate = 90c, Packet of crisps = 70c **4.** Adult ticket costs €10, Student ticket costs €5 **5.** Phone credit = €10, Sandwich = €4 **6.** 1st number, $x = 2$, 2nd number, $y = -1$ **7.** (i) Concert ticket costs €60 (ii) The credit card charge is €5 **8.** (i) Cost of a pen = €2 (ii) Cost of a notebook = €3 **9.** 1500 children went to the fair, 700 adults went to the fair. **10.** (i) $x + y = 12, 3x - y = 4$ (ii) $x = 4, y = 8$ **11.** (i) $a + b = 10, 4a - 2b = 4$ (ii) $a = 4, b = 6$ **12.** (i) $x + y = 40; x - y = 4.6$ (ii) $x = 22.3; y = 17.7$ **13.** (i) $2x + y = 50; 7x - \frac{y}{2} = 75$ (ii) $x = 12.5; y = 25$ **14.** (i) $4x - \frac{y}{2} = \frac{13}{2} = 6.5; \frac{x+3}{2} - \frac{y}{3} = \frac{3}{2} = 1.5$ (ii) $x = 2; y = 3$ **15.** (i) $2x + 3y = 47.50; x + 2y = 27.50$ (ii) Adult ticket costs €12.50; concession ticket costs €7.50 **16.** (i) $x + 4y = 2.00; 2x + 3y = 1.90$ (ii) The cost of a banana is 32 cents; the cost of an apple is 42 cents **17.** (ii) $x + y - 10 = y + \frac{x}{3}; y + \frac{x}{3} = 60$ (iii) $y = 55°; x = 15°$ **18.** (i) $x + y = 30; x = \frac{y}{4}$ (ii) Width of rectangle = 6 cm; Length of rectangle = 24 cm (iv) 144 cm^2 **19.** (i) $(x - y) = 110°$, as opposite angles in a parallelogram are equal. (ii) $(x - 3y) = 70°$, as adjacent angles in a parallelogram sum to 180°. (iii) $x - y = 110; x - 3y = 70$ (iv) $x = 130°; y = 20°$

Revision Activity 10

1. (a) 55° (b) $\frac{x}{2} + 2y - 10 = 55; x + y = 55$ (c) $y = 25°; x = 30°$ **2.** (a) $2x + y = 8.10; 4x + 4y = 18$ (b) $x = 3.60; y = 0.90$ (c) €0.90 (d) €3.60 **3.** (a) $37x + 8y = 423.65;$ $37x + 11y = 462.50$ (b) (i) €8.65 (ii) €12.95 **4.** (a) $5x + y = 16;$ $x + 2y = 5$ (b) $x = 3; y = 1$ (c) (i) 3 points (ii) 1 point **5.** (a) $x + y = 4; 3x - y = 0$ (b) $x = 1; y = 3$ (d) (i) 1 m (ii) 3 m (e) 3 m^2 **6.** (a) $x + y = 30; 6x + 8y = 216$ (b) $x = 12; y = 18$ (c) 12 (d) 18 **7.** (c) 4 days (d) Company A

Exam-style Questions

1. $x = -3; y = -4$ **2.** A car costs €2.10 to go through the M50 toll; a small van costs €2.90 to go through the M50 toll. **3.** (a) (i) 5 (ii) 1 (b) Teams who win consistently receive more points for a win, which encourages winning. With the new system, the ratio of wins to draws is higher, which rewards a victory more and might encourage a team to go for a win.

Chapter 11

Activity 11.1

1. (ii) 15 km/h **2.** (ii) Yes (iii) 40 km/h **3.** (ii) Yes (iii) 10 km/h **4.** (i) Mary **5.** Car 1: 60 km/h; Car 2: 30 km/h **6.** (i) 45 km/h (ii) 54 km/h (iii) 60 km/h (iv) 25 km/h **7.** (i) from the slopes of the graphs; Bob 5 km/h, Cathy 3 km/h **8.** (i) 8 km (ii) 20 min

Activity 11.2

1. 50 km/h; 60 km/h; 3 hours; 80 seconds; 9 km; 2.5 m **2.** (i) 2.5 h (ii) 1.25 h (iii) 2.5 h **3.** (i) 3 h (ii) 122.5 km **4.** (i) 15 m/s (ii) 20 m/s (iii) 10 m/s (iv) 35 m/s **5.** (i) 54 km/h (ii) 36 km/h **6.** (i) 0.4 h (ii) 4.5 km/h (iii) 0.45 km **7.** (i) 24 min (ii) 6 min **8.** (i) 7 h (ii) 60 min

Activity 11.3

1. (i) 60 km/h (ii) 12:40 **2.** (i) 50 km/h (ii) 80 km/h (iii) 72.5 km/h **3.** 66 km/h **4.** 50 km/h **5.** (i) 48 min (ii) 70 km/h (iii) 34 km/h **6.** (i) 15 min (ii) 12 min (iii) 17.78 km/h **7.** 24 km/h **8.** 48 km/h

Activity 11.4

1. (ii) 100 km/h (iii) 25 km **2.** (i) 5 minutes (ii) 5 minutes (iii) 100 km/h (iv) 20 minutes (v) $33\frac{1}{3}$ km **3.** (ii) 25 km/h (iii) 15 minutes (iv) 6.25 km **4.** (ii) 60 km/h (iii) 5 km **5.** (i) 5 minutes (ii) 20 km/h (iii) 10 minutes (i.e. $\frac{1}{6}$ of an hour). (iv) $3\frac{1}{3}$ km **8.** (i) 60 km/h (ii) 3 minutes (iii) 100 km/h (iv) 3.3 km (vi) 68.9 km/h **9.** (ii) 144 km/h **10.** 4 seconds

Activity 11.5

1. (i) 10 minutes (ii) 4 km (iii) His speed on the way to the shop is slower than on his return journey. **2.** (i) At 12.00 pm (ii) At 4.20 pm (iii) 6 km (iv) 12.45 pm and 3.45 pm (v) From 3.20 pm to 4.20 pm (vi) From 1.40 pm to 2.20 pm **3.** (i) 40 minutes and 30 minutes (ii) She was travelling at the same speed on both parts of the journey towards Cahir. (iii) 30 minutes (iv) 72 km/h **4.** (i) 0.75 km (ii) 2 minutes (iii) 2 km (iv) Her walking speed is obviously much slower than the car. **6.** (i) A is the tortoise. B is the hare. **7.** (ii) The slope of Mary's graph is greater than the slope of John's. (iii) Slope of Mary's graph = her speed = $\frac{200}{20}$ = 10 m/sec. Slope of John's graph = his speed = $\frac{200}{25}$ = 8 m/sec. Units used are m/sec. **8.** Most likely answer: Susan has decided to stop for two hours at a location 10 km from home. **10.** (i) 620 m approximately in 30 seconds approximately (ii) 450 m approximately (iii) 40 m approximately (iv) No, because the graph is not a straight line. **11.** A → 2, B → 3, C → 4, D → 1 **14.** 1D, 2E, 3A, 4B, 5F, 6G, 7C **15.** 1A, 2D, 3B, 4C **16.** 1E, 2C, 3A, 4B, 5D **17.** B **18.** A(ii), B(iii), C(i)

Revision Activity 11

1. 7 km/h slower **2.** (a) 0.55 km/min (b) E to F: speed = 0.7 km/min (c) D to E: speed = 0.2 km/min (d) 0.44 km/min **3.** 9.75 km/h **4.** 1188 km/h **5.** (a) 3 stops (b) 4.5 km (c) Two (d) $5\frac{1}{3}$ km/h (e) 8 km/h

Exam-style Questions

1. (a) D **2.** 63 km

Chapter 12

Activity 12.1

1. (a) (ii) yes (iii) output = input + 2 (b) (ii) No (iii) output ⩾ input (c) (ii) yes (iii) output = 2(input) (d) (ii) yes (iii) output = $(\text{input})^2$ (e) (ii) No (iii) output ⩽ input **2.** (ii) output = $\pm\sqrt{\text{input}}$ (iii) This relation is not a function **3.** (i) {(1,1), (2,4), (3,3), (4,2), (5,16), (6,6), (7,7), (8,4), (9,6), (10,5)} (ii) Is a function (iii) {1, 2, 3, 4, 5, 6, 7, 8, 9, 10} (iv) {1, 2, 3, 4, 5, 6, 7, 16} (v) {1, 2, 3, 4, 5, 6, 7, 16} **4.** (i) {(Tom, 56%), (Pat, 43%), (Ann, 78%), (Cora, 89%), (Tim, 81%)} (iii) {Tom, Pat, Ann, Cora, Tim} (iv) {43, 56, 78, 81, 89, 100} (v) {43, 56, 78, 81, 89} **5.** (ii) It is a function **6.** (i) This relation is a function (ii) output = input + 2 (iii) Domain = {–2, –1, 0, 1, 2}, Codomain = {0, 1, 2, 3, 4}, Range = {0, 1, 2, 3, 4} **7.** (i) This relation is not a function **8.** (i) This relation is a function (ii) output = $(\text{input})^2$ (iii) Domain = {–3, –2, 1, 2, 3}, Codomain = {1, 4, 8, 9, 11}, Range = {1, 4, 9} **9.** (i) This relation is not a function **10.** (i) This relation is a function (ii) output = $(\text{input})^2 + 2$ (iii) Domain = {–5, –2, 0, 2, 3}, Codomain = {2, 6, 11, 12, 27}, Range = {2, 6, 11, 27} **11.** This relation is not a function **12.** (i) 12 cm^2, 27 cm^2, 48 cm^2, 75 cm^2 (ii) {(2, 12), (3, 27), (4, 48), (5, 75)} **13.** (i) 4 cm^2, 16 cm^2, 36 cm^2, 64 cm^2

(ii) {(2, 4), (4, 16), (6, 36), (8, 64)} **14.** (i) 5 cm^2, 10 cm^2, 15 cm^2, 20 cm^2 (ii) {(2, 5), (4, 10), (6, 15), (8, 20)}

Activity 12.2

1. (i) –5 (ii) 7 (iii) 3 (iv) 2 (v) –8 **2.** (ii) €80, €160, €240, €320 **3.** (i) –4 (ii) 0 (iii) –3 (iv) –3 (v) 0 **4.** {4, 7, 10, 13} **6.** (i) 8 (ii) –1 (iii) 24 (iv) 7 (v) 0 **8.** (i) $f(x) = x + 5$ (ii) $f(x) = 2x + 9$ (iii) $f(x) = 3x - 7$ (iv) $f(x) = x^2 - 2$ (v) $f(x) = x^2 - 2x + 3$ **9.** (i) 5 m/s (iii) 25 m/s (v) 55 m/s (vi) 85 m/s (vii) 105 m/s **10.** (i) {–1, 2, 7, 14, 23} **11.** (i) {4, 5, 7, 10, 14} **12.** (i) {–1, 1, 5, 11}

Revision Activity 12

1. (a) 13 (b) 17 **2.** (a) 7 (b) –13 **3.** (a) 17 (b) 7 **4.** (a) 18 (b) 28 **5.** (a) 21 (b) 16 **6.** (b) {1, 2, 3, 4} (c) {a, b, c} (d) Yes **7.** (b) {1, 2, 3} (c) {5, 8, 9, 10} (d) This relation is not a function **8.** (b) {1, 4, 5, 7} (c) {3, 6, 8, 9} (d) This relation is a function **9.** (b) This relation is a function **10.** (c) This relation is a function

Exam-style Question

1. (a) 1 (b) (i) $t^2 - 3t$ and $4t^2 - 2t - 2$ (ii) $t = \frac{2}{3}$, $t = -1$

Chapter 13

Activity 13.1

5. (ii) The slope of $f(x) = x$ is 1 and the slope of $h(x) = 2x$ is 2 (iii) The y-intercepts are both (0, 0) (iv) a straight line **6.** (iii) –5 **7.** (iii) 2 **8.** (i) $x = -1.5$ (ii) $y = 3$ (iii) $y = 1$ (iv) $y = 5$ (v) $x = -2$ **9.** (i) $x = 6$ (ii) $y = 6$ (iii) $y = 2$ (iv) $y = 4.5$ (v) $x = 2$ **10.** (i) $x = 3.5$ (ii) $y = -7$ (iii) $y = -5$ (iv) $x = 2.5$ (v) $x = 2$ **11.** (i) $x = 0$ (ii) $y = 0$ (iii) $y = 3$ (iv) $y = -3$ (v) $x = 0.67$

Activity 13.2

1. (i) 35 (ii) 8 (iii) $t^2 + 2t$ and $t^2 + 4t + 3$ (iv) $t = -\frac{3}{2}$ **2.** (i) $k = -2$ (ii) $x = 0$ or $x = -\frac{3}{4}$ **3.** (ii) (0.5, 10.5) (iii) $x < 0.5$ (iv) $x > 0.5$ (v) $x = 0.5$ **4.** (ii) 4 (iii) $x = 0.6$, $x = 2.9$ (iv) $x = 0.15$, $x = 3.35$ (v) $0.15 < x < 3.35$, $x \in \mathbb{R}$ **5.** (i) $3b - c = 18$ Equation 1; $2b + c = -8$ Equation 2 (ii) $b = 2$; $c = -12$ (iii) (0, –12) (iv) (2.6, 0) and (–4.6, 0) **6.** (i) $5 = c$ (ii) $3a - b = 3$ Equation 1; $5a + b = 5$ Equation 2 (iii) $a = 1$; $b = 0$ **7.** (ii) $c = -12$ (iii) $x^2 + 2x - 12$ **8.** (i) (a) $x = \frac{1}{2}$ or $x = -3$ (b) $x = 2$ (c) $x = 0$ or $x = 3$ (ii) Graph 1 corresponds to $h(x)$; Graph 3 corresponds to $g(x)$; Graph 5 corresponds to $f(x)$ **9.** (iii) $x = -5.3$ and $x = 2.3$ **10.** (ii) (a) 6.1 (b) $x = -2$ and $x = 1.5$ (c) $\{-2 \leq x \leq 1.5\}$

Activity 13.3

1. (i) $l = 140 - 2x$ (iii) (a) 2450 m^2 (b) 1650 m^2 **2.** (ii) (a) 61 metres (b) 41 metres (c) $t_1 \approx 0.6s$, $t_2 \approx 6.4s$ **3.** (i) $x = 2$ (ii) Find where the graph of $f(x) = 2x^2 + 25x - 58$ cuts the positive x-axis. (iii) $x = 2$ **4.** (iv) Approximately 3.2 seconds (v) 3.16 sec (vi) $h = 45$ m (vii) 7.75 sec **5.** (i) 0 m above ground (iii) 18 seconds (v) 9 seconds (vi) 405 metres **6.** (i) $w = 18 - x$ (ii) Length of the inner section = $(x - 3)$ m; Width of the inner section = $(15 - x)$ m (v) 36 m^2 **7.** (i) €420 (ii) €$(520 - 20n)$ (iii) $520n - 20n^2$ (v) The company makes a loss of €2400 if they take 30 people on the tour. (vii) $n = 0$ or $n = 26$ (viii) $n = 13$ (ix) €3380 **8.** (ii) The relationship between height and time is linear. (iii) Tank A: 2 cm/s; Tank B: –2 cm/s (v) (50, 0) means that after 50 seconds the volume of Tank B is zero. (vi) Tank A: $h = 15 + 2t$, h = height of water in cm, t = time in seconds; Tank B: $h = 100 - 2t$, h = height of water in cm, t = time in seconds (vii) 21.25 sec; 57.5 cm **9.** (ii) $21000x - 500x^2$ (iii) $x = 0$ or $x = 42$ (v) x = €21; €220,500 (vi) €16 (vii) €12,500 (viii) No

Activity 13.4

1. (iv) (0, 1) (v) y is increasing (vi) $3^{10} = 59049$; $3^{20} = 3486784401$; $3^{30} = 2.058911321 \times 10^{14}$ **2.** (i) 3 (ii) x (iii) The exponent (iv) The base 3 (v) Real numbers $\mathbb{R}$ (vi) There are no values (vii) All the positive real numbers (viii) As x decreases the output gets closer and closer to 0 but never equals 0. (ix) No **3.** (iii) (0, 2) (iv) $2(3^{10}) = 118098$; $2(3^{20}) = 6975568802$ **4.** (ii) $x = 2$ **5.** (ii) 262144 **6.** (i) 50 (ii) 136221 **7.** (i) $k = 2$; $a = 3$ (ii) 4374 **8.** Graph C: $f(x)$; Graph B: $g(x)$; Graph A: $h(x)$; Graph D: $j(x)$ **9.** (i) $a = 4$; $b = 3$ (ii) $1.129718146 \times 10^{12}$ (iii) 1.1×10^{12} (iv) 1.1 billion bacteria (taking 1 billion to be 1 million million) (v) $t = 10.052$ hours **10.** (ii) $x = -0.2$ and 3.1 (iii) $k \approx 1.89$ (iv) $g(k) \approx 29$

Activity 13.5

2. (iii) y-intercepts are at 0, –2, –4, and –5 respectively. **8.** $f(x) = (x + 1)^2 - 3$; $g(x) = (x - 2)^2 - 3$ **9.** (i) $k = +3$ (ii) (a) (3, –4) (b) $x = 3$ **10.** (i) $h = 2$ (ii) (a) (–2, 3) (b) $x = -2$

Revision Activity 13

1. (a) $b = 1$, $c = -6$ (b) $x = -1.5$ **3.** (b) $x = 0.4$ and $x = 1.9$ (c) $k \approx 1.3$. Using the calculator, $k \approx 1.26$ (d) $g(1.3) \approx 13.5$ **4.** (b) (i) 160 (ii) 320 (c) No **5.** (a) Production cost = €5000, and total revenue = €5000 (c) $-x^2 + 60x - 500$ (d) A loss of €500 (e) $x = 10$ and $x = 50$ (g) 30 items (h) €400 **6.** (b) Between 4 and 5 seconds (c) 4.45 seconds (e) 2 sec (f) About 4 seconds (g) $0 \leq t \leq 4.45$, $t \in \mathbb{R}$ (h) $0 \leq h \leq 30$, $h \in \mathbb{R}$

Exam-style Questions

1. (a) $5a - b = 29$ Equation 1; $2a + b = -1$ Equation 2 (b) $a = 4$; $b = -9$ (c) (0, –9) (d) (1.6, 0) and (–5.6, 0) **3.** (b) Roots of $f(x)$: $x = -4$; $x = 0$; Roots of $g(x)$: $x = 1$; $x = 5$ (d) $h = +5$ (e) $x = 5$ **4.** (a) $f(x)$: $x = \frac{3}{2}$, $x = -2$; $g(x)$: $x = 3$; $h(x)$: $x = 0$, $x = 2$ (b) $f(x)$: Diagram 3; $g(x)$: Diagram 5; $h(x)$: Diagram 2

Chapter 14

Activity 14.1

1. (iii) 10 (iv) 20 (v) $T_n = 2n$ **2.** (iii) 22 (iv) $T_n = 3n + 1$ (v) Position 12 **3.** (i) 17, 20, 23 (iii) $T_n = 3n + 2$ **4.** (ii) $T_n = 2n + 2$ (iii) 202 (iv) Stage 16 **5.** $T_n = 3n + 1$ **6.** (iii) $n + 1$ (iv) $T_n = 5n + 8$ (v) $T_n = 6n + 9$ **7.** (vi) $A = 10 + 2w$ (vii) €50 **8.** (vi) $M = 10w + 50$ (vii) €1090

Activity 14.2

1. (iii) The number of weeks times 6, plus 15 (iv) $S = 15 + 6w$ (v) No (vi) No (vii) €75 **2.** (iii) No **3.** (i) €55 (vi) 20 weeks (vii) I do not agree with Lucy. **4.** (i) Aaron is saving more (iv) 2 (v) Aaron's **5.** (ii) 8 km (iii) 3 miles **6.** (i) €10 (ii) Yes (iii) Yes (iv) The amount that Joe gets paid is directly proportional to the number of hours he works. **7.** (ii) 4 (iii) B, 40 m (v) $d = 80 + 10t$ (vi) $d = 40 + 20t$

Activity 14.3

1. (ii) 3, 9, 19, 33, 51 (iii) Second difference = 4 **2.** (i) 1, 3, 7, 13, 21, 31, … (ii) 1, 5, 11, 19, 29, 41, … (iii) 2, 4, 10, 20, 34, 50, … (iv) 3, 6, 12, 21, 33, 48, … (v) 4, 9, 16, 25, 36, 49, … **4.** (iv) 2 (v) Green tiles = 2 times the stage number (vi) Blue tiles = the square of the stage number (vii) Total tiles = $2 + 2n + n^2$ **6.** (iv) 3 (v) Number of green tiles = 4 times the stage number (vi) Number of blue tiles = the square of the stage number (vii) Total tiles = $3 + 4n + n^2$

Activity 14.4

1. (ii) (a) $n^2 + n$ (b) $n^2 + 2n + 2$ (c) $n^2 + 3n + 2$ (d) $2n^2 + n$ **2.** (iii) n^2 **3.** (iiii) $n(n + 1)$ or $n^2 + n$ (iv) 72 **4.** (iii) $(n + 2)(n + 3)$ or $n^2 + 5n + 6$ (iv) 156 **5.** $n(n + 2) + 2$ or $n^2 + 2n + 2$ **6.** (ii) perimeter: $4n + 2$ (iii) Area: $(n + 1)(n)$ (iv) same area; perimeter = $6n$ **7.** (ii) $4n + 8$ (iii) Area: $n(n + 2) + 2$

Activity 14.5

6. (i) Graph 1 is $y = 3^x$, Graph 2 is $y = 2^x$ (iii) 3 (v) 4
7. Graph 1 is experiment A, Graph 2 is experiment C, Graph 3 is experiment B **8.** (iii) €8
9. (iii) 18,446,744,070,000,000,000 cent = €184,467,440,700,000,000

Revision Activity 14

1. (a) €25 (d) 16 (e) €7 (f) I agree with Kevin
4. S1 – F3 – G2 ; S2 – F4 – G3 ; S3 – F5 – G4 ; S4 – F1 – G5 : S5 – F2 – G1 **5.** 60

Exam-style Question

1. (b) $8n - 4$ (c) $n^2 + (n - 1)^2$ or $2n^2 - 2n + 1$
(d) Quadratic pattern, as the formula has a highest power of 2 on the variable.

Chapter 15

Activity 15.1

1. (i) {22, 24, 26, 28} (ii) 4 (iii) {22, 24, 26}, {22, 24, 28}, {22, 26, 28}, {24, 26, 28} **2.** (i) {a, h, p, y} (ii) 4 (iii) {h}, {a}, {p}, {y}
3. (i) {51, 53, 55, 57, 59, 61, 63, 65, 67, 69} (ii) {Saturday, Sunday} (iii) {Blue, Yellow, Red} (iv) {Green, White, Orange} (v) {a, e, g, l, m, o, p, r} **4.** (i) 10 (ii) 2 (iii) 3 (iv) 3 (v) 8 **5.** (i) $\{x \mid x$ is a divisor of 12$\}$ (ii) $\{x \mid x$ is a letter in the word 'surprise'$\}$ (iii) $\{x \mid x$ is a multiple of 5 which is less than 50$\}$ (iv) $\{x \mid x$ is an even number less than 15$\}$ **6.** (i) The null set which is a subset of all sets (ii) The set of whole numbers from 1 to 10 (iii) The set of 4 boys' names beginning with A (iv) The set of 5 European languages **7.** (i) {a, e, h, l, n, p, t} (ii) {a, c, e, h, t} (iii) {a, c, e, h, l, n, p, t} (iv) {a, e, h, t}
8. (i) (a) {1, 2, 3, 4, 5, 6, 7, 8, 10, 12} (b) {2, 4, 6} (ii) (a) 7 (b) 6 (c) 10 (d) 3 **9.** (ii) (a) {10, 12, 14, 15, 16, 18, 20, 22, 24, 25} (b) {10, 20}

Activity 15.2

1. (ii) {3, 4, 7, 8, 9} **2.** (i) {1, 2, 3, 4, 5, 6} (ii) {1, 2, 3, 5} (iii) {4, 6} (iv) {4, 6} **3.** (i) {b, d, f, g, h} (ii) {a, f, g, h, i} (iii) {f, g, h} (iv) {a, i} **4.** (ii) (a) {2, 3, 4, 6, 8, 9, 10} (b) {6} (c) {1, 3, 5, 7, 9} (d) {1, 2, 4, 5, 7, 8, 10} (e) {1, 5, 7} (f) {1, 2, 3, 4, 5, 7, 8, 9, 10} (g) {2, 4, 8, 10} (h) {3, 9} (iii) (a) 7 (b) 9 **5.** (ii) (a) {a, b, c, d, f, h} (b) {b, d} (c) {a, c, e, g} (d) {e, f, g, h} (e) {e, g} (f) {a, c, e, f, g, h} (g) {f, h} (h) {a, c} (i) {a, b, c, d, e, g} (j) {b, d, e, f, g, h}
6. (i) (a) {2, 4, 6, 8, 10, 12} (b) {3, 6, 9, 12, 15} (c) {2, 3, 4, 6, 8, 9, 10, 12, 15} (d) {2, 3, 4, 8, 9, 10, 15} (e) {2, 4, 8, 10} (ii) (a) $G \cap H = \{6, 12\}$ (b) $6 \in H$ (c) $G \setminus H = \{2, 4, 8, 10\}$ (d) $G \cup H = \{2, 3, 4, 6, 8, 9, 10, 12, 15\}$ (e) $3 \notin G$ (f) $\{3, 9, 15\} \subset H$ **7.** (ii) (a) {1, 4, 6, 8, 9, 10, 12, 14, 15} (b) {3, 5, 7, 11, 13} (c) {4, 6, 8, 10, 12, 14} (d) {1, 9, 15} (e) {2}

Activity 15.3

1. (ii) 13 **2.** (ii) 4 **3.** (ii) 9 **4.** (i) 30 (ii) 21 (iii) 33 **5.** (ii) 10
6. (i) The students in the class who have blue eyes and/or wear glasses. (ii) The students in the class who have blue eyes and wear glasses. (iii) The students in the class who neither have blue eyes nor wear glasses. **7.** 7 **8.** (i) 18 (ii) 5
9. (ii) 6 **10.** 7 **11.** 15 **12.** (i) 27 (ii) 69 **13.** (i) 8 (ii) 35
14. (i) 1 sometimes true; 2 never true; 3 Always true; 4 Always true (ii) For example: True for {1, 2} and {3, 4}; False for {1, 2} and {1,3}

Activity 15.4

1. (i) {a, d, e, g, i, m, r} (ii) {a, g, n} (iii) { } (iv) {a, e, g, i, m} (v) {e, i, m} (vi) {a, g} (vii) {e} **2.** (i) {2, 3, 4, 10} (ii) {3, 7, 9, 10, 11} (iii) {2, 7, 8, 10, 12} (iv) {2, 3, 4, 7, 8, 10, 12,} (v) {3} (vi) {1, 5, 6, 8, 12} (vii) {4} (viii) {3, 7, 10} (ix) {7} **3.** (i) {1, 4} (ii) {1, 4, 5, 6} (iii) { } **5.** (ii) (a) {h, g, c, i, f, n, l, j, k} (b) {h, g, c, l, j, k} (c) {a, b, m, d} (d) {a, b, d, e, m} (e) {m} (iii) (a) 1 (b) 3 (c) 11 **6.** (i) 7 (ii) 2 (iii) Prime Numbers
7. (ii) (a) 6 (b) 10 (c) 1 (d) 8 (e) 11 (f) 5

8. (ii) (a) {n, u, m, e, r, i, c, a, l, y} (b) {m, i, r, a, c, l, e} (c) {r, a, l, y} (d) {c, e, i, m, n, u} (e) {a, e, l, m, r} (f) {n, m, e, i, c, u, r, l, y} (g) {n} (h) {a, e, l, m, n, r, y}
9. (i) Students in the class who are afraid of either mice or spiders. (ii) Students in the class who are afraid of mice and wasps. (iii) Students in the class who are afraid of wasps but not spiders. (iv) Students in the class who are afraid of mice and spiders but are not afraid of wasps. (v) Students in the class who are not afraid of mice or spiders or wasps.
10. (i) The number of people who own a pet or like dogs but don't have pet insurance. (ii) The number of people who own a pet, like dogs and have pet insurance. (iii) The number of people who have pet insurance, but excluding people who both own a pet and also like dogs. (iv) The number of people who don't have a pet or like dogs or have pet insurance. **11.** (ii) 9 (iii) (a) 49 (b) 51 (c) 78 (d) 61

Activity 15.5

1. (ii) Yes **4.** (i) Distributive property of union over intersection (ii) Commutative property of intersection (iii) Associative property of intersection (iv) Distributive property of intersection over union (v) Commutative property of union (vi) Associative property for union **5.** (i) The people who are both married and own a car or who own their own home. (ii) The people who own their own home and own a car or who own their own home and are married. (iii) The people who own a car or their own home or are married. **6.** (i) (a) {1, 2, 3, 4, 5, 6} (b) {5, 6} (c) {1, 2, 3, 4, 5, 6} (ii) $(P \cup Q) \cap (P \cup R)$

Activity 15.6

1. (ii) 169 (iii) 2 **2.** (ii) 2 (iii) 12 **3.** (i) 13 (ii) 13 (iii) 54 (iv) 28 (v) 39 (vi) 20 (vii) 90 (viii) 0 **4.** (ii) 6 (iii) 12
5. (ii) 3 **6.** (ii) 15 (iii) 57 **7.** (i) 3 (ii) 44 **8.** (i) 15 (ii) 88
9. (i) $x = 4$, $y = 3$ (ii) 30 members **10.** (i) $y = 1$, $x = 3$ (iii) 33

Revision Activity 15

1. (a) (i) {a, b, c, d, e, f} (ii) {e, f, g, h, i} (iii) {a, b, c, d, e, f, g, h, i} (iv) {e, f} (v) {a, b, c, d} (b) (i) 6 (ii) 5 (iii) 9 (iv) 2 (v) 4
2. (b) 370 **3.** (a) 29 (b) 27 (c) 22 **4.** (b) $p + q + d - c$
5. (b) (i) {b, c, e, f} (ii) {b, c, e, f, h, i, k, l} (iii) {a, b, c, d, e, f, g, i, j, k} (iv) {a, d, e, g, i, k} (v) {h, j, l} (vi) {h, j, l} (d) Distributive property of intersection over union
6. (a) True (b) False (c) False (d) False (e) True (f) True (g) True (h) False (i) True (j) True (k) False (l) False
7. (a) {1, 2, 3, 4, 5, 6, 8, 9, 10, 11, 12, 13, 14, 16, 17, 18, 19, 20} (b) {5, 7, 9, 14, 15, 17, 19, 20} (c) {2, 4, 8, 12} (d) {3, 13} (e) {1, 10, 16, 18} (f) {2, 3, 12, 13} (g) {3} (h) {2, 12} (i) {5, 6, 9, 11, 13, 14, 17, 19, 20} (j) {1, 2, 4, 5, 6, 7, 8, 9, 10, 11, 12, 13, 14, 15, 16, 17, 18, 19, 20}
9. (b) 7 (c) 36%

Exam-style Questions

1. (b) $P \setminus (E \cup O)$, $P \cap E \cap O$, $E \cap O$, $(E \cap O) \setminus P$ (c) $\frac{1}{5}$
2. (b) Incorrect statements: (iii) or (v) (c) 5

Chapter 16

Activity 16.1

1. (i) $t = 2s - a$ (ii) $t = p - 5q$ (iii) $t = \frac{x}{w}$ (iv) $t = rk$ (v) $t = \frac{f}{gh}$ (vi) $t = \frac{y}{w} + d$ **2.** (i) $w = \frac{A}{l}$ (ii) $a = \frac{F}{m}$ (iii) $d = \frac{T}{f}$ (iv) $F = PA$ (v) $m = \frac{W}{g}$ (vi) $t = \frac{W}{P}$ **3.** (i) $x = \sqrt{\frac{a}{b}}$ (ii) $x = d - e(s - q)$ (iii) $x = a^2 - g$ (iv) $x = 2p + 2d$ (v) $x = \sqrt{\frac{y - qs^2}{r}}$ (vi) $x = \sqrt{\frac{w}{s - u - t}}$ **4.** (i) $h = \frac{E}{mg}$ (ii) $m = \frac{E}{c^2}$ (iii) $a = \frac{v^2 - u^2}{2s}$ (iv) $M = \frac{4\pi^2R^3}{GT^2}$ (v) $u = \frac{2s - at^2}{2t}$ (vi) $r = \sqrt{\frac{A}{\pi}}$ (vii) $d = \sqrt{\frac{Gm_1m_2}{F}}$ (viii) $r = \sqrt{\frac{3V}{\pi h}}$ (ix) $g = \frac{4\pi^2 l}{T^2}$ **5.** (i) $b = \frac{c}{a - p}$ (ii) $b = \frac{2u}{s + u}$

(iii) $b = \frac{y}{3c-1}$ (iv) $b = \frac{w}{1-k}$ (v) $b = \frac{e}{c^4-1}$ **6.** (i) $I = \frac{qw}{y}$
(ii) $I = \frac{u}{(p-s)}$ **7.** (i) $l = \sqrt{A}$ (ii) $R = \sqrt[3]{\frac{GMT^2}{4\pi^2}}$ **8.** (i) $w = \frac{p+4}{3}$
(ii) $w = \frac{p}{(5-bu)}$

Activity 16.2

1. (i) $K = 310.15$ (ii) $C = K - 273.15$ (iii) $C = 33$
2. (i) $h = \frac{A}{a}$ (ii) $a = \frac{A}{h}$ (iii) 18 cm **3.** (i) $a = \frac{2A}{h}$ (ii) 10 m
4. (i) $b = \sqrt{c^2 - a^2}$ (ii) $b = 4$ **5.** (i) $u = v - at$ (ii) 10 *m/s*
6. (i) $m = \frac{F}{a}$ (ii) 700 **7.** (i) $r = \sqrt[3]{\frac{3V}{4\pi}}$ (ii) 7.6 cm **8.** (i) $R = \frac{V}{I}$
(ii) 6 ohms **9.** (i) $r = \sqrt{\frac{3V}{\pi h}}$ (ii) 5 **10.** (i) $F = \frac{9C}{5} + 32$
(ii) 84.2° **11.** (i) $m = \rho V$ (ii) 3000 g

Revision Activity 16

1. (a) $A = \frac{F}{P}$ (b) $\frac{W}{m} = g$ (c) $Pt = W$ (d) $\frac{Fd^2}{Gm_1} = m_2$
(e) $h = \frac{E}{mg}$ (f) $c = \sqrt{\frac{E}{m}}$ (g) $u = \sqrt{v^2 - 2as}$ (h) $a = \frac{2s - 2ut}{t^2}$
(i) $R = \sqrt[3]{\frac{T^2GM}{4\pi^2}}$ (j) $\frac{T^2g}{4\pi^2} = l$ **2.** (a) $\sqrt[3]{\frac{3V}{4\pi}} = r$ (b) 6051.9 km
3. (a) $\sqrt{\frac{2E}{m}} = v$ (b) 2 m/s **4.** (a) $h = \frac{A}{2\pi r} - r$ (b) 10.5 cm
5. (a) $\sqrt{\frac{2W}{c}} = v$ (b) 228 *v*

Exam-style Questions

1. (a) $\frac{10}{3}$ (b) As the denominator increases, the value of the fraction decreases, so an increase in *P* means a decrease in *M*.
(c) $P = \frac{1}{M} - S$ or $\frac{1 - MS}{M}$ **2.** (a) 1 280 000 Joules (b) $\sqrt{\frac{2W}{C}} = V$

Chapter 17

Activity 17.1

2. (i) $\frac{1}{6}$ (ii) $\frac{1}{18}$ (iii) $\frac{1}{36}$ (iv) $\frac{1}{9}$ **3.** (i) €7.80 (ii) €15
(iii) €8 (iv) 3 **4.** only part (iii) **6.** (i) €12.80 (ii) €13.60
(iii) €1.50 **7.** Answer (iv) **8.** (iv) smallest = $\frac{1}{4}$
9. Tanya is not correct. **10.** (i) $\frac{4}{6}$ (ii) $\frac{8}{12}$ **13.** (i) 4 (ii) $1\frac{1}{2}$
(iii) $3\frac{2}{3}$ **14.** A: 1 square B: 2 squares C: 8 squares
D: 4 squares **15.** $\frac{7}{10}$ **16.** (i) $\frac{5}{8}$ kg (ii) $\frac{5}{24}$ kg **17.** (i) $\frac{5}{7}$ (ii) $\frac{7}{5}$

Activity 17.2

1. (i) a^9 (ii) a^4 (iii) a^2 (iv) a^{12} (v) a^9b^6 (vi) a^5b^{20} **2.** $\frac{a^7}{a^7} = 1$
3. $\frac{a^0}{a^5} = \frac{1}{a^5}$ **4.** 5 **5.** $\frac{1}{36}$ **6.** 1 **7.** 4 **8.** $\frac{1}{5}$ **9.** 3 **10.** $\frac{1}{3}$
11. 10 **12.** $\frac{1}{10}$ **13.** 10 **14.** 2 **15.** $\frac{2}{3}$ **16.** 4 **17.** 3 **18.** 27
19. 8 **20.** $\frac{1}{10}$ **21.** 1 **22.** 6 **23.** 3 **24.** 3 **25.** $\frac{1}{3}$ **26.** 5
27. 25 **28.** $\frac{4}{9}$ **29.** $\frac{64}{729}$ **30.** $\frac{3}{4}$ **31.** $\frac{81}{256}$ **32.** $\frac{2}{3}$ **33.** $\frac{8}{27}$
34. $\frac{8}{27}$ **35.** $\frac{13}{5}$ **36.** $\frac{2}{5}$ **37.** $\frac{4}{25}$ **38.** $\frac{16}{625}$ **39.** $\frac{16}{9}$ **40.** $\frac{343}{125}$
41. $\frac{64}{343}$ **42.** (i) $x^{\frac{1}{2}}$ (ii) $x^{\frac{3}{2}}$ (iii) $x^{\frac{3}{2}}$ (iv) $x^{\frac{1}{4}}$ (v) $x^{\frac{5}{6}}$
43. (i) False (ii) True (iii) False (iv) False (v) False (vi) False
(vii) False **44.** $2^{\frac{5}{2}}$ **45.** $3^{\frac{11}{2}}$ **46.** $5^{\frac{3}{2}}$

Activity 17.3

1. (i) $x = 3$ (ii) $x = 6$ (iii) $x = 3$ (iv) $x = 3$ (v) $x = 5$ (vi) $x = 1$
(vii) $x = 7$ (viii) $x = 8$ **2.** (i) $x = 6$ (ii) $x = 4$ (iii) $x = \frac{3}{2}$
(iv) $x = 2$ (v) $x = 8$ (vi) $x = 1$ (vii) $x = 13$ (viii) $x = 3$ **3.** $x = 5$
4. $x = 3$ **5.** $x = 4$ **6.** (i) 729 (ii) 3^4 (iii) $x = -10$ **7.** (i) 2
(ii) $2^{\frac{1}{2}}$ (iii) $x = 2\frac{1}{2}$ **8.** (i) (a) 2^3 (b) 2^2 (ii) $x = 3$ **9.** (i) (a) 3^5
(b) $3^{\frac{3}{2}}$ (ii) $x = 7$ **10.** (i) 2^5 (ii) $x = 3$ **11.** (i) $5^{\frac{3}{2}}$ (ii) $x = -\frac{3}{2}$
12. $p = -\frac{1}{4}$ **13.** $n = -2$ **14.** $n = -3$

Activity 17.4

1. $x = \frac{2}{9}$ **2.** $x = \frac{3}{9}$ **3.** $x = \frac{45}{99}$ **4.** $x = \frac{23789}{99999}$
5. $x = \frac{5489}{999}$ **6.** $x = \frac{323}{999}$ **7.** $x = \frac{13}{9}$ **8.** No
9. π. Its digits never repeat

Activity 17.5

3. (i) $9\sqrt{5}$ (ii) $8\sqrt{7} + 5\sqrt{3}$ (iii) 30 (iv) –20 (v) $12\sqrt{14}$
(vi) –30 **4.** (i) $13\sqrt{2}$ (ii) $7\sqrt{13} + \sqrt{6}$ (iii) 120 (iv) $-3\sqrt{10}$
(v) $-12\sqrt{34}$ (vi) –105 **5.** (i) $3\sqrt{5}$ (ii) $2\sqrt{6}$ (iii) $3\sqrt{7}$ (iv) $10\sqrt{2}$
(v) $6\sqrt{2}$ (vi) $2\sqrt{2}$ **6.** (i) $\frac{3}{4}$ (ii) $16\sqrt{2}$ (iii) $4\sqrt{5}$ (iv) $5\sqrt{5}$
(v) $3\sqrt{7}$ **7.** (i) $7\sqrt{3}$ (ii) $4\sqrt{5}$ (iii) $7\sqrt{2}$ (iv) $4\sqrt{7}$ **8.** (i) $p = 9$
(ii) $p = 2$ (iii) $p = 16$ (iv) $p = 2$ **9.** (i) 24 (ii) –24 (iii) $18\sqrt{14}$
(iv) –216 (v) $6\sqrt{35}$ **10.** 41 **11.** (i) 7 (ii) 44 (iii) 1
(iv) $27 + 10\sqrt{2}$ **12.** (i) 25 (ii) 5 **13.** $1 + 3\sqrt{10}$ **14.** $3^{\frac{3}{2}}$
16. $8 - 9\sqrt{2}$ **17.** $\frac{\sqrt{2}}{2}$ **18.** $\frac{2\sqrt{3}}{3}$ **19.** (i) $\sqrt{3} + \frac{\sqrt{6}}{3}$
(ii) $\frac{\sqrt{10}}{2} - \frac{\sqrt{2}}{2}$ (iii) $\sqrt{5} - \frac{\sqrt{15}}{5}$

Activity 17.6

1. 3.85×10^9 **2.** (i) 7.6×10^2 (ii) 4.62×10^3 (iii) 2.5×10^7
(iv) 3.15×10^5 (v) 1.075×10^9 (vi) 6.3×10^{13} **3.** 8.3812×10^{-26}
4. (i) 8.6×10^{-4} (ii) 4.62×10^{-3} (iii) 2.7×10^7 (iv) 3.26×10^{-7}
(v) 1.077×10^9 (vi) 7.8×10^{-8} **5.** €(5.3×10^9) **6.** (i) 630 000
(ii) 0.000 092 (iii) 3 450 000 (iv) 0.000 29 (v) 823 000 000
(vi) 0.000 003 3 (vii) 0.001 **7.** 1.2×10^{14} kg **8.** 1×10^{-5}
9. 2.5×10^{-6} **10.** (i) 8.42×10^3 (ii) 1.35×10^4 (iii) 9.7×10^2
(iv) 1.7×10^{-2} (v) 3.9×10^{-3} (vi) 4.9993×10^{-2}
11. (i) 4.16×10^{13} km (ii) 3.5×10^6 km **12.** 2×10^{-6}
13. (i) 8.6×10^7 (ii) 2.7×10^{-1} (iii) 2.08×10^2 (iv) 9.9×10^0
14. (i) 2×10^3 (ii) 3.7×10^8 (iii) 8×10^2 (iv) 1.4×10^7
15. (i) 3.1×10^2 (ii) 1.1×10^2 (iii) 1.22×10^{-1} **16.** 5.3×10^6
17. 1.089×10^5 km **18.** 3.52×10^{-2} **19.** 2.03×10^6 km

Activity 17.7

1. 2, 3, 5, 7, 11, 13, 17, 19, 23, 29, 31, 37, 41, 43, 47 **2.** $2^3 \times 3^2$
3. (i) 6 = 3 + 3; 8 = 3 + 5; 10 = 5 + 5; 12 = 5 + 7; 14 = 7 + 7; 16 = 3 + 13 (ii) 86 = 43 + 43 **4.** 3 and 5; 5 and 7; 11 and 13; 17 and 19; 29 and 31; 41 and 43; 59 and 61; 71 and 73;
7. Always even **9.** Always even **11.** Always odd
14. Always even **15.** Always odd **17.** Always even
18. Sometimes even, sometimes odd

Revision Activity 17

1. (a) 1.5×10^8 (b) (i) 3.40; 1.73; 2.97; 1.60; 1.57; 3.50
2. (a) 5.188 (b) 6.56 (c) 10 **3.** (a) $\frac{1}{49}$; 9 (b) 1.68×10^7
4. $3^{\frac{5}{2}}$ **5.** 2^1 **6.** $30\sqrt{2} - 48$ **7.** (a) 512 (b) 16 **8.** $n = 0$
9. (a) 2^{12} (b) 2^5 **10.** $3^{\frac{3}{2}}$

Exam-style Questions

1. (ii) $\sqrt{5}$ is an irrational number; it cannot be written as a fraction. **2.** (a) –7.3 is negative and is not a whole number.

Chapter 18

Activity 18.1

1. (i) A: Very unlikely; B: Very likely; C: Very likely; D: Evens chance; E: Impossible **2.** (i) 500 (ii) 500 (iii) 0 **3.** (i) $\frac{1}{2}$ (ii) $\frac{1}{4}$ (iii) 0.3 (iv) 80% **4.** (i) 0.4 (ii) 0.6 **5.** (ii) 80 (iii) $\frac{1}{4}$ (iv) $\frac{1}{80}$ **6.** (i) (a) 0 (b) 1 (c) $\frac{1}{2}$ (ii) (c) A number from 1 to 6 inclusive turns up. **7.** (i) 0.5 (ii) 0.5005, 0.4995 (iii) 0.5 **8.** (i) $\frac{1}{6}$ (iii) Yes **9.** $\frac{4}{27}$ **10.** (i) C (ii) $\frac{1}{2}$ or 50% (iii) 0 (iv) B (v) A (vi) Add 2 yellow counters (vii) 9 or more (viii) No (ix) 45 red counters, 30 blue counters **11.** (i) $\frac{1}{3}$ (ii) Add 2 green balls (iii) 8 balls of another colour (iv) Add 4 balls of colour red/blue **12.** (ii) (a) Group Y (b) 78 times (c) $\frac{128}{175}$ **13.** (i) $\frac{15}{32}$ (ii) $\frac{17}{32}$ **14.** (i) $\frac{4}{11}$ (ii) $\frac{7}{11}$ **15.** (i) 6 (ii) (W, W), (W, B), (B, W), (B, B), (C, W), (C, B) **16.** (i) $\frac{3}{7}$ (ii) $\frac{2}{3}$ (iii) $\frac{5}{18}$ (iv) $\frac{5}{8}$ **17.** (i) $\frac{1}{8}$ (ii) $\frac{1}{8}$ **18.** $\frac{16}{25} = 0.64$ **19.** (i) 2, 3, 4; 2, 4, 3; 3, 2, 4; 3, 4, 2; 4, 2, 3; 4, 3, 2 (ii) $\frac{1}{6}$ (iii) $\frac{1}{3}$ **20.** (i) 16 (ii) $\frac{1}{16}$ (iii) $\frac{1}{4}$ (iv) $\frac{3}{4}$ **21.** (i) $\frac{17}{96}$ (ii) $\frac{47}{96}$ (iii) $\frac{1}{8}$ (iv) $\frac{59}{96}$ **22.** (ii) $\frac{35}{76}$ (iii) $\frac{83}{152}$ (iv) $\frac{31}{69}$ (v) $\frac{19}{41}$ **23.** (i) $\frac{1}{6}$ (ii) + (iii) The number 4 appeared 179 times. **24.** (i) 0.25 **25.** 0.375

Activity 18.2

1. (i) (a) (H, H); (H, T); (T, H); (T, T) (c) (ii) $\frac{1}{4}$ (iii) 200 times (iv) This is not likely (v) 50–50 chance **2.** (ii) 36 possible outcomes (iii) No (iv) (a) Not fair (b) $\frac{2}{3}$ (c) $\frac{1}{3}$ (v) Give Callum a win if 7 is the outcome **3.** (i) $\frac{1}{2}$ (ii) $\frac{1}{3}$ (iii) $\frac{1}{2}$ (iv) $\frac{1}{3}$ **4.** (i) $\frac{1}{2}$ (iv) Incorrect **5.** (ii) $\frac{1}{12}$ (iii) $\frac{1}{6}$ (iv) Not very likely **6.** (iii) $\frac{1}{8}$ (iv) $\frac{7}{8}$ (v) $\frac{1}{2}$ **7.** (i) $\frac{3}{5}$ **8.** (ii) $\frac{1}{8}$ (iii) $\frac{1}{2}$ (iv) $\frac{1}{2}$ **9.** (ii) $\frac{1}{16}$ **10.** (i) $\frac{1}{8}$ (ii) $\frac{1}{4}$ **11.** (iii) $\frac{1}{6}$ **12.** (ii) $\frac{1}{12}$ (iii) $\frac{1}{6}$ (iv) $\frac{1}{3}$ **13.** (i) Ben is incorrect (ii) Chloe is also incorrect **14.** (ii) 0.94 (iii) 0.06 **15.** (ii) $\frac{1}{4}$ (iii) $\frac{1}{4}$ (iv) $\frac{1}{2}$

Activity 18.3

1. (i) 12 (ii) $\frac{3}{7}$ (iii) $\frac{1}{4}$ **2.** (ii) (a) $\frac{5}{26}$ (b) $\frac{11}{26}$ (c) $\frac{145}{442}$ **3.** (ii) $x = 16$ (iii) $\frac{1}{20}$ (iv) $\frac{1}{40}$ **4.** (ii) 0.8 **5.** (ii) $\frac{2}{27}$ (iii) $\frac{19}{54}$ (iv) $\frac{31}{54}$

Revision Activity 18

2. (b) 23 (c) $\frac{1}{36}$ (d) 0 **3.** (a) (i) 55% (ii) 16% (c) (i) 240 (ii) 6720 (iii) 1280 **4.** (a) $\frac{3}{7}$ (b) $\frac{1}{4}$ (c) $\frac{3}{28}$ (d) $\frac{1}{4}$ **5.** (a) $\frac{1}{7}$ (b) $\frac{1}{49}$ (c) $\frac{1}{49}$ **6.** (a) $\frac{2}{5}$ (b) $\frac{3}{20}$ (c) $\frac{1}{4}$ **7.** (a) $\frac{2}{3}$ (b) $\frac{1}{6}$ (c) $\frac{1}{3}$

Exam-style Questions

1. (b) (i) 3 (ii) $\frac{5}{12}$ **2.** (a) $\frac{1}{100}$ (b) 10% (c) 84%

Chapter 19

Activity 19.1

1. (i) 30 (v) 0.3 **3.** (ii) 90 cm (iii) 162 cm (iv) 165 cm **4.** (ii) 30 families (iii) 4 (iv) 20% (v) 0.2 **5.** (i) 20 (ii) 24 cm (iii) 50% (iv) 0.5

Activity 19.2

4. (ii) Q1: Categorical nominal, Q2: Categorical nominal, Q3: Categorical nominal, Q4: Numerical continuous, Q5: Numerical discrete, Q6: Categorical ordinal, Q7: Categorical ordinal

Activity 19.3

1. (i) Mean = 2.33 **2.** (i) 4.58 = 5 people (ii) 4.58 is not a natural number **3.** (ii) 2.42 = 2 cars (iii) 2 (iv) 2 (v) 2 **4.** 84 years **5** 35 hours **6.** 32 years **7.** 168 cm **8.** (i) 28 (ii) 6.5 (iii) 4.5 (iv) 4 **9.** (i) 45 (ii) 83 (iii) 76 (iv) 45 (v) Median **10** (i) 14 (ii) Michelle is better than Fiachra **11.** (i) Median is 9 (ii) Mode is 9 (iii) You cannot give the range **12.** The mean, median and mode can all be applied to numerical data. The only measure of central tendency which can be applied to categorical data is the mode.

Activity 19.4

1. (i) 49 years (ii) 67% (iii) 26 (iv) 0 **2.** (i) 165 to 170 cm (ii) 165 to 170 cm (iii) 166 cm **3.** (i) 60% (ii) 55–70 marks; 59.8 (iii) 59 marks **4.** (ii) 20–25 years (iii) 7% (iv) 34.09 years; 34.32 years **5.** (ii) €28,750 **6.** (iii) 100 kg (iv) 96 kg (v) $(100 - y)$ kg **7.** (i)13 (ii) 87.5% (iii) €45.20

Activity 19.5

1. 10 **2.** (i) 60° (ii) Electricity: €30.00 Fuel: €20.00 Other: €50.00 Food: €80.00 **3.** (i) 30 (iv) 0.7 **7.** (iii) $\frac{9}{24}$ = 0.375 = 37.5% **9.** (i) A little: 21, fairly concerned: 5.1 = 5, not at all: 3, very concerned: 0.9 = 1 **13.** (i) 150° (ii) 1440 (iii) 600

Activity 19.6

1. (ii) 5–10 (iii) 11 (iv) $\frac{11}{32}$ = 34.38% = 0.34 **2.** (ii) 2–4 hours (iii) Skewed right (iv) 13 (v) $\frac{13}{100}$ **3.** (i) €4–€8 (ii) €12 (iii) €30–€40 (iv) €40 **4.** (ii) 12 cm (iii) 23–26 cm (iv) 5 (v) $\frac{1}{6}$ **5** (ii) 25 cm (iii) 175–180 cm (iv) 18 (v) $\frac{3}{4}$ = 0.75 = 75% **6.** (ii) 35 cm (iii) 165–170 cm (iv) 6 (v) 0.25

Activity 19.7

2. (ii) 12 people at John's party, 39 people at Saoirse's party. (iii) The ages of people at John's party are from 28 to 40 which is a range of 12 years. The ages of people at Saoirse's party are from 0 to 92 years which is a range of 92 years. (iv) John's party mode: 29, median: 31, mean: 32; Saoirse's party mode: 34 and 58, median 37, mean 42 **3.** (ii) Yes. One student was absent. (iii) Test 1 max: 100, min: 5, range: 95; median: 58, mean: 58; Test 2 max: 100, min: 35, range: 65; median: 73; mean: 70 **4.** (i) 21 students on the first day and 22 students on the second day.

Revision Activity 19

1. (a) 50 (b) The minimum time interval was 90–100 minutes and the maximum time interval was 190–200 minutes. (e) 120 to 130 minutes (f) 129 minutes (g) 120–130 minutes **3.** (a) 824 schools (b) No **6.** (a) Q1 with histogram B, Q2 with histogram C and Q3 with histogram A **7.** (a) (i) 34 (ii) 28.5 (iii) 26.4 (c) Mode = 31, Median = 25.5, Mean = 23.4 **9.** (b) 77 actors, 77 actresses (c) actors 62 years; actresses 67 years (d) Median = 47 years (e) Median 39 years **10.** (b) 2–4 hours (c) 6.5 hours

Exam-style Questions

1. (b) 38 people; 30 people (c) Mean or mode **2.** (a) 1460 (b) 30% (c) 108°

Chapter 20

Activity 20.1

1. (i) [*PQ*] matches with [*ST*], [*QR*] matches with [*TV*], [*PR*] matches with [*SV*] **2.** [*AB*] matches with [*DE*], [*BC*] matches with [*EF*], [*AC*] matches with [*DF*] **3.** (i) [*AB*] and [*DE*], [*BC*] and [*EF*], [*AC*] and [*DF*] (ii) [*PQ*] and [*SV*], [*QR*] and [*TV*], [*PR*] and [*ST*] (iii) [*LN*] and [*RS*], [*LM*] and [*PS*], [*MN*] and [*RP*] (iv) [*AB*] and [*YZ*], [*AC*] and [*XZ*], [*BC*] and [*XY*] **4.** 15 **5.** (i) 2 (ii) $x = 8$, $y = 10$ **6.** (i) 1.5 (ii) 18 (iii) 10.8 (iv) 6 **7.** (iii) 12.09 m **8.** 16.67 m **9.** 450 cm **10.** (ii) 8.37 m **11.** (i) ΔAEF is similar to ΔACB (ii) $|AF| = 7.62$ cm, $|AC| = 22.86$ cm, $|BC| = 9$ cm **12.** (iii) $|HE| = 50$ **13.** (i) $x = 4.05$ (ii) $x = 4.99$ **14.** (iii) 2.3 cm **16.** (ii) $\frac{|AC|}{|AB|} = \frac{|DC|}{|AD|}$ (iii) $|DC| = 8$

Activity 20.2

1. (i) $x = 4$ (ii) $x = 5$ **2.** 480 m **3.** (ii) $|AG| = |GE| = |ED| = |BH| = |HF| = |FC|$ (iii) $|BM| = |ME|$ (iv) $|GN| = |NC|$ (v) 1.2 m (vi) 2.33 m (vii) 16.26 m **4.** (i) $x = 6$ (ii) $x = \frac{35}{4}$ (iii) $x = \frac{33}{10}$ (iv) $x = \frac{24}{5}$ (v) $x = 5$ (vi) $x = \frac{130}{9}$ **5.** (i) 5 : 3 (ii) 8 : 5 (iii) 3 : 8 **6.** (ii) $x = 7.5$ **7.** $x = \frac{15}{4}$; $y = \frac{48}{5}$ **8.** $w = \frac{35}{9}$ m **10.** (ii) $|KR| = |RW| = |TU| = |UV|$ **11.** (i) 4.5

Activity 20.3

2. (i) $|OA| = |OC| = |OE| = |OD|$ (ii) 10 (iii) *OAC* (iv) [*CE*] and [*AD*] (v) 78.54 units^2 **3.** (i) $|OA| = |OC| = |OH| = |OK|$ (ii) *OAC*, *OHK* (iii) $|\angle OAC| = |\angle OCA|$ (iv) $|\angle OHK| = |\angle OKH|$ **4.** (i) 60° (ii) 55° (iii) 34° (iv) 100° (v) 90° (vi) 70° (vii) 51° (viii) 120° **5.** (i) 50° (ii) 50° **6.** (i) $\theta = 75°$ (ii) $\theta = 50°$ (iii) $\theta = 130°$ (iv) $\theta = 90°$ (v) $\theta = 61°$ (vi) $\theta = 60°$ (vii) $\theta = 45°$ (viii) $\theta = 50°$ **7.** (i) 140° (ii) 30° **8.** (i) 100° (ii) 40° **10.** (i) 20° (ii) 55° **14.** 119.5°

Revision Activity 20

1. 13.2 m **4.** (a) 4 (c) $\frac{24}{5}$

Exam-style Questions

1. (a) $\alpha = 40°$ (b) $\beta = 70°$ (c) $\gamma = 110°$

Chapter 21

Activity 21.1

1. (a): (i) *a* (ii) *b* (iii) *c* (b): (i) *c* (ii) *b* (iii) *a* (c): (i) *a* (ii) *c* (iii) *b* (d): (i) *b* (ii) *c* (iii) *a* **2.** (i) Hypotenuse = [*AC*] (ii) Adjacent to α: [*AB*] (iii) Opposite to α: [*BC*] (iv) Adjacent to β: [*BC*] (v) Opposite to β: [*AB*] **3.** (i) Opposite to θ: [*AC*], Adjacent to θ: [*BC*], Hypotenuse: [*AB*] (ii) Opposite to θ: [*XZ*], Adjacent to θ:[*XY*], Hypotenuse: [*YZ*] (iii) Opposite to θ: [*QR*], Adjacent to θ: [PQ], Hypotenuse: [*PR*]. **4.** (a): (i) 4 (ii) 3 (iii) 5 (b): (i) 5 (ii) 12 (iii) 13 (c): (i) 20 (ii) 21 (iii) 29 **5.** (iii) Yes (iv) Yes (v) Yes **6.** (iv) Yes (v) Yes (vi) Yes

Activity 21.2

1. (i) $\frac{12}{13}$ (ii) $\frac{5}{13}$ (iii) $\frac{12}{5}$ (iv) $\frac{5}{13}$ (v) $\frac{12}{13}$ (vi) $\frac{5}{12}$ **2.** (i) 10 (ii) (a) $\frac{6}{10}$ (b) $\frac{8}{10}$ (c) $\frac{6}{8}$ (d) $\frac{8}{10}$ (e) $\frac{6}{10}$ (f) $\frac{8}{6}$ **3.** (i) 25 (ii) (a) $\frac{7}{25}$ (b) $\frac{24}{25}$ (c) $\frac{7}{24}$ (d) $\frac{24}{25}$ (e) $\frac{7}{25}$ (f) $\frac{24}{7}$ **4.** (i) 0.7431 (ii) 0.4540 (iii) 0.9848 (iv) 0.9511 (v) 3.0777 (vi) 0.3090 **5.** (i) not true (ii) not true (iii) not true (iv) not true **6.** (i) 13 (ii) (a) $\frac{5}{13}$ (b) $\frac{12}{13}$ (c) $\frac{5}{12}$ (d) $\frac{12}{13}$ (e) $\frac{5}{13}$ (f) $\frac{12}{5}$ **7.** (i) (a) $\frac{y}{x}$ (b) $\frac{y}{x}$ (c) $\frac{z}{x}$ (d) $\frac{z}{x}$ (ii) $\tan A = \frac{y}{z}$; $\tan B = \frac{z}{y}$; tan *A* is the reciprocal of tan *B* **8.** $|AC| = 6 \tan 30°$ **9.** (ii) $\cos A = \frac{\sqrt{51}}{10}$ **11.** Statement (ii) is correct; Statement (iv) is correct **12.** (i) 4.9 cm (ii) $|CR| = 1.7$ cm; $|BQ| = 3.6$ cm; $|AP| = 4.6$ cm (v) The value of the sine of an angle can never exceed 1 **13.** (i) $|OR| = 6.5$ cm; $|OQ| = 4.6$ cm; $|OP| = 2.3$ cm (iv) The value of the cosine of an angle can never exceed 1 **14.** (iii) Yes

Activity 21.3

1. $x = 9.830$ **2.** $y = 15.321$ **3.** $p = 25.981$ **4.** $x = 27.475$ **5.** $x = 4.663$ **6.** $x = 76.604$ **7.** (i) $|BC| = 8.391$, $|AC| = 13.054$ (ii) $\sin 50° = \frac{10}{|AC|}$, so $|AC| = 13.054$ **8.** $|PQ| = 12.586$ $|QR| = 19.581$ **9.** (i) $x = 13.210$ (ii) $x = 5.393$ **10.** (i) $x = 30.642$ (ii) $|BC| = 8.210$ **11.** (i) $|PR| = 10.392$ (ii) $|RS| = 3.782$

Activity 21.4

1. (i) $A = 10°$ (ii) $\alpha = 80°$ (iii) $\beta = 30°$ (iv) $\theta = 60°$ (v) $\beta = 45°$ (vi) $\beta = 45°$ (vii) $\alpha = 45°$ (viii) $\beta = 30°$ (ix) $\beta = 60°$ **2.** (i) $\alpha = 19°$ (ii) $\beta = 78°$ (iii) $\theta = 23°$ (iv) $\alpha = 56°$ (v) $\beta = 10°$ (vi) $\beta = 80°$ (vii) $\alpha = 63°$ (viii) $\beta = 27°$ (ix) $\beta = 30°$ (x) $\alpha = 30°$ **3.** (i) $\alpha = 53°$, $\beta = 37°$, missing side = 5 (ii) $\alpha = 28°$, $\beta = 62°$, missing side = 17 (iii) $\beta = 53°$, $\alpha = 37°$, missing side = 16 **4.** (i) 16.26° (ii) 16.26° (iii) 16.26° **5.** (i) $29^2 = 21^2 + 20^2$ (ii) $\theta = 46.4°$, $\alpha = 43.6°$ **6.** (i) (a) $A = 61.93°$ (b) $A = 61.93°$ (c) $A = 61.93°$ **7.** $A = 80°$ $B = 10°$ $x = 61$ **8.** $B = 24°$ $A = 66°$ $x = 10.93$ **9.** $A = 65°$, $y = 11.79$ $x = 13.01$ **10.** $B = 40°$, $A = 50°$ $x = 7.81$ **11.** $A = 49°$, $B = 41°$, $x = 2.65$ **12.** $B = 35°$, $A = 55°$, $x = 1.73$ **13.** $y = x\sqrt{3} - 2\sqrt{3}$

Activity 21.5

1. (i) α (ii) α would increase in size. (iii) 19.20 m **3.** 10 m **4.** 96.17 m **5.** (ii) 1.84 m **6.** (i) $\angle A$ (ii) $\angle A$ and $\angle C$ (iii) $|\angle C| = 35°$, $\angle B = 55°$ (iv) 87.17 m **7.** $\angle C$ **8.** (i) The angle has increased (ii) The exterior angle equals the sum of the two interior opposite angles. (iii) $|\angle D| = |\angle A| + |\angle E|$ $|\angle D| = |\angle C| + |\angle E|$ **9.** 63.49 m

Activity 21.6

1. (ii) $|AC| = \sqrt{2}$ units **2.** (iii) $\sqrt{3}$ units **3.** (i) $x = 2\sqrt{2}$ (ii) $x = \frac{5\sqrt{3}}{2}$ (iii) $x = 1$ (iv) $x = 3\sqrt{3}$ **4.** $b = 6$; $a = 6$; $\theta = 45°$ **6.** $x = 6$ **7.** (i) $|CBD| = 90°$ (ii) Radius = 5 **10.** (i) $\sin 2A = \frac{\sqrt{3}}{2}$; $2\sin A = 1$ (ii) $\sin 2A \neq 2\sin A$ **11.** (i) 1 (ii) 1

Activity 21.7

1. $h = 4.01$ m **2.** 104.96 m **3.** 2.82 m **4.** 39.99 m **5.** (ii) 337.25 m **6.** 15.2 m **7.** (i) $\theta = 68.56°$ (ii) 75° 45′ (iii) 12.56 m **8.** 5° 43′ **9.** (i) $h = x\sqrt{3}$ (ii) $h = (20 - x)\frac{1}{\sqrt{3}}$ (iii) $x = 5$ (iv) $h = 8.66$ m **10.** (i) $|OQ| = |OR| = |OP|$ (ii) $|\angle PRQ| = 90°$ (iii) $x = \frac{15}{2\sqrt{3}}$ m **12.** (i) $|AB| = 2.403$ m (ii) 10.30 m (iii) 3.79 m **13.** (iv) 20 m (v) 15 m

Revision Activity 21

1. (a) $x = 7.2$ m (b) $x = 9.45$ cm; $y = 22.06$ cm **3.** (a) 30° (b) 45° **5.** (a) $h = x\sqrt{3}$ (b) 10.4 m **6.** (b) 125 m

Exam-style Questions

1. (a) Not correct (b) Correct (c) Not correct
2. Suurhusen is the most tilted

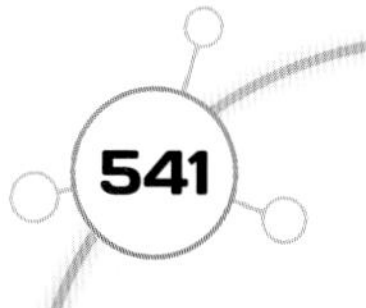

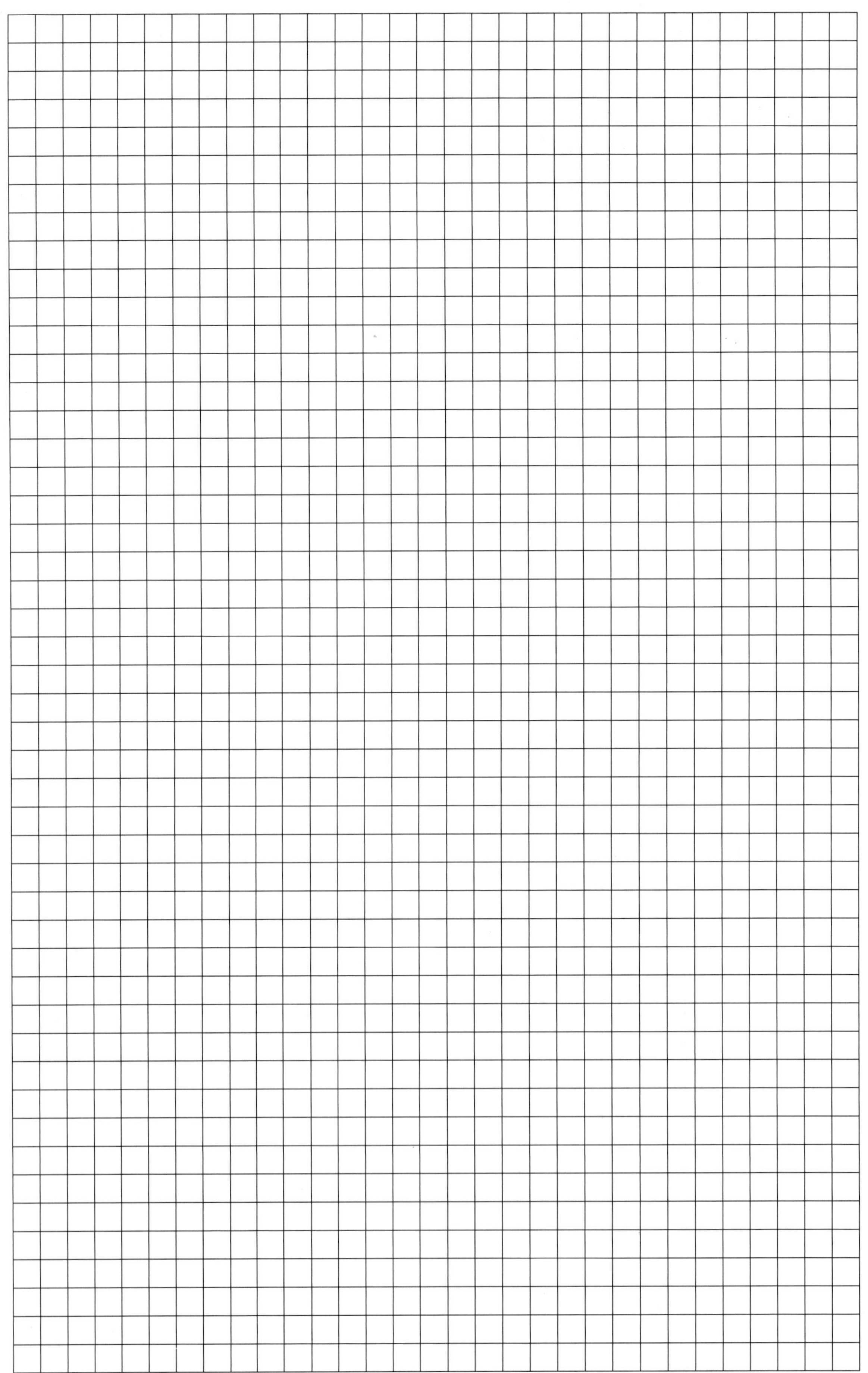

545